ArtScroll Tanach Series®

A traditional commentary on the Books of the Bible

Rabbi Nosson Scherman / Rabbi Meir Zlotowitz

General Editors

A PROJECT OF THE

Mesorah Heritage Foundation

Translation and Commentary by
Rabbi Yosef Weinberger

Edited by
Yaacov Dovid Shulman

An Overview:
'Samuel and a New Era in Israel'
by
Rabbi Nosson Scherman

shmuel I

I SAMUEL: / A NEW TRANSLATION WITH A COMMENTARY ANTHOLOGIZED FROM TALMUDIC, MIDRASHIC, AND RABBINIC SOURCES.

Published by

Mesorah Publications, ltd

FIRST EDITION
First Impression ... June 2011

Published and Distributed by
MESORAH PUBLICATIONS, LTD.
4401 Second Avenue / Brooklyn, N.Y 11232

Distributed in Europe by
LEHMANNS
Unit E, Viking Business Park
Rolling Mill Road
Jarow, Tyne & Wear, NE32 3DP
England

Distributed in Australia and New Zealand
by **GOLDS WORLDS OF JUDAICA**
3-13 William Street
Balaclava, Melbourne 3183
Victoria, Australia

Distributed in Israel by
SIFRIATI / A. GITLER — BOOKS
6 Hayarkon Street
Bnei Brak 51127

Distributed in South Africa by
KOLLEL BOOKSHOP
Ivy Common
105 William Road
Norwood 2192, Johannesburg, South Africa

THE ARTSCROLL TANACH SERIES®
SHMUEL I / I SAMUEL

ISBN 10: 1-4226-1091-8 / ISBN 13: 978-1-4226-1091-6

Typography by CompuScribe at ArtScroll Studios, Ltd.
Bound by Sefercraft, Quality Bookbinders, Ltd., Brooklyn N.Y. 11232

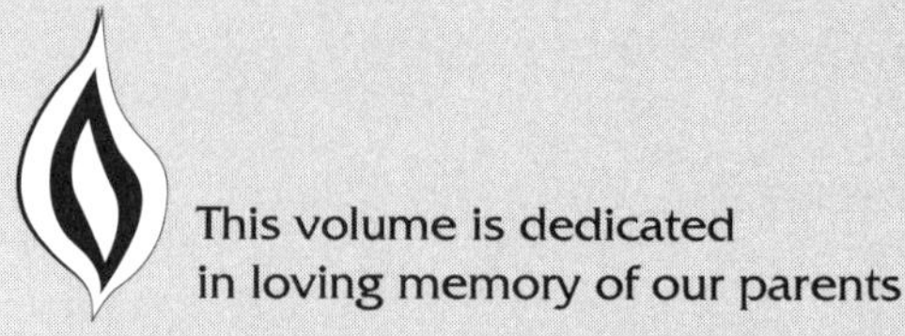

This volume is dedicated
in loving memory of our parents

Pinches and Chava Feldman ע״ה

פנחס דוד בן מיכאל ע״ה

נפטר כ״ב תמוז תשמ״ה

חוה בת יצחק ע״ה

נפטרה כ״ג אייר תשנ״א

George and Jean Brookenthal ע״ה

גדליה בן חיים יצחק ע״ה

נפטר כ״ד כסלו תש״נ

זלטא בת פסח ע״ה

נפטרה א׳ כסלו תשנ״ד

The Feldmans were survivors. They came to Detroit with their three children and a powerful determination to preserve the Yiddishkeit of their past. Pinches began as a union painter carrying his equipment on buses. When illness forced him out of the union, he continued working as an independent painter, and devoted himself to his shul as gabbai and organizer of minyanim. He would visit the cemetery before festivals to help people recite the Keil Malei. Chava worked for a caterer. Their income was small, but there was always enough for tzedakah and to make chessed an essential part of their lives. She tendered shul luncheons for the benefit of our brethren in Israel. Every family Yom Tov and other gathering was in their home. They lived for their children and grandchildren — and took pride in them. Their efforts bore fruit.

The Brookenthals lived modestly and honestly in Detroit. George (Gedaliah) left his family of eleven as a youngster and lived with relatives in Toledo, working as a tool and die maker. Jean (Zlata) came to America as a teenager and worked in a clothing store in Detroit. She taught herself to read and speak English and imbued her children with her love of learning. George became a union painter in Detroit, where he and Jean married and raised their two children. He enjoyed sports and she enjoyed cooking and was an avid reader. Most of all, they enjoyed their children. They were loving and adoring parents, who richly earned their nachas from children and grandchildren.

Paul and Bella Brookenthal

⸎ Publisher's Preface

We are proud to present this volume to those who wish to attain a new level of understanding of the Book of *I Samuel.* This comprehensive treatment, many years in the making, assembles what may well be an unprecedented array of Talmudic, Midrashic, and Rabbinic commentaries on this *sefer*. It follows the pattern of some of the most respected works in the ArtScroll Tanach Series, such as the anthologized commentary on *Bereishis*. This volume offers an extended, detailed, phrase-by-phrase commentary that is unique in its thoroughness. In addition, it presents a broad selection of interpretations from the Talmud and Midrash, as well as homiletic teachings from sages of many centuries.

The deservedly popular Rubin Edition of the Early Prophets, on the other hand, introduces and explains the topics of the Books, and provides the reader with a very good, but general understanding of the chapters and verses, as well as a discussion of many subjects that, on the surface, are hard to understand.

RABBI YOSEF WEINBERGER, in this work, has complied an anthologized commentary that will be studied and consulted far into the future by people who want a thorough understanding of the Book. Rabbi Weinberger is known to, and admired by, ArtScroll's readership for his work on volume 2 of *Mishlei* / Proverbs. We are proud to present the work of such a distinguished teacher and scholar to the Torah public, and we look forward to publishing his future volumes.

⁂

The Book of *I Samuel* marks a turning point in Jewish history. It begins with the miraculous birth of Samuel and his emergence as the leader of his generation after the destruction of the Tabernacle at Shiloh, and the capture of the Ark by the Philistines. Samuel led the people to new heights and, when they demanded a king, God instructed him to anoint Saul as the first Jewish king. But he fell short, and Samuel anointed David as Saul's eventual successor and the founder of the Messianic dynasty. With Samuel, there began a new role for the prophets as the moral and spiritual leaders of Israel.

Over twenty years ago, RABBI MENDEL GELDWERTH ז״ל, a legendary teacher and a great *talmid chacham,* began work on an erudite and copious commentary on all aspects of this Book. Unfortunately, his unpublished work covers only the first fifteen chapters of *I Samuel.* Rabbi Weinberger had permission to refer to and quote Rabbi Geldwerth's manuscript, as needed. For this permission we are grateful to his son, our good friend RABBI LIPA GELDWERTH.

In the years since the ArtScroll Series was born, in 1976, we have had the privilege to publish over 1,500 titles, spanning Tanach, Tefillah, Halachah, Talmud, Midrash, and Jewish history. The "ArtScroll Library" now comprises over 1,500 titles, including such classics as the Schottenstein Hebrew and English Editions of Talmud Bavli and Yerushalmi, the Kleinman Editions of Midrash Rabbah and Kitzur Shulchan Aruch, and a host of other works that are enhancing Jewish life throughout the world. The public's enthusiastic acceptance of such volumes testifies to the growing thirst for literature that is loyal to the eternity of Torah.

Words are not adequate to express our gratitude to Hashem for allowing us to be a vehicle for bringing His word to His people. May this blessing continue with the fulfillment of the prophecy that there will be a hunger, *not a hunger for bread nor a thirst for water, but to hear the words of Hashem* (*Amos* 8:11), speedily in our days.

Rabbi Meir Zlotowitz / Rabbi Nosson Scherman

Sivan 5771 / June 2011

⸙ Author's Preface

מה אשיב לה׳ כל תגמולוהי עלי

What an honor and a privilege it is to have been given the opportunity to join the illustrious roster of ArtScroll writers whose anthologized commentaries on *Tanach* have been made available to the Torah world! Knowing whom that list includes, I am humbled and I thank Hashem for permitting me to produce this volume.

I benefited enormously from the wellsprings of Torah and leadership personified by RABBI MEIR ZLOTOWITZ. Aside from his unstinting warmth, encouragement, patience, and personal friendship, his *sefarim* have been a role model for me with regard to commentaries on *Nach*. He is the founding father of the ArtScroll anthology, and I sought to emulate the flowing, reader-friendly style of his commentaries to the *Megillos* and *Chumash*. My gratitude to him is boundless.

What the public knows about the masterful writings and speaking talents of my father-in-law, RABBI NOSSON SCHERMAN, is but a fraction of his multifaceted attributes. In addition to providing clarity of thought and sage advice, he is also, behind the scenes, an exceptionally humble, loving, and caring father and zeidy, whose unpretentious presence never ceases to inspire. May he, along with my mother-in-law, שתחי׳, enjoy many years of continued good health and *nachas* from all of us.

While preparing this work, I consulted a *talmid chacham* of note, RABBI SHMUEL MOELLER, for whom the study of *Tanach* is a passion, and he directed me to a number of very helpful volumes. Many thanks, Reb Shmuel, and much *hatzlachah* on your *Nach shiurim*.

In the process of preparing this publication I was privileged to have available to me the unpublished commentary on fifteen chapters of *Shmuel* of *Mori v'Rabbi* HARAV HAGAON RAV MENDEL GELDWERTH זצ״ל. This extraordinary commentary is a rich tapestry spanning *dikduk* and Halachah, *Aggadah* and *machshavah*, and I drew from it often. It is unfortunate for us and for posterity that

this work was never completed. Rav Geldwerth was renowned as an extraordinary *talmid chacham* and scholar, as well as a legendary *mechanech* whose impact on his *talmidim* was enduring. I am proud to be included among them.

The incredible work of RABBI SHIMON KRASNER of Baltimore, *Sefer Nachalas Shimon*, presents encyclopedic essays on Halachah and *Aggadah* related to *Sifrei Neviim*. I used his well-researched and well-organized volumes regularly. He has done a great service to the *Nach* student and we thank him for that.

I also gained much from *Mishbetzos Zahav*, a recent masterpiece by RAV SHABSI SHEFTEL WEISS of Yerushalayim. יישר חילו לאורייתא.

My gratitude goes to the editor, REB YAAKOV DOVID SHULMAN, who, once again, has structured my thoughts and presented them in a clear, readable fashion.

As always, the ArtScroll staff blends professionalism with genuine warmth and friendliness. REB MENDY HERZBERG is a pleasure to work with, as he gets the job done efficiently, while spicing it with his sweet, amiable personality. Reb Mendy, I look forward to continued projects together.

I am very grateful to the "ArtScroll team," which comprises many enormously talented and dedicated people. RABBI SHEAH BRANDER continues to set the standard in design, beauty, and "user-friendliness" in Torah publications. AVROHOM YITZCHAK DEUTSCH insured the accuracy of the Hebrew text and quotes. MRS. ESTIE DICKER typed, paginated, and entered corrections. Others who typed with skill and attention to detail were MRS. ESTHER FEIERSTEIN, and MRS. TOBY GOLDZWEIG. MRS. FAIGIE WEINBAUM and MRS. MINDY STERN proofread and made valuable comments and suggestions.

No words can adequately express my feelings of admiration and appreciation toward my parents, RABBI MOSHE YAAKOV שליט"א and MRS. ROSALIE ע"ה WEINBERGER. They have been the quintessential parents, making their children their first priority, and sparing no effort or resource in directing us in the paths of Torah. My father is an erudite writer who left his comments and editorial imprint on this work as well. Any accomplishments that we, their children, bring about will be to them the ultimate repayment for their efforts, that have always been channeled toward that goal.

My wife MALKY is the perfect life partner and deserves enormous credit for her remarkable balancing act, juggling her roles as principal, consultant, daughter, wife, mother, and grandmother with wisdom, poise, and dignity. May Hashem grant our joint wish that we merit to

see our children develop into accomplished Jews who are dedicated to the service of Hashem and study Torah with utmost dedication.

Finally, I thank Hashem for allowing me to have my lot among those who dwell in the tent of Torah.

Yosef Weinberger

Sivan 5771 / June 2011

An Overview — Samuel and a New Era in Israel

I. The Title

Abarbanel raises an interesting question about the title of the Book of *Samuel.* His answer will not only explain the rather simple matter of choice of title, it will also give us an insight into the nature and purpose of the Book.

On the surface, one might say that the Book is named for its author, but this is not so.

On the surface, one might say that the Book is named for its author, but this is not so. First, Samuel was also the author of the Books of *Joshua* and *Judges* (*Bava Basra* 14b), but they are not named for him. The other Books of the Early Prophets — *Joshua, Judges,* and *Kings* — are named for their subject matter, rather than their authors. Furthermore, although we refer to *I Samuel* and *II Samuel* as two separate Books, the Sages consider them to be one big Book. Samuel wrote less than half of both Books of *Samuel* (his death is recorded in 25:1 of this volume); the rest was written by the prophets Nathan and Gad the Seer (ibid.), but it is not named for them.

At first glance, it would seem that the major focus of the complete Book of Samuel is on Saul and David, not Samuel.

Of course, several Books are named for their authors, such as Isaiah, Jeremiah, and Ezekiel, but the reason for that is obvious: they all deal almost exclusively with the prophecies and experiences of their namesakes; but at least at first glance, it would seem that the major focus of the complete Book of *Samuel* is on Saul and David, not Samuel. Abarbanel notes that the importance of the king, as leader of the nation, would suggest that the Book be named for Saul, the very first king, or David, the greatest of all the kings and the most prominent player of the entire Book. Similarly, even though the Book of *Kings* has much to say about the great prophets Elijah and Elisha, it derives its name from the sovereigns of the nation, the kings of Judah and the Ten Tribes.

His Profound Influence

He was the one whom God commanded to anoint Saul and David, so whatever they accomplished can be ascribed to Samuel's initiatives.

Abarbanel's first and primary reason for the title is that, in its most profound sense, the entire Book — including what is popularly known as *II Samuel* — is about Samuel himself. He was the one whom God commanded to anoint Saul and David to be kings, so whatever they accomplished in their personal roles as leaders of the nation can be ascribed to Samuel's initiatives, just as the exploits of children can be credited to their parents. In further discussing this subject, Abarbanel highlights the origin and personal greatness of Samuel. He was born in purity in response to the earnest, holy — in many ways prophetic — prayer of Hannah, a barren woman. His entire life was dedicated to the service of God, first in the Sanctuary at Shiloh, and later in his personal sanctuary of dedicated service to God and Israel. He grew up in a time when *the word of HASHEM* [i.e., prophecy] *was scarce . . . [prophetic] vision was not widespread* (3:1), but Samuel elevated himself and his generation to the point where he earned the gift of prophecy (ibid., v. 21), and he had countless disciples who became prophets thanks to his inspiration and teaching. Even the newly anointed King Saul, a non-prophet, was inspired to prophesy when he came into the proximity of Samuel's disciples (see Ch. 10).

Samuel elevated himself and his generation to the point where he earned the gift of prophecy and he had countless disciples who became prophets thanks to his inspiration and teaching.

Like Moses and Aaron

So great did Samuel become that he is compared to Moses and Aaron:

> מֹשֶׁה וְאַהֲרֹן בְּכֹהֲנָיו וּשְׁמוּאֵל בְּקֹרְאֵי שְׁמוֹ קֹרְאִים אֶל-ה׳ וְהוּא יַעֲנֵם בְּעַמּוּד עָנָן יְדַבֵּר אֲלֵיהֶם שָׁמְרוּ עֵדֹתָיו וְחֹק נָתַן-לָמוֹ
>
> *Moses and Aaron were among His priests, and Samuel among those who invoke His Name. They called upon HASHEM and He answered them. In a pillar of cloud He spoke to them; they obeyed His testimonies and whatever decree He gave them* (*Psalms* 99:6-7).

In its plain meaning, the above passage says that just as God accepted the prayers of Moses and Aaron, so too, He accepted the prayers of Samuel, as we will see in the course of this Book. The Vilna Gaon finds

another dimension in this expression of Samuel's equivalence to his two illustrious predecessors. The Sages teach that the throat of Moses was the conduit through which the *Shechinah* itself, as it were, made itself heard. So too, in describing the Yom Kippur service in the Temple, the Mishnah states that God's Ineffable Name יוֹצֵא מִפִּי כֹּהֵן גָּדוֹל, *emanated from the mouth of the Kohen Gadol* (*Mishnah Yoma* 6:2), implying that the Name emanated of its own accord, not that the High Priest uttered it himself. As the Kohen Gadol, Aaron was the one who initiated this phenomenon.

The Sages teach that the throat of Moses was the conduit through which the Shechinah itself, as it were, made itself heard.

Scripture indicates that Samuel, too, was of this extraordinary spiritual stature. When Samuel addressed Israel and told the people how, whenever they repented, God sent saviors countless times to redeem them from enemy domination, the prophet gave examples:

Scripture indicates that Samuel, too, was of this extraordinary spiritual stature.

וַיִּשְׁלַח ה׳ אֶת־יְרֻבַּעַל וְאֶת־בְּדָן וְאֶת־יִפְתָּח וְאֶת־שְׁמוּאֵל וַיַּצֵּל אֶתְכֶם מִיַּד אֹיְבֵיכֶם מִסָּבִיב

So H*ASHEM sent Jerubaal [i.e., Gideon] and Bedan [i.e., Samson] and Jephthah and Samuel and He rescued you from the hand of your enemies from all around, and you dwelt in security* (12:11).

Strange, is it not, that in listing the saviors, Samuel speaks of himself in third person? It would have been more logical for him to have said וְאוֹתִי, *and [God sent] me.* From this third-person reference, Vilna Gaon deduces that Samuel was not the speaker, but that the voice of God was emanating from his throat. It is in this sense that the verse in *Psalms* equates Samuel with Moses and Aaron (*Kol Eliyahu, Psalms* 99). It is entirely appropriate that the one who inaugurated a new epoch in the history of Israel should be a prophet of such stature.

It is entirely appropriate that the one who inaugurated a new epoch in the history of Israel should be a prophet of such stature.

II. The New Role of the Prophet

Seers and Prophets

The emergence of Samuel was more than the story of a great man who led his generation and anointed the first two kings of Israel. Samuel marked a turning

He inaugurated an era when prophecy became widespread, a phenomenon that continued for nearly five centuries.

point, a revolutionary new era, in Jewish history. As noted above, he inaugurated an era when prophecy became widespread, a phenomenon that continued for nearly five centuries, until the destruction of the First Temple. The Sages state that there were twice as many prophets during those centuries as the number of Jews who left Egypt (*Megillah* 14a).

More important than sheer numbers was the new role of the prophet.

More important than sheer numbers was the new role of the prophet. It was foreshadowed in the incident that led Saul to meet Samuel for the first time (Ch. 9). The donkeys of Saul's father, Kish, were lost, and Saul was sent to try and find them. The search was fruitless, and Saul wanted to go back home, but his attendant told him that "there is a man of God in this city . . . perhaps he will tell us upon which road we should travel" (9:6). Then Scripture adds a parenthetical comment:

> לְפָנִים בְּיִשְׂרָאֵל כֹּה־אָמַר הָאִישׁ בְּלֶכְתּוֹ לִדְרוֹשׁ אֱלֹהִים לְכוּ וְנֵלְכָה עַד־הָרֹאֶה, כִּי לַנָּבִיא הַיּוֹם יִקָּרֵא לְפָנִים הָרֹאֶה
>
> *Formerly in Israel, this is what someone said when he went to inquire of God: "Let us go to the 'seer,' " for "the prophet" of today was formerly called "the seer"* (9:9).

Why did Scripture find it necessary just now to tell us that the title of a prophet had changed? What was the role of a seer, and what was the role of a prophet?

What is the difference between a prophet and a seer? And why did Scripture find it necessary just now — when Saul was about to be anointed as the first Jewish king — to tell us that the title of a prophet had changed? What was the role of a seer, and what was the role of a prophet?

A New Mission

Rabbi Yaakov Kamenetsky explains that this verse indicates a seminal crossroads in Jewish history. The Book of *Samuel* marks the change from the rule of Judges to the rule of Kings. Eli the Kohen Gadol was the Judge when Samuel, his eventual successor, was born. Samuel was the last Judge. The post was not hereditary; as the Book of *Judges* shows, the Judges were appointed by God, based on personal merit and righteousness. Throughout the nearly four centuries of the Judges, there was no case of a leader who was sinful,

and certainly not of one who descended to idolatry. To the contrary, the Judges were chosen by God to pull the nation back from the muck of idol worship. During those years, the leadership of the Judge was, by and large, not only temporal but spiritual. The nation did not need to turn elsewhere for spiritual leadership, nor did its Judge need a spiritual mentor to guide him.

The leadership of the Judge was, by and large, not only temporal but spiritual. The nation did not need to turn elsewhere for spiritual leadership.

That was about to change in the time of Samuel. The era of monarchy was at hand. The monarchy was hereditary, and — as catalogued in the sad history of the Books of *Kings* and *Chronicles* — many of the kings sinned grievously and ultimately caused Israel's downfall and exile. First came the split between the Davidic Kingdom of Judah and the northern Kingdom of the Ten Tribes. The schism deepened until there were civil wars between the northern and southern cousins. The Ten Tribes, led by their kings, were awash in idolatry, and even many of the kings of Judah followed suit. Both kingdoms paid dearly for the transgressions of their kings.

Kings could not be the moral and spiritual leaders of the nation, as the Judges had been.

Kings could not be the moral and spiritual leaders of the nation, as the Judges had been. In a hereditary monarchy, there was no guarantee that even a king as righteous as Hezekiah would be succeeded by a righteous successor — and, indeed, Hezekiah was succeeded by Manassah, one of Judah's most evil kings. The role of moral and spiritual leadership could not be entrusted to kings; that role had to be assumed by prophets. Thus, in the Book of *Samuel* and especially in the following Books, we find the prophets assuming a new authority and prominence. They inspired the people, admonished the kings, and sought to prove by means of miracles that Hashem alone is the true God and that the fashionable idols were worthless.

The prophets inspired the people, admonished the kings, and sought to prove that Hashem alone is the true God.

This change of role is implicit in the terms רֹאֶה, "seer" and נָבִיא, "prophet." A seer, as the name implies, sees things that others do not. An individual could ask him for guidance in how to come closer to God, and the seer, with his insight, could penetrate to the seeker's essence and tell him which course is best for him and help him navigate the challenges. On the most mundane level, a seer could "see" the location

of lost donkeys. But he was not responsible to tell the leader of the nation what he should or should not do. Such leaders had been chosen by God and they could be trusted to know what He wanted of them.

Mentor to Rulers

The word navi, or prophet, is derived from the Hebrew word נִיב, speech, because it is his function to convey the word of God.

A prophet is different. The word *navi,* or prophet, is derived from the Hebrew word נִיב, *speech,* because it is his function to convey the word of God. Thus, until Samuel's time, a prophet was a seer; beginning with Samuel, he was a *navi.* Samuel not only anointed Saul, he guided him and admonished him — and finally he had the unhappy assignment of telling him that God had found him unworthy of the throne. After the deaths of Samuel and Saul, the prophet Nathan became David's prophetic mentor. As the decades went on, such august figures as Elijah, Elisha, Isaiah, Jeremiah, and Ezekiel became the central figures of their generation, overshadowing the kings they advised, helped, and admonished.

Just as he inaugurated the era of the monarchy, so he introduced the new form of Jewish leadership.

In this sense, Samuel is more than the towering figure who led and shaped the nation during his tenure. Just as he inaugurated the era of the monarchy, so he introduced the new form of Jewish leadership. To a very great extent, the paradigm that temporal rulers in Israel must answer to the spiritual leaders who represent the word of God continued down the centuries.

Samuel transmitted the direct word of God, while the Torah leaders of the exile must rely on judgment that is conditioned by knowledge of all areas of the Written and Oral Torah.

Throughout our history, Jews have had leaders who interacted with governments and undertook responsibility for their communities. When those leaders were loyal to the Torah, they sought and accepted guidance from the great Torah scholars and *tzaddikim* of their time. The concept behind this subservience is the same now as it was in the time of Samuel, although, admittedly, Samuel transmitted the direct word of God, while the Torah leaders of the exile must rely on judgment that is conditioned by knowledge of all areas of the Written and Oral Torah, and their totally objective striving to apply it to the situations at hand. As the Mussar masters have expressed it, when such classic early commentators as the *Rashba* or the *Rosh* write נִרְאֶה לִי, *it seems to me,* it does not mean that they are merely expressing an opinion for which they have no

proof. To the contrary, the entire Torah is their proof, because their thought processes have been shaped by their uncompromising dedication to understand and interpret the Torah.

The Book of Samuel is very aptly named for him. He is the one who set all of its events in motion.

In summary, the Book of *Samuel*, although it could be argued that most of it does not deal directly with the prophet, is very aptly named for him. He is the one who set all of its events in motion, and beyond that he also set the precedent for the future relationship between kings and prophets. From his time onward, Jewish heads of state would be guided by the counsel of the prophets and by others who could speak in the Name of God, as they understood His word from the Torah. There were kings who let themselves be guided, such as David and Hezekiah. There were others who were too evil or too arrogant, such as Jeroboam and Ahab. The Books of *Kings* and *Chronicles* narrate the fates of both. Suffice it to say that the wicked kings brought disaster upon themselves and upon the nation.

There were kings who let themselves be guided, such as David and Hezekiah. There were others who were too evil or too arrogant, such as Jeroboam and Ahab.

III. Kingship*

The Torah's Prologue

It is illustrative of the role of the Jewish king that the Torah seems to anticipate the danger that comes with ceding power to a human being. The passage commanding Israel to ask for a king (*Deuteronomy* 17:14-20) is preceded by a passage that commands the nation to be subservient to the court (ibid., vs. 8-13). When disputes arise you are to go to the authorities who are in office in your time — and not say that they are inferior to the judges of an earlier generation — and you are to abide by their rulings: *According to the teaching that they will teach you and according to the judgment that they will say to you, shall you do; you shall not deviate from the word that they will tell you, right or left* (v. 11).

So vital was it to uphold the authority of the court that if an acknowledged, senior, respected elder

This portion of the Overview is based primarily on the Commentary on Chumash of Rabbi Samson Raphael Hirsch.

publicly repudiated its ruling, he could incur the death penalty. The seeming harshness of this law is understandable when one considers that serious insubordination by such a sage undermines the authority of the court and can lead to anarchy. As the sages put it, there would be two Torahs in Israel. Anarchy itself is a deplorable situation, but when it stems from refusal to accept the judgment of the court as ordained by God, it is worse. It constitutes rebellion against God, and can lead to the undoing of the nation itself, as happened during the reigns of the idolatrous kings of the Ten Tribes.

Serious insubordination by such a sage undermines the authority of the court and can lead to anarchy.

Leadership and Humility

An illustration of the importance of this principle is found in the case of a halachic dispute between two historic sages (*Mishnah Rosh Hashanah* 2:8-9). Rabban Gamliel was the *Nasi,* the leader of the nation and the head of the court. According to his calculation of the lunar cycle and the testimony of witnesses who claimed to have seen the new moon, Rabban Gamliel declared Rosh Chodesh Tishrei. But Rabbi Yehoshua, an equally great sage, held that Rabban Gamliel's calculation was wrong and therefore the witnesses were either mistaken or lying. Rabbi Yehoshua declared that he would observe the next day as Rosh Chodesh. This meant that there would be two versions of the calendar; Rabban Gamliel and his followers would observe one day as Yom Kippur and Rabbi Yehoshua and his followers would observe the next day. This dichotomy would continue through the centuries and, theoretically, such disputes could be repeated and make a shambles of the calendar.

This meant that there would be two versions of the calendar. This dichotomy would continue through the centuries and make a shambles of the calendar.

Rabban Gamliel commanded Rabbi Yehoshua to "desecrate" his own Yom Kippur by making a public appearance before the *Nasi* carrying his staff and belongings. Understandably, Rabbi Yehoshua was chagrined and upset, not because of the public humiliation, but because, according to his calculation, he would be transgressing the commandment not to carry articles in a public domain on Yom Kippur. His great disciple Rabbi Akiva comforted him. Rabbi Akiva adduced Scriptural proof that the decision of Rabban Gamliel's

court was binding, even on those who were sure it was wrong. Furthermore, Rabbi Akiva argued, if the ruling of Rabban Gamliel's court could be set aside because a qualified sage disagreed, every court decision from the time of Moses could be called into question. Rabbi Yehoshua accepted Rabbi Akiva's reasoning and, on the day of "his" Yom Kippur, he appeared before Rabban Gamliel carrying his staff and pouch, confident that he was obeying the Torah.

Come in peace, my master and my disciple: my master in wisdom, and my disciple because you have accepted my decision.

Rabban Gamliel stood up and kissed Rabbi Yehoshua, saying, "Come in peace, my master and my disciple: my master in wisdom, and my disciple because you have accepted my decision."

The king had a major role in the nation, but he had to be guided by God's word as conveyed by the prophet and the Sanhedrin.

Clearly, a man of Rabban Gamliel's greatness was not motivated by a desire to win a power struggle with an influential adversary. As *Nasi*, it was his responsibility to uphold the authority of the court and keep the nation from splitting into factions. The same applies to the relationship between the king, the prophet, and the court. As we will see below, the king had a major role in the nation, but he had to be guided by God's word as conveyed by the prophet and by the Halachah, as decided by the Sanhedrin.

Hierarchy of Values

As noted above, before stating the commandment of the monarchy, the Torah presents a passage stating the absolute authority of the court. By doing so, the Torah places the royal scepter in its proper context. The king's power is very great. Powerful though he may be, however, and though the entire nation may owe him its allegiance, he remains subject to the higher authority of God, His prophet, and His Sanhedrin.

It is not the role of the king of Israel to conquer the Land and secure Israel's possession of it.

The commandment to have a king states clearly that the mitzvah takes effect only after the Land was conquered and settled: "*When you come to the Land that* H*ASHEM*, *your God, gives you,* וִירִשְׁתָּהּ וְיָשַׁבְתָּה בָּהּ, *and you possess it and settle in it* (*Deuteronomy* 7:14). In commenting on this verse, R' Hirsch writes, "These words, which introduce the section on the king, state unequivocally at the very outset that it is not the role of the king of Israel to *conquer the Land and secure Israel's possession of it.* It is *not* his role to build up

power to be used externally. For it is God who gives the Land to Israel," and with His help they will defeat their enemies, as Moses promised over and over again in the Book of *Deuteronomy.* To accomplish this, Israel does not need a king. All it needs to do to possess and settle its Promised Land is to be God's people and remain loyal to Him and His Torah; then, by being victorious over its own base instincts, it would be victorious over its enemies.

All it needs to do to possess and settle its Promised Land is to be God's people and remain loyal to Him and His Torah.

According to the Halachah, the commandment to appoint a king would take effect only after the Land was conquered and divided among the tribes and families (*Kiddushin* 37b). But if the king was not needed until after the wars of conquest, when the nation was at peace, what was his function? And what does the Torah mean when it says that Israel will desire a king *like all the nations that are around me* (*Deuteronomy* 17:14) — if it is a commandment, why does it depend on the nation's desire? And why should God's chosen nation seek to emulate *all the nations that are around me* — is that not a contradiction to Israel's Divine calling to be unique?

But if the king was not needed until after the wars of conquest, when the nation was at peace, what was his function?

Like Other Nations

R' Hirsch writes that nations institute governments of whatever sort — monarchies, democracies, or oligarchies — to unify and organize the nation for the greatest good of the people. The primary goal is defense, but not far behind are conquest, commerce, and prosperity, as the case may be. Israel is no different from its neighbors in wanting a head of state to foster its interests, but its interests are unlike theirs. The surrounding countries needed kings to organize and lead armies, as we find throughout *Tanach* that Israel was constantly forced to defend itself against foreign invaders.

Israel is no different from its neighbors in wanting a head of state to foster its interests, but its interests are unlike theirs.

Like all nations, Israel would also need a leader who would unite it and organize its citizens to strive toward its national goal. But its goal was unique to the nation of God. In the words of R' Hirsch:

> You, too, will feel the need for national unity in order to obtain the greatest possible good for yourself, but you deem this good to lie solely

in the most complete fulfillment of the Torah *in your own midst*. For this purpose, you, too, will seek to establish national unity by means of subordination to one head of state. But the function of your head of state will be to stand out as the first among all Jews loyal to the Torah — to shine forth personally in all the moral nobility of this allegiance to the Torah. Imbued with the spirit of your mission, he will seek to win over all hearts and minds to this spirit, in thought, word, and deed. With the power of his word, his personal example, and his personal prestige, he will combat anything that would violate this spirit. You are to place all your resources at his command so that he may fight for and defend your national mission internally.

Your head of state will stand out as the first among all Jews loyal to the Torah — to shine forth in allegiance to the Torah.

The Moral Commander

That goal could not be achieved as long as Israel was fighting wars of conquest with the Canaanite nations, because at such a time all but the most spiritual Jews would have looked at their king as a commander in chief who was to be their leader in battle, not as their moral role model. That is why a monarchy in Israel would have to wait until the Land — all of it — was possessed and settled.

But this condition had not been met. As Scripture laments, the Jews did not complete the conquest of the land, and the result was tragic. Moses had warned that if any Canaanites were permitted to remain, they would be constant sources of pain and harrassment (*Numbers* 33:55). Joshua echoed this warning on the last day of his life (*Joshua* 23:12-13). Unfortunately, Canaanite idolaters *were* allowed to remain, with the result that their religious perversion infiltrated Israel, and idolatry became a national cancer. Therefore, as Rabbi Yehudah put it (*Sifre*):

Moses had warned that if any Canaanites were permitted to remain, they would be constant sources of pain and harrassment.

Unfortunately, Canaanite idolaters were allowed to remain.

> *The people were commanded by Scripture to request a king . . . why then were they punished [when they did so] in the days of Samuel?* לְפִי שֶׁהִקְדִּימוּ עַל יָדָם, *because they acted too soon.*

The people of Israel demanded a royal field marshal to lead them in battle. Samuel responded, "HASHEM, your God, is your King!"

Instead of following leaders who would remove the Canaanite influence from the Land, the people of Israel demanded a royal field marshal to lead them in battle; as they said when they presented their petition to Samuel, they feared attack by the king of Ammon, and they needed a king to lead and defend them. At such a time and to such a demand, Samuel responded, *"HASHEM, your God, is your King!"* (12:12). When Samuel lamented to God that the people had repudiated him, Samuel, despite his grueling and unselfish service to them, God responded, *"It is not you whom they have rejected, but it is Me whom they have rejected from reigning over them"* (8:7).

Had they waited until the right time, a request for a king would have been not a rejection, but a validation of the leadership of Samuel and the sovereignty of God, for their request would have represented a sincere desire to strive for closeness to God and to do so by having a leader who would unite them in this quest.

Tragedy Without a King

The Book of *Judges* concludes with two of the most tragic episodes in the period of the Judges. The first is פֶּסֶל מִיכָה, *Micah's Molten Image,* in which a substantial portion of the tribe of Dan succumbed to idolatry (*Judges* Chs. 17,18). The second is פִּלֶגֶשׁ בְּגִבְעָה, *the Concubine in Gibeah,* in which an atrocity in the town of Gibeah led to national revulsion and a civil war with 80,000 casualties (ibid. Chs. 19-21). The two incidents demonstrated a lack of faith in God and perverted morality — exactly the sort of deficiencies that a king would be responsible to combat. And about both tragedies Scripture says no less than four times, that there was no king in Israel, as if to groan that such things could happen to a holy nation when it lacked a strong leader:

The two incidents demonstrated a lack of faith in God and perverted morality — exactly the sort of deficiencies that a king would be responsible to combat.

> בַּיָּמִים הָהֵם אֵין מֶלֶךְ בְּיִשְׂרָאֵל אִישׁ הַיָּשָׁר בְּעֵינָיו יַעֲשֶׂה
>
> *In those days there was no king in Israel; a man would do whatever was proper in his eyes* (*Judges* 17:6, 21:25; see also 18:1, 19:1).

Samuel had begun the task of uniting the people

and bringing them close to their Torah-ordained goal. What would have happened if the people had not made their premature demand for a king? We do not know. Perhaps Samuel would have completed the task of preparing the people for the monarchy by finally ridding the Land of the Canaanite nations. Perhaps in his time or in the time of one of his successors the nation would have been made ready to have a king in the role that God had intended. Be that as it may, the people demanded a king, and the era of the hereditary monarchy came into existence.

What would have happened if the people had not made their premature demand for a king? We do not know.

This Book and those that follow tell the story of that era and the prophets whom God sent to guide the kings and the nation. No longer would these spiritual giants be merely "seers." They would be "prophets," who would transmit the word of God to their own generations and all the succeeding ones until our time.

The great founder and leader of the Frankfurt *kehillah* that was transplanted to Washington Heights, Rabbi Yosef Breuer, would often ask students if they studied *Tanach*. Usually the answer was no. He would ask, "Have David and Isaiah nothing to teach you?" Indeed, they have much to teach us. The Book of *Samuel* sets the stage for a new era in the history of the Jewish people, and this masterful commentary enables us to begin absorbing its lessons.

"Have David and Isaiah nothing to teach you?" Indeed, they have much to teach us.

Rabbi Nosson Scherman

Adar Sheni 5771 / March 2011

shmuel I

א וַיְהִי֩ אִ֨ישׁ אֶחָ֜ד מִן־הָרָמָתַ֛יִם צוֹפִ֖ים מֵהַ֣ר אֶפְרָ֑יִם

Introduction

The Book of *Samuel* begins, appropriately, with a portrayal of the unusual circumstances leading to the birth of its title figure. We are introduced to Samuel's illustrious parents and apprised of their deeds, piety, and intense prayer, in whose merit Samuel was born.[1]

I

Elkanah's Pilgrimage

1. וַיְהִי — *There was.*

וַיְהִי literally means *"and there was"* (the initial letter *vav* means *and*). In our translation, we elide the *and*, following *Radak*, who maintains that the *vav* is merely a linguistic convention that indicates no direct connection to the preceding text of the Book of *Judges*.[2] *Radak* does acknowledge a connection between the concluding episode of *Judges* and the opening verses of *Samuel;* however, he claims that it cannot be derived from the word וַיְהִי.

Rashi is apparently of the contrary opinion and to indicate the continuity between the two Books cites the opening mishnah of *Pirkei Avos*: *Moses acquired the Torah at Sinai and transferred it to Joshua, and Joshua [transferred it] to the Elders, and the Elders to the Prophets.* Until this point, Scripture documented the periods of Moses (the *Pentateuch*), Joshua (the Book of *Joshua*), and the Elders (the Book of *Judges*). Now it begins to describe the period of the Prophets, the first one being Samuel.[3]

Abarbanel agrees with *Rashi* and *Metzudos* that the letter *vav* plays a connective function. However, he cites a different rationale for the placement of *Samuel*, one that he derives from the Midrash (*Vayikra Rabbah* 32:6). The final few chapters of the Book of *Judges* describe the horrific incident of the concubine in Gibeah, an episode that had catastrophic consequences for the Jewish nation, and which implicated (among others) a Levite from Mt. Ephraim. In order to protect the reputation of the Levites, as well as of the inhabitants of Mt. Ephraim, that narrative is immediately followed by the portrayal of Elkanah, a pious and exemplary Levite from Mt. Ephraim, who fathered Samuel, the great benefactor of the Jewish people.

The narration of the concubine of Gibeah is directly preceded by the description of the idol of Micah, which also describes a Levite who spent time on Mt. Ephraim (*Ralbag*).

אִישׁ אֶחָד — *A certain man.*

This unconventional phrase literally means "one man," implying that this man was "one of a kind" — i.e., uniquely

1. Like two other barren women, Sarah and Rachel, Samuel's mother Hannah was *remembered* by God and she conceived on Rosh Hashanah (*Rosh Hashanah* 10b). Thus the Torah portion describing Sarah's conception is read on the first day of Rosh Hashanah, and the *Haftarah* of that day is taken from the present narrative (*Megillah* 31a).

2. Having elaborated on this concept at the beginning of *Joshua, Radak* briefly reiterates it here.

3. *Rashi's* explanation is consistent with his interpretation of the same word, וַיְהִי, with which the Book of *Joshua* opens, which he sees as being directly related to the end of *Chumash*. *Metzudos* (ibid.) expresses this idea more explicitly.

It is noteworthy that although Samuel authored both the Books of *Judges* and *Samuel* (see *Bava Basra* 14b), the two Books were separated in order to distinguish between the period of the Elders and the period of the Prophets (*R' Yaakov Kamenetsky*, cited by *Mishbetzos Zahav*).

[1] *There was a certain man from Ramathaim-zophim, from Mount Ephraim,*

great. Our Sages derive from this that Elkanah was a Torah leader unparalleled in his time (*Bamidbar Rabbah* 10:5).

Malbim comments that the word אֶחָד, *one*, implies that Elkanah was uniquely distinguished in having been the father of the illustrious Samuel.

According to *Ahavas Yehonasan*, this phrase emphasizes the contrast between Elkanah and the Levite involved in the episode of the concubine of Gibeah, and as such reads the verse as stating, "There was [however], one Levite from Mt. Ephraim [who reached exalted heights]" (*Me'am Loez*).

מִן־הָרָמָתַיִם צוֹפִים — *From Ramathaim-zophim.*

The Talmudic Sages and subsequent commentators raise many questions regarding the name of Elkanah's hometown. Among them are:

❒ Are both רָמָתַיִם and צוֹפִים parts of the name, or is one perhaps a modifying adjective?

❒ Why does the word רָמָתַיִם contain the duplicating suffix תַיִם? Were there possibly two such towns?

❒ Why is there a deviation from the commonly used name רָמָה (see v. 19 below)?

In responding to these questions, various monumental facts are derived. The first three mentioned below are introduced in the Talmud (*Megillah* 14a).

The word רָמָתַיִם derives from רָם, *high*, referring to a tall mountain. רָמָתַיִם — which literally means *two heights* — therefore means *two tall mountains*. The root of צוֹפִים is צוֹפֶה, *gaze*. Thus, רָמָתַיִם צוֹפִים can be read as *two high peaks that gaze at each other*, i.e., they were close and symmetrical. Elkanah lived on one of those peaks (*Radak*), referred to in the singular by the word רָמָתָה (*Maharsha*).

Abarbanel entertains the notion that Elkanah's wives, Hannah and Peninnah, each lived on a separate peak.

Approaching the verse homiletically, the Talmud (*ibid.*) splits the word רָמָתַיִם into two numerical units. The first letter of רָמָתַיִם, the *reish*, has the numerical value of 200. The remainder of the word may be read as מָאתַיִם, which also means 200 (see *Maharsha, Chidushei Aggados, Megillah* 14a). Thus, Elkanah was one of 200 seers of his generation who prophesied for the Jewish people (see *Maharsha ibid.*).[1]

According to this explanation, the word צוֹפֶה, *gaze*, is also a reference to a *prophet* for, as Scripture relates later, *for "the prophet" of today was formerly called "the seer"* (9:9).

The word רָמָתַיִם can also be understood as providing information about Elkanah's ancestry. He traced his lineage to *those who stand at the height of the world:* these being the three sons of Korah, one of whom, Abiasaf, was Elkanah's paternal ancestor. When the earth swallowed Korah and his followers after their mutiny against Moses, Korahs' sons' last-minute remorse saved them. God established an elevated position for them in Gehinnom, where they stood and sang praises to Him (*Megillah* ibid.; *Yalkut Shimoni;* see *Rashi* to *Psalms* 42:1; also see *Sanhedrin* 110a and *Rashi* there). Following this interpretation, the word צוֹפִים retains its meaning of *prophets*, since these sons of Korah were indeed prophets.

1. This mention of 200 prophets clearly disputes the oft-quoted statement that there were 48 male prophets in the Biblical era: one of those prophets being, incidentally, Elkanah (for the full list, see *Rashi* on *Megillah* ibid.).

The Talmud resolves this contradiction by stating that there were many thousands of prophets during Biblical times; however, only 48 of them delivered prophecies that contained lessons germane for all generations.

וּשְׁמוֹ אֶלְקָנָה בֶּן־יְרֹחָם בֶּן־אֱלִיהוּא בֶּן־תֹּחוּ
ב בֶּן־צוּף אֶפְרָתִי: וְלוֹ שְׁתֵּי נָשִׁים שֵׁם אַחַת
חַנָּה וְשֵׁם הַשֵּׁנִית פְּנִנָּה וַיְהִי לִפְנִנָּה יְלָדִים
ג וּלְחַנָּה אֵין יְלָדִים: וְעָלָה הָאִישׁ הַהוּא מֵעִירוֹ

Ralbag suggests that the word רָמָתַיִם connotes no duality. Rather, just as an inhabitant of Egypt was a מִצְרִי and many were מִצְרִיִּים, an individual from רָמָה was a רָמָתִי, and many were רָמָתִיִּים, or, also, רָמָתַיִם.

Ralbag adds that these רָמָתִיִּים may have been referred to as צוֹפִים, because they descended from a man named צוּף, as the verse goes on to relate. *Malbim* supports this idea by noting that the genealogy listed here ends with צוּף.

מֵהַר אֶפְרָיִם — *From Mount Ephraim.*

As previously mentioned, Elkanah was actually a Levite, descending from Korah, who was a member of the family of Kohath. They had been allotted portions of land on Mt. Ephraim (*Joshua* 21:21; *Radak*; see also *Malbim*).

וּשְׁמוֹ אֶלְקָנָה — *Whose name was Elkanah.*

Although there is no clear indication of Elkanah's tribal affiliation in the Book of *Samuel*, it is universally agreed that he was an offspring of Korah's son, Abiasaf.[1]

The assertion that Elkanah was a prophet and, as such, an exalted personality, is supported by the phrase, וּשְׁמוֹ אֶלְקָנָה — *and his name was Elkanah* — for, as the Midrash states, in Scripture the phraseology *his name was* indicates the introduction of a righteous man (*Bamidbar Rabbah* 10:5).[2]

In addition, *Abarbanel* asserts that Elkanah's very name testifies to his piety, for it means אֵל קָנָה, *God has acquired [him as His private possession].*[3]

בֶּן־יְרֹחָם בֶּן־אֱלִיהוּא בֶּן־תֹּחוּ בֶּן־צוּף — *Son of Jeroham, son of Elihu, son of Tohu, son of Zuph.*

In the parallel passage in *Chronicles* (*I Chronicles* 6:11,12,19) the names Elihu, Tohu, and Zuph appear slightly altered.

אֶפְרָתִי — *From the land of Ephraim.*

Noting that the verse already stated that Elkanah came from Mt. Ephraim, *Radak* concludes that this phrase refers not to Elkanah but to his ancestor Zuph. The family had resided in the land of Ephraim for many generations.

Rashi states — basing himself on a Midrash — that אֶפְרָתִי is related to אַפִּרְיוֹן, *esteemed*, and thus may be translated as *an honorable man* — an apt reference to Elkanah (see ArtScroll *Ruth* 1:2).[4]

2. שֵׁם אַחַת חַנָּה — *One's name was Hannah.*

Our Sages remark that Hannah was Elkanah's first wife, and that due to her initiative he took a second wife. Hannah's motivation was the same as that of the Matriarchs Sarah and Rachel in their day: to selflessly help her husband father a child despite the suffering

1. The details of his genealogy may be found in *I Chronicles* (6:7-12, 19-23).

2. Conversely, the phrase "... *was his name*" — e.g., "Goliath was his name" — indicates the opposite. See also *ArtScroll Esther* 2:5.

3. Further on (2:27), Elkanah is referred to as אִישׁ־אֱלֹהִים, *a man of God*, a glorious appellation otherwise applied only to Moses.

4. *Kli Yakar* quotes a Midrash (*Midrash Shocher Tov*) that sheds further light on this topic. Jacob gave Ephraim the blessing that praiseworthy people would be associated with his name. Hence, we learn: אֶלְקָנָה ... אֶפְרָתִי; וְדָוִד בֶּן־אִישׁ אֶפְרָתִי (17:12), and so forth. (See also *Ruth Rabbah* 2:5, as well as *Kli Yakar's* beautiful exposition on how Ephraim's humility earned him this honor.)

whose name was Elkanah, son of Jeroham, son of Elihu, son of Tohu, son of Zuph, from the land of Ephraim. [2] *He had two wives; the name of one was Hannah and the name of the second was Peninnah. Peninnah had children, but Hannah had no children.* [3] *This man would ascend from his city*

that the acquisition of a rival wife would cause her, in the hope that God would then reward her by granting her children of her own (*Yalkut Shimoni*).

Malbim substantiates this assertion on the basis of the phrase, שֵׁם אַחַת, "the name of one," which deviates noticeably from the standard phrase, שֵׁם הָאַחַת, *the name of one of them* (as in, for example, שֵׁם הָאַחַת שִׁפְרָה וְשֵׁם הַשֵּׁנִית פּוּעָה, *the name of one of them was Shifrah and the name of the second was Puah* [*Exodus* 1:15]). "The name of one" implies that there was originally only one wife — i.e., Hannah.

Kli Yakar[1] adds that even after Elkanah married Peninnah, he retained a special affection for Hannah (see v. 5). Thus, in his eyes she remained אַחַת, *one*, or *unique* (as in the phrase, אַחַת הִיא יוֹנָתִי תַמָּתִי, *Unique is My perfect dove* [*Song of Songs* 6:9]; see also *Megillah* 28a regarding *Numbers* 28:4).[2]

Kli Yakar offers another interpretation of the word אַחַת, *one*. Just as the reference to Elkanah as אִישׁ אֶחָד, *a certain man*, lit., *one man* (v. 1), indicates his greatness, so too does אַחַת here allude to the uniqueness of Hannah's character.

וּלְחַנָּה אֵין יְלָדִים — *But Hannah had no children.*

The Midrash and various commentators state that Hannah was barren, suffering from a physiological defect that prevented her from having children. Thus *Yalkut Shimoni* sees an allusion to Hannah in the verse, מוֹשִׁיבִי עֲקֶרֶת הַבַּיִת אֵם־הַבָּנִים שְׂמֵחָה, *He transforms the barren wife into a glad mother of children* [*Psalms* 113:9].[3]

However, *Abarbanel* notes that the present verse describes Hannah simply as אֵין יְלָדִים, she *had no children*, and he contends, accordingly, that there was nothing physically wrong with her. Only Providential intervention *closed her womb* (verse 5).[4]

3. וְעָלָה — *Would ascend.*

Our translation is based on *Rashi*, who renders this word in the recurring

1. *Kli Yakar* on Prophets (which is cited extenstively in this volume) was written by R' Shmuel Laniado. It should not be confused with *Kli Yakar* on *Chumash*, written by R' Shlomo Ephraim Lunchitz.

2. It may be that because Elkanah exhibited a preference for Hannah, God awarded Peninnah children first. This would be similar to the case of Leah and Rachel and their relationship with Jacob (*Ralbag*, end of Chapter 7).

3. *Rema MiPanu* mentions in *Gilgulei Nishamos* that Elkanah was a *gilgul* (*reincarnation*) of Lemech (see *Genesis* 4:19, 20, and *Rashi* ad loc.), and Hannah was a *gilgul* of his wife Zilah, who was sterilized and could not bear children, while Peninnah was a *gilgul* of his other wife Adah, who bore children. Thus, Hashem removed the effects of the sterilizing drug, allowing Hannah to bear children.

4. The Talmud attributes God's purpose in inflicting childlessness on some righteous people to His desire to hear their prayers (*Yevamos* 64a).

Rabbi Elie Munk explains that "then the child who would be born would be much more than a gift of nature. He would be born at the price of tears from his mother and supplication from his righteous father. He would be designated from birth as being the child of Providence" (*The Call of the Torah*, *Genesis* 11:30).

present tense, in accord with the grammatical rule that he explicates in *Genesis* (29:3), that such verbs can be presented either in the past or future tense.

וְעָלָה הָאִישׁ הַהוּא מֵעִירוֹ — *This man would ascend from his city.*

Malbim notes that the term, הָאִישׁ הַהוּא, *this man,* implies that Elkanah was alone in this endeavor. Elkanah was the only man *of his city* to regularly make the excursion to Shiloh. Because — as the end of the verse relates — the priests who served there were the sons of Eli (see 2:12-17), whose turpitude was infamous, most people chose to avoid them. This explanation illuminates the apparently gratuitous mention of Eli's two sons at this point.

Although, as *Abarbanel* and *Malbim* comment, Elkanah too suffered the discomforts of dealing with these two corrupt individuals, he remained scrupulously conscientious in discharging his halachic obligations.

מֵעִירוֹ — *From his city.*

This word is ostensibly superfluous. As mentioned above, *Malbim* connects it to הָאִישׁ הַהוּא to deduce that he was the only one from his city who went.

Ralbag employs מֵעִירוֹ to resolve a perplexity. Why did Elkanah only go to Shiloh מִיָּמִים יָמִימָה, *once a year,* rather than for each of the three pilgrimage festivals? *Ralbag* states that he did in fact travel three times a year; however, only once a year did he bring along his wives and children (who were exempt from the obligation of the festival pilgrimage). In support of this view, *Ralbag* reads the phrase, וְעָלָה הָאִישׁ הַהוּא מֵעִירוֹ מִיָּמִים יָמִימָה, as stating that *Once a year, he would completely vacate from his city, leaving none of his household behind.*[1]

Our Sages relate that Elkanah was committed to influencing other Jews to make the holiday pilgrimages too, and as such never went on the same route more than once, so that his impressive entourage would always attract new adherents (*Rashi; Yerushalmi Berachos* 9:5).

According to the commentator to *Talmud Yerushalmi,* this is implied in the word, מֵעִירוֹ, *from his city.* The only part of the trip that Elkanah regularly repeated was *from his city.*[2]

מִיָּמִים יָמִימָה — *From year to year.*

We follow the most widely accepted rendering of these words. In support of this translation, *Radak* refers to the

1. *Ralbag* (following Chapter 7) and *Abarbanel* assert that Elkanah brought his extended family with him to Shiloh even though many of them were halachically exempt from going.

He did so for two reasons. First, he believed that an exposure to the Temple rituals would secure their unequivocal faith. Second, this gathering of the entire family would ensure the attainment of a jubilant spirit. It is therefore presumable that the family would go on Succos, the joyous peak of the year, described by Scripture as "the time of our joy."

2. The Sages laud Elkanah for adapting this meritorious custom.

Yalkut Shimoni describes in detail the fanfare with which Elkanah surrounded this communal journey. He would bring his entire extended family into the streets of the city to sleep there overnight (*Kli Yakar* sees this as alluded to in the word מֵעִירוֹ, *from his city*; see also *Radak, Ein Yaakov* to *Yerushalmi Berachos* ibid.).

When the residents asked them why they were doing so, they responded, "We are on our way to Shiloh, the source of Torah and mitzvos. Won't you join us?" Many Jews would weep in a spirit of repentance and accompany them.

God told Elkanah that as a reward for having influenced so many Jews to walk upon the proper path, he would be given a son who would also educate the Jewish people and lead them on the path of righteousness. Particularly, since Elkanah circled from city to city to bring Jews to the pilgrimage, he merited to have Samuel, who would circle from city to city to judge the Jews (see below, 6:16, *Me'am Loez* ad loc.).

from year to year to prostrate himself and to bring offerings to HASHEM, *Master of Legions,*

identical phrase used in a verse describing the Passover routine: וְשָׁמַרְתָּ אֶת־הַחֻקָּה הַזֹּאת לְמוֹעֲדָהּ מִיָּמִים יָמִימָה, *You shall observe this decree at its designated time from year to year* (*Exodus* 13:10).

Metzudos points out that the word יָמִים (literally, *days*) is often used to refer to a year, as in the phrase, יָמִים תִּהְיֶה גְאֻלָּתוֹ, *The [period of] redemption [for a residential house in a walled city] shall be a year* (*Leviticus* 25:29; see also *Kesubos* 57b).

This translation is supported by verse 7, which explicitly states that וְכֵן יַעֲשֶׂה שָׁנָה בְשָׁנָה, *This is what [Elkanah] would do year after year* (*Abarbanel*).

When did Elkanah make his annual trip?

Midrash Shmuel states that it was for Shavuos.

Another Midrash, pointing out that the phrase, מִיָּמִים יָמִימָה — *once a year* — is found both here and in regard to Passover (as we saw earlier), concludes that it occurred on Passover.

Ralbag and *Abarbanel* presume that it took place on Succos (see footnote 1 on p. 6).

Finally, *Shnei Luchos HaBris*, on the basis of the Talmudic teaching that Hannah was "remembered" on Rosh Hashanah, assumes that it was then that she supplicated God, and therefore concludes that Elkanah's yearly excursion took place on Rosh Hashanah (see *Mishbetzos Zahav*).

As previously mentioned, *Ralbag* maintains that Elkanah traveled to Shiloh on each pilgrimage festival. The view that Elkanah went to Shiloh three times a year is supported by a tradition recorded in the *Talmud Yerushalmi* that [Elkanah] would lead the Jews on the footsteps of their [festival] pilgrimage (*Berachos* 9:5).

Those commentators who state that Elkanah went to Shiloh only once a year offer varying rationales for his absence during the other occasions. For instance, *Panim Yafos* suggests that the mandate to appear three times a year took effect only after the Temple in Jerusalem was inaugurated (see *Ramban* to *Deuteronomy* 16:11, see also *Nachalas Shimon* for an exhaustive review of this subject).

Rashi quotes *Targum Yonasan's* rendering of מִיָּמִים יָמִימָה as *from designated time to designated [time]* — i.e., from holiday to holiday, the implication being that Elkanah visited Shiloh three times a year, in accordance with the Torah's demands.

לְהִשְׁתַּחֲוֹת — *To prostrate himself.*

Based on *Targum*, we translate לְהִשְׁתַּחֲוֹת literally as *to prostrate himself*, a common gesture of respect upon arriving at a holy site (*Ralbag*).

However, the Sages and most commentators understand לְהִשְׁתַּחֲוֹת to be a figurative reference to prayer (for prayer was generally accompanied by prostrating oneself [*Malbim*]). Thus, the verse is telling us that Elkanah came to the Sanctuary to pray.

Ralbag comments that although prayer is acceptable even when performed at home, it is preferable when performed in the Holy Temple.

וְלִזְבֹּחַ — *And to bring offerings.*

The appropriate festival offerings (*Radak, Ralbag*).

לְהִשְׁתַּחֲוֹת וְלִזְבֹּחַ לַה׳ צְבָאוֹת — *To prostrate himself and to bring offerings to* HASHEM, *Master of Legions.*

Malbim observes that two subsequent references to Elkanah's visits to Shiloh (verses 1:21 and 2:19) mention *offerings* but not *prayer*. He infers from this that Elkanah's initial purpose in going to Shiloh was to beg for Hannah to conceive, a task whose necessity eventually ceased. This is also evident from the unusual usage here of the name ה׳ צְבָאוֹת, HASHEM, *Master of Legions*, which is the same formula that Hannah used in her prayer (verse 11; see commentary).

בְּשִׁלֹה וְשָׁם שְׁנֵי בְנֵי־עֵלִי חָפְנִי וּפִנְחָס כֹּהֲנִים
ד לַיהוָה: וַיְהִי הַיּוֹם וַיִּזְבַּח אֶלְקָנָה וְנָתַן לִפְנִנָּה
ה אִשְׁתּוֹ וּלְכָל־בָּנֶיהָ וּבְנוֹתֶיהָ מָנוֹת: וּלְחַנָּה
יִתֵּן מָנָה אַחַת אַפָּיִם כִּי אֶת־חַנָּה אָהֵב
ו וַיהוָה סָגַר רַחְמָהּ: וְכִעֲסַתָּה צָרָתָהּ גַּם־כַּעַס

From this text our Sages draw a number of conclusions regarding the relative significance of prayer and sacrificial offerings. For instance, Rabbi Yitzchak states that the fact that לְהִשְׁתַּחֲוֹת precedes לִזְבֹּחַ indicates that prayer is superior to sacrifice. Another opinion derives that prayer is equal to all of the sacrifices together (*Yalkut Shimoni;* see also *Radak; Berachos* 32b).

בְּשִׁלֹה — *In Shiloh.*

During the 14 years that Joshua was engaged in conquering and apportioning the Land of Israel, the Tabernacle stood in the city of Gilgal, from which it was transferred to Shiloh (*Joshua* 18:1; see commentary to ArtScroll *Yehoshua*). For 369 years, the Tabernacle in Shiloh served as the focal point of the Jews' service to God (*Zevachim* 118b), until it was subsequently located in Nob and Gibeon.

During the periods that the Tabernacle was in Gilgal, Nob, and Gibeon, it was permissible to offer certain sacrifices on a private altar. However, while the Tabernacle was in Shiloh, ritual sacrifices had to be offered there exclusively (ibid. 112b).

וְשָׁם שְׁנֵי בְנֵי־עֵלִי חָפְנִי וּפִנְחָס — *Where the two sons of Eli — Hophni and Phinehas.*

Upon mentioning Elkanah's sacrifices, the verse introduces us to these two priests, whose practices in regard to offerings will shortly be related (*Radak*).

Seemingly, this is mentioned here to emphasize that one of the reasons that the Jews had become lax in ascending to Shiloh was because of the unscrupulous behavior of the sons of Eli (see below, Ch. 2), which deterred people from coming. Still, Elkanah succeeded in influencing the masses to ignore the discomfort and make the pilgrimage (*Be'er Moshe, Mishbetzos Zahav;* see *Radak* below, 2:24).

עֵלִי — *Eli.*

Eli, a Kohen from the family of Ithamar (son of Aharon), was both High Priest and Judge of the Jewish people. In addition, Eli was one of the 48 primary prophets (*Rashi, Megillah* 14a; see footnote on page 3), and in the chain of transmission of the Torah from Moses through the generations, he represents the link just prior to Samuel (*Rambam,* Introduction to *Mishneh Torah*).

⸎ Hannah's Pain

4. וַיְהִי הַיּוֹם — *It happened on the day.*

According to Rabbi Yehoshua ben Levi, this is a reference to Shavuos (*Midrash Shmuel;* see above, v. 3). *Zayis Ra'anan* explains that הַיּוֹם — *the day* — implies a holiday that lasts just one day which is, of course, Shavuos.

וַיִּזְבַּח אֶלְקָנָה וְנָתַן לִפְנִנָּה אִשְׁתּוֹ ... מָנוֹת — *Elkanah brought offerings that he gave portions to Peninnah, his wife ...*

"[Proper] gladness [on a holiday] is aroused only with meat [from a peace-offering]" (*Pesachim* 109a). Since a husband is responsible for gladdening his wife, Elkanah gave his wives portions of meat (*Malbim*).

5. וּלְחַנָּה יִתֵּן — *But to Hannah he gave.*

Although the word יִתֵּן, *he gave,* is generally used to indicate the future tense, *Radak* finds precedence for usage of such words in the past tense (citing the phrase, אָז יַבְדִּיל מֹשֶׁה, *Then Moses set aside* [*Deuteronomy* 4:41]).

in Shiloh, where the two sons of Eli — Hophni and Phinehas — were Kohanim to HASHEM.

[4] It happened on the day that Elkanah brought offerings that he gave portions to Peninnah, his wife, and to all her sons and daughters. [5] But to Hannah he gave a double portion, for he loved Hannah and HASHEM had closed her womb.

[6] Her rival [Peninnah] provoked her again and

מָנָה אַחַת אַפָּיִם — *A double portion.*

The Sages and commentators differ in their interpretations of אַפָּיִם (lit., *faces*), which is an obscure description of Hannah's portion.

Our translation, based on *Yalkut Shimoni,* is closest to the literal meaning of the word, rendering "faces" as a figurative way of saying *twofold.*

However, how can a single phrase describe something as both אַחַת, *one,* and אַפָּיִם, *double?*

One answer to this question is to say that in accord with *Metzudos'* translation, אַחַת here means not "one" but "unique," or else to translate it as "exquisite" (as in אַחַת הוּא יוֹנָתִי תַמָּתִי, *Unique is My perfect dove* [*Song of Songs* 6:9]; see commentary to verse 1, אִישׁ אֶחָד, and to verse 2, שֵׁם אַחַת חַנָּה). Accordingly, the phrase may be translated as מָנָה אַחַת אַפָּיִם, *two special portions.* (However, *Metzudos* explains the word אַפָּיִם differently.)

Targum translates מָנָה אַחַת אַפָּיִם as *a choice portion,* something that, as *Rashi* states, would be received with a cheerful expression of the *face* (אַפָּיִם).

Ralbag offers two possible explanations of אַפָּיִם. One is that Elkanah offered Hannah a choice — i.e., between a plump and a lean portion. Alternatively, *Ralbag* proposes that Elkanah sat with Hannah *face-to-face* to demonstrate intimacy and a regard for her welfare. This explains why he realized that she had refrained from eating.

The word אַפָּיִם is often used in reference to *wrath,* as in the phrase, חֲרוֹן אַף. Accordingly, *Radak* states that Elkanah offered Hannah a מָנָה אַחַת, *a desirable portion* — אַפָּיִם — in order to appease her *exasperation.*

Conversely, *Radak* quotes his father's explanation that אַפָּיִם refers not to Hannah but to Elkanah, who was *angry* and dejected that he could serve Hannah no more than one portion, for he yearned to have children from her.

כִּי אֶת־חַנָּה אָהֵב וַה׳ סָגַר רַחְמָהּ — *For he loved Hannah and HASHEM had closed her womb.*

In order to soothe Hannah's grief, Elkanah exhibited his solicitude by offering her an especially honorable portion of meat (*Metzudos*).

Ahavas Yehonasan explains the sequence of this verse as follows. Cognizant that God delays the ability of the righteous to have children because He desires their supplications (*Yevamos* 64a; see above, verse 2), Elkanah loved Hannah precisely *because* "Hashem had closed her womb."

6. צָרָתָהּ — *Her rival* (*Peninnah*).

In a polygamous marriage, each wife is considered to be a צָרָה, *rival,* to her co-wives. The root of צָרָה is צַר, *enemy* (as in אִישׁ צַר וְאוֹיֵב [*Esther* 7:6]), for women in this situation generally dislike one another (see *Yevamos* 118a).

וְכִעֲסַתָּה צָרָתָהּ גַּם כַּעַס — *Her rival provoked her again and again.*

Rashi understands the phrase גַּם־כַּעַס to imply continuity and regularity.

Abarbanel sees in this verse an allusion to an interesting psychological phenomenon. Peninnah perturbed Hannah

ז בַּעֲבוּר הַרְּעִמָהּ כִּי־סָגַר יהוה בְּעַד רַחְמָהּ: וְכֵן יַעֲשֶׂה
שָׁנָה בְשָׁנָה מִדֵּי עֲלֹתָהּ בְּבֵית יהוה כֵּן תַּכְעִסֶנָּה
ח וַתִּבְכֶּה וְלֹא תֹאכַל: וַיֹּאמֶר לָהּ אֶלְקָנָה אִישָׁהּ חַנָּה
לָמֶה תִבְכִּי וְלָמֶה לֹא תֹאכְלִי וְלָמֶה יֵרַע לְבָבֵךְ

regarding petty matters unrelated to her infertility. Since Hannah was constantly embittered because of her misfortune, she reacted resentfully even to trivial annoyances.

The Sages tell us that Peninnah teased Hannah by asking her, "Have you bought a coat for your older grown son or a shirt for your younger son?" In the morning, she would ask Hannah, "Won't you wash your sons' faces before they go to school?" and at noon she would inquire, "Hannah, aren't you waiting for your sons to return from school?"

Also, when Elkanah distributed portions of the sacrifices, Peninnah would interject, "Give this son of mine his share," and "You haven't served this one yet" (*Pesikta*).

Metzudos describes הַרְּעִמָהּ as a synonym for זָעֵף, *depressed* (as in the description of Pharaoh's two imprisoned servants, וְהִנָּם זֹעֲפִים [*Genesis* 40:6]), and compares it to רָעֲמוּ פָּנִים, *their countenances were aggrieved* (*Ezekiel* 27:35).

Targum Yonasan renders הַרְּעִמָהּ as לְאַקְנָיוּתָהּ, *to engage her envy*.

Rashi, presumably associating the word with רַעַם, *thunder* (see commentary to ArtScroll *Ezekiel* ibid.), renders הַרְּעִמָהּ as *to stormily complain*. Accordingly, our Sages teach that God stated, "Just as thunder is always followed by rain, so will I assure that Hannah's complaints will be followed by the blessing of a child" (cf. *Midrash Shmuel*).

The Talmud relates that Peninnah was a righteous woman with an altruistic goal. Her intention in afflicting Hannah was בַּעֲבוּר הַרְּעִמָהּ, *to induce her to intensify her prayers*, so that God would accept them (*Bava Basra* 16a). This interpretation is supported by the phrase that introduces Peninnah: וְשֵׁם הַשֵּׁנִית פְּנִנָּה (verse 2), *and the name of the second*, for this formula indicates the introduction of a righteous person (*Ahavas Yehonasan*; see commentary above, verse 1).

But if Peninnah's motives were pure, why did eight of her sons die in retribution for tormenting Hannah? (*Midrash Shmuel*; see 2:5 and commentary for details).

Alshich contends that Peninnah's motives were essentially benign; but she was also impelled by a subtle trace of jealousy, because Elkanah's love for Hannah was greater than his love for her. Thus: וְכִעֲסַתָּה צָרָתָהּ, *her rival provoked her*, refers to the pain that she afflicted on Hannah, motivated by jealousy, and גַּם־כַּעַס בַּעֲבוּר הַרְּעִמָהּ, *provoked her again and again in order to irritate her*, is the pain that she caused Hannah in order to induce her to pray.

Me'am Loez (citing *Nachlas Reuven*) suggests that Peninnah erred in misjudging Hannah's character. Although Hannah was childless because God longed for her prayers, Peninnah suspected that Hannah was being punished for her sins and tried to induce her to repent. For her unwarranted judgment of Hannah, Peninnah was punished.

Sefer Chassidim (Chapter 48a) cites Peninnah as an example of a person with pure intentions who miscalculates and thus sins. Although such a person will be rewarded for his noble intentions, he also incurs discipline. (Other such instances include Uzza's mishap with the Holy Ark [*II Samuel* Ch. 6] and Jacob's concealment of Dinah from Esau [see *Rashi* on *Genesis* 32:23; see also *Nachalas Shimon*, Ch. 31].)

Rabbi Chaim Shmulevitz derives a profound concept from this episode. Just as a person sustains a burn if he touches fire, even if his intentions are positive, causing someone else pain — even for a virtuous reason — causes him to suffer tragic repercussions (*Sichos Mussar* 5731:24).

כִּי־סָגַר ה׳ בְּעַד רַחְמָהּ — *For HASHEM had closed her womb.*

The word בְּעַד in this phrase indicates

again in order to irritate her, for HASHEM had closed her womb. [7]This is what he would do year after year, and whenever she [Peninnah] would go up to the House of HASHEM, she would provoke her; she [Hannah] would cry and not eat. [8]Elkanah, her husband, said to her, "Hannah, why do you cry and why do you not eat? Why is your heart broken?

that Hashem had formed a closure before Hannah's womb (*Rashi*).[1]

7. וְכֵן יַעֲשֶׂה — *This is what he would do.*

The word יַעֲשֶׂה, *what he would do,* necessarily refers to Elkanah: he would pacify Hannah with especial affection (*Rashi, Metzudos*).

Abarbanel, however, maintains that this phrase alludes to Peninnah: every year, when the family ascended to the House of Hashem, she would provoke Hannah. (Although the phrase literally speaks of what *he* would do, *Abarbanel* cites other cases in which a male pronoun refers to a female.)

מִדֵּי עֲלֹתָהּ בְּבֵית ה׳ כֵּן תַּכְעִסֶנָּה — *Whenever she (Peninnah) would go up to the House of HASHEM, she would provoke her.*

As Scripture has already related, the friction between Hannah and Peninnah was exacerbated by Elkanah's distribution of portions of sacrificial meat during their pilgrimage to the House of Hashem (*Radak, Abarbanel*).

According to the Talmud's assertion that Peninnah intended to inspire Hannah to intensify her prayer, the ideal place to do this was the Sanctuary, where such petitions were speedily accepted (*Malbim, Abarbanel*).[2]

וַתִּבְכֶּה וְלֹא תֹאכַל — *She [Hannah] would cry and not eat.*

Excessive weeping made Hannah lose her appetite (*Metzudos*).

Alternatively, the Sages cite this verse to bolster the idea that when a person is in distress, crying has a satiating effect that removes the need to eat (a concept that they derive from the verse, הָיְתָה־לִּי דִמְעָתִי לֶחֶם יוֹמָם וָלָיְלָה, *For me, my tears were sustenance day and night* [*Psalms* 42:4; *Midrash Shmuel; Midrash Tehillim; Eichah Rabbah* 1:22]).

8. לָמֶה תִבְכִּי — *Why do you cry?*

Me'am Loez asserts that crying and grief often induce infertility.

וְלָמֶה לֹא תֹאכְלִי וְלָמֶה יֵרַע לְבָבֵךְ — *And why do you not eat? Why is your heart broken?*

Elkanah reminded Hannah that it was inappropriate to act so dejected because eating from the festival peace-offerings is a great privilege, and because one is obligated to be joyful on a festival (*Abarbanel*).

1. Unlike this verse, the preceding verse did not contain the word בְּעַד.

Kli Yakar observes that בְּעַד can mean *because of,* and on the basis of that offers the following exposition. The present verse offers Peninnah's perspective — i.e., that *HASHEM obstructed [passage of children] because of her womb.* That is to say, because Elkanah favored Hannah over Peninnah, Hannah was punished insofar as her own womb caused itself to be obstructed.

The previous verse, however, presented the proper, objective description of Hannah's childlessness: simply, *HASHEM had closed [Hannah's] womb* — through no fault of her own.

2. The verse employs the phrase, בְּבֵית ה׳, *in the House of HASHEM,* rather than *to the House of HASHEM.* From this, *Kli Yakar* derives that Peninnah's vexations were restricted to the period of time that she spent in the Temple area itself; otherwise, she maintained a civil disposition.

ט הֲלוֹא אָנֹכִי טוֹב לָךְ מֵעֲשָׂרָה בָּנִים: וַתָּקָם חַנָּה
אַחֲרֵי אָכְלָה בְשִׁלֹה וְאַחֲרֵי שָׁתֹה וְעֵלִי הַכֹּהֵן יֹשֵׁב
י עַל־הַכִּסֵּא עַל־מְזוּזַת הֵיכַל יהוה: וְהִיא מָרַת נָפֶשׁ

הֲלוֹא אָנֹכִי טוֹב לָךְ מֵעֲשָׂרָה בָּנִים — *Am I not better to you than ten sons?*

"Isn't my affection for you worth more than even 10 sons whom you might have borne?" (*Targum, Radak*).

The number 10 is a common representation for *many* (*Radak*).

However, *Rashi* understands the number 10 to refer specifically to Peninnah's sons, and states that Elkanah consoled Hannah, *I love you more than [I love Peninnah's] ten sons.*

Although women are exempt from the obligation of having children, women generally desire sons to take care of them — in the language of our Sages, as a staff for support in their old age, and as a shovel with which to bury them after they pass away (*Yevamos* 65b).

Thus, Elkanah consoled Hannah by asserting that אָנֹכִי טוֹב לָךְ מֵעֲשָׂרָה בָּנִים, *I can [provide those services] better than ten sons [could]* (*Malbim*).

Midrash Shmuel observes that Elkanah did not use the conventional word for I, אֲנִי, but rather אָנֹכִי, a reference to Hashem, as in (*Exodus* 20:2): אָנֹכִי ה׳ אֱלֹהֶיךָ, *I am* HASHEM, *your God.* With this, Elkanah implied that the knowledge that Hashem is with you should console you and cause all pain to subside (*Mishbetzos Zahav*).

◆§ Hannah's Prayer and Vow

Hannah, who was not only saintly but a prophetess (*Megillah* 14a), undoubtedly prayed with the utmost adherence to halachah and with deep devotion. Her approach to God and her choice of words were carefully planned and her sincerity unwavering. The Talmud (*Berachos* 30-31) exhaustively analyzes the following description of her prayer, from which it draws many lessons: some in regard to her fascinating methods of negotiating with God, and others pertaining to the laws of prayer.

9. וַתָּקָם חַנָּה — *Hannah arose.*

Having realized from Elkanah's conciliatory remarks that he had abandoned hope of her ever bearing children and thus had ceased praying on her behalf, Hannah saw that she must herself pray with the utmost urgency (*Malbim*).

אַחֲרֵי אָכְלָה בְשִׁלֹה וְאַחֲרֵי שָׁתֹה — *After eating in Shiloh and after drinking.*

Although Hannah sorrowfully abstained from eating, she nevertheless did eat a minimal amount of food in order to sustain herself (*Metzudos*). Also, considering the fact that this was either a festival or Rosh Hashanah, it may have been prohibited for her to fast (see *Pnei Yehoshua* to *Kesubos* 65a).

Abarbanel suggests that Hannah was calmed by Elkanah's sympathy and then was persuaded to eat.

Ralbag, however, sees no change in Hannah's attitude and abstinence from food and drink. Thus, Hannah states further on to Eli, יַיִן וְשֵׁכָר לֹא שָׁתִיתִי, *I have drunk neither wine nor strong drink* (verse 15). Accordingly, *Ralbag* states, the present verse is referring to her companions' eating and drinking.

Rashi seemingly concurs with this interpretation, for he states that the word אָכְלָה should not be read with a מַפִּיק ה which would have added the feminine possessive implication — "her eating" — but rather the ה is simply an appendage to the word and is indiscriminate of gender. Thus, the subject of these actions was left vague but, by implication, were Elkanah and his company.[1]

1. The Talmud (*Kesubos* 65a, according to *Tosafos* and *Maharsha*) explains this extra letter ה as being functionally similar to the מַפִּיק ה (albeit not completely — see *Shitah Mekubetzes* ibid.). Thus,

Am I not better to you than ten sons?"
9 Hannah arose after eating in Shiloh and after drinking; and Eli the Kohen was sitting on the chair, near the doorpost of the Sanctuary of HASHEM. *10 She was feeling bitter,*

וְעֵלִי הַכֹּהֵן יֹשֵׁב עַל־הַכִּסֵּא — *And Eli the Kohen was sitting on the chair.*

The unusual spelling of the word יֹשֵׁב, *sitting,* which makes the exegetic reading יָשַׁב, *he sat down,* possibly leads our Sages to state that Eli had been *seated* — i.e., appointed — on that day as High Priest (*Midrash Shmuel*).

Similarly, *Rashi* states that Eli had that day been inaugurated as national judge, or governor.

וְעֵלִי הַכֹּהֵן יֹשֵׁב עַל־הַכִּסֵּא עַל־מְזוּזַת הֵיכַל ה׳ — *And Eli the Kohen was sitting on the chair, near the doorpost of the Sanctuary of* HASHEM.

Although it is ordinarily forbidden to sit in the Temple Courtyard, there is a view that the Kohen Gadol is permitted to do so. *Midrash Shocher Tov* (Chapter 7) finds evidence for that view here (*Radak, Ralbag*).[1]

עַל־מְזוּזַת הֵיכַל ה׳ — *Near the doorpost of the Sanctuary of* HASHEM.

This phrase implies that Eli was *chief of the judicial body,* for similar terminology is used to describe scholars: e.g., לִשְׁמֹר מְזוּזֹת פְּתָחָי, *To watch the doorposts of my entrances* (*Proverbs* 8:34; *Me'am Loez,* citing *Midrash HaCheifetz*).

Why didn't Hannah ask Eli to pray on her behalf as per the Talmud's advice? (*Bava Basra* 116a). *Chasam Sofer* (*Derashos* Vol. II) suggests that since Eli had bad fortune in regard to children, as his children were not like him, his blessing may have had the adverse effect and extend that fortune to her as well.

10. וְהִיא מָרַת נָפֶשׁ — *She was feeling bitter.*

The potency of prayer is augmented when it comes from a brokenhearted individual whose devotion is pure and sincere. Although praying in a state of despondency is considered to be improper, that is only if a person is upset about matters extrinsic to his prayer. However, if his concern about a situation induces him to intensify his entreaties for relief, such a prayer is ideal (*Divrei Malkiel*; see *Nachalas Shimon*).

וַתִּתְפַּלֵּל עַל־ה׳ — *And she prayed to* HASHEM.

The phrase עַל־ה׳, literally, *on* HASHEM, is a variation of the more common אֶל ה׳, "to Hashem." *Ralbag* suggests that עַל־ה׳ means that Hannah faced westward, toward the innermost Sanctuary, which housed the Holy Ark.

Kli Yakar states that this phrase may be translated as *regarding [matters of]*

אַחֲרֵי אָכְלָה means *after her eating.* The words וְאַחֲרֵי שָׁתֹה, on the other hand, do not refer to a female.

According to this understanding, the verse may be read, *After [Hannah's time of] eating in Shiloh and after [his or their] drinking,* from which we may infer that Hannah did not drink wine. The Talmud concludes from this that it is improper for a woman to overindulge in wine (see *Mishnah Berurah* 170:13).

1. This seems to contradict the oft-quoted doctrine that, with the exception of the kings of the Davidic dynasty, this restriction applies to everyone, even the Kohen Gadol (cf. *Sotah* 40b, *Tosafos* ibid.).

Rema MiPanu suggests that a special dispensation for the Kohen Gadol (in particular for Eli, who was also chief judge) existed prior to the time that the members of the Davidic dynasty constructed the Holy Temple in Jerusalem (*Asarah Ma'amaros;* see *Nachalas Shimon, Mishbetzos Zahav*).

יא וַתִּתְפַּלֵּל עַל־יהוה וּבָכֹה תִבְכֶּה׃ וַתִּדֹּר נֶדֶר
וַתֹּאמַר יהוה צְבָאוֹת אִם־רָאֹה תִרְאֶה ׀ בָּעֳנִי
אֲמָתֶךָ וּזְכַרְתַּנִי וְלֹא־תִשְׁכַּח אֶת־אֲמָתֶךָ
וְנָתַתָּה לַאֲמָתְךָ זֶרַע אֲנָשִׁים וּנְתַתִּיו לַיהוה

HASHEM. Hannah's yearning to bear children was not a selfish one; rather, she wished to bring a son into the world who would perform good deeds and glorify God's Name.

Alternatively, she prayed on behalf of Hashem's Holy Name that she should not need to use the tactic of being forced to drink *sotah* waters (see below) which would cause His Name to be erased (*Mishbetzos Zahav,* from *R' Meir Premishlaner*).[1]

וּבָכֹה תִבְכֶּה — *Weeping continuously.*

Hannah wept because the *gates of tears* are never locked (*Berachos* 32b; *Ralbag*).

R' Chaim Volozhiner, cited by *R' Yosef Zundel of Salant,* derives from here that although weeping is inappropriate on Rosh Hashanah, if it comes by itself, one is not expected to suppress it.

11. וַתִּדֹּר נֶדֶר — *She made a vow.*

Our forefather Jacob introduced the practice of making a vow to God at a critical moment in one's life. Doing so is laudable and helps assure the success of one's prayers (*Genesis* 28:20; see Stone *Chumash* ibid.; *Bereishis Rabbah* 70).

צְבָאוֹת — *Master of Legions.*

The Talmud tells that this is the first time that this appellation of God was ever used. (The narration in verse 3 uses this term, but of course only after Hannah had already done so.) The Sages homiletically interpret Hannah's petition to God to mean, "Of all the multitudes of legions that You created in the universe, is it so difficult for You to give me one son?" (*Berachos* 31b).

Alternatively, Hannah pleaded, "Master of the Universe, You created two legions: one in heaven and one on earth. In heaven, Your host neither multiply nor die. On earth, Your host both procreate and die. Allow me one or the other: either to be like Your host on earth and procreate, or else like those in heaven so that I will never die" (*Rashi*).

רָאֹה תִרְאֶה — *If You take note.*

On the basis of the phrase, רָאֹה תִרְאֶה, literally, *see, You will see,* the Talmud (ibid.) states that Hannah challenged God in the following sensational manner: "רָאֹה — *If You will see* my pain and grant me a child, fine. But if You do not, then תִרְאֶה —*You will see* what I will do. I will seclude myself with another man

1. The Talmud (*Berachos* 31a) comments on the words וַתִּתְפַּלֵּל עַל־ה' that Hannah, in her bitterness, spoke harsh, confrontational words to Hashem, as it were. *Maharsha* explains this as a reference to the various surprising words of negotiation that she used, such as her threat to conceal herself and be forced to drink *sotah* waters, or her wondering why Hashem gave her breasts (v. 13). *Michtav MeEliyahu* (Vol. IV) elucidates this act. Only someone with intentions as pure as Hannah's could be excused for such a thing. Hannah's only concern was that the generation had fallen to the level of evil that produced the idol of Micah and the concubine in Gibeah. Sensing the "pain of Hashem's Presence," as it were, Hannah felt that there was a desperate need for someone to raise the spiritual level of the nation and to establish Jewish kings who would instill law and order in the nation. Her sincerity can be seen from her prayer of thanks (cf. 2:1-10, which shows her interest in Hashem's glory and in the establishment of the Messianic dynasty). Accordingly, she merited with this prayer that her מַזָּל, *predetermined destiny,* should change from her being one who was not naturally able to bear children to becoming the mother of one of the greatest prophets in history.

and she prayed to H*ASHEM*, *weeping continuously.*
[11]*She made a vow and said, "*H*ASHEM*, *Master of Legions, if You take note of the suffering of Your maidservant, and You remember me, and do not forget Your maidservant, and give Your maidservant male offspring, then I shall give him to* H*ASHEM*

so that my husband will suspect me of being unfaithful to him. He will then force me to drink the *sotah* water, which will prove my innocence. Following that ordeal, I will be rewarded with a child, as per the Scriptural promise: *then she shall be proven innocent and she shall bear seed"* (*Numbers* 5:28).[1]

אֲמָתֶךָ — *Your maidservant.*

Hannah describes herself as a "maidservant" three times in this verse. The Talmud (ibid.) states that she was alluding to the three primary commandments incumbent upon women: the laws of family purity, taking *challah* from dough, and lighting the Sabbath candles, regarding which they are scrutinized with especial care on perilous occasions.

Desperately, Hannah cried out to God, "Have I violated any of these?"

וּזְכַרְתַּנִי וְלֹא־תִשְׁכַּח — *And You remember me, and do not forget.*

Remember me, and send me sons; *and do not forget,* but send me daughters (*Midrash Shmuel*).

זֶרַע אֲנָשִׁים — *Male offspring.*

Our translation is fairly literal, in line with the interpretation of *Radak* and *Metzudos.*

The Sages describe in detail the particular attributes that Hannah requested for her son. From the word אֲנָשִׁים, *Midrash Shmuel* homiletically deduces that she asked for a son who would possess wisdom, understanding, prophecy, righteousness, and eminence. If questioned about the apparent extravagance of her request, Hannah would simply respond, "This is for God's sake."

According to one version, she specifically requested "offspring that would blend among other men," i.e., of average height, weight, complexion, and intelligence. This way, he would not attract attention, which could cause עַיִן הָרָע, *the evil eye* of envy.

וּנְתַתִּיו לַה׳ — *Then I shall give him to* H*ASHEM.*

Targum (and *Metzudos*) state that Hannah's vow begins at this point. She selflessly promises that if her prayer is granted, she will present her son to God for unconditional service.[2]

1. The commentators pose the question of how Hannah could have threatened to engage in such a scheme, which would have forced her to seclude herself with a man other than her husband, an act that is halachically proscribed.

Most offer the suggestion that she would have secluded herself in a manner that, while technically not a transgression, would have required her to undergo the *sotah*-water ordeal (for instance, she might have secluded herself with another man while her husband was in the same city — *Hafla'ah, Netziv*).

2. *Rashi*'s commentary is somewhat vague. His explanation of וּנְתַתִּיו לַה׳ should seemingly be translated as *that he should be fit to be given to* H*ASHEM*, indicating that this phrase constitutes part of Hannah's prayer. In addition, *Rashi* renders וּמוֹרָה as Hannah's prayer that her son should *fear* no one, not as a commitment to make him a *nazir.*

That being the case, although the verse opens with the phrase, *she made a vow,* it seemingly does not express any vow.

But (based on a comment made by *Radak*) we can translate *Rashi*'s explanation of וּנְתַתִּיו לַה׳

יב כָּל־יְמֵי חַיָּיו וּמוֹרָה לֹא־יַעֲלֶה עַל־רֹאשׁוֹ: וְהָיָה
כִּי הִרְבְּתָה לְהִתְפַּלֵּל לִפְנֵי יהוה וְעֵלִי שֹׁמֵר אֶת־
יג פִּיהָ: וְחַנָּה הִיא מְדַבֶּרֶת עַל־לִבָּהּ רַק שְׂפָתֶיהָ
נָּעוֹת וְקוֹלָהּ לֹא יִשָּׁמֵעַ וַיַּחְשְׁבֶהָ עֵלִי לְשִׁכֹּרָה:

וּמוֹרָה לֹא־יַעֲלֶה עַל־רֹאשׁוֹ — *And a razor shall not come upon his head.*

The Sages (*Nazir* 66a) offer differing renditions of this phrase.

Rabbi Nehorai translates מוֹרָה as *a razor,* contending that Hannah promised to offer her anticipated son as a *nazir.* (From this, *Ralbag* sees support for the view that a person who as much as makes a vow to shave his hair implies, and thus effects, all the other Nazirite prohibitions — i.e., eschewing wine and avoiding contamination by corpses [see *Nazir* 36].) Rabbi Nehorai points out that the word מוֹרָה is used in regard to Samson to unambiguously refer to *a razor* [*Judges* 13:5].[1]

Rabbi Yose disagrees with Rabbi Nehorai and maintains that מוֹרָה as used here derives from the word יִרְאָה, *fear* (even though מוֹרָא, *fear,* is ordinarily spelled with the letter א). Accordingly, Hannah was praying for a son who would be so immersed in the fear of God that he would not even be able to imagine fearing anyone else (*Malbim*).

Rabbi Nehorai, however, refutes this interpretation by citing the episode in which Samuel (Hannah's son) expressed his apprehension, "How can I go? If Saul hears, he will kill me" (16:2). If Rabbi Nehorai is correct, how could Samuel fear a mere mortal?

Netziv (*Meromei Sadeh, Nazir* 66) defends Rabbi Yose's view by claiming that fearing no one but God does not exclude a case in which Samuel's life would be placed in danger (see *Nachalas Shimon* 3a for further justifications of Rabbi Yose's view).

❧ Eli's Misjudgment and Subsequent Blessing

12. וְהָיָה כִּי הִרְבְּתָה לְהִתְפַּלֵּל — *It happened as she continued to pray.*

Citing this verse, *Talmud Yerushalmi* presents diametrically opposing views on the efficacy of lengthy prayer.

One sage states that because Hannah הִרְבְּתָה לְהִתְפַּלֵּל, *continued to pray,* her supplication was immediately accepted. Another opinion, however, based on the verse, וּדְבַר־שְׂפָתַיִם אַךְ־לְמַחְסוֹר, *[superfluous] words of the lips lead only to deficiency* (*Proverbs* 14:23), posits that by praying at length Hannah eventually made a comment that curtailed Samuel's lifetime. She asked that her son וְיָשַׁב שָׁם עַד־עוֹלָם, *shall settle there forever* (verse 22). However, the phrase עַד־עוֹלָם in regard to Levites refers to 50 years. Thus,

so that it constitutes the beginning of Hannah's vow: *Then I shall give him.*

According to this, *Rashi* is incorporating into his commentary the dialogue from the Midrash that we presented earlier, in which Hannah defended her petition for a wise, righteous son with this very phrase: וּנְתַתִּיו לַה׳, *[I request a special son, because] then I shall give him to HASHEM.*

1. *Radak* asks how Hannah could have imposed the laws of *nezirus* upon her son, since only a father is halachically empowered to do so (*Nazir* 28b.).

In his *Eitz HaChaim, Mahari Chagiz* explains that when Elkanah told Hannah, עֲשִׂי הַטּוֹב בְּעֵינַיִךְ, *Do what is good in your eyes* (verse 23), he in effect authorized all the details of Hannah's vow.

Alternatively, *Kol HaRamaz* states that Hannah merely intended to train her son to adhere to the Nazirite strictures, hoping that when he came of age he would accept them of his own volition.

all the days of his life, and a razor shall not
come upon his head."
[12] *It happened as she continued to pray*
before H*ASHEM* *that Eli observed her mouth.*
[13] *Hannah was speaking from her heart*
— only her lips moved, but her voice was
not heard — so Eli thought she was drunk.

Samuel only reached the age of 52 — 2 years until he was weaned, plus 50 years of service in the Tabernacle.

וְעֵלִי שֹׁמֵר אֶת־פִּיהָ — *That Eli observed her mouth.*

Our translation of שֹׁמֵר follows *Metzudos.* Eli watched Hannah in order to hear what she was saying, and thus noticed that she was speaking inaudibly.

Targum and *Rashi,* on the other hand, translate שֹׁמֵר as *awaited* (as in: וְאָבִיו שָׁמַר אֶת־הַדָּבָר, *and his father waited for the matter [Genesis* 37:11]). Accordingly, they render פִּיהָ as *her words* (*Radak*), and the text may thus be read, *and Eli waited for her speech [to end].* (*Rabbi A. J. Rosenberg* [*Judaica Press*] explains that *Targum* apparently avoids the more literal translation because it implies that Eli was gazing at Hannah.)

13. מְדַבֶּרֶת עַל־לִבָּהּ — *Was speaking from her heart.*

Radak (based on *Targum*) understands this phrase as a reference to Hannah's concentration. This phrase serves as a source for the halachah that a person must focus on the words of prayer.

Metzudos renders עַל־לִבָּהּ, literally, *on her heart,* as אֶל לִבָּהּ, ***to*** *her heart* — i.e., silently.

Our Sages homiletically interpret this phrase as meaning that Hannah "spoke *about* her heart" — i.e., she commented that all the limbs on the body had a purpose. For what purpose was she given breasts? Were they not to breast-feed?! (*Berachos* 31b).[1]

רַק שְׂפָתֶיהָ נָּעוֹת וְקוֹלָהּ לֹא יִשָּׁמֵעַ — *Only her lips moved, but her voice was not heard.*

Hannah's exemplary style of devotion remains the ordained manner of Jewish prayer. A person must form the words with his lips, but his voice should not be inaudible (*Berachos* 31a), so that his confession of sinful behavior will remain private (*Sotah* 32b).

There are differing opinions as to whether a person should be able to hear his own voice. The generally accepted view is that one should; however, failing that, one has still fulfilled his obligation (*Mishnah Berurah* 101:5).[2]

וַיַּחְשְׁבֶהָ עֵלִי לְשִׁכֹּרָה — *So Eli thought she was drunk.*

On the basis of this verse, the Talmud states that it is forbidden to pray while intoxicated (*Berachos* 31a).

1. She mentioned only breasts and not the womb or other limbs involved in the process of birth. Possibly, she meant that she would love to bear a child, but if that were not possible, let her at least be given someone else's son whom she could breast-feed and influence him to fear Hashem. The fact that a child is influenced by the one who feeds him is evidenced from many sources (see *Tos. Avodah Zarah* 10b; *Tanchuma Yashan* in *Vayeira* 38; addenda to *Mishbetzos Zahav*).

2. *Rema MiPanu* derives an additional restriction from Hannah's behavior. The phrase, רַק שְׂפָתֶיהָ נָּעוֹת, *only her lips moved,* implies that when a person prays, no other part of his body should move.

This view is cited by *Magen Avraham,* which disputes that of *Rema* (*Orach Chaim* 48). *Magen Avraham's* halachic conclusion is that a person should engage in whichever practice he finds more conducive to concentrating (*Mishnah Berurah* ibid. §5).

יד וַיֹּאמֶר אֵלֶיהָ עֵלִי עַד־מָתַי תִּשְׁתַּכָּרִין
טו הָסִירִי אֶת־יֵינֵךְ מֵעָלָיִךְ: וַתַּעַן חַנָּה וַתֹּאמֶר
לֹא אֲדֹנִי אִשָּׁה קְשַׁת־רוּחַ אָנֹכִי וְיַיִן וְשֵׁכָר
לֹא שָׁתִיתִי וָאֶשְׁפֹּךְ אֶת־נַפְשִׁי לִפְנֵי יהוה:
טז אַל־תִּתֵּן אֶת־אֲמָתְךָ לִפְנֵי בַּת־בְּלִיָּעַל

Rashi suggests that Eli was suspicious of Hannah because it was unusual for people to pray inaudibly. *Maharsha* (*Berachos* 31a) raises the obvious question: Since praying quietly is halachically mandated, how could doing so not have been customary? *Maharsha* thus explains that Eli judged Hannah to be drunk because of the unusual length of her prayer (see above).

In defense of *Rashi*'s suggestion, *Teshuvah MeAhavah* offers the following explanation. The extraneous words, וְקוֹלָהּ לֹא יִשָּׁמֵעַ, *but her voice was not heard*, imply that Hannah went beyond the letter of the law, so that her voice was inaudible even to herself (see above). It was this unusual behavior that led Eli to suspect the influence of alcohol. *Sh'lah* suggests that since it was Rosh Hashanah, Eli felt that she should have been praying aloud (see *Shulchan Aruch Orach Chaim* 582:9). Hannah explained that she had not been praying the regular text of prayer, but she was expressing her own private petition for children, which must be done quietly even on Rosh Hashanah. (See *Nachalas Shimon* for other arguments in defense of *Rashi*.)[1]

14. וַיֹּאמֶר אֵלֶיהָ עֵלִי עַד־מָתַי תִּשְׁתַּכָּרִין — *Eli said to her, "How long will you be drunk?"*

From here we learn that if a person sees another Jew acting improperly, he is obligated to rebuke him (*Berachos* ibid.). This is the case even if that behavior is only prohibited by Rabbinic decree (*Tosafos, Berachos* 31b).

הָסִירִי אֶת־יֵינֵךְ — *Remove your wine from yourself!*

Regain sobriety by sleeping, taking a walk, or other means (see *Eruvin* 64b; *Metzudos*).

But what was the point of this directive? Hannah was no longer drinking, and there are no easy antidotes for intoxication. To answer this question, *Abarbanel* offers a novel approach. Eli didn't intend to solve the immediate problem of Hannah's apparent intoxication. Rather, he meant to offer a solution to what he perceived to be an ongoing vice. He thus advised Hannah to completely abstain from drinking in the future. This proposal is similar to Maimonides' suggestion that a person who wishes to correct an improper habit should go to the opposite extreme, and only afterward gravitate toward the golden mean.

15. לֹא אֲדֹנִי — *No, my lord,*

Our translation follows *Radak* and *Metzudos*, who place a comma after לֹא, *no*, and interpret the phrase to mean, "No, my lord, it is not as you suspect that I am drunk; rather, I am a woman of aggrieved spirit."

1. Basing himself on an old text of *Rashi*, the *Vilna Gaon* suggests an original theory to explain Eli's misjudgment. Bewildered by Hannah's behavior, Eli consulted the *Urim VeTumim*. On his breastplate, the letters ה,כ,ש,ר were illuminated (of the letters spelling out the names of the Jewish tribes engraved onto the twelve semiprecious stones), and in that Eli saw a confirmation of his suspicion, for he read them as שִׁכֹּרָה: *a drunken woman.*

But when he confronted Hannah with this accusation, she replied, לֹא אֲדֹנִי, and as our Sages interpret her answer, *You are not my master in this matter, and the Divine Spirit is not with you here* (*Berachos* 31b). You, she told him, have erred in your interpretation, for you should have read the letters as spelling out the word, כְּשָׂרָה: *like Sarah.*

Hannah, in other words, was beseeching God to give her a child just as Sarah had prayed for a child.

[14] *Eli said to her, "How long will you be drunk? Re-move your wine from yourself!"* [15] *Hannah answered and said, "No, my lord, I am a woman of aggrieved spirit. I have drunk neither wine nor strong drink, and I have poured out my soul before* HASHEM. [16] *Do not deem your maidservant to be a base woman*

The Talmud, however, renders לֹא אֲדֹנִי without the comma, translating it as, *You are not my master [in this matter].* Why? Because by judging Hannah improperly, Eli showed that he lacked Divine Inspiration (*Berachos* 31b; *Rashi*).

From this, the Talmud derives an important principle governing interpersonal relations. A person unjustly accused of wrongdoing must clearly state his innocence. This is comparable to the concept, *You should remain innocent [in the eyes of] God and Israel* (*Numbers* 32:22): a person must avoid even the appearance of impropriety.

לֹא אֲדֹנִי אִשָּׁה קְשַׁת־רוּחַ אָנֹכִי — *No, my lord, I am a woman of aggrieved spirit.*

According to *Targum,* Hannah was explaining that her behavior was not that of a drunkard but rather that of a woman experiencing great pain.

Abarbanel, however, understands קְשַׁת־רוּחַ to mean *an ill-tempered woman,* and rearranges the text to read, אֲדֹנִי לֹא אִשָּׁה קְשַׁת־רוּחַ אָנֹכִי וְיַיִן וְשֵׁכָר לֹא שָׁתִיתִי, *My lord, I am not an irascible woman nor have I drunk ...* Hannah maintained that her actions were not the outcome of drinking alcohol or of a hot temper (the symptoms of the two being somewhat similar in nature).

וְיַיִן וְשֵׁכָר לֹא שָׁתִיתִי — *I have drunk neither wine nor strong drink.*

Neither young wine nor aged wine (*Targum*).

וָאֶשְׁפֹּךְ אֶת־נַפְשִׁי לִפְנֵי ה׳ — *And I have poured out my soul before* HASHEM.

"And since I am communicating only with Hashem, why would I raise my voice for others to hear?" (*Metzudos*).

Kli Yakar understands the last two phrases to be correlated as follows: יַיִן וְשֵׁכָר לֹא שָׁתִיתִי וָאֶשְׁפֹּךְ אֶת־נַפְשִׁי, *I would never have drunk wine and [subsequently] prayed under the influence of alcohol!*

Prayer is referred to here as a pouring out of the soul. *R' Aharon Kotler* explains that the word נֶפֶשׁ, *soul,* means *will* (see *Genesis* 23:8). When one prays, he is dedicating his entire will to Hashem, expressing the realization that Hashem controls everything and the man who prays knows that only Hashem's will will prevail (*Mishnas R' Aharon,* Vol. IV).

16. אַל־תִּתֵּן אֶת־אֲמָתְךָ לִפְנֵי בַּת־בְּלִיָּעַל — *Do not deem your maidservant to be a base woman.*

Do not suspect me of entering the Sanctuary while intoxicated (*Metzudos*).

Hannah refers to a person who prays while intoxicated as "base," and Scripture uses the same terminology to describe a person who worships idols (*Deuteronomy* 13:14). The Talmud thus employs the exegetical concept of *gezeirah shavah* to conclude that praying while intoxicated is tantamount to worshiping idols (*Berachos* 31b).[1]

Targum (followed by *Rashi*) interprets this verse differently. It understands *a base woman* as Hannah's reference to Peninnah, and translates the verse as follows: *Do not embarrass your maidservant in the presence of*

1. *Rashba* (in *Ein Yaakov*) offers the following rationale for this concept. Alcohol confuses the mind and inhibits its rational processes, making it relatively easy for a person to entertain heretical thoughts. A person who worships God while drunk runs the risk of allowing certain images that might well constitute genuine idolatry to impinge upon his service.

יז כִּֽי־מֵרֹ֥ב שִׂיחִ֛י וְכַעְסִ֖י דִּבַּ֥רְתִּי עַד־הֵֽנָּה׃ וַיַּ֧עַן
עֵלִ֛י וַיֹּ֖אמֶר לְכִ֣י לְשָׁל֑וֹם וֵֽאלֹהֵ֤י יִשְׂרָאֵל֙ יִתֵּן֙
יח אֶת־שֵׁ֣לָתֵ֔ךְ אֲשֶׁ֥ר שָׁאַ֖לְתְּ מֵעִמּֽוֹ׃ וַתֹּ֕אמֶר
תִּמְצָ֧א שִׁפְחָתְךָ֛ חֵ֖ן בְּעֵינֶ֑יךָ וַתֵּ֨לֶךְ הָאִשָּׁ֤ה
לְדַרְכָּהּ֙ וַתֹּאכַ֔ל וּפָנֶ֥יהָ לֹא־הָֽיוּ־לָ֖הּ עֽוֹד׃

[Peninnah,] the wicked woman [by calling me a drunkard, for she will rejoice in my disgrace].

בְּלִיָּעַל — *A base woman.*

The word בְּלִיָּעַל is a conjunction of the two words בְּלִי עוֹל, *without a yoke* — i.e., a person unrestrained by God's laws.

כִּי־מֵרֹב שִׂיחִי וְכַעְסִי דִּבַּרְתִּי עַד־הֵנָּה — *For it is out of much grievance and anger that I have spoken until now.*

Rashi explains that Hannah was excusing her harsh language to Eli: "I am speaking under the influence of grief and anger."

According to *Targum*, Hannah was defending her lengthy prayer. Hence, "I was relating in prayer *the many [incidents of] jealousy and anger [instigated by my co-wife].*"

Abarbanel, in line with his rendering of the previous verse, reads the passage as saying, *Do not deem your maidservant to be a woman of evil temperament by saying that I have spoken under the influence of vile loquacity and anger. That is not the case, for I have only come to pour out my heart to God.*

17. וַיַּעַן עֵלִי וַיֹּאמֶר לְכִי לְשָׁלוֹם — *Eli then answered and said, "Go in peace."*

From here we learn that a person who falsely accuses someone must pacify and bless him (*Berachos* 31b).

The Talmud states that when blessing someone on his departure, one should say, לֵךְ לְשָׁלוֹם, *Go in peace*, not לֵךְ בְּשָׁלוֹם, *Go with peace*, the latter being appropriate for departing from a deceased individual (*Berachos* 64a).

לְכִי לְשָׁלוֹם — *Go in peace.*

Abarbanel suggests that Eli continued to doubt Hannah's blameless character, and therefore conveyed the instructive, if politely phrased, message, לְכִי לְשָׁלוֹם, *Leave in peace.* Eli was referring to Hannah's conflict with Peninnah and encouraging her to avoid taking issue with Peninnah and instead to place her complete trust in God, so that the *God of Israel will grant ...*

וֵאלֹהֵי יִשְׂרָאֵל — *The God of Israel.*

Kli Yakar points out that this is a variation on the standard וַה׳ יִתֵּן, *May Hashem give*, and offers the enlightening explanation that Eli was notifying Hannah that Hashem would respond to her specifically in His aspect of God of Israel, the Jewish people, and as such she would bear the future leader and shepherd of His people.

Alternatively, Eli noted that Hannah was emulating Jacob, who initiated the practice of vowing to God in a time of need with his commitment of אִם־יִהְיֶה אֱלֹהִים עִמָּדִי, *If God will be with me ...* (*Genesis* 28:20). Thus, Eli reassured Hannah, ... אֱלֹהֵי יִשְׂרָאֵל יִתֵּן. *The God of Israel* — i.e., Jacob — *will [respond to your vow] and grant ...*

יִתֵּן אֶת־שֵׁלָתֵךְ — *Will grant your request.*

As previously stated (see verse 3), Eli was a prophet; therefore, this encouraging statement was actually a prophecy (*Rashi, Radak*).[1]

1. The *Imrei Emes* wonders: How is it possible that moments ago, Eli suspected Hannah of overdrinking, and now he immediately tells her that her prayers have been answered? He explains that it is the nature of a leader to sense the pain of his subjects (see *Berachos* 28a). Eli had not sensed her anguish at all. Initially, he assumed that she was drunk. After she told

— for it is out of much grievance and anger that I
have spoken until now." 17 *Eli then answered and*
said, "Go in peace. The God of Israel will grant
your request that you have made of Him." 18 *She*
said, "May your maidservant find favor in your
eyes." Then the woman went on her way and she
ate, and no longer had the same look on her face.

Metzudos, however, understands Eli's words as no more than a personal supplication that her request be fulfilled.

אֶת־שֵׁלָתֵךְ — *Your request.*

The word שְׁאֵלָה, *request,* is generally spelled with an א. The absence of the א here homiletically refers to a child (*Rashi*), for it is reminiscent of the word שִׁלְיָה, *placenta* (as in וּבְשִׁלְיָתָהּ הַיּוֹצֵת מִבֵּין רַגְלֶיהָ, *and her offspring that is discharged from between her feet* [*Deuteronomy* 28:57]). This Midrashically based exegesis is further testimony to Eli's Divine Inspiration, for he was aware of the burden of Hannah's prayer, even though she hadn't revealed it to him (*Kli Yakar*).

Midrash Shmuel compares שֵׁלָתֵךְ to the word שָׁלָל, *spoils.* Accordingly, Eli was implying, "The son that you raise will collect many spoils — i.e., much knowledge — from the Torah."

18. תִּמְצָא שִׁפְחָתְךָ חֵן בְּעֵינֶיךָ — *May your maidservant find favor in your eyes.*

Following the interpretation that Eli's proclamation of the previous verse, "The God of Israel will grant your request" (see above), was a prayer, Hannah now asked Eli to continue to pray on her behalf. Now, feeling assured that Eli's prayers would be answered, she ate. According to the interpretation that Eli's statement was a prophecy, Hannah here expressed her gratitude for already having found favor in his eyes (*Radak*).

However, although *Rashi* understands Eli's remark as having been prophetic, he nevertheless interprets this verse to be expressing Hannah's plea, "May your maidservant find favor in your eyes [so that you will continue to] *plead* for mercy [on my behalf]." But why, if Eli had already prophetically assured Hannah of a positive outcome, did she continue to seek assurance? *Rabbi A. J. Rosenberg* answers that even when a blessing has been granted (*Berachos* 4a), a person's sins can abrogate it.

וַתֵּלֶךְ הָאִשָּׁה לְדַרְכָּהּ — *Then the woman went on her way.*

Midrash Shmuel comments that the word לְדַרְכָּהּ, *on her way,* alludes to the *way of women* (*Genesis* 31:35) — i.e., menstruation. *Kli Yakar* comments that this was the first time that she experienced the phenomenon, and this supports the notion that until this point she lacked the physical capacity to bear children (see above, v. 2).

וּפָנֶיהָ לֹא־הָיוּ־לָהּ עוֹד — *And no longer had the same look on her face.*

Hannah no longer wore a dejected expression (*Rashi* and the majority of commentators).[1]

him that she was actually just aggrieved, he understood that the only remaining reason that he wouldn't sense her pain was because her prayers had already been answered and she had nothing to worry about (*Mishbetzos Zahav*).

1. The commentators are largely in agreement that Hannah's change of mood was based on the optimistic anticipation that her prayers had been accepted. But how could Hannah have adapted such an attitude, since our Sages frown upon assurance in the efficacy of one's prayer?

יט וַיַּשְׁכִּמוּ בַבֹּקֶר וַיִּשְׁתַּחֲווּ לִפְנֵי יהוה וַיָּשֻׁבוּ וַיָּבֹאוּ
אֶל־בֵּיתָם הָרָמָתָה וַיֵּדַע אֶלְקָנָה אֶת־חַנָּה אִשְׁתּוֹ
כ וַיִּזְכְּרֶהָ יהוה: וַיְהִי לִתְקֻפוֹת הַיָּמִים וַתַּהַר חַנָּה וַתֵּלֶד
בֵּן וַתִּקְרָא אֶת־שְׁמוֹ שְׁמוּאֵל כִּי מֵיהוה שְׁאִלְתִּיו:

Midrash Shmuel states that Hannah's face had previously resembled that of a monkey, a condition from which she was now healed.

Kli Yakar explains that her features had withered from old age (*Yalkut Shimoni* 80 states that Hannah was 130 years old); at this point, her youthful countenance returned.

☙ The Birth of Samuel

19. וַיַּשְׁכִּמוּ בַבֹּקֶר — *They arose early in the morning.*

Our Sages state that a person leaving the Sanctuary for home should do so only in the morning (*Sifrei, Parshas Re'eh* 181, on the verse וּפָנִיתָ בַבֹּקֶר וְהָלַכְתָּ לְאֹהָלֶיךָ, *Turn back in the morning and go to your tents* [*Deuteronomy* 16:7]). Elkanah and his family were acting in compliance with this instruction (*Abarbanel*).

וַיִּשְׁתַּחֲווּ לִפְנֵי ה׳ — *And prostrated themselves before* HASHEM.

According to *Kli Yakar*, Hannah and Elkanah realized that Hannah's menstrual flow meant that her prayer had been accepted, and they prostrated themselves as an expression of gratitude.[1]

וַיָּבֹאוּ אֶל־בֵּיתָם הָרָמָתָה וַיֵּדַע אֶלְקָנָה אֶת־חַנָּה — *And they came to their home, to Ramah. Elkanah knew Hannah.*

The word וַיֵּדַע, *and he knew*, is commonly used to refer to marital relations (as in וְהָאָדָם יָדַע אֶת־חַוָּה אִשְׁתּוֹ, *Now the man had known his wife Eve* [*Genesis* 4:1]). This verse points out that Elkanah returned home before having relations with Hannah. The Talmud (*Kesubos* 65a) derives from this the rule of modesty that prohibits a guest from marital relations.[2,3]

וַיִּזְכְּרֶהָ ה׳ — *And* HASHEM *remembered her.*

Hashem "remembered" Hannah — i.e., for her benefit (*Metzudos*).

Utilizing the hermeneutical tool of גְּזֵרָה שָׁוָה, the Talmud associates this verse with Scripture's reference to *remembrance* in the context of Rosh Hashanah, which is שַׁבָּתוֹן זִכְרוֹן תְּרוּעָה, *a day of rest, remembering the [shofar] blowing* (*Leviticus* 23:24). This is the source of the oft-quoted assertion that Hannah was "remembered" on Rosh Hashanah (*Rosh Hashanah* 10b, 11a).[4]

20. וַיְהִי לִתְקֻפוֹת הַיָּמִים וַתַּהַר חַנָּה — *And it*

(See *Berachos* 32b and *Tosafos* ad loc.)

Chasam Sofer offers a profound suggestion. Hannah was aware that the most she could do was pray. Once she did so to the best of her ability, she adapted an unwavering trust that whatever God decided would be for the best.

1. Prostrating oneself to God is a meritorious act that expresses humility, subservience, and acceptance of His sovereignty. The Midrash states that God took note of Hannah only in the merit of her prostrating herself before Him (*Bereishis Rabbah* 56:2; see *Rashash*).

2. This rule has practical application in a case in which a couple is not provided with a completely private room. Even in a private room, they must use their own linen (*Orach Chaim* 240:13).

3. This derivation is obviously incongruous with the previously quoted Midrashic statement that Hannah had just experienced her menstrual period (*Nachalas Shimon*).

4. For a discussion of whether Hannah conceived on Rosh Hashanah or whether God at that time decreed that she would conceive, see *Nachalas Shimon*.

[19] *They arose early in the morning and prostrat-*
ed themselves before HASHEM; *then they returned*
and came to their home, to Ramah. Elkanah knew
Hannah his wife and HASHEM *remembered her.*
[20] *And it happened with the passage of the pe-*
riod of days that Hannah had conceived, and
she gave birth to a son. She named him Samuel,
for [she said,] "I requested him from HASHEM."

happened with the passage of the period of days that Hannah had conceived.

Although the verse apparently states that this "period of days" preceded Hannah's conception, *Radak* maintains that this period refers to the gestation period following her conception. *Radak* finds precedence for this assertion in similar instances of grammatical usage. (For instance, וַתַּהַר, lit., *and she became pregnant,* at times indicating a previously established status: *she had already been pregnant.*)

וַיְהִי לִתְקֻפוֹת הַיָּמִים — *And it happened with the passage of the period of days.*

Targum interprets this as referring to the completion of the gestation period.

On the basis of this verse, the Talmud makes an interesting physiological observation. A normal gestation period is nine months, although some babies are fully developed after seven months. A nine-month gestation lasts an *entire* nine months. Contrarily, from this verse we see otherwise in regard to a seven-month gestation. The phrase לִתְקֻפוֹת הַיָּמִים, *with the passage of the period of days,* more literally means *the seasons of days.* The Talmud reads *seasons* as denoting two seasons of the year (the minimum of a multiple), and *days* as denoting two days (again, the minimum of a multiple). Thus, we can calculate as follows: *seasons* refers to two seasons, each three months long (totaling six months), and *days* refers to two *days.* Accordingly, the gestation period for Samuel extended for only two days into the seventh month.[1]

וַתִּקְרָא אֶת־שְׁמוֹ שְׁמוּאֵל כִּי מֵה׳ שְׁאִלְתִּיו — *She named him Samuel, for [she said,] "I requested him from* HASHEM."

If Hannah named her baby in honor of the fact that "מֵה׳ שְׁאִלְתִּיו," why didn't she name him שָׁאוּל, *Saul?*

Ralbag dismisses this question by citing other precedents — such as the cases of Noah and Reuben — in which people were not precise in naming their children.

Radak suggests that Samuel is a conjunction of שָׁאוּל מֵאֵל, *requested from God.*

The only difference between the names Saul and Samuel is the addition of the letter *mem* to the latter. *Me'am Loez* quotes an interpretation that the letter *mem* in Samuel connotes King David, whom Samuel would anoint and whose reign lasted 40 years, the numerical value of the letter *mem.*[2]

1. According to *Teshuvos Rivash* 446, 447, even six months and a day suffice (see *Nachalas Shimon* 6:5).

2. *Chasam Sofer* offers an interesting solution to this question. Until Hannah's day, we have evidence of two men having been named Saul. Saul was the name of one of the royal descendants of Esau (*Genesis* 36:37), who was presumably an evil man. And one of the names of the infamous Zimri ben Salu was Saul ben HaC'naanis (*Sanhedrin* 82b).

In adherence to the precept that one should not call one's child by the name of a wicked person (*Yoma* 38b), Hannah refrained from using the name Saul. (Naming one's child Saul became permissible only following the precedence of the righteous King Saul — see *Pnei Yehoshua; Kesubos* 104b.)

כא וַיַּעַל הָאִישׁ אֶלְקָנָה וְכָל־בֵּיתוֹ לִזְבֹּחַ לַיהוָה
כב אֶת־זֶבַח הַיָּמִים וְאֶת־נִדְרוֹ׃ וְחַנָּה לֹא עָלָתָה
כִּי־אָמְרָה לְאִישָׁהּ עַד יִגָּמֵל הַנַּעַר וַהֲבִאֹתִיו
וְנִרְאָה אֶת־פְּנֵי יְהוָה וְיָשַׁב שָׁם עַד־עוֹלָם׃
כג וַיֹּאמֶר לָהּ אֶלְקָנָה אִישָׁהּ עֲשִׂי הַטּוֹב בְּעֵינַיִךְ
שְׁבִי עַד־גָּמְלֵךְ אֹתוֹ אַךְ יָקֵם יְהוָה אֶת־דְּבָרוֹ
וַתֵּשֶׁב הָאִשָּׁה וַתֵּינֶק אֶת־בְּנָהּ עַד־גָמְלָהּ אֹתוֹ׃

Midrash Shmuel says that every day a heavenly voice would spread across the world, proclaiming that a righteous man is going to arise whose name is Samuel. Naturally, every boy who was born was named Samuel (see below, v. 23).

21. וַיַּעַל הָאִישׁ אֶלְקָנָה — *The man Elkanah ascended.*

When the time came for his ascent to offer sacrifices (*Metzudos*).

לִזְבֹּחַ — *To bring ...*

Malbim points out that, in contrast to verse 3, this time Elkanah is not described as having *prostrated himself*. This supports *Malbim*'s contention that Elkanah originally prostrated himself as part of his prayers for Hannah to have a child, something that was no longer necessary.

זֶבַח הַיָּמִים — *The annual offering.*

Our translation follows the interpretation of מִיָּמִים יָמִימָה in verse 3 above.

Targum renders זֶבַח הַיָּמִים as *the offering of the holiday*.

נִדְרוֹ — *His vow.*

Rashi understands this to refer to Elkanah's vows to offer sacrifices that he had made since the last holiday. Elkanah now brought these animals to the altar, in adherence to the law that a person is obliged to fulfill all of his vows by the time of the coming pilgrimage holiday (*Rosh Hashanah* 6a).

Radak maintains that this is a specific reference to Elkanah's vow to God that he made in gratitude for the birth of Samuel.

22. וְחַנָּה לֹא עָלָתָה — *But Hannah did not ascend.*

She did not go to Shiloh that year (*Metzudos*).

The Talmud (*Chagigah* 6a) cites this verse in the course of a discussion regarding a woman's obligation to participate in the joyous holiday festivities and a man's obligation to bring his young boys to join in the pilgrimage. That passage seemingly indicates that both women and young boys are exempt. However, the Talmud concludes that this verse cannot be cited as a proof text for that contention, because in this specific case Hannah sensed that Samuel had an unusually delicate nature and was afraid that traveling to Shiloh would be injurious to him.

כִּי־אָמְרָה לְאִישָׁהּ עַד יִגָּמֵל הַנַּעַר וַהֲבִאֹתִיו — *As she told her husband, "When the child is weaned, then I will bring him."*

Hannah envisioned that after Samuel came to the Sanctuary, he would remain there for the rest of his life (*Ralbag*).

Malbim adds that Hannah understood this to have been a part of her vow to God — i.e., that once Samuel appeared at the Sanctuary, he would not leave it. This is implicit in the verse, וְנִרְאָה אֶת־פְּנֵי ה׳ וְיָשַׁב שָׁם עַד־עוֹלָם, *and he shall appear before HASHEM, and shall settle there forever.*

עַד יִגָּמֵל הַנַּעַר — *When the child is weaned.*

This refers to a 24-month nursing period (*Rashi*). (The reading in *Rashi* of 22

[21]*The man Elkanah ascended with his entire
household to bring to HASHEM the annual offering
and his vow.* [22]*But Hannah did not ascend, as she
told her husband, "When the child is weaned, then
I will bring him, and he shall appear before HASHEM
and shall settle there forever."* [23]*Elkanah her husband said to her, "Do what is good in your eyes;
remain until you wean him — but may HASHEM fulfill His word." So the woman remained and nursed
her son until she weaned him.*

months is apparently an erroneous text.)

עַד־עוֹלָם — *Forever.*

All the days of his life (*Radak*).

Metzudos explains עַד־עוֹלָם to refer to all the days of Eli's life, during which Samuel would serve Eli.

Midrash Shmuel understands עַד־עוֹלָם, *forever,* to mean the extent of the "world" of a Levite in his service of God, which is to say 50 years, for when a Levite reached that age he retired from the Temple service.[1] Indeed, *Rashi* affirms, Samuel lived 50 years past his 2 years of nursing. As previously mentioned, our Sages take Hannah to task for having overextended her prayers and thereby unwittingly curtailed Samuel's lifetime.

23. עֲשִׂי הַטּוֹב בְּעֵינַיִךְ — *Do what is good in your eyes.*

Although Elkanah would have preferred his family to join his pilgrimage so as to make the joy of the festival complete, he deferred to Hannah's decision (*Me'am Loez*).

Legally, a husband has the right to void his wife's vows. Here, however, Elkanah officially demonstrated his consent (*Malbim*).

אַךְ יָקֵם ה׳ אֶת־דְּבָרוֹ — *But may HASHEM fulfill His word.*

Hannah had requested זֶרַע אֲנָשִׁים, *male offspring,* a child who would live to serve God, and Eli had prophesied that this would come to pass. Elkanah now prayed that Hashem would keep that promise (*Rashi, Radak*).

Kli Yakar explains that although the boy was already born, all of the specific qualities inherent in the phrase זֶרַע אֲנָשִׁים, *male offspring* (see commentary to v. 11), had not yet been realized.[2]

Malbim refers to Chapter 2, in which Hannah prophesies about Samuel's future as the leader and savior of the Jewish people. It is those "words of Hashem," states *Malbim*, for whose realization Elkanah prayed.

Rashi quotes a fascinating *Midrash Shmuel* on this verse. Every day, a voice from heaven (a *bas kol*) proclaimed that an extraordinarily righteous person would be born whose name would be Samuel. Naturally, all

1. *Kli Yakar* sees grammatical support for this Midrashic teaching from the text. The conventional expression for *forever* is לְעוֹלָם. עַד־עוֹלָם, literally, *until a world*, suggests a specific span of time.

2. In particular, by implication Hannah requested that Samuel should be *a powerful man* (*Berachos* 32b).

With this understanding, *Me'am Loez* offers the following clever interpretation of Elkanah's words to Hannah: "*Remain until you wean him. But let HASHEM fulfill His word,* so that Samuel will be a strong man capable of making the trip to the Sanctuary on his own."

כד וַתַּעֲלֵהוּ עִמָּהּ כַּאֲשֶׁר גְּמָלַתּוּ בְּפָרִים שְׁלֹשָׁה וְאֵיפָה
אַחַת קֶמַח וְנֵבֶל יַיִן וַתְּבִאֵהוּ בֵית־יהוה שִׁלוֹ וְהַנַּעַר
כה נָעַר: וַיִּשְׁחֲטוּ אֶת־הַפָּר וַיָּבִאוּ אֶת־הַנַּעַר אֶל־עֵלִי:

mothers named their sons Samuel. However, as each son grew older, people would say, "This cannot be *the* Samuel." When Hannah's Samuel was born and began to mature, however, everyone acceded that he was the one. Accordingly, Elkanah prayed for the fulfillment of the promise made by that heavenly voice.

According to all of the above interpretations, the antecedent of דְּבָרוֹ, *His word*, is God (i.e., God should keep His word).

Metzudos, however, states that דְּבָרוֹ here means the words spoken about Samuel. Elkanah told Hannah, "Bringing Samuel to the Sanctuary is in your hands; however, whether וְיָשַׁב שָׁם עַד־עוֹלָם, *that he remains there forever*, is up to him." Therefore, Elkanah prayed, אַךְ יָקֵם ה׳ אֶת־דְּבָרוֹ, *May* HASHEM *[inspire the heart of the boy so that he will choose to fulfill] the prediction about him.*

◆§ The Fulfillment of Hannah's Vow

Hannah's maternal selflessness is legendary. She sacrificed her natural desires to nurture and monitor her child's development, and sent him as early as possible to the sacred confines of the Sanctuary, where he would perform the service of Hashem. Hannah was the ultimate "joyful mother of children" (*Psalms* 113:9), whose actions proved that she had longed for a child not in order to satisfy her emotional desires but rather for the sake of the glory of God (*Abarbanel, Me'am Loez*).

24. וַתַּעֲלֵהוּ עִמָּהּ — *She brought him up with her.*

Kli Yakar notes the conspicuous absence of Elkanah's name in this passage, and concludes that after Samuel was weaned, Hannah brought him to the Sanctuary alone.

Kli Yakar admits that verse 11 in the following chapter — וַיֵּלֶךְ אֶלְקָנָה הָרָמָתָה עַל־בֵּיתוֹ, *Elkanah then went to Ramah, to his house* — seemingly contradicts this thesis. However, he explains that verse as meaning that Elkanah went on a pilgrimage, visited Samuel, and left him at the Sanctuary with Eli.

Radak seemingly disagrees with *Kli Yakar's* contention, however, on the basis of the following verse: וַיִּשְׁחֲטוּ ... וַיָּבִאוּ, *They slaughtered, ... they brought*, which apparently refers to both Elkanah and Hannah.

בְּפָרִים שְׁלֹשָׁה — *With three bulls.*

Metzudos states that all three bulls were offered as sacrifices. As *Me'am Loez* expounds, Hannah brought one on behalf of Elkanah, one on her own behalf, and one on behalf of Samuel.

Radak disagrees, however, and claims that Hannah brought bulls, flour, and wine, offering some on the altar, and leaving some to be consumed by herself and her family. *Radak* supports his claim on the basis of the following verse: וַיִּשְׁחֲטוּ אֶת הַפָּר, *They slaughtered the bull* — a single bull — on its own, not as part of a group.

וְאֵיפָה אַחַת קֶמַח — *One ephah of flour.*

An *ephah* is a dry measure equal to three *seah*, which, when sifted, provide the three-tenths of an *ephah* of the *fine flour* meal-offering that accompanies a bull sacrifice (*Rashi*; see *Numbers* 15:9).[1]

וַתְּבִאֵהוּ בֵית־ה׳ שִׁלוֹ — *She brought him to the house of* HASHEM *in Shiloh.*

1. *Abarbanel* understands *Rashi* to be stating that there was an *ephah* per bull — i.e., a total of three *ephos*. This is in accord with the opinion that all three bulls were sacrificed.

However, *Rashi's* comment may be understood to be congruent with *Radak's* opinion that only one bull was offered, necessitating the use of only one *ephah*.

[24]*She brought him up with her when she weaned him, with three bulls, one ephah of flour, and a flask of wine; she brought him to the house of* HASHEM *in Shiloh, though the child was still tender.* [25]*They slaughtered the bull, and brought the child to Eli.*

The Talmud (*Zevachim* 118a) contrasts this designation of the Sanctuary in Shiloh as a *house* with its description in *Psalms* as מִשְׁכַּן שִׁלוֹ, the *tent of Shiloh* (*Psalms* 78:60). The Talmud explains that the Tabernacle in Shiloh bore similarities to both a house and a tent. Its walls were made of stone like a house — anticipating the permanent structure of the Temple in Jerusalem — whereas its roof was tentlike, made of curtains, and in that regard resembled the original desert Tabernacle (*Zevachim* 112b).

וְהַנַּעַר נָעַר — *Though the child was still tender.*

Although Samuel was still young, Hannah had no hesitation in bringing him to the Sanctuary in order to fulfill her vow (*Metzudos, Ralbag*).

Most commentators follow Targum's rendering of נָעַר as יָנִיק, *young.*

Some, however, see in the word נָעַר a reference to Samuel's early intellectual maturity.

Radak sees the word as having the meaning of "shaking off"; just as a farmer shakes off the inferior part of the flax, so did Samuel shake off all evil and choose only good.

Malbim extrapolates the meaning of this word from its root עֵר, *awake;* the boy's intelligence, morals, and personal characteristic traits had already *awoken,* i.e., had made themselves apparent.

25. וַיִּשְׁחֲטוּ אֶת־הַפָּר — *They slaughtered the bull.*

They slaughtered the bull as an *offering.*

וַיָּבִאוּ אֶת־הַנַּעַר אֶל־עֵלִי — *And brought the child to Eli.*

They brought the child to show Eli that his prophecy had been fulfilled (*Rashi*).

According to *Metzudos,* who states that Eli's words above (v. 17) had not been prophecy but prayer, the boy was brought to show Eli the product of his supplications.

According to *Radak,* Samuel's parents now presented Samuel to Eli as his educational charge and disciple.

However, these three interpretations do not answer an obvious question: Why are the slaughtering of the bull and Samuel being brought to Eli mentioned in the same verse? Was one event causative of the other?[1]

In order to answer this question, the Talmud (*Berachos* 31b) narrates an amazing incident that occurred at the time. The first bull was meant to be offered as a sacrifice. When Elkanah sent someone to summon a Kohen to slaughter it, Samuel asked him, "Why do you need a Kohen? The slaughtering may be performed by a non-Kohen." Soon thereafter, when Samuel was brought to Eli, Eli asked him for the source of this contention. Samuel responded that in its description of offering sacrifices, the Pentateuch mentions the Kohen only as necessary to accept the blood of the slaughtered animal — implying that the slaughtering itself need not be performed by a Kohen (*Leviticus* 1:5). Eli answered, "Your logic is accurate, but you are deserving of death for having

1. *Malbim* explains this contiguity as follows. Samuel was introduced to Eli during the process of the sacrifice to indicate that just as the bull was a burnt-offering dedicated completely to Hashem, so too would Samuel be totally dedicated to the service of God.

כו וַתֹּאמֶר בִּי אֲדֹנִי חֵי נַפְשְׁךָ אֲדֹנִי אֲנִי הָאִשָּׁה
כז הַנִּצֶּבֶת עִמְּכָה בָּזֶה לְהִתְפַּלֵּל אֶל־יהוה: אֶל־הַנַּעַר
הַזֶּה הִתְפַּלָּלְתִּי וַיִּתֵּן יהוה לִי אֶת־שְׁאֵלָתִי אֲשֶׁר
כח שָׁאַלְתִּי מֵעִמּוֹ: וְגַם אָנֹכִי הִשְׁאִלְתִּהוּ לַיהוה כָּל־
הַיָּמִים אֲשֶׁר הָיָה הוּא שָׁאוּל לַיהוה וַיִּשְׁתַּחוּ שָׁם

issued a legal ruling in the presence of your teacher."[1]

When Hannah heard what had occurred, she came screaming, אֲנִי הָאִשָּׁה הַנִּצֶּבֶת עִמְּכָה בָּזֶה, *"I am the woman who was standing by you [praying for this boy] ..."* Eli tried to console her, "Let me punish him, and then I will pray that you have a son even greater than he." Hannah responded, "No, אֶל־הַנַּעַר הַזֶּה הִתְפַּלָּלְתִּי, *This is the child that I prayed for."*

A number of perplexities arise from this story. First, how could the 2-year-old Samuel have been held responsible for having violated the law, since he was not yet legally accountable for his actions? *Maharsha* explains that the Heavenly Court may at times determine that a child is sufficiently mature to be considered liable for his actions.

Another obvious question is how Eli could have retractejmnd his legal ruling simply because of Hannah's appeal.

Ahavas Yehonasan offers a brilliant solution to this problem. He states that issuing a halachic ruling in the presence of one's mentor is prohibited because the student is presumed to be so overcome with awe in his teacher's presence that he cannot concentrate sufficiently to issue a proper finding. Hannah thus stated, "אֶל־הַנַּעַר הַזֶּה הִתְפַּלָּלְתִּי, *I prayed for this boy,* so that וּמוֹרָה לֹא־יַעֲלֶה עַל־רֹאשׁוֹ, *fear of humans should not affect him."* Accordingly, Samuel should be exempt from the prohibition against issuing a halachic ruling in the presence of one's teacher. (For further discussion of a variety of issues regarding this episode, see *Nachalas Shimon* 8.)

26. The burden was now on Hannah to persuade Eli to accept this exceptionally young but capable student. Hannah presented her case by describing the miraculous circumstances that led to Samuel's birth, indicating that he was clearly a product of heartfelt prayer. The immediacy of God's response to Hannah's petition and the amazing precision with which Samuel fulfilled the details of Hannah's request were grounds enough to recognize his uniqueness and accept him at his young age (*Malbim*).

וַתֹּאמֶר בִּי אֲדֹנִי — *She said, "Please, my lord! ..."*

Make him your disciple!

Our translation follows *Targum*, which renders בִּי, *please*, as a polite form of entreaty (see *Ramban, Genesis* 43:20).

Ibn Ezra (ibid.) understands this phrase as a compressed way of saying, "I am the responsible party, so you have the right to do to me as you please — but please hear my plea!" (See below 25:24.) Accordingly, Hannah was notifying Eli that it was through *her* vow that Samuel would be placed in the service of the Sanctuary (*R' Mendel Geldwerth*).

Abarbanel interprets בִּי as meaning *through me* — i.e., Hannah stated, "It is through my prayers that this child exists; thus, it is my privilege to dedicate him to the Sanctuary."

חֵי נַפְשְׁךָ — *By your life.*

Hannah asked Eli to swear by his own life that he would give the boy his close attention (*Metzudos*).

1. *Tosafos* points out that although Samuel had not yet learned anything from Eli, he was already prohibited from issuing any halachic decisions in Eli's presence, for Eli was the recognized leader of the generation, and Samuel had come with the intention of accepting Eli's tutelage.

[26] *She said, "Please, my lord! By your life, my lord, I am the woman who was standing by you here praying to HASHEM.* [27] *This is the child that I prayed for; HASHEM granted me my request that I asked of Him.* [28] *Furthermore, I have dedicated him to HASHEM — all the days that he lives he is dedicated to HASHEM." He then prostrated himself to HASHEM.*

Mahari Kara understands the verse to mean that Hannah herself swore by his life that she was the woman who had earlier prayed in Eli's presence for a child.

Alternatively, *Mahari Kara* quotes an opinion that this phrase is a blessing, "May your soul live long," that Hannah made prior to her plea.

אֲנִי הָאִשָּׁה הַנִּצֶּבֶת עִמְּכָה בָּזֶה — *I am the woman who was standing by you here.*

The word עִמְּכָה, *together with you,* apparently cannot be taken literally, since Eli had been sitting during Hannah's prayer (*Radak, Metzudos*; see v. 9).

The Sages, however, state that when Eli realized that Hannah was praying he rose to his feet. From this, our Sages learn that one is not allowed to sit idly within four cubits of somebody who is reciting the *Shemoneh Esrei* (*Berachos* 31b). [The unusual spelling of עִמְּכָה (instead of עִמְּךָ) is not unique — see *Exodus* 13:16, 15:11, and *Numbers* 22:23 (*Radak*).]

בָּזֶה — *Here.*

Our translation of this unclear word (lit., *by this*) follows *Metzudos.*

Radak, on the other hand, translates בָּזֶה as *for [the sake of] this [boy].*

27. אֶל־הַנַּעַר הַזֶּה הִתְפַּלָּלְתִּי — *This is the child that I prayed for.*

"He perfectly matches the description of the son that I had imagined" (*Malbim*).

Following the Midrashic interpretation of this episode, *Rashi* renders the phrase as, "Do not attempt to appease me by saying that this boy will die and you will pray for another, because I prayed specifically for him."

Maharsha states that Hannah preferred to keep this boy because she had earned him with the merit of her supplications, and he therefore represented the embodiment of her fervent prayer.

28. אָנֹכִי הִשְׁאִלְתִּהוּ — *I have dedicated him.*

Literally, as *Rashi* states, הִשְׁאִלְתִּהוּ means "I have lent him," as a person sends his son to serve his own teacher. Following the Talmud's interpretation, *Rashi* asserts that Hannah implored, "You may not have Samuel punished, for I have lent him to Hashem, and Hashem must return him to me."

הוּא שָׁאוּל — *He is dedicated.*

Midrash Shmuel comments that a spark of Divine Inspiration entered Hannah's speech, and with these words she alluded to King Saul, implying that as long as Samuel lived, Saul would remain alive as well. (This came about in response to Samuel's petition that he not live to see the demise of his own handiwork, which included Samuel's anointing of Saul — *Taanis* 5b.)

וַיִּשְׁתַּחוּ שָׁם לַה' — *He then prostrated himself to HASHEM.*

Who prostrated himself?

Rashi states that it was either Samuel or Elkanah.

Metzudos specifies that it was Samuel, prostrating himself as an expression of his gratitude to God for having stationed him among the servants of God.

Radak states that if indeed the verse is referring to Samuel, he bowed simply

ב/א א לַיהוָה׃ וַתִּתְפַּלֵּל חַנָּה
וַתֹּאמַר עָלַץ לִבִּי בַּיהוָה רָמָה קַרְנִי בַּיהוָה
רָחַב פִּי עַל־אוֹיְבַי כִּי שָׂמַחְתִּי בִּישׁוּעָתֶךָ׃

Mahari Kara disagrees with both views and contends that this verse is referring to Eli, who prostrated himself upon hearing the glad news that his blessing of Hashem had been fulfilled.

because his parents were teaching him how to properly comport himself. Alternatively, if it was Elkanah, he prostrated himself in the course of requesting permission to depart from the Sanctuary.

II

☙ Hannah's Prayer and Song

Our Sages regard Hannah's expression of gratitude as one of history's great prophetic songs. In its literal sense, it is a poetic testimony to God's impeccable justice and the dependence of human existence on Divine Providence, but it has other dimensions as well, which are explicated by the multifaceted interpretations provided by the commentators.

The Talmud finds evidence in this chapter that Hannah was one of history's seven prophetesses (*Megillah* 14a; see comm. verse 1), and *Targum Yonasan* elucidates the prophetic implications of her words.[1]

We will offer comments on both the direct meaning and prophetic import of this song.

1. וַתִּתְפַּלֵּל חַנָּה וַתֹּאמַר ... — *Then Hannah prayed and said ...*

Only the tenth and last verse of this paean to God is, technically speaking, a prayer — i.e., a supplication.

Metzudos explains that before addressing Hashem in prayer Hannah wished to express her praise (see *Berachos* 32a).

According to *Kli Yakar*, Hannah's encomium expressed her confidence that her petition, when she did offer it, would not go unanswered. King David articulated a similar hopefulness when he stated, מְהֻלָּל אֶקְרָא ה׳, *With praises I call unto* H*ASHEM* (*II Samuel* 22:4).[2]

עָלַץ לִבִּי בַּה׳ — *My heart exults in* H*ASHEM*.

Hannah's heart, which had been previously broken, was transformed and experienced exultation (*Mahari Kara*).

With these words, Hannah was alluding and responding to Elkanah's query, לָמֶה תִבְכִּי ... וְלָמֶה יֵרַע לְבָבֵךְ — *Why do you cry? ... Why is your heart broken?* (1:8) (*Abarbanel*).

A Midrash points out that the numerical value of the word עָלַץ, *exults*, is 190, and relates that Hannah was saying, "Abraham and Sarah were given a son when they were, respectively, 100 years old and 90 years old; therefore, I rejoice." *Kli Yakar* explains that Hannah believed that she had greater reason to rejoice than had Abraham and Sarah, since she had borne a child at the age of 130.

רָמָה קַרְנִי בַּה׳ — *My pride has been raised through* H*ASHEM*.

1. The *Vilna Gaon* also explains Hannah's prayer as a sweeping prophetic view of Jewish history, from Abraham until Messiah. See *R' Shlomo Brevda's* treatment of the Vilna Gaon's commentary on this prayer.

2. The Midrash (*Yalkut Shimoni*) shows that Hannah paraphrased each of the eighteen blessings of our *Shemoneh Esrei*, and deduces that since Hannah prayed eighteen blessings, it must be that women are obligated to pray. (However, for actual practice, see *Shulchan Aruch Orach Chaim* 106:1, *Magen Avraham*, and *Mishnah Berurah*.)

2/1 1 Then Hannah prayed and said:
My heart exults in HASHEM,
my pride has been raised through HASHEM;
my mouth is opened wide against my antagonists,
for I rejoice in Your salvation.

The word קֶרֶן, literally *horn,* is often used to represent strength. It is an appropriate metaphor because the horn is the highest part of the animal and its source of strength in combat (*Radak*).

Metzudos understand this phrase as meaning that Hannah "raised her horns" in victory over her antagonists — Peninnah and her children — who would no longer be able to harass her.

רָחַב פִּי עַל־אוֹיְבַי — *My mouth is opened wide against my antagonists.*

This is a reference to Peninnah (*Rashi*).

Until now, Hannah had been like a silent sheep, afraid to open its mouth (*Metzudos*).

According to *Abarbanel,* Hannah was responding to Eli's previous rebuke of her silent prayer (above, 1:14), telling him that now she could speak proudly and openly.

כִּי שָׂמַחְתִּי בִּישׁוּעָתֶךָ — *For I rejoice in Your salvation.*

Hannah's joy in her deliverance was enhanced by the fact that it came from Hashem (*Metzudos*).

Hannah expressed her satisfaction that her salvation came in the form of a sensational miracle that demonstrated God's omnipotence (*Malbim*).

◈ The Prophetic Implications of This Verse

Targum states that the phrase עָלַץ לִבִּי בַּה׳, *My heart exults in HASHEM,* is a prophecy that during the days of Samuel, the Jews would be redeemed from the Philistines.

Ralbag comments that Hannah was referring specifically to the fact that Samuel would remove the idols of Baal and Ashtaros and the Jews would return to serve Hashem alone. Hence, she stated, עָלַץ לִבִּי בַּה׳, *My heart exults in HASHEM* — i.e., in Hashem alone.

According to *Targum,* Hannah's reference to קַרְנִי, *my horn,* means that she prophetically saw her Levite descendants holding musical instruments and making music in the Holy Temple.

Our Sages also associate this reference to a *horn* with the anointing of kings, as follows.

Samuel anointed King Saul with a flask of oil (see below, 10:1), and King Yehu was similarly anointed (*II Kings* 9:1-3). But Samuel anointed King David with a horn of oil (see 16:1) and King Solomon was similarly anointed (*I Kings* 1:39). Hannah's exclamation that her horn — and not her flask — was raised meant that the dynasties of King David and Solomon would extend for posterity, whereas the kingdoms of King Saul and King Yehu would not (*Megillah* 14a).[1] Accordingly, the Talmud cites this to prove Hannah's prophetic power.

Targum associates the phrase רָחַב פִּי עַל־אוֹיְבַי with the incident when the Philistines returned the captured Ark to the Israelites (Chapter 6). Prophetically, Hannah *widened her mouth* in song and praise *over* the salvation from *her enemies.*

1. The horn is something that lasts long, so its "products" had longevity, as opposed to the earthenware flask, which breaks easily, as did its "products" (*Mussar HaNeviim*).

ב אֵין־קָדוֹשׁ כַּיהוָה כִּי־אֵין בִּלְתֶּךָ וְאֵין צוּר
ג כֵּאלֹהֵינוּ: אַל־תַּרְבּוּ תְדַבְּרוּ גְּבֹהָה גְבֹהָה יֵצֵא עָתָק
מִפִּיכֶם כִּי אֵל דֵּעוֹת יהוה °וְלֹא נִתְכְּנוּ עֲלִלוֹת: °וְלוֹ ק׳

2. אֵין־קָדוֹשׁ כַּה׳ — *There is none as holy as* Hashem.

The word קָדוֹשׁ, *holy*, generally connotes a state in which one is separate from the restrictions of earthliness.

Mahari Kara understands it here as a reference to God's all-pervasive power and sovereignty.

אֵין־קָדוֹשׁ כַּה׳ כִּי־אֵין בִּלְתֶּךָ — *There is none as holy as* Hashem, *for there is none besides You.*

The flow and reasoning of this verse are perplexing, for the totally exclusive statement אֵין בִּלְתֶּךָ, *there is none besides You,* makes it unnecessary to say *there is none as holy as* Hashem; since He is the only one, there is obviously none who can compare to Him. *Metzudos* rectifies this by adding כִּי־אֵין בּוֹרֵא בִּלְתֶּךָ — You are the *sole Creator,* and therefore there cannot be anyone as holy as You, for the product cannot possibly reach the level of its producers.

Malbim provides a profound interpretation of this verse. We are generally accustomed to associating holiness with separation from earthly matters (thus, angels are holy). But since Hashem is constantly involved in everything that exists, how appropriate is it to refer to Him as "holy"? With the words אֵין־קָדוֹשׁ כַּה׳, *there is none as holy as* Hashem, Hannah addresses this question by stating that His holiness is unique. And in what sense? Hannah's next words provide the answer: כִּי־אֵין בִּלְתֶּךָ, *for there is none besides You;* all of the world is part of Him and completely dependent on Him. Hashem is separate from created entities in the sense that they are as nothing in regard to Him, and were He not to infuse them with life they would cease to exist.

כִּי־אֵין בִּלְתֶּךָ — *For there is none besides You.*

The Talmud understands this phrase homiletically as אֵין לְבַלּוֹתֶךָ — *no one causes You to wither.* The objects that a person produces can outlast him, because he, the older creature, begins to wither before the newer ones. By contrast, Hashem outlasts everything (*Berachos* 10a).

וְאֵין צוּר כֵּאלֹהֵינוּ — *And there is no Rock like our God.*

When referring to God, the word צוּר, *Rock,* represents His might (see *Deuteronomy* 32:4).

Radak and *Ralbag* thus explain Hannah's expression as indicating that Hashem's power is incomparable, since He can alter natural systems at will, thereby, for example, presenting a child to a physically barren women.

The Talmud, however, reads צוּר as צַיָּר, *painter* or *sculptor* (*Berachos* ibid.). Whereas an artist can at most create an image but cannot invest it with life, Hashem can create a form within another form (a fetus inside its mother's womb) and then infuse it with a soul and a variety of physical functions.[1]

◆§ The Prophetic Implications of This Verse

According to *Targum,* this verse alludes to the episode in which, after the Assyrian king Sennacherib laid siege to Jerusalem and made blasphemous remarks, all of his soldiers died in one

1. The *Ponevezher Rav* explains the idea that Hashem is the greatest painter as follows. The test of a good painter is to see how lifelike his products appear. Similarly, Hashem created this world, with all its enticing pleasures. Their "value" is really a worthless figment of people's imagination, yet Hashem made them appear as if they have "life" (*Mishbetzos Zahav*).

[2] *There is none as holy as* HASHEM,
for there is none besides You,
and there is no Rock like our God.
[3] *Do not abound in speaking*
[with] arrogance upon arrogance,
let not haughtiness come from your mouth;
for HASHEM *is the God of thoughts, and [men's]*
deeds are accounted by Him.

night (*II Kings* Ch. 19). At that time, all of the nations exclaimed, אֵין קָדוֹשׁ כַּה׳ כִּי אֵין בִּלְתֶּךָ, *There is none as holy as* HASHEM, *for there is none besides You,* and the Jews exulted, אֵין צוּר כֵּאלֹהֵינוּ, *There is no Rock like our God.*

3. אַל־תַּרְבּוּ תְדַבְּרוּ גְּבֹהָה גְבֹהָה — *Do not abound in speaking [with] arrogance upon arrogance.*

People who enjoy periods of success should not grow arrogant and make disparaging remarks about those less fortunate than they. Hannah is referring specifically to Peninnah (*Rashi*).

אַל ... יֵצֵא עָתָק מִפִּיכֶם — *Let not haughtiness come from your mouth.*

The negative command אַל at the beginning of the verse (there translated as *Do not*) applies to this phrase as well.

עָתָק literally means *strong;* hence, strong speech. Alternatively, it can mean *devious, words stripped of truth* (*Rashi*).

Me'am Loez quotes an interpretation that translates עָתָק as *excessive.* Thus, the verse means, Do not pain your fellow human beings with needless words that remind them of their deficiencies. Do not burden a poor man by stressing what he lacks, nor a barren woman ...

כִּי אֵל דֵּעוֹת ה׳ וְלוֹ נִתְכְּנוּ עֲלִלוֹת — *For* HASHEM *is the God of thoughts, and [men's] deeds are accounted by Him.*

Our translation follows *Rashi.* Accordingly, Hannah is warning haughty individuals that they will have to give a reckoning for their hurtful intentions and deeds.

The phrase וְלוֹ נִתְכְּנוּ עֲלִלוֹת has the word לא written (*ksiv*) with an א, *not;* yet traditionally this word is read (*kri*) as though it were written with a ו, *by him.* Following the common Rabbinic practice of drawing from both meanings, *Radak* offers the following interpretation:

לֹא נִתְכְּנוּ עֲלִלוֹת means that no actions of man can be realized without God's consent. לוֹ נִתְכְּנוּ עֲלִלוֹת indicates that God is ultimately in control of all that a human being can accomplish.

According to *Me'am Loez,* this idea flows directly from the fact that כִּי אֵל דֵּעוֹת ה׳, HASHEM *is the God of thoughts.* Man's actions are based on his intellectual ability. Since God is אֵל דֵּעוֹת. *the God of thoughts,* i.e., in control of human minds, לוֹ נִתְכְּנוּ עֲלִלוֹת, *[men's] deeds are accounted by Him* — i.e., He determines the success of all human deeds.

Another interpretation quoted by *Me'am Loez* is that Hannah was exclaiming, "Let not the haughty person assume that his success means that he has met with God's approval, כִּי אֵל דֵּעוֹת ה׳, *for* HASHEM *is a God of deep and hidden considerations,*" which are often incomprehensible to man.[1]

1. *Kli Yakar* sees in this verse an allusion to the philosophical concept of הַכֹּל צָפוּי וְהָרְשׁוּת נְתוּנָה, *All* [future occurrences and actions] *are foreseen* [by Hashem, yet] *the freedom* [of choice] *is granted* [to man to act as he wishes] (*Avos* 3:19). Many have pondered this concept, and the text here reiterates it. Although it may be difficult for human comprehension, אֵל דֵּעוֹת ה׳,

ד קֶשֶׁת גִּבֹּרִים חַתִּים וְנִכְשָׁלִים אָזְרוּ חָיִל:
ה שְׂבֵעִים בַּלֶּחֶם נִשְׂכָּרוּ וּרְעֵבִים חָדֵלוּ עַד־
עֲקָרָה יָלְדָה שִׁבְעָה וְרַבַּת בָּנִים אֻמְלָלָה:

◆§ The Prophetic Implications of This Verse

Targum interprets this verse as warning Nebuchadnezzar and other oppressors of the Jews not to speak proudly or blasphemously, for one day there will be retribution against them.

◆§ Man's Fluctuating Fortunes

In the following five verses, Hannah addresses the unstable nature of the human condition. A person experiencing success should not feel self-assured, for the vicissitudes of this world are fluctuating and hold many surprises.

4. קֶשֶׁת גִּבֹּרִים חַתִּים — *The bow and the mighty are broken.*

This phrase literally reads, "the bow of the mighty is broken." However, that presents a grammatical problem, for the adjective חַתִּים, *broken*, is written to modify a plural noun. Our translation is that of *Radak*, who replaces the word *of* with *and.*

Ralbag renders this phrase as "The powerful men, with bow in hand, were broken."

Malbim suggests that קֶשֶׁת, *bow*, is a singular collective noun referring to many "bows," similar to "sheep" and "fish" in English, and as found in the verse, וַיְהִי־לִי שׁוֹר וַחֲמוֹר, *I have acquired oxen and donkeys*, which literally reads "I have acquired an ox and a donkey" (*Genesis* 32:6).

◆§ The Prophetic Implications of This Verse

Targum reads this verse as predicting the fate of the Macedonian Greeks, whose power would suddenly be broken in their confrontation with the weak family of the Hasmoneans.

5. שְׂבֵעִים בַּלֶּחֶם נִשְׂכָּרוּ וּרְעֵבִים חָדֵלוּ — *The sated ones are hired out for bread, while the hungry ones cease to be so.*

Wealthy people suddenly grew hungry and had to toil for their sustenance, whereas those who had been laboring for their food grew prosperous (*Rashi*).

עַד־עֲקָרָה יָלְדָה שִׁבְעָה וְרַבַּת בָּנִים אֻמְלָלָה — *While the barren woman bears seven, the one with many children becomes bereft.*

The woman who bore many children will bury them (*Rashi*).

Most commentators state that Hannah is here speaking of herself and Peninnah. While she bore seven children, Peninnah's children were dying.[1]

However, verse 21 states that Hannah gave birth to only five children (three sons and two daughters).

Many solutions to this apparent contradiction have been offered, among them the following:

❒ *Radak* understands the number *seven* as a conventional expression meaning "many," as in the verse, וְיָסַפְתִּי לְיַסְּרָה ...

HASHEM *is God Who knows* [the future], yet לוֹ נִתְכְּנוּ עֲלִלוֹת, *He still takes an account of man's decisions* and לֹא נִתְכְּנוּ עֲלִלוֹת, *human execution is not altered* [by God's foresight]. See *Rambam, Hilchos Teshuvah* 5:5; ArtScroll *Pirkei Avos* ad loc.

1. When Abraham was told that Isaac would be born, he said, "O that Ishmael might live before You" (*Genesis* 17:18). *Be'er Mayim Chaim* explains that just as Peninnah's children died when Hannah bore hers, Abraham was concerned that since Hagar pained Sarah by bringing attention to the fact that she and not Sarah had a child, Ishmael would die when Isaac was born. Abraham's prayer was accepted.

[4]*The bow and the mighty are broken,*
while the foundering are girded with strength.
[5]*The sated ones are hired out for bread,*
while the hungry ones cease to be so;
while the barren woman bears seven,
the one with many children becomes bereft.

אֶתְכֶם שֶׁבַע עַל־חַטֹּאתֵיכֶם — *... then I shall punish you further sevenfold for your sins* (*Leviticus* 26:18).

❒ *Midrash Shmuel* (quoted by *Rashi*) cites the opinions of two Talmudic Sages.

Rabbi Nehemiah states that when each of Hannah's first four children was born, two of Peninnah's 10 children (see 1:8) died. When Hannah became pregnant with her fifth, Peninnah feared that she would lose her remaining two children. She prostrated herself at Hannah's feet and begged for mercy. Hannah prayed on their behalf and saved their lives; thus, they are considered as her own children. That brings the total to seven.

Rabbi Yehudah states that the verse here is referring to the two grandsons that Hannah lived to see, for grandchildren are considered to be like children.

❒ *Pesikta Rabbasi* offers identical explanations. However, it attributes the first interpretation to the Sages (and not Rabbi Nehemiah), and the second to Rabbi Nehemiah (and not Rabbi Yehudah). It then adds another solution in the name of Rabbi Yehudah. In *Psalms* (99:6), Samuel is equated with Moses and Aaron. Accordingly, Samuel is here calculated as two people.[1]

❒ *Rashi* points out that the numerical value of שִׁבְעָה, *seven*, is equal to that of שְׁמוּאֵל, *Samuel* (377). Thus, the word *seven* is not meant to be taken literally but as an allusion to Samuel.

The Prophetic Implications of This Verse

Radak sees in this verse a prophecy regarding the tribulations of the Jewish nation in its exile among idolaters. Hannah compares Israel to a barren woman[2] and the other nations to a woman with many children. One day, the other nations' success will cease and the Jewish nation will rise to glory.

Targum Yonasan associates the first half of this verse with the downfall of Haman and his children, which was accompanied by Mordecai and Esther's sudden attainment of wealth.

Along those lines, the Talmud homiletically reads שְׂבֵעִים בַּלֶּחֶם נִשְׂכָּרוּ as שִׁבְעִים בַּלֶּחֶם נִשְׂכָּרוּ, *"seventy* are hired out for bread." After the demise of Haman and 10 of his sons, 70 of his sons remained alive; they were reduced to penury and had to beg for bread (*Megillah* 15b).

According to *Targum*, the latter half of this verse prophesies that after having been as desolate as a barren woman, Jerusalem will once again be widely

1. Clearly, according to this answer, we are forced to say that the five children mentioned in v. 21 were *in addition* to Samuel. This is actually quite feasible since the births of these five seem to be recorded as an outgrowth of Eli's blessing, which came long after Samuel's birth. However, according to the previous two answers quoted by *Midrash Shmuel*, it would seem likely that the five children of verse 21 included Samuel.

2. As does Isaiah in the verse, רָנִּי עֲקָרָה לֹא יָלָדָה, *Sing out, O barren one who has not given birth* (*Isaiah* 54:1).

ו יְהוָה מֵמִית וּמְחַיֶּה מוֹרִיד שְׁאוֹל וַיָּעַל:
ז יְהוָה מוֹרִישׁ וּמַעֲשִׁיר מַשְׁפִּיל אַף־מְרוֹמֵם:
ח מֵקִים מֵעָפָר דָּל מֵאַשְׁפֹּת יָרִים אֶבְיוֹן
לְהוֹשִׁיב עִם־נְדִיבִים וְכִסֵּא כָבוֹד יַנְחִלֵם
כִּי לַיהוָה מְצֻקֵי אֶרֶץ וַיָּשֶׁת עֲלֵיהֶם תֵּבֵל:

populated, whereas bustling Rome will be destroyed.[1]

6. ה׳ מֵמִית וּמְחַיֶּה — *Hashem brings death and gives life.* Seemingly, the verse should first have stated that Hashem gives life and only then that He brings death.

Radak explains that during a life-threatening crisis, Hashem chooses either to bring a person death or to allow him an extension of life.[2]

Alshich views this verse as a justification of the fact that on occasion Hashem brings a virtuous man death at a relatively young age, whereas He gives a long life to a wicked man. The early death of the virtuous man is a prerequisite to a glorious afterlife — a reward denied the wicked man.

The assembly of Korah is listed among those infamous groups that lost their share in the World to Come (*Sanhedrin* 108a). Rabbi Eliezer contends that Hannah's words, ה׳ מֵמִית וּמְחַיֶּה, *Hashem brings death and gives life,* are to be understood as a prayer on their behalf: "Hashem, You Who bring death, bring life [in the World to Come]!" As the *Talmud Yerushalmi* elaborates, the company of Korah was sinking gradually into an eternal abyss until Hannah petitioned for them and saved them.[3]

◆§ The Prophetic Implications of This Verse

Targum (as quoted by *Radak* and *Ralbag*) considers this a prophecy regarding the revivification of the dead.

7. ה׳ מוֹרִישׁ וּמַעֲשִׁיר — *Hashem impoverishes and makes rich.*

A person who internalizes this fact will not grow arrogant when he gains wealth nor worried if he grows impoverished, for he will know that his circumstances may be altered at any time (*Ralbag*).

Alshich points out that often a righteous man's poverty is his wealth in a deeper sense, for it cleanses him in preparation for the next world.

מַשְׁפִּיל אַף־מְרוֹמֵם — *He humbles and He elevates.*

1. *Bereishis Rabbah* (72:1) interprets this verse in regard to Rachel and Leah. שְׂבֵעִים בַּלֶּחֶם נִשְׂכָּרוּ, [Leah], who had already been *satiated* [with children], *still did business* (by exchanging her *dudaim* for the privilege of having Jacob spend the night in her tent), וּרְעֵבִים חָדֵלּוּ [contrary to Rachel], who was childless [*the hungry one*], yet forfeited that opportunity [*ceases to be so*]. [As a result] עַד־עֲקָרָה יָלְדָה שִׁבְעָה, the עֲקֶרֶת הַבַּיִת, *primary wife* [Leah], *had seven children,* while רַבַּת בָּנִים אֻמְלָלָה, [Rachel], who should have had *many children, remained unfortunate* (see *Yefeh Toar*).

2. *Kli Yakar* comments that it is most appropriate that this follows the previous verse, which alluded to Hannah's last-minute supplication to save the lives of Peninnah's last two children.

3. *Kli Yakar* provides an interesting insight to clarify why Hannah went out of her way specifically for the sake of Korah and his group. *Rashi* (to *Numbers* 16:7) quotes *Midrash Tanchuma* that ascribes Korah's mistake to his inspired knowledge that the great prophet Samuel would be his descendant, and he erroneously assumed that that was proof that he would prevail. *Kli Yakar* asserts that Hannah felt somewhat guilty that her son Samuel was thus indirectly responsible for Korah's rebellion and death. This emotion aroused Hannah to pray for their ascension.

6 HASHEM brings death and gives life,
He lowers to the grave and raises up.
7 HASHEM impoverishes and makes rich,
He humbles and He elevates.
8 He raises the needy from the dirt,
from the trash heaps He lifts the destitute,
to seat [them] with nobles, and He will endow
them with a seat of honor —
for HASHEM's are the pillars of the earth,
and upon them He set the world.

This phrase literally means, "He humbles, He even elevates."

Radak explains that more energy is required to raise something than to lower it.

Metzudos understands this phrase as connected to the earlier statement that שְׂבֵעִים בַּלֶּחֶם נִשְׂכָּרוּ וּרְעֵבִים חָדֵלּוּ, *The sated ones are hired out for bread, while the hungry ones cease to be so* (v. 5). In a dramatic turn of events, the hungry individual can be raised so high that he is exalted *even* above the man who had been sated and who must now hire himself out to the formerly hungry individual.

The word אַף can also be translated as *anger*. Accordingly, *Midrash Tanchuma* states that the anger that Hashem directs against one person to impoverish him elevates another person. For instance, when Hashem wanted the tribes of Reuben and Gad to become wealthy, he exercised His revenge on Midian by taking away their cattle, and He transferred it to those tribes (see *Numbers* Chs. 31,32).

Kli Yakar translates אַף־מְרוֹמֵם as *with wrath, He elevates.* Sometimes God elevates a person but with wrath — i.e., in order to cast him down from a higher place — as He did to Haman.

8. מֵקִים מֵעָפָר דָּל מֵאַשְׁפֹּת יָרִים אֶבְיוֹן — *He raises the needy from the dirt, from the trash heaps He lifts the destitute.*

A person who is דַּל, *needy,* is not as poor as someone who is an אֶבְיוֹן, *destitute,* who is so hungry that he desires anything (*Metzudos*)

Mahari Kara suggests that the destitute person lacks clothing and so he seeks shelter and warmth amid the trash heaps.

לְהוֹשִׁיב עִם־נְדִיבִים וְכִסֵּא כָבוֹד יַנְחִלֵם — *To seat [them] with nobles, and He will endow them with a seat of honor.*

The contrast is remarkable: A person from the lowest stratum of society will be raised to the highest circles. *Ralbag* states that Hannah is referring to her own marvelous leap from childlessness to bearing Samuel, who would be an esteemed leader of the Jews.

Midrash Shmuel associates this verse with the stories of Joseph and Daniel, each of whom was transferred from sorrowful circumstances to a position of power and honor.

וְכִסֵּא כָבוֹד יַנְחִלֵם — *And He will endow them with a seat of honor.*

The word יַנְחִלֵם, *endow them,* is generally associated with inheritance. Hashem raises the pauper to such a respectable level that the populace perceives him as having inherited this honor from his presumably prestigious family (*Metzudos*).

כִּי לַה׳ מְצֻקֵי אֶרֶץ וַיָּשֶׁת עֲלֵיהֶם תֵּבֵל — *For HASHEM's are the pillars of the earth, and upon them He set the world.*

ט רַגְלֵ֤י °חסידו יִשְׁמֹ֔ר וּרְשָׁעִ֖ים בַּחֹ֣שֶׁךְ יִדָּ֑מּוּ (°חֲסִידָיו ק׳)
י כִּֽי־לֹ֥א בְכֹ֖חַ יִגְבַּר־אִֽישׁ׃ יְהֹוָ֞ה יֵחַ֣תּוּ °מריבו (°מְרִיבָיו ק׳)

Hannah offers a rationale for God's distribution of glory. Since He fashioned the world, He can do with it as He pleases (*Mahari Kara, Metzudos*).

Targum Yonasan understands this verse as addressing the concept of reward and punishment. Knowing of the righteous deeds of the downtrodden, Hashem raises them לְהוֹשִׁיב עִם־נְדִיבִים, *to seat them with righteous people*, for Hashem knows the hidden deeds of people and therefore, לַה׳ מְצֻקֵי אֶרֶץ, *HASHEM has made the pangs [of Gehinnom] in the earth* for them. As for noble people, וַיָּשֶׁת עֲלֵיהֶם תֵּבֵל, *[God] has established the World [to Come] for them.*

The Talmud (*Yoma* 38b) interprets מְצֻקֵי אֶרֶץ, *pillars of the earth*, as a reference to righteous people. It derives homiletically that Hashem foresaw that there would be few such people in the world; thus, He spread them out throughout history, placing one in every generation, וַיָּשֶׁת עֲלֵיהֶם תֵּבֵל, *he predicated the [ongoing existence of the] world upon them.*

וַיָּשֶׁת עֲלֵיהֶם תֵּבֵל — *And upon them He set the world.*

תֵּבֵל refers specifically to the *inhabited* world.

9. רַגְלֵי חֲסִידָיו יִשְׁמֹר וּרְשָׁעִים בַּחֹשֶׁךְ יִדָּמּוּ — *He guards the steps of His devout ones, but the wicked are stilled in darkness.*

A person might mistakenly attribute the shifting of people's fortunes to a lack of resolution on Hashem's part. Hannah here affirms that all changes in a person's situation are deserved, because they reflect that person's attitude toward God (*Abarbanel*). God protects those who trust in Him. As for those who do not, they are left in the dark to rely upon their own devices (*Malbim*).

Ramban (to *Job* 36:7) explains that Hashem's protection of man is dependent on how connected his mind is to Hashem's presence. If one lives with Hashem, then he will often be saved from situations that are naturally perilous. However, if one does not live with consciousness of Hashem, then his "darkness" will cause him to be subjected to the natural perils of the world, without protection (see *Sifsei Chaim, Emunah V'Hashgachah*).

רַגְלֵי חֲסִידָיו יִשְׁמֹר — *He guards the steps of His devout ones.*

According to the majority of commentators, this means that God protects a devout person from the troubles of this world, and subjects the wicked person to retribution in this world at the proper time.

וּרְשָׁעִים בַּחֹשֶׁךְ יִדָּמּוּ — *But the wicked are stilled in darkness.*

The translation of יִדָּמּוּ as *stilled* (as in the verse, וַיִּדֹּם אַהֲרֹן, *and Aaron was silent, Leviticus* 10:3), is that of *Radak*.

This word may also be translated as *cut off* (*Radak, Metzudos*).

כִּי־לֹא בְכֹחַ יִגְבַּר־אִישׁ — *For not through strength does man prevail.*

Man's fate is not dependent upon his own strength, but on Divine responses to his behavior (*Metzudos*).

Targum, however, sees this verse as a reference to Gehinnom. Hashem will save devout people from its punishments while the corrupt will be consigned to its doom.

The Talmud (*Yoma* 38b) derives a number of crucial philosophical postulates from this phrase.

The spelling of the word חֲסִידָו, *His devout ones*, allows for the meaning, *His devout one*. Second, the word רַגְלֵי, *the steps of*, may be translated as *because of* (as in the verse וַיְבָרֶךְ ה׳ אֹתְךָ לְרַגְלִי, *HASHEM blessed you because of me; Genesis* 30:30, *Rashi* ad loc.). This phrase may thus

9 He guards the steps of His devout ones,
but the wicked are stilled in darkness;
for not through strength does man prevail.
10 Hashem — may those who contend with Him
be shattered,

be read, *Because of His devout one, He maintains the world.* Hashem maintains the existence of the world even for the sake of a single righteous individual.

Rabbi Yochanan states that once a person has avoided sinning for the majority of his life, Hashem safeguards him so that he will never sin again.[1] The word רַגְלֵי, *steps,* literally means *feet,* which are at the end of a person's body, and Rabbi Yochanan reads it as referring to *the end.* Hence he translates the phrase רַגְלֵי חֲסִידָיו יִשְׁמֹר as *He will guard the end [of the life] of His devout ones* (*Rashi* ibid.).

Alternatively, once a person has twice restrained himself from a particular transgression, he will no longer succumb to that temptation. In this understanding of this phrase, the word רַגְלֵי is understood to mean *times* (as in the verse, כִּי הִכִּיתָנִי זֶה שָׁלֹשׁ רְגָלִים, *that you struck me these three times — Numbers* 22:28, *Rashi* ibid.). The phrase may thus be translated as *after two times, He shields His pious one.*

These last two interpretations apply only to iniquities associated with material temptations; however, a person must always guard himself against falling prey to lack of faith (*Me'am Loez*).[2]

כִּי־לֹא בְכֹחַ יִגְבַּר־אִישׁ — *For not through strength does man prevail.*

This phrase recalls our Sages' definition of strength: אֵיזֶהוּ גִבּוֹר הַכּוֹבֵשׁ אֶת יִצְרוֹ, *Who is strong? One who subdues his personal inclination* (*Pirkei Avos* 4:1; see *Midrash Shmuel*).[3]

10. This is the only verse in Hannah's song that makes a request of God, pleading for God's glory to be revealed as a result of His visiting judgment upon transgressors and giving sovereignty to His chosen kingdom, the Davidic dynasty.

Some commentators interpret this prayer as pertaining to Samuel.

ה' יֵחַתּוּ מְרִיבָיו — *Hashem — may those who contend with Him be shattered.*

1. In a novel interpretation of this statement, *Maharsha* (to *Moed Katan* 28a) explains that Hannah alluded here to her own son Samuel and places his relatively short lifespan of 52 years in a complimentary light. Assuming "majority" means approximately two-thirds (see *Berachos* 48a), *Maharsha* says that after the initial 20 years of one's life, for which he is not held responsible in the Heavenly Court, he is generally allotted 50 years, two-thirds of which is 32. Accordingly, once one lives 52 years without sin, he is assured never to sin. Thus, even if Samuel would have lived longer, he would surely never have sinned.

2. Otherwise, these Talmudic statements would contradict the warning of the Mishnah in *Avos* (2:5) that one should not trust himself until the day of his death, as in the case of Yochanan who served as Kohen Gadol for 80 years, and then became a heretic.

As an alternative solution, these Talmudic statements assure only that one will be protected from inadvertent sins. Of course, one still has free choice to sin intentionally. Accordingly, Scripture here says that the *foot* of the righteous will be protected, because, with regard to the damages done by an animal (see *Bava Kamma* 2b), the רֶגֶל, *foot,* represents אֵין כַּוָּנָתוֹ לְהַזִּיק, *unintentional damage* (*Mussar HaNeviim;* see also *Mishnas R' Aharon,* Vol. II p. 166).

3. See the Midrash in its entirety for its exegesis of this verse in connection with Joseph and Potiphar's wife. See too *Kli Yakar's* treatment of that Midrash.

°עָלָיו ק׳

°עלו בַּשָּׁמַיִם יַרְעֵם יהוה יָדִין אַפְסֵי־אָרֶץ
וְיִתֶּן־עֹז לְמַלְכּוֹ וְיָרֵם קֶרֶן מְשִׁיחוֹ׃
יא וַיֵּלֶךְ אֶלְקָנָה הָרָמָתָה עַל־בֵּיתוֹ וְהַנַּעַר
הָיָה מְשָׁרֵת אֶת־יהוה אֶת־פְּנֵי עֵלִי הַכֹּהֵן׃

Those who attack righteous people are in effect contending with Hashem (*Radak*).

In its enumeration of various types of punishment meted out to those engaged in different types of iniquity, the Talmud (*Rosh Hashanah* 16b-17a) cites this verse in referring to the worst group of evildoers, who are sentenced to eternal damnation. This group includes: heretics who use the words of Torah for evil (such as Zadok and Baithus); slanderers who get pagan governments to wrongfully confiscate Jewish property; non-believers who deny that Torah is Divine, dispute the doctrine of the revivification of the dead, or insult Torah scholars; those who instigate mass evil (such as Jeroboam); and powerful community financiers who impose unwarranted and excessive fear on the congregation. These people are considered to be God's opponents because their evil precipitated the destruction of the Temple (*Maharsha*; see *Rambam, Hilchos Teshuvah* 3:6).

Our translation of יֵחַתּוּ as *shattered* follows *Metzudos*.

However, *Mahari Kara* renders this word as *frightened* (as in the verse, וַיְהִי חִתַּת אֱלֹהִים, *There fell a Godly terror, Genesis* 35:5).

עָלָיו — *Against them.*

עָלָיו literally means *against him*, but here refers to every single individual in a group (*Mahari Kara*).

עָלָיו בַּשָּׁמַיִם יַרְעֵם — *Let the heavens thunder against them.*

May the heavens produce frightening noises in order to confuse them and cause them to panic. This thunder alludes to various forms of punishment that descend from heaven (*Radak*).

ה׳ יָדִין אַפְסֵי־אָרֶץ — *May* Hashem *judge to the ends of the earth.*

May He judge even those who try to escape His grasp by traveling to the far corners of the world (*Radak*).

Since this song of Hannah deals with Hashem's just distribution of worldly possessions and concludes with the mention of judgment, it is associated with Rosh Hashanah, the Day of Judgment. The Talmud (*Berachos* 29a) thus states that the nine blessings of the Rosh Hashanah *Mussaf* prayer correspond to the nine utterances of Hashem's Name in this song. Also, Hannah conceived on Rosh Hashanah (see commentary above, 1:19).

וְיָרֵם קֶרֶן מְשִׁיחוֹ — *And raise the pride of His anointed one.*

קֶרֶן, literally, *horn*, is often used as a symbol of strength or pride (see verse 1).

◆§ The Prophetic Implications of This Verse

Targum explains that מְרִיבָיו, *those who contend*, are people who persecute the Jewish nation. Hannah here prays for Hashem to punish them. The phrase ה׳ יָדִין אַפְסֵי־אָרֶץ, *May* Hashem *judge to the ends of the earth*, refers in particular to Magog and predatory nations that will come from the far corners of the world.

Ralbag and *Metzudos* explain this verse as alluding to episodes that occurred in the course of Samuel's lifetime, as follows.

ה׳ יֵחַתּוּ מְרִיבָיו, Hashem *— may those who contend with Him be shattered.* May Hashem shatter the Philistines when they set out to war with Samuel.

עָלָיו בַּשָּׁמַיִם יַרְעֵם, *Let the heavens thunder against them.* After Samuel's sacrificial offering elicited Hashem's mercy, Hashem's thunderous noise

let the heavens thunder against them.
May HASHEM judge to the ends of the earth;
may He give power to His king and raise the
pride of His anointed one.
11 *Elkanah then went to Ramah, to his house,*
while the boy served HASHEM before Eli the Kohen.

threw the Philistines into turmoil and eventually led to their defeat (7:10).

ה׳ יָדִין אַפְסֵי־אָרֶץ, *May HASHEM judge to the ends of the earth.* This may be translated as *May HASHEM aid [my son Samuel] when he travels from place to place to judge the Jews* (7:16).

וְיִתֶּן־עֹז לְמַלְכּוֹ, *May He give power to His king.* May Hashem grant strength to Saul, whom Samuel would anoint and whose kingdom Samuel would personally experience.

וְיָרֵם קֶרֶן מְשִׁיחוֹ, *And raise the pride of His anointed one.* The "anointed one" is King David; Samuel anointed him but did not live to see his reign. (See verse 1 regarding the usage of a horn in David's anointing.)

◆§ The Iniquity of Eli's Sons

Following Hannah's profound and inspiring tribute to Hashem and His impeccable recompense to every individual for his deeds, which the Talmud refers to with the phrase, בְּמִדָּה שֶׁאָדָם מוֹדֵד בָּהּ מוֹדְדִין לוֹ, *According to the measure with which one measures, so is it measured for him* (*Sotah* 8b-14a; *Sanhedrin* 90a), Scripture presents an account of such retribution in the story of Eli's sons.

11. וַיֵּלֶךְ אֶלְקָנָה הָרָמָתָה עַל־בֵּיתוֹ — *Elkanah then went to Ramah, to his house.*

The phrase עַל בֵּיתוֹ literally means *on his house*, but *Targum* renders it as אֶל בֵּיתוֹ, *to his house.*

Ralbag translates this phrase as *for the sake of his house* — i.e., to tend to the needs of his household. Elkanah would have remained to train Samuel himself, for it is a father's responsibility to teach his son (see *Deuteronomy* 6:7, 11:19; *Kiddushin* 29a). However, since he had to provide for his household, he entrusted Samuel to Eli's tutelage.[1]

וְהַנַּעַר הָיָה מְשָׁרֵת אֶת־ה׳ — *While the boy served HASHEM.*

He learned Torah and the manner of worshiping God.

אֶת־פְּנֵי עֵלִי הַכֹּהֵן — *Before Eli the Kohen.*

Eli instructed Samuel on how to serve Hashem (*Radak*).

Targum renders this phrase as *during the lifetime of Eli the Kohen.*[2]

This verse emphasizes that Samuel took care to acquaint himself only with Eli, and avoided any ties with Eli's corrupt sons (*Kli Yakar*).

The *Talmud Yerushalmi* (*Eruvin* 5:1) notes that although Samuel was serving Eli, he is described as serving Hashem. The Talmud derives from this that serving a Torah scholar is tantamount to worshiping before the Divine Presence. As *Rabbi A. J. Rosenberg* elucidates,

1. In the Talmud (*Yoma* 2a), בֵּיתוֹ, *his house*, is often a reference to one's wife. Accordingly, *R' M. D. Vali* (cited by *Mishbetzos Zahav*) suggests that this verse emphasizes that although Hannah had just experienced a prophetic revelation, she did not become conceited, and when they returned home, Elkanah was still עַל־בֵּיתוֹ, *over his wife*, i.e., she had as much respect for him as before (see also *Maharsha* to *Berachos* 61a).

2. *Mishbetzos Zahav* understands that this emphasizes that even though Samuel was a young man fit to teach Torah, he still remained a "lad" studying under his mentor Eli as long as the latter lived (see *Tosafos, Gittin* 84b, regarding Rabbi Yochanan).

יב-יג וּבְנֵי עֵלִי בְּנֵי בְלִיָּעַל לֹא יָדְעוּ אֶת־יְהֹוָה׃ וּמִשְׁפַּט
הַכֹּהֲנִים אֶת־הָעָם כָּל־אִישׁ זֹבֵחַ זֶבַח וּבָא נַעַר
הַכֹּהֵן כְּבַשֵּׁל הַבָּשָׂר וְהַמַּזְלֵג שְׁלֹשׁ־הַשִּׁנַּיִם
יד בְּיָדוֹ׃ וְהִכָּה בַכִּיּוֹר אוֹ בַדּוּד אוֹ בַקַּלַּחַת אוֹ
בַפָּרוּר כֹּל אֲשֶׁר יַעֲלֶה הַמַּזְלֵג יִקַּח הַכֹּהֵן בּוֹ
כָּכָה יַעֲשׂוּ לְכָל־יִשְׂרָאֵל הַבָּאִים שָׁם בְּשִׁלֹה׃

based on *Mesillas Yesharim* (Ch. 26), "A Torah scholar is one who cleaves to the Almighty in his thoughts at all times, so that even his mundane deeds become holy. Therefore serving him is tantamount to serving in the sanctuary."

Abarbanel states that since Samuel was studying under Eli in preparation for a life of engaging in God's service, he is considered to have already been serving God.

12. וּבְנֵי עֵלִי בְּנֵי בְלִיָּעַל — *The sons of Eli were lawless men.*

The word בְּלִיָּעַל, *lawless*, is a conjunction of two words: בְּלִי עוֹל, *without a yoke*, meaning, "without the constraints of law" (see above, 1:16).

Although the phrase בְּנֵי בְלִיָּעַל literally means *sons of a lawless person*, it in no way implicates their father Eli. Rather, it indicates that although they were the children of a saintly man, their personalities gave the impression that they were the descendants of an unscrupulous person.

Alshich points out that a person's spiritual success is not necessarily dependent on his exposure to the virtuous environment that his parents provide, but may be due to his parents' merits. Thus ... וַיֵּלֶךְ אֶלְקָנָה, *Elkanah went*, and left Samuel. Nevertheless, וְהַנַּעַר הָיָה מְשָׁרֵת, *the boy served* God — Samuel flourished. Yet on the other hand, וּבְנֵי עֵלִי בְּנֵי בְלִיָּעַל, *the sons of Eli were lawless men*, even though they were under their father's constant guidance.

לֹא יָדְעוּ אֶת־ה׳ — *They did not recognize* H*ASHEM*.

According to the Midrash, Eli's sons first succumbed to their gluttonous desires (see below), and that corruption led them to then cast off the yoke of the Kingdom of Heaven, so that לֹא יָדְעוּ אֶת־ה׳, *they did not recognize* H*ASHEM*. (Similarly, the word בְּלִיָּעַל elsewhere appears in association with idolatry: יָצְאוּ אֲנָשִׁים בְּנֵי־בְלִיַּעַל, *Lawless men have emerged*, *Deuteronomy* 13:14 [*Midrash Shmuel* 6:1].)

Abarbanel, however, sees the sons' deterioration proceeding in the opposite direction. It is was not their gluttony that brought them to impiety but rather their weak faith that induced them to sin in the Sanctuary.

According to *Targum*, לֹא יָדְעוּ אֶת־ה׳, means that Eli's sons did not fear Hashem. *Radak* interprets this to mean that they abused their priestly prerogatives.[1]

13. וּמִשְׁפַּט הַכֹּהֲנִים אֶת־הָעָם — *This was the practice of the Kohanim with the people.*

The custom described here was not the Biblically ordained practice but an illegitimate ritual that the sons of Eli instituted.

1. *Maharsha* (to *Shabbos* 55b) contends that the sons of Eli would not have been labeled בְּנֵי בְלִיַּעַל were it not for their involvement in immoral behavior (see below, v. 22, comm.), just as we find the term בְּנֵי בְלִיַּעַל associated with such conduct in regard to the episode of the concubine in Gibeah (*Judges* 19:22, 20:13).

[12]The sons of Eli were lawless men; they did not recognize HASHEM.

[13]This was the practice of the Kohanim with the people: When any person would slaughter a sacrifice, the Kohen's attendant would come while the meat was cooking, with a three-pronged fork in his hand. [14]He would thrust it into the pot or the cauldron or the pan or the kettle, and everything the fork would bring up the Kohen would take with it. This is what they would do with all the Israelites who would come there, to Shiloh.

14. וְהִכָּה בַכִּיּוֹר ... — *He would thrust it into the pot ...*

He would thrust it into the pot in a ravenous manner, exhibiting irreverence for the holy vessels (*Me'am Loez*).

Kli Yakar states that he would thrust the fork so deeply into the meat, with the intention of grabbing the absolute maximum, that it would pierce the meat and scrape the base of the pot.

The Torah dictates that the Kohen is entitled only to the breast and thigh of a peace-offering. Anything that Eli's sons took in excess of that was thievery.[1]

בַכִּיּוֹר אוֹ בַדּוּד אוֹ בַקַּלַּחַת אוֹ בַפָּרוּר — *The pot or the cauldron or the pan or the kettle.*

Each type of utensil was used for a different-size animal. The Kohanim were indiscriminate regarding the size of the offering, and took as much meat from a small animal as from a large one (*Malbim*).

כָּכָה יַעֲשׂוּ לְכָל־יִשְׂרָאֵל הַבָּאִים שָׁם בְּשִׁלֹה — *This is what they would do with all the Israelites who would come there, to Shiloh.*

They did not take any less from a pauper or from a person with a large family (*Malbim*), nor did they show any self-restraint before distinguished people or people who had traveled long distances to come to Shiloh (*Kli Yakar*).

Notwithstanding the sharp condemnation in these verses, some sources say that Hophni and Phinehas were actually on a high spiritual level, and the charges against them were only commensurate with their exalted level, as in the case of Nadab and Abihu. (In fact, *Rema MiPanu* says that they were reincarnations of Nadab and Abihu.) *Zohar* says that they took only from offerings that Kohanim were entitled to, so they were *not* guilty of thievery. Their sin was that they took the service of offerings lightly. It is also possible that, initially, their seizing of meat was done out of love for the mitzvah (see *Chullin* 133a), except that the masses took it as gluttony, and that caused a lack of regard for the sanctity of the offerings among the people (*Mishbetzos Zahav*).

It is further noteworthy that the Midrash (*Bereishis Rabbah* 54:4) refers to Hophni and Phinehas as צַדִּיקִים, *righteous men* (see below, 4:12, footnote).

1. *Nachalas Shimon* cites *Teshuvos Amudei Ohr* (#120) who explains that the improper actions of Eli's sons were based on erroneous interpretations of law. In this case, he reasons that they thought they were entitled to the three priestly gifts: the foreleg, jaws, and maw (see *Deuteronomy* 18:3). Their mistake was that those gifts apply only to privately owned animals, but not to sacred offerings.

טו גַּם בְּטֶרֶם יַקְטִרוּן אֶת־הַחֵלֶב וּבָא | נַעַר הַכֹּהֵן
וְאָמַר לָאִישׁ הַזֹּבֵחַ תְּנָה בָשָׂר לִצְלוֹת לַכֹּהֵן
טז וְלֹא־יִקַּח מִמְּךָ בָּשָׂר מְבֻשָּׁל כִּי אִם־חָי: וַיֹּאמֶר
אֵלָיו הָאִישׁ קַטֵּר יַקְטִירוּן כַּיּוֹם הַחֵלֶב וְקַח לְךָ
כַּאֲשֶׁר תְּאַוֶּה נַפְשֶׁךָ וְאָמַר | °לו כִּי עַתָּה תִתֵּן °לא ק׳
יז וְאִם־לֹא לָקַחְתִּי בְחָזְקָה: וַתְּהִי חַטַּאת הַנְּעָרִים
גְּדוֹלָה מְאֹד אֶת־פְּנֵי יְהוָה כִּי נִאֲצוּ הָאֲנָשִׁים אֵת
יח מִנְחַת יְהוָה: וּשְׁמוּאֵל מְשָׁרֵת אֶת־פְּנֵי יְהוָה נַעַר

15. גַּם בְּטֶרֶם יַקְטִרוּן אֶת־הַחֵלֶב — *Even before they would burn the fat.*

Originally, Eli's sons sinned by gluttonously taking meat that was not rightfully theirs. At least, however, they waited until the Jew bringing the offering had burned the fat upon the altar — a waiting period required by halachah before the Kohen takes his meat (see *Leviticus* 7:31, *Rashi* ad loc. based on *Toras Kohanim* 16:4).

What followed, as described in this verse, constituted an even graver sin, and ratifies our Sages' warning (in *Avos* 4:2) that עֲבֵרָה גוֹרֶרֶת עֲבֵרָה, *one sin leads to another sin.* Now Eli's sons no longer waited but sent an attendant to obtain the meat immediately (*Alshich*). Why? The answer is that were they to wait, the Jew might have begun cooking the meat, but they wanted it raw so that they might roast it (*Radak*).

תְּנָה בָשָׂר לִצְלוֹת — *Give some meat for roasting.*

The attendant persuaded the reluctant Jew to submit the meat by claiming that they would not eat it until later (*Mussar HaNeviim*).

It is possible that this was a lie — that they intended to eat the meat before the fats were offered on the altar (*Radak*). It is a matter of dispute whether only the eating before the sacrifice was burned on the altar was prohibited, or whether taking their portion at that time was also a sin, since it was not yet legally theirs (see *Nachalas Shimon* 10:2).

Malbim adds that the attendant would argue that the Jew would benefit twofold from giving the meat raw: (a) he wouldn't have to bother cooking it, and (b) he could give the meat that he wanted to instead of having the attendant take whatever meat he wanted with his fork out of the pot.

וְלֹא־יִקַּח מִמְּךָ בָּשָׂר מְבֻשָּׁל כִּי אִם־חָי — *He will not take cooked meat from you, but only raw [meat].*

In this case, the Kohen would not take cooked meat; on other occasions, however, he did so (as described above, vs. 13-14) (*Radak*).

Alternatively, the attendant was lying. After he took the raw meat, he came back later and seized the cooked meat as well.

16. וְקַח לְךָ כַּאֲשֶׁר תְּאַוֶּה נַפְשֶׁךָ — *And then take for yourself whatever your soul desires.*

The Jew would tell the attendant, "Wait until after the fats are burned on the altar, and then I will give you the meat as you prefer it, raw or cooked."

וְאָמַר לֹא — *But [the attendant] would say, "No."*

The word לו is written (*ksiv*) with a ו, meaning *to him,* but is traditionally read (*kri*) as if with an א, meaning *No.* Both interpretations are valid *(Radak).*

וְאִם־לֹא לָקַחְתִּי בְחָזְקָה — *Or else I will take it by force.*

[15]*Even before they would burn the fat [upon the*
altar] the Kohen's attendant would come and say to
the man who was bringing the offering, "Give some
meat for roasting for the Kohen; he will not take
cooked meat from you, but only raw [meat]." [16]*The*
man would say, "Let them first burn the fat [upon
the altar] and then take for yourself whatever your
soul desires." But [the attendant] would say, "No;
give it now, or else I will take it by force." [17]*The sin*
of the attendants was very great before H*ASHEM*, *for*
the men had disgraced H*ASHEM's offering.*
[18]*Samuel was serving before* H*ASHEM* — *a lad*

The Talmud (*Sanhedrin* 58b) derives from here that even if a person merely threatens violence he is considered a sinner. As the following verse testifies, *The sin of the attendants was very great.*

17. כִּי נִאֲצוּ הָאֲנָשִׁים אֵת מִנְחַת ה׳ — *For the men had disgraced* H*ASHEM's offering.*

The lads, or attendants, sinned in enabling the transgressions of the men — i.e., Eli's sons.

These attendants engaged in their sinful behavior because they were influenced by Eli's sons' disparaging attitude toward the ritual services.

God granted the Kohanim their priestly prerogatives so that they would be able to devote themselves to serving Him. With their display of greedy self-indulgence, Eli's sons desecrated that entire institution (*Ralbag*).

נִאֲצוּ — *Had disgraced.*

נִאֲצוּ literally means *angered.* The word is used here because a person who expresses contempt for another brings him to anger (*Metzudos*).

מִנְחַת ה׳ — H*ASHEM's offering.*

The word מִנְחָה, *offering,* can refer to a specific type of offering or to offerings in general; it is here used in the latter sense (*Metzudos*).

☙ The Stark Contrast Between Samuel and Eli's Sons

Scripture now interrupts its narrative of the evil behavior of Eli's sons with four verses that laud Samuel and describe his swift development as a servant of Hashem. This indicates the stark contrast between Samuel and Eli's sons, and implicitly commends Samuel for not having been influenced by them.

18. וּשְׁמוּאֵל מְשָׁרֵת אֶת־פְּנֵי ה׳ — *Samuel was serving before* H*ASHEM.*

Unlike Eli's sons, who were preoccupied with culinary delights and the pursuit of shameful pleasures, Samuel busied himself learning Torah and studying the Levitical duties, including the mastery of vocal and instrumental music.

Unlike verse 11, this verse makes no mention of Samuel serving Eli. *Metzudos* understands this to mean that Samuel had become independent of Eli's instruction.

נַעַר — *A lad.*

Although young people usually spend time together and influence one another, Samuel was unaffected by the mischief of the Kohanim's attendants (*Abarbanel*).

חָגוּר אֵפוֹד בָּד — *Girded with a linen robe.*

יט חָגוּר אֵפוֹד בָּד׃ וּמְעִיל קָטֹן תַּעֲשֶׂה־לּוֹ אִמּוֹ
וְהַעַלְתָה לוֹ מִיָּמִים | יָמִימָה בַּעֲלוֹתָהּ אֶת־אִישָׁהּ
כ לִזְבֹּחַ אֶת־זֶבַח הַיָּמִים׃ וּבֵרַךְ עֵלִי אֶת־אֶלְקָנָה
וְאֶת־אִשְׁתּוֹ וְאָמַר יָשֵׂם יהוה לְךָ זֶרַע מִן־
הָאִשָּׁה הַזֹּאת תַּחַת הַשְּׁאֵלָה אֲשֶׁר שָׁאַל לַיהוָה
כא וְהָלְכוּ לִמְקֹמוֹ׃ כִּי־פָקַד יהוה אֶת־חַנָּה וַתַּהַר

Rashi states that this *ephod* and the robe of the following verse were, respectively, a large and a small robe.

Other commentators (see *Metzudos, Abarbanel*) draw parallels between these garments and those of the same name worn by the High Priest (*Exodus* Ch. 28).

The commentators generally agree that both the אֵפוֹד and מְעִיל were worn exclusively by individuals who wished to distinguish themselves in some capacity of Divine service (*Ralbag, Metzudos;* see also 22:18, *II Samuel* 6:14). *Rambam* (*Hil. Klei HaMikdash* 10:13) derives from here that prophets would wear linen robes to show that they reached the level of the High Priest, who could speak with Divine Inspiration through his *Ephod* and Breastplate.

חָגוּר — *Girded.*

This implies that there was a strap attached to the *ephod*, which fastened it securely to his body, similar to the *Ephod* of the High Priest (*Mahari Kara,* however, translates חָגוּר in this verse as *enclothed*).

19. וּמְעִיל קָטֹן תַּעֲשֶׂה־לּוֹ אִמּוֹ — *His mother would make him a small robe.*

This robe was only long enough to match Samuel's height. *Me'am Loez* explains that typically a robe dragged on the floor. Hannah made a shorter robe that wouldn't impede Samuel's movement in order to train him to act swiftly before Eli.

This type of garment was generally worn by adults, but Hannah made one for Samuel out of her love for him and because he was occupying himself with God's service (*Mahari Kara; Radak*).

Ralbag asserts that the *ephod* of the previous verse was worn on top of this robe.

תַּעֲשֶׂה — *Would make him.*

A recurring verb may be represented in the past tense or — as here — in the future tense (see comm. 1:3).

וְהַעַלְתָה לוֹ מִיָּמִים יָמִימָה — *And bring it up to him from year to year.*

Abarbanel (and *Metzudos*) states that as Samuel grew older and taller, Hannah made him a new robe every year.

Radak, however, states that Hannah made only one robe, which she would bring with her for Samuel to wear only in honor of the festival. In order to be sure that he would not wear it otherwise, she would take it back with her. (According to this explanation, מִיָּמִים יָמִימָה means from *holiday to holiday;* see *Targum*, commentary above, 1:3.)

This latter explanation is supported by *Midrash Tanchuma* (*Emor* 63b), which states that Samuel wore the same robe throughout his lifetime (presumably, it grew miraculously in proportion to his growth) and was buried with it. This explains why, in the scene where Samuel is raised in necromancy (28:14), he is wearing such a robe.

Rashi (ad loc.) adds that when the dead are revived, they will wear the same garments in which they had been buried (see *Job* 38:14; *Rashi* ad loc.).

בַּעֲלוֹתָהּ אֶת־אִישָׁהּ לִזְבֹּחַ אֶת־זֶבַח הַיָּמִים — *When she came up with her husband to slaughter the annual offering.*

girded with a linen robe. [19] *His mother would make him a small robe and bring it up to him from year to year, when she came up with her husband to slaughter the annual offering.* [20] *Then Eli would bless Elkanah and his wife and say, "May* HASHEM *grant you offspring from this woman," because of the request that he had made of* HASHEM, *and they would return to [Elkanah's] place.* [21] *For* HASHEM *had remembered Hannah, and she conceived*

Their purpose in ascending was not to lay eyes on their son but to bring offerings to God (*Kli Yakar*).

(Regarding the nature of the annual offering, see above 1:3,21).

20. וּבֵרַךְ עֵלִי אֶת־אֶלְקָנָה וְאֶת־אִשְׁתּוֹ — *Then Eli would bless Elkanah and his wife.*

When Eli saw Samuel's maturation into a virtuous person, both in his dealings with God and with his fellow men, he was inspired to bless Samuel's parents with more such offspring.

יָשֵׂם ה׳ לְךָ זֶרַע מִן־הָאִשָּׁה הַזֹּאת — *May* HASHEM *grant you offspring from this woman.*

Eli thus implicitly expressed his recognition of Hannah's merits (*Midrash Shmuel*).

Targum renders זֶרַע, *offspring,* as בְּנִין כְּשֵׁרִין, *worthy children.*

תַּחַת הַשְּׁאֵלָה אֲשֶׁר שָׁאַל לַה׳ — *Because of the request that he had made of* HASHEM.

This is a reference to Elkanah and Hannah's intense prayer for a child, which had led to the birth of Samuel. In the merit of that prayer, they should be blessed with more children (*Abarbanel*).[1]

Some commentators render the word שְׁאֵלָה as *loan.* Eli saw that Elkanah and Hannah had forfeited any personal benefits from Samuel by "loaning" him to the service of Hashem (see 1:28). In reward for their selflessness, and to satisfy their need for children at home to aid them in their old age, Eli blessed them with more children (*Radak, Metzudos*).

וְהָלְכוּ לִמְקֹמוֹ — *And they would return to [Elkanah's] place.*

They would immediately return after receiving Eli's blessing, confident that it would be fulfilled. They also had to go home in order to engage in marital relations, which they could not do as guests in Shiloh (*Metzudos;* see above, 1:19).

Abarbanel interprets the phrase וְהָלְכוּ לִמְקֹמוֹ, *and they would return to [Elkanah's] place,* as part of Eli's blessing. Thus, Eli told them: יָשֵׂם ה׳ לְךָ זֶרַע, *May* HASHEM *grant you offspring,* תַּחַת הַשְּׁאֵלָה אֲשֶׁר שָׁאַל לַה׳, *in place of the loan [Samuel] whom [Elkanah] gave to* HASHEM, וְהָלְכוּ לִמְקֹמוֹ, *who will go about in [Elkanah's] place.*

21. כִּי־פָקַד ה׳ אֶת־חַנָּה — *For* HASHEM *had remembered Hannah.*

Elkanah and Hannah's confidence in Eli's blessing was in place, because indeed Hashem did remember her and she bore three sons and two daughters (*Radak*).

1. See *Kli Yakar* for a discussion of why Eli referred to this prayer as Elkanah's by using the masculine verb אֲשֶׁר שָׁאַל, *that he requested,* whereas it was actually Hannah who had initiated it.

וַתֵּלֶד שְׁלֹשָׁה־בָנִים וּשְׁתֵּי בָנוֹת וַיִּגְדַּל הַנַּעַר
כב שְׁמוּאֵל עִם־יְהוָה׃ וְעֵלִי זָקֵן מְאֹד
וְשָׁמַע אֵת כָּל־אֲשֶׁר יַעֲשׂוּן בָּנָיו לְכָל־יִשְׂרָאֵל וְאֵת
אֲשֶׁר־יִשְׁכְּבוּן אֶת־הַנָּשִׁים הַצֹּבְאוֹת פֶּתַח אֹהֶל
כג מוֹעֵד׃ וַיֹּאמֶר לָהֶם לָמָּה תַעֲשׂוּן כַּדְּבָרִים הָאֵלֶּה

וַתֵּלֶד שְׁלֹשָׁה־בָנִים — *And gave birth to three sons.*

(As to whether the children mentioned here include Samuel, see above, verse 5, commentary and footnote.)

וַיִּגְדַּל הַנַּעַר שְׁמוּאֵל עִם־ה׳ — *And the boy Samuel grew up with* H*ASHEM*.

But the other children remained with their parents.

☙ Eli's Rebuke

22. וְעֵלִי זָקֵן מְאֹד — *Eli became very old.*

According to *Metzudos,* this verse mentions Eli's old age to indicate that, as an elderly man, he lacked the strength to properly rebuke his sons.

Alshich suggests that because Eli's health was fragile, people were hesitant to complain to him about his sons' behavior. As a result, he was sheltered from the knowledge of the depth of their iniquity.

Radak mentions that Eli's body quivered uncontrollably and he was therefore unfit to engage in the priestly service (*Chullin* 24b). Because he was no longer constantly on the Sanctuary premises, his sons were able to act unhindered.

According to *Midrash Tanchuma* (*Parashas Chayei Sarah*), Eli grew so angry at his sons that he suffered a premature decline and the symptoms of old age.

אֵת כָּל־אֲשֶׁר יַעֲשׂוּן בָּנָיו — *All that his sons were doing*

I.e., forcibly taking meat to which they were not entitled.

וְאֵת אֲשֶׁר־יִשְׁכְּבוּן אֶת־הַנָּשִׁים — *And that they would lie with the women.*

There is much discussion and diversity among the Sages and commentators in interpreting this crime.

According to one view (cited by *Rashi*), this statement is to be understood literally: Eli's sons committed adultery in the Sanctuary Courtyard.

A Talmudic authority states (*Shabbos* 55b) that only Hophni was guilty of this behavior. His brother Phinehas was implicated because he failed to protest.

However, further on we learn of a reproof delivered by a man of God to Eli regarding his sons (verses 27-29), which complains only of their disgracing the sacrifices. If they were guilty of adultery, a more abhorrent offense, why didn't the man of God mention that as well (*Ralbag; Talmud Yerushalmi, Kesubos* 13:1)? Furthermore, the *Zohar* finds it inconceivable that Kohanim could have engaged in such depravity.

Due to objections of this nature, the Talmud (ibid.) concludes that this accusation is not to be taken literally. What, then, was the nature of Eli's sons' enormity? Several answers have been proposed.

A woman who has become ritually contaminated, due either to a discharge or to having given birth, must undergo a purification process, which is completed when she offers a pair of birds as a sacrifice. The women would bring their offerings to Shiloh and wait for Eli's sons to offer them. (Although the women were not legally obligated to wait, they did so because they knew that Eli's sons were not trustworthy — see *Rashi, Shabbos* ibid.; *Nachalas Shimon* 12.) Eli's sons took their time offering these bird offerings, for they instead gave precedence to animal offer-

and gave birth to three sons and two daugh-
ters. And the boy Samuel grew up with HASHEM.
[22] *Eli became very old. He heard about all that*
his sons were doing to all of Israel, and that
they would lie with the women who congregated
at the entrance of the Tent of Meeting, [23] *so he*
said to them, "Why do you do such things?

ings, which provided them with more meat (*Rif, Ein Yaakov*).[1] As a result, the women had to sleep overnight in the Temple area. This prevented them from being able to spend the night with their husbands, and that is considered tantamount to Eli's sons having committed adultery with them.

Three other views read the phrase וְאֵת אֲשֶׁר־יִשְׁכְּבוּן אֶת־הַנָּשִׁים not as *and that they would lie with the women,* but more literally, as *and that they would cause the women to lie down.*

Metzudos offers the view that Eli's sons' sin consisted in forcing these women to sleep overnight away from their husbands.

Malbim states that Eli's sons' procrastination led to men and women sleeping at the Sanctuary site unattended, which led at times to immodest behavior.[2]

Finally, the nature of Eli's sons' sin may be that they went to sleep in comfortable beds at home while these women were forced to sleep at the Sanctuary (*Nachalas Shimon* from *Amudei Ohr*).

הַצֹּבְאוֹת — *Congregated.*

According to this translation, which is based on *Radak,* צֹבְאוֹת is related to צָבָא, *army,* a group of people from disparate parts who assemble at a central meeting point.

Targum renders הַצֹּבְאוֹת as *who came to pray.*

אֹהֶל מוֹעֵד — *The Tent of Meeting.*

This term is generally used in connection with the Tabernacle and not the Temple, which was not a tent but a permanent building. The Sanctuary in Shiloh was, like the Tabernacle, covered by curtains (1:24), and thus, the term *Tent* of Meeting is applicable here as well (*Radak*).

23. כַּדְּבָרִים הָאֵלֶּה — *Such things.*

In this phrase, the prefix כּ, meaning, *such,* indicates that Eli told his sons that

1. Notwithstanding the apparent sharp condemnation of the sons of Eli for delaying the offering of the birds, *Chasam Sofer* (*Parashas Nitzavim*) says that they were actually involved in studying Torah, and didn't interrupt their studies to accommodate the women. Accordingly, Scripture above says that they were כֹּהֲנִים לַה׳, *Kohanim "to* HASHEM*"* (1:3), implying that they were indeed scrupulous, but only in matters involving Hashem, such as learning Torah; however, they were wanting in their interpersonal activities.

2. This sheds light on the Talmud's statement that Shiloh was ultimately destroyed because of immorality (*Yoma* 9a). If indeed all the sons of Eli did was to delay the women, which is only *tantamount* to adultery, would that be enough to cause the destruction of Shiloh? Ben Yehoyada raises this point. Following *Malbim,* it could be that the delay caused *others* to be involved in immoral behavior, which was grounds for destruction (*Mishbetzos Zahav*). Ben Yehoyada says that since the leaders, whom the masses looked up to, did things that were "like" adultery, it dulled the senses of the people and caused general attraction to real adultery among the masses. *Netziv* supports this idea, and says that people *suspected* the sons of Eli of delaying the women's offerings for the purpose of adultery. The fact that such a suspicion was possible proves that the generation was weak in that area.

אֲשֶׁר אָנֹכִי שֹׁמֵעַ אֶת־דִּבְרֵיכֶם רָעִים מֵאֵת כָּל־הָעָם
כד אֵלֶּה: אַל בָּנָי כִּי לוֹא־טוֹבָה הַשְּׁמֻעָה אֲשֶׁר אָנֹכִי
כה שֹׁמֵעַ מַעֲבִרִים עַם־יהוה: אִם־יֶחֱטָא אִישׁ לְאִישׁ
וּפִלְלוֹ אֱלֹהִים וְאִם לַיהוה יֶחֱטָא־אִישׁ מִי יִתְפַּלֶּל־לוֹ
וְלֹא יִשְׁמְעוּ לְקוֹל אֲבִיהֶם כִּי־חָפֵץ יהוה לַהֲמִיתָם:

even if the damaging reports about their behavior were not entirely true, neither could it be that they were completely fabricated. Thus, he asked them, "Why do you engage in deeds similar to these things that have been reported?" (*Malbim*).

מֵאֵת כָּל־הָעָם אֵלֶּה — *From all these people.*

It could not be argued that the accusations were libelous, because not one person *from all these people* stood up to defend Eli's sons (*Malbim*).

From this verse, *Midrash Shmuel* derives that if a person wishes to tell someone about a compliment he heard about him, he should say who expressed the compliment. However, if he is (for good reasons) notifying someone of derogatory information that he heard about him, he should not say from whom he heard it.[1]

24. אַל בָּנָי —*No, my sons.*

Eli told his sons not to continue committing these trespasses (*Metzudos*).

Abarbanel translates אַל בָּנָי as *you are not acting as my sons*. The fact that they were the sons of Eli, a prestigious Jewish leader, magnified the desecration of God's Name (*Me'am Loez*).

מַעֲבִרִים עַם־ה' — *HASHEM's people passing on.*

מַעֲבִרִים, *passing on*, means that they were spreading information, as in the verse, וַיַּעֲבִירוּ קוֹל בַּמַּחֲנֶה, *they proclaimed throughout the camp* (*Exodus* 36:6, *Rashi*).

Radak, however, translates מַעֲבִרִים עַם ה' as *you are removing HASHEM's people* — i.e., you are preventing them from coming to bring their offerings.

The word מַעֲבִרִים may also be understood to refer to the removal of Eli's sons from their priestly positions. (See *Midrash Shmuel; Talmud Yerushalmi, Sanhedrin* Chapter 2; Responsa of *Chasam Sofer, Orach Chaim* 41.)

There is some controversy regarding the spelling of the word מַעֲבִרִים. The Talmud (*Shabbos* 55b) spells it מעברם, deleting the last י. (See *Rashi* and *Tosafos* ad loc.)

25. Eli ends his reproof of his sons with a desperate reminder that the only way to escape God's judgment is by engaging in repentance.

וּפִלְלוֹ — *Tries him.*

Most commentators associate the word וּפִלְלוֹ with judgment (as in the verse, וְנָתַן בִּפְלִלִים, *he shall pay by order of the judges* — *Exodus* 21:22), and thus translate it as *tries him*.

Targum, however, renders וּפִלְלוֹ as וְיִפְלֵי, *to separate*, i.e., the judge will solve the litigants' dispute. This may be related to the phrase כִּי יַפְלִא, *who shall dissociate* (*Numbers* 6:2; see also *Job* 31:11, *Targum* ad loc.).

וּפִלְלוֹ אֱלֹהִים — *A judge tries him.*

The word אֱלֹהִים, generally a reference to God, may also be used to refer to a judge (as in the verse, וְנִקְרַב בַּעַל־הַבַּיִת אֶל־הָאֱלֹהִים, *then the householder shall approach the court* — *Exodus* 22:7).

1. It is not clear why this is considered merely a matter of דֶּרֶךְ אֶרֶץ. To name the source of the shameful information to the face of the one who was spoken about should constitute genuine רְכִילוּת. [Even though the informer had reason to convey the information, it still causes ill will between the two parties (see *Chofetz Chaim, Laws of Rechilus* 1:3).

For I hear of your evil deeds from all these
people. 24 *No, my sons! — for the report that I*
hear Hashem*'s people passing on is not good.* 25 *If*
man sins against man, a judge tries him; but if
he sins against Hashem*, who can speak in his*
defense?" But they would not listen to their
father's voice, for Hashem *desired to kill them.*

The commentators differ in their translation of the word here.

אִם־יֶחֱטָא אִישׁ לְאִישׁ וּפִלְלוֹ אֱלֹהִים וְאִם לַה׳ יֶחֱטָא־אִישׁ מִי יִתְפַּלֶּל־לוֹ — *If man sins against man, a judge tries him, but if he sins against* Hashem*, who can speak in his defense?*

Our translation represents the interpretation of *Rashi, Mahari Kara, Radak,* and *Ralbag.* If a person gets involved in a dispute with his fellow man, an unbiased judge can settle their disagreement. But when a person has a dispute with Hashem, Hashem acts as both plaintiff and judge; as such He does not attempt to find mitigating factors on behalf of the person but instead exacts strict judgment (*Ralbag*). Accordingly, the phrase מִי יִתְפַּלֶּל־לוֹ is to be translated not as *who can speak in his defense* but rather as *who will pray on his behalf?*[1]

Metzudos renders אֱלֹהִים as *God*, and reads this verse as presenting an *a fortiori* (*kal v'chomer*) argument. אִם יֶחֱטָא אִישׁ לְאִישׁ וּפִלְלוֹ אֱלֹהִים, *If a man sins against man [and the case is adjudicated in a court of law, if] God [isn't satisfied with the judge's decision, He] will [alter] the judgment,* אִם לַה׳ יֶחֱטָא־אִישׁ מִי יִתְפַּלֶּל־לוֹ, *[surely] in a case where a man sins against* Hashem*, who will conduct the trial [if not God Himself]?*

According to *Metzudos,* therefore, the words וּפִלְלוֹ and יִתְפַּלֵּל derive from the same root, meaning *judged.*

The Talmud (*Yoma* 87a) offers another interpretation of this verse. The Mishnah states that if a person has harmed someone else he must pacify his victim before he can gain atonement from God. Hence, this verse states, אִם־יֶחֱטָא אִישׁ לְאִישׁ וּפִלְלוֹ, *If man will sin against man and conciliate him* (פִּלְלוֹ from תְּפִלָּה, *pray,* or beg forgiveness), *[then]* אֱלֹהִים, *God [will forgive him].* וְאִם לַה׳ יֶחֱטָא־אִישׁ מִי יִתְפַּלֶּל־לוֹ, *But if he sins against* Hashem*, what will effect his conciliation? [Only repentance and good deeds.]*

וְלֹא יִשְׁמְעוּ לְקוֹל אֲבִיהֶם כִּי־חָפֵץ ה׳ לַהֲמִיתָם — *But they would not listen to their father's voice, for* Hashem *desired to kill them.*

Usually God sends a sinner a measure of inspiration to repent. However, Eli's sons had (like Pharaoh) descended to such a level of depravity that Hashem decided to obstruct any avenues of penitence that might have been open to them.

One reason is that God perceived that even if Eli's sons would accept their father's rebuke, they would not be sincere (*Radak; Rashi* makes a similar comment regarding Pharaoh; see *Exodus* 7:3).

Besides that, God was disappointed

1. There seems to be a variant text of *Targum* on this phrase. *Mahari Kara* quotes *Targum* to say מַן יִבְעֵי וְיִשְׁתְּבֵיק לֵיהּ, which is translated as we have mentioned, "Who will pray so that he will be acquitted?" *Radak's* text, which is printed in our version of *Targum,* reads as מִמַּן יִבְעֵי וְיִשְׁתְּבֵיק לֵיהּ, implying "From whom may [the criminal] request to arrange for his acquittal?"

כו וְהַנַּעַר שְׁמוּאֵל הֹלֵךְ וְגָדֵל וָטוֹב גַּם עִם־יהוה
וְגַם עִם־אֲנָשִׁים׃
כז וַיָּבֹא אִישׁ־אֱלֹהִים אֶל־עֵלִי וַיֹּאמֶר אֵלָיו כֹּה
אָמַר יהוה הֲנִגְלֹה נִגְלֵיתִי אֶל־בֵּית אָבִיךָ

by Eli's sons' attitude toward the ritual service in general. To teach future generations of Kohanim to recognize the sanctity of that service, Hashem blocked their path to repentance (*Ralbag*).

This punishment would also serve the goal of impressing upon the people the severity of sin and the reality of retribution (see *Rambam, Hilchos Teshuvah* 6:3).

Some of the sins in which Eli's sons engaged were those in which there is an element that particularly impedes repentance (see *Rambam's Hilchos Teshuvah* Chapter 4). One such impediment is instigating others to sin, something that they did insofar as they openly showed their contempt for the ritual service. Another impediment is difficulty in making amends. Gaining atonement for the sin of stealing the meat of offerings would require their reimbursing their victims, an all-but-impossible task (*Kli Yakar*).

Midrash Shmuel quotes a *Sifrei*, which poses a contradiction between the present verse, which states that Hashem desired the death of Eli's sons, and *Ezekiel* 18:32, in which Hashem proclaims: לֹא אֶחְפֹּץ בְּמוֹת הַמֵּת ... וְהָשִׁיבוּ וִחְיוּ, *I do not desire the death of a person dying ... Repent and live!*[1]

Sifrei explains that only prior to the sealing of a sinner's judgment does Hashem prefer that he repent. However, the decree that Eli's sons die had already been sealed.[2]

26. וָטוֹב — *And improving.*

Targum interprets this to mean that he gained a good reputation. In this he further distinguished himself from Eli's sons, who had grown extremely unpopular (*Malbim*).

וְגַם עִם־אֲנָשִׁים — *And with people.*

Often, pious individuals retreat into a reclusive way of life, which may alienate others. However, although Samuel was in a state of constant spiritual growth, that did not deter him from interacting with the common people and gaining their approbation (*Kli Yakar*).

Samuel's fine reputation was so well established that Eli's sons too honored him, never suspecting that it was he who had denounced them to Eli (*Abarbanel, Metzudos*).[3]

Sh'lah (to *Parashas Korach*) comments that this verse can be understood in light of the words of the Sages that Samuel was equivalent to Moses and Aharon (*Berachos* 31b, based on *Psalms* 99:6). Moses was "on good terms with Hashem" as he was called אִישׁ־הָאֱלֹהִים, *the man of God* (*Psalms* 90:1). Aaron was known to be on good terms with people, as he was the peacemaker (*Pirkei Avos* 1:12). Here, Samuel is described with both of those attributes.

◆§ Judgment Against Eli

After Eli's attempt to persuade his sons to repent proved futile, Hashem dispatched a messenger to inform him of the punishment that his family would incur.

1. See also ibid. v. 23.

2. Regarding the potency of repentance after the Divine decree is sealed, see *Rosh Hashanah* 16-18; *Tosafos, Niddah* 70b ד״ה כאן בעושה תשובה; *Maharal* ad loc.; *Nachalas Shimon* 13:2.

3. Eli's sons would have taken offense if they knew that Samuel's testimony had sparked Eli's reproof. Nevertheless, it is still unclear why Samuel would keep that a secret. Clearly, such reproof was in place, and it was Samuel's responsibility to notify Eli, who was in a position to deliver it.

[26] *But the boy Samuel kept growing and improving, both with* HASHEM *and with people.*

[27] *A man of God came to Eli and said to him: Thus said* HASHEM, *"Did I [not] appear to your ancestor's family*

27. וַיָּבֹא אִישׁ־אֱלֹהִים — *A man of God came.*

Sifrei (as quoted by *Rashi* and *Radak*) identifies this man as Elkanah. Elkanah was one of the 48 primary prophets (*Seder Olam; Rashi, Megillah* 14a; see above, 1:1 comm.). Only ten men were honored with the title *man of God* (among them Moses and Samuel [*Seder Olam*]).

Ralbag disagrees, pointing out that there is no clear Scriptural evidence that Elkanah was a prophet. He instead suggests that this "man of God" was Phinehas the son of Elazar (see *Numbers* Ch. 25), who was known to have been alive at this time.

Malbim, however, refutes that idea, since Phinehas ben Elazar was not qualified to deliver this prophecy, because he would personally benefit from it. The proclamation that the priestly leadership would be taken away from Eli's family (the descendants of Aaron's son Ithamar) meant that it would be transferred to Phinehas' family (the descendants of Aaron's son Elazar).

At any rate, why didn't God communicate directly with Eli?

Ralbag proposes that although Eli was the recognized prophet of the era, since he was old and feeble, he had ceased to prophesy.

Kli Yakar states that Hashem demonstrated humility in choosing not to inform Eli directly of His impending judgment but instead sent an emissary.

הֲנִגְלֹה נִגְלֵיתִי — *Did I [not] appear?*

God began by asking, *Did I appear to your ancestor's family when they were in Egypt?* Clearly, He did. What, then, was the purpose of this question?

Radak explains that this was a rhetorical device used as a dramatic introduction.

Radak also cites another explanation — that of his father — which sees this as the introduction to a question that is only completed in verse 29: "Did I appear ... in order to have you scorn My offering and My gifts ...?"

According to *Rashi*, the prophet was implying, "Do you realize that God bestowed all of those benefits upon your ancestor Aaron?"

Malbim reads this verse as follows: "Did I appear to your ancestor's family [for them to be priests on behalf of the nation of] Egypt and [as ministers] to the house of Pharaoh? [Of course not!]"

הֲנִגְלֹה נִגְלֵיתִי אֶל־בֵּית אָבִיךָ ... — *Did I [not] appear to your ancestor's family?*

The commentators agree that Hashem was reminding Eli that his ancestor Aaron had prophesied in Egypt. The prophecy alluded to here is quoted in *Ezekiel* (20:7): אִישׁ שִׁקּוּצֵי עֵינָיו הַשְׁלִיכוּ וּבְגִלּוּלֵי מִצְרַיִם אַל־תִּטַּמָּאוּ, *Every man, cast away the idols of his eyes, and with the idols of Egypt do not defile yourselves.*

Rashi (ibid.) states that even before Hashem appeared to Moses at the burning bush, Aaron was warning his brethren in Egypt to purify themselves of idol worship.

Ralbag elaborates on the meaning of the prophet's message to Eli as follows: "I first chose Aaron as a prophet and then added to his prestige by appointing him as Kohen Gadol. How then could you rebel against Me?"

The Talmud (*Megillah* 29a) homiletically derives from this verse a crucial philosophical doctrine. The word נִגְלֵיתִי (literally, *appeared*) may be associated with the word גָּלוּת, *exile*. Hence, Hashem was testifying that wherever the Jewish nation traveled throughout

כח בְּהְיוֹתָם בְּמִצְרַיִם לְבֵית פַּרְעֹה: וּבָחֹר אֹתוֹ
מִכָּל־שִׁבְטֵי יִשְׂרָאֵל לִי לְכֹהֵן לַעֲלוֹת עַל־
מִזְבְּחִי לְהַקְטִיר קְטֹרֶת לָשֵׂאת אֵפוֹד לְפָנָי
וָאֶתְּנָה לְבֵית אָבִיךָ אֶת־כָּל־אִשֵּׁי בְּנֵי יִשְׂרָאֵל:
כט לָמָּה תִבְעֲטוּ בְּזִבְחִי וּבְמִנְחָתִי אֲשֶׁר צִוִּיתִי מָעוֹן
וַתְּכַבֵּד אֶת־בָּנֶיךָ מִמֶּנִּי לְהַבְרִיאֲכֶם מֵרֵאשִׁית

their many exiles, His Holy Presence accompanied them. As the verse states, נִגְלֵיתִי אֶל־בֵּית אָבִיךָ בִּהְיוֹתָם בְּמִצְרַיִם, *I have gone into exile with your ancestors in Egypt.*

לְבֵית פַּרְעֹה — *[Enslaved] to the house of Pharaoh.*

The word *enslaved* is added by *Targum* to avoid an awkwardness of language.

According to *Malbim*'s interpretation of the verse, however, there is no awkwardness (see above).

28. וּבָחֹר אֹתוֹ מִכָּל־שִׁבְטֵי יִשְׂרָאֵל — *And choose him from among all the tribes of Israel.*

Based on this verse, *Midrash HaCheifetz* (cited by *Me'am Loez*) relates that when Jacob's sons arrived in Egypt, they conferred to decide who should be their leader. They began by eliminating Judah, for his designated time for leadership would begin only when the Sanhedrin would come into effect. As they continued deliberating, a cloud came to them and told them that leadership should be assumed by the tribe of Levi.

Alshich relates that originally all firstborns were destined to serve as priests. After the sin of the Golden Calf, the tribe of Levi was chosen מִכָּל שִׁבְטֵי יִשְׂרָאֵל, which may be translated as *in exchange for [the firstborn of] all the tribes of Israel.*

לַעֲלוֹת עַל־מִזְבְּחִי — *To ascend My altar.*

God gave the Kohanim the privilege of setting foot on His holy altar (*Kli Yakar*).

Targum interprets לַעֲלוֹת as לְהַעֲלוֹת, *to raise up [offerings].*

לָשֵׂאת אֵפוֹד — *To wear an Ephod.*

The *Ephod* was one of Aaron's priestly garments.

Ralbag understands this to be a reference to the spirit of prophecy, for the *Ephod* carried the *Urim VeTumim*, which provided a means of direct communication with Hashem.[1]

וָאֶתְּנָה לְבֵית אָבִיךָ אֶת־כָּל־אִשֵּׁי בְּנֵי יִשְׂרָאֵל — *And [didn't] I give your ancestor's family all the fire-offerings of the Children of Israel?*

Recognizing their status as representatives of and intermediaries between God and His nation, God rewarded the Kohanim with the privilege of receiving a portion of the sacrifices.

כָּל־אִשֵּׁי — *All the fire-offerings.*

This is a reference to the remainders of the offerings, which are reserved for the Kohanim (*Mahari Kara*).

The word אִשֵּׁי, *fire-offerings*, connotes that the Kohen's portion belonged to Hashem and should thus have been consumed on the altar fire, but Hashem chose to share His portion with the Kohanim (*Malbim*).

29. לָמָּה תִבְעֲטוּ — *Why do you scorn ...?*

תִּבְעֲטוּ literally means *kick*, an explicit sign of disparagement (*Radak*).

1. See footnote to 1:13.

when they were in Egypt [enslaved] to the house
of Pharaoh, [28] and choose him from among all the
tribes of Israel to be a Kohen to Me, to ascend My
altar, to burn incense, to wear an Ephod before me;
and [didn't] I give your ancestor's family all the
fire-offerings of the Children of Israel? [29] Why do
you scorn My animal-offering and My meal-offering
which I have commanded [to be brought in My]
dwelling place, and you honor your sons more than
Me, to fatten yourselves from the choicest parts

לָמָּה תִבְעֲטוּ בְּזִבְחִי וּבְמִנְחָתִי — *Why do you scorn My offering and My meal-offering?"*

After God had enriched Eli's family with prophecy, glory, and special gifts, how could they despise His service?[1]

The prestige of Eli's family was based on administering the offerings. Should they fail to accord that service respect, their own honor would be diminished (*Malbim*).

וַתְּכַבֵּד אֶת־בָּנֶיךָ מִמֶּנִּי — *And you honor your sons more than Me.*

God held Eli responsible for not sufficiently discouraging his sons' corruption (see below, 3:13).

Although it would appear that Eli did all he could to reform his sons, *Abarbanel* (among other commentators) claims that Eli addressed them too gently. He should have yelled at them (*Radak*, or even struck them; *Aggadas Bereishis*). *Radak* (below, 3:13) says that his rebuke came too late; he was old and they no longer feared him.

Netziv (*Emek HaNetziv; Korach*) states that although Eli rebuked his sons for taking too much meat and for encouraging breaches of modesty (see above, verse 22), he failed to rebuke them for eating the meat before the fats were burned. Thus, the man of God now specified that particular sin.[2]

לְהַבְרִיאֲכֶם — *To fatten yourselves.*

Alternatively, לְהַבְרִיאֲכֶם may be translated as *to dine* (*Rashi*).

According to either reading, the prophet was referring to Eli's sons' practice of eating before the fats were burned (verse 15).

The second person form of לְהַבְרִיאֲכֶם, *to fatten yourselves,* implicates Eli in having partaken of such meals. It is not possible that he was able to altogether avoid eating the food that his sons ate (*Radak*).

1. *Reishis Chochmah* (*Shaar HaYirah* Ch. 14) derives from here that if one has been blessed with wisdom or wealth, or a miracle had been done for him, he becomes obligated to serve Hashem on a higher level, in order not to be considered ungrateful.

2. *Sefer Chassidim* (#757) brings a story that sheds light on Eli's guilt. An elderly man, who had regularly led the services in his congregation during Rosh Hashanah and Yom Kippur, refused that honor toward the end of his life. Upon inquiry, he explained that if he would be the *chazzan* the last year of his life, then his son would automatically inherit the position. "My son," he said, "is not worthy of the task. Let the congregation hire a particular pious man (whom he named) while I'm alive, so that he should continue after my death." *Sefer Chassidim* continues that Eli was punished because he should have sensed this problem and appointed righteous Kohanim to officiate while he was healthy. His failure to do so was tantamount to aiding the iniquity of his sons.

ל כָּל־מִנְחַת יִשְׂרָאֵל לְעַמִּי: לָכֵן נְאֻם יהוה אֱלֹהֵי
יִשְׂרָאֵל אָמוֹר אָמַרְתִּי בֵּיתְךָ וּבֵית אָבִיךָ יִתְהַלְּכוּ
לְפָנַי עַד־עוֹלָם וְעַתָּה נְאֻם־יהוה חָלִילָה לִּי
לא כִּי־מְכַבְּדַי אֲכַבֵּד וּבֹזַי יֵקָלּוּ: הִנֵּה יָמִים בָּאִים

לְעַמִּי — *Before My people.*

Rashi reads this word as though it directly follows the phrase וַתְּכַבֵּד אֶת־בָּנֶיךָ מִמֶּנִּי, *and you honor your sons more than Me.* Thus, it means that Eli tolerated his son's sinning in the sight of the people.

Metzudos, however, interprets this passage without rearranging the order of words: *You honor your sons more than Me by fattening yourselves with the choicest parts of every offering of Israel, [which should have been offered] to find favor for My people, and not to satisfy your greed.*

30. The fate of Eli's family is now being read before him. As one would predict, the first punitive measure mentioned is the removal of the prestigious privilege of High Priesthood. This retribution reflected not only on Eli and his lineage, but the entire pedigree of Kohanim from which Eli descended. It is important to preface that after the tragic death of Nadab and Abihu (*Leviticus* 10:2), who died without offspring, Aaron was left with two sons, Elazar and Ithamar, who remained the progenitors of the entire legacy of priesthood. Eli was a descendant of Ithamar, while Phinehas was the son of Elazar.

אָמוֹר אָמַרְתִּי בֵּיתְךָ וּבֵית אָבִיךָ יִתְהַלְּכוּ לְפָנַי עַד־עוֹלָם — *I had indeed said that your family and your father's family would walk before Me forever.*

Rashi offers two historically informative interpretations of this passage, particularly focusing on the double-worded phrase אָמוֹר אָמַרְתִּי (literally, *saying I had said*). In the first, *Rashi* mentions that Hashem twice assigned authority to the family of Ithamar. When appointing leaders of the families of Levi's sons Gershon and Merari, these two groups were assigned to Ithamar (see *Numbers* 4:28,33). The second appointment was when Eli, Ithamar's descendant, became High Priest.

The second version of *Rashi* details some of the fluctuations of priestly leadership. Immediately after the passing of Aaron, the mantle of High Priesthood was passed to Elazar (*Numbers* 20:28). During the episode of the Concubine in Gibeah (see *Judges* Ch. 19-21), dereliction in regard to many commandments was rampant, and the blame was placed on Phinehas son of Elazar who should have traveled from city to city to rebuke the populace. As a result, High Priesthood was removed from Elazar's family in favor of Eli, who was from Ithamar. Hence, אָמוֹר אָמַרְתִּי refers to the two contrasting appointments that Hashem had thus far made regarding the High Priesthood.

בֵּית אָבִיךָ — *Your father's family.*

This refers to the descendants of Ithamar (*Metzudos*).

עַד־עוֹלָם — *Forever.*

When God allots a position of authority, He does so for posterity (*Rashi, Mahari Kara*).

חָלִילָה לִּי כִּי־מְכַבְּדַי אֲכַבֵּד וּבֹזַי יֵקָלּוּ — *Far be it from Me [to do so]; for I honor those who honor Me, and those who scorn Me will be accursed.*

This means that the post of Kohen Gadol would be removed from Eli's lineage and returned to the family of Phinehas. (Although Phinehas had been found wanting in the episode of the concubine, he had earlier gained great merit when he had honored Hashem during the incident involving Zimri [*Numbers,* Ch. 25].)

of all the offerings of Israel, before My people?"
30 Therefore, [this is] the word of HASHEM, God
of Israel: "I had indeed said that your family
and your father's family would walk before Me
forever — but now" — the word of HASHEM —
"far be it from Me [to do so]; for I honor those
who honor Me, and those who scorn Me
will be accursed. 31 Behold, days are coming

This transfer took place in the time of King Solomon. The Kohen Gadol at the time was Ebiathar, from the family of Ithamar. The post was taken from him (*I Kings* 2:27) and given to Zadok, a descendant of Phinehas (ibid. verse 35; *Rashi*).

חָלִילָה לִּי — *Far be it from Me.*

Our translation, based on *Metzudos,* follows the common rendering of חָלִילָה as related to חוּלִּין, *base* or *shameful.* It would be shameful for God to allow Eli's family to remain in office.

Targum, however, renders this phrase as קוּשְׁטָא אִינוּן דִּינַי, *Truthful are My judgments. Targum Onkelos* offers the same reading in regard to a phrase in *Genesis* 18:25. In both cases, this word is applied to God, and thus the translation presented is not literal but reverent. (See *Shaarei Aharon* ad loc., ArtScroll *Bereishis* comm.)

כִּי־מְכַבְּדַי אֲכַבֵּד — *For I honor those who honor Me.*

Ben Zoma refers to this verse to support his statement, אֵיזֶהוּ מְכֻבָּד? הַמְכַבֵּד אֶת הַבְּרִיּוֹת, *Who is honored? He who honors others* (*Pirkei Avos* 4:1). Since man was created in the image of God (*Genesis* 1:27), a person who honors others is in effect honoring God, and God will therefore honor him (*Me'am Loez*).

כִּי־מְכַבְּדַי אֲכַבֵּד וּבֹזַי יֵקָלּוּ — *For I honor those who honor Me, and those who scorn Me will be accursed.*

Hashem actively honors those who honor Him, but passively removes His providence from those who scorn Him (*Rashi*).

Also, it is a signal mark of Hashem's humility that although He actively punishes someone who curses a righteous man, מְקַלֶּלְךָ אָאֹר, *he who curses you, I will curse* (*Genesis* 12:3), He does not actively avenge His own honor (*Bereishis Rabbah* 39:12).[1]

Mahari Kara, however, disagrees with the view that Hashem remains passive when insulted. Rather, he sees the word יֵקָלּוּ, *will be accursed,* as meaning that Hashem will directly punish the malefactor, and this is in fact evident from the words that begin the following verse: ...הִנֵּה יָמִים בָּאִים וְגָדַעְתִּי, *Behold, days are coming, when I shall cut off ....*

יֵקָלּוּ — *Will be accursed.*

Mahari Kara associates the word יֵקָלּוּ with קְלָלָה, *curse.*

Radak, however, relates the word to קָלוֹן, *disgrace.*

31. הִנֵּה יָמִים בָּאִים — *Behold, days are coming.*

This curse would not take place immediately but during the reign of King Solomon, with the appointment of Zadok (*Radak*).

1. Accordingly, it is also inappropriate for anyone, even a scholar, to defend his own honor and punish one who insults him, as he should emulate Hashem. *Shulchan Aruch* rules (*Yoreh Deah* 243:9) that although a scholar has the *right* to excommunicate someone who dishonored him, it is not praiseworthy for him to do so (*Mussar HaNeviim*).

וְגָדַעְתִּי֙ אֶת־זְרֹ֣עֲךָ֔ וְאֶת־זְרֹ֖עַ בֵּ֣ית אָבִ֑יךָ מִֽהְי֥וֹת
לב זָקֵ֖ן בְּבֵיתֶֽךָ׃ וְהִבַּטְתָּ֙ צַ֣ר מָע֔וֹן בְּכֹ֥ל אֲשֶׁר־
יֵיטִ֖יב אֶת־יִשְׂרָאֵ֑ל וְלֹֽא־יִהְיֶ֥ה זָקֵ֛ן בְּבֵיתְךָ֖
לג כָּל־הַיָּמִֽים׃ וְאִ֗ישׁ לֹֽא־אַכְרִ֤ית לְךָ֙ מֵעִ֣ם
מִזְבְּחִ֔י לְכַלּ֥וֹת אֶת־עֵינֶ֖יךָ וְלַאֲדִ֣יב אֶת־נַפְשֶׁ֑ךָ

וְגָדַעְתִּי אֶת־זְרֹעֲךָ — *When I shall cut off your arm ...*

The arm is a symbol of strength. The unwarranted strength flaunted by Eli's sons in seizing sacrificial meat (verse 16) would come to an end.

According to *Radak*, the *strength* referred to here is a reference to long life, as is evident from the end of the verse.

מִהְיוֹת זָקֵן בְּבֵיתֶךָ — *From there being any old person in your family.*

Since Eli's sons had hastened to grab meat before its proper time, the end of their lives and the lives of their descendants would be hastened (*Mahari Kara*). (See also *Rashi*, verse 32.)

Verse 33 explicitly states that Eli's descendants would die young. The commentators thus assume that the word זָקֵן must here be referring to something other than old age.

Thus, *Mahari Kara* quotes a Midrash that זָקֵן here is a reference to the post of Kohen Gadol.

Metzudos notes that the word זָקֵן, *elder*, is often used to describe a leader, and thus derives from this phrase that no position of authority would be allotted to Eli's descendants. This, *Me'am Loez* explains, would prevent Eli's family from further abusing the privileges of power.

The word זָקֵן can also refer to a sage. A verse states, וְהָדַרְתָּ פְּנֵי זָקֵן, *You shall honor the presence of an elder* (*Leviticus* 19:32), and our Sages explain that the word זָקֵן, *elder*, here is an abbreviation for זֶה קָנָה חָכְמָה, *This man has acquired wisdom* — i.e., a sage. The present passage thus means that no descendant of the house of Eli would ever be a sage on the Sanhedrin (*Sanhedrin* 14a).[1]

32. God's penalties mirror a person's offenses. In this verse in particular, we see some illustrations of this concept.

וְהִבַּטְתָּ צַר מָעוֹן — *You will see a rival [Kohen in My] dwelling place.*

Just as a woman views her co-wife as a צָרָה, a *rival* (see 1:6 and comm.), similarly, Eli will view the other families of Kohanim as his competition.

Targum renders צַר, as צַעַר, *pain*, and translates, *You will see the agony [that your family will endure for the sins they committed] in My dwelling place.*

Even though the word וְהִבַּטְתָּ, *you will see*, is in the singular, it applies not to Eli but to his children, for Eli himself did not experience this (*Metzudos*).

Mahari Kara points out that the pain of וְהִבַּטְתָּ צַר, *you will see a rival*, is described as occurring in מָעוֹן, God's *dwelling place*, in direct compensation for the fact that Eli's sons had despised the offerings that God had commanded מָעוֹן, *for [His] dwelling place* (verse 29).

Holy sites repel evil and desecration; thus, the Courtyard itself cried out, "Remove the sons of Eli, who contaminated the Temple of Hashem" (*Pesachim* 57a).

בְּכֹל אֲשֶׁר־יֵיטִיב אֶת־יִשְׂרָאֵל — *Throughout all the good [times] that He will bring upon Israel.*

1. Rabbi Yochanan made numerous attempts to have Rabbi Chanina and Rabbi Hoshaya ordained, but in vain. When Rabbi Yochanan expressed his frustration at his failure, they informed him that they descended from Eli and consequently their ordination was being blocked (ibid.).

when I shall cut off your arm and the arm of your father's family, from there being any old person in your family. [32] *And you will see a rival [Kohen in My] dwelling place throughout all the good [times] that He will bring upon Israel, but there will be no elder in your family for all time.* [33] *But I will not [completely] cut off any of your men from upon My altar, to make your eyes pine and your soul sad;*

During King Solomon's reign, the Temple was built and the Jews lived securely and comfortably, with an abundance of luxuries (*Rashi*). Since Eli's family had enjoyed a gluttonous existence at the expense of the Jewish people, now they would witness the tranquility of Jews but would be prevented from sharing in it (*Mahari Kara*).

Instead, they would have to struggle to earn a living (*Malbim*).

In this vein, *Ralbag* interprets the beginning of the verse, וְהִבַּטְתָּ צַר, as *you will watch* [the bounty of the Jews] *from a constrained position*. Eli's sons' self-indulgence led to a situation in which their descendants would lack in the midst of plenty.

Radak and *Metzudos* state that Eli's descendants would be distressed by their lack of authority in the Temple.

וְלֹא־יִהְיֶה זָקֵן ... — *But there will be no elder.*

Kli Yakar reads this as a continuation of the previous phrase, בְּכֹל אֲשֶׁר יֵיטִיב אֶת־יִשְׂרָאֵל, *throughout all the good [times] that He will bring upon Israel*, and translates as follows: *All of the good [times] that He will bring upon Israel [will include the fact that] there will be no elder in your house all the days*. No one of the house of Eli would attain a position of authority from which to harass the people.

33. וְאִישׁ לֹא־אַכְרִית לְךָ מֵעִם מִזְבְּחִי — *But I will not [completely] cut off any of your men from upon My altar.*

This verse indicates the increasing severity of God's judgment. Hashem preferred, as it were, for Eli's family to live in anguish rather than cease to exist, which would constitute a lesser punishment (*Radak*).

Ralbag paraphrases this verse as, "They will serve in the Sanctuary and experience the feeling of degradation as low-ranking Kohanim; for that reason, they will die only after reaching the age of 18, so that they may have the ego-crushing experience of being in such a humble position."

Malbim reads this verse in accordance with his theme that Eli's descendants would be placed under financial constraints. Let no one think that they would then go out and search alternative terms of livelihood. They would remain downtrodden and low-ranking Kohanim in the Temple.

לְכַלּוֹת אֶת־עֵינֶיךָ — *To make your eyes pine.*

This phrase implies an unrequited longing (*Metzudos; see Deuteronomy* 28:65, *Rashi*).

Targum renders לְכַלּוֹת as לְחַשָּׁכָא, *darken*.

Although the possessive pronoun of עֵינֶיךָ, *your eyes*, is in the singular, it is addressed not to Eli but to his descendants, who are closely identified with him (*Metzudos, Radak*).

וְלַאֲדִיב אֶת־נַפְשֶׁךָ — *And your soul sad.*

The root of the word וְלַאֲדִיב, *sad*, is generally spelled with the ד before the א, as in *Deuteronomy* (ibid.): דַאֲבוֹן נָפֶשׁ. This is one of a group of words whose

לד וְכָל־מַרְבִּית בֵּיתְךָ יָמוּתוּ אֲנָשִׁים: וְזֶה־לְּךָ
הָאוֹת אֲשֶׁר יָבֹא אֶל־שְׁנֵי בָנֶיךָ אֶל־חָפְנִי
לה וּפִינְחָס בְּיוֹם אֶחָד יָמוּתוּ שְׁנֵיהֶם: וַהֲקִימֹתִי
לִי כֹּהֵן נֶאֱמָן כַּאֲשֶׁר בִּלְבָבִי וּבְנַפְשִׁי יַעֲשֶׂה

letters can be rearranged (other examples are שִׂמְלָה and שַׂלְמָה [*garment*], and כֶּבֶשׂ and כֶּשֶׂב [*lamb*]; *Mahari Kara*).

וְכָל־מַרְבִּית בֵּיתְךָ יָמוּתוּ אֲנָשִׁים — *And all those raised in your house will die as [young] men.*

They will die just as they arrive at manhood. The grief over the loss of a fully grown son is greater than that over the loss of a child (*Rashi*).

In particular, they would die at the age of 18 (see *Rashi* 3:12).

Generally, the word אִישׁ (pl. אֲנָשִׁים, as it appears here) connotes the age 13, but here it refers to the ideal age of marriage, which, our Sages state (*Avos* 5:2), is 18 (*Nachalas Shimon*, quoting *Gilyonei HaShas; R' Yaakov Emden).*

Me'am Loez observes that the initial letters of this phrase — וְכָל־מַרְבִּית בֵּיתְךָ יָמוּתוּ — may be rearranged to form the word יִבּוּם, *Levirate marriage*. In such a marriage, the widow of a childless man marries his brother. The implication here is that these young descendants of Eli would marry but die before fathering children.

According to the responsa of *Chavos Yair* 152, this decree of early death applied equally to the women.

However, it is a basic tenet of the Jewish faith that an individual is not punished for the sins of his forebears, as expressed in the verse, אִישׁ בְּחֶטְאוֹ יוּמָתוּ, *a man should be put to death for his own sin* (*Deuteronomy* 24:16), meaning only for his own sin and not that of someone else. How then could it be that the descendants of Eli and his sons would be subjected to this suffering?[1]

Ralbag and *Radak* (to *Ezekiel* Ch. 18) discuss this issue and conclude that this decree applied only to those of Eli's descendants who did not properly amend their ancestors' evil ways.[2]

And indeed, the Talmudic literature demonstrates that it was possible for Eli's descendants to escape this dreadful punishment.

Thus, we learn that Rabbah and Abaye, two Amoraic giants who are pillars of the Talmudic tradition, were both descendants of Eli. Nevertheless, Rabbah lived until the age of 40 because he toiled in learning Torah, and Abaye lived until the age of 60, because in addition to learning Torah, he was also intensively involved in deeds of kindness (*Rosh Hashanah* 18a; see *Rashi, Tosafos* ad loc.).[3]

1. *Sefer HaIkarim* (*Maamar Revii*, Ch. 13) draws from this incident that if one's sin caused חִלּוּל ה׳, *desecration of HASHEM's Name*, and brought masses to sin, there is an exception to the rule, and children may die because of their parent's sin (cited by *Mishbetzos Zahav*).

2. For a comprehensive exposition of this topic, see *Nachalas Shimon* 13; ArtScroll *Ezekiel* 18:2, comm. and footnote.

3. Although Scripture clearly negates the possibility of atonement through the normal track of sin-offerings, as it is written (3:14): אִם־יִתְכַּפֵּר עֲוֹן בֵּית־עֵלִי בְּזֶבַח וּבְמִנְחָה, *the sin of the house of Eli would never be atoned for by offering or meal-offering*, nevertheless, it may be cleansed through Torah study or benevolence. As *Maharsha* (*Yevamos* 105a) explains, there are three pillars of the world: Torah, service of God, and kind deeds (*Pirkei Avos* 1:2). For Eli's family, which desecrated the holy service, to be atoned via offerings would have been impossible. This is based on the principle of אֵין קָטֵגוֹר נַעֲשֶׂה סַנֵּגוֹר, *the prosecutor cannot become the defense attorney* — i.e., the very ritual whose abuse was their sin could not be the vehicle to salvage their fate. However, the other two pillars, Torah and kind deeds, were still available to them and helped them earn more years.

and all those raised in your house will die as [young] men. [34]*This [will be] the sign for you: that which will befall your two sons, Hophni and Phinehas — they will both die on the same day.* [35]*And I will appoint for Myself a faithful Kohen, who will do as is in My heart and in My desire,*

The Talmud also tells of a Jerusalem family whose children died at the age of 18 — a family that, Rabban Yochanan ben Zakkai realized, were descended from Eli. He advised them to learn Torah and indeed they ceased to die young. Henceforth, they became known as "Yochanan's family" (*Rosh Hashanah* ibid.).

Also, *Bereishis Rabbah* (59:1) tells of a city named Mamlah, all of whose inhabitants were black haired, for no one lived long enough for his hair to turn white. When Rabbi Meir visited that city, he informed its inhabitants that they were no doubt the descendants of Eli; he advised them to devote themselves to charitable deeds, in keeping with the verse, עֲטֶרֶת תִּפְאֶרֶת שֵׂיבָה בְּדֶרֶךְ צְדָקָה תִּמָּצֵא, *The crown of splendor is old age; it can be found on the road of charity* (*Proverbs* 16:31).[1]

Talmud Yerushalmi (*Sanhedrin* 1:2) teaches that the descendants of Eli could achieve long life through prayers. See below, 3:14.

34. וְזֶה־לְּךָ הָאוֹת — *This [will be] the sign for you.*

When Eli would witness the death of his two sons on the same day, that would indicate that the curses would indeed come to pass (*Rashi*)

Malbim (as well as *Rashi* below, 3:12) understands this to mean that the death of Hophni and Phinehas would signal the onset of the curses (with the exception of the removal of the post of Kohen Gadol, as Ebiathar retained that position until the reign of King Solomon).

Radak (verse 35) disagrees and contends that the curses took effect only when Zadok was appointed Kohen Gadol.

35. כֹּהֵן נֶאֱמָן — *A faithful Kohen.*

The commentaries agree that this is a reference to Zadok, who replaced Ebiathar as Kohen Gadol during the reign of King Solomon, as described in the verse, הַכֹּהֲנִים הַלְוִיִּם בְּנֵי צָדוֹק אֲשֶׁר שָׁמְרוּ אֶת־מִשְׁמֶרֶת מִקְדָּשִׁי בִּתְעוֹת בְּנֵי־יִשְׂרָאֵל מֵעָלַי, *The Levite priests, the children of Zadok, who protected the safeguard of My Sanctuary when the Children of Israel strayed from Me* (*Ezekiel* 44:15).

בִּלְבָבִי וּבְנַפְשִׁי — *In My heart and in My desire.*

Targum renders this phrase as כְּמֵימְרִי וְכִרְעוּתִי, *as per My command and My will.*

Mahari Kara explains this to mean that Zadok would perform the sacrificial services exactly as God deemed proper.

נֶפֶשׁ literally means *soul.* The soul of a mitzvah is a person's intent to fulfill God's command in a holy way, an intent that vastly outweighs the value of the mechanical execution of God's commandments. Hashem desires a person who invests his thoughts into his deeds of service (*Malbim*).

Kli Yakar adds that this phrase alludes to a person who ponders the service of Hashem until he grows sensitive enough to do God's will without needing to be commanded.

1. This is yet another example of Hashem's practice of מִדָּה כְּנֶגֶד מִדָּה, *measure-for-measure* reward. When one prolongs another's life by giving charity, he has earned an extension to his own life span (*Me'am Loez*).

וּבָנִיתִי לוֹ בַּיִת נֶאֱמָן וְהִתְהַלֵּךְ לִפְנֵי־מְשִׁיחִי
לו כָּל־הַיָּמִים: וְהָיָה כָּל־הַנּוֹתָר בְּבֵיתְךָ יָבוֹא
לְהִשְׁתַּחֲוֺת לוֹ לַאֲגוֹרַת כֶּסֶף וְכִכַּר־לָחֶם
וְאָמַר סְפָחֵנִי נָא אֶל־אַחַת הַכְּהֻנּוֹת לֶאֱכֹל פַּת־

וּבָנִיתִי לוֹ בַּיִת נֶאֱמָן — *And I will build for him a faithful house.*

The word נֶאֱמָן, *faithful*, here implies stability and endurance (*Radak, Metzudos*). Zadok's lineage retained the post of Kohen Gadol for hundreds of years. (The names of their generations until the time of Ezra are documented in *I Chronicles* [Chapter 5].)

Mahari Kara interprets the phrase בַּיִת נֶאֱמָן, *a faithful house*, as referring to the Temple. Implicit in this prophecy was the demise of the Sanctuary in Shiloh.

וְהִתְהַלֵּךְ לִפְנֵי־מְשִׁיחִי כָּל־הַיָּמִים — *And he will walk before My anointed one all the days.*

מְשִׁיחִי, *My anointed one*, is a reference to the Jewish kings. In Zadok's case, this refers to King Solomon (*Abarbanel*). The Kohen Gadol should spend time with the king, so that they will be comrades (*Radak, Metzudos;* see also *Zechariah* 6:13).

Radak derives from here that whenever the king and the Kohen Gadol meet, the Kohen Gadol must go to the king.[1] There is one exception: when the king consults the *Urim VeTumim* (see above, 1:13 fn), he goes to the Kohen Gadol.

36. יָבוֹא לְהִשְׁתַּחֲוֹת לוֹ — *Will come to bow down to him.*

They will come to the Kohen Gadol, who will be of the family of Zadok.

Targum translates לְהִשְׁתַּחֲוֹת not literally but as לְאִשְׁתַּפָּלָא, *to humble himself,* connoting that Eli's descendants would have to humiliate themselves in order to attain even a minimal amount of money and food.

לַאֲגוֹרַת כֶּסֶף — *For a small coin.*

Most commentators assume that the word לַאֲגוֹרַת, *coin*, is related to גֵּרָה, a small silver coin (*Exodus* 30:13; see *Rashi* ad loc.); therefore, the letter א is not a part of the root of the word.

In keeping with that view, *Targum* translates לַאֲגוֹרַת as לְמָעָא — מָעָא being the Aramaic for גֵּרָה.

Mahari Kara, however, associates אֲגוֹרַת with the Aramaic word אַגְרָא, *payment,* in which the א is part of the root. According to this, Eli's descendants would bow down before the Kohen Gadol in order to *earn* a small amount of silver.

וְכִכַּר־לָחֶם — *Or a loaf of bread.*

This is the common translation of כִּכַּר־לָחֶם (*Metzudos*).

In the present instance, however, *Targum* renders this phrase as פִּיתָא דְלַחְמָא, which *Radak* explains as meaning a *morsel* of bread. This is in keeping with the phrase פַּת־לָחֶם at the end of the verse, which indeed means *a morsel of bread.*

There are two puzzling elements to this verse. First, the request for bread is mentioned twice — a seeming redundancy. Also, the first half of the verse refers to a yearning for money and a *loaf of bread,* whereas the second half elides the reference to money and refers to a request for *a morsel of bread. Metzudos* interprets these peculiarities to mean that initially the remnant of Eli's family would bow to the Kohen Gadol in the hope of receiving money and a loaf of bread. Eventually, they would desperately request to be allowed to work in the Temple on a priestly shift in order to at the very least acquire a *morsel* of bread.

1. The implication that the office of the king ranks higher than that of the High Priest is not necessarily accurate. See *Rambam, Hil. Melachim* 2:5; *Nachalas Shimon* 31:11.

and I will build for him a faithful house, and he
will walk before My anointed one all the days.
36 *And it shall be that anyone left over of your*
family will come to bow down to him for a small
coin or a loaf of bread, and will say, 'Please attach
me to one of the priestly divisions to eat a morsel
of bread.'"

סְפָחֵנִי נָא — *Please attach me.*

Radak translates סְפָחֵנִי as *attach.*

Similarly, *Targum* renders it as *count me in.*

Mahari Kara, and *Rashi* as well, render it as *absorb me* [among the Kohanim] — implying that their status would be secondary to the other Kohanim (see *Sotah* 5b; *Rashi* ad loc.).

Kli Yakar exegetically associates סְפָחֵנִי with סַפַּחַת, one of the afflictions of *tzaraas* (*Leviticus* 13:2), and draws three parallels between poverty and *tzaraas*: (a) Both are sorrowful predicaments; (b) both necessitate constant dependence on others; and (c) both are difficult to heal.

סְפָחֵנִי נָא אֶל־אַחַת הַכְּהֻנּוֹת — *Please attach me to one of the priestly divisions.*

This is a reference to the 24 *watches* of the Kohanim, which took turns performing the Temple service (see *Rambam, Hil. Klei HaMikdash* Ch. 4). *Netziv* (*Haamek Davar, Deuteronomy* 18:6) explains that although the Kohanim were divided into 24 groups, there were still scattered Kohanim from small families that didn't belong to any division, and therefore technically had no obligation to come to serve. Still, if they would come to serve, the Torah directs the Kohanim to allow them to serve together with whichever group was present. This was the destiny of Eli's family.

Kli Yakar reads אַחַת הַכְּהֻנּוֹת as *the special priestly privilege;* namely, those that involve grains necessary for man's sustenance. Eli's descendants would be so hungry that they would yearn for bread, and luxuries such as meat would not even enter their imagination. This came about measure-for-measure, in response to the fact that Eli's sons were overcome by their appetite for meat.

Me'am Loez quotes a comment in *Eliyahu Zuta* that this episode demonstrates that if a person marries with sordid financial motives, eventually his wife will cause him to be dependent on others.

Apparently, this means that Eli's sons married unworthy women for their money. These women corrupted them, thus bringing about their downfall and descent into dire poverty.

III

וְזָרַח הַשֶּׁמֶשׁ וּבָא הַשָּׁמֶשׁ — *And the sun rises and the sun sets* (*Ecclesiastes* 1:5). Even before the sun of Eli set, [Hashem] raised the sun of Samuel (*Kiddushin* 72b).

Proper leadership is an integral factor in a nation's survival and well-being. In Hashem's infinite wisdom and compassion, He saw to it that each generation would be supplied with its share of righteous people who would serve as examples for the populace. So exactly are these righteous people distributed that the Talmud lists many instances in which a pious individual was born on the very day that the leader of the previous generation died. As King Solomon signifies in the verse from *Ecclesiastes* quoted above, this insures that the world will not be devoid of any meritorious souls.

The present chapter describes such "changing of the guard," as Eli's decline coincides with the rising of the new shining sun, Samuel.

א לָחֶם: וְהַנַּעַר שְׁמוּאֵל מְשָׁרֵת
אֶת־יהוָה לִפְנֵי עֵלִי וּדְבַר יהוה הָיָה יָקָר בַּיָּמִים
ב הָהֵם אֵין חָזוֹן נִפְרָץ: וַיְהִי בַּיּוֹם הַהוּא וְעֵלִי שֹׁכֵב
בִּמְקוֹמוֹ °ועינו הֵחֵלּוּ כֵהוֹת לֹא יוּכַל לִרְאוֹת:

°וְעֵינָיו ק׳

◆§ The Inception of Samuel's Prophecy

1. וְהַנַּעַר שְׁמוּאֵל מְשָׁרֵת אֶת־ה׳ לִפְנֵי עֵלִי — *The lad Samuel was serving* HASHEM *before Eli.*

Why does the chapter open with a repetition of information that had already been amply provided in the previous chapter? Various commentators speak to this issue, relating it to the focal theme of the chapter — the onset of Samuel's prophecy — which is marked by the incident in which he mistakes a Divine summons for a human voice.

Abarbanel thus derives from the opening phrase of this verse two reasons for how Samuel could have so erred. First, as a young *lad* Samuel failed to immediately grasp what was transpiring. Second, since Samuel was constantly serving Eli, he assumed that the voice calling him was that of Eli.

Kli Yakar understands this opening phrase to be praising Samuel for not having eavesdropped on the colloquy presented at the end of the previous chapter between *the man of God* and Eli. Hence, he translates וְהַנַּעַר שְׁמוּאֵל מְשָׁרֵת אֶת־ה׳ as *[However,] the lad Samuel [heard none of this because he was in the Sanctuary for one purpose only:] to serve* HASHEM.

וְהַנַּעַר שְׁמוּאֵל — *The lad Samuel.*

A bit of chronology is in place here. From a superficial reading of the text, it appears as if soon after Samuel arrived in Shiloh, while he was yet a *lad,* he received this prophecy, and it was realized soon after with the destruction of Shiloh and the death of Eli and his sons. However, following *Seder Olam,* as well as what can be gleaned from the Talmud (*Zevachim* 118b, *Temurah* 14b), a period of 40 years passed from the day Hannah prayed for Samuel, when Eli was first appointed judge, until he died and was succeeded by Samuel. Accordingly, Chapters 2 and 3, although there is no clear mention of it, spanned 37 years. Thus, if Samuel's prophecy came immediately prior to its fulfillment, it seems inaccurate to call Samuel, who was now 39 years old, a lad. *Abarbanel* holds that, indeed, Samuel was presently still young, and this prophecy came to him many years before its realization. This would be supported by the fact that 3:2 reports that Eli's eyes had *begun* to weaken, and by the time he died, his eyes had already "become motionless" (below, 4:15). Accordingly, fulfillment of the prophecy that Samuel was about to receive was not imminent. As a possible alternative, we may say that many years of Samuel's studying under Eli had already passed in Ch. 2 (see vs. 22, 26), and Scripture refers to Samuel here as a lad only figuratively, because he still humbled himself before Eli (see *Exodus* 33:11), or because he had not yet experienced prophecy.

לִפְנֵי עֵלִי — *Before Eli.*

Metzudos explains לִפְנֵי to mean *before* in a temporal sense. Samuel had taken such strides in his spiritual development that he now responded to the Divine duty even before Eli did so.

וּדְבַר ה׳ הָיָה יָקָר — *The word of* HASHEM *was scarce.*

Targum renders יָקָר as *covered,* and *Rashi* renders it as *withheld,* both translations implying that people were not commonly exposed to prophecy. Thus, neither Samuel nor Eli immediately realized that the voice Samuel heard was a prophetic revelation (*Mahari Kara*).

[1] *The lad Samuel was serving HASHEM before Eli. The word of HASHEM was scarce in those days; vision was not widespread.* [2] *It happened one day that Eli was lying in his place; his eyes had begun to become dim, he could not see.*

אֵין חָזוֹן נִפְרָץ — *Vision was not widespread.*

חָזוֹן, *vision,* is universally understood to be an analogue for נְבוּאָה, *prophecy.* This designation for prophecy, although unusual, is congruent with the statement that כִּי לַנָּבִיא הַיּוֹם יִקָּרֵא לְפָנִים הָרֹאֶה, *for "the prophet" of today was formerly called "the seer"* (9:9).

The two words are not entirely synonymous, however. A נָבִיא, *prophet,* acted to deliver God's teachings and reproof to the nation. A רוֹאֶה, *seer,* or חוֹזֶה, *visionary,* on the other hand, although he received the information in the same way as a prophet, functioned primarily to foretell the future or (as in the case of Saul in Chapter 9) to help people recover lost objects. Apparently, this verse teaches that even the prevalence of visionaries was limited. (See Overview to ArtScroll *Joshua, Prophets and Prophecy,* for an extensive exposition on this subject.)

The word נִפְרָץ, *widespread* — but literally, *breached* — implies that those who experienced prophecy did not make their experiences known. With this, *Me'am Loez* resolves a seeming contradiction between this verse and the Talmud's assertion that Elkanah was one of 200 seers of his generation (*Megillah* 14a; see *Maharsha* ad loc.; comm. 1:1). These 200 *visionaries* kept their visions to themselves.

Expounding on the metaphor of the "breach," *Malbim* compares prophecy to a river with high banks. Even if a small breach is made in the banks, a powerful torrent rushes through, spreading water in great abundance.

The word of Hashem is like water. Samuel's arrival allowed the waters of prophecy to breach their banks, so that prophecy poured forth vigorously and even inspired others (cf. verse 21; see comm. וַיֹּסֶף ה' לְהֵרָאֹה בְשִׁלֹה, כִּי־נִגְלָה ה' אֶל־שְׁמוּאֵל, *HASHEM once again appeared in Shiloh, for HASHEM appeared to Samuel in Shiloh*).

Because the Jews of the era preceding Samuel worshiped idols, they were deprived of the benefits of Divine Inspiration. This, our Sages state, is the meaning of the verse, וְנֶפֶשׁ רְמִיָּה תִרְעָב, *The deceitful soul* — i.e., the soul that serves idols and is deceitful to God — *will be starved* (*Proverbs* 19:15; Introduction to *Ruth Rabbah* 2).

2. וַיְהִי בַּיּוֹם הַהוּא — *It happened one day.*

בַּיּוֹם הַהוּא literally means *on that day.* This incident occurred in the same 24-hour period that *the man of God* had informed Eli of his family's impending doom (*Mahari Kara* and *Ralbag*).

This repetition impressed Eli with the awareness that his family's doom was imminent, as Hashem was ready and eager to execute it (*Malbim*; compare to Pharaoh's dreams, *Genesis* 41:32).

However, *Targum* simply renders בַּיּוֹם הַהוּא as *during those days.*

Since this episode took place during the night, we see that nighttime may be referred to as יוֹם, lit., *day* (*Radak*).

וְעֵלִי שֹׁכֵב בִּמְקוֹמוֹ — *That Eli was lying in his place.*

Eli was bedridden due to his poor eyesight, and Samuel was thus accustomed to serve him when summoned. Accordingly, Samuel responded to the heavenly voice by running to Eli (*Mahari Kara*).

וְעֵינָיו הֵחֵלּוּ כֵהוֹת — *His eyes had begun to become dim.*

Samuel's initiation into leadership began with the inception of the decline of Eli's health (*Malbim*). Now that the time

ג וְנֵר אֱלֹהִים טֶרֶם יִכְבֶּה וּשְׁמוּאֵל שֹׁכֵב בְּהֵיכַל
ד יהוה אֲשֶׁר־שָׁם אֲרוֹן אֱלֹהִים: וַיִּקְרָא יהוה
ה אֶל־שְׁמוּאֵל וַיֹּאמֶר הִנֵּנִי: וַיָּרָץ אֶל־עֵלִי וַיֹּאמֶר
הִנְנִי כִּי־קָרָאתָ לִּי וַיֹּאמֶר לֹא־קָרָאתִי שׁוּב שְׁכָב

for his removal had arrived, Eli's eyes grew weak. בַּיּוֹם הַהוּא, *on that very day,* Samuel's sun began to rise (*Kli Yakar*).

Abarbanel explains that since Samuel saw a sudden change in Eli's health, he was concerned and jumped to Eli's aid as soon as he heard a voice calling him.

Radak suggests that עֵינָיו הֵחֵלּוּ כֵהוֹת, *his eyes had begun to become dim,* figuratively means that the Divine spirit had begun to leave Eli, setting the stage for Samuel to take his place.

Midrash Shmuel uses this incident to illustrate the contention that a person who raises a wicked child will suffer from dimmed eyesight, as had occurred to Isaac. Thus, Scripture mentions Eli's dimmed eyesight apropos of God's denunciation of Eli's dissolute sons (*Radak*).

3. וְנֵר אֱלֹהִים טֶרֶם יִכְבֶּה — *The lamp of God had not yet gone out.*

The flames of the Menorah, which would remain lit from dusk to dawn, had not yet gone out — i.e., dawn had not yet arrived. Most commentators infer that this episode occurred toward the end of the night. (*Metzudos* adds that not even one of the flames had been extinguished.)

The reason Scripture mentions that the light of the Menorah was still burning may be to explain how it was possible for prophecy to come during nighttime. *Ibn Ezra* (*Numbers* 8:2) derives from the juxtaposition of a verse about prophecy (ibid. 7:89) to one about the Menorah, that when the area is lit with a candle, prophecy may come at night (see *Ramban,* who disagrees; *Mishbetzos Zahav*).

In the latter part of the night, a person's mind and soul are purified and cleansed of the previous day's distracting thoughts; therefore, this time is most conducive for communication with the Divine (*Malbim*).

The Talmud's remark, cited at the beginning of this chapter that Samuel's era began even before that of Eli terminated, is based on this phrase (see *Kiddushin* 72b): נֵר אֱלֹהִים, *the lamp of HASHEM,* may be understood as a reference not only to the Menorah but to the soul, as in the verse, נֵר ה׳ נִשְׁמַת אָדָם, *A lamp of HASHEM is the soul of a man* (*Proverbs* 20:27). Hence, we may understand this verse to be stating that *Even before Eli's soul had been extinguished, Samuel was lying in the Temple of HASHEM ....*

וּשְׁמוּאֵל שֹׁכֵב בְּהֵיכַל ה׳ — *And Samuel was lying — in the Temple of HASHEM.*

This literal translation presents a problem explicated by the Talmud and alluded to by the commentators, which is that only a member of the Davidic royal dynasty may sit or lie down in the Sanctuary area.

The Talmud (*Kiddushin* 78b) explains the text by parsing it so that the words בְּהֵיכַל ה׳ — *in the Temple of HASHEM* — refer to the initial phrase of the verse, and that וּשְׁמוּאֵל שֹׁכֵב is a parenthetical clause, and thus: *The lamp of HASHEM had not yet gone out — at the time that Samuel was lying [in his place] — in the Temple of HASHEM.*

Targum solves this issue by parsing the verse so that וּשְׁמוּאֵל שֹׁכֵב, *Samuel was lying,* reads as the completion of one thought, and בְּהֵיכַל ה׳, *in the Temple of HASHEM,* begins a new clause. Thus, it translates, *Samuel was lying [in the Levitical quarters; while] in the Temple of HASHEM, [a voice was heard].*

Metzudos supports this contention and specifies that the *Temple of HASHEM*

[3]The lamp of God had not yet gone out — and Samuel was lying — in the Temple of HASHEM where the Ark of God was.

[4]HASHEM called to Samuel, and he said, "Here I am."
[5]He ran to Eli and said, "Here I am, for you called me."
But he said, "I did not call; go back and lie down,"

refers to the Holy of Holies, where, as the verse states, *was housed the Ark of God* (and which was the usual site from where the voice of God emanated — see *Exodus* 25:22).

These interpretations of the text are substantiated by the cantillation marks. The word שֹׁכֵב is marked by an *esnachta,* which denotes a pause, one that disengages וּשְׁמוּאֵל שֹׁכֵב from בְּהֵיכַל ה׳ (*Radak*).

4. וַיִּקְרָא ה׳ אֶל־שְׁמוּאֵל — *HASHEM called to Samuel.*

Eli was stationed inside the Temple, whereas the Levitical quarters where Samuel slept were outside the Temple area (see *Middos* 1:9). Yet the voice that emanated from the Holy of Holies bypassed Eli, so that only Samuel heard it. This miraculous conveyance of sound is alluded to as well in the verse, יַרְעֵם אֵל בְּקוֹלוֹ נִפְלָאוֹת, *Through His voice, God gives wondrous sounds* (*Job* 37:5; *Midrash Shmuel*).[1]

וַיֹּאמֶר הִנֵּנִי — *And he said, "Here I am."*

Samuel responded in order to notify Eli that he was not asleep (*Malbim*).

Rashi points out (in *Genesis* 22:1) that this response is that of the devout, and connotes humility and readiness.

5. וַיֹּאמֶר הִנְנִי כִּי־קָרָאתָ לִּי — *And said, "Here I am, for you called me."*

In order not to startle Samuel, Hashem called him using Eli's voice. Also, this informed Samuel that he had earned the privilege of prophecy because he had heeded Eli's voice (*Me'am Loez*).

וַיֹּאמֶר לֹא־קָרָאתִי שׁוּב שְׁכָב — *But he said, "I did not call; go back and lie down."*

Eli assumed that the voice that Samuel heard was a figment of his imagination (*Abarbanel*).

1. There is some controversy as to the nature of this sound and as to prophetic communication in general.

In his *Moreh Nevuchim, Rambam* contends that the recipient of a prophetic communication does not receive it through normal sensory channels — i.e., by hearing physical sounds. Rather, the prophecy is a completely mental communication sensed solely in the mind. There are, however, a variety of forms in which the prophet may envision this communication. Sometimes, as in this case, he imagines the prophetic voice as if it were a regular, familiar, human voice.

Accordingly, *Rambam* explains that since Samuel was ignorant of prophetic revelation, he did not associate his experience with prophecy and therefore assumed that Eli was calling him.

Abarbanel disagrees sharply with *Rambam*'s contention and claims that at times prophecy may be communicated through sound waves and impinge upon the eardrum; hence, Samuel's error.

But why did Hashem choose to appear to Samuel in a misleading manner?

Abarbanel explains that Hashem wanted Samuel to tell Eli the details of this prophecy. Had Eli not known that Samuel was receiving a prophetic message and had he not forced Samuel to reveal it, Samuel would not have dared do so.

Malbim adds that this prophecy was not meant to induce Samuel to influence Eli's family to repent, since God's decree against Eli's family had already been sealed and could not be rescinded (*Rosh Hashanah* 18a). Rather, it was meant only to deliver information to Samuel, who had the prerogative of choosing whether or not to divulge it. Therefore, had Samuel not experienced this confusion and consulted with Eli, he would not have told Eli about the prophecy.

ו וַיֵּלֶךְ וַיִּשְׁכָּב׃ וַיֹּסֶף יהוה קְרֹא עוֹד שְׁמוּאֵל וַיָּקָם
שְׁמוּאֵל וַיֵּלֶךְ אֶל־עֵלִי וַיֹּאמֶר הִנְנִי כִּי קָרָאתָ לִי
ז וַיֹּאמֶר לֹא־קָרָאתִי בְנִי שׁוּב שְׁכָב׃ וּשְׁמוּאֵל טֶרֶם
ח יָדַע אֶת־יהוה וְטֶרֶם יִגָּלֶה אֵלָיו דְּבַר־יהוה׃ וַיֹּסֶף
יהוה קְרֹא־שְׁמוּאֵל בַּשְּׁלִשִׁית וַיָּקָם וַיֵּלֶךְ אֶל־עֵלִי
וַיֹּאמֶר הִנְנִי כִּי קָרָאתָ לִי וַיָּבֶן עֵלִי כִּי יהוה קֹרֵא
ט לַנָּעַר׃ וַיֹּאמֶר עֵלִי לִשְׁמוּאֵל לֵךְ שְׁכָב וְהָיָה אִם־
יִקְרָא אֵלֶיךָ וְאָמַרְתָּ דַּבֵּר יהוה כִּי שֹׁמֵעַ עַבְדֶּךָ
י וַיֵּלֶךְ שְׁמוּאֵל וַיִּשְׁכַּב בִּמְקוֹמוֹ׃ וַיָּבֹא יהוה וַיִּתְיַצַּב

According to *Abarbanel* and *Malbim*, Eli responded sternly, for he believed that Samuel was allowing his imagination to run riot. *Kli Yakar*, however, disputes the idea that Eli would have grown angry.

6. וַיָּקָם שְׁמוּאֵל וַיֵּלֶךְ אֶל־עֵלִי — *So Samuel arose and went to Eli.*

Having been abashed by Eli's initial sharp reaction, the second time Samuel was summoned he did not run to him (*Abarbanel*). He also had no reason to call הִנְנִי before appearing before Eli (as he had done the first time), for that was only to inform Eli that he was awake — something that Eli already knew this time (*Malbim*).

וַיֹּאמֶר לֹא־קָרָאתִי בְנִי שׁוּב שְׁכָב — *But he said, "I did not call, my son; go back and lie down."*

Now that this incident occurred a second time, Eli suspected that Samuel had truly heard a voice, and so this time, he spoke more softly and referred to Samuel as *my son* (*Abarbanel*).

Realizing that Samuel might be experiencing a prophetic revelation, Eli took care not to upset him, knowing that any trace of dejection could disturb it (*Malbim*).

7. וּשְׁמוּאֵל טֶרֶם יָדַע אֶת־ה׳ — *Samuel had not yet known* H*ASHEM*.

This statement is inserted between the second and third of Hashem's summonses to Samuel in order to explain why, although Eli was beginning to perceive what was happening, Samuel remained oblivious (*Abarbanel*).

וּשְׁמוּאֵל טֶרֶם יָדַע אֶת־ה׳ וְטֶרֶם יִגָּלֶה אֵלָיו דְּבַר־ה׳ — *Samuel had not yet known* H*ASHEM, and the word of* H*ASHEM had not yet been revealed to him.*

טֶרֶם יָדַע אֶת־ה׳ means that Samuel was not yet familiar with the phenomenon of the voice heard in prophecy (*Rashi*).

Alternatively, he did not yet know the science of Godliness. Had he been familiar with that science, he would have understood and recognized the voice of prophecy. טֶרֶם יִגָּלֶה אֵלָיו tells that he had not had any personal experiences (*Radak*).

8. וַיָּקָם וַיֵּלֶךְ אֶל־עֵלִי — *And he arose and went to Eli.*

This verse testifies to Samuel's patience and devotion: he continued to go to Eli even after the awkward reactions with which he was received the previous two times (*Abarbanel*).

וַיָּבֶן עֵלִי כִּי ה׳ קֹרֵא לַנָּעַר — *Then Eli realized that* H*ASHEM was calling the lad.*

Eli concluded that the voice was that of Hashem for two reasons: first, because Samuel had been summoned three times and was thus definitely awake and not dreaming, and second, because no one

so he went and lay down. [6] *HASHEM continued to*
call again, "Samuel!" so Samuel arose and went to
Eli and said, "Here I am, for you called me." But
he said, "I did not call, my son; go back and lie
down." [7] *Samuel had not yet known HASHEM, and*
the word of HASHEM had not yet been revealed to
him. [8] *HASHEM continued to call, "Samuel!" a third*
time, and he arose and went to Eli and said, "Here
I am, for you called me." Then Eli realized that
HASHEM was calling the lad.
[9] *Eli said to Samuel, "Go and lie down; and if*
He calls you, you should say, 'Speak, HASHEM, for
Your servant is listening.'" Samuel went and lay
down in his place. [10] *HASHEM came and appeared,*

else who could have called was present (*Radak*).

Ibn Ezra states that Eli realized what was happening because Samuel heard the voice, whereas he did not: a circumstance that could be explained only if this were a communication from the Divine (*Numbers* 7:89, *Rashi* ad loc.; see comm. verse 4).

9. לֵךְ שְׁכָב — *Go and lie down.*

On the two previous occasions, Eli had told Samuel, שׁוּב שְׁכָב, *"Go back and lie down,"* implying, "Go back to sleep." This time, however, Eli was aware that Samuel would not be able to sleep while anxiously awaiting the voice of Hashem, and so he said he said לֵךְ שְׁכָב, "Go and lie down" (*Kli Yakar*).

10. וַיָּבֹא ה׳ — *HASHEM came.*

In Chapter 2, we discussed God's exacting dynamics of reward and punishment.

The Midrash makes reference to that measure-for-measure system to explain why Hashem came to Samuel rather than having Samuel meet with Him in a place of His own designation. This is in contrast to the fact that Hashem caused Moses to go to the Sanctuary to hear Hashem's voice (*Numbers* 7:89).

In the latter case, state our Sages, Hashem was responding to Moses' actions — i.e., to the fact that when he judged the Jews he remained in his place and had them come to him (*Exodus* 18:13). Samuel, on the other hand, later in his career traveled to the Jews throughout the land of Israel to judge them (below, 7:16). In recompense for this behavior, when Hashem wished to speak with Samuel, He came to Samuel (*Shemos Rabbah* 16:4, citing *Proverbs* 16:11, פֶּלֶס וּמֹאזְנֵי מִשְׁפָּט לַה׳, *A scale and just balances are HASHEM's ...*; see *Maharzu* there).

וַיִּתְיַצַּב — *And appeared.*

Radak understands this to mean that a vision appeared before Samuel's eyes.

Abarbanel disagrees, however, and indeed infers from the phrase, וַיִּקְרָא כְפַעַם־בְּפַעַם, *and called as the other times,* that there was no change between this and the previous communications. Accordingly, וַיִּתְיַצַּב means that *[HASHEM's voice returned and] presented itself [to Samuel's ears].*

וַיִּקְרָא כְפַעַם־בְּפַעַם שְׁמוּאֵל | שְׁמוּאֵל וַיֹּאמֶר
יא שְׁמוּאֵל דַּבֵּר כִּי שֹׁמֵעַ עַבְדֶּךָ: וַיֹּאמֶר
יהוה אֶל־שְׁמוּאֵל הִנֵּה אָנֹכִי עֹשֶׂה דָבָר בְּיִשְׂרָאֵל
יב אֲשֶׁר כָּל־שֹׁמְעוֹ תְּצִלֶּינָה שְׁתֵּי אָזְנָיו: בַּיּוֹם הַהוּא
אָקִים אֶל־עֵלִי אֵת כָּל־אֲשֶׁר דִּבַּרְתִּי אֶל־בֵּיתוֹ
יג הָחֵל וְכַלֵּה: וְהִגַּדְתִּי לוֹ כִּי־שֹׁפֵט אֲנִי אֶת־בֵּיתוֹ
עַד־עוֹלָם בַּעֲוֹן אֲשֶׁר־יָדַע כִּי־מְקַלְלִים לָהֶם בָּנָיו

שְׁמוּאֵל שְׁמוּאֵל — *Samuel, Samuel!*

With this, Samuel became a member of an elite group — the others being Abraham, Jacob, and Moses — whom Hashem addressed by repeating their names. The Midrash (*Bereishis Rabbah* 56:7) explains that this implies both love[1] and urgency. In addition, the Sages comment that this repetition testifies to the recipients' humility. *Samuel was the same Samuel* before and after Hashem communicated with him prophetically (*Tosefta, Berachos* 1:15; see ArtScroll *Genesis* 22:11, comm.).

וַיֹּאמֶר שְׁמוּאֵל דַּבֵּר כִּי שֹׁמֵעַ עַבְדֶּךָ — *And Samuel said, "Speak, for Your servant is listening."*

Why didn't Samuel respond as Eli had told him to with the words, *"Speak, HASHEM"*?

The Talmud (*Shabbos* 113b) commends Samuel for being cautious not to utter Hashem's Name. He did this because he feared that this may not be the voice of Hashem but rather that of an angel (*Yalkut Shimoni)* or even that of a demon (see *Radak*) (*Shabbos* 113b). Samuel was skeptical for two reasons: Prophecy was uncommon in those days, and he did not consider himself worthy of receiving a prophetic communication (*Ralbag*).

Radak suggests that Samuel was certain that this was the voice of Hashem, but he was afraid to utter Hashem's Name in the course of experiencing a prophetic vision.

11. הִנֵּה אָנֹכִי עֹשֶׂה דָבָר בְּיִשְׂרָאֵל — *Behold, I am going to do [such] a thing in Israel.*

This is a reference to two incidents: the Philistines' capture of the Holy Ark[2] (Chapter 4; *Midrash Shmuel*), and the great loss of life that the Jews suffered in their war against the Philistines (*Abarbanel*).

תְּצִלֶּינָה שְׁתֵּי אָזְנָיו — *Both of his ears will ring.*

תְּצִלֶּינָה, *will ring,* derives from צֶלְצְלִים, *cymbals* (*Rashi*). When someone will hear of the terrible tragedies that will befall the Jews, his ears will ring as if they heard a crash of cymbals (see *Psalms* 150:5; *Tamid* 3:8).

Alternatively, *Metzudos* renders תְּצִלֶּינָה as *shudder*.

12. בַּיּוֹם הַהוּא אָקִים אֶל־עֵלִי — *On that day, I will fulfill for Eli.*

On the very same day that the calamity occurs and makes people's ears ring,

1. *Mishbetzos Zahav* comments that only this time did Hashem repeat his name as a gesture of love, because this was the first time that Samuel realized Hashem was calling.

2. The Ark contained the Holy Tablets, and was the site of the Divine Presence that had previously been at Mount Sinai. Thus, it represented the influence of Torah. The fact that the Midrash singles out the capture of the Ark as the event that would make all ears ring — notwithstanding the other tragedies that were to occur — illustrates how central the value of Torah was to every Jew (*R' Aharon Kotler, Mishnas Rav Aharon*, Vol. III).

and called as the other times, "Samuel, Samuel!"
and Samuel said, "Speak, for Your servant is
listening."
11 *HASHEM said to Samuel, "Behold, I am going to*
do [such] a thing in Israel that when anyone hears
about it, both of his ears will ring. 12 *On that day, I*
will fulfill for Eli all that I have spoken concerning
his house, beginning to destroy. 13 *I have told him*
that I am executing judgment against his house
forever for the sin [he committed] that he was
aware that his sons were blaspheming themselves

God will begin to execute His sentence against the family of Eli (*Radak*).

אֶל־בֵּיתוֹ — *Concerning his house.*

Although אֶל־בֵּיתוֹ literally means *to his house*, it is to be understood as עַל בֵּיתוֹ, *concerning his house* (*Radak*).

הָחֵל וְכַלֵּה — *Beginning to destroy.*

Our translation follows *Mahari Kara*, who renders these words as if they said הָחֵל לְכַלֵּה.

Literally, however, this phrase means, *I will begin* and *I will completely [destroy]*. Many commentators thus understand it to mean, "I *will begin [to place a curse upon Eli's family] and then eventually I will continue and complete [the curse]*."

The beginning refers to the death of Eli's sons, Hophni and Phinehas, on the selfsame day (as mentioned above, 2:34). וְכַלֵּה implies the complete fulfillment of that judgment — i.e., that all of Eli's offspring would suffer from an early death (*Rashi*).

According to *Ralbag*, however, וְכַלֵּה refers to the murder of the Kohanim of Nob, who were Eli's descendants (see below, 22:19).

13. וְהִגַּדְתִּי לוֹ — *I have told him.*

Because Eli failed to take action upon hearing from *the man of God*, Hashem repeated His prophecy to Samuel (*Kli Yakar*).

מְקַלְלִים לָהֶם — *Were blaspheming themselves.*

The phrase should have read, *were blaspheming Me*; however, the verse expresses itself euphemistically out of a sense of reverence for God (*Rashi*).[1]

Abarbanel, however, understands this phrase literally. With their unscrupulous actions, Eli's sons cursed themselves in the sense that they brought about their own tragic end. Thus, Scripture implies that even though Eli knew the suicidal effects of their deeds, he still failed to censure them.

Ralbag renders מְקַלְלִים לָהֶם בָּנָיו as *[the Jews] cursed [Eli's] sons*. However, this clearly deviates from the simple meaning of the phrase.

The word קְלָלָה (lit., *blaspheming* or *cursing*) derives from קַל, *light* or *derisive*. Although Eli's sons did not actually curse, their actions exhibited a lack of reverence for Hashem (*Rashi*; see above, 2:30, וּבֹזַי יֵקָלּוּ and comm.).

Alternatively, *Targum* renders מְקַלְלִים as *angering*.

1. This is one of eighteen such euphemisms found in Scripture (*Radak*; some are listed in *Yalkut Shimoni*). See ArtScroll *Genesis* 18:22, comm. and footnote, for an elaboration on this topic.

יד וְלֹא כִהָה בָּם: וְלָכֵן נִשְׁבַּעְתִּי לְבֵית עֵלִי אִם־
יִתְכַּפֵּר עֲוֹן בֵּית־עֵלִי בְּזֶבַח וּבְמִנְחָה עַד־
טו עוֹלָם: וַיִּשְׁכַּב שְׁמוּאֵל עַד־הַבֹּקֶר וַיִּפְתַּח
אֶת־דַּלְתוֹת בֵּית־יְהוָה וּשְׁמוּאֵל יָרֵא מֵהַגִּיד
טז אֶת־הַמַּרְאָה אֶל־עֵלִי: וַיִּקְרָא עֵלִי אֶת־שְׁמוּאֵל
יז וַיֹּאמֶר שְׁמוּאֵל בְּנִי וַיֹּאמֶר הִנֵּנִי: וַיֹּאמֶר מָה
הַדָּבָר אֲשֶׁר דִּבֶּר אֵלֶיךָ אַל־נָא תְכַחֵד מִמֶּנִּי
כֹּה יַעֲשֶׂה־לְּךָ אֱלֹהִים וְכֹה יוֹסִיף אִם־תְּכַחֵד

וְלֹא כִהָה בָּם — *And he did not censure them.*

Eli failed to censure his sons even after he received God's prophecy (*Abarbanel;* see above).

For greater elaboration on why Eli was held responsible for his son's iniquities, see comm. 2:29.

כִהָה — *Censure.*

Our translation follows *Midrash Shmuel.*

Rashi, however, renders this verse as *[Eli] did not darken [his son's] faces,* whether by removing them from their post, or, as *Metzudos* suggests, by shouting at them and publicly shaming them.

According to *Radak,* כִהָה means to *restrain.*

Mussar HaNeviim comments that Hashem was admonishing Eli for not living up to the ideals of the tribe of Levi. At the denouement of the incident of the Golden Calf, the Levites were lauded for not having favored their relatives in defending Hashem's honor (*Exodus* 32:27). By not rebuking his sons, Eli failed to emulate his ancestors.

14. וְלָכֵן נִשְׁבַּעְתִּי לְבֵית עֵלִי אִם־יִתְכַּפֵּר ... עַד־עוֹלָם — *Therefore I have sworn concerning the house of Eli ... would never be atoned for.*

The *man of God* had delivered the Divine message to Eli regarding everything that would occur to his family. Nevertheless, Eli had failed to censure his sons and impress upon them the severity of the situation. Thus, Hashem now told Samuel that He would strengthen His judgment with an *oath* — something that would render His decision almost impossible to retract (see *Rosh Hashanah* 18a).

From here, the Sages learn that a decree to which Hashem has sworn cannot be revoked (ibid.).

אִם־יִתְכַּפֵּר עֲוֹן בֵּית־עֵלִי בְּזֶבַח וּבְמִנְחָה עַד־עוֹלָם — *That the sin of the house of Eli would never be atoned for by offering or meal-offering.*

However, atonement might be achieved via other means: i.e., via Torah study and kind deeds (ibid.).

This is because Torah study and kind deeds are preferable to offerings and have a greater spiritual impact (*Ralbag*). For instance, whereas sacrificial worship atones for sins, Torah study can protect a person from even the temptation to sin (*Sotah* 21a) (*Me'am Loez*). (For further explanation on how Eli's descendants escaped this decree, see above, 2:33, comm. and footnote.)

Talmud Yerushalmi (*Sanhedrin* 1:2) understands the implication to be that they could not atone through offerings, but only through prayer — which is considered greater than offerings — could they atone. The Talmud cites one such incident in which Rav Kahana, a descendant of Eli, merited long life through prayer. See also *Midrash Shmuel.*

and he did not censure them. [14]*Therefore I have*
sworn concerning the house of Eli that the sin
of the house of Eli would never be atoned for by
animal-offering or meal-offering.''
[15]*Samuel lay until the morning, when he*
opened the doors of the House of HASHEM*; and*
Samuel was fearful of relating the vision to Eli.
[16]*Eli called Samuel and said, ''Samuel, my son!''*
and he said, ''Here I am.'' [17]*He said, ''What is*
the word that He spoke to you? Please do not
withhold from me! Such shall God do to you
and such shall He do further, if you withhold

Abarbanel, alternatively, interprets אִם־ יִתְכַּפֵּר עֲוֹן בֵּית עֵלִי בְּזֶבַח וּבְמִנְחָה עַד־עוֹלָם as meaning that *the sin of Eli would never be atoned for because of [how his sons had disgraced] the offering and meal-offering.*

☙ Eli Accepts Judgment

15. וַיִּשְׁכַּב שְׁמוּאֵל עַד־הַבֹּקֶר וַיִּפְתַּח אֶת־ דַּלְתוֹת בֵּית־ה׳ — *Samuel lay until the morning, when he opened the doors of the House of* HASHEM.

Rather than going to Eli immediately after experiencing this prophecy, Samuel remained in bed (*Abarbanel*); however, he did not sleep (*Kli Yakar*).

Even with the arrival of morning, he did not approach Eli. Instead, he went about his regular Levitical duty as gatekeeper (*Radak; Mahari Kara*).

וּשְׁמוּאֵל יָרֵא מֵהַגִּיד אֶת־הַמַּרְאָה אֶל־עֵלִי — *And Samuel was fearful of relating the vision to Eli.*

God had not commanded Samuel to convey the message of the prophecy to Eli; he thus chose to conceal it (see verse 4, comm. and footnote).

16. וַיִּקְרָא עֵלִי אֶת־שְׁמוּאֵל — *Eli called Samuel.*

Eli understood that Samuel's prophecy bode poorly for him, for two reasons: first, Eli had already received evil tidings from *the man of God;* second, לֵב יוֹדֵעַ מָרַּת נַפְשׁוֹ, *[A person's] heart [intuitively] knows the bitterness of his soul* — i.e., his impending fate (*Proverbs* 14:10; *Malbim*).

שְׁמוּאֵל בְּנִי — *Samuel, my son!*

By calling Samuel "my son," Eli implied that he considered him to be his true and spiritual progeny. Although Hophni and Phinehas, his physical offspring, would die early, his real descendant, Samuel, would live (*Kli Yakar*).

17. כֹּה יַעֲשֶׂה־לְּךָ אֱלֹהִים וְכֹה יוֹסִיף — *Such shall God do to you and such shall He do further.*

This is a common Scriptural formulation of imprecation (*Radak, Ralbag*), implying extreme punishment.

The Sages, however, presume that Eli accurately intuited the burden of Samuel's prophecy, and they thus read his words literally: *[The curse that was intended for me] such shall God do to you* — i.e., your children will not follow in your footsteps and will thus be ineligible to inherit your position (*Midrash Shmuel*).

This curse was fulfilled, for Samuel's children did not live up to the standards that he set for them (see below, 8:3; *Shabbos* 56a), even though Samuel acceded to Eli's request and informed him

יח מִמֶּנִּי דָּבָר מִכָּל־הַדָּבָר אֲשֶׁר־דִּבֶּר אֵלֶיךָ: וַיַּגֶּד־לוֹ
שְׁמוּאֵל אֶת־כָּל־הַדְּבָרִים וְלֹא כִחֵד מִמֶּנּוּ וַיֹּאמַר
יט יְהוָה הוּא הַטּוֹב °בעינו יַעֲשֶׂה: וַיִּגְדַּל שְׁמוּאֵל וַיהוָה °בְּעֵינָיו ק׳
כ הָיָה עִמּוֹ וְלֹא־הִפִּיל מִכָּל־דְּבָרָיו אָרְצָה: וַיֵּדַע
כָּל־יִשְׂרָאֵל מִדָּן וְעַד־בְּאֵר שָׁבַע כִּי־נֶאֱמָן שְׁמוּאֵל
כא לְנָבִיא לַיהוָה: וַיֹּסֶף יְהוָה לְהֵרָאֹה בְשִׁלֹה כִּי־

of the prophecy. The Talmud derives from this that even a conditional curse uttered by a scholar is realized in one way or another, even if the condition is not met (*Makkos* 11a).

18. וַיַּגֶּד־לוֹ שְׁמוּאֵל אֶת־כָּל־הַדְּבָרִים — *Samuel told him all the words.*

Samuel did not paraphrase the prophecy but related its exact words.

וַיֹּאמַר ה׳ הוּא הַטּוֹב בְּעֵינָיו יַעֲשֶׂה — *[Eli] said, "He is HASHEM; He will do what is good in His eyes."*

With this, Eli expressed his acceptance of God's judgment. Insofar as the Name of Hashem may be pronounced as אֲדֹנָי, *Midrash Shmuel* explains Eli's exclamation to mean, אָדוֹן הוּא, *He is the Master* and Proprietor of all, and therefore no one can object to anything that He does.[1]

However, Eli made use here of the sacred four-letter Name of Hashem (י־ה־ו־ה — the Tetragrammaton), which represents God's attribute of mercy. Hence, the phrase may be translated as ה׳ הוּא הַטּוֹב, *He is ever-compassionate,* בְּעֵינָיו יַעֲשֶׂה, *everything, His eyes [see], that He does is good [although our eyes may not perceive this].*

Samuel's prophecy contained a *measure of pity* lacking in the words delivered by *the man of God;* namely, that atonement could be attained by means of Torah and kind deeds. Eli responded to this *measure of pity* with the words, ה׳ הוּא הַטּוֹב בְּעֵינָיו יַעֲשֶׂה *[May the merciful] HASHEM fulfill this good tiding* (*Me'am Loez*).

Malbim comments that with these words Eli acknowledged God's *oath* and abandoned hope of appeasing Him: הַטּוֹב בְּעֵינָיו יַעֲשֶׂה *[clearly,] HASHEM wants to do this.*

☙ Samuel Emerges as Leader

19. וַיִּגְדַּל שְׁמוּאֵל — *Samuel grew up.*

He grew in wisdom and the fear of God (*Metzudos*).

וַה׳ הָיָה עִמּוֹ — *And HASHEM was with him.*

Samuel was constantly accompanied by the Divine Spirit (*Malbim*).

In Chapter 2 (2:11), Samuel was described as serving Hashem by means of serving Eli (see comm.). The present verse, in contrast, implies that Samuel no longer required an intermediary to maintain his attachment with Hashem (*Alshich*).

וְלֹא־הִפִּיל מִכָּל־דְּבָרָיו אָרְצָה — *He did not cast any of his words to the ground.*

Hashem did not allow even Samuel's casual statements to go unfulfilled (*Radak*).

Literally, these words state that God *did not allow any of his words to fall to the ground.*

Even the words that Samuel spoke

1. Citing *Arizal, Chomas Anach* says that Eli was a גִּלְגּוּל, *reincarnation,* of Aharon. Accordingly, there is a similarity seen here in that Eli accepts the judgment of the death of his two sons, as did Aharon (see *Leviticus* 10:3). This is consistent with the words of *Rema MiPanu (Gulgulei Neshamos* §57) that Hophni and Phinehas were reincarnations of Aharon's sons Nadab and Abihu (*Mishbetzos Zahav*).

from me anything from the word that He spoke to
you!" 18 *Samuel told him all the words and did not*
withhold from him. [Eli] said, "He is H*ASHEM; He*
will do what is good in His eyes."
19 *Samuel grew up, and* H*ASHEM was with him; He*
did not cast any of his words to the ground. 20 *All of*
Israel, from Dan to Be'er-sheba, knew that Samuel
was faithful as a prophet to H*ASHEM.*
21 *[Thus]* H*ASHEM once again appeared in Shiloh, for*

after he "fell to the ground" (i.e., after he died) did not go unfulfilled. This is a reference to the episode in which Samuel's spirit told Saul that "you and your sons will join me" (below, 28:19; *Midrash Shmuel*).

According to *Kli Yakar*, וְלֹא־הִפִּיל מִכׇּל־דְּבָרָיו אָרְצָה means that Hashem did not allow any of His *own* words to go unfulfilled. This is a reference to the Midrashic teaching that before Samuel was born, a Divine voice proclaimed that a righteous man named Samuel would come into the world (see comm. 1:23).

Abarbanel understands וְלֹא־הִפִּיל as referring not to God but to Samuel. Samuel was a man of such exactitude and integrity that he never let any of his words go unaccounted for; everything that he said was premeditated and absolutely honest. An important prerequisite to experiencing prophecy is a refined and perfected character. Samuel's meticulous behavior, which was the expression of such a character, persuaded people that he was a genuine prophet.

20. וַיֵּדַע כׇּל־יִשְׂרָאֵל ... כִּי־נֶאֱמָן שְׁמוּאֵל לְנָבִיא לַה׳ — *All of Israel ... knew that Samuel was faithful as a prophet to* H*ASHEM.*

The fact that Hashem fulfilled all of Samuel's words substantiated his standing as a prophet. In fact, *Rambam* (*Hil. Yesodei HaTorah* 10:1-3) uses this verse to illustrate the differences between a prophet, whom we are commanded to believe, and a magician or diviner, whom we may not believe. A prophet is substantiated when, after numerous tests, *all* his predictions come true. Contrarily, diviners are sometimes accurate and sometimes not (*Mishbetzos Zahav*).

Malbim comments that the people understood that Samuel was not like private prophets, who employed their inspiration solely in the service of their own spiritual and Godly pursuits. Rather, he was sent as an emissary from Hashem to the people.

מִדָּן וְעַד־בְּאֵר שָׁבַע — *From Dan to Be'er-sheba.*

Dan is a city at the northern border of the Land of Israel, whereas Be'er Sheba is at the south (see *Joshua* 19:2,47; see ArtScroll edition, maps on pp. 375, 391). This phrase is commonly used in Scripture to refer to the entire Jewish commonwealth.

נֶאֱמָן — *Faithful.*

Even when Samuel later reproved the Jews, they sensed his concern and loved him (*Me'am Loez*).

Metzudos renders נֶאֱמָן as *permanent* (as above, 2:35; see comm.). In contrast to other prophets, whose inspiration came only on occasion, Samuel regularly attained a prophetic state.

21. וַיֹּסֶף ה׳ לְהֵרָאֹה בְשִׁלֹה — *[Thus]* H*ASHEM once again appeared in Shiloh.*

In contrast to the pre-Samuel era, when אֵין חָזוֹן נִפְרָץ, *vision was not widespread* (above, verse 1; see comm.), with Samuel's emergence into greatness, prophecy grew commonplace.

א נִגְלָה יְהוָה אֶל־שְׁמוּאֵל בְּשִׁלוֹ בִּדְבַר יְהוָה׃ וַיְהִי
דְבַר־שְׁמוּאֵל לְכָל־יִשְׂרָאֵל וַיֵּצֵא יִשְׂרָאֵל°
לִקְרַאת פְּלִשְׁתִּים לַמִּלְחָמָה וַיַּחֲנוּ עַל־הָאֶבֶן
ב הָעֵזֶר וּפְלִשְׁתִּים חָנוּ בַאֲפֵק׃ וַיַּעַרְכוּ פְלִשְׁתִּים

According to *Abarbanel*, the Divine Spirit came upon Samuel in such an abundance that he was able to pour it onto others as well (as in *Numbers* 11:17). Hence וַיֹּסֶף ה׳ לְהֵרָאֹה, *In addition,* H*ASHEM appeared [to many people]* in Shiloh in the manner of a short *appearance*, a glimpse (*Malbim*), כִּי־נִגְלָה ה׳ אֶל־שְׁמוּאֵל בְּשִׁלוֹ בִּדְבַר ה׳, *for* H*ASHEM appeared to Samuel in Shiloh with the word of* H*ASHEM*.

Samuel rose to an exalted position as prophet and leader even during Eli's lifetime (*Ralbag*).

בְּשִׁלֹה — *In Shiloh.*

What is the significance of the fact that Samuel's prophecy occurred in Shiloh? And why is this repeated twice?

Kli Yakar suggests that Hashem originally wished to abandon the Sanctuary at Shiloh because of the disgrace that Eli's sons had brought upon it. Its saving grace was the fact that God had appeared to Samuel there. Accordingly, וַיֹּסֶף ה׳ לְהֵרָאֹה בְשִׁלֹה, H*ASHEM [only continued] to appear in Shiloh*, כִּי נִגְלָה ה׳ אֶל־שְׁמוּאֵל בְּשִׁלוֹ, *because He had previously appeared to Samuel in Shiloh.*

Midrash Shmuel observes that the second time Shiloh is spelled with a ו. As *R' Shlomo Buber* comments, this indicates that the latter word implies בְּשֶׁלוֹ, *Because of him* (Samuel). Hashem appeared in Samuel's merit.

בִּדְבַר ה׳ — *With the word of* H*ASHEM*.

According to *Radak*, this refers to the opening verse of the coming chapter, in which, he contends, God *commands* the Jews to wage war against the Philistines (4:1). See comm. below.

Along the same lines, *Kli Yakar* explains the flow of this verse as follows, וַיֹּסֶף ה׳ לְהֵרָאֹה בְשִׁלֹה, H*ASHEM now reappeared in Shiloh* to send the Jews to their fateful confrontation with the Philistines, כִּי־נִגְלָה ה׳ אֶל־שְׁמוּאֵל, because H*ASHEM had already revealed Himself to Samuel* and informed him of the impending tragedy that would occur (in verse 11: ... הִנֵּה אָנֹכִי עֹשֶׂה דָבָר בְּיִשְׂרָאֵל, *Behold, I am going to do such a thing in Israel ...*"). The time had now arrived for that prophecy to be realized.

IV

וְאִם־בְּזֹאת לֹא תִשְׁמְעוּ לִי ... וַהֲשִׁמּוֹתִי אֶת־מִקְדְּשֵׁיכֶם וְלֹא אָרִיחַ בְּרֵיחַ נִיחֹחֲכֶם, *If despite this you will not heed Me ... I will make your sanctuaries desolate; I will not savor your satisfying aromas* (*Leviticus* 26:27,31).

Israel is a nation that can survive and blossom only when it enjoys a close proximity to God's presence and to His sanctified sites. So exigent is this need that in the Levitical curse, in which God warns the Jews of the desolation and destruction that would result if they were to stray from the proper path, He threatens that He will abrogate His "sanctuaries" and end the sacrificial service, a threat that carries much weight with a nation whose spiritual lifeline depends on the Divine Presence. Foremost among the elements of the sanctuaries and that service was the Ark of God, which represents the Crown of Torah.

Accordingly, when — as occurs in the present chapter — the Jewish people experienced a spiritual descent and were in desperate need of renewal, they were

HASHEM appeared to Samuel in Shiloh, with the word of HASHEM.

4/1-2

1 *The word of Samuel befell all of Israel.*
Israel went out to war against the Philistines. They encamped at Eben-ezer, while the Philistines encamped at Aphek. 2 *The Philistines arrayed*

made aware of the urgency of their predicament by being deprived of the Ark. This alerted them to the fact that they could not take for granted the hallowed gift of proximity to the Divine, but had to deserve it.

As we will see, the Ark was so much a part of the lives of the Jewish people that the news of its loss caused the death of two valuable souls.

◆§ War Against the Philistines

1. וַיְהִי דְבַר־שְׁמוּאֵל לְכָל־יִשְׂרָאֵל — *The word of Samuel befell all of Israel.*

The forthcoming details of this chapter will describe that tragedy (*Rashi*, as followed by most commentators).

However, as mentioned in our comments on the previous verse (3:21), *Radak* explains this verse differently. God sent Samuel with a prophecy *commanding* the Jews to battle the Philistines.[1] According to *Radak*, the text should thus be understood as follows: *The word of Samuel came to all of Israel [directing them to wage war]. And [therefore] Israel went out ...*

Abarbanel objects to *Radak*'s interpretation, stating that it is unlikely that Samuel's first public prophecy would have resulted in disaster — something that would have severely inhibited the Jews' trust in him.[2] Rather, the Jews waged war against the Philistines without seeking advice (this despite their awareness of the availability of the *Urim VeTumim* [see comm. to 1:13] and of Samuel's prophetic abilities — *Ralbag*).

Abarbanel offers as an alternative understanding of the verse: וַיְהִי דְבַר־שְׁמוּאֵל לְכָל־יִשְׂרָאֵל וַיֵּצֵא יִשְׂרָאֵל, *The word of Samuel* — his prophecy regarding the tragic events that would occur subsequent to the Jews' confrontation with the Philistines — *was [known] to all of Israel. [Yet] Israel [ignored it and fearlessly] went out ...*

Although Scripture does not clearly delineate how much time passed since the beginning of Ch. 3, it is noteworthy that Samuel was already 39 years old at this juncture (see Timeline in Appendix).

וַיַּחֲנוּ עַל־הָאֶבֶן הָעֵזֶר — *They encamped at Eben-ezer.*

Samuel named this site Eben-ezer only later on (see 7:12), after the Jews defeated the Philistines. Nevertheless, the chronicler of the Book of *Samuel*

1. A battle that ended in their defeat. Another such incident occurred during the episode of the Concubine in Gibeah (*Judges* 20:23), when a prophecy was sent to direct Jews to their defeat.

2. *Kli Yakar* defends *Radak*'s view by stating that Samuel's initial prophecy was the prediction of the tragedy that the Jews would suffer at the hands of the Philistines. In his second prophecy, he directed them to engage the Philistines in battle.

Presumably, *Kli Yakar* means to say that Samuel's prophetic call to attack the Philistines would be properly understood by the Jews as God's decision that they must go forward to meet their condign fate, and that together these two prophecies would lead the Jews to develop an appropriate awe and trust in his word.

לִקְרַאת יִשְׂרָאֵל וַתִּטֹּשׁ הַמִּלְחָמָה וַיִּנָּגֶף יִשְׂרָאֵל
לִפְנֵי פְלִשְׁתִּים וַיַּכּוּ בַמַּעֲרָכָה בַּשָּׂדֶה כְּאַרְבַּעַת
ג אֲלָפִים אִישׁ׃ וַיָּבֹא הָעָם אֶל־הַמַּחֲנֶה וַיֹּאמְרוּ זִקְנֵי
יִשְׂרָאֵל לָמָּה נְגָפָנוּ יהוה הַיּוֹם לִפְנֵי פְלִשְׁתִּים
נִקְחָה אֵלֵינוּ מִשִּׁלֹה אֶת־אֲרוֹן בְּרִית יהוה

chooses to anachronistically refer to it by that name here (*Rashi, Radak*).

2. וַתִּטֹּשׁ הַמִּלְחָמָה — *And the battle spread.*

Targum renders this phrase, *The [soldiers] spread out.*

Alternatively, *Abarbanel* translates וַתִּטֹּשׁ הַמִּלְחָמָה as *And the battle was left behind* — i.e., the Jewish soldiers retreated, an action that constituted the proximate cause of their defeat (*Sotah* 44b).

3. וַיָּבֹא הָעָם אֶל־הַמַּחֲנֶה — *The people came to the camp.*

This refers to the soldiers who had engaged in battle. They now returned to join those who had not yet fought (*Metzudos*) in order to regroup and return to the battlefield (*Malbim*).

וַיֹּאמְרוּ זִקְנֵי יִשְׂרָאֵל לָמָּה נְגָפָנוּ ה׳ — *And the elders of Israel said, "Why did Hashem smite us ...?"*

The elders did not suspect the Jews of malfeasance but assumed that the Jews lacked a sufficient measure of merit to evoke God's providential protection and sought to gain God's support by taking the Ark into battle (*Abarbanel*).

נִקְחָה אֵלֵינוּ מִשִּׁלֹה אֶת־אֲרוֹן בְּרִית ה׳ — *Let us take with us from Shiloh the Ark of the Covenant of Hashem.*

Just as Hashem takes heed of the Ark and will surely save it from the hands of the Philistines, reasoned the elders, so too would He protect the Jewish people (*Abarbanel, Malbim*).

The Jews had learned of this concept from the words that Moses would utter when the Ark was transported — וַיְהִי בִּנְסֹעַ הָאָרֹן וַיֹּאמֶר מֹשֶׁה קוּמָה ה׳ וְיָפֻצוּ אֹיְבֶיךָ וְיָנֻסוּ מְשַׂנְאֶיךָ מִפָּנֶיךָ, *When the Ark would journey, Moses said, "Arise, Hashem, and let Your foes be scattered; let those who hate You flee from before You"* (*Numbers* 10:35) — as well as from a number of miraculous incidents recorded in *Joshua*, Chapters 3 and 6, in which the Ark escorted the Jews through miraculous experiences.

However, their reasoning was faulty, for the Ark is not a magical and indiscriminate savior; it protects only those who uphold its covenant (*Malbim*).

נִקְחָה אֵלֵינוּ מִשִּׁלֹה — *Let us take with us from Shiloh.*

Kli Yakar states that this seemingly superfluous reference to Shiloh indicates that the Jews blamed Eli's sons' corruption for their defeat, and decided to remove the Ark from Shiloh, which was the place of their blasphemy and which was clouded in iniquity. The Jews' primary intention was to salvage the Ark from disgrace. They would never have taken the Ark with the sole intention of bringing it to the battlefront; once, however, it was in transit, they decided to do so.

אֲרוֹן בְּרִית ה׳ — *The Ark of the Covenant of Hashem.*

The Tannaim (*Talmud Yerushalmi, Shekalim* 6:1) and early commentators (*Rashi, Ramban*, and *Abarbanel*, et al.) debate whether one or two Arks existed and, if there were two, which was taken into the battle under discussion.[1]

According to Rabbi Yehudah bar Ilai, two Arks existed: one constructed by

4/3 *themselves opposite Israel and the battle*
spread. Israel was smitten before the Philis-
tines; they slew about four thousand men in the
battlefield.
3 *The people came to the camp, and the*
elders of Israel said, "Why did HASHEM *smite us*
today before the Philistines? Let us take with us
from Shiloh the Ark of the Covenant of HASHEM,

Bezalel, which housed the original Torah scroll and which remained always in the Holy of Holies, and one constructed by Moses, which contained the shards of the broken Tablets and accompanied the Jews into battle.

The Sages disagree and maintain that there was only one Ark, which was never removed from the Holy of Holies, with the present exception, which resulted in its captivity.

Of those who claim that there were two Arks, the majority agree that the Ark taken into battle was that of Bezalel, and that this constituted a transgression of God's ordinance (*Rashi, Deuteronomy* 10:1; but see *Sifrei, Parashas Eikev* 11:10; *R' Bachya, Deuteronomy* 10:1; *Nachalas Shimon* 14:9,10). Among the Scriptural sources quoted by each opinion to substantiate its claim, some are from this chapter, and we will indicate them.

לָמָּה נְגָפָנוּ ה׳ — *Why did* HASHEM *smite us?*

Why did the Jews suffer defeat in battle and the loss of the Ark to the Philistines?

Abarbanel offers five explanations:

(1) As evidenced from Samuel's rebuke in Chapter 7 (7:3) — *Remove the foreign gods ...* — idolatry among the Jews was rampant, particularly that of the Idol of Mihah (*Judges*, Chapters 17,18).

When the Jews worship idols, Divine judgment is imposed on them and on the sacred sites and objects that they have forsaken (see *Leviticus* 26:19,31; see also the prefatory remarks to this chapter).

The perspective that idolatry caused the destruction of Shiloh and the capture of the Ark is stated explicitly in *Psalms* 78:58-61.

(2) The sins of Eli's sons, who had jurisdiction over the Ark, caused it to be exiled. This may be inferred from verse 4, where the Ark is mentioned adjacent to their names.

(3) The unauthorized removal of the Ark from its place and its relocation to a battlefield evinced a lamentable lack of reverence for the Ark. (Removal of the Ark should have been approved by the prophet Samuel or by consultation with the *Urim VeTumim*.)

(4) After having lost the battle, the Jews should have engaged in repentance and prayer. The Jews' failure to engage in sober introspection was itself a serious offense that brought tragedy upon themselves and upon the Ark.

(5) Hashem wanted to demonstrate the holiness of the Ark not only to the Jewish people but to the foreign nations and statesmen as well. The frightening events that took place in the presence of the Ark — both in Philistia (Chapter 5) and upon its return to the people of Israel (Chapter 6) — demonstrated its unique and hallowed nature.

1. For an elaborate treatment of this controversy, see *Abarbanel* and *Nachalas Shimon* 14.

ד וְיָבֹא בְקִרְבֵּנוּ וְיֹשִׁעֵנוּ מִכַּף אֹיְבֵינוּ: וַיִּשְׁלַח
הָעָם שִׁלֹה וַיִּשְׂאוּ מִשָּׁם אֵת אֲרוֹן בְּרִית־
יהוה צְבָאוֹת יֹשֵׁב הַכְּרֻבִים וְשָׁם שְׁנֵי בְנֵי־עֵלִי
ה עִם־אֲרוֹן בְּרִית הָאֱלֹהִים חָפְנִי וּפִינְחָס: וַיְהִי
כְּבוֹא אֲרוֹן בְּרִית־יהוה אֶל־הַמַּחֲנֶה וַיָּרִעוּ כָל־
ו יִשְׂרָאֵל תְּרוּעָה גְדוֹלָה וַתֵּהֹם הָאָרֶץ: וַיִּשְׁמְעוּ
פְלִשְׁתִּים אֶת־קוֹל הַתְּרוּעָה וַיֹּאמְרוּ מֶה קוֹל
הַתְּרוּעָה הַגְּדוֹלָה הַזֹּאת בְּמַחֲנֵה הָעִבְרִים וַיֵּדְעוּ

◆§ The Ark Enters the Scene

4. אֲרוֹן בְּרִית־ה׳ צְבָאוֹת יֹשֵׁב הַכְּרֻבִים — *The Ark of the Covenant of* HASHEM, *Master of Legions, Who dwells atop the Cherubim.*

Generally, the reference to Hashem as the *Master of Legions* alludes to His authority over the celestial legions. Here, however, *Radak* explains it as a reference to human armies: God can bring victory to those whom He loves and defeat to His enemies.

Cherubim refers to the images that constituted part of the *Kapores,* the cover of the Ark that stood in the Holy of Holies (*Exodus* 25:17-22).[1] It was from the space between the Cherubim that Hashem's voice emanated when He spoke to Moses. They are thus associated with Hashem's presence and representative of the idea that Hashem is close to those who conform to His ideals. Scripture's mention of the Cherubim emphasizes this, and reminds us that Hashem would have wanted to defend the Jews, but their sins caused their downfall (*Radak*).

Kli Yakar disagrees and maintains that ה׳ צְבָאוֹת here refers to God as the Master of Heavenly Legions, understanding the verse to be stating that HASHEM *[dwells] among the Heavenly Legions and dwells atop the Cherubim [but at present He is not amid the Jews].*

וְשָׁם שְׁנֵי בְנֵי־עֵלִי עִם־אֲרוֹן בְּרִית הָאֱלֹהִים — *And the two sons of Eli ... were there along with the Ark of the Covenant of God.*

Eli's sons carried the Ark themselves (*Metzudos*). *Radak* says that Scripture's emphasis that Eli's sons were at the Ark's site is to make clear that they were largely responsible for the impending calamity (*Radak*; see verse 3, comm. from *Abarbanel*).

God's Providence arranged for Hophni and Phinehas — who, as Kohanim, would otherwise not have gone to a battlefield — to accompany the soldiers to war, so that the prophecy of their demise on one day (2:34) could be realized. Indeed, the Jews did not want them to come, but they insisted on doing so (see *Kli Yakar* above, verse 3).

According to *Me'am Loez,* Eli's sons did not necessarily carry the Ark themselves but did not object to its being taken.

אֲרוֹן בְּרִית הָאֱלֹהִים — *The Ark of the Covenant of God.*

At this point, the Ark is associated with the name *Elokim,* which represents God as a strict judge. (By contrast, at the beginning of this verse and in the following verse, it is associated with the name Hashem.) The meaning of this is

1. This supports the notion that the Ark brought into battle was clearly the one from the Holy of Holies, which did not usually escort them to battle. This may comply with either opinion mentioned above (see v. 3).

that He may come in our midst and save us from
the hands of our enemies!''
4 *So the people sent to Shiloh and carried from*
there the Ark of the Covenant of H*ASHEM*, *Master*
of Legions, Who dwells atop the Cherubim, and the
two sons of Eli — Hophni and Phinehas — were
there along with the Ark of the Covenant of God.
5 *When the Ark of the Covenant of* H*ASHEM arrived*
at the camp, all of Israel sounded a great shofar
blast and the ground shook.
6 *The Philistines heard the sound of the blast and*
they said, ''What is the sound of this great blast in
the camp of the Hebrews?'' And they became aware

that in regard to Eli's sons, the Ark was a source of the due process of Divine law (*Kli Yakar*).

5. וַיָּרִעוּ כָל־יִשְׂרָאֵל תְּרוּעָה גְדוֹלָה — *All of Israel sounded a great shofar blast.*

The Jews raised a clamor upon the arrival of the Ark (*Metzudos*).

Me'am Loez cites an opinion that the Jews sounded trumpets, in accordance with the procedure described in *Numbers* 10:9: וְכִי־תָבֹאוּ מִלְחָמָה בְּאַרְצְכֶם עַל־הַצַּר הַצֹּרֵר אֶתְכֶם וַהֲרֵעֹתֶם בַּחֲצֹצְרֹת, *When you go to wage war in your Land against an enemy who oppresses you, you shall sound short blasts of the trumpets ...*

Following these two interpretations, the Jews did nothing wrong.

Abarbanel, however, considers this shofar blast to have been a significant transgression. He explains that these were outcries of victory, based on the Jews' assumption that the Ark would save them as it had at the battle of Jericho (*Joshua* Chapter 6). But at Jericho the Jews had been commanded not to utter a sound until the wall sank (ibid. verse 10); until then, they were obligated to engage in silent prayer. Because the Jews now ignored the imperative to pray but instead engaged in hasty and premature celebration, they were punished.

Abarbanel's contention is supported by the statement in *Tanna DeVei Eliyahu* (cited by *Me'am Loez*, verse 3) that the entire Jewish nation let out an empty shout — i.e., one devoid of repentance (*Mussar HaNeviim*). This is alluded to by Jeremiah in the verse, *She raised up her voice against Me; therefore I hated her* (*Jeremiah* 12:8).

וַתֵּהֹם הָאָרֶץ — *And the ground shook.*

This is an exaggeration indicating that the sounds could be heard at a distance by the Philistines (*Metzudos*).

Kli Yakar derives from this phrase that only the ground shook; not, however, the heavens, where the shofar blasts were ignored.

6. וַיֹּאמְרוּ — *And they said.*

They questioned one another (*Metzudos*).

מֶה קוֹל הַתְּרוּעָה הַגְּדוֹלָה הַזֹּאת בְּמַחֲנֵה הָעִבְרִים — *What is the sound of this great blast in the camp of the Hebrews?*

That is to say, ''Since we are winning the war, why are the Jews celebrating?'' (*Kli Yakar*).

הָעִבְרִים — *The Hebrews.*

Jews are commonly referred to as

ז כִּי אָרוֹן יהוה בָּא אֶל־הַמַּחֲנֶה: וַיִּרְאוּ הַפְּלִשְׁתִּים
כִּי אָמְרוּ בָּא אֱלֹהִים אֶל־הַמַּחֲנֶה וַיֹּאמְרוּ
אוֹי לָנוּ כִּי לֹא הָיְתָה כָּזֹאת אֶתְמוֹל שִׁלְשֹׁם:
ח אוֹי לָנוּ מִי יַצִּילֵנוּ מִיַּד הָאֱלֹהִים הָאַדִּירִים
הָאֵלֶּה אֵלֶּה הֵם הָאֱלֹהִים הַמַּכִּים אֶת־מִצְרַיִם
ט בְּכָל־מַכָּה בַּמִּדְבָּר: הִתְחַזְּקוּ וִהְיוּ לַאֲנָשִׁים

עִבְרִים because their ancestor Abraham came from עֵבֶר הַנָּהָר, *across the river.*

7. וַיִּרְאוּ הַפְּלִשְׁתִּים — *The Philistines were afraid.*

For generations, the nations of the world maintained their fear of the God of Israel, Who had split the Sea of Reeds, at which time the Jews had said, חִיל אָחַז יֹשְׁבֵי פְּלָשֶׁת, *terror gripped the dwellers of Philistia ...* (*Exodus* 15:14), a fear that Rahab had described to the Jewish spies (*Joshua* 2:9-11; *Me'am Loez*).

בָּא אֱלֹהִים אֶל־הַמַּחֲנֶה — *God has come to the camp.*

That is to say, the Ark came with the Jews to war (*Metzudos*; see verse 8, comm.).

Kli Yakar offers an alternative interpretation. Had the Ark appeared prior to the first battle, they would have expected to be defeated by God with minimal losses. Now, however, the Philistines exclaimed, "Woe unto us that He did not come then, but has come now seeking revenge. Who can withstand their God when He avenges His people's suffering, as He did in Egypt ...?"

8. מִיַּד הָאֱלֹהִים הָאַדִּירִים הָאֵלֶּה — *From the hand of this mighty God.*

The adjectives and verbs in this verse that apply to God are written in the plural form, because, simply, the word אֱלֹהִים, God, is also in the plural (*Metzudos*). However, other commentators are not satisfied with that explanation, presumably because Scripture generally employs the singular form in such instances.

Me'am Loez thus advances the alternative explanation that as polytheists the Philistines could not fathom the concept of a single God, particularly after witnessing the diversity of plagues inflicted upon Egypt.

אוֹי לָנוּ מִי יַצִּילֵנוּ מִיַּד הָאֱלֹהִים הָאַדִּירִים — *Woe to us! Who will save us from the hand of this mighty God?*

The Philistines' frightened reaction lends support to the opinion that there was only one Ark that had never before been removed from the Sanctuary. If there were another Ark that regularly accompanied the Jews in war, the Philistines would not have cried out in panic, "There was never such a thing before" (*Shekalim* 6:1; *Korban HaEidah* ad loc.).[1]

1. Rabbi Yehudah bar Ilai could defend his thesis that there were two Arks by stating that the Philistines were terrified because this was the first time that Bezalel's Ark — which normally remained in the Sanctuary — had ever been brought out.

The Sages, however, could question the force of this argument by asking why that should have frightened the Philistines so completely. After all, if the Philistines were accustomed to seeing an Ark of some sort, they should not have been so thoroughly terrified when seeing that of Bezalel (*Yefeh Mareh*; see *Nachalas Shimon* 14).

Some commentators agree with Rabbi Yehudah bar Ilai that there were two Arks. However, they imply that the Ark that usually escorted the Jews to war was brought out this time as well. This should not have been an unusual sight to the Philistines, and so the Sages express surprise that the Philistines would have been taken aback. (However, the view of these commentators is problematic for a number of reasons [see *Radak* on verse 4].)

that the Ark of HASHEM had come to the camp.
7 The Philistines were afraid, as they said, "God
has come to the camp!" And they said, "Woe to
us, for such a thing had not happened yesterday
or the day before! 8 Woe to us! Who will save us
from the hand of this mighty God? This is the
God Who struck the Egyptians with all kinds of
plagues in the wilderness! 9 Be strong; be men,

אֵלֶּה הֵם הָאֱלֹהִים הַמַּכִּים אֶת־מִצְרַיִם בְּכָל־מַכָּה בַּמִּדְבָּר — *This is the God Who struck the Egyptians with all kinds of plagues in the wilderness.*

The Philistines recalled an instance in which God had come to the aid of the Jews.

Malbim explains the Philistines' thinking as follows: We cannot rest assured that God's strength is limited to pestilence or water-related plagues, for He smote the Egyptians בְּכָל־מַכָּה, *with all kinds of plagues.* Nor can we assure ourselves that God's power is restricted to Egypt, for מַכִּים אֶת־מִצְרַיִם בְּכָל־מַכָּה בַּמִּדְבָּר, *He sent His plagues both in Egypt and in the wilderness.*

בַּמִּדְבָּר — *In the wilderness.*

This word is perplexing because the plagues occurred in Egypt.

Rashi explains that this refers to the plagues that struck the Egyptians at the Sea of Reeds, which was in the wilderness. There God's afflictions were most severe, for there both fathers and sons died (*Mahari Kara*), as well as Pharaoh and his army (*Ralbag*).

According to *Malbim* (cited above), the verse emphasizes that God sent plagues both in Egypt and in the wilderness.

Targum resolves this issue by inserting a phrase: *and who performed wonders for His nation in the wilderness.*

Radak quotes his father who deviates from the usual translation of בַּמִּדְבָּר, *in the wilderness,* and renders it *with his speech,* relating it to the word דִּבּוּר (cf. *Song of Songs* 4:3). The Philistines thus exclaimed, "If God wreaked such havoc in Egypt merely *with His speech,* how much more destruction will He cause now that He Himself has come."

9. הִתְחַזְּקוּ וִהְיוּ לַאֲנָשִׁים — *Be strong; be men.*

That is to say, Be brave and courageous (*Metzudos*).

Malbim explains that the Philistines denied that the God of the Jews preceded or created the world, and thus believed that it is possible upon occasion for mortal human beings to overcome Him in battle. They therefore encouraged each other, "Be men! For if you act like timid animals, you will definitely not prevail."

In the previous verse the Philistines' attitude was fearful. What changed between these two verses?

The Sages explain that there were three groups of Philistines: the worthy, the evil, and the brave.

The worthy among them said, מִי יַצִּילֵנוּ מִיַּד הָאֱלֹהִים הָאַדִּירִים הָאֵלֶּה, *Who will save us from the hand of this mighty God?*

The evil among them insolently responded, אֵלֶּה הֵם הָאֱלֹהִים הַמַּכִּים אֶת־מִצְרַיִם בְּכָל־מַכָּה בַּמִּדְבָּר — *Their God has already smitten the Egyptians with all [of His ten] plagues [and He has no more plagues to use against us].*[1]

1. Hashem answered them, "You will see that I will bring upon you a plague that has never been seen before in the world" — i.e., hemorrhoids; see below, 5:6 and comm.

פְּלִשְׁתִּים פֶּן תַּעַבְדוּ לָעִבְרִים כַּאֲשֶׁר עָבְדוּ
י לָכֶם וִהְיִיתֶם לַאֲנָשִׁים וְנִלְחַמְתֶּם: וַיִּלָּחֲמוּ
פְלִשְׁתִּים וַיִּנָּגֶף יִשְׂרָאֵל וַיָּנֻסוּ אִישׁ לְאֹהָלָיו
וַתְּהִי הַמַּכָּה גְּדוֹלָה מְאֹד וַיִּפֹּל מִיִּשְׂרָאֵל
יא שְׁלֹשִׁים אֶלֶף רַגְלִי: וַאֲרוֹן אֱלֹהִים נִלְקָח וּשְׁנֵי
יב בְנֵי־עֵלִי מֵתוּ חָפְנִי וּפִינְחָס: וַיָּרָץ אִישׁ־בִּנְיָמִן
מֵהַמַּעֲרָכָה וַיָּבֹא שִׁלֹה בַּיּוֹם הַהוּא וּמַדָּיו

The brave among them encouraged them and said, "Be strong; be men ..." (*Rashi*, from *Midrash Shmuel; Tosefta Sotah* 9:5).[1]

פֶּן תַּעַבְדוּ לָעִבְרִים כַּאֲשֶׁר עָבְדוּ לָכֶם — *Lest you become enslaved to the Hebrews as they have been enslaved to you!*

Apparently, the Jews had recently been subservient to the Philistines (*Ralbag*).

This invigorating talk spoke to the pride of the Philistines. They said, "If we lose this battle, we will be enslaved to the Hebrews, who had been our slaves, and thus we will be slaves to slaves" (*Kli Yakar*).

According to *Malbim*, these words imply, "If you are brave, then even if you will not gain victory and enslave Jews, you will at least avoid being subjugated to them."

וִהְיִיתֶם לַאֲנָשִׁים וְנִלְחַמְתֶּם — *Be men and fight!*

This repetition is puzzling. *Malbim* interprets it to mean: "Even if you lose the war, at least your egos will not be shattered, for you will go down to defeat as brave men, not as cowards."

Kli Yakar observes that the word וִהְיִיתֶם is literally in the past tense: *you were men.* Accordingly, he explains that these words served to excite the Philistines by reminding them of their previous victory.[2]

◆§ Tragic Consequences

10. וַיִּלָּחֲמוּ פְלִשְׁתִּים — *So the Philistines fought.*

This encouragement was so persuasive that the Philistines initiated the fighting (*Me'am Loez*).

וַיָּנֻסוּ אִישׁ לְאֹהָלָיו וַתְּהִי הַמַּכָּה גְּדוֹלָה מְאֹד — *And they ran, every man to his tents. The blow was very great.*

Abarbanel attributes even the first defeat to the fact that the Jews retreated (see above, verse 2).

However, *Malbim* states that the first time they retreated in an orderly fashion to prepare for further battle (see verse 3). This time, however, they dispersed in a confused and chaotic manner, which was clearly the cause for the magnitude of their defeat (*Malbim; Sotah* 44b).

וַתְּהִי הַמַּכָּה גְּדוֹלָה מְאֹד — *The blow was very great.*

This is a reference to the great number of soldiers who perished in such a short period of time (*Me'am Loez*).

11. וַאֲרוֹן אֱלֹהִים נִלְקָח — *The Ark of God was taken.*

1. This is one of several verses in Scripture that contain confusing combinations of quotes that must be properly sorted and attributed.

2. It is true that the ו at the beginning of the word should act as a ו הַהִפּוּךְ, transforming the word to the future tense. *Kli Yakar*, however, seems to infer a contrast between the use of the same word near the beginning of the verse — וִהְיוּ — which clearly implies a command in the future tense, to prove that וִהְיִיתֶם may be read with a conjunctive ו in the past tense.

O Philistines, lest you become enslaved to the
Hebrews as they have been enslaved to you! Be
men and fight!"
10 *So the Philistines fought. Israel was smitten*
and they ran, every man to his tents. The blow was
very great: Thirty thousand foot soldiers fell from
Israel; 11 *the Ark of God was taken; and the two*
sons of Eli — Hophni and Phinehas — died.
12 *A Benjamite man ran from the battle-*
front and came to Shiloh that day, his clothing

Thus, Samuel's prophecy (above, 3:11) was fulfilled.

Kli Yakar points out that the verse states that the Ark *was taken* rather than that the Philistines took it. This indicates that it was God's will that the Ark be captured; the Philistines were merely puppets executing His will.

Kli Yakar observes that this time the Ark is not described as being the Ark of the Covenant. The "covenant" refers to the Tablets of the Covenant that it contained (see *Exodus* 34:28, *Deuteronomy* 9:9). Even while the Ark was in captivity, Saul rescued the Tablets (as the Midrash teaches — see below). Thus, only the empty Ark (divested of its "covenant") spent an extended period of time in captivity.

וּשְׁנֵי בְנֵי־עֵלִי מֵתוּ חָפְנִי וּפִינְחָס — *And the two sons of Eli — Hophni and Phinehas — died.*

They both died on the same day, as prophesied by the *man of God* (2:34) and by Samuel (3:12).

Although the verse does not specify the manner of their demise, *Psalms* indicates that they died violently: *His priests fell by the sword* (*Psalms* 78:64). (See *Rashi* ad loc.; see also *Targum* below, 4:17, which states that Hophni and Phinehas *were murdered. Rashi* (below, 17:8) says that Goliath killed them, as is evident from the words added parenthetically to *Targum.*)

☙ Eli is Notified — and Dies

12. וַיָּרָץ אִישׁ־בִּנְיָמִן מֵהַמַּעֲרָכָה וַיָּבֹא שִׁלֹה בַּיּוֹם הַהוּא — *A Benjamite man ran from the battlefront and came to Shiloh that day.*

Malbim describes how everyone retreated and escaped in a confused manner to hide in caves and the like except for this Benjamite, who, having witnessed the episode, ran to Shiloh to deliver the news.

Midrash Shmuel informs us that this man was Saul (who would later become king of Israel). The Midrash apparently makes its inference from the mention of his tribe, which implies a reference to a known personality of Benjamin. When Saul heard that the Tablets had been seized, he ran to Goliath (below, 17:4), snatched the Tablets from him, and ran with them back to Shiloh.[1]

Our Sages present three views as to the length that Saul ran that day. All agree that the

1. Now that the Jews possessed the Tablets but not the Ark, they should presumably have had to build a new Ark — something that *Minchas Chinuch* (Commandment 95:9) implies that they did. It is surprising, however, that Scripture makes no mention of this.

Even if a temporary Ark had been built, we must conclude from the description of the pomp and fanfare glorifying the return of the Ark (see Chapter 7; *II Samuel* Chapter 6) that the original Ark constructed by Bezalel retained a primary sanctity and returned to its previous position. (See *Nachalas Shimon* 15.)

יג קְרֻעִ֔ים וַאֲדָמָ֖ה עַל־רֹאשֽׁוֹ׃ וַיָּב֗וֹא וְהִנֵּ֣ה עֵ֠לִי יֹשֵׁ֨ב
עַֽל־הַכִּסֵּ֜א °יך דֶּ֚רֶךְ מְצַפֶּ֔ה כִּֽי־הָיָ֤ה לִבּוֹ֙ חָרֵ֔ד עַ֖ל
אֲר֣וֹן הָאֱלֹהִ֑ים וְהָאִ֗ישׁ בָּ֚א לְהַגִּ֣יד בָּעִ֔יר וַתִּזְעַ֖ק
יד כָּל־הָעִֽיר׃ וַיִּשְׁמַ֤ע עֵלִי֙ אֶת־ק֣וֹל הַצְּעָקָ֔ה וַיֹּ֕אמֶר
מֶ֛ה ק֥וֹל הֶהָמ֖וֹן הַזֶּ֑ה וְהָאִ֣ישׁ מִהַ֔ר וַיָּבֹ֖א וַיַּגֵּ֥ד
טו לְעֵלִֽי׃ וְעֵלִ֕י בֶּן־תִּשְׁעִ֥ים וּשְׁמֹנֶ֖ה שָׁנָ֑ה וְעֵינָ֣יו
טז קָ֔מָה וְלֹ֥א יָכ֖וֹל לִרְאֽוֹת׃ וַיֹּ֨אמֶר הָאִ֜ישׁ אֶל־עֵלִ֗י
אָנֹכִי֙ הַבָּ֣א מִן־הַֽמַּעֲרָכָ֔ה וַאֲנִ֕י מִן־הַֽמַּעֲרָכָ֖ה
נַ֣סְתִּי הַיּ֑וֹם וַיֹּ֕אמֶר מֶֽה־הָיָ֥ה הַדָּבָ֖ר בְּנִֽי׃

°יַד ק׳

distance between the battlefront and Shiloh was 60 *mil* (a *mil* is approximately one mile).

According to one opinion, Saul was at the battlefront when he heard about the Tablets. He retrieved them and ran 60 *mil* to Shiloh.

According to a second opinion, he was in Shiloh when he received the news. He ran to the battlefront and back to Shiloh, for a total of 120 *mil*.

Yet a third opinion contends that Saul was first at the battlefield. He escaped the calamitous massacre and ran to Shiloh, where he heard about the Tablets. He ran back to the battlefront, seized the Tablets, and brought them back to Shiloh, for a total of 180 *mil*.

According to all opinions, Saul exhibited great prowess and unusual speed. Thus, after Saul died, David eulogized him, מִנְּשָׁרִים קַלּוּ וּמֵאֲרָיוֹת גָּבֵרוּ, *[He was] swifter than eagles, stronger than lions* (*II Samuel* 1:23; *Me'am Loez*).[1]

וּמַדָּיו קְרֻעִים ... — *His clothing ripped ...*

He did so in mourning over the tragedy that had befallen the Ark and the Jewish people (*Metzudos*).

13. יַד דֶּרֶךְ — *Next to the road.*

According to the written text, which uses the word יַךְ, *hit*, *Eli's* heart was anxiously palpitating (*Radak*). (We find a similar usage in the verse, וַיַּךְ לֵב־דָּוִד אֹתוֹ, *David's heart was beating [violently inside] him* [*I Samuel* 24:6; see *Metzudos* ad loc.].) Accordingly, the complete phrase is יַךְ דֶּרֶךְ מְצַפֶּה *[His heart] was beating [rapidly] in the manner of one who is anxiously awaiting* (*Kli Yakar*).

According to tradition, however, this word is to be read as יַד (lit., *hand*), meaning *at the place of* or *next to.*

מְצַפֶּה — *Looking out.*

Our translation follows *Targum* (as well as *Ralbag*), which relates מְצַפֶּה to הַצֹּפִים, *gazers* or *watchers* (see below, 14:16).

Other commentators, such as *Radak*, interpret מְצַפֶּה as *anxiously and hopefully awaiting.*

כִּי־הָיָה לִבּוֹ חָרֵד עַל אֲרוֹן הָאֱלֹהִים — *For his heart was fearful about the Ark of God.*

Although Eli was informed of the impending death of his two sons, his sole concern was the welfare of the Ark. Later on it was the tragic information about the Ark, not about his two sons, that brought about his death (verse 18; *Ralbag*).

1. There must be an underlying reason that it was Saul in particular who engaged in this venture. *Me'am Loez* (citing *Chaim Tovim*) explains as follows: The Midrash (*Bereishis Rabbah* 54:4) says that when Abraham made a covenant with Abimelech and offered seven sheep, Hashem was upset and stated that as a result Abimelech's descendants (the Philistines) would kill seven of Abraham's righteous descendants: Samson, Hophni, Phinehas, Saul, and Saul's three sons. Now that Hophni and Phinehas had died, Saul perhaps sensed that his time had come, and he therefore engaged in this risky maneuver in order to earn himself some saving grace.

ripped and dirt upon his head. [13]*When he came*
Eli was seated in a chair next to the road, looking
out, for his heart was fearful about the Ark of God.
The man arrived to inform the city, and the entire
city cried out. [14]*Eli heard the sound of the outcry*
and said, "What is the commotion of this mul-
titude?" And the man hastened — he came and
told Eli. [15]*Now Eli was ninety-eight years old; his*
eyes had become motionless and he could not see.
[16]*The man said to Eli, "I am the one who came*
from the battlefront. And I ran from the battlefront
today."[Eli] said, "What is the report, my son?"

וְהָאִישׁ בָּא לְהַגִּיד בָּעִיר — *The man arrived to inform the city.*

Eli was seated just outside the city gates (*Targum* inserts this fact, evident from verse 18, into its rendering of the present verse). Eli sat near the road upon which people could be expected to return from the battleground, awaiting their reports. *The man,* however — Saul — who was escaping, went in a roundabout way and entered the city from the opposite direction so he first informed the city residents of the news (*Abarbanel; Malbim*).

וַתִּזְעַק כָּל־הָעִיר — *And the entire city cried out.*

They burst into wails of grief and lamentation (*Metzudos*).

14. וְהָאִישׁ מִהַר וַיָּבֹא וַיַּגֵּד לְעֵלִי — *And the man hastened — he came and told Eli.*

No one else wished to deliver the tragic news to Eli, and so Saul himself was impelled to do so.

Since the commotion caused by his report had spread throughout the city, Saul assumed that Eli already knew the general outline of what had happened and only wanted to hear the details. Thus — as God had arranged it — Saul now broke the story to Eli suddenly, whereas he would otherwise have delivered it slowly and with sensitivity (*Malbim*).

15. וְעֵינָיו קָמָה — *His eyes had become motionless.*

Functioning eyes are constantly in motion. But Eli's eyes, which had ceased to see, were motionless (*Metzudos*).

Abarbanel, however, renders קָמָה as *weakened.*

There seems to be a grammatical flaw in this verse, because עֵינָיו, *eyes,* is in the plural, whereas קָמָה, *had become motionless,* is in the singular. *Mahari Kara* resolves this by explaining that עֵינָיו means *each of his eyes.* According to *Malbim,* this phrase can be translated as *his eyesight had stopped.*

וְלֹא יָכוֹל לִרְאוֹת — *And he could not see.*

Thus, Eli did not see Saul's ripped clothing and the dirt on his head. He was therefore utterly stunned when he heard Saul's report (*Malbim*).

16. אָנֹכִי הַבָּא מִן־הַמַּעֲרָכָה — *I am the one who came from the battlefront.*

Me'am Loez suggests that when Eli summoned Saul, he mistakenly took him for a local resident who had heard the news. Thus, Saul now introduced himself as an eyewitness.

אָנֹכִי הַבָּא מִן־הַמַּעֲרָכָה וַאֲנִי מִן הַמַּעֲרָכָה נַסְתִּי הַיּוֹם — *I am the one who came from the battlefront. And I ran from the battlefront today.*

This redundancy implies that Saul came from the battlefront twice; it thus

יז וַיַּ֨עַן הַֽמְבַשֵּׂ֜ר וַיֹּ֗אמֶר נָ֤ס יִשְׂרָאֵל֙ לִפְנֵ֣י פְלִשְׁתִּ֔ים וְגַ֛ם
מַגֵּפָ֥ה גְדוֹלָ֖ה הָיְתָ֣ה בָעָ֑ם וְגַם־שְׁנֵ֨י בָנֶ֜יךָ מֵ֗תוּ חָפְנִי֙
יח וּפִ֣ינְחָ֔ס וַאֲר֥וֹן הָאֱלֹהִ֖ים נִלְקָֽחָה׃ וַיְהִ֞י כְּהַזְכִּיר֣וֹ ׀
אֶת־אֲר֣וֹן הָאֱלֹהִ֗ים וַיִּפֹּ֣ל מֵֽעַל־הַ֠כִּסֵּא אֲחֹ֨רַנִּ֜ית
בְּעַ֣ד ׀ יַ֣ד הַשַּׁ֗עַר וַתִּשָּׁבֵ֤ר מַפְרַקְתּוֹ֙ וַיָּמֹ֔ת כִּֽי־זָקֵ֥ן
הָאִ֖ישׁ וְכָבֵ֑ד וְה֛וּא שָׁפַ֥ט אֶת־יִשְׂרָאֵ֖ל אַרְבָּעִ֥ים שָׁנָֽה׃

supports the view that he ran 180 *mil* that day (see above, verse 12): from the battlefront to Shiloh, back to the battlefront to seize the Tablets, and back again to Shiloh (*Kli Yakar*).

17. וַיַּעַן הַמְבַשֵּׂר — *The bearer of the tidings answered him.*

The present use of the term מְבַשֵּׂר, *bearer of tidings,* is puzzling because generally that word is used in reference to good news.

Radak maintains simply that the word may also be used in the case of bad news.

Kli Yakar, however, contends that Saul intended to relate the good news that he had returned the Tablets.[1]

נָס יִשְׂרָאֵל לִפְנֵי פְלִשְׁתִּים וְגַם מַגֵּפָה גְדוֹלָה הָיְתָה בָעָם וְגַם־שְׁנֵי בָנֶיךָ מֵתוּ חָפְנִי וּפִינְחָס וַאֲרוֹן הָאֱלֹהִים נִלְקָחָה — *Israel ran from before the Philistines; and there was a great blow among the people; also, your two sons — Hophni and Phinehas — died; and the Ark of God was taken!*

See above, comm. to verse 2 and verse 10, from *Sotah* 44b.

This is seemingly not in accord with the previous description of events, in which the capture of the Ark is mentioned before the death of the Eli's sons (verse 11).

Malbim contends that the events occurred in the sequence reported by Saul.

Abarbanel, however, explains that in his report to Eli, Saul displayed great wisdom rearranging the sequence of events in ascending order of severity, so as to first report those items that would be less upsetting to Eli (*Me'am Loez*).

וַאֲרוֹן הָאֱלֹהִים נִלְקָחָה — *And the Ark of God was taken.*

Radak observes that the word אָרוֹן,

1. *Kli Yakar* offers an alternative approach to explain why Saul was considered a bearer of good news.

The Midrash quotes the opening of *Psalms* 79 — מִזְמוֹר לְאָסָף אֱלֹהִים בָּאוּ גוֹיִם בְּנַחֲלָתֶךָ, *A song of Assaf, to God! The nations have entered into your estate* — and asks why it is called a *song,* when it should more properly have been called a *lament.*

The Midrash explains with a parable. A poor girl's earthenware jug fell into a well, and she began to cry. A princess came by, and by chance her golden jug fell into that same well, as a result of which the poor girl smiled. She explained, "No one would bother retrieving my inexpensive vessel, but now that the golden jug has also fallen into the well, whoever retrieves it will retrieve mine too."

In this verse, Assaf implies that God, Who would descend to the bowels of the earth to retrieve the Temple's gates, would also raise up his father, Korah, who had been swallowed by the earth. (See prefatory remarks to ArtScroll *Psalms* 79.)

Similarly, says *Kli Yakar,* Saul intended to bring Eli encouraging news by conveying the idea that just as God would avenge the capture of the Ark, so too would He avenge the souls of the slaughtered Jews.

Me'am Loez adds that before Saul had a chance to express this idea, Eli fell backward and died.

[17] *The bearer of the tidings answered him saying, "Israel ran from before the Philistines; and there was a great blow among the people; also, your two sons — Hophni and Phinehas — died; and the Ark of God was taken!"* [18] *As soon as he mentioned the Ark of God, [Eli] fell backward out of his chair, opposite the site of the city gate, breaking his neck, and he died, for the man was old and heavy. He had judged Israel for forty years.*

Ark, can be either masculine or feminine. In this verse, it is treated as feminine, whereas in verse 11 it is treated as masculine. (See *Rashi* to *Genesis* 32:9 for other examples).

18. וַיְהִי כְּהַזְכִּירוֹ אֶת־אֲרוֹן הָאֱלֹהִים — *As soon as he mentioned the Ark of God.*

Only when Eli heard that the Ark had been seized did he react with such stunned heartache — so much so that he fell backward. The news of the other calamities, even the death of his sons, did not cause him such a degree of distress. See footnote above, 3:11.

וַיִּפֹּל מֵעַל־הַכִּסֵּא אֲחֹרַנִּית — *He fell backward out of his chair.*

Because Eli had not concerned himself sufficiently with his posterity — i.e., with what he would leave *behind* — and so he had failed to rebuke his children properly, he died by falling *backward*. Also, due to his timidity in dealing with his sons' misdeeds, Eli failed to secure his family's "seat" of High Priesthood. Therefore, he met his demise by falling out of his chair (*Me'am Loez*). Thus, we may here intuit a Divine measure-for-measure retribution.

מַפְרַקְתּוֹ — *His neck.*

Radak explains that the neck is called מַפְרֶקֶת, for this word is related to פְּרָקִים, *sections*, since the neck is composed of vertebrae.

Alternatively, *Me'am Loez* cites an opinion that מַפְרֶקֶת refers to the entire spine, likewise because it is composed of a chain of vertebrae.

כִּי־זָקֵן הָאִישׁ — *For the man was old.*

And his body was frail.

וְכָבֵד — *And heavy.*

Old age made mobility difficult for Eli. Therefore, he was unable to tilt his body to avoid falling on his neck (*Metzudos*).

Alternatively, *Radak* suggests that he literally weighed a lot and this aggravated his fall and caused his death.

וְהוּא שָׁפַט אֶת־יִשְׂרָאֵל אַרְבָּעִים שָׁנָה — *He had judged Israel for forty years.*

This piece of information seems awkwardly out of place.

Simply understood, on the occasion of Eli's death, Scripture offers a brief, positive description of his lifework (*Abarbanel*).

Alternatively, *Abarbanel* suggests that the toil that Eli exerted as Chief Judge contributed to his weakness as he aged, and this was a factor in his death.

Me'am Loez explains this verse as a penetrating depiction of the tragedy of Eli's life: After he had filled this prestigious position of Judge for 40 years, his life ended suddenly in this violent, disastrous manner. This augmented the wound that the Jewish people incurred that day, for after losing the war and the Ark, they also lost the great leader who had judged them for 40 years (*Kli Yakar*).

יט וְכַלָּתוֹ אֵשֶׁת־פִּינְחָס הָרָה לָלַת וַתִּשְׁמַע אֶת־
הַשְּׁמֻעָה אֶל־הִלָּקַח אֲרוֹן הָאֱלֹהִים וּמֵת
חָמִיהָ וְאִישָׁהּ וַתִּכְרַע וַתֵּלֶד כִּי־נֶהֶפְכוּ עָלֶיהָ
כ צִרֶיהָ: וּכְעֵת מוּתָהּ וַתְּדַבֵּרְנָה הַנִּצָּבוֹת עָלֶיהָ
אַל־תִּירְאִי כִּי־בֵן יָלָדְתְּ וְלֹא עָנְתָה וְלֹא־
כא שָׁתָה לִבָּהּ: וַתִּקְרָא לַנַּעַר אִי כָבוֹד לֵאמֹר

The date on which these tragedies occurred was the 10th of Iyar, and *Shulchan Aruch* (*Orach Chaim* 580:2, from *Megillas Taanis*) records it as a day on which it is commendable to fast.

The Talmud (*Zevachim* 118b) relates that the death of Eli led to the destruction of the Tabernacle in Shiloh, where it had stood for 369 years (see comm. above, 1:3).

This destruction is only alluded to in Scripture in the verse: וַיִּטֹּשׁ מִשְׁכַּן שִׁלוֹ, *He abandoned the Tabernacle of Shiloh* (*Psalms* 78:60).

The Sages discuss prophecies that predicted this destruction (*Bereishis Rabbah* 54:4, *Megillah* 16b, *Rashi* to *Genesis* 45:14) and the iniquities that brought it about (*Yoma* 9a). (However, as *Chasam Sofer* points out [*Parashas Re'eh*], even if sins had not contributed to the Tabernacle's destruction it would have needed to be destroyed anyway, so that the Temple in Jerusalem might be built [see *Nachalas Shimon* 31:13].)

From Shiloh, the Tabernacle was transferred to Nob.

◆§ The Wife of Phinehas Gives Birth and Dies

19. הָרָה לָלַת — *Was soon to give birth.*

Most commentators agree that לָלַת derives from the word לָלֶדֶת, *to give birth* (with an elided ד).

Alshich suggests that since the letter ד is spelled דלי"ת, related to the word דֶּלֶת, *door*, the missing letter ד in לָלַת symbolizes that the "door" of her womb was closed — i.e., she was not yet due to give birth.

Conversely, *Ralbag* assumes that לָלַת means *complete*, implying that her gestation period had ended and she was ready for birth.

The grammarian Menachem associates לָלַת with יְלָלָה, *wailing*. This would imply either that all labor pains evoke screams (*Radak*), or that this birth in particular was accompanied by excessive pain and bitter cries (*Rashi*).

וַתִּשְׁמַע אֶת־הַשְּׁמֻעָה אֶל־הִלָּקַח אֲרוֹן הָאֱלֹהִים וּמֵת חָמִיהָ וְאִישָׁהּ — *And when she heard the news about the capture of the Ark of God and [that] her father-in-law died, and her husband ...*

People related the news items in the order of their significance, mentioning the most important one first (*Malbim*).

Kli Yakar, however, suggests that whoever reported these events to Phinehas' wife intended to begin with what would presumably be the least severe in her eyes. However, as a virtuous woman, she was most disturbed by the news about the Ark; and she was further perturbed by the assumption made by this person.

כִּי־נֶהֶפְכוּ עָלֶיהָ צִרֶיהָ — *For her labor pains came upon her.*

נֶהֶפְכוּ literally means *changed* or *reversed* and may simply mean that her labor pains began suddenly. This is related to the shifting of the fetus that typically accompanies the beginning of the birth process (*Me'am Loez*).

Alternatively, *Me'am Loez* explains that the emotional pain from the tidings changed into (i.e., induced) contractions.

According to these interpretations, since the labor pains came unexpectedly,

[19] *His daughter-in-law, the wife of Phinehas, was*
soon to give birth, and when she heard the news
about the capture of the Ark of God and [that] her
father-in-law died, and her husband, she crouched
down and gave birth, for her labor pains came upon
her. [20] *As she was about to die, those standing around*
her spoke to her, "Fear not, for you have borne a
son!" But she did not answer, and she did not take
it to her heart. [21] *She called the boy Ichabod saying,*

she was unable to concentrate on proper birthing methods and this resulted in her death (*Ralbag*).

Following *Rashi*, however, נֶהֶפְכוּ implies that the nature of her labor pains was different — presumably, more severe — than normal, and that caused her death.

Abarbanel explains that her labor pains and contractions ceased after the baby was born but before the placenta was released from her body, and that was the cause of her death.

צִרֶיהָ — *Labor pains.*

The word צִרֶיהָ derives from צִירִים, *hinges* (see *Bechoros* 45a). Labor pains result when the tight bonds of the womb loosen [and tighten] to allow for the passage of the baby, just as hinges loosen to allow passage through a door (*Metzudos*).

20. *Midrash Shmuel* lists Phinehas' wife as one of three noble women who died in childbirth, the other two being Rachel (*Genesis* 35:18) and Michal (*II Samuel* 6:23).

Although our Sages list three sins punished with death in childbirth (i.e., negligence with the laws of family purity, *challah*, and Shabbos candle-lighting [*Shabbos* 31b]), we should not assume that a woman who has suffered such a fate was guilty of any of these sins, for when God so wills, even the most righteous of women can also suffer that misfortune (*Yefeh Toar* on *Bereishis Rabbah* 82:7).

אַל־תִּירְאִי כִּי־בֵן יָלָדְתְּ — *Fear not, for you have borne a son!*

These women thought that she might be worried due to her knowledge of the axiom that when a person dies, his entire family should also fear death. Their glad tidings served to remind her that the antidote against this potential hazard is the birth of a son in the family *(R' Yaakov Padanki)*.

Me'am Loez explains that the women intended to console her by pointing out that she would have a son who would carry on her husband's name and memory.

וְלֹא עָנְתָה וְלֹא־שָׁתָה לִבָּהּ — *But she did not answer, and she did not take it to her heart.*

The depth and severity of the tragedy was so great that she could not be consoled.

21. וַתִּקְרָא לַנַּעַר אִי כָבוֹד — *She called the boy Ichabod.*

In so doing, she exhibited her disregard for the women's sympathy. Had she accepted their consolation, she would have called the boy Raphael, meaning *God heals* (*R' Yaakov Padanki*, see above).

אִי כָבוֹד — *Ichabod.*

Most commentators understand this to mean אִי כָבוֹד, *there is no glory.*

Alternatively, *Radak* renders this name as אֵי כָבוֹד, *Where is the glory?*, and *Me'am Loez* relates it to אוֹי לְכָבוֹד, *Woe is to the glory* [*that is gone*]*!*

לֵאמֹר — *Saying.*

Ichabod's very name will *say* and

ד/כב גָּלָ֥ה כָב֛וֹד מִיִּשְׂרָאֵ֖ל אֶל־הִלָּקַח֙ אֲר֣וֹן הָאֱלֹהִ֔ים
כב וְאֶל־חָמִ֖יהָ וְאִישָֽׁהּ׃ וַתֹּ֕אמֶר גָּלָ֥ה כָב֖וֹד מִיִּשְׂרָאֵ֑ל
כִּ֥י נִלְקַ֖ח אֲר֥וֹן הָאֱלֹהִֽים׃
ה/א־ג א וּפְלִשְׁתִּים֙ לָֽקְח֔וּ אֵ֖ת אֲר֣וֹן הָאֱלֹהִ֑ים וַיְבִאֻ֛הוּ
ב מֵאֶ֥בֶן הָעֵ֖זֶר אַשְׁדּֽוֹדָה׃ וַיִּקְח֤וּ פְלִשְׁתִּים֙ אֶת־אֲר֣וֹן
הָאֱלֹהִ֔ים וַיָּבִ֥יאוּ אֹת֖וֹ בֵּ֣ית דָּג֑וֹן וַיַּצִּ֥יגוּ אֹת֖וֹ אֵ֥צֶל
ג דָּגֽוֹן׃ וַיַּשְׁכִּ֣מוּ אַשְׁדּוֹדִים֙ מִֽמָּחֳרָ֔ת וְהִנֵּ֣ה דָגוֹן֙ נֹפֵ֤ל
לְפָנָיו֙ אַ֔רְצָה לִפְנֵ֖י אֲר֣וֹן יהוה֑ וַיִּקְחוּ֙ אֶת־דָּג֔וֹן

testify that at the time of his birth, the glory of Israel went into exile.

וְאֶל־חָמִיהָ וְאִישָׁהּ — *And because of [the deaths of] her father-in-law and her husband.*

The commentators state that the loss of Eli's son Phinehas contributed to the entire nation's exile and loss of glory.

This supports the contention that Phinehas was a righteous man and died only because he did not object to Hophni's deeds (*Shabbos* 55b; see above, 2:12). Indeed, Phinehas was so worthy that the High Priests were his descendants until the time of Solomon, when the curse upon the family was fully realized.

22. This verse is perplexing for two reasons: first, its repetitious mention of the seizure of the Ark, and second, its conspicuous failure to mention the deaths of her father-in-law and husband.

Radak explains that this shows that the principal loss of glory inhered in the exile of the Ark.

Abarbanel interprets the flow of this and the previous verse as follows. Phinehas' wife called her son Ichabod without providing an explanation for having done so.

The women in attendance, thinking to explicate her assumed intentions, said, "He is called Ichabod because glory has been exiled from Israel, due to the capture of the Ark and the deaths of her father-in-law and husband." But with her last breath, Phinehas' wife objected, "[No, that is not what I had in mind.] Glory has departed from Israel because [— and only because —] the Ark of God has been captured." With this, she demonstrated enormous strength of character, for although in her weakness she had not expressed any joy upon the birth of her son, she gathered the energy to defend the glory of the Ark.[1]

1. *Malbim* explains this puzzling verse in a very profound way.

He considers the capture of the Ark (which housed the Torah and Tablets) as the symbolic exile of the Written Torah, and the death of Eli and his sons, who were notable scholars, as symbolizing the diminished potency of the Oral Torah (which is contained solely in the minds of its students).

In the last verse of this chapter, Phinehas' wife spoke of the two tragedies as one, attributing the illustrious title "Ark" both to the actual Ark in which the written Tablets were contained and to Eli and his sons, on whose hearts the contents of the Oral Torah were carved (as in *Proverbs* 3:3).

By equating these "Arks," she aroused the people's deep sorrow.

In a similar spirit, our Sages teach, "How foolish are those Babylonians who stand up for [and revere] a Torah scroll, but do not stand up for a great [Talmudic] scholar [who contains the precepts of the Oral Law]" (*Makkos* 22b).

See also *Meshech Chochmah, Leviticus* 16:1-3, for his understanding of why the Ark was considered Israel's glory.

4/22 *"Glory has been exiled from Israel," because of the capture of the Ark of God and because of [the deaths of] her father-in-law and her husband. [22] And she said, "Glory has been exiled from Israel, for the Ark of God has been captured."*

5/1-3 *[1] The Philistines had taken the Ark of God and brought it from Eben-ezer to Ashdod. [2] The Philistines took the Ark of God and brought it to the House of Dagon, placing it next to Dagon. [3] The Ashdodites arose early the next day and behold, Dagon had fallen upon its face to the ground, before the Ark of HASHEM. So they took Dagon*

V

By capturing the Ark as if it were a defeated soldier, the Philistines exhibited abundant disdain not only for the Ark but for the invincible God Whom it represented.

Because the Philistines' overweening pride persuaded them to claim sole credit for their victory, Hashem deemed it necessary to remind them that it was ultimately He Who had smitten the Jews, and that He could subject them to the same fate.

The manner in which He delivered this message to the Philistines punctured their bloated egos and cast them down from their self-erected pedestals (*Abarbanel*). Also, His admonition attained a second goal as well: the return of the Ark to the people of Israel.

◆§ Judgment Against the Philistines' God

2. וַיָּבִיאוּ אֹתוֹ בֵּית דָּגוֹן וַיַּצִּיגוּ אֹתוֹ אֵצֶל דָּגוֹן — *And brought it to the House of Dagon, placing it next to Dagon.*

Dagon, the Philistines' god, had human features from its head to its navel, and below that the torso of a fish. Hence the name דָּגוֹן, derived from דָּג, *fish* (*Radak*). *Me'am Loez* suggests that the Philistines worshiped a god in this form because its hybrid physiology indicated their belief in its sovereignty over both seas and land.

The Sages differ in their explanation of why the Philistines stationed the Ark next to their idol.

Rabbi Yochanan accredits the Philistines with having honored the Ark by placing it in their shrine, next to their deity. However, although the Philistines meant well, they were punished, for by equating Hashem with their idol, they clearly insulted Hashem's glory (*Kli Yakar*).

Reish Lakish disagrees and argues that if it had been their intent to honor the Ark, God would not have subjected them to such terrific punishment (as will be described in this chapter). Rather, he suggests the Philistines meant to degrade the Ark, and so they put it next to their idol to indicate the Ark's supposed subservience to that idol (*Midrash Shmuel*).

3. וְהִנֵּה דָגוֹן נֹפֵל לְפָנָיו אַרְצָה לִפְנֵי אֲרוֹן ה׳ — *And behold, Dagon had fallen upon its face to the ground, before the Ark of HASHEM.*

Dagon had been standing alongside the Ark and facing the door. Thus, if it had fallen by happenstance, it would

ד וַיָּשִׁבוּ אֹתוֹ לִמְקוֹמוֹ: וַיַּשְׁכִּמוּ בַבֹּקֶר מִמָּחֳרָת
וְהִנֵּה דָגוֹן נֹפֵל לְפָנָיו אַרְצָה לִפְנֵי אֲרוֹן יהוה
וְרֹאשׁ דָּגוֹן וּשְׁתֵּי | כַּפּוֹת יָדָיו כְּרֻתוֹת אֶל־הַמִּפְתָּן
ה רַק דָּגוֹן נִשְׁאַר עָלָיו: עַל־כֵּן לֹא־יִדְרְכוּ כֹהֲנֵי דָגוֹן
וְכָל־הַבָּאִים בֵּית־דָּגוֹן עַל־מִפְתַּן דָּגוֹן בְּאַשְׁדּוֹד עַד
ו הַיּוֹם הַזֶּה: וַתִּכְבַּד יַד־יהוה אֶל־הָאַשְׁדּוֹדִים
וַיְשִׁמֵּם וַיַּךְ אֹתָם °בעפלים אֶת־אַשְׁדּוֹד וְאֶת־גְּבוּלֶיהָ:

°בַּטְּחֹרִים ק׳

have fallen toward the door and not toward the Ark.

Even if it did fall sideways toward the Ark, it would have fallen onto its side. The fact that it lay face down before the Ark was therefore a clearly supernatural miracle; one, however, that the Philistines willfully ignored, interpreting it as an accident (*Malbim*).

Me'am Loez, pointing out that נֹפֵל, *falling*, is in the present tense, understands Dagon to have fallen in a manner that portrayed ongoing submission toward the Ark (cf. וְהָמָן נֹפֵל עַל־הַמִּטָּה, *Haman was prostrated on the couch* [*Esther* 7:8]).

וַיָּשִׁבוּ אֹתוֹ לִמְקוֹמוֹ — *And returned it to its place.*

The verse does not state that the Philistines *lifted* the Ark, but rather that they *returned* it, implying that the Ark had traveled a considerable distance across the room and needed to be returned to its place — a further demonstration that this was no random mishap (*Malbim*).

4. וַיַּשְׁכִּמוּ בַבֹּקֶר מִמָּחֳרָת — *They arose early the next morning.*

Having been shaken by the events of the previous day, the Philistines awoke early to inspect the well-being of their idol in its shrine (*Kli Yakar, Me'am Loez*).

וְהִנֵּה דָגוֹן נֹפֵל לְפָנָיו אַרְצָה לִפְנֵי אֲרוֹן ה׳ וְרֹאשׁ דָּגוֹן וּשְׁתֵּי כַּפּוֹת יָדָיו כְּרֻתוֹת אֶל־הַמִּפְתָּן — *Dagon had fallen upon its face to the ground, before the Ark of* H*ASHEM*, *and Dagon's head and two hands were severed, [lying] upon the threshold.*

Malbim sees this verse as describing a double miracle.

First, the idol was found a second time lying prone before the Ark; second, its head and hands were scattered across the threshold. A reconstruction of what had occurred led the Philistines to the supposition that first the idol had fallen toward the door, where its head and hands had broken off, and that it had then turned and fallen toward the Ark.

Had the head and hands been found in front of the Ark, the Philistines would have incorrectly concluded that the Ark had battled the idol and chopped off its head and hands. The fact that these shards were found at the shrine's entrance showed that they had broken off by themselves (*Malbim*).

According to *Me'am Loez*, this verse indicates the idol's impotence. Its broken hands and head showed it to be incapable of acting and thinking, and the fact that its hands and head landed at the threshold, which corresponds to the mouth, indicated its inability to speak.

רַק דָּגוֹן נִשְׁאַר עָלָיו — *Only Dagon's [body] remained intact.*

Literally, *only Dagon remained intact.* With its head and hands severed, only the fishlike torso of the idol, which served as the source of its name, remained.

5. עַל־כֵּן לֹא־יִדְרְכוּ כֹהֲנֵי דָגוֹן ... — *This is why the priests of Dagon ... do not tread ...*

They considered it a hallowed place (*Metzudos*).

Although they did not tread upon the

and returned it to its place. [4] *They arose early the next*
morning and [again] Dagon had fallen upon its face
to the ground before the Ark of HASHEM*, and Dagon's*
head and the two palms of its hands were severed,
[lying] upon the threshold; only Dagon's [body] re-
mained intact. [5] *(This is why the priests of Dagon and*
all those who come to the House of Dagon do not tread
upon the threshold of Dagon in Ashdod to this day.)
[6] *The hand of* HASHEM *then became heavy against*
the Ashdodites, and He devastated them; He struck
them — Ashdod and its surrounding areas — with
hemorrhoids.

threshold, they did not trouble themselves to jump over it but only stepped over it.

On the other hand, when the Jews engaged in idol worship, they were even stricter than the gentiles. Thus, states the prophet Zephaniah, God rebuked them, וּפָקַדְתִּי עַל כָּל־הַדּוֹלֵג עַל־הַמִּפְתָּן, *I will take issue with anyone who leaps over the threshold* (*Zephaniah* 1:9; *Midrash Shmuel*).

Since the verse has informed us that the common man refrained from treading upon the threshold, what need was there to state that the priests did so as well? In line with the Midrash quoted above, *Kli Yakar* explains that even these priests did no more than avoid treading upon the threshold, whereas idolatrous Jews would enthusiastically jump over it.

The verse may be understood as presenting an additional contrast between the behavior of the Philistines and that of the Jews; it reflected poorly on the Jews. When the Philistines' idol was damaged, they instituted a new procedure to commemorate its downfall; yet when the Jews lost their treasured Ark, they failed to even attempt to retrieve it (*Me'am Loez*).[1]

☙ The Plague of Hemorrhoids

6. וַתִּכְבַּד יַד־ה׳ אֶל־הָאַשְׁדּוֹדִים — *The hand of* HASHEM *then became heavy against the Ashdodites.*

After Hashem's two attacks on Dagon failed to elicit a change of heart in the Philistines, Hashem extended His judgment directly against the people by afflicting their bodies.

Hashem's initial attack was restricted to the population of Ashdod. There, states *Kli Yakar*, the disease manifested itself as a relatively mild illness, and thus the verse makes use of God's Name of mercy, the Tetragrammaton.

וַיַּךְ אֹתָם בַּטְּחֹרִים — *He struck them with hemorrhoids.*

However, according to *Rashi* this was a torturous and degrading plague

1. This verse is quoted by the Talmud (*Avodah Zarah* 42b) in regard to a dispute concerning idolatrous objects.

It is a universally accepted dictum that deriving benefit from such an object is prohibited unless a gentile who worships it has nullified its validity. But what if the idol broke by itself?

In such a case, Rabbi Yochanan states, it retains its prohibited status, and to support his thesis he cites the case of Dagon: although the statue broke, its followers did not tread on the threshold of its shrine, indicating that they continued to view it as a deity.

Reish Lakish, on the other hand, contends that if an idol broke by itself, its worshipers may be assumed to have nullified it. He too cites the case of Dagon, and claims that the Philistines lost faith in the idol itself and instead attributed sanctity to the threshold.

ז וַיִּרְאוּ אַנְשֵׁי־אַשְׁדּוֹד כִּי־כֵן וְאָמְרוּ לֹא־יֵשֵׁב
אֲרוֹן אֱלֹהֵי יִשְׂרָאֵל עִמָּנוּ כִּי־קָשְׁתָה יָדוֹ עָלֵינוּ
ח וְעַל דָּגוֹן אֱלֹהֵינוּ: וַיִּשְׁלְחוּ וַיַּאַסְפוּ אֶת־כָּל־
סַרְנֵי פְלִשְׁתִּים אֲלֵיהֶם וַיֹּאמְרוּ מַה־נַּעֲשֶׂה
לַאֲרוֹן אֱלֹהֵי יִשְׂרָאֵל וַיֹּאמְרוּ גַּת יִסֹּב אֲרוֹן
אֱלֹהֵי יִשְׂרָאֵל וַיַּסֵּבּוּ אֶת־אֲרוֹן אֱלֹהֵי יִשְׂרָאֵל:

in which mice would enter the sufferer's anus, dislocate his intestines, and drag them from his body.[1]

Other commentators understand the plague as having been a physical ailment. According to *Ralbag*, for instance, it was an extremely painful disease that occasioned the loss of much blood.[2]

בַּטְּחֹרִים — *With hemorrhoids.*

This is an example of a verse in which a word is written in one form (בעפלים)ut read differently. (An identical instance appears in *Deuteronomy* 28:27.)

According to the Talmud (*Megillah* 25b), the word טְחֹרִים has a more delicate connotation than עפלים; both words, however, refer to the anus (*Rashi* ad loc.).

Alternatively, *Radak* explains טְחֹרִים to be the name of the disease and עפלים to be a euphemism referring to the lower extremities. The root of the word עפלים is עפל, *hidden* — i.e., a concealed place of the body (see *II Kings* 5:24).

Others understand עפלים to mean a *storage place*, for digested food is stored in the intestines (*Mahari Kara*).

Not only was this plague a source of physical pain for the Philistines, even more distressing, it was a source of shame. Some commentators see the plague alluded to in the verse, וַיַּךְ־צָרָיו אָחוֹר חֶרְפַּת עוֹלָם נָתַן לָמוֹ, *He smote his oppressors on their backs; He gave them an everlasting disgrace* (*Psalms* 78:66; see *Rashi* ad loc.).

Me'am Loez states that this affliction was meant to deflate the egotism of the Philistines, who were wallowing in the glory of their prowess, and to remind them of the frailty of a human being, "who is composed of many cavities, such that if but one of them were to be ruptured, it would be impossible for him to survive."

Mishbetzos Zahav suggests that since

1. *Rashi*'s explanation is based on *Midrash Shocher Tov* (which is quoted by *Yalkut Shimoni*).

According to this Midrash, the Philistines initially claimed that Hashem had exhausted all his plagues in Egypt (see above, 4:8 and comm.). To counter this assertion, Hashem brought a novel plague upon them, one that had never previously existed. Whenever a Philistine defecated, rodents would crawl up from beneath the ground to extract his intestines.

The Philistines began to excrete into pails or other vessels that would block the passage of the rodents. But the rodents addressed the pails: "We are emissaries of God and you are His creations. Show respect for your Creator." As a result, the pails cracked and allowed the rodents to pass through. This, states the Midrash, is an example of a case in which Hashem allowed the soft to overpower the firm.

2. According to *Abarbanel*, part of the degradation associated with this plague was that it consisted of phenomena reminiscent of menstruation: excruciating pain and blood flowing from the lower extremities.

This implied that the Philistines' victory could not be attributed to their physical prowess, for they were no stronger than women. Rather, their victory was due to God's providence alone (*Abarbanel*).

[7]*The men of Ashdod saw that it was so, and they said, "Let the Ark of the God of Israel not stay with us, for its hand has been hard against us and against Dagon, our god."* [8]*They summoned and gathered all the governors of the Philistines to them, and they said, "What shall we do about the Ark of the God of Israel?" They replied, "Let the Ark of the God of Israel be transferred to Gath." So they transferred the Ark of the God of Israel.*

the Philistines seized the Ark, which was based in the innermost part of the Sanctuary, they were smitten in their most private places.

7. ... וַיִּרְאוּ אַנְשֵׁי־אַשְׁדּוֹד כִּי־כֵן וְאָמְרוּ — *The men of Ashdod saw that it was so, and they said ...*

Kli Yakar points out two anomalies in this verse. The first is the superfluous word אַנְשֵׁי, *the men of* (unlike the briefer and more conventional designation הָאַשְׁדּוֹדִים, *the Ashdodites*, employed in the previous verse), and the second is the use of the word וְאָמְרוּ for *and they said*, rather than the conventional וַיֹּאמְרוּ.

Kli Yakar explains that the word אַנְשֵׁי often implies *distinguished people* (see *Rashi* on *Numbers* 13:3). Its use here indicates that the individuals who realized that this plague was due to the capture of the Ark were the most noble of the Philistines.

The word וְאָמְרוּ can be understood as referring to an act that had taken place some time ago. The sensitivity of these relatively noble Philistines had been aroused quite early (at which time they had exclaimed, "Who will save us from this mighty God?" — above, 4:8). Accordingly, the word וְאָמְרוּ implies that from the very beginning they had said that the Ark should be returned.

כִּי־קָשְׁתָה יָדוֹ עָלֵינוּ וְעַל דָּגוֹן אֱלֹהֵינוּ — *For its hand has been hard against us and against Dagon, our god.*

In this verse, *us* refers not to the Philistines as a whole, but only to the residents of Ashdod. Although they recognized that the afflictions they were undergoing were a punishment for their seizure and detainment of the Ark, the Ashdodites mistakenly believed that all they had to do to end the plague was to transfer it to another Philistine city (*Kli Yakar*).

8. גַּת יִסֹּב אֲרוֹן אֱלֹהֵי יִשְׂרָאֵל — *Let the Ark of the God of Israel be transferred to Gath.*

The word יִסֹּב, *transfer*, implies movement of a significant distance (see *Exodus* 13:18). The Ashdodites moved the Ark to a distant city so that if the plague broke out there, it would be an unambiguously supernatural event and not attributable to natural contagion (*Malbim*).

Kli Yakar points out that the Philistines did not use the term גַּת הָסֵבּוּ, *Transfer it to Gath*, but rather גַּת יִסֹּב, *it will be transferred to Gath*. This was an unintentional prophecy, insofar as it indicated that the Ark would itself transfer the same plague to Gath that it had brought to Ashdod.

גַּת — *To Gath.*

Literally, *Gath*. The absence of the prefix לְ, *to*, is common (*Radak*).

ט וַיְהִ֗י אַחֲרֵי֙ | הֵסַ֣בּוּ אֹת֔וֹ וַתְּהִ֨י יַד־יְהוָ֤ה | בָּעִיר֙
מְהוּמָה֙ גְּדוֹלָ֣ה מְאֹ֔ד וַיַּךְ֙ אֶת־אַנְשֵׁ֣י הָעִ֔יר מִקָּטֹ֖ן
°טְחֹרִים ק׳ י וְעַד־גָּד֑וֹל וַיִּשָּׂתְר֥וּ לָהֶ֖ם °עפלים׃ וַֽיְשַׁלְּח֛וּ אֶת־
אֲר֥וֹן הָאֱלֹהִ֖ים עֶקְר֑וֹן וַיְהִ֗י כְּב֞וֹא אֲר֤וֹן הָאֱלֹהִים֙
עֶקְר֔וֹן וַיִּזְעֲק֨וּ הָֽעֶקְרֹנִ֜ים לֵאמֹ֗ר הֵסַ֤בּוּ אֵלַי֙ אֶת־
יא אֲרוֹן֙ אֱלֹהֵ֣י יִשְׂרָאֵ֔ל לַהֲמִיתֵ֖נִי וְאֶת־עַמִּֽי׃ וַֽיִּשְׁלְח֡וּ
וַיַּאַסְפוּ֩ אֶת־כָּל־סַרְנֵ֨י פְלִשְׁתִּ֜ים וַיֹּאמְרוּ֩ שַׁלְּח֨וּ
אֶת־אֲר֜וֹן אֱלֹהֵ֤י יִשְׂרָאֵל֙ וְיָשֹׁ֣ב לִמְקֹמ֔וֹ וְלֹֽא־
יָמִ֥ית אֹתִ֖י וְאֶת־עַמִּ֑י כִּֽי־הָיְתָ֤ה מְהֽוּמַת־מָ֙וֶת֙
בְּכָל־הָעִ֔יר כָּבְדָ֥ה מְאֹ֛ד יַ֥ד הָאֱלֹהִ֖ים שָֽׁם׃
°בַּטְּחֹרִים ק׳ יב וְהָֽאֲנָשִׁים֙ אֲשֶׁ֣ר לֹא־מֵ֔תוּ הֻכּ֖וּ °בעפלים וַתַּ֛עַל
ו/א א שַׁוְעַ֥ת הָעִ֖יר הַשָּׁמָֽיִם׃ וַיְהִ֛י

9. וַיְהִי אַחֲרֵי הֵסַבּוּ אֹתוֹ — *After they transferred it ...*

God's punishment of Gath was harsher than had been that of Ashdod, because its residents insisted on retaining the Ark. Accordingly, Scripture relates, the residents of Gath suffered a number of novel punishments: the מְהוּמָה גְּדוֹלָה, *great commotion,* which instilled an augmented fear; מִקָּטֹן וְעַד־גָּדוֹל, *from young to old* — the plague in Gath affected everyone; and finally (as will be discussed below) the symptoms of the disease were especially severe (*Malbim*). Indeed, in Gath the plague of hemorrhoids grew fatal.[1]

וַיִּשָּׂתְרוּ לָהֶם טְחֹרִים — *And they were internally stricken with hemorrhoids.*

The word וַיִּשָּׂתְרוּ may be read as וַיִּסָּתְרוּ, implying something *concealed.*

Most commentators understand this to mean that in Gath the hemorrhoids reached a more internal area of the intestinal tract, causing greater pain and becoming more difficult to heal (*Rashi, Ralbag*). *Mahari Kara* explains the implication of this verse to be that those who were not struck with the *panic of death* were afflicted with hemorrhoids.

10. וַיְשַׁלְּחוּ אֶת־אֲרוֹן הָאֱלֹהִים — *Then they sent the Ark of God.*

Since the Philistine governors had previously convened and agreed to the idea of transferring the Ark, the people of Gath did so without again consulting the governors (*Malbim*).

וַיִּזְעֲקוּ הָעֶקְרֹנִים לֵאמֹר הֵסַבּוּ אֵלַי — *The people of Ekron cried out saying, "They have transferred to me."*

Because this phrase was spoken by each individual, it is expressed in the singular — i.e., *to me,* not *to us* (*Me'am Loez*).

לַהֲמִיתֵנִי וְאֶת־עַמִּי — *To kill me and my people.*

According to *Radak,* this statement was made by the city's public representatives.

11. וַיִּשְׁלְחוּ וַיַּאַסְפוּ אֶת־כָּל־סַרְנֵי פְּלִשְׁתִּים

1 The word אַחֲרֵי, *after,* implies the passage of a period of time (as opposed to אַחַר, which means *immediately afterward;* see *Rashi* to *Genesis* 15:1). Hashem deliberately delayed unleashing the plague upon the residents of Gath, waiting for them to first grow smug and self-assured that the plague in Ashdod had been a natural phenomenon (*Kli Yakar*).

[9] *It was after they transferred it that the hand of*
HASHEM was [set] against the city, [causing] a great
commotion; He struck the people of the city, from
small to great, and they were internally stricken
with hemorrhoids. [10] *They then sent the Ark of God*
to Ekron. It happened when the Ark of God arrived
in Ekron that the people of Ekron cried out saying,
"They have transferred to me the Ark of the God
of Israel, to kill me and my people!"

[11] *So they summoned and gathered all the gov-*
ernors of the Philistines and said [to them], "Send
away the Ark of the God of Israel. Let it return to
its place and not kill me and my people!" For there
was a panic of death in the whole city; the hand of
God was very heavy there. [12] *The people who did*
not die were stricken with hemorrhoids, and the
cry of the city ascended to heaven.

וַיֹּאמְרוּ — *So they summoned and gathered all the governors of the Philistines and said [to them].*

One might initially assume that the word וַיֹּאמְרוּ, *and they said,* refers to the governors — i.e., *so they summoned and gathered all of the governors of the Philistines, who said ... .* The latter part of the statement, "and not kill me and my people," shows that this was spoken by the public representatives of Ekron as they addressed the governors (*Abarbanel;* see *Kli Yakar*).

כִּי־הָיְתָה מְהוּמַת־מָוֶת בְּכָל־הָעִיר — *For there was a panic of death in the whole city.*

According to *Kli Yakar,* even before the Ark arrived the people of Ekron cried out that they did not want it, since there *had been a panic of death* in the city of Gath, an experience that they did not wish to undergo (*Kli Yakar*).

More conventionally, *the whole city* refers to Ekron. It was there that the severity of the punishment reached its apogee, with masses of people dying as soon as the Ark arrived (*Malbim*). In *Abarbanel's* words, there was no house that did not contain a corpse.

Originally, the plague had been relatively mild. But after the Philistines did not return the Ark to its rightful custodians, *the hand of God — Elokim — was very heavy* — this Divine Name indicating God's aspect of strict judgment (*Kli Yakar*).

All instances of *panic,* including that described here, are associated with thunderous sounds (cf. 7:10): וַיַּרְעֵם ה׳ בְּקוֹל־גָּדוֹל בַּיּוֹם הַהוּא עַל־פְּלִשְׁתִּים וַיְהֻמֵּם, *HASHEM then thundered with a great noise on that day against the Philistines and confounded them* (*Rashi*).

12. וַתַּעַל שַׁוְעַת הָעִיר הַשָּׁמָיִם — *And the cry of the city ascended to heaven.*

According to *Metzudos,* this is a figure of speech, implying that the people's outcries were very great.

However, *Kli Yakar* understands this verse literally. The Philistines' bitter outcries were heard in heaven, and this resulted in the removal of the Ark from their territory and subsequent relief from the plague.

אֲרוֹן־יהוָה בִּשְׂדֵה פְלִשְׁתִּים שִׁבְעָה חֳדָשִׁים:
ב וַיִּקְרְאוּ פְלִשְׁתִּים לַכֹּהֲנִים וְלַקֹּסְמִים לֵאמֹר
מַה־נַּעֲשֶׂה לַאֲרוֹן יהוָה הוֹדִעֻנוּ בַּמֶּה
ג נְשַׁלְּחֶנּוּ לִמְקוֹמוֹ: וַיֹּאמְרוּ אִם־מְשַׁלְּחִים
אֶת־אֲרוֹן אֱלֹהֵי יִשְׂרָאֵל אַל־תְּשַׁלְּחוּ אֹתוֹ
רֵיקָם כִּי־הָשֵׁב תָּשִׁיבוּ לוֹ אָשָׁם אָז תֵּרָפְאוּ

VI

מִזְמוֹר שִׁירוּ לַה׳ שִׁיר חָדָשׁ כִּי־נִפְלָאוֹת עָשָׂה הוֹשִׁיעָה־לּוֹ יְמִינוֹ וּזְרוֹעַ קָדְשׁוֹ
A psalm: Sing to HASHEM a new song, for He has done wonders; His own right hand and His holy arm have helped him (Psalms 98:1).

The Midrash (*Bereishis Rabbah* 54:4) sees the events of Chapter 6 alluded to in this verse. Even when God deemed it necessary to send His Holy Ark — עֻזּוֹ, *His strength* (see *Psalms* 78:61) — into captivity in order to send the Jewish people a message of His disapprobation, He did not abandon it. Rather, he waited for the Jews to come to its rescue. When they did not do so, however,[1] God Himself returned the Ark in a spectacular manner, demonstrating to the world His all-encompassing power and His concern for the eternally sanctified Ark.

☙ The Decision to Return the Ark

1. בִּשְׂדֵה פְלִשְׁתִּים — *In the land of the Philistines.*

Our translation follows *Metzudos*, which interprets the word שְׂדֵה, lit., *field*, as *the land*.

Me'am Loez, however, renders this word literally, and explains that after the Ark's presence brought devastation to the residents of the cities to which it was brought, the Philistines placed it in an uninhabited field; this did not suffice, however, and the plague continued.

שִׁבְעָה חֳדָשִׁים — *For seven months.*

Not until seven months of suffering passed — during which time the Ark was relocated several times — did the Philistines acknowledge that the plague was due to their holding it in captivity.

These seven months during which the Jews lost possession of the Ark, states the Midrash (*Bereishis Rabbah* 54:4), corresponded to Abraham's unwarranted gift of seven ewes to the Philistine king, Abimelech (*Genesis* 21:30).[2]

2. וַיִּקְרְאוּ פְלִשְׁתִּים לַכֹּהֲנִים וְלַקֹּסְמִים — *The Philistines called upon the priests and the sorcerers.*

The Philistines consulted their priests

1. To God's acute disappointment (as it were) — see comm. to verse 13.

2. Commentators explain that Abraham was held accountable for making a covenant, which was an act of self-protection, that was unauthorized by Hashem. Accordingly, hundreds of years later, when the Jewish people again made an unauthorized attempt at self-protection — the transporting of the Ark — again involving the Philistines, Hashem remembered Abraham's error and the retribution was measure for measure. Incidentally, the episode of Ch. 6 seems to have a historical precedent. When Sarah was abducted by Abimelech, king of Philistia (*Genesis* Ch. 20), the punishment involved their bodily cavities (ibid. v. 18, *Bava Kamma* 92a), and they were forced to send Sarah back with gifts. This is an example of מַעֲשֵׂה אָבוֹת סִימָן לְבָנִים., *The deeds of the forefathers act as historical symbols for what would happen to their descendants* (see *Ramban, Genesis* 12:6). Here too, the Philistines abducted something precious and sacred, and were punished at their bodily cavities, and again had to atone with gifts (*Sig V'Siach B'Neviim*).

6/1-3

[1] *The Ark of HASHEM had been in the land of the*
Philistines for seven months. [2] *The Philistines*
called upon the priests and the sorcerers, saying,
"What shall we do about the Ark of HASHEM? In-
form us how we should send it [back] to its place!"
[3] *They replied, "If [you] are sending [back] the*
Ark of the God of Israel, you must not send it [back]
empty-handed, but you must certainly send back
a guilt-offering to Him. Then you will be healed,

and sorcerers to determine how to pacify God and thus end the bitter plague.

Commentators extrapolate from the response that the Philistines still remained in doubt as to whether the plague befalling them was God's punishment for having seized the Ark.

They thus turned to the sorcerers, who were knowledgeable about supernatural events, and asked them, מַה־נַּעֲשֶׂה לַאֲרוֹן ה׳ — *What shall we do about the Ark of HASHEM* — i.e., shall we return it or not?

If they should return it, then they had a second question dealing with proper religious protocol, which they addressed to the priests: הוֹדִעֻנוּ בַּמֶּה נְשַׁלְּחֶנּוּ לִמְקוֹמוֹ, *Inform us how we should send it away.* How exactly should we do so? Should we send it on an animal-drawn carriage or should we have people carry it on their shoulders? Should it be accompanied by a gift or not? (*Abarbanel, Malbim*).

3. וַיֹּאמְרוּ אִם־מְשַׁלְּחִים אֶת־אֲרוֹן אֱלֹהֵי יִשְׂרָאֵל אַל־תְּשַׁלְּחוּ אֹתוֹ רֵיקָם — *They replied, "If you are sending [back] the Ark of the God of Israel, you must not send it [back] empty-handed."*

The answer to the Philistines' first question — as to whether or not to send back the Ark — also expressed a doubt regarding the need to return it — *"if you* are sending back the Ark." Indeed, part of the plan was to test the Ark with the nursing cows (verses 7-9) to determine if Divine intervention was involved, and if there was a need to return it.

Accordingly, the second issue — how to send it back — was answered first, because for that there was a more definitive answer. Hence, "We're not sure if we must return the Ark, but if we do, we must definitely send a gift." In addition, the discussion about the nature of the proposed gift had to precede the test with the nursing cows (*Malbim*).

Me'am Loez suggests that the priests and sorcerers opposed the idea of returning the Ark, and that they offered their advice for how to do so grudgingly and reluctantly — i.e., *if* you insist on sending back the Ark, against our better judgment, you must not send it empty-handed ...

Alternatively, *Kli Yakar* explains that they responded in a deferential manner, leaving the decision to the Philistine officers, and offering only information on how to return it should those officers choose to do so.

אָשָׁם — *A guilt-offering.*

This constituted an acknowledgment of their criminal behavior (*Rashi*).

Mishbetzos Zahav suggests that the suggestion to send the tribute (as well as the manner in which it was eventually sent) sought to effect a קִדּוּשׁ ה׳, *sanctifying of HASHEM's Name,* which is the sole option to atone for the חִלּוּל ה׳, *desecration of His Name,* that they had caused, as per the words of *Rabbeinu Yonah* (*Shaarei Teshuvah* 1:47, 4:5).

אָז תֵּרָפְאוּ — *Then you will be healed.*

If the Ark were returned without a

ד וְנוֹדַע לָכֶם לָמָּה לֹא־תָסוּר יָדוֹ מִכֶּם: וַיֹּאמְרוּ
מָה הָאָשָׁם אֲשֶׁר נָשִׁיב לוֹ וַיֹּאמְרוּ מִסְפַּר סַרְנֵי
פְלִשְׁתִּים חֲמִשָּׁה °עפלי זָהָב וַחֲמִשָּׁה עַכְבְּרֵי °טְחֹרֵי ק׳
ה זָהָב כִּי־מַגֵּפָה אַחַת לְכֻלָּם וּלְסַרְנֵיכֶם: וַעֲשִׂיתֶם
צַלְמֵי °עפליכם וְצַלְמֵי עַכְבְּרֵיכֶם הַמַּשְׁחִיתִם °טְחֹרֵיכֶם ק׳
אֶת־הָאָרֶץ וּנְתַתֶּם לֵאלֹהֵי יִשְׂרָאֵל כָּבוֹד
אוּלַי יָקֵל אֶת־יָדוֹ מֵעֲלֵיכֶם וּמֵעַל אֱלֹהֵיכֶם

tribute, the priests and sorcerers told their interlocutors, the Philistines would only be avoiding future damage but they would not gain atonement for having captured it; practically speaking, that would mean that those who were already struck by the plague would continue to be afflicted. If, however, they would appease God by sending a gift, then even those presently stricken by the plague would be healed (*Abarbanel*).

וְנוֹדַע לָכֶם לָמָּה לֹא־תָסוּר יָדוֹ מִכֶּם — *And you will realize why His hand would not turn away from against you.*

Then, when the Philistines were healed, they would understand with a surety that the plague had remained as long as they had retained the Ark (*Radak*).

Alternatively, *Rashi* explains the verse to mean, *Then you will be healed and you will be aware [that* Hashem *had brought about this plague — for] why shouldn't His hand turn away from you then?* — i.e., His hand will definitely turn aside and grant the Philistines relief.

4. מִסְפַּר סַרְנֵי פְלִשְׁתִּים — *According to the number of Philistine governors.*

Their names were, as listed in *Joshua* 13:3, Aza, Ashdod, Ashkelon, Gath, and Ekron (*Rashi*).

חֲמִשָּׁה טְחֹרֵי זָהָב וַחֲמִשָּׁה עַכְבְּרֵי זָהָב — *Five golden [images of] hemorrhoids and five golden mice.*

This would serve as an expression of their remorse and as their acknowledgment that God had caused their suffering (*Radak*).

As *Malbim* explains, every plague is a metaphoric reflection of the sin that brought it about. Accordingly, their strategy was to rectify their sin by using, for a hallowed purpose, the same object that was their penalty, i.e., in the form of a contribution to the Jews. The choice of the phrase אֲשֶׁר נָשִׁיב לוֹ, lit., *that we shall return to Him*, supports the idea that the Philistines were sending something that represented direct acknowledgment of their sin.

חֲמִשָּׁה עַכְבְּרֵי זָהָב — *Five golden mice.*

This provides a Scriptural basis for the Midrashic teaching that the plague of hemorrhoids involved rodents as well (as described above, 5:6; *Mahari Kara, Radak*).

Me'am Loez suggests that the gift of golden mice represented the Philistines' recognition that God had brought about the plague, for even the mice altered their behavior to submit to His will.

כִּי־מַגֵּפָה אַחַת לְכֻלָּם וּלְסַרְנֵיכֶם — *For the same plague is upon all [of you] and upon your governors.*

A group of hemorrhoids and a group of mice were sent: one group representing the governors and the other representing their provinces (*Abarbanel*).

לְכֻלָּם — *All [of you].*

This is a grammatical anomaly; more conventionally, the word would read כֻּלְּכֶם (see *Mahari Kara, Radak*).

and you will realize why His hand would not turn
away from against you."
4 So they said, "What is the guilt-offering that
we should send back to Him?" They answered,
"According to the number of Philistine governors
— five golden [images of] hemorrhoids and five
golden mice; for the same plague is upon all [of
you] and upon your governors. 5 Make images of
your hemorrhoids and images of your mice, which
are demolishing the country, and give them as hom-
age to the God of Israel; perhaps He will alleviate
His hand from upon you and from upon your gods

5. וַעֲשִׂיתֶם צַלְמֵי טְחֹרֵיכֶם — *Make images of your hemorrhoids.*

This is an elaboration of the previous verse (*Mahari Kara*).

As we will see in verse 18, there is some controversy as to how many golden mice and hemorrhoids were fashioned.

One opinion claims that the number of golden hemorrhoids and mice corresponded to the number of towns in Philistia, many more than five. Following that interpretation, *Mahari Kara* understands the end of the previous verse and the beginning of the present verse to run together, as follows: כִּי־מַגֵּפָה אַחַת לְכֻלָּם וּלְסַרְנֵיכֶם, *Since a plague occurred that affected all of you as it did the governors,* וַעֲשִׂיתֶם צַלְמֵי טְחֹרֵיכֶם וְצַלְמֵי עַכְבְּרֵיכֶם, *form [as many of the] images of your hemorrhoids and images of your mice [as you need and include them with the governors' five].*

הַמַּשְׁחִיתִם אֶת־הָאָרֶץ — *Which are demolishing the country.*

This implies that in addition to the plague of the hemorrhoids, the mice consumed and destroyed the produce of the land (*Mahari Kara, Malbim*).

Metzudos renders אֶת־הָאָרֶץ as *the people of the land.*

וּנְתַתֶּם לֵאלֹהֵי יִשְׂרָאֵל כָּבוֹד — *And give them as homage to the God of Israel.*

When Hashem sent fiery serpents to bite the Jews in the wilderness, Moses fashioned a copper serpent to remind the Jews that it is Hashem Who strikes and heals, and thus inspired their repentance (*Numbers* 21:6-9). Similarly, the sorcerers understood that a golden representation of the plague would remind the Philistines that they had been struck by God's hand and that when the Philistines repented God would grant them relief.

אוּלַי יָקֵל אֶת־יָדוֹ מֵעֲלֵיכֶם — *Perhaps He will alleviate His hand from upon you.*

This statement is more hesitant than that of verse 3 — אָז תֵּרָפְאוּ, *Then you will be healed* — because it implies that the priests now hoped, although diffidently, for even more than they had wished in verse 3.

Abarbanel explains that here the priests implied that if the Philistines paid proper tribute to the God of Israel they might earn such a degree of His favor that He would refrain from subjecting them to other military defeats and plagues.

Alternatively, *Kli Yakar* suggests that in this verse the priests expressed their hope that the formation of these images, even before they were delivered, would evoke relief, for it would

ו וּמֵעַל אַרְצְכֶם׃ וְלָמָּה תְכַבְּדוּ אֶת־לְבַבְכֶם כַּאֲשֶׁר
כִּבְּדוּ מִצְרַיִם וּפַרְעֹה אֶת־לִבָּם הֲלוֹא כַּאֲשֶׁר
ז הִתְעַלֵּל בָּהֶם וַיְשַׁלְּחוּם וַיֵּלֵכוּ׃ וְעַתָּה קְחוּ וַעֲשׂוּ
עֲגָלָה חֲדָשָׁה אֶחָת וּשְׁתֵּי פָרוֹת עָלוֹת אֲשֶׁר
לֹא־עָלָה עֲלֵיהֶם עֹל וַאֲסַרְתֶּם אֶת־הַפָּרוֹת
בָּעֲגָלָה וַהֲשֵׁיבֹתֶם בְּנֵיהֶם מֵאַחֲרֵיהֶם הַבָּיְתָה׃

demonstrate the Philistines' submission to God.

וּמֵעַל אַרְצְכֶם — *And from upon your land.*

The judgment had affected the produce of the land as well.

Me'am Loez explains that the plague had taken such a toll on Philistia that it developed a reputation as a land that devours its inhabitants, and many people fled its borders.

According to *Kli Yakar*, the priests were predicting that if the Philistines did not soon offer a guilt-offering, the plague would spread to all of Philistia.

6. וְלָמָּה תְכַבְּדוּ אֶת־לְבַבְכֶם — *Why should you harden your hearts?*

Because the Philistines retained a measure of skepticism that the plague represented God's retribution for their having captured the Ark, they were thus uneasy with the idea of sending it back unconditionally, an action that would be irreversible. Sensing their hesitation, the priests now urged them, וְלָמָּה תְכַבְּדוּ אֶת־לְבַבְכֶם, "Why should you harden your hearts ...?" Nevertheless, they offered a method of returning the Ark that would alleviate the Philistines' concern (*Ralbag*).

How could the priests have accused the Philistines of hardening their hearts, since the Philistines had already requested, מַה־נַּעֲשֶׂה לַאֲרוֹן ה׳ הוֹדִעֻנוּ בַּמֶּה נְשַׁלְּחֶנּוּ לִמְקוֹמוֹ, *What shall we do about the Ark of Hashem? Inform us how we should send it [back] to its place* (verse 2).

As mentioned previously (verse 3), *Abarbanel* explains by parsing that phrase as two questions. First, מַה־נַּעֲשֶׂה לַאֲרוֹן ה׳, *What should we do about the Ark of Hashem?* — i.e., should we send the Ark back or not? And second, בַּמֶּה נְשַׁלְּחֶנּוּ לִמְקוֹמוֹ, *How should we send it?* That is to say, if we do send the Ark, how should it be transported?

The priests responded by bringing up another point: "If you are sending back the Ark ... you must not send it back without an accompanying gift" (verse 3). This occasioned a dialogue as to what should accompany the Ark. After that was dealt with, the priests reprimanded the Philistines for doubting the exigency of returning the Ark.

Verses 7-9 will relate the priests' response to the question of how to send the Ark.

הִתְעַלֵּל בָּהֶם — *He mocked them.*

Our translation follows *Mahari Kara* as well as *Rashi* to *Exodus* 10:2 (see *Stone Chumash* ad loc.).

Radak renders הִתְעַלֵּל as *performed acts of destruction.*

הֲלוֹא כַּאֲשֶׁר הִתְעַלֵּל בָּהֶם וַיְשַׁלְּחוּם וַיֵּלֵכוּ — *Did it not happen that when He mocked them, they had to send [the Israelites] forth, and they left?*

Malbim explains that the Philistines assumed that even if God did have a hand in afflicting them with the plague, it nevertheless resembled natural illnesses that were limited in scope and eventually were healed. The priests therefore reminded them that Pharaoh had also waited for an end to the Egyptians' suffering but that God sent plague after plague until Pharaoh was eventually forced to send the Jews away.

and from upon your land. 6 *Why should you harden*
your hearts as Egypt and Pharaoh hardened their
hearts? Did it not happen that when He mocked
them they had to send [the Israelites] forth, and they
left? 7 *So now, take [materials] and make one new*
wagon, and [take] two nursing cows upon whom a
yoke was never placed, and tie the cows to the wagon,
and send their calves back home from behind them.

◆§ The Test of the Cows

In order to confirm that the plague meant that God was avenging the honor of the Ark and wanted the Philistines to return it to the Jews, the priests and sorcerers devised a scheme whereby the Ark would return to the Jews only if God performed a miracle. If no miracle were to take place, they would assume that the plague was a natural phenomenon and, accordingly, retain the Ark.

7. קְחוּ — *Take [materials].*

That is to say, take wood (*Metzudos*).

קְחוּ וַעֲשׂוּ עֲגָלָה חֲדָשָׁה אַחַת — *Take [materials] and make one new wagon.*

The wagon should be new, because only utensils that have never been used for mundane purposes should be employed in the service of sanctified objects (*Radak;* see *Rambam, Hil. Beis HaBechirah* 1:20).[1]

According to *Malbim*, the condition that the wagon be new was part of the test designed by the priests and sorcerers, for it is more difficult for cows to lead a new wagon than one that has been broken in.

Me'am Loez suggests that a new wagon would be more likely to successfully arrive at its destination.

וּשְׁתֵּי פָרוֹת עָלוֹת — *And two nursing cows.*

עָלוֹת means *nursing*, as in *Genesis* 33:13 (see *Rashi* ad loc.).

Under ordinary circumstances, a nursing cow will not pull a wagon, for two reasons. First, such a cow will generally not accept a burden (*Malbim*). Second, it will not willingly accept separation from its suckling.

אֲשֶׁר לֹא־עָלָה עֲלֵיהֶם עֹל — *Upon whom a yoke was never placed.*

The cows had never experienced the strain of pulling a wagon, and for this reason too, they could be expected to resist the task, or at least tarry in its fulfillment (*Rashi*).

Radak explains that this condition also served as a means of showing respect for the Ark; even the cows should not have previously been employed for a mundane purpose.

וַאֲסַרְתֶּם אֶת־הַפָּרוֹת בָּעֲגָלָה וַהֲשֵׁיבֹתֶם בְּנֵיהֶם מֵאַחֲרֵיהֶם הַבָּיְתָה — *And tie the cows to the wagon, and send their calves back home from behind them.*

This, the most radical aspect of the test, created a condition under which it would be all but impossible for the cows to willingly leave.

1. The priests advised the Philistines to both *take* and *make*.

The word קְחוּ, *take*, implies מִקָּח, a *sale* (see *Kiddushin* 2a). In other words, the materials of which the wagon is made should be legally purchased, for when something is used for a holy mission, great care must be taken to see to it that it was honestly acquired (see *Succah* 30a; *Kli Yakar*).

And make: buying a ready-made wagon would not have sufficed; rather, it had to be constructed with its hallowed purpose in mind.

ח וּלְקַחְתֶּ֞ם אֶת־אֲר֣וֹן יהוה וּנְתַתֶּ֤ם אֹתוֹ֙ אֶל־הָ֣עֲגָלָ֔ה
וְאֵ֣ת ׀ כְּלֵ֣י הַזָּהָ֗ב אֲשֶׁ֨ר הֲשֵׁבֹתֶ֥ם לוֹ֙ אָשָׁ֔ם תָּשִׂ֥ימוּ
ט בָאַרְגַּ֖ז מִצִּדּ֑וֹ וְשִׁלַּחְתֶּ֥ם אֹת֖וֹ וְהָלָֽךְ׃ וּרְאִיתֶ֗ם
אִם־דֶּ֨רֶךְ גְּבוּל֤וֹ יַעֲלֶה֙ בֵּ֣ית שֶׁ֔מֶשׁ ה֚וּא עָ֣שָׂה לָ֔נוּ
אֶת־הָרָעָ֥ה הַגְּדוֹלָ֖ה הַזֹּ֑את וְאִם־לֹ֗א וְיָדַ֙עְנוּ֙ כִּ֣י
י לֹ֤א יָדוֹ֙ נָ֣גְעָה בָּ֔נוּ מִקְרֶ֥ה ה֖וּא הָ֥יָה לָֽנוּ׃ וַיַּעֲשׂ֤וּ
הָאֲנָשִׁים֙ כֵּ֔ן וַיִּקְח֗וּ שְׁתֵּ֤י פָרוֹת֙ עָל֔וֹת וַיַּאַסְר֖וּם
יא בָּעֲגָלָ֑ה וְאֶת־בְּנֵיהֶ֖ם כָּל֥וּ בַבָּֽיִת׃ וַיָּשִׂ֛מוּ אֶת־אֲר֥וֹן
יהוה אֶל־הָעֲגָלָ֑ה וְאֵ֣ת הָאַרְגַּ֗ז וְאֵת֙ עַכְבְּרֵ֣י הַזָּהָ֔ב
יב וְאֵ֖ת צַלְמֵ֥י טְחֹרֵיהֶֽם׃ וַיִּשַּׁ֨רְנָה הַפָּר֜וֹת בַּדֶּ֗רֶךְ

The fact that the cows were first tied to the wagon before their calves were *sent back home* accentuated the cows' distress and natural unwillingness to leave (*Kli Yakar*).

8. וּלְקַחְתֶּם אֶת־אֲרוֹן ה׳ — *Then take the Ark of* HASHEM.

Kli Yakar observes that, as a sign of respect for the Ark, the cows were harnessed and prepared for travel before the Ark was loaded onto the wagon so that there would be no delay. (The Torah similarly commands that the poles with which the Ark was carried must always remain in place, so that there should never be any delay in its transport.)

אֶל־הָעֲגָלָה — *Onto the wagon.*

Radak states that the word אֶל, lit., *to*, is to be read as having the meaning, עַל, *onto*, and cites other instances of such usage.

Alternatively, *Radak* interprets אֶל־הָעֲגָלָה as בָּעֲגָלָה, *into the wagon.*

וְשִׁלַּחְתֶּם אֹתוֹ — *Send it forth.*

Escort it respectfully (*Me'am Loez*).

וְהָלָךְ — *And it will go.*

See if it will go by itself; do not allow anyone to lead it (*Metzudos*).

9. אִם־דֶּרֶךְ גְּבוּלוֹ יַעֲלֶה בֵּית שֶׁמֶשׁ — *If it ascends by the road to its boundary, toward Beth-shemesh.*

If the team of cows chooses the ascending road, which requires more effort than a descending incline (*Me'am Loez*), and if it travels directly toward Beth-shemesh, which is the closest community under Jewish sovereignty (*Ralbag*), then we will know beyond the shadow of a doubt that the plague had been Divinely wrought.

10. וַיַּעֲשׂוּ הָאֲנָשִׁים כֵּן וַיִּקְחוּ שְׁתֵּי פָרוֹת עָלוֹת — *The men did so; they took two nursing cows.*

This verse seems redundant.

According to *Kli Yakar*, וַיַּעֲשׂוּ הָאֲנָשִׁים כֵּן, *the men did so*, alludes to the fact that the Philistines constructed a new wagon and acquired previously unyoked cows, these being, as stated above, gestures of respect for the Ark (see above, verse 7).

וְאֶת־בְּנֵיהֶם כָּלוּ בַבָּיִת — *And secured their calves at home.*

כָּלוּ, *secured*, derives from the word כֶּלֶא, *prison* (see *I Kings* 22:27); such a missing א is not uncommon (*Radak*).

Alternatively, כָּלוּ means to *restrain*, as in לֹא־יִכְלֶה מִמְּךָ, *will not withhold from you* (*Genesis* 23:6; *Rashi* to *Avodah Zarah* 24b).

12. וַיִּשַּׁרְנָה הַפָּרוֹת בַּדֶּרֶךְ — *The cows set out on the direct road.*

[8]*Then take the Ark of* H*ASHEM and place it onto
the wagon, and put the golden objects that you
are sending back to Him as a guilt-offering in
a box at its side. Send it forth and it will go.*
[9]*Then you will see: If it ascends by the road to
its boundary, toward Beth-shemesh, then it was
He Who brought upon us all this great evil; but
if not, we will know that His hand did not afflict
us, but it was all by chance that this befell us.''*
[10]*The men did so; they took two nursing
cows and tied them to the wagon, and secured
their calves at home.* [11]*They placed the Ark
of* H*ASHEM onto the wagon, along with the box
and the golden mice and their images of hemorrhoids.* [12]*The cows set out on the direct road —*

Our translation, rendering וַיִּשַּׁרְנָה as derived from יָשָׁר, *straight,* is in line with the verse's further elaboration that the cows went on a direct route toward Beth-shemesh.

The Sages (*Avodah Zarah* 24b, *Bereishis Rabbah* 54:4), however, homiletically relate וַיִּשַּׁרְנָה to שִׁירָה, *song,* and derive from this verse that as the cows brought the Ark back to the Land of Israel they sang in praise of Hashem and the Ark.[1]

Drawing on the literal meaning of וַיִּשַּׁרְנָה, which implies *direct,* our Sages further derive that while singing, the cows turned their heads toward the Ark behind them in a gesture of respect.[2]

According to the interpretation of *Maharzu* (*Bereishis Rabbah* ibid.), the Midrash also interprets וַיִּשַּׁרְנָה as being cognate with the Aramaic שָׁרָן, *release,* implying that the cows loosened their harnesses so that they could face the Ark.

The commentators point out the unusual grammatical structure of the word וַיִּשַּׁרְנָה. A word that possesses the suffix נָה (which indicates the feminine plural) generally has a ת as a prefix. Thus the word should have read וַתִּשַּׁרְנָה (as in וַתִּגַּשְׁןָ וַתִּשְׁתַּחֲוֶיןָ [*Genesis* 33:6]). Yet here the word begins with a י, which generally indicates the masculine.

Rashi deduces from this that not only did the female cows sing praise but that their abandoned male calves did as well. And *Maharsha* (*Avodah Zarah* 24b) adds that the latter faced the Ark as it departed. (*Mahari Kara,* however, sees no such special meaning in this gram-

1. *Ritva* (to *Avodah Zarah* 24b) comments that this miraculous phenomenon is alluded to in the list of supernatural items created at the twilight of Sabbath eve (*Pirkei Avos* 5:8), incorporated into the mention of *the mouth of [Balaam's] donkey.*

2. Based on a Midrashic teaching (*Bamidbar Rabbah* 5:8), *Rambam* rules that the Levites who carried the Ark had to constantly face the Ark (*Hil. Klei HaMikdash* 2:13).

Rashash suggests that the source of this ruling is the present incident (*Bamidbar Rabbah* ibid.; see *Nachalas Shimon* 31:14).

עַל־דֶּ֫רֶךְ בֵּית שֶׁמֶשׁ בִּמְסִלָּה אַחַת הָלְכוּ הָלֹךְ
וְגָעוֹ וְלֹא־סָרוּ יָמִין וּשְׂמֹאול וְסַרְנֵי פְלִשְׁתִּים
יג הֹלְכִים אַחֲרֵיהֶם עַד־גְּבוּל בֵּית שָׁמֶשׁ: וּבֵית
שֶׁמֶשׁ קֹצְרִים קְצִיר־חִטִּים בָּעֵמֶק וַיִּשְׂאוּ אֶת־
עֵינֵיהֶם וַיִּרְאוּ אֶת־הָאָרוֹן וַיִּשְׂמְחוּ לִרְאוֹת:

matical construction, and states that it simply serves to indicate the feminine.)

☙ What Did the Cows Sing?

Our Sages disagree as to the text of the cows' praise.

Some maintain that they sang the Song of the Sea of Reeds (*Exodus* Chapter 15) which states, חִיל אָחַז יֹשְׁבֵי פְּלָשֶׁת, *Terror gripped the dwellers of Philistia* (ibid. verse 14). They base that claim on the usage in the present verse of the word וְגָעוֹ, *lowing,* which resembles the words of the phrase, in the Song of the Sea of Reeds, כִּי גָאֹה גָּאָה, *for He is exalted above the arrogant* (ibid. verse 1) — i.e., above the Philistines and their god, Dagon. (The letters א and ע are often treated interchangeably.) The tribulations of the Philistines were in many ways similar to those of the Egyptians at the Sea of Reeds: in both cases, God took vengeance upon the Jews' oppressors as He saved the Jews, so that even the gentiles acclaimed His omnipotence.

Other Sages offer alternative opinions regarding the cows' praise, identifying verses from *Isaiah* and *Psalms* as their text.[1]

According to yet another view, the cows composed their own paean in ecstatic recognition of the majestic glory being showered upon the Ark. They sang, *"Sing with joy, sing with joy, O [Ark of] cedar [wood], be elevated by your great splendor — [O Ark] wrapped in golden adornments, praiseworthy for [containing] the [Torah] scroll of the Inner Sanctuary, glorified with the ornament of ornaments."*[2]

Further drawing upon the word וַיִּשַּׁרְנָה, the Midrash states that when God heard this beautiful song, He explained, "[Moses,] son of Amram, worked so hard to teach the art of song, yet you [cows] have sung on your own יְיַשֵּׁר חֵילְכֶם, *May your strength be firm* (literally, *straight*)!"

עַל־דֶּרֶךְ בֵּית שֶׁמֶשׁ — *On the road to Beth-shemesh.*

Beth-shemesh was populated by Jews (*Rashi*).

הָלֹךְ וְגָעוֹ — *Lowing as they went.*

1. According to one version, they sang (*Isaiah* 12:4): וַאֲמַרְתֶּם בַּיּוֹם הַהוּא הוֹדוּ לַה׳ קִרְאוּ בִשְׁמוֹ הוֹדִיעוּ בָעַמִּים עֲלִילֹתָיו, *And you will say on that day, "Give thanks to* H*ASHEM*, *declare His Name, make His acts known among the peoples ..."*

The "acts" refers to the miracles that Hashem exhibited in honor of the Ark. Thus, upon returning the Ark and stationing it in the City of David (see *II Samuel* Ch. 6), King David sang a song of praise to Hashem that begins with those very words: הוֹדוּ לַה׳ קִרְאוּ בִשְׁמוֹ (*I Chronicles* 16:8-36). *Rashi* (ad loc.) explains how the words of that hymn are designed to praise Hashem for the wondrous deeds that He did regarding the Ark. *Rashi* cites one opinion of *Bereishis Rabbah* (54:4) that it was these words in *Chronicles* that were sung by the cows, and that King David instituted that it be said every day before the Ark. Indeed, it is still our custom to recite these words at the beginning of our *Shacharis* prayer.

2. *Yefeh To'ar* (*Bereishis Rabbah* ad loc.) explains that this song celebrates four aspects of the Ark: (1) its material makeup (*cedar*), (2) its exquisite workmanship (*splendor*), (3) its beautiful decoration (*golden coverings*), and (4) its distinguished purpose (*for [containing] the [Torah] scroll*).

on the road to Beth-shemesh — on a single road did
they go, lowing as they went, and they did not veer
right or left. The governors of the Philistines went
behind them until the border of Beth-shemesh.
13 *[The people of] Beth-shemesh were reaping*
the wheat harvest in the valley; they raised their
eyes and saw the Ark, and they rejoiced to see [it].

Abarbanel states that the cows were lamenting their forced separation from their calves. Nevertheless, they did not stray from the path but continued devotedly toward Beth-shemesh (*Mahari Kara*).

Me'am Loez comments that a great lesson can be learned from the actions of these cows. Even when a person is subject to crises and difficulties in his relationship with his children, he should continue to joyously serve Hashem.

Alternatively, the lowing of the cows was an expression of the awe that they felt regarding the Ark and the importance of their mission (*Me'am Loez*).

וְלֹא־סָרוּ יָמִין וּשְׂמֹאול — *And they did not veer right or left.*

Considering the Midrash (quoted above) that the cows' faces were turned toward the Ark, it is fascinating to imagine them as they proceeded on an unswerving path (*Kli Yakar*).

וְסַרְנֵי פְלִשְׁתִּים הֹלְכִים אַחֲרֵיהֶם — *The governors of the Philistines went behind them.*

They came to witness the unbelievable spectacle (*Ralbag*).

Kli Yakar states that they came to tender respect to the Ark, and supports his opinion by pointing out that the term אַחֲרֵיהֶם, *behind them*, refers to a masculine object — presumably the Ark, which is grammatically masculine.

The Ark's Arrival at Beth-shemesh

13. וַיִּשְׂאוּ אֶת־עֵינֵיהֶם — *They raised their eyes.*

The Ark was coming down from the mountain to the valley of Beth-shemesh (*Me'am Loez*).

וַיִּרְאוּ אֶת־הָאָרוֹן וַיִּשְׂמְחוּ לִרְאוֹת — *And saw the Ark, and they rejoiced to see [it].*

Although no clear misdeed is evident from the text, the reaction of the people of Beth-shemesh to the arrival of the Ark was considered to be gravely inappropriate (as we will soon see). Most commentators find the allusion to the people's error in this verse.

According to *Rashi*, in their joy the people lost their sense of awe: a failing that was especially egregious in that it so starkly contrasted with the respect that the Philistines were according the Ark (*Me'am Loez*).

According to the Midrash (*Bamidbar Rabbah* 5:9, quoted here by *Mahari Kara* and *Radak*) the Jews gazed upon the Ark as it was "exposed," which is to say, without its special coverings. *Radak* adds that, even worse, they opened the Ark to look inside. Both of these actions violated the Biblical prohibition, וְלֹא־יָבֹאוּ לִרְאוֹת כְּבַלַּע אֶת־הַקֹּדֶשׁ, *But [the Levites] shall not come and look as the holy [vessels] are inserted [in their wrappings]* (*Numbers* 4:20; see *Rashbam* ad loc.).

The Talmud (*Sotah* 35a) asserts that the people of Beth-shemesh sinned in that they did not even pause from their reaping to honor the Ark's arrival.[1]

Malbim explains that instead of experiencing a spiritual elation, which would have compelled them to stop their work and properly escort the Ark to its place,

1. To understand why the Talmud was not satisfied with the interpretation of the Midrash, which seems plausible and is based on a clear Biblical command, see *Nachalas Shimon* 17.

יד וְהָעֲגָלָה בָּאָה אֶל־שְׂדֵה יְהוֹשֻׁעַ בֵּית־הַשִּׁמְשִׁי
וַתַּעֲמֹד שָׁם וְשָׁם אֶבֶן גְּדוֹלָה וַיְבַקְּעוּ אֶת־
עֲצֵי הָעֲגָלָה וְאֶת־הַפָּרוֹת הֶעֱלוּ עֹלָה
טו לַיהוָה׃ וְהַלְוִיִּם הוֹרִידוּ | אֶת־
אֲרוֹן יהוה וְאֶת־הָאַרְגַּז אֲשֶׁר־אִתּוֹ אֲשֶׁר־בּוֹ
כְלֵי־זָהָב וַיָּשִׂמוּ אֶל־הָאֶבֶן הַגְּדוֹלָה וְאַנְשֵׁי בֵית־
שֶׁמֶשׁ הֶעֱלוּ עֹלוֹת וַיִּזְבְּחוּ זְבָחִים בַּיּוֹם הַהוּא
טז לַיהוָה׃ וַחֲמִשָּׁה סַרְנֵי־פְלִשְׁתִּים רָאוּ וַיָּשֻׁבוּ
יז עֶקְרוֹן בַּיּוֹם הַהוּא׃ וְאֵלֶּה

the Jews were merely curious to see this out-of-the-ordinary procession.

According to another Talmudic opinion, the Jews addressed the Ark disrespectfully: "Until now, who angered you that you refrained from saving yourself, and now who appeased you that you decided to return?"[1]

14. וַתַּעֲמֹד שָׁם וְשָׁם אֶבֶן גְּדוֹלָה — *And stopped there, where there was a large rock.*

The cows walked directly into the field of a man named Joshua and halted at a large rock, which had been Divinely prepared for that very purpose (*Malbim*), and the people saw this as a sign that they should bring an offering (*Me'am Loez*).

וַיְבַקְּעוּ אֶת־עֲצֵי הָעֲגָלָה — *They chopped the wood of the wagon.*

Generally speaking, wood that has been made use of may not serve as fuel for an offering (*Menachos* 22a). However, this was not a problem here, since the only use this wood had served was of a sacred character (see above, verse 7; *Meshech Chochmah, Vayikra* 22:27; see *Nachalas Shimon*).

Thus, the people intended to use the wood as fuel for the offering which, having been employed for a sacred purpose, could not be used to any mundane ends (*Abarbanel*).

Malbim comments that the use of the wood and cows for the sake of an offering must have been done with the permission of the Philistine governors, who were the rightful owners.

וְאֶת־הַפָּרוֹת הֶעֱלוּ עֹלָה לַה׳ — *And offered up the cows as an elevation-offering to* H*ASHEM*.

Although the Torah states that only a male animal may be sacrificed as an elevation-offering (*Leviticus* 1:3), in this case female animals were brought. This was permissible because after the destruction of Shiloh, the use of private altars was legitimate, and a female

1. According to another Midrashic interpretation, the fault of the people of Beth-shemesh lay not in their unenthusiastic welcome of the Ark but in the fact that for months they had made no attempt to retrieve it.

God said, "If one of you lost a chicken, wouldn't he search everywhere for it? Yet My Ark was captured by the Philistines and no one paid any mind." Presumably, the author of this view had the understanding that for the right price, or that following the plague of hemorrhoids, the Philistines would have returned the Ark if requested to do so. The people of Beth-shemesh in particular were held responsible for failing to make this request because they were most closely situated to Philistia (*Bereishis Rabbah* 54:4, *Yefeh To'ar*).

[14]*The wagon came to the field of Joshua, a Beth-shemeshite, and stopped there, where there was a large rock. They chopped the wood of the wagon, and offered up the cows as an elevation-offering to* HASHEM.

[15]*The Levites had unloaded the Ark of* HASHEM *and the box that was with it, in which were the golden objects, and placed them upon the large rock. The people of Beth-shemesh offered up elevation-offerings and slaughtered feast-offerings on that day to* HASHEM. [16]*The five Philistine governors saw [all this] and returned to Ekron on that day.*

elevation-offering may be sacrificed on such an altar (*Avodah Zarah* 24b).

According to one Tannaic view, a gentile's animal may not be brought as an offering. In line with that view, the present offering made use of a limited, temporary dispensation made possible by the miraculous conditions associated with the arrival of the cows (ibid.; *Rashi* ad loc.). Alternatively, it was not the Jews who brought this offering but the Philistine governors (*Radak*, based on *Yerushalmi Avodah Zarah* 2:1).

15. וְהַלְוִיִּם הוֹרִידוּ אֶת־אֲרוֹן ה׳ — *The Levites had unloaded the Ark of* HASHEM.

This of course took place before the wood was chopped (see previous verse) (*Kli Yakar*).

וְאֶת־הָאַרְגַּז אֲשֶׁר־אִתּוֹ — *And the box that was with it.*

The Jews honored the Philistines' gift by placing it next to the Ark (*Kli Yakar*).

The Talmud relates that from this point onward, the box sent by the Philistines remained adjacent to the Ark, even when the Ark was placed in the Inner Sanctuary of the Holy Temple. The Torah scroll which, as the Torah prescribes (*Deuteronomy* 31:26), was to be placed at the side of the Ark, was situated on top of this box (*Bava Basra* 14a). And when King Josiah hid the Ark, he hid this box along with it (*Yoma* 52b).

Ben Yehodaya comments that only the empty box was placed near the Ark, not the golden ornaments that had been inside it.

וְאַנְשֵׁי בֵית־שֶׁמֶשׁ הֶעֱלוּ עֹלוֹת — *The people of Beth-shemesh offered up elevation-offerings.*

This was in addition to the cows (*Metzudos*).

16. וַחֲמִשָּׁה סַרְנֵי־פְלִשְׁתִּים רָאוּ — *The five Philistine governors saw [all this].*

They saw that God had indeed returned the Ark to Israel in a miraculous manner (*Metzudos*).

וַיָּשֻׁבוּ עֶקְרוֹן בַּיּוֹם הַהוּא — *And returned to Ekron on that day.*

As *Malbim* points out, this constituted another miraculous element of this wondrous episode. The governors' entire round trip, including their stay at Beth-shemesh to watch the offerings, was completed in one day.

Kli Yakar suggests that either they experienced a miraculously rapid passage in both directions, or that the Ark, which "carried its carriers" (*Sotah* 35a), brought them to Beth-shemesh with supernatural velocity.

טְחֹרֵי הַזָּהָב אֲשֶׁר הֵשִׁיבוּ פְלִשְׁתִּים אָשָׁם
לַיהוָה לְאַשְׁדּוֹד אֶחָד לְעַזָּה אֶחָד לְאַשְׁקְלוֹן
יח אֶחָד לְגַת אֶחָד לְעֶקְרוֹן אֶחָד׃ וְעַכְבְּרֵי
הַזָּהָב מִסְפַּר כָּל־עָרֵי פְלִשְׁתִּים לַחֲמֵשֶׁת
הַסְּרָנִים מֵעִיר מִבְצָר וְעַד כֹּפֶר הַפְּרָזִי וְעַד |
אָבֵל הַגְּדוֹלָה אֲשֶׁר הִנִּיחוּ עָלֶיהָ אֵת אֲרוֹן
יְהוָה עַד הַיּוֹם הַזֶּה בִּשְׂדֵה יְהוֹשֻׁעַ בֵּית־הַשִּׁמְשִׁי׃
יט וַיַּךְ בְּאַנְשֵׁי בֵית־שֶׁמֶשׁ כִּי רָאוּ בַּאֲרוֹן יְהוָה

17-18. These two verses do not clearly indicate the quantity of gifts that the Philistines sent.

Radak and *Mahari Kara* maintain that the five hemorrhoids and five mice that the priests and sorcerers suggested (above, verse 4 — see comm. to verse 5) are referred to here: וְאֵלֶּה טְחֹרֵי הַזָּהָב, *These are the golden hemorrhoids* etc., לְאַשְׁדּוֹד אֶחָד, *one for Ashdod*, etc., totaling five — וְעַכְבְּרֵי הַזָּהָב מִסְפַּר כָּל־עָרֵי פְלִשְׁתִּים לַחֲמֵשֶׁת הַסְּרָנִים, *as well as golden mice [corresponding to] the amount of [major] cities of Philista* — [which were five] *[also corresponding] to the five governors.* (The governors are mentioned separately, because this gift served as an atonement for them as well.)

Then, states *Radak*, beginning with the words מֵעִיר מִבְצָר, *from fortified city*, Scripture relates that in addition to these five hemorrhoids and five mice, the other Philistine localities contributed one golden hemorrhoid and one mouse each. They did so in order to alleviate their fears that five golden hemorrhoids and five golden mice would not suffice to appease God. According to this interpretation, the conjunction ו is implied before the phrase מֵעִיר מִבְצָר, [*from fortified city*], and the verse must be read as stating **וּמֵעִיר** מִבְצָר, *and from the fortified city ....*

Other commentators contend that the Philistines sent a total of five hemorrhoids but a greater number of mice. Verse 17 should thus be read, וְאֵלֶּה טְחֹרֵי הַזָּהָב, *These are the golden hemorrhoids* — i.e., there were five and no more. On the other hand, regarding the golden mice, verse 18 relates that וְעַכְבְּרֵי הַזָּהָב מִסְפַּר כָּל־עָרֵי פְלִשְׁתִּים, *the amount of golden mice corresponded to all of the Philistine cities* — i.e., each city contributed a mouse — לַחֲמֵשֶׁת הַסְּרָנִים, *[these cities being governed] by the five governors,* מֵעִיר מִבְצָר ... *[who ruled over all areas, including] the fortified city* (*Abarbanel, Malbim*). Our translation follows this latter interpretation.

The Philistines donated more mice than hemorrhoids because they suffered especially from the mice (*Me'am Loez*).

Kli Yakar presents a third opinion: that the Philistines gave nothing beyond the amount suggested by the sorcerers: five mice and five hemorrhoids.

אָבֵל הַגְּדוֹלָה — *The Great Stone.*

This is the *large rock* mentioned in verse 14. The word for *rock* is here written with a ל instead of a נ (an interchange that occurs elsewhere as well — *Rashi*). This change is particularly apt because the word *rock* spelled with a ל — אָבֵל — can be read as *mourning*, referring, therefore, to the subsequent mourning that occurred (as described in the following verse).

וְעַד אָבֵל הַגְּדוֹלָה — *Until the Great Stone.*

[17] *These are the golden hemorrhoids that the Philistines sent as a guilt-offering to* HASHEM: *for Ashdod
one; for Gaza one; for Ashkelon one; for Gath one;
for Ekron one;* [18] *and golden mice corresponding to the
number of all Philistine cities of the five governors,
[who ruled] from fortified city until the open village,
until the Great Stone, upon which they placed the
Ark of* HASHEM, *which to this day is in the field of
Joshua the Beth-shemeshite.*

[19] *And He smote some of the men of Beth-
shemesh because they peered into the Ark of* HASHEM.

That is to say, all of the cities and villages of the Philistines, coming right up to the border of the land of Israel — where the Great Stone was located — contributed gifts.

Kli Yakar explains וְעַד אָבֵל הַגְּדוֹלָה as meaning that *governors escorted the Ark and the gifts] until [they arrived at] the Great Stone,* following which the governors returned to Philistia.

According to these interpretations, וְעַד אָבֵל הַגְּדוֹלָה constitutes the end of the opening phrase of the verse. *Abarbanel* disagrees, however, and sees it as constituting the beginning of the second phrase of the verse. Thus, the verse is to be translated, *As well as golden mice corresponding to the number of all of the [major] cities of Philistia, [also corresponding] to the five governors — from fortified city to the open village. And even the large stone upon which they placed the Ark of* HASHEM *[became a famous landmark and can be recognized] to this day [just as the field of Joshua].*

☙ Rerouting the Ark to Kiriath-je'arim

19. וַיַּךְ בְּאַנְשֵׁי בֵית־שֶׁמֶשׁ — *And he smote some of the men of Beth-shemesh.*

Only after Scripture relates that the Philistine governors went home does it report about what happened to the residents of Beth-shemesh. Hashem didn't want the governors to see the punishment of the people of Beth-shemesh so that they shouldn't say that the Ark kills Jews just as it does Philistines. Therefore, He waited until they left (*Alshich*).

כִּי רָאוּ בַּאֲרוֹן ה׳ — *Because they peered into the Ark of* HASHEM.

As described above (see comm. to verse 13), the people treated the arrival of the Ark disrespectfully. The term רָאוּ, *they saw,* can imply a disdainful gaze, as in אַל־תִּרְאוּנִי שֶׁאֲנִי שְׁחַרְחֹרֶת, *Do not view me with contempt despite my swarthiness* (*Song of Songs* 1:6; *Rashi* on *Sotah* 35a).

According to *Malbim,* whenever the verb רְאִיָּה, *seeing,* is followed by a word with the prefix ב, רְאִיָּה is to be understood as a long and analytical stare; one that, when applied to the Ark, indicates a lack of reverence.

As mentioned, *Radak* claims that the Jews not only gazed unlawfully at the Ark, but opened it to look inside. He supports that claim on the basis of the fact that the present verse employs the phrase, רָאוּ בַּאֲרוֹן, *peered into the Ark,* rather than רָאוּ הָאָרוֹן, *they peered at the Ark.*

וַיַּךְ בָּעָם שִׁבְעִים אִישׁ חֲמִשִּׁים אֶלֶף אִישׁ וַיִּתְאַבְּלוּ
כ הָעָם כִּי־הִכָּה יהוה בָּעָם מַכָּה גְדוֹלָה׃ וַיֹּאמְרוּ אַנְשֵׁי
בֵית־שֶׁמֶשׁ מִי יוּכַל לַעֲמֹד לִפְנֵי יהוה הָאֱלֹהִים
כא הַקָּדוֹשׁ הַזֶּה וְאֶל־מִי יַעֲלֶה מֵעָלֵינוּ׃ וַיִּשְׁלְחוּ
מַלְאָכִים אֶל־יוֹשְׁבֵי קִרְיַת־יְעָרִים לֵאמֹר הֵשִׁבוּ
פְלִשְׁתִּים אֶת־אֲרוֹן יהוה רְדוּ הַעֲלוּ אֹתוֹ אֲלֵיכֶם׃

וַיַּךְ בָּעָם שִׁבְעִים אִישׁ חֲמִשִּׁים אֶלֶף אִישׁ — *He struck among them seventy men, fifty thousand men.*

This phrase clearly requires elucidation. How many casualties were there? Why is the word *men* mentioned twice?

Some commentators include this phrase among those that are conjunctive even though they lack an explicit ו, *and;* hence, it means that God struck 50,000 and 70 men (*Radak, Mahari Kara*). However, this does not explain why the verse mentions the word *men* twice.

Targum explicates that the verse is referring to 70 elders and 50,000 common people. The Talmud explains this to mean either that 70 extraordinary men died, each of whom was as worthy as 50,000 ordinary men, or that 50,000 men died, each of whom was as worthy as an entire body of the Sanhedrin, which is composed of 70 judges (*Sotah* 35b).

Malbim explains that 50,000 men lived in Beth-shemesh, of whom 70 perished. Although the phrase is to be translated as *70 out of 50,000 died,* the prefix מ, *out of,* is elided in order to teach that the people were so devastated by the loss of their brethren that they felt as if they had all perished.

וַיִּתְאַבְּלוּ הָעָם כִּי־הִכָּה ה׳ בָּעָם מַכָּה גְדוֹלָה — *The people mourned because Hashem had smitten the people with a great blow.*

The people mourned on two accounts. First, כִּי־הִכָּה ה׳ בָּעָם, *for Hashem had smitten the people,* God had exhibited His wrath and condemnation of the people of Beth-shemesh, and second, because of the מַכָּה גְדוֹלָה, *the greatness of [their] loss* (*Kli Yakar*).

20. וַיֹּאמְרוּ אַנְשֵׁי בֵית־שֶׁמֶשׁ מִי יוּכַל לַעֲמֹד לִפְנֵי ה׳ — *And the people of Beth-shemesh said, "Who can [possibly] stand before Hashem?"*

Abarbanel interprets this verse as describing a heretofore unmentioned reason for the tragedy that befell the inhabitants of Beth-shemesh. According to him, this statement was *before* the Ark arrived. Aware of the terrible affliction that the Philistines had suffered at the hands of the Ark, the residents of Beth-shemesh fearfully exclaimed, *"Who can possibly stand before Hashem ... and to whom can we pass on the Ark?"* They were punished for not sanctifying themselves with proper devotion and dedication so as to act as hosts for the Ark.

However, a more literal explanation of the verse is that, having experienced God's strict judgment, the inhabitants of Beth-shemesh wondered who could possibly continue to bear His scrutiny. "Even the most noble among us," they stated, "have died. Who among those who remain alive will be able to properly adhere to the level of holiness that the task of guarding the Ark demands?" (*Metzudos*).

לִפְנֵי ה׳ הָאֱלֹהִים הַקָּדוֹשׁ הַזֶּה — *Before Hashem, this Holy God?*

Targum adds, *before the Ark of Hashem, this Holy God?*

הַקָּדוֹשׁ — *Holy.*

The Ark's holiness was unaffected by the defiled environment of Philistia.

Alternatively, the word הַקָּדוֹשׁ, *the holy,* implies that God was publicly sanctified

He struck among them seventy men, fifty thousand men. The people mourned because HASHEM *had smitten the people with a great blow.* [20] *And the people of Beth-shemesh said, "Who can [possibly] stand before* HASHEM, *this Holy God? To whom among us can [the Ark] ascend?"* [21] *They then sent emissaries to the inhabitants of Kiriath-je'arim, saying, "The Philistines have returned the Ark of* HASHEM. *Come down and bring it up unto yourselves."*

when the men of Beth-shemesh died in consequence of not having maintained a proper standard of behavior. This same idea is expressed in the verse, בִּקְרֹבַי אֶקָּדֵשׁ, *I will be sanctified through those who are nearest me* (*Leviticus* 10:3; *Rashi* ad loc.; *Kli Yakar*).

וְאֶל־מִי יַעֲלֶה מֵעָלֵינוּ — *To whom among us can [the Ark] ascend?*

Mahari Kara adds a pause after the word מִי, rendering the phrase, *"To whom [can we send the Ark? Just let it] be removed from our midst."*[1]

21. וַיִּשְׁלְחוּ מַלְאָכִים אֶל־יוֹשְׁבֵי קִרְיַת־יְעָרִים לֵאמֹר הֵשִׁבוּ פְלִשְׁתִּים אֶת־אֲרוֹן ה׳ — *They then sent emissaries to the inhabitants of Kiriath-je'arim, saying, "The Philistines have returned the Ark of* HASHEM."

Both Beth-shemesh and Kiriath-je'arim belonged to the territory of the tribe of Judah. The residents of Beth-shemesh chose to transfer the Ark a short distance to members of their own tribe. They then assured the residents of Kiriath-je'arim that there was no reason to fear that the nearby Philistines would attempt to recapture the Ark, since they had just willingly returned it (*Malbim*).

הַעֲלוּ אֹתוֹ אֲלֵיכֶם — *Bring it up unto yourselves.*

Beth-shemesh was situated in a valley, a location not befitting the honor of the Ark. The residents of Beth-shemesh thus told the inhabitants of Kiriath-je'arim that the Ark would be better placed with them, since they were situated at a higher altitude.

VII

הֶחָפֹץ אֶחְפֹּץ מוֹת רָשָׁע נְאֻם אֲדֹנָי אֱלֹהִים הֲלוֹא בְּשׁוּבוֹ מִדְּרָכָיו וְחָיָה — *"Do I desire at all the death of the wicked man?" — the word of the Lord* HASHEM/*Elohim — "Is it not rather his return from his ways, so that he may live?"* (*Ezekiel* 18:23)

The Jewish people, whom God chose to sanctify His Name, are under His exacting scrutiny. Time after time they fell short of fulfilling His precise demands and they immediately met with the painful consequences of their failures.

Yet, in the course of time, God has dispatched many prophets and preachers to remind the Jews that His hand is always "extended to accept penitents" and recall them to their task.

Thus, when the Israelites accorded the Holy Ark scant respect — considerably less than had the Philistines — Samuel instructed them how to regain God's favor so that His providence might again shield them upon the Holy Land.

1. *Mahari Kara* supports his interpretation by citing the *Targum* (a version apparently different from the one we possess).

א וַיָּבֹאוּ אַנְשֵׁי | קִרְיַת יְעָרִים וַיַּעֲלוּ אֶת־אֲרוֹן
יהוה וַיָּבִאוּ אֹתוֹ אֶל־בֵּית אֲבִינָדָב בַּגִּבְעָה
וְאֶת־אֶלְעָזָר בְּנוֹ קִדְּשׁוּ לִשְׁמֹר אֶת־אֲרוֹן
ב יהוה: וַיְהִי מִיּוֹם שֶׁבֶת הָאָרוֹן
בְּקִרְיַת יְעָרִים וַיִּרְבּוּ הַיָּמִים וַיִּהְיוּ עֶשְׂרִים שָׁנָה

The present chapter is the last to describe the pre-monarchic Jewish commonwealth and Samuel in the role of the sole authority over the nation. He is afterward described chiefly as inaugurating Saul and David into kingship and offering them guidance, although he continued to judge the Jewish nation until his death.

⇶ The Israelites Repent

1. וַיָּבֹאוּ אַנְשֵׁי קִרְיַת יְעָרִים — *So the men of Kiriath-je'arim came.*

Upon learning that they had the opportunity to host the Ark, the entire populace of Kiriath-je'arim traveled to Beth-shemesh to pay their respects (*Malbim*).

Kli Yakar notes that in the previous verse, emissaries were sent only to יוֹשְׁבֵי קִרְיַת יְעָרִים, *the inhabitants of Kiriath-je'arim,* which, he explains, were those that were involved בְּישׁוּבָהּ שֶׁל עִיר, *with the settlements of the city,* i.e., the city council. This response, however, came from אַנְשֵׁי קִרְיַת יְעָרִים, *the men* of the city, i.e., *all* its inhabitants, for everyone wanted a share in this special privilege.

אֶל־בֵּית אֲבִינָדָב בַּגִּבְעָה — *To the house of Abinadab on the hill.*

This phrase specifically identifies an Abinadab in Kiriath-je'arim who lived on a hill, as distinct from any other man of that name (*Radak*).

Alternatively, there was but one man named Abinadab in Kiriath-je'arim. He owned two houses, one of which was located on a hill, and this one was chosen to house the Ark, for it was more isolated, which created the need for a guard (*Malbim, Kli Yakar*).

Me'am Loez observes that the Jews placed the Ark in a house built high on a hill in accordance with the principle that a synagogue should be housed in a community's tallest edifice (*Shabbos* 11a; *Shulchan Aruch, Orach Chaim* 150:2).

Interestingly, they did not bring the Ark to Nob, where the Tabernacle stood. It seems that they considered the destruction of Shiloh a result of the disrespect they had shown by moving the Ark to the battlefield. Therefore they resolved now to limit its transport. Aware that the Tabernacle would not be in Nob permanently, they preferred to bring the Ark to a place where it could stay until the Temple would be built (*Ezras Kohanim,* cited by *Mishbetzos Zahav*).

קִדְּשׁוּ — *They designated.*

The word קִדְּשׁוּ, *designated,* indicates a person or object set aside and dedicated solely to a single purpose (*Malbim*).

לִשְׁמֹר אֶת־אֲרוֹן ה׳ — *To guard the Ark of Hashem.*

That is to say, to maintain the site's ritual purity and physical cleanliness (*Radak*).

According to *Metzudos,* the guard was charged with preventing anyone from looking upon the Ark in an illicit fashion (see above, 6:13).

The Ark arrived in Kiriath-je'arim, accompanied by the Philistines' gift of golden representations of mice.

The *Chachmei Ashkenaz* (Sages of Germany) point out that, by way of marking the city's hosting of these mice, God miraculously caused the women of the city to bear

1 **S**o the men of Kiriath-je'arim came and brought up the Ark of HASHEM, and they brought it to the house of Abinadab on the hill, and they designated Elazar his son to guard the Ark of HASHEM.

2 From the time the Ark was stationed at Kiriath-je'arim there ensued many days, they were twenty years,

sextuplets, just as mice bear an average of six offspring in a litter (*Me'am Loez*).

2. וַיְהִי מִיּוֹם שֶׁבֶת הָאָרוֹן בְּקִרְיַת יְעָרִים ... וַיִּנָּהוּ כָּל־בֵּית יִשְׂרָאֵל אַחֲרֵי ה' — *From the time the Ark was stationed at Kiriath-je'arim ... the entire House of Israel was drawn after HASHEM.*

Having witnessing God's exacting punishment of Eli's sons for their sins and the might that He displayed against the Philistines (*Rashi*), and having seen the puissant holiness of the Ark — which avenged itself on those who disrespected it and protected those who honored it (*Malbim*) — the Jews were infused with an awe of Hashem, and were inspired to repent.

וַיִּרְבּוּ הַיָּמִים — *There ensued many days.*

The word יָמִים, *days,* implies a period of tranquility, one that the Jews earned because they diligently maintained the proper environment of sanctity for the Ark (*Me'am Loez*).

וַיִּהְיוּ עֶשְׂרִים שָׁנָה — *They were twenty years.*

During the first 10 of these years, Samuel was the universally accepted sole leader of the Jewish nation.

In the following year, Samuel ruled in conjunction with King Saul.

Then Samuel severed his relationship with Saul and for 2 years King Saul reigned alone (15:35; see *Rashi, Zevachim* 115b).

Following that time, David began his rule, during the first 7 years of which the capital city was Hebron (*I Kings* 2:11).

Thus a total of 20 years passed. At the end of that time, King David transferred the Ark from Kiriath-je'arim to the home of Obed-edom the Gittite (*II Samuel* Chapter 6; *Seder Olam,* quoted by *Zevachim* 118b; see Timeline in Appendix).[1]

According to this chronology, as presented by *Seder Olam,* the period of the Jews' repentance occurred during these 20 years.

Abarbanel rejects this understanding of the verse based on two observations regarding the text, and offers an alternative explanation.

First, states *Abarbanel,* the length of the Ark's stay in Kiriath-je'arim is unrelated to the Jews' penitence, and thus the two topics should not have appeared in the same verse.

Second, since the verse specifically states that 20 years passed, it is supererogatory for it to characterize them as *many days.*

Thus, *Abarbanel* reinterprets the verse to mean that the Jews began their process of spiritual rehabilitation only 20 years after the Ark arrived in Kiriath-je'arim.

Thus, according to this understanding of the verse, the length of 20 years and the Jews' process of repentance are indeed interrelated.

In regard to *Abarbanel's* second point, according to this understanding it is indeed relevant to characterize the period of 20 years as *many days,* in order to underscore the point that the Jews waited an absurdly long amount of time before beginning their process of repentance.[2]

1. During this 20-year period, the Tabernacle stood in Nob until the destruction of that site (which occurred at the same time as Samuel's death), at which time it was transferred to Gibeon.

2. According to this, Samuel's lifetime extended past these initial 20 years, and the Ark remained in Kiriath-je'arim much longer than 20 years — until King David removed it after 7 years of his reign (see *II Samuel,* Chapter 6).

וַיִּנָּהוּ כָּל־בֵּית יִשְׂרָאֵל אַחֲרֵי יהוה: וַיֹּאמֶר ג
שְׁמוּאֵל אֶל־כָּל־בֵּית יִשְׂרָאֵל לֵאמֹר אִם־בְּכָל־
לְבַבְכֶם אַתֶּם שָׁבִים אֶל־יהוה הָסִירוּ אֶת־אֱלֹהֵי
הַנֵּכָר מִתּוֹכְכֶם וְהָעַשְׁתָּרוֹת וְהָכִינוּ לְבַבְכֶם
אֶל־יהוה וְעִבְדֻהוּ לְבַדּוֹ וְיַצֵּל אֶתְכֶם מִיַּד
פְּלִשְׁתִּים: וַיָּסִירוּ בְּנֵי יִשְׂרָאֵל אֶת־הַבְּעָלִים וְאֶת־ ד
הָעַשְׁתָּרֹת וַיַּעַבְדוּ אֶת־יהוה לְבַדּוֹ: וַיֹּאמֶר ה
שְׁמוּאֵל קִבְצוּ אֶת־כָּל־יִשְׂרָאֵל הַמִּצְפָּתָה

Kli Yakar defends the chronology as presented in *Seder Olam* and responds to *Abarbanel's* two observations as follows.

First, *Kli Yakar* states, the period of 20 years is mentioned in the same verse as the Jews' repentance to note that the Ark remained in one place and the process of repentance was consistently successful despite frequent changes of leadership.

Second, this period is described as *many days* because of those many changes of authority.

Kli Yakar further suggests that it took the entire 20 years until כָּל־בֵּית יִשְׂרָאֵל, *the entire House of Israel,* participated in the process of repentance.

וַיִּנָּהוּ — *Was drawn.*

The Jews were inspired by Samuel, who traveled from city to city in order to judge and rebuke them (*Rashi*).

Rashi mentions two alternative translations of the word וַיִּנָּהוּ. Either *they wailed,* i.e., they mourned their sinful deeds and thus repented, *after* Hashem, or *they gathered to perform the service of* HASHEM.

כָּל־בֵּית יִשְׂרָאֵל — *The entire House of Israel.*

This included the women. The word בַּיִת, *house,* often refers to women (see *Rashi, Exodus* 19:3; *Shabbos* 118b).

3. וַיֹּאמֶר שְׁמוּאֵל אֶל־כָּל־בֵּית יִשְׂרָאֵל — *Samuel said to the entire House of Israel.*

This phrase can also be translated as *Samuel spoke to every House of Israel.* That was indeed Samuel's custom: rather than wait for people to seek his counsel, he would journey from one locale to another until he spread his influence across the entire land of Israel (*Kli Yakar*).

הָסִירוּ אֶת־אֱלֹהֵי הַנֵּכָר — *Remove the foreign gods.*

Complete repentance demands a rigorous renunciation of one's evil habits and a firm resolve to lead a more righteous life. Both the renunciation and the resolve must exist internally, in one's heart and mind, and externally, in one's deeds.

Thus, the verse states: הָסִירוּ אֶת־ אֱלֹהֵי הַנֵּכָר מִתּוֹכְכֶם, *Remove the foreign gods from your midst* — i.e., renounce the evil that is entrenched in your hearts and minds; וְהָעַשְׁתָּרוֹת, *and the [practice of serving the idol] Ashtaroth* — amend your past deeds. Following that, וְהָכִינוּ לְבַבְכֶם אֶל־ה׳, *Direct your hearts to* HASHEM, resolve to turn your hearts and minds to God; וְעִבְדֻהוּ לְבַדּוֹ, *serving Him alone* in your deeds (*Malbim*).

וְיַצֵּל אֶתְכֶם מִיַּד פְּלִשְׁתִּים — *Then He will rescue you from the hand of the Philistines.*

As our Sages teach, when a person accepts the yoke of Torah, the yoke of government is removed from him (*Pirkei Avos* 3:6; *Me'am Loez*).

Abarbanel adds: "Do not think that because the Philistines honored the

during which the entire House of Israel was drawn
after HASHEM. [3]*Samuel said to the entire House of*
Israel, saying, "If you are returning unto HASHEM
with all your hearts, then remove the foreign gods
and the Ashtaroth from your midst, and direct your
hearts to HASHEM, *serving Him alone; then He will*
rescue you from the hand of the Philistines." [4]*So*
the Children of Israel removed the Baalim and the
Ashtaroth, and served HASHEM *alone.*
[5]*Then Samuel said, "Gather all of Israel to Mizpah,*

Ark Hashem will favor them in their confrontation with you; when you dedicate yourselves to Hashem, He will protect you from all adversity."

4. ... וַיָּסִירוּ בְּנֵי יִשְׂרָאֵל — *So the Children of Israel removed ...*

Malbim, following his thoughts on the previous verse, comments that the prophet testifies only about the practical, discernible changes that they made (both regarding their past deeds and their resolve for the future). However, as for the needed internal improvements in their hearts and minds, only Hashem is aware.

הַבְּעָלִים — *The Baalim.*

This is the commonly used title of a particular type of idol worship. One theory is that it is a generic term that is used for many idols (such as Baal-zebub, *II Kings* 1:2). It is thus related to the word בַּעַל, *owner, master,* or *guardian* (*Me'am Loez*). Thus, this general reference echoes that of the previous verse, אֱלֹהֵי הַנֵּכָר, *the foreign gods.*

בְּעָלִים can also be understood as referring to clusters of stars, which were worshiped as deities.

Finally, בְּעָלִים might also refer to a carved depiction of the male anatomy with which women performed lewd acts. According to this reading, בַּעַל derives from בְּעִילָה, *intercourse.* In this regard, the term זְנוּת (lit., *straying* — usually involving promiscuity) is often used to describe the actions of an idol worshiper (as in *Exodus* 34:15; *Me'am Loez, Kli Yakar*).

5. וַיֹּאמֶר שְׁמוּאֵל קִבְצוּ אֶת־כָּל־יִשְׂרָאֵל — *Then Samuel said, "Gather all of Israel."*

The glory of the Jewish people is augmented when they gather together. As Moses said, וַיְהִי בִישֻׁרוּן מֶלֶךְ בְּהִתְאַסֵּף רָאשֵׁי עָם יַחַד שִׁבְטֵי יִשְׂרָאֵל, *[God] became King over Jeshurun when the heads of the nation gathered — the tribes of Israel in unity* (*Deuteronomy* 33:5; *Me'am Loez*).

הַמִּצְפָּתָה — *To Mizpah.*

Mizpah was the site of Joshua's victory against the coalition of northern Canaanite kings (*Joshua* 11:38).

Radak conjectures that in recognition of the notable victory that God granted the Israelites in Mizpah, Joshua built an altar there and established that location as a site of assembly and public prayer.[1]

The ruins of the Tabernacle in Shiloh presumably retained a significant level of sanctity after the Tabernacle had stood there 369 years. Why then did Samuel not gather the Jews there?

The Midrash explains that although Shiloh did possess great sanctity, it was exceeded by that of Mizpah, insofar as the latter was situated on land upon which the Temple

1. Mizpah is also mentioned as a gathering place in *Judges* 11:11, 20:1, and below, 10:17.

ו וְאֶתְפַּלֵּל בַּעַדְכֶם אֶל־יְהוָה: וַיִּקָּבְצוּ הַמִּצְפָּתָה
וַיִּשְׁאֲבוּ־מַיִם וַיִּשְׁפְּכוּ | לִפְנֵי יְהוָה וַיָּצוּמוּ בַּיּוֹם
הַהוּא וַיֹּאמְרוּ שָׁם חָטָאנוּ לַיהוָה וַיִּשְׁפֹּט שְׁמוּאֵל
ז אֶת־בְּנֵי יִשְׂרָאֵל בַּמִּצְפָּה: וַיִּשְׁמְעוּ פְלִשְׁתִּים כִּי־
הִתְקַבְּצוּ בְנֵי־יִשְׂרָאֵל הַמִּצְפָּתָה וַיַּעֲלוּ סַרְנֵי־
פְלִשְׁתִּים אֶל־יִשְׂרָאֵל וַיִּשְׁמְעוּ בְּנֵי יִשְׂרָאֵל וַיִּרְאוּ

would eventually be constructed (see *Rashi, Deuteronomy* 33:12).[1]

One might also ask why the Jews did not assemble at Nob, the site of the Tabernacle at that time. A possible answer is that Nob was presumably not large enough to accommodate them all.[2]

וְאֶתְפַּלֵּל בַּעַדְכֶם אֶל־ה׳ — *And I will pray to* HASHEM *for you.*

After encouraging the people to better their ways, Samuel felt that the time had come to ask God to help them repent and protect them from further tribulations (see *Nachalas Shimon* 31:16 from *Beis Elokim*).

6. וַיִּשְׁאֲבוּ־מַיִם וַיִּשְׁפְּכוּ לִפְנֵי ה׳ — *They drew water and poured it out before* HASHEM.

This was a symbolic gesture of submission to God. It was as if the Jews were saying, "We are before You as water which is poured out" (*Rashi*).[3]

Ralbag and *Radak* explain this outpouring of water literally and state that it indicated that the Jews had cleansed themselves of their sins and thus gained atonement.

Targum (as also *Yerushalmi Taanis* 2:7), on the other hand, seems to understand this reference figuratively as meaning that the Jews remorsefully poured forth their hearts like water.

According to *Abarbanel,* this verse means to say that the Jews poured forth their tears before Hashem in fervent prayer.

Midrash Shmuel interprets the verse to mean that the Jews drew forth *words of Torah.* This presumably echoes the Talmudic axiom that water is symbolic of Torah (*Bava Kamma* 17a).

וַיֹּאמְרוּ שָׁם חָטָאנוּ לַה׳ — *They said there, "We have sinned to* HASHEM*!"*

Talmud Yerushalmi (ibid.) states that Samuel "donned the cloak of all the Jews" — i.e., he acted as their defense attorney (*Me'am Loez*) — and exclaimed, "Master of the worlds, do You demand more of a person than his admission, 'I have sinned'? The Jews are confessing, 'We have sinned' — won't You forgive them?"

From this, *Kli Yakar* extrapolates three crucial lessons.

First, the Jews confessed as a whole — i.e., "*We* have sinned." From this, we learn that Jews should confess as a congregation, for the merits of the many are more potent that those of any individual.

1. This was a strip of land belonging to the tribe of Judah that extended into the territory of the tribe of Benjamin. (As for why Benjamin earned the right to have the Temple in his portion, see *Onkelos, Genesis* 49:27; *Deuteronomy* 33:12, *Rashi* ad loc.)

2. The above is *Rabbi Yaakov Padanki's* explanation (published together with the commentary of *Abarbanel*) of a puzzling passage in *Midrash Shmuel,* one that *Radak* quotes and leaves unsolved. See *Mishbetzos Zahav.*

3. *Beis Meir* (*Orach Chaim* 583) comments that this idea is the basis for *Tashlich* — the custom of going to a body of water on Rosh Hashanah. The sight of water can arouse a person's sense of humility, which is a necessary precursor to repentance.

and I will pray to HASHEM for you." 6 *So they gath-*
ered at Mizpah. They drew water and poured it out before HASHEM and fasted on that day; they said there, "We have sinned to HASHEM!" And Samuel judged the Children of Israel at Mizpah.
7 *The Philistines heard that the Children of Israel*
had gathered together at Mizpah, and the governors of the Philistines came up against Israel. The Children of Israel heard and were afraid

Second, we learn from this corporate confession that every Jew must feel a sense of responsibility for another Jew's misdeeds. As our Sages state, כָּל יִשְׂרָאֵל עֲרֵבִים זֶה בָּזֶה, *All of Israel are guarantors for one another.*

Third, Samuel stated that the Jews *are saying* — in the present tense. This indicates that the Jews constantly repeated their confession; this too is a commendable practice worthy of emulation.

Interpreting the text somewhat homiletically, *Kli Yakar* states that because the Jews felt guilty over the destruction of Shiloh and the exile of the Ark, they exclaimed, שָׁם חָטָאנוּ לַה׳, *"There* [in Shiloh] *we sinned against HASHEM* "and thus brought about its downfall.

וַיִּשְׁפֹּט שְׁמוּאֵל אֶת־בְּנֵי יִשְׂרָאֵל — *And Samuel judged the Children of Israel.*

Samuel focused on resolving interpersonal disputes, facilitating the process in which a person who had wronged another repaired the damage he had done and gained forgiveness, this being a necessary precursor to atonement (*Yoma* 85b; *Rashi, Me'am Loez*).

Radak states that the Jews confessed their sins there, and Samuel meted out the appropriate punishment.

◆§ The Philistines Attack and God's Miraculous Salvation

7. וַיִּשְׁמְעוּ פְלִשְׁתִּים כִּי־הִתְקַבְּצוּ בְנֵי־יִשְׂרָאֵל הַמִּצְפָּתָה — *The Philistines heard that the Children of Israel had gathered together at Mizpah.*

The Philistines were cognizant of the special providence that the Jews enjoyed when they assembled at Mizpah (*Abarbanel*). They thus assumed that the purpose of that gathering was to wage war against them, and grew furious (*Metzudos*). To demonstrate that they did not fear a Jewish attack, they decided to strike first. Their fearless preparation for battle aroused the apprehension of the Israelites, especially since they vividly recalled how their last confrontation with the Philistines had resulted in their abject defeat (*Kli Yakar*).

According to *Me'am Loez*, however, the Philistines knew the real reason for the Jews' assembly, and decided to take advantage of the Jews' vulnerability as they were congregated and preoccupied with prayer, in order to launch a surprise attack against them.

וַיַּעֲלוּ סַרְנֵי־פְלִשְׁתִּים אֶל־יִשְׂרָאֵל — *And the governors of the Philistines came up against Israel.*

Whereas at the beginning and end of the verse the Jews are referred to as בְּנֵי יִשְׂרָאֵל, at this point they are referred to simply as יִשְׂרָאֵל, *Israel*. Apparently, the Philistines, still flushed with the glory of their previous victory, planned to destroy not just *the Children of Israel* convened in Mizpah but to erase the very name of *Israel* from the face of the earth (*Kli Yakar*).

ח מִפְּנֵי פְלִשְׁתִּים: וַיֹּאמְרוּ בְנֵי־יִשְׂרָאֵל אֶל־שְׁמוּאֵל
אַל־תַּחֲרֵשׁ מִמֶּנּוּ מִזְּעֹק אֶל־יהוה אֱלֹהֵינוּ
ט וְיֹשִׁעֵנוּ מִיַּד פְּלִשְׁתִּים: וַיִּקַּח שְׁמוּאֵל טְלֵה
חָלָב אֶחָד °ויעלה עוֹלָה כָּלִיל לַיהוה וַיִּזְעַק
שְׁמוּאֵל אֶל־יהוה בְּעַד יִשְׂרָאֵל וַיַּעֲנֵהוּ יהוה:

°וַיַּעֲלֵהוּ ק׳

8. אַל־תַּחֲרֵשׁ מִמֶּנּוּ — *Do not be silent ... on our behalf.*

Although the phrase אַל־תַּחֲרֵשׁ is typically used in a causative sense — i.e., "Do not cause [someone else] to be silent" — it is nevertheless grammatically acceptable, also, as "Don't be silent" (*Mahari Kara, Radak*). *Kli Yakar* suggests that they said, "Don't cause God to be silent; [avoid that] by crying out to [Him]."

וְיֹשִׁעֵנוּ מִיַּד פְּלִשְׁתִּים — *That He save us from the hand of the Philistines.*

Malbim states that the Israelites were so overwhelmed by fear that they felt unable to fight on their own behalf and requested that Hashem save them without their participation.

9. טְלֵה חָלָב אֶחָד — *One suckling lamb.*

Samuel chose a small, young animal that could be quickly sacrificed, for the Philistine army was swiftly approaching. *Be'er Moshe* (citing *Teshuvos Radvaz*) explains that Samuel hinted that just as the suckling is completely dependent on its mother, so too the Jewish people place their full trust only in Hashem, so that He should hear their prayers and save them from the Philistines.

The word אֶחָד, *one*, seems redundant (and considering the Midrash that says that it was female [see below], the word אֶחָד is grammatically inappropriate; it should have said אַחַת). *Kli Yakar* understands the word to denote מְיוּחָד, *special*, i.e., of superior quality (see comm. to 1:1).

Although Samuel offered this sacrifice on behalf of the Jewish nation, he took the animal from his own flock, so as not to make use of public funds (*Bamidbar Rabbah* 18:10, *Maharzu*). This was consistent with his practice of eschewing all benefit from others (see below, v. 17, 12:3, *Berachos* 10b).

וַיַּעֲלֵהוּ עוֹלָה — *And offered it up ... as an elevation-offering.*

Samuel had to offer this sacrifice in order to reach a level of prophecy and connection with God that would make it possible for his prayer to gain acceptance (*Ralbag*).

The elevation-offering is the most cherished of sacrifices because it is completely offered to Hashem. In addition, it has the property of attaining atonement for sinful thoughts. The Israelites had reached such an elevated level of repentance that, Samuel realized, the only misdeed of theirs that could have precipitated this war was that of indulging in iniquitous thoughts (*Me'am Loez*).

As mentioned earlier, after the destruction of the Tabernacle site in Shiloh, it was permissible to construct a private altar (even though a public altar stood in Nob), to which many of the regulations pertaining to Temple and public-altar offerings did not apply.

Thus, although the Torah prescribes that the animal brought as an elevation-offering must be male (*Leviticus* 1:3), Samuel apparently offered a female. This may be derived from the fact that the word וַיַּעֲלֵהוּ — whose read version (*kri*) is translated, *and [Samuel] offered him up* — is spelled without a ו at the end, so it may be read as וַיַּעֲלֶהָ, *and [Samuel] offered her up.* The Talmud (*Avodah Zarah* 24b) refers to this as the source for the idea that a female elevation-offering may

of the Philistines. 8The Children of Israel
said to Samuel, "Do not be silent from crying out on our behalf to HASHEM, our God, that
He save us from the hand of the Philistines."
9Samuel took one suckling lamb and offered it
up entirely as an elevation-offering to HASHEM;
Samuel cried out to HASHEM on behalf of Israel and
HASHEM answered him.

be offered on a private altar.

Our Sages note three other ways in which this offering deviated from the parameters of a normative offering.

The word כָּלִיל, *entirely,* implies that even the hide of the offering was burned, whereas normally the hide of an elevation-offering is divided among the Kohanim.

Based on the phrase, טְלֵה חָלָב, *suckling lamb,* our Sages state that this sheep was below the minimal age of seven days (see *Leviticus* 22:27).

Also, although normally only a Kohen may perform this hallowed service, Samuel, who was not a Kohen, performed it (*Yerushalmi Megillah* 1:12; *Midrash Shmuel; Vayikra Rabbah* 22:9).

However, the *Yerushalmi* (*Avodah Zarah* 2:1) and other sources deny that these peculiarities shed light on the regulations governing a private sacrifice. Rather, Samuel made use of a הוֹרָאַת שָׁעָה, *a temporary, limited ruling,* from which no precedents may be derived (see above, 6:14, comm.).[1]

וַיַּעֲנֵהוּ ה׳ — *And HASHEM answered him.*

Possibly, a heavenly fire descended and consumed the offering (*Radak*), and this persuaded Samuel that God would save the Jews (*Metzudos*).

Alternatively, after Samuel heard the thunderous sounds (described in the following verse), he knew that God had accepted his prayer (*Radak*).

1. In a very perplexing Midrash, the Sages seemingly refer to this offering as a source for the idea that "use of a private altar is permissible only when sanctioned by a prophet" (*Midrash Shmuel, Vayikra Rabbah* 22:9, *Bamidbar Rabbah* 14:1, *Yerushalmi Megillah* 1:11,12).

Commentators (see *Rashash, Vayikra Rabbah* 22:9) wonder how that rule can be applicable to an offering that was brought during the time of the Tabernacle at Nob, when all private altars are permitted. That law is relevant, for example, to the offering of Elijah (*I Kings* Ch. 18), which was brought after the construction of Solomon's Temple, when the use of private altars was forbidden.

Abarbanel maintains that even when private altars were permitted — as in Samuel's day — offerings had to be brought by a prophet.

Radak explicates this to mean that the first offering sacrificed on a private altar had to be brought by a prophet.

According to *Maharzu* (*Bamidbar Rabbah* 14:1), an offering that was congregational in nature, such as the one brought by Samuel, must always be brought only at the public altar. Only a prophet could authorize such an offering on a private altar.

Careful analysis of the *Yerushalmi* (*Megillah* 1:11,12) (according to *Korban HaEidah*) indicates that there may have been an error in the text of some Midrashim and the Sages never intended to use the present instance to support the idea that prophetic authorization was necessary. The discussion of prophetic authorization had been concluded. The reference to Samuel's offering applied to the next Mishnah, which teaches that private altars are permissible, unconditionally, after Shiloh's destruction.

י וַיְהִי שְׁמוּאֵל מַעֲלֶה הָעוֹלָה וּפְלִשְׁתִּים נִגְּשׁוּ
לַמִּלְחָמָה בְּיִשְׂרָאֵל וַיַּרְעֵם יהוה | בְּקוֹל־גָּדוֹל בַּיּוֹם
הַהוּא עַל־פְּלִשְׁתִּים וַיְהֻמֵּם וַיִּנָּגְפוּ לִפְנֵי יִשְׂרָאֵל׃
יא וַיֵּצְאוּ אַנְשֵׁי יִשְׂרָאֵל מִן־הַמִּצְפָּה וַיִּרְדְּפוּ אֶת־
יב פְּלִשְׁתִּים וַיַּכּוּם עַד־מִתַּחַת לְבֵית כָּר׃ וַיִּקַּח שְׁמוּאֵל
אֶבֶן אַחַת וַיָּשֶׂם בֵּין־הַמִּצְפָּה וּבֵין הַשֵּׁן וַיִּקְרָא
אֶת־שְׁמָהּ אֶבֶן הָעָזֶר וַיֹּאמַר עַד־הֵנָּה עֲזָרָנוּ יהוה׃
יג וַיִּכָּנְעוּ הַפְּלִשְׁתִּים וְלֹא־יָסְפוּ עוֹד לָבוֹא בִּגְבוּל
יִשְׂרָאֵל וַתְּהִי יַד־יהוה בַּפְּלִשְׁתִּים כֹּל יְמֵי שְׁמוּאֵל׃

10. וַיְהִי שְׁמוּאֵל מַעֲלֶה הָעוֹלָה וּפְלִשְׁתִּים נִגְּשׁוּ — *Samuel was offering up the elevation-offering when the Philistines approached.*

The somewhat unusual wording, וּפְלִשְׁתִּים נִגְּשׁוּ, *when the Philistines approached* (in contrast to the more conventional וַיִּגְּשׁוּ פְלִשְׁתִּים) contains the implication that the Philistines began their assault even as Samuel was engaged in bringing his offering. Still, Samuel did not pause; rather, in an extraordinary exhibition of unwavering trust in Hashem, he continued performing the ceremony.[1]

וַיַּרְעֵם ה׳ בְּקוֹל־גָּדוֹל — *HASHEM then thundered with a great noise.*

Hannah alluded to this episode in her prophetic paean: עָלָיו בַּשָּׁמַיִם יַרְעֵם, *Let the heavens thunder against them* (above, 2:10; see comm. ad loc.).

Ralbag and *Abarbanel* maintain that this thunder was accompanied by fiery flames that burned before the eyes of the Philistines. (The presumable source for this claim is the verse in *Psalms,* which refers to this incident, וַיַּרְעֵם בַּשָּׁמַיִם ה׳ וְעֶלְיוֹן יִתֵּן קֹלוֹ בָּרָד וְגַחֲלֵי־אֵשׁ, *HASHEM thundered at them in the heavens, the Most High gave forth His voice — hail and fiery coals* [18:14] [see *Mahari Kara, II Samuel* 22:14].)

According to *Ralbag,* God made it possible for the Israelites as well to hear these thunderous sounds, so as to reinforce their faith.

Kli Yakar adds that whereas the Philistines heard these sounds as an unbearably loud, disorienting noise, the Israelites heard it at a tolerable volume. This miracle is alluded to in the verse, יַרְעֵם אֵל בְּקוֹלוֹ נִפְלָאוֹת, *God thunders marvelously with His voice* (Job 37:5) — He can project a sound that exists simultaneously at different decibel levels.

בַּיּוֹם הַהוּא — *On that day.*

Throughout the entire day (*Kli Yakar*).

וַיִּנָּגְפוּ לִפְנֵי יִשְׂרָאֵל — *So that they were defeated by Israel.*

Just as the Israelites had requested of God (see above, verse 8), the Philistines began to flee of their own accord. All that the Israelites had to do was chase and kill them (*Malbim*).

11. וַיֵּצְאוּ אַנְשֵׁי יִשְׂרָאֵל — *The men of Israel went out.*

Not all of the Jews chased after the Philistines; only the אֲנָשִׁים, the *powerful men* (*Kli Yakar*).

מִתַּחַת לְבֵית כָּר — *Beneath Beth-car.*

The *Targum* and *Rashi* render this phrase as *at the foot of the plains.*

12. וַיִּקַּח שְׁמוּאֵל אֶבֶן אַחַת — *Samuel then*

1. In contrast with the later behavior of Saul; see below, 14:19 (*Kli Yakar*).

[10] *Samuel was offering up the elevation-offering
when the Philistines approached for the battle
with Israel. HASHEM then thundered with a great
noise on that day against the Philistines and
confounded them, so that they were defeated by
Israel.* [11] *The men of Israel went out of Mizpah
and pursued the Philistines, striking them down
until beneath Beth-car.* [12] *Samuel then took one
rock and placed it between Mizpah and the cliff
and called it Eben-ha'ezer (the Rock of Help),
saying, "HASHEM helped us until here."*

[13] *The Philistines were humbled and no longer
continued to enter the borders of Israel; and the
hand of HASHEM was against the Philistines all the
days of Samuel.*

took one rock.

Samuel built a monument so that passersby would recite the appropriate blessing. Those who had witnessed the miracle would state, בָּרוּךְ שֶׁעָשָׂה לִי נֵס בַּמָּקוֹם הַזֶּה, *Blessed is He Who performed a miracle for me at this place*, and those of future generations would state, בָּרוּךְ שֶׁעָשָׂה נִסִּים לַאֲבוֹתֵינוּ בַּמָּקוֹם הַזֶּה, *Blessed is He Who performed miracles for our forefathers at this place* (*Berachos* 54a; *Shulchan Aruch, Orach Chaim* 218; *Me'am Loez*).

הַשֵּׁן — *The cliff.*

Our translation follows *Rashi.*

Radak avers that this was the proper name of the site — *Hashein* — designated as such because it was a cliff.

עַד־הֵנָּה עֲזָרָנוּ ה׳ — *HASHEM helped us until here.*

Until this point, Hashem's salvation was clearly evident, for the Philistines retreated without the Israelites even having lifted a sword. Beyond this point, when the Israelites pursued the Philistines, the Hand of Hashem was camouflaged by their actions (*Metzudos, Malbim*).

13. וַיִּכָּנְעוּ הַפְּלִשְׁתִּים — *The Philistines were humbled.*

They were humbled by their fear (*Kli Yakar*).

וַתְּהִי יַד־ה׳ בַּפְּלִשְׁתִּים — *And the hand of HASHEM was against the Philistines.*

The Israelites crossed the Philistine border to repossess the cities that the Philistines had taken (as detailed in the next verse) (*Metzudos*).

Targum renders וַתְּהִי יַד־ה׳ בַּפְּלִשְׁתִּים as *the fear of HASHEM lay upon the Philistines.*

כֹּל יְמֵי שְׁמוּאֵל — *All the days of Samuel.*

A national leader is responsible for the internal well-being of the state and for its security against external threats. Samuel was successful in both regards: the Jews achieved a sound judicial system (verses 15,17) and attained peace with the Philistines and Amorites (verses 13,14; *Malbim*).

Unfortunately, this ideal condition did not continue throughout Samuel's life. When he grew old and was no longer able to travel in order to judge and reprove the Jewish people, they again began to sin; in consequence, they forfeited their special Divine protection, as a result of which the Philistines were again able to invade their

יד וַתָּשֹׁבְנָה הֶעָרִים אֲשֶׁר לָקְחוּ־פְלִשְׁתִּים מֵאֵת
יִשְׂרָאֵל ׀ לְיִשְׂרָאֵל מֵעֶקְרוֹן וְעַד־גַּת וְאֶת־
גְּבוּלָן הִצִּיל יִשְׂרָאֵל מִיַּד פְּלִשְׁתִּים וַיְהִי שָׁלוֹם
טו בֵּין יִשְׂרָאֵל וּבֵין הָאֱמֹרִי: וַיִּשְׁפֹּט שְׁמוּאֵל
טז אֶת־יִשְׂרָאֵל כֹּל יְמֵי חַיָּיו: וְהָלַךְ מִדֵּי שָׁנָה
בְּשָׁנָה וְסָבַב בֵּית־אֵל וְהַגִּלְגָּל וְהַמִּצְפָּה וְשָׁפַט

territory (see Chapter 13).

As we will later see, the Jews requested a king specifically so that he would guard them against these Philistine incursions (see below, 9:16). This request angered Hashem, for had they refrained from sinning they would have merited Hashem's safekeeping, and the need for a king would never have developed (*Radak*).

14. וַתָּשֹׁבְנָה הֶעָרִים — *The cities ... reverted.*

As described in the beginning of *Judges* (1:18), these cities had been conquered by the tribe of Judah and were apparently afterward captured by the Philistines (*Radak*).

וְאֶת־גְּבוּלָן — *Their surrounding areas.*

Metzudos explains that the Jews regained control over גְּבוּלָן, literally, *their borders,* and were now in a position to repulse further Philistine raids.

וַיְהִי שָׁלוֹם בֵּין יִשְׂרָאֵל וּבֵין הָאֱמֹרִי — *There was peace between Israel and the Amorites.*

This is a reference to the Amorites who were not conquered by the first Israelites to arrive in the Holy Land (see *Judges* 1:34-36).

Scripture makes no mention of war between the Amorites and the Jews. Presumably, however, the Amorites were a hostile force until the Jews subdued the Philistines, following which the Amorites sued for peace (*Radak*).

Kli Yakar suggests that the Israelites and Amorites had been competing for limited space (see *Judges* 1:34). Now that Israel reconquered the cities that the Philistines had seized so that its territory expanded, that dispute was resolved.

◆§ Samuel's Unique System of Judgment

15. The statement that "there was peace" precedes this verse, in order to indicate that peace prevails in the merit of justice (*Me'am Loez*).

כֹּל יְמֵי חַיָּיו — *All the days of his life.*

This statement cannot be accepted literally, for obviously Samuel did not judge during his entire lifetime — i.e., from the moment of his birth to that of his death.

Rather, Samuel started his career as Chief Judge as an adult, with the death of Eli (whose own 40 years' career as Chief Judge began just prior to Samuel's conception; see above, 1:9, *Rashi* ad loc.).

Most commentators explain this phrase to mean that once Samuel began to judge, he did not cease doing so until his death — a period of 13 years. (According to this, Samuel was 39 years of age when Eli died, and he lived to the age of 52 [*Taanis* 5b].)

Abarbanel elaborates on this point. Samuel's lifetime extended through the events regarding King Saul and King David of the following chapters, and his death is not mentioned until Ch. 25 (v. 1). Prior to describing the monarchy of Saul, the present verse encapsulates Samuel's career. Accordingly, it states that Samuel judged *all the days of his life* until his death, and even during his last two years, when Saul was already ruling as king.

Our Sages, however, interpret this verse as inclusive of the beginning of Samuel's life. It is true that Samuel did

[14]*The cities that the Philistines had taken from Israel reverted to Israel, from Ekron to Gath; and Israel rescued their surrounding areas from the hand of the Philistines. Furthermore, there was peace between Israel and the Amorites.*

[15]*Samuel judged Israel all the days of his life.* [16]*He would travel year after year, circling to Beth-el, Gilgal, and Mizpah, and judging*

not literally judge from the moment of his birth; however, he was given Divine recompense as though that were indeed the case.

This idea is reflected in the following Midrashim regarding the Levites.

According to one Midrash (*Bamidbar Rabbah* 3:10), Scripture states that the members of the Levitical family of Kehath from the age of one month and older were שֹׁמְרֵי מִשְׁמֶרֶת הַקֹּדֶשׁ, *the guardians of the charge of the sanctity* (*Numbers* 3:28). The explanation for this is that Hashem rewarded them for their service as if they had served all their lives. (This was due to the fact that although the family of Kehath suffered many casualties because of the danger involved in carrying the Ark, they nevertheless rushed enthusiastically to carry the Ark.)

A similar passage in *Numbers* (3:15) directs Moses to count the members of the tribe of Levi from the age of one month and up. Although Levites at that age were clearly not involved in the Tabernacle service, Hashem included them in the census so that they would be rewarded as if they had served their entire lives (*Bamidbar Rabbah* 3:8).

In the same way, Samuel (himself a Levite from the family of Kehath — see above, comm. to 1:1) was credited for his deeds, including his role as judge, as if he had performed them *all of his life* (*Bamidbar Rabbah* 3:8,10, as explained by *Kli Yakar*).[1]

Me'am Loez cites two alternative explanations of this verse.

(a). Samuel's sole profession was the Torah. Since he was focused on the goal of judging Israel, he is considered as if he had done so for his entire life.

(b). From the time that Samuel was 2 years old and brought to Eli in Shiloh, he began to act as a decisor of Torah law for 50 years until his death. (Significantly, the numerical value of the word כֹּל in כֹּל יְמֵי חַיָּיו, *all the days of his life*, is 50.)

16. וְהָלַךְ מִדֵּי שָׁנָה בְּשָׁנָה — *He would travel year after year.*

Samuel did so in order to save the Jewish people the trouble of traveling to him (*Malbim*).

The choice of the word הָלַךְ, *went*, implies that Samuel journeyed slowly and patiently. Although traveling makes most people tense and anxious, Samuel judged every case carefully and deliberately, in accordance with the Mishnaic dictum, הֱווּ מְתוּנִים בַּדִּין, *Be deliberate in judgment* (*Pirkei Avos* 1:1; *Me'am Loez*).

וְסָבַב בֵּית־אֵל וְהַגִּלְגָּל וְהַמִּצְפָּה — *Circling to Beth-el, Gilgal, and Mizpah.*

Samuel chose these particular loca-

1. Yet another Midrash (*Midrash Tehillim* 92) states that every Levite is enlisted in the heavenly army while still in his mother's womb.

The source of this idea is the fact that Jocheved, daughter of Levi, is accounted one of the seventy souls who arrived in Egypt together with Jacob, even though at the time she still reposed in her mother's womb (*Genesis* 46:26, *Rashi*; *Bamidbar Rabbah* 3:8).

יז אֶת־יִשְׂרָאֵל אֵת כָּל־הַמְּקוֹמוֹת הָאֵלֶּה: וּתְשֻׁבָתוֹ
הָרָמָתָה כִּי־שָׁם בֵּיתוֹ וְשָׁם שָׁפָט אֶת־יִשְׂרָאֵל
וַיִּבֶן־שָׁם מִזְבֵּחַ לַיהוָה:

tions because each one was suffused with the Divine Presence throughout Jewish history.

Gilgal was the first home for the Tabernacle after Joshua brought the Israelites into the land of Israel (see *Joshua* 5:10, *Zevachim* 112b), where it remained for 14 years. (Gilgal was also the site where Samuel later crowned King Saul [below, 11:14,15].)

This mention of Beth-el is actually (according to *Abarbanel*) a reference to Shiloh, which is sometimes given this designation because it hosted the Sanctuary for 319 years (Beth-el literally means *House of God*; see *Judges* 21:24, *Abarbanel*).

Mizpah, as mentioned above (verse 6), was a place of Jewish assembly, and attracted a special Godly influence (*Abarbanel*).

וְשָׁפַט אֶת־יִשְׂרָאֵל — *And judging Israel.*

Jews from the surrounding areas would come for judgment (*Kli Yakar*).

In correcting others, Samuel was performing the Biblical commandment הוֹכֵחַ תּוֹכִיחַ אֶת־עֲמִיתֶךָ, *you shall reprove your fellow* (*Leviticus* 19:17).

This passage raises the question of whether a Jew is obligated to actively look for people acting improperly in order to correct them, as did Samuel.

Sdei Chemed (Vol. 6, *Asifas HaDinim*, letter *Hei*, 2) discusses this issue and concludes that whereas a private individual is not obligated to seek out such occasions, the leader of the generation (as well as the head of a household in his home) is responsible to search out people's iniquities and reform them (see *Nachalas Shimon*).

As mentioned previously, Samuel's father Elkanah used to travel about in order to influence people to go on pilgrimage to Jerusalem (see above, 1:3), and therefore merited to have a son who would perform the noble and greatly lauded act of touring Israel to spread Torah.

Samuel was rewarded "measure for measure" for his personal service. Just as Samuel traveled to the Jewish people, so too did Hashem come to Samuel to speak with him (*Shemos Rabbah* 16:4; see above, 3:10 and comm.).

17. וּתְשֻׁבָתוֹ הָרָמָתָה — *Then he would return to Ramah.*

Why must Scripture inform us of this seemingly slight detail?

One answer is that — unlike many judges and lecturers — Samuel was beloved not only by those whom he met briefly on his travels, but also at home by the people who knew him best; he did not travel merely because of a lack of popularity in his hometown. (His success in dealing with people has been documented above [2:26].) Accordingly, he was always welcome to *return to Ramah.*

Also, this verse teaches that after all of Samuel's strenuous circuits, in which he surely met some difficult trials and obstacles, he always *returned to Ramah* as pure and sinless as he had been on his departure. In a similar spirit, the Talmudic sage, Rav, would pray before judging cases, וּלְוַאי שֶׁתְּהֵא בִּיאָה כִּיצִיאָה, *May my return be as my going forth,* i.e., may I not deliver any erroneous judgment (*Sanhedrin* 7b; *Me'am Loez*).

הָרָמָתָה — *To Ramah.*

See above, 1:1 and comm., and 1:19.

כִּי־שָׁם בֵּיתוֹ — *For his home was there* (lit., *in Ramah*)

Our Sages apply the word שָׁם, *there,* homiletically to the cities mentioned in the previous verse: Wherever [Samuel] would go, *there was his home* (*Berachos* 10b, *Nedarim* 38a; see *Kli Yakar* and *Maharsha* to *Nedarim* 38a). That is to say,

7/17 *Israel in all these places.* 17 *Then he would return to Ramah, for his home was there, and there he would judge Israel. And there he built an altar to HASHEM.*

he would pitch his own tent and carry his own utensils.[1] This was part of Samuel's policy of not benefiting from others, even when he was entitled to do so. As Samuel himself proclaimed, the animals that he used for public offerings and the donkey upon which he rode during his many journeys were supplied by his own funds (below, 12:3, *Bamidbar Rabbah* 18:10).[2]

The Talmud (*Berachos* ibid.) explains that a public figure may benefit from the public if he wishes to do so, as did Elisha (*II Kings* Ch. 4), or choose to eschew such aid, as did Samuel, without fear of suspected haughtiness or ill feelings (*Rashi*).

Mishbetzos Zahav comments that it is possible that Samuel wished to differentiate himself from Eli's sons. They sinned by taking too much from others; Samuel went to the other extreme, by not accepting even what he was entitiled to.

The issue of whether Rabbinic scholars may accept public funds to facilitate their work is the subject of a major controversy amid the halachic decisors. In the process of this discourse, *Rambam* states that no proof can be adduced from the case of Elisha, for he received no regular stipend but, at most, occasional meals (*Pirkei Avos* 4:5).

The prevalent custom, concludes *Rema*, is to permit scholars to make use of public funds, although a person who refrains from doing so is highly commendable (*Yoreh De'ah* 246:21; see *Rema, Shach, Taz,* ibid.; *Nachalas Shimon* 31:24).

וְשָׁם שָׁפָט אֶת־יִשְׂרָאֵל — *And there he would judge Israel.*

וְשָׁם, *and there,* clearly refers to Ramah. Even after returning home from his exhausting travels, Samuel's homecoming was not for relaxation (*Malbim*); rather, he would continue to judge the local people and others who came to him in Ramah because they didn't live near the cities of his tour (*Radak*). When there was a lull in this activity, Samuel did not sit idle but וַיִּבֶן־שָׁם מִזְבֵּחַ לַה׳, *he built there an altar to HASHEM,* so as never to interrupt his service (*Malbim, Kli Yakar*).

Me'am Loez notes that the phrase, וְשָׁם שָׁפָט אֶת־יִשְׂרָאֵל, *[even] there he would judge Israel,* teaches that although Samuel was a national figure, he did not ignore the residents of his hometown but judged them as well. In addition, although he was personally acquainted with them, he judged them with scrupulous impartiality.

וַיִּבֶן־שָׁם מִזְבֵּחַ לַה׳ — *And there he built an altar to HASHEM.*

This phrase provides conclusive proof that during the period that the Tabernacle stood in Nob, offerings on private altars were permitted (*Yerushalmi Megillah* 1:12; see above, comm. to verse 9, 6:14).

1. The Talmud (*Nedarim* 38a) derives from here that Samuel was wealthy.

2. *Chofetz Chaim* provides a novel homiletical approach to this verse. Samuel's focus in life was always הָרָמָתָה — regarding דְּבָרִים הָעוֹמְדִים בְּרוּמוֹ שֶׁל עוֹלָם, *matters that are in the heights of the world* (spiritual pursuits), כִּי שָׁם בֵּיתוֹ, *because his "house,"* or permanent dwelling, is in the eternal spiritual world, not in this transient world.

In a similar vein, *Torah Bar Nash* cites the *Vilna Gaon,* who says that the word שָׁמַיִם, *heaven,* derives from the world שָׁם, *there,* because from anyone's perspective, heaven is far away. Accordingly, although Samuel's travels did not offer him much in the area of delicacies and gastronomical pleasures, he was satisfied with simple provisions כִּי־שָׁם בֵּיתוֹ, *because his "home"* was שָׁם, in the heavens, i.e., his mind was in the eternal world.

א וַיְהִי כַּאֲשֶׁר זָקֵן שְׁמוּאֵל וַיָּשֶׂם אֶת־בָּנָיו שֹׁפְטִים
ב לְיִשְׂרָאֵל: וַיְהִי שֶׁם־בְּנוֹ הַבְּכוֹר יוֹאֵל וְשֵׁם
ג מִשְׁנֵהוּ אֲבִיָּה שֹׁפְטִים בִּבְאֵר שָׁבַע: וְלֹא־הָלְכוּ
בָנָיו °בדרכו וַיִּטּוּ אַחֲרֵי הַבָּצַע וַיִּקְחוּ־שֹׁחַד °בִּדְרָכָיו ק׳

VIII

1. Since Samuel was no longer well enough to travel throughout the Land of Israel and judge the people, he divided his circuit into two halves, which he assigned to his two sons (*Malbim*).

וַיְהִי כַּאֲשֶׁר זָקֵן שְׁמוּאֵל — *When Samuel grew old ...*

The Talmud (*Taanis* 5b) relates that Samuel died at the relatively young age of 52 (see Timeline in Appendix); however, he aged prematurely and appeared to be elderly. The reason for this is as follows. After Saul sinned and God sentenced him to die, Samuel prayed that Saul's kingdom not end within his own lifetime, so that he should not witness the failure of his handiwork. This meant that Samuel had to die at the age of 52, prior to the date that God had chosen for David's ascension to the crown. Samuel's death at such an early age might lead people to believe that he had been punished for having committed some moral offense. To avoid this supposition, God caused Samuel to age prematurely (over a period of years — *Me'am Loez*), so that it would appear as if he died an old man.

Kli Yakar finds an allusion to this idea in the phrase כַּאֲשֶׁר זָקֵן שְׁמוּאֵל, *when Samuel grow old*, which can also mean *as if Samuel grew old* — i.e., it seemed *as if* he had aged.

Abarbanel, however, reads this verse literally and states that Samuel lived to be 70 or 80 years old. *Abarbanel* thus disputes the premises upon which the Sages calculate Samuel's age (see Timeline in Appendix). For instance, one factor that the Sages refer to in determining Samuel's age is the period of time that the Ark was in Kiriath-je'arim. The Sages state that the Ark remained there for exactly 20 years. However, *Abarbanel* points out that a precise reading of Scripture (7:2) permits the conclusion that the Ark was there much longer — and thus Samuel was much older than the Sages allow. Of course, as *Kli Yakar* succinctly states, we heed the words of the Sages, "whose waters we drink."

וַיָּשֶׂם אֶת־בָּנָיו שֹׁפְטִים לְיִשְׂרָאֵל — *He appointed his sons judges over Israel.*

The fact that Samuel appointed his sons judges shows that they were worthy of the role. *Me'am Loez* qualifies this by stating that indeed, initially they were fit, and only with the passage of time did they grow somewhat corrupt and no longer deserved it.

Derashos HaRan, however, disagrees, and states that although they were not as pious as their father, they never ceased being worthy of the position. (Thus, the Jews' subsequent request that Samuel's sons be replaced by a king was unwarranted.)

Why did Samuel choose his sons in particular? Is there a rule of inheritance regarding a Rabbinic position such as Samuel's? *Rambam* (*Hil. Melachim* 1:7) rules that, indeed, not only is the throne of a king inherited, but any appointed position of leadership is also passed on to one's offspring, as long as they follow in his footsteps.[1]

Chasam Sofer (*Teshuvos, Orach Chaim* #12), however, disputes this view, and states that only a position of secular rulership may be bequeathed as an inheritance. However, a position of sanctity — such as a Rabbinic post — is not transfer-

1. *Rambam*'s ruling is based on *Sifrei* (*Kesef Mishneh*).

[1] *When Samuel grew old, he appointed his sons*
judges over Israel. [2] *The name of his firstborn*
son was Joel and the name of his second was Abijah;
they were judges in Beer-sheba. [3] *But his sons did*
not follow his ways. They were swayed by profit;

able to one's children (with the exception of the role of Kohen Gadol). Accordingly, Samuel had his sons replace him not because they had an intrinsic legal right to the post but because he considered them the most qualified men available.

However, even according to this view, it is possible that one's offspring have legal *preference* over anyone else, as long as they are worthy (see *Mishnas Yaavetz, Yoreh Deah* #36; *Mishbetzos Zahav;* see also *Nachalas Shimon* #18).

2. וַיְהִי שֶׁם־בְּנוֹ הַבְּכוֹר יוֹאֵל וְשֵׁם מִשְׁנֵהוּ אֲבִיָּה — *The name of his firstborn son was Joel and the name of his second was Abijah.*

Verse 3 will describe Samuel's sons as having engaged in scurrilous behavior, and that is already hinted at now. Thus, the present verse does not refer to Abijah conventionally as הַמִּשְׁנֶה, *the second,* but as מִשְׁנֵהוּ, *his second.* This emphatic possessive pronoun indicates that when Joel's corruption grew apparent, the people thought that Samuel's second son would be better, but he followed in his brother's footsteps (*Maharzu, Bamidbar Rabbah* 10:5).

Ultimately, however, both sons repented, and that too is alluded to in the syntax of this verse, which states, "his name was ..." (as opposed to "... was his name") — a phraseology that refers specifically to a righteous person (Midrash; see above, 1:1).

This is alluded to as well in *I Chronicles* (6:13), where Samuel's older son is called וַשְׁנִי, a word derived from שִׁינּוּי, *change* — because he changed for the better (*Maharzu*). Indeed, he became a prophet: Joel, son of Pethuel, whose prophecies are recorded in *Trei Asar* (see *Yalkut* ibid. for why Samuel was called Pethuel). As for Abijah, the Midrash (*Yalkut Shimoni, Joel* 1:1) notes that the word used here, מִשְׁנֵהוּ, *his second,* can also mean *to change,* and thus indicates homiletically that he too *changed* his ways. And the word מִשְׁנֵהוּ also implies a *pair* — i.e., the two sons were similar — which is to say that like Joel, Abijah eventually received Divine inspiration (*Maharzu*).

שֹׁפְטִים בִּבְאֵר שָׁבַע — *They were judges in Beer-sheba.*

Beer-sheba is the southernmost city of the land of Israel (see *II Samuel* 17:11).

Ralbag suggests that since the aging Samuel could no longer travel that far south, he stationed his sons there.

Radak holds this choice of venue against the sons. Not only did they fail to circulate throughout the land but they settled at its farthest bounds, forcing Jews in need of adjudication to make a long and wearying journey.

Kli Yakar derives from the verse's two seemingly superfluous usages of the word שֵׁם, *name,* that these sons were judges in name only. Although they sought the prestige of the judgeship, they did not possess the requisite concern for the poor and suffering.

3. This was a fulfillment of Eli's curse that just as his own sons had not maintained his standard, so would those of Samuel (see above, 3:17). Although this curse was made contingent on conditions that did not eventuate, it nevertheless retained its potency (*Makkos* 11a).

This verse indicates that Samuel's sons committed serious offenses. Our Sages, however, interpret the verse figuratively, in a way that mitigates the severity of their sins.

We will first present the literal explanations of these words as per the commentators, and then the Midrashic interpretations.

וַיִּטּוּ אַחֲרֵי הַבָּצַע — *They were swayed by profit.*

ד וַיַּטּוּ מִשְׁפָּט: וַיִּתְקַבְּצוּ כֹּל זִקְנֵי
ה יִשְׂרָאֵל וַיָּבֹאוּ אֶל־שְׁמוּאֵל הָרָמָתָה: וַיֹּאמְרוּ אֵלָיו

Targum renders בֶּצַע, *profit,* as *dishonest money.*

Radak, however, understands בֶּצַע to simply mean that they were attracted to profit, which led them to accept bribes. Scripture states that a judge must be a שׂוֹנֵא בָּצַע (*Exodus* 18:21) — he must *hate money* (not just illicit gains), and be satisfied with his lot.

The verb ויט is used twice in this verse, with different vowelizations: the first time reflexively, to indicate that they *were swayed* by the desire for money, and the second time causatively, to state that they caused justice to be *swayed* or *perverted* (*Rashi*).

וַיִּקְחוּ־שֹׁחַד וַיַּטּוּ מִשְׁפָּט — *They took bribes, and they perverted justice.*

Malbim comments that although initially Samuel's sons were swayed by legal means of gaining profit, that eventually led them to accept bribes and pervert justice (see *Deuteronomy* 16:19; *Ralbag*).

We now list some of the views of our Sages regarding the misdeeds of Samuel's sons.

❐ In contrast to Samuel, who traveled among the people to judge them, his sons stayed in their own place (*Shabbos* 56a). This is implicit in the words, וְלֹא־הָלְכוּ בָנָיו בִּדְרָכָיו, they *did not follow in his ways,* which can be understood hyper-literally to mean that they did not go upon the pathways that he had traveled (*Maharsha*). Their motivation was to provide more business for their court officials and scribes who received payment for their services. This is what is meant by their being drawn to profit.

Whether or not Samuel's sons were obligated to travel in order to judge the people seems to be a matter of dispute among the halachic decisors.

Some state, based on this verse, that they were indeed responsible to do so (see *Tur, Choshen Mishpat* #9, *Bach* #8; *Bach* adds that nowadays this obligation no longer applies).

Others consider Samuel's behavior to have been an act of exceptional piety and not mandatory upon his sons. Their behavior was held against them only because they should have maintained his exemplary standards (*Meiri; Derishah;* see *Nachalas Shimon* 18:1).[1]

❐ They were Levites and requested that the people give them their tithes. Since they were highly respected, no one refused them and, as a result, the poor Levites were left with nothing (*Shabbos* 56a).

❐ They forcibly took more than their share of tithes (ibid.).

❐ They accepted favors from people who subsequently came to them for judgment, which was considered tantamount to bribery. Whether this was legally prohibited or merely unseemly is the subject of dispute (see *Birkei Yosef, Choshen Mishpat* 9:12).

❐ According to *Midrash Shmuel* (7:4), they judged people who had previously

1. *Mishbetzos Zahav* adds an interesting insight. The nation at that time "judged its judges" (*Ruth* 1:1) —meaning that the people criticized their judges (*Bava Basra* 15b) and demanded the highest standards of conduct from them. The people found a man worthy of their standards in Samuel. Because he took nothing from them — not even his traveling expenses — they did not suspect him of accepting bribes, and they accepted his reproach and his judgments. During such a time, it was incumbent upon Samuel's sons to emulate his example. The fact that they did not do so was considered comparable to accepting bribes.

they took bribes and they perverted justice.
[4] *All the elders of Israel then gathered together*
and came to Samuel, to Ramah. [5] *They said to him,*

brought them tithes, which gave the appearance of bribery (*Pnei Moshe*).

❐ A Midrash (*Bereishis Rabbah* 85:12) relates that Samuel's sons would interrupt courtroom proceedings when they saw a passing caravan in order to engage in business. *Kli Yakar* elucidates the nature of this sin: when at work, judges may not allow themselves to be distracted by personal business concerns. Samuel's sons' behavior thus constituted a perversion of justice, although one that was inadvertent, since it was due to their being distracted.

Why didn't Samuel reprove them for their actions? Why weren't they punished like the sons of Eli?

Abarbanel raises these questions and provides two answers. One is that their actions were not done publicly, as were the sins of Eli's sons. It is even possible that Samuel was unaware of them. Also, Eli's sons failed in their mission as Kohanim, a Divinely appointed position, in a way that made them deserving of death. Samuel's sons were appointed by their father, and their sin of bribery is not punishable by death. They were justly punished with the loss of their positions of authority, and, when Samuel heard about it, he told the people (below, 12:2) וּבָנַי הִנָּם אִתְּכֶם, *and as for my sons, here they are with you,* implying that the people should not absolve them on his account but punish them.

4. *Malbim* suggests that as a result of the perversion of justice implemented by Samuel's sons, the Jews were once again subjugated to the Philistines, from whom they had been liberated during Samuel's jurisdiction. Thus, the Jews now gathered to seek a solution to this servitude.

◆§ Jewish Monarchy

To understand the next few verses, an extensive introduction is in place. This episode, involving the Israelites' demand for a monarch and the extremely negative, yet yielding, response that they received, is a most intriguing one. Various questions must be answered in shedding light upon this topic. Among them:

❐ There is an explicit discussion in the Torah (*Deuteronomy* 17:14-20; see below) governing the appointment of a Jewish king. Is the Torah stating a command, or merely an option?

❐ Whether it is mandatory or optional, it is clearly permissible. Why, then, were the Jews so severely criticized for requesting it?

❐ Furthermore, if they erred by requesting a king, why did Hashem oblige in fulfilling their wish?

We will address these issues one at a time. We begin by citing and analyzing the verses in *Deuteronomy* that discuss the appointment of kings.

כִּי־תָבֹא אֶל־הָאָרֶץ אֲשֶׁר ה׳ אֱלֹהֶיךָ נֹתֵן לָךְ וִירִשְׁתָּהּ וְיָשַׁבְתָּה בָּהּ וְאָמַרְתָּ אָשִׂימָה עָלַי מֶלֶךְ כְּכָל־הַגּוֹיִם אֲשֶׁר סְבִיבֹתָי. שׂוֹם תָּשִׂים עָלֶיךָ מֶלֶךְ אֲשֶׁר יִבְחַר ה׳ אֱלֹהֶיךָ בּוֹ מִקֶּרֶב אַחֶיךָ תָּשִׂים עָלֶיךָ מֶלֶךְ ..., *When you come to the Land that HASHEM, your God, gives you, and you possess it and settle in it, and you say, "I will set a king over myself, like all the nations that are around me," you shall surely set over yourself a king whom HASHEM, your God, shall choose; from among your brethren shall you set a king over yourself* (*Deuteronomy* 17:14,15).

According to the Talmudic sage, Rabbi Yehudah, these verses mandate that the Jews appoint a king, as one of three missions that they had to accomplish upon their arrival in the Land of

Israel.[1] His counterpart, Rabbi Nehorai, however, disagrees. He derives from the phrase, וְאָמַרְתָּ אָשִׂימָה עָלַי מֶלֶךְ, *and you say, "I will set a king over myself...,"* that appointing a king is dependent upon the Jews proclaiming that they want one (*Sanhedrin* 20b).

Rambam cites Rabbi Yehudah's view as being halachically authoritative (*Hil. Melachim* 1:1).

Ramban, however, is troubled by the phrase, *like all the nations that are around me*, in which the Jews seemingly express a desire to emulate other nations — something that the Torah would surely not endorse. *Ramban* thus seemingly moves in the direction of Rabbi Nehorai's interpretation and concludes that the passage is predictive of the future, i.e., the time will come when Jews will petition to have a king like all other nations (a reference to the current episode of Samuel's generation). When that happens, they are to appoint a king in accordance with the conditions stipulated by the Torah.[2]

Many sources seem to support the view that it is advantageous to the Jews to have a monarch. Throughout the Book of *Judges*, reference is made to the people's corruption since *during those days, there was no king in Israel* (17:6, cf. 18:1,19:1,21:25). The prophecies about Messianic times focus on a king from the Davidic dynasty. And *Rabbeinu Bachya* states that in the Kabbalistic literature, *kingdom* is the fourth leg of the esoteric Chariot, which is represented on earth by the king of Israel, whose presence is therefore essential.

However, *Abarbanel* disagrees and states that the Jewish nation should avoid the institution of the monarchy. He explains that a king fulfills three functions: he wages war, passes legislation, and punishes criminals. But these functions are already fulfilled in the Torah system: God conducts the wars of the nation (see *Deuteronomy* 33:29), the Torah presents a system of legislation, and judges punish wrongdoers and maintain a civil society (ibid. 16:18, 17:8-13). The existence of a monarchy, therefore, is undesirable and is permitted by the Torah only to mitigate the Jews' evil inclination, which would otherwise find expression in even more egregious behavior. In this, it is similar to the law that allows a Jewish soldier to have relations with a "captured beautiful woman" (*Deuteronomy* 21:10-15; see *Rashi* ad loc.), so as to provide a permissible outlet for an otherwise uncontrollable desire.

Ohr HaChaim presents another interpretation of these verses. There are two types of monarch: an improper king, who rules based on his own ideas and wages war relying on his own strength, and a proper king, who is a trustworthy servant of Hashem and earns God's grace on behalf of His people, adding honor and glory to Israel. Both types are alluded to in the passage from *Deuteronomy*. The words, *And you say, "I will set a king over myself, like all the nations ...,"* refer to the improper type of king, and the words, *You shall surely set over yourself a king whom HASHEM, your God, will choose*, refer to the proper, God-fearing king.

Ohr HaChaim's reading of this passage is in line with the opinion of Rabbi Yehudah that appointing a king is mandatory. Furthermore, *Ohr HaChaim* adds that Rabbi Nehorai too may hold the view that although there is no intrinsic obligation to install a king, if the Jews demand a king, then they are obligated to do so.

Why did Samuel and Hashem admonish the Israelites for requesting a king? According to *Abarbanel*, the reason is simple: the institution of the

1. If that is the case, why didn't Joshua or the subsequent Judges install a king? *Kli Yakar* (to Prophets) explains that the command was to take effect only when the Jews had the wherewithal to do so, but generations of Joshua and his successor Judges were occupied with conquering and settling the Land of Israel.

2. This view is shared by *Ibn Ezra*.

monarchy is intrinsically undesirable, especially for the Jews. In line with the approach of *Ohr HaChaim*, the Jews may be understood to have requested the wrong type of king.

But according to those who maintain that the appointment of a king is permissible and perhaps even obligatory, why did Samuel and then Hashem react angrily to the Jews' supplication?

According to *Sifrei*, the problem with the Jews' request lay in their motive, as revealed by their request, *Now, appoint for us a king to judge us, like all the nations* (v. 5), which implies that they wanted a king who would permit idol worship. Thus, Hashem responded to Samuel, *[Just as] they abandoned Me and worshiped the gods of others, so are they doing to you as well!* (v. 8).

Similarly, *Ralbag* explains that the Jews wanted a king who would rule in accordance with his own whims — as gentile kings did — and not in accordance with Torah law.

Many commentators (among them *Rashi* and *Radak*) contend that the Israelite elders petitioned properly, but that the common people demanded a sovereign who would be *like all the nations* (see *Sanhedrin* 20b). Thus, those presenting this request are referred to repeatedly as הָעָם, *the people*. In so doing, they demonstrated a lack of trust in Hashem's protection (*Radak*).

Some explain that the Jews were wrong to request a king within the lifetime of Samuel, a prophet who ruled justly and who had led the people to military victory. By rejecting such a man, they were in effect rejecting Hashem Himself (v. 7).[1] *Ramban* (to *Genesis* 49:10) adds that Hashem accordingly punished the Jews by not giving them a permanent king. Instead, He coronated King Saul, who did not descend from the tribe of Judah and whose kingdom was therefore short-lived.

Derashos HaRan (*Derush* #11) explains that the Jews erred in requesting a king who would judge them on a day-to-day basis, for that would usurp the role of the Sanhedrin, whose function was to rule and judge according to Torah law. They should have instead requested a king who would restrict himself to maintaining a civil society and passing and enforcing laws germane to the time.

A novel approach is advanced by *Kli Yakar* on the *Chumash*. He explains that the Torah specifically commands the Jews to request אָשִׂימָה עָלַי מֶלֶךְ, *I will set a king over myself* — a king to whom *they* will be completely subservient. The Jews, however, stated, שִׂימָה־לָּנוּ מֶלֶךְ, *Appoint for us a king* (v. 5), implying that he would be subject to *their* will. Hashem responded by presenting them with a description of the king's absolute authority, ending with the statement that the king יִמְלֹךְ עֲלֵיהֶם, *will reign over them* (v. 9). The Jews subsequently admitted their error and agreed that כִּי אִם־מֶלֶךְ יִהְיֶה עָלֵינוּ, *There shall be a king over us* (v. 19) — a king to whom they would be subservient.

If the Jews erred in their request for a king, why did Hashem fulfill it?

According to one view, in making this request the Jews demonstrated their unreadiness to place their complete trust in Hashem. Recognizing this, Hashem allowed them to establish a substitute in the form of a human monarch. This is in accordance with the principle that people have freedom of choice, even if they choose the wrong thing (see *Ramban*, *Numbers* 13:2; *Chovos HaLevavos*, Preface to *Shaar HaBitachon*).

Be'er Moshe suggests that the Jews' request was granted for two reasons. First, they ultimately repented and asked for a king who would rule *over* them — i.e., whose Torah authority they would unreservedly accept (as per *Kli Yakar*, above). Second, they stated that they wanted a king who would וְנִלְחַם אֶת־מִלְחֲמוֹתֵינוּ, *fight our wars* (v. 20), making it clear that they did not want the king to usurp the role of the Sanhedrin but who would act within his authority as the nation's military commander.

1. *Maharsha* (to *Sanhedrin* 20b) traces this explanation to a *Tosefta* (*Sanhedrin* 4:3).

הִנֵּה֙ אַתָּ֣ה זָקַ֔נְתָּ וּבָנֶ֕יךָ לֹ֥א הָלְכ֖וּ בִּדְרָכֶ֑יךָ
עַתָּ֗ה שִֽׂימָה־לָּ֥נוּ מֶ֛לֶךְ לְשָׁפְטֵ֖נוּ כְּכָל־הַגּוֹיִֽם׃
ו וַיֵּ֤רַע הַדָּבָר֙ בְּעֵינֵ֣י שְׁמוּאֵ֔ל כַּאֲשֶׁר֙ אָֽמְר֔וּ
תְּנָה־לָּ֥נוּ מֶ֖לֶךְ לְשָׁפְטֵ֑נוּ וַיִּתְפַּלֵּ֥ל שְׁמוּאֵ֖ל אֶל־
ז יהוָֽה׃ וַיֹּ֤אמֶר יהוה֙ אֶל־שְׁמוּאֵ֔ל
שְׁמַע֙ בְּק֣וֹל הָעָ֔ם לְכֹ֥ל אֲשֶׁר־יֹאמְר֖וּ אֵלֶ֑יךָ כִּ֣י לֹ֤א

Earlier we cited the view that it was specifically הָעָם, *the common people,* who petitioned improperly for a king. The verse that closes this passage refers to אַנְשֵׁי יִשְׂרָאֵל, *the "men" of Israel* (v. 22), indicating that now the people were acting in accordance with the standards expected of the nation *of Israel,* and presented their petition properly.

5. הִנֵּה אַתָּה זָקַנְתָּ — *Behold! You are old.*

According to *Metzudos,* the Jews were complaining that Samuel was too weak to function as their judge.

Arugas HaBosem homiletically interprets this verse to mean that the nation complained that Samuel was out of touch with the times, the proof being that בָנֶיךָ לֹא הָלְכוּ בִּדְרָכֶיךָ, even *your sons did not follow your ways.*[1]

שִׂימָה־לָּנוּ מֶלֶךְ — *Appoint for us a king.*

See *Kli Yakar* in the preface to Jewish Monarchy. *Rabbeinu Bachya* comments on the commandment (*Deuteronomy* 17:15), שׂוֹם תָּשִׂים עָלֶיךָ מֶלֶךְ, that the word שׂוֹם is a surprising choice to denote "appoint." It should have said תְּמַנֶּה or תָּקִים. The word שׂוֹם can be homiletically understood to allude to the word סַם, *drug.* Some drugs heal and enhance life, whereas others cause death. Similarly, depending on the goals of those requesting a king, a monarchy can be either life-sustaining or destructive.

6. וַיֵּרַע הַדָּבָר בְּעֵינֵי שְׁמוּאֵל כַּאֲשֶׁר אָמְרוּ תְּנָה־לָּנוּ מֶלֶךְ לְשָׁפְטֵנוּ — *It was wrong in Samuel's eyes that they said, "Give us a king to judge us."*

There are two discrepancies between the language of this and the previous verse.

First, the previous verse states that the Jews requested שִׂימָה־לָּנוּ מֶלֶךְ, *appoint for us a king,* but in his reiteration here, Samuel changes this to תְּנָה־לָּנוּ מֶלֶךְ , *give us a king.*

Second, whereas the previous verse states that the Jews asked for a king לְשָׁפְטֵנוּ כְּכָל־הַגּוֹיִם, *to judge us, like all the nations,* this verse states only לְשָׁפְטֵנוּ, *to judge us,* and omits the words כְּכָל־הַגּוֹיִם, *like all the nations.*

Be'er Moshe explains the first discrepancy in accordance with the view of *Derashos HaRan* (cited above) that a Jewish king may not act as a judge, for that role belongs exclusively to the Sanhedrin. Samuel was upset that the Jews were requesting a king לְשָׁפְטֵנוּ, *to judge us.* Although they had used the word שִׂימָה, *appoint,* they did not mean it in the way that the Torah does (in *Deuteronomy* 17:15), which allows a king only to exercise his limited prerogatives. Rather, Samuel indicated to them, they wanted him to תְּנָה, *give,* them a king, in the sense expressed by the verse שֹׁפְטִים וְשֹׁטְרִים תִּתֶּן־לְךָ, *You shall **give** yourselves judges and officers* (ibid. 16:18) — i.e., they wanted a king who would have the power vested in a judge.

Malbim addresses the second discrepancy. There are two types of king: one who rules according to Torah law and values, and one who fabricates his own legal system and culture. When the Jews

1. Citing these words, *Mishbetzos Zahav* adds that *Chasam Sofer* wrote in his will, "Never say that times have changed."

"Behold! You are old, and your sons did not follow your ways. So now appoint for us a king to judge us, like all the nations."

6 *It was wrong in Samuel's eyes that they said, "Give us a king to judge us," and Samuel prayed to HASHEM.*

7 *HASHEM said to Samuel, "Listen to the voice of the people in all that they say to you, for it is not*

requested in v. 5, שִׂימָה־לָּנוּ מֶלֶךְ לְשָׁפְטֵנוּ כְּכָל־הַגּוֹיִם, it could be understood either way. They could have meant: שִׂימָה־לָּנוּ מֶלֶךְ כְּכָל־הַגּוֹיִם — לְשָׁפְטֵנוּ, *Appoint for us a king like all nations — to judge us [according to the Torah].* Thus, not rejecting Hashem, but only seeking a replacement for Samuel, with whose manner of judgment they were dissatisfied. Or, they could have meant, *Appoint for us a king who will judge us like all the nations* — i.e., who will establish his own laws and judicial system, and thus they were rejecting Hashem. In this verse, Samuel expresses his favorable judgment of their intent, quoting them as having said that they wanted a king לְשָׁפְטֵנוּ, *to judge us,* implying that they meant the former version, not that they sought a justice system like that of the nations. In the next verse, Hashem informs him that he was mistaken. It was not you that they rejected but Me.

Kli Yakar states that Samuel was upset for two reasons. First, the Jews had the temerity to ask him to his face for a replacement. Second, they requested that Samuel find them a king, rather than asking that Hashem Himself make the choice

וַיִּתְפַּלֵּל שְׁמוּאֵל אֶל־ה׳ — *And Samuel prayed to HASHEM.*

Samuel prayed that he be prophetically inspired to know how to answer them (*Radak; Metzudos*).

According to *Kli Yakar,* Samuel prayed to Hashem not to consider their request sinful.

7. וַיֹּאמֶר ה׳ אֶל־שְׁמוּאֵל שְׁמַע בְּקוֹל הָעָם לְכֹל אֲשֶׁר־יֹאמְרוּ אֵלֶיךָ כִּי לֹא אֹתְךָ מָאָסוּ כִּי־אֹתִי מָאֲסוּ — *HASHEM said to Samuel, "Listen to the voice of the people in all that they say to you, for it is not you whom they have rejected, but it is Me Whom they have rejected."*

How is the fact that the Jewish people rejected not only Samuel but Hashem Himself a reason for him to heed their request?

Metzudos explains Hashem to be saying, "If you cannot bring yourself to continue to act on behalf of the Jewish people after they have rejected you, consider that it is not you whom they have rejected but Myself."

Malbim provides a momentous comment. As mentioned earlier, Samuel originally thought that the Jews were requesting a king who would judge them in accordance with the way of the Torah, until Hashem informed him that they were requesting human leadership in preference to Divine providence. Hashem now tells Samuel that if the Jews choose to trust solely in the protection of mortal man, then so be it. This is consistent with the concept presented by *Chovos HaLevavos* (Preface to *Shaar HaBitachon*) that Hashem leaves a person in the care of whatever power he chooses to rely on — be it his intelligence, his strength, his financial resources, nature, the king, or Hashem (see *Ramban, Numbers* 13:2).

Citing *R' Shlomo Alkabetz, Kli Yakar* explains this verse as follows. Although, generally speaking, Hashem does not punish a Jew for an evil intent, idolatry is an exception. However, if a Jew

ח אֹתְךָ מָאָסוּ כִּי־אֹתִי מָאֲסוּ מִמְּלֹךְ עֲלֵיהֶם׃ כְּכָל־
הַמַּעֲשִׂים אֲשֶׁר־עָשׂוּ מִיּוֹם הַעֲלֹתִי אֹתָם מִמִּצְרַיִם
וְעַד־הַיּוֹם הַזֶּה וַיַּעַזְבֻנִי וַיַּעַבְדוּ אֱלֹהִים אֲחֵרִים כֵּן
ט הֵמָּה עֹשִׂים גַּם־לָךְ׃ וְעַתָּה שְׁמַע בְּקוֹלָם אַךְ כִּי־
הָעֵד תָּעִיד בָּהֶם וְהִגַּדְתָּ לָהֶם מִשְׁפַּט הַמֶּלֶךְ אֲשֶׁר
י יִמְלֹךְ עֲלֵיהֶם׃ וַיֹּאמֶר שְׁמוּאֵל אֵת כָּל־דִּבְרֵי
יא יְהוָה אֶל־הָעָם הַשֹּׁאֲלִים מֵאִתּוֹ מֶלֶךְ׃ וַיֹּאמֶר

is punished for such an intent, even before he commits the act, an onlooker may question Divine justice, which will result in a desecration of Hashem's Name. For this reason, in the incident of the Golden Calf, Aaron encouraged the Jews to make the Calf. Since they had already formulated their idolatrous plans and earned their punishment, it would be best that they sin explicitly, so that everyone would understand the reason for their punishment. In the present case, Hashem considered the Jews' request for a king as containing a trace of idol worship, because it constituted a rejection of His leadership — thus, it would be better to fulfill their request, so that any punishment they suffered would be clearly understood by all.

לֹא אֹתְךָ מָאָסוּ כִּי־אֹתִי מָאֲסוּ מִמְּלֹךְ עֲלֵיהֶם — *It is not you whom they have rejected, but it is Me Whom they have rejected from reigning over them.*

Targum translates כִּי־אֹתִי מָאֲסוּ *but it is My service that they have despised.*

The Jews should not have asked for a monarch, since Hashem was their king; thus, their request constituted a rejection of Him (*Abarbanel*).

Kli Yakar explains that by requesting a replacement for Samuel, who was Hashem's prophet and emissary, the Jews were in effect rejecting Hashem Himself.

Maharam Schiff (in his *Derashos* found after *Maseches Chullin*) explains that Samuel understood the Jews to be rejecting him because they suspected him of accepting bribes. Hashem informed him that, to the contrary, they did not want him as judge precisely because he did *not* accept bribes. It was not he whom they were rejecting but the Torah's system of honest and impartial justice.

8. כְּכָל־הַמַּעֲשִׂים אֲשֶׁר־עָשׂוּ ... — *Like all their deeds that they have done ...*

Their rejection of Hashem was not something new — they had been choosing other gods for a long time (*Metzudos*).

כֵּן הֵמָּה עֹשִׂים גַּם־לָךְ — *So are they doing to you, as well.*

Radak understands לָךְ, lit., *to you,* as *with you.* Although you are with them and have rescued them from their enemies and established their might so that they have almost no wars to fight, they still rebelled against Hashem and requested a king.

Mishbetzos Zahav sees in this verse support for the words of the Sages that denying the good done by one's fellowman is tantamount to denying the good done by Hashem.

9. וְעַתָּה שְׁמַע בְּקוֹלָם — *And now, heed their voice.*

This phrase seems superfluous, as it substantially already appeared in verse 7. *Abarbanel* explains that this is not a new command, but rather a message that although Samuel will grant their request, he must make sure to warn them.

Kli Yakar suggests that Hashem repeated His command to hasten Samuel to the task, and calm the people's grievances.

you whom they have rejected, but it is Me Whom
they have rejected from reigning over them. [8]*Like*
all their deeds that they have done from the day I
brought them up from Egypt until this day — they
abandoned Me and worshiped the gods of others. So
are they doing to you, as well. [9] *And now, heed their*
voice, but be sure to warn them and tell them about
the protocol of the king who will reign over them."
[10]*Samuel told all the words of* HASHEM *to the*
people who had requested a king of him.

אַךְ כִּי־הָעֵד תָּעִיד בָּהֶם וְהִגַּדְתָּ לָהֶם מִשְׁפַּט הַמֶּלֶךְ אֲשֶׁר יִמְלֹךְ עֲלֵיהֶם — *But be sure to warn them and tell them about the protocol of the king who will reign over them.*

In the following verses, Samuel describes this protocol, which consists of a list of property and personnel that the king may appropriate for his use.

The Talmud (*Sanhedrin* 20b) cites two opinions regarding this protocol.

Rabbi Yose says that it was the king's lawful prerogative, sanctioned by the Torah. Rabbi Yehudah disagrees and says that it comprised an unlawful abuse of power.

Rashi apparently interprets this verse in accordance with Rabbi Yose, for he comments that Hashem was telling Samuel to inform the people that it would be proper for them to venerate the king.

Ralbag and *Metzudos* follow the view of Rabbi Yehudah, and explain that Samuel intended to warn the people that the king was liable to seize undue power.

Malbim agrees and adds that the phrase מִשְׁפַּט הַמֶּלֶךְ, *the protocol of the king*, implies a subjective whim on the part of the king, as opposed to the legally sanctioned behavior referred to in the phrase מִשְׁפַּט הַמְּלֻכָה, *the protocol of the kingship* (below, 10:25).

Abarbanel also accepts Rabbi Yehudah's view, arguing that these rules could not have been sanctioned for we find no source for them in the Torah.

However, *Nachalas Shimon* questions this argument of *Abarbanel* by citing a number of authorities who do find an allusion in the Torah to the promulgation of this protocol. Thus, *Rashbam* (*Bava Basra* 99b) states that the verse, לְבִלְתִּי רוּם־לְבָבוֹ מֵאֶחָיו, *so that [the king's] heart does not grow haughty over his brethren* (*Deuteronomy* 17:20), implies that the king is to wield considerable authority ***over*** *his brethren. Kli Yakar* suggests that the emphatic phrase, שׂוֹם תָּשִׂים, *you shall surely set [over yourself a king]* (ibid. 17:15), connotes an all-encompassing subservience to the king.

10. וַיֹּאמֶר שְׁמוּאֵל אֵת כָּל־דִּבְרֵי ה׳ אֶל־הָעָם ... — *Samuel told all the words of* HASHEM *to the people.*

He told them that Hashem knows their thoughts and understands that they are asking for a king in the model of the non-Jewish nations (*Malbim*) and that He considers this a rejection not only of Samuel but of Himself as well (*Abarbanel*).

אֶל־הָעָם — *To the people.*

Since (as mentioned above), it was only the common people whose petition was improper, this message was directed specifically at them (*Me'am Loez*).

הַשֹּׁאֲלִים מֵאִתּוֹ מֶלֶךְ — *Who had requested a king of him.*

This phrase is seemingly superfluous. The emphasis on the word מֵאִתּוֹ, *of him,*

זֶה יִהְיֶה מִשְׁפַּט הַמֶּלֶךְ אֲשֶׁר יִמְלֹךְ עֲלֵיכֶם אֶת־
בְּנֵיכֶם יִקָּח וְשָׂם לוֹ בְּמֶרְכַּבְתּוֹ וּבְפָרָשָׁיו וְרָצוּ
יב לִפְנֵי מֶרְכַּבְתּוֹ: וְלָשׂוּם לוֹ שָׂרֵי אֲלָפִים וְשָׂרֵי
חֲמִשִּׁים וְלַחֲרֹשׁ חֲרִישׁוֹ וְלִקְצֹר קְצִירוֹ וְלַעֲשׂוֹת
יג כְּלֵי־מִלְחַמְתּוֹ וּכְלֵי רִכְבּוֹ: וְאֶת־בְּנוֹתֵיכֶם יִקָּח
יד לְרַקָּחוֹת וּלְטַבָּחוֹת וּלְאֹפוֹת: וְאֶת־שְׂדוֹתֵיכֶם
וְאֶת־כַּרְמֵיכֶם וְזֵיתֵיכֶם הַטּוֹבִים יִקָּח וְנָתַן לַעֲבָדָיו:
טו וְזַרְעֵיכֶם וְכַרְמֵיכֶם יַעְשֹׂר וְנָתַן לְסָרִיסָיו וְלַעֲבָדָיו:

implies that the Jews requested a king of *Samuel,* because they were upset that his sons demanded fees for their scribes and attendants. They would soon learn that the king would demand much more than that, and while they had the right to ask that Samuel's sons not assume roles of leadership, they would not have the right to ask that the king's sons abdicate their roles, because the monarchy is an inherited position (*Me'am Loez*).

11. וַיֹּאמֶר זֶה יִהְיֶה מִשְׁפַּט הַמֶּלֶךְ — *He said, "This will be the protocol of the king."*

The phrase זֶה יִהְיֶה, *this will be,* rather than simply זֶה, *this is,* supports the opinion of Rabbi Yehudah that this protocol did not exist in the Torah but would be established by the king when he gained power (*Kli Yakar*).

According to *Abarbanel,* the phrase מִשְׁפַּט הַמֶּלֶךְ, *the protocol of the king,* but which literally means *the justice of the king,* is here meant in an ironic manner, because these rules exemplified the very opposite of justice. The king that the Jews yearned for would not perform the righteous deeds of their dreams. Rather, his brand of "justice" would consist of ugly acts of abuse.

וְשָׂם לוֹ בְּמֶרְכַּבְתּוֹ וּבְפָרָשָׁיו וְרָצוּ לִפְנֵי מֶרְכַּבְתּוֹ — *And place them in his chariots and cavalry, and they will run before his chariot.*

The king would subject them to demeaning obligations.

12. וְלָשׂוּם לוֹ שָׂרֵי אֲלָפִים וְשָׂרֵי חֲמִשִּׁים — *He will appoint for himself captains of thousands and captains of fifty.*

Although these seem like distinguished positions, respectable people are not interested in assuming this type of authority (*Abarbanel*).

Many people have a general aversion to involvement with any type of governmental responsibility (*Metzudos*).

וְלַחֲרֹשׁ חֲרִישׁוֹ וְלִקְצֹר קְצִירוֹ — *To plow his furrow and to reap his harvest.*

Even trained professionals would be forced to work on behalf of the king, rather than in their own fields.

Radak states that although the king could draft the people to work for him, they would be paid for their labor. *Abarbanel* points out that this reflects Rabbi Yose's opinion that these verses list the king's legal rights, which place certain restrictions and obligations upon him.

13. *Rambam* (*Hil. Melachim* 4:4), who accepts Rabbi Yose's view that the Torah authorizes the king to impose the "protocol" described here, understands the present verse to mean that the king may take Jewish girls as wives or even as concubines (wives without the formal commitment of a *kesubah*), and then use them as perfumers, cooks, or bakers.

לְרַקָּחוֹת — *Perfumers.*

This may also refer to any professions involved with spices (*Me'am Loez*).

[11] *He said, "This will be the protocol of the king*
who will reign over you: He will take away your
sons and place them in his chariots and cavalry,
and they will run before his chariot; [12] *he will*
appoint for himself captains of thousands and
captains of fifty, to plow his furrow and to reap
his harvest, and to produce his implements of
battle and the furnishings of his chariot. [13] *He will*
take your daughters to be perfumers, cooks, and
bakers. [14] *Your best fields, vineyards, and olive*
trees he will confiscate, and give to his servants.
[15] *He will take a tenth of your grain and vines,*
and present them to his officers and servants.

14. וְאֶת־שְׂדוֹתֵיכֶם וְאֶת־כַּרְמֵיכֶם וְזֵיתֵיכֶם הַטּוֹבִים יִקָּח — *Your best fields, vineyards, and olive trees he will confiscate.*

These three items — fields, vineyards, and olive trees — produce grain, grapes, and olives, which represent the people's primary source of sustenance (*Radak*).

יִקָּח וְנָתַן לַעֲבָדָיו — *He will confiscate and give to his servants.*

This implies that the king will take whatever field he desires. Certainly, according to Rabbi Yehudah, there is concern that he may do so. However, the fact that Scripture mentions that he will give these properties to his servants rather than keep them for himself suggests that, in accordance with the view of Rabbi Yose, the king is exercising his lawful rights, which impose certain restrictions on him (see *Tosafos, Sanhedrin* 20b; see, however, *Rashi, II Samuel* 9:9). *Radak* adds that the king may not keep the field itself but only its produce, should he need it for his soldiers when they go to war. Even then, if he takes more than a tenth (as mentioned in the following verse), he must reimburse the owner.

Radak supports the idea that a king may not take another's field for himself by citing the episode of Ahab, whom God punished when he took Navoth's vineyard (*I Kings* Ch. 21).

Tosafos (ibid.), however, offer a variety of alternative reasons for why Ahab was punished. Among these are:

❒ Only a king who fulfills two conditions may take a private citizen's field: (1) He has been Divinely chosen, and (2) he rules over the entire Jewish nation. Ahab complied with neither criterion.

❒ The king may take only fields far from the city limits.

❒ He may take only a field from a person who bought it, not from a person who inherited it from his ancestors.

❒ Ahab wanted to use the vineyard for the purpose of idolatry.

15. After the Levites receive their tithe, the king will be authorized to take another tenth for himself (*Radak*).

The previous verse referred to wartime conditions, when the king may distribute the *best fields, vineyards, and olive trees* to his soldiers. The present verse refers to a tithe that the king may take and distribute to any of his officers or servants (*Kli Yakar*).

Abarbanel, who follows Rabbi Yehudah's view that this protocol is unlawful, understands the present verse to

טז וְאֶת־עַבְדֵיכֶם וְאֶת־שִׁפְחוֹתֵיכֶם וְאֶת־בַּחוּרֵיכֶם
הַטּוֹבִים וְאֶת־חֲמוֹרֵיכֶם יִקָּח וְעָשָׂה לִמְלַאכְתּוֹ׃
יז-יח צֹאנְכֶם יַעְשֹׂר וְאַתֶּם תִּהְיוּ־לוֹ לַעֲבָדִים׃ וּזְעַקְתֶּם
בַּיּוֹם הַהוּא מִלִּפְנֵי מַלְכְּכֶם אֲשֶׁר בְּחַרְתֶּם לָכֶם
יט וְלֹא־יַעֲנֶה יהוָה אֶתְכֶם בַּיּוֹם הַהוּא׃ וַיְמָאֲנוּ
הָעָם לִשְׁמֹעַ בְּקוֹל שְׁמוּאֵל וַיֹּאמְרוּ לֹּא כִּי
כ אִם־מֶלֶךְ יִהְיֶה עָלֵינוּ׃ וְהָיִינוּ גַם־אֲנַחְנוּ כְּכָל־
הַגּוֹיִם וּשְׁפָטָנוּ מַלְכֵּנוּ וְיָצָא לְפָנֵינוּ וְנִלְחַם אֶת־
כא מִלְחֲמֹתֵנוּ׃ וַיִּשְׁמַע שְׁמוּאֵל אֵת כָּל־דִּבְרֵי הָעָם

be pointing out that by taking tithes the king would be arrogating to himself the sanctity of the Levites.

16. Because the king will treat his own servants like idle noblemen, he will take the people's servants to do his work. Similarly, the king will allow his donkeys to rest and instead make use of those of the people (*Malbim*).

Me'am Loez adds that this will result in the people being deprived of the wherewithal to work their fields.

17. צֹאנְכֶם יַעְשֹׂר — *He will take a tenth of your flock.*

The king will thus take even more than a Levite, who receives only a share of grain, wine, and oil (*Abarbanel*).

Radak adds that "flock" here refers to both sheep and cattle.

וְאַתֶּם תִּהְיוּ־לוֹ לַעֲבָדִים — *And you will be his slaves.*

The people themselves will be pressed into the king's service.

According to *Rambam* (*Hil. Melachim* 4:1), this verse functions as the source that allows a king to levy taxes.

18. וּזְעַקְתֶּם בַּיּוֹם הַהוּא מִלִּפְנֵי מַלְכְּכֶם אֲשֶׁר בְּחַרְתֶּם לָכֶם וְלֹא־יַעֲנֶה ה׳ אֶתְכֶם — *On that day you will cry out because of your king whom you have chosen for yourselves — but* H*ASHEM* *will not answer you.*

The people will cry out because of the heavy load that the king has placed upon them (*Ralbag*), but it will be too late to cast off his yoke (*Malbim*). Hashem will not respond to them, because they had previously disregarded His warning that this would happen (*Ralbag, Metzudos*).

וְלֹא־יַעֲנֶה ה׳ אֶתְכֶם בַּיּוֹם הַהוּא — *But* H*ASHEM* *will not answer you on that day.*

The repetition of the phrase, בַּיּוֹם הַהוּא, *on that day,* implies that only on that day will God not answer them, since they brought this fate upon themselves. Ultimately, however, Hashem will exact judgment upon the king for having oppressed the people — even if they do not cry out (*Kli Yakar*).

19. וַיְמָאֲנוּ הָעָם לִשְׁמֹעַ בְּקוֹל שְׁמוּאֵל וַיֹּאמְרוּ לֹּא — *But the people refused to listen to the voice of Samuel. They said, "No!"*

The people refused to accept Samuel's denunciation of the idea that they accept a king (*Metzudos*).

According to *Akeidah*, they responded that the glum picture that Samuel painted was wrong. The king would not abuse them but judge them honestly, and he would gloriously lead them to military victory.

As we have mentioned above, some commentators understand these words to connote that the Jews retracted their improper petition, שִׂימָה־לָּנוּ מֶלֶךְ, *Give us a king* (i.e., one whom they could ma-

16 *He will take your servants and maidservants
and your best young men and your donkeys and
press them into his service.* 17 *He will take a tenth
of your flock, and you will be his slaves.* 18 *On that
day you will cry out because of your king whom
you have chosen for yourselves — but* HASHEM *will
not answer you on that day."* 19 *But the people refused to listen to the voice of Samuel. They said,
"No! There shall be a king over us,* 20 *and we will
be like all the other nations; our king will judge
us, and go forth before us, and he will fight our
wars!"*
21 *Samuel heard all the words of the people and*

nipulate; above v. 5), and now requested מֶלֶךְ יִהְיֶה עָלֵינוּ, *a king over us.* Thus, God accepted their request (*Kli Yakar* on *Chumash; Be'er Moshe*).

Similarly, *Malbim* explains that the people altered their request to ask for a king who would judge not according to his whim but according to Torah law.

20. וְהָיִינוּ גַם־אֲנַחְנוּ כְּכָל־הַגּוֹיִם — *And we will be like all the other nations.*

Many commentators understand the Jews to be implying that even if the king will overburden and abuse them, they will be no worse than other nations, and it will be worthwhile to pay such a price in return for his judging them, unifying them, and leading them in battle (*Ralbag, Abarbanel, Metzudos*).

According to *Kli Yakar*, the Jewish people did not mean that they wanted to be like other nations. On the contrary, they were saying that once they had a king, even if they were to slip and begin to act like the other nations, then וּשְׁפָטָנוּ מַלְכֵּנוּ, *our king will judge us,* the king would steer them back on track.

וּשְׁפָטָנוּ מַלְכֵּנוּ — *Our king will judge us.*

He will follow the direction of the Torah judges.

Alternatively, the word וּשְׁפָטָנוּ, *will judge us,* implies that the king will take up the Jews' cause and exact justice against their enemies (*Radak*).

וְיָצָא לְפָנֵינוּ וְנִלְחַם אֶת־מִלְחֲמֹתֵנוּ — *And go forth before us, and fight our wars!*

With this, the Jews alluded to the fact that preceding Judges such as Eli had not led them into battle, nor had Samuel done so of late (*Abarbanel*). *Meshech Chochmah* adds that as a Nazirite (see *Nazir* 66a), Samuel was not accustomed to leaving the Land of Israel. The Jews wanted a leader who would stand at the head of their troops wherever they were.

וְנִלְחַם אֶת־מִלְחֲמֹתֵנוּ — *And fight our wars!*

We render וְנִלְחַם as *he will fight.* However, this word can also be translated as ***we** will fight* (*Radak*).

The word מִלְחֲמֹתֵינוּ, *our wars,* connotes that the king will not take credit for the victories but attribute them to the people (*Malbim*).

21. וַיִּשְׁמַע שְׁמוּאֵל אֵת כָּל־דִּבְרֵי הָעָם — *Samuel heard all the words of the people.*

ח/כב כב וַיְדַבְּרֵם בְּאָזְנֵי יהוה׃ וַיֹּאמֶר
יהוה אֶל־שְׁמוּאֵל שְׁמַע בְּקוֹלָם וְהִמְלַכְתָּ לָהֶם
מֶלֶךְ וַיֹּאמֶר שְׁמוּאֵל אֶל־אַנְשֵׁי יִשְׂרָאֵל לְכוּ
ט/א-ב א אִישׁ לְעִירוֹ׃ וַיְהִי־אִישׁ
°מִבִּנְיָמִין ק׳ °מבן ימין וּשְׁמוֹ קִישׁ בֶּן־אֲבִיאֵל בֶּן־צְרוֹר בֶּן־
ב בְּכוֹרַת בֶּן־אֲפִיחַ בֶּן־אִישׁ יְמִינִי גִּבּוֹר חָיִל׃ וְלוֹ־הָיָה

22. וְהִמְלַכְתָּ לָהֶם מֶלֶךְ — *Crown a king for them.*

According to *Kli Yakar* (to *Chumash*), the verse should have stated that the Jews will have a king crowned *upon* them — i.e., a king who would have absolute Torah authority. But since the authority of the king ultimately depends upon the people's acceptance of him, Hashem told Samuel that the king would be crowned *for them* — i.e., subject to their approval.

וַיֹּאמֶר שְׁמוּאֵל אֶל־אַנְשֵׁי יִשְׂרָאֵל לְכוּ אִישׁ לְעִירוֹ — *Samuel told the men of Israel, "Go, each man to his city."*

Realizing that the people had placed the matter in his hands, Samuel told them to return to their homes and await a reply, because Hashem and not he would choose their king (*Abarbanel*).

According to *Me'am Loez*, Samuel was wary of accepting suggestions for the king because people would tend to recommend their relatives, rather than candidates most suitable for the position. Thus, he told them to go home and there await news of the decision.

According to *Malbim* and *Kli Yakar*, Samuel sensed the positive shift in the people's tone, and so he spoke to Hashem on their behalf.

Malbim adds that Samuel acknowledged that he was not competent to serve as the military commander that the Jews desired because his was a different type of leadership, one based on receiving Divine aid. Thus, he no longer considered it an affront to his honor that they asked for a replacement.

וַיְדַבְּרֵם בְּאָזְנֵי ה׳ — *And repeated them to* HASHEM.

According to *Radak*, Samuel prayed that Hashem would answer him regarding their request.

Kli Yakar, however, disagrees. He notes that previously (v. 6) Samuel was explicitly described as having *prayed*. At that time, he was disappointed with the Jews' attitude and he asked Hashem not to hold it against them. But now he merely *spoke*. Seeing that the Jews had changed for the better, he had no need to pray and so he merely repeated their words to Hashem.

IX

גְּדֹל הָעֵצָה וְרַב הָעֲלִילִיָּה אֲשֶׁר־עֵינֶיךָ פְקֻחוֹת עַל־כָּל־דַּרְכֵי בְּנֵי אָדָם ..., *[You who are] great in counsel and mighty in deed, Your eyes are cognizant of all the ways of mankind* .... (*Jeremiah* 32:19).

How fascinating are the ways of Hashem, Who weaves together all human deeds — both those that are manifestly significant and those that are seemingly trivial — in such a way that all of our experiences are threads in the Grand Tapestry that ultimately brings fame and glory to God's Holy Name.

This chapter gives us a glimpse of this phenomenon.

repeated them to H*ASHEM.*

[22] H*ASHEM told Samuel, "Listen to their voice, and crown a king for them." Samuel told the men of Israel, "Go, each man to his city."*

[1] *There was a man of Benjamin whose name was Kish, son of Abiel, son of Zeror, son of Becorath, son of Aphiah, son of a distinguished Benjamite — a mighty man of valor.* [2] *He had a*

◆§ Introduction of Saul

If the Book of *Samuel* were arranged in a strict chronological sequence, it would at this point relate Hashem's message to Samuel regarding His choice of monarch. That message, however, does not appear until verse 15. Instead, Scripture first introduces us to Saul, describing his genealogy and the incident that led to his convocation with Samuel.

The Midrash (*Esther Rabbah* 5:4) makes reference to this interruption as a common Scriptural technique. After the text sets the stage for the introduction of a major figure, it provides us with background information about him. A similar procedure is employed in introducing Moses (*Exodus* 3:1), David (below, 17:12), and Mordechai (*Esther* 2:5).

1. וַיְהִי־אִישׁ מִבִּנְיָמִין — *There was a man of Benjamin.*

In the Hebrew, the word מִבִּנְיָמִין is written as two words — בן ימין — meaning, literally, *from the son of the right hand.*

When Rachel gave birth to Benjamin she called him בֶּן אוֹנִי (*Genesis* 35:18) — *son of my pain* (*Rashi*) or *son of my mourning* (*Ibn Ezra, Rambam*), but Jacob changed that to בִּנְיָמִין, *son of the right hand,* for the right hand represents strength and success (*Ramban*). By writing *Benjamin* as two words, our verse wishes to avoid any association with Rachel's version, which is reminiscent of the infamous incident of the concubine of Gibeah (see *Rashi, Numbers* 26:34), and specifically relates Saul to the prowess of Jacob's version (*Me'am Loez*).

Alternatively, the word *Benjamin* is written as two words in order to intimate that Saul earned the right to the throne through bravery and dedication in snatching the Holy Tablets from Goliath (see above, 4:12, *Rashi*). Since the Tablets were given מִימִינוֹ, *from [God's] right hand* (*Deuteronomy* 33:2), the present verse alludes to Saul as descending from בִּנְיָמִין, a *son of the right hand* (*Kli Yakar*).

וּשְׁמוֹ קִישׁ בֶּן־אֲבִיאֵל — *Whose name was Kish, son of Abiel.*

Although this verse states that Kish's father was named Abiel, in the parallel history in *I Chronicles* (8:33), Kish's father is called Ner.

The Midrash (*Vayikra Rabbah* 9:2) resolves this contradiction by stating that Kish's father was indeed Abiel (as in the present verse). He was known as Ner, however — lit., *candle* — because he used to light lamps along the dark roads leading to the study halls. God rewarded his concern for the populace by granting him a grandson who became king and, as such, similarly concerned himself with attending to the people's needs (*Me'am Loez*).

However, a verse further on (14:50,51) lists Ner not as Abiel's father but as his son.

Radak suggests the following explanation. Abiel, who was referred to as Ner because of his noble practice of lighting lamps, had two sons: one named Kish and the other, like himself, Ner.

בֶּן וּשְׁמוֹ שָׁאוּל בָּחוּר וָטוֹב וְאֵין־אִישׁ מִבְּנֵי יִשְׂרָאֵל טוֹב מִמֶּנּוּ מִשִּׁכְמוֹ וָמַעְלָה גָּבֹהַּ מִכָּל־הָעָם׃

(The unusual circumstance of a father and son possessing the same name is discussed by *Nachalas Shimon* [31:21].)

Kli Yakar adds that although a father naming his son by his own name presents a halachic difficulty, that was not the case here, since Abiel was only called Ner as an informal nickname, whereas his son's official name was Ner.[1]

2. וּשְׁמוֹ שָׁאוּל — *Named Saul.*

As mentioned before (1:1), this phraseology is reserved for righteous people.

בָּחוּר וָטוֹב — *Exceptional and handsome.*

בָּחוּר, lit., *choice*, means that Saul's deeds were exceptional (*Metzudos*).

The word בָּחוּר also implies *youth.* Accordingly, *Malbim* explains בָּחוּר וָטוֹב as meaning that although Saul was still young, at an age when most people are drawn after the passionate pursuit of life's pleasures, Saul displayed an exceptional maturity in his relations with God and with man.[2]

וְאֵין־אִישׁ מִבְּנֵי יִשְׂרָאֵל טוֹב מִמֶּנּוּ — *No one in Israel was better than he.*

No one, not even the elders, possessed character traits superior to his (*Malbim*). The Midrash (*Bamidbar Rabbah* 9:24), however, understands the words that follow to be qualifying this statement: No one in Israel was better than him. In all areas? No. מִשִּׁכְמוֹ וָמַעְלָה גָּבֹהַּ מִכָּל־הָעָם, *from his shoulders and up he was taller than any of the people,* i.e., his advantage over all Jews was only in terms of physical height. He was not, however, the tallest in spiritual terms, for when Samuel told him that he had lost the crown, the prophet said, וּנְתָנָהּ לְרֵעֲךָ הַטּוֹב מִמֶּךָּ, *[God] has given [your kingdom] to your fellow who is better than you* (below, 15:28; *Me'am Loez*).

מִשִּׁכְמוֹ וָמַעְלָה גָּבֹהַּ מִכָּל־הָעָם — *From his shoulders and up, he was taller than any of the people.*

The Talmud (*Sotah* 10a) lists five individuals each of whom was blessed with heavenly perfection in a specific limb, and each of whom was ultimately stricken in that very limb (presumably because of the blemish of conceit — *Kli Yakar*). One of these individuals was Saul; his neck was his distinguishing feature and he met his demise by the sword (at his neck; *Rashi*; below, 31:4).[3]

The location "between the shoulders" has particular significance for the tribe of Benjamin, which was blessed by Jacob with the words, וּבֵין כְּתֵפָיו שָׁכֵן, *[God] will rest between his shoulders* (*Deuteronomy* 33:12) — an

1. Alternatively, Abiel was given the sobriquet Ner only after his son Ner had been born.

2. However, a simple calculation indicates that Saul was in his 50's or 60's at this time. Saul ruled for less than three years, following which his fourth son Ish-bosheth took the throne over the house of Israel at the age of 40 (*II Samuel* 2:10; see *Abarbanel* to 8:1 above).

3. *Sefer Avodas P'nim* suggests that when it says "from his shoulders and above he was higher than the whole nation," it figuratively implies that regarding all the body functions that are based above the shoulder, i.e., thoughts, eyesight, hearing, and speech, he was more pure than any other Jew. This is consistent with the statement of the Sages that he was "like a one-year-old that hasn't tasted sin" (see below, 13:1). He was called שָׁאוּל, which means "borrowed," because Hashem was a "borrower," as it were, who has כָּל הֲנָאָה שֶׁלּוֹ, i.e., *He derives benefit without paying for it* (*Bava Metzia* 34a). This means that Saul sought no pleasure from this world. A borrower is responsible even for accidental occurrences to the item; so too, Hashem took "responsibility," as it were, to protect Saul from accidental damage, both to his body and soul (cited by *Mishbetzos Zahav*).

9/2 *son named Saul who was exceptional and handsome; no one in Israel was better than he. From his shoulders and up, he was taller than any of the people.*

allusion to the fact that the Temple was built upon the portion of the tribe of Benjamin (*Rashi*). Accordingly, Saul — of the tribe of Benjamin — was endowed with supremacy "above his shoulders" (*Maharam Schiff, Derushim Nechmadim* after *Maseches Chullin; Be'er Moshe*).

◈ The Choice of Saul as King

As mentioned above, Saul was chosen king due in part to the merit of his worthy grandfather Ner, who lit candles for the public (see v. 1), and due to his own noble and heroic rescue of the Tablets.

The commentators cite as well Saul's dedication and persistence in seeking his father's donkeys (just as Moses and David proved their worthiness in their exemplary care of their sheep [*Me'am Loez*]).

From the first two verses of this chapter, *Abarbanel* derives four indicators that made Saul the proper candidate for king at that time.

(a) His father was a גִּבּוֹר חָיִל, a *powerful warrior*. A person of such caliber often imbues his children with bravery and confidence. Saul inherited his father's courage and was thus fit to lead his people in war.

(b) The name שָׁאוּל means *borrowed*, prophetically connoting that his reign would be temporary.

(c) Saul was בָּחוּר וָטוֹב — his impeccable character qualified him as a person who would rule according to the Torah's prescription.

(d) Saul was ... מִשִּׁכְמוֹ וָמַעְלָה גָּבֹהַּ. His physique commanded respect and subservience.

There were also a number of reasons that a member of the tribe of Benjamin should be king.

With the appointment of a king, the Jews were required to fulfill the commandment to eradicate Amalek (*Sanhedrin* 20b). This could be done only by a descendant of Rachel[1] — of which Saul, as a member of the tribe of Benjamin, was one (*Me'am Loez*).

Abarbanel has a different explanation. Benjamin was the smallest of the Jewish tribes; in addition, it was downtrodden following the casualties and disgrace that it suffered during the incident of the *concubine in Gibeah* (*Judges* Ch. 19-21). A king was chosen from Benjamin in order, first, to insure that the king of Israel would trust in God and not in the size of his tribe and, second, to boost the tribe's morale.

But how could anyone but a descendant of Judah become king? *Ramban* (*Genesis* 49:10) explains Jacob's blessing of his sons, לֹא־יָסוּר שֵׁבֶט מִיהוּדָה, *The scepter shall not depart from Judah,* to mean that Jacob endowed Judah and his descendants with the exclusive and eternal possession of the kingship. Accordingly, states *Ramban*, many years later, when the righteous Hasmoneans set up a royal dynasty, since they were of the tribe of Levi it foundered and eventually dissolved.

That being the case, how did Hashem appoint Saul of the tribe of Benjamin as the Jews' first king? Ramban explains that in response to the ill-timed nature of the Jews' request for a king (see above, Ch. 8), Hashem sent them a ruler whose kingdom would last only a brief while. As the verse states, אֶתֶּן־לְךָ מֶלֶךְ בְּאַפִּי וְאֶקַּח בְּעֶבְרָתִי, *I gave you a king in*

1. See *Meshech Chochmah, Deuteronomy* 29:3; but see also *Bava Basra* 123b, which refers to *descendants of Joseph.*

ג וַתֹּאבַדְנָה הָאֲתֹנוֹת לְקִישׁ אֲבִי שָׁאוּל וַיֹּאמֶר
קִישׁ אֶל־שָׁאוּל בְּנוֹ קַח־נָא אִתְּךָ אֶת־אַחַד
ד מֵהַנְּעָרִים וְקוּם לֵךְ בַּקֵּשׁ אֶת־הָאֲתֹנֹת׃ וַיַּעֲבֹר
בְּהַר־אֶפְרַיִם וַיַּעֲבֹר בְּאֶרֶץ־שָׁלִשָׁה וְלֹא מָצָאוּ
וַיַּעַבְרוּ בְאֶרֶץ־שַׁעֲלִים וָאַיִן וַיַּעֲבֹר בְּאֶרֶץ־יְמִינִי
ה וְלֹא מָצָאוּ׃ הֵמָּה בָּאוּ בְּאֶרֶץ צוּף וְשָׁאוּל אָמַר

My anger and took [him] away in My fury (*Hosea* 13:11).[1]

Abarbanel, however, strongly disputes *Ramban's* thesis, and raises pointed questions, such as why is there no mention of the tribe of Judah in the *Deuteronomic* paragraph regarding the commandment to appoint a king (17:14-20), and, when Solomon sinned, why was his kingship partially transferred to Jeroboam of the tribe of Ephraim, rather than to a deserving member of the tribe of Judah (see *I Kings* Chs. 11,12)?

Abarbanel therefore contends that Jacob never gave Judah exclusive rights to the throne. The promise that *the scepter shall not depart from Judah* simply meant that Judah would always retain some level of leadership. Alternatively, the word שֵׁבֶט, *tribe*, can be translated as *staff* (see *Leviticus* 27:32), and Jacob was implying that although the tribe of Judah would frequently be "stricken by the staff" — i.e., suffer the pains of exile — it would nonetheless produce great scholars and teachers.

Thus, Judah was never awarded the sole right to the monarchy, and Samuel's anointing of Saul was complete and unreserved (as in 13:13, quoted in fn. below).

But *Kli Yakar* defends *Ramban's* view and resolves *Abarbanel*'s challenges. *Kli Yakar* explains that Jacob's prophecy that *the scepter shall not depart from Judah* was not intended to be "an integral part of the commandment to appoint a king, but simply a blessing and designation as the preferred tribe for monarchy." In regard to the partial transfer of Solomon's sovereignty to Jeroboam, Jacob's prophecy allowed for some measure of the kingdom to be removed from Judah's control.

◆§ The Search for the Donkeys

Scripture now relates the means whereby Hashem brought Saul to Samuel and to the throne — demonstrating an instance of how seemingly trivial incidents play a crucial role in furthering God's Master Plan.

3. וַתֹּאבַדְנָה הָאֲתֹנוֹת לְקִישׁ אֲבִי שָׁאוּל — *The donkeys of Kish, Saul's father, were lost.*

The verse should have more idiomatically stated that the donkeys were lost מִקִּישׁ, *from Kish*. The actual phraseology — לְקִישׁ, *for Kish* — indicates that the donkeys were lost *for the sake of Kish*, and the superfluous characterization of him as אֲבִי שָׁאוּל, *Saul's father*, shows more specifically that this was in connection with Saul — i.e., so that Saul would become king (*Malbim*).

The use of this phrase also indicates that Saul would be provided with an opportunity to perform the commandment of honoring his father, the merit of which would help him earn the kingship (*Kli Yakar*).

1. Samuel later rebuked Saul, כִּי עַתָּה הֵכִין ה׳ אֶת־מַמְלַכְתְּךָ אֶל־יִשְׂרָאֵל עַד עוֹלָם, *Up to now, [had you not sinned], Hashem would have established your kingdom over Israel forever* (below, 13:13). But that meant that Saul would have remained king of Rachel's descendants, or that he would have reigned as subordinate to the Judean king.

[3] [One day] the donkeys of Kish, Saul's father,
were lost, and Kish said to Saul his son, "Please
take one of the attendants with you, get up and go;
search for the donkeys."
[4] He passed through Mount Ephraim and he
passed through the land of Shalishah, but they did
not find [them]; they passed through the land of
Shaalim, but they were not there; and he passed
through the land of the Benjamite but they did
not find them. [5] They came to the land of Zuph
and Saul said to his attendant who was with him,

קַח־נָא אִתְּךָ אֶת־אַחַד מֵהַנְּעָרִים — *Take one of the attendants with you.*

Under normal circumstances, the lad should have been sent on his own to pursue the donkeys. Hashem put this idea into Kish's mind (*Malbim*).

Although Saul eventually took two lads to escort him (for which he is later commended — below, 28:8; see *Vayikra Rabbah* 26:7), at this point he was exceedingly shy and humble, and so followed his father's orders and took only one (*Me'am Loez*).

וְקוּם לֵךְ — *Get up and go.*

לֵךְ, *Go,* would have sufficed. קוּם was an unintentional prophecy, implying that Saul would experience קִימָה, *an uplifting.* Also, the last three letters of the phrase, קוּם לֵךְ spell out the word, מֶלֶךְ, *king* (*Me'am Loez*).

4. וַיַּעֲבֹר בְּאֶרֶץ־שָׁלִשָׁה ... — *And he passed through the land of Shalishah.*

Targum renders בְּאֶרֶץ־שָׁלִשָׁה as *the southern land.*

It is not normal for donkeys to wander so far; the fact that they did so constituted a part of God's Providential intervention, leading Saul to search for them far and wide (*Malbim*).

וַיַּעֲבֹר ... וְלֹא מָצָאוּ וַיַּעַבְרוּ ... וָאַיִן ... וַיַּעֲבֹר ... וְלֹא מָצָאוּ — *And he passed ... but they could not find [them]. They passed .. but they were not there .. and he passed ... but they did not find them.*

In regard to *the land of Shalishah* and *the land of Yemini*, the verse states that ***he*** *passed* and *they did not find them*. In regard to the *land of Shaalim*, however, the verse states that *they passed*, in the plural and concludes that *they were not there.*

Malbim suggests that when Saul and his lad came to *the land of Shalishah* and *the land of Yemini*, they had some evidence that the donkeys were there. They therefore split up and individually combed the area but *they did not find* [what they though was there]. But in *the land of Shaalim*, where they had no indication that the donkeys were close at hand, they searched together, and the donkeys simply *weren't there.*

5. בְּאֶרֶץ צוּף — *To the land of Zuph.*

Our translation follows *Ralbag*, who states that Zuph is another name for Ramah, Samuel's birthplace,[1] which was named after one of Samuel's ancestors (above, 1:1).

Targum renders בְּאֶרֶץ צוּף as *the land where there was a prophet*, deriving צוּף from the word צוֹפֶה, [prophetic] *seer.*[2]

1. See above, 1:1, where it is called רָמָתַיִם צוֹפִים.

2. See below, v. 9. See also comm. to 1:1 רָמָתַיִם צוֹפִים.

לְנַעֲרוֹ אֲשֶׁר־עִמּוֹ לְכָה וְנָשׁוּבָה פֶּן־יֶחְדַּל אָבִי
ו מִן־הָאֲתֹנוֹת וְדָאַג לָנוּ: וַיֹּאמֶר לוֹ הִנֵּה־נָא אִישׁ־
אֱלֹהִים בָּעִיר הַזֹּאת וְהָאִישׁ נִכְבָּד כֹּל אֲשֶׁר־יְדַבֵּר
בּוֹא יָבוֹא עַתָּה נֵלְכָה שָּׁם אוּלַי יַגִּיד לָנוּ אֶת־
ז דַּרְכֵּנוּ אֲשֶׁר־הָלַכְנוּ עָלֶיהָ: וַיֹּאמֶר שָׁאוּל לְנַעֲרוֹ
וְהִנֵּה נֵלֵךְ וּמַה־נָּבִיא לָאִישׁ כִּי הַלֶּחֶם אָזַל
מִכֵּלֵינוּ וּתְשׁוּרָה אֵין־לְהָבִיא לְאִישׁ הָאֱלֹהִים

פֶּן־יֶחְדַּל אָבִי מִן־הָאֲתֹנוֹת וְדָאַג לָנוּ — *Lest my father stop thinking about the donkeys and worry about us!*

That is to say, his fear for our welfare will override his concern for the donkeys (*Rashi*).

The Sages state that as Judah earned the status of royalty because of his humility (*Genesis* 44:33), Saul merited to be king due to his modesty. They also cite the phrase וְדָאַג **לָנוּ**, *he will worry about us,* as evidence of Saul's humility, for with it he equated the attendant with himself (*Tosefta, Berachos* 4:16).

Kli Yakar adds that Saul exhibited modesty earlier in the verse as well when he stated לְכָה וְנָשׁוּבָה, *"Come, let us return,"* which connoted, "You lead the way."

6. וְהָאִישׁ נִכְבָּד — *And the man is esteemed.*

Truly honorable people respect others (*Avos* 4:1). Thus, Saul told his attendant that this man, who was truly esteemed, would undoubtedly be courteous, patient, and honest (*Mahari Kara*).

Similarly, *Targum* renders the word נִכְבָּד as *who prophesies truthfully.*

כֹּל אֲשֶׁר־יְדַבֵּר בּוֹא יָבוֹא — *Everything he says is certain to occur.*

Following *Targum,* who translates נִכְבָּד as *a truthful prophet,* this phrase seems redundant.

Radak explicates that since prophecy was scarce at that time (above, 3:1), whereas soothsayers of other sorts — e.g., necromancers — were often inaccurate, the lad found it necessary to state that this prophet's predictions were truthful.

Kli Yakar understands these words to say that not only does Samuel predict the future but that Hashem conforms to his behest. (This idea is alluded to in the verse, וְתִגְזַר־אֹמֶר וְיָקָם לָךְ, *You would utter a decree and it would be done* (*Job* 22:28.)

אוּלַי יַגִּיד לָנוּ אֶת־דַּרְכֵּנוּ אֲשֶׁר־הָלַכְנוּ עָלֶיהָ — *Perhaps he will tell us upon which road we should travel.*

Literally, the phrase דַּרְכֵּנוּ אֲשֶׁר־הָלַכְנוּ עָלֶיהָ means *the road upon which we have traveled. Rashi* explicates, *Perhaps he will [help us locate the donkeys, which were the reason that] we traveled on this road.*

Other commentators interpret this inversion to teach that the curious happenstance of their having traveled so long and far for donkeys, which usually do not stray very far, caused the servant to realize that there was some underlying, deeper dynamic at work. He said, *Perhaps [the man of God] will tell us [the real purpose] of our having taken the road that we have traveled* (*Likkutei Yekarim, Alshich, Be'er Moshe*).

According to *Abarbanel,* the lad intended to test Samuel's abilities: *If he can retrace for us the [complex] route on which we traveled, [then he is genuine].*

Kli Yakar adds that this idea is implicit in the words אוּלַי יַגִּיד לָנוּ, *Perhaps he will be able to tell us [without our even asking] . . . ,* which is indeed what happened (see below, v. 20).

"Come, let us return, lest my father stop thinking about the donkeys and worry about us!" [6] *But [the attendant] said to him, "Behold now, there is a man of God in this city, and the man is esteemed; everything he says is certain to occur. Let us go there now; perhaps he will tell us upon which road we should travel."*
[7] *Saul replied to his attendant, "Behold, if we go, what shall we bring to the man, for the bread is gone from our vessels and we have no gift to bring to the man of God.*

7. וּמַה־נָּבִיא לָאִישׁ — *What shall we bring to the man?*

That is to say, if the man of God will charge a fee, what can we give him (*Targum*)? Saul was not aware that Samuel did not accept payment for his services (see above, 7:17; *Rashi*), and he thought that it was the general policy of prophets to charge a fee, as did the sorcerers of his time (*Radak*).

כִּי הַלֶּחֶם אָזַל מִכֵּלֵינוּ — *For the bread is gone from our vessels.*

That is to say, if we had bread, we could at least give him that (*Metzudos*).

Although bread is a seemingly inappropriate gift for a man of God, *Me'am Loez* suggests that Saul and his attendant conjectured that he would distribute it to the needy. In general, *Me'am Loez* states, the prophets gave the poor the token gifts that they received.

Radak, based on *Targum*, explains that Saul did not intend to offer Samuel bread, but meant to say, "We have no money, for even our bread is gone and we have no funds to replenish it."

וּתְשׁוּרָה — *And ... [a] gift.*

Our translation follows *Mahari Kara*. *Rashi*, based on *Targum*, relates תְּשׁוּרָה to יוֹשֶׁר, *proper*, and thus renders תְּשׁוּרָה as *something fitting*.

Alternatively, *Rashi* quotes the grammarian Menachem, who states that תְּשׁוּרָה has the same root as אֲשׁוּרֶנּוּ, *I see it* (*Numbers* 23:9). Accordingly, תְּשׁוּרָה is a *token of vision* — meaning, a gift that allows one to see and be seen by an eminent person, such as a king. Similarly, on the pilgrimage festivals, וְלֹא־יֵרָאוּ פָנַי רֵיקָם, *[the Jews] should not be seen before Me empty-handed* (*Exodus* 23:15).

It is clear from the present verse, as well as other sources, that a person would customarily bring a gift to a prophet or Rabbi upon seeking his advice, blessing, or other aid. The Talmud likens a tribute given to a Torah scholar to the presentation of *bikkurim, first fruits* (*Kesubos* 105b). It is true that Samuel did not as a rule accept gifts; others, however, did (see *Berachos* 10b).

What was the purpose of such a gift?

As we have seen, *Menachem* (quoted by *Rashi*) explains it to be a gesture of respect.

According to *Malbim*, a gift constitutes payment for the sage's time and effort. The value of the present should thus be proportionate to the stature of the adviser, the gravity of the matter, the time and trouble needed to solve it, and the social status of the inquirer.

However, considering the fact that Saul and his servant gave a mere quarter of a shekel, *Ralbag* states that this payment could not be intended to either benefit or honor the prophet. He therefore states that this gratuity was meant to help the prophet focus and thus evoke Divine inspiration. That is why Isaac asked Esau to "make me delicacies ... so that my soul may bless you ..." (*Genesis* 27:4; see ArtScroll ed.). Thus,

ח מָה אִתָּנוּ׃ וַיֹּסֶף הַנַּעַר לַעֲנוֹת אֶת־שָׁאוּל
וַיֹּאמֶר הִנֵּה נִמְצָא בְיָדִי רֶבַע שֶׁקֶל כָּסֶף וְנָתַתִּי
ט לְאִישׁ הָאֱלֹהִים וְהִגִּיד לָנוּ אֶת־דַּרְכֵּנוּ׃ לְפָנִים |
בְּיִשְׂרָאֵל כֹּה־אָמַר הָאִישׁ בְּלֶכְתּוֹ לִדְרוֹשׁ אֱלֹהִים
לְכוּ וְנֵלְכָה עַד־הָרֹאֶה כִּי לַנָּבִיא הַיּוֹם יִקָּרֵא
י לְפָנִים הָרֹאֶה׃ וַיֹּאמֶר שָׁאוּל לְנַעֲרוֹ טוֹב דְּבָרְךָ

the purpose of the gift is not to benefit the recipient but rather the person presenting it — in this present case.

As it happened, however, the gift was unnecessary — Samuel's mind was already focused on the choice of king, and even before Saul arrived with his gift he received a prophecy about him.

Finally, *Me'am Loez* states that the custom of presenting a gift was meant to express esteem and appreciation for the words of the prophet (in fact, when a person must pay for something, he often values it more). Similarly, in the times of Hillel, one had to pay to enter the study hall of Shmaya and Avtalyon (*Yoma* 35b).[1]

מָה אִתָּנוּ — *What do we have with us?*

Yefeh Kol (based on *Shir HaShirim Rabbah* 4:8:2) notes the specificity of the words "man *of God*." Combining this with the fact that the next verse tells that the attendant did not have a quarter shekel, he interprets Saul as saying, "[We have a small amount for a gift] but not one befitting the *man of God.*" His attendant's response (4.8) implies, "I have a quarter shekel — and [although that is a pittance,] I will give it to the man of God, [and he will accept it anyway]" (see also *Maharzu* ad loc.).

Targum renders this as, *What can we do?*

8. הִנֵּה נִמְצָא בְיָדִי — *Behold! I have ...*

The word הִנֵּה, *behold*, implies that the servant had only just now discovered this coin (*Me'am Loez*).

See *Yefeh Kol*, who interprets this phrase otherwise.

רֶבַע שֶׁקֶל כָּסֶף — *A quarter of a silver shekel.*

This is equivalent to a *zuz* (*Targum*).

וְנָתַתִּי לְאִישׁ הָאֱלֹהִים — *I will give it to the man of God.*

וְנָתַתִּי is written in the singular, indicating that the servant recognized that although such a small amount would not be an appropriate gift if it came from a prestigious person such as Saul, it would suffice as the gift of a mere servant.

We have already mentioned *Ralbag's* contention that the amount of the gift was irrelevant, for it was meant solely to serve as a means of arousing the prophetic abilities of the man of God.

Abarbanel maintains that Saul and his servant underestimated Samuel's greatness and were unaware that this small amount was insufficient.

9. ... לְפָנִים בְּיִשְׂרָאֵל — (*Formerly in Israel ...*

As implied by the parentheses, these are not the words of the servant but those of the narrator of the Book of *Samuel*.

Abarbanel appeals to this verse to support his theory regarding the final authorship of the Book of *Samuel*. The Sages credit Samuel as the author up to the section following his death (which

1. Regarding the question of whether a Talmudic scholar may accept donations to support himself while he studies, see *Rema, Yoreh Deah* 246:21, with *Shach* and *Taz*. See also *Nachalas Shimon* 31:24.

What do we have with us?" [8] *The attendant spoke up once more to Saul, and said, "Behold! I have a quarter of a silver shekel with me. I will give it to the man of God and he will tell us about our way."*

[9] *(Formerly in Israel, this is what someone said when he went to inquire of God: "Let us go to the seer"; for "the prophet" of today was formerly called "the seer.")*

[10] *Saul said to his attendant, "You have spoken well;*

was written by Gad the Seer [*Bava Basra* 14b]). However, states *Abarbanel,* the Book of *Samuel* was redacted, with some additional comments, by a later figure — probably Jeremiah or Ezra. *Abarbanel* understands this verse as stating that in the days of that later redactor, a prophet was called a *prophet,* whereas in the earlier days of Samuel and Saul he was known as a *seer* (see *Abarbanel* here and his introduction to *Joshua*).

Radak, however, contends that Samuel narrated this verse. He interprets the verse as teaching that in the days preceding those of Samuel and Saul a man of God was known as a *seer.* Nowadays, however, in the era of Saul and Samuel, such a man is called either a *prophet* (a concept popularized by Samuel himself; see below) or a *seer.*

What is the purpose of this information, and why is it presented particularly at this point?

Abarbanel explains that this information prefaces Saul's use of the term *seer* in the upcoming conversation (v. 11).

Malbim sees this information as shedding light on the previous few verses. Should one wonder about Saul's seemingly trivial use of a prophet and leader to inquire about his father's lost donkeys, Scripture explains that originally the primary function of a Godly man was indeed as a *seer* who was expected to aid individuals in their personal endeavors, such as finding their belongings. The concept of a prophet serving and chastising the congregation at large was as yet uncommon. When that grew prevalent during Samuel's days, the *seer's* title changed to נָבִיא, *prophet* — a word alluding to speech, as in the phrase, נִיב שְׂפָתָיִם, *the speech of the lips* (*Isaiah* 57:19). The man of God's primary function was transformed to that of delivering public speeches meant to arouse the masses to repentance.

Me'am Loez adds that in earlier days a person blamed his problems — such as the loss of an object — on his personal imperfections, and thus went to the *seer,* who gazed into the inner recesses of his soul, in order through him to *inquire of God* on where to improve. But now people had ceased to do so, and so the *seers* had to go forth to lecture the people.

Finally, *Kli Yakar* offers a novel explanation. Having introduced the custom of the תְּשׁוּרָה, the *viewer's tribute* (see *Menachem* above, v. 7), Scripture parenthetically clarifies that the supplicant was not paying for the privilege of viewing the prophet. Rather, he was coming *to inquire of* and *see God* via the *seer,* who perceives God and His message. For that, he had to bring a tribute.

10. וַיֹּאמֶר שָׁאוּל לְנַעֲרוֹ טוֹב דְּבָרְךָ — *Saul said to his attendant, "You have spoken well."*

Here we see another of Saul's exemplary attributes: he did not hesitate to take advice from a person whose stature was lower than his own (*Me'am Loez*).

לְכָ֣ה | נֵלֵ֑כָה וַיֵּלְכוּ֙ אֶל־הָעִ֔יר אֲשֶׁר־שָׁ֖ם אִ֥ישׁ
יא הָאֱלֹהִֽים׃ הֵ֗מָּה עֹלִים֙ בְּמַעֲלֵ֣ה הָעִ֔יר וְהֵ֙מָּה֙ מָצְא֣וּ
נְעָר֔וֹת יֹצְא֖וֹת לִשְׁאֹ֣ב מָ֑יִם וַיֹּאמְר֣וּ לָהֶ֔ן הֲיֵ֥שׁ בָּזֶ֖ה
יב הָרֹאֶֽה׃ וַתַּעֲנֶ֧ינָה אוֹתָ֛ם וַתֹּאמַ֥רְנָה יֵּ֖שׁ הִנֵּ֣ה לְפָנֶ֑יךָ
מַהֵ֣ר | עַתָּ֗ה כִּ֤י הַיּוֹם֙ בָּ֣א לָעִ֔יר כִּ֣י זֶ֧בַח הַיּ֛וֹם לָעָ֖ם
יג בַּבָּמָֽה׃ כְּבֹאֲכֶ֨ם הָעִ֜יר כֵּ֣ן תִּמְצְא֣וּן אֹת֗וֹ בְּטֶ֨רֶם֩
יַעֲלֶ֤ה הַבָּמָ֙תָה֙ לֶאֱכֹ֔ל כִּ֛י לֹֽא־יֹאכַ֥ל הָעָ֖ם עַד־בֹּא֑וֹ

לְכָה וְנֵלְכָה — *Come, let us go.*

Our translation follows *Targum.* Literally, the phrase reads, "Go, let us go." This supports the idea that the attendant offered to present the meager gift as if he were the one making the inquiry. Saul consented by saying לְכָה, *Go [and offer the tribute,] and [then]* וְנֵלְכָה, *we will both [be there to hear his advice]* (*Malbim, Kli Yakar*).

Saul Encounters Samuel

11. בְּמַעֲלֵה הָעִיר — *The ascent to the city.*

That is to say, the road leading up to the city (*Metzudos*).

וְהֵמָּה מָצְאוּ נְעָרוֹת — *They encountered some girls.*

The word מָצְאוּ, *encountered,* literally means *found,* and usually implies something unexpected, such as when one comes upon a מְצִיאָה, a *lost object,* but literally *a find. Kli Yakar* explains the novelty of the meeting, in that this was not the regular time for girls to go forth to draw water. Thus, this encounter constituted part of the Divine plan shaping Saul's experiences.

Rabbi Akiva teaches that "whoever comes to a city and encounters girls coming toward him will be successful in his endeavors — as in the cases of Eliezer (*Genesis* 24:15), Jacob (ibid. 29:6), Moses (*Exodus* 2:16), and Saul" (*Pirkei D'Rabbi Eliezer*).

Accordingly, *Kli Yakar* suggests וְהֵמָּה מָצְאוּ to mean that *They found [success] as the girls were going out ...*

הֲיֵשׁ בָּזֶה הָרֹאֶה — *Is this where the seer is?*

Alternatively, *Is the seer here now, [or is he traveling to judge the people]?* (*Kli Yakar*).

12. יֵּשׁ — *It is [the case] ...*

According to *Midrash Shmuel,* the word יֵּשׁ, *it is [the case],* alludes to a heavenly cloud, as in the verse, וְיֵשׁ אֲשֶׁר יִהְיֶה הֶעָנָן, *It would be the case that the clouds would be...* (*Numbers* 9:21). Accordingly, the girls' reply meant, "When you see the cloud representing the Divine Presence hovering over a doorway of a house, you will know that to be the domicile of the holy man."

This, states the Midrash, is alluded to in the verse, מֹשֶׁה וְאַהֲרֹן בְּכֹהֲנָיו וּשְׁמוּאֵל בְּקֹרְאֵי שְׁמוֹ ... בְּעַמּוּד עָנָן יְדַבֵּר אֲלֵיהֶם — *Moses and Aaron were among His priests, and Samuel among those who invoke His Name ... In a pillar of cloud He spoke to them* (*Psalms* 99:6,7).

הִנֵּה לְפָנֶיךָ מַהֵר — *He is just ahead of you. Hurry ...*

The girls showed Saul that Samuel's house was standing directly before him (*Metzudos*).

At the beginning of the verse, the girls addressed אוֹתָם, *them,* both Saul and his attendant. But לְפָנֶיךָ, *ahead of you,* and the next word מַהֵר, *hurry,* are stated in the singular, for the girls now addressed only Saul.

Radak explains that the girls focused solely on Saul, because he was clearly the more esteemed of the two men.

come, let us go.'' So they went to the city where
the man of God was. 11 *As they were climbing the*
ascent to the city they encountered some girls go-
ing out to draw water, and they said to them, ''Is
this where the seer is?'' 12 *They answered them*
saying, ''It is. Behold, he is just ahead of you.
Hurry now, for he came to the city today, for the
people are bringing a feast-offering today at the
High Place. 13 *As you enter the city, so will you*
find him before he ascends to the High Place to
eat, for the people will not eat before he comes,

According to *Kli Yakar,* they spoke only to Saul so as to gaze upon him (v. 13).[1]

מַהֵר עַתָּה — *Hurry now.*

In the following verse, the girls will explain why Saul should hurry (*Abarbanel, Malbim*).

כִּי הַיּוֹם בָּא לָעִיר — *For he came to the city today.*

According to *Malbim,* in this phrase the girls indicated why Samuel would be accessible just now: because he had just arrived, the local people would probably not bother him immediately; on the other hand, since Saul was a guest he would be given the privilege of gaining access to him.

כִּי זֶבַח הַיּוֹם לָעָם — *For the people are bringing a feast-offering today.*

This idiosyncratic phraseology (rather than the more conventional כִּי זֶבַח לָעָם הַיּוֹם), implies that the people were celebrating a זֶבַח הַיּוֹם, an annual *feast-offering* specific to that day (*Metzudos*).

Kli Yakar (based on *Bamidbar Rabbah* 18:10) states that Samuel prepared this feast from his own funds after God sent him the prophecy that the future monarch would arrive today.

Radvaz interprets (*Teshuvos* Vol. II, 679; v. 24 — see footnote) one of the Talmudic Sages as stating that no offering was brought. Rather, זֶבַח here refers to the slaughter of an unsanctified animal (as in *Deuteronomy* 12:21).

בַּבָּמָה — *At the High Place.*

As mentioned earlier, during the era that the Tabernacle was in Nob, offerings were permitted on a *High Place* — i.e., a private altar (see above, 6:15).

Targum renders הַבָּמָה as *the circular house.* This is synonymous with a *banquet hall.* Similarly, a place to dine is called מְסִיבָּה, *a circle,* because celebrants would typically sit in a circle (*Radak*).

13. כֵּן תִּמְצְאוּן אֹתוֹ — *So will you find him.*

The word כֵּן, *so,* literally means *truthfully* (see *Genesis* 42:11; כֵּנִים אֲנַחְנוּ), and thus lends the phrase the meaning, *[You will] definitely [find him]* (*Mahari Kara*).

כִּי לֹא־יֹאכַל הָעָם עַד־בֹּאוֹ — *For the people will not eat before he comes.*

With this, the girls explained why they were pressuring Saul to hurry. "Since the people will not eat before Samuel arrives, he will not want to keep them waiting. So if you do not meet him now, you may miss him. And

1. Neither *Radak* nor *Kli Yakar* explains why the girls again address both Saul and his attendant in the next verse.

כִּֽי־הוּא֙ יְבָרֵ֣ךְ הַזֶּ֔בַח אַחֲרֵי־כֵ֖ן יֹאכְל֣וּ הַקְּרֻאִ֑ים
יד וְעַתָּ֣ה עֲל֔וּ כִּֽי־אֹת֥וֹ כְהַיּ֖וֹם תִּמְצְא֥וּן אֹתֽוֹ׃ וַֽיַּעֲל֖וּ
הָעִ֑יר הֵ֗מָּה בָּאִים֙ בְּת֣וֹךְ הָעִ֔יר וְהִנֵּ֤ה שְׁמוּאֵל֙
טו יֹצֵ֣א לִקְרָאתָ֔ם לַעֲל֖וֹת הַבָּמָֽה׃ וַֽיהוָ֔ה
גָּלָ֖ה אֶת־אֹ֣זֶן שְׁמוּאֵ֑ל י֣וֹם אֶחָ֔ד לִפְנֵ֥י בֽוֹא־שָׁא֖וּל
טז לֵאמֹֽר׃ כָּעֵ֣ת ׀ מָחָ֗ר אֶשְׁלַ֣ח אֵלֶיךָ֮ אִ֚ישׁ מֵאֶ֣רֶץ

if you think that you may wait until tomorrow,"כִּי־אֹתוֹ כְהַיּוֹם תִּמְצְאוּן אֹתוֹ, *you will find him only* ***today,*** for tomorrow he will travel to judge the people, or else return home to Ramah" (*Abarbanel*).

כִּי־הוּא יְבָרֵךְ הַזֶּבַח — *Since he blesses the sacrifices.*

Samuel was awarded the honor of reciting the blessing on the food — thus discharging the others present of that obligation — and then distributing the food (*Targum, Rashi*).

As implied by the words יְבָרֵךְ הַזֶּבַח, *blesses the sacrifice,* the verse is referring specifically not to a *blessing of enjoyment* but rather to a *blessing recited on performing a commandment* — i.e., on eating the meat of a sacrifice. The text of that blessing was: ... אֲשֶׁר קִדְּשָׁנוּ בְּמִצְוֹתָיו וְצִוָּנוּ לֶאֱכוֹל אֶת הַזָּבַח ..., *Who has sanctified us with His commandments, and commanded us to eat from the offering.* (For sources regarding the existence of such a commandment, see *Rashi, Berachos* 48b *and Pesachim* 59a; *Nachalas Shimon* 22:2.)[1]

The Talmud (*Berachos* 48b) cites this verse to demonstrate the concept of reciting a blessing before a meal. Although the specific formulations of the blessings are of relatively late Rabbinic origin (see *Berachos* 20b, *Rashi*), this verse functions as an אַסְמַכְתָּא, *a support,* which corroborates the legislation of the Sages.

The fact that the people of Samuel's era recited blessings should not be surprising. As *Netziv* writes (*Haamek She'eilah* 137:4), generally speaking the Sages' ordinances merely ratified long-standing custom.[2]

כִּי־אֹתוֹ כְהַיּוֹם תִּמְצְאוּן אֹתוֹ — *For you will find him as surely as it is day.*

Our translation follows *Rashi.*

As mentioned, *Abarbanel* interprets this verse to mean, *You will find him here only today.*

Mahari Kara renders this phrase as *On a day such as this [when there is a public offering] you will find him, [because he is not traveling].*

One immediately notes the wordiness of this reply to Saul's question, particularly of its closing words (although not according to *Abarbanel*'s interpretation). Although these girls were asked only if the seer were available, they spoke at great length, offering much unsolicited information (*Maharsha*; see *Berachos* 48b and *Yalkut Shimoni* 108).

According to one view, the lengthiness of their response may be attributed to the general tendency of women to be verbose.

Another opinion — one that the

1. *Radak* comments that Samuel first recited the familiar blessing on bread — הַמּוֹצִיא לֶחֶם מִן הָאָרֶץ —but that the verse makes no mention of that because it is focusing specifically on the main part of the meal, which was the offering.

2. It is perplexing, however, that the Talmud refers to this verse to demonstrate the necessity of reciting *blessings on enjoyment* (see *Mechilta, Parashas Bo*), since the verse describes an instance of an altogether different type of blessing: one recited *over the performance of a commandment.* This issue is raised by *Maharsha, Pnei Yehoshua, Tzlach,* and *Maharatz Chayes.* For a digest of their answers, see *Nachalas Shimon* 22:1.

since he blesses the offering; only afterward do the invited guests eat. Now go up, for you will find him as surely as it is day." 14 *So they ascended to the city. As they were entering the city, behold, Samuel was coming out toward them, to go up to the High Place.*

15 *Now* HASHEM *had revealed in Samuel's ear, one day before Saul had come, saying,* 16 *"At this time tomorrow I will send a man to you from the land of*

Talmud itself offers — is that the girls deliberately prolonged their speech in order to gaze at Saul's handsome mien (see above, v. 2; v. 12 הִנֵּה לְפָנֶיךָ). Others dispute this, stating that such a characterization besmirches these girls with the accusation of engaging in lewd behavior, for just as a man may not gaze at a woman who is not his wife, so may a woman not gaze at a man who is not her husband.

Kli Yakar defends this characterization and denies that such behavior is opprobrious. The girls were gazing at Saul in order to admire God's handiwork. Although a man may not stare at a woman with such intent, the opposite is permitted. (Evidence that a woman may gaze at a man if her intentions are not salacious may be gleaned from the fact that Rabbi Yochanan had the custom of lingering outside the ritual bathhouse so that women would gaze at him on their way out and bear children like him [*Berachos* 20a].)

Indeed, a number of contemporary halachic authorities state that when a woman's intentions are not prurient and there is no danger that she will come to harbor illicit thoughts, she may gaze at a man (see *Igros Moshe, Even HaEzer* Vol. 1 §69; see also *Nachalas Shimon* 21)

Another explanation of the girls' volubility is that it was Divinely engineered so that Samuel and Saul would not meet a moment too soon. God had told Samuel on the previous day (v. 16) that כָּעֵת מָחָר, *at this time tomorrow* [exactly — *Malbim*], a man will come who will become the king. Samuel was the ruler of the Jews; as soon as he crowned Saul, leadership of the Jewish people would change hands. Since that precise moment had not arrived and since there is a principle that *a new regime cannot encroach for even a split second on that of its predecessor,* Saul's arrival had to wait a few moments. Hashem thus caused the girls to extend their answer (unbeknownst to them — *Maharsha*) in order to delay this fateful meeting.

14. וְהִנֵּה שְׁמוּאֵל יֹצֵא לִקְרָאתָם — *Behold, Samuel was coming out toward them.*

Although Samuel was on his way to the High Place, it was Divinely arranged that he should be walking in the direction of Saul and his attendant — *toward them* — because the time for him to meet Saul had arrived (*Malbim, Kli Yakar*).

Alternatively, *Kli Yakar* suggests that Samuel was, in fact, walking with the intention of meeting Saul.

15. *Alshich* comments that Hashem revealed to Samuel about Saul's arrival one day before so that they should prepare a feast and invite dignitaries, and when Saul would come they would be seated already and he would be seated at the head. This would show that it was all Hashem's plan. Thus, Samuel had already announced that he was awaiting the arrival of a righteous man who would recite the blessing. Apparently, the girls sensed that this man who was seeking the seer was the very man that the assembled were waiting for, so they encouraged him to go quickly because they were waiting for *him.*

בִּנְיָמִ֔ן וּמְשַׁחְתּ֤וֹ לְנָגִיד֙ עַל־עַמִּ֣י יִשְׂרָאֵ֔ל וְהוֹשִׁ֥יעַ
אֶת־עַמִּ֖י מִיַּ֣ד פְּלִשְׁתִּ֑ים כִּ֤י רָאִ֙יתִי֙ אֶת־עַמִּ֔י כִּ֛י
יז בָּ֥אָה צַעֲקָת֖וֹ אֵלָֽי׃ וּשְׁמוּאֵ֖ל רָאָ֣ה אֶת־שָׁא֑וּל
וַיהוָ֣ה עָנָ֔הוּ הִנֵּ֤ה הָאִישׁ֙ אֲשֶׁ֣ר אָמַ֣רְתִּי אֵלֶ֔יךָ
יח זֶ֖ה יַעְצֹ֥ר בְּעַמִּֽי׃ וַיִּגַּ֥שׁ שָׁא֛וּל אֶת־שְׁמוּאֵ֖ל בְּת֣וֹךְ
הַשָּׁ֑עַר וַיֹּ֙אמֶר֙ הַגִּֽידָה־נָּ֣א לִ֔י אֵי־זֶ֖ה בֵּ֥ית הָרֹאֶֽה׃
יט וַיַּ֤עַן שְׁמוּאֵל֙ אֶת־שָׁא֔וּל וַיֹּ֙אמֶר֙ אָנֹכִ֣י הָרֹאֶ֔ה

16. לְנָגִיד — *To be ruler.*

Kli Yakar notes that the verse refers only to a נָגִיד, *ruler,* and not to a מֶלֶךְ, *king,* indicating that God had authorized Samuel to crown Saul only because ... רָאִיתִי אֶת־עַמִּי, *I have seen [the distress of] My people,* and that Saul's reign would be temporary.

וְהוֹשִׁיעַ אֶת־עַמִּי מִיַּד פְּלִשְׁתִּים — *And he will save My people from the hands of the Philistines.*

As mentioned earlier, the Jews remained independent only when they adhered to Samuel's directions (see 7:13-15). After Samuel aged and was no longer able to chastise the Jews, however, they regressed and once again fell into the hands of the Philistines (see below, 13:3; *Radak*).

כִּי רָאִיתִי אֶת־עַמִּי ... — *For I have seen My people.*

Targum reads this phrase as, *For I have seen the distress of my people.* Alternatively, *Radak* cites a version of *Targum* that reads, *For I have seen the disgrace of my people.*

In either reading, Hashem sent the Jews a king to save them from subjugation to the Philistines.

Abarbanel disputes this interpretation.[1] He argues that Hashem was perfectly capable of subduing the Philistines without a king, and would not have ordered Samuel to appoint a monarch for that purpose. Accordingly, *Abarbanel* explains the verse as follows: כִּי רָאִיתִי אֶת־עַמִּי, *For I have seen My people [and their ill-advised desire for a king],* כִּי בָאָה צַעֲקָתוֹ אֵלָי, *because their cries for a king have come to Me [and I have reluctantly decided to honor their request]* (see Preface above).

17. וַה׳ עָנָהוּ — *Hashem spoke to him.*

The word עָנָהוּ usually means *answered him.* Here, however (as in a number of other cases), it may be rendered as *spoke to him in a raised voice* (*Mahari Kara*).

Radak opines that this word indicates that God conveyed this message to Samuel via the normal mode of prophecy.

Kli Yakar maintains the ordinary translation: *answered.* When Samuel saw Saul, he asked himself, "Could this man approaching me be the one?" Hashem thus *answered* his query positively.

זֶה יַעְצֹר בְּעַמִּי — *This one will rule over My people.*

The word עוֹצֵר, usually translated as *to restrict* or *to restrain,* is here rendered as *to rule. Radak* finds precedence for such usage in *Judges* (18:7): יוֹרֵשׁ עֶצֶר, *an heir to the throne.*

The commentators explain that a ruler is responsible for restraining the army from dispersing and for *restricting* the populace from engaging in evil (*Rashi*) and unacceptable behavior (*Radak*); as a result, the people are protected against the depredations of their enemies (*Malbim*).

Targum translates זֶה יַעְצֹר בְּעַמִּי as *This*

1. Consistent with his views on Jewish monarchy in general — see Preface, Ch. 8.

Benjamin; you shall anoint him to be ruler over My
people Israel, and he will save My people from the
hands of the Philistines — for I have seen [the dis-
tress] of My people, since its cry has come before Me."
17 *When Samuel saw Saul, HASHEM spoke to him,*
"This is the man of whom I said to you, 'This
one will rule over My people.'"
18 *Saul moved*
close to Samuel inside the [city] gate and said,
"Tell me, please, which is the house of the seer?"
19 *Samuel answered Saul, saying, "I am the seer!*

one will [remove and] suppress [any foreign power from taking] over my people.

18. וַיִּגַּשׁ שָׁאוּל אֶת־שְׁמוּאֵל — *Saul moved close to Samuel.*

Our translation reflects the generally accepted understanding of וַיִּגַּשׁ as *moved closer*. Accordingly, the word אֶת — usually an untranslated connector — here substitutes for אֶל, *to* (*Radak*; see *Genesis* 44:18).

Malbim, however, suggests that the word אֶת connotes passivity, as opposed to אֶל, which connotes activity. Thus, Saul approached Samuel, but before he reached him, Samuel stepped up to Saul. Thus, it was Samuel who reached Saul, not the opposite.

According to *Targum*, וַיִּגַּשׁ here does not mean *moved closer*, but rather *reached* or *encountered*. Therefore אֶת retains its more conventional meaning.

אֵי־זֶה בֵּית הָרֹאֶה — *Which is the house of the seer?*

It may well be that Saul suspected that he was speaking to Samuel himself, but phrased his question as he did because it would not have been proper to ask outright, "Are you the seer?" (*Me'am Loez*).

19. וַיֹּאמֶר אָנֹכִי הָרֹאֶה — *Saying, "I am the seer."*

On a simple level, Samuel's statement showed no lack of humility, since Samuel was compelled to answer Saul's question and couldn't just ignore it (*Radak*).

The Sages, however, state that God discovered a subtle trace of pride in Samuel's response, for *HASHEM scrutinizes the deeds of the righteous [and disciplines them even for a flaw] the size of a hair's-breadth* (*Yevamos* 121b).

Hashem thus rebuked Samuel, "Do you consider yourself to be a seer? I will show you that you do not always see." Years later, God sent Samuel to anoint one of the sons of Jesse as king (after Saul lost Divine favor), and Samuel erroneously assumed that it would be Jesse's oldest son, Eliab. God told him (below, 16:7), אַל־תַּבֵּט אֶל־מַרְאֵהוּ ... כִּי מְאַסְתִּיהוּ כִּי לֹא אֲשֶׁר יִרְאֶה הָאָדָם ..., *Do not look at his appearance ... for I have rejected him. For it is not as man sees ....* As *Be'er Moshe* explains, this was direct retribution (מִדָּה כְּנֶגֶד מִדָּה) for Samuel's error. By identifying himself as the seer, he implied that he foresaw Hashem's choice of Saul as king, and he was shown at the appointing of King David that he wouldn't recognize the chosen individual until the very last minute.

How then should Samuel have responded?

Radak states that he should have answered, "Ask someone else." *Kli Yakar* suggests that אָנֹכִי, *"It is I,"* would have sufficed. *Be'er Moshe* explains that Samuel was held responsible not for actual conceit, but for מֵיחֱזֵי כְּיוֹהֲרָא, an *apparent* haughtiness, misleading to someone who would have heard Samuel's answer but not Saul's question.

עֲלֵה לְפָנַי הַבָּמָה וַאֲכַלְתֶּם עִמִּי הַיּוֹם וְשִׁלַּחְתִּיךָ
כ בַבֹּקֶר וְכֹל אֲשֶׁר בִּלְבָבְךָ אַגִּיד לָךְ׃ וְלָאֲתֹנוֹת
הָאֹבְדוֹת לְךָ הַיּוֹם שְׁלֹשֶׁת הַיָּמִים אַל־תָּשֶׂם אֶת־
לִבְּךָ לָהֶם כִּי נִמְצָאוּ וּלְמִי כָּל־חֶמְדַּת יִשְׂרָאֵל הֲלוֹא
כא לְךָ וּלְכֹל בֵּית אָבִיךָ׃ וַיַּעַן שָׁאוּל וַיֹּאמֶר
הֲלוֹא בֶן־יְמִינִי אָנֹכִי מִקְּטַנֵּי שִׁבְטֵי יִשְׂרָאֵל
וּמִשְׁפַּחְתִּי הַצְּעִרָה מִכָּל־מִשְׁפְּחוֹת שִׁבְטֵי בִנְיָמִן
כב וְלָמָּה דִּבַּרְתָּ אֵלַי כַּדָּבָר הַזֶּה׃ וַיִּקַּח שְׁמוּאֵל
אֶת־שָׁאוּל וְאֶת־נַעֲרוֹ וַיְבִיאֵם לִשְׁכָּתָה וַיִּתֵּן

Me'am Loez derives a number of important guidelines from this exchange. For instance, a person who wishes to discuss or quote his students should not speak of "my student" but rather of "one of the students at the yeshivah." Also, a rabbi should never discuss his installation as *rabbi*, but rather his appointment to public service.

Incidentally, *Arizal* says that a נָבִיא, *prophet*, is a much higher level than a רוֹאֶה, *seer*. As implicit from the verse above (v. 9), *previously* prophets were called seers, but Samuel raised the spiritual status and he was indeed fit to be called a prophet. Thus, by referring to himself as a seer, he was actually belittling himself, and still he was punished (*Chomas Anach*).

עֲלֵה לְפָנַי הַבָּמָה וַאֲכַלְתֶּם עִמִּי — *Go up before me to the High Place, and you shall eat with me.*

Kli Yakar notes that in the present and following verse, Samuel addresses only Saul, with the exception of the invitation, וַאֲכַלְתֶּם, *you shall eat*, which is phrased in the plural. This indicates that only Samuel's invitation to the meal was addressed to both Saul and his servant. Everything else he said was meant for Saul alone.

וְשִׁלַּחְתִּיךָ — *I will send you away.*

It is not proper to depart from a great man without taking formal leave (*Metzudos*).

וְכֹל אֲשֶׁר בִּלְבָבְךָ אַגִּיד לָךְ — *And I will tell you whatever you desire.*

That is to say, any questions that you may have on your mind, whether in regard to Torah or to any other topic (*Malbim*).

Samuel was not referring here to the whereabouts of the donkeys, which would be discussed separately (*Abarbanel*).

Me'am Loez suggests that Saul, feeling the distress of the Jewish nation and aware of their request for a king, suspected that he was a candidate for the position, a supposition that Samuel confirmed: כֹּל אֲשֶׁר בִּלְבָבְךָ אַגִּיד לָךְ, *I will notify you of the appointment that you were thinking of.*

Abarbanel, who previously stated that Saul and his attendant intended to test Samuel by checking if he could retrace their route for them (see v. 8), interprets the verse in the context of that understanding: וְכֹל אֲשֶׁר בִּלְבָבְךָ אַגִּיד לָךְ, *I will gladly tell you of all the places that you have been.*

20. וְלָאֲתֹנוֹת הָאֹבְדוֹת לְךָ הַיּוֹם שְׁלֹשֶׁת הַיָּמִים — *As for the donkeys that have been lost to you for three days.*

Targum reckons these three days from the time that Saul and his attendant began their search, not from the time that the donkeys were lost.

The verse speaks of the donkeys

Go up before me to the High Place, and you shall eat with me today. I will send you away in the morning, and I will tell you whatever you desire.
[20] As for the donkeys that have been lost to you for three days — do not concern yourself over them, for they have been found. Besides, to whom does all the desirable property in Israel belong, if not to you and to all your father's family?"
[21] Saul answered, saying, "But I am only a Benjamite, and I am from the smallest of the tribes of Israel, and furthermore my family is the youngest of all the families of the tribe of Benjamin; why, then, have you spoken to me in this way?"
[22] Samuel then took Saul and his attendant and brought them into the chamber. He gave

הָאֹבְדוֹת לְךָ, *that have been lost to you,* although they belonged to Saul's father. *Kli Yakar* explains that since Saul's father had already retrieved them, the donkeys were lost only to Saul during these three days.

R' Chaim Palagi sees in this verse a hint to the Talmudic law that an animal that is roaming is considered *lost* after three days (*Bava Metzia* 30b; see specific details ad loc.).

וּלְמִי כָּל־חֶמְדַּת יִשְׂרָאֵל הֲלוֹא לְךָ — *Besides, to whom does all the desirable property in Israel belong, if not to you?*

In these words, Samuel hinted that Saul would be king and master of the entire national wealth, and thus need not concern himself with mere donkeys.

חֶמְדַּת יִשְׂרָאֵל, *desirable property in Israel,* refers to the Jews' material goods: their vineyards and farmlands (*Mahari Kara*).

According to *Me'am Loez,* כָּל־חֶמְדַּת יִשְׂרָאֵל — lit., *all the desires of Israel* — refers to a monarchy, the true object of Israel's desire.

21. וַיַּעַן שָׁאוּל וַיֹּאמֶר — *Saul answered, saying ...*

Saul immediately understood Samuel's hint, and in his humility argued that for various reasons, he was unworthy of the task. As mentioned earlier, one of Saul's outstanding traits that earned him the crown was his modesty.

הֲלוֹא בֶן־יְמִינִי אָנֹכִי מִקְּטַנֵּי שִׁבְטֵי יִשְׂרָאֵל — *But I am only a Benjamite and I am from the smallest of the tribes of Israel.*

The population of the tribe of Benjamin had been significantly diminished during the tragedy of the incident of the concubine in Gibeah.

Some commentaries see two independent statements in this statement. "First of all," Saul said, "I am not from Judah, the tribe known to be destined for royalty (see above, v. 2; *Ramban, Abarbanel*). Aside from that, I am from Benjamin, the smallest of all the tribes."

☙ Samuel Honors Saul

22. וַיְבִיאֵם לִשְׁכָּתָה — *And brought them into the chamber.*

The High Place (v. 12) was the building; the לִשְׁכָּה, *chamber,* was the room in which the banquet was held.

לָהֶם מָקוֹם בְּרֹאשׁ הַקְּרוּאִים וְהֵמָּה כִּשְׁלֹשִׁים
כג אִישׁ: וַיֹּאמֶר שְׁמוּאֵל לַטַּבָּח תְּנָה אֶת־הַמָּנָה
אֲשֶׁר נָתַתִּי לָךְ אֲשֶׁר אָמַרְתִּי אֵלֶיךָ שִׂים אֹתָהּ
כד עִמָּךְ: וַיָּרֶם הַטַּבָּח אֶת־הַשּׁוֹק וְהֶעָלֶיהָ וַיָּשֶׂם |
לִפְנֵי שָׁאוּל וַיֹּאמֶר הִנֵּה הַנִּשְׁאָר שִׂים־לְפָנֶיךָ
אֱכֹל כִּי לַמּוֹעֵד שָׁמוּר־לְךָ לֵאמֹר הָעָם קָרָאתִי

וַיִּתֵּן לָהֶם מָקוֹם בְּרֹאשׁ הַקְּרוּאִים — *He gave them a place at the head of the guests.*

It was evident from the seating arrangement which guests were especially prominent (*Rashi*). It is thus noteworthy that Saul's attendant, a mere lad, was seated at the head of the table. According to *Malbim*, this constituted a mark of respect for Saul, following the principle that the *servant of a king [commands homage just as] the king does.*

In addition, the attendant had played a major role in bringing Saul there (*Me'am Loez*).

Kli Yakar suggests, furthermore, that Samuel sat Saul's attendant in the immediate vicinity of Saul to teach Saul his first lesson of leadership: that he should equate himself with even the humblest members of society, in order that, as the Torah states, לְבִלְתִּי רוּם־לְבָבוֹ מֵאֶחָיו *his heart not grow haughty over his brethren* (*Deuteronomy* 17:20).

Another alternative, offered by *Kli Yakar*, is that the attendant was not being accorded any honor. Rather, it was a common practice to seat the attendant of a prominent man before him so that he might more easily serve him.

וְהֵמָּה כִּשְׁלֹשִׁים אִישׁ — *Who were some thirty men.*

Only the most esteemed people were invited to this feast (*Malbim*).

23. Having learned prophetically of Saul's imminent arrival, Samuel told the cook to reserve a special portion for him. After all the other guests were seated, Samuel would place Saul at the head of the table and publicly present him with this choice portion (*Abarbanel*).

This would serve two purposes. First, Samuel would honor Saul, and second, he would demonstrate that he had foreseen Saul's arrival (*Malbim*).

אֲשֶׁר נָתַתִּי לָךְ — *That I gave you.*

The fact that Samuel personally chose and handled this portion of meat added to the prestige that Samuel would accord Saul (*Kli Yakar*).

24. וַיָּרֶם הַטַּבָּח אֶת־הַשּׁוֹק — *So the cook lifted up the thigh.*

He raised it up in a grand manner, in what was a common gesture of obeisance performed when serving people of eminence (*Abarbanel*).

Malbim maintains that this portion was equivalent to the *breast and thigh* offered to the priests in the Temple (see below). Although at a private altar these portions were not allotted to priests (*Zevachim* 119b), they were nonetheless considered select portions and were awarded to the person who recited the blessing. In this case, Samuel assigned that privilege to Saul. In addition, just as the breast and thigh were raised as part of the service in the Temple (*Leviticus* 7:30-34), it was customary to raise them even at a private altar.

אֶת־הַשּׁוֹק וְהֶעָלֶיהָ — *The thigh and what was on it.*

The Talmud (*Avodah Zarah* 25a) offers three interpretations of the term הֶעָלֶיהָ, *what was on it:*

(a). **The אַלְיָה,** *tail.* This view is presumably based on the fact that the letters א and ע are often used interchangeably (*Me'am Loez*). The tail is considered

them a place at the head of the invited guests, who were some thirty men. [23] *Samuel said to the cook, "Bring the portion that I gave you, about which I told you, 'Keep it with yourself.' "* [24] *So the cook lifted up the thigh and what was on it, and placed it before Saul. [Samuel] then said, "This is the portion that was set aside. Put it before yourself — eat; for it was reserved for you when I told [the cook how many] people I had invited."*

to be עָלֶיהָ, *on [the thigh],* because it is attached to the animal's body slightly higher than the thigh.[1]

(b) **The חָזֶה,** *breast.* The breast is referred to as being עָלֶיהָ, *upon [the thigh],* because it was placed on top of the thigh during the "waving" ceremony.

According to this opinion, the choice of portion contained an implicit message that the king must maintain a strong heart to withstand his adversaries (*Me'am Loez*)

(c) **The כַּף הַיָּרֵךְ,** *hip-socket.* This is right above the thigh and is thus described as עָלֶיהָ, *upon it. Targum* and *Rashi* follow this opinion.

Accordingly, a king must race forward enthusiastically on behalf of his nation (*Me'am Loez*).

וַיֹּאמֶר הִנֵּה הַנִּשְׁאָר שִׂים־לְפָנֶיךָ אֱכֹל כִּי לַמּוֹעֵד שָׁמוּר־לְךָ לֵאמֹר הָעָם קָרָאתִי — *[Samuel] then said, "This is the portion that was set aside. Put it before yourself — eat; for it was reserved for you when I told [the cook how many] people I had invited."*

This statement is vague and cryptic, and the commentators offer varying interpretations regarding who made it and exactly what it is meant to convey.

Our translation follows *Rashi,* who explains that Samuel delivered this entire statement, telling Saul that this portion had been reserved for him and that he should therefore not hesitate to eat it.

Most commentators, however, following the flow of the verse (which mentions only the cook), assume that the cook delivered this statement.

Mahari Kara, who is one of these commentators, explains the message much the same as *Rashi* does. As the cook gave Saul his portion, he told Saul not to be concerned that he was getting someone else's piece because הִנֵּה הַנִּשְׁאָר, *This is the portion that was set aside.* שִׂים־לְפָנֶיךָ אֱכֹל, *Put it before yourself — eat,* כִּי לַמּוֹעֵד שָׁמוּר־לְךָ, *for it was reserved for you,* לֵאמֹר הָעָם קָרָאתִי, *when [Samuel] told [me,] "I have invited the people [to come in honor of an esteemed person, and this portion is for him."]*

Other opinions claim that the entire quote, including the latter part regarding the extending of invitations, was made by the cook about himself, since he was authorized to figure out the amount of guests and invite them. Thus, he said, אֱכֹל כִּי לַמּוֹעֵד שָׁמוּר־לְךָ, *Eat, for it was reserved for you,* לֵאמֹר הָעָם קָרָאתִי, *when I* — i.e., the cook — *calculated the [number of] people that I had invited.*

But what is the meaning of הַנִּשְׁאָר, *the portion that was set aside?*

Some say, as *Mahari Kara* above, that the cook meant to reassure Saul that

1. Since this animal was presumably brought as an offering, albeit on a private altar, it seems incongruous that Saul could have been served the tail, as that part is burned with the fats on the altar (*Leviticus* 3:9). See *Teshuvos Radvaz* Vol. II §679; *Nachalas Shimon* 22:3. See above, v. 12.

כה וַיֹּאכַל שָׁאוּל עִם־שְׁמוּאֵל בַּיּוֹם הַהוּא: וַיֵּרְדוּ
מֵהַבָּמָה הָעִיר וַיְדַבֵּר עִם־שָׁאוּל עַל־הַגָּג:
כו וַיַּשְׁכִּמוּ וַיְהִי כַּעֲלוֹת הַשַּׁחַר וַיִּקְרָא שְׁמוּאֵל
°הַגָּגָה ק׳ אֶל־שָׁאוּל °הגג לֵאמֹר קוּמָה וַאֲשַׁלְּחֶךָּ וַיָּקָם
כז שָׁאוּל וַיֵּצְאוּ שְׁנֵיהֶם הוּא וּשְׁמוּאֵל הַחוּצָה: הֵמָּה
יוֹרְדִים בִּקְצֵה הָעִיר וּשְׁמוּאֵל אָמַר אֶל־שָׁאוּל
אֱמֹר לַנַּעַר וְיַעֲבֹר לְפָנֵינוּ וַיַּעֲבֹר וְאַתָּה עֲמֹד

no one was going to go hungry on his account — הִנֵּה הַנִּשְׁאָר, *this piece is set aside for you* (*Me'am Loez*).

Abarbanel, on the other hand, explains that the cook intended to preclude any suspicions that he was serving Saul leftovers: ... הִנֵּה הַנִּשְׁאָר, *This is reserved [for you from yesterday — it was not accumulated from any leftovers].*

According to *Kli Yakar*, the cook feared that Saul would suspect that he was giving Saul his own portion and thus refuse to eat. The cook therefore showed Saul what was left in the pot and said הִנֵּה הַנִּשְׁאָר, *This is what is left [for me], and so you may eat to your heart's content.*

Malbim, consistent with his belief that the portions served were the *breast and thigh* (see above), claims that those parts are called נִשְׁאָר, *remains*, because they may be considered *God's leftovers*, insofar as the owner "sacrifices" these pieces to Hashem, and Hashem in turn allots them to the Kohanim. Accordingly, when the cook served Saul, he told him, הִנֵּה הַנִּשְׁאָר, *Here are the remains.*

וַיֹּאכַל שָׁאוּל עִם־שְׁמוּאֵל בַּיּוֹם הַהוּא — *So Saul ate with Samuel on that day.*

The feast lasted the entire day (*Malbim*).

25. וַיֵּרְדוּ — *When they descended.*

They descended at nighttime (*Malbim*).

וַיְדַבֵּר עִם־שָׁאוּל — *He spoke with Saul.*

Scripture does not reveal what Samuel and Saul spoke about. *Rashi* explains that Samuel instructed Saul to fear God. (See *Deuteronomy* 17:19.)

According to *Kli Yakar* and *Malbim*, Samuel and Saul discussed the mystic secrets of the Torah and other Divine topics.

Abarbanel, consistent with his approach (as described above, vs. 6,19), states that Samuel retraced for Saul all of his experiences since he had set out to seek the donkeys.

עַל־הַגָּג — *On the rooftop.*

This was the roof of Samuel's house (*Metzudos*).

Perhaps they went onto the roof because *the walls have ears* (*Midrash*) and, as they were discussing private and secretive issues, they wished to avoid being overheard (*Kli Yakar*).

Be'er Moshe states that Samuel imparted a crucial lesson to Saul by taking him to the roof. Our Sages teach that a roof represents the trait of arrogance (see *Pesichta D'Eichah Rabbasi* :24). In a Jewish monarchy, the king has earned no right to power, for he is no more than Hashem's representative; therefore, humility is a basic prerequisite. As the Torah states clearly, לְבִלְתִּי רוּם־לְבָבוֹ מֵאֶחָיו, *[The king's] heart [should] not become haughty over his brethren* (*Deuteronomy* 17:20). By taking Saul to the roof, Samuel communicated to him that even the slightest trace of arrogance on the part of the king threatens the survival of the monarchy.

Conversely, *Me'am Loez* suggests that by bringing Saul to the roof, Samuel hinted that although Saul had a humble disposition, a king must act firmly and dominantly (although without arrogance).

26. וַיַּשְׁכִּמוּ וַיְהִי כַּעֲלוֹת הַשַּׁחַר — *They arose early [the next morning], and at daybreak ...*

So Saul ate with Samuel on that day.
[25]*When they descended from the High Place to the city, he spoke with Saul on the rooftop.* [26]*They arose early [the next morning], and at daybreak Samuel called Saul to the roof, saying, "Arise, I will send you off." So Saul arose and the two of them — he and Samuel — went outside.* [27]*As they were going down at the edge of town, Samuel said to Saul, "Tell the attendant to go on ahead of us"; so he passed ahead. "You stand here*

They arose in the middle of the night and studied Torah until daybreak (*Me'am Loez*).

וַיִּקְרָא שְׁמוּאֵל אֶל־שָׁאוּל הַגָּגָה — *Samuel called Saul to the roof.*

Kli Yakar assumes that Samuel regularly slept on the roof. After they spoke in the evening, Saul went down into the house, and at daybreak Samuel called him back up to the roof.

Kli Yakar further explains that Saul was probably eager to return to his father, who was presumably worried about him. However, he could not leave without permission from Samuel, and Samuel would not want him to go until it grew light (as the Talmud advises, travelers should set out during the day — *Pesachim* 2a). Immediately at daybreak (or possibly a bit before, as may be inferred from the כ, *around*, of כַּעֲלוֹת הַשַּׁחַר, *around daybreak*), Samuel summoned Saul and told him to prepare for his departure.

קוּמָה וַאֲשַׁלְּחֶךָּ — *Arise, I will send you off.*

Metzudos renders וַאֲשַׁלְּחֶךָּ as *I will escort you,* as in *Genesis* 18:16: וְאַבְרָהָם הֹלֵךְ עִמָּם לְשַׁלְּחָם, *Abraham walked with them to escort them.*

וַיֵּצְאוּ שְׁנֵיהֶם הוּא וּשְׁמוּאֵל הַחוּצָה — *And the two of them — he and Samuel went outside.*

Samuel escorted Saul because he wanted to anoint him outside of the city in an isolated area, since אֵין הַבְּרָכָה מְצוּיָה אֶלָּא בְּדָבָר הַסָּמוּי מִן הָעַיִן, *Blessing* (i.e., *success*) *prevails only in matters concealed from the [public] eye* (*Bava Metzia* 42a; *Kli Yakar*).

27. וּשְׁמוּאֵל אָמַר אֶל־שָׁאוּל אֱמֹר לַנַּעַר ... — *Samuel said to Saul, "Tell the attendant ..."*

Samuel did not speak to the attendant himself, for it is not proper to tell someone else's attendant what to do (*Abarbanel*).

Alternatively, Samuel did not want the attendant to sense that anything extraordinary was occurring, which he would have if Samuel himself had ordered him away. However, he might attribute Saul's sending him away to nothing more than Saul's belief that Samuel wants to discuss something of a confidential nature with him.

וְיַעֲבֹר לְפָנֵינוּ — *To go on ahead of us.*

To a place distant enough that he should be unable to hear our conversation (*Rashi*).

וַיַּעֲבֹר — *So he passed ahead.*

Mahari Kara notes that Scripture elides Saul's command to his attendant, mentioning only that the servant obeyed.

Metzudos, however, states that there was no such command; when the attendant heard Samuel speaking to Saul, he immediately left of his own volition.

וְאַתָּה עֲמֹד — *You stand ...*

After recording the attendant's immediate obedience, Scripture returns to Samuel's instructions to Saul.

א כַּיּוֹם וְאַשְׁמִיעֲךָ אֶת־דְּבַר אֱלֹהִים׃ וַיִּקַּח שְׁמוּאֵל אֶת־פַּךְ הַשֶּׁמֶן וַיִּצֹק עַל־רֹאשׁוֹ וַיִּשָּׁקֵהוּ

עֲמֹד — *Stand.*

Samuel told Saul that what he had to tell him was of such importance that he must stand still in order to properly concentrate. (Similarly, when the time comes to recite the *Shema,* which involves a declaration of allegiance to God's sovereignty, a traveler must stand still for the essential first few verses [*Berachos* 13b].)

עֲמֹד כַּיּוֹם — *Stand here now.*

Our translation, rendering כַּיּוֹם — lit., *as day* — as *now,* follows *Metzudos.*

Malbim explains the phrase to mean, *It is as clear as day that you will rise to royalty and success.*

Me'am Loez suggests that just as the light of the coming day will grow ever brighter, so too will Saul's kingdom continuously shed more light upon the nation.

According to *Abarbanel,* Samuel told Saul to await the arrival of sunrise, at which point he would anoint him, for Saul's kingdom should commence with strength, like "the powerfully rising sun" (*Judges* 5:31).

X

The role of a Jewish monarch is a demanding one, particularly in the diversity of its often-conflicting responsibilities.

The role requires strength and courage, yet at the same time humility and compassion. It requires firm confidence and decisiveness blended with a deep trust in, and loyalty to, the will of God. It requires an elevated sense of spirituality, yet also a keen sensitivity to the smallest details of life and the concerns of simple people, so that one may evaluate each of life's trials with its many subtle facets in order to make wise decisions.

This chapter, which describes Saul's inauguration, illustrates his possession of these requirements, and relates how he initially maintained an almost perfect balance between them.

⇐§ Samuel Anoints Saul and Gives Him Prophetic Signs

1. ... וַיִּקַּח שְׁמוּאֵל — *Then Samuel took ...*

Rambam cites this verse to illustrate the rubric that a Jewish king can be appointed only via the authority of a prophet. There is another prerequisite as well, states *Rambam,* which is that this appointment must meet with the approval of the High Court of seventy elders (*Hil. Melachim* 1:3).

Presumably, Samuel consulted with these elders prior to anointing Saul, although Scripture makes no mention of that meeting (*Me'am Loez*).

אֶת־פַּךְ הַשֶּׁמֶן — *A flask of oil.*

Saul and Yehu[1] were both anointed from an earthenware flask, which breaks easily and, once broken, cannot be repaired — and their reigns did not extend for posterity. David and Solomon, on the other hand, were anointed from a horn, which is solid and long-lasting — and their dynasty did extend for posterity (below, 16:1; *I Kings* 1:39; *Maharsha* on *Megillah* 14a; see above, comm. to 2:1).

הַשֶּׁמֶן — *Of oil.*

The שֶׁמֶן הַמִּשְׁחָה, *anointment oil,* was composed of a formula that came from the days of Moses (*Exodus* 30:22-34), and had been used to consecrate the priests and the vessels of the Tabernacle.

1. Regarding Yehu, see *II Kings* 9:1-3.

now and I will let you hear the word of God."

10/1 [1] *Then Samuel took a flask of oil and poured some onto [Saul's] head, and he kissed him.*

In addition, this oil was to be used to consecrate those kings belonging to the Davidic dynasty exclusively (*Kereisos* 5b). In light of this last criterion, *Radak* denies that Saul was anointed with this oil. Rather, he was anointed with balsam oil.

Rashi and *Tosafos* (*Kereisos* ad loc.), however, contend that the limitation of the anointment oil to Davidic kings began only after the appointment of King David; Saul thus could have been anointed with it, and indeed was (see also *Rambam, Hil. Melachim* 1:7; *Nachalas Shimon* 23:1).

Oil symbolizes humility, a trait that a righteous king must possess (*Be'er Moshe*).

In addition, anointing the king with oil expressed the prayer that his leadership would rise to the greatest heights, just as oil does not mix with other liquids but rises to the top (*Me'am Loez*).

וַיִּצֹק עַל־רֹאשׁוֹ — *And poured some onto [Saul's] head.*

Scripture mentions only the pouring of oil on his head. Typically, at any anointment ceremony, this was either preceded by or followed by a smearing of oil on his forehead, which, in the case of a king, was done in the configuration of a crown (*Kereisos* ibid., *Horayos* 12a).

This anointment process invested Saul with a new spirit, explained by *Malbim* as power and confidence and by *Abarbanel* as sanctity and godliness.

Since this anointment was of major national significance, why didn't Samuel perform it in public?

Abarbanel suggests that Samuel still intended to draw lots to determine whom God had chosen as ruler, and thus anointing Saul in public would cast doubt on the probity of the casting of lots.

But that begs a new question: since Samuel intended to cast lots, why did he first anoint Saul? The answer is that he did so in order to infuse Saul with godliness and transform him into a "new man" (see verses 9-10).

According to *Kli Yakar*, Samuel anointed Saul privately in accordance with the concept that success devolves upon matters that are concealed (see *Bava Metzia* 42a). This precaution was particularly germane in Saul's case, for his appointment was potentially contentious, since he belonged to the tribe of Benjamin and not to Judah, the tribe designated for royalty.

Additionally, had this anointment been performed in the public eye, the facts of its being performed (a) with an earthenware flask and (b) without the anointing oil (see above) would have made the people immediately aware that this monarchy would be temporary (*Malbim*).

וַיִּשָּׁקֵהוּ — *And he kissed him.*

Kissing is appropriate only on three occasions: (a) upon greeting someone after a protracted separation (see *Exodus* 4:27); (b) upon parting from someone (see *Ruth* 1:14); and (c) at an inauguration such as this one (*Bereishis Rabbah* 70:12).

Yefeh Toar (ad loc.) explains that with this kiss Samuel demonstrated that Saul was a great person worthy of the people's love.

In addition, with this kiss Samuel communicated that although he had previously opposed the Jews' request for a king he trusted Saul in that role (*Daas Sofrim*).

Malbim states that this kiss linked Samuel's spirit to that of Saul and instilled an element of sanctity into him, which prepared him for the experience of prophecy.

וַיֹּאמֶר הֲלוֹא כִּי־מְשָׁחֲךָ יהוה עַל־נַחֲלָתוֹ לְנָגִיד׃
ב בְּלֶכְתְּךָ הַיּוֹם מֵעִמָּדִי וּמָצָאתָ שְׁנֵי אֲנָשִׁים
עִם־קְבֻרַת רָחֵל בִּגְבוּל בִּנְיָמִן בְּצֶלְצַח וְאָמְרוּ
אֵלֶיךָ נִמְצְאוּ הָאֲתֹנוֹת אֲשֶׁר הָלַכְתָּ לְבַקֵּשׁ
וְהִנֵּה נָטַשׁ אָבִיךָ אֶת־דִּבְרֵי הָאֲתֹנוֹת וְדָאַג לָכֶם
ג לֵאמֹר מָה אֶעֱשֶׂה לִבְנִי׃ וְחָלַפְתָּ מִשָּׁם וָהָלְאָה

וַיֹּאמֶר הֲלוֹא כִּי־מְשָׁחֲךָ ה׳ — *He said, "It is indeed the case that HASHEM has anointed you."*

Our translation follows *Metzudos,* which renders הֲלוֹא as בֶּאֱמֶת, *indeed.* Accordingly, the word כִּי, which can be translated in a variety of ways (*Rosh Hashanah* 3a; see *Rashi* to *Genesis* 18:15), is rendered here as אֲשֶׁר, *that.*

Mahari Kara, on the other hand, translates כִּי as *because,* and inserts [I have done this to you], *because God has anointed you....*

Radak comments that the word הֲלוֹא is often used as an expression to confirm something and inspire those involved.

כִּי־מְשָׁחֲךָ ה׳ — *HASHEM has anointed you.*

Abarbanel offers three reasons that God did not leave the election of a king to a popular vote: (a) to avoid strife; (b) a king must be an exceptionally noble person with no evil tendencies of any sort, and that is something that only God can judge; (c) if the people had chosen Saul, he might have been tempted to flatter the people and make biased decisions.

עַל־נַחֲלָתוֹ — *Over His inheritance.*

The Jewish people are God's *inheritance.*

Also, the word נַחֲלָה, *inheritance,* generally refers to real estate. A ruler of the Jews is placed in control of Hashem's holy land (*Daas Sofrim*).

לְנָגִיד — *As ruler.*

As mentioned above (9:16), the word נָגִיד, *ruler,* implies a temporary leader. Thus, Samuel subtly connotes: the reason for using a flask containing balsam oil and not a horn containing anointment oil is because you are being appointed only as a נָגִיד (*Kli Yakar*).

2. בְּלֶכְתְּךָ הַיּוֹם מֵעִמָּדִי ... — *When you leave me today ...*

In order to help Saul believe in his newly acquired royal status and in the fact that God Himself had chosen him king, Samuel told Saul three experiences that he would undergo that very day.

עִם־קְבֻרַת רָחֵל בִּגְבוּל בִּנְיָמִן בְּצֶלְצַח — *Near Rachel's Tomb, within the border of Benjamin, in Zelzah.*

Literally translated, עִם־קְבֻרַת רָחֵל means *at Rachel's Tomb.* This is obviously problematic, because Rachel was buried in Bethlehem (or Efrath — *Genesis* 35:19), which is located in the portion of Judah, not Benjamin (see *Micah* 5:1).

Our translation follows *Mahari Kara,* who reads the word עִם as *near,* and indeed, Bethlehem is near the border of Judah and Benjamin. (The purpose of mentioning Rachel's Tomb will be discussed below.)

Alternatively, *Tosefta* (*Sotah* 11:7, cited by *Rashi*) understands Samuel's message as follows: "The men are currently at Rachel's Tomb. As you leave here, they will also start traveling, and you will meet them at Zelzah, which is in Benjamin's portion." (See also *Bereishis Rabbah* 82:9, *Rashash, Yefeh Toar.*)

בְּצֶלְצַח — *In Zelzah.*

This name can be divided into two

He said, "It is indeed the case that HASHEM *has anointed you as ruler over His inheritance.* [2]*When you leave me today you will meet two men near Rachel's Tomb, within the border of Benjamin, in Zelzah. They will tell you that the donkeys that you went to seek were found, and that your father has set aside the matter of the donkeys and has begun to worry about you, saying, 'What shall I do about my son?'*

[3]*Then you will travel from there and beyond*

words: צֵל, *shade*, and צַח, *white* or *clear*. Accordingly, *Rashi* homiletically interprets that as a reference to Jerusalem (which was in the portion of Benjamin). Jerusalem is God's dwelling, which may also be referred to as His *shade*, and God is referred to as *pure* (*Song of Songs* 5:10; see *Rashi, Joshua* 15:8, *and* ibid. 18:28).

Me'am Loez states that each detail of this seemingly unnecessary description represents one of the merits whereby Saul attained the crown.

1. Rachel's Tomb recalls the merit of Saul's ancestor Rachel, and is reminiscent of the fact that she gave birth to Benjamin in the Land of Israel.

2. The verse's reference to *the border of Benjamin* recalls the fact that Benjamin was the sole son of Jacob to be born in the Land.

3. Zelzah can be interpreted to mean, "the dark shade is clearly illuminated." This recalls Saul's grandfather, Ner, who lit candles on dark roadways for the public weal (see above, 9:1, comm.).

4. Finally, the verse continues with a reference to the lost donkeys, an oblique reference to Saul's fulfillment of the command to honor one's parents, for in the course of his journey to find his father's donkeys he endangered his life.

וְהִנֵּה נָטַשׁ אָבִיךָ אֶת־דִּבְרֵי הָאֲתֹנוֹת — *And that your father has set aside the matter of the donkeys ...*

According to *Radak*, Saul's father set aside the issue of the donkeys even before they were found and instead began worrying about Saul.

Metzudos disagrees and explains instead that only after the donkeys were found and Saul's father was relieved of his worry about them was he overwhelmed by a much greater worry: the well-being of Saul.

וְדָאַג לָכֶם לֵאמֹר מָה אֶעֱשֶׂה לִבְנִי — *And has begun to worry about you, saying, "What shall I do about my son?"*

Abarbanel observes that the word לָכֶם, *about you*, is in the plural. This implies that Kish was concerned for both Saul and the attendant, yet his impassioned outcry was only for his son.[1]

3. וְחָלַפְתָּ מִשָּׁם וָהָלְאָה — *Then you will travel from there and beyond.*

1. *R' Yisrael Salanter* in *Eitz Pri*, cites this verse to illustrate a monumental emotional concept. At times, a person may have subconscious feelings that he himself is not aware of, but that surface at a moment of truth. For example, although a person may show more active affection for a student than for his son, particularly if the student follows in his path and the son does not, still, if there were to be a fire, he would instinctively save his son first because of his deeper, albeit unknown, love for his son. Thus, although Saul's father, on a conscious level, was דָאַג לָכֶם — worried about both of you, still Scripture testifies that לֵאמֹר מָה אֶעֱשֶׂה לִבְנִי — subconsciously he was still more concerned about his son.

וּבָ֨אתָ עַד־אֵל֣וֹן תָּב֔וֹר וּמְצָא֣וּךָ שָּׁ֗ם שְׁלֹשָׁ֤ה אֲנָשִׁים
עֹלִ֥ים אֶל־הָאֱלֹהִ֖ים בֵּֽית־אֵ֑ל אֶחָ֞ד נֹשֵׂ֣א ׀ שְׁלֹשָׁ֣ה
גְדָיִ֗ים וְאֶחָ֙ד נֹשֵׂ֜א שְׁלֹ֙שֶׁת֙ כִּכְּר֣וֹת לֶ֔חֶם וְאֶחָ֥ד נֹשֵׂ֖א
ד נֵֽבֶל־יָֽיִן׃ וְשָׁאֲל֥וּ לְךָ֖ לְשָׁל֑וֹם וְנָתְנ֣וּ לְךָ֔ שְׁתֵּי־לֶ֖חֶם
ה וְלָקַחְתָּ֖ מִיָּדָֽם׃ אַ֣חַר כֵּ֗ן תָּבוֹא֙ גִּבְעַ֣ת הָאֱלֹהִ֔ים

This encounter in the Plain of Tabor would be the second of the three signs predicted by Samuel.

וְחָלַפְתָּ, *you shall travel,* in itself means that Saul would move on. What then is the necessity for the added words מִשָּׁם וָהָלְאָה, *from there and beyond?*

Me'am Loez suggests that וְחָלַפְתָּ connotes *you shall change* (see *Genesis* 31:7); after Saul experienced the first sign, it would be incumbent upon him to "become a new man" (verse 6). Accordingly, מִשָּׁם וָהָלְאָה instructs him to *travel forward.*

Similarly, *Kli Yakar* understands וְחָלַפְתָּ as a prediction that after Saul saw the fulfillment of the first sign, his spirit would be *re-invigorated* with the recognition of the reality of his new position, and that with this revitalized spirit he would *travel onward* from there to the Plain of Tabor (see below).

וּבָאתָ עַד־אֵלוֹן תָּבוֹר — *And come to the Plain of Tabor.*

According to *Kli Yakar* (see above), this name recollects Mount Tabor, one of the peaks that God rejected as a site for the giving of the Torah because of its height and haughtiness (*Midrash Shocher Tov* 68:9). Samuel was thus imparting a covert message to Saul: "Now that you have grown enthusiastic about ruling the Jewish people, you must remember the lesson of Mount Tabor and suppress any possible arrogance."

וּמְצָאוּךָ — *Then you will be met by.*

The previous verse referred to Saul's meeting other men with the term, וּמָצָאתָ, *you will meet,* for he would come upon them as he was traveling.

In this verse, the verb used to describe Saul's encounter with others is וּמְצָאוּךָ, *you will be met by,* for these men would be traveling as well, so that they would come across Saul on the road.

עֹלִים אֶל־הָאֱלֹהִים בֵּית־אֵל — *On their way to [worship] God at Beth El.*

Targum Yonasan inserts: *on their way to [bow down to] God ...*

Originally known as Luz, Beth-el was where Jacob established a monument to God and proclaimed, *This stone which I have set up as a pillar shall become a house of God* (28:22). Notwithstanding the Midrashic assertion that Jacob was referring to Jerusalem (see *Rashi, ibid. v.* 17), the literal meaning of that verse is that Jacob established Beth-el as a holy place of prayer.

In subsequent periods of history during which private altars were permitted, Beth-el was a choice location for offerings. In addition, many prophets came to Beth-el to be spiritually inspired and learn about heavenly decrees, for Beth -el was, in Jacob's words, *the gate of heaven* (*Genesis* 28:17; *Radak*).

Also, it was at Beth-el that Jacob was told that kings would descend from him, which was a reference to Saul and his son Ish-bosheth (see *Genesis* 35:11, *Rashi* ad loc.). Possibly, for that reason, Beth-el was mentioned here (*Mishbetzos Zahav*).

According to *Metzudos*, Beth-el mentioned here is actually a reference to Shiloh, which had previously been the site of the Tabernacle.

and come to the Plain of Tabor, then you will be met by three men on their way to [worship] God at Beth-el — one carrying three kids, one carrying three loaves of bread, and one carrying a container of wine. [4]*They will greet you and give you two breads, which you should take from them.* [5]*After that you will arrive at the Hill of God,*

4. וְשָׁאֲלוּ לְךָ לְשָׁלוֹם — *They will greet you.*

They will greet Saul respectfully, apparently aware that he is destined for leadership (*Daas Sofrim*).

וְנָתְנוּ לְךָ שְׁתֵּי־לֶחֶם — *And give you two breads.*

Considering the fact that these three men had only three loaves of bread, it seems unreasonable to expect that they would give two of them to Saul and his attendant, leaving only one for themselves.

According to *Abarbanel*, however, this is indeed what happened, and their unexpected behavior showed that they miraculously recognized Saul's royal status (*Kli Yakar, Daas Sofrim*).

Alternatively, *Kli Yakar* states that the men broke off two *pieces* of bread. Accordingly, this constituted a message for Saul: "Do not be too proud to accept gifts as humble as the broken pieces of bread of a poor man's meal."

Radak observes that in verse 3 *Targum Yonasan* renders כִּכְּרוֹת לֶחֶם, *loaves of bread*, as פִּתִּין דִלְחֵם, and in verse 4 translates לֶחֶם, *bread*, as גְּרִיצָן דִלְחֵם. *Radak* interprets these, respectively, as large loaves and small loaves[1] (apparently, the smaller loaves were not mentioned in verse 3 because of their relative insignificance). Thus, the men gave Saul two smaller loaves, but retained the larger loaves for themselves.

שְׁתֵּי־לֶחֶם — *Two breads.*

שְׁתֵּי, *two*, is the feminine form. The word לֶחֶם, *bread*, is sometimes grammatically considered masculine and sometimes feminine (see above, 9:7: הַלֶּחֶם אָזַל, which is masculine; see also *Tosafos, Menachos* 94a; *Tosafos Yom Tov, Menachos* 11:1).

וְלָקַחְתָּ מִיָּדָם — *Which you should take from them.*

Samuel felt it necessary to instruct Saul to take the bread because he knew that Saul was not accustomed to accepting gifts (see above, 9:7; *Daas Sofrim*).

Samuel did not give Saul any food for the road, but instead assured him that he would be offered bread on the way (*Daas Sofrim*).

5. אַחַר כֵּן — *After that ...*

This is the third and last of the prophetic signs that Samuel gave to Saul.

גִּבְעַת הָאֱלֹהִים — *The Hill of God.*

This is a reference to Kiriath-je'arim, where the Holy Ark was stationed (7:1,2; *Targum, Rashi*).[2]

1. *Exodus* 29:23 makes a similar distinction.

2. *Me'am Loez* comments on the significance of the three locations of Saul's encounters.

a. **Zelzah** was, some say, Jerusalem; that site reminded him to place his full trust in God, Whose Presence resides in Jerusalem.

b. **Tabor** was the site of the Jewish victory against Sisera (*Judges* 4:6), and therefore served as a source of strength and encouragement.

c. **Kiriath-je'arim** was the home of the Ark, which housed the Holy Tablets, representing the Torah. Saul's encounter there was meant to arouse in him a strong dedication to Torah.

אֲשֶׁר־שָׁם נְצִבֵי פְלִשְׁתִּים וִיהִי כְבֹאֲךָ שָׁם הָעִיר
וּפָגַעְתָּ חֶבֶל נְבִיאִים יֹרְדִים מֵהַבָּמָה וְלִפְנֵיהֶם
ו נֵבֶל וְתֹף וְחָלִיל וְכִנּוֹר וְהֵמָּה מִתְנַבְּאִים׃ וְצָלְחָה
עָלֶיךָ רוּחַ יהוה וְהִתְנַבִּיתָ עִמָּם וְנֶהְפַּכְתָּ לְאִישׁ
ז אַחֵר׃ וְהָיָה כִּי °תבאינה הָאֹתוֹת הָאֵלֶּה לָךְ

°תָּבֹאנָה ק׳

אֲשֶׁר־שָׁם נְצִבֵי פְלִשְׁתִּים — *Where the Philistine officials are stationed.*

As mentioned above, after Samuel grew old and was less active (see above, 7:14, 9:16), the Philistines regained some control over the Jews, and stationed officials at strategic locations around the land of Israel.

Daas Sofrim states that the Philistine officials allowed the prophets to carry on at will, for they were still somewhat humbled by their recollection of the tribulations that they had suffered on account of the Ark (Chapter 5).

Kli Yakar disagrees, stating that the Philistines' intent in placing their soldiers near the Ark was to demonstrate an insolent disregard for Jewish sensibilities.

In addition, the Philistines intended to instill in those Jews who visited the Ark a fear of themselves that would dispel any spiritual inspiration. Possibly, Samuel mentioned these Philistines to impress upon Saul the concept that he must not be frightened by them but join with the prophets with joy and confidence.

Radak comments that Saul received a Divine spirit at this location for two reasons: (a) Prophetic Inspiration came via the presence of the Ark, and (b) the presence of the Philistine officials impressed upon him the need to eventually remove them from power.

וּפָגַעְתָּ חֶבֶל נְבִיאִים — *You will encounter a band of prophets.*

Based on *Targum, Radak* concludes that these were disciples of the primary prophets of the generation.

Scripture's comment that prophecy was scarce in those days (3:1) refers specifically to the pre-Samuel era. With the emergence of Samuel, a new group of prophets came forward (*Ralbag, Abarbanel;* see comm. to 3:1,21).

Me'am Loez quotes a Midrash stating that this band of prophets was composed of all those who had been named Samuel following a Divine proclamation that a prophet would be born with the name of Samuel (see above).

וְלִפְנֵיהֶם נֵבֶל וְתֹף וְחָלִיל וְכִנּוֹר — *Preceded by [musicians playing on] a lyre, drum, flute, and harp.*

A person can prophesy only in an atmosphere of joy, and that may be induced by music. Similarly, Scripture tells of Elisha that וְהָיָה כְּנַגֵּן הַמְנַגֵּן וַתְּהִי עָלָיו יַד־ה׳, *as the musician played, the hand of* Hashem *came upon him* (*II Kings* 3:15; see *Rambam, Hil. Yesodei HaTorah* 7:4).

נֵבֶל וְתֹף וְחָלִיל וְכִנּוֹר — *Lyre, drum, flute, and harp.*

For an elaborate description of the lyre, drum, and harp, see comm. to *ArtScroll Tehillim* 33:2, 150:3,4.

וְהֵמָּה מִתְנַבְּאִים — *And they will be prophesying.*

Prophecy refers to the word of God — in this case, Divinely inspired praise of God (*Targum*); it does not necessarily involve foretelling the future.

Abarbanel contends that grammatically the word מִתְנַבְּאִים does not mean *prophesying* but rather *preparing themselves* for prophecy.

6. וְצָלְחָה עָלֶיךָ רוּחַ ה׳ — *The spirit of* Hashem *will then pass over you.*

The nation will witness that Jewish kings do not attain the throne as do other monarchs — through bloody

where the Philistine officials are stationed. It
shall be that when you arrive at the city you
will encounter a band of prophets descending
from the High Place, preceded by [musicians
playing on] a lyre, drum, flute, and harp, and
they will be prophesying. 6 *The spirit of HASHEM*
will then pass over you, and you will prophesy
with them, and you will be transformed into an-
other person. 7 *After these signs come upon you,*

battles and revolutions — but rather by the word of God (*Me'am Loez*).

רוּחַ ה׳ — *The spirit of HASHEM.*

Sometimes, as in this verse, *Targum* translates רוּחַ ה׳ as **רוּחַ נְבוּאָה מִן קֳדָם ה׳**, *a spirit of prophecy from HASHEM* (see also *Judges* 3:10; below, 16:13). In other instances, it translates this phrase as a **רוּחַ גְּבוּרָה מִן קֳדָם ה׳**, *a spirit of strength from HASHEM* (*Judges* 6:34, 11:29).

Daas Sofrim explains that although *the spirit of HASHEM* manifests itself in different ways, it generally constitutes a wave of Godly inspiration that helps a person perform tasks with extraordinary perfection. See *Abarbanel* below, 11:6.

Later, when Scripture describes how *the spirit of HASHEM* was removed from Saul (below, 16:14), *Targum* renders the phrase not as a *spirit of prophecy* but as *a spirit of might.*

Possibly, this change indicates that the present verse describes Saul receiving two aspects of *the spirit of HASHEM*: a one-time *spirit of prophecy* that lasted for a short time, and a *spirit of might* that remained with him longer. Alternatively, even then the spirit of prophecy remained with him, and only the רוּחַ גְּבוּרָה of leadership was retracted (*Daas Sofrim*).

Malbim explains רוּחַ ה׳ even here as a *spirit of might* — a Divine sense of confidence and fearlessness.

According to *Abarbanel*, this verse describes a three-part process that Saul was to go through: first, he would have רוּחַ ה׳, a desire to prophesy; second, וְהִתְנַבִּיתָ עִמָּם, he was told to act upon that desire and attempt to prophesy; and third, וְנֶהְפַּכְתָּ לְאִישׁ אַחֵר, he would succeed in doing so.

וְהִתְנַבִּיתָ עִמָּם — *And you will prophesy with them.*

It was specifically עִמָּם, *with them*, the other prophets, that Saul prophesied. At times, even a person who is intrinsically incapable of prophesying can absorb some of the spirit of prophecy from others (*Kli Yakar*).

וְנֶהְפַּכְתָּ לְאִישׁ אַחֵר — *And you will be transformed into another person.*

As *Rambam* states, "Prophecy occurs only with very wise men who possess strength of character ... When a person perfects all of his character traits ... possesses an accurate understanding ... sanctifies himself and distances himself from the way of the masses ... and focuses his mind constantly ... on gazing at the wisdom of Hashem ... [then] a holy spirit will rest upon him ... and he will reach the exalted level of the angels ... He is transformed into another person and understands that he is no longer the same as he had been before. Rather, he has been elevated beyond the high ranks of other wise men. As the verse states, 'You will prophesy with them, and you will be transformed into another person'" (*Hil. Yesodei HaTorah* 7:1).

7. וְהָיָה כִּי תָבֹאנָה הָאֹתוֹת הָאֵלֶּה לָךְ — *After these signs come upon you.*

Once these signs that Samuel predicted came true, Saul would know that

י/ח

עֲשֵׂה לְךָ אֲשֶׁר תִּמְצָא יָדֶךָ כִּי הָאֱלֹהִים עִמָּךְ׃
ח וְיָרַדְתָּ לְפָנַי הַגִּלְגָּל וְהִנֵּה אָנֹכִי יֹרֵד אֵלֶיךָ לְהַעֲלוֹת
עֹלוֹת לִזְבֹּחַ זִבְחֵי שְׁלָמִים שִׁבְעַת יָמִים תּוֹחֵל
עַד־בּוֹאִי אֵלֶיךָ וְהוֹדַעְתִּי לְךָ אֵת אֲשֶׁר תַּעֲשֶׂה׃

Samuel's proclamation must also be true (*Rashi*).

Kli Yakar, however, rejects the notion that Saul would require verification to authenticate Samuel's prophecy. Rather, these signs presented Saul with lessons to assimilate before coming to the throne.

Abarbanel, utilizing *Kli Yakar's* approach, distinguishes three spheres in which Saul would be involved, regarding which each of these signs provided guidance.

The first sphere is that of personal matters and family obligation, and was alluded to by the first sign that Samuel predicted (v. 2), concerning Saul's search for his father's donkeys. Samuel concluded his words there with the instruction, וְחָלַפְתָּ מִשָּׁם וָהָלְאָה, *Move on from there and beyond;* no longer could Saul busy himself with such matters, as the burden of the entire nation lay upon him.

The second sphere is that of responsibilities to the nation. That corresponded to Samuel's second sign (vs. 3,4), which taught not to be possessive of others' belongings (and not take anything until it is offered). Furthermore, he should satisfy himself with the bare necessities of life, such as bread, and not indulge in excessive consumption of meat and wine. As Solomon writes, אַל לַמְּלָכִים שְׁתוֹ־יָיִן, *It is not proper for kings to drink [much] wine* (*Proverbs* 31:4).

The third sphere is that of devotion and attachment to God, which Samuel's third sign alluded to, reminding Saul of the ultimate purpose of man's life: to consecrate oneself to and bond with God. The presence of the Philistine officials acted as a reminder that Saul must, as a spiritually growing person, eradicate God's enemies. Also וְהִתְנַבִּיתָ עִמָּם, *you should prophesy with them* — Saul must rise above the mortal realm into spiritual, Godly spheres.

עֲשֵׂה לְךָ אֲשֶׁר תִּמְצָא יָדֶךָ — *Prepare yourself [for leadership] as best as you can.*

Targum renders this phrase as *Make yourself royal garments* — and, *Rashi* adds, other royal paraphernalia.

Mahari Kara suggests that this verse authorized Saul to wage war against the Philistines and against Nahash the Ammonite (11:9) (as we do not find such authorization stated anywhere else). Thus, the phrase תִּמְצָא יָדֶךָ (lit., *your hands will find*) refers to battle, as in the verse, כַּאֲשֶׁר מָצְאָה יָדִי לְמַמְלְכֹת הָאֱלִיל, *Just as my hand has overpowered* (literally, *found*) *the kingdoms of the false god* (*Isaiah* 10:10).

According to *Radak*, these words are to be understood literally: You may now do whatever you please, for Hashem is with you. *Daas Sofrim* elaborates that Samuel did not assign any particular mission to Saul. Rather, it would be Saul's prerogative to determine what must be done. Saul's authority was expanded insofar as he was given *carte blanche* to do as he chose. Yet it remained limited, because he could perform only actions naturally within his reach, as opposed to the Messiah, who will possess supernatural powers with which to effect judgment and avenge injustice.

8. As soon as Saul was appointed monarch, he was given his first test. Although granted broad authority, he must still abide by the directions of the prophet, who represents the word of God. Under the most trying circumstances, he must realize that ultimately he himself is no more than an agent of God.

This verse seems to be discussing a trivial matter — one that, however, will play a significant role in Saul's destiny.

וְיָרַדְתָּ לְפָנַי הַגִּלְגָּל ... שִׁבְעַת יָמִים תּוֹחֵל ... — *Then you shall go down to Gilgal ahead of me...You shall wait for seven days...*

The commentators disagree as to when this rendezvous in Gilgal occurred. Scripture mentions two incidents

prepare yourself [for leadership] as best as you can, for God is with you. 8 *Then you shall go down to Gilgal ahead of me; behold! I will go down to you, to offer burnt-offerings, to slaughter peace-offerings. You shall wait for seven days until I come to you and I will inform you what you are to do."*

involving Samuel and Saul that occurred in Gilgal. First, Samuel gathered the nation there to renew the coronation of Saul and bring peace-offerings (11:14,15). In Chapter 13, Saul gathers an army in Gilgal to fight the Philistines (v. 4), and it is then that the instruction to wait seven days for Samuel is expected to be fulfilled (see vs. 8-11).

Were these two separate episodes, or did they take place during one extended visit to Gilgal?

According to the timeline presented in *Seder Olam*, these were two separate episodes, and the war against the Philistines took place during the second year of Saul's reign. (And thus, *Mahari Kara* asserts, Samuel's statement now was prophetic, for at the time that he made it there were no immediate plans to go to Gilgal.)

Rashi and *Metzudos* agree that these were two separate episodes. Thus, they understand Samuel to be informing Saul that when, in the distant future, he would go to Gilgal to wage war against the Philistines he must first wait seven days until Samuel would arrive.

However, *Radak*, *Abarbanel*, and *Malbim* state that both episodes in Gilgal took place at the same time. Samuel officially crowned Saul in Gilgal and then told Saul that he was leaving for a seven-day period, and instructed Saul to await his return.

In a strikingly original interpretation, *Daas Sofrim* suggests that Samuel did not tell Saul to go to Gilgal. Rather, Samuel said that if Saul should ever require Samuel's counsel, the two of them should meet at Gilgal (rather than have either party travel to the other, which might constitute a slight to the dignity of the traveler). Samuel said, "Notify me when you wish to see me, and then wait seven days until I arrive. To distract people's attention from our meeting, when I arrive we will bring offerings." This idea is supported by the phrases: וְיָרַדְתָּ לְפָנַי ... אָנֹכִי יֹרֵד אֵלֶיךָ, *You will go down before me ... I will go down to you* — implying that each of them traveled to the other.

וְהִנֵּה אָנֹכִי יֹרֵד אֵלֶיךָ — *Behold! I will go down to you.*

Following the view that Samuel and Saul went to Gilgal only once, the phrase, וְיָרַדְתָּ לְפָנַי הַגִּלְגָּל, *then you shall go down to Gilgal ahead of me*, refers to Samuel and Saul's journey to Gilgal for the purpose of engaging in the coronation ceremony. Then Samuel prepared to take his leave, promising Saul, אָנֹכִי יֹרֵד אֵלֶיךָ, *I will come down to you*, referring to Samuel's return after a seven-day departure.

Kli Yakar sees in the word וְהִנֵּה, *and behold*, an unwitting prophecy. Samuel intimated, "On the seventh day, when you are about to lose patience and hope, be aware that I will suddenly appear" — but this admonition, as it turned out, was to no avail.

שִׁבְעַת יָמִים תּוֹחֵל עַד־בּוֹאִי אֵלֶיךָ — *Wait for seven days until I come to you.*

Samuel intimated that during this period Saul should not bring any offerings, for Samuel would do so after he returned (*Metzudos*).

וְהוֹדַעְתִּי לְךָ אֵת אֲשֶׁר תַּעֲשֶׂה — *And I will inform you what you are to do.*

Mahari Kara interprets this phrase as meaning that Samuel would tell Saul how to bring the offerings.

ט וְהָיָה כְּהַפְנֹתוֹ שִׁכְמוֹ לָלֶכֶת מֵעִם שְׁמוּאֵל וַיַּהֲפָךְ־
לוֹ אֱלֹהִים לֵב אַחֵר וַיָּבֹאוּ כָּל־הָאֹתוֹת הָאֵלֶּה
י בַּיּוֹם הַהוּא: וַיָּבֹאוּ שָׁם הַגִּבְעָתָה וְהִנֵּה
חֶבֶל־נְבִאִים לִקְרָאתוֹ וַתִּצְלַח עָלָיו רוּחַ אֱלֹהִים
יא וַיִּתְנַבֵּא בְּתוֹכָם: וַיְהִי כָּל־יוֹדְעוֹ מֵאִתְּמוֹל שִׁלְשׁוֹם
וַיִּרְאוּ וְהִנֵּה עִם־נְבִאִים נִבָּא וַיֹּאמֶר
הָעָם אִישׁ אֶל־רֵעֵהוּ מַה־זֶּה הָיָה לְבֶן־קִישׁ
יב הֲגַם שָׁאוּל בַּנְּבִיאִים: וַיַּעַן אִישׁ מִשָּׁם וַיֹּאמֶר

According to *Malbim*, this phrase means that Samuel would tell Saul how to wage war against the Philistines. Although Samuel had said that Saul may act as he pleases, on this occasion he must accept instruction.

Why did Samuel choose to tell Saul at this point that he will have to wait seven days, rather than wait until they came to Gilgal? *Radak* explains that by speaking to Saul about becoming king and about waiting for seven days in the same conversation, Samuel was intimating that only if Saul could refrain from acting impulsively and succumbing to impatience would he succeed. Therefore, Samuel concluded his words, וְהוֹדַעְתִּי לְךָ אֵת אֲשֶׁר תַּעֲשֶׂה, *[After this test], I will be able to properly predict what you will do* — i.e., whether or not Saul will succeed as king.

Metzudos understands this phrase to mean that after the seven days passed, Samuel would specify Saul's responsibilities as king. However, Samuel was angered by Saul's failure to wait properly, and thus did not follow through with this intent.

◌§ Saul's Metamorphosis and Prophecy

9. וְהָיָה כְּהַפְנֹתוֹ שִׁכְמוֹ לָלֶכֶת מֵעִם שְׁמוּאֵל וַיַּהֲפָךְ־לוֹ אֱלֹהִים לֵב אַחֵר — *As soon as [Saul] turned away to depart from Samuel, God transformed him with a new heart.*

Although Samuel had thought that God would transform Saul's heart only after the realization of the three signs, God did so immediately (*Abarbanel*).

וְהָיָה כְּהַפְנֹתוֹ שִׁכְמוֹ לָלֶכֶת ... — *As soon as [Saul] turned away to depart.*

Me'am Loez cites an opinion that Saul acted improperly by turning his back to the prophet; he should rather have retreated facing Samuel, like a student taking leave of his teacher (see *Yoma* 53b; *Rambam, Hil. Talmud Torah* 5:6; *Nachalas Shimon* 31:26). In acting as he did, Saul deviated from his normally humble manner.

וַיַּהֲפָךְ־לוֹ אֱלֹהִים לֵב אַחֵר — *God transformed him with a new heart.*

God gave Saul a spirit of royal bravery (*Rashi*).

Just as the heart of an individual determines the state of his body, so does the heart of a king affect the state of the hearts of the people. Solomon thus writes, פַּלְגֵי־מַיִם לֶב־מֶלֶךְ בְּיַד־ה׳ עַל־כָּל־אֲשֶׁר יַחְפֹּץ יַטֶּנּוּ, *Like streams of water is the heart of a king in the hand of* H*ASHEM*, *wherever He wishes, so does He direct it* (*Proverbs* 21:1). If God chooses to impress an idea upon the hearts of the people, He will use the "heart of the king" as a medium through which to do so. Hence, Scripture here relates the metamorphosis of Saul's heart from a private one to a public one (*Malbim*).

10. וַיָּבֹאוּ שָׁם הַגִּבְעָתָה — *They arrived there at the Hill.*

[9] *As soon as [Saul] turned away to depart from Samuel, God transformed him with a new heart and all these signs came about on that day.*

[10] *They arrived there at the Hill and behold! a band of prophets was opposite him. The spirit of God passed over him, and he prophesied among them.* [11] *All those who had known him from yesterday and before then saw that behold! he was prophesying along with the prophets, and they said one to another, "What is this that has happened to the son of Kish? Is Saul also among the prophets?"* [12] *A man spoke up from there and said,*

This is the third sign predicted by Samuel, which Scripture describes in detail, for it was of particular significance (*Abarbanel*).

11. מֵאִתְּמוֹל שִׁלְשׁוֹם — *From yesterday and before then.*

שִׁלְשׁוֹם literally means *the day before yesterday* (*Metzudos*).

וְהִנֵּה עִם־נְבִאִים נִבָּא — *Behold! he was prophesying along with the prophets.*

Had Saul been prophesying alone, the people may have doubted the authenticity of his prophecy, but since they saw that he had been accepted by the other prophets, they could not doubt his credibility (*Daas Sofrim*).

מַה־זֶּה הָיָה לְבֶן־קִישׁ הֲגַם שָׁאוּל בַּנְּבִיאִים — *What is this that has happened to the son of Kish? Is Saul also among the prophets?*

The people were stunned by Saul's sudden transformation. *Malbim* explains that there are two prerequisites for achieving prophecy. First, a person must possess the requisite inborn propensities, and second, he must exert great effort to isolate and sanctify himself in order to purify his soul. The people who saw Saul believed, erroneously, that the potential prophet's inborn abilities must be inherited from his father; they therefore asked, מַה־זֶּה הָיָה לְבֶן־קִישׁ, *What is this that has happened to the son of Kish?*, for they knew that Kish, honorable man that he was, was no prophet. Then, those who were familiar with Saul מֵאִתְּמוֹל שִׁלְשׁוֹם, *from yesterday and before then*, and knew that he had not spent his days in solitude and meditation asked, הֲגַם שָׁאוּל בַּנְּבִיאִים, *Is Saul also among the prophets?* — i.e., how did he reach such heights so quickly?

Kli Yakar alternatively interprets the words מַה־זֶּה הָיָה לְבֶן־קִישׁ, *What is this that has happened to the son of Kish?*, as an expression of surprise that Saul had attained prophecy without entering into seclusion. A person who chooses to consecrate himself, they thought, must isolate himself even from his parents. (That is why, for example, before following Elijah, Elisha requested, וַיֹּאמֶר אֶשְּׁקָה־נָּא לְאָבִי וּלְאִמִּי וְאֵלְכָה אַחֲרֶיךָ, *Please let me kiss my father and mother, and then I shall go after you* [*I Kings* 19:20].) Since the people knew that Saul was still very much in contact with his father, they asked, *What is this that happened to the son of Kish?*

The *Zohar* (*Parashas Terumah*) attributes the people's surprise to the fact that Saul simultaneously acquired the throne and prophecy, a privilege that had been previously awarded to no other man but Moses.

וּמִ֥י אֲבִיהֶ֑ם עַל־כֵּן֙ הָיְתָ֣ה לְמָשָׁ֔ל הֲגַ֥ם שָׁא֖וּל
יג־יד בַּנְּבִאִֽים׃ וַיְכַל֙ מֵֽהִתְנַבּ֔וֹת וַיָּבֹ֖א הַבָּמָֽה׃ וַיֹּ֩אמֶר֩
דּ֨וֹד שָׁא֜וּל אֵלָ֗יו וְאֶל־נַעֲר֛וֹ אָ֥ן הֲלַכְתֶּ֖ם וַיֹּ֣אמֶר
לְבַקֵּשׁ֙ אֶת־הָ֣אֲתֹנ֔וֹת וַנִּרְאֶ֥ה כִי־אַ֖יִן וַנָּב֥וֹא אֶל־
טו שְׁמוּאֵֽל׃ וַיֹּ֖אמֶר דּ֣וֹד שָׁא֑וּל הַגִּֽידָה־נָּ֣א לִ֔י מָֽה־
טז אָמַ֥ר לָכֶ֖ם שְׁמוּאֵֽל׃ וַיֹּ֤אמֶר שָׁאוּל֙ אֶל־דּוֹד֔וֹ הַגֵּ֤ד
הִגִּיד֙ לָ֔נוּ כִּ֥י נִמְצְא֖וּ הָאֲתֹנ֑וֹת וְאֶת־דְּבַ֤ר הַמְּלוּכָה֙
יז לֹֽא־הִגִּ֣יד ל֔וֹ אֲשֶׁ֖ר אָמַ֥ר שְׁמוּאֵֽל׃ וַיַּצְעֵ֨ק

12. וּמִי אֲבִיהֶם — *And who is the father of [the other prophets]?*

It should not be surprising that Saul joined this band, for the other prophets were also of undistinguished parentage. Prophecy does not run in families (*Rashi*).

A person who sees a proselyte who wishes to study Torah should not dismiss him saying, "This person who used to eat carcasses, torn animals, rodents, and insects now wants to learn Torah!" As the verse states, וּמִי אֲבִיהֶם *And who is the father of [the other prophets]?*; regarding Torah, inheritance is not a factor (*Tosefta Bava Metzia* 3:14; see also *Avos* 2:17).

Targum renders וּמִי אֲבִיהֶם as *Who is their mentor?* — i.e., who supplies them with the spirit of prophecy? It is God, and He can do the same for Saul.

According to *Kli Yakar*, the question וּמִי אֲבִיהֶם refers to Saul, and אֲבִיהֶם refers to a progenitor in a general sense. Thus, *Who is the ancestor of this man?* The answer is that it is Abiel, who installed streetlights to make it easier for the public to learn Torah (see comm. 9:1); thus, by virtue of Abiel's merits, Saul earned the ability to prophesy.

עַל־כֵּן הָיְתָה לְמָשָׁל הֲגַם שָׁאוּל בַּנְּבִאִים — *It thus became an aphorism: "Is Saul also among the prophets?"*

Any sudden and unexpected rise to spiritual prominence recollects this aphorism (*Mahari Kara*).

The words עַל־כֵּן (lit., *therefore*), as well as the positioning of this phrase immediately after the man's response, seem out of place. *Abarbanel* and *Malbim* solve this problem. In the previous verse, the people had expressed two sources of bewilderment: first, that Saul lacked a heritage of prophecy, and second, that he had not secluded himself to bring prophecy upon himself (see *Malbim* above). After the anonymous "man" effectively refuted the former, because prophecy is not hereditary, the only source for surprise was that of Saul's own credentials; hence, what became an aphorism was *only* הֲגַם שָׁאוּל בַּנְּבִאִים.

13. וַיְכַל מֵהִתְנַבּוֹת — *Then he ceased prophesying.*

Daas Sofrim infers that Saul cased prophesying entirely, with one exception later on in his career, in the course of his pursuit of David (below, 19:23,24).

וַיְכַל מֵהִתְנַבּוֹת וַיָּבֹא הַבָּמָה — *Then he ceased prophesying and arrived at the High Place.*

The word בָּמָה is at times used in regard to a private altar (which was then permitted). Accordingly, we can contrast Saul from the rest of the band of prophets. They used the altar, which represents devoted service and prayer, as a prepatory stage to arouse themselves to the spirit of holiness that is fit for prophecy. Hence, Samuel told Saul, וּפָגַעְתָּ חֶבֶל נְבִיאִים יֹרְדִים מֵהַבָּמָה ... וְהֵמָּה מִתְנַבְּאִים, *You will encounter a band of prophets descending from the*

"And who is the father of [the other prophets]?"
It thus became an aphorism: "Is Saul also among
the prophets?" 13 *Then he ceased prophesying and*
arrived at the High Place.
14 *Saul's uncle said to him and his attendant,*
"Where did you go?" He replied, "To look for the
donkeys, but when we saw that they were gone
we went to Samuel." 15 *Saul's uncle said, "Tell me*
now what Samuel said to you." 16 *Saul answered*
his uncle, "He told us that the donkeys had been
found," but he did not tell him about the matter of
the kingship of which Samuel had spoken.

בָּמָה ... *and they will be prophesying.* Contrarily, Saul was imbued with a spontaneous flow of prophecy; he thus capitalized on the experience and went to the בָּמָה, in order to involve himself in intense service and prayer (*Malbim*).

◆§ Saul's Modesty

14. ... וַיֹּאמֶר דּוֹד שָׁאוּל — *Saul's uncle said to him ...*

Either Saul's uncle chanced upon Saul at the site of the High Place (*Mahari Kara*) or Saul actually went home and met his uncle there (a detail that Scripture omits) (*Radak*). According to either version, Saul's uncle apparently noticed a change in Saul's nature and inquired as to its cause (*Me'am Loez*).

Malbim adds that Saul's uncle understood that Saul had engaged in prophecy. Aware that the other prophets drew the potency of their experiences from their propinquity to Samuel, he asked if Saul too had spent time with Samuel. Saul answered affirmatively, but left his uncle with the impression that he had met Samuel solely in regard to the donkeys, and made no mention of his new status.

Scripture's purpose in documenting this dialogue is to teach us about Saul's humility (v. 16; *Mahari Kara*).

דּוֹד שָׁאוּל — *Saul's uncle.*

Presumably, this was Ner, the brother of Saul's father Kish and father of Abner, who was to become Saul's general (see 14:50,51).

וַיֹּאמֶר לְבַקֵּשׁ אֶת־הָאֲתֹנוֹת — *He replied, "To look for the donkeys."*

Although Saul's uncle addressed this question to Saul and his attendant, the attendant properly remained silent and allowed his master to respond (*Kli Yakar*).

16. וְאֶת־דְּבַר הַמְּלוּכָה לֹא־הִגִּיד לוֹ אֲשֶׁר אָמַר שְׁמוּאֵל — *But he did not tell him about the matter of the kingship of which Samuel had spoken.*

Our translation follows most commentaries, who rearrange the order of the text as if it said, וְאֶת דְּבַר הַמְּלוּכָה אֲשֶׁר אָמַר שְׁמוּאֵל לֹא הִגִּיד לוֹ. The textual form would have implied that "he didn't tell as Samuel had spoken," or warned, but there is no clear evidence of such a warning.

As *Abarbanel* sees it, however, the fact that Samuel sent away Saul's attendant before anointing him indicates that he meant Saul to keep his royal status a secret (9:27). Thus *Abarbanel* reads the verse in its textual order (see *Alshich, Chomas Anach*).

The Talmud (*Megillah* 13b) praises Saul for keeping silent and attributes

יח שְׁמוּאֵל֙ אֶת־הָעָ֔ם אֶל־יְהוָ֖ה הַמִּצְפָּֽה׃ וַיֹּ֣אמֶר ׀
אֶל־בְּנֵ֣י יִשְׂרָאֵ֗ל כֹּֽה־אָמַ֤ר יהוה֙ אֱלֹהֵ֣י יִשְׂרָאֵ֔ל
אָנֹכִ֛י הֶעֱלֵ֥יתִי אֶת־יִשְׂרָאֵ֖ל מִמִּצְרָ֑יִם וָאַצִּ֣יל
אֶתְכֶם֙ מִיַּ֣ד מִצְרַ֔יִם וּמִיַּד֙ כָּל־הַמַּמְלָכ֔וֹת
יט הַלֹּחֲצִ֖ים אֶתְכֶֽם׃ וְאַתֶּ֨ם הַיּ֜וֹם מְאַסְתֶּ֣ם אֶת־
אֱלֹהֵיכֶ֗ם אֲשֶׁר־ה֨וּא מוֹשִׁ֣יעַ לָכֶם֮ מִכָּל־רָעוֹתֵיכֶ֣ם
וְצָרֹתֵיכֶם֒ וַתֹּ֣אמְרוּ ל֔וֹ כִּֽי־מֶ֖לֶךְ תָּשִׂ֣ים עָלֵ֑ינוּ
וְעַתָּ֗ה הִֽתְיַצְּבוּ֙ לִפְנֵ֣י יהוה לְשִׁבְטֵיכֶ֖ם וּלְאַלְפֵיכֶֽם׃

that self-control to his virtue of צְנִיעוּת, *privacy,* or *modesty* in shunning the publicity of his exalted position.

The Talmud (ibid.) relates that Saul's ancestor Rachel also possessed this trait of צְנִיעוּת (see *Rashi, Rashash* ad loc.); she thus merited to have among Saul's progeny another person who displayed that trait: Esther. In all cases, the characteristic of צְנִיעוּת is closely associated with restraining one's speech, particularly in regard to divulging secrets (see *Bereishis Rabbah* 71:5).

The *Zohar* states that the merit of controlling one's speech is so great that it results in Divine Inspiration, as was the case with both Saul and Esther.

Even according to *Abarbanel*'s contention that Saul was ordered to keep his inauguration a secret, Saul's silence is still considered praiseworthy, for most people would not have been able to resist the urge to share such momentous news with someone such as a trusted family member. Alternatively, Saul could have understood that he may not tell the attendant, but to notify his relatives would be permissible. He withstood this temptation and was accordingly praised (*Daas Sofrim*).

☙ God's Public Selection of Saul

17. וַיַּצְעֵק שְׁמוּאֵל — *Samuel gathered.*

The word וַיַּצְעֵק, *gathered,* is related to the word צְעָקָה, *scream,* because often the congregating of the masses is accomplished through *screaming* (*Radak*).

אֶל ה׳ הַמִּצְפָּה — *To* H*ASHEM at Mitzpah.*

As previously mentioned (7:5), Mitzpah had been the site of an altar and house of prayer where the Jews had gathered, since the time of Joshua's miraculous victory there (*Joshua* 11:1-8) (*Radak*).

Metzudos comments that this assemblage was considered אֶל ה׳, *to* H*ASHEM*, because God's Presence rests on a gathering of the majority of the populace.

18. כֹּה־אָמַר ה׳ ... — *Thus said* H*ASHEM* ...

This was Hashem's response to the Israelites' initial request for a king (*Radak*).

Abarbanel explains that Samuel did not intend to rebuke the Jews at this juncture for demanding a king; that admonition would come later (Chapter 12). His more modest purpose was to preclude any misunderstanding that God Himself had reconsidered and concluded that it would be beneficial for the Jews to have a king. On the contrary, Samuel here stresses that since, after their petition, he had ordered them to go home to their cities (8:22), he now reassembled them in accordance with *their* request.

אָנֹכִי הֶעֱלֵיתִי ... וּמִיַּד כָּל־הַמַּמְלָכוֹת ... — *I brought Israel up ... and from the hand of all the kingdoms.*

Hashem emphasizes that He Himself saved the Jews from Egypt, without the aid of a human king, and if anyone should think that God had since had a

[17] *Samuel gathered the people to* H*ASHEM at Miz-*
pah. [18] *He said to the Children of Israel, "Thus*
said H*ASHEM, the God of Israel: 'I brought Israel*
up from Egypt. I rescued you from the hand of
Egypt and from the hand of all the kingdoms that
oppressed you. [19] *Today you have rejected your*
God, Who saves you from all your calamities and
troubles, and you said to Him, "Only place a king
over us!" Now stand before H*ASHEM, according to*
your tribes and your thousands.'"

change of heart regarding appointing a king, Hashem adds, וּמִיַּד כָּל־הַמַּמְלָכוֹת הַלֹּחֲצִים אֶתְכֶם, *and from the hand of all the kingdoms that oppressed you,* implying that "I have *continued* to protect you from all of your oppressors, to this very moment. The phrase הַלֹּחֲצִים אֶתְכֶם, *that oppressed you,* is literally written in the present tense — i.e., *those who are at present oppressing you* (*Malbim, Kli Yakar*).

19. מְאַסְתֶּם אֶת־אֱלֹהֵיכֶם — *You have rejected your God.*

Targum renders this phrase as *You have rejected the service of your God.*

רָעוֹתֵיכֶם וְצָרֹתֵיכֶם — *Your calamities and troubles.*

Calamities are natural misfortunes, whereas *troubles* are caused by one's enemies. A mortal king can protect the populace only against human enemies, not against natural disasters; nevertheless, the Jews preferred a human king to the rule of God (*Malbim*).

Daas Sofrim suggests that רָעוֹת are the people's evil deeds, which God helps them overcome by sending them prophets and by punishing them. The Jews preferred a human king to accomplish that task as well.

וַתֹּאמְרוּ לוֹ — *And you said to Him.*

Samuel considered the brazen complaints made to him as if they had been spoken directly to God (*Daas Sofrim*).

Radak cites a number of commentators who interpret לוֹ, *to Him,* as if it were written לֹא, *no.* In other words, לֹא, כִּי־מֶלֶךְ תָּשִׂים עָלֵינוּ, *"No! Only place a king over us!"* (as in 8:19).

הִתְיַצְּבוּ לִפְנֵי ה׳ — *Stand before* H*ASHEM.*

According to *Radak, before* H*ASHEM* indicates that the choosing of a king was made in an environment of holiness, specifically, in the presence of the Kohen Gadol and through the medium of the *Urim VeTumim*[1] (and possibly in the presence of the Ark as well). This was a public display, and as such confirmed to the nation that God had chosen Saul, and thus there could be no jealousy among the tribes or surprise that someone other than a member of the tribe of Judah had been chosen. According to those commentators who state that Saul was chosen by means of casting lots (see next verse), possibly these lots were cast in the presence of the *Urim VeTumim* (*Metzudos*).

לְשִׁבְטֵיכֶם וּלְאַלְפֵיכֶם — *According to your tribes and your thousands.*

According to the view that Samuel cast lots, first, a tribe was chosen by lot,

1. The *Urim VeTumim* were [a parchment slipped into] the Kohen Gadol's breastplate. Messages were transmitted through the illumination of specific letters carved into the twelve stones in the breastplate; see *Stone Chumash, Exodus* 28:30; see above, fn. 1 on p. 18.

כ וַיַּקְרֵב שְׁמוּאֵל אֵת כָּל־שִׁבְטֵי יִשְׂרָאֵל וַיִּלָּכֵד
כא שֵׁבֶט בִּנְיָמִן: וַיַּקְרֵב אֶת־שֵׁבֶט בִּנְיָמִן °למשפחתו
וַתִּלָּכֵד מִשְׁפַּחַת הַמַּטְרִי וַיִּלָּכֵד שָׁאוּל בֶּן־קִישׁ
כב וַיְבַקְשֻׁהוּ וְלֹא נִמְצָא: וַיִּשְׁאֲלוּ־עוֹד בַּיהוָֹה הֲבָא
עוֹד הֲלֹם אִישׁ   וַיֹּאמֶר יְהוָֹה הִנֵּה־
כג הוּא נֶחְבָּא אֶל־הַכֵּלִים: וַיָּרֻצוּ וַיִּקָּחֻהוּ מִשָּׁם

°לְמִשְׁפְּחֹתָיו ק׳

and then a family of that tribe. אַלְפֵיכֶם, *thousands*, refers to these families, for each tribe was divided genealogically into groups of thousands (*Metzudos;* see *Exodus* 18:21, *Numbers* 1:16).

20. וַיִּלָּכֵד שֵׁבֶט בִּנְיָמִן — *And the tribe of Benjamin was singled out.*

Scripture doesn't define what method was used for election. According to *Rashi,* it was via a lottery, whereas *Radak* contends that it was chosen by the *Urim VeTumim.* Some commentators assume that both methods were used. This may be explained in one of two ways:

(a) This procedure was similar to that whereby the territories of the Land of Israel were distributed. Joshua consulted the *Urim VeTumim* and then drew lots, which ratified the decisions of the *Urim VeTumim* (*Bava Basra* 122a; see ArtScroll *Joshua* 14:2; *Abarbanel*).

(b) This ceremony was modeled on the procedure employed in the case of Achan, who stole from the banned property of Jericho. Joshua first used the *Urim VeTumim* to determine the offender's tribe, and then cast lots to narrow down the search to families and then to the individual (*Pirkei D'Rabbi Eliezer* Ch. 38; *Rashi, Joshua* 7:16,17; *Radak, Joshua* 7:14). Here too, perhaps, the *Urim VeTumim* were used only to single out the tribe of Benjamin.

וַיַּקְרֵב שְׁמוּאֵל אֵת כָּל־שִׁבְטֵי יִשְׂרָאֵל — *Samuel then brought all the tribes of Israel near.*

Possibly, this means that Samuel gathered representatives of each tribe (*Daas Sofrim*).

Metzudos renders this phrase as *[Samuel] brought the names of all the tribes [before the Urim VeTumim in order to draw the lottery]* (see above).

וַיִּלָּכֵד — *Was singled out.*

The root of וַיִּלָּכֵד (לכד) means to *conquer* or *seize* (see *Numbers* 21:32). Following *Metzudos,* the lot upon which the name of Benjamin appeared was *seized* in that it was held in the hand of the lot-drawer.

Me'am Loez states that the prospect of being ceremonially honored was so repulsive to Saul that he felt as if he had been trapped (see *Horayos* 10b). Indeed, as soon as he heard that the Matar family had been chosen, he escaped and hid among the baggage.

21 וַיְבַקְשֻׁהוּ וְלֹא נִמְצָא — *They searched for him, but he was not found.*

Presumably, Samuel told Saul to come to Mitzpah, and Saul knew that a lottery would be held that would confirm his appointment. Since he found it uncomfortable to be in the public eye, before the expected announcement of his election he sought to hide (*Daas Sofrim*).

◆§ Saul's Emergence as Monarch and the Nation's Mixed Reaction

22. וַיִּשְׁאֲלוּ־עוֹד בַּה׳ — *They asked* HASHEM *further.*

They asked by means of the *Urim VeTumim* (*Metzudos*).

הֲבָא עוֹד הֲלֹם אִישׁ — *Has the man arrived here as yet?*

Our translation follows *Radak* and *Mahari Kara,* who render עוֹד — lit.,

[20]Samuel then brought all the tribes of Israel
near, and the tribe of Benjamin was singled out.
[21]Then he brought the tribe of Benjamin near ac-
cording to its families, and the Matrite family
was singled out; [eventually] Saul son of Kish was
singled out. They searched for him but he was not
found. [22]They then asked HASHEM *further, "Has*
the man arrived here as yet?"

And HASHEM *replied, "He is hidden among the*
baggage." [23]They ran and took him from there,

more, or *else* — as עֲדַיִן, *yet,* and who translate אִישׁ, *a man,* as if it read הָאִישׁ, *the man.*

Abarbanel avoids the novel translation and renders: *Is any other man expected to come [who has not yet arrived]?* That too requires a grammatical adjustment: הֲבָא, *has [he] come?,* must be read as הֲיָבֹא, *Will [he] come?*

Metzudos avoids all these grammatical difficulties by translating the phrase as, *Has any other man come here [who happens not to be standing here now]?*

הֲלֹם — *Here.*

The word הֲלֹם is often used to connote royalty (see *Zevachim* 102a).

הִנֵּה־הוּא נֶחְבָּא אֶל־הַכֵּלִים — *He is hidden among the baggage.*

The word אֶל — usually *to* — here means *in* or *among.* In his haste to shun leadership and honor, Saul escaped to the house where people had left their bags, and hid among them.

Alternatively, כֵּלִים — which literally means *utensils* — may refer to agricultural instruments such as plows (*Abarbanel*).

Midrash Tanchuma (*Leviticus* §3) translates כֵּלִים as *garments* and applies this to the *Urim VeTumim.* When Saul heard that he had been chosen king, he exclaimed, "Maybe I'm not worthy of royalty! First consult the *Urim VeTumim* to see if I am worthy and if not, then leave me alone." The people inquired as Saul had requested, and he hid awaiting the response.[1]

The Midrash (ibid.) refers to Saul's hiding

1. This Midrash is consistent with *Rashi's* statement (v. 20) that Samuel publicly chose Saul as king by means of casting lots. That having occurred, Saul now sought the endorsement of the *Urim VeTumim* as well.

This Midrash can also be understood as consistent with the view that Samuel had initially used the *Urim VeTumim* solely to identify the tribe of Benjamin. Now Saul asked Samuel to consult with the *Urim VeTumim* to identify the individual who should be king.

However, according to *Radak,* who states that originally the *Urim VeTumim* had been used to choose Saul, or according to *Abarbanel,* who assumes that the *Urim VeTumim* and the lottery had been employed simultaneously, this verse would be describing a second appeal to the *Urim VeTumim.* What would be the purpose of that?

Possibly, Saul needed to be reassured that he would acquit himself honorably as king. Although Samuel's first inquiry of the *Urim VeTumim* determined that Saul should be appointed king, it did not assure Saul that he would succeed in that demanding position.

Similarly, in the episode of the Concubine in Gibeah, when the tribes inquired of the *Urim VeTumim* whether to battle against Benjamin, they twice received positive replies, yet twice they were beaten. Thus, they first asked, *Who among us should advance first* to battle against Benjamin? (*Judges* 20:18), and were simply told that Judah should be at the vanguard. After they suffered a colossal defeat, they again approached the *Urim VeTumim* and

וַיִּתְיַצֵּב בְּתוֹךְ הָעָם וַיִּגְבַּהּ מִכָּל־הָעָם מִשִּׁכְמוֹ
כד וָמָעְלָה: וַיֹּאמֶר שְׁמוּאֵל אֶל־כָּל־הָעָם הַרְּאִיתֶם
אֲשֶׁר בָּחַר־בּוֹ יהוה כִּי אֵין כָּמֹהוּ בְּכָל־הָעָם וַיָּרִעוּ
כה כָל־הָעָם וַיֹּאמְרוּ יְחִי הַמֶּלֶךְ: וַיְדַבֵּר
שְׁמוּאֵל אֶל־הָעָם אֵת מִשְׁפַּט הַמְּלֻכָה וַיִּכְתֹּב
בַּסֵּפֶר וַיַּנַּח לִפְנֵי יהוה וַיְשַׁלַּח שְׁמוּאֵל אֶת־
כו כָּל־הָעָם אִישׁ לְבֵיתוֹ: וְגַם־שָׁאוּל הָלַךְ לְבֵיתוֹ

to illustrate one of King Solomon's classic lessons. גַּאֲוַת אָדָם תַּשְׁפִּילֶנּוּ וּשְׁפַל־רוּחַ יִתְמֹךְ כָּבוֹד, *A man's pride will bring him low, but a lowly spirit will support [his] honor* (*Proverbs* 29:23): A person who flees honor will be pursued by honor, whereas a person who pursues honor will find that it flees from him. Thus, although Saul fled honor, he became king; Gideon's son Abimelech, on the other hand, pursued honor and lost it (*Judges* Ch. 9).

However, although Saul was initially reluctant to accept the crown, later on he clung to it so jealously that he even attempted to kill his rival David. As *Avos D'Rabbi Nassan* (10) observes, as difficult as it is to ascend to a high rank, descending from that rank, once achieved, is equally hard.

23. וַיִּתְיַצֵּב בְּתוֹךְ הָעָם — *And he stood in the midst of the people.*

Now that Saul was removed from seclusion, he realized that he must present himself properly, and he stood in a majestic manner (*Daas Sofrim*).

Kli Yakar observes that even now, Saul maintained his modest disposition, as he stood בְּתוֹךְ הָעָם, *in the midst of the people*, and didn't seek the limelight.

וַיִּגְבַּהּ מִכָּל־הָעָם מִשִּׁכְמוֹ וָמָעְלָה — *He was taller than any of the people from his shoulders upward.*

Saul had a royal appearance (*Abarbanel*).

Daas Sofrim states that the people had no way of gauging Saul's character, and could only be impressed by his visibly regal features.

24. הַרְּאִיתֶם אֲשֶׁר בָּחַר־בּוֹ ה׳ — *Have you seen [the one] whom* HASHEM *has chosen?*

That is to say, have you taken sufficient heed to contemplate and appreciate that Hashem has chosen a most appropriate figure? (*Metzudos*).

כִּי אֵין כָּמֹהוּ בְּכָל־הָעָם — *That there is none like him among all the people.*

According to *Radak*, Samuel's words spoke to Saul's visible qualities: "Don't you realize that the extraordinary height and stately appearance of this man will help arouse the masses' respect?"

Other commentators state that Samuel alluded to Saul's ethical and spiritual greatness as well. According to *Me'am Loez*, Samuel said, "Did any other one of you hide lest he be chosen as king? This man's supreme modesty makes him fit for the throne" (see also *Kli Yakar*).

יְחִי הַמֶּלֶךְ — *May the king live!*

This exclamation became a standard salutation, expressed at an inauguration or when pledging one's allegiance (see *II Samuel* 16:16, *I Kings* 1:25).

Targum renders יְחִי הַמֶּלֶךְ as *Let the king succeed!*

asked, *Should I once again approach for war?* (ibid. v. 23). Hashem responded affirmatively, but again they were decisively beaten.

They then inquired a third time, but this time asked specifically if they would prevail in battle (see ibid. v. 28, *Radak* ad loc.), and this time God answered that particular question: *Go up, for tomorrow I shall deliver them into your hand* (see *Yoma* 73; below, 23:9-12; 30:8).

and he stood in the midst of the people. He was
taller than any of the people from his shoulders
upward. 24 *Samuel said to all the people, "Have you*
seen [the one] whom HASHEM has chosen, that there
is none like him among all the people?" And all the
people shouted, saying, "May the king live!"
25 *Samuel then told the people the protocol of the*
kingship. He wrote it in a book and placed it before
HASHEM. Then Samuel sent away all the people, ev-
eryone to his home. 26 *Saul, too, went to his home,*

25. וַיְדַבֵּר שְׁמוּאֵל אֶל־הָעָם אֵת מִשְׁפַּט הַמְּלֻכָה — *Samuel then told the people the protocol of the kingship.*

Following *Radak,* the same list of kingly prerogatives mentioned above (8:9-17) when the people demanded a king were repeated here as a reminding warning at the moment of the king's inauguration (*Abarbanel*). *Targum,* by using the same translation for the words מִשְׁפַּט הַמְּלֻכָה here as he used above for the words מִשְׁפַּט הַמֶּלֶךְ (8:9), seems to comply with this opinion. As mentioned above, there is a Tannaic disagreement regarding whether those powers listed in Chapter 8 were legal monarchial rights, or only hypothetical, though illegal, abuses of sovereignty.

Abarbanel and *Malbim,* siding with the latter view, prefer to interpret that although previously, Samuel had intended to warn the people of the possibility of a tyranny, at this juncture, he actually taught them the authentic, Torah-based, royal protocol, including the people's obligation to fear and obey the king. *Malbim* notes the distinction of the words מִשְׁפַּט הַמֶּלֶךְ, which implies the list of a particular king's illicit whims, and the term used here מִשְׁפַּט הַמְּלֻכָה, which refers to the authentic protocol.

וַיִּכְתֹּב בַּסֵּפֶר — *He wrote it in a book.*

Samuel wrote this protocol down so that it would be clearly recorded, which would help assure that the structure of the Jewish monarchy would in no way be influenced by that of other nations (*Daas Sofrim*).

וַיַּנַּח לִפְנֵי ה׳ — *And placed it before HASHEM.*

It was placed in the Ark (*Radak*) or near the Ark (Ralbag), so that it might serve as an accessible testimony to kings of future generations (*Mahari Kara*).

וַיְשַׁלַּח אֶת־כָּל־הָעָם אִישׁ לְבֵיתוֹ — *Then Samuel sent away all the people, everyone to his home.*

The people had anticipated hearing Saul deliver an inaugural address, but when it was not forthcoming Samuel sent them home (*Daas Sofrim*).

Alternatively, *Alshich* understands that Samuel sent the people home in order to bring tributary gifts for Saul.

According to *Me'am Loez,* Samuel dispersed the assembly so as to avoid attracting the attention of the Philistines, who would surely attack if they heard that the Jews were appointing a king.

26. וְגַם־שָׁאוּל הָלַךְ לְבֵיתוֹ — *Saul, too, went to his home.*

Saul realized that his leadership had not been unanimously recognized (as we will see in the next verse); in fact, only a scarce few demonstrated strong support for him. Thus, he chose to es-

י/כז גִּבְעָתָה וַיֵּלְכוּ עִמּוֹ הַחַיִל אֲשֶׁר־נָגַע אֱלֹהִים
כז בְּלִבָּם: וּבְנֵי בְלִיַּעַל אָמְרוּ מַה־יֹּשִׁעֵנוּ זֶה וַיִּבְזֻהוּ
יא/א א וְלֹא־הֵבִיאוּ לוֹ מִנְחָה וַיְהִי כְּמַחֲרִישׁ: וַיַּעַל

chew the role of monarch until he could gather a more widespread allegiance, a goal that he reached after he defeated Nahash the Ammonite in battle (Ch. 11; *Radak, Abarbanel*).

הַחַיִל אֲשֶׁר־נָגַע אֱלֹהִים בְּלִבָּם — *The army of those whose heart was inspired by [the fear of] God.*

We follow the literal meaning of חַיִל as *army*.

Daas Sofrim interprets the entire phrase, הַחַיִל אֲשֶׁר־נָגַע אֱלֹהִים בְּלִבָּם, as *the army [of soldiers who had previously fought in wars and] were inspired by the fear of God [were the first to volunteer their military services on behalf of Saul].*

Targum, on the other hand, renders הַחַיִל as *some [members] of the nation.*

אֲשֶׁר־נָגַע אֱלֹהִים בְּלִבָּם — *Whose heart was inspired by [the fear of] God.*

Our translation of this phrase, which literally means *whose heart God touched,* paraphrases *Targum,* which states that these people were motivated by a genuine desire to honor God's chosen king (*Metzudos*).

Radak offers an alternative translation: *whose heart was inspired by God to be attracted to him* — i.e., God placed an allegiance to Saul into the hearts of certain individuals. (*Radak,* however, acknowledges that the following verse, which implies that those who did not follow Saul were completely *base men* who had no fear of God, seems to support *Targum's* reading.)

Kli Yakar explains this phrase to mean that God-fearing people always experience a connection to God (unlike the wicked). Thus, נָגַע אֱלֹהִים בְּלִבָּם, *God is [always] able to "touch" their hearts.*

27. ... וּבְנֵי בְלִיַּעַל — *But base men ...*

As mentioned above (1:16, 2:12), בְלִיַּעַל is a conjunction of the words בְּלִי עוֹל, *without a yoke* — i.e., unrestricted by the word of God. *Targum* renders this term as וּבְנֵי רִשְׁעָא, *wicked men.*

The term בְלִיַּעַל is applied here appropriately, since these men's refusal to recognize the authority of a Divinely appointed king was tantamount to casting off the yoke of God's kingdom (*Kli Yakar*).

Me'am Loez suggests that these people preferred an anarchic society.

Daas Sofrim comments that the fact that these men were not moved by God's public election of Saul constituted sufficient grounds to label them בְּנֵי בְלִיַּעַל.

מַה־יֹּשִׁעֵנוּ זֶה — *How can this person save us?*

Since Saul was descended from the youngest of the tribes and came from a relatively small family, these men thought that he would lack the widespread support that a new ruler requires (*Abarbanel*).

According to *Malbim,* previously these very same people had requested a king in order to escape the regulations of the Torah. They assumed that a king would legitimize their corrupt habits and govern according to the loose codes of other nations. Now, having seen that the ruler had been chosen by God and that only the more pious people followed him, they complained, "How can this person help *us*?"

וַיִּבְזֻהוּ — *They ridiculed him.*

They mocked him publicly (as is evident from the episode in the next chapter, v. 12; *Daas Sofrim*).

וְלֹא־הֵבִיאוּ לוֹ מִנְחָה — *And did not bring him a tribute.*

10/27 *to Gibeah, and with him went all the army of those whose heart was inspired by [the fear of] God.*
27 *But base men said, "How can this person save us!" They ridiculed him and did not bring him a tribute; still, he remained mute.*

It was customary to bring a gift to a new ruler, and many people had already done so (*Radak*). These בְּנֵי בְלִיַּעַל refrained from bringing gifts in order to demonstrate their disdain (*Daas Sofrim*).

Targum renders וְלֹא־הֵבִיאוּ לוֹ מִנְחָה as *They did not come to greet him;* i.e., they did not show the new leader the most basic courtesy.

Abarbanel explains the significance of their contempt. A king must be chosen by God and accepted by the people. This is implicit in the verse, שׂוֹם תָּשִׂים עָלֶיךָ מֶלֶךְ, *You shall surely set over yourself a king [and accept him]*, אֲשֶׁר יִבְחַר ה׳ אֱלֹהֶיךָ בּוֹ, *whom* H*ASHEM*, *your God, shall choose* (*Deuteronomy* 17:15).

Accordingly, the people's allegiance is crucial, and this was particularly the case in regard to the coronation of the first Jewish monarch.

To attain that allegiance, God employed supernatural methods. When that failed, He arranged for the war with Nahash (Ch. 11), in order to instill in the Jewish people the requisite awe of the monarchy.

וַיְהִי כְּמַחֲרִישׁ — *Still, he remained mute.* Saul ignored them (*Mahari Kara*).

Metzudos comments that the word חֵרֵשׁ can denote either *deaf* or *mute.* Hence, Saul either refused to *hear* or refused to *respond.*

The Talmud informs us that Saul acted incorrectly, because a king is obligated to demand proper respect (*Kiddushin* 32b). He was punished for this misapplied humility by being placed in predicaments that eventually led to his downfall (*Yoma* 22b, *Rashi;* see 15:17).

Mishbetzos Zahav notes that *Rambam* considers it *optional* for a king to kill a rebel (*Hil. Melachim* 3:8). Nevertheless, at times when such humility will undermine the nation's respect for the throne, the king *must* act resolutely. Also, *Chida* says that the king has only the option *not* to kill, but he is required to take some action to punish renegades. Furthermore, it could be that Saul was not *punished;* however, since he now showed that he lacked the firm nature necessary for rulership, it was taken from him (see Ch. 15).

Mishbetzos Zahav adds that Saul possibly rationalized that since he was not yet accepted by the masses, his status as king was not yet solidified, and he wasn't yet mandated to penalize rebels. He was wrong because it was only a few "yokeless" individuals who didn't recognize his authority, and it was his job to suppress them.[1]

כְּמַחֲרִישׁ — *Mute.*

The word מַחֲרִישׁ implies the causative — i.e., *to make mute. Me'am Loez* suggests that Saul's passivity silenced his detractors, who were left with no one against whom to struggle.

1. Amidst the discussion about Saul's failure to take action, the *Talmud* (*Yoma* 22b) states that any scholar who doesn't "take revenge like a snake" is not considered a scholar. Although the Torah prohibits revenge (*Leviticus* 19:18), he is still expected to keep it in his heart, and, as *Rashi* explains, not object if someone else avenges his honor. Thus, it is possible that Scripture here emphasizes that Saul erred when he acted כְּמַחֲרִישׁ, *as if deaf*, and totally ignored it. Moreso, later, when people offered to kill those who lacked respect for Saul, Saul did not allow it (below, 11:12,13), thus failing to comply with this ruling (*Bihyos HaBoker*, cited by *Mishbetzos Zahav*).

נָחָשׁ הָֽעַמּוֹנִי וַיִּחַן עַל־יָבֵישׁ גִּלְעָד וַיֹּאמְרוּ כָּל־
אַנְשֵׁי יָבֵישׁ אֶל־נָחָשׁ כְּרָת־לָנוּ בְרִית וְנַעַבְדֶךָּ׃
ב וַיֹּאמֶר אֲלֵיהֶם נָחָשׁ הָעַמּוֹנִי בְּזֹאת אֶכְרֹת לָכֶם
בִּנְקוֹר לָכֶם כָּל־עֵין יָמִין וְשַׂמְתִּיהָ חֶרְפָּה עַל־כָּל־
ג יִשְׂרָאֵל׃ וַיֹּאמְרוּ אֵלָיו זִקְנֵי יָבֵישׁ הֶרֶף לָנוּ שִׁבְעַת

XI

1. וַיַּעַל נָחָשׁ הָעַמּוֹנִי — *Then Nahash the Ammonite went up.*

Targum explicates that Nahash was *king* of the Ammonites.

Nahash's name — literally, *snake* — alludes to the evil that he meant to perpetrate (as described in the following verses). He was כְּמוֹ־פֶתֶן חֵרֵשׁ יַאְטֵם אָזְנוֹ, *like a deaf viper that closes its ears* (*Psalms* 58:5) to pleas for mercy (*Abarbanel*).

וַיִּחַן עַל־יָבֵישׁ גִּלְעָד — *And besieged Jabesh-gilead.*

Angered by the Jews' appointment of a king, Nahash sought to instigate a war against them (*Malbim*). *Daas Sofrim* adds that Nahash was contemptuous of Saul's appointment because it was done in an unconventional manner and because Saul was not known as a warrior.

Jabesh-gilead was a convenient target because it was near the border of Ammon (*Daas Sofrim*). *Malbim* suggests as well that Nahash chose to humiliate Jabesh-gilead because it belonged to Saul's tribe of Benjamin. Following the episode of the concubine in Gibeah, the men of Benjamin went there to marry (*Judges* 21:12), and subsequently the property of their wives passed into their hands. Nahash theorized that by humiliating Jabesh-gilead, he would be indirectly humiliating the king of Israel himself.

Kli Yakar assumes that the inhabitants of Jabesh-gilead were the base men who had scorned Saul (10:27). They deserved the opprobrium that Nahash would soon heap upon their heads; furthermore, in an instance of poetic justice, this episode would lead Saul — the man whom they had derided as ineffectual — to prove his valor.

These men were attacked by a man named "Snake" because they had slandered Saul, just as fiery snakes had attacked the Jews of an earlier generation for having slandered Hashem and Moses (*Numbers* 21:5,6).

וַיֹּאמְרוּ כָּל־אַנְשֵׁי יָבֵישׁ אֶל־נָחָשׁ ... — *And all the people of Jabesh said to Nahash...*

They all joined in this frightened declaration. Not one believed that they would succeed in resisting Nahash militarily, or that they would gain any advantage by approaching Saul (*Daas Sofrim*).

כְּרָת־לָנוּ בְּרִית וְנַעַבְדֶךָּ — *Seal a covenant with us and we will serve you.*

Fearful of being slaughtered, they asked Nahash, as the king of Ammon, to enter into a treaty with them (*Metzudos*), even though — as *Me'am Loez* points out — doing so is prohibited by the Torah (see *Deuteronomy* 23:7).

Be'er Moshe comments that their failure to immediately seek Saul's aid proves that their request for a king to lead and protect them had been insincere.

2. וַיֹּאמֶר אֲלֵיהֶם נָחָשׁ הָעַמּוֹנִי בְּזֹאת אֶכְרֹת לָהֶם בִּנְקוֹר לָכֶם כָּל־עֵין יָמִין — *But Nahash the Ammonite replied to them, "On this [condition] will I seal [a covenant] with you: when each right eye of yours is put out."*

Nahash felt that he had no reason to make a treaty; in his eyes he had already defeated them. He was ready to negotiate only if he could disgrace the Jews by poking out the eyes of the residents of Jabesh-gilead. Their inability to prevent this would effectively demonstrate his

1 Then Nahash the Ammonite went up and besieged
*Jabesh-gilead, and all the people of Jabesh said
to Nahash, "Seal a covenant with us, and we will
serve you."* 2 *But Nahash the Ammonite replied to
them, "On this [condition] I will seal [a covenant]
with you: when each right eye of yours is put out.
It will be a sign of shame for all of Israel."* 3 *The elders of Jabesh replied to him, "Delay [attacking] us*

superiority over the entire Jewish nation (*Malbim*).

Nahash intended this harsh condition literally (*Rashi*). By demanding humiliation and disgrace of the Jews rather than requesting something of tangible benefit to him, such as silver or gold, he demonstrated his wanton cruelty (*Abarbanel*). The Jews were thus forcibly reminded — in the most literal way — of the Torah's warning that any gentiles that they allowed to live on their land would be *as barbs in their eyes* (*Numbers* 33:55; *Me'am Loez*).

The Midrash, however, diverges from the literal meaning of Nahash's threat and presents a number of metaphorical interpretations.

Rashi cites a Midrash (*Midrash Shmuel* 14:7) that Nahash intended to burn the Torah. He alluded to it as the *right* eye because it was given by Hashem's *right* hand (*Deuteronomy* 33:3). Nahash's hostility to the Torah originated in the fact that it prohibits Jews from marrying Ammonite converts (ibid. 23:4).

Chomas Anach states that Nahash was objecting not to the Torah's ban on marriage with Ammonite converts but to its prohibition against entering into a treaty with the nation of Ammon. Now that the Jews of Jabesh-gilead proposed to forge a covenant with him, he intimated that he would agree only if they burn the Torah that contains this commandment (ibid. 23:7).[1]

Another Midrash (*Midrash Shmuel* 14:7) interprets the *right eye* as a reference to Israel's expert slingers and archers, who were viewed as precious as the eyes of the Jewish people. They are referred to specifically as *the right eye* because they would aim by sighting their target with the right eye (*Siddur HaGra; Mishbetzos Zahav*).

Finally, a Midrash (ibid.) avers that this *eye* represents the Sanhedrin, which comprises *the eyes of the assembly* (*Numbers* 15:24).

עֵין יָמִין — *Right eye.*

There are two grammatical anomalies in this phrase. First, although the noun עַיִן, *eye*, is feminine, the modifying adjective, יָמִין, is masculine. Second, the vowelization of עֵין indicates the possessive — i.e., *the eye of*. Therefore, the precise translation of this phrase must be *the eye of the right side* (*Radak*).

וְשַׂמְתִּיהָ חֶרְפָּה עַל־כָּל־יִשְׂרָאֵל — *It will be a sign of shame for all of Israel.*

It will be a source of shame to the

1. *Chomas Anach*'s comment is consistent with *Rashi*'s version of the Midrash, which states that Nahash wanted to burn the entire Torah. Our text of the Midrash states that he wanted to uproot only the passage about the prohibition to marry Ammonites.

Kli Yakar comments that our text of the Midrash seems to reflect the verse more precisely than does *Rashi*'s explanation, for putting out an eye is analogous to removing a commandment from the Torah. *Kli Yakar* thus suggests that *Rashi* possessed a version of the Midrash that was emphasizing the word כָּל in כָּל־עֵין יָמִין, *the entire right eye*, implying that Nahash wished to uproot the *entire* Torah.

יָמִים וְנִשְׁלְחָה מַלְאָכִים בְּכֹל גְּבוּל יִשְׂרָאֵל וְאִם־
ד אֵין מוֹשִׁיעַ אֹתָנוּ וְיָצָאנוּ אֵלֶיךָ: וַיָּבֹאוּ הַמַּלְאָכִים
גִּבְעַת שָׁאוּל וַיְדַבְּרוּ הַדְּבָרִים בְּאָזְנֵי הָעָם וַיִּשְׂאוּ
ה כָל־הָעָם אֶת־קוֹלָם וַיִּבְכּוּ: וְהִנֵּה שָׁאוּל בָּא אַחֲרֵי
הַבָּקָר מִן־הַשָּׂדֶה וַיֹּאמֶר שָׁאוּל מַה־לָּעָם כִּי
ו יִבְכּוּ וַיְסַפְּרוּ־לוֹ אֶת־דִּבְרֵי אַנְשֵׁי יָבֵישׁ: וַתִּצְלַח
רוּחַ־אֱלֹהִים עַל־שָׁאוּל °בשמעו אֶת־הַדְּבָרִים
ז הָאֵלֶּה וַיִּחַר אַפּוֹ מְאֹד: וַיִּקַּח צֶמֶד בָּקָר וַיְנַתְּחֵהוּ

°כְּשָׁמְעוֹ ק׳

Israelites that the weakness of Jabesh-gilead forced its inhabitants to enter into a treaty with Ammon (*Ralbag*) and that the nation as a whole was unable to succor its beleaguered countrymen (*Metzudos*).

3. וַיֹּאמְרוּ אֵלָיו זִקְנֵי יָבֵישׁ הֶרֶף לָנוּ שִׁבְעַת יָמִים — *The elders of Jabesh replied to him, "Delay [attacking] us for seven days."*

The elders realized that Nahash wished to demonstrate that the nation of Israel was powerless to act on behalf of the inhabitants of Jabesh-gilead. They thus argued that if he took immediate action he would defeat his own purpose, for the nation would claim that it had failed to act solely because it had been ignorant of his deeds. To prevent the Jews as a whole from being able to make this claim he must give them the opportunity to defend Jabesh-gilead; then, should they fail to answer his challenge, they would be thoroughly discredited (*Akeidah, Abarbanel*).

According to *Ralbag*, Nahash agreed to the elders' request because he sought a pretext to wage war against the entire nation of Israel in order to conquer its land.

וְאִם־אֵין מוֹשִׁיעַ אֹתָנוּ — *If there is no one to save us.*

Kli Yakar notes that מוֹשִׁיעַ, *save*, is written in the singular. Unlike the common people of Jabesh-gilead, who had scant regard for Saul, the elders trusted that Hashem would help them through the agency of their new king. Thus, in this phrase they were alluding to Hashem.

וְיָצָאנוּ אֵלֶיךָ — *Then we will go out to you.*

If Nahash's threat to put out the right eye of the Jews of Jabesh-gilead is to be understood literally, then this phrase means, "We will go out and submit to your demand." If, however, he was threatening to destroy the Torah — in whole or in part — then it is unimaginable that the Jews of Jabesh-gilead would submit. Accordingly, they meant, "If no one comes to our aid, we will be forced to go out to wage war against you" (*Kli Yakar*).

4. וַיָּבֹאוּ הַמַּלְאָכִים גִּבְעַת שָׁאוּל וַיְדַבְּרוּ הַדְּבָרִים בְּאָזְנֵי הָעָם ... — *When the messengers arrived at Gibeath-shaul and reported these words to the people...*

The messengers went to Gibeath Shaul to meet Saul (*Abarbanel*). However, because he was not present (as we will see in the following verse), they conveyed their information to others (*Kli Yakar*).

5. וְהִנֵּה שָׁאוּל בָּא אַחֲרֵי הַבָּקָר מִן־הַשָּׂדֶה — *Just then, Saul came in from the field behind the cattle.*

This means, states *Rashi*, that Saul came at the time of day that the cattle return from the fields; as king, he himself would not have been herding livestock (*Abarbanel*).

for seven days while we send messengers through-
out all the Land of Israel. If there is no one to
save us, then we will go out to you [and submit].''
4 *When the messengers arrived at Gibeath-*
shaul and reported these words to the people,
all the people raised their voices and wept. 5 *Just*
then, Saul came in from the field behind the
cattle, and Saul said, "Why are the people cry-
ing?" They told him the words of the men from
Jabesh. 6 *The spirit of God rested upon Saul when*
he heard these things, and he became very angry.
7 *He took a pair of oxen and cut them into pieces,*

Radak disagrees and reads the verse literally. Since Saul's monarchy had not been universally recognized — possibly due to the insults hurled at him by base people — he had returned to his former avocation (*Metzudos*).

Mussar HaNeviim accepts *Radak*'s claim and states that doing so eventually cost Saul the monarchy. Once he had been anointed king, he should not have allowed the contemptuous words of vile men to influence him, but should have immediately undertaken the affairs of state.

According to *Malbim*, Saul arrived together with the herdsmen leading their cattle; thus, it was natural for him to make use of the cattle (as we will see in verse 7) in response to this dismal news.

Kli Yakar comments that we see here an application of the principle that *the gates of tears are never locked*. As soon as the Jewish people began to cry, their salvation arrived.

וַיֹּאמֶר שָׁאוּל מַה־לָּעָם כִּי יִבְכּוּ — *And Saul said, "Why are the people crying?"*

Had Saul been acting as king, he would not have had to ask why they were crying. Because the heart of the king is one with the heart of the nation, he would have naturally resonated to their tribulations (*Mishbetzos Zahav*).

6. וַתִּצְלַח רוּחַ־אֱלֹהִים עַל־שָׁאוּל — *The spirit of God rested upon Saul.*

Targum renders רוּחַ־אֱלֹהִים, *spirit of God*, as *a spirit of strength*. *Abarbanel* explains, based on *Rambam's Moreh Nevuchim*, that this is Divine Inspiration (the most basic form of prophecy), which manifests itself as superior capability.

כְּשָׁמְעוֹ אֶת־הַדְּבָרִים הָאֵלֶּה ... — *When he heard these things...*

Although this was Saul's first opportunity to display his strength, he was motivated not by egotism but by the desire to uphold the dignity of the Jewish nation.

According to the view that Nahash sought to disgrace the Torah, the phrase הַדְּבָרִים הָאֵלֶּה, *these things*, alludes to the Torah (as in *Exodus* 34:27), and implies that Saul's purpose was to avenge the honor of the Torah (*Kli Yakar*).

וַיִּחַר אַפּוֹ מְאֹד — *And he became very angry*

Anger serves a function for the spirit of strength, by arousing it (*Abarbanel*).

7. וַיִּקַּח צֶמֶד בָּקָר וַיְנַתְּחֵהוּ — *He took a pair of oxen and cut them into pieces.*

With this, Saul made the point that

וַיְשַׁלַּח בְּכָל־גְּבוּל יִשְׂרָאֵל בְּיַד הַמַּלְאָכִים |
לֵאמֹר אֲשֶׁר אֵינֶנּוּ יֹצֵא אַחֲרֵי שָׁאוּל וְאַחַר
שְׁמוּאֵל כֹּה יֵעָשֶׂה לִבְקָרוֹ וַיִּפֹּל פַּחַד־יהוה עַל־
ח הָעָם וַיֵּצְאוּ כְּאִישׁ אֶחָד: וַיִּפְקְדֵם בְּבֶזֶק וַיִּהְיוּ בְנֵי־

just as an ox dies if its lifeline is cut, so too would the nation cease to exist if it did not maintain its lifeline — that being its unity and commitment to mutual assistance (*Malbim*).

The act of dividing the carcass and dispersing its parts was reminiscent of the incident of the concubine at Gibeah, in which the body of the woman was cut and distributed (*Judges* 19:29). Saul deliberately chose to arouse that association in people's minds in order to unnerve them and rouse them to action (*Daas Sofrim*).

The Midrash (*Yalkut Shimoni*) comments that, seeing the necessity of defending the Israelite nation, Saul unhesitatingly offered his own pair of oxen — notwithstanding, *Me'am Loez* adds, his previous concern for his father's donkeys, which indicates that he was, generally speaking, solicitous of the integrity of his property. This was in contradistinction to Samuel's admonishment that the king may confiscate whatever property he chooses (Ch. 8) (*Mishbetzos Zahav*).

בְּיַד הַמַּלְאָכִים — *With the messengers.*

These were the men who had come from Jabesh-gilead (*Metzudos*).

אֲשֶׁר אֵינֶנּוּ יֹצֵא ... — *Whoever does not go out...*

These words were spoken in the present rather than the future tense in order to connote that the Jews must set forth immediately (*Kli Yakar*).

אַחֲרֵי שָׁאוּל וְאַחַר שְׁמוּאֵל — *After Saul and after Samuel.*

Since not all of the Jews had accepted Saul as king, he added that if they hesitated to follow him, they should at least follow Samuel (*Radak*). *Abarbanel* adds that Saul mentioned Samuel because the latter had previously led the Jews to victory against the Philistines (Saul, on the other hand, had no military experience).

Although he mentioned Samuel, Saul placed his own name first because the fear of the king should exceed that of the prophet (*Chomas Anach*).

The words אַחֲרֵי and אַחַר, both of which mean *after*, are associated in this verse with, respectively, Saul and Samuel. אַחֲרֵי denotes a significant distance, whereas אַחַר denotes closer proximity (in either space or time) (see *Rashi, Genesis* 15:1). Thus, Saul implied that he would proceed well in advance of the army, with Samuel following behind him, close to the people. Saul wished the people to proceed in close proximity to Samuel so that they would be able to demonstrate their respect for him (*Kli Yakar*).

According to *Mishbetzos Zahav*, however, Samuel did not participate in this war (see *Ramban, Genesis* 49:18); the statement that the people would go *after Samuel* means that they would heed his advice.

כֹּה יֵעָשֶׂה לִבְקָרוֹ — *So shall be done to his oxen.*

If the people refused to unite, then their own oxen would be cut to pieces, in a form of measure-for-measure justice (*Malbim*).

It is not clear whether Saul meant that he would slaughter the oxen or that God would strike them with pestilence. Such statements, comments *Abarbanel*, possess maximum impact when they remain ambiguous.

Tiferes Yisrael (to *Middos* 1:2) assumes that Saul threatened to kill the

which he sent with the messengers throughout the Land of Israel, saying, "Whoever does not go out after Saul and after Samuel [to battle], so shall be done to his oxen." A dread of HASHEM fell upon the people and they went forth as one man.
8 *He counted them at Bezek, and the Children*

people's animals, and he derives from this the principle that if an item is destroyed in the course of the imposition of a fine or penalty, that is considered to have occurred for a constructive purpose and does not involve the transgression of בַּל תַּשְׁחִית, *unjustified destructiveness.*

וַיִּפֹּל פַּחַד־ה׳ עַל־הָעָם — *A dread of HASHEM fell upon the people.*

The people dreaded not the loss of their cattle but the possibility that by failing to obey they would be rebelling against the anointed one of Hashem (*Abarbanel*).

Daas Sofrim adds that they reacted with awe to the events that were transpiring, as they saw the unfolding of the new period of monarchy and the acceptance of the king's rulership.

The Four Letter Name of God used here connotes the Attribute of Compassion. The people were shaken with joy and fear as they witnessed the kindness of Hashem, Who was about to save them and establish a sovereign for them (*Kli Yakar*).

וַיֵּצְאוּ כְּאִישׁ אֶחָד — *And they went forth as one man.*

They went forth quickly and in common accord (*Metzudos*).

Malbim adds that they accepted Saul's exhortation that they maintain their unity, for they understood that just as when a person is ill each limb feels his pain, so too each man must feel the pain of his fellow Jew.

8. וַיִּפְקְדֵם בְּבָזֶק — *He counted them at Bezek.*

Simply understood, Bezek is the name of a place. *Rashi*, however, cites two homiletic Midrashic interpretations: that this word refers to earthenware shards (*Yoma* 22b) or to pebbles (*Tanchuma Ki Sisa* 9). Because taking a head count of Jews is forbidden, Saul collected either a shard or a pebble from each, and counted these.[1]

Based on the present incident, the Talmud (*Yoma* ibid.) rules that counting Jews is prohibited even for the purpose of performing a mitzvah.[2] (Later, when David disregarded this interdiction and instructed Joab to take a head count of the Jews, a severe pestilence eventuated [*II Samuel* Ch. 24].)

The concept of not taking a head count appears in the Torah (*Exodus* 30:12) following the incident of the golden calf, when God instructed Moses to take a census by collecting half-shekels.Only in that specific instance were half-shekels required, in order to atone for the sin of the golden calf; otherwise, any object may be used (*Ohr HaChaim*).

1. What difference does it make whether one counts heads or an object? *Yaaros Devash* suggests that a Jew is always better off when viewed as a member of the nation, for when he is counted as an individual, his every deed is scrutinized from heaven and the Attribute of Justice may be aroused. In a head count, a Jew is singled out; in the counting of a pooled collection of objects, he is subsumed within the group (cited by *Mussar HaNeviim*).

2. Regarding the question of why the Talmud traces the prohibition to the present episode and not to that described in the *Chumash*, see *Maharsha* (ibid.) and *Nachalas Shimon* 25.

יִשְׂרָאֵל֙ שְׁלֹ֣שׁ מֵא֣וֹת אֶ֔לֶף וְאִ֥ישׁ יְהוּדָ֖ה שְׁלֹשִׁ֥ים
ט אָֽלֶף׃ וַיֹּאמְר֞וּ לַמַּלְאָכִ֣ים הַבָּאִ֗ים כֹּ֣ה תֹאמְר֗וּן
לְאִישׁ֙ יָבֵ֣ישׁ גִּלְעָ֔ד מָחָ֕ר תִּהְיֶה־לָכֶ֥ם תְּשׁוּעָ֖ה °בחם
הַשָּׁ֑מֶשׁ וַיָּבֹ֣אוּ הַמַּלְאָכִ֗ים וַיַּגִּ֛ידוּ לְאַנְשֵׁ֥י יָבֵ֖ישׁ
י וַיִּשְׂמָֽחוּ׃ וַיֹּֽאמְרוּ֙ אַנְשֵׁ֣י יָבֵ֔ישׁ מָחָ֖ר נֵצֵ֣א אֲלֵיכֶ֑ם
יא וַעֲשִׂיתֶ֣ם לָּ֔נוּ כְּכָל־הַטּ֖וֹב בְּעֵינֵיכֶֽם׃ וַיְהִ֣י
מִֽמָּחֳרָ֗ת וַיָּ֨שֶׂם שָׁא֣וּל אֶת־הָעָם֮ שְׁלֹשָׁ֣ה רָאשִׁים֒
וַיָּבֹ֤אוּ בְתוֹךְ־הַֽמַּחֲנֶה֙ בְּאַשְׁמֹ֣רֶת הַבֹּ֔קֶר וַיַּכּ֥וּ אֶת־
עַמּ֖וֹן עַד־חֹ֣ם הַיּ֑וֹם וַיְהִ֤י הַנִּשְׁאָרִים֙ וַיָּפֻ֔צוּ וְלֹ֥א
יב נִשְׁאֲרוּ־בָ֖ם שְׁנַ֥יִם יָֽחַד׃ וַיֹּ֤אמֶר הָעָם֙ אֶל־שְׁמוּאֵ֔ל מִ֚י
הָאֹמֵ֔ר שָׁא֖וּל יִמְלֹ֣ךְ עָלֵ֑ינוּ תְּנ֥וּ הָאֲנָשִׁ֖ים וּנְמִיתֵֽם׃

°כְּחֹם ק׳

וַיִּהְיוּ בְנֵי־יִשְׂרָאֵל שְׁלֹשׁ מֵאוֹת אֶלֶף וְאִישׁ יְהוּדָה שְׁלֹשִׁים אָלֶף — *The Children of Israel were three hundred thousand, and the men of Judah, thirty thousand.*

The tribe of Judah was traditionally counted separately because of its prominence (*Abarbanel*) and because of the preeminence of its soldiers (*Daas Sofrim*).

The word אִישׁ — translated here as *men*, but literally *man* — is associated with Judah to indicate that this tribe was more unified than were the others; i.e., it stood as one man. Perhaps it is for this reason that it was treated separately (*Kli Yakar*).

9. וַיֹּאמְרוּ — *They said.*

This is a reference to Samuel and Saul (*Kli Yakar*).

כֹּה תֹאמְרוּן לְאִישׁ יָבֵישׁ גִּלְעָד — *So shall you tell the people of Jabesh-gilead.*

The word used for *people* is אִישׁ — literally, *man*, meaning, any inhabitant of Jabesh-gilead (*Metzudos*). *Kli Yakar* adds that some residents of Jabesh-gilead may have fled the city in fear, and the messengers were charged to deliver their information to each such individual.

Alternatively, the messengers spoke only to the most distinguished *man* of Jabesh-gilead — i.e., the governor — in order to maintain the confidentiality of their communication.

כְּחֹם הַשָּׁמֶשׁ — *By the time the sun gets hot.*

This means at the sun's strongest point, which is noon (*Metzudos*).

Mishbetzos Zahav notes that according to the Talmud (*Berachos* 27a) the "heat of the sun" refers to four hours after sunrise, or approximately 10:00 a.m. This would seem to contradict verse 11, which states that the war ended at חֹם הַיּוֹם, *the heat of the day*, which, according to the Talmud (ibid.), refers to noon. Possibly it grew clear in the morning that the Ammonites would not succeed in overpowering the Jews, and at noon the Jews' military victory was completed.

This phrase is read (*kri*) differently than it is written (*ksiv*). Although it is written בְּחֹם הַשָּׁמֶשׁ, *with the heat of the sun*, it is ready כְּחֹם הַשָּׁמֶשׁ, *approximately at the heat of the sun*, which allows for the designation of the time of day to be imprecise.

וַיַּגִּידוּ לְאַנְשֵׁי יָבֵישׁ וַיִּשְׂמָחוּ — *They told the people of Jabesh, and they rejoiced.*

They rejoiced when the messengers arrived on the seventh and final day of

of Israel were three hundred thousand, and the men
of Judah, thirty thousand. [9]They said to the messengers who had come, "So shall you tell the people
of Jabesh-gilead, 'Tomorrow there will be a salvation
for you by the time the sun gets hot.' " The messengers came and told the people of Jabesh, and they
rejoiced. [10]So the people of Jabesh said [to Nahash],
"Tomorrow we will go forth to you, and you may do
to us whatever seems good in your eyes."

[11]It was on the next day that Saul set the people
into three companies, and they entered the camp [of
the Ammonites] at the approach of dawn, and they
struck down Ammon by the time the day became hot.
There were survivors but they scattered; there did
not remain of them two [men] together. [12]The people
then said to Samuel, "Who is it that said, 'Will Saul
reign over us?' Deliver these men and we will put
them to death!"

their reprieve (*Kli Yakar*).

10. מָחָר נֵצֵא אֲלֵיכֶם — *Tomorrow we will go forth to you.*

This message was deliberately delivered ambiguously. The Ammonites understood the men of Jabesh to mean that they would surrender, but they really meant that they would come out to fight (*Abarbanel*).

11. וַיָּשֶׂם שָׁאוּל אֶת־הָעָם שְׁלֹשָׁה רָאשִׁים — *Saul set the people into three companies.*

They attacked from three vantage points (*Daas Sofrim*).

בְּאַשְׁמֹרֶת הַבֹּקֶר — *At the approach of dawn.*

Nighttime is divided into three equal watches (see *Berachos* 3a), of which this was the third and last (*Metzudos*). Saul chose to attack at night for two reasons: one, to catch the Ammonites off-guard, and two, because his men would thus avoid the enervating heat of the sun (*Daas Sofrim*).

וַיַּכּוּ אֶת־עַמּוֹן עַד־חֹם הַיּוֹם — *They struck down Ammon by the time the day became hot.*

Saul had said that he would save Jabesh-gilead *by the time the sun gets hot* (v. 9). However, there is no discrepancy here, for the word *day* is sometimes used to denote the sun (*Metzudos*).[1]

וַיְהִי הַנִּשְׁאָרִים וַיָּפֻצוּ — *There were survivors but they scattered.*

Radak renders this as, *There were some who survived because they scattered.*

12. וַיֹּאמֶר הָעָם אֶל־שְׁמוּאֵל מִי הָאֹמֵר שָׁאוּל יִמְלֹךְ עָלֵינוּ תְּנוּ הָאֲנָשִׁים וּנְמִיתֵם — *The people then said to Samuel, "Who is it that said, 'Will Saul reign over us?' Deliver these men and we will put*

1. See also *Mishbetzos Zahav* above (v. 9).

יג וַיֹּאמֶר שָׁאוּל לֹא־יוּמַת אִישׁ בַּיּוֹם הַזֶּה כִּי הַיּוֹם
יד עָשָׂה־יהוה תְּשׁוּעָה בְּיִשְׂרָאֵל: וַיֹּאמֶר
שְׁמוּאֵל אֶל־הָעָם לְכוּ וְנֵלְכָה הַגִּלְגָּל וּנְחַדֵּשׁ
טו שָׁם הַמְּלוּכָה: וַיֵּלְכוּ כָל־הָעָם הַגִּלְגָּל וַיַּמְלִכוּ

them to death.''

Having witnessed this victory, which was clearly due to God's miraculous assistance and Saul's merits, the people sought those who had initially rejected Saul (*Rashi; Metzudos*), in order to kill them as rebels (*Malbim*).

We translate the phrase שָׁאוּל יִמְלֹךְ עָלֵינוּ — *Will Saul reign over us?* — as a rhetorical question, in accord with the majority of commentators.

Be'er Moshe, however, understands it to be a declarative sentence: *Who is it that said, ''Saul will rule over us!''* — i.e., Saul alone, independent of God. Those people had sought a government solely under the aegis of a human monarch. But today the people realized that their real king is Hashem, and that the role of the human sovereign is to obey Him and enforce His Torah.

13. וַיֹּאמֶר שָׁאוּל לֹא־יוּמַת אִישׁ בַּיּוֹם הַזֶּה — *But Saul said to them, ''Let no man be put to death this day.''*

Samuel agreed with those who wished to punish the miscreants, but Saul objected (*Daas Sofrim*).

לֹא יוּמַת אִישׁ בַּיּוֹם הַזֶּה כִּי הַיּוֹם עָשָׂה־ה׳ תְּשׁוּעָה בְּיִשְׂרָאֵל — *Let no man be put to death this day, for today* Hashem *has wrought salvation in Israel.*

It would be inappropriate to execute anyone on this joyous day of victory (*Metzudos*).

Mishbetzos Zahav mentions that this is reminiscent of the incident at the time of the giving of the Torah in which Nadab and Abihu gazed inappropriately at the sacred vision of God; although they deserved death, Hashem postponed their execution so as not to disturb the celebratory nature of the day (*Rashi, Exodus* 24:10).

It is not clear whether Saul had these men killed later or pardoned them altogether (*Ralbag*).

Some commentators state that he let them live, and understand his statement here as his rationale for doing so.

According to *Daas Sofrim*, the purpose of killing these men would have been to demonstrate the puissance of the king; now that this magnificent victory had established his authority, it was no longer necessary to do so, so it would be better to show compassion and forgiveness.

Malbim states that the word הַיּוֹם, *today*, indicates that Saul's rulership was universally recognized only today; thus, those men who had opposed Saul prior to this time could not technically be considered rebels.

Finally, *Kli Yakar* suggests that in his humility Saul was suggesting that those who had questioned his ability to rule were right, because today it was clear that Hashem and not he had brought about a great salvation. Therefore God was the true King of the Jews, not Saul.

Nevertheless, the Talmud (*Yoma* 22b; cf. *Rashi* there) condemns Saul for having improperly ceded his honor now and in a previous incident (10:27), and states that this ultimately resulted in his losing the throne.

Although *Rambam* rules that a king is not obligated to put a rebel to death (*Hil. Melachim* 3:8), Saul should have done so in this case, for these men had undermined the entire enterprise of his regency, and executing them would have established a proper awe for the throne.

Chida states that although a king is

[13]*But Saul said to them, "Let no man be put to*
death this day, for today HASHEM *has wrought sal-*
vation in Israel."
[14]*Then Samuel said to the people, "Come and let*
us go to Gilgal, and let us renew the kingdom there."
[15]*So all the people went to Gilgal: there they made*

not obligated to kill renegades, he *is* expected to penalize them; Saul's failure to take any action at all cost him the kingdom.

According to *Mishbetzos Zahav*, God was not punishing Saul; rather, Saul's failure to take a strong stand indicated that he was unqualified to serve as king.

עָשָׂה־ה׳ תְּשׁוּעָה לְיִשְׂרָאֵל — *HASHEM has wrought salvation in Israel.*

This phrase can be read, *HASHEM has wrought salvation for the sake of Israel.* Whereas the Jews celebrated Saul as the immediate source of their victory (v. 12), he stated that Hashem saved them on their own behalf.

14. לְכוּ וְנֵלְכָה — *Come and let us go.*

According to *Daas Sofrim,* this phrase implies that Samuel did not order the people to go but merely invited them to proceed of their own accord.

לְכוּ וְנֵלְכָה הַגִּלְגָּל — *Come and let us go to Gilgal.*

As mentioned above (10:8), some commentators understand that Samuel's statement to the people, *Let us go to Gilgal,* was independent of his earlier command to Saul to go to Gilgal and await his arrival (ibid.). The present statement involved all the people and not just Saul, and it took place before the incident in which Saul alone was required to go to Gilgal (*Mahari Kara*). Others understand that Saul came to Gilgal now for the coronation, and after Samuel left, the king was to wait seven days for the prophet's return (see above).

Why did Samuel choose Gilgal? A number of reasons are advanced.

First, since the Jews were commanded to appoint a king after they entered the Land of Israel (*Sanhedrin* 21b) and they came initially to Gilgal (*Joshua* 4:19), it stands to reason that they would perform that rite there.

Also, when Joshua had entered the land he had placed the Ark and Tabernacle there, rendering it a sacred site (*Radak, Kaftor VaFerach*).

It is true that the Tabernacle was currently situated in Nob, and one might have thought that Saul should thus be crowned there. Nevertheless, Gilgal was still preferable because it was more centrally located since, being near the Jordan River, it was easily accessible to the tribes of Reuben and Gad, who lived east of the Jordan.

Citing *Rema MiPano, Mishbetzos Zahav* adduces another reason that Samuel chose not to coronate Saul in Nob: he foresaw that Saul would eventually kill the Kohanim of Nob (Ch. 22); thus, it would be an inauspicious omen for his kingdom to be inaugurated there.

At any rate, it is possible that the Ark was brought to Gilgal for the occasion (*Abarbanel*).

וּנְחַדֵּשׁ שָׁם הַמְּלוּכָה — *And let us renew the kingdom there.*

Now that everyone consented to Saul's rule, it would be proper for him to be newly crowned.

According to *Be'er Moshe,* the Jews' initial request for a king had been motivated by improper considerations. Now that they understood that a Jewish ruler's role is to act as a representative of the kingdom of Hashem, they had to again formally accept his rule.

שָׁם אֶת־שָׁאוּל לִפְנֵי יהוה בַּגִּלְגָּל וַיִּזְבְּחוּ־שָׁם
זְבָחִים שְׁלָמִים לִפְנֵי יְהוָה וַיִּשְׂמַח שָׁם שָׁאוּל

א וְכָל־אַנְשֵׁי יִשְׂרָאֵל עַד־מְאֹד׃ וַיֹּאמֶר
שְׁמוּאֵל אֶל־כָּל־יִשְׂרָאֵל הִנֵּה שָׁמַעְתִּי בְקֹלְכֶם
לְכֹל אֲשֶׁר־אֲמַרְתֶּם לִי וָאַמְלִיךְ עֲלֵיכֶם מֶלֶךְ׃
ב וְעַתָּה הִנֵּה הַמֶּלֶךְ ׀ מִתְהַלֵּךְ לִפְנֵיכֶם וַאֲנִי זָקַנְתִּי
וָשַׂבְתִּי וּבָנַי הִנָּם אִתְּכֶם וַאֲנִי הִתְהַלַּכְתִּי לְפָנֵיכֶם

15. וַיַּמְלִכוּ שָׁם אֶת־שָׁאוּל לִפְנֵי ה׳ — *There they made Saul king before HASHEM.*

This is described as having taken place *before HASHEM* because the Divine Presence rests wherever the majority of the Jewish people congregate (*Metzudos*).

This verse does not make mention of the fact that the Jews were renewing Saul's sovereignty but focuses on the far more significant fact that this time he was made king *before HASHEM* (*Kli Yakar*).

Daas Sofrim adds that the people acknowledged that Hashem was responsible for their victory and admitted in general their dependence on His aid.

וַיִּשְׂמַח שָׁם שָׁאוּל וְכָל־אַנְשֵׁי יִשְׂרָאֵל — *And there Saul, as well as all the men of Israel, rejoiced.*

Because the people were now spiritually elevated, they are not described as כָּל־הָעָם, *all the people*, but are given the more respectful sobriquet, אַנְשֵׁי יִשְׂרָאֵל, *the men of Israel* (*Be'er Moshe*).

Daas Sofrim conjectures that Samuel's name is omitted here because he did not share the others' level of joy. He knew that this salvation would have come from Hashem even without a king, which would have resulted in even greater glory to Hashem.

XII

In this chapter, which relates the shift from Samuel's leadership to Saul's reign, Samuel speaks to the nation in order to explicate the ideals and philosophy of Jewish leadership. First and foremost, the king and his constituents must recognize that their ultimate allegiance is to God. The king is the bearer of God's Majesty; as such, it is his responsibility to safeguard the nation's righteousness and guide the people in Hashem's way.

In the incident of the rebellion of Korah, these guidelines of Jewish leadership were challenged (see *Numbers* Ch. 16). It is thus appropriate that the present chapter, which records how Samuel — a descendant of Korah — corrected his ancestor's error and presented the Torah's perspective, is read as the *Haftarah* for *Parashas Korah.*

1. וַיֹּאמֶר שְׁמוּאֵל אֶל־כָּל־יִשְׂרָאֵל — *Then Samuel said to all of Israel.*

It is apparent from verse 3 below that Saul was present during this talk. This supports the supposition that Samuel delivered it during the gathering at Gilgal described in the previous chapter.

Samuel first gave the people time to rejoice in their victory over Ammon. Only then did he rebuke them for having requested a king — utilizing the occasion to remind them, *inter alia*, not to take such victories for granted (*Daas Sofrim*).

The implication of the word וַיֹּאמֶר, *he said*, as opposed to וַיְדַבֵּר, *he spoke*, is that Samuel addressed the people gently.

Saul king before HASHEM *in Gilgal, and there they slaughtered feast peace-offerings before* HASHEM*; and there Saul, as well as all the men of Israel, rejoiced exceedingly.*

12/1-2

[1] *Then Samuel said to all of Israel, "Behold!*
I have hearkened to your voice, to every-
thing that you have said to me, and I have ap-
pointed a king over you. [2] *And now, behold! —*
the king goes before you, but I have grown old
and gray. As for my sons, here they are with
you. And as for me, I have walked before you

הִנֵּה שָׁמַעְתִּי בְקֹלְכֶם לְכֹל אֲשֶׁר־אֲמַרְתֶּם לִי וָאַמְלִיךְ עֲלֵיכֶם מֶלֶךְ — *Behold! I have hearkened to your voice, to everything that you have said to me, and I have appointed a king over you.*

The commentators wonder why Samuel repeated his reproof of the people for requesting a king. *Abarbanel* explains that Samuel's previous reproof might have been interpreted as an attempt to prevent the Jews from removing him from his position of leadership. Now that he had already given them a king, he could no longer be suspected of such a motive.

Abarbanel and *Malbim* observe that with these words Samuel criticized the people for having rejected him. The phrase, לְכֹל אֲשֶׁר־אֲמַרְתֶּם לִי, *to everything that you have said to me,* may be read as *everything that you have said about me* — i.e., they had complained that he was too old to lead and that his sons were unworthy of replacing him.

Mishbetzos Zahav adds that Samuel now felt assured that the people would heed his reproof. Since they had already attained their goal, their passion had subsided and they were amenable to critique. So is it with every sinful deed; after it is over, the perpetrator's passion dies down and he grows painfully aware of the depth to which he had descended (see *Tanchuma, Balak* 7; *Ohr HaChaim, Bereishis* 3:7).

The word כֹּל, *everything,* alludes to the Jews' three requests: a king who (a) was *fit* (לָנוּ מֶלֶךְ, *a king [fit] for us;* above, 8:5); (b) would be chosen quickly (עַתָּה, *now,* ibid.); and (c) would be appointed by Samuel (*Kli Yakar*).

2. הִנֵּה הַמֶּלֶךְ מִתְהַלֵּךְ לִפְנֵיכֶם — *Behold! The king goes before you.*

With these words, Samuel reminded the people that he had appointed a king who had the self-confidence and strong convictions to go before them, i.e., to lead them, rather than being led by them (*Me'am Loez*).

וַאֲנִי זָקַנְתִּי וָשַׂבְתִּי — *But I have grown old and gray.*

זִקְנָה, growing old, precedes שֵׂיבָה, turning gray. Thus, our Sages associate old age with the age of 60 and gray hair with the age of 70 (*Avos* 5:25). Samuel was telling the people that he had grown old and, furthermore, had reached the age of being hoary (*Abarbanel*).

According to the view of our Sages that Samuel died at the age of 52, his words here indicate that he had grown prematurely old.

וּבָנַי הִנָּם אִתְּכֶם — *As for my sons, here they are with you.*

Radak understands this phrase to

ג מִנְּעֻרַי עַד־הַיּוֹם הַזֶּה: הִנְנִי עֲנוּ בִי נֶגֶד יהוה וְנֶגֶד
מְשִׁיחוֹ אֶת־שׁוֹר | מִי לָקַחְתִּי וַחֲמוֹר מִי לָקַחְתִּי

mean that Samuel was presenting his sons as teachers to whom the people could turn for Torah rulings that they had learned from him.

Abarbanel explains that Samuel told the people that they might judge his sons as they saw fit.

According to *Kli Yakar*, Samuel was implying that the people should show their appreciation for his leadership by fulfilling the needs of his children.

Me'am Loez suggests that before Samuel began to rebuke the people for having chosen a king, he wished to assure them that he had no intention of unseating Saul. First, he told them, *the king goes before you* — i.e., Saul's position as king was firmly established. Second, *I have grown old and gray* — Samuel was too aged to desire to lead the people. And third, *as for my sons, here they are with you* — Samuel was not seeking a leadership position for any of his sons, because they had already been removed from authority. They were now no different from any other citizen.

Metzudos adds that the phrase, וּבָנַי הִנָּם אִתְּכֶם, *as for my sons, here they are with you*, may be read as, "*as for my sons, here they are with you* in their desire to serve the king."

In his subsequent words, וַאֲנִי הִתְהַלַּכְתִּי לִפְנֵיכֶם מִנְּעֻרַי עַד־הַיּוֹם הַזֶּה, *I have led you from my youth until this day*, Samuel was implying that the people were familiar enough with him to know that he was telling the truth and that he harbored no ulterior motives.

Mahari Kara interprets this verse as being part of Samuel's rebuke of the people. In the words, *I have grown old and gray*, he was telling them that he had aged prematurely because of his toil on their behalf. The people might defend their request for a king with the claim that Samuel was too feeble to lead them. But if so, *as for my sons, here they are with you* — the people should have accepted the leadership of his sons. And any complaint on their part that Samuel had overburdened the people was certainly not true — for, as the next verse tells, he had taken nothing from them.

According to *Ahavas Yehonasan*, Samuel blamed his premature aging on the fact that the people had requested a king. Samuel had prayed that his handiwork — i.e., the appointment of the king — not be disqualified during his lifetime. This meant that he must pass away before Saul was unseated (see above, 8:1 comm.).

According to *Ri Padanki* (cited by *Me'am Loez*), this verse constitutes a preface to the coming verse, in which Samuel cleared his name of having seized property illicitly. People might state that he did not take this property because he recognized that he did not deserve it. To the contrary, he asserted, *I have grown old and gray* — he had toiled so hard on the nation's behalf that he had grown prematurely old. And he challenged the people to refute his selflessness, [confident that they could not do so, and that] they would have to acknowledge his integrity. Since they now had a king and there was no longer any reason for them to fear Samuel, that acknowledgment could only be interpreted as being an honest appraisal.

3. הִנְנִי עֲנוּ בִי — *Here I am; testify about me.*

In accord with the dictum that a person must be demonstrably blameless before correcting others, Samuel now prefaced his reproof of the people by declaring that he had been honest and selfless in his dealings with them (*Me'am Loez*).

Since this was a generation that "judged its judges" — i.e., that cast

from my youth until this day. ³*Here I am; testify about me in the presence of* HASHEM *and in the presence of His anointed: Whose ox have I taken? Whose donkey have I taken?*

aspersions on anyone who rebuked it (*Bava Basra* 15b) — Samuel felt it necessary to demand every individual's acknowledgment that he had no claims against him [i.e., Samuel] (the Brisker Rav).

Samuel made this statement נֶגֶד מְשִׁיחוֹ, *in the presence of His anointed* — i.e., Saul. It was the common practice for a new monarch to investigate whether the previous ruler had accepted bribes. Samuel now performed this inquiry to clear himself of suspicion (*Abarbanel*).

Also, since Samuel's sons had been accused of acting dishonestly and accepting bribes, Samuel wished to clarify that he himself was not suspected of such activities (*Mussar HaNeviim*).

According to *Daas Sofrim*, since the era of Judges was now coming to a close, Samuel was making a general statement about the probity of the vast majority of the Judges. Also, this statement would serve as a moral lesson and exemplar for the incoming era of monarchy, challenging the kings to maintain a similar standard of integrity.

נֶגֶד ה׳ — *In the presence of* HASHEM.

This phrase means that the Holy Ark was present (*Abarbanel*).

Kli Yakar suggests that Samuel's statement, הִנְנִי עֲנוּ בִי נֶגֶד ה׳, *Here I am; testify about me in the presence of* HASHEM, implies that should anyone have the audacity to testify falsely against Samuel in the presence of Hashem, he would make good that person's claim, no matter what the cost. This explains the reason for our Sages' inference from this phrase that Samuel was wealthy (*Yalkut Shimoni*).

נֶגֶד ה׳ וְנֶגֶד מְשִׁיחוֹ — *In the presence of* HASHEM *and in the presence of His anointed.*

Samuel was telling the people that they had no need to refrain from pressing their claims in a desire to passively flatter him, because they were standing before Hashem, Who prohibits flattery. Nor need they fear his revenge if they testified against him, because their king Saul was present, who would protect them and impose justice (*Malbim*).

אֶת־שׁוֹר מִי לָקַחְתִּי וַחֲמוֹר מִי לָקַחְתִּי — *Whose ox have I taken? Whose donkey have I taken?*

Legally, Samuel had the right to use public funds for the oxen that he offered to God when he pleaded on the people's behalf and when he appointed their king, and for the donkey that he rode on when traveling as judge. Nevertheless, he refrained from doing so and used his own funds instead (*Midrash Tanchuma, Korah* 7).[1]

Also, Samuel had the right to take a donkey from Saul's property in order to travel to him and inform him that his father's donkeys had been found, but he did not do so (*Ahavas Yehonasan*).

Ahavas Yehonasan comments that in using the phrase, "Whose donkey have I taken?" Samuel intended to correct the sin of his ancestor Korah, whose actions had forced Moses to state similarly, לֹא חֲמוֹר אֶחָד מֵהֶם נָשָׂאתִי, *I have not taken even a single donkey of theirs* (*Numbers* 16:15).

1. *Daas Sofrim* derives from *Rashi* (to *Nedarim* 38a) that Samuel refrained from using public funds because he was wealthy. However, a leader who is not wealthy may not refrain from acting on behalf of the masses in order to avoid spending their money. *Daas Sofrim* comments that it is not clear that all halachic authorities concur with this ruling.

וְאֶת־מִ֣י עָשַׁ֗קְתִּי אֶת־מִ֣י רַצּ֔וֹתִי וּמִיַּד־מִ֙י
לָקַ֣חְתִּי כֹ֔פֶר וְאַעְלִ֥ים עֵינַ֖י בּ֑וֹ וְאָשִׁ֖יב לָכֶֽם׃
ד וַיֹּ֣אמְר֔וּ לֹ֥א עֲשַׁקְתָּ֖נוּ וְלֹ֣א רַצּוֹתָ֑נוּ וְלֹֽא־לָקַ֥חְתָּ
ה מִיַּד־אִ֖ישׁ מְאֽוּמָה׃ וַיֹּ֨אמֶר אֲלֵיהֶ֜ם עֵ֧ד יְהוָ֣ה
בָּכֶ֗ם וְעֵ֤ד מְשִׁיחוֹ֙ הַיּ֣וֹם הַזֶּ֔ה כִּ֛י לֹ֥א מְצָאתֶ֖ם
ו בְּיָדִ֣י מְא֑וּמָה וַיֹּ֖אמֶר עֵֽד׃ וַיֹּ֣אמֶר

וְאֶת־מִי עָשַׁקְתִּי אֶת־מִי רַצּוֹתִי — *Whom have I robbed? Whom have I coerced?*

Our translation of רַצּוֹתִי as *coerced* follows *Targum. Rashi,* however, renders this verb as *Whom have I shattered?*

According to *Radak,* אֶת־מִי עָשַׁקְתִּי refers to monetary damage, and אֶת־מִי רַצּוֹתִי to physical damage.

The Sages associate the word רַצּוֹתִי with רָצוֹן, *will.* Samuel was stating that he would not even rent someone else's animal [since he could not be sure of that person's willing consent]. Our Sages state that Samuel went even beyond Moses' scrupulousness. Moses would not force anyone to rent him his donkey, but Samuel would not rent a donkey even if the owner gave his consent, since the owner might have been too embarrassed to refuse (*Nedarim* 38a, *Ran* ad loc.).

Mussar HaNeviim adds that Samuel acted in this way because he had seen the punishment that Eli's sons had incurred for engaging in morally questionable behavior.

וּמִיַּד־מִי לָקַחְתִּי כֹפֶר וְאַעְלִים עֵינַי בּוֹ — *From whom have I taken redemption-money that I should avert my eyes from him?*

Samuel asked rhetorically: From whom have I accepted bribes in order to avoid rendering a judgment against him.

Following *Metzudos,* we render the word כֹּפֶר as *redemption-money.*

This word may also be related to וְכָפַרְתָּ, *you should cover* (see *Genesis* 6:14), because bribery covers the truth (*Me'am Loez*).

Our Sages state that a person who accepts bribes ages prematurely. Samuel wished to make it clear that his premature aging was due to other factors (see above, v. 2) (*Ahavas Yehonasan*).

Ahavas Yehonasan cites the halachic ruling that a person who shames a Torah scholar must pay a fine (see *Rambam, Hil. Talmud Torah* 6:12), which the scholar may himself collect. Samuel was saying that although some people had embarrassed him, he had not insisted on collecting this fine. The next phrase, וְאַעְלִים עֵינַי בּוֹ, *that I should avert my eyes from him,* means that Samuel made sure not to gaze at such people, for he did not want the psychic power in his eyes to harm them (as opposed to other great men, who did use their eyes in such a manner; see *Berachos* 58a).

According to *Radak,* וְאַעְלִים עֵינַי בּוֹ means that Samuel promised that if anyone felt too intimidated to speak, Samuel would ease the man's discomfort by turning his eyes away from him.

וְאָשִׁיב לָכֶם — *And I shall make restitution to you.*

Metzudos understands this phrase as meaning that Saul would respond to every individual's claim.

As in the phrase, *in the presence of Hashem,* we see from here as well that Samuel promised to pay any claim made against him (*Rashi*). From this (as stated above), the Sages derive that Samuel was a wealthy man (*Yalkut Shimoni*).

Whom have I robbed? Whom have I coerced? From
whose hand have I taken redemption-money that I
should avert my eyes from him? And I shall make
restitution to you."
4 *And they said, "You have not robbed us; you*
have not coerced us; and you have not taken any-
thing from any person's hand."
5 *So he said to them, "HASHEM is your witness,*
and His anointed one is a witness this day, that
you have not found anything in my hand." And
they said as one, "A witness!"

4. וְלֹא־לָקַחְתָּ מִיַּד־אִישׁ מְאוּמָה — *You have not taken anything from any person's hand.*

The people acknowledged that, because he did not want to benefit from anyone, Samuel had not even accepted gifts (*Malbim*).

Kli Yakar observes that in the beginning of the verse, the people spoke of themselves in the plural — *us* — but the final clause expresses itself in the singular — מִיַּד־אִישׁ, *from the hand of any man*. The people acknowledged that not only did Samuel not derive benefit from the community at large but he did not even take anything from a single individual.

5. וַיֹּאמֶר אֲלֵיהֶם עֵד ה׳ בָּכֶם וְעֵד מְשִׁיחוֹ — *So he said to them, "HASHEM is your witness and His anointed one is a witness."*

Above (v. 3), we cited the comment of the Brisker Rav that before rebuking the people Samuel needed to gain their acknowledgment that he was clear of any wrongdoing. The Talmud (*Sanhedrin* 29a) rules that even if a person admits to monetary liability in front of witnesses, he can withdraw that admission unless he has explicitly stated, "You are my witnesses." Accordingly, states the Brisker Rav, in order for the people's acknowledgment to be valid they had to elucidate their acceptance of Hashem and Saul as witnesses.

כִּי לֹא מְצָאתֶם בְּיָדִי מְאוּמָה — *That you have not found anything in my hand.*

This included even items that a court must sometimes hold until a dispute is resolved or information is gathered (*Me'am Loez*).

וַיֹּאמֶר עֵד — *And they said as one, "A witness!"*

Our translation follows *Radak*, who explains the singular construction of the word *witness* as meaning that the nation spoke as one.

The word וַיֹּאמֶר literally means *and he said. Mahari Kara* suggests that this refers to the singular noun יִשְׂרָאֵל, *Israel*.

Alternatively, states *Mahari Kara*, it was Saul who spoke, since he, the *anointed one*, had been asked to testify.

Our Sages teach that it was God Who spoke. If so, this is one of three instances in which a Divine voice confirmed a claim (*Makkos* 23b).

Midrash Shmuel adds that Hashem was saying, "Whereas human beings can testify only to what is revealed to them, I can testify even to what is concealed from them."

Mussar HaNeviim adds that it was necessary for Hashem to testify so that no one should later claim that the people's acknowledgment was insincere and motivated by shame or fear.

שְׁמוּאֵל אֶל־הָעָם יהוה אֲשֶׁר עָשָׂה אֶת־מֹשֶׁה
וְאֶת־אַהֲרֹן וַאֲשֶׁר הֶעֱלָה אֶת־אֲבֹתֵיכֶם מֵאֶרֶץ
ז מִצְרָיִם: וְעַתָּה הִתְיַצְּבוּ וְאִשָּׁפְטָה אִתְּכֶם
לִפְנֵי יהוה אֵת כָּל־צִדְקוֹת יהוה אֲשֶׁר־עָשָׂה
ח אִתְּכֶם וְאֶת־אֲבוֹתֵיכֶם: כַּאֲשֶׁר־בָּא יַעֲקֹב
מִצְרָיִם וַיִּזְעֲקוּ אֲבֹתֵיכֶם אֶל־יהוה וַיִּשְׁלַח
יהוה אֶת־מֹשֶׁה וְאֶת־אַהֲרֹן וַיּוֹצִיאוּ אֶת־
אֲבֹתֵיכֶם מִמִּצְרַיִם וַיֹּשִׁבוּם בַּמָּקוֹם הַזֶּה:

6. ה׳ אֲשֶׁר עָשָׂה אֶת־מֹשֶׁה וְאֶת־אַהֲרֹן — *HASHEM, Who produced Moses and Aaron.*

This verse is somewhat ambiguous, as it merely describes some acts of Hashem, and it is not clear why this prefaces Samuel's words of rebuke. We will elucidate the phrase, and then explain the context of the verse.

The word עָשָׂה literally means *made*. *Radak* explains this to mean that Hashem raised and taught Moses and Aaron. According to *Rashi*, the verb עָשָׂה implies that He prepared Moses and Aaron to be His emissaries. A Midrash (*Shir HaShirim Rabbah* 4:5) understands this word to mean that Hashem created Moses and Aaron solely in honor of and for the sake of the Jews.

Targum renders this phrase as *HASHEM, Who performed great acts through Moses and Aaron.*

Metzudos follows this interpretation, and sees these words as part of Samuel's preface to his rebuke of the people for having requested a king. The people knew what Hashem had done through Moses and Aaron — i.e., He had miraculously redeemed their ancestors from Egypt. They should therefore have considered that since the Jewish people had always survived without a king, there had been no need for them to demand a king now.

Abarbanel also explains this verse to be a part of their rebuke for their having rejected Hashem's providential leadership. Samuel reminds them that Hashem created Moses and Aaron as special people: their very births were supernatural (*Abarbanel* does not clarify how Aaron's birth was supernatural), and they were groomed to perform miracles for the Jews of their time. This also explains why Hashem is described as the One Who raised them from Egypt, rather than as the Creator of the world.

Ahavas Yehonasan states that Samuel was telling the people that since the redemption from Egypt had occurred in the merit of the Jews' trust in Hashem, this generation should have emulated that trust and not requested a king.

Daas Sofrim states that Samuel was rebuking the people for having urged their ideas regarding the installation of a king on Hashem. In the past, Hashem had appointed leaders such as Moses and Aaron without the people's initiative. Just as Hashem had taken the Jews out of Egypt and saved them from other tribulations without their suggestions, so too should this generation have waited for Hashem to choose the perfect king.

Radak understands this verse to mean that Samuel was identifying God as the Witness Who had confirmed his statement in the previous verse.

Samuel now explicitly identified that voice as having emanated from God (*Malbim*).

By confirming that Hashem had appointed Moses and Aaron as the Jewish people's leaders, Samuel corrected the sin of his ancestor Korah, who had

*[6] Samuel then said to the people, "[It is] HASHEM,
Who produced Moses and Aaron, and Who brought
your forefathers up from the land of Egypt. [7] And
now, stand erect, and I shall enter into judgment
with you before HASHEM, concerning all the righteous
deeds of HASHEM that He has done with you and
with your forefathers. [8] When Jacob came to Egypt
and your forefathers cried out to HASHEM, HASHEM
sent Moses and Aaron, and they brought your forefathers out of Egypt, and settled them in this place.*

questioned the validity of their authority (see Preface) (*Mishbetzos Zahav*).

7. וְאִשָּׁפְטָה אִתְּכֶם לִפְנֵי ה׳ אֵת כָּל־צִדְקוֹת ה׳ — *And I shall enter into judgment with you before HASHEM, concerning all the righteous deeds of HASHEM.*

Samuel informed the people that he would remind them of the many miracles that Hashem had performed for the Jews even when they had no king (*Mahari Kara*).

And this was the case, Samuel left unsaid but meant the people to realize, despite the fact that the Jews had sinned (*Radak*).

Daas Sofrim comments that the word צִדְקוֹת, *righteous deeds*, refers to charitable actions that one is not obligated to perform.

Malbim states that after criticizing the Jews for having rejected him, Samuel went on to censure their rejection of Hashem as their King. What flaw could they possibly have found in Him?

אִתְּכֶם וְאֶת־אֲבֹתֵיכֶם — *With you and with your forefathers.*

Samuel first mentioned אִתְּכֶם, *you*, and only then אֲבֹתֵיכֶם, *your forefathers*. This implies that when a generation of Jews is troubled (*you*), their *forefathers* also suffer in their graves; and when they are saved, their forefathers are relieved. Therefore, whatever Hashem did for *you* he also did for your forefathers.

The Talmud (*Arachin* 17a) derives from this verse that not even Abraham, Isaac, and Jacob (the Jews' *forefathers)* would escape censure were God to judge them — meaning, were He to investigate whether they deserved the favors that He had performed for them (*Maharsha*).

8. כַּאֲשֶׁר־בָּא יַעֲקֹב מִצְרָיִם וַיִּזְעֲקוּ אֲבֹתֵיכֶם — *When Jacob came to Egypt and your forefathers cried out.*

Actually, the Jews did not cry out until some generations following the death of Jacob, when they were forced to do hard labor and otherwise persecuted. Samuel abridged the narrative for the sake of brevity (*Radak*).

Daas Sofrim raises the possibility that Samuel spoke in greater detail, but Scripture omitted the details of his speech that were unnecessary for future generations.

וַיִּזְעֲקוּ — *Cried out.*

Although the Jews cried out, Samuel implied, they did not ask for a king, and Hashem saved them through prophets (*Abarbanel*).

וַיִּשְׁלַח ה׳ אֶת־מֹשֶׁה וְאֶת־אַהֲרֹן וַיּוֹצִיאוּ אֶת־אֲבֹתֵיכֶם מִמִּצְרַיִם וַיֹּשִׁבוּם בַּמָּקוֹם הַזֶּה — *HASHEM sent Moses and Aaron, and they brought your forefathers out of Egypt, and settled them in this place.*

Moses and Aaron did not literally settle the Jews in the Land of Israel, because they themselves did not enter it. However, since it was their leadership that made the Jewish people worthy of

ט וַיִּשְׁכְּחוּ אֶת־יהוה אֱלֹהֵיהֶם וַיִּמְכֹּר אֹתָם
בְּיַד סִיסְרָא שַׂר־צְבָא חָצוֹר וּבְיַד־פְּלִשְׁתִּים
י וּבְיַד מֶלֶךְ מוֹאָב וַיִּלָּחֲמוּ בָּם: וַיִּזְעֲקוּ אֶל־
יהוה °ויאמר חָטָאנוּ כִּי עָזַבְנוּ אֶת־יהוה
וַנַּעֲבֹד אֶת־הַבְּעָלִים וְאֶת־הָעַשְׁתָּרוֹת וְעַתָּה
יא הַצִּילֵנוּ מִיַּד אֹיְבֵינוּ וְנַעַבְדֶךָּ: וַיִּשְׁלַח יהוה
אֶת־יְרֻבַּעַל וְאֶת־בְּדָן וְאֶת־יִפְתָּח וְאֶת־שְׁמוּאֵל

°וַיֹּאמְרוּ ק׳

entering the Land, they are credited as though they had done so (*Radak*).

Alternatively, this process is accredited to them since they initiated it (*Daas Sofrim*).

9. וַיִּשְׁכְּחוּ אֶת־ה׳ אֱלֹהֵיכֶם — *But they forgot* H*ASHEM their God.*

Targum renders this phrase as *They forgot to serve* H*ASHEM.*

Daas Sofrim comments that throughout the period of the Judges, when the Jews' service of Hashem lapsed it was due not to a rebellious attitude, but because they forgot their ideals and did not properly interpret their history.

וַיִּמְכֹּר אֹתָם ... — *So He delivered them.*

With these words, Samuel pointed out the clear manifestation of Divine Providence throughout Jewish history. When the Jews sinned, they immediately experienced retribution; when they repented and prayed for aid, they were immediately saved (*Malbim*).

בְּיַד סִיסְרָא שַׂר־צְבָא חָצוֹר וּבְיַד־פְּלִשְׁתִּים וּבְיַד מֶלֶךְ מוֹאָב — *Into the hand of Sisera, general of the army of Hazor, and into the hand of the Philistines, and into the hand of the king of Moab.*

This is not a complete list of those who fought against the Jews. These three enemies were apparently those who subdued the Jews most completely. They are listed in order of severity, in descending order (*Daas Sofrim*).

In regard to the Philistines, no individual is mentioned, because they had no single overall ruler (ibid.).

וַיִּלָּחֲמוּ בָּם — *And they battled them.*

In each case to which the verse alludes there was a battle, followed by Hashem delivering the Jews into their enemies' hand (*Metzudos*).

Alternatively, the verse alludes to a broader range of battles. In some instances the Jews were delivered into the hands of their enemies — for instance, in the incidents involving Sisera and the Philistines during Samson's time. In other instances, however, an enemy would battle the Jews but without gaining victory, such as the king of Moab and the Ammonites in Jephthah's time (*Malbim*).

10. וַיִּזְעֲקוּ אֶל־ה׳ — *Then they cried out to* H*ASHEM.*

Yet even then, Samuel implicitly rebuked his audience, the Jews of earlier generations did not request a king (*Abarbanel*).

וַיֹּאמְרוּ — *And [they] said.*

The written version (*ksiv*) is וַיֹּאמֶר, *and he said,* connoting an individual's repentance, whereas the verbalized version (*kri*) is וַיֹּאמְרוּ, *and they said,* implying collective repentance (*Radak*).

וְעַתָּה הַצִּילֵנוּ מִיַּד אֹיְבֵינוּ וְנַעַבְדֶךָּ — *But now, rescue us from the hand of our enemies, and we will worship You!*

The people should have first promised to worship God and then asked Him to rescue them. Apparently, belief in the power of idols was so pervasive that God needed to save the Jews before they would commit themselves to serving Him (*Daas Sofrim*).

⁹But they forgot HASHEM, their God, so He delivered them into the hand of Sisera, general of the army of Hazor, and into the hand of the Philistines, and into the hand of the king of Moab; and they battled them. ¹⁰Then they cried out to HASHEM, and said, 'We have sinned! For we have forsaken HASHEM, and we have worshiped the Baalim and the Ashtaroth; but now, rescue us from the hand of our enemies, and we will worship You.' ¹¹So HASHEM sent Jerubaal and Bedan and Jephthah and Samuel,

11. יְרֻבַּעַל — *Jerubaal.*

"Jerubaal" may be read as a compilation of two words: *yariv baal,* "he battles against Baal." This is a reference to Gideon (*Judges* Chs. 6-9), who fought against the acolytes of Baal (*Rosh Hashanah* 25a).

This name had originally been assigned to Gideon by these acolytes with the intended meaning, "May Baal battle [him]" (*Judges* 6:32). After Gideon defeated them, Scripture chose to keep this name, in praise of his victory (*Maharsha*).

בְּדָן — *Bedan.*

This word is an abbreviation of בֶּן דָּן, *son of Dan,* and refers to Samson, who came from the tribe of Dan.

Although Samson was chronologically preceded by Jephthah, Scripture mentions him first because he was on a greater spiritual level than was Jephthah (*Radak*).

Maharsha specifies that this can be seen from the fact that Samson's actions are alluded to in the *Chumash* (see *Genesis* 49:16-19, *Rashi* ad loc.), whereas those of Jephthah are not.

Rema MiPanu (in *Gilgulei Neshamos*) states that Samson was a reincarnation of Nadab and Abihu. Accordingly, Samson is referred to as בְּדָן, whose letters rearranged form the name *Nadab.*

וְאֶת־שְׁמוּאֵל — *And Samuel.*

Since Samuel was speaking, he should have said, "and me."

Radak explains Samuel's usage by stating that it was common at times for people to speak of themselves in the third person. We see this in *Genesis* (4:23) — "Wives of Lemech, listen to my speech" — and in the language of certain prophets.

Additionally, *Radak* cites a Midrashic comment (*Shocher Tov* 90:4) that at times Samuel prophesied without knowing what he was saying. On such occasions the word of Hashem that spoke through him referred to "Samuel" and not to "me."[1]

Alternatively, Samuel spoke about himself in the third person to show that he had no personal agenda in rebuking the Jewish people and was not concerned for his own dignity (cited by *Me'am Loez*).

1. Thus, it was the word of Hashem that now came from Samuel's throat. This phenomenon also occurred in regard to Moses (see *Zohar, Pinchas* 232) and in regard to Aaron when he pronounced the Holy Name of Hashem.

The *Vilna Gaon* (*Kol Eliyahu*) homiletically interprets the phrase מֹשֶׁה וְאַהֲרֹן בְּכֹהֲנָיו וּשְׁמוּאֵל בְּקֹרְאֵי שְׁמוֹ — literally, *Moses and Aaron were among his priests and Samuel was among those who invoke His Name* (*Psalms* 99:6) — as meaning that Hashem spoke through the throats of these three men: Moses, Aaron *among his priests* (i.e., when performing his priestly duties), and Samuel *among those who invoke his [own] name* (i.e., when he said "Samuel" instead of "me") (cited by *Mishbetzos Zahav*).

וַיַּצֵּל אֶתְכֶם מִיַּד אֹיְבֵיכֶם מִסָּבִיב וַתֵּשְׁבוּ בֶּטַח:
יב וַתִּרְאוּ כִּי נָחָשׁ מֶלֶךְ בְּנֵי־עַמּוֹן בָּא עֲלֵיכֶם וַתֹּאמְרוּ
לִי לֹא כִּי־מֶלֶךְ יִמְלֹךְ עָלֵינוּ וַיהוָה אֱלֹהֵיכֶם
יג מַלְכְּכֶם: וְעַתָּה הִנֵּה הַמֶּלֶךְ אֲשֶׁר בְּחַרְתֶּם
אֲשֶׁר שְׁאֶלְתֶּם וְהִנֵּה נָתַן יהוָה עֲלֵיכֶם מֶלֶךְ:

אֶת־יְרֻבַּעַל וְאֶת־בְּדָן וְאֶת־יִפְתָּח וְאֶת־שְׁמוּאֵל — *Jerubaal and Bedan and Jephthah and Samuel.*

These four figures were all Judges. The first three — Jerubaal, Bedan, and Jephtah — are listed in descending order of the miracles and [level of] prophecy associated with them. Samuel should have headed the list, for he was greater than the others. However, in his humility he mentioned himself last. Samuel chose not to mention the judge and prophetess Deborah because she was a woman, and he could influence his audience without having to do so (*Abarbanel*).

Mahari Kara states that although Samuel mentioned the Jews' victories against Sisera and the king of Moab, he did not mention Deborah or Ehud — who had, respectively, led the Jews to those victories — because his humility prevented him from comparing himself to them.

Alternatively, *Abarbanel* suggests that the four Judges whom Samuel mentioned represent four types of people. Gideon was a prophet of relatively low stature; Samson was not particularly intelligent; Jephthah was intelligent; and Samuel was a prominent prophet and judge. Samuel thus implied that Hashem was able to bring salvation through all kinds of leaders, without the Jews requiring a king.[1]

Of the six men whom Samuel mentioned, Moses, Aaron, and Samuel were among Jewish history's greatest rulers, and Gideon, Samson, and Jephthah were among the least qualified. What they all had in common was that each was the undisputed leader of his generation. Similarly, the Jews of every generation must respect and follow their leader just as if he were the greatest prophet. In our Sages' words, "Jephthah in his generation is like Samuel in his generation" (*Rosh Hashanah* 25b).

וַיַּצֵּל אֶתְכֶם — *And He rescued you.*

The singular usage of this verb underscores the fact that it was not the various Judges but Hashem Himself Who rescued the Jews, using the Judges as His agents. Also, in referring to אֶתְכֶם, *you*, Samuel pointed out that those now listening to him had themselves experienced some of these victories firsthand (*Abarbanel*).

וַיַּצֵּל אֶתְכֶם מִיַּד אֹיְבֵיכֶם מִסָּבִיב וַתֵּשְׁבוּ בֶּטַח — *And He rescued you from the hand of your enemies from all around, and you dwelt in security.*

Following his interpretation of v. 9,

1. *Ahavas Yehonasan* explains that Samuel listed these Judges to refute the claim that until now there had never been an appropriate candidate for the throne. Each one of these four individuals fulfilled at least one of the criteria mentioned by the Sages as befitting a monarch, as follows.

a. As a descendant of Joseph, Gideon satisfied the requirement that the first king of Israel had to be a descendant of Rachel.

b. Samson possessed the might that a king must have.

c. A person in a position of authority should have some flaw in his background to keep him from growing arrogant (see *Yoma* 22b), and Jephthah was the son of a harlot.

d. Lest they claim that the appointment of a king, which had to precede the building of the Temple, had to wait until after the destruction of Shiloh, Samuel's reign began after Shiloh.

Thus, each of these men was a valid candidate to be king, but Hashem said that the time was not ripe as of yet.

and He rescued you from the hand of your en-
emies from all around, and you dwelt in security.
12 *But when you saw that Nahash, king of the*
Children of Ammon, came upon you, you said
to me, 'No, but a king shall reign over us!' But
HASHEM, your God, is your King!
13 *"And now, here is the king whom you*
have chosen, whom you have requested;
and behold, HASHEM has set a king over you.

Malbim explains that *He rescued* speaks of the cases in which God rescued the Jews from nations that had subdued them, and *you dwelt in security* refers to cases in which gentile nations battled against them unsuccessfully.

12. וַתִּרְאוּ כִּי נָחָשׁ מֶלֶךְ בְּנֵי־עַמּוֹן בָּא עֲלֵיכֶם וַתֹּאמְרוּ לִי לֹא כִּי־מֶלֶךְ יִמְלֹךְ עָלֵינוּ — *But when you saw that Nahash, king of the Children of Ammon, came upon you, you said to me, "No, but a king shall reign over us!"*

With this request, Samuel told the people, they were different from the previous generations, which were satisfied when a Judge led them in battle as Hashem's emissary (*Metzudos*).

However, a glance at the previous chapters shows that Nahash attacked the Jews only *after* Saul had been appointed king.

Abarbanel explains Samuel's words here as meaning that the Jews should have interpreted Nahash's attack as God's retribution against them for having requested a king. In consequence of Nahash's attack, they should have regretted their actions and supplicated Hashem to rescue them. Instead, they intensified their expectation that their human king would save them, without realizing that Hashem is their real Sovereign, Who could rescue them without the agency of a human being.

According to *Kli Yakar,* this verse teaches that even before Saul was appointed king, the Jews learned that Nahash was mobilizing his troops against them. They should then have repented, prayed, and trusted in the leadership of Hashem, Who could have saved them through Samuel. Had they done so, Nahash would not have attacked. Instead, however, they requested the aid of a human king, whose leadership in repulsing Nahash they then required.

13. וְעַתָּה הִנֵּה הַמֶּלֶךְ אֲשֶׁר בְּחַרְתֶּם אֲשֶׁר שְׁאֶלְתֶּם — *And now, here is the king whom you have chosen, whom you have requested.*

The people chose Saul king after his military victory, following which they received Hashem's approbation of their decision. Therefore, the matter was final (*Metzudos*).

The word שְׁאֶלְתֶּם also implies "borrowed." The reign of Saul was "borrowed" from that of the Davidic dynasty. (This also explains Saul's name, which can be understood as meaning "borrowed" [*Ahavas Yehonasan*].)

וְהִנֵּה נָתַן ה׳ עֲלֵיכֶם מֶלֶךְ — *And behold, HASHEM has set a king over you.*

In this verse, Samuel refers to the king as having been chosen both by the people and by God. Initially — independently and against Hashem's will — the people chose to have a king. Afterward, he was given to them by Hashem in that He chose the individual who would become king.

Malbim explains this verse as a preface to the upcoming verses. If the people would influence their king to follow

יד אִם־תִּירְאוּ אֶת־יְהוָה וַעֲבַדְתֶּם אֹתוֹ וּשְׁמַעְתֶּם
בְּקוֹלוֹ וְלֹא תַמְרוּ אֶת־פִּי יְהוָה וִהְיִתֶם גַּם־
אַתֶּם וְגַם־הַמֶּלֶךְ אֲשֶׁר־מָלַךְ עֲלֵיכֶם אַחַר יְהוָה
טו אֱלֹהֵיכֶם: וְאִם־לֹא תִשְׁמְעוּ בְּקוֹל יְהוָה וּמְרִיתֶם
אֶת־פִּי יְהוָה וְהָיְתָה יַד־יְהוָה בָּכֶם וּבַאֲבֹתֵיכֶם:
טז גַּם־עַתָּה הִתְיַצְּבוּ וּרְאוּ אֶת־הַדָּבָר הַגָּדוֹל הַזֶּה
יז אֲשֶׁר יְהוָה עֹשֶׂה לְעֵינֵיכֶם: הֲלוֹא קְצִיר־חִטִּים
הַיּוֹם אֶקְרָא אֶל־יְהוָה וְיִתֵּן קֹלוֹת וּמָטָר וּדְעוּ
וּרְאוּ כִּי־רָעַתְכֶם רַבָּה אֲשֶׁר עֲשִׂיתֶם בְּעֵינֵי יְהוָה

in Hashem's ways, then he would be Hashem's chosen one and function as a vehicle for His glory. If, however, the people would influence him to ignore Hashem's will, the king would be no more than the vehicle of their desires, and they would suffer the consequences.

14. ...אִם־תִּירְאוּ אֶת ה׳ — *If you will fear* H*ASHEM*...

This verse is ambiguous because, at first glance, the words וִהְיִתֶם גַּם־אַתֶּם וְגַם הַמֶּלֶךְ אֲשֶׁר־מָלַךְ עֲלֵיכֶם אַחַר ה׳ אֱלֹקֵיכֶם, *you and the king who rules over you will follow after* H*ASHEM*, *your God*, seem like part of the stipulation that they will behave properly. Accordingly, the verse never concludes what will happen if they keep the condition.

Following *Rashi*, we interpret this verse as stating a condition followed by a reward. The condition is, *If you will fear* H*ASHEM* *and serve Him and hearken to His voice and not rebel against the word of* H*ASHEM*. The reward is, *Then you and also the king who rules over you will follow only* H*ASHEM*, *your God*, i.e., the Jews and their king will survive and follow Hashem for a long period of time.

Abarbanel also interprets the latter part of the verse as a reward. The Jews will enjoy the prestige and glory of Hashem; just as He is One, so they will be His unique nation. Also, the Jews will follow Hashem into war, and He will go before them and fight their battle.

Following *Malbim*, the second clause of this verse — *then you and also* ... — states that if the Jews fear Hashem and so forth, Hashem will be their true Sovereign, Whom both they and their human king will follow. Then their king will have justified his position.

According to *Radak*, however, the entire verse is to be read as a set of conditions that follow from the previous verse. Thus, Hashem has set a king over you *to save you if you will follow* H*ASHEM* *and serve Him and hearken to His voice and not rebel against the word of* H*ASHEM*, *and you and also the king who rules over will follow after* H*ASHEM*, *your God*...

וּשְׁמַעְתֶּם בְּקוֹלוֹ וְלֹא תַמְרוּ אֶת־פִּי ה׳ — *And hearken to His voice and not rebel against the word of* H*ASHEM*.

The word *hearken* refers to keeping the positive commandments and *not rebel* to avoiding transgression of the negative commandments (*Malbim*).

Daas Sofrim suggests that וּשְׁמַעְתֶּם בְּקוֹלוֹ, *and hearken to His voice*, implies that the people should heed the words of the prophets.

15. וְהָיְתָה יַד־ה׳ בָּכֶם וּבַאֲבֹתֵיכֶם — *Then the hand of* H*ASHEM* *will be against you and against your fathers*.

Targum interprets this phrase to

14 *If you will fear* HASHEM *and serve Him and hearken*
to His voice and not rebel against the word of HASHEM*,*
then you and also the king who rules over you will
remain [following] after HASHEM*, your God.* 15 *But if*
you do not hearken to the voice of HASHEM*, and you*
rebel against the word of HASHEM*, then the hand of*
HASHEM *will be against you and against your fathers.*
16 *"Even now, stand erect and see this great thing*
that HASHEM *will bring about before your eyes.* 17 *Is*
today not the wheat harvest season? I shall call to
HASHEM *and He will set forth thunder and rain; then*
you will recognize and see how great is your wick-
edness, that you performed in the eyes of HASHEM*,*

mean that Hashem would turn His hand against the present generation of Jews just as He had turned it against their fathers (*Targum*).

Radak explains *fathers* to be a figurative reference to the king (as in *Genesis* 45:8 — *He made me a father to Pharaoh*).

Rashi cites the Talmud's interpretation of this verse — that the hand of Hashem would bring about the desecration of the Jews' fathers' graves (*Yevamos* 63b). As *Daas Sofrim* explains, when their descendants sin, this element of punishment and disgrace is placed on the ancestors for not having properly prepared the foundations of the following generation.

Kli Yakar states (based on a comment of the Sages) that when a generation suffers or rebels against God, then its *fathers* in their graves are pained as well. *Sefer Chassidim* (607, cited by *Me'am Loez*) states that at times parents suffer pain in their graves, and this functions as a mechanism whereby their children gain redemption.

16. גַּם־עַתָּה הִתְיַצְּבוּ וּרְאוּ אֶת־הַדָּבָר הַגָּדוֹל הַזֶּה — *Even now, stand erect and see this great thing.*

As described in the following verses, Samuel was about to pray to God to cause rain to fall out of season. By showing the Jews that he could alter nature with his prayer, Samuel would demonstrate that despite the infirmities of age, he could have gained military victory with his power of prayer, and thus the Jews should not have requested a king during his lifetime.

According to *Abarbanel*, Samuel meant this miraculous occurrence to lead the people to understand why, if Hashem was opposed to their request for a king, He had nevertheless appointed Saul — even arranging that the choice be made through the *Urim VeTumim.* Rain during the harvest season is harmful to the crop, yet Hashem honored Samuel's request. This showed that, in keeping with the principles of free will, at times Hashem gives people what they want, despite deleterious consequences.

אֲשֶׁר ה׳ עֹשֶׂה לְעֵינֵיכֶם — *That* HASHEM *will bring about before your eyes.*

Samuel's rebuke of the people was apparently not sufficient to change their decision to rely on a human king. They would require a miracle to remind them that ultimately they are subject to Hashem's will (*Malbim, Daas Sofrim*).

17. הֲלוֹא קְצִיר־חִטִּים הַיּוֹם אֶקְרָא אֶל־ה׳ וְיִתֵּן קֹלוֹת וּמָטָר וּדְעוּ וּרְאוּ כִּי־רָעַתְכֶם רַבָּה — *Is today not the wheat harvest season? I*

יח לִשְׁא֥וֹל לָכֶ֖ם מֶֽלֶךְ׃ וַיִּקְרָ֤א
שְׁמוּאֵל֙ אֶל־יְהֹוָ֔ה וַיִּתֵּ֧ן יְהֹוָ֛ה קֹלֹ֥ת וּמָטָ֖ר
בַּיּ֣וֹם הַה֑וּא וַיִּירָ֨א כָל־הָעָ֥ם מְאֹ֛ד אֶת־יְהֹוָ֖ה
יט וְאֶת־שְׁמוּאֵֽל׃ וַיֹּאמְר֨וּ כָל־הָעָ֜ם אֶל־שְׁמוּאֵ֗ל
הִתְפַּלֵּ֧ל בְּעַד־עֲבָדֶ֛יךָ אֶל־יְהֹוָ֥ה אֱלֹהֶ֖יךָ וְאַל־

shall call to HASHEM and He will send forth thunder and rain. Then you will recognize and see how great is your wickedness.

The wheat harvest occurs in the summer, when rain normally does not fall in the Land of Israel (*Radak*). Rainfall at that time is harmful, as it prevents the cut wheat from drying, and can even ruin it (see *Taanis* 2b, 12b). Samuel told them that although Hashem does not seek to punish the Jews for no reason, he would heed Samuel's prayer and alter nature to demonstrate His displeasure at their having requested a king (*Mahari Kara*).

Had the Jewish people been worthy, Samuel was implying, Hashem would have rejected his prayer (later editions of *Mahari Kara*).

The commentators offer a number of explanations of the message that God intended to convey with this miracle.

❒ Rain is beneficent when it falls at the proper time, and harmful when it falls at the wrong time. Similarly, Hashem had planned to provide the Jewish people with a king at the proper time, which would have been propitious. However, they requested a king prematurely — while Samuel was alive and while they were still benefiting from God's supernatural protection. They thus deserved censure (*Malbim*).

❒ Farmers expend enormous effort in growing their crops. They feel anguish if, subsequent to all their toil, the crops are damaged by unseasonable rain. So too, Hashem expended much effort, as it were, in redeeming the Jews from Egypt and settling them in the Land of Israel. How great was His anguish, as it were, in that they asked for a king, expressing their desire to imitate the surrounding nations (*Mussar HaNeviim*).

❒ The Talmud states that rain is withheld due to the sin of thievery (*Taanis* 7b). According to one view, the people had requested a king because they rejected the possible rule of Samuel's sons, whom they suspected of greed. Samuel wished to show that his sons were innocent. If they had been guilty, there would have been a drought; yet [not only did rain fall in its proper time] but it fell even during the summer season (*Ahavas Yehonasan*).

❒ *Akeidas Yitzchak* (*Shaar* 95) states that when summer rain mitigates the heat, it creates a short-lived joy; in the long run, however, it creates sorrow because it damages the crops. Samuel thus intimated that although a king may bring short-term benefits — in particular, a sense of security — in the long term, his rule is harmful.

Along these lines, *Abarbanel* explains the phrase, רָעַתְכֶם רַבָּה אֲשֶׁר עֲשִׂיתֶם בְּעֵינֵי ה׳, *How great is your wickedness that you performed in the eyes of HASHEM*, as meaning that although the Jews did not appreciate the pitfalls inherent in the appointment of a king, Hashem had the eyes to see the harmful consequences of their deeds.

18. וַיִּתֵּן ה׳ קֹלֹת וּמָטָר בַּיּוֹם הַהוּא — *And HASHEM sent forth thunder and rain on that day.*

Because there was no intimation of rain such as the presence of clouds, the

in requesting a king for yourselves."
[18] *Then Samuel called to HASHEM, and HASHEM set forth thunder and rain on that day; and all the people greatly feared HASHEM and Samuel.*
[19] *All the people then said to Samuel, "Pray on behalf of your servants to HASHEM, your God, that we not*

farmers were preparing to harvest the wheat. But now thunder clapped and rain descended suddenly. This immediate response of God to Samuel's prayer instilled fear in the hearts of the people (*Abarbanel*).

וַיִּירָא כָל־הָעָם מְאֹד — *And all the people greatly feared.*

The word כָּל, *all,* includes even those scorners who had previously mocked the installation of Saul as king, with the words, מַה־יֹּשִׁעֵנוּ זֶה, *How can this person save us?* (above, 10:27; *Radak*).

The Talmud states that thunder was created to straighten out the crookedness in the human heart and inspire it to fear Hashem (*Berachos* 59a), exactly as occurred here.

אֶת־ה׳ וְאֶת־שְׁמוּאֵל — *HASHEM and Samuel.*

Targum renders this phrase as *they feared HASHEM and the words of Samuel.*

According to *Abarbanel,* the people now recognized the evil inherent in their rejection of Hashem and Samuel.

Be'er Moshe comments that the phrase *all the people greatly feared HASHEM and Shmuel* is similar to וַיַּאֲמִינוּ בַּה׳ וּבְמֹשֶׁה עַבְדּוֹ, *they had faith in HASHEM and in Moses His servant* (*Exodus* 14:31). The Midrash (*Mechilta*) asks, "Isn't it obvious that if they believed in Moses they believed in Hashem?" and answers that if a person believes in God's trusted shepherd, it is considered as though he believes in God Himself. The same idea, states *Be'er Moshe,* applies to the present verse.

19. וַיֹּאמְרוּ כָל־הָעָם אֶל־שְׁמוּאֵל הִתְפַּלֵּל בְּעַד־עֲבָדֶיךָ — *All the people then said to Samuel, "Pray on behalf of your servants."*

The people realized that it was too late to unseat the king. Their only option was to pray, or to have Samuel pray, that even under these circumstances they should be able to elevate themselves and serve Hashem properly (*Daas Sofrim*).

הִתְפַּלֵּל בְּעַד־עֲבָדֶיךָ אֶל־ה׳ אֱלֹהֶיךָ — *Pray on behalf of your servants to HASHEM, your God.*

The people realized that they had erred twice: once in rejecting Hashem and once again in rejecting Samuel. Therefore, they now requested that Samuel pray *to HASHEM, your God.* With the words *to HASHEM,* they were referring to their hope that Hashem would forgive their affront against Him. By referring to *your God,* they were asking Samuel to forgive their having sinned against him, for without his forgiveness, Samuel's God would avenge his honor. In order to earn Samuel's forgiveness, the people humbled themselves before him and referred to themselves as *your servants* (*Kli Yakar*).

In regard to the phrase אֱלֹהֶיךָ, *your God,* in which the word *your* is singular, *Be'er Moshe* observes that Hashem is only rarely referred to as the God of an individual. In particular, this occurs in regard to Abraham, Isaac, Jacob, Joshua (*Joshua* 1:17), Samuel, David (*II Samuel* 24:3), Solomon (*I Kings* 2:3), Elijah (ibid. 17:12) and Isaiah (*II Kings* 19:4). Each of these individuals was so closely attached to Hashem that he became a "chariot of the Divine Presence," as it were, and thus merited that distinction.

נָמוּת כִּי־יָסַפְנוּ עַל־כָּל־חַטֹּאתֵינוּ רָעָה לִשְׁאֹל
כ לָנוּ מֶלֶךְ: וַיֹּאמֶר שְׁמוּאֵל אֶל־
הָעָם אַל־תִּירָאוּ אַתֶּם עֲשִׂיתֶם אֵת כָּל־הָרָעָה
הַזֹּאת אַךְ אַל־תָּסוּרוּ מֵאַחֲרֵי יהוה וַעֲבַדְתֶּם
כא אֶת־יהוה בְּכָל־לְבַבְכֶם: וְלֹא תָּסוּרוּ כִּי | אַחֲרֵי
הַתֹּהוּ אֲשֶׁר לֹא־יוֹעִילוּ וְלֹא יַצִּילוּ כִּי־תֹהוּ הֵמָּה:

The truth is that every Jew has the potential to reach this exalted level. As the verse states, שׁוּבָה יִשְׂרָאֵל עַד ה׳ אֱלֹהֶיךָ, *Return, Israel, to* HASHEM*, your God* (*Hosea* 14:2).

וְאַל־נָמוּת — *That we not die.*

They realized that they deserved to die for having requested a king (*Abarbanel*).

כִּי יָסַפְנוּ עַל־כָּל־חַטֹּאתֵנוּ רָעָה לִשְׁאֹל לָנוּ מֶלֶךְ — *For to all of our sins we have added evil, by requesting a king for ourselves.*

Samuel rebuked the Jews for having requested a king. Now they acknowledged that they had *added evil* — committed other wrongs — as well. This is in accordance with the precept that עֲבֵרָה גוֹרֶרֶת עֲבֵרָה, *one sin drags along another* (*Avos* 4:2; *Mishbetzos Zahav*).

Kehillas Yaakov explains this *added evil* to have been their rejection of Samuel. Had they committed only the sin of rejecting God, they would have prayed on their own behalf. In regard to their sin against Samuel they knew that they could not earn Hashem's atonement without first gaining Samuel's forgiveness. Therefore, they required Samuel's intervention, [for if he interceded on their behalf, that would prove that he had forgiven them].

Mishbetzos Zahav adds that this idea is hinted at in an earlier verse: אִם־יֶחֱטָא אִישׁ לְאִישׁ וּפִלְלוֹ אֱלֹהִים, *If man sins against man, a judge tries him* (2:25). The word וּפִלְלוֹ, *tries him*, may also mean *prays for him*. This implies that after a judge concluded a civil case, he would pray on behalf of the litigants. Accordingly, the people asked Samuel to pray on their behalf.

Abarbanel observes that the people did not say, *to all of our sins we have added sins* but rather *to all of our sins we have added evil*. This follows his approach that aside from the sin of rejecting Hashem, the actual request for a king was רָעָה, harmful to them.

20. וַיֹּאמֶר שְׁמוּאֵל אֶל־הָעָם אַל־תִּירָאוּ — *Samuel said to the people, "Fear not."*

The ethical teachers describe two types of fear of God. One is the fear of Divine punishment, and the other, which is more exalted and commendable, is called יִרְאַת הָרוֹמְמוּת, a fear of God's exalted Being. Had the people exhibited the latter trait, Samuel would not have told them, *Fear not*. But since their concern was only that they might be punished — "lest we will die" — he told them that they need not fear death for this sin (*Daas Sofrim*).

Had Hashem been angry at the Jews without a root cause, then the people would have reason to fear that they were out of favor with Him. However, since His wrath could easily be traced to the fact that they had sinned, it was clear that if they repented His anger would disappear (*Malbim*).

Kli Yakar comments that since the people were cognizant of their sins and regretted them, they need not fear. There would be cause for worry only if they forgot their sins.

אַתֶּם עֲשִׂיתֶם אֵת כָּל־הָרָעָה הַזֹּאת — *You have done all this evil.*

die; for to all of our sins we have added evil, by
requesting a king for ourselves."
[20]*Samuel said to the people, "Fear not. You*
have done all this evil — but do not turn away
from following HASHEM, *rather serve* HASHEM
with all your heart. [21]*Do not turn away for*
[that would be to] pursue futilities that can-
not avail and cannot rescue, for they are futile.

They did evil in requesting a king (*Radak*).

Metzudos explains that Samuel was telling the Jews that although the king whom they had requested could not be removed, as long as they did not stray from God, their sin inherent in requesting a king would be forgiven.

Following his approach, *Abarbanel* explains that although the people had harmed themselves by requesting a king, that request would not be considered sinful if they did not stray from Hashem.

Targum renders the phrase, אַתֶּם עֲשִׂיתֶם אֵת כָּל־הָרָעָה הַזֹּאת, *you have done all this evil*, as *you brought about all this evil drought*. [According to this view, God punished the Jews for requesting a king by causing a drought to occur.]

אַךְ אַל־תָּסוּרוּ מֵאַחֲרֵי ה׳ — *But do not turn away from following* HASHEM.

Me'am Loez (citing *Divrei Yedidyah*) states that after Samuel alluded to the appointment of Moses and Aaron (see v. 8), the people expressed the worry that just as the followers of Korah were destroyed for rejecting Moses, so too would they would be destroyed for [rejecting Samuel]. Samuel reassured them that if they served Hashem properly, they would not suffer such a fate.

וַעֲבַדְתֶּם אֶת־ה׳ — *Rather, serve* HASHEM.

The people had expressed their remorse and willingness to subjugate themselves to Samuel by calling themselves עֲבָדֶיךָ, *your servants*. Samuel now responded that he was not concerned for the honor they might give him and had no interest in their becoming his servants. Rather, he only wanted them to serve Hashem (*Me'am Loez*, from *Alshich*).

21. This verse is somewhat ambiguous for two reasons: (1) The word כִּי usually means *because*, but it does not seem to be stating a reason for anything; and (2) why the repetition of the words כִּי־תֹהוּ? *Daas Sofrim* comments that this verse is deliberately cryptic because it is referring to idol worship, and it wishes to avoid a lengthy description of its degraded nature.

Our translation of this verse presents its simplest interpretation, based on *Metzudos*. According to this, the verse is stating, "Do not turn after idols, which is tantamount to turning after worthlessness, because they cannot help and are thus futile."

Targum seems to render כִּי not as *because*, but as *rather* or *instead*, and he extends the word לֹא of the beginning of the verse to the words כִּי אַחֲרֵי הַתֹּהוּ as well. Thus, "Do not stray [from the service of Hashem] and [do not serve idols], which are futile and cannot avail ..."

According to *Me'am Loez*, Samuel was warning the Jews that if they strayed from actively serving Hashem, they would not be able to maintain a morally neutral position, because once a person turns away from Hashem, he will inevitably end up following "futilities" — [i.e., idols].

כב כִּ֠י לֹֽא־יִטֹּ֤שׁ יהוה֙ אֶת־עַמּ֔וֹ בַּעֲב֖וּר שְׁמ֣וֹ הַגָּד֑וֹל כִּ֚י
כג הוֹאִ֣יל יהוה לַעֲשׂ֥וֹת אֶתְכֶ֛ם ל֖וֹ לְעָֽם׃ גַּ֣ם אָנֹכִ֗י
חָלִ֤ילָה לִּי֙ מֵחֲטֹ֣א לַיהוה מֵחֲדֹ֖ל לְהִתְפַּלֵּ֣ל
בַּעַדְכֶ֑ם וְהוֹרֵיתִ֣י אֶתְכֶ֔ם בְּדֶ֥רֶךְ הַטּוֹבָ֖ה וְהַיְשָׁרָֽה׃
כד אַ֣ךְ ׀ יְר֣אוּ אֶת־יהוה וַעֲבַדְתֶּ֥ם אֹת֛וֹ בֶּאֱמֶ֖ת בְּכָל־

According to *Kli Yakar*, Samuel was addressing people who might be tempted to experiment with idolatry. Since they would eventually come to see its futility, there would be no point in making that experiment in the first place.

Kehillas Yaakov clarifies the repetition of the word תֹּהוּ, *futility*, by explaining that the first instance expresses the *prohibition* against serving idols, and the second underscores the idea that even if it weren't prohibited, it would be irrational to involve oneself in an exercise in futility.

22. כִּי לֹא־יִטֹּשׁ ה׳ אֶת־עַמּוֹ בַּעֲבוּר שְׁמוֹ הַגָּדוֹל — *Because* HASHEM *will not forsake His people, for the sake of His great Name.*

With this verse, Samuel explains why the people need not worry that they will die for their actions. It is true that they may be unworthy; however, since Hashem has chosen them as His nation, it would be a desecration of His Name to destroy them, since the other nations would claim that He forsook the Jews because He was unable to protect them. This argument was also advanced by Moses (*Exodus* 14:15,16) and Joshua (*Joshua* 7:9).

The Midrash makes it clear that Hashem's commitment to maintain the existence of the Jewish people in order to prevent a desecration of His Name applies whether or not they are deserving (*Ruth Rabbah* 2:11, *Esther Rabbah* 7:12).

לֹא יִטֹּשׁ — *Will not forsake.*

Our translation follows *Metzudos.*

Targum renders this phrase as *shall not distance.*

כִּי הוֹאִיל ה׳ לַעֲשׂוֹת אֶתְכֶם לוֹ לְעָם — *For* HASHEM *has sworn to make you a people for Him.*

Our translation of הוֹאִיל as *sworn* follows *Rashi.*

Targum translates this word as *willed.*

The translation of this word is the subject of a Midrashic dispute (*Midrash Shmuel*), in which three interpretations are presented: *began, slept* (alternatively, *rested*), or *swore.*

Kehillas Yaakov explains each one. First, a commitment is particularly believable after a person has begun to keep it. Since Hashem already *began* to protect us from our enemies, He will surely continue to do so.

Second, the relationship of Hashem to the Jewish people is comparable to that of a groom and his bride. Since Hashem has brought the Jews into His Land as a groom brings home his bride, He must fulfill His responsibility of עוֹנָה (time spent together) by causing His Divine Presence to *rest* in their midst on a regular basis.

Third, this would not suffice were the Jews to have to worry that their sins would nullify the commitment, but since in the past Hashem *swore* unconditionally to keep the Jews as a nation, He was now bound, as it were, to fulfill His oath.

23. גַּם אָנֹכִי חָלִילָה לִּי מֵחֲטֹא לַה׳ מֵחֲדֹל לְהִתְפַּלֵּל בַּעַדְכֶם — *And I too — far be it from me to sin against* HASHEM *and refrain from praying on your behalf.*

Samuel told the people that once they did what was expected of them — to repent — how could he not do what was expected of him — to pray on their behalf? (*Rashi*).

22 Because H*ASHEM* *will not forsake His people,*
for the sake of His great Name; for H*ASHEM* *has*
sworn to make you for a people for Him. *23 And I*
too — far be it from me to sin against H*ASHEM* *and*
refrain from praying on your behalf; rather, I shall
instruct you in the good and proper path. *24 Only*
fear H*ASHEM* *and serve Him faithfully, with all*

Abarbanel explains the word גַּם, *too,* as implying that just as Hashem forgives an affront to His honor, so too would Samuel forgive the disrespect that he had endured.

According to *Kli Yakar,* Samuel was implying that since it was Hashem's will not to forsake the Jews, he himself would be considered a sinner should he fail to do what he could for them.

The Talmud (*Berachos* 12b) derives from this verse that a person who is able to pray on behalf of someone else but fails to do so is a sinner.

Be'er Moshe derives from the Talmud's statement that there are circumstances under which a person is not able to pray [on someone else's behalf]. In the present case, before the people repented, it never occurred to Samuel to do so. This obliviousness is considered to be a type of inability (see *Rashi, Jeremiah* 15:1).

A Midrash (*Bamidbar Rabbah* 19:23) derives from this verse that a person who refuses to forgive another who had sinned against him but is now seeking forgiveness is himself considered to be a sinner. *Rambam* adds that not to forgive under such circumstances is a form of cruelty (*Hil. Teshuvah* 2:10; *Rema, Orach Chaim* 606:1; and *Mesillas Yesharim, Shaar HaNekius* Ch. 10).

We may derive from this verse that after forgiving his former perpetrator, a person who had been harmed should then pray on the perpetrator's behalf. *Mishbetzos Zahav* explains the reason for this. A heavenly judgment is aroused against someone who has sinned against another. As the verse states, וְהָאֱלֹהִים יְבַקֵּשׁ אֶת־נִרְדָּף, *God always seeks [to take the side of] the pursued* (*Ecclesiastes* 3:15). In order for that judgment to be removed, when the former perpetrator seeks to make amends, his victim must pray on his behalf.

וְהוֹרֵיתִי אֶתְכֶם בְּדֶרֶךְ הַטּוֹבָה וְהַיְשָׁרָה — *Rather, I shall instruct you in the good and proper path.*

טוֹבָה, *good,* refers to the goal, whereas יְשָׁרָה, *proper,* refers to the means of reaching it.

The people might think that since Samuel was praying on their behalf they could rebel against God without adverse consequences. Samuel thus intimated that nothing would help them if they did not remain on the right path (*Abarbanel*).

מֵחֲטֹא לַה׳ מֵחֲדֹל לְהִתְפַּלֵּל בַּעַדְכֶם וְהוֹרֵיתִי אֶתְכֶם — *To sin against* H*ASHEM* *and refrain from praying on your behalf; rather, I shall instruct you.*

Malbim understands these words of Samuel to mean that he would be sinful were he to refrain from performing either of the two things that he would normally do for their protection: praying on their behalf and instructing them.

24. וַעֲבַדְתֶּם אֹתוֹ בֶּאֱמֶת — *And serve Him faithfully.*

Serving Hashem "faithfully" — literally, *with truth* — means "willingly": with the consent and cooperation of all of one's faculties (*Daas Sofrim*).

יב/כה כה לְבַבְכֶם כִּי רְאוּ אֵת אֲשֶׁר־הִגְדִּל עִמָּכֶם: וְאִם־הָרֵעַ
תָּרֵעוּ גַּם־אַתֶּם גַּם־מַלְכְּכֶם תִּסָּפוּ:
יג/א א בֶּן־שָׁנָה שָׁאוּל בְּמָלְכוֹ וּשְׁתֵּי שָׁנִים מָלַךְ עַל־יִשְׂרָאֵל:

כִּי רְאוּ אֵת אֲשֶׁר־הִגְדִּל עִמָּכֶם — *For look at how much He has done for you.*

This refers to the great favors that God bestowed upon that generation, as well as upon its ancestors (*Abarbanel*).

It can also refer to the fact that God forgave the people's sin (*Metzudos*).

According to *Kli Yakar*, Samuel was alluding to the Great Name of Hashem. Hashem had associated that Name with the Jews by doing great things on their behalf. Were they to sin, that Name would be desecrated.

Radak states that אֲשֶׁר־הִגְדִּל עִמָּכֶם, *how much He has done for you*, refers to the miraculous rain that fell during the harvest season, which confirmed God's ability to do whatever He wishes — the awareness of which should lead the Jews to fear Him.

25. וְאִם־הָרֵעַ תָּרֵעוּ — *But if you act wickedly.*

The repetition of the word wicked (הָרֵעַ תָּרֵעוּ) intimates that one sin draws another in its wake (*Kli Yakar*).

Alternatively, it alludes to continuity of sin, which is usually the cause for a punishment of such dimensions (*Daas Sofrim*).

גַּם־אַתֶּם גַּם־מַלְכְּכֶם תִּסָּפוּ — *Both you and your king will perish.*

The phrase *your king* implies that if the people sinned the king would be held responsible for not having properly guided them (*Radak*).

In this phrase, the word גַּם, *both*, is repeated. Literally, it reads *both you, both your king*. This indicates that at times the nation influences the king to do evil, and at other times the opposite is the case. Should either occur, all parties will perish (*Kli Yakar, Kehillas Yaakov*).

תִּסָּפוּ — *Will perish.*

This translation follows *Metzudos*.

Daas Sofrim suggests that the word תִּסָּפוּ may be traced to סוּפָה, *storm* (see *Isaiah* 29:6). After a period in which repentance is anticipated, if it does not come, Hashem may send His punishment as a sudden, destructive storm.

XIII

אֵלֶּה בָרֶכֶב וְאֵלֶּה בַסּוּסִים וַאֲנַחְנוּ בְּשֵׁם־ה׳ אֱלֹהֵינוּ נַזְכִּיר. הֵמָּה כָּרְעוּ וְנָפָלוּ וַאֲנַחְנוּ קַמְנוּ וַנִּתְעוֹדָד, *Some with chariots and some with horses — but we call out in the Name of HASHEM, our God. They bowed and fell — but we arose and were invigorated* (*Psalms* 20:8,9).

In this verse, King David describes the Jewish nation's unique focus at times of war, one that has made it possible for the Jews to survive all challenges — a focus not on conventional tactics but on trust in ה׳ אִישׁ מִלְחָמָה, *HASHEM, the Master of War* (*Exodus* 15:3).

This chapter describes the preparations for a battle in which that trust was tested and, ultimately, strengthened. It was tested because under duress Saul lost sight of the presence of the Supreme Warrior — a relatively minor lapse but one that, since he was the nation's spiritual leader, had severe repercussions. And that trust was ultimately strengthened because that battle, in which the odds weighed heavily against the Jews, ended in accordance with King David's formula: *but we arose and were invigorated.*

Saul's Army

1. In order to understand the commentators' explanations of Verse 1, we must familiarize ourselves with four possible timelines describing the leadership of Samuel and Saul, as provided in four

12/25 *your hearts, for look at how much He has done*
for you. [25] *But if you act wickedly, both you and*
your king will perish."

13/1-2 [1] *During the first year of Saul's reign (he*
reigned over Israel for two years), [2] *Saul*

versions of *Seder Olam*, a seminal historical record authored by the Tanna, Rabbi Yose ben Chalafta.

These timelines are as follows.

(1) According to the Talmud's version of *Seder Olam*, Samuel ruled alone for 10 years; for the next year, he and Saul ruled together; and for 2 years after that, Saul ruled alone (*Temurah* 15a, *Zevachim* 118b).

Accordingly, Saul reigned for a total of 3 years, one of them jointly with Samuel.

(2) Contemporary editions of *Seder Olam* state that Samuel ruled alone for 10 years; and then he and Saul ruled together for 2 years.

(3) Further on in the text, *Seder Olam* states that Samuel ruled alone for 11 years, and then together with Saul for 1 year. (This chronology is the most difficult to justify, for it is inconsistent with the present verse, which states that Saul was king for at least 2 years.)

(4) *Rashi* (to *Taanis* 5b) quotes *Seder Olam* as stating that Saul's reign began midway through Samuel's 11th year, and that he ruled afterward for 2 more years. (This seems to be an amalgam of the other versions.)

Although some versions of *Seder Olam* claim that Saul ruled alone without Samuel for some period, all seem to agree that Samuel was alive for most of that period, and died only four months before Saul did (*Rashi, Temurah* 15a; *Taanis* 5b).

For more information regarding this chronology, see comm. above, on 8:1, and Timeline in Appendix.

בֶּן־שָׁנָה שָׁאוּל בְּמָלְכוֹ — *During the first year of Saul's reign ...*

All of the commentators agree that this phrase cannot be understood literally — reading, as it does, *Saul was one year old when he became king.*

Our translation follows an interpretation offered by *Rashi*: the episode that will be described in this chapter occurred *during the first year of Saul's reign*. The verse then parenthetically states that Saul's entire reign lasted two years. This is consistent with version 2 of *Seder Olam*.[1]

Alternatively, *Radak* suggests that this verse is referring to Samuel's installation of Saul in Gilgal, as described in the previous chapter. *Saul was king for one year* — i.e., he was privately anointed by Samuel. Then he was publicly declared king in Gilgal, following which *he reigned another two years*. This is consistent with version 1 of *Seder Olam*.

The *Vilna Gaon* (on *Rashi, Temurah* 15a) understands this verse exactly coincident with version 1 above. He reads the verse as stating, *After Saul had reigned for one year* together with Samuel, *he reigned for two years* alone. (Although Samuel was alive during most of those two years [see Preface], he disassociated himself from Saul because of the latter's errors [see below, 15:35; *Rashi, Zevachim* 118b].)[2]

Targum and the Talmud (*Yoma* 22b, cited by *Rashi*) interpret the phrase בֶּן־שָׁנָה

1. The significance of this episode having occurred in Saul's first year will be discussed in our commentary on verse 2.

2. According to this version of *Seder Olam*, Saul was a blameless king for one year. Toward the end of that year, he erred twice (as described in Chapters 13 and 15). His subsequent persecution

ב וַיִּבְחַר־לוֹ שָׁאוּל שְׁלֹשֶׁת אֲלָפִים מִיִּשְׂרָאֵל וַיִּהְיוּ
עִם־שָׁאוּל אַלְפַּיִם בְּמִכְמָשׂ וּבְהַר בֵּית־אֵל וְאֶלֶף
הָיוּ עִם־יוֹנָתָן בְּגִבְעַת בִּנְיָמִין וְיֶתֶר הָעָם שִׁלַּח אִישׁ
ג לְאֹהָלָיו: וַיַּךְ יוֹנָתָן אֵת נְצִיב פְּלִשְׁתִּים אֲשֶׁר בְּגֶבַע
וַיִּשְׁמְעוּ פְּלִשְׁתִּים וְשָׁאוּל תָּקַע בַּשּׁוֹפָר בְּכָל־הָאָרֶץ

שָׁאוּל בְּמָלְכוֹ as intimating that, *upon being anointed king,* Saul was as innocent and free of sin *as a one-year-old child.*[1] Although Saul would now err and lose his right to leadership, until this point he had been perfectly righteous (*Maharsha*).

The Talmud (ibid.) mentions that a person is eligible to serve as a public leader only if he has a "container of rodents hanging behind him" — i.e., some sort of disrepute in his or his family's past — for awareness of this shortcoming will inhibit any tendency toward arrogance. Because Saul's history was spotless, his leadership did not last. Accordingly, *Alshich* explains the verse as follows: *[Because] Saul was as [free of sin] as a one-year-old, his reign lasted only two years.*

Radak cites the *Talmud Yerushalmi's* comment on this verse — that when a person is appointed to a position of political leadership he is forgiven his sins and thus becomes as sinless as a 1-year-old (*Bikkurim* 3:3). (The same applies to a scholar who rises to a Rabbinic position and to a bridegroom on his wedding day.)

Mussar HaNeviim quotes *Rambam's* grandson Rabbi Saadia as rendering בֶּן־שָׁנָה as *52 years old,* for the numerical value of בֶּן is 52.

2. וַיִּבְחַר־לוֹ שָׁאוּל — *Saul chose.*

Saul picked these men from all of the Israelites who had gathered in Gilgal (*Radak*) — particularly, from the soldiers who had fought with him against Nahash (*Daas Sofrim*).

Saul chose these men for a distinctive quality that they possessed — that being physical strength (*Ralbag*) or piety (*Kli Yakar*).

שְׁלֹשֶׁת אֲלָפִים מִיִּשְׂרָאֵל — *Three thousand [troops] from Israel.*

This is quite a small fighting force (see above, 11:8).

Malbim suggests that Saul dedicated his first year as king (see above, verse 1, comm.) to developing a rapport with the people, and as such eschewed engaging in warfare.[2]

of David and his mental afflictions (רוח רָעָה) all occurred within a span of two years.

Abarbanel, however, rejects the idea that all of the episodes described from Chapter 16 until the end of *I Samuel* occurred within a span of two years, and assumes that Saul reigned for considerably longer (a view shared by *Ralbag*).

Following a lengthy discourse regarding the chronology of the era, *Abarbanel* concludes that Saul ruled for a total of 17 years. Verse 1 relates that a year after Saul was anointed king, he was publicly installed in Gilgal, following which he reigned for 2 more years, until David was anointed (Chapter 16). In actuality, however, in addition to those two years he remained king for 14 more years; however, these are not documented by Scripture because they were such a painful time for Saul, during which he pursued David even as he was cognizant of having lost the throne.

Rabbeinu Yeshayah interprets similarly, saying that after David was anointed during Saul's reign, it was as if his kingdom were void and it was considered "a kingdom without a crown."

1. The Talmud (ibid.) relates that Rav Nachman bar Yitzchak interpreted the verse as implying that Saul was "soiled with dirt and feces," as is common for 1-year-olds. Frightening angels then appeared in Rav Nachman's dreams until he retracted and apologized.

2. Similarly, a person in the first year of his marriage or who has built a new house must avoid involvement in the public sphere (see *Deuteronomy* 24:5).

chose three thousand [troops] from Israel — with
Saul were two thousand at Michmas and at Mount
Beth-el, and one thousand were with Jonathan at
Gibeath-benjamin; and the rest of the people he
sent home, each man to his tent.
3 *Jonathan slew the Philistine commissioner*
in Geba, and the Philistines heard [about it].
Saul had the shofar blown throughout the land,

Daas Sofrim explains that Saul wanted to avoid initiating his reign with war. Alternatively, he was hesitant to provoke the Philistines by building a large army.

וַיִּהְיוּ עִם־שָׁאוּל — *With Saul were.*

These men were available to serve Saul at a moment's notice (*Metzudos*).

אַלְפַּיִם בְּמִכְמָשׂ וּבְהַר בֵּית־אֵל — *Two thousand at Michmas and at Mount Beth-el.*

That is to say, 1,000 at Michmas and 1,000 at Mount Beth-el, for Saul wished to divide his time between these two locations (*Malbim*).

בְּמִכְמָשׂ — *At Michmas.*

Minchas Shai contends that more accurate versions of the text spell מִכְמָשׂ with a שׂ — thus, *Michmas* (as in *Isaiah* 10:28). In *Ezra* (2:27) and *Nehemiah* (7:31), the word is spelled with a ס, also pronounced Michmas.

יוֹנָתָן — *Jonathan.*

Jonathan was Saul's oldest son (below, 14:49). It is interesting to observe that Scripture does not identify Jonathan as Saul's son until verse 16.

וְיֶתֶר הָעָם שִׁלַּח אִישׁ לְאֹהָלָיו — *And the rest of the people he sent home.*

He did so in order not to overburden the Israelites with military service (*Ralbag*).

Alternatively, he trusted that God could protect the Jews with a small army as easily as with a large one (*Me'am Loez*).

◆§ Jonathan's Provocative Offense

3. וַיַּךְ יוֹנָתָן אֵת נְצִיב פְּלִשְׁתִּים — *Jonathan slew the Philistine commissioner.*

Jonathan's motive in assassinating the commissioner was to instigate a rebellion that would liberate the Israelites of their subservience to the Philistines (see above, 10:5; *Abarbanel*).

Malbim asserts that Jonathan did not confer with his father before performing this deed. *Daas Sofrim* agrees but, finding it hard to believe that Jonathan would deliberately plan such an attack on his own, assumes that he acted on the spur of the moment, possibly in response to a Philistine provocation.

נְצִיב פְּלִשְׁתִּים — *The Philistine commissioner.*

This man had been appointed to govern and collect taxes (*Abarbanel*).

בְּגֶבַע — *In Geba.*

According to *Rashi* and *Ralbag*, Geba is identical to *Gibeath-benjamin* (v. 2).

Radak, however, contends that these were two different places, and supports that claim by citing *Joshua* (18:24, 28).

However, Scripture previously clearly stated that the Philistine commissioners were stationed in Gibeath Ha-Elokim (10:5). Possibly, there was more than one set of commissioners on Benjamin's territory.

וְשָׁאוּל תָּקַע בַּשּׁוֹפָר בְּכָל־הָאָרֶץ — *Saul had the shofar blown throughout the land.*

Saul sent emissaries to blow the shofar; he himself did not leave Gilgal (*Radak*).

ד לֵאמֹר יִשְׁמְעוּ הָעִבְרִים: וְכָל־יִשְׂרָאֵל שָׁמְעוּ
לֵאמֹר הִכָּה שָׁאוּל אֶת־נְצִיב פְּלִשְׁתִּים וְגַם־
נִבְאַשׁ יִשְׂרָאֵל בַּפְּלִשְׁתִּים וַיִּצָּעֲקוּ הָעָם אַחֲרֵי
ה שָׁאוּל הַגִּלְגָּל: וּפְלִשְׁתִּים נֶאֶסְפוּ | לְהִלָּחֵם עִם־
יִשְׂרָאֵל שְׁלֹשִׁים אֶלֶף רֶכֶב וְשֵׁשֶׁת אֲלָפִים פָּרָשִׁים
וְעָם כַּחוֹל אֲשֶׁר עַל־שְׂפַת־הַיָּם לָרֹב וַיַּעֲלוּ וַיַּחֲנוּ
ו בְמִכְמָשׂ קִדְמַת בֵּית־אָוֶן: וְאִישׁ יִשְׂרָאֵל רָאוּ כִּי
צַר־לוֹ כִּי נִגַּשׂ הָעָם וַיִּתְחַבְּאוּ הָעָם בַּמְּעָרוֹת

לֵאמֹר — *Announcing.*

After the shofar was blown, an announcement was made describing the events and their implications (*Daas Sofrim*).

יִשְׁמְעוּ הָעִבְרִים — *Let the Hebrews hear.*

Let the Israelites know that we have rebelled, and prepare — either for Philistine retaliation (*Rashi*) or for battle (*Radak, Ralbag*).

הָעִבְרִים — *The Hebrews.*

Generally, Scripture refers to the Jews as יִשְׂרָאֵל, *Israelites.* We earlier saw the term עִבְרִים, *Hebrew,* used by the Philistines (above 4:6,9), presumably in a derogatory manner, the implication being that they originated from עֵבֶר הַנָּהָר, *across the river* (see *Joshua* 24:2) and were thus not native to the land. Also, the word עִבְרִי implies a Jewish slave (*Deuteronomy* 15:12); hence, the Philistines' comments, פֶּן תַּעַבְדוּ לָעִבְרִים כַּאֲשֶׁר עָבְדוּ לָכֶם, *lest you become enslaved to the Hebrews as they have been enslaved to you* (4:9).

Saul meant to incite the people's fury by reminding them of the contemptuous epithet with which the Philistines referred to them (*Kli Yakar*).

4. הִכָּה שָׁאוּל אֶת־נְצִיב פְּלִשְׁתִּים — *Saul has slain the Philistine commissioner.*

A false rumor spread — either that Saul himself had committed the assassination, or that Jonathan had acted upon Saul's command (*Radak*).

Alternatively, the story was accurately transmitted, but responsibility was attributed to Saul either because he was king (*Metzudos*) or because he summoned the army to Gilgal (*Me'am Loez*).

וְגַם־נִבְאַשׁ יִשְׂרָאֵל בַּפְּלִשְׁתִּים — *And Israel has become despicable in the eyes of the Philistines.*

Had an insignificant individual committed this act, the Philistines might not have been aroused to retaliate against the entire nation. However, since Saul was said to have committed the offense, the Philistines would seek vengeance against all of Israel (*Malbim*).

נִבְאַשׁ — *Despicable.*

Our translation of נִבְאַשׁ — literally, *malodorous* — is that of *Radak,* who defines this word as describing an object that has decayed and grown repulsive (see *Exodus* 7:18, 8:10).

According to *Rashi,* נִבְאַשׁ implies *hatred.*

Targum renders נִבְאַשׁ יִשְׂרָאֵל בַּפְּלִשְׁתִּים as *Israel has provoked the Philistines.*

וַיִּצָּעֲקוּ — *And the people were summoned.*

This is related to the word צְעָקָה, *an urgent cry.* The passive form, וַיִּצָּעֲקוּ, denotes the gathering of the people in response to an outcry (*Metzudos*).

הַגִּלְגָּל — *At Gilgal.*

As we have previously mentioned (10:8, 11:14), *Radak* and *Abarbanel* state that Saul had remained in Gilgal since his

announcing, "Let the Hebrews hear." 4 *All Israel*
heard [the announcement], saying, "Saul has slain
the Philistine commissioner, and Israel has be-
come despicable in the eyes of the Philistines,"
and the people were summoned to Saul at Gilgal.
5 *The Phil-istines gathered to wage war against*
Israel, with thirty thousand chariots, six thousand
cavalry, and soldiers as numerous as the sand
of the seashore. They went up and encamped
at Michmas, east of Beth-aven. 6 *The men of Is-*
rael saw that they were in trouble, for the people
were hard pressed; and the people hid in caves

public installation there. When Samuel told him, וְיָרַדְתָּ לְפָנַי הַגִּלְגָּל ... שִׁבְעַת יָמִים תּוֹחֵל עַד־בּוֹאִי אֵלֶיךָ, *"Then you shall go down to Gilgal ahead of me ...You shall wait for seven days until I come to you"* (above, 10:8), he meant that after the installation he would leave, while Saul remained and awaited his return.

Rashi, however, disassociates the inauguration ceremony from this gathering in Gilgal. Accordingly, in Chapter 10, Samuel prophesied that one day in the future Saul would be stationed at Gilgal; at that time, he should wait seven days for Samuel to come and join him.

5. שְׁלֹשִׁים אֶלֶף רֶכֶב — *Thirty thousand chariots.*

The Philistines were apparently gripped by an irrational fear, for the enormous offensive that they were preparing to launch was vastly disproportionate to the feeble army of the subjugated Israelite nation, particularly since the latter had no access to iron weapons (below, v. 19).

וְעָם — *And soldiers.*

The word עָם, literally *nation* or *masses,* here implies soldiers, as in the previous verse.

Daas Sofrim suggests that the word עָם can be understood in its literal sense: confident multitudes of Philistine civilians followed their army in the hope of gathering the spoils of the Israelites.

וַיַּחֲנוּ בְמִכְמָשׂ — *And encamped at Michmas.*

This itself further frightened the Israelites, for the massive Philistine army was poised just opposite Saul's camp (v. 2) (*Malbim*).

According to *Daas Sofrim,* however, Saul's troops at Michmas had left to join his assemblage at Gilgal, and the Philistines found Michmas to be abandoned.

בֵּית־אָוֶן — *Beth-aven.*

As evident from *Joshua* 7:2 and 18:12-13, Beth-aven was a city just east of Beth-el, bordering the territories of Benjamin and Ephraim. In *Hosea* (4:15, 5:8, 10:5), the name Beth-aven, which literally means *House of Iniquity,* is disparagingly applied to Beth-el, which was the site of one of the idolatrous golden calves set up by Jeroboam.

☙ The Israelites Fear War

6. וְאִישׁ יִשְׂרָאֵל רָאוּ כִּי צַר־לוֹ כִּי נִגַּשׂ הָעָם — *The men of Israel saw that they were in trouble, for the people were hard pressed.*

The phrase reads literally, *Each man of Israel — they saw that it is in trouble.*

The majority of commentators state that כִּי צַר־לוֹ — *that it was in trouble* — refers to the nation.

ז וּבַחֲוָחִים וּבַסְּלָעִים וּבַצְּרִחִים וּבַבֹּרוֹת: וְעִבְרִים
עָבְרוּ אֶת־הַיַּרְדֵּן אֶרֶץ גָּד וְגִלְעָד וְשָׁאוּל עוֹדֶנּוּ
ח בַגִּלְגָּל וְכָל־הָעָם חָרְדוּ אַחֲרָיו: °וייחל שִׁבְעַת
יָמִים לַמּוֹעֵד אֲשֶׁר שְׁמוּאֵל וְלֹא־בָא שְׁמוּאֵל
ט הַגִּלְגָּל וַיָּפֶץ הָעָם מֵעָלָיו: וַיֹּאמֶר שָׁאוּל הַגִּשׁוּ
י אֵלַי הָעֹלָה וְהַשְּׁלָמִים וַיַּעַל הָעֹלָה: וַיְהִי כְּכַלֹּתוֹ

°וַיּוֹחֶל ק׳

Kli Yakar, however, rejects this on the basis of three peculiarities. First, the singular word לוֹ, *it*, conflicts with the plural word רָאוּ, *they saw*. Second, *each man of Israel* is an unusual reference to the nation. And third, כִּי נִגַּשׂ הָעָם, *for the people were hard pressed*, seems redundant.

Kli Yakar thus offers the following novel rendering of the verse: וְאִישׁ יִשְׂרָאֵל רָאוּ, *All Israel in unison understood*, כִּי צַר־לוֹ, *that it pained him* — i.e., Saul (the antecedent having been mentioned at the end of the previous verse) — כִּי נִגַּשׂ הָעָם, *that the people* of Israel *had pressed forward* so soon, for he had wanted them to wait for seven days. And therefore וַיִּתְחַבְּאוּ הָעָם, *the nation hid* from Saul.

כִּי נִגַּשׂ הָעָם — *For the people were hard pressed.*

Targum and the majority of commentators interpret הָעָם, *the people*, as a reference to Israel. Therefore, the verb נִגַּשׂ is in the passive form.

Abarbanel, however, interprets *the people* as referring to the Philistines, and reads נִגַּשׂ in the active form — thus, *the Philistines pressed on.*

נִגַּשׂ — *Pressed.*

This word is related to נֹגְשָׂיו, *taskmasters* (*Exodus* 3:7) and לֹא־יִגֹּשׂ, *he shall not pressure* (*Deuteronomy* 15:2).[1]

וּבַחֲוָחִים — *And in fortresses.*

Our translation follows *Targum.*

Rashi, however, relates חֲוָחִים to חוֹחִים, *thorns* (*Song of Songs* 2:2). The verse thus means that the Jews hid amidst clumps of thorns.

וּבַצְּרִחִים — *And in towers.*

Radak translates צְרִיחַ as an *elevated place* or *fortress.*

Rashi interprets the word to mean *a well-concealed forest area.*

7. וְעִבְרִים עָבְרוּ אֶת־הַיַּרְדֵּן — *Some Hebrews [even] crossed the Jordan.*

Saul's men split into three groups. Some found hiding places in which to conceal themselves, some crossed to the eastern side of the Jordan River, and some ran to Saul in Gilgal (*Radak*).

וְעִבְרִים עָבְרוּ — *Hebrews crossed.*

Malbim suggests that this refers to a specific group of Jews who were called עִבְרִים and not יִשְׂרָאֵל because they were situated עֵבֶר הַיַּרְדֵּן, just *beyond the Jordan*, on its western bank, allowing them easy access to escape to the eastern side.

As mentioned above (4.3), the appellation עִבְרִים was a derogatory reference to the Jews, associating them with servility. These people deserved that epithet, for they fled like weak, panic-stricken slaves (*Daas Sofrim*).

Metzudos and *Kli Yakar* note Scripture's play on words in the phrase, וְעִבְרִים עָבְרוּ.

וְשָׁאוּל עוֹדֶנּוּ בַגִּלְגָּל — *Saul was still in Gilgal.*

Saul was patiently awaiting Samuel's arrival, as per Samuel's instructions (*Mahari Kara*).

וְכָל־הָעָם חָרְדוּ אַחֲרָיו — *And all the people hurried after him.*

The word חֲרָדָה literally means *trembling* or *apprehension*. Hence, *the people fearfully hurried after [Saul]* (*Rashi*).

1. The word נִגַּשׂ is *unrelated* to נִגַּשׁ with a שׁ, which means *drew near.*

and in fortresses and in rocks and in towers and in
pits. [7] *Some Hebrews [even] crossed the Jordan to the*
land of Gad and Gilead. Saul was still in Gilgal, and
all the people [who remained] hurried after him. [8] *He*
waited seven days, for the time that Samuel [had set];
but Samuel had not arrived at Gilgal, so the people
began to disband from him. [9] *So Saul said, "Bring me*
the elevation-offering and the peace-offering!" and
he offered up the elevation-offering. [10] *It was just as*

Rendering this verse more literally, *Mahari Kara* states that first Saul was gripped by fear, and then *the people* [who were with him] *joined him in that fear.*

Following *Rashi*'s view that these people had not previously been with Saul, why did they come to him now?

According to *Abarbanel*, the people came to complain and blame Saul for having created this precarious situation.

Metzudos states, on the other hand, that the people came to Saul in order to assist him.

Malbim explains that they came to persuade Saul to leave his station in Gilgal and prepare for war.

Kli Yakar avers that the people sensed his patience and confidence in following Samuel's command and waiting for him, and they came to support and protect him.

◆§ Saul's Error

8. Samuel had enjoined Saul to wait for him in Gilgal for seven days, at which time Samuel would come and bring elevation-offerings and peace offerings (10:8), as well as instruct Saul. That juncture had arrived now, and the upcoming verses relate how Saul dealt with that mission.

לַמּוֹעֵד אֲשֶׁר שְׁמוּאֵל ... — *For the time that Samuel ...*

This line is clearly a fragmentary phrase, which must be completed.

Rashi suggests either *for the time that Samuel [had set]*, or *for the time [of] Samuel. Targum* amends the phrase to *for the time that Samuel [had mentioned to him].*

As we will see, one of the explanations for Saul's error was his assumption that he was required to wait only until the *beginning* of the seventh day. The seventh day had arrived, but Samuel had until the end of the day to appear (*Malbim*).

Accordingly, *Kli Yakar* remarks, Scripture deliberately left this phrase vague, implying that this was the intended day of his arrival but his deadline had not come yet.

וְלֹא־בָא שְׁמוּאֵל — *But Samuel had not arrived.*

Me'am Loez emphasizes the enormity of the Divine test confronting Saul, who clearly faced strong pressures and could easily rationalize not waiting for Samuel.

וַיָּפֶץ הָעָם מֵעָלָיו — *So the people began to disband from him.*

The people began to leave, fearing Philistine attack (*Ralbag*), and attributing Samuel's absence to a lack of Divine protection, as they did not understand the depth of God's test (*Kli Yakar*).

In particular, *Daas Sofrim* states, they interpreted Samuel's failure to appear as an expression of his opposition to their having prepared for war without consulting him, and they therefore believed that their efforts would fail.

9. וַיֹּאמֶר שָׁאוּל הַגִּשׁוּ אֵלַי הָעֹלָה וְהַשְּׁלָמִים — *So Saul said, "Bring me the elevation-*

לְהַעֲלוֹת הָעֹלָה וְהִנֵּה שְׁמוּאֵל בָּא וַיֵּצֵא שָׁאוּל
יא לִקְרָאתוֹ לְבָרְכוֹ: וַיֹּאמֶר שְׁמוּאֵל מֶה עָשִׂיתָ
וַיֹּאמֶר שָׁאוּל כִּי־רָאִיתִי כִּי־נָפַץ הָעָם מֵעָלַי
וְאַתָּה לֹא־בָאתָ לְמוֹעֵד הַיָּמִים וּפְלִשְׁתִּים
יב נֶאֱסָפִים מִכְמָשׂ: וָאֹמַר עַתָּה יֵרְדוּ פְלִשְׁתִּים אֵלַי
הַגִּלְגָּל וּפְנֵי יהוה לֹא חִלִּיתִי וָאֶתְאַפַּק וָאַעֲלֶה
יג הָעֹלָה: וַיֹּאמֶר שְׁמוּאֵל אֶל־שָׁאוּל נִסְכָּלְתָּ

offering and the peace-offering!''

Since Samuel had notified the people that upon his arrival he would bring offerings, they had prepared the animals. Now that Samuel tarried, Saul decided to bring these offerings himself (*Radak*). His purpose (as we will see — v. 12) was to gain Hashem's favor and sanctify himself before entering into battle.[1]

In addition, *Ralbag* adds, Saul hoped that bringing these offerings would imbue him with a spirit of prophecy.

וַיַּעַל הָעֹלָה — *And he offered up the elevation-offering.*

Although Saul was not a Kohen, he was permitted to bring an offering, for any Jew may officiate at a private altar (*Zevachim* 118a, *Rashi*). Rationalizing on Saul's behalf, *Malbim* explains that Saul thought that waiting for the offering was not included in Samuel's command, but only that he should wait for Samuel's arrival to receive further direction.

◆§ Samuel Reproves Saul

11. וַיֹּאמֶר שְׁמוּאֵל מֶה עָשִׂיתָ — *Samuel said, ''What have you done?''*

Samuel apparently realized — possibly via prophecy (*Radak*) — that Saul had brought offerings, and reminded Saul that he had said that *he* would do so (*Rashi*).

Samuel's style of reproof is reminiscent of Hashem's rebuke of Adam (*Genesis* 3:9) and Cain (ibid. 4:9), in which He began with an inquiry, so that they would not be too frightened to reply (*Rashi* ad loc.).

Samuel's question carried a sharp and incriminating tone (*Daas Sofrim*).

Had Saul immediately acknowledged his guilt (as David did when confronted with his guilt — *II Samuel* 12:13), he would have suffered a less severe punishment (*Kli Yakar*).

11.-12. In these two verses Saul presents a four-part defense of his actions, outlined by *Malbim* as follows.

(a) כִּי־רָאִיתִי כִּי־נָפַץ הָעָם מֵעָלַי — *Because I saw that the people were disbanding from me.*

Saul was afraid to be left alone.

(b) וְאַתָּה לֹא־בָאתָ לְמוֹעֵד הַיָּמִים — *And you had not arrived by the appointed time of the day.*

Saul assumed that, following the principle that *part of a day is considered like an entire day* (*Pesachim* 4a), he had waited the prescribed seven days and was now free to act on his own.

(c) וּפְלִשְׁתִּים נֶאֱסָפִים מִכְמָשׂ. וָאֹמַר עַתָּה יֵרְדוּ פְלִשְׁתִּים אֵלַי הַגִּלְגָּל וּפְנֵי ה׳ לֹא חִלִּיתִי — *And that the Philistines were gathering at Michmas, and I thought, ''Now the Philistines will descend upon me to Gilgal and I have not supplicated before Hashem.''*

Saul could not countenance entering into battle without having first brought offerings.

(d) וָאֶתְאַפַּק וָאַעֲלֶה הָעֹלָה — So *I withheld*

1. Similarly, Samuel had offered sacrifices before the Jews' victory at Eben-ha'ezer; see above, 7:9.

he finished offering up the elevation-offering when behold! Samuel arrived, and Saul went forth to greet him.

11 *Samuel said, "What have you done?"*

Saul said, "Because I saw that the people were disbanding from me and you had not arrived by the appointed time of the day, and that the Philis-tines were gathering at Michmas, 12 *and I thought, 'Now the Philistines will descend upon me to Gil-gal and I have not supplicated before* HASHEM,*' so I withheld [my natural inclination] and offered up the elevation-offering."*

13 *Samuel said to Saul, "You have acted foolishly!*

[my natural inclination] and offered up the elevation-offering.

Malbim understands Saul to be saying, "After all this, I *only* brought the offering, which I assumed was not in violation of your command. I *held back* from going to battle, which was what I understood your directive to be."

וּפְנֵי ה׳ לֹא חִלִּיתִי — *And I have not supplicated before* HASHEM.

Generally, prayers were accompanied by offerings (*Radak*). It seems to have been Saul's supreme challenge to weigh the value of some exceedingly noble deed against the word of the prophet. A similar decision is placed before him in dealing with Amalek (Ch. 15). Here, Saul was placed in a dilemma: although Samuel had told him to wait, how could he possibly go to war without properly sanctifying himself and praying? (*Daas Sofrim*).

לֹא חִלִּיתִי — *I have not supplicated.*

This phrase implies distress in a time of peril. The same term is used in *Exodus* 32:11 — וַיְחַל מֹשֶׁה — describing how *Moses pleaded* on behalf of the Jews after they made the golden calf. It is related to the word חוֹלֶה, a *diseased person,* who cries out in pain.

וָאֶתְאַפַּק — *So I withheld.*

This word implies strengthening one's resolve so as to act against one's natural tendencies (*Radak*). Saul explained that in offering the sacrifices he was not following his intrinsic inclination. On the contrary, his preference had been to wait for Samuel, but he made a rational decision that he must bring an offering for the sake of attaining victory.

According to *Mahari Kara,* Saul told Samuel, *I had already restrained myself [long enough from bringing the offerings; I then decided that the time had come to go to save my people, and so] I offered the elevation-offering* (see also *Daas Sofrim*).

As we have already seen, *Malbim* interprets וָאֶתְאַפַּק as *I refrained [from going to war].*

Without question, Saul had been placed under extreme pressure, and his response was far from reprehensible. Nonetheless, Hashem expects more than this of a Jewish monarch, for his primary mission — to be Hashem's emissary — requires him to punctiliously fulfill God's every word.

13. **נִסְכָּלְתָּ** — *You have acted foolishly!*

You thought that you were wise to engage in logical rationalization, but

לֹא שָׁמַרְתָּ אֶת־מִצְוַת יהוה אֱלֹהֶיךָ אֲשֶׁר צִוָּךְ כִּי
עַתָּה הֵכִין יהוה אֶת־מַמְלַכְתְּךָ אֶל־יִשְׂרָאֵל עַד־
יד עוֹלָם: וְעַתָּה מַמְלַכְתְּךָ לֹא־תָקוּם בִּקֵּשׁ יהוה לוֹ

the opposite was true. God requires not your calculations but your obedience (*Abarbanel*).

Saul's lack of trust that Samuel would come on time was tantamount to a denial of Samuel's prophecy, and thus a rejection of his authority (*Radak*).

לֹא שָׁמַרְתָּ אֶת־מִצְוַת ה׳ — *You did not keep the commandment of* HASHEM.

Disobedience to the word of a prophet is, in effect, a transgression of God's commandment. As the verse states, נָבִיא מִקִּרְבְּךָ מֵאַחֶיךָ כָּמֹנִי יָקִים לְךָ ה׳ אֱלֹהֶיךָ אֵלָיו תִּשְׁמָעוּן, *A prophet from your midst, from your brethren, like me [Moses], shall* HASHEM, *your God, establish for you — to him shall you hearken* (*Deuteronomy* 18:15), and God himself states, וְנָתַתִּי דְבָרַי בְּפִיו, *I will place My words in his mouth* (ibid v. 18).

אֲשֶׁר צִוָּךְ — *As He commanded you.*

There were two reasons that Saul was so severely chastised, possibly more so than if he had been delinquent in regard to any other commandment. First, this command had been directed specifically to him, and second, this was the first such directive that he had received (*Abarbanel*).

Daas Sofrim comments that the words אֲשֶׁר צִוָּךְ, as *He commanded you,* themselves constitute an implied reproof: "You should have realized that these were not my (Samuel's) words but Hashem's."

☙ What Exactly Was Saul's Sin?

Abarbanel list three misdeeds for which Saul was held accountable:

1. Although during this time period, any individual was permitted to bring offerings on a private altar, Saul was specifically told that Samuel would bring them this time, not he.

2. Saul took action during the seventh day, mistakenly thinking that he need only wait until that seventh day began. (And even according to the view that this understanding was correct, Samuel had instructed him, עַד־בּוֹאִי אֵלֶיךָ, *until I come to you* [above, 10:8], meaning that Saul must wait even if Samuel delayed beyond the seven days.)

3. Samuel had told Saul, *I will inform you what you are to do* (ibid.); i.e., Saul should not plan any military strategy without Samuel, for Hashem wished to bring about a miraculous victory (as indeed occurred; see Ch. 14). God wanted Saul to place his full trust in Him and not in any military prowess. Saul's fear of the approaching Philistine army as his own troops were dispersing showed that he lacked this trust.

As mentioned above, it was not only Saul's errors that condemned him but his decision to act on the basis of his calculations rather than to adhere to the directive of the prophet, for that betrayed a lack of faith in the word of God. Also, considering that this was Saul's very first mission as king, that failure was especially egregious (*Abarbanel*).

כִּי עַתָּה הֵכִין ה׳ אֶת־מַמְלַכְתְּךָ אֶל־יִשְׂרָאֵל עַד־עוֹלָם — *[Until] now,* HASHEM *[would have] established your kingdom over Israel forever.*

Literally, עַתָּה הֵכִין means, *now [He] has established.* Our translation follows *Rashi,* who inserts, *[until] now,* HASHEM *[would have] established.*

Malbim and *Metzudos* render this phrase as, *Now, [if you would have passed this test], He would have established.*

According to *Abarbanel,* the word עַתָּה, *now,* implies immediacy. Thus, he translates the phrase as *So soon after* HASHEM *has established your kingdom, [you have rebelled].*

Daas Sofrim understands the word עַתָּה

You did not keep the commandment of HASHEM, *your God, as He commanded you. [Until] now* HASHEM *[would have] established your kingdom over Israel forever,* [14] *but now your kingdom shall not endure.* HASHEM *has sought*

as indicating that the time had been ripe for Saul's kingdom to flourish.

הֵכִין — *Established.*

The word הֵכִין can also mean *prepared.* As such, it implies that Hashem prepared the crown for Saul on condition that he would pass these tests (*Daas Sofrim*).

אֶל־יִשְׂרָאֵל — *Over Israel.*

אֶל־יִשְׂרָאֵל literally means *to Israel,* or *for Israel.* (More conventionally, this phrase would read עַל־יִשְׂרָאֵל, *over Israel.*) The phrase connotes that Saul's greatness was congruent with the spiritual level of the Jewish people, and that he was thus fit to be their king (*Daas Sofrim*). (See also *Ramban* below.)

הֵכִין ה׳ אֶת מַמְלַכְתְּךָ אֶל־יִשְׂרָאֵל עַד־עוֹלָם — HASHEM *[would have] established your kingdom over Israel forever.*

When God assigns a person a position of leadership, it will be passed on to his progeny as well unless he grows arrogant (*Zevachim* 102a, *Rashi*; see also *Deuteronomy* 17:20; *Rambam, Hil. Melachim* 1:7).

But how could Saul, a descendant of Benjamin, have been the progenitor of a Jewish monarchy, since that privilege was reserved for the tribe of Judah (as in the verse, לֹא־יָסוּר שֵׁבֶט מִיהוּדָה, *The scepter shall not part from Judah* [*Genesis* 49:10])?

We have already discussed this issue (see comm. 9:1) and will briefly review those points relevant to the interpretation of the present verse.

Ralbag understands עַד־עוֹלָם not as *forever* but as *for a long time.* Similarly, when Hannah stated that וְיָשַׁב שָׁם עַד־עוֹלָם, *[Samuel] shall settle there forever* (above, 1:22), she obviously did not mean that literally (see comm. ad loc.).

Ramban (to *Genesis* ibid.) states that if Saul had not sinned, his progeny would have maintained a limited leadership. Possibly they would have ruled over Rachel's descendants or else maintained a position of authority subordinate to that of the Judean king. Thus, Saul and his progeny would have been kings אֶל־יִשְׂרָאֵל, *for Israel,* but not עַל־יִשְׂרָאֵל, *over [the entirety of] Israel.*

14. וְעַתָּה מַמְלַכְתְּךָ לֹא־תָקוּם — *But now your kingdom shall not endure.*

Not only did Saul lose the privilege of bequeathing his monarchy to his offspring, but his own rule would be cut short as well (*Malbim*).

For a king to merit long life and a long-lasting dynasty, he must *observe all the words of the Torah ... and not stray from the commandment* (cf. *Deuteronomy* 17:19,20), the latter phrase intimating that he must obey the words of a prophet (*Rashi*).

Malbim sees this phrase as expressing sharp reproof. Because Saul had not placed his trust in Hashem but planned his own military strategy, it was now מַמְלַכְתְּךָ, *your kingdom* only; it was no longer Hashem's kingdom and would not endure.

As in the previous verse, *Abarbanel* reads וְעַתָּה, *and now,* as indicating immediacy. Thus, he renders וְעַתָּה מַמְלַכְתְּךָ לֹא־תָקוּם as *very soon, your kingdom will no longer endure.*

◆§ Was This One Misdeed Sufficient to Strip Saul of His Throne?

The present text implies that it was. However, many other sources indicate otherwise.

First and foremost, when Saul sinned in regard to eradicating Amalek, Hashem

אִישׁ כִּלְבָבוֹ וַיְצַוֵּהוּ יהוה לְנָגִיד עַל־עַמּוֹ כִּי לֹא
טו שָׁמַרְתָּ אֵת אֲשֶׁר־צִוְּךָ יהוה׃ וַיָּקָם שְׁמוּאֵל
וַיַּעַל מִן־הַגִּלְגָּל גִּבְעַת בִּנְיָמִן וַיִּפְקֹד שָׁאוּל אֶת־

stated, נִחַמְתִּי כִּי־הִמְלַכְתִּי אֶת־שָׁאוּל לְמֶלֶךְ, *I have reconsidered My having made Saul king* (below, 15:11), implying that until that point, Saul's position was assured. Furthermore, the Talmud (*Yoma* 22b) ratifies that Saul lost his kingdom for one sin only: that of failing to wipe out Amalek.

This issue is addressed by many commentators and we cite a variety of their solutions.

Tosafos Yeshanim (*Yoma* ibid.) claims that if Saul had failed only in Gilgal, he would have been removed from office but his children would have retained the throne. After the Amalek incident, however, leadership was taken from them as well.

Radak (below, 15:28) suggests the opposite. At Gilgal, Saul forfeited the possibility of establishing a dynasty; his own reign, however, might have extended for a long period of time. It was after the Amalek incident that he lost his own rights to the throne as well.

Radak (ibid.) offers an alternative approach. After the incident at Gilgal, it would still have been feasible for Saul to have regained his good standing. When he repeated his misdeed (the similarity of the Gilgal and Amalek episodes will be discussed further on), he sealed his doom.

Maharsha (*Yoma* ibid.) contends that the sin at Gilgal was not a sufficiently grave offense for Saul to lose the throne, and Samuel's words to Saul merely constituted a warning that if he would not do Hashem's will, he would then forfeit the sovereignty. When Saul repeated his offenses, Hashem Himself deprived him of the throne.

Along these lines, *Daas Sofrim* interprets Samuel's statement here, מַמְלַכְתְּךָ לֹא־תָקוּם *your kingdom shall not endure*, as a prediction: "Although your actions have not yet sealed your fate, it seems inevitable that your weaknesses will lead you to fall again."

The *Brisker Rav* explains that a Divine decree about something bad can be retracted, but not about something good (see *Rambam, Hil. Yesodei HaTorah* 10:4). Since, at Gilgal, Hashem decreed that Saul would lose his kingdom, the decree could have been reversed. However, after the incident with Amalek, Samuel prophesied that Hashem has "torn the kingship of Israel from upon you ... and has given it to your fellow ..." (below, 15:28). Since that prophecy implied a promise that David would ascend to the throne, it could no longer be retracted.

For not heeding the word of the prophet, Saul deserved to die (*Abarbanel*). As the verse states, וְהָיָה הָאִישׁ אֲשֶׁר לֹא־יִשְׁמַע אֶל־דְּבָרַי אֲשֶׁר יְדַבֵּר בִּשְׁמִי אָנֹכִי אֶדְרֹשׁ מֵעִמּוֹ, *And it shall be that the man who will not hearken to [Hashem's] words that [the prophet] shall speak in My name, I will exact from him* (*Deuteronomy* 18:19).

In this regard, our Sages state that Saul met his violent end because of five iniquities, one of them being his behavior at Gilgal (*Midrash Shmuel* 24:7; *Vayikra Rabbah* 26:7). (*Rashi* cites that Midrash in his commentary on the verse, וַיָּמָת שָׁאוּל בְּמַעֲלוֹ אֲשֶׁר־מָעַל בַּה׳ עַל־דְּבַר ה׳ אֲשֶׁר לֹא־שָׁמָר, *Saul died because of the betrayal by which he betrayed Hashem, because of the command of Hashem that he did not keep [I Chronicles* 10:13].)

בִּקֵּשׁ ה׳ לוֹ... — *Hashem has sought...*

This is written in the past tense, for Hashem had already chosen a successor, although Samuel was not yet aware of his identity (*Rashi*). *Mishbetzos Zahav* explains that since in Hashem's realm there is no difference between past and future, for He sees everything without regard to time, prophetic statements

a man after His own heart and appointed him as a ruler over His people, because you have not observed that which HASHEM *has commanded you."*
15 *Then Samuel arose and went up from Gilgal to Gibeath-benjamin.*

are often given in the past tense, as if they had already occurred. This emphasizes that the matter is final, as if it has already been carried out. See *Radak, Psalms* 3:5, 4:2, 21:3.

אִישׁ כִּלְבָבוֹ — *A man after His own heart.*

That is to say, a man who will perform Hashem's will (*Targum*).

Kli Yakar interprets this phrase homiletically to mean *a man like his own heart* — i.e., a man whose external behavior reflects his inner character (see *Berachos* 28a).

In v. 12, Saul claims, as *Rashi* explains, that his heart had told him to wait for Samuel, but he "forced himself" to bring the offering against his will, apparently because of pressure from the masses. Accordingly, we suggest that Hashem chose אִישׁ כִּלְבָבוֹ, a man who follows the convictions of his own heart and does not bend to political pressure (*Mishbetzos Zahav*, citing *Rav C.Z. Ullman*).

Midrash Shocher Tov (1:3) tells that King David took pride in Hashem's reference to him as אִישׁ כִּלְבָבוֹ, *a man after His own heart* — i.e., a man who emulates God. David stated, "Just as my Creator avoids unseemly speech (see *Genesis* 7:8, *Pesachim* 3a), so do I. I thus wrote the phrase, אַשְׁרֵי־הָאִישׁ אֲשֶׁר לֹא הָלַךְ בַּעֲצַת רְשָׁעִים, *Praiseworthy is the man who has not walked in the counsel of the wicked*, rather than אָרוּר הָאִישׁ אֲשֶׁר הָלַךְ, *Cursed is the man who has walked*" (*Psalms* 1:1).

וַיְצַוֵּהוּ ה׳ לְנָגִיד עַל־עַמּוֹ — *And appointed him as a ruler over His people.*

God decreed that David should be ruler (*Metzudos*).

However, *Daas Sofrim* interprets this phrase as a reference to Saul. Hashem had appointed Saul, who had initially been *a man like His heart*. But now Hashem sought his replacement כִּי לֹא שָׁמַרְתָּ אֵת אֲשֶׁר־צִוְּךָ ה׳, *because you have not observed that which* HASHEM *has commanded you*, and not due to a commitment to assign royalty to the tribe of Judah or the like (*Daas Sofrim*).

◆§ Opposing Camps Prepare for War

15. וַיָּקָם שְׁמוּאֵל — *Then Samuel arose.*

Originally, Samuel intended to inform Saul in Gilgal אֵת אֲשֶׁר תַּעֲשֶׂה, *what you are to do. Radak* interprets this to mean that Samuel would inform Saul of the fate of his monarchy, which was directly dependent on his performance at Gilgal. Thus, Samuel did as he had promised (verse 14).

However, most commentators explain that Samuel intended to give Saul advice on how to wage war against the Philistines. Following that understanding, we must conclude that Samuel was so disappointed in Saul's failure that he decided not to offer him that advice (*Metzudos* 10:8).

וַיָּקָם שְׁמוּאֵל וַיַּעַל מִן־הַגִּלְגָּל גִּבְעַת בִּנְיָמִן — *Then Samuel arose and went up from Gilgal to Gibeath-benjamin.*

Most commentators agree that Saul accompanied Samuel to Gibeath-benjamin. Although this fact is not mentioned, it is self-evident, insofar as Saul had been in Gilgal for the sole purpose of meeting with Samuel (*Ralbag*).

Additionally, Jonathan was stationed in Gibeath-benjamin (above, v. 2), and the following verse relates that Saul and Jonathan were together in Geba-benjamin, which is presumably another name for Gibeath-benjamin.

Daas Sofrim suggests that Saul went to Gibeath-benjamin to join forces with Jonathan, and that Samuel accompanied

יג/טז־יט

טז הָעָם֙ הַנִּמְצְאִ֣ים עִמּ֔וֹ כְּשֵׁ֥שׁ מֵא֖וֹת אִֽישׁ׃ וְשָׁא֞וּל
וְיוֹנָתָ֣ן בְּנ֗וֹ וְהָעָם֙ הַנִּמְצָ֣א עִמָּ֔ם יֹשְׁבִ֖ים בְּגֶ֣בַע בִּנְיָמִ֑ן
יז וּפְלִשְׁתִּ֖ים חָנ֥וּ בְמִכְמָֽשׂ׃ וַיֵּצֵ֧א הַמַּשְׁחִ֛ית מִמַּחֲנֵ֥ה
פְלִשְׁתִּ֖ים שְׁלֹשָׁ֣ה רָאשִׁ֑ים הָרֹ֨אשׁ אֶחָ֥ד יִפְנֶ֛ה אֶל־
יח דֶּ֥רֶךְ עָפְרָ֖ה אֶל־אֶ֥רֶץ שׁוּעָֽל׃ וְהָרֹ֨אשׁ אֶחָ֜ד יִפְנֶ֗ה
דֶּ֚רֶךְ בֵּ֣ית חֹר֔וֹן וְהָרֹ֨אשׁ אֶחָ֤ד יִפְנֶה֙ דֶּ֣רֶךְ הַגְּב֔וּל
יט הַנִּשְׁקָ֛ף עַל־גֵּ֥י הַצְּבֹעִ֖ים הַמִּדְבָּֽרָה׃ וְחָרָשׁ֙
לֹ֣א יִמָּצֵ֔א בְּכֹ֖ל אֶ֣רֶץ יִשְׂרָאֵ֑ל כִּֽי־°אמר פְּלִשְׁתִּ֔ים

°אָמְר֣וּ ק׳

him so that no one should have an inkling of their confrontation in Gilgal.

Kli Yakar, however, maintains that Samuel and Saul went in different directions, and that Geba-benjamin and Gibeath-benjamin are two different cities.

וַיִּפְקֹד שָׁאוּל אֶת־הָעָם הַנִּמְצְאִים עִמּוֹ כְּשֵׁשׁ מֵאוֹת אִישׁ — *Saul counted the people who were [still] found with him, about six hundred men.*

The rest had dispersed out of fear (*Rashi, Ralbag*).

16. וְשָׁאוּל וְיוֹנָתָן בְּנוֹ וְהָעָם הַנִּמְצָא עִמָּם יֹשְׁבִים בְּגֶבַע בִּנְיָמִן — *Saul and his son Jonathan and the people who were found with them were staying in Geba-benjamin.*

Although they originally split into two camps (above, v. 2), they decided to join forces and stay together because they were so few in number (*Abarbanel*).

וּפְלִשְׁתִּים חָנוּ בְמִכְמָשׂ — *While the Philistines were encamped at Michmas.*

The narrative returns to the military theatre (cf. verse 5).

Saul had much to fear, as his already minuscule army had been greatly reduced and the Philistines were camped in close proximity (*Malbim*).

17. הַמַּשְׁחִית — *The raiding party.*

This consisted of strong warriors armed with swords and spears (*Radak*).

According to *Rashi* (below v. 23), they were marauders sent to plunder enemy cities.

יִפְנֶה — *Turned.*

This word is written in the future tense, as constant or recurring action words often are; hence, it may be rendered, *the first group was constantly turning* (see above, 1:7).

Alternatively, Saul saw these raiders preparing to charge in that direction (*Daas Sofrim*).

עָפְרָה — *Ophrah.*

Presumably, this is the Ophrah listed in *Joshua* as being one of the cities of Benjamin (18:23).

אֶרֶץ שׁוּעָל — *The land of Shual.*

Targum renders this as *the southern land.*

It was possibly called אֶרֶץ שׁוּעָל because it contained an abundance of שׁוּעָלִים, *foxes* (*Abarbanel*).

18. בֵּית חֹרוֹן — *Beth-horon.*

The territory of Ephraim had two cities named, respectively, Beth-horon and Upper Beth-horon (*Joshua* 16:3, 16:5). The geographical information provided in *Joshua* indicates that the present verse is referring to Beth-horon. This city was located along the southern border, which separated Ephraim from Benjamin and was therefore closer than was Upper Beth-horon to the other cities mentioned in this chapter.

דֶּרֶךְ הַגְּבוּל — *The border road.*

That is to say, the border between the land of Israel and the Philistines (*Daas Sofrim*).

*Saul counted the people who were [still] found
with him, about six hundred men.* 16 *Saul and his son
Jonathan and the people who were found with them
were staying in Geba-benjamin, while the Philistines were encamped at Michmas.* 17 *A raiding party
went forth from the Philistine camp in three companies — one company turned toward the road to
Ophrah, to the land of Shual;* 18 *one company turned
toward the road to Beth-horon; and one company
turned toward the border road, which is visible [to
a person] in the Zeboim Valley, toward the desert.*
19 *Now there was no smith to be found anywhere
in the entire Land of Israel, for the Philistines said,*

הַנִּשְׁקָף עַל־גֵּי הַצְּבֹעִים — *Which is visible [to a person] in the Zeboim Valley.*

A person standing in Zeboim Valley could see the border (*Metzudos*).

גֵּי הַצְּבֹעִים — *Zeboim Valley.*

The valley carried that name because it contained an abundance of a creature called the צָבוּעַ.

Targum renders this as אַפְעַיָא, Aramaic for אֶפְעֶה, an animal occasionally mentioned in Scripture (e.g. *Isaiah* 30:6), and referred to by the Talmud as אַפָּא (*Bava Kamma* 16a; see *Radak*).

In his commentary on *Isaiah* (ibid.), *Rashi* defines the אֶפְעֶה as a species of viper, of which there exists only one male and one female, which procreate once every 70 years. *Rashi* to *Bereishis Rabbah* (7:4) classifies the צָבוּעַ as a serpent.

Rashi also refers to the צָבוּעַ as a bird [*Bereishis Rabbah* ibid.] and, in his commentary on this verse, as a crawling mammal with a malicious nature. There is evidence that *Rashi* identifies it more specifically with the *bardelos* (see *Bava Metzia* 24a) or polecat (see *Yoma* 84a, *Rashi* משכא דאפא).

At any rate, all seem to agree that this creature's name derives from the root word צֶבַע, *dye*, because it is many-colored.

הַמִּדְבָּרָה — *Toward the desert.*

The border road turned toward the desert (*Metzudos*).

◆§ Saul's Arms Disadvantage

19. וְחָרָשׁ לֹא יִמָּצֵא בְּכֹל אֶרֶץ יִשְׂרָאֵל — *Now there was no smith to be found anywhere in the entire Land of Israel.*

The Philistines had maintained their hold over Israel for many years, going back to the times of Samson and Eli. Although the Jews experienced a measure of relief following Samuel's victory at Eben-ha'ezer (Ch. 7), after Samuel grew elderly the Philistines regained their authority (see above, 7:13, 10:5).

In order to prevent rebellion, the Philistines forbade Israelite blacksmiths from forging swords and spears, to that end preventing them from working with iron altogether, so that farming had to be conducted with tools made of wood, such as olive wood (*Daas Sofrim*).

Jewish warriors instead used the inferior weapons of bows and arrows and stone-slinging devices (*I Chronicles* 12:2). Yet, despite the disadvantage to which this subjected them, they achieved victory, for *not through sword and spear does HASHEM grant salvation, for unto HASHEM is the battle* (below, 17:47).

כ פֶּן יַעֲשׂוּ הָעִבְרִים חֶרֶב אוֹ חֲנִית: וַיֵּרְדוּ כָל־
יִשְׂרָאֵל הַפְּלִשְׁתִּים לִלְטוֹשׁ אִישׁ אֶת־מַחֲרַשְׁתּוֹ
כא וְאֶת־אֵתוֹ וְאֶת־קַרְדֻּמּוֹ וְאֵת מַחֲרֵשָׁתוֹ: וְהָיְתָה
הַפְּצִירָה פִים לַמַּחֲרֵשֹׁת וְלָאֵתִים וְלִשְׁלֹשׁ
כב קִלְּשׁוֹן וּלְהַקַּרְדֻּמִּים וּלְהַצִּיב הַדָּרְבָן: וְהָיָה בְּיוֹם
מִלְחֶמֶת וְלֹא נִמְצָא חֶרֶב וַחֲנִית בְּיַד כָּל־הָעָם
אֲשֶׁר אֶת־שָׁאוּל וְאֶת־יוֹנָתָן וַתִּמָּצֵא לְשָׁאוּל

Ralbag comments that there had always been a shortage of iron in the land of Israel, such that Jews had traditionally resorted to the Philistines for their iron works.

Even Philistine blacksmiths were prohibited from working in Israelite territory, lest they produce weapons for the Israelites.

וְחָרָשׁ לֹא יִמָּצֵא — *Now there was no smith to be found.*

Literally, this phrase reads, *a smith should not be found.* The verse apparently quotes the text of the Philistines' decree (*Kli Yakar*).

כִּי־אָמְרוּ פְלִשְׁתִּים פֶּן יַעֲשׂוּ הָעִבְרִים חֶרֶב אוֹ חֲנִית — *For the Philistines said, "Lest the Hebrews produce a sword or spear."*

The Philistines' purpose was to prevent rebellion.

Chomas Anach adds that the tone of this declaration was spiteful and irreverent, as if to say: "Why do you need swords and spears? Doesn't your God fight your battles?" Accordingly, there was an element of חִלּוּל ה׳, *desecration of God's Name,* in this prohibition as well.

20. וַיֵּרְדוּ כָל־יִשְׂרָאֵל הַפְּלִשְׁתִּים — *So all the Israelites would have to go down to the Philistines.*

Literally, this phrase reads, *There went down all Israel, the Philistines.*

Targum renders הַפְּלִשְׁתִּים as *to the Land of the Philistines.*

However, *Kli Yakar* objects to this on two grounds: first, the phrase lacks the prefix ל, *to;* and second, the ה prefix, *the,* in הַפְּלִשְׁתִּים is superfluous. *Kli Yakar* therefore reads the phrase as *all the Philistine Israelites went down.* That is to say, the Israelites who lived along the Philistine border were known as "Philistine Israelites," and they would go to the Philistines to sharpen their tools, unlike other Jews, who sharpened their own tools (as described in the following verse).

מַחֲרַשְׁתּוֹ — *His plowshare.*

The *plowshare* is the iron blade used in plowing.

Targum, however, renders מַחֲרַשְׁתּוֹ as a *goad,* which drives the cattle drawing the plow.

אֵתוֹ — *His spade.*

Our translation follows *Radak,* who states that an אֵת is used in digging. Other interpreters render אֵתוֹ as a *peg* that attaches oxen to each other and to the yoke (*Targum*), a *coulter* (*Rashi*) (an iron peg that functions in the plowing process — see *Bava Metzia* 80a, *Rashi* ad loc.), or a *pruning knife* (*Shitah Mekubetzes, Bava Metzia* ibid.).

קַרְדֻּמּוֹ — *His axe.*

Radak cites an opinion that the קַרְדּוֹם is a set of *tongs.*

A mishnah (*Avos* 4:7) associates קַרְדּוֹם with digging rather than wood-chopping; accordingly, it would be translated as a *spade.*

מַחֲרֵשָׁתוֹ — *His hoe.*

The root of this word, חוֹרֵשׁ, shows an association with plowing.

Radak (based on *Targum*) explains it

"Lest the Hebrews produce a sword or spear."
[20](So all the Israelites would have to go down to
the Philistines, each man to sharpen his plowshare
and his spade, his axe and his hoe. [21]*There was*
a multi-grooved file that was used to [sharpen]
hoes, spades, three-pronged pitchforks, and
axes, and for setting the peg of an ox-goad.)
[22]*Thus it was on the day of war that there was*
not to be found sword or spear in the posses-
sion of any of the people who were with Saul
and Jonathan; but they could be found with Saul

to be a tool that creates furrows in the ground.

Other commentators (*Radak* among them) also relate מַחֲרַשְׁתּוֹ to the word חָרָשׁ, *blacksmith*, of the previous verse, and interpret it as a tool used in carving wood or stone.

21. וְהָיְתָה הַפְּצִירָה פִים לַמַּחֲרֵשֹׁת — *There was a multi-grooved file that was used to [sharpen] hoes.*

Those who did not wish to make their way to the Philistines would use this file to sharpen their tools (*Rashi*).

According to *Abarbanel*, they did not use the file as a sharpener but transformed it into the above-listed agricultural tools.

וְהָיְתָה הַפְּצִירָה פִּים — *There was a multi-grooved file.*

The word פְּצִירָה means *much* or *many*, as in וַיִּפְצַר־בָּם מְאֹד, *[Lot] urged [the angels] very much* (*Genesis* 19:3), and פִּים is derived from פֶּה, *mouth*, Hence, פְּצִירָה פִּים is an object with many "mouths" — i.e., grooves.(*Radak*).

וְלִשְׁלֹשׁ קִלְּשׁוֹן — *Three-pronged pitchforks.*

According to *Radak*, this tool was used to move hay or fertilizer.

According to *Targum*, this was a tool used by launderers to spread out freshly laundered clothing (*Radak*).

וּלְהַקַּרְדֻּמִּים — *And axes.*

The formation of this word is slightly unusual. Generally, when the prefix לְ, בְּ, or כְּ is combined with a definite article (which would carry a ה), the prefix substitutes for the ה; hence, we would have expected וְלַקַּרְדֻּמִּים (*Radak*).

וּלְהַצִּיב הַדָּרְבָן — *And for setting the peg of an ox-goad.*

The goad had to be filed so that it could be inserted into the wooden handle (*Rashi*). This item was not mentioned in the previous verse, presumably because it was relatively easier to sharpen with the file and did not necessitate a trip to Philistine territory.

According to *Targum*, this is identical with the *goad* mentioned in the previous verse.

22. וְהָיָה בְּיוֹם מִלְחֶמֶת — *Thus it was on the day of war.*

The choice of the word וְהָיָה rather than וַיְהִי for *thus it was* implies that this situation was ongoing — whenever the Israelites had to engage in warfare, they lacked iron weapons.

וַתִּמָּצֵא לְשָׁאוּל — *But they could be found with Saul.*

The Sages disagree as to how Saul received this weapon. Some say that it was brought to him by an angel, and others that it was brought to him by Hashem Himself. At any rate, he possessed them through supernatural means (*Rashi*).

כג וּלְיוֹנָתָן בְּנוֹ: וַיֵּצֵא מַצַּב פְּלִשְׁתִּים אֶל־מַעֲבַר
א מִכְמָשׁ: וַיְהִי הַיּוֹם
וַיֹּאמֶר יוֹנָתָן בֶּן־שָׁאוּל אֶל־הַנַּעַר נֹשֵׂא כֵלָיו לְכָה
וְנַעְבְּרָה אֶל־מַצַּב פְּלִשְׁתִּים אֲשֶׁר מֵעֵבֶר הַלָּז
ב וּלְאָבִיו לֹא הִגִּיד: וְשָׁאוּל יוֹשֵׁב בִּקְצֵה הַגִּבְעָה

The next chapter (verse 34) describes how Saul demonstrated some of the rules of animal slaughtering to his troops. Specifically, the Midrash explains, he showed them the appropriate length of the slaughtering blade. God rewarded Saul by providing him with a blade with which to do battle (*Bamidbar Rabbah* 10:1).

When David eulogized Saul and Jonathan, he said, אֵיךְ נָפְלוּ גִבּוֹרִים וַיֹּאבְדוּ כְּלֵי מִלְחָמָה, *How have the mighty fallen and the weapons of war gone to waste!* (*II Samuel* 1:27). David bemoaned the loss of their weapons, for they had been miraculously furnished (*Me'am Loez*).

וַתִּמָּצֵא — *But they could be found.*

Literally, *it could be found.* According to *Kli Yakar,* there was only one weapon available, which Saul and Jonathan shared.

23. מַצַּב פְּלִשְׁתִּים — *A Philistine garrison.*

Our translation follows *Rashi,* who describes a מַצַּב as a group of soldiers stationed for protection against enemy attack. Thus, the word may be related to נִצָּב, *standing.*

Abarbanel, based on *Targum,* translates מַצַּב as נְצִיב, an *army officer.*

Radak renders מַצַּב as does *Abarbanel,* but reads the word as a collective noun, referring to a group of officers.

אֶל־מַעֲבַר מִכְמָשׁ — *Toward the Michmas pass.*

Michmas and Geba were located on the peaks of two opposite mountains. The Philistines were stationed on Michmas, and Saul and his troops on Geba. The Philistine garrison, possibly sensing Saul's weakness due to his meager numbers and deficient weaponry, went on the offensive and approached the valley — the *pass* — in the direction of Geba (*Rashi*).

XIV

כִּי־בְךָ אָרֻץ גְּדוּד, וּבֵאלֹהַי אֲדַלֶּג־שׁוּר, *For with You, I smash a troop, and with my God, I leap over a wall* (*Psalms* 18:30).

In this verse, King David describes the attitude that a Jewish monarch must adapt when he enters into battle. By placing his trust solely in God, he may hope to overcome any obstacle and prevail even over the bleakest conditions.

In this chapter, which records the military exploits of two of Israel's greatest warriors, Saul and Jonathan, we are shown how each step in a battle must proceed: every action must obey Hashem's command, and the credit for victory must be attributed to Him alone. In addition, a Jewish commander must detect and rectify any shortcomings among his troops, just as weapons are inspected prior to embarking onto the battlefield — for when the army conforms to Hashem's expectations, it may reasonably expect to attain victory.

◈ Jonathan's Bold Advance

1. וַיְהִי הַיּוֹם — *It happened one day.*

According to *Malbim,* this is a reference to the specific day discussed in the previous verse — that upon which the Philistine garrison set forth.

יוֹנָתָן בֶּן־שָׁאוּל — *Jonathan son of Saul.*

The relationship between Jonathan

13/23 *and his son Jonathan.* [23] *A Philistine garrison went forth toward the Michmas Pass.*

14/1-2 [1] ***I****t happened one day that Jonathan son of Saul said to the attendant who bore his armor, "Come, let us cross over to the Philistine garrison that is on that side," but he did not tell his father.*

[2] *Saul was staying at the outskirts of Gibeah,*

and his father is noted here again, in order to indicate that Jonathan was a loyal and trustworthy son, although in this instance he acted without his father's consent (*Daas Sofrim*).

הַנַּעַר נֹשֵׂא כֵלָיו — *The attendant who bore his armor.*

Young, up-and-coming warriors were commonly enlisted to serve as armor-bearers. For instance, David was appointed Saul's armor-bearer (below, 16:21) and Joab's armor-bearers were among David's heroic warriors (*II Samuel* 23:37; *Daas Sofrim*).

לְכָה וְנַעְבְּרָה אֶל־מַצַּב פְּלִשְׁתִּים — *Come, let us cross over to the Philistine garrison.*

Kli Yakar suggests that in stating *Let us cross*, Jonathan equated his status with that of his attendant and in so doing emulated his father Saul's modest behavior (Chapter 9, vs. 5-10, see comm. ad loc.). This also explains why Jonathan is here called *son of Saul*.

Jonathan was clearly exposing himself to peril. Perhaps he felt the need to do so because his previous action — the assassination of a Philistine governor — had elicited the Philistines' military mobilization (above, 13:3; *Chomas Anach*).

וְנַעְבְּרָה — *Let us cross over.*

At the moment, the Jews were encamped on the south side of Geva. Since Michmas, where the Philistines were stationed, was north of Geva (v. 5), Jonathan merely intended to move to Geva's northern side so as to directly face the Philistine garrison (*Malbim*).

מֵעֵבֶר הַלָּז — *On that side.*

The word הַלָּז, *that*, more so than the more common הַזֶּה, *this*, denotes something directly opposite the speaker that he can point to.

According to *Rashi*, Jonathan was expressing a wish to cross the gorge separating the two mountains.

וּלְאָבִיו לֹא הִגִּיד — *But he did not tell his father.*

Jonathan did not think it necessary to inform his father because he did not plan to advance into the Philistine camp, but was making a relatively insignificant move (*Malbim*).

Alternatively, so thoroughly did Jonathan trust in Hashem's salvation that he saw no reason to confide in anyone. Thus he also refrained from seeking the counsel of the *Urim VeTumim* (see above, 1:13 with comm.) and from asking other soldiers to come to his assistance if necessary (*Me'am Loez*).

Daas Sofrim compares Jonathan's actions to those of a prophet whose word, as Jeremiah says, *is like a burning fire in [his] heart, stored in [his] bones — which, though [he] might struggle to contain, [he] cannot* (*Jeremiah* 20:9). Jonathan sensed that he would be successful in this battle, which he saw as being Divinely orchestrated. As such, he did not divulge his plans to Saul, knowing that Saul would raise objections.

2. וְשָׁאוּל יוֹשֵׁב בִּקְצֵה הַגִּבְעָה — *Saul was staying at the outskirts of Gibeah.*

Because Saul had only 600 men with

תַּ֚חַת הָֽרִמּ֔וֹן אֲשֶׁ֖ר בְּמִגְר֑וֹן וְהָעָם֙ אֲשֶׁ֣ר עִמּ֔וֹ
ג כְּשֵׁ֥שׁ מֵא֖וֹת אִֽישׁ׃ וַאֲחִיָּ֣ה בֶן־אֲחִט֡וּב אֲ֠חִי
אִיכָב֨וֹד ׀ בֶּן־פִּֽינְחָ֜ס בֶּן־עֵלִ֨י כֹּהֵ֧ן יְהוָ֛ה בְּשִׁלֹ֖ה
ד נֹשֵׂ֣א אֵפ֑וֹד וְהָעָם֙ לֹ֣א יָדַ֔ע כִּ֥י הָלַ֖ךְ יוֹנָתָֽן׃ וּבֵ֨ין
הַֽמַּעְבְּר֜וֹת אֲשֶׁ֨ר בִּקֵּ֤שׁ יֽוֹנָתָן֙ לַעֲבֹר֙ עַל־מַצַּ֣ב
פְּלִשְׁתִּ֔ים שֵֽׁן־הַסֶּ֤לַע מֵהָעֵ֙בֶר֙ מִזֶּ֔ה וְשֵֽׁן־הַסֶּ֥לַע
מֵהָעֵ֖בֶר מִזֶּ֑ה וְשֵׁ֤ם הָֽאֶחָד֙ בּוֹצֵ֔ץ וְשֵׁ֥ם הָאֶחָ֖ד סֶֽנֶּה׃

him, he was apprehensive about approaching the Philistines, and thus camped on the southern side of Gibeah, at Migron (*Malbim*).

According to *Abarbanel*, Saul was situated at one end of Gibeah and Jonathan at the other; that is why Saul was unaware of Jonathan's actions.

תַּחַת הָרִמּוֹן — *Under the pomegranate tree.*

This phrase, reminiscent of the phrase, אִישׁ תַּחַת גַּפְנוֹ וְתַחַת תְּאֵנָתוֹ, *Each man under his grapevine and under his fig tree* (*I Kings* 5:5), connotes a sense of tranquil trust in Hashem (*Kli Yakar*).

כְּשֵׁשׁ מֵאוֹת אִישׁ — *About six hundred men.*

This is the same amount mentioned above (13:15). Although the Philistines were preparing for battle, no additional Jewish soldiers joined Saul (*Radak*).

3. וַאֲחִיָּה בֶן־אֲחִטוּב אֲחִי אִיכָבוֹד — *And Ahijah son of Ichabod's brother Ahitub.*

Ahitub, father of Ahijah, was another son of Phinehas, presumably older than Ichabod, as the latter was born after his father's death (above, 4:17,19,21). Still, Ahitub is referred to as Ichabod's brother because until this point, Ichabod is the only son of Phinehas with whom we are familiar (*Radak*). *Radak* suggests an alternative explanation for the mention of Ichabod here. He had been given his name — which means *lack of honor* — after the Jews' accumulated sins led to their devastating defeat at the hands of the Philistines, with the concomitant capture of the Ark. Scripture mentions him here to contrast between that defeat and the present moment, in which a righteous man was Kohen Gadol and the Israelites were about to win a miraculous, unexpected victory.

וַאֲחִיָּה בֶן־אֲחִטוּב אֲחִי אִיכָבוֹד בֶּן־פִּינְחָס — *And Ahijah — son of Ichabod's brother Ahitub, son of Phinehas.*

Ahijah was a righteous man. The fact that Scripture records his genealogy until his grandfather Phinehas indicates that Phinehas himself must have been an upstanding Jew. Had that not been the case, he would have been subject to the imprecation, יַכְרֵת ה׳ לָאִישׁ אֲשֶׁר יַעֲשֶׂנָּה עֵר וְעֹנֶה מֵאָהֳלֵי יַעֲקֹב וּמַגִּישׁ מִנְחָה לַה׳, *May* Hashem *eliminate from the man who [sins] any child and descendant from the tents of Jacob, and anyone who might present an offering to* Hashem (*Malachi* 2:12). Therefore, the sins ascribed to Phinehas (2:22) cannot be understood literally (*Shabbos* 55b).

בֶּן־עֵלִי — *Son of Eli.*

The fact that Ahijah's ancestry is traced back to Eli, who is known to have been noble and righteous, shows that Ahijah shared those traits (*Daas Sofrim*).

כֹּהֵן ה׳ בְּשִׁלֹה — *The Kohen of* Hashem *at Shiloh.*

These words refer to Eli. Ahijah could not have served at Shiloh, since it was destroyed at the time of Eli's death (see comm. above, 4:18).

נֹשֵׂא אֵפוֹד — *Who wore the Ephod.*

This garment, worn exclusively by the

under the pomegranate tree that is in Migron, along
with the people who were with him, about six hun-
dred men, 3 *and Ahijah, son of Ichabod's brother Ahi-*
tub, son of Phinehas, son of Eli the Kohen of HASHEM
at Shiloh, who wore the Ephod. The people did not
know that Jonathan had gone.
4 *Between the passes that Jonathan wanted to cross*
to the Philistine garrison there was a rocky precipice
on one side and a rocky precipice on the other side;
one was named Bozez and the other was named Seneh.

Kohen Gadol (cf. *Exodus* 28),[1] was attached to the breastplate containing the *Urim VeTumim*, via which Hashem's word was solicited (see *Exodus* ibid. v. 30; *Ralbag*).

According to *Malbim*'s view that Jonathan attacked the Philistines on the spur of the moment, had he planned this offensive he would have now consulted with the *Urim VeTumim*.

Ahijah is introduced here to foreshadow Saul's subsequent consultation with the *Urim VeTumim* following that attack (v. 18; *Abarbanel*).

וְהָעָם לֹא יָדַע כִּי הָלַךְ יוֹנָתָן — *The people did not know that Jonathan had gone.*

This includes Jonathan's men — had they known, they would have joined him (*Radak*).

4. וּבֵין הַמַּעְבְּרוֹת — *Between the passes.*

Targum renders מַעְבְּרוֹת as the plural of מַעֲבַר (*pass*, as in Michmas *Pass* [13:23]). Although in some ways more dangerous than that principal passageway, these unfrequented pathways possessed the advantage of being relatively inconspicuous (*Malbim*).

Rashi, on the other hand, identifies מַעְבְּרוֹת as the plural of the word עֵבֶר, *side*, which appears later in the verse. Thus, בֵּין הַמַּעְבְּרוֹת, *between the passes*, refers to the two *sides* of the gorge, each of which had a rock precipice, as we will see.

עַל־מַצַּב פְּלִשְׁתִּים — *To the Philistine garrison.*

Literally, the phrase states *upon the Philistine garrison*, connoting Jonathan's aspiration to assail the Philistines (*Daas Sofrim*).

שֵׁן־הַסֶּלַע מֵהָעֵבֶר מִזֶּה וְשֵׁן־הַסֶּלַע מֵהָעֵבֶר מִזֶּה — *There was a rocky precipice on one side and a rocky precipice on the other side.*

In order for Jonathan to reach the other side of the valley, he had to descend a cliff on the south and then scale a cliff on the north on his hands and feet (as described further on, v. 13), with prodigious bravery (*Abarbanel*).

שֵׁן־הַסֶּלַע — *A rocky precipice.*

A שֵׁן, literally *a tooth*, is a stone jutting out of the mountainside (see above, 7:12).

מֵהָעֵבֶר מִזֶּה...מֵהָעֵבֶר מִזֶּה — *On one side... on the other side.*

The Hebrew idiom — literally, *on this side ... on this side* — describes the viewpoints of an observer on each side (*R' Mendel Geldwerth*).

וְשֵׁם הָאֶחָד בּוֹצֵץ וְשֵׁם הָאֶחָד סֶנֶּה — *One was named Bozez and one was named Seneh.*

The fact that these precipices had names indicates that they were unusually tall peaks (*Malbim*).

1. The fact that Ahijah was Kohen Gadol shows that God's curse against Eli's offspring attaining that position (above, 2:30) had not yet taken effect.

ה הַשֵּׁן הָאֶחָד מָצוּק מִצָּפוֹן מוּל מִכְמָשׂ וְהָאֶחָד
ו מִנֶּגֶב מוּל גָּבַע: וַיֹּאמֶר יְהוֹנָתָן אֶל־הַנַּעַר ׀
נֹשֵׂא כֵלָיו לְכָה וְנַעְבְּרָה אֶל־מַצַּב הָעֲרֵלִים
הָאֵלֶּה אוּלַי יַעֲשֶׂה יהוה לָנוּ כִּי אֵין לַיהוה
ז מַעְצוֹר לְהוֹשִׁיעַ בְּרַב אוֹ בִמְעָט: וַיֹּאמֶר לוֹ נֹשֵׂא
כֵלָיו עֲשֵׂה כָּל־אֲשֶׁר בִּלְבָבֶךָ נְטֵה לָךְ הִנְנִי עִמְּךָ
ח כִּלְבָבֶךָ: וַיֹּאמֶר יְהוֹנָתָן הִנֵּה אֲנַחְנוּ

שֵׁם הָאֶחָד... וְשֵׁם הָאֶחָד — *One was named... and one was named.*

When listing two items, Scripture sometimes refers to the second as הַשֵּׁנִי, *the second* (as in *Numbers* 11:26, 28:4), and sometimes as הָאֶחָד, *one* (as here and as in *Exodus* 18:4; *Ibn Ezra* to *Exodus* ibid.)

בּוֹצֵץ — *Bozez.*

Targum renders this as *slippery spot.*

סֶנֶּה — *Seneh.*

Following the *Targum*, this name implies *a trodden area.*

5. This verse can be understood in two ways, both interpretations portraying the same reality.

According to the first explanation, one precipice rose on the northern side of the valley and extended northward toward Michmas, and the other precipice rose on the southern side of the valley and extended southward toward Geba (*Rashi*).

Alternatively, one precipice jutted out from the southern mountain toward the north and the other emerged from the northern mountain of Michmas. *Malbim* seems to understand the verse in this latter fashion.

מָצוּק — *Jutted out.*

Literally, מָצוּק means *rising on a steep incline* (*Rashi*). Similarly, in Mishnaic Hebrew a צוק is a high-sloped peak (see *Bava Metzia* 36b, 93b, and *Rashi* ad loc.).

Targum, however, renders מָצוּק as *visible.*

6. וַיֹּאמֶר יְהוֹנָתָן אֶל־הַנַּעַר נֹשֵׂא כֵלָיו לְכָה וְנַעְבְּרָה — *Jonathan said to the attendant, his armor-bearer, "Come, let us cross over."*

This verse repeats Jonathan's words to his attendant recorded earlier (14:1). After having interrupted the narrative to describe the topography of the area, Scripture marks its return to the story by repeating Jonathan's words (*Metzudos*).

Abarbanel, however, disagrees and states that Jonathan repeated himself — possibly because his attendant had failed to respond, a failure that Jonathan ascribed to apprehension, and which he countered by reiterating his words and adding an expression of trust in Hashem.

According to *Malbim* (above), only now did Jonathan make the decision to advance upon the Philistines.

Kli Yakar points out that originally when Jonathan proposed crossing over, he spoke only of פְּלִשְׁתִּים אֲשֶׁר מֵעֵבֶר הַלָּז *Philistines who are on the other side*, who were not yet visible to him. At that time, he planned only to spy on their position. Now that he had advanced and was able to see them — as indicated by his words הָעֲרֵלִים הָאֵלֶּה, *these uncircumcised ones* — he decided to move forward.

וַיֹּאמֶר יְהוֹנָתָן — *Jonathan said.*

From the time that Jonathan is introduced (in Chapter 13) until Chapter 18, his name is spelled without a ה — with two exceptions, this being one (*Radak* above, 13:3). The ה is added here so as

5 One precipice jutted out on the north, facing Mich-
mas, and the other was on the south, facing Geba.
6 Jonathan said to the attendant, his armor-
bearer, "Come, let us cross over to the garrison of
these uncircumcised ones. Perhaps HASHEM *will act*
on our behalf, for nothing prevents HASHEM *from*
saving, whether through many or through few."
7 His armor-bearer said to him, "Do whatever you
desire. Choose your direction; I am with you as
you desire." 8 Jonathan said, "Behold! — we are

to combine with the י in order to connote Hashem's Name. This reflects the fact that Jonathan's God-inspired bravery and spirit evoked his subsequent remarkable success in battle (*Daas Sofrim*).

אֶל־מַצַּב הָעֲרֵלִים הָאֵלֶּה — *To the garrison of these uncircumcised ones.*

In order to arouse his attendant's trust in God, Jonathan emphasized the contrast between the uncircumcised Philistine idolaters and themselves, guardians of the Divine covenant, whose loyalty to God should evoke His favor so that יַעֲשֶׂה ה׳ לָנוּ, *HASHEM will act on our behalf* (*Abarbanel*).

אוּלַי יַעֲשֶׂה ה׳ לָנוּ — *Perhaps HASHEM will act on our behalf.*

This phrase — literally, *do for us* — is fragmentary. *Targum* explicates, *Perhaps HASHEM will perform [a miracle] on our behalf.*

כִּי אֵין לַה׳ מַעְצוֹר לְהוֹשִׁיעַ בְּרַב אוֹ בִמְעָט — *For nothing prevents HASHEM from saving, whether through many or through few.*

☙ Relying on a Miracle

It is axiomatic that although Hashem is in control of all events, He generally allows them to proceed in accordance with natural law (see *Ramban, Genesis* 6:14). It is therefore incumbent upon man to act within the framework of that law with a cognizance of the fact that Hashem *could* bring about the results with or without his contribution (*Chovos HaLevavos, Shaar HaBitachon* Ch. 3). Yet Jonathan's words indicate that he was relying on a miracle.

Daas Sofrim conjectures that Jonathan was prophetically aware that he would succeed.

Alternatively, Jonathan calculated that there was no natural way whereby his father's army, severely limited in numbers and weaponry, could withstand the mighty war machine of the Philistines. Accordingly, the Jews' only chance lay in God's miraculous intervention. And once they required a miracle, Jonathan reasoned, it would make no difference whether it were performed בְּרַב, *through many*, i.e., six hundred soldiers, or בִמְעָט, *through few*, the two of them (*Kli Yakar*).

7. נֹשֵׂא כֵלָיו — *Armor-bearer.*

Until this point, Scripture referred to the armor-bearer as נַעַר, literally, *lad*. Here, when he demonstrated courage, that deprecating epithet is abandoned and he is called simply נֹשֵׂא כֵלָיו, *the armor-bearer* (*Daas Sofrim*).

עֲשֵׂה כָּל־אֲשֶׁר בִּלְבָבֶךָ — *Do whatever you desire.*

The armor-bearer sensed that Jonathan would not have embarked upon such a risky venture were he not Divinely inspired. Literally, this phrase reads, *Do whatever is in your heart*, for the heart perceives a deeper reality that

ט עִבְרִים אֶל־הָאֲנָשִׁים וְנִגְלִינוּ אֲלֵיהֶם: אִם־כֹּה
יֹאמְרוּ אֵלֵינוּ דֹּמּוּ עַד־הַגִּיעֵנוּ אֲלֵיכֶם וְעָמַדְנוּ
י תַחְתֵּינוּ וְלֹא נַעֲלֶה אֲלֵיהֶם: וְאִם־כֹּה יֹאמְרוּ עֲלוּ
עָלֵינוּ וְעָלִינוּ כִּי־נְתָנָם יהוה בְּיָדֵנוּ וְזֶה־לָּנוּ הָאוֹת:
יא וַיִּגָּלוּ שְׁנֵיהֶם אֶל־מַצַּב פְּלִשְׁתִּים וַיֹּאמְרוּ פְלִשְׁתִּים
הִנֵּה עִבְרִים יֹצְאִים מִן־הַחֹרִים אֲשֶׁר הִתְחַבְּאוּ־שָׁם:

is concealed from the physical eye. The armor-bearer was eager to commit himself, because he realized that a man of Jonathan's spiritual stature could trust the perceptions of his heart.

He did not conclude with the words, לְבָבִי כִּלְבָבֶךָ, *My heart is like your heart,* for he himself did not share Jonathan's vision. Rather, he said, הִנְנִי עִמְּךָ כִּלְבָבֶךָ, *I am prepared to be with you according to the perceptions of your heart* (*Malbim*).

9. וְעָמַדְנוּ תַחְתֵּינוּ וְלֹא נַעֲלֶה אֲלֵיהֶם — *We will stay where we are and not go up to them.*

If the Philistines were prepared to step forward and initiate battle, that would testify to their confidence and show that they were likely to prevail (*Rashi*), particularly because it is usually the pursuer who is victorious (*Ralbag*).

וְעָמַדְנוּ תַחְתֵּינוּ — *We will stay where we are.*

But even if pursued, Jonathan would not retreat, for doing so might endanger Saul (*Daas Sofrim*).

10. וְאִם־כֹּה יֹאמְרוּ עֲלוּ עָלֵינוּ וְעָלִינוּ כִּי־נְתָנָם ה׳ בְּיָדֵנוּ — *But if they say this: "Come up upon us," then we will go up, for* H*ASHEM will have delivered them into our hand.*

Rashi explains that if the Philistines feared leaving their position, that would show that notwithstanding their immense military advantage, they were gripped by a dread of Hashem and were thus likely to be easily defeated.

Abarbanel disagrees with this understanding, however, and describes Jonathan not as making a strategically-based decision but as seeking an omen. If the Philistines responded, עֲלוּ עָלֵינוּ, *Come up upon us,* that would constitute a message from God implying that he and his attendant would rise above and defeat the Philistines.

◆§ Jonathan's Omen From a Legal Perspective

Jonathan's basing his decision on a fabricated omen is seemingly at odds with the Torah prohibition against the practice of divination: לֹא תְנַחֲשׁוּ (*Leviticus* 19:26). Indeed, the Talmud (*Chullin* 95b) cites Jonathan's omen in that context.[1] A person who devises and heeds an omen, *Rambam* legislates, is punishable by lashes (*Hil. Avodas Kochavim* 11:4).

How then could Jonathan have relied on a sign?

Furthermore, *Radak* adds that if Jonathan had acted wrongly, Hashem would not have rewarded him by helping him gain victory.

A variety of solutions to this problem have been proffered, of which we will here cite a few.

❒ According to *Tosafos* (*Chullin* ibid.), Jonathan was not relying on an omen.

1. *Any omen that is not as that of Eliezer, servant of Abraham* (when he chose a wife for Isaac — see *Genesis* 24:12-14), *and, Jonathan son of Saul, is not an omen.*

In referencing this teaching, *Rambam* omits the example of Jonathan. This may be because that example did not appear in *Rambam*'s version of the Talmud, or because he justified Jonathan's actions (see below), and therefore omitted that case (*Kesef Mishneh*).

crossing over to the men, and we will show ourselves
to them. [9] *If they say this to us, 'Halt until we reach*
you!' we will stay where we are and not go up to
them. [10] *But if they say this: 'Come up upon us!'*
then we will go up, for HASHEM *will have delivered*
them into our hand, and that will be our sign!"
[11] *So the two of them showed themselves to the*
Philistine garrison, and the Philistines said, Look!
The Hebrews are emerging from the holes where
they were hiding!"

He had already decided to take action, and he used this sign only as a means of motivating his armor-bearer.

❒ *Chidushei HaRan* states that the Torah only prohibits an omen unrelated to the choice being made — such as saying that if one's bread falls from one's hand, that is a sign of bad luck. If, however, the sign is logically related to the decision, then seeking such a sign is permissible — like someone considering the weather in deciding whether or not to travel. In this case, as *Rashi* explains, the Philistines' reaction would clearly indicate whether they were confident or fearful.

Accordingly, when the Talmud cites this case as an example of using an omen, that is only insofar as the level to which one relies on the sign. Thus, Eliezer and Jonathan's actions were permitted; only if one would completely depend on a non-logical omen to the same degree that they did would he be transgressing God's commandment.

❒ According to *Radak*, omens are prohibited only if they reflect commonly accepted superstitious belief. However, a person is permitted to devise a sign to aid him in making a decision. Thus, the Talmud's citation of Jonathan does not mean to state that his action was impermissible. On the contrary, the Talmud's use of Jonathan's incident is to teach that it is appropriate to rely *only* on an omen that has been clearly stipulated in advance. A disquieting incident that has not been specified in advance only appears like a bad omen, and should be given no credence.

Rama assumes that *Radak*'s interpretation of the verse is coincident with the opinion of *Raavad* [and in opposition to that of *Rambam*], and *Rema* cites these as two valid opinions regarding the use of omens (*Yoreh Deah* 179:4).

❒ *Maharal* (*Gur Aryeh, Genesis* 24:14) maintains that Eliezer and Jonathan would have been sinning if not for the fact that they acted for the sake of a mitzvah: in Eliezer's case, finding a wife for Isaac, and in Jonathan's case, defending and saving the Jewish people.

❒ *Bach* (*Yoreh Deah* 179) assumes that Eliezer and Jonathan were permitted to act as they did because they were motivated by a Divine spirit and trust in Hashem's salvation (Eliezer was acting on behalf of Abraham, and Jonathan on behalf of the Jewish people; see *Daas Sofrim* above).

❒ *Sforno* (*Genesis* ibid.) states that Eliezer and Jonathan's omens did not constitute sorcery but were rather a type of prayer to Hashem.

11. הִנֵּה עִבְרִים יֹצְאִים מִן־הַחֹרִים אֲשֶׁר הִתְחַבְּאוּ־שָׁם — *Look! The Hebrews are emerging from the holes where they were hiding!*

The Philistines erroneously assumed that Jonathan was one of the cowardly

יב וַיַּעֲנוּ אַנְשֵׁי הַמַּצָּבָה אֶת־יוֹנָתָן | וְאֶת־נֹשֵׂא
כֵלָיו וַיֹּאמְרוּ עֲלוּ אֵלֵינוּ וְנוֹדִיעָה אֶתְכֶם
דָּבָר וַיֹּאמֶר יוֹנָתָן אֶל־נֹשֵׂא
כֵלָיו עֲלֵה אַחֲרַי כִּי־נְתָנָם יהוה בְּיַד יִשְׂרָאֵל:
יג וַיַּעַל יוֹנָתָן עַל־יָדָיו וְעַל־רַגְלָיו וְנֹשֵׂא כֵלָיו אַחֲרָיו
וַיִּפְּלוּ לִפְנֵי יוֹנָתָן וְנֹשֵׂא כֵלָיו מְמוֹתֵת אַחֲרָיו:
יד וַתְּהִי הַמַּכָּה הָרִאשֹׁנָה אֲשֶׁר הִכָּה יוֹנָתָן וְנֹשֵׂא
כֵלָיו כְּעֶשְׂרִים אִישׁ כְּבַחֲצִי מַעֲנָה צֶמֶד שָׂדֶה:

soldiers who had initially fled the battlefield and sought refuge in shelters (above 13:6). This magnifies the miracle of the Philistines' fear and defeat, as they didn't realize that they were being challenged by mighty warriors. They thought that Jonathan was among the cowards, yet they reacted with fear (*Malbim*).

12. וַיַּעֲנוּ — *Called out.*

Generally, the word וַיַּעֲנוּ is translated as *they responded*. In the present case, where this word introduces a dialogue, it indicates speech in a raised voice (*Rashi*). Nonetheless, *Targum* renders *and they responded*, apparently considering their words to be a response to Jonathan's bold appearance.

אַנְשֵׁי הַמַּצָּבָה — *The men of the garrison.*

Most commentators understand הַמַּצָּבָה just as מַצַּב פְּלִשְׁתִּים, to the *Philistine garrison* (above, 13:23). *Targum*, however, here renders אַנְשֵׁי הַמַּצָּבָה as *the guards of the camp* (*Radak*).

וַיֹּאמְרוּ עֲלוּ אֵלֵינוּ — *Saying, "Come up to us."*

This response gave Jonathan the confidence that his actions met with the approbation and support of God.

However, the Philistines' response did not fulfill his most optimistic hopes. As *Kli Yakar* observes, Jonathan had spoken of the Philistines saying עֲלוּ עָלֵינוּ, *Come up upon us*. However, they actually said עֲלוּ אֵלֵינוּ, *Come up to us*. Had the Philistines used Jonathan's phraseology, that would have indicated their surrender to Jonathan and his armor-bearer. In that case, indeed, as Jonathan put it (v. 10) כִּי־נְתָנָם ה׳ בְּיָדֵנוּ, *HASHEM [would have] delivered [the Philistines] into our hands*. But the Philistines' actual statement, עֲלוּ אֵלֵינוּ, *Come up to us*, indicated to Jonathan that he would only initiate the victory, which would be completed by the Israelite forces. With this understanding, therefore, he told his armor bearer, עֲלֵה אַחֲרַי כִּי־נְתָנָם ה׳ בְּיַד יִשְׂרָאֵל, *Come up after me, for HASHEM has delivered them into the hand of Israel.*

וְנוֹדִיעָה אֶתְכֶם דָּבָר — *We have something to tell you!*

The Philistines spoke mockingly (*Metzudos*).

Malbim comments that these words were Divinely placed in their mouths and had a deeper meaning of which they themselves were unaware: *"We have an important message to tell you:* that we fear you and if you attack you will gain victory" — a message that Jonathan immediately comprehended and acted upon.

וַיֹּאמֶר יוֹנָתָן — *Jonathan then said...*

Immediately prior to the words וַיֹּאמֶר יוֹנָתָן, *Jonathan then said*, some texts contain an indentation (*Minchas Shai*). This teaches that Jonathan paused in order to thank Hashem for His imminent salvation (*Me'am Loez*).

13. וַיַּעַל יוֹנָתָן עַל־יָדָיו וְעַל־רַגְלָיו — *Jonathan*

14/12-14

[12] *The men of the garrison called out to Jonathan
and his armor-bearer, saying, "Come up to us! We
have something to tell you!" Jonathan then said to
his armor-bearer, "Come up after me, for* HASHEM
has delivered them into the hand of Israel!" [13] *Jonathan then climbed up on his hands and feet, with
his armor-bearer behind him, and [the Philistines]
fell before Jonathan, while his armor-bearer slew
people behind him.* [14] *The first blow that Jonathan
and his armor-bearer dealt [killed] about twenty
men within about [the area of] half a furrow of a
pair [of oxen plowing] in a field.*

then climbed up on his hands and feet.

Jonathan had to use his hands for support because the incline was steep and slippery (*Radak;* see above, v. 4 בּוֹצֵץ).

Mahari Kara explains that Jonathan climbed along the rocks and precipices, using his hands to pull himself up the stones. He chose that more dangerous route because he knew that the Philistines would be expecting him to climb the paths that were less steep and were waiting there for battle.

Rashi, however, interprets עַל־יָדָיו וְעַל־רַגְלָיו, *on his hands and feet,* as a figure of speech that means *quickly and with all his might.*

וְנֹשֵׂא כֵלָיו אַחֲרָיו — *With his armor-bearer behind him.*

Normally a prince's armor-bearer precedes him, so that in case of an attack the prince would have the opportunity to escape. Jonathan relinquished that privilege out of his deep trust in Hashem — and in that merit he prevailed (*Kli Yakar*).

וְנֹשֵׂא כֵלָיו מְמוֹתֵת אַחֲרָיו — *While his armor-bearer slew people behind him.*

Some commentators explain that the armor-bearer dispatched those whom Jonathan had not stricken (*Mahari Kara, Abarbanel*).

Others understand the verse to mean that Jonathan's blows were not enough to kill the Philistines, and so the armor-bearer would deliver the coup de grace (*Metzudos*).

The armor-bearer was armed only with arrows or slingshots (above, 13:22). Either he used these or he killed the Philistines with their own swords (*Daas Sofrim*).

14. כְּעֶשְׂרִים אִישׁ כְּבַחֲצִי מַעֲנָה צֶמֶד שָׂדֶה — *About twenty men within about [the area of] half a furrow of a pair [of oxen plowing] in a field.*

Although the Philistines were crowded together and should have been able to unite and overpower Jonathan, he still managed to kill them (*Rashi*).

In addition, the description of the area in terms of a furrow implies that the Philistines were assembled in an organized row and should have easily been able to strike back, yet in their agitation failed to do so (*Kli Yakar*).

כְּבַחֲצִי מַעֲנָה — *Half a furrow.*

The mishnah (*Oholos* 17:1) states that a standard furrow is 100 cubits. Half a furrow was thus 50 cubits (*Me'am Loez*).

צֶמֶד — *A pair.*

Targum inserts, *of oxen.*

שָׂדֶה — *A field.*

Targum inserts, *in a field.*

טו וַתְּהִי֩ חֲרָדָ֨ה בַמַּחֲנֶ֤ה בַשָּׂדֶה֙ וּבְכָל־הָעָ֔ם הַמַּצָּב֙
וְהַמַּשְׁחִ֔ית חָרְד֖וּ גַּם־הֵ֑מָּה וַתִּרְגַּ֣ז הָאָ֔רֶץ וַתְּהִ֖י
טז לְחֶרְדַּ֥ת אֱלֹהִֽים׃ וַיִּרְא֤וּ הַצֹּפִים֙ לְשָׁא֔וּל בְּגִבְעַ֖ת
יז בִּנְיָמִ֑ן וְהִנֵּ֧ה הֶהָמ֛וֹן נָמ֖וֹג וַיֵּ֥לֶךְ וַהֲלֹֽם׃ וַיֹּ֣אמֶר
שָׁא֗וּל לָעָם֙ אֲשֶׁ֣ר אִתּ֔וֹ פִּקְדוּ־נָ֣א וּרְא֔וּ מִ֖י הָלַ֣ךְ
מֵעִמָּ֑נוּ וַֽיִּפְקְד֔וּ וְהִנֵּ֛ה אֵ֥ין יוֹנָתָ֖ן וְנֹשֵׂ֥א כֵלָֽיו׃
יח וַיֹּ֤אמֶר שָׁאוּל֙ לַאֲחִיָּ֔ה הַגִּ֖ישָׁה אֲר֣וֹן הָאֱלֹהִ֑ים

15. וַתְּהִי חֲרָדָה בַמַּחֲנֶה — *Then a great terror took hold in the camp.*

Assuming that they were under massive attack, the Philistines panicked and began to mistake each other for Jewish soldiers (*Abarbanel*).

הַמַּצָּב וְהַמַּשְׁחִית חָרְדוּ גַּם־הֵמָּה — *The raiding party and the garrison, too, were terrified.*

These were generally brave and well-armed warriors (*Radak, Metzudos*).

וַתִּרְגַּז הָאָרֶץ — *The very ground trembled.*

Most commentators understand this as hyperbole meaning that the soldiers trembled (*Radak, Metzudos*; see *Chullin* 90b for similar instances).

Abarbanel, however, conjectures that these words might be taken literally. In order to arouse terror among the Philistines, God caused the very earth to shake.

וַתְּהִי לְחֶרְדַּת אֱלֹהִים — *And a God-inspired terror took hold.*

Our translation reflects the view of the majority of commentators, who (like *Targum*) understand this fear as having been caused by God. Otherwise, the Philistines would not have been afraid of the poorly-armed, diminutive Israelite army (*Radak*). This assumption is supported by a Midrash (*Bereishis Rabbah* 81:4) that describes this as one of three episodes in which the efforts of a gentile nation to wage war against the Israelites were suppressed by Hashem even before they began.

Daas Sofrim, however, understands this verse as stating that the Philistines feared not the Jews but God.

And *Metzudos* contends that this phrase means simply *a great fear* and that here, as elsewhere, when Scripture wishes to express a superlative it uses the Divine appellation אֵל or אֱלֹהִים (as in וַעֲנָפֶיהָ אַרְזֵי־אֵל, *and its branches became mighty cedars* — literally, *cedars of God* [*Psalms* 80:11]).

☙ Saul Continues the Rout of the Philistines

16. וַיִּרְאוּ הַצֹּפִים לְשָׁאוּל — *Saul's sentries saw.*

This phrase is read as if it said הַצֹּפִים אֲשֶׁר לְשָׁאוּל — *the sentries that were Saul's ...*

וְהִנֵּה הֶהָמוֹן נָמוֹג — *That behold! the multitude [of Philistines] was scattering...*

As long as an army is stable, confident, and unified, it is referred to as a single collective, such as "the camp," or "the nation." However, when confusion and havoc prevail, it is referred to as a disorganized הָמוֹן, a *multitude*, for its unitary nature has been lost (*Malbim*).

Me'am Loez adds that the word הָמוֹן is related to מְהוּמָה, *confusion.*

נָמוֹג — *Scattering.*

Our translation follows *Rashi.*

Targum renders this word as *broken*, and *Mahari Kara*, citing the grammarian *Menachem*, translates it as *dissolved* or *plagued* (see *Exodus* 15:15, נָמֹגוּ; *Rashi*).

וַיֵּלֶךְ וַהֲלֹם — *And approaching them.*

This difficult phrase literally reads,

[15] *Then a great terror took hold in the camp, on*
the field, and among all the people; the raiding
party and the garrison, too, were terrified. The
very ground trembled and a God-inspired terror
took hold.
[16] *Saul's sentries at Gibeath-benjamin saw that,*
behold! the multitude [of Philistines] was scatter-
ing and approaching them. [17] *Saul said to the people*
who were with him, "Check and see who has gone
forth from us." They checked and behold! — Jona-
than and his armor-bearer were not [there]. [18] *Saul*
then said to Ahijah, "Bring near the Ark of God,"

and he went and halom.

Rashi translates *halom* as *here.* The ו following the word וַיֵּלֶךְ, *and he went,* implies a steady movement toward הֲלֹם, *here,* thus forming the phrase *coming close.* This is similar to הָלוֹךְ וְחָסוֹר, *continuously diminishing* (*Genesis* 8:15).

Targum interprets הֲלֹם as *shattered* — as in the verse וְהָלְמָה סִיסְרָא, *and [Jael] shattered Sisera* (*Judges* 5:26). Thus, וַיֵּלֶךְ וַהֲלֹם means *continuously becoming shattered.*

Malbim translates the phrase *he went and he came close.* In their utter confusion, some Philistines ran away from the Israelites and others toward them. This confused the Israelites, who could not determine whether the Philistines were fleeing or attacking.

17. פִּקְדוּ־נָא וּרְאוּ מִי הָלַךְ מֵעִמָּנוּ — *Check and see who has gone forth from us.*

Saul understood that the behavior of the Philistine soldiers had been triggered by an attack upon them, and he investigated to learn who had launched it.

פִּקְדוּ — *Check.*

Alternatively, פִּקְדוּ may be translated as *count,* as in the verse פְּקֹד אֶת־בְּנֵי לֵוִי, *Count the sons of Levi* (*Numbers* 3:15; *Mahari Kara*).

18. הַגִּישָׁה אֲרוֹן הָאֱלֹהִים — *Bring near the Ark of God.*

Saul wished to consult the *Urim VeTumim* — which Ahijah the Kohen Gadol carried in his breastplate — a procedure that was customary before going into battle (see *Berachos* 3b), and he apparently wished to do so in the presence of the Ark, the resting place of God's Presence (*Metzudos*).[1]

According to some commentators, the *Urim VeTumim* were at that time stored in the Ark, and for that reason the Ark had to be brought to Saul (*Ralbag, Radak*).

The *Talmud Yerushalmi* cites a disagreement among the Sages regarding the Holy Ark. One opinion contends that there were two Arks: one that remained in the Sanctuary and one that escorted the Jews to war. Support for this theory is derived from the

1. The Talmud states (*Yoma* 73a) that when the *Urim VeTumim* are consulted, the Kohen Gadol must face the Heavenly presence.

Rashi explains that he faces the *Urim VeTumim,* upon which God's Holy Name is written.

Rambam (*Hil. Klei HaMikdash* 10:11), on the other hand, states that the Kohen Gadol faces the Ark. That understanding may be based on this verse, which implies that the presence of the Ark is essential when making such an inquiry. See *Nachalas Shimon* 31:35.

כִּֽי־הָיָה אֲרוֹן הָאֱלֹהִים בַּיּוֹם הַהוּא וּבְנֵי יִשְׂרָאֵֽל׃
יט וַיְהִי עַד דִּבֶּר שָׁאוּל אֶל־הַכֹּהֵן וְהֶהָמוֹן אֲשֶׁר
בְּמַחֲנֵה פְלִשְׁתִּים וַיֵּלֶךְ הָלוֹךְ וָרָב וַיֹּאמֶר
כ שָׁאוּל אֶל־הַכֹּהֵן אֱסֹף יָדֶךָ׃ וַיִּזָּעֵק שָׁאוּל וְכָל־
הָעָם אֲשֶׁר אִתּוֹ וַיָּבֹאוּ עַד־הַמִּלְחָמָה וְהִנֵּה
הָֽיְתָה חֶרֶב אִישׁ בְּרֵעֵהוּ מְהוּמָה גְּדוֹלָה מְאֹֽד׃
כא וְהָעִבְרִים הָיוּ לַפְּלִשְׁתִּים כְּאֶתְמוֹל שִׁלְשׁוֹם

present verse. Since the Ark of God that had previously been captured by the Philistines (above, Ch. 4) was presently housed in Kiriath-je'arim (above, 7:1), the Ark described in this verse must have been a different one. The opposing opinion states that there was only one Ark; if so, the Ark mentioned in this verse was simply a container in which the Kohen Gadol's vestments were stored (see above, comm. 4:3).[1]

Saul intended to make three inquiries: (1) What was the fate of Jonathan? (2) What were the prospects of war against the Philistines? and (3) Was the confusion in the enemy camp genuine or an artifice designed to lure the Jews into battle? (*Ralbag, Abarbanel*).

כִּי־הָיָה אֲרוֹן הָאֱלֹהִים בַּיּוֹם הַהוּא וּבְנֵי יִשְׂרָאֵל — *For the Ark of God was [there] on that day with the Children of Israel.*

Rashi makes sense of this cryptic statement by inserting the word *there* — thus, *for the Ark of God was [there] on that day.*

Targum renders the ו of וּבְנֵי יִשְׂרָאֵל as *with* — i.e., *with the Children of Israel,* rather than the usual translation *and.*

Kli Yakar adds that the verse states that the Ark was *with the Children of Israel* rather than merely that it was *there,* in order to clarify that although proper reverence for the Ark required that the Jews keep a minimal distance from it, they nevertheless stayed close to it in order to prevent it from being recaptured by the Philistines, as in their previous encounter (Ch. 4).

19. וְהֶהָמוֹן אֲשֶׁר בְּמַחֲנֵה פְלִשְׁתִּים וַיֵּלֶךְ הָלוֹךְ וָרָב — *The multitudes that were in the Philistine camp grew more and more.*

According to *Radak, more and more* means that the Philistine multitudes grew increasingly broken.[2] Since they appeared confused and defeated, Saul felt that there was no longer any need to consult the *Urim VeTumim* — nor, for that matter, any time to do so, as the moment was ripe to strike and secure victory.

Mahari Kara, on the other hand, explains this phrase as meaning *whose multitudes were growing larger and larger* and approaching the Israelites, filling Saul with foreboding and the sense that there was no time to consult the *Urim VeTumim.*

Following the translation (v. 16) of הָמוֹן as *tumult,* this verse reads, *The tumult that was in the Philistine camp increased* (*Radak*).

1. In order to inquire of the *Urim VeTumim,* the Kohen Gadol had to be clothed in his eight special vestments. The question thus arises: How could Ahijah have worn those at the battlefield, since they may be worn only in the Temple (*Yoma* 69a)?

Teshuvos Imrei Yosher answers that the lives of Jonathan and his armor-bearer were presumed to be in danger, and therefore that prohibition was waived. See *Nachalas Shimon* 31:35.

2. *Radak* supports his insertion of the word *broken* from his version of *Targum,* although in our printed texts that word does not appear.

for the Ark of God was [there] on that day with
the Children of Israel. [19] *But as Saul was speak-*
ing to the Kohen, the multitudes that were in the
Philistine camp grew more and more, so Saul told
the Kohen, "Stay your hand!"
[20] *Saul and the entire people with him were*
summoned and came into the battle. And behold!
every [Philistine] man's sword was turned against
his colleague — a very great panic! [21] *And the*
Hebrews who had sided with the Philistines from
yesterday and earlier, who had come up with them

אֱסֹף יָדֶךָ — *Stay your hand.*

אֱסֹף, *stay*, is related to אֲסִיפָה, *gathering*. Hence, Saul told Ahijah, *Stay your hand* and refrain from consulting the *Urim VeTumim.*

But *Targum* renders אֱסֹף יָדֶךָ as *Bring close the Ephod*, which contained the *Urim VeTumim* — apparently, in order to consult them. This is perplexing, for Saul's request to bring the *Urim VeTumim* was already recorded in the previous verse. Also, if Saul did consult the *Urim VeTumim*, why doesn't Scripture tell us its response? A possible explanation is that Saul was telling the Kohen to bring the *ephod* close not in order to consult the *Urim VeTumim* but in order to conceal it in the Ark (*Radak*).

Saul's decision not to consult the *Urim VeTumim* at the advent of battle is listed as one of the five errors that he made that cost him his kingdom and his life (*Midrash Shmuel* 24:7; *Vayikra Rabbah* 26:7). The Sages see a reference to this idea in the verse, וְלֹא־דָרַשׁ בַּה׳ וַיְמִיתֵהוּ — *he did not seek [the counsel of]* HASHEM, *and He killed him* (*I Chronicles* 10:14).

One Midrash seems to imply that not only did Saul fail to consult the *Urim VeTumim*, but he is taken to task also for abandoning it and running away (*Midrash Shocher Tov* 27:2; *Pesikta Rabbasi* Ch. 8).

20. When the Israelites arrived to engage in battle, they discovered that the war was being fought without them (*Abarbanel*).

וַיִּזָּעֵק — *Were summoned.*

Targum renders וַיִּזָּעֵק as *were gathered* — i.e., they were called to come together (*Radak;* see above, 13:4).

וְהִנֵּה הָיְתָה חֶרֶב אִישׁ בְּרֵעֵהוּ — *And behold! every [Philistine] man's sword was turned against his colleague.*

In their panic, the Philistines mistook their fellow soldiers for Jews (*Radak*).

Alternatively, conflicts regarding the proper strategy and a desperation to escape caused the Philistines to turn against one another (*Daas Sofrim*).

21. This verse is interpreted by the commentators in two distinct ways. Our translation represents the more commonly accepted version, which we explain first, followed by the second version, which is advanced by *Ralbag.*

וְהָעִבְרִים הָיוּ לַפְּלִשְׁתִּים — *And the Hebrews who had sided with the Philistines.*

They sided with the Philistines either willingly, out of fear (*Rashi*), or after having been forcibly conscripted into the Philistine army (*Ralbag, Radak*).

Radak states that these were Jews who had made their homes in Philistine territory and were therefore considered Philistine citizens, subject to military service.

אֲשֶׁר עָלוּ עִמָּם בַּמַּחֲנֶה סָבִיב וְגַם־הֵמָּה לִהְיוֹת
כב עִם־יִשְׂרָאֵל אֲשֶׁר עִם־שָׁאוּל וְיוֹנָתָן: וְכֹל אִישׁ
יִשְׂרָאֵל הַמִּתְחַבְּאִים בְּהַר־אֶפְרַיִם שָׁמְעוּ כִּי־נָסוּ
פְלִשְׁתִּים וַיַּדְבְּקוּ גַם־הֵמָּה אַחֲרֵיהֶם בַּמִּלְחָמָה:
כג וַיּוֹשַׁע יהוה בַּיּוֹם הַהוּא אֶת־יִשְׂרָאֵל וְהַמִּלְחָמָה
כד עָבְרָה אֶת־בֵּית אָוֶן: וְאִישׁ־יִשְׂרָאֵל נִגַּשׂ בַּיּוֹם
הַהוּא וַיֹּאֶל שָׁאוּל אֶת־הָעָם לֵאמֹר אָרוּר הָאִישׁ
אֲשֶׁר־יֹאכַל לֶחֶם עַד־הָעֶרֶב וְנִקַּמְתִּי מֵאֹיְבַי

אֲשֶׁר עָלוּ עִמָּם בַּמַּחֲנֶה סָבִיב — *Who had come up with them in the camp all around.*

They had come to the battlefield as part of the Philistine fighting forces.

סָבִיב may be translated as meaning that they remained *on the outskirts* of the camp, in order to avoid entering into conflict with their brethren (*Radak*).

Malbim understands the word סָבִיב to mean that they were not expected to engage in battle — rather, they worked as auxiliary soldiers supplying food and other provisions.

וְגַם־הֵמָּה לִהְיוֹת עִם־יִשְׂרָאֵל אֲשֶׁר עִם־שָׁאוּל וְיוֹנָתָן — *And they, too, [turned] to join the Israelites who were with Saul and Jonathan.*

The word *turned* is supplied by *Targum.*

The words וְגַם־הֵמָּה, *and they too,* seem superfluous; particularly the ו — *and. Ralbag* thus offers an altogether different explanation of the verse. וְהָעִבְרִים, *The Hebrews* who had until now been frightened by the Philistines' overpowering army, הָיוּ לַפְּלִשְׁתִּים כְּאֶתְמוֹל שִׁלְשׁוֹם, *reverted to their prior attitude toward the Philistines* as it had been in the days when Samuel had subjugated the Philistines (see Ch. 7), אֲשֶׁר עָלוּ עִמָּם בַּמַּחֲנֶה סָבִיב, *and now rose against them all around their camp* and smote them, וְגַם־הֵמָּה לִהְיוֹת עִם־יִשְׂרָאֵל — *and in addition even they* — the Philistines — *seemed to be siding with the Israelites,* in that they began killing one another.

22. וַיַּדְבְּקוּ — *Gave chase.*

The word וַיַּדְבְּקוּ is related to דָּבֵק, *attached.* They pursued the Philistines and, as *Radak* translates, *apprehended* them.

According to *Me'am Loez,* וַיַּדְבְּקוּ means that the Jews *attached themselves* single-mindedly to the pursuit of victory. In this regard, *Me'am Loez* cites *Rambam*'s legislation (*Hil. Melachim* 7:15) that a Jewish soldier is expected to completely set aside all his other concerns — even those for his wife and children — in order to dedicate himself completely to fighting.

23. וְהַמִּלְחָמָה עָבְרָה אֶת־בֵּית אָוֶן — *And the battle passed by Beth-aven.*

Targum clarifies this statement to mean that *the [soldiers engaged in] battle passed by Beth-aven* in their pursuit of the Philistines. Apparently, Beth-aven was situated at the border and the battle moved into Philistine territory (*Me'am Loez*).

Malbim, on the other hand, renders this phrase as *the battle was past at Beth-aven* — i.e., it came to an end there. Since the Philistines disbanded, there was no more point in fighting them.

◆§ Saul's Oath — and Jonathan's Transgression

24. וְאִישׁ־יִשְׂרָאֵל נִגַּשׂ בַּיּוֹם הַהוּא — *The people of Israel were hard-pressed on that day.*

in the camp all around, they, too, [turned] to join the
Israelites who were with Saul and Jonathan. [22] *All*
the men of Israel who were hiding in Mount Ephraim
heard that the Philistines were running away,
and they too gave chase after them in the battle.
[23] *So HASHEM saved Israel on that day and the battle*
passed by Beth-aven. [24] *The people of Israel were hard-*
pressed on that day, and Saul adjured the people, say-
ing, "Cursed be the man who shall eat food until the
evening, when I shall be avenged of my enemies."

The people applied pressure to themselves, so eager were they to capitalize on their sudden and miraculous advantage and consummate their victory.

Some commentators, however, explain the pressure on the people as having resulted from Saul's curse and their pangs of hunger (*Radak, Mahari Kara*). Accordingly, the words, וַיֹּאֶל שָׁאוּל אֶת־הָעָם, should be translated as *Saul had already adjured the nation [not to eat]* (*Radak*).

Malbim, according to whom the Israelites had already ceased to fight (v. 23), understands this phrase as the rationalization for their actions. Since the Israelites had no personal motivation to fight, but were in battle only *because they were pressured* by Saul, they were happy to take a break when they saw that victory was inevitable. Accordingly, the verse adds that Saul used the oath to pressure them to complete the task and return to battle.

וַיֹּאֶל שָׁאוּל אֶת־הָעָם — *Saul adjured the people.*

The word וַיֹּאֶל, from אָלָה, *curse* or *oath*, implies a restrictive oath accompanied by the threat of punishment.

The word וַיֹּאֶל can also mean *he desired* (as in *Exodus* 2:21). Saul made this oath freely and not under any compulsion (*Abarbanel*).

See *Radak* above.

אָרוּר הָאִישׁ אֲשֶׁר־יֹאכַל לֶחֶם עַד־הָעֶרֶב — *Cursed be the man who shall eat food until the evening.*

The purpose of this provision was to prevent the Jews from occupying themselves with eating at the expense of pursuing the war; alternatively, it meant to imbue them with the merit of a fast (*Malbim*).

The issue of whether a person in a perilous situation may fast if that might weaken him is discussed in *Nachalas Shimon* 31:37. See below, v. 30.

In v. 27 Scripture calls this adjuration שְׁבוּעָה, an *oath*. Clearly, then, one can proclaim an *oath* using the term אָרוּר (*Shevuos* 36a). In fact, *Ran* cites this verse as *Rambam's* source (*Hil. Shevuos* 2:2-4) that an oath has some validity even without mention of Hashem's Name (see *Kesef Mishneh* ad loc.)

But how could this oath have been binding, since there is no record that the Jews accepted it? This question is particularly germane in regard to Jonathan, who was not even present when it was imposed. Also, since violating an oath is not a capital crime, how is it that Saul considered executing Jonathan (below, v. 44)?

In his essay *Mishpat HaCherem* (published in *Chidushei HaRamban* after Tractate *Gittin*), *Ramban* states that this adjuration was not merely an oath but rather a *cherem*, a *ban*. In this regard, the Torah states, כָּל־חֵרֶם אֲשֶׁר יָחֳרַם מִן־הָאָדָם לֹא יִפָּדֶה מוֹת יוּמָת, *Any condemned person who has been banned*

כה וְלֹא־טָעַם כָּל־הָעָם לָחֶם: וְכָל־הָאָרֶץ בָּאוּ בַיָּעַר
כו וַיְהִי דְבַשׁ עַל־פְּנֵי הַשָּׂדֶה: וַיָּבֹא הָעָם אֶל־הַיַּעַר
וְהִנֵּה הֵלֶךְ דְּבָשׁ וְאֵין־מַשִּׂיג יָדוֹ אֶל־פִּיו כִּי־יָרֵא
כז הָעָם אֶת־הַשְּׁבֻעָה: וְיוֹנָתָן לֹא־שָׁמַע בְּהַשְׁבִּיעַ
אָבִיו אֶת־הָעָם וַיִּשְׁלַח אֶת־קְצֵה הַמַּטֶּה אֲשֶׁר
בְּיָדוֹ וַיִּטְבֹּל אוֹתָהּ בְּיַעְרַת הַדְּבָשׁ וַיָּשֶׁב יָדוֹ אֶל־פִּיו

from mankind shall not be redeemed; he shall be put to death (*Leviticus* 27:29). From this we learn that (a) the king or Sanhedrin have the power to effect such a *cherem* in the presence of the majority of the Jewish people; (b) such a *cherem* is binding on every individual, even without his acceptance of it; and (c) its violation is punishable by death.[1]

אֲשֶׁר־יֹאכַל לֶחֶם — *Who shall eat food.*

Most commentators understand the word לֶחֶם — literally, *bread* — as a reference to food in general, and יֹאכַל, *shall eat*, as including tasting, even if the food is not swallowed.

Kli Yakar, however, suggests that Saul specifically prohibited the swallowing of bread (possibly because only preparation for a meal that includes bread distracts one from war — see *Malbim*). However, the Israelites, fearful of transgressing this oath, refrained from even tasting any food.

וְלֹא־טָעַם כָּל־הָעָם לָחֶם — *So the entire people did not taste food.*

Although they were exhausted, the people obeyed Saul's command punctiliously. This shows their obedience to Saul, and thus undercuts his claim in the next chapter that he lacked the power to protest effectively when the people took sheep from Amalek (see 15:9,15,24); had he objected, they would have undoubtedly obeyed (*Me'am Loez*).

25. וְכָל־הָאָרֶץ — *Then all [the people of] the land.*

The obvious insertion — *the people of* — is made by *Targum*.

וַיְהִי דְבַשׁ עַל־פְּנֵי הַשָּׂדֶה — *Where there was honey on the surface of the field.*

Most commentators, *Targum* among them, render יַעַר as *forest* and describe the דְּבַשׁ, *nectar*, as *bee honey*. *Rashi*, however, assumes that the דְּבַשׁ was *cane sugar*.[2] Following *Rashi*'s lead, *Metzudos* translates יַעַר as the *cane* in which the דְּבַשׁ — the *sugar* — grows (see also v. 27).

Rashi himself translates יַעְרַת הַדְּבַשׁ of v. 27 that way. Here, however, he does not explicitly deviate from *Targum's* translation of יַעַר in this verse nor in the next verse (see, however, *Radak*).

According to *Ralbag*, this episode involved honey from beehives, and according to *Radak*, honey from honeycombs.

26. וַיָּבֹא הָעָם — *The people came.*

There is a seeming redundancy. *Me'am Loez* states that *all [the people of] the land* referred to in the previous verse were civilians (who were not obligated to fast) whereas *the people* of this verse refers specifically to the soldiers.

הֵלֶךְ דְּבָשׁ — *An oozing of honey.*

The word הֵלֶךְ, *oozing*, derives from הוֹלֵךְ, *to go* — the fluid flowed freely along the surface of the field (*Radak*).

1. For further elaboration of this topic, as well as a clarification of an oath that does not mention God's Name, see *Nachalas Shimon* 27.

2. The sweet extract of any plant is called דְּבַשׁ — *Rashi* to *Leviticus* 2:11.

14/25-27 *So the entire people did not taste food.* [25] *Then all [the people of] the land came into the forest, where there was honey on the surface of the field.* [26] *The people came to the forest and behold! there was an oozing of honey, but no one put his hand to his mouth, for the people feared the oath.*

[27] *But Jonathan had not heard when his father adjured the people, so he stretched out the edge of the staff that was in his hand, and dipped it into the cane of the sugar; he then brought his hand*

Targum, however, renders הֵלֶךְ as *a row*, similar to a straight road on which one is הוֹלֵךְ, *goes* (*Ralbag*). There was such an abundance of honey that it formed a row. Alternatively, the beehives in which the honey was produced were arranged in rows (*Ralbag*).

Although the honey was abundant and readily available, the Jews refrained from taking even the smallest amount (*Malbim*).

וְאֵין־מַשִּׂיג יָדוֹ אֶל־פִּיו — *But no one put his hand to his mouth.*

No one put his hand to the honey and then to his mouth (*Radak*).

כִּי־יָרֵא הָעָם אֶת־הַשְּׁבֻעָה — *For the people feared the oath.*

They feared not punishment so much as violating an oath; even those who could have eaten without being detected refrained from doing so (*Daas Sofrim*).

27. וְיוֹנָתָן לֹא־שָׁמַע בְּהַשְׁבִּיעַ אָבִיו — *But Jonathan had not heard when his father adjured ....*

Although Jonathan was not present, he was still subject to his father's oath, as is evident from the following verses.

Ralbag suggests that Jonathan should have noticed that his fellow soldiers were abstaining from eating and inquired as to the cause (see also *Ramban, Mishpat HaCherem*).

בְּיַעְרַת הַדְּבָשׁ — *Into the cane of the sugar.*

This is *Rashi*'s interpretation. The contention that יַעַר can be translated as *cane*, which is similar to a reed, is supported by Onkelos' rendering of וַתָּשֶׂם בַּסּוּף, *she placed it among the reeds* (*Exodus* 2:3), as וְשַׁוִּיתָהּ בְּיַעֲרָא. Also, the verse in *Song of Songs* (5:1) אָכַלְתִּי יַעְרִי עִם־דִּבְשִׁי, is translated by *Rashi* as *I ate my cane together with my nectar* (i.e., the sugar that grows inside it).

Rashi's interpretation is shared by *Tosafos* (*Berachos* 36b s.v. ברטובא) and *Rosh* (*Berachos* Ch. 6:6). Many halachic authorities rule that since sugar cane is called יַעַר, sugar should require the blessing recited on fruit. However, this is not the prevalent custom (see *Tur Orach Chaim* 202, *Shulchan Aruch Orach Chaim* 202:15, and commentators).

Targum renders יַעְרַת הַדְּבָשׁ as קִינָא דְדוּבְשָׁא, which is either a *beehive* (קִינָא is cognate to קַן צִפּוֹר, a *bird's nest* — *Mahari Kara*), or *honeycomb* (which is arranged in the form of קָנִים, *reeds* — *Radak*).

The Talmud supports the interpretation of דְּבַשׁ as beehoney and uses this verse as the basis of significant halachic rulings (*Shabbos* 95a, *Bava Basra* 66a, 80b).[1]

1. For an explanation of how *Rashi* deals with this exegesis, see *Yeish Seder LaMishnah*, cited in the Artscroll Edition of Mishnayos *Sheviis* 10:7.

כח °ותראנה עֵינָיו: וַיַּעַן אִישׁ מֵהָעָם וַיֹּאמֶר הַשְׁבֵּעַ
הִשְׁבִּיעַ אָבִיךָ אֶת־הָעָם לֵאמֹר אָרוּר הָאִישׁ אֲשֶׁר־ °וַתָּאֹרְנָה ק׳
כט יֹאכַל לֶחֶם הַיּוֹם וַיָּעַף הָעָם: וַיֹּאמֶר יוֹנָתָן עָכַר
אָבִי אֶת־הָאָרֶץ רְאוּ־נָא כִּי־אֹרוּ עֵינַי כִּי טָעַמְתִּי
ל מְעַט דְּבַשׁ הַזֶּה: אַף כִּי לוּא אָכֹל אָכַל הַיּוֹם הָעָם
מִשְּׁלַל אֹיְבָיו אֲשֶׁר מָצָא כִּי עַתָּה לֹא־רָבְתָה
לא מַכָּה בַּפְּלִשְׁתִּים: וַיַּכּוּ בַּיּוֹם הַהוּא בַּפְּלִשְׁתִּים

וַתָּאֹרְנָה עֵינָיו — *And his eyes lit up.*

The קְרִי, the oral version of this word, וַתָּאֹרְנָה, is related to אוֹר, *light*, whereas the כְּתִיב — the written version — וַתִּרְאֶנָה, derives from רוֹאֶה, *to see*. Both lend themselves to the same interpretation: Jonathan's eyes were blurred and weakened from hunger and exhaustion; when he tasted the honey, however, he was invigorated and his vision restored (*Radak*).

28. וַיַּעַן — *Called out.*

See above, v. 12.

וַיָּעַף הָעָם — *And the people have become weary.*

These words are part of the quote of the soldier. He testified that although they had all grown weary, they had nonetheless remained loyal to the king's oath (*Radak*).

Abarbanel, however, questions how one man could have spoken on behalf of everyone, and instead attributes these words to the narrative.

29. עָכַר אָבִי אֶת־הָאָרֶץ — *My father has distressed the land.*

The word עָכַר is related to מַיִם עֲכוּרִים, *cloudy waters*. By imposing a fast on the soldiers, Jonathan claimed, Saul had confused their minds and made it impossible for them to achieve a maximal victory (*Rashi*).

Kli Yakar comments that Jonathan fully trusted Hashem and attributed all of the war's developments to His Providence. Thus, he did not really think that Saul's decision to impose a fast had limited their potential for success. Had he thought so, he would have expressed himself in far more forceful language.

רְאוּ־נָא כִּי־אֹרוּ עֵינַי — *See now how my eyes lit up.*

Jonathan supported his contention by citing his own experience (*Abarbanel*).

The Talmud states (*Yoma* 83b) that a person suffering from *bulmos*, a dangerous condition caused by extreme hunger that dims one's eyesight, should be fed honey or sweets, which will restore his vision.

The present episode speaks of a somewhat similar disorder, but one not as dire. Had Jonathan been suffering from actual *bulmos*, he would have been exempt from the oath (*Maharsha*).

◆§ Was It Wrong for Jonathan to Dispute His Father's Word?

Generally speaking, a son should not expressly disagree with his father, nor a student challenge the halachic decisions of his mentor (during the lifetimes of the father or mentor). However, this stipulation is waived when the son or disciple possesses clear evidence that serious damage may result from the ruling of his father or mentor. Even then, however, he should first present his superior's reasoning and only then his own.

Thus Jonathan — Saul's son and presumably his student as well — could only dispute his father's position in that manner. This is what is emphasized

to his mouth and his eyes lit up. [28]*Then one of the*
people called out and said, "Your father has adjured
the people saying, 'Cursed be the man who eats
food today,' and the people have become weary."
[29]*Jonathan said, "My father has distressed the*
land. See now how my eyes lit up when I tasted
just a bit of this honey; [30]*surely, if the people had*
eaten today of the spoils of their enemy that they
have acquired, would there not now have been an
even greater blow against the Philistines?"
[31]*The people smote the Philistines on that day,*

here. Jonathan, in disagreeing with his father, clarifies his justification — "see now how my eyes lit up ...". In v. 31, Scripture defends Jonathan with the words וַיָּעַף הָעָם מְאֹד, *the people were very weary,* and under these extenuating circumstances, Jonathan was permitted to openly dispute his father (*Me'am Loez*).

Ralbag, however, faults Jonathan's approach, claiming that he shamed his father unduly.

30. אַף כִּי לוּא אָכֹל אָכַל הַיּוֹם הָעָם — *Surely, if the people had eaten today.*

The word אַף is usually rendered *even* or *also.* However, when it is paired with the word כִּי (אַף כִּי — here translated as *surely*), it introduces a קַל וָחוֹמֶר, a *kal v'chomer* (or *a fortiori*) inference (see *Rashi* to *Ezekiel* 14:21, *Proverbs* 15:11). Thus, Jonathan argued, since a mere taste of honey had sufficed to revive him, then surely if the people had eaten an entire meal they would have been significantly more fit to engage in battle.

However, according to *Kli Yakar* — which states that Jonathan was not blaming Saul for any deficiency in the prosecution of the war — the phrase אַף כִּי is to be translated as *even.* Thus he translates the passage as: עָכַר אָבִי אֶת־הָאָרֶץ, *My father has unduly pained the soldiers* by making them fast... אַף כִּי — *even though* לוּא אָכֹל אָכַל — *if they would have eaten...* לֹא־רָבְתָה מַכָּה בַּפְּלִשְׁתִּים — *there would not have been [any change] in the blow to the Philistines.*

לוּא — *If.*

Generally spelled without an א', this word usually indicates *if only.*

מִשְּׁלַל אֹיְבָיו — *Of the spoils of their enemy.*

Saul's command that the people fast could not have been motivated by a desire to save the time that would have been invested in preparing a meal, since the enemy spoils would have provided the Jews with more than enough readily available food (*Malbim*).

כִּי־עַתָּה לֹא־רָבְתָה מַכָּה בַּפְּלִשְׁתִּים — *Would there not now have been an even greater blow against the Philistines?*

This is a rhetorical question (*Rashi* and *Radak*). The word עַתָּה, *now,* implies, "if that would have been the case..." (as above [13:13], in *Genesis* [31:42, 43:10], and elsewhere).

According to *Abarbanel,* however, these words are not a rhetorical question but a statement: כִּי־עַתָּה, *for now* [that the Israelite troops have not eaten], לֹא־רָבְתָה מַכָּה בַּפְּלִשְׁתִּים, *there was not as much of a blow against the Philistines* [as there would have been if they would have eaten].

According to *Kli Yakar,* this phrase

לב מִמִּכְמָשׂ אַיָּלֹנָה וַיָּעַף הָעָם מְאֹד: °ויעש
הָעָם אֶל-°°שלל וַיִּקְחוּ צֹאן וּבָקָר וּבְנֵי
בָקָר וַיִּשְׁחֲטוּ־אָרְצָה וַיֹּאכַל הָעָם עַל־הַדָּם:
לג וַיַּגִּידוּ לְשָׁאוּל לֵאמֹר הִנֵּה הָעָם חֹטְאִים
לַיהוָה לֶאֱכֹל עַל־הַדָּם וַיֹּאמֶר בְּגַדְתֶּם גֹּלּוּ־
לד אֵלַי הַיּוֹם אֶבֶן גְּדוֹלָה: וַיֹּאמֶר שָׁאוּל פֻּצוּ

°וַיַּעַט ק׳
°°הַשָּׁלָל ק׳

means that even if the Jews had eaten, they would *not* have gained greater success, for battle is in the hands of Hashem — *nothing prevents* HASHEM *from saving...* (above, v. 6).

According to *Malbim* (above), Jonathan was stating that the time spent in eating would have been more than compensated by the renewed strength that it would have given the Jews, and the advantage that would have resulted at the war front.

☙ What Are the Halachic Ramifications of Jonathan's Argument?

Ralbag states that Jonathan's words here are seemingly not in accord with his earlier exclamation that *nothing prevents* HASHEM *from saving...* (above, v. 6), and he deems this latter statement as mistaken.

However (as mentioned above — see comm. above, v. 6), it is this second view that is generally accepted in Jewish practice and perspective — i.e., that a person must acknowledge the natural course of events and act in accordance with them. Thus, *Sefer Chassidim* (618), based on Jonathan's words, teaches that a person engaged in a life and death struggle may not engage in a private fast, lest he grow too weak to prevail. The source for this assertion is apparently a *Tosefta* (*Taanis* 2:11).

The Talmud (*Taanis* 22b), on the other hand, seems to rule that fasting under such circumstances is permitted.

However, there may be no contradiction between the two passages, for the latter statement may be referring to people who are not in danger but who wish to fast on behalf of others (see *Shiltei HaGiborim, Taanis* Ch. 3, *Nachalas Shimon* 31:37).

In conclusion, the *Shulchan Aruch* (*Orach Chaim* 571:3) prohibits fasting when involved in battle with gentiles (although he suggests that [those under attack] should commit themselves to fasting after they are saved). It is noteworthy that *Rambam* (*Hil. Melachim* 8:1) rules that if Jewish soldiers enter gentile territory and are hungry, they may even eat nonkosher food if nothing else is available, which further accentuates the importance of eating while at war.

31. מִמִּכְמָשׂ אַיָּלֹנָה וַיָּעַף הָעָם מְאֹד — *From Michmas to Aijalon; and the people were very weary.*

Michmas was the headquarters of the Philistine army (see above, 13:16).

Targum renders אַיָּלוֹן as *the Plain of Aijalon* (as it does Aijalon Valley in *Joshua* [10:12]). This city was located in the region of Dan (ibid. 19:42), in the western region of the Land of Israel, near the Philistine border (see *II Chronicles* 28:18).

Ralbag states that there was a significant distance between Michmas and Aijalon, and the long pursuit exhausted the soldiers.

Conversely, *Abarbanel* assumes that Aijalon was close to Michmas, yet still the soldiers grew weary; this confirmed Jonathan's contention that it is extremely taxing for soldiers to pursue the enemy without eating.

☙ The Nation's Sin and Saul's Redress

In the following verses, Scripture

from Michmas to Aijalon; and the people were
very weary. 32 *The people swooped down upon the*
spoils, and took sheep, cattle, and young cattle.
They slaughtered them on the ground; and the
people ate with the blood. 33 *They told Saul, saying,*
"Behold! — the people are sinning to HASHEM *by*
eating with the blood!"
He said, "You have transgressed. Roll over to me
a large boulder today." 34 *Saul said, "Spread out*

describes how the people transgressed לֶאֱכֹל עַל־הַדָּם, *eating with the blood* — and how Saul educated them and directed them to act properly

The text lends itself to varying interpretations. We will begin by summarizing the different explanations of the transgression and of how Saul corrected the people with the help of a stone. Then we will show how each of the interpretations is derived from the text.

The most obvious place to seek elucidation regarding the sin of "eating with the blood" is the Torah's prohibition: לֹא תֹאכְלוּ עַל־הַדָּם, *You shall not eat over the blood* (*Leviticus* 19:26). That prohibition is itself subject to many interpretations, both in the Talmud and in the writings of the classical commentators. We will cite only those that lend themselves to understanding the verses here.[1]

❐ Because the verse appears adjacent to the prohibition against belief in heathen omens (v. 10), many commentators (*Ralbag, Ramban* [to *Leviticus* 19:26], *Radak, Rambam* [*Moreh Nevuchim* III:46]) state that it comes to interdict an ancient heathen custom of using blood in order to engage in divination. Specifically, the heathens would slaughter animals and drain their blood into a pool, in the belief that demons would come and drink from the blood. They would then eat the meat with the goal of forming a bond with the demons, so that the latter would inform them of future events. According to this explanation, the words לֹא תֹאכְלוּ עַל־הַדָּם are rendered, *Do not eat over the blood.*

Ramban states that in the present instance the people were so terrified of the Philistines and desperate for a glance into the future that, although Saul would soon consult the *Urim VeTumim,* they sinned by performing this ritual.

Abarbanel, however, refuses to believe that the nation really believed in this superstition. Rather, the people were famished and thus rushed to eat near the pooled blood. Although their intentions were not paganistic, the Torah's prohibition was nonetheless breached.

In response to the troops' behavior — of either actual divination with blood or of engaging in behavior reminiscent of such divination — Saul set up a large stone (v. 33) to serve as a slaughtering area located at a distance from where the troops camped to eat (*Ramban, Abarbanel*).

❐ The Talmud interprets this verse as an interdiction against eating the meat of a slaughtered animal before the final flickers of life have left it (*Sanhedrin* 63a). The word דָּם, *blood,* is often used as a reference to life — thus, עַל־הַדָּם

1. Although *you shall not eat over the blood* would seem to refer to the prohibition against eating blood, there is universal agreement that this is not the case, since that prohibition is stated explicitly elsewhere (*Leviticus* 7:26).

may be rendered, *in the presence of its lifeblood*.[1]

In the present instance, the famished troops disregarded this law (*Rambam* to *Leviticus* ibid. *Radal* to *Vayikra Rabbah* 25:8). Saul thus rectified the situation by having them slaughter the animals on top of a large stone, so that during the delay entailed by bringing the meat down, the last sparks of the animal's life would be extinguished (*Me'am Loez*).

❒ According to another view offered by the Talmud (*Sanhedrin* ibid.), the Torah's prohibition refers specifically to eating the meat of an offering before the blood service has been completed. Thus עַל־הַדָּם means *in the presence of the blood*, i.e., *while the blood is still in the sprinkling utensil.*

In the present instance, states *Rashi* (citing the Sages), the troops were bringing peace-offerings, and in their haste to relieve their hunger pangs ate before the blood service.[2] Thus, Saul made use of a large stone to serve as an altar[3] (private altars were permitted during that period — see above, 6:14) on which to sprinkle the blood.

❒ *Rashi's* interpretation, based on the verse וַיִּקְחוּ צֹאן וּבָקָר וּבְנֵי בָקָר *and [they] took sheep, cattle, and young cattle* (v. 32), is that the people sinned by slaughtering אֹתוֹ וְאֶת־בְּנוֹ בְּיוֹם אֶחָד, *a mother and her offspring on the same day* (*Leviticus* 22:28).

Accordingly, Saul required the troops to bring their animals to the large stone where he himself would inspect them to prevent them from violating that transgression (see *Kli Yakar*).

However, it is difficult to reconcile this explanation with the phrase וַיֹּאכַל הָעָם עַל־הַדָּם, *the people ate with the blood* — since the prohibition of bringing a mother and her offspring has nothing to do with either blood or eating.

❒ According to *Radak*, in their haste to eat, the soldiers failed to elevate the animal during the slaughtering process. Instead, וַיִּשְׁחֲטוּ־אָרְצָה, *they slaughtered while [the animals were] on the ground*, preventing the blood from properly draining, so that it remained absorbed in the meat. Thus, when the people ate the meat, they transgressed the prohibition against consuming blood (*Leviticus* 7:26). Accordingly עַל־הַדָּם means *with the blood* (just as עַל־מְרֹרִים means *with bitter herbs — Exodus* 12:8).

Saul introduced the large stone upon which to elevate the animals during the slaughtering process to allow the blood to properly drain from the body.[4]

❒ On the basis of a Talmudic discussion (*Zevachim* 120a), *Kli Yakar* suggests that the people sinned by slaughtering offerings at night. The reference to blood is reminiscent of the Torah's equation of the similar offense of slaughtering offerings outside of the Tabernacle with bloodshed (*Leviticus* 17:4).

1. This is similar to לֹא־תִשְׁחַט עַל־חָמֵץ דַּם־זִבְחִי, *Do not slaughter my blood-offering while in the possession of leavened food* (*Exodus* 34:25).

2. Although *Rashi* cites a Talmudic or Midrashic text to that effect, that text is seemingly no longer extant.

3. The use of a single stone as a place of worship is the subject of controversy.

Sifrei, cited by *Rashi* (*Deuteronomy* 16:22), cites the verse וְלֹא־תָקִים לְךָ מַצֵּבָה, *And you shall not erect for yourselves a pillar* (ibid.), as prohibiting the worship of Hashem on a one-stone pillar.

In light of Scripture's testimony (below, v. 35) that Saul built an altar, *Pardes Yosef* (*Parashas Vayetzei*) states that he hewed the stone spoken of here into smaller pieces and built an altar with them.

Rashbam (*Deuteronomy* ibid.) and *Rambam* (*Hil. Avodah Zarah* 6:6) interpret the prohibition of מַצֵּבָה differently, avoiding this issue altogether. See *Nachalas Shimon* 28:4.

4. This interpretation finds considerable support in *Vayikra Rabbah* 25:8 (see *Maharzu*; see *Radal* ad loc.).

Saul thus brought the stone to serve as an altar הַיּוֹם, *during the day.*

32. וַיַּעַט הָעָם — *The people swooped down.*

Our translation of the קְרִי, the oral tradition, follows *Rashi*, who relates וַיַּעַט to עַיִט, a *bird of prey* (*Genesis* 15:11). The ravenous soldiers hastily grabbed what food they could, like birds of prey. Since this impugns the dignity of the Jewish soldiers, the word appears in the כתיב, the written text, as וַיַּעַשׂ, *accumulated* (see *Genesis* 31:1, *Rashi* ad loc.; 41:47, *Targum* ad loc.; *Radak*, *Daas Sofrim*).

Targum, alternatively, renders וַיַּעַט as *they turned*, and *Ibn Ezra* (to *Song of Songs* 1:7) translates וַיַּעַט הָעָם אֶל־הַשָּׁלָל as *the nation mixed into the booty.*

וַיִּקְחוּ צֹאן וּבָקָר וּבְנֵי בָקָר — *And took sheep, cattle, and young cattle.*

בְּנֵי בָקָר, literally *offspring of cattle*, generally implies juvenility, as in *Genesis* 18:7. It is similar to בְּנֵי יוֹנָה, *young doves* (*Leviticus* 1:14, *Rashi; Mahari Kara*).

As mentioned in the preface to verses 32-34, *Rashi* derives from this phrase that the people transgressed the prohibition against slaughtering אֹתוֹ וְאֶת־בְּנוֹ בְּיוֹם אֶחָד, *mother and offspring on the same day.*

וַיִּשְׁחֲטוּ־אָרְצָה — *They slaughtered them on the ground.*

Following *Radak* (above), the people failed to elevate the animals, thus preventing the proper drainage of blood.

According to the interpretation cited by *Rashi* that the people ate prior to sprinkling blood, וַיִּשְׁחֲטוּ־אָרְצָה means that *they slaughtered* [an offering] *on the ground* and not in the presence of an altar (*Mahari Kara*).

The other interpretations note no specific significance to the fact that the animals were slaughtered *on the ground.*

וַיֹּאכַל הָעָם עַל־הַדָּם — *And the people ate with the blood.*

See preface above.

All of the commentators agree that the fast imposed by Saul had by this time come to an end.

33. וַיַּגִּידוּ לְשָׁאוּל — *They told Saul.*

It is common for Scripture to use a pronoun without specifying its antecedent (see *Rashi* to *Genesis* 48:2).

בְּגַדְתֶּם — *You have transgressed.*

Transgressed is the reading of *Metzudos*. However, the more common meaning of this word is *betrayal* or *disloyalty.*

According to the interpretations that claim that the Jews' offense involved the misuse of sanctified meat (such as eating offerings before the blood service), it would indeed be appropriate to use בְּגִידָה in the sense of *disloyalty*, which is an apt characterization of the misuse of materials dedicated to the Temple.

That meaning is also consistent with *Ralbag*'s view that the sin involved participation in pagan superstition, for any practice that draws a person away from the Torah constitutes a betrayal of God (*Kli Yakar*).

Ramban (to *Leviticus* 19:26) characterizes the Jews' behavior as a betrayal of God in that they stooped to seek revelations from a lowly, idolatrous source even as God was performing a miraculous salvation and granting them victory.

Daas Sofrim states that the fact that the Jews neglected halachah in any area of their lives after God had performed such supernatural deeds on their behalf was a *betrayal*. Accordingly, any of the interpretations would tolerate that translation.

גֹּלּוּ־אֵלַי הַיּוֹם אֶבֶן גְּדוֹלָה — *Roll over to me a large boulder today.*

Saul wished to stop the people from sinning and to rectify their behavior. The specific function of the boulder, according to the views of the various commentators, was discussed in the Preface.

הַיּוֹם — *Today.*

Radak explains that הַיּוֹם does not necessarily denote daytime but should rather be translated as *at this time* (as

בָעָם וַאֲמַרְתֶּם לָהֶם הַגִּישׁוּ אֵלַי אִישׁ שׁוֹרוֹ
וְאִישׁ שְׂיֵהוּ וּשְׁחַטְתֶּם בָּזֶה וַאֲכַלְתֶּם וְלֹא־
תֶחֶטְאוּ לַיהוָה לֶאֱכֹל אֶל־הַדָּם וַיַּגִּשׁוּ כָל־הָעָם
לה אִישׁ שׁוֹרוֹ בְיָדוֹ הַלַּיְלָה וַיִּשְׁחֲטוּ־שָׁם׃ וַיִּבֶן
שָׁאוּל מִזְבֵּחַ לַיהוָה אֹתוֹ הֵחֵל לִבְנוֹת מִזְבֵּחַ
לו לַיהוָה׃ וַיֹּאמֶר שָׁאוּל נֵרְדָה אַחֲרֵי
פְלִשְׁתִּים לַיְלָה וְנָבֹזָּה בָהֶם | עַד־אוֹר הַבֹּקֶר

in the verse, יוֹם־צָעַקְתִּי בַלַּיְלָה נֶגְדֶּךָ, *at a time* — literally, *day* — *when I cry in the night before you* [*Psalms* 88:2]).

Thus, in the evening,[1] as soon as the fast came to an end, the people began slaughtering animals, and Saul directed them to stop and take instruction from him.

However, the Talmud (*Zevachim* 120a) reads הַיּוֹם literally as *day*, meaning that the animals were slaughtered during the day, and thus sees this as contradicting the following verse, which states that the animals were slaughtered at night.

The Talmud offers several solutions to this contradiction. According to one opinion, all offerings, even on a private altar, must be slaughtered during the day; the animals slaughtered at night were therefore not offerings but unsanctified animals (חוּלִין). The opposing opinion maintains that the present verse is referring specifically to offerings originally dedicated to be brought on the main altar in the Sanctuary at Nob — these must be slaughtered by day. As for offerings on private altars, these may be slaughtered at night as well (provided that they were originally dedicated as private altar offerings).

34. הַגִּישׁוּ אֵלַי אִישׁ שׁוֹרוֹ וְאִישׁ שְׂיֵהוּ וּשְׁחַטְתֶּם בָּזֶה — *Let each man bring to me his ox and each man his sheep, and you shall slaughter [them] here.*

Saul wished to supervise in order to ensure that his troops would not sin (as explained above).

וּשְׁחַטְתֶּם בָּזֶה — *And you shall slaughter [them] here.*

Targum and commentators translate בָּזֶה as *here.*

Literally, however, בָּזֶה means *with this*, or *at this.* The Sages interpret this unusual term as meaning *with this knife*, and from this they draw two halachic conclusions.

First, Saul began by inspecting the slaughtering knife to see if it was halachically fit.[2] The Talmud thus derives that a qualified halachic expert must inspect the knife before an animal is slaughtered (*Chullin* 17b).[3] Second, Saul showed the men that the proper length of a slaughtering knife is 14 fingerbreadths — 14 being the numerical value of בָּזֶה (*Vayikra Rabbah* 25:8).

As mentioned above, since Saul was so meticulous regarding these rules, he was rewarded by being granted miraculous possession of a sword at a time when

1. See the following verse.

2. The word בָּזֶה may be understood to comprise the acrostic of the phrase, בְּסַכִּין זֶה הַבָּדוּק — *with this inspected knife* (*Chomas Anach*).

3. Nowadays, this regulation has been relaxed because only skilled experts who are themselves competent to inspect the knives are employed to engage in slaughtering (*Shulchan Aruch Yoreh Deah* 18:17).

among the people and say to them, 'Let each man
bring to me his ox and each man his sheep, and
you shall slaughter [them] here and eat them, so
that you not sin unto HASHEM by eating with the
blood.' " So each man of the people brought his ox
with him that night, and they slaughtered them
there. 35 *Saul built an altar to HASHEM; [with] this,*
he began to build altars to HASHEM.
36 *Saul said, "Let us go down after the Philistines*
at night and let us plunder them until the morning's

such weapons were banned by the Philistines (above, 13:22; *Vayikra Rabbah* ibid.).

◆§ The Chase Is Curtailed Due to the Absence of Divine Guidance

35. אֹתוֹ הֵחֵל לִבְנוֹת מִזְבֵּחַ לַה׳ — *[With] this, he began to build altars to HASHEM.*

The word אֹתוֹ, *[with] this,* literally means *him* or *this,* the antecedent of that pronoun being unclear.

Rashi and *Radak* understand this pronoun as referring to the new altar that Saul built: this was the first altar that he ever erected, for those that he had used in the past (such as in Gilgal [above, 13:9]), had been previously constructed (*Radak*). (To make this translation clear, we follow *Metzudos* in adding the word *with.*)

Ralbag and *Abarbanel* associate this verse with the large stone of verse 33. Saul meant the boulder to serve as the foundation for an altar. He was unable to build that altar immediately, for he was in the middle of a military offensive against the Philistines. After routing the Philistines that night, he returned and completed the altar as a memento marking the miraculous victory, and to give thanks to Hashem for His kindness. Hence, the verse may be translated אֹתוֹ, *with that stone,* הֵחֵל לִבְנוֹת מִזְבֵּחַ לַה׳, *he began to build an altar to HASHEM.*[1]

The Midrash (*Vayikra Rabbah* 25:5, *Bamidbar Rabbah* 10:1) states that אֹתוֹ refers to Saul, and explains the verse as telling that Saul was the first person to build an altar to Hashem.

But what of the many individuals who built altars prior to Saul, among them Noah, Abraham, Isaac, and Jacob? The Midrash provides two answers. One is that Saul was the first leader to build an altar for the sake of the entire nation. Alternatively, he was so dedicated to the institution of proper animal slaughter (see above, vs. 32-34), which is a prerequisite to bringing offerings, that he is given credit as if he were the first to build an altar to Hashem.

Radak too sees אֹתוֹ as referring to Saul (on the basis of another Midrash), and reads the verse as follows: *[Saul only] began to build an altar to HASHEM;* after he set down the first stone, it was completed by others.

36. וְנָבֹזָּה בָהֶם — *And let us plunder them.*

Our translation represents the conventional translation of נָבֹזָּה, as *Metzudos* renders it. The *Targum* however, translates *let us kill,* which corresponds to the words that follow, וְלֹא־נַשְׁאֵר בָּהֶם אִישׁ, *let us not let any man of them remain.*

1. *Ralbag* states that אֹתוֹ can refer to אֶבֶן even though אֹתוֹ is masculine and אֶבֶן generally is feminine, as such inconsistent pairing appears across *Tanach.* (See *Rashi* to *Genesis* 32:9. Also see *Genesis* 28:22, וְהָאֶבֶן הַזֹּאת, *this stone* [feminine], יִהְיֶה, *will be* [masculine].)

וְלֹא־נַשְׁאֵר בָּהֶם אִישׁ וַיֹּאמְרוּ כָּל־הַטּוֹב בְּעֵינֶיךָ
עֲשֵׂה וַיֹּאמֶר הַכֹּהֵן נִקְרְבָה הֲלֹם אֶל־
לז הָאֱלֹהִים: וַיִּשְׁאַל שָׁאוּל בֵּאלֹהִים הַאֵרֵד אַחֲרֵי
פְלִשְׁתִּים הֲתִתְּנֵם בְּיַד יִשְׂרָאֵל וְלֹא עָנָהוּ בַּיּוֹם
לח הַהוּא: וַיֹּאמֶר שָׁאוּל גֹּשׁוּ הֲלֹם כֹּל פִּנּוֹת הָעָם וּדְעוּ
לט וּרְאוּ בַּמָּה הָיְתָה הַחַטָּאת הַזֹּאת הַיּוֹם: כִּי חַי־יהוה
הַמּוֹשִׁיעַ אֶת־יִשְׂרָאֵל כִּי אִם־יֶשְׁנוֹ בְּיוֹנָתָן בְּנִי

וַיֹּאמֶר הַכֹּהֵן נִקְרְבָה הֲלֹם אֶל־הָאֱלֹהִים — *The Kohen then said, "Let us approach God at this point."*

Ahijah, the Kohen Gadol, who had been prevented from consulting the *Urim VeTumim* at the onset of this battle (above, v. 19), now suggested that Saul seek Divine counsel before proceeding further.

Saul's words, נֵרְדָה אַחֲרֵי פְלִשְׁתִּים לַיְלָה, *Let us go down after the Philistines at night,* imply that the night had arrived. How then could Ahijah have suggested consulting the *Urim VeTumim,* since they may be questioned only during the day (*Baal HaTurim* to *Exodus* 28:15)? Some explain that this was a dire, perhaps even life-threatening, situation, and so consulting the *Urim VeTumim at night* was permitted (see *Nachalas Shimon* 31:38).

However, *Teshuvos She'eilas Shlomo* §4 states that this discussion, including Saul's words נֵרְדָה ... לַיְלָה, *Let us go down ... at night,* may have taken place earlier during the day, as Saul was preparing for the upcoming evening. Thus, immediately after speaking with Ahijah and while it was still day Saul consulted the *Urim VeTumim* (as the following verse states, בַּיּוֹם הַהוּא, *on that day*).

Possibly, after Scripture describes how the troops offered sacrifices at night in v. 34, it goes back here to describe what had happened the previous day (as the Torah is not necessarily written in chronological order).

Alternatively, the conversation with Ahijah and the inquiry of the *Urim VeTumim* took place during the day following those nighttime sacrifices.

נִקְרְבָה הֲלֹם אֶל־הָאֱלֹהִים — *Let us approach God at this point.*

Targum renders this as, *Let us approach [God] at this point and seek God's word.*

37. הַאֵרֵד אַחֲרֵי פְלִשְׁתִּים הֲתִתְּנֵם בְּיַד יִשְׂרָאֵל — *Shall I go down after the Philistines? Will You deliver them into the hand of Israel?*

Saul posed two questions in quick succession, for an answer to the first question alone would not have sufficed, as Saul had doubtless learned from the precedent of the Concubine at Gibeah (*Judges* 20:18). At that time, the Jews had asked only if they should go to war but not if they would be victorious and they were answered in the affirmative, but they then sustained a terrific loss (*Shevuos* 35b).

Yet what of the Talmud's dictum (*Yoma* 73a) that one may pose only one question at a time to the *Urim VeTumim*?

Possibly, Saul felt that the circumstances of the moment allowed for the presentation of two questions (see *Yoma* 73b regarding David).

Alternatively, first Saul posed a question about himself: *Shall I go down*? When there was no response, it occurred to him that he might be answered in the merit of the nation, so he added, הֲתִתְּנֵם בְּיַד יִשְׂרָאֵל, *Will You deliver them into the hand of Israel?* (*Daas Sofrim*).

וְלֹא עָנָהוּ — *But He did not answer him.* *Targum* renders this as *He did not*

light; let us not let any man of them remain."
And [the people] answered, "Whatever is good
in your eyes, do!"
The Kohen then said, "Let us approach God at
this point." 37 *So Saul asked of God: "Shall I go*
down after the Philistines? Will You deliver them
into the hand of Israel?" But He did not answer
him on that day.
38 *Saul said, "Draw near to here, all you*
captains of the people, and find out and see
through whom this sin occurred today. 39 *For*
as H*ASHEM*, *the Savior of Israel, lives, even if*
[the sin] is found to be with my son Jonathan,

accept his prayers.

☙ Investigation and Conviction Via Lots

38. Saul immediately realized that the refusal of the *Urim VeTumim* to answer him must be due to some sin.

כׇּל פִּנּוֹת הָעָם — *All you captains of the people.*

The word פִּנּוֹת literally means *corners.*

An אֶבֶן הַפִּנָּה, *cornerstone,* connotes a significant (*Rashi*) and foundational (*Daas Sofrim*) element; in the present context, a *corner* is to be understood as a significant and foundational member of the troops: i.e., a *captain* or *leader* (*Targum, Rashi, Radak*).

Also, the word פִּנָּה is related to פּוֹנֶה, *to face,* indicating that everyone turned to these people for guidance (*Kli Yakar*).

Abarbanel, hewing more closely to the literal meaning of the word, explains that Saul addressed the troops who stood at all corners of the encampment.

וּדְעוּ וּרְאוּ — *And find out and see.*

This seemingly redundant phrase is used to indicate an attainment of knowledge so tangible that it is tantamount to sensory sight (*R' Mendel Geldwerth*).

Kli Yakar suggests that דְעוּ, *find out,* and רְאוּ, *see,* represent two different phases of the investigation. First, the people must *find out* what crime was committed; second, they must *see* and understand why God responded by refusing to answer Saul. Subsequent investigation showed that Jonathan had failed to listen to the חֵרֶם, *ban,* and as such was subject to the "silent treatment." God's ignoring their inquiry of the *Urim VeTumim* thus provided the appropriate מִדָּה כְּנֶגֶד מִדָּה — just and fit punishment.

הַיּוֹם — *Today.*

The miraculous victories of the preceding days showed that Hashem had then looked favorably upon the Jews; thus, Saul understood that God's silence must indicate that a sin had been recently committed (*Abarbanel*).

39. חַי־ה׳ — *For as* H*ASHEM* *lives.*

This formula is a type of binding oath (one that Hashem Himself used at the episode of the sin of the spies — *Numbers* 14:21).

אִם־יֶשְׁנוֹ בְּיוֹנָתָן בְּנִי — *Even if [the sin] is found to be with my son Jonathan.*

Simply understood, Saul had no inkling that Jonathan was guilty. He mentioned Jonathan's name only to

מ כִּ֣י מ֣וֹת יָמ֑וּת וְאֵ֥ין עֹנֵ֖הוּ מִכָּל־הָעָֽם׃ וַיֹּ֣אמֶר אֶל־
כָּל־יִשְׂרָאֵ֗ל אַתֶּם֙ תִּֽהְיוּ֙ לְעֵ֣בֶר אֶחָ֔ד וַאֲנִי֙ וְיוֹנָתָ֣ן
בְּנִ֔י נִֽהְיֶ֖ה לְעֵ֣בֶר אֶחָ֑ד וַיֹּאמְר֤וּ הָעָם֙ אֶל־שָׁא֔וּל
מא הַטּ֥וֹב בְּעֵינֶ֖יךָ עֲשֵֽׂה׃ וַיֹּ֣אמֶר שָׁא֔וּל אֶל־
יְהוָ֛ה אֱלֹהֵ֥י יִשְׂרָאֵ֖ל הָ֣בָה תָמִ֑ים וַיִּלָּכֵ֧ד יוֹנָתָ֛ן וְשָׁא֖וּל
מב וְהָעָ֥ם יָצָֽאוּ׃ וַיֹּ֣אמֶר שָׁא֔וּל הַפִּ֕ילוּ בֵּינִ֕י וּבֵ֖ין יוֹנָתָ֣ן

demonstrate his impartiality and his unbending determination to see justice done (*Abarbanel*). He may have mentioned Jonathan in particular only out of anticipation that if he were the guilty party, it would arouse many to speak in his defense because he had initiated the rout against the Philistines (*Malbim*). Thus, he referred to God as ה׳ הַמּוֹשִׁיעַ אֶת־יִשְׂרָאֵל, *HASHEM, the Savior of Israel* implying that no credit for salvation — nor amnesty — will be awarded to any man, for victory is solely in the hands of God (*Kli Yakar*).

According to a Midrash (*Pirkei D'Rabbi Eliezer* — 38; see also *Tanchuma Vayeishev* 2, *Yalkut Shimoni* 117), when Saul saw that the Philistines began to augment their war efforts, he understood that someone had violated the interdiction against eating. As he gazed at the stones of the *Choshen* on the Kohen Gadol's breast, where the names of all the tribes were inscribed, he noticed that the radiance of Benjamin's stone had dimmed. Thus, he knew that the culprit came from his own tribe of Benjamin.

In an alternative interpretation, *Abarbanel* suggests that Saul was informed of Jonathan's infraction by the soldier who saw him tasting the honey (v. 28). Saul did not directly accuse Jonathan, however, preferring instead to cast lots. Possibly he foresaw that the people would come to Jonathan's defense, yet made a noble impression by threatening to kill even his own son.

כִּי מוֹת יָמוּת — *He shall surely die.*

As mentioned above (v. 24), *Ramban* (in *Mishpat HaCherem*) states that the king was authorized to institute a חֵרֶם, *ban*, the violation of which was punishable by death. As the verse states, כָּל־חֵרֶם אֲשֶׁר יָחֳרַם מִן־הָאָדָם לֹא יִפָּדֶה מוֹת יוּמָת, *Any condemned person who has been banned from mankind shall not be redeemed; he shall be put to death* (*Leviticus* 27:29). Accordingly, Saul presumed that this ban had been violated.

Daas Sofrim offers an alternative opinion. It was standard military procedure to execute a soldier for any misdeed committed in the midst of war — either because that soldier's sinful presence might undesirably influence his fellow soldiers or because it might evoke heavenly displeasure with the army.

כִּי מוֹת יָמוּת — *That he shall surely die!*

The word כִּי, *that*, seems superfluous. *Kli Yakar* suggests that Saul wanted to avoid reference to a death sentence, which would be פִּתְחוֹן פֶּה לְשָׂטָן, "giving ideas to the Satan," since even a conditional condemnation pronounced by a wise man is fulfilled (*Makkos* 11a). Saul thus stated, כִּי אִם־יֶשְׁנוֹ בְּיוֹנָתָן בְּנִי, *even if the sin is found to be with my son Jonathan,* כִּי מוֹת יָמוּת, *that will then lead me to decree that he should be put to death.*

40. Saul now cast lots to determine who the guilty party was. Similarly, in years past, Joshua had cast lots (in his case, as specifically directed to do so by Hashem) to determine whose guilt had led to a military defeat (*Joshua* 7:14).

Although Saul was not acting at Hashem's command, he cast lots in the presence of the Ark and with specific knowledge about the manner of lots, so that the outcome was providentially orchestrated (see *Nachalas Shimon*

he shall surely die!" But no one of all the people
answered him. 40 *He then said to all Israel, "You*
will be on one side and I and my son Jonathan will
be on the other side [and let the lot be conducted]."
The people said to Saul, "Do what is proper in
your eyes."
41 *Saul said to* HASHEM, *"God of Israel, produce*
a flawless [verdict]!" [The side of] Jonathan and
Saul was singled out, and the people were absolved.
42 *Then Saul said, "Cast [a lot] between me and*

31:39). Thus, no proof can be derived from here as to whether or not one may in general draw lots to determine a person's guilt or innocence (as the gentiles did in the episode of Jonah — *Jonah* 1:7; *Sefer Chassidim* 701. See also *Sefer Chassidim* 679, *Mishbetzos Zahav*).

אַתֶּם תִּהְיוּ לְעֵבֶר אֶחָד וַאֲנִי וְיוֹנָתָן בְּנִי נִהְיֶה לְעֵבֶר אֶחָד — *You will be on one side and I and my son Jonathan will be on the other side.*

Regarding the translation of אֶחָד — literally, *one* — as *the other*, see above, v. 4.

Normally, casting lots would identify the tribe of the perpetrator, then his extended family, then his household, and finally the man himself (as occurred in the case of Joshua).

Possibly, Saul acted as he did because he already possessed evidence that Jonathan was to blame (see above).

Alternatively, Saul intended to show that he was unbiased and therefore equated himself and his son — the king and the prince — with the rest of the masses. If the latter would have been drawn, he would have proceeded as Joshua did (*Abarbanel*).

Kli Yakar comments that when Saul mentioned the name of Jonathan as a possible culprit (v. 39), no one rose to his defense. Saul may have understood that as incriminating evidence, and thus elected to perform the lot in this manner.

Saul's inclusion of himself in the lottery seems to imply that he left room for the possibility that a misdeed of his own — whether his failure to heed Samuel's directive (Ch. 13) or some other offense — had caused the *Urim VeTumim* to remain silent (*Abarbanel*).

41. וַיֹּאמֶר שָׁאוּל אֶל ה׳ — *Saul said to* HASHEM.

Saul recited a short prayer that this casting of lots should reveal the truth (*Abarbanel*).

From here we learn that anyone who casts lots should first offer such a supplication (*Sefer Chassidim* 679).

אֱלֹהֵי יִשְׂרָאֵל — *God of Israel.*

Saul meant to elicit God's special love for the people of Israel, so that no innocent person would be convicted (*Kli Yakar*).

הָבָה תָמִים — *Produce a flawless [verdict]!*

הָבָה means *give* (*see Genesis* 29:21) or *give forth.* תָמִים is related to תָּם, *complete* or *truthful.* Thus, Saul implored, "Although You have not responded through the *Urim VeTumim*, please allow the lottery to serve as a vehicle for the Divine message" (*Abarbanel*).

וַיִּלָּכֵד יוֹנָתָן וְשָׁאוּל וְהָעָם יָצָאוּ — *[The side of] Jonathan and Saul was singled out, and the people were absolved.*

For some perplexing reason, this verse contains two indications that Jonathan himself was singled out by the first round of lots. First, the word וַיִּלָּכֵד, *singled out*, is a singular word that appears

מג בְּנִי וַיִּלָּכֵד יוֹנָתָן: וַיֹּאמֶר שָׁאוּל אֶל־יוֹנָתָן הַגִּידָה
לִּי מֶה עָשִׂיתָה וַיַּגֶּד־לוֹ יוֹנָתָן וַיֹּאמֶר טָעֹם טָעַמְתִּי
בִּקְצֵה הַמַּטֶּה אֲשֶׁר־בְּיָדִי מְעַט דְּבַשׁ הִנְנִי אָמוּת:
מד וַיֹּאמֶר שָׁאוּל כֹּה־יַעֲשֶׂה אֱלֹהִים וְכֹה יוֹסִף כִּי־
מה מוֹת תָּמוּת יוֹנָתָן: וַיֹּאמֶר הָעָם אֶל־שָׁאוּל הֲיוֹנָתָן
יָמוּת אֲשֶׁר עָשָׂה הַיְשׁוּעָה הַגְּדוֹלָה הַזֹּאת
בְּיִשְׂרָאֵל חָלִילָה חַי־יהוה אִם־יִפֹּל מִשַּׂעֲרַת
רֹאשׁוֹ אַרְצָה כִּי־עִם־אֱלֹהִים עָשָׂה הַיּוֹם הַזֶּה
מו וַיִּפְדּוּ הָעָם אֶת־יוֹנָתָן וְלֹא־מֵת: וַיַּעַל

next to the word *Jonathan*, meaning *he was singled out*. And second, the cantillation notes necessitate a pause between *Jonathan* and *Saul* (*Me'am Loez*).

42. וַיִּלָּכֵד יוֹנָתָן — *[The side of] Jonathan ... was singled out.*

Although Jonathan had not heard Saul imposing a fast on the troops, he should have realized that no one was eating and inquired into the matter. Alternatively (as he himself admitted by justifying himself [v. 29,30]), if he would have been aware of the oath he would not have fasted anyway.

However, *Abarbanel* (as understood by *Daas Sofrim*) contends that Jonathan was not singled out as the guilty part. To the contrary, the testimony of the casting of lots was that Jonathan was innocent, for the words הָבָה תָמִים can be rendered as *set forth a faultless [person]*. Rather, the *Urim VeTumim* remained unresponsive due to Saul's misdeed.

43. מֶה עָשִׂיתָה — *What have you done?*

That is to say, "What crime have you committed?"

הִנְנִי אָמוּת — *I am prepared to die.*

This is *Abarbanel*'s rendering.

Targum translates this phrase as, *I deserve to die.*

Kli Yakar suggests that אָמוּת simply means, *I will die* — i.e., Jonathan chose not to contest his death sentence, for even if Saul let him live, Hashem would take his life in some other way. Thus, although Jonathan had previously defended his behavior, he now accepted the casting of lots as a Divine decree (*Malbim*).

However, *Mahari Kara* renders הִנְנִי אָמוּת as an astonished rhetorical question: *Am I to die [for sinning unwittingly]?*

44. כֹּה־יַעֲשֶׂה אֱלֹהִים וְכֹה יוֹסִף — *So shall God do and so shall He do further.*

Targum renders כֹּה־יַעֲשֶׂה ה׳ as *So shall God do to me*. This common formula for an oath is understood by the majority of commentators as a general imprecation.

Abarbanel, on the other hand, understands it as directly relevant to this case. Thus, he reads the verse as follows: *So shall God do* — So shall He continue to ignore my inquiries — *if Jonathan is not put to death.*[1]

מוֹת תָּמוּת יוֹנָתָן — *For you must surely die, Jonathan.*

Already convinced of Jonathan's guilt, Saul inferred from the unresponsiveness of the *Urim VeTumim* that Jonathan had sinned against God; and since this was presumably God's message, Saul believed that he lacked the authority to forgive him, painful as it may be (*Hamaspik* 48).

1. Eli spoke the same phrase to Samuel — see above, 3:17.

my son Jonathan," and Jonathan was singled out.
43 *Saul said to Jonathan, "Tell me, what have you*
done?" And Jonathan told him, and he said, "I did indeed taste a bit of nectar from the tip of the staff that was in my hand; I am prepared to die."
44 *So Saul said, "So shall God do and so shall He*
do further [if I do not carry out my oath], for you must surely die, Jonathan."
45 *But the people said to Saul, "Shall Jonathan*
die, he who has achieved this great salvation for Israel? A sacrilege! — as Hashem *lives, not a hair of his head shall fall to the ground, for he has acted for God's sake this day!" So the people redeemed Jonathan and he did not die.*

Jonathan seems to be sentenced here based on his own testimony. This is similar to the case of Achan, who was also discovered via lots, and subsequently admitted guilt (*Joshua* 7:18-20). *Rambam* (*Hil. Sanhedrin* 18:16) writes that the execution of Achan based on his own admission was either a temporary suspension of Torah law, or it was based on the special authority of the king. Possibly, the same can be said here. See *Mishbetzos Zahav.*

✎ Jonathan Is Vindicated — but the War Ends

45. חָלִילָה — *A sacrilege!*

The word חָלִילָה is related to the words חוּלִין, *profanation,* and חִילּוּל, *desecration.* (See above, 2:30; *Genesis* 18:25.)

חַי־ה׳ — *As* Hashem *lives.*

A formula of an oath, as above, v. 39.

אִם־יִפֹּל מִשַּׂעֲרַת רֹאשׁוֹ אַרְצָה — *Not a hair of his head shall fall to the ground.*

This is a commonly used expression, and implies that no harm should be done.

The word שַׂעֲרָה means a single hair (as opposed to שֵׂעָר, *a mass of hair*), and the prefix מ, *of,* implies a part of one strand of hair. Thus, not even a *part* of a single hair shall fall.

כִּי־עִם־אֱלֹהִים עָשָׂה הַיּוֹם הַזֶּה — *For he has acted for God's sake this day.*

Since, with undaunted trust in God, Jonathan had risked his life by entering a perilous situation on behalf of the Jews, it was inconceivable that he had sinned intentionally; thus, he must have been unaware of the oath (*Radak, Metzudos*; see below).

Me'am Loez adds that the words כִּי־עִם־אֱלֹהִים עָשָׂה imply that the fact that Jonathan's eyes lit up demonstrated Hashem's approval of his deeds.

Targum paraphrases כִּי־עִם־אֱלֹהִים עָשָׂה as *God knows that he acted [unintentionally].*

וַיִּפְדּוּ הָעָם אֶת־יוֹנָתָן וְלֹא־מֵת — *So the people redeemed Jonathan and he did not die.*

The word *redeemed* connotes that the people gave something in exchange for Jonathan's life. According to one Midrash, they contributed his weight in gold (*Midrash Shmuel* 17:3, *Yalkut Shimoni* 118), and another (*Pirkei D'Rabbi Eliezer* 38) maintains that they brought an elevation-offering on his behalf.

However, most interpretations of this verse understand וַיִּפְדּוּ to mean that the people rescued Jonathan from death by means of some legal defense.

The following are a few of these interpretations.

שָׁאוּל מֵאַחֲרֵי פְּלִשְׁתִּים וּפְלִשְׁתִּים הָלְכוּ
מז לִמְקוֹמָם: וְשָׁאוּל לָכַד הַמְּלוּכָה עַל־יִשְׂרָאֵל
וַיִּלָּחֶם סָבִיב | בְּכָל־אֹיְבָיו בְּמוֹאָב | וּבִבְנֵי־עַמּוֹן

❒ As mentioned above, *Targum* explains that the people argued that Jonathan had acted unintentionally.

But why then did they mention Jonathan's part in the great victory, which seems irrelevant?

Radak (citing his father) explains that they were saying that after Jonathan had performed such a heroic, self-sacrificing deed, they would be ungrateful indeed were they not to seek to vindicate him.

Metzudos (as cited above) explains the people to be saying that it was unimaginable that, after having performed such a noble act, Jonathan would have sinned intentionally.

Also, the fact that Hashem performed a miracle via Jonathan constitutes evidence of his innocence, for Hashem does not manifest wonders through unscrupulous men (*Ramban* [*Mishpat HaCherem; Deuteronomy* 27:29] and *Abarbanel*).[1]

If indeed Jonathan was vindicated because he had been unaware, why didn't the *Urim VeTumim* respond to Saul?

As noted earlier, *Ralbag* considers Jonathan as having been culpable of two other sins: having spoken disrespectfully of his father, and not having investigated why the troops were not eating.

Also, having eaten and realized that he had inadvertently violated his father's oath, Jonathan should have pleaded with Saul to annul that oath, which would have gained him retroactive exoneration (*Malbim*).

Rav Saadiah Gaon (cited by *Radak*), however, contends that Hashem considered Jonathan completely innocent. Hashem refrained from answering Saul's inquiry via the *Urim VeTumim* in order to make the incident of Jonathan's eating universally known, so that the people would defend and vindicate him. Otherwise, there might be a few people who knew that Jonathan had eaten but did not know that he had been unaware of the oath, and who would then claim that the prince was getting privileged protection from punishment.

Abarbanel maintains that Hashem's decision not to respond to Saul via the *Urim VeTumim* had nothing to do with Jonathan's actions. Rather, Saul himself was to blame, in that he had failed to heed Samuel's directions at Gilgal.

❒ According to *Rashi,* Jonathan was vindicated because the people annulled Saul's vow retroactively through the legal mechanism of פֶּתַח חֲרָטָה, *an element of regret,* on the part of the one who uttered the oath.[2]

❒ *Ramban* (*Mishpat HaCherem*) contends that Saul's imposition of a fast had not been an *oath* but rather a חֵרֶם, a *ban* (see above, v. 24), and that the king or Sanhedrin that enacts such a ban has the authority to forgive or undo their own ban without the mechanism of *an element of regret.*

❒ A Midrash (cited in *Midrash Shmuel* 17:3 and *Yalkut Shimoni* 118) states that the people exonerated Jonathan because he ate only honey, whereas Saul's oath specified לֶחֶם, *bread.* Saul's intention may have been to prohibit all food (לֶחֶם can mean food in general — see *Rashi, Genesis* 31:54), but since Jonathan was unaware of that intention, he was not liable to the death penalty (*Zayis Ra'anan*; see *Nachalas Shimon* 29:1:4).

❒ Another Midrash (ibid.) justifies Jonathan on the grounds that he *tasted* food, whereas Saul only prohibited *eating.*[1]

46. וַיַּעַל שָׁאוּל מֵאַחֲרֵי פְּלִשְׁתִּים — *Saul then went back up from [chasing] after the Philistines.*

1. The fact that this miraculous deliverance occurred before the incident with the honey does not void this idea; see *Radal* to *Pirkei D'Rabbi Eliezer* 38:136.

2. Regarding the possibility of annulling an oath after its time limit has transpired, see *Nachalas Shimon* 29:1:2.

[46] *Saul then went back up from [chasing] after the*
Philistines, and the Philistines went to their place.
[47] *Saul consolidated the kingdom over Israel.*
He waged war against all his enemies all around
— with Moab and with the Children of Ammon

Saul withdrew his attack.

Because the Jews had not received the approval of the *Urim VeTumim*, Saul feared that they did not deserve victory. Although Jonathan had been vindicated, there might nevertheless be some other charge against them (*Radak*).

According to *Abarbanel* (above, v. 45), Saul suspected that he himself was guilty of a misdeed, and that this might hinder the Jews' military success.

Alternatively, during the time that Saul spent casting lots, the Philistines withdrew, and Saul felt it would be futile to pursue them (*Radak*).

◆§ Saul's Valor

47. וְשָׁאוּל לָכַד הַמְּלוּכָה — *Saul consolidated the kingdom.*

The word לָכַד — here rendered *consolidated* by *Radak* — literally means *seized* or *captured*.

Now that the Israelites had rid themselves of the last remnants of Philistine rule, Saul was able to gain uncontested control (*Malbim*).

Abarbanel adds that Saul now began to behave in a regal manner, in contrast to his previous humble disposition, when he would walk behind the cattle (above, 11:5).

According to *Daas Sofrim*, Saul now took the opportunity to organize the government so that all areas of the kingdom would come under his authority.

Targum renders וְשָׁאוּל לָכַד הַמְּלוּכָה as *Saul flourished as king.*

The Midrash explains that the use of the unusual word לָכַד implies that Saul deserved the throne due to his humility, modesty, piety, fear of sin, beneficence, concern for other Jews' belongings, and commitment to Torah study (*Bamidbar Rabbah* 11:3, *Midrash Shmuel* 17:4, *Pesikta Rabbasi* 15:3).

Conversely, *Alshich* understands לָכַד to connote that Saul's acquisition of the crown was improper, since the right to that office was reserved for Judah's descendants.

וַיִּלָּחֶם סָבִיב בְּכָל־אֹיְבָיו — *He waged war against all his enemies all around.*

This phrase sets the stage for the war against Amalek.

The Torah mandates, וְהָיָה בְּהָנִיחַ ה׳ אֱלֹהֶיךָ לְךָ מִכָּל־אֹיְבֶיךָ מִסָּבִיב... תִּמְחֶה אֶת־זֵכֶר עֲמָלֵק, *It shall be that when* H*ASHEM*, *you God, gives you rest from all your enemies all around... you shall wipe out the memory of Amalek* (*Deuteronomy* 25:19). A Jewish monarchy and the eradication of Amalek are interdependent. As soon as Saul's monarchy was stabilized, he was responsible to undertake this mission (*Mahari Kara*).[2]

בְּכָל־אֹיְבָיו — *Against all his enemies.*

The nations listed in this verse bordered the Land of Israel, and had for many generations been the greatest enemies of the Jews. However, since the days of Joshua some of them had not engaged in any battle against the Jewish people (at least, none that is recorded). Possibly, they now initiated war out of

1. Because tasting does not qualify as eating or drinking, it does not require the recitation of a blessing and is not prohibited during a fast day (ibid.).

But what is the definition of tasting? For instance, is it necessary to spit out the food? Is eating less than a certain amount of food called tasting? Such questions, the subject of much controversy, are discussed at length in *Nachalas Shimon* 29, and in *Mishbetzos Zahav*).

2. When he failed in this endeavor, he lost the right to lead, and his successor was anointed in his lifetime.

וּבֶאֱד֡וֹם וּבְמַלְכֵ֥י צוֹבָה֙ וּבַפְּלִשְׁתִּ֔ים וּבְכֹ֥ל אֲשֶׁר־
מח יִפְנֶ֖ה יַרְשִֽׁיעַ׃ וַיַּ֣עַשׂ חַ֔יִל וַיַּ֖ךְ אֶת־עֲמָלֵ֑ק וַיַּצֵּ֥ל אֶת־
מט יִשְׂרָאֵ֖ל מִיַּ֥ד שֹׁסֵֽהוּ׃ וַיִּֽהְיוּ֙ בְּנֵ֣י שָׁא֔וּל
יוֹנָתָ֥ן וְיִשְׁוִ֖י וּמַלְכִּי־שׁ֑וּעַ וְשֵׁם֙ שְׁתֵּ֣י בְנֹתָ֔יו שֵׁ֚ם
נ הַבְּכִירָה֙ מֵרַ֔ב וְשֵׁ֥ם הַקְּטַנָּ֖ה מִיכַֽל׃ וְשֵׁם֙ אֵ֣שֶׁת שָׁא֔וּל
אֲחִינֹ֖עַם בַּת־אֲחִימָ֑עַץ וְשֵׁ֤ם שַׂר־צְבָאוֹ֙ אֲבִינֵ֔ר

envy and fear. At any rate, they were soon subdued by Saul (*Daas Sofrim*).

וּבְכֹל אֲשֶׁר־יִפְנֶה יַרְשִׁיעַ — *Wherever he turned, he inspired terror.*

Our rendering of יַרְשִׁיעַ, *he inspired terror*, follows *Radak*.

Mahari Kara translates this word as *he consumed* or *destroyed*, and *Ibn Ezra* (to *Job* 34:49) as *he prevailed.*

Ralbag renders יַרְשִׁיעַ in its conventional sense of *he did evil* and attributes the phrase to Saul's enemies — thus, *anyone who turned* [against Israel] *to perform villainous deeds....*

One implication of the word יַרְשִׁיעַ is *to do badly*. The Sages thus homiletically derive that although Saul was an accomplished Torah scholar, because he did not teach Torah to others, he did not merit to have his halachic decisions accepted (*Eruvin* 53a,b; *Sanhedrin* 93b).

48. וַיַּעַשׂ חָיִל — *He assembled an army.*

Our translation follows *Targum* and *Rashi*.

Abarbanel, rendering חַיִל as *strength* (see above, 9:1), translates וַיַּעַשׂ חָיִל as *he exhibited great strength*, וַיַּךְ אֶת־עֲמָלֵק *in striking Amalek*, a nation known to be composed of powerful men.

Translating חַיִל as *wealth* (as in *Exodus* 18:21, *Rashi*), *Daas Sofrim* explains that וַיַּעַשׂ חָיִל is a reference to the material wealth that Saul amassed in battle (as described in David's elegy — *II Samuel* 1:24).

וַיַּךְ אֶת־עֲמָלֵק — *And struck Amalek.*

Radak understands this as a reference to the war that Saul was to wage with Amalek at Hashem's behest (as described in the following chapter).

Abarbanel, however, contends that this verse refers to Saul's prior battles against Amalek.

וַיַּצֵּל אֶת־יִשְׂרָאֵל מִיַּד שֹׁסֵהוּ — *And he rescued Israel from the hand of its oppressor.*

Malbim understands this as a critique. Saul's goal in his war against Amalek was *only* to save Israel from its oppressor, *not* to fulfill the command to eradicate Amalek, which he therefore failed to do, as described in the next chapter (see also *Abarbanel*).

Metzudos — who, like *Abarbanel*, assumes that this battle with Amalek preceded that described in Ch. 15 — explains the verse to be saying that at present Saul's sole purpose was to protect Israel. Only later, after having been specifically commanded to do so, did he attempt to exterminate Amalek.

❧ Saul's Immediate Family

49. Scripture now introduces us to the names of Saul's children, wife, and the general of his army. This listing of names is a gesture of respect to the king. In addition, these personalities will appear in upcoming events (*Ralbag*).

וַיִּהְיוּ בְּנֵי שָׁאוּל יוֹנָתָן וְיִשְׁוִי וּמַלְכִּי־שׁוּעַ — *And the sons of Saul were Jonathan, Ishvi, and Malchi-shua.*

There exist some inconsistencies regarding the names of Saul's sons. When describing the death of Saul and his sons, Scripture (below, 31:2) names Jonathan, Malchi-shua and — in place of Ishvi — Abinadab. In *I Chronicles* (8:33), Saul is described as having not three but four sons: Jonathan, Malchi-shua, Abinadab,

and with Edom and with the kings of Zobah and
with the Philistines; wherever he turned he in-
spired terror. [48] *He assembled an army and struck*
Amalek, and he rescued Israel from the hand of its
oppressor.
[49] *And the sons of Saul were Jonathan, Ishvi, and*
Malchi-shua; and the names of his two daughters
— the name of the older one [was] Merab, and the
name of the younger one [was] Michal; [50] *the name*
of Saul's wife [was] Ahinoam daughter of Ahimaaz;
the name of the leader of his army [was] Abiner,

and Eshbaal. Again, Ishvi's name is omitted. Furthermore, these three sources fail to mention Ish-bosheth, who is elsewhere mentioned explicitly as Saul's son (and who in fact became Saul's successor [see *II Samuel* 2:8-10]).

The most generally accepted explanation of these discrepancies is that of *Radak*.[1] He states that Ishvi was also called Abinadab, and Eshbaal was also called Ish-bosheth. (It is common for Scripture to use different names to refer to one person.) The name of Ish-bosheth (Eshbaal) is omitted in the present verse, which lists only those who went to war.[2]

Kli Yakar adds that everyone mentioned in this verse had some connection with Saul's war effort (which is why Saul's general — although not a member of his family — is mentioned here).

Thus, Saul's wife was named Ahinoam because of her pleasant (*noam*) attitude in supporting her husband's military action on behalf of Hashem. As for Saul's daughters, they were promised as wives to victorious warriors (see below, 18:17-27).

According to *Abarbanel*, Scripture lists here only those who were not destined to succeed Saul to the throne. Since details of Ish-bosheth's reign are clearly documented below (*II Samuel* Chs. 2-4), there was no reason to mention him here.

Metzudos suggests an alternative solution to explain the inconsistencies in the listing of Saul's sons.

First, Ishvi, Ish-bosheth, and Eshbaal are three names for the same person. He is not mentioned in Ch. 31 — which records the death of Saul and his sons — because he did not perish during the war. As for Abinadab, who is mentioned in Ch. 31 and in *Chronicles*, he was possibly not yet born at this point, and so is not mentioned here.[3]

Two other sons of Saul are named in *II Samuel* 21:8: Armoni and Mephibosheth. Presumably, since they were born to Saul's concubine Ritzpah they were not deserving of princely rank and were therefore omitted from the lists cited above (*R' Mendel Geldwerth)*

50. וְשֵׁם אֵשֶׁת שָׁאוּל אֲחִינֹעַם — *The name of Saul's wife was Ahinoam.*

Abarbanel conjectures that Ahinoam was the mother of the three sons mentioned in the previous verse, but not of Ish-bosheth, and it is for that reason that his name was omitted.

אֲבִינֵר — *Abiner.*

There is a shorter form of that name, *Abner*, which is more commonly used.

According to *Pirkei D'Rabbi Eliezer* (33), Abiner's mother was the woman

1. See also the *Vilna Gaon* to *Seder Olam* Ch. 13.
2. Ish-bosheth did not go to war because he was involved in the study of Torah (*Kli Yakar*).
3. This theory is feasible only if we accept the view that Saul's reign lasted considerably longer than two years (see above, 13:1, *Abarbanel*), so that Abinadab could have grown old enough to fight during Saul's monarchy (*R' Mendel Geldwerth*).

יד/נא־נב
נא בֶּן־נֵר דֹּוד שָׁאוּל: וְקִישׁ אֲבִי־שָׁאוּל וְנֵר אֲבִי־
נב אַבְנֵר בֶּן־אֲבִיאֵל: וַתְּהִי הַמִּלְחָמָה
חֲזָקָה עַל־פְּלִשְׁתִּים כֹּל יְמֵי שָׁאוּל וְרָאָה
שָׁאוּל כָּל־אִישׁ גִּבּוֹר וְכָל־בֶּן־חַיִל וַיַּאַסְפֵהוּ
טו/א
א אֵלָיו: וַיֹּאמֶר שְׁמוּאֵל אֶל־שָׁאוּל אֹתִי
שָׁלַח יהוה לִמְשָׁחֲךָ לְמֶלֶךְ עַל־עַמּוֹ עַל־יִשְׂרָאֵל

who practiced necromancy in En-dor (below, 28:7).

Besides being a great warrior, Abner was a man of extraordinary physical prowess and an outstanding scholar (see *Koheles Rabbah* 9:11).

51. וְקִישׁ אֲבִי־שָׁאוּל — *And Saul's father Kish.*

The fact that Scripture sometimes refers to Kish as *the father of Saul* and other times calls Saul *the son of Kish* illustrates that they were equal in intelligence, and also that Kish, like Saul, was a man of great stature (*Koheles Rabbah* 2:9, *Chidushei Radal*).

וְקִישׁ אֲבִי־שָׁאוּל וְנֵר אֲבִי־אַבְנֵר בֶּן־אֲבִיאֵל — *And Saul's father Kish and Abner's father Ner were sons of Abiel.*

In the course of relating Saul's offspring, Scripture mentions his genealogy.

Also, having stated that Ner was Saul's uncle, the verse now informs us of the nature of that relationship: their fathers were brothers (*Abarbanel*). Although written in the singular, בֶּן־אֲבִיאֵל — literally, *the son of Abiel* — the phrase refers to both Kish and Ner.

Kli Yakar suggests that Scripture states בֶּן־אֲבִיאֵל in the singular form, seemingly applying only to Ner, in order to indicate that Kish merited having a son who became king because of his own humility, in that he made himself secondary to his brother so that it appeared that Ner was the only son of Abiel.[1]

בֶּן־אֲבִיאֵל — *Sons of Abiel.*

As noted earlier (9:1), Abiel is called Ner in *I Chronicles* (8:33, 9:39). Here he is called by his original name, probably in order to avoid confusing him with his son Ner.

52. עַל־פְּלִשְׁתִּים — *Against the Philistines.*

The choice of the word עַל — lit., *upon* — connotes either that Saul's army always had the upper hand (*Kli Yakar*), or that the Israelites generally initiated battle (*Daas Sofrim*).

וַתְּהִי הַמִּלְחָמָה חֲזָקָה עַל־פְּלִשְׁתִּים כֹּל יְמֵי שָׁאוּל — *The war against the Philistines was intense all the days of Saul.*

As this verse appears immediately prior to the episode of the war with Amalek, *Me'am Loez* suggests that it serves as somewhat of a justification for Saul's not having initiated war against Amalek until he was explicitly directed to do so. It was because he was often preoccupied with the war against the Philistines.

וְרָאָה שָׁאוּל — *Whenever Saul saw.*

Although the verb in this form usually indicates the future tense, *Rashi* explains that here it designates the present tense.

כָּל־אִישׁ גִּבּוֹר וְכָל־בֶּן־חַיִל — *Any mighty warrior or military strategist.*

Generally, both of these terms imply strength. The contrast presented in our translation between גִּבּוֹר and בֶּן־חַיִל is the *Targum's*.

Ralbag renders גִּבּוֹר as a man of power and military know-how, and בֶּן־

1. Saul too was noted for his humility (see above, Ch. 9).

14/51-52 *son of Saul's uncle Ner;* [51] *and Saul's father Kish*
and Abner's father Ner were sons of Abiel.
[52] *The war against the Philistines was intense all*
the days of Saul. Whenever Saul saw any mighty
warrior or military stategist, he would take him to
himself [into his army].

15/1 [1] *Samuel said to Saul, "HASHEM sent me to anoint*
you as king over His people, over Israel,

חַיִל as someone who has already proven his skills and has enjoyed success in a battle.

Kli Yakar suggests that the בֶּן־חַיִל was a righteous, pious man who amassed an "army" (חַיִל) of protective merits.

XV

Chapter 15 carries the potential for the fulfillment of one of the most essential goals of the Jewish people, the eradication of the nation of Amalek, and the frustration and disappointment when the nation fell just short of accomplishing it. It shows the high standards that God expects of His emissaries, and how even the greatest of men may be blinded by hardly detectable biases as he sets forth to do God's will. It is a major turning point in the history of the Jews, as Saul's reign begins its decline, preparing to make room for the destined Jewish Monarch, David.[1]

Saul's Mission to Eradicate Amalek

1. אֹתִי שָׁלַח ה׳ לִמְשָׁחֲךָ לְמֶלֶךְ — *HASHEM sent me to anoint you as king.*

... and just as you witnessed the fulfillment of *that* mission and the truth of *that* prophecy, although it may have initially seemed far-fetched, you should also not hesitate to believe in the authenticity and feasibility of this mission, to completely eradicate Amalek, which may also appear somewhat radical (*Metzudos*).

The Kabbalist Rabbi Chaim Vital teaches that in this short phrase, Samuel clearly illustrates five different elements of the significance of this anointment.

אֹתִי — *I.* God sent His most trusted servant, **Samuel**, to appoint Saul.

שָׁלַח ה׳ — *HASHEM sent me.* **Hashem** Himself chose Saul to be king.

לִמְשָׁחֲךָ — *To anoint you.* **Saul** specifically was chosen as the most worthy emissary to execute God's will.

לְמֶלֶךְ — *As king.* The appointment itself — to be **king** — is of great importance.

עַל־עַמּוֹ עַל־יִשְׂרָאֵל — *Over His people, over Israel.* The people whom Saul represented, **Israel**, are God's chosen nation (*Me'am Loez*).

לִמְשָׁחֲךָ לְמֶלֶךְ — *To anoint you as king.*

This is an essential introduction to the command to eradicate Amalek, since, as the Talmud states (*Sanhedrin* 20b), the establishment of Jewish monarchy is a prerequisite to the task of destroying Amalek, which implies that one of the primary goals of the king must be to fulfill that task. Thus, it is implicit in Hashem's own commitment to erase Amalek that He is entrusting His king with its execution, as Moses proclaimed, כִּי־יָד עַל־כֵּס קָהּ מִלְחָמָה לַה׳ בַּעֲמָלֵק, *For [HASHEM's] Hand* (His oath) *is upon the Throne of God* — represented by the Jewish monarch — and He commands

1. When *Parashas Zachar*, which recalls the commandment to erase Amalek, is read in the synagogue, this chapter serves as the *Haftarah*.

ב וְעַתָּה שְׁמַע לְקוֹל דִּבְרֵי יהוה: כֹּה
אָמַר יהוה צְבָאוֹת פָּקַדְתִּי אֵת אֲשֶׁר־עָשָׂה
עֲמָלֵק לְיִשְׂרָאֵל אֲשֶׁר־שָׂם לוֹ בַּדֶּרֶךְ בַּעֲלֹתוֹ

him to wage *a war of HASHEM against Amalek* (*Exodus* 17:16, *Rabbeinu Bachya* ibid.).

The idea that waging war against Amalek is the responsibility of the king is also expressed in *Numbers* 24:7: וְיָרֹם מֵאֲגַג מַלְכּוֹ, *His king shall be exalted over Agag.*[1]

Thus, considering the central role that the war against Amalek plays in the agenda of the king, it seems logical that were he to fall short of this expectation, he would prove unworthy of his position, and therefore lose it.

עַל־עַמּוֹ עַל־יִשְׂרָאֵל — *Over His people, over Israel.*

It was Saul's responsibility to promote the Jews' interests, protect their honor, and avenge any injustices that had been perpetrated against them (*Abarbanel*).

The word עַמּוֹ, *His nation,* indicates that Saul must be aware that the nation is not his but God's. He himself is therefore not a potentate who can make arbitrary decisions but a servant of the Divine will (*Rav Hirsch*).

וְעַתָּה שְׁמַע לְקוֹל דִּבְרֵי ה' — *So now hear the sound of HASHEM's words.*

Samuel intimated that as king, Saul must execute the royal mandate — i.e., to destroy Amalek (*Radak*).

Rashi infers from וְעַתָּה, *and now* — that Samuel was implying, "Last time — in Gilgal (see Ch. 13) — you acted foolishly. This time, take care."

We have previously cited the Talmud's statement that Samuel requested that his handiwork, i.e., the kingdom of Saul, should not be annulled during his lifetime. Accordingly, when Saul was sentenced to die, Samuel's life had to be cut short so that he would die earlier (*Taanis* 5b). Accordingly, Samuel tells Saul that since "Hashem sent *me* to anoint you" ... please obey His command so that my life span should not be affected by your failure (*Mishbetzos Zahav,* from *R' Adrabi*).

לְקוֹל דִּבְרֵי ה' — *The sound of HASHEM's words.*

This phrase often denotes a prophetic message (see *Rashi, Deuteronomy* 13:5; *Daas Sofrim*).

Our Sages teach that at one point David's general Joab killed the Amalekite males but allowed the females to live (see *I Kings* 11:15,16). He explained that his teacher had taught him the verse from *Deuteronomy,* תִּמְחֶה אֶת־זָכָר עֲמָלֵק, *Erase the males — zachar — of Amalek* (25:19). But the phrase actually reads תִּמְחֶה אֶת זֵכֶר־עֲמָלֵק, *Erase the memory — zeicher — of Amalek* (*Bava Basra* 21).

To prevent Saul from engaging in such misreading, Samuel said: שְׁמַע לְקוֹל דִּבְרֵי ה', *Hear the sound of HASHEM's words.* Saul should not only read the commandment from a Torah scroll, which lacks vowels, but he should instead *hear* the proper pronunciation of the words (*Me'am Loez,* from *Nachalas Reuven*).

2. כֹּה אָמַר ה' — *So said HASHEM.*

Although the commandment to eradicate Amalek is clearly indicated in *Deuteronomy* (25:19), and was one of the missions that the Jewish people were commissioned to perform upon entering the Land of Israel, nevertheless no individual was responsible to perform it until specifically directed to do so by a prophet, as is clearly evident from this verse (*Chidushei HaGriz al HaTorah,* p. 108). Thus, *Rambam* does not state that every Jew is required to kill individual Amalekites (unlike his ruling regarding the seven Canaanite nations (*Hil. Melachim* 5:4,5). This also clarifies why

1. This verse is cited by *Rambam* (*Hil. Melachim* 1:2) in reference to the Talmudic edict (*Sanhedrin* 20b) that the war against Amalek must be preceded by the appointment of a Jewish king. The Talmud itself cites another source; see *Lechem Mishneh* ad loc.

so now hear the sound of HASHEM's words. 2 *So said HASHEM, Master of Legions, 'I have remembered what Amalek did to Israel — [the ambush] he emplaced against him on the way, as he went up*

no one after Saul has ever attempted to eradicate Amalek.[1]

In the Torah's mandate to eradicate Amalek, a prerequisite is mentioned: *When HASHEM, your God, gives you rest from all your enemies all around* (*Deuteronomy* ibid.). Accordingly, *Netziv* (to *Parashas Re'eh*) says that since the Jews had not yet completed their conquest of the seven Canaanite nations, the Biblical command to destroy Amalek was not yet applicable, and this particular command was directed only to Saul. *Rambam* (in his introduction to Mishnah) seems to share this view.

צְבָאוֹת — *Master of Legions*

This appellation, which implies that God is the Master of an army at war, as it were, is used in conjunction with His performance of retributive war against he world's evil-doers (*Shemos Rabbah* 3:6; *Midrash Tanchuma, Parashas Shemos*).

פָּקַדְתִּי — *I have remembered.*

The word פָּקַדְתִּי is distinguished from זָכַרְתִּי, which is the more commonly used word for "I remembered," in that פְּקִידָה is generally associated with the concept of retribution (as in *Exodus* 20:5, 32:34; *Mahari Kara*; *Radak*).

Midrash Shmuel homiletically associates the word פָּקַדְתִּי with פִּקָּדוֹן, the Talmudic term for an item deposited by its owner in another's custody, to be returned later. Sarah deposited a bundle of mitzvos with God, and in consequence וַה׳ פָּקַד אֶת שָׂרָה, *HASHEM remembered Sarah* (*Genesis* 21:1) so that she bore Isaac. As for Amalek, they deposited a bundle of thorns with God — i.e., they attacked the Israelites in the wilderness. Therefore, God repaid them with a bundle of thorns.[2]

This Midrash imparts the idea that the system of reward and punishment follows the laws of cause and effect: one takes from the system whatever one has put into it (*Yefeh Toar* to *Bereishis Rabbah* 53:5). *Kli Yakar* observes that Amalek's deeds were directed against God Himself (see *Abarbanel* below); thus, God attended to Amalek Himself, as it were.

לְיִשְׂרָאֵל — *To Israel.*

Abarbanel systematically deduces that Amalek's goal in waging war with Israel was not for national pride, nor imperialism. Rather, they had two motives in attacking Israel. The first was (as mentioned earlier) its desire to diminish the awe of Hashem. By reducing the fear that had gripped all the nations of the world after Hashem's miraculous feats in Egypt, Amalek drastically minimized Hashem's glory for many generations to come, for which it was now about to be held accountable (*Kli Yakar*).

The second was its desire to take out upon the Jews its bitter hatred against Jacob, who had stolen the patriarchal

1. *S'mag* rules that at present there is no mandate to destroy Amalek; that obligation will return only upon the arrival of the Mashiach and the reconquest of the Land of Israel.

Moadim U'Zemanim (162) adds that this commandment applies only when one has the ability to eradicate Amalek. Following Saul's failure, many survivors of Amalek escaped and were scattered across the globe, such that it will not be possible for us to find them all until the Mashiach arrives. See *Nachalas Shimon* 30:6.

Chinuch §604 (*Mossad HaRav Kook* edition), however, considers it the obligation of every Jew to kill any Amalekite that he can, at every place and time.

2. What are these thorns? According to *Be'er Moshe*, they are the righteous Jews who protect the nation of Israel, just as thorns protect a vineyard. Thus, it is through the noble deeds of the righteous that Jews prevail and succeed in subduing Amalek.

ג מִמִּצְרָיִם: עַתָּה לֵךְ וְהִכִּיתָה אֶת־עֲמָלֵק
וְהַחֲרַמְתֶּם אֶת־כָּל־אֲשֶׁר־לוֹ וְלֹא תַחְמֹל עָלָיו
וְהֵמַתָּה מֵאִישׁ עַד־אִשָּׁה מֵעֹלֵל וְעַד־יוֹנֵק

blessings from Amalek's ancestor, Esav.

Thus, Samuel alludes to both. In v. 1, he says שְׁמַע לְקוֹל דִּבְרֵי ה׳, *hear the sound of* H*ASHEM's words,* as He wishes to avenge His own Honor, and here, פָּקַדְתִּי אֵת אֲשֶׁר־עָשָׂה עֲמָלֵק לְיִשְׂרָאֵל, *I have remembered what Amalek did to Israel.* As *Kli Yakar* observes, Samuel did not speak of what Amalek did לִבְנֵי יִשְׂרָאֵל, *to the Children of Israel,* but rather לְיִשְׂרָאֵל, *to Israel,* alluding to Jacob, who is also called Israel.

A Midrash (cited by *Kli Yakar*) offers another reason for Amalek's hatred of Jacob. Amalek's mother, Timna, was a noblewoman of Seir (see *Genesis* 36:12, *Rashi*), who desired to attach herself in marriage to the descendants of Abraham and Isaac; however, Jacob refused her. She was subsequently accepted as a concubine for Esau's son Eliphaz, but this rejection by Jacob rankled in her heart; thus, after she mothered Amalek, she commanded him to capitalize on the Israelites' laxness in Torah performance and avenge her shame. Accordingly, we see again that Amalek's hostility was directed at *Israel,* i.e., our patriarch Jacob.

בַּדֶּרֶךְ בַּעֲלֹתוֹ מִמִּצְרָיִם — *On the way, as he went up from Egypt.*

Amalek could not have had motives of conquest in attacking the Jews, since they were בַּדֶּרֶךְ, *on the road,* and homeless. Nor could Amalek have been concerned for its security, as Israel was בַּעֲלֹתוֹ מִמִּצְרָיִם, *coming up from Egypt,* and nowhere near the land of the Amalekites. By process of elimination, Amalek must have come to diminish Hashem's glory and to express their hatred for the descendants of Jacob (*Abarbanel, Malbim*).

The word בַּדֶּרֶךְ, *on the way,* is reminiscent of the episode in which Amalek's father Eliphaz pursued Jacob when he was travelling from Haran, and stole all of his possessions (see *Genesis* 29:11, *Rashi; Me'am Loez*).

3. עַתָּה לֵךְ וְהִכִּיתָה אֶת־עֲמָלֵק — *Now go and strike down Amalek.*

We can cite three reasons that Samuel directed this commandment specifically to Saul.

First, Saul was king, and according to some authorities commandments involving war, such as the eradication of Amalek, are incumbent upon a unified nation and thus upon its executive — i.e., the king.

Second, he was a descendant of the matriarch Rachel, and tradition has it that Amalek will fall only to such an individual.[1]

And finally, he came from the tribe of Benjamin — which, *Chomas Anach* states, possesses an especial strength in fighting the offspring of Esau, because Benjamin was the only son of Jacob who did not bow to Esau (*Genesis* 33:6,7).

וְהִכִּיתָה אֶת־עֲמָלֵק וְהַחֲרַמְתֶּם אֶת־כָּל־אֲשֶׁר־לוֹ וְלֹא תַחְמֹל עָלָיו וְהֵמַתָּה... — *And strike down Amalek and destroy everything he has. Have no pity on him — kill...*

The word וְהִכִּיתָה, *strike down,* is often used to indicate a fatal blow. Yet Samuel follows that directive with the word וְהֵמַתָּה, *kill. Kli Yakar* suggests that there was a two-step process. The Jews were to inflict a mortal blow — but not one that would kill immediately. First the Amalekites were to witness וְהַחֲרַמְתֶּם אֶת־כָּל־אֲשֶׁר־לוֹ — all their belongings being destroyed and they were helpless to prevent it, and then the Jews should kill them.

1. Joshua, Mordechai, and Esther — who also battled Amalek — were descendants of Rachel as well.

from Egypt. 3 Now go and strike down Amalek and destroy everything he has. Have no pity on him — kill man and woman alike, infant and suckling alike, ox

וְהַחֲרַמְתֶּם — *And destroy.*

Targum renders this as וּתְגַמַּר, *and completely destroy.*

Radak, on the other hand, quotes his father to the effect that וְהַחֲרַמְתֶּם means to *ban*. Hence, Samuel told Saul to first prohibit all benefit from Amalekite property, and then to destroy it.

◆§ Why Were the Jews to Destroy Amalek's Property?

According to *Abarbanel*, Amalek's property was destroyed in order to make it clear that the sole purpose of this war was to avenge Amalek's attack on Hashem and Israel in the wilderness.[1]

Rashi (to *Deuteronomy* 25:19), on the other hand, explains that the property was destroyed so that no one would allude to Amalek even by reference to — for instance — "an animal of Amalek." This would be in keeping with the tenor of the command, *You shall wipe out the memory of Amalek* (see *Deuteronomy* 25:19: see *Mechilta* [*Parashas Beshalach*], as well as *Midrash Eichah* [Ch. 3]).

Rashi (here) states that the Jews were commanded to kill the animals in particular because the Amalekites would by means of sorcery disguise themselves as animals.

Midrash Eichah adds that even the trees of Amalek were to be destroyed. This may imply that (although it is not evident from the present verse) inanimate objects as a whole were subject to this command.[2]

Rambam does not record any commandment to destroy the property of Amalek (either in his *Mishneh Torah* or *Sefer HaMitzvos*). It is apparently his view that the directive to destroy the property was applicable only to Saul and does not constitute a part of the Biblical command.

The fact that וְהַחֲרַמְתֶּם, *and you shall destroy*, is a command in the plural supports the opinion that the commandment to destroy Amalek applies to all individuals throughout the ages, and not just to the king (see above).

וְלֹא תַחְמֹל עָלָיו — *Have no pity on him.*

Eventually, Saul did have pity (v. 9). With this warning, Samuel precluded any defense on Saul's behalf (*Radak*).

Kli Yakar explains וְלֹא תַחְמֹל as *Do not seek a mild means of death* for them.

This mandate was difficult for the Jewish people to accept, since they are naturally merciful, particularly since they could not have foreseen what evil might come of pitying Amalek — e.g., the birth of Haman generations later (*Daas Sofrim*).

◆§ Was Peace With Amalek an Option?

The Torah dictates that before waging war, Israel must offer its opponent peace under prescribed conditions (*Deuteronomy* 20:10-18).

Rashi (ad loc.) states that in the case of a mandatory war, such as that waged against the seven Canaanite nations or against Amalek, it is not necessary or appropriate to do so.

Rambam (*Hil. Melachim* 6:4) disagrees, and rules that this offer must be made in all circumstances. *Kesef Mishneh* explains that a gentile nation that sues for peace must agree to accept the seven Noahide laws. Once it does so, it becomes an upright descendant of Noah and no longer retains its original status — as, for instance, Canaan or Amalek.

1. Similarly, Mordechai and Esther abstained from the spoils of their enemies (*Esther* 9:10).
2. Mordechai too apparently refrained from taking even inanimate spoils (ibid.).

ד מִשּׁוֹר וְעַד־שֶׂה מִגָּמָל וְעַד־חֲמוֹר׃ וַיְשַׁמַּע
שָׁאוּל אֶת־הָעָם וַיִּפְקְדֵם בַּטְּלָאִים מָאתַיִם אֶלֶף
ה רַגְלִי וַעֲשֶׂרֶת אֲלָפִים אֶת־אִישׁ יְהוּדָה׃ וַיָּבֹא
ו שָׁאוּל עַד־עִיר עֲמָלֵק וַיָּרֶב בַּנָּחַל׃ וַיֹּאמֶר שָׁאוּל

וְהֵמַתָּה מֵאִישׁ עַד־אִשָּׁה מֵעוֹלֵל וְעַד־יוֹנֵק — *Kill man and woman alike, infant and suckling alike.*

Rashi (to *Deuteronomy* 25:19) states that the present verse elaborates on the more generally expressed command delivered by Moses: תִּמְחֶה אֶת־זֵכֶר עֲמָלֵק, *Wipe out the memory of Amalek* (see also *Ibn Ezra* ad loc.).

Amalek's venomous hatred was so deeply engraved in its character that leaving any descendant alive would have constituted too great a risk (*Daas Sofrim*).

◆§ Saul's Falls Short of Expectation

4. וַיְשַׁמַּע שָׁאוּל — *Saul had all the people summoned.*

The word וַיְשַׁמַּע, *summoned*, is related to שׁוֹמֵעַ, *to hear*, and means, literally, *to make hear*. Thus, the people were assembled by means of public proclamations (*Rashi*). Following the *Targum*, who renders וַיְשַׁמַּע שָׁאוּל as *and Saul gathered*, the convening was for the purpose of heeding his command, hence the term וַיְשַׁמַּע (*Radak*).

This term clearly possesses a less anxious tone than Saul's previous calls for assembly, וַיִּצָּעֲקוּ (above, 13:4) and וַיִּזָּעֵק (above, 14:20). Since no present danger existed (*Daas Sofrim*), the people were easily motivated to take part in avenging Hashem's honor against Amalek (*Ahavas Yehonasan*).

וַיִּפְקְדֵם בַּטְּלָאִים — *And he counted them through lambs.*

Literally, the word *telaim* is the name of a place (*Tosafos Yeshanim, Yoma* 22b; *Radak*), one referred to in *Joshua* (15:24) as Telem (*Metzudos*). However, if the present verse were referring to that location, the word order would have been different — i.e., וַיְשַׁמַּע שָׁאוּל אֶת־הָעָם בַּטְּלָאִים וַיִּפְקְדֵם, *Saul had all the people summoned to Telaim, and [there] he counted them* (*Kli Yakar*).

The Talmud (*Yoma* ibid.) thus concludes that *telaim* serves here not as a proper noun but as a reference to Saul's sheep; he distributed one to each Israelite, and then counted the sheep. His purpose in so doing was to conduct a census without counting heads, which is prohibited even for the purpose of a mitzvah.[1]

The fact that Saul had so many sheep at his disposal shows that after being anointed king he became wealthy. The Talmud (ibid.) cites this fact to illustrate the idea that a person appointed to a position of public fiscal responsibility grows affluent.

This indication of Saul's wealth makes it clear that when he later took the spoils of Amalek he could not excuse himself on the grounds of poverty (*Malbim*).

Targum Yonasan states that the sheep were *paschal lambs*. This translation is subject to two interpretations.

According to *Radak*, the census was conducted just before Passover at Nob, the site of the large altar where people brought their *pesach*-offerings.[2] Thus,

1. Previously, Saul had used shards to count the people.

2. Why did God bring about the war against Amalek with such a census, at just this time?

Ahavas Yehonasan explains that Amalek is described as the *first of nations* (*Numbers* 24:20) and Nissan is the first month of the year, whose zodiacal sign is the sheep. Thus, the Amalekites, who were strong believers in astrology, saw a correspondence between themselves,

and sheep alike, camel and donkey alike.' "
[4]Saul had all the people summoned, and he
counted them through lambs: two hundred thou-
sand infantrymen, and the men of Judah were
ten thousand. [5]Saul came to the city of Amalek,
and he fought [them] in the valley. [6]Saul said

instead of counting heads, they tallied lambs and then gathered information on how many individuals were registered for each lamb (*Mahari Kara*). *Radak* assumes that the *Targum's* interpretation is consistent with the Talmud's contention that Saul distributed the sheep for the census.

Abarbanel, however, explains that even according to *Targum*, the census did not necessarily take place immediately prior to Passover. Rather, long before that, Saul distributed sheep for the purpose of taking the census (as the Talmud states), and later on these sheep were offered as paschal lambs.

מָאתַיִם אֶלֶף רַגְלִי — *Two hundred thousand infantrymen.*

Chasam Sofer wonders how there were so few, since every Jew is required to participate in the command to destroy Amalek. He assumes that all others returned from the war because their sins did not allow them to participate (see *Deuteronomy* 20:8, *Rashi* ad loc.).

אֶת־הָעָם ... אֶת־אִישׁ יְהוּדָה — *The people ... the men of Judah.*

Again, the soldiers of Judah are counted separately. See above, 11:8.

5. וַיָּרֶב בַּנָּחַל — *And he fought [them] in the valley.*

Our translation is in accord with *Rashi's* view that וַיָּרֶב is related to רִיב, *argument* or *battle*.

According to *Radak*, on the other hand, the word וַיָּרֶב is related to אָרַב, to *ambush*.

Mahari Kara cites the view that וַיָּרֶב is related to רְבָבָה (lit., ten-thousands) *multitudes* — i.e., Saul mobilized tens of thousands of soldiers.

According to *Malbim*, Saul looked for a pretext to engage in battle so that the Jews would not appear to be launching an unprovoked attack. He thus staged an argument over the proprietorship of a border valley. But, adds *Malbim*, Saul erred in doing so; he should have candidly stepped forward to avenge Hashem's honor.

Abarbanel states that נַחַל here means not *valley* but *river*. Accordingly, the Amalekites attempted to prevent Saul's troops from benefiting from the water of a certain river, and the Israelites fought to gain access to it.

The Sages too reject the notion that Saul battled Amalek at a valley, because of sources that describe Amalek's territory as consisting of mountainous land (*Maharsha* to *Yoma* 22b). Instead, they offer a homiletic approach to this verse that is of major significance.

The Torah prescribes an atonement procedure involving an עֶגְלָה עֲרוּפָה, a *decapitated heifer*, in the case of a murder to which there were no witnesses (see *Deuteronomy* 21:1-9). The elders of the city nearest to where the corpse was discovered perform this

Nissan, and sheep. Hashem therefore ordained that their demise should come about in that month and through the use of sheep.

It is noteworthy that according to some, the ultimate eradication of Amalek is destined to occur on the 14th of Nissan, the date of the *pesach*-offering (see *Mishbetzos Zahav*).

אֶל־הַקֵּינִי לְכוּ סֻּרוּ רְדוּ מִתּוֹךְ עֲמָלֵקִי פֶּן־אֹסִפְךָ
עִמּוֹ וְאַתָּה עָשִׂיתָה חֶסֶד עִם־כָּל־בְּנֵי יִשְׂרָאֵל
בַּעֲלוֹתָם מִמִּצְרָיִם וַיָּסַר קֵינִי מִתּוֹךְ עֲמָלֵק׃

ritual, in a *valley*. וַיָּרֶב בַּנָּחַל can thus be said to mean that Saul *deliberated* — either with himself (*Rashi*) or with God (*Midrash Shmuel*) — in regard to the concept evoked by that *valley* ceremony. Saul said, "If the Torah demands atonement for the violent death of one soul, how much more will I be held accountable for the destruction of an entire nation. Furthermore, if the Amalekite men sinned, why do the animals and children deserve to die?"

But a heavenly voice responded, אַל תְּהִי צַדִּיק הַרְבֵּה, *Do not be overly righteous* — i.e., Do not be more righteous than your Creator (*Ecclesiastes* 7:16; *Yoma* 22b).[1]

Tosafos Yeshanim (*Yoma* 22b) states that Saul's sin is significantly mitigated — so much so that it assumes the character of an unintentional misdeed — by the fact that his logic persuaded him that he was acting correctly.

Yet how could he have so blatantly erred and equated the death of a Jew with the eradication of this vicious nation?

Kli Yakar suggests that Saul no more than momentarily questioned Hashem's command, but then rejects this idea and states instead that when Saul began his attack, various Amalekites became proselytes, leading Saul to wonder whether he should save them.[2]

Iyun Yaakov, however, denies that Saul had any qualms about killing Amalekites. Rather, he thought that following the war, he should bring offerings to atone for the lives that he had taken, and for that purpose he reserved some of the choice Amalekite animals.

6. וַיֹּאמֶר שָׁאוּל אֶל־הַקֵּינִי — *Saul said to the Kenite.*

Ralbag paraphrases this phrase as stating that *Saul had already said to the Kenite* — i.e., this had occurred prior to the battle with Amalek that Scripture began to describe in the previous verse.

Abarbanel, on the other hand, prefers to maintain the chronological flow of the text, and explains that after that initial battle in the valley, Saul paused to advise the Kenites to take leave, following which he resumed the war.

הַקֵּינִי — *The Kenite.*

The identity of the Kenite nation, which was in possession of one of the ten territories promised by God to Abraham (*Genesis* 15:19), is the subject of Tannaic dispute (*Bava Basra* 56a). However, what is clear — as we learn from Scripture — is that when the Jews inhabited the Holy Land the Kenite nation was composed of the descendants

1. Why is the ceremony of the decapitated heifer alluded to by the specific element of the *valley*, in particular a נַחַל אֵיתָן, a *harsh valley*, that cannot yield crops?

The Talmud (*Sotah* 46a) explains that the symbolism of the valley — particularly a נַחַל אֵיתָן — a *harsh valley* that cannot yield crops — is that such an infertile area served as a reminder that the murder victim could no longer have children.

Saul may have been concerned that destroying the people of Amalek would prevent worthwhile descendants from coming into the world. Indeed, his concern was warranted — for, as our Sages teach, the descendants of Haman taught Torah in Bnei Brak (*Sanhedrin* 96b). Nonetheless, it was wrong of Saul to second-guess a direct command from Hashem (*Me'am Loez*).

2. See *Nachalas Shimon* 30:2, which deals with the parameters of this issue.

15/6 *to the Kenite, "Go, withdraw, descend from among the Amalekite, lest I destroy you with them; for you acted kindly to all the Children of Israel when they went up from Egypt." So the Kenite withdrew from among Amalek.*

of Jethro, Moses' father-in-law (who was referred to as *the Kenite* [*Judges* 1:16]).

The Kenites led a nomadic life-style.[1] They inhabited Jericho temporarily (see *Judges* 1:16, *Rashi*), following which they left and settled south of Arad — itself in the south of the land — in order to study Torah under the tutelage of Jabez (another name for Othniel, son of Kenaz [*Terumah* 16a]). *Rashi* states that *Arad* is identical with *Amalek*. In other words, the Kenites territory touched on that of Amalek. Concerned that he might unwittingly strike the Kenites, Saul thus suggested that they leave the battle area.

לְכוּ סֻרוּ רְדוּ — *Go, withdraw, descend.*

Saul used these three words to emphasize the urgency of the matter (*Daas Sofrim*).

וְאַתָּה עָשִׂיתָה חֶסֶד עִם־כָּל־בְּנֵי יִשְׂרָאֵל — *For you acted kindly to all the Children of Israel.*

Rashi, paraphrasing the Talmud (*Berachos* 63b), understands this as a reference to the feast that Jethro ate together with Moses, Aharon, and all the elders of Israel (*Exodus* 18:12). Accordingly, Jethro is accredited as being the host of that meal, and, as the Talmud (ibid.) elaborates, since he benefited Torah scholars, he is considered to have bestowed kindness upon the entire nation, even though his intentions were for his own honor.

However, *Maharsha* states that the Talmud is referring to Jethro's command to his daughters to invite Moses to eat with them (*Exodus* 2:20). That being the case, the kindness that Jethro did for *all the Children of Israel* was to protect their savior Moses from Pharaoh's sword. A Midrash (*Vayikra Rabbah* 34:8) supports *Maharsha's* version and emphasizes that although Jethro acted in gratitude for Moses' assistance to his daughters, his kindness was repaid. One who performs kindness not out of obligation will surely be rewarded.

Alternative explanations of Jethro's kindness to the Israelites include his joy upon their successes (*Exodus* 18:9), his advice to them to appoint multiple judges (ibid. 18:21,22; *Ralbag, Abarbanel*), and his service to them as a guide in the wilderness (*Numbers* 10:31; *Mahari Kara*).

וְאַתָּה עָשִׂיתָה חֶסֶד — *For you acted kindly.*

With these words, Saul contrasted the deeds of Amalek with those of the Kenite. It would be unjust for the Jews to treat the malevolent Amalek and the beneficent Kenite in the same manner — particularly since it was Jethro who had helped the Israelites establish their justice system (*Abarbanel, Malbim, Ahavas Yehonasan*).

According to one Talmudic opinion, the narration of Jethro's arrival appears out of chronological order, and is placed adjacent to the description of the war against Amalek (*Avodah Zarah* 24b). This illustrates that just as we recall the evil of Amalek in order to avenge it, so too do we remember the goodness of Jethro in order to reciprocate it (*Ibn Ezra, Exodus* 18:1; *Radak, Judges* 1:16; see also *Tosafos* to *Avodah Zarah* 24b).

1. One example is that of the children of Jehonadab, son of Rechab, who descended from Jethro (*Jeremiah* 35:7; see *I Chronicles* 2:55).

ז וַיַּךְ שָׁאוּל אֶת־עֲמָלֵק מֵחֲוִילָה בּוֹאֲךָ שׁוּר אֲשֶׁר
ח עַל־פְּנֵי מִצְרָיִם׃ וַיִּתְפֹּשׂ אֶת־אֲגַג מֶלֶךְ־עֲמָלֵק
ט חָי וְאֶת־כָּל־הָעָם הֶחֱרִים לְפִי־חָרֶב׃ וַיַּחְמֹל
שָׁאוּל וְהָעָם עַל־אֲגָג וְעַל־מֵיטַב הַצֹּאן וְהַבָּקָר

7. וַיַּךְ שָׁאוּל אֶת־עֲמָלֵק — *Saul struck down Amalek.*

Although Saul's rout of Amalek tends to be forgotten amidst the discussion of his shortcomings, it was indeed a significant historical event, predicted by Balaam (*Numbers* 24:7), in which Israel's first king defeats Agag, king of Amalek. This campaign was followed by further victories by King David (below, Ch. 30; see *I Kings* 11:16) and by the tribe of Simon (*I Chronicles* 4:43), which eradicated the last remnants of Amalek as a cohesive group.

מֵחֲוִילָה בּוֹאֲךָ שׁוּר — *From Havilah to the approach to Shur.*

This stretch of land served as the dwelling-place of Ishmael's descendants (*Genesis* 25:18). Possibly, the Amalekites settled here peaceably among their Ishmaelite cousins; alternatively, they seized the area (*Radak*).

בּוֹאֲךָ שׁוּר — *To the approach to Shur.*

Literally, this phrase means *until you arrive at Shur* — addressing a person familiar with the area (*Radak*).

The Israelites' first encampment after the splitting of the Sea of Reeds was in the wilderness of Shur (*Exodus* 15:22). Presumably, this was in the vicinity of where Amalek attacked them at that time. Thus, the words בּוֹאֲךָ שׁוּר homiletically imply that the nation of Amalek met its demise in the same area that years earlier *you* — the Israelites — *arrived at Shur* from Egypt (*Kli Yakar*).

8. וְאֶת־כָּל־הָעָם הֶחֱרִים לְפִי־חָרֶב — *And he destroyed all the people by the edge of the sword.*

Not long after this, David engaged in battle with the Amalekites (Ch. 30). Evidently, therefore, some Amalekites survived this encounter. Either they escaped, or else they had not been in the vicinity of this battle (*Daas Sofrim*).

9. וַיַּחְמֹל שָׁאוּל וְהָעָם — *Saul, as well as the people, took pity.*

Although the people had various reasons for allowing survivors, their underlying motivation was one of misplaced pity.

Saul's compassion in this instance contrasts shockingly with his brutal slaughter of the innocent populace of Nob (below, 22:19), where he exterminated man and beast, young and old alike, exactly as he was commanded to do to Amalek. This contrast leads the Midrash to comment that a person who is merciful when he should be cruel will eventually be cruel when mercy is called for (*Koheles Rabbah* 7:16). Furthermore, a person who shows pity when he should be stern will be set upon by the Attribute of Judgment — as occurred when Saul and his three sons were killed by the sword.[1]

Malbim, an authority on Scriptural synonyms, differentiates between three words indicating pity: רחם, חס, and חמל.

רַחֵם describes an emotional discomfort at beholding a fellow human's pain or death. חָס and חָמַל are used also in regard to the destruction of property. חָס refers to the emotional feeling of one who can't bear to see the destruction of something *he* could have used. By contrast, חֶמְלָה is an intellectual feeling that applies even when one could not have had *personal* benefit from the item, but is upset to see it wasted, since it is wrong to put to waste what someone may have benefited from. Hashem's warning to Saul made no mention of רַחֵם and חָס, because it is natural for someone to *feel* pity while executing a command to destroy something of

1. Presumably, this is because the Attribute of Judgment takes revenge for having been ignored.

*[7] Saul struck down Amalek, from Havilah to
the approach to Shur, which is alongside Egypt.
[8] He captured Agag, king of Amalek, alive, and
he destroyed all the people by the edge of the
sword. [9] Saul, as well as the people, took pity
on Agag, on the best of the sheep, the cattle,*

value. Rather, Hashem warned against חֶמְלָה (above v. 3), for that would mean a calculated, rational disagreement with Hashem's decision to destroy, considering it wasteful. With the word וַיַּחְמֹל Scripture testifies that that was Saul's error, and for that he lost the opportunity to repent.

In the phrase, וַיַּחְמֹל שָׁאוּל וְהָעָם — *Saul, as well as the people, took pity* — the verb is in the singular. *Kli Yakar* suggests that in actuality only the nation sinned (as Saul himself later testified [v. 15]). However, Saul was implicated in its guilt because he did not veto its actions.

וְהָעָם — *As well as the people.*

Midrash Shmuel states that this is a veiled reference to Doeg HaAdomi, a Torah scholar and head of the Sanhedrin who served as Saul's adviser and who instigated various offenses, the worst being the massacre at Nob (Ch. 22). He is called הָעָם, *the nation,* because his intelligence and scholarship equaled that of the entire nation, and also because his influence over the people and over Saul was so great.

According to *Be'er Moshe,* it was Doeg who decided to salvage Agag and the livestock; Saul was incriminated because he failed to protest (see *Kli Yakar* above).

In verse 4, הָעָם, *the people,* and אִישׁ יְהוּדָה, *the men of Judah,* are mentioned separately. Accordingly, *Meshech Chochmah* (*Genesis* 49:8) notes that Scripture here testifies that only the עָם, *the people,* were guilty — but the troops of Judah were not involved in setting aside Amalekite animals. Since the eradication of Amalek is directly dependent on the existence of an Israelite monarch (see above, v. 1), and the Judahites were faithful to their mission against Amalek, they merited the kingship. Jacob alluded to this by telling his son Judah (*Genesis* ibid.): יָדְךָ בְּעֹרֶף אֹיְבֶיךָ, *[Since] your hand will be at your enemies' nape,* יִשְׁתַּחֲווּ לְךָ בְּנֵי אָבִיךָ, *your brothers will prostrate themselves to you.*

עַל אֲגָג — *On Agag.*

Abarbanel speculates that Agag was spared because he was handsome and impressive-looking.

Ahavas Yehonasan infers from verse 33, כֵּן־תִּשְׁכַּל מִנָּשִׁים אִמֶּךָ, *so shall your mother be childless among women,* that only Agag's mother was an Amalekite and not his father. Following the Talmudic principle (*Yevamos* 78b, *Kiddushin* 67a) that a gentile child's nationality follows that of his *father,* Agag was legally not an Amalekite at all. Thus, Saul felt justified in leaving him alive. However, suggests *Nachalas Shimon* 30:13 (based on *Moadim U'Zemanim*), this was an error: because Agag was the Amalekite king, sparing him violated the Torah's directive to erase any recollection of Amalek (see *Deuteronomy* 25:19). *Mishbetzos Zahav* draws the opposite conclusion. Since Saul seems to have left Agag's mother alive, it appears that *she* was not of Amalekite descent, but only his father.

וְעַל־מֵיטַב הַצֹּאן ... — *On the best of the sheep...*

As mentioned above (v. 3), the Torah does not specify the commandment to destroy Amalek's animals. *Rashi* understands that it is implicit in זֵכֶר עֲמָלֵק, *the memory of Amalek* (*Deuteronomy* 25:19).

According to *Minchas Chinuch* (604) the requirement stated here to kill the animals was a limited directive given to Samuel at this instance only. Thus,

וְהַמִּשְׁנִים וְעַל־הַכָּרִים וְעַל־כָּל־הַטּוֹב וְלֹא אָבוּ
הַחֲרִימָם וְכָל־הַמְּלָאכָה נְמִבְזָה וְנָמֵס אֹתָהּ
י הֶחֱרִימוּ: וַיְהִי דְּבַר־
יא יהוה אֶל־שְׁמוּאֵל לֵאמֹר: נִחַמְתִּי כִּי־הִמְלַכְתִּי
אֶת־שָׁאוּל לְמֶלֶךְ כִּי־שָׁב מֵאַחֲרַי וְאֶת־דְּבָרַי לֹא
הֵקִים וַיִּחַר לִשְׁמוּאֵל וַיִּזְעַק אֶל־יהוה כָּל־הַלָּיְלָה:

many commentators maintain that Saul considered Samuel's order to kill the animals as Samuel's own initiative and not the will of God, and thus not binding on him.[1]

וְהַמִּשְׁנִים — *The fatted bulls.*

Most commentators render וְהַמִּשְׁנִים as *animals of superior quality,* yet there are different versions for the word's source.

Rashi relates the word to מִשְׁנֶה, *double,* for these animals contained a double portion of flesh and fat.

According to *Radak,* the word is an re-arrangement of שְׁמָנִים, *fatted.*

Alternatively, *Radak* suggests that it comes from שָׁנָה, *year,* as the animals were within their first year, or from שְׁנַיִם, *two,* since they were second-born to their mothers (such animals usually being stronger than the firstborn).

Malbim states that מִשְׁנִים were of *secondary* quality compared to מֵיטַב, *the best.* Thus, the best and the mediocre livestock remained alive, whereas the worst were destroyed.

Finally, *Mahari Kara* cites an interpretation of מִשְׁנִים as *choice horses* (see *Genesis* 41:43).

וְהַמִּשְׁנִים וְעַל־הַכָּרִים — *And the fatted bulls, and the fatted sheep.*

Alternatively, וְהַמִּשְׁנִים and הַכָּרִים both refer to fatted sheep. The difference between the two is that the מִשְׁנִים ate on their own, whereas the כָּרִים were force-fed. Alternatively, the מִשְׁנִים were within their first year, and the כָּרִים were older (*Radak*).

הַמְּלָאכָה — *Livestock.*

Literally, מְלָאכָה means *work.* Thus, our translation, which is that of *Radak,* renders הַמְּלָאכָה as any productive animal — either one that works or one whose wool may be sheared.

Ibn Ezra (*Genesis* 33:14) explains that anything that man can produce or acquire through his work, including *money,* is considered מְלָאכָה (see also *Ramban* to *Exodus* 36:6).

נְמִבְזָה וְנָמֵס — *The inferior and wretched.*

נְמִבְזָה, *inferior,* a feminine adjective, refers to the feminine noun מְלָאכָה; and נָמֵס, *wretched,* a masculine adjective, refers to the masculine noun מִקְנֶה, *livestock* (*Radak*).

וְכָל־הַמְּלָאכָה נְמִבְזָה וְנָמֵס אֹתָהּ הֶחֱרִימוּ — *But the inferior and wretched livestock, that they did destroy.*

Even what they did was not in fulfillment of Hashem's mandate, since they killed certain animals only because they were inferior (*Abarbanel*).

1. *Ner Mitzvah* cites *Rambam* (*Sefer HaMitzvos: Mitzvos Asei* 173) as stating that, with the exception of a direct command from Hashem, a king's word is more authoritative than that of a prophet.

According to *Kli Chemdah,* killing the animals would ordinarily have violated the Torah's prohibition against hurting animals. Whereas a prophet may override that prohibition with good cause, Saul reasoned that here there was no room for such dispensation, since such a mass slaughter would only instill within the Israelites the trait of cruelty. See also *Be'er Moshe* and *Mishbetzos Zahav* for alternative versions of Saul's rationalization.

the fatted bulls, the fatted sheep, and on all that
was good; and they were not willing to destroy
them; but the inferior and wretched livestock, that
they did destroy.

10 *The word of Hashem then came to Samuel, say-*
ing, 11 *"I have reconsidered My having made Saul*
king, for he has turned away from Me and has
not fulfilled My word!" Samuel was aggrieved [by
this] and he cried out to Hashem the entire night.

◆§ Rebuke and Judgment of Saul

11. נִחַמְתִּי כִּי־הִמְלַכְתִּי אֶת־שָׁאוּל לְמֶלֶךְ — *I have reconsidered My having made Saul king.*

The word נִחַמְתִּי indicates a change of heart — in this case irrevocable because, when Hashem's will is removed from something, it ceases to exist (*Malbim*).

More conventionally, נִחַמְתִּי means *I am consoled*. In keeping with that meaning of the word, Hashem said, "My consolation is that I crowned [only] Saul and did not promise the kingdom to his descendants" (*Kli Yakar*).

כִּי־שָׁב מֵאַחֲרַי וְאֶת־דְּבָרַי לֹא הֵקִים — *For he has turned away from Me and has not fulfilled My word.*

Saul's loss of the kingship had been decreed earlier at the incident of Gilgal (13:13-14). His repentance at that time might have brought him atonement, were it not for this second offense. (See comm. above for alternative approaches.)

Abarbanel incorporates both of Saul's failings into this verse: כִּי־שָׁב מֵאַחֲרַי, *he has turned away from Me,* refers to Gilgal, and דְּבָרַי לֹא הֵקִים, *has not fulfilled My word,* to his Amalekite mission.

According to *Malbim*, however, the entire phrase applies to Saul's present failure. וְאֶת־דְּבָרַי לֹא הֵקִים incriminates Saul for inaction, while כִּי־שָׁב מֵאַחֲרַי, *he has turned away from Me,* implies that Saul's failure was due to a calculated decision to act contrary to Hashem's directive, and that drastically deepened the level of his guilt.

"Following Hashem" implies emulating His attributes — i.e., pitying those worthy of compassion and punishing those who deserve judgment. When Saul employed mercy in place of judgment, שָׁב מֵאַחֲרַי, *he turned away from [Hashem's ways].*

וַיִּחַר לִשְׁמוּאֵל — *Samuel was aggrieved.*

Although generally used to indicate a burning anger, וַיִּחַר sometimes implies sorrow or mental suffering (see *Genesis* 45:5, *Numbers* 16:15), and that is its likely meaning here as well.

Nonetheless, some commentators follow the conventional meaning of the word: Samuel had invested so much love and exerted so much effort in molding Saul and establishing his kingdom that Saul's failure now frustrated and angered him (*Abarbanel, Mahari Kara*).

וַיִּזְעַק אֶל־ה׳ — *And he cried out to Hashem.*

Although Samuel was angry with Saul, he cried out in prayer on his behalf (*Mahari Kara*).

The *Zohar* (Vol. II 19:2) states that the verb וַיִּזְעַק, *and he cried out* (like צְעָקָה), indicates a state in which the supplicant is so agitated that he cannot articulate his feelings in words, but simply cries out. This heartfelt outcry comes closer to Hashem than any other prayer.

The Talmud (*Taanis* 5b), however, tells that Samuel did express himself in words, as follows: "Master of the Universe, You equated me with Moses and Aharon (see *Psalms* 99:6). Just as their protege, Joshua, was not incapacitated during their lifetimes, so too may

יב וַיַּשְׁכֵּם שְׁמוּאֵל לִקְרַאת שָׁאוּל בַּבֹּקֶר וַיֻּגַּד
לִשְׁמוּאֵל לֵאמֹר בָּא־שָׁאוּל הַכַּרְמֶלָה וְהִנֵּה מַצִּיב
לוֹ יָד וַיִּסֹּב וַיַּעֲבֹר וַיֵּרֶד הַגִּלְגָּל: יג וַיָּבֹא שְׁמוּאֵל
אֶל־שָׁאוּל וַיֹּאמֶר לוֹ שָׁאוּל בָּרוּךְ אַתָּה לַיהוָֹה
יד הֲקִימֹתִי אֶת־דְּבַר יהוָֹה: וַיֹּאמֶר שְׁמוּאֵל וּמֶה קוֹל־
הַצֹּאן הַזֶּה בְּאָזְנָי וְקוֹל הַבָּקָר אֲשֶׁר אָנֹכִי שֹׁמֵעַ:

my protege Saul not lose his kingdom during my lifetime." Were it not for Samuel's petition, Saul would have died immediately; instead, this prayer extended his reign for another two and a half years.

12. וַיַּשְׁכֵּם שְׁמוּאֵל ... בַּבֹּקֶר — *Samuel arose early in the morning.*

Our patriarchs and prophets — Abraham (*Genesis* 22:3), Jacob (ibid. 28:18), Moses (*Exodus* 34:4), and Joshua (*Joshua* 3:1) — enthusiastically began their undertakings early in the morning. Here Samuel did the same, his deed being particularly noteworthy since he had been awake all night praying (*Me'am Loez*).

In this case, Samuel was preparing to perform the mitzvah of rebuke (*Daas Sofrim;* see *Mechilta Bo, Yalkut Shimoni* 432).

וַיֻּגַּד לִשְׁמוּאֵל — *It had been told to Samuel.*

He had been informed via Divine inspiration (*Kli Yakar*).

הַכַּרְמֶלָה — *To the Carmel.*

Carmel is a city in Judah's territory (*Joshua* 15:55), not far from Gilgal.

Rashi, however (as we will see below), cites a Midrash that *Carmel* here refers to Mount Carmel, which was situated a considerable distance from Gilgal, at the northwestern end of the land of Israel.

וְהִנֵּה מַצִּיב לוֹ יָד — *And set up for himself a place [for an altar].*

Our translation follows *Rashi,* who cites a Midrash associating מַצִּיב with an altar (as in וַיַּצֶּב־שָׁם מִזְבֵּחַ, *He set up there an altar* [*Genesis* 33:20]).[1]

According to *Ralbag,* Saul established a place in which to serve Hashem and offer thanks for his military victory.

Targum, on the other hand, translates this verse to the effect that Saul established a site at Carmel for the distribution of the spoils.

Radak states that this site served as a resting place for his army.

1. The altar located at Mount Carmel was subsequently demolished by the corrupt kings of Israel (a commonwealth composed of the northern ten tribes). Elijah rebuilt it in the course of his challenge to the prophets of the idol Baal, and he brought his offering upon it at that time (*I Kings* 18:30, see *Rashi* ad loc.).

Scripture refers there to the altar as מִזְבַּח ה׳ הֶהָרוּס, *the ruined altar of HASHEM.* Some commentators explain that Elijah corrected the error of Saul and thereby "rebuilt" what was ruined by Saul. Saul weakened the people's trust in the word of Hashem and the prophets, and Elijah strengthened them (*Mishbetzos Zahav*).

Shevet HaLevi says that while Mount Sinai was chosen for the giving of the Torah because of its humility, Mount Tabor and Mount Carmel were rejected because of their haughtiness. Nevertheless, they were chosen for the battle against Sisera (*Judges* Ch. 4) and Elijah's repudiation of the idol Baal (*I Kings* Ch. 18) respectively. The reason for this is that whereas humility is appropriate for Torah study, to battle the Torah's enemies, one must "raise his heart in the way of Hashem" (*II Chronicles* 17:6), and "kosher haughtiness" is appropriate for such an undertaking. Thus, since Saul failed in not standing up to the people, his altar at Mount Carmel was ruined, until Elijah restored it.

15/12-14

[12] *Samuel arose early in the morning to meet Saul.*
(It had been told to Samuel, saying, "Saul came
to the Carmel and set up for himself a place [for
an altar]. He turned and descended to Gilgal.")
[13] *When Samuel came to Saul, Saul said to him,*
"Blessed are you to H*ASHEM! I have fulfilled the*
word of H*ASHEM."*
[14] *Samuel said, "And what is this sound of the*
sheep in my ears and the sound of the cattle that
I hear?"

According to all of the above interpretations, the word יָד — usually, *hand* — is *a place*, as in *Deuteronomy* 23:13 (see *Sifrei* 257).

Malbim, however, reads יָד simply as *hand*, and he suggests that מַצִּיב is related to מַצֵּבָה, *monument* (as in וַיַּצֶּב לוֹ בְחַיָּיו אֶת־מַצֶּבֶת, *[Absalom] had erected the monument* [*II Samuel* 18:18]). Thus, Saul erected a monument to commemorate his victory, upon which was placed the image of a *hand*, symbolizing strength.

וַיִּסֹּב וַיַּעֲבֹר וַיֵּרֶד הַגִּלְגָּל — *He turned and descended to Gilgal.*

This constituted part of the message that Samuel received via Divine inspiration. Saul left Carmel and descended to Gilgal in order to bring offerings there.

Although Saul could have brought offerings on a private altar wherever he wished, he chose Gilgal in honor of the fact that it had been the first site of the Sanctuary in the Holy Land (*Radak*).

Ralbag and *Abarbanel* contend that *Saul set up for himself a place [for an altar]* not in Carmel but Gilgal. They thus translate the verse, וְהִנֵּה מַצִּיב לוֹ יָד, *[Since he wanted] to set up for himself a place [for an altar]*, וַיִּסֹּב וַיַּעֲבֹר וַיֵּרֶד הַגִּלְגָּל, *he turned and descended to Gilgal.*

13. וַיָּבֹא שְׁמוּאֵל אֶל־שָׁאוּל — *When Samuel came to Saul*, in Gilgal.

בָּרוּךְ אַתָּה לַה׳ הֲקִימֹתִי אֶת דְּבַר־ה׳ — *Blessed are you to* H*ASHEM! I have fulfilled the word of* H*ASHEM.*

Saul assumed that he had fulfilled God's word; since it had been delivered to him through Samuel, he called upon Hashem to bless him (*Abarbanel*).

As he joyously welcomed Samuel, Saul was complacent and self-confident (*Me'am Loez*). Ironically, however, Saul's praise of himself — *I have fulfilled the word of* H*ASHEM* — was the exact opposite of Hashem's assessment of his conduct: *he has ... not fulfilled My word* (v. 11; *R' Mendel Geldwerth*).[1]

14. וַיֹּאמֶר שְׁמוּאֵל — *Samuel said.*

The verse does not say that Samuel spoke to Saul. Rather, he was so disappointed with Saul that he did not direct his words to him but spoke as if to himself (*Kli Yakar*).

וּמֶה קוֹל־הַצֹּאן הַזֶּה ... — *And what is this sound of the sheep ...*

This style of rebuke — reminiscent of Hashem's castigation of Adam (*Genesis*

1. In his *Ner Yisrael*, Rabbi Yisrael of Rizhin gives Saul's false claim a redeeming prophetic quality. The Talmud (*Shabbos* 88a) states that following Haman's downfall, the Jews enthusiastically re-committed themselves to the Torah. Thus, Saul's decision to leave Haman's ancestor Agag alive indirectly "fulfilled the word of Hashem."

טו וַיֹּאמֶר שָׁאוּל מֵעֲמָלֵקִי הֱבִיאוּם אֲשֶׁר חָמַל
הָעָם עַל־מֵיטַב הַצֹּאן וְהַבָּקָר לְמַעַן זְבֹחַ לַיהוָה
טז אֱלֹהֶיךָ וְאֶת־הַיּוֹתֵר הֶחֱרַמְנוּ׃ וַיֹּאמֶר
שְׁמוּאֵל אֶל־שָׁאוּל הֶרֶף וְאַגִּידָה לְּךָ אֵת
אֲשֶׁר דִּבֶּר יְהוָה אֵלַי הַלָּיְלָה °ויאמרו לוֹ
יז דַּבֵּר׃ וַיֹּאמֶר שְׁמוּאֵל הֲלוֹא אִם־קָטֹן אַתָּה
בְּעֵינֶיךָ רֹאשׁ שִׁבְטֵי יִשְׂרָאֵל אָתָּה וַיִּמְשָׁחֲךָ יְהוָה

°וַיֹּאמֶר ק׳

3:9) and Cain (ibid. 4:9) — involves asking a rhetorical question that invites the listener to admit his guilt and repent (*Daas Sofrim*).

Targum reads the phrase as, *If you have indeed fulfilled [HASHEM's word], what is the sound of the sheep...*

According to *Abarbanel*, this was a request for information, for Samuel had not been Divinely apprised of the nature of Saul's sin. Thus, his first indication of what it was came when he heard the sheep.

קוֹל־הַצֹּאן ... וְקוֹל הַבָּקָר — *The sound of the sheep ... and the sound of the cattle.*

According to the view that Saul had distributed the spoils in Carmel, he had saved some of it to offer on the altar in Gilgal.

Me'am Loez states that the *sound of the sheep* may be read as referring to the sound of young Jewish children in the time of Haman crying out to Hashem like bleating sheep (see *Me'am Loez, Esther; Selichos, Taanis Esther*). Accordingly, Samuel was implicitly rebuking Saul, "If you had done as you were told, why would I prophetically perceive the cries of panic brought about by Agag's descendant?"

As mentioned above, the Amalekites were able to transform themselves into animals. Accordingly, *Shevet HaLevi* explains that Samuel says to Saul, "You hear only sheep and cattle, but I am able to detect, through Divine inspiration, the sounds of humans." Scripture later tells of Amalekites who attacked the city of Ziklag (below, Ch. 30). Since that incident occurred soon after this one, and Saul killed all Amalekites except for Agag, those Amalekites must have been those who had transformed themselves into sheep to escape the wrath of Israel. Although the people saved these animals to bring as offerings, they must have delayed long enough for them to escape and transform themselves back into prople (*Siach Mordechai*, cited by *Mishbetzos Zahav*).

15. מֵעֲמָלֵקִי הֱבִיאוּם... — *I have brought them from the Amalekite.*

Saul argued that the Jews intended to offer these animals to God.

Saul inadvertently undid his own justification with this response. He assumed that the objection to allowing the animals to live was that doing so would perpetuate the name of Amalek. However, thought Saul, this should not be a problem, since these animals would soon be brought as offerings. Yet in his answer to Samuel, *I have brought them from the Amalekite*, he himself perpetuated the name of Amalek (HaRav Yaakov Padanki, whose commentary is published together with that of *Abarbanel*).

אֲשֶׁר חָמַל הָעָם — *For the people took pity.*

Saul shifted the blame onto the people.

According to some, his claim was justified. Nevertheless, he should have made an effort to stop them; since he had not, he should have accepted responsibility for their actions (*Me'am Loez*).

לְמַעַן זְבֹחַ לַה׳ — *In order to bring them as offerings to HASHEM.*

Their purpose was solely for the sake of heaven (*Radak*).

The Talmud (*Avodah Zarah* 24b) discusses the halachic aspects of attaining

15 Saul said, "I have brought them from the
Amalekite, for the people took pity on the best
of the sheep and cattle in order to bring them
as offerings to HASHEM, your God, but we have
destroyed the remainder."
16 Samuel said to Saul, "Desist, and I shall tell
you what HASHEM spoke to me last night."
He said to him, "Speak."
17 Samuel said, "Is this not so? — Though you
may be small in your own eyes, you are the head of
the tribes of Israel; and HASHEM has anointed you

animals from gentiles for the purpose of offering them to God. One opinion states that this is permissible, and cites the present instance, in which Saul intended to use Amalekite animals as offerings. However, a second view states that he meant only to sell the animals and use the funds to obtain offerings. Thus, he took only מֵיטָב, *the best*, which he would be able to sell quickly. The Jerusalem Talmud (*Avodah Zarah* 2:1) states that no evidence can be adduced from this episode, since Saul acted incorrectly.

However, *Rambam* (*Hil. Issurei Mizbe'ach* 3:15) does cite this episode to conclude that a person may use animals obtained from a gentile as an offering.

אֱלֹהֶיךָ — *Your God.*

By associating Samuel with God, Saul accorded him a high degree of honor. The greater a person is, the more appropriate it is to associate God's Name with him (*Radak*).

וְאֶת־הַיּוֹתֵר הֶחֱרַמְנוּ — *But we have destroyed the remainder.*

They destroyed whatever could not have served as an offering (*Metzudos*).

When mentioning this deed, Saul made it a point to include himself.

16. הֶרֶף — *Desist.*

Targum and *Rashi* render הֶרֶף as *wait* (see above, 11:3). Here it does not indicate a delay but rather Samuel's disappointment in Saul's self-vindication; he thus sharply cut him off with the peremptory command, *Wait!*

Metzudos relates הֶרֶף to רִפְיוֹן, *weaken* (as in *Deuteronomy* 9:14), imbuing it with a similar implication: *Weaken your hold on your words and stop talking.*

Malbim adds that Samuel halted Saul's self-justification because, as a denial of his manifest guilt, it was in itself a serious malefaction.

Abarbanel, however, understands the use of this word entirely differently. According to him, with it Samuel formally petitioned Saul as monarch for the right to speak.

וַיֹּאמֶר לוֹ דַּבֵּר — *He said to him, "Speak."*

The קְרִי, the oral version, has וַיֹּאמֶר, *he said*, implying that only Saul spoke. However, the כְּתִיב, the written version, is וַיֹּאמְרוּ, *they said*, implying that the elders of the nation answered together with Saul (*Radak*).

17. אִם־קָטֹן אַתָּה בְּעֵינֶיךָ רֹאשׁ שִׁבְטֵי יִשְׂרָאֵל אָתָּה — *Though you may be small in your own eyes, you are the head of the tribes of Israel.*

In response to Saul's statement that *the people took pity*, Samuel told Saul that this was no time for humility and submissiveness. Saul was held responsible for performing Hashem's will, even if that required him to ignore popular

יח לְמֶלֶךְ עַל־יִשְׂרָאֵל׃ וַיִּשְׁלָחֲךָ יהוה בְּדָרֶךְ
וַיֹּאמֶר לֵךְ וְהַחֲרַמְתָּה אֶת־הַחַטָּאִים אֶת־עֲמָלֵק
יט וְנִלְחַמְתָּ בוֹ עַד־כַּלּוֹתָם אֹתָם׃ וְלָמָּה לֹא־
שָׁמַעְתָּ בְּקוֹל יהוה וַתַּעַט אֶל־הַשָּׁלָל וַתַּעַשׂ
כ הָרַע בְּעֵינֵי יהוה׃ וַיֹּאמֶר

opinion. If he failed to command the people properly, he would be held accountable for their misdeeds (*Radak*).

The Talmud (*Yoma* 22b) attributes Saul's downfall to his failure to demand that the people pay him the respect due to a king (above, 10:27). By not doing so, he in effect relinquished not only his own honor but that of the nation as well, and thus that of Hashem (*Be'er Moshe*).

The eyes of a nation look toward its leader to provide a model of ethical conduct. For example, אִם הַכֹּהֵן הַמָּשִׁיחַ יֶחֱטָא לְאַשְׁמַת הָעָם, *If the anointed priest will sin, [that will lend] to the guilt of the nation* (*Leviticus* 4:3), for the people will emulate him (*Ta'ama D'Kra*).

Thus, Samuel chastised Saul, "You may feel justified in considering your sin to be minor. But you are the king, and thus your deeds have ramifications that affect everyone" (*Mussar HaNeviim*).

Targum (cited by *Rashi*) makes reference to a Talmudic tradition (*Sotah* 37a) that the tribe of Benjamin was the first to jump into the Sea of Reeds. Samuel thus told Saul, "Although you may consider yourself weak, remember that you attained the monarchy in the merit of your forefathers, who were *the leaders of the tribes of Israel.*" Just as they assumed the role of leadership, so — implied Samuel — should Saul.

Mussar HaNeviim adds that the Talmud (ibid.) states that the Benjaminites jumped in despite being stoned by the ministers of the tribe of Judah. So too, Saul should not concern himself with public opinion when obeying Hashem's command.

וַיִּמְשָׁחֲךָ ה׳ לְמֶלֶךְ — *And Hashem has anointed you to be king.*

Even if Saul had been elected, he would have to exercise his authority over the people; how much more must he do so since he had been chosen by Hashem Himself (*Abarbanel*).

18. וַיִּשְׁלָחֲךָ ה׳ — *Hashem sent you.*

Saul's guilt was especially egregious because Hashem had assigned this mission specifically to him (*Daas Sofrim*). Thus, he had no right to yield to the will of the people (*Abarbanel*).

בְּדָרֶךְ — *On the way.*

The simple understanding of this word is "on a mission."

Abarbanel sees in this term an allusion to the דֶּרֶךְ, *road*, in which Amalek initially confronted the Jewish people, as it says, זָכוֹר אֵת אֲשֶׁר־עָשָׂה לְךָ עֲמָלֵק בַּדֶּרֶךְ בְּצֵאתְכֶם מִמִּצְרָיִם, *Remember what Amalek did to you on the way when you were leaving Egypt* (*Deuteronomy* 25:17; see above, v. 2).

אֶת־הַחַטָּאִים אֶת־עֲמָלֵק — *The sinners, Amalek.*

The word הַחַטָּאִים can be translated either as *sinners* or as *sins* (unlike the word חוֹטְאִים, which means only *sinners*). The use of this word implies that Amalek embodies the essence of sin, for which reason it must be eradicated (*Be'er Moshe*). The same word appears in the verse, יִתַּמּוּ חַטָּאִים מִן־הָאָרֶץ, *Sinners will cease from the earth* (*Psalms* 104:35), a verse that the *Zohar* applies to Amalek (see *Berachos* 10a).

Rambam (*Hil. Melachim* 6:4) rules that were the people of Amalek to accept the seven Noahide laws and make peace with the Jews, there would be no commandment to kill them. The *Brisker Rav* finds support for this from here. The halachos pertaining to

to be king over Israel. 18 *HASHEM sent you on the way, and He said, 'Go, destroy the sinners, Amalek, and wage war with him until you have exterminated them.'* 19 *Why did you not obey the voice of HASHEM? You rushed after the spoils, and you did what was evil in the eyes of HASHEM."*

Amalek are in effect only as long as they fit the description of הַחַטָּאִים, *the sinners.*

וְהַחֲרַמְתָּה אֶת־הַחַטָּאִים אֶת־עֲמָלֵק וְנִלְחַמְתָּ בוֹ עַד־כַּלּוֹתָם אֹתָם — *Destroy the sinners, Amalek, and wage war with him until you have exterminated them.*

The verse initially speaks of *the sinners* in the singular — בּוֹ, *with him,* and then in the plural אֹתָם, *them. Kli Yakar* explains *the sinners* as referring to Amalek and to Agag. Hence, the verse may be read as follows: וְנִלְחַמְתָּ בוֹ, *Wage war with [Agag],* and in so doing, you will כַּלּוֹתָם אֹתָם, *exterminate them* — the nation. That is to say, once Saul destroyed Agag, the morale of the nation would have plummeted and they could have been easily defeated.

עַד־כַּלּוֹתָם אֹתָם — *Until you have exterminated them.*

Our translation, which follows *Radak,* renders כַּלּוֹתָם as *you have exterminated them.* The word may be divided into two: כַּלּוֹת, *you* (singular) *have exterminated,* plus the suffix ם, which denotes *them.* The following word, אֹתָם, *them,* merely adds emphasis.

However, *Rashi* rejects this redundancy. Instead, he reads כַּלּוֹתָם as *they* — i.e., the nation — *have exterminated.*

19. In his sharp reproach, Samuel made three points (*Malbim*), as follows.

וְלָמָּה לֹא־שָׁמַעְתָּ בְּקוֹל ה׳ — *Why did you not obey the voice of HASHEM?*

When a person is sent on a mission, he may, under normal circumstances, choose to modify its particulars, since he understands its general scope. However, in regard to a heavenly mission, the depths of whose every nuance a person cannot comprehend, he must follow orders punctiliously (*Malbim*).

וַתַּעַט אֶל־הַשָּׁלָל — *You rushed after the spoils.*

וַתַּעַט is related to הָעַיִט, *birds of prey* (*Genesis* 15:11), which swoop down to devour their quarry. See above, 14:32.

Although Saul blamed the people for having taken the spoils, God held him responsible for not having objected.

Also, notwithstanding Saul's rationalization that the animals had been saved solely so that they might be offered to Hashem, Samuel implied here that the underlying motivation was greed (*Abarbanel, Malbim*).

R' Eliyahu Dessler (*Michtav MeEliyahu* Vol. V) says that although, on a conscious level, Saul though that he wanted to save animals as offerings — for a spiritual purpose — subconsciously his concern was his discomfort with the materialistic waste of those animals. He was held accountable for those underlying feelings (see also *Mishnas R' Aharon* Vol. I, p. 187).

וַתַּעַשׂ הָרַע בְּעֵינֵי ה׳ — *And you did what was evil in the eyes of HASHEM.*

Although Saul's fault was, simply understood, a failure to act, Samuel incriminated him for having actively done wrong. Because Saul had diminished the Biblical mandate to eliminate all Amalek, his performance was considered to be

1. The Torah prohibits re-interpreting a commandment by diminishing it and performing less than the actual specifications — e.g., wearing *tzitzis* on three corners of a garment.

שָׁא֣וּל אֶל־שְׁמוּאֵ֗ל אֲשֶׁ֤ר שָׁמַ֙עְתִּי֙ בְּק֣וֹל יְהוָ֔ה וָאֵלֵ֕ךְ
בַּדֶּ֖רֶךְ אֲשֶׁר־שְׁלָחַ֣נִי יְהוָ֑ה וָאָבִ֗יא אֶת־אֲגַג֙ מֶ֣לֶךְ
כא עֲמָלֵ֔ק וְאֶת־עֲמָלֵ֖ק הֶחֱרַֽמְתִּי׃ וַיִּקַּ֨ח הָעָ֧ם מֵהַשָּׁלָ֛ל
צֹ֥אן וּבָקָ֖ר רֵאשִׁ֣ית הַחֵ֑רֶם לִזְבֹּ֛חַ לַיהוָ֥ה אֱלֹהֶ֖יךָ
כב בַּגִּלְגָּֽל׃ וַיֹּ֣אמֶר שְׁמוּאֵ֗ל הַחֵ֤פֶץ לַֽיהוָה֙
בְּעֹל֣וֹת וּזְבָחִ֔ים כִּשְׁמֹ֖עַ בְּק֣וֹל יְהוָ֑ה הִנֵּ֤ה שְׁמֹ֙עַ֙

evil in the eyes of Hashem (*Malbim*).[1] In fact, since he was told to kill all the Amalekites, and he didn't, it is as if he acted on his own, and even those that he killed are simply considered to have been unjustly murdered (see *Sefer Chofetz Chaim al HaTorah*).

According to *Abarbanel*, at this point Samuel was not yet aware that Saul had also spared Agag, and noticed only the live animals, so he made mention only of that.

20. וַיֹּאמֶר שָׁאוּל אֶל־שְׁמוּאֵל אֲשֶׁר שָׁמַעְתִּי בְּקוֹל ה׳ — *Saul said to Samuel, "But I did heed the voice of* HASHEM.*"*

Notwithstanding Samuel's acerbic condemnation, Saul maintained his innocence.

Radak states that with these words Saul interrupted Samuel's rebuke. Accordingly, the word אֲשֶׁר does not bear its common meaning — *that* or *since* — but indicates the rejoinder, *Yes, [I did heed the word of* HASHEM*]*.

Alternatively, *Radak* translates אֲשֶׁר conventionally and explains that Saul was elaborating on his previous joyous exclamation, הֲקִימֹתִי אֶת־דְּבַר ה׳, *I have fulfilled the word of* HASHEM (v. 13). Now he added אֲשֶׁר שָׁמַעְתִּי בְּקוֹל ה׳ וָאֵלֵךְ בַּדֶּרֶךְ, *in that I heeded the voice of* HASHEM *and walked on the path...*

Kli Yakar, seeking to find some element in אֲשֶׁר שָׁמַעְתִּי, that is not included in his previous statement, translates אֲשֶׁר as כַּאֲשֶׁר, *when* or, *as soon as*. Thus, Saul attempts to accentuate his self-justification by stating that he reacted to Hashem's command with alacrity.

וָאָבִיא אֶת־אֲגַג — *I brought Agag.*

Although Saul had not yet killed Agag, he had not committed an irrevocable offense, for that responsibility could still be discharged (*Radak*).

According to *Abarbanel*, Saul defended his decision to leave the king alive by saying that he had done so in order to humiliate him — a common procedure in Biblical days (see *Judges* 1:7).

21. צֹאן וּבָקָר — *Sheep and cattle.*

Saul here made two points. First, he reiterated that it was not he but the people who had taken the spoils. Second, he added that their intentions were noble, for they took only kosher animals, with the intent to offer them to God. Had the Israelites been satisfying their material desires, they would have taken camels and donkeys as well (*Kli Yakar*).

רֵאשִׁית הַחֵרֶם — *The best of that which was to be destroyed.*

Our translation of רֵאשִׁית — literally, *first* — as *best*, follows *Rashi* (as in רֵאשִׁית דְּגָנְךָ, *the best of your grain* [*Deuteronomy* 18:4]).

Targum renders רֵאשִׁית הַחֵרֶם as *before the cherem*. This may be translated in one of two ways: *before the destruction*, or (in the view of *Radak*'s father [above, v. 3]), *before the ban [on Amalek's property]*. The people assumed that they were permitted to dedicate Amalekite livestock to Hashem before the ban went into effect (*Radak; Klei Chemdah, Parashas Ki Setzei*).

In the introduction to *Teshuvos Oneg Yom Tov*, the author offers an alternative approach to *Targum's* translation.

20 Saul said to Samuel, "But I did heed the voice
of HASHEM, and I did walk the path on which
HASHEM sent me! I brought Agag, king of Amalek,
and I destroyed Amalek! 21 The people took sheep
and cattle from the spoils — the best of that which
was to be destroyed — in order to bring offerings
to HASHEM, your God, in Gilgal."
22 Samuel said, "Does HASHEM delight in eleva-
tion-offerings and feast-offerings as in obedience
to the voice of HASHEM? Behold! to obey [is better]

God's directive to eradicate Amalek's possessions would take effect only after all of the Amalekites were killed. Saul purposely left Agag alive so that the Jews would still retain the opportunity to offer animals from Amalekite flocks. Thus רֵאשִׁית הַחֵרֶם means *before the destruction [of the people]. Oneg Yom Tov* adds that from a purely halachic perspective, Saul was right. He was condemned because he had sought a way to evade the simple meaning of God's orders.

לִזְבֹּחַ לַה׳ אֱלֹהֶיךָ בַּגִּלְגָּל — *In order to bring offerings to HASHEM, your God, in Gilgal.*

As mentioned previously, upon coming to the the Land of Israel, the Jews had set up the Sanctuary in Gilgal. Although the Sanctuary was at this point in Nob, Gilgal remained a cherished place and an appropriate location for spiritual elevation (*Radak*).

In *Doros HaRishonim* (Vol. VI, Chs. 33,34), however, Rabbi Yehudah HaLevi states that the Sanctuary was still located in Gilgal (and he cites this passage as confirmation of that claim). It was only after this episode that Saul, bitter and frustrated, deemed the place as unpropitious for him and transferred it to Nob.

22. ... וַיֹּאמֶר שְׁמוּאֵל — *Samuel said ...*

After Samuel dismissed Saul's explanation that he had saved the animals to offer them to God, Saul repeated that assertion. Samuel now responded that even if that were the case, the Jews were still at fault (*Abarbanel*).

... הַחֵפֶץ ה׳ בְּעֹלוֹת וּזְבָחִים — *Does HASHEM delight in elevation-offerings and feast-offerings ...*

Samuel began with a rhetorical question in order to impress the obvious and undeniable nature of his argument on Saul (*Daas Sofrim*). Then, for further emphasis, he answered the question himself.

הַחֵפֶץ ה׳ בְּעֹלוֹת וּזְבָחִים כִּשְׁמֹעַ בְּקוֹל ה׳ — *Does HASHEM delight in elevation-offerings and feast-offerings as in obedience to the voice of HASHEM?*

Offerings are a vehicle through which a person humbles himself before Hashem and commits himself to Hashem's service. How hypocritical it therefore is for a person insubordinate to Hashem's decrees to bring an offering.

Indeed, throughout the generations the prophets denounced the Jews for offering sacrifices that were not accompanied by submission to God that involved a high level of purity of thought (*Rambam, Moreh Nevuchim* Vol. III, Ch. 32).

Ralbag adds that offerings are generally brought to attain atonement. Hashem would much rather that a person not sin and thereby avoid the necessity for bringing an offering in the first place.

כג מִזֶּבַח טוֹב לְהַקְשִׁיב מֵחֵלֶב אֵילִים: כִּי חַטַּאת־קֶסֶם
מֶרִי וְאָוֶן וּתְרָפִים הַפְצַר יַעַן מָאַסְתָּ אֶת־דְּבַר יהוה
כד וַיִּמְאָסְךָ מִמֶּלֶךְ: וַיֹּאמֶר שָׁאוּל אֶל־שְׁמוּאֵל
חָטָאתִי כִּי־עָבַרְתִּי אֶת־פִּי־יהוה וְאֶת־דְּבָרֶיךָ

הִנֵּה שְׁמֹעַ מִזֶּבַח טוֹב — *Behold! to obey [is better] than a choice offering.*

Our translation follows *Mahari Kara*, according to whom טוֹב means *choice* and modifies זֶבַח, *offering*. He comments that the cantillation supports this reading, in that it associates טוֹב with מִזֶּבַח.

Rashi, however, translates טוֹב as *better* and renders this phrase as *to obey is better than an offering.*

According to *Kli Yakar*, the choice offering mentioned here is a peace-offering, which is offered not to atone for sin but to bring a person closer to Hashem. Genuine obedience is a greater virtue than even such an offering.

HaAkeidah (*Shaar* 42) explains the מ prefix in מִזֶּבַח not as *than* but as *from*. Therefore, הִנֵּה שְׁמֹעַ מִזֶּבַח טוֹב means, *Behold, the good [that comes] from an offering is primarily submissiveness.* שֶׁאָמַרְתִּי וְנַעֲשָׂה רְצוֹנִי, [Hashem says,] "for I spoke and My will was done" (*Rashi, Exodus* 29:18).

לְהַקְשִׁיב מֵחֵלֶב אֵילִים — *To be attentive than the fat of rams.*

... that are brought on the altar.

Simply understood, this phrase repeats — and thus emphasizes — the import of the previous phrase, *to obey is better than a choice offering* (*Metzudos*).

Targum renders הַקְשִׁיב as *to obey the voice of prophets.*

Daas Sofrim explains the repetition to imply two parts of obedience. He must be a שֹׁמֵעַ, *a listener*, which means he must try to understand the depths of what is being said in order to *obey*; second, he must be מַקְשִׁיב, pay close attention to the specific words of the speaker, and understand precisely the ramifications of what he heard, rather than drawing his own conclusions.

23. In rebuking Saul, Samuel draws a series of analogies between Saul's misdeeds and serious offenses against God. To properly understand the textual meaning of the analogy, we must first translate some of the words individually, and then explain the entire phrase.

קֶסֶם — *Sorcery.*

Sorcery has various forms, but in particular involves foretelling the future. It is prohibited by the Torah (*Deuteronomy* 18:10-14) because it exhibits a lack of trust in Hashem.

Saul had succeeded in eradicating different forms of sorcery from the Jewish midst (below, 28:3). Possibly, Samuel alluded to that in the rebuke to imply that just as Saul was zealous about that sin, so he should have avoided rebelliousness (*Ohel David*, cited by *Mishbetzos Zahav*).

וְאָוֶן וּתְרָפִים — *And the iniquity of idolatry.*

The word אָוֶן, a general term denoting *evil* (*Proverbs* 6:12), is sometimes used specifically to indicate idol worship (see *Hosea* 4:15).

תְּרָפִים are images worshiped as deities (see *Genesis* 31:19,30). Thus, simply speaking, the two words אָוֶן and תְּרָפִים are synonyms, repeated for emphasis. *Ralbag* sees the ו — *and* — conjunction here as extraneous, and translates the phrase as וְאָוֶן תְּרָפִים, *the iniquity of idolatry.*

הַפְצַר — *Verbosity.*

The word הַפְצַר implies *excess* in general and, more specifically, an over-insistence on expressing one's will (see *Genesis* 33:11). According to *Targum*, this refers to Saul's addition to Samuel's instructions — i.e., his plan to offer Amalekite animals. Other commentators understand הַפְצַר as Saul's repeated and insistent justifications of his actions.

than a choice offering, to be attentive than the fat
of rams. 23 *For rebelliousness is like the sin of sor-*
cery, and verbosity is like the iniquity of idolatry.
Because you have rejected the word of HASHEM, *He*
has rejected you as king!"
24 *Saul said to Samuel, "I have sinned, for I have*
transgressed the word of HASHEM *and your word,*

כִּי חַטַּאת־קֶסֶם מֶרִי וְאָוֶן וּתְרָפִים הַפְצַר — *For rebelliousness is like the sin of sorcery, and verbosity is like the iniquity of idolatry.*

כִּי חַטַּאת־קֶסֶם מֶרִי — *for rebelliousness is like the sin of sorcery.* A person engages in sorcery when he lacks trust in Hashem: he may then worry, seek fortune-tellers, and in general disobey Hashem's orders (*Radak*).

וְאָוֶן וּתְרָפִים הַפְצַר — *and verbosity is like the iniquity of idolatry.* Just as an idol is something baseless and empty, so too is a guilty person's self-vindication baseless and empty (*Metzudos*).

Radak reads כִּי חַטַּאת, *for rebelliousness,* as כְּחַטַּאת, *like a sin.* Thus, he translates כְּחַטַּאת־קֶסֶם מֶרִי as, *Just as sorcery is a great sin, so is rebelliousness a great sin.*

He describes the word כְּחַטַּאת as modifying the second phrase as well: i.e., *Just as idolatry is a great sin, so is verbosity a great sin.*

In *Metzudos'* view, the prefix כ is not apt since Samuel's misdeeds were not analogous to but literally equivalent to *rebelliousness* and *idolatry* (see *Targum*). (Similarly, *Rashi* states that the punishment for the two is equivalent.)

The verse first mentions sorcery, which is punishable by lashes, and then the graver infraction of idolatry, which is a capital crime. Saul's initial rebelliousness was comparable to sorcery; his subsequent insistent self-justification was tantamount to idolatry. It was because of his refusal to admit guilt that Saul's eventual repentance could not salvage his kingship (*Sefer HaIkarim* 4:26).

וַיִּמְאָסְךָ מִמֶּלֶךְ — *He has rejected you as king.*

As mentioned earlier, when Saul disobeyed Samuel at Gilgal, he was told מַמְלַכְתְּךָ לֹא־תָקוּם, *Your kingdom shall not endure* (13:14), implying that although he would continue to be king his children would not inherit the throne. Now that Saul was rejected, his own regime would be shortened as well (*Ralbag*).

The phrase, וַיִּמְאָסְךָ מִמֶּלֶךְ may be read as *He rejected you from [the time you became] king* — from the moment that Saul became king, he began to lose favor in Hashem's eyes.

Alternatively, מִמֶּלֶךְ means *because you were king;* i.e., as a result of being monarch Saul grew arrogant, and that brought about his downfall (*Abarbanel*).

24. וַיֹּאמֶר שָׁאוּל אֶל־שְׁמוּאֵל חָטָאתִי כִּי־עָבַרְתִּי אֶת־פִּי־ה׳ וְאֶת־דְּבָרֶיךָ — *Saul said to Samuel, "I have sinned, for I have transgressed the word of* HASHEM *and your word."*

After Samuel's repeated chastisements, Saul finally admitted his guilt. In doing so, he referred separately to having disobeyed Hashem's words and Samuel's words.

According to *Abarbanel,* this indicates that Saul refused to acknowledge that all of Samuel's words were a prophetic message from Hashem. He continued instead to maintain that he had satisfied Hashem's command, confessing only that he had failed to adhere to Hashem's word according to what he perceived as Samuel's interpretations of and additions to Hashem's word. This further angered Samuel.

כה כִּ֤י יָרֵ֙אתִי֙ אֶת־הָעָ֔ם וָאֶשְׁמַ֖ע בְּקוֹלָֽם׃ וְעַתָּ֕ה שָׂ֥א נָ֖א
כו אֶת־חַטָּאתִ֑י וְשׁ֣וּב עִמִּ֔י וְאֶשְׁתַּחֲוֶ֖ה לַיהוָֽה׃ וַיֹּ֤אמֶר
שְׁמוּאֵל֙ אֶל־שָׁא֔וּל לֹ֥א אָשׁ֖וּב עִמָּ֑ךְ כִּ֣י מָאַ֙סְתָּה֙ אֶת־
דְּבַ֣ר יהוה וַיִּמְאָסְךָ֣ יהוה מִהְי֥וֹת מֶ֖לֶךְ עַל־יִשְׂרָאֵֽל׃

Contrarily, *Metzudos* understands Saul's mention of וְאֶת־דְּבָרֶיךָ, *and your word*, as a reference to Samuel's repeated attempts to make Saul aware of his misdeeds. Saul now expressed his recognition that his stubbornness had intensified his guilt, and expressed sincere regret for his defiance.

כִּי יָרֵאתִי אֶת־הָעָם — *For I feared the people.* Saul acknowledged that his misinterpretation of God's command had been rooted in an unconscious desire to satisfy the masses, or, as noted earlier, Doeg HaAdomi.

A Midrash (*Shemos Rabbah* 26:3) says that because Joshua descended from Joseph, who feared Hashem (*Genesis* 42:18), he was chosen to overcome Amalek (*Exodus* 17:9), the nation that did not fear Hashem (*Deuteronomy* 25:18). Accordingly, Saul now revealed that the reason he didn't merit to eradicate Amalek was because he had some trace of fear of the nation, which detracted from his fear of Hashem (*Mishnas Rav Aharon* Vol. III).

25. וְעַתָּה — *But now.*

Now that I have repented, I deserve to be forgiven (*Metzudos*).

שָׂא נָא אֶת־חַטָּאתִי — *Please forgive my sin.*

The word שָׂא — literally, *carry* or *remove* — is often used to imply atonement (see *Exodus* 10:17, 34:7).

Understandably, Samuel could not forgive Saul's sin, as that is solely the prerogative of Hashem (see *Psalms* 130:4, *Isaiah* 43:25). *Malbim* explains that after Saul confessed to having sinned against Hashem and against Samuel, he first requested that Samuel pardon him, as interpersonal sins can be atoned for only after gaining the forgiveness of the victim. Only afterward did he ask Samuel to join him as he prostrated himself in an attempt to earn Hashem's pardon.

וְשׁוּב עִמִּי — *And return with me.*

Apparently, Samuel and Saul held this discussion in a secluded place and Saul was now preparing to return to the people. Samuel's accompaniment of Saul would testify to God's satisfaction with Saul as before, when Samuel had anointed Saul (above, 9:26, 11:15; *Me'am Loez*).

26. לֹא אָשׁוּב עִמָּךְ כִּי מָאַסְתָּה אֶת־דְּבַר ה׳ ... וַיִּמְאָסְךָ ה׳ — *I will not return with you, for you have rejected the word of* HASHEM, *and* HASHEM *has rejected you.*

With these words, Samuel implied, "How can I return with you if Hashem Himself has rejected you? My show of support would be tantamount to rebelling against Him" (*Abarbanel, Metzudos*).

Also, according to *Abarbanel*, Samuel refused to accompany Saul because he was angered by Saul's presumption that Samuel had fabricated some of the details of his instructions to Saul. Samuel now rebuked him, "*You have rejected the word of* HASHEM" — i.e., all that Samuel said had come from God.

וַיִּמְאָסְךָ ה׳ מִהְיוֹת מֶלֶךְ עַל־יִשְׂרָאֵל — HASHEM *has rejected you from being king over Israel.*

Earlier, Samuel had stated simply, וַיִּמְאָסְךָ מִמֶּלֶךְ, *He has rejected you as king* (v. 23). The addition of עַל־יִשְׂרָאֵל connotes that now that Saul had been rejected, the nation had to be informed (*Daas Sofrim*).

According to *R' Yitzchak Hutner*, Saul's loss of the throne was merely a symptom of the more profound punishment that he suffered: his spiritual level

*for I feared the people and I hearkened to their
voice.* [25]*But now, please forgive my sin and return
with me, and I will prostrate myself to* HASHEM.''
[26]*Samuel said to Saul, ''I will not return with you,
for you have rejected the word of* HASHEM *and*
HASHEM *has rejected you from being king over Israel!''*

was lowered so that he was no longer fit to remain king (*Pachad Yitzchak, Yom Kippur* 11:8).

◈§ Why Was Saul Punished With the Forfeiture of His Kingship, Unlike David?

The commentators discuss at length why Saul's failure to destroy Amalek cost him the kingship — particularly since he committed only this one iniquity, whereas David, who sinned twice (in regard to Uriah and to taking a census), did not forfeit the throne.[1]

One of the most widely accepted explanations is that Saul's mission to destroy Amalek was a responsibility specifically to him as king. His failure, due to his self-confessed fear of the people, showed a lack of leadership crucial to the success of a king. David's errors, on the other hand, were of a private nature and not associated with his role as king (*Sefer HaIkarim* 24:4; see also *Malbim*). Furthermore, since Saul failed in missions that were directed specifically to him (the incident at Gilgal was also of that nature), his failure was viewed as a delinquency in monarchial duties, whereas David's crime pertained to a mitzvah of universal application, so he was judged as a common man would be (*Sefer HaIkarim*).

Alternatively, Saul was held accountable because he did not confess immediately but insisted on his righteousness. Such an attitude is the opposite of penitence. By contrast, when David was confronted with his sin, he immediately accepted responsibility, with the exclamation חָטָאתִי, *I have sinned* (*II Samuel* 12:13; *Sefer HaIkarim, Maharsha*).

Sefer Chassidim 362 writes that David would have been subject to the same judgment as Saul had it not been for the fact that he performed many great deeds that brought honor to Hashem, such as his preparations for the construction of the Temple and his heroic acts on behalf of the needy.

Some explain that since Saul was of a pure nature and had a predisposition to do good (see above, 13:1), the tarnish of his sin was irreversible (*Arizal, Shaar HaGilgulim*). Also, Saul's sin altered his nature from good to bad. By contrast, David's predisposition was for evil. He overcame it and channeled his attributes for good, so he was forgiven for his relatively few misdeeds (*Vilna Gaon* to *Proverbs* 22:6, *Ohr HaChaim* to *Deuteronomy* 33:1).

Since royalty was the prerogative of the tribe of Judah, Saul possessed the kingship on loan, as it were (indeed, *Saul* means *borrowed*). Thus, even slight misconduct on his part sufficed for the kingdom to be removed from him and transferred to its rightful holder (*Maharal, Gevuros* HASHEM Ch. 9).

More specifically, some suggest that Saul had been appointed king solely so that he might exterminate Amalek (see *Bava Basra* 123b). When he failed to do so, his claim to the throne ceased (*Me'am Loez*).

Hashem had made His very throne dependent on the eradication of Amalek (see *Exodus* 17:16, *Rashi*). Thus, when Saul failed in his task to uphold God's throne, he lost his own throne (*Alshich*).

Saul's intention had been for the good: to enhance Hashem's glory by sparing the sheep for offerings. But by so doing, he prevented Hashem from fulfilling His oath to eradicate Amalek; thus, he deserved to lose his throne.[2]

1. See *Yoma* 22b for a discussion of why some sins are not taken into consideration for the purposes of this comparison.

2. In this regard, a local governor once asked Rabbeinu Tam to explain why Saul lost his throne, whereas David did not.

Rabbeinu Tam answered with a story that illustrated this theme.

A certain French king was once captured by the king of an Arabian country who demanded

כז וַיִּסֹּב שְׁמוּאֵל לָלֶכֶת וַיַּחֲזֵק בִּכְנַף־מְעִילוֹ
כח וַיִּקָּרַע: וַיֹּאמֶר אֵלָיו שְׁמוּאֵל קָרַע יהוה אֶת־
מַמְלְכוּת יִשְׂרָאֵל מֵעָלֶיךָ הַיּוֹם וּנְתָנָהּ לְרֵעֲךָ
כט הַטּוֹב מִמֶּךָּ: וְגַם נֵצַח יִשְׂרָאֵל לֹא יְשַׁקֵּר

After Saul sinned, a tangible trace of his sin remained in the existence of the remaining Amalekites. Thus, in line with the idea that מְעֻוָּת לֹא־יוּכַל לִתְקֹן, *A perverted thing cannot be corrected* (*Ecclesiastes* 1:15), his misdeed could not be completely erased (see *Chagigah* 9a; *Nachalas Binyamin*, cited by *Nachalas Shimon* 30:10).

God decreed an end to Saul's kingdom, and He immediately chose David as his successor, and that could not be annulled (see below, vs. 28, 29; *Meshech Chochmah, Brisker Rav;* see above, 13:14).

27. וַיַּחֲזֵק בִּכְנַף־מְעִילוֹ וַיִּקָּרַע — *But [Saul] grabbed the hem of his tunic, and it tore.*

This verse leaves unclear whose tunic was torn and who tore it. *Midrash Shmuel* cites two opinions regarding whose tunic it was. If it was Samuel's, commentators differ regarding who did the tearing.

According to *Rashi*, Saul accidentally ripped Samuel's tunic. Saul was clinging desperately to Samuel's garment, anticipating the shame he would suffer if the prophet appeared before the Jews without him. When Samuel continued walking, it tore.

According to *Radak*, however, Samuel tore his own tunic as a sign of mourning. Our text of the Midrash supports this, for it adds, "Such is the way of the righteous: to exhibit pain when the work of their hands do not properly develop."[1]

The alternative version of the Midrash is that Samuel ripped Saul's tunic, and in so doing indicated that his kingship would be ripped away from him (as he specifically stated in the following verse). Samuel also hinted that whoever would rip Saul's tunic in the future would be his successor. Thus, when David did so later on, Saul told him, "I know that you will certainly reign" (below, 24:21).

בִּכְנַף־מְעִילוֹ — *The hem of his tunic.*

According to the view that the ripped tunic was that of Samuel, it was probably the one that his mother Hannah had made for him (above, 2:19), and which constituted an integral feature of his appearance (see below, 28:14).

The word כָּנָף literally means *wing* or *corner* (see *Numbers* 15:38). Following *Rashi*'s understanding of the High Priest's מְעִיל as a shirt-like cloak (*Exodus* 28:4), it seems likely that this is similar, and the כָּנָף then must be the hem. *Ramban* (ibid. 28:31) disagrees with *Rashi* and maintains that the מְעִיל was a four-cornered robe, similar to our טַלִּית קָטָן, and cites this verse as support to his view, since the verse mentions the *corner* of the מְעִיל.[2]

a significant ransom for his release. Since the French king did not have the funds available, his captor allowed him to go home and send him the money.

The French king agreed, and when he returned home, he immediately dispatched a messenger with the funds. On the way, this emissary was offered a chance to buy a certain province on behalf of the king, which he did with the ransom money.

When the French king learned of this, he was furious, for although the messenger meant to advance the king's interests, he caused the king to transgress his oath. And so he sentenced him to death by hanging (*Me'am Loez*).

1. *Mussar HaNeviim* explains that Samuel perceived Saul's being stripped of his glory as an element of Saul's death, and thus ripped his own clothing in an act of mourning.

2. In fact, *R' Tzadok HaKohen* says that since Saul failed in regard to destroying Amalek, about which the Torah commands to *remember* (*Deuteronomy* 25:17), the corner of his garment was ripped to remind him of the *tzitzis*, which is the mitzvah that arouses memory (*Numbers* 15:39; *Resisei Lailah*).

[27] *Samuel then turned away to leave, but [Saul]*
grabbed the hem of his tunic, and it tore. [28] *Sam-*
uel said to him, "HASHEM has torn the king-
ship of Israel from upon you this day, and has
given it to your fellow who is better than you.
[29] *Moreover, the Eternal One of Israel does not lie*

וַיִּקָּרַע — *And it tore.*

This passive verb supports the idea that the garment was ripped unintentionally. However, *Kli Yakar*, following the view that the garment was deliberately torn, states that it ripped apart with miraculous ease, as if by itself.

קְרִיעָה, *ripping*, results in two shortened portions. The tearing of the tunic indicated that Saul would be left with a shortened term of office and that his son Ish-bosheth would succeed him with another short reign (*Alshich*).

28. וַיֹּאמֶר אֵלָיו שְׁמוּאֵל קָרַע ה׳ אֶת־מַמְלְכוּת יִשְׂרָאֵל מֵעָלֶיךָ הַיּוֹם — *Samuel said to him, "HASHEM has torn the kingship of Israel from upon you this day."*

This prophecy was irreversible, for two reasons.

First, although a prophecy that a tragedy will occur can ordinarily be reversed, that is not the case if it is accompanied by a symbolic action (*Ramban, Genesis* 12:6, cited by *Malbim*). Second, a prophecy to benefit someone cannot be revoked, and this prophecy benefited David.

Following Saul's misdeeds at Gilgal, Samuel had notified him that his kingship would cease (above, Ch. 13). *Radak* offers two explanations of what the present rebuke, following the failure to exterminate Amalek, added.

First, directly after the events at Gilgal, Saul could have repented and gained atonement; now that he had sinned again, however, his fate was sealed.

Second, at Gilgal, the monarchy had been taken from Saul's offspring, but he himself could have remained king for a long while. Now, even that was curtailed (for other explanations, see comm. 13:14).

וּנְתָנָהּ לְרֵעֲךָ הַטּוֹב מִמֶּךָּ — *And has given it to your fellow who is better than you.*

Previously, Saul was described in the phrase (above, 9:2) אֵין־אִישׁ מִבְּנֵי יִשְׂרָאֵל טוֹב מִמֶּנּוּ, *No one in Israel was better than he.* Now he lost that distinction, and his throne would pass on to the better man.

Saul was not notified who that would be. He eventually had reason to suspect that it was David, but did not know for sure until he summoned Samuel from the grave (below, 28:17).

· *Ahavas Yehonasan* comments that Saul's successor would be "better" than Saul in that he would be aware of Saul's errors and subsequent punishment.[1]

Midrash Esther Rabbah (4:9) notes that Saul's kingship was returned to his descendant Esther with terminology similar to that of the present verse: וּמַלְכוּתָהּ יִתֵּן הַמֶּלֶךְ לִרְעוּתָהּ הַטּוֹבָה מִמֶּנָּה *And let the king confer [Vashti's] royal estate upon another who is better than she* (*Esther* 1:19).

29. נֵצַח יִשְׂרָאֵל — *The Eternal One of Israel.*

Most of the commentators state that נֵצַח יִשְׂרָאֵל (a phrase unique to this verse) refers to Hashem.

The word נֵצַח conveys various shades of endurance: *victory* (*I Chronicles* 29:11), *perpetuity* (*II Samuel* 2:26, *Psalms* 13:2, 103:9), *strength* (*Lamentations* 3:18), and *lifeblood* (*Isaiah* 63:3).

Our translation of נֵצַח follows that of *Abarbanel* and *Malbim*. *Targum* and *Rashi*, on the other hand, render נֵצַח

1. David's superiority was not necessarily apparent. *Midrash Tehillim* (27:2) relates that the angels asked why David was more deserving than Saul. Hashem told them that in Gilgal Saul had failed to wait for the *Urim VeTumim* (above, 14:18-20), whereas David would refuse to enter into battle without their advice (see *II Samuel* 5:22,23).

ל וְלֹא יִנָּחֵם כִּי לֹא אָדָם הוּא לְהִנָּחֵם: וַיֹּאמֶר
חָטָאתִי עַתָּה כַּבְּדֵנִי נָא נֶגֶד־זִקְנֵי עַמִּי וְנֶגֶד
יִשְׂרָאֵל וְשׁוּב עִמִּי וְהִשְׁתַּחֲוֵיתִי לַיהוָה אֱלֹהֶיךָ:
לא וַיָּשָׁב שְׁמוּאֵל אַחֲרֵי שָׁאוּל וַיִּשְׁתַּחוּ שָׁאוּל
לב לַיהוָה: וַיֹּאמֶר שְׁמוּאֵל הַגִּישׁוּ אֵלַי אֶת־אֲגַג
מֶלֶךְ עֲמָלֵק וַיֵּלֶךְ אֵלָיו אֲגַג מַעֲדַנֹּת וַיֹּאמֶר אֲגָג אָכֵן

יִשְׂרָאֵל as נִצְחוֹנוֹ שֶׁל יִשְׂרָאֵל, *the Triumphant One of Israel* — an allusion to Hashem as the Victor over Amalek (despite Saul's failure).[1]

Ralbag understands this appellation as the *Strength, Hope, and Life-support of Israel.*

Radak, however, applies the word נֵצַח not to God but to the Jews' *everlasting* royalty — which is to say, the Davidic dynasty.

וְגַם נֵצַח יִשְׂרָאֵל לֹא יְשַׁקֵּר וְלֹא יִנָּחֵם — *Moreover, the Eternal One of Israel does not lie and does not relent.*

Rashi, basing himself on *Targum,* explains this verse as anticipating a plea by Saul. "You may hope to repent and thereby regain your kingship," Samuel told Saul, "but that is no longer possible, for Hashem has promised your throne to someone else, and He will not renege on that commitment."

Although Hashem may renounce a troubling prophecy, He will not withdraw a favorable assurance. Therefore, Saul's fate was sealed.

Rambam (*Hil. Yesodei HaTorah* 10:4) states that this guideline may be used to test an untried prophet. If he issues a dire prediction that fails to materialize, that does not disqualify him, since Heaven may rescind such a judgment when the people engage in sincere repentance — as occurred, for instance, in the case of Jonah and the people of Nineveh (see *Jonah*). However, if a positive prophecy does not materialize, the prophet is revealed to be a fraud.

According to *Abarbanel* and *Malbim,* the appellation of Hashem as נֵצַח יִשְׂרָאֵל, *the Eternal One of Israel,* indicates one of the distinctions between God and man. Mortal man is in flux. His speech may at times contradict his thoughts, he exaggerates, rethinks his plans, and his passions wax and wane. On the other hand, נֵצַח יִשְׂרָאֵל is *unchanging,* for God is constant and unaffected by time. Thus, any promises He made that he would deprive Saul of the kingship are final, because לֹא יְשַׁקֵּר, *he will not exaggerate,* וְלֹא יִנָּחֵם, *and will not relent.*

Radak renders וְגַם not as *moreover* but as *yet* or *nevertheless,* and (as noted above) interprets נֵצַח יִשְׂרָאֵל as referring not to Hashem but to the eternal, royal monarchy of Israel. (The subject, Hashem, is carried over from the previous verse.) Hence, the verse states that although Hashem took the throne of Israel from Saul — to whom He had not promised a perpetual kingship — וְגַם נֵצַח יִשְׂרָאֵל לֹא יְשַׁקֵּר, *nevertheless, He will not forsake the eternity of Israel,* but will establish a secure and enduring monarchy through the house of David, since that eternal state was reserved for him — וְלֹא יִנָּחֵם, *and [God] will not renege* on that commitment.

וְלֹא יִנָּחֵם — *And does not relent.*

We do find verses that describe God as expressing regret; in this very chapter, He is quoted as saying, נִחַמְתִּי כִּי־הִמְלַכְתִּי אֶת־שָׁאוּל לְמֶלֶךְ, *I have reconsidered My having made Saul king* (above, v. 11). However, that is due to a change in man's attitude (*Abarbanel*).

כִּי לֹא אָדָם הוּא לְהִנָּחֵם — *For He is not a human being that He should relent.*

1. This expression is also quoted in *Midrash Tehillim* (13:1).

and does not relent, for He is not a human that He should relent."

30 *He said, "I have sinned. Now, please honor me in the presence of the elders of my people and in the presence of Israel; return with me, and I shall prostrate myself to HASHEM, your God."*
31 *So Samuel returned after Saul, and Saul prostrated himself before HASHEM.*

32 *Samuel then said, "Bring me Agag, king of Amalek."*

Agag went to him in chains, and Agag said, "Alas,

In contrasting God and man, Samuel considers it natural for man to *regret*, but not to lie. Thus, he gave mankind more credit than the gentile prophet Balaam, whose similar contrasts read: לֹא אִישׁ אֵל וִיכַזֵּב וּבֶן־אָדָם וְיִתְנֶחָם, *God is not a man that He should be deceitful, nor a son of a man that He should relent* (*Numbers* 23:19; *Daas Sofrim, R' Mendel Geldwerth*).

30. וַיֹּאמֶר חָטָאתִי — *He said, "I have sinned."*

This time, Saul acknowledged guilt without the previous modifications. As *Abarbanel* comments, he thus accepted the prescribed penalty.

עַתָּה כַּבְּדֵנִי — *Now, please honor me.*

Although I have sinned, עַתָּה, *now* that you are already here with me, it would be proper for you to escort me as I return to the people (*Metzudos*).

Daas Sofrim avers that Saul, who had not long ago shown an aversion to personal honor, could not have intended this for his own glory. Rather, he was concerned that if Samuel did not return with him that would constitute a slight to the Jewish monarchy and to the Jewish people (see also *Mahari Kara*).

However, some commentators take Saul to task for seeking honor at a time like this. *Abarbanel*, for instance, points out that even though Saul admitted guilt, he still did not request atonement but rather honor, and that is all he received (*Abarbanel*).

31. וַיָּשָׁב שְׁמוּאֵל אַחֲרֵי שָׁאוּל — *So Samuel returned after Saul.*

Seeing that Saul was embarrassed to appear alone before the masses, Samuel granted him this last request and escorted him (*Ralbag*).

In particular, he honored Saul's position as king by following *after* him (*Abarbanel*).

Other commentators, however, interpret the verse in the opposite fashion: וַיָּשָׁב שְׁמוּאֵל אַחֲרֵי שָׁאוּל — Samuel turned *away* from Saul, so as not to follow him, and thus denied him the honor for which he had pleaded (*Me'am Loez*).

וַיִּשְׁתַּחוּ שָׁאוּל לַה׳ — *And Saul prostrated himself before HASHEM.*

Saul gave thanks for God's kindness and for delivering his enemy into his hand (*Abarbanel*).

◆§ Samuel Completes the Task — and Disassociates From Saul

32. וַיֹּאמֶר שְׁמוּאֵל הַגִּישׁוּ אֵלַי אֶת־אֲגַג מֶלֶךְ עֲמָלֵק וַיֵּלֶךְ אֵלָיו — *Samuel then said, "Bring me Agag, king of Amalek." Agag went to him.*

Samuel did not think that Agag would willingly walk to his death, so he commanded that he forcibly be brought to him. Surprisingly, Agag chose to walk, even, according to some interpretations, in a stately manner (*Alshich*).

וַיֵּלֶךְ אֵלָיו אֲגַג מַעֲדַנֹּת — *Agag went to him in chains.*

Our translation of מַעֲדַנֹּת as

לג סָר מַר־הַמָּוֶת: וַיֹּאמֶר שְׁמוּאֵל כַּאֲשֶׁר שִׁכְּלָה
נָשִׁים חַרְבֶּךָ כֵּן־תִּשְׁכַּל מִנָּשִׁים אִמֶּךָ וַיְשַׁסֵּף
לד שְׁמוּאֵל אֶת־אֲגָג לִפְנֵי יהוה בַּגִּלְגָּל: וַיֵּלֶךְ

chains represents *Rambam's* view (Commentary to *Mishnayos, Keilim* 20:7, mentioned also by *Radak*). This word is used in a similar fashion in *Job*: הַתְקַשֵּׁר מַעֲדַנּוֹת כִּימָה, *Did you tie up the bond of Pleiades* (38:31)? *Rambam* explains that only Agag's hands were shackled, for he would have found it difficult to walk with fettered feet.

Targum, however, renders מַעֲדַנֹּת altogether differently, as *with pleasure* (as in *Genesis* 49:20 and *Proverbs* 29:17). Agag was thus *delighted* — or, in *Malbim's* words, even *joyous* — since he preferred death to life (*Radak*).

In one of his classic novellae, *R' Yitzchak Hutner* (*Pachad Yitzchak, Purim* 29) explains Agag's ideology based on a conflation of these two interpretations of מַעֲדַנֹּת: Agag was both chained and delighted. The people of Amalek believed that man's actions are predetermined, thus "chained"; therefore, Agag had no reason to be bitter about his death. On the contrary, he took pride in attributing, albeit incorrectly, even man's actions to Hashem's choice.

The Jewish people, on the other hand, believe in free will. The ultimate victory of the nation of Israel over Amalek will signify a sanctification of Hashem's Name associated with the triumph of the awareness that man can emerge victorious from his inner struggles.

וַיֹּאמֶר אֲגָג אָכֵן סָר מַר־הַמָּוֶת — *And Agag said, "Alas, the bitterness of death approaches."*

The word סָר, *approaches*, conventionally indicates the opposite: *leaving, going away*. *Rashi* (*Exodus* 3:3) and *Ibn Ezra* (ibid., *Genesis* 19:2, *Exodus* 25:2) point out that the word may convey the meaning of *movement* from one spot to another. In such a case, the verb can assume the meaning of *approaching* (*R' Mendel Geldwerth*).

Rashi and *Radak* render the word סָר here in that meaning: the bitterness of death, stated Agag, had approached and overwhelmed him.

Others, however, understand סָר in its conventional sense. Agag thus stated, *The bitterness of death has left me* (*Pirkei D'Rabbi Eliezer*, Ch. 49). As a descendant of royal stock accustomed to honor, he suffered from the degradation of being a prisoner of war. Under such circumstances, death would come as sweet relief (*Abarbanel*).

Malbim echoes this general interpretation of Agag's mood, but translates מַר as *substitute* (as in *Leviticus*, וְלֹא יָמִיר אֹתוֹ, *he shall not substitute it* [27:10]). Accordingly, מַר־הַמָּוֶת means the *substitute for death* — i.e., servitude. Agag thus exclaimed, "Servitude, that substitute for death, has now thankfully been removed."

According to *Ralbag*, when Agag was brought before Samuel, he sensed Samuel's saintliness and thus assumed that Samuel would have mercy on him and let him live. Thus, he said, "The bitterness of my anticipated death has just left."

Chida (*Chomas Anach*) interprets the verse similarly. Agag had been afraid that he would be killed by a lowly soldier or executioner, which would have slighted his dignity. When he saw Samuel, he felt honored that the highest-ranking figure in Israel would be the one to end his life; thus, the bitterness of death was ameliorated.

Ahavas Yehonasan offers yet another explanation of this phrase. According to an old Talmudic tradition (*Megillah* 13a), during the last night that Agag remained alive, he cohabited with a maiden, who conceived the forebear of Haman. Sensing that he had prepared the way for a progeny who would, he thought, avenge his death (*Kli Yakar*), he exclaimed, "Now, the bitterness of death has abated."

Based on the principle that a שׂ and ס are interchangeable (see *Rashi* above, 5:9), *Targum* renders סָר as שַׂר, *lord*. Hence, Agag exclaimed, אָכֵן שַׂר מַר־

the bitterness of death approaches."
[33] Samuel said, "Just as your sword made women
childless, so shall your mother be childless among
women!" And Samuel hewed Agag in pieces before
HASHEM in Gilgal.

הַמָּוֶת, *Indeed, my lord, death is bitter.*

The Midrash (*Midrash Shmuel* 18:6, *Eichah Rabbah*, end of Ch. 3) also interprets שַׂר as *lord*. Thus, as Agag beheld the preparations being made for a torturous, gory execution (see below, v. 33), he lamented, "Is this the bitter manner of dispatching a prince?"

According to another Midrash, סָר is related to סֵרוּס, *emasculation*. Accordingly, in direct retribution for what the Amalekites had done to the Hebrews as they left Egypt (see *Rashi*, *Deuteronomy* 25:18), Samuel castrated Agag (*Midrash Shmuel* ibid.).

33. וַיֹּאמֶר שְׁמוּאֵל כַּאֲשֶׁר שִׁכְּלָה נָשִׁים חַרְבֶּךָ כֵּן־תִּשְׁכַּל מִנָּשִׁים אִמֶּךָ — *Samuel said, "Just as your sword made women childless, so shall your mother be childless among women!"*

Hearing Agag bemoan the bitterness of death, Samuel retorted that it was no more than the fate that Agag had inflicted upon his helpless victims.

כַּאֲשֶׁר שִׁכְּלָה נָשִׁים חַרְבֶּךָ — *Just as your sword made women childless.*

The word שִׁכְּלָה generally is understood to mean the loss of offspring (*Rashi* to *Genesis* 27:45, and as is evident from the latter part of this verse). These were the mothers of Agag's victims (*Mahari Kara*).

Ralbag and *Rashi*, however, render the phrase as *Just as your sword left women widowed*. According to *Ralbag*, this was literally the case: Agag killed Jewish men. *Rashi*, however, understands it to imply that the women lost their men as husbands in the sense that the latter were castrated (see above).

כֵּן־תִּשְׁכַּל מִנָּשִׁים אִמֶּךָ — *So shall your mother be childless among women.*

R' Chaim Vital interprets, so shall your mother become childless through the efforts of women, referring to Esther, who brought about the death of her descendants Haman and his sons.

See also *Ahavas Yehonasan*, cited above, v. 9.

וַיְשַׁסֵּף שְׁמוּאֵל אֶת־אֲגָג — *And Samuel hewed Agag in pieces.*

The word וַיְשַׁסֵּף is unique to this verse. Based on *Targum's* rendering, most authorities associate it with a hewing motion similar to that used in the chopping of wood. Also, Samuel's emphasis on retribution indicates that he used a sword, which was what Agag had used when he made women childless.

Rashi cites a Midrash (*Eichah Rabbah* 3) that Agag was drawn and quartered (see *Matnos Kehunah*, *Maharzu*). According to another Midrash (ibid.), Samuel peeled off Agag's flesh and fed it to ostriches. (*Yefeh Nof* sees this as based on the idea that the word שִׁיסוּף, is combined of שְׁסַע, *to split*, and עוֹף, *bird.*)

Even in his old age, Samuel was able to execute Agag with the ease of a person chopping wood (*Abarbanel*). The purpose of this gory means of execution was to send a chilling warning to other nations not to attack the Jewish people (*Ralbag*).

According to one opinion, Samuel was a Nazirite and therefore forbidden to contaminate himself by contact with a corpse (see above, 1:11). The commentators thus discuss how he could have performed this execution. See *Nachalas Shimon* 3:1, *Mishbetzos Zahav*.

לִפְנֵי ה׳ בַּגִּלְגָּל — *Before HASHEM in Gilgal.*

This occurred near the altar.

Alternatively, according to some, the

טו/לה שְׁמוּאֵל הָרָמָתָה וְשָׁאוּל עָלָה אֶל־בֵּיתוֹ גִּבְעַת
לה שָׁאוּל: וְלֹא־יָסַף שְׁמוּאֵל לִרְאוֹת אֶת־שָׁאוּל
עַד־יוֹם מוֹתוֹ כִּי־הִתְאַבֵּל שְׁמוּאֵל אֶל־שָׁאוּל וַיהוָה
א נִחָם כִּי־הִמְלִיךְ אֶת־שָׁאוּל עַל־יִשְׂרָאֵל: וַיֹּאמֶר
טז/א יְהוָה אֶל־שְׁמוּאֵל עַד־מָתַי אַתָּה מִתְאַבֵּל אֶל־
שָׁאוּל וַאֲנִי מְאַסְתִּיו מִמְּלֹךְ עַל־יִשְׂרָאֵל מַלֵּא קַרְנְךָ

Sanctuary was at that time in Gilgal, and this occurred there (see above, v. 21).

Samuel acted *before* H*ASHEM* — he was not motivated by political purposes but solely by the desire to do Hashem's will (*R' Mendel Geldwerth.*)

34. גִּבְעַת שָׁאוּל — *Gibeath-shaul.*

Possibly, Gibeath-benjamin (above, 13:2) was renamed Gibeath-shaul after Saul built his palace there.

Alternatively, this was a different city, which Saul built (*Radak*).

וַיֵּלֶךְ שְׁמוּאֵל הָרָמָתָה וְשָׁאוּל עָלָה אֶל־בֵּיתוֹ — *Samuel went to Ramah, and Saul went up to his home.*

This austere statement leaves the impression that the two men departed without any expression of cordiality and that, with a mutual feeling of estrangement, each was inclined to keep his distance from the other (*R' Mendel Geldwerth*).

35. וְלֹא־יָסַף שְׁמוּאֵל לִרְאוֹת אֶת־שָׁאוּל — *Samuel never again saw Saul.*

Samuel did not seek out Saul. However, the two men did meet by chance, as is evident from the narrative of Chapter 19. Possibly, if the present verse is to be taken literally, even at that meeting Samuel avoided looking at Saul (*Abarbanel*).

According to *Kli Yakar*, the words וְלֹא־יָסַף שְׁמוּאֵל — lit., *Samuel did not continue* — imply that Samuel may have met with Saul, but not as a continuation of their previous meetings, for the spirit of conviviality had dissipated.

עַד־יוֹם מוֹתוֹ — *Until the day of his death.*

After his death, however, when Samuel was summoned by the necromancer, he did come to Saul (below, 28:12; *Abarbanel*).

Considering the opinion of most authorities that Saul's reign lasted only two and a half years and that Samuel died before Saul's kingship ended, this was a brief span of time (*Daas Sofrim*).

כִּי־הִתְאַבֵּל שְׁמוּאֵל אֶל־שָׁאוּל וַה׳ נִחָם כִּי־הִמְלִיךְ אֶת־שָׁאוּל — *For Samuel mourned over Saul. And* H*ASHEM reconsidered His having made Saul king.*

The word כִּי, *for*, applies to the entire rest of the verse. Hashem stood by His decision to reject Saul, and in so doing disregarded Samuel's grief over the fall of his protege, the first king of Israel. Cognizant that seeing Saul now would only aggravate his heartache, Samuel chose to avoid him (*Metzudos*).

XVI

בִּרְצוֹת ה׳ דַּרְכֵי־אִישׁ גַּם־אוֹיְבָיו יַשְׁלִם אִתּוֹ — *When* H*ASHEM favors a man's ways, even his foes will make peace with him* (*Proverbs* 16:7).

Sometimes, in accordance with Hashem's will, a person's enemy unwittingly acts as a catalyst to further his success. This chapter, which presents a major event in Jewish history, introduces us to David and to the dawn of his eternal dynasty. As is

15/34-35 [34] *Samuel went to Ramah, and Saul went up to his home at Gibeath-shaul.* [35] *Samuel never again saw Saul until the day of his death, for Samuel mourned over Saul. And* H*ASHEM reconsidered His having made Saul king over Israel.*

16/1 [1] *H*ASHEM *said to Samuel, "How long will you mourn over Saul, when I have rejected him from reigning over Israel? Fill your horn with*

evident from the Book of *Psalms,* David spent much of his life fleeing or defending himself against various opponents — prominent among them King Saul and his advocate Doeg HaAdomi.

In the second half of this chapter, we begin to see the unfolding of Hashem's plan for the emergence of David's glory, as it is unintentionally facilitated by the actions of Saul and Doeg.

◆§ Samuel Is Dispatched to Anoint a New King

1. וַיֹּאמֶר ה׳ אֶל־שְׁמוּאֵל עַד־מָתַי אַתָּה מִתְאַבֵּל אֶל־שָׁאוּל וַאֲנִי מְאַסְתִּיו מִמְּלֹךְ עַל־יִשְׂרָאֵל — *H*ASHEM *said to Samuel, "How long will you mourn over Saul, when I have rejected him from reigning over Israel?"*

Since Hashem had decreed the cessation of Saul's reign, it was inappropriate for Samuel to mourn as extensively as he did (*Metzudos*). *Mishbetzos Zahav* explicates that no one is more merciful than Hashem, Who is the source of mercy (*Chovos HaLevavos, Shaar HaBitachon* Ch. 3). Thus Samuel's mourning could not have come from compassion, but from his disappointment in the failure of his handiwork (see above, 8:1). Hashem told Samuel that he must be prepared to accept that loss in deference to Hashem's decision to reject Saul. Furthermore, since a loyal servant of Hashem will love whom He loves and dislike whom He dislikes, Samuel should have no reason to mourn.

Malbim explains that Samuel may have been distraught either by the magnitude of the loss of Saul as king or by the vacuum of leadership caused by Saul's absence. In regard to the former issue, Hashem told Samuel that the loss of Saul was not a cause for grief since Hashem had rejected him; in regard to the latter issue, Hashem told him that there would be an immediate successor.

The phrase מִתְאַבֵּל אֶל־שָׁאוּל literally means *mourn to Saul.* More conventionally, the preposition should have been עַל — *on,* or *over.* Some commentators derive from this unusual usage the view that Samuel's extensive mourning was predicated upon his belief that his heartfelt prayer could undo God's decree. The word אֶל — *to* —implies "toward an end," and may thus be understood to mean that Samuel *mourned [with a view of having the kingship returned] to Saul.* Hashem responded that such an approach was futile, for two reasons. First, אֲנִי מְאַסְתִּיו, *I have rejected him,* and there was no hope of changing God's resolve (*Kli Yakar*), and second, לֵךְ אֶשְׁלָחֲךָ, *Go forth — I shall send you* [to anoint David] (below). Since God had determined to transfer sovereignty

שֶׁמֶן וְלֵךְ אֶשְׁלָחֲךָ֙ אֶל־יִשַׁ֣י בֵּֽית־הַלַּחְמִ֔י כִּֽי־
ב רָאִ֧יתִי בְּבָנָ֛יו לִ֖י מֶֽלֶךְ׃ וַיֹּ֤אמֶר שְׁמוּאֵל֙ אֵ֣יךְ אֵלֵ֔ךְ

to David, His decision [to take it from Saul] could not be retracted (*Be'er Moshe*).

Mishbetzos Zahav suggests that Hashem told Samuel not to mourn because Hashem was sending him on a prophetic mission to anoint the new king, and a person cannot be Divinely inspired when he is not in a state of joy (see *Shabbos* 30b, *Tosafos* to *Kiddushin* 38a).

מַלֵּא קַרְנְךָ שֶׁמֶן — *Fill your horn with oil.*

This horn was either a man-made vessel shaped like a horn (*Metzudos*) or else an actual ram's horn (*Daas Sofrim*). In either case, it was designated to administer the sanctified anointment oil, whose formula is described in *Exodus* (30:22-25).

This horn was stored in the Inner Sanctuary, together with the vessels that held the anointment oil. Although Scripture mentions only that Kohanim and sanctified vessels are to be anointed with this oil, sources teach that it was used as well as to anoint kings of the Davidic dynasty.

The act of anointing a king had to be performed by a prophet. The oil was poured on his head, then smeared in the form of a crown between his eyebrows, and the remainder again poured on his head. The amount of oil used was the amount that filled the horn (*Radak*).

Hannah alluded to this horn in her prophetic song when she stated רָמָה קַרְנִי בַּה' — *My pride (lit., horn) has been raised through* HASHEM (2:1). This implied that only the king whom her son Samuel would anoint with the horn would enjoy an extensive reign, whereas the reign of those whose anointments were made with a flask — i.e., Saul and Jehu — would not last long (*Megillah* 14a).

וְלֵךְ אֶשְׁלָחֲךָ — *And go forth — I shall send you.*

Hashem chose Saul in response to and as a way of satisfying the will of the people. In that case, He did not send the prophet to anoint the king as His emissary, but had the prospective king go to the prophet. In this case, when Hashem chose the candidate to represent His kingdom without reference to the will of the people, He sent the prophet to the king (*Malbim*).

The use of two verbs in this phrase — *go forth* and *I shall send you* — seems self-contradictory, for the command *Go forth* implies that the prophet is to proceed on his own, whereas *I shall send you* connotes that he will be acting as God's messenger. *Chomas Anach* (based on the words of *Arizal* in *Likkutei Torah*) explains this discrepancy as follows. The Midrash (*Bereishis Rabbah* 3:6) states that Hashem does not attach His Name to an evil decree. *Yefeh Toar* explains that this is because He does not want people to suffer; however, people bring suffering upon themselves. Thus, when Hashem requests that something evil be done, He tells the prophet to act as if he were acting independently. Accordingly, *Go forth* implies that the prophet shall of his own initiative bring misfortune upon Saul by divesting him of his kingdom, which will have the effect of causing the spirit of Hashem to depart from him (v. 14). The second phrase, *I shall send you*, does expressly state Hashem's involvement, for it refers to the good fortune of David.

אֶל־יִשַׁי בֵּית־הַלַּחְמִי — *To Jesse the Bethlehemite.*

Jesse belonged to the tribe of Judah. His father, Oved, was the son of Boaz and Ruth (see *Ruth* Ch. 4).

Jesse was a highly respected Torah scholar (see below, 17:12), and one of the eight "officers" mentioned in the Book of *Micah* (5:4) who, our Sages teach, will help save the Jews at the time of the

oil and go forth — I shall send you to Jesse the Bethlehemite, for I have seen for Myself a king among his sons." [2] *Samuel asked, "How can I go?*

ultimate redemption (*Succah* 52b). Our Sages also state that he is one of four people who never sinned and who died only because death had been decreed upon all of mankind after the serpent induced Adam to transgress (*Bava Basra* 17a).

The Bethlehemite means that Jesse resided in the Judean city of Bethlehem, where his grandfather Boaz had lived (see *Ruth*). In Hebrew, Bethlehem is written as two words: Beth-lehem. Following the rules of Hebrew usage, the article ה — "the," referring to Jesse as *the Bethlehemite* — is placed before the second word, thus בֵּית־הַלַּחְמִי (*Rashi*).

Midrash Shmuel states that the word *Lehem* as used here — [literally, "bread" or "food"] — refers to Torah (as per *Proverbs* 9:5), and teaches that Jesse was a Torah scholar.

כִּי־רָאִיתִי בְּבָנָיו לִי מֶלֶךְ — *For I have seen for Myself a king among his sons.*

The word רָאִיתִי — *I have seen* — implies that David's fitness for kingship was not readily apparent and only Hashem detected it.

Also, Hashem initially left the identity of the specific son concealed for two reasons: first, to indicate that Jesse's entire household was spiritually distinguished, and second, to teach the types of flaws that disqualify a person from sitting on the throne, as we will see (*Daas Sofrim*).

Kli Yakar states that the word בְּבָנָיו — *among his sons* — can be read as ב׳ בָּנָיו, meaning, *his two sons*: David and his brother Eliab, who also initially fulfilled the qualifications to be king. This may be inferred from the phrase מְאַסְתִּיהוּ — *I have rejected [Eliab]* (below, v. 7; see *Pesachim* 66b), which indicates that he had originally been fit. This explanation is consistent with King David's description of the selection of the king as a three-step process (*I Chronicles* 28:4): first the tribe of Judah was chosen, then the family of Jesse, and finally David among the sons of Jesse (*Brisker Rav*).

Alternatively, *Kli Yakar* suggests that *among his sons* refers to the descendants of David who would reign after him.

לִי מֶלֶךְ — *For Myself a king.*

The new king would not be like Saul, who had disobeyed Hashem, but a king for Hashem who would heed His commands (*Radak*). Furthermore, when Hashem had chosen Saul, He had done so in response to the people's request, and so He had chosen someone of whom they would approve: a tall, impressive man. This time, Hashem alone would determine the criteria for the choice of king (*Malbim*).

The purpose of a Jewish king is to act as Hashem's representative and lead the people to follow in His ways. Ultimately, all of the honor that the king receives is channeled to Hashem. Thus, the proper king humbles himself before the Ark (*II Samuel* Ch. 6). This is the meaning of the phrase לִי מֶלֶךְ — *for Myself a king* (*Be'er Moshe*). Because David was prepared to abase himself before Hashem, his kingdom would long endure. In fact, a Midrash states that whatever the Torah associates with the word לִי will enjoy everlasting existence — first in this world and then in the next.

Kli Yakar adds that this phrase may be translated as "a king over Me," as it were. This is based on the concept that "the righteous man decrees, and Hashem fulfills his decrees" (*Taanis* 23a). King David himself alluded to this מוֹשֵׁל בָּאָדָם צַדִּיק, *God rules over mankind, but the righteous man rules over God* (*II Samuel* 23:3, as interpreted in *Moed Katan* 16b).

וְשָׁמַע שָׁאוּל וַהֲרָגָנִי וַיֹּאמֶר יהוה עֶגְלַת בָּקָר
ג תִּקַּח בְּיָדֶךָ וְאָמַרְתָּ לִזְבֹּחַ לַיהוה בָּאתִי: וְקָרָאתָ

2. וַיֹּאמֶר שְׁמוּאֵל אֵיךְ אֵלֵךְ וְשָׁמַע שָׁאוּל וַהֲרָגָנִי — *Samuel asked, "How can I go? If Saul finds out, he will kill me."*

Presumably, Samuel was concerned that Saul would view his anointing another man king as a seditious offense punishable by death. Samuel feared that Saul would not believe that Hashem had directly commissioned him to do so (*R' Chaim Kanievsky*, quoted by *Mishbetzos Zahav*).

Ritva (to *Yevamos* 65b) states that Samuel's lack of faith in Saul was unwarranted and unworthy, and so Hashem now told Samuel to offer a heifer as an atonement sacrifice.

The Talmud articulates the principle that a person performing a mitzvah will not be harmed. However, that is true only when danger is not prevalent (*Pesachim* 8b). Otherwise, *Radak* explains, Hashem expects that even righteous people and prophets will not rely on miracles.[1]

It is true that other prophets, such as Moses and Jeremiah, did fearlessly enter certain dangerous situations. *Malbim* explains that in those instances they performed their missions publicly in order to persuade people of Hashem's omnipotence; thus, they could reasonably expect that Hashem would protect them. In this case, however, Samuel was sent on a secret mission, so he could not rely on a miracle, and any miracle that did occur would be for his sake alone and as such would diminish his store of merits.

Alternatively, *Malbim* suggests, Samuel was not worriedly questioning Hashem's command. Rather, his question אֵיךְ אֵלֵךְ — *How can I go?* — may be read as *In what manner shall I go?* That is to say, should he make a public display of the anointing, in which case he could expect God to perform miracles to further his mission if necessary, or should he go in a secretive manner, in which case he would require a miracle for his sake alone should Saul attempt to kill him?

As noted earlier (v. 1), *Arizal* states that God's command, לֵךְ, *Go forth*, directed Samuel to act independently to end Saul's kingdom, and אֶשְׁלָחֲךָ, *I shall send you*, was a Divine mission to anoint David. Accordingly, Samuel's question, אֵיךְ אֵלֵךְ, *How can I go?* relates to the former, and indicates that Samuel was worried only about his mission to end Saul's kingdom, since in that case he was not acting directly on behalf of Hashem.

Kli Yakar also focuses on *How can I go*, and writes that Samuel was concerned that Saul would be upset that he was going to the prospective king, rather than having the latter come to him, as had occurred in the case of Saul's anointment. Hashem told Samuel that if he set out with the intent of offering a sacrifice, Saul could not protest if, once arrived, he also anointed the prospective king.

Rav M.D. Vali (cited by *Mishbetzos Zahav*) observes that Samuel was only concerned with how he would *go* to David, when the Divine spirit would still be resting upon Saul. Samuel would have no reason to worry on his return, because by then the spirit would have left Saul (v. 14).

According to *Abarbanel*, Samuel was not concerned that Saul would harm him. Rather, he preferred not to anoint David, since that would invalidate Saul's kingdom, which he had himself estab-

1. So also states *Chovos HaLevavos* (*Shaar HaBitachon* Ch. 4). See, however, Rambam's *Eight Chapters* Ch. 7; *Chesed Avraham* ad loc.; *Kovetz Maamarim* of *R' Elchonon Wasserman*; *Nachalas Shimon* #32.

If Saul finds out he will kill me."

HASHEM said, "Take a heifer and say, 'I have come to bring an offering to HASHEM.' [3]Invite

lished. As for his stated fear of Saul, that was merely a pretext to avoid going.

Kli Yakar suggests that when Samuel said וַהֲרָגָנִי, *he will kill me,* he was euphemistically expressing his fear that Saul might kill the newly chosen successor or himself.

In her prayer (above, 1:1), Hannah stated regarding Samuel, וּמוֹרָה לֹא־יַעֲלֶה עַל־רֹאשׁוֹ, *no morah shall come upon his head.* According to one Talmudic authority, this is to be translated as "No fear shall come upon his head." That is to say, Samuel would not fear anyone. Another authority points out that Samuel did fear Saul. According to this view, the word וּמוֹרָה in Hannah's blessing means not *fear* but a *razor;* therefore, with these words Hannah was committing Samuel to be a nazirite (*Nazir* 66a). (See comm. ad loc., *Nachalas Shimon* 32:5.)

וַיֹּאמֶר ה׳ עֶגְלַת בָּקָר תִּקַּח בְּיָדֶךָ וְאָמַרְתָּ לִזְבֹּחַ לַה׳ בָּאתִי — *HASHEM said, "Take a heifer and say, 'I have come to bring an offering to HASHEM.' "*

At that time, it was permitted to offer sacrifices on private altars (*Radak*).

Abarbanel states that Samuel would commonly go to a particular site to rebuke the Jews or give [public] thanks to Hashem, and announce that he had come to bring an offering.

Malbim comments that although Samuel could himself have devised the excuse that he was going to offer a sacrifice, he preferred not to tell a falsehood. Therefore, he waited for Hashem to suggest this ruse. Now that he was commanded to bring an offering, it was true that he was going to do so.

Although Samuel was telling the truth — since he was in fact going to bring an offering — his omission of the fact that his principal motivation was to anoint a new king constituted a deviation from the truth (*Maharsha*). Thus, the Talmud derives from this verse that, when necessary, it is a mitzvah to diverge from the truth in order to bring about or maintain peace (*Yevamos* 65b). Not all lies are permitted, however. For instance, a blatant lie may be prohibited (*Aruch LaNer*) as well as lying about one's plans for the future (*Sefer Chassidim* 426, *Magen Avraham* 156; see also *Nachalas Shimon* 32, *Mishbetzos Zahav*).

The fact that Hashem told Samuel to offer this information without waiting to be asked indicates that telling a falsehood to bring about peace is not only permitted but mandatory (*Kli Yakar*).

עֶגְלַת בָּקָר תִּקַּח בְּיָדֶךָ — *Take a heifer.*

In a novel approach to this verse, *Ralbag* (citing *R' Shlomo HaNasi*) suggests that the heifer was intended to mislead people into thinking that a murdered corpse had been found [in a field] and that Samuel was planning to perform the ritual of the *eglah arufah,* the *decapitated heifer* (see *Deuteronomy* 21:1-9). This was meant to send an implicit message to Saul that just as the heifer would determine the identity of the murderer (see *Targum Yonasan* to ibid. 21:8), Saul should not think that if he killed Samuel, his guilt would remain undetected.

Earlier, Saul's error in showing mercy to the Amalekite animals had been derived from his understanding of the law of the *decapitated heifer* (see above, 15:5). Samuel's evocation of that law would remind Saul to show mercy to Samuel (*Mussar HaNeviim*).

Radak explains that Hashem told Samuel, "I initially planned for you to anoint the new king privately. Now, however, that you are afraid that Saul will kill you, you must sacrifice the heifer in a public forum, and let us see who will kill you."

לְיִשַׁי בַּזָּבַח וְאָנֹכִי אוֹדִיעֲךָ אֵת אֲשֶׁר־תַּעֲשֶׂה
ד וּמָשַׁחְתָּ לִי אֵת אֲשֶׁר־אֹמַר אֵלֶיךָ׃ וַיַּעַשׂ שְׁמוּאֵל
אֵת אֲשֶׁר דִּבֶּר יהוה וַיָּבֹא בֵּית לָחֶם וַיֶּחֶרְדוּ
ה זִקְנֵי הָעִיר לִקְרָאתוֹ וַיֹּאמֶר שָׁלֹם בּוֹאֶךָ׃ וַיֹּאמֶר ׀
שָׁלוֹם לִזְבֹּחַ לַיהוה בָּאתִי הִתְקַדְּשׁוּ וּבָאתֶם
אִתִּי בַּזָּבַח וַיְקַדֵּשׁ אֶת־יִשַׁי וְאֶת־בָּנָיו וַיִּקְרָא
ו לָהֶם לַזָּבַח׃ וַיְהִי בְּבוֹאָם וַיַּרְא אֶת־אֱלִיאָב וַיֹּאמֶר
ז אַךְ נֶגֶד יהוה מְשִׁיחוֹ׃ וַיֹּאמֶר

3. וְאָנֹכִי אוֹדִיעֲךָ אֵת אֲשֶׁר־תַּעֲשֶׂה וּמָשַׁחְתָּ לִי אֵת אֲשֶׁר־אֹמַר אֵלֶיךָ — *I will then tell you what to do, and you shall anoint for Me the one whom I shall tell you.*

Hashem delayed identifying the proposed king so that all would see that he chose only David from among Jesse's sons, since the prophecy would come to Samuel in the presence of Jesse and his family (*Radak*).

God's response to Samuel expressed an implied rebuke for a certain measure of hubris. Samuel had previously stated אָנֹכִי הָרֹאֶה, *I am the seer* (above, 9:19). Hashem wished to show him that not even he could foresee which of Jesse's son would be chosen (*Kli Yakar*).

Furthermore, Hashem wanted to demonstrate that the choice of prospective king was not a natural phenomenon, in which case Eliab would have been chosen — as the oldest or as the most physically imposing — and so He arranged events so that Samuel would himself choose Eliab and then be corrected (*Kli Yakar*).

Alternatively, until that time it was not yet clear that Eliab would be rejected and David chosen. Eliab's flaw of anger had not yet developed fully enough to disqualify him and David still required more time to perfect himself. Hashem's decision became final only upon Samuel's arrival at Jesse's house (*Kli Yakar*).

Daas Sofrim states that all of these introductory events preceding the anointing of David were clouded in mystery and secrecy so that even those closest to him would not be aware of his capability to be king. This fits into a broader pattern of episodes eventually leading to David's birth that seem antithetical to the development of a holy monarch. These include the conception of David's ancestor Moab (*Genesis* 19:30-38), the union of his later forebears Judah and Tamar (ibid. Ch. 38), and the story of his great-grandparents, Boaz and Ruth. These incidents were meant to fool Satan into thinking that no sanctity could come from such a background. Had Satan known that Hashem's kingdom was in the process of formulation, he would have done all he could to prevent it (*Chofetz Chaim al HaTorah*).[1]

4. וַיֶּחֶרְדוּ זִקְנֵי הָעִיר לִקְרָאתוֹ וַיֹּאמֶר שָׁלֹם בּוֹאֶךָ — *The elders of the city hurried nervously toward him, and one said, "Do you come in peace?"*

Our translation of וַיֶּחֶרְדוּ as *hurried nervously* follows *Rashi*. Literally, the word means *tremble* (see *Genesis* 27:33).

The *Targum* renders this phrase as *[they] gathered toward him.*

Radak suggests that the elders

1. This concept is treated elaborately in the Overview to the ArtScroll edition of the Book of *Ruth*. See also below, v. 11.

Jesse to the feast; I will then tell you what to do,
and you shall anoint for Me the one whom I shall
tell you.''
4 *So Samuel did as* H*ASHEM had spoken, and he*
arrived in Bethlehem. The elders of the city hur-
ried nervously toward him, and one said, ''Do
you come in peace?'' 5 *And he answered, ''Peace.*
To bring an offering to H*ASHEM have I come. Pre-*
pare yourselves and join me at the feast.'' And
he invited Jesse and his sons, calling them to
the feast.
6 *And it was upon their arrival that Samuel*
saw Eliab; he said, ''Surely, before H*ASHEM is His*
anointed one.''

trembled out of fear that Samuel had come because someone had sinned, and so they asked if all was well. *Be'er Moshe* explains that, accordingly, it was the Torah scholars who approached him, regarding whom the verse states, שִׁמְעוּ דְּבַר־ה׳ הַחֲרֵדִים אֶל־דְּבָרוֹ, *Listen to the words of* H*ASHEM, you who tremble regarding His word* (*Isaiah* 66:5; *Bava Metzia* 33b). Samuel responded that they had no reason to worry, for he came only to offer a sacrifice.

According to *Malbim*, when the elders saw Samuel arriving with a heifer, they trembled out of fear that a corpse had been found, because they thought that he wished to perform the ritual of the *eglah arufah* (see *Ralbag* above). Accordingly, they stepped forward, as it is their responsibility to perform that mitzvah (*Deuteronomy* 21;3).

וַיֹּאמֶר שָׁלֹם בּוֹאֶךָ — *And one said, ''Do you come in peace?''*

The word וַיֹּאמֶר, *and he said,* is singular because only one man, the greatest of the elders, spoke on their behalf. Possibly, this was Jesse (*Radak*). *Be'er Moshe* suggests that the singular verb means that the elders joined together as one to greet Samuel.

6. וַיֹּאמֶר אַךְ נֶגֶד ה׳ מְשִׁיחוֹ — *He said, ''Surely, before* H*ASHEM is His anointed one.''*

According to *Rashi,* Samuel did not speak these words aloud but rather had the thought that Eliab is God's choice to be king. *Chomas Anach* adds that Samuel would not have expressed his conjecture audibly, since he was commanded to choose whomever Hashem would designate.

Radak, however, considers it possible that Samuel spoke his thoughts aloud.

אַךְ נֶגֶד ה׳ מְשִׁיחוֹ — *Surely, before* H*ASHEM is His anointed one.*

The simplest understanding of this verse is that Samuel was stating that the man whom Hashem wished him to anoint as king was standing before him (see *Rashi* to *II Chronicles* 11:18).

Radak interprets this phrase as the prayer, *May* H*ASHEM's anointed one always be before Him,* implying that Hashem should be with him and support him.

Kli Yakar suggests that the word נֶגֶד

יהוָ֜ה אֶל־שְׁמוּאֵ֗ל אַל־תַּבֵּ֧ט אֶל־מַרְאֵ֛הוּ וְאֶל־גְּבֹ֥הַּ
קוֹמָת֖וֹ כִּ֣י מְאַסְתִּ֑יהוּ כִּ֣י ׀ לֹ֗א אֲשֶׁ֤ר יִרְאֶה֙ הָֽאָדָ֔ם כִּ֤י
ח הָֽאָדָם֙ יִרְאֶ֣ה לַעֵינַ֔יִם וַיהוָ֖ה יִרְאֶ֥ה לַלֵּבָֽב׃ וַיִּקְרָ֤א
יִשַׁי֙ אֶל־אֲבִ֣ינָדָ֔ב וַיַּעֲבִרֵ֖הוּ לִפְנֵ֣י שְׁמוּאֵ֑ל וַיֹּ֕אמֶר
ט גַּם־בָּזֶ֖ה לֹֽא־בָחַ֥ר יְהוָֽה׃ וַיַּעֲבֵ֥ר יִשַׁ֖י שַׁמָּ֑ה וַיֹּ֕אמֶר
י גַּם־בָּזֶ֖ה לֹא־בָחַ֥ר יְהוָֽה׃ וַיַּעֲבֵ֥ר יִשַׁ֛י שִׁבְעַ֥ת בָּנָ֖יו

as used here is similar to its usage in the phrase שִׁוִּיתִי ה׳ לְנֶגְדִּי תָמִיד, *I have set* Hashem *before me always* (*Psalms* 16:8). Samuel saw that Eliab possessed a constant awareness that he stood before Hashem; such a person, Samuel assumed, must be Hashem's choice as king.

Radak explains that Eliab, like Saul, was a handsome, tall man, and Samuel assumed that Hashem chose such men to be king because people tend to respect and fear them.

Radak also offers the explanation that Samuel was speaking not about Eliab but about Saul, and making a final plea on his behalf. Samuel stated that Hashem's anointed one — i.e., Saul — was handsomer and taller than Eliab. Hashem's response also referred to Saul: "Do not look at his appearance or at his tall stature, for I have rejected him" (v. 7).

Ralbag, however, rejects this interpretation, since in v. 8 Hashem says of Abinadab, "Hashem has not chosen this one either," implying a previous discussion about Eliab (see *Abarbanel*, who defends *Ralbag*).

Midrash Tanchuma (cited by *Abarbanel*) states that Samuel prophesied correctly that Eliab's family would play a role in the palace. However, he erred in thinking that this would be Eliab. Actually, it was Eliab's daughter, who became the queen when she married Rehoboam, son of Solomon (*II Chronicles* 11:18).

7. כִּי מְאַסְתִּיהוּ — *For I have rejected him.*

Although Hashem had initially considered Eliab to be a candidate for the throne, He ultimately rejected him (*Pesachim* 66b), due to Eliab's tendency toward anger, as we will see in 17:28. Although that incident had yet to occur, Hashem was aware of Eliab's bad temper (*Rashi, Pesachim* ibid.).

Although, generally, Hashem does not judge a person according to his future deeds, Eliab's rejection was not a punishment, but a recognition that his trace of anger made him unfit to be king, for one cannot be master over a nation if he is not even master over himself (*R' Elyah Lopian*, cited by *Sifsei Chaim, Moadim* Vol. II).

According to *Abarbanel*, מְאַסְתִּיהוּ does not mean *I have rejected him* but rather *I have rejected it* — that is to say, Hashem rejected the idea that a man's appearance and height are relevant to whether he should be considered a candidate for the throne, since the tall and imposing Saul had strayed from God's will.

כִּי לֹא אֲשֶׁר יִרְאֶה הָאָדָם — *For it is not as man sees.*

As mentioned above, Samuel had previously referred to himself as a *seer* (above, 9:19). Hashem now showed him that he could not see everything (*Sifrei*, cited by *Rashi*). Following *Rashi*'s view that Samuel had never verbalized his thought that Eliab was the prospective king, the rebuke was only in his mind and no one else knew about it (*Chomas Anach*).

כִּי הָאָדָם יִרְאֶה לַעֵינַיִם וַה׳ יִרְאֶה לַלֵּבָב — *Man sees what his eyes behold, but*

[7]*But* HASHEM *said to Samuel, "Do not look at
his appearance or at his tall stature, for I have
rejected him. For it is not as man sees — man sees
what his eyes behold, but* HASHEM *sees into the
heart."* [8]*Jesse then called Abinadab and brought
him before Samuel, but he said, "*HASHEM *has not
chosen this one either."* [9]*Then Jesse brought Shammah, but [Samuel] said, "*HASHEM *has not chosen
this one either."* [10]*Jesse presented his seven sons*

HASHEM sees into the heart.

Our translation follows *Targum*, which explains that since man uses his physical eyes to see, he can perceive only externals. Hashem, on the other hand, perceives a man's internal thoughts.

Metzudos renders this phrase as *A man can see whether another person's eyes are pleasant, but he cannot see into that person's heart.*

Literally, הָאָדָם יִרְאֶה לַעֵינַיִם means, *man sees into the eyes.* Indeed, physician's look into the eyes as part of their diagnosis. A discerning person can perceive someone else's internal state of being by gazing into his eyes, which are the "window of the soul." Accordingly, the prophet can indeed see a person's traits through his eyes, but Hashem sees more than these traits. He perceives the *heart* and can thus detect even roots of bad traits that have not yet developed, such as Eliab's temper, which did not manifest itself until later on (see 17:28; *Sifsei Chaim, Middos V'Avodas* HASHEM, Vol. I).

Although Eliab's deeds were righteous, Hashem perceived a flaw in his heart (*Daas Sofrim*). From this, the Talmud derives the aphorism that רַחֲמָנָא לִיבָּא בָּעֵי, *HASHEM desires the [purity of] heart* (*Sanhedrin* 106b).

The heart is the seat of a person's desires. The Jewish king's mission is to teach the people to subdue their desires to the will of Hashem. Because a bad temper is not merely a character flaw, it indicates that someone has not managed to place Hashem's will over his own, and is therefore not qualified to be king (*Sifsei Chaim, Moadim*, Vol. II).

8. וַיֹּאמֶר גַּם־בָּזֶה לֹא־בָחַר ה׳ — *But he said, "HASHEM has not chosen this one either."*

Samuel knew that he was not the intended king because Hashem said nothing to Samuel (*Radak*).

Unlike Eliab, Abinadab and the other brothers had never been possible candidates, and so the word "rejected" is not used in reference to them (*Daas Sofrim*).

9. שַׁמָּה — *Shammah.*

Elsewhere, Shammah's name is given as שִׁמְעָה, *Shim'ah* (*II Samuel* 13:3, *I Chronicles* 2:13).

10. שִׁבְעַת בָּנָיו — *His seven sons.*

Including David, Jesse had eight sons (see also below, 17:12). In *Chronicles* (2:15), however, David is listed as Jesse's seventh and last son. It is possible that one son died without children, and so the list in *Chronicles*, which is transmitting information of purely genealogical interest, does not mention him (*Rashi* below, 17:12).

Rashi (to *I Chronicles* 1:1) explains the discrepancy by stating that Scripture typically lists family members until it reaches the prominent individual who is its primary subject, and stops there. Accordingly, David was the seventh of eight sons. When the verse in Chronicles reached him — the "jewel it was seeking," in *Rashi*'s words (ibid. 2:15), it

לִפְנֵי שְׁמוּאֵל וַיֹּאמֶר שְׁמוּאֵל אֶל־יִשַׁי לֹא־
יא בָּחַר יהוה בָּאֵלֶּה: וַיֹּאמֶר שְׁמוּאֵל אֶל־יִשַׁי
הֲתַמּוּ הַנְּעָרִים וַיֹּאמֶר עוֹד שָׁאַר הַקָּטָן
וְהִנֵּה רֹעֶה בַּצֹּאן וַיֹּאמֶר שְׁמוּאֵל אֶל־יִשַׁי
שִׁלְחָה וְקָחֶנּוּ כִּי־לֹא נָסֹב עַד־בֹּאוֹ פֹה:

came to an end.

Finally, Ibn Ezra (cited by *Radak* to *Chronicles*) suggests that one of Jesse's sons was born of a different mother, and the list in Chronicles mentions only the sons who had both the same father and mother.

11. וַיֹּאמֶר שְׁמוּאֵל אֶל־יִשַׁי הֲתַמּוּ הַנְּעָרִים — *Samuel said, "Are these all the youths?"*

Samuel knew that there had to be at least one other son, because Hashem had told him that He would choose the candidate, and He had not yet given any indication of having done so (*Malbim*).

וַיֹּאמֶר עוֹד שָׁאַר הַקָּטָן וְהִנֵּה רֹעֶה בַּצֹּאן — *And he said, "The youngest one is still left; he is tending the sheep."*

Generally, the word *left* is written in the passive form, נִשְׁאַר, connoting "left behind." The active verb used here — שָׁאַר — indicates that David remained behind on his own volition. This may be because he was the youngest and therefore somewhat timid, and also because he was busy tending the sheep (*Malbim*).

Alternatively, *Alshich* states that he stayed behind out of humility.

הַקָּטָן — *The youngest one.*

In the next chapter (v. 14), Scripture repeats that David was the youngest. The Hebrew for *the youngest one* literally means "small," and the Midrash (*Sifrei, Yalkut Shimoni*) interprets it to mean "humble." Thus, even after David left his flocks of sheep to become king, he remained humble.

According to *Radak* (to *I Chronicles* 2:15), David had one brother younger than himself, Elihu (mentioned in *I Chronicles* 27:18). Nevertheless, because of his humility, David was called "the small one."

וְהִנֵּה רֹעֶה בַּצֹּאן — *He is tending the sheep.*

The *Zohar* states that because David was very wise and knew how to properly tend sheep, to which the Jewish people are compared (see *Ezekiel* 34:31, 36:38), God chose him to be king. A compassionate shepherd carries a newborn sheep in his arms behind its mother so that it will not grow tired. So too, a leader of Israel must lead the people with compassion.

The Midrash teaches (*Shemos Rabbah* 2:2) that Hashem tests whether his "righteous ones" (*Psalms* 11:5) are fit to be leaders by making them shepherds. When David tended his sheep, he would first feed the youngest sheep tender grass, then feed the oldest sheep fresh grass, and finally feed the strongest sheep the toughest grass. Since he knew how to tend to each sheep's individual needs, Hashem appointed him to do the same for the people of Israel. Thus, we read in *Psalms*, וַיִּבְחַר בְּדָוִד עַבְדּוֹ וַיִּקָּחֵהוּ מִמִּכְלְאֹת צֹאן. מֵאַחַר עָלוֹת הֱבִיאוֹ לִרְעוֹת בְּיַעֲקֹב עַמּוֹ וּבְיִשְׂרָאֵל נַחֲלָתוֹ, *He chose David, His servant, and took him from the sheep' corrals. From behind the nursing ewes He brought him to tend to Jacob, His nation, and to Israel, His inheritance* (78:70,71).

וַיֹּאמֶר שְׁמוּאֵל אֶל־יִשַׁי שִׁלְחָה וְקָחֶנּוּ כִּי־לֹא נָסֹב עַד־בֹּאוֹ פֹה — *Samuel said to Jesse, "Send and bring him, for we will not*

before Samuel, but Samuel said to Jesse, "Hashem
has not chosen these." 11 *Samuel said, "Are these*
all the youths?" And he said, "The youngest one is
still left; he is tending the sheep." Samuel said to
Jesse, "Send and bring him, for we will not sit [to
dine] until he arrives here."

sit [to dine] until he arrives here."

From these verses, it appears that Jesse forgot about David and thus neglected to send for him. Moreover, even after he acknowledged David's existence in response to Samuel's questioning him, he still proposed that they sit down to eat without first calling David.

Jesse certainly knew that Samuel had come as a prophet and emissary of Hashem to anoint one of his sons as king. Why then did he act in this fashion?

A number of sources[1] address this issue, in the course of which they also deal with some puzzling comments that David makes about himself in *Psalms*. For example, David says, הֵן־בְּעָווֹן חוֹלָלְתִּי וּבְחֵטְא יֶחֱמַתְנִי אִמִּי, *Behold, in iniquity was I fashioned, and in sin did my mother conceive me* (*Psalms* 51:7). To what iniquity and sin is he referring? Also, David says מוּזָר הָיִיתִי לְאֶחָי וְנָכְרִי לִבְנֵי אִמִּי, *I became an alien to my brothers, and a stranger to my mother's sons* (*Psalms* 69:9). Why was that the case?

We will here present a compilation of these sources which, although they differ in details, are generally consistent with each other.

As we have seen, Ruth's marriage to Boaz was marred by controversy, since she descended from Moab and the Torah prohibits Moabites to marry into the Jewish nation (*Deuteronomy* 23:4). Boaz headed a court that ruled that this prohibition applied only to Moabite males, not females, and thus he permitted himself to marry Ruth. Yet doubts still remained, particularly when Boaz died the day after his marriage, which was interpreted as a sign of Divine disapproval.

Thus, although Oved, Jesse, and Jesse's sons were respected Jews, some question as to their Jewish status still lingered.

Therefore, after having fathered six sons, Jesse began to suspect that he was a Moabite and forbidden to remain married to a Jewish woman, and he accordingly separated himself from her.

After a few years passed, he wanted to have more children, and so devised the following plan. He had a non-Jewish maidservant, whom he proposed to marry in the following manner. He would free her on condition that he was not a Moabite, so that she might become a full-fledged Jew, and he would then marry her. Should he be a Moabite, that act of manumission would be void. Then he would marry her as a gentile; their children would not have the status of Moabites, and they would be converted to Judaism.

Hearing this proposal, the maidservant felt sorry for Jesse's wife. She agreed to the proposal but apprised Jesse's wife of the plan; on the wedding night, the two women secretly exchanged places (as Rachel and Leah had done). Thus, that night Jesse unknowingly caused

1. *Yalkut HaMechiri* to *Psalms* (18:22 [*Yalkut HaMechiri* is a 14th-century work by R' Machir bar Abba Mari of Provence]); *Kli Yakar* citing *R' Shlomo Alkabetz; Rema MiPanu* in *Asarah Ma'amaros, Ma'amar Chikur Din* 3:10; *Chida; Veyeivk Yosef* by *R' Aryeh Leib Friedman; Sifsei Kohen;* and *Sefer HaTodaah* by *R' Eliyahu KiTov.*

יב וַיִּשְׁלַח וַיְבִיאֵהוּ וְהוּא אַדְמוֹנִי עִם־יְפֵה עֵינַיִם וְטוֹב
רֹאִי וַיֹּאמֶר יהוה קוּם מְשָׁחֵהוּ כִּי־זֶה הוּא:

his first wife and not the maidservant to conceive.[1]

When Jesse's wife grew visibly pregnant, apparently from an adulterous relationship, her sons thought she was liable to the death penalty, but Jesse calmed them. As for the child, who was David, he was considered to be illegitimate, and since he was viewed as an embarrasssment to the family, he was sent into the wilderness as a shepherd, away from the public eye.

David's mother did not reveal the facts of the matter so as not to embarrass Jesse and not to reveal what the maid had done. As a result, David was estranged by his brothers, as expressed by the verse, מוּזָר הָיִיתִ לְאֶחָי, *I became an alien to my brothers*, in which the word for *alien*, מוּזָר, is similar to the word מַמְזֵר, *mamzer*. They believed that וּבְחֵטְא יֶחֱמַתְנִי אִמִּי, *in sin did my mother conceive me*. They disassociated themselves from him and suspected him of every sort of wrongdoing. They did not consider him their brother, and Jesse did not consider him his son.

Until he was 28, David tended the sheep in the wilderness and his father and brothers expected to hear that a lion or bear had slaughtered him. But instead of growing bitter, he spent those years attaching himself to Hashem, singing His praises, accepting humiliation and accepting Hashem's will, and associated with sages until he developed into an exceptional Torah scholar.

When Samuel arrived, therefore, Jesse saw no reason to summon David, since he did not realize that David was his son. Only after his other sons were not chosen did Jesse begin to wonder if Samuel was referring to David. Finally, when David came and Samuel anointed him, Jesse understood what had happened. He realized that David was his child, and was holy, pure, and fit to be king.

Now Jesse's mother cried out of joy that her secret had been revealed and that her shame was removed. She proclaimed אֶבֶן מָאֲסוּ הַבּוֹנִים הָיְתָה לְרֹאשׁ פִּנָּה, *The stone despised by the builders has become the cornerstone* (*Psalms* 118:22). The word for "builders," בּוֹנִים, can be homiletically read as בָּנִים, "sons."

12. וְהוּא אַדְמוֹנִי עִם־יְפֵה עֵינַיִם — *He was ruddy, with fair eyes.*

David's ruddy complexion aroused Samuel's concern that he would be a murderer, since the color red is associated with bloodshed. If so, he would be like Esau, who was also ruddy. Therefore, Hashem notified Samuel that unlike Esau, David would spill blood only under two conditions: when doing so was halachically permissible, and with the sanction of the Sanhedrin (*Midrash Shmuel*).[2]

Mussar HaNeviim adds that the phrase יְפֵה עֵינַיִם, *fair eyes*, alludes to the Sanhedrin, which is considered to be the *eyes of the assembly* (*Numbers* 15:24).

David utilized his natural tendency to spill blood solely to rid the world of evil, which is the purpose of the Davidic kingdom (*Mishbetzos Zahav*).

The *Vilna Gaon* cites this as an ex-

1. Thus, David was born from a union in which the man mistakes the woman whom he has impregnated, a circumstance that generally results in spiritual damage to the offspring (see *Nedarim* 20b). This issue with regard to David (and also to Reuben, who was conceived by Leah when Jacob thought he had married Rachel) is discussed by *Rema MiPano*. See also *Magen Avraham, Orach Chaim* 240:9; *Birkei Yosef* ad loc.; *Nachalas Shimon* 39:3).

2. Thus, when David justifiably had Uriah the Hittite put to death, he was censured because he had failed to consult with the Sanhedrin (*Shabbos* 56a; *Mussar HaNeviim*).

[12]*He sent and brought him. He was ruddy, with fair eyes and a pleasing appearance.* HASHEM *said, "Arise and anoint him, for this is he!"*

ample of the dictum, חֲנֹךְ לַנַּעַר עַל־פִּי דַרְכּוֹ, *Train a youth according to his way* (*Proverbs* 22:6). Parents cannot change their child's nature. Their job, rather, is to channel the child's tendencies to the good.

Malbim explains similarly that David's ruddiness indicated the character of a person prepared to spill blood, yet his *fair eyes and pleasing appearance* indicated a clear mind and self-control.

With his clear mind, David directed his tendency to spill blood for the sole purpose of eradicating evil; and, when appropriate, he exercised compassion (*Me'am Loez*).

According to *Yalkut HaMechiri* (see above, v. 11), David's brothers were sure that he was an illegitimate child because his ruddy complexion made him seem the son of a father other than their own. But in fact, he was ruddy because at the time of conception Jesse's thoughts had been on the maidservant rather than on his wife.

וְטוֹב רֹאִי — *And a pleasing appearance.*

The *Vilna Gaon* (to *Proverbs* 11:22) states that a person's character, which is seated in his heart, is displayed in his appearance. Therefore, David's appearance was pleasing, because it expressed his internal traits, which were good.

On the basis of this description of David, the Midrash (*Vayikra Rabbah* 20:1) states that when people would look at him they would recall the Torah that they had learned. Some explain this to mean that since David's every action was based on the Torah, seeing him would remind people of how to act (*Mussar HaNeviim*). Others state that the glow of David's face had the power to spiritually illuminate those who saw him, so that they recalled the Torah stored in their memories (*Be'er Moshe;* see *Eruvin* 13b).

Me'am Loez translates טוֹב רֹאִי not as *a pleasing appearance* but as *good vision.* Even if David determined that someone deserved the death penalty, he would let the man live should his vision show him that he might be the progenitor of a righteous offspring — as occurred, for instance, in the case of Shimei son of Gera (see *Yalkut Shimoni* 151).

קוּם מְשָׁחֵהוּ כִּי־זֶה הוּא — *Arise and anoint him, for this is he!*

The word קוּם, *arise,* calls upon others to act with alacrity (*Radak*). A Midrash (*Tanchuma*) teaches that Hashem said, "My anointed one is standing here, yet you remain seated. Stand up and anoint him!"

According to tradition, a blank space is inserted in the middle of this verse, before the words וַיֹּאמֶר ה׳ קוּם מְשָׁחֵהוּ — HASHEM *said, "Arise and anoint him." Me'am Loez* states that this signifies the beginning of a new phase in Jewish history: the advent of the Davidic kingdom. Alternatively, this indicates that when Samuel saw David's ruddiness he hesitated, until Hashem told him, *Arise . . . .*

כִּי־זֶה הוּא — *For this is he!*

He is the one whom Hashem sent Samuel to anoint and who would have an everlasting dynasty.

The word זֶה, *this,* is used to refer to something that is tangibly perceptible, whereas the word הוּא, *he* (in the third person), refers to something not directly present. With this paradoxical expression, Hashem was telling Samuel that just as David was visibly *pleasant looking,* so were his imperceptible inner traits good and pleasant (see *Berachos* 28a). Unlike Eliab, David had a heart as pure as his outer appearance (*Be'er Moshe; Mussar HaNeviim*).

The Talmud derives from this verse

יג וַיִּקַּח שְׁמוּאֵל אֶת־קֶרֶן הַשֶּׁמֶן וַיִּמְשַׁח אֹתוֹ בְּקֶרֶב
אֶחָיו וַתִּצְלַח רוּחַ־יהוה אֶל־דָּוִד מֵהַיּוֹם הַהוּא
יד וָמָעְלָה וַיָּקָם שְׁמוּאֵל וַיֵּלֶךְ הָרָמָתָה: וְרוּחַ יהוה
סָרָה מֵעִם שָׁאוּל וּבִעֲתַתּוּ רוּחַ־רָעָה מֵאֵת יהוה:
טו וַיֹּאמְרוּ עַבְדֵי־שָׁאוּל אֵלָיו הִנֵּה־נָא רוּחַ־אֱלֹהִים
טז רָעָה מְבַעִתֶּךָ: יֹאמַר־נָא אֲדֹנֵנוּ עֲבָדֶיךָ לְפָנֶיךָ

that only *this* man and his descendants should be anointed with the special anointing oil (*Horayos* 11b).

13. וַיִּקַּח שְׁמוּאֵל אֶת־קֶרֶן הַשֶּׁמֶן וַיִּמְשַׁח אֹתוֹ — *Samuel took the horn of oil and anointed him.*

A Midrash relates that Samuel had previously attempted to anoint David's brothers, but as he began to pour the oil, it flowed away from them. When David arrived, the oil poured onto him of its own volition. David later said of this, וַתָּרֶם כִּרְאֵים קַרְנִי בַּלֹּתִי בְּשֶׁמֶן רַעֲנָן, *You raised my horn as a re'eim; I was saturated with fresh oil* (*Psalms* 92:11).

Some commentators find evidence for this Midrash in the fact that when Samuel anointed Saul the verse states explicitly that Samuel poured the oil, whereas it does not do so here (*Kli Yakar*).

Also, the fact that Samuel is here described as having taken the horn, a seemingly irrelevant detail, implies that he did no more than take the horn. The following word וַיִּמְשַׁח, *anointed*, must then apply to Hashem (*Alshich*).

Hashem said of this incident, מָצָאתִי דָּוִד עַבְדִּי בְּשֶׁמֶן קָדְשִׁי מְשַׁחְתִּיו, *I found David My servant; with My holy oil I anointed him* (*Psalms* 89:21) (*Be'er Moshe*).

According to *Yalkut HaMechiri*, when David arrived, the oil in Samuel's horn began to bubble up. As Samuel poured it onto David's head, it hardened and turned into precious stones and jewels, while the horn remained full and overflowing; Jesse and his sons looked on, trembling in fear.

בְּקֶרֶב אֶחָיו — *In the midst of his brothers.*

This indicates that David was the choicest of Jesse's sons (*Radak*).

Malbim suggests that Samuel wanted a quorum of ten present at this momentous occasion — since the Divine Presence rests on ten adult males (*Avos*) — and so he anointed David in the presence of Jesse and his other sons (including David and Samuel, that came to ten).

Abarbanel, however, assumes that Samuel would not have anointed David so publicly. Samuel singled David out only *in the midst of his brothers*, and then anointed him privately, with no one present, but possibly his father.

וַתִּצְלַח רוּחַ־ה׳ אֶל־דָּוִד — *And the spirit of* HASHEM *passed over David.*

The Targum states that this *spirit* was a spirit of prophecy.

According to *Rashi*, it was a spirit of strength.

All seem to agree that immediately after his anointment, David was charged with some sort of Divine inspiration that gave him wisdom, strength, and confidence to kill a lion and bear and defeat Goliath, the ability to play pleasing music, the talent to compose the *Psalms*, and success in his every endeavor (*Radak, Abarbanel, Ralbag*).

We translate וַתִּצְלַח as *passed*, in accordance with *Metzudos*. This word is usually associated with success.

Kli Yakar adds that the verb *passed over* implies that (as we will see in the following verse), the spirit was *transferred* from Saul to David. This also explains why the verse states אֶל־דָּוִד, which we translated as *over David*,

[13]*Samuel took the horn of oil and anointed him in
the midst of his brothers, and the spirit of HASHEM
passed over David from that day on. Then Samuel
arose and went to Ramah.*
[14]*The spirit of HASHEM departed from Saul, and
he was tormented by an evil spirit from HASHEM.*
[15]*Saul's servants said to him, "Behold now! an
evil spirit from God torments you.* [16]*Let our lord
tell your servants [who are] before you [that] they*

but which literally means *to David* (*Mishbetzos Zahav*).

☙ Saul's Change of Spirit and the Antidote to Counter It

14. וְרוּחַ ה׳ סָרָה מֵעִם שָׁאוּל — *The spirit of HASHEM departed from Saul.*

Because two kings cannot rule simultaneously (see *Chullin* 60b), as soon as this spirit — which included the expansive inspiration of the heart necessary to function as king and national judge — descended upon David, it left Saul (*Abarbanel*).

In two previous instances — when the spirit of Hashem had descended upon Saul (see above, 10:10) and in the previous verse — Targum translated this phrase as *a spirit of prophecy*. Here, however, Targum renders it as a *spirit of strength*. *Daas Sofrim* suggests that even now [some measure of prophecy] remained with Saul. He continued to participate in wars and lead the nation. However, he lacked the power to dispel his worries.

וּבִעֲתַתּוּ רוּחַ־רָעָה מֵאֵת ה׳ — *And he was tormented by an evil spirit from HASHEM.*

This spirit filled Saul with fear and depression, and he obsessively dwelled on the fact that he had lost the kingdom.

Abarbanel explains that Hashem did not actually afflict Saul with an evil spirit. Rather, Saul's present state of mind came as a result of the removal of the Divine spirit, which was considered as if an evil spirit came from Hashem.

Kli Yakar compares Saul's experience with contamination that affects the body after a person's soul departs. This is caused by impure forces called *klipos*, or "husks." Such "husks" seek to attach themselves to holy entities but find the concentration of holiness in a living Jew overwhelming. However, they can attach themselves to his body after his soul has gone. Similarly, when the Divine spirit left Saul, these husks attached themselves to him and caused him great anxiety. The idea of bringing a musician was to arouse in Saul a spirit of prophecy, which would attach him again to the Divine and banish the evil spirit.

Radak states that this spirit frightened Saul so thoroughly that he was not responsible for his thoughts, emotions, and actions. Thus (as we will see in the coming chapters), Saul engaged in behaviors that do not seem consistent with the great and righteous person that we have previously learned about [in particular, his persecution of David]. When our Sages list Saul's failings, they do not mention his irrational attacks against David. Apparently, these were not held against Saul because at these times he was not in a rational state of mind (*Mishbetzos Zahav*).

15. רוּחַ־אֱלֹהִים רָעָה — *An evil spirit from God.*

The phrase רוּחַ־אֱלֹהִים is translated here literally as *spirit from God*. However, often the word אֱלֹהִים is used to denote something exceptionally large

יְבַקְשׁוּ אִישׁ יֹדֵעַ מְנַגֵּן בַּכִּנּוֹר וְהָיָה בִּהְיוֹת עָלֶיךָ
יז רֽוּחַ־אֱלֹהִים רָעָה וְנִגֵּן בְּיָדוֹ וְטוֹב לָךְ׃ וַיֹּאמֶר
שָׁאוּל אֶל־עֲבָדָיו רְאוּ־נָא לִי אִישׁ מֵיטִיב לְנַגֵּן
יח וַהֲבִיאוֹתֶם אֵלָי׃ וַיַּעַן אֶחָד מֵהַנְּעָרִים וַיֹּאמֶר הִנֵּה
רָאִיתִי בֵּן לְיִשַׁי בֵּית הַלַּחְמִי יֹדֵעַ נַגֵּן וְגִבּוֹר חַיִל

and strong (as above, 14:15). Thus this phrase may be translated as *a mighty evil spirit* (*Metzudos*).

16. אִישׁ יֹדֵעַ מְנַגֵּן בַּכִּנּוֹר — *A man who knows how to play the harp.*

Our translation of יֹדֵעַ מְנַגֵּן as *who knows how to play* reflects one of *Radak*'s interpretations. However, according to this, the phrase is awkward, since it literally means *knows playing,* and should more properly state יוֹדֵעַ לְנַגֵּן, *knows how to play.* Thus, *Radak* offers an alternative interpretation of this phrase. The people should seek a person who possesses two qualities. First, יֹדֵעַ, *he knows* and understands the wisdom of music; second, and more particularly, מְנַגֵּן בַּכִּנּוֹר, he *can play the harp.*

Kli Yakar prefers the latter interpretation, because he understands that the purpose of this music was to arouse Divine inspiration (as in the case of Elisha — see *II Kings* 3:15), and so the man must be not merely a musician, but must know how to use music to drive away the evil spirit. Thus, the verse states as well, וְנִגֵּן בְּיָדוֹ, *he will play [the harp] with his hand.* This implies that his musical skills must be so natural that his hands will play by themselves, leaving his mind free to attach itself to holiness.

According to *Malbim,* the objective of the music was to divert Saul's mind and heart from depression to more joyous thoughts and feelings.

17. רְאוּ־נָא לִי אִישׁ מֵיטִיב לְנַגֵּן — *Seek now for me someone who plays well.*

Saul made the additional request: רְאוּ־נָא לִי, *Seek now for me.* Since Saul was king, it would be proper to get someone particularly suited for him, and that was someone who מֵיטִיב לְנַגֵּן, *plays well,* someone who possesses a strong sensitivity for the nuances of music and is able to compose songs that arouse and inspire the soul (*Malbim*).

18. וַיַּעַן אֶחָד מֵהַנְּעָרִים וַיֹּאמֶר — *One of the young men spoke up and said.*

The Talmud (*Sanhedrin* 93b) states that the word אֶחָד — *one* — refers to a person who is unique, and that was Doeg HaAdomi, a Torah scholar who was called אַבִּיר הָרֹעִים אֲשֶׁר לְשָׁאוּל — *the chief of Saul's shepherds* (below, 21:8) — the appellation, our Sages state, accorded to the chief justice.

We see elsewhere that Doeg was jealous of David and consistently opposed him. There is one incident to this effect recorded in Scripture: the episode in which Doeg instigated the murder of the Kohanim of Nob because they had protected David (Ch. 22). Aside from that, our Sages cite many instances in which Doeg incited Saul against David.

In this passage, Doeg is apparently praising David. Nevertheless, our Sages understand Doeg's intentions to have been malevolent and refer to his ostensible high praise as לְשׁוֹן הָרַע, *evil speech;* it was an artful slander (*Sanhedrin* 93b). Doeg's intent, they explain, was to arouse Saul's jealousy against David in the hope that Saul would eventually kill him. In this Doeg succeeded.

Why do the Sages attribute such a base motive to this seemingly sincere statement of praise? One answer is that they very logically interpret the deeds of the righteous positively and the deeds of the wicked negatively. Since we find

should seek a man who knows how to play the
harp, so that when the evil spirit from God is upon
you, he will play [the harp] with his hand and it
will be well with you.'' 17 *So Saul said to his ser-*
vants, ''Seek now for me someone who plays well
and bring him to me.'' 18 *One of the young men*
spoke up and said, ''Behold! I have seen a son of
Jesse the Bethlehemite, he knows how to play, is a
mighty man of valor

later in the Book that Doeg hated David, slandered him, and sought to disqualify him, here too his intentions were doubtless malign. Although we are generally enjoined to judge people favorably, that principle does not apply to a person who has a record of doing evil (see *Rabbeinu Yonah* to *Avos* 1:6; *Chofetz Chaim, Hil. Lashon Hara* 4:7; see also *Mishbetzos Zahav*, who clarifies this point with a parable).

Maharsha explains that Doeg's words constituted slander because they consisted of over-profuse praise, something against which the Talmud warns, since it tends to eventually result in disparagement (*Bava Basra* 164b; see *Chofetz Chaim, Hil. Lashon Hara* 9:1).

The spirit of melancholy that engulfed Saul was part of Hashem's plan to bring David into the palace and eventually make him acting king (*Ralbag*).

It is one of Hashem's marvels that the very person whose endorsement brought David to serve Saul — causing David to become a military hero, gain the love of the nation, and eventually become king — was none other than his greatest enemy, Doeg. Similarly, in an earlier generation Hashem manipulated events so that Pharaoh, who feared the birth of the Jews' savior and thus decreed that all Jewish boys be thrown into the river (*Exodus* 1:22), raised that savior — Moshe — as his own son in his palace, where Moshe learned to be a leader (*Mishbetzos Zahav*).

מֵהַנְּעָרִים — *Of the young men.*

Although Doeg was a highly respected Torah scholar and head of the Sanhedrin, Scripture calls him a *young man*. This was literally true — Doeg lived only to the age of 34.

Besides that, this term is possibly meant to belittle him. Alternatively, it means that, like a youthful servant, he devoted himself wholly to fulfilling his master's desires (*Daas Sofrim*).

Kli Yakar homiletically associates this word with the verb נער, *shaken*, as it appears in the expression, מְנוּעָר מִן הַמִּצְוֹת (as found in *Sotah* 46b) — "shaken loose of mitzvos." That is to say, although Doeg was learned, he did not fear Hashem.

יֹדֵעַ נַגֵּן וְגִבּוֹר חַיִל — *He knows how to play, is a mighty man of valor.*

The Talmud and Midrash homiletically interpret every phrase in the following description of David as referring to different aspects of his Torah scholarship. *Maharsha* finds support for this interpretation in the fact that Saul was advised to bring someone who could play the *harp* (v. 16), but Doeg did not mention the harp. Also since Doeg mentioned many qualities irrelevant to musicianship, we can infer that he was not discussing musical ability, but something else entirely — and that was Torah.

We will first explain this description in accordance with the simple meaning

וְאִישׁ מִלְחָמָה וּנְבוֹן דָּבָר וְאִישׁ תֹּאַר וַיהוָה עִמּוֹ׃
יט וַיִּשְׁלַח שָׁאוּל מַלְאָכִים אֶל־יִשָׁי וַיֹּאמֶר שִׁלְחָה אֵלַי
כ אֶת־דָּוִד בִּנְךָ אֲשֶׁר בַּצֹּאן׃ וַיִּקַּח יִשַׁי חֲמוֹר לֶחֶם
וְנֹאד יַיִן וּגְדִי עִזִּים אֶחָד וַיִּשְׁלַח בְּיַד־דָּוִד בְּנוֹ אֶל־
כא שָׁאוּל׃ וַיָּבֹא דָוִד אֶל־שָׁאוּל וַיַּעֲמֹד לְפָנָיו וַיֶּאֱהָבֵהוּ

of the words and afterward present the Sages' interpretation.

גִּבּוֹר חַיִל — *A mighty man of valor.*

This connotes a combination of physical strength and fearlessness. This description was based on Doeg's knowledge that David had successfully defeated a lion and bear that had come to attack his flock (see below, 17:34) (*Radak*).

וְאִישׁ מִלְחָמָה — *And a man of war.*

Radak and *Ralbag* understand this to mean that David understood military strategy and was experienced in battle.

However, *Rav M.D. Vali* finds it difficult to believe that as a shepherd David participated in battle. He instead suggests that this description too was based on David's having overcome the lion and bear. Anyone who could fearlessly approach a wild beast and defeat it had the potential to become an outstanding warrior (cited by *Mishbetzos Zahav*).

וּנְבוֹן דָּבָר — *He understands a matter.*

He considers matters fairly and sagaciously (*Ralbag*), and offers sound advice (*Targum*).

וְאִישׁ תֹּאַר — *He is a handsome man.*

This phrase literally means *a man of form.* The implication is that his *form* — or appearance — is pleasing (*Targum*).

וַה' עִמּוֹ — *And Hashem is with him.*

He is successful in all that he does (*Radak*).

Ralbag adds that a successful person has a beneficent influence on those around him, and so David's presence might cause Saul's evil spirit to depart.

יֹדֵעַ נַגֵּן וְגִבּוֹר חַיִל וְאִישׁ מִלְחָמָה וּנְבוֹן דָּבָר וְאִישׁ תֹּאַר וַה' עִמּוֹ — *He knows how to play, is a mighty man of valor and a man of war, he understands a matter, he is a handsome man, and Hashem is with him.*

Although Saul had only requested a musician, these other characteristics were relevant in that they would make David fit to serve successfully in the palace (*Radak*).

There may have been others who know how to play the harp proficiently, but David was chosen because he also possessed these other attributes.

Abarbanel explains that it was highly unusual to find all of these traits in one person — particularly so since some of them are usually exclusive of one another, as follows:

יֹדֵעַ נַגֵּן — *Knows how to play.* It is unusual to find a shepherd who is wise, yet David had mastered the intricacies of music.

גִּבּוֹר חַיִל — *A mighty man of valor.* Although musicians are generally weak, David was powerful

אִישׁ מִלְחָמָה — *A man of war.* It is surprising that a shepherd should be trained in warfare. It is equally surprising that a warrior should interest himself in song.

נְבוֹן דָּבָר — *Understands a matter.* Musicians generally develop their creative imaginations and not their logical faculties. Yet David had a sharp legal mind.

אִישׁ תֹּאַר — *A handsome man.* Although singers usually do not have impressive physiques, David did.

וַה' עִמּוֹ — *And Hashem is with him.* Musicians and good-looking people are often lascivious, yet David feared

and a man of war, he understands a matter, he is a
handsome man, and HASHEM is with him."
19 *Saul sent messengers to Jesse, and said, "Send*
me David your son who is with the sheep." 20 *Jesse*
took a donkey [laden with] bread, a jug of wine, and
one kid, and sent it with his son David, for Saul. 21 *Da-*
vid came to Saul and stood before him. He loved him

Hashem and acquired His aid.

As stated above, the Talmud relates each of these six characteristics to Torah learning, as follows.

יֹדֵעַ נַגֵּן — *He knows how to play,* i.e., David knew how to pose a question properly. And, notes *Ben Yehoyada,* citing the aphorism of R' Shlomo ibn Gabirol, a correctly phrased question is half the answer.

גִּבּוֹר חַיִל — *A mighty man of valor,* i.e., he knew how to reply to questions, clearly and concisely (*Ben Yehoyada*).

אִישׁ מִלְחָמָה — *A man of war,* i.e., he could hold his own in the vigorous give and take of Torah disputation (see *Kiddushin* 30b).

נְבוֹן דָּבָר — *He understands a matter,* i.e., he could draw the proper conclusions from what he learned.

אִישׁ תֹּאַר — *A handsome man,* i.e., he could defend his views.

וַה' עִמּוֹ — *And HASHEM is with him,* i.e., the halachah followed David's view in all matters.

As Doeg made mention of each trait, Saul responded, "My son Jonathan possesses that quality as well," but when Doeg stated that the halachah is always in accord with David, Saul fell silent. He reflected that the halachah was not always in accord with his own views (see above, 14:47), and this aroused his jealousy of David.

The fact that a person's halachic decisions are universally accepted does not necessarily reflect on his brilliance or scholarship. Rather, that is solely in accord with God's will. We find this to be the case in regard to Beis Hillel and Beis Shamai (*Eruvin* 13b) and in more contemporary cases as well, when certain views prevail even though the proofs supporting them are relatively insubstantial (see *Urim VeTumim* 25; *Teshuvos Chasam Sofer* on *Even HaEzer,* Vol. II #102; *Mishbetzos Zahav).*

There is a greater likelihood that a person's halachic decisions will be accepted when he is unusually humble (*Chida;* see *Eruvin* ibid.). Hashem proclaims that He and an arrogant man cannot be together (*Sotah* 5a); from this we may infer that when a person is humble, then וַה' עִמּוֹ, *HASHEM is with him,* and so the halachah is in accord with his views.

[In Biblical times,] halachic authorities generally came from the tribes of Levi and Issachar. Since David was from neither of these tribes, Saul understood that since the halachah was in accord with David, an exception was being made in his case — and the reason was that heaven considered David to be the true monarch. This too aroused Saul's envy (*Chomas Anach,* citing *R' Frimo*).

20. חֲמוֹר לֶחֶם — *A donkey [laden with] bread.*

Our translation is in accord with the *Targum.*

Alternatively, *Radak* renders this phrase as *a heap of bread* (see *Exodus* 8:10).

Bread might seem like a commonplace item to send to a king. However, the name of Jesse's town, Bethlehem, literally means "house of bread," implying that its wheat was of exceptional quality (*Me'am Loez*).

טז/כב־כג

כב מְאֹד וַיְהִי־לוֹ נֹשֵׂא כֵלִים: וַיִּשְׁלַח שָׁאוּל אֶל־יִשַׁי
לֵאמֹר יַעֲמָד־נָא דָוִד לְפָנַי כִּי־מָצָא חֵן בְּעֵינָי:
כג וְהָיָה בִּהְיוֹת רוּחַ־אֱלֹהִים אֶל־שָׁאוּל וְלָקַח דָּוִד
אֶת־הַכִּנּוֹר וְנִגֵּן בְּיָדוֹ וְרָוַח לְשָׁאוּל וְטוֹב לוֹ וְסָרָה
א מֵעָלָיו רוּחַ הָרָעָה: וַיַּאַסְפוּ פְלִשְׁתִּים אֶת־
מַחֲנֵיהֶם לַמִּלְחָמָה וַיֵּאָסְפוּ שֹׂכֹה אֲשֶׁר לִיהוּדָה
ב וַיַּחֲנוּ בֵּין־שׂוֹכֹה וּבֵין־עֲזֵקָה בְּאֶפֶס דַּמִּים: וְשָׁאוּל
וְאִישׁ־יִשְׂרָאֵל נֶאֶסְפוּ וַיַּחֲנוּ בְּעֵמֶק הָאֵלָה וַיַּעַרְכוּ
ג מִלְחָמָה לִקְרַאת פְּלִשְׁתִּים: וּפְלִשְׁתִּים עֹמְדִים
אֶל־הָהָר מִזֶּה וְיִשְׂרָאֵל עֹמְדִים אֶל־הָהָר מִזֶּה

יז/א־ג

וַיִּשְׁלַח בְּיַד־דָּוִד בְּנוֹ אֶל־שָׁאוּל — *And sent it with his son, David, for Saul.*

It was customary to bring a tribute when coming to a distinguished personage (*Malbim*).

21. וַיְהִי־לוֹ נֹשֵׂא כֵלִים — *And he became his armor-bearer.*

This was considered a dignified position, although not necessarily befitting someone of David's accomplishments (*Daas Sofrim*).

23. וְרָוַח לְשָׁאוּל וְטוֹב לוֹ — *Saul would feel relieved and it would be well with him.*

Not only would the disturbances leave him but he would even feel happy (*Malbim*).

XVII

לֹא בְּחֶרֶב וּבַחֲנִית יְהוֹשִׁיעַ ה׳, *Not through sword and spear does* H*ASHEM grant salvation* (below v. 47).!

This chapter demonstrate the principle that we must seek to understand Scripture according to the interpretations of the Sages and traditional commentators. The story of David and Goliath has been sensationalized and been used as a metaphor for myriad cases of an underdog triumphing over a superior opponent, whether in sports, business, or politics. It is widely portrayed as an example of the fallacy that brute strength and armor are always superior to agility and strategy. As a result, its true lesson as understood by the Sages has been distorted beyond description.

A careful study of this chapter, however, reveals that none of this is so, and that David's prowess was simply the hand of Hashem acting in this world.

After having described how David utilized his musical talents in the king's court, Scripture in this chapter goes on to relate how David acted as a *mighty man of valor and a man of war* (above, v. 18) (*Malbim*).

1. וַיַּאַסְפוּ פְלִשְׁתִּים אֶת־מַחֲנֵיהֶם לַמִּלְחָמָה — *The Philistines assembled their camps for war.*

After the spirit of Hashem departed from Saul, the Jews were left vulnerable, and the Philistine enemy, which had not long before been routed by Jonathan, regained the confidence to wage war (*Malbim*).

Me'am Loez states that the Philistines may have heard that Saul was suffering from anxiety and unable to offer adequate leadership, and thus decided to attack.

16/22-23 *very much, and he became his armor-bearer.* 22 *Saul*
sent to Jesse, saying, "Let David stand before me,
for he has found favor in my eyes." 23 *And it hap-*
pened that whenever the evil spirit from God was
upon Saul, David would take the harp and play [it]
with his hand, and Saul would feel relieved and it
would be well with him, and the evil spirit would
depart from him.

17/1-3 1 *The Philistines assembled their camps for war;*
they gathered at Socoh, which belongs to
Judah; they encamped between Socoh and Aze-
kah, in Ephes-dammim. 2 *So Saul and the people*
of Israel assembled themselves; they encamped
in the Terebinth Valley, and they arranged for
war against the Philistines. 3 *The Philistines were*
standing on the mountain on one side and Israel
was standing on the mountain on the other side,

וַיֵּאָסְפוּ שֹׂכֹה אֲשֶׁר לִיהוּדָה — *They gathered at Socoh, which belongs to Judah.*

They had the audacity to assemble on Judean territory (*Malbim*).

בְּאֶפֶס דַּמִּים — *In Ephes-dammim.*

The word בְּאֶפֶס, *in Ephes,* may be translated as *for nothing.* The Philistine soldiers were ordinarily paid. In this instance, however, they were so eager to go to war that they volunteered their services (see also *Judges* 5:19) (*Me'am Loez*).

In *I Chronicles* (11:13), this site is called פַּס־דַּמִּים, *Pas-dammim.* The word [*pas* means "strip of land," and] *dammim* is related to *adom,* which means *red.* Thus, this name may be translated as *Red Field* — i.e., red with the blood that was spilled there (*Ruth Rabbah* 5:1).

Alternatively, *pas* derives from פָּסַק and may be rendered as *ceased.* If so, the name means *The Red Ceased* — the bloodshed came to an end because the Philistines fled (ibid.).

3. וְיִשְׂרָאֵל עֹמְדִים אֶל־הָהָר מִזֶּה — *And Israel was standing on the mountain on the other side.*

The Israelite soldiers initially camped in the Terebinth Valley, but now those who prepared for battle ascended the adjoining mountain toward the Philistine camp (*Radak*).

וּפְלִשְׁתִּים עֹמְדִים אֶל הָהָר מִזֶּה וְיִשְׂרָאֵל עֹמְדִים אֶל־הָהָר מִזֶּה — *The Philistines were standing on the mountain on one side and Israel was standing on the mountain on the other side.*

From the Midrashic treatment of this verse, we glean that this confrontation was more than a battle between two armies; it was a conflict between good and evil. Thus *Aggudas Bereishis* (Ch. 50) finds the underlying meaning of the conflict in the narrative's use of the word זֶה, *this,* as follows: the Philistines were on הָהָר מִזֶּה, *this side of the mountain,* depending on Goliath who is referred to

ד וְהַגַּיְא בֵּינֵיהֶם: וַיֵּצֵא אִישׁ־הַבֵּנַיִם מִמַּחֲנוֹת
פְּלִשְׁתִּים גָּלְיָת שְׁמוֹ מִגַּת גָּבְהוֹ שֵׁשׁ אַמּוֹת
ה וָזָרֶת: וְכוֹבַע נְחֹשֶׁת עַל־רֹאשׁוֹ וְשִׁרְיוֹן קַשְׂקַשִּׂים
הוּא לָבוּשׁ וּמִשְׁקַל הַשִּׁרְיוֹן חֲמֵשֶׁת־אֲלָפִים
ו שְׁקָלִים נְחֹשֶׁת: וּמִצְחַת נְחֹשֶׁת עַל־רַגְלָיו

as זֶה, *this one* (v. 25), and the Israelites were on הָהָר מִזֶּה, *this side of the mountain*, putting their hopes on David, who was also called זֶה (16:12).

The Philistines were supported by Satan, who is also referred to as זֶה (*Job* 6:3), and Israel was supported by ministering angels, each of which is called זֶה (*Isaiah* 6:3). Satan contended that the Jews still desreved to be punished for the sin of the Golden Calf, about which its worshipers said זֶה אֱלֹהֶיךָ, *this is your god* (*Nehemiah* 9:18), to which the angels retorted that Israel had used the same word in an eloquent expression of gratitude: זֶה אֵלִי וְאַנְוֵהוּ, *This is my God and I will build Him a Sanctuary* (*Exodus* 15:2).

וְהַגַּיְא בֵּינֵיהֶם — *And the valley was between them.*

This particular word for *valley* evokes the memory of Moses, who was buried in a valley named similarly גַּי (*Deuteronomy* 34:6). *Aggadas Bereishis* (ibid.) states that David grew apprehensive about confronting Goliath, so Hashem reminded him of Moses, who had prophesied that a descendant of Judah — i.e., David — would defeat his enemies. As the verse states, יָדָיו רָב לוֹ וְעֵזֶר מִצָּרָיו תִּהְיֶה, *His hands will fight on his behalf, and You will help him against his enemies* (*Deuteronomy* 33:7).

4. וַיֵּצֵא אִישׁ־הַבֵּנַיִם — *The champion went forth.*

The literal meaning of the phrase, אִישׁ־הַבֵּנַיִם — *the champion* — is *the man of the middle.* This implies that Goliath left his camp and stood between the two armies. The word is preceded by the definite article in order to indicate that he was the Philistine warrior par excellence, or because he was called that because of this incident (*Daas Sofrim*).

The Talmud (*Sotah* 42b) presents a variety of homiletical interpretations of this phrase.

❒ The word בֵּינַיִם may be related to בִּנְיָן, *building.* Goliath was perfectly structured, without a single blemish.

❒ He was tall and mighty as a building.

❒ This word may be related to the word בֵּין, *between*, i.e., Goliath was the average among his four brothers.

Maharsha understands this to mean that he was of average height.

❒ אִישׁ הַבֵּינַיִם may be translated as *a man from among.* The night after Orpah declined to accompany her mother-in-law Naomi to the land of Israel (see *Ruth* 1:14), she consorted with many men (and, according to one tradition, with a dog as well), as a result of which she conceived Goliath. Thus, he was *a man [conceived] from among [many]* (*Rashi*).

❒ *Targum* renders הַבֵּינַיִם as מִבֵּינֵיהֶם, *from among them.* It thus translates the phrase וַיֵּצֵא אִישׁ־הַבֵּנַיִם as *a man went forth from among them.*

גָּלְיָת שְׁמוֹ — *Goliath was his name.*

The formula "... was his name" (rather than "his name was ...") is used to describe a wicked man (*Bamidbar Rabbah* 10:5; see comm. above 1:1).

The name גָּלְיָת is associated with the word גִּילוּי, meaning *revealed.* The Talmud (ibid.) states that Goliath spoke with גִּילוּי פָּנִים, *a revealed face*, which is to say, insolently, because he in effect challenged Hashem to battle (see below, v. 8).

Our Sages teach that during the war against the Philistines in the time of Eli,

and the valley was between them.

[4]The champion went forth from the Philistine camps, Goliath was his name, from Gath; his height six cubits and one span. [5]A copper helmet was on his head, and he was wearing a coat of mail; the weight of the coat was five thousand copper shekels. [6]A copper shield was on his legs

Goliath had captured the Holy Tablets from the Ark, which Saul subsequently recovered (*Midrash Shmuel;* see above, 4:12). Goliath had also killed Eli's sons Hophni and Phinehas (see *Targum* below, v. 8).

מִגַּת — *From Gath.*

Gath was one of the five major Philistine cities (see above, Chs. 5,6).

The name Gath means *winepress.* The Talmud (ibid.) homiletically comments that just as anyone may tread on a winepress, so too whoever wanted to could consort with Goliath's mother Orpah.

גָּבְהוֹ שֵׁשׁ אַמּוֹת וָזָרֶת — *His height was six cubits and one span.*

A span is the distance from the thumb to the little finger (*Metzudos*), and is equal to half a cubit (see *Rashbam, Exodus* 28:16). Assuming a cubit to be just under 2 feet, Goliath was nearly 13 feet high. Scripture mentions the span to indicate that it is providing Goliath's exact height, and not an exaggeration (*Daas Sofrim*).

The purpose of describing Goliath in such detail is to praise David, who was not afraid to do battle with him (*Sotah* 42b). In fact, as we will see (v. 7), Scripture does not even describe half of Goliath's might.

When Ruth came to Boaz's threshing-floor, he gave her six measures of barley (*Ruth* 3:15). This indicated that six righteous men would descend from her, each of whom would be praised with six descriptions (*Ruth Rabbah* 7:2; see above, 16:18; *Isaiah* 11:2 et al.). One of these was David, who incorporated the number six into his service of Hashem (see *II Samuel* 6:5,13,19; *Be'er Moshe* ad loc.). Orpah could have received these blessings as well, but she turned her back on them and received instead a corresponding six measures of contamination. Accordingly, her descendant Goliath was six cubits tall (*Arizal* in *Sefer HaLikkutim*). We also find that Goliath's brother had six fingers on each hand and six toes on each foot (*II Samuel* 21:20), and according to one tradition, Orpah bore six illegitimate sons, all of whom were slain by David and his soldiers (*Zohar Chadash, Ruth* 816) (*Be'er Moshe*).

5. וְכוֹבַע נְחֹשֶׁת עַל־רֹאשׁוֹ — *A copper helmet was on his head.*

According to *Abarbanel,* the helmet did not cover Goliath's forehead. However, others dispute this (see below, v. 49).

וְשִׁרְיוֹן קַשְׂקַשִּׂים הוּא לָבוּשׁ — *And he was wearing a coat of mail.*

This consisted of linked iron rings covered with scales, similar to those of a fish, to provide protection against swords and spears (*Rashi, Metzudos*).

וּמִשְׁקַל הַשִּׁרְיוֹן חֲמֵשֶׁת־אֲלָפִים שְׁקָלִים נְחֹשֶׁת — *The weight of the coat was five thousand copper shekels.*

This was exceedingly heavy and could be worn only by a very powerful man (*Ralbag, Abarbanel*).

6. וּמִצְחַת נְחֹשֶׁת עַל־רַגְלָיו — *A copper shield was on his legs.*

מִצְחָה — *greaves* — is related to the word מֵצַח, which means *forehead.* Our translation follows *Radak,* who states that this was a leg shield that resembled golden or silver ornaments that girls would wear on their foreheads.

According to *Rashi,* this was a shield that was attached to the helmet at the

°וְעֵץ ק׳

ז וְכִידוֹן נְחֹשֶׁת בֵּין כְּתֵפָיו: °וחץ חֲנִיתוֹ כִּמְנוֹר
אֹרְגִים וְלַהֶבֶת חֲנִיתוֹ שֵׁשׁ־מֵאוֹת שְׁקָלִים בַּרְזֶל
ח וְנֹשֵׂא הַצִּנָּה הֹלֵךְ לְפָנָיו: וַיַּעֲמֹד וַיִּקְרָא אֶל־מַעַרְכֹת
יִשְׂרָאֵל וַיֹּאמֶר לָהֶם לָמָּה תֵצְאוּ לַעֲרֹךְ מִלְחָמָה
הֲלוֹא אָנֹכִי הַפְּלִשְׁתִּי וְאַתֶּם עֲבָדִים לְשָׁאוּל
ט בְּרוּ־לָכֶם אִישׁ וְיֵרֵד אֵלָי: אִם־יוּכַל לְהִלָּחֵם אִתִּי

forehead, covering the nose and extending down to the feet.

וְכִידוֹן נְחֹשֶׁת בֵּין כְּתֵפָיו — *And a copper neck-guard was between his shoulders.*

The word כִּידוֹן is elsewhere translated as *javelin* (cf. *Joshua* 8:26).

Rashi states that this was a neck-guard shaped like a javelin and attached to the helmet, extending between the shoulders.

Verse 45 seemingly lists the כִּידוֹן as one of Goliath's weapons. Accordingly, *Radak* understands it to be a javelin placed between Goliath's shoulders, as he held other weapons in his hands.

Me'am Loez cites a view that the כִּידוֹן was a shield protecting Goliath's shoulders.

7. וְעֵץ חֲנִיתוֹ כִּמְנוֹר אֹרְגִים — *The shaft of his spear was like a weaver's beam.*

Scripture further illustrates the huge extent of the giant's trappings. The circumference of the shaft equaled that of a beam on which weavers roll their material (*Mahari Kara*) — that material being the unwoven warp (*Metzudos*).

The word עֵץ, *shaft*, is written (*k'siv*) as חֵץ, *arrow*, since it was shaped like an arrow (*Abarbanel*).

The Talmud (*Sotah* 42b) associates חֵץ with the word חֲצִי, meaning *half*, and derives from this that Scripture does not describe even half of Goliath's strength, because it is prohibited to praise an evil man. Scripture states the little that it does only in order to denote David's heroism.

וְלַהֶבֶת חֲנִיתוֹ — *And the blade of his spear.*

The word לַהֶבֶת, *blade*, literally means *flame*. When the blade was sharpened it shone as brightly as a flame (*Metzudos*).

שֵׁשׁ־מֵאוֹת שְׁקָלִים בַּרְזֶל — *Six hundred iron shekels.*

Each type of metal (copper, iron, silver, and so forth) was weighed by a different standard, although they were all called "shekel" — e.g., the copper shekel, the iron shekel, the silver shekel, and so forth (*Radak*).

וְנֹשֵׂא הַצִּנָּה הֹלֵךְ לְפָנָיו — *The shield-bearer walked before him.*

According to *Abarbanel*, the shield-bearer held the shield until Goliath went to fight, at which time he would take it himself.

Metzudos states that the shield-bearer held up the shield during the battle to protect Goliath from harm. This further emphasizes the miracle that allowed David's stone to penetrate all Goliath's protective paraphernalia (*Me'am Loez*).

8. לָמָּה תֵצְאוּ לַעֲרֹךְ מִלְחָמָה — *Why are you going forth to wage war?*

The word *you* is in the plural. Goliath asked why all of the Israelites were going to war, since they could end this conflict by selecting one man to represent them in a duel (*Rashi*).

הֲלוֹא אָנֹכִי הַפְּלִשְׁתִּי וְאַתֶּם עֲבָדִים לְשָׁאוּל — *Am I not the Philistine, while you are the servants of Saul?*

Goliath said that although he was an ordinary Philistine soldier, he had accomplished much on the battlefield, whereas the Israelite king had yet to prove his valor in battle (*Rashi*).

According to a text added to *Targum*,

and a copper neck-guard was between his shoul-
ders. [7]The shaft of his spear was like a weavers'
beam and the blade of his spear [weighed] six hun-
dred iron shekels. The shield-bearer walked before
him. [8]He stood and called out to the battalions of
Israel and said to them, "Why are you going forth
to wage war? Am I not the Philistine, while you
are the servants of Saul? Choose yourselves a man
and let him come down to me! [9]If he can fight me

Goliath said, "I am the Philistine who killed Hophni and Phinehas, the sons of Eli, and who seized the Ark and brought it to our god Dagon. At every Philistine war, I fought at the front and was victorious, leaving behind casualties like the dust of the land."

According to one view, Goliath demanded specifically to battle Saul (see below). Since he was an officer, whereas the soldiers were mere servants, they should send Saul forward so that this confrontation would take place between two equals (*Me'am Loez*).

Abarbanel, however, understands the phrase אָנֹכִי הַפְּלִשְׁתִּי, *I am the Philistine*, to indicate that although Goliath was a high-ranking officer who would ordinarily not duel an opponent who was not of equal rank, he was in this instance prepared to do so.

Some commentators derive from the words אָנֹכִי הַפְּלִשְׁתִּי, *I am the Philistine*, that Goliath was representative of the Philistine nation in that both were the product of extreme promiscuity (see *Genesis* 10:14, *Rashi* ad loc.; *Midrash Tanchuma, Vayeishev* 1; *Be'er Moshe*).

וְאַתֶּם עֲבָדִים לְשָׁאוּל — *While you are the servants of Saul.*

According to *Abarbanel*, Goliath was implying that the Jews had nothing to lose. Should they win, their situation would remain as before; should he win, on the other hand, they would simply change their allegiance from Saul to Goliath.

בְּרוּ־לָכֶם אִישׁ — *Choose yourselves a man.*

Simply understood, Goliath meant any man. *Rashi*, however, understands that he meant Saul.

The Talmud (*Sotah* 42b) states that in his arrogance, Goliath challenged Hashem Himself, Who is called אִישׁ מִלְחָמָה, *Man of War* (*Exodus* 15:3).

Maharsha explains that the word אִישׁ — one of several synonyms in Hebrew meaning *man* — has the connotation of a powerful being and thus refers here to Hashem. Also, since this confrontation took place on the mountaintop, Goliath's words וְיֵרֵד אֵלָי, *let him come down to me*, can only be understood as referring to a being descending from heaven.

The Talmud adds that Hashem responded that although Goliath wanted to fight against a *man*, God would send him to his demise through the hands of a בֶּן־אִישׁ, *son of a man* (below, v. 12), who was not known as a warrior but only as his father's son (*Maharsha*).

וְיֵרֵד אֵלָי — *And let him come down to me.*

The Talmud (ibid.) cites this as one of the instances in which Goliath inadvertently predicted his own fate, for this phrase may be interpreted to mean, "He will subdue me" (*Rashi, Kli Yakar*).

9. אִם־יוּכַל לְהִלָּחֵם אִתִּי ... וְאִם־אֲנִי אוּכַל־לוֹ ... — *If he can fight me ... but if I can defeat him ...*

וְהִכָּנִי וְהָיִינוּ לָכֶם לַעֲבָדִים וְאִם־אֲנִי אוּכַל־לוֹ
וְהִכִּיתִיו וִהְיִיתֶם לָנוּ לַעֲבָדִים וַעֲבַדְתֶּם אֹתָנוּ׃
י וַיֹּאמֶר הַפְּלִשְׁתִּי אֲנִי חֵרַפְתִּי אֶת־מַעַרְכוֹת
יִשְׂרָאֵל הַיּוֹם הַזֶּה תְּנוּ־לִי אִישׁ וְנִלָּחֲמָה יָחַד׃
יא וַיִּשְׁמַע שָׁאוּל וְכָל־יִשְׂרָאֵל אֶת־דִּבְרֵי הַפְּלִשְׁתִּי
יב הָאֵלֶּה וַיֵּחַתּוּ וַיִּרְאוּ מְאֹד׃ וְדָוִד בֶּן־אִישׁ
אֶפְרָתִי הַזֶּה מִבֵּית לֶחֶם יְהוּדָה וּשְׁמוֹ יִשַׁי וְלוֹ

Abarbanel cites the view of gentile scholars that Goliath was challenging the Jews to a formal duel, which was a customary manner of settling a dispute between two countries in the belief that the result would be divinely determined. *Abarbanel,* however, takes issue with this premise and argues that such a duel must assure conditions of equality, which were lacking in the present instance. Rather, Goliath's challenge was simply meant to insult the Jews and demonstrate his superiority.

Malbim agrees that Goliath meant to insult the Jews, but he also believes that initially Goliath did propose a duel. The Jews had previously been subjects of the Philistines — when they chose their own king, the Philistines viewed that as seditious. Goliath now wished to force the Jews to renew their allegiance with the Philistines. The Jews, however, declined this challenge because they did not want to risk the fate of the nation on the vagaries of one's man's abilities. Thus, following Goliath's challenge, as presented in this verse, they responded — [although that is not reported in the text] — that they preferred a regular battle between two nations.

Yaaros Devash also wonders about the purpose of this duel and how the success or failure of one warrior would be the deciding factor in the war. He also questions why it would be disgraceful for the entire nation of Israel to lose such a duel in view of the fact that Israel does not take pride in physical strength. Every nation's fate is dependent upon its king, whose own fate is determined by his *mazal,* his astrological fortunes. There is one exception — the Jewish nation, which transcends the influence of the stars, and whose king receives his fortune directly from the Heavenly throne. However, that applies only to a king of the Davidic dynasty.

Goliath came to challenge the Jews only at this point (and not earlier when Jonathan had attacked the Philistines; see Ch. 14), because he saw that his fortunes were now ascendant. If Saul, their king, were able to defeat him now when the constellations pointed to Goliath's success, that would prove that Israel is above all the signs of the zodiac. However, if Goliath were to triumph, that would prove that Israel was not protected by God but were, like all other nations, subject to the influence of the zodiac. Goliath was unaware, however, that even if Israel as a whole is less worthy, its kings of the Davidic line transcend the influence of the zodiac.

10. We insert the word *saying* in accordance with the *Targum.*

Metzudos [does not insert the word *saying* into the text, but] explains that Goliath implied that since he had disgraced the Jews by calling them cowards, they must defend their honor — and the way to do that was to send a representative to fight him.

Malbim [too does not insert the word *saying* into the verse.] According to his understanding, after Goliath challenged

and kill me, we will be slaves to you; but if I defeat him and kill him, you will be slaves to us and serve us."
10 Then the Philistine said, "I have disgraced the battalions of Israel this day, [saying,] 'Give me a man and we will fight together.' "
11 Saul and all Israel heard these words of the Philistine, and they were terrified and greatly afraid.
12 David was the son of a certain Ephrathite from Bethlehem [in] Judah; his name was Jesse and he had

the Jews to a formal duel and they declined, he made a new demand: *Give me a man and we will fight together* — but this time without the protocol of a formal duel.

It was this ultimatum that impelled David to respond.

11. וַיֵּחַתּוּ וַיִּרְאוּ מְאֹד — *They were terrified and greatly afraid.*

Not long before, Saul had seen his son Jonathan single-handedly defeat an entire Philistine garrison. How is it that he now feared this single blaspheming soldier?

Kli Yakar explains that this fear was one expression of the evil spirit that had affected Saul (*Kli Yakar*).

Alternatively, although Goliath may have *thought* that he was challenging Hashem, he never said so explicitly. On the contrary, he said "I have disgraced the battalions *of Israel*," not "I have disgraced Hashem." Goliath continued, "He will not come to your defense, because you are out of favor, since you failed to eradicate Amalek." Thus Goliath implied that Hashem would not exact revenge against him because he had not been blasphemous. This aroused fear in Saul and his people. David, however, understood Goliath's true intent: by disgracing the people of God, he would in effect be deriding God Himself (v. 26).

12. וְדָוִד בֶּן־אִישׁ אֶפְרָתִי — *David was the son of a certain Ephrathite.*

According to *Abarbanel*, this verse introduces David's rise to prominence and so appropriately provides background information about his family. *Radak* explains that this and the following verses explain how it happened that David came to the battlefield.

Malbim adds that Scripture is explaining why David did not come to the battlefield sooner despite his awareness of his physical prowess and what he could contribute to the war effort.

אֶפְרָתִי הַזֶּה מִבֵּית לֶחֶם יְהוּדָה — *A certain Ephrathite from Bethlehem [in] Judah.*

The city of Bethlehem is situated in a region called Ephrath (*Rashi*).

A Midrash states that the word אֶפְרָתִי — *Ephratite* — is an appellation used to describe a distinguished person (see above, 1:1).

From this verse, the Talmud (*Sotah* 11b) derives that David descended from Miriam, who was also called Ephrath (*I Chronicles* 2:19). This substantiated Hashem's promise to her that she would be the progenitor of kings (see *Exodus* 1:21, *Rashi* ad loc.).

הַזֶּה — *A certain.*

This indicates that Jesse was a well-known figure (*Metzudos*).

According to *Radak*, the word הַזֶּה refers to David, and the verse should be read as stating, *This David [who was introduced in the previous chapter] was the son of an Ephratite.*

וּשְׁמוֹ יִשַׁי — *His name was Jesse.*

The formula "his name was ..." (rather than "... was his name") is used

שְׁמֹנָ֥ה בָנִ֖ים וְהָאִישׁ֙ בִּימֵ֣י שָׁא֔וּל זָקֵ֖ן בָּ֥א בַאֲנָשִֽׁים׃
יג וַיֵּ֨לְכ֜וּ שְׁלֹ֤שֶׁת בְּנֵֽי־יִשַׁי֙ הַגְּדֹלִ֔ים הָלְכ֥וּ אַֽחֲרֵי־
שָׁא֖וּל לַמִּלְחָמָ֑ה וְשֵׁ֣ם ׀ שְׁלֹ֣שֶׁת בָּנָ֗יו אֲשֶׁ֤ר הָֽלְכוּ֙
בַּמִּלְחָמָ֔ה אֱלִיאָ֣ב הַבְּכ֔וֹר וּמִשְׁנֵ֙הוּ֙ אֲבִ֣ינָדָ֔ב
יד וְהַשְּׁלִשִׁ֖י שַׁמָּֽה׃ וְדָוִ֖ד ה֣וּא הַקָּטָ֑ן וּשְׁלֹשָׁה֙ הַגְּדֹלִ֔ים
טו הָלְכ֖וּ אַחֲרֵ֥י שָׁאֽוּל׃ וְדָוִ֛ד הֹלֵ֥ךְ וָשָׁ֖ב מֵעַ֣ל שָׁא֑וּל
טז לִרְע֛וֹת אֶת־צֹ֥אן אָבִ֖יו בֵּֽית־לָֽחֶם׃ וַיִּגַּ֣שׁ הַפְּלִשְׁתִּ֔י
יז הַשְׁכֵּ֣ם וְהַעֲרֵ֑ב וַיִּתְיַצֵּ֖ב אַרְבָּעִ֥ים יֽוֹם׃ וַיֹּ֨אמֶר

to describe a righteous man (*Bamidbar Rabbah* 10:5; see v. 4).

וְלוֹ שְׁמֹנָה בָנִים — *And he had eight sons.*

Only seven sons are listed in *I Chronicles* (2:15). Possibly, one died without children, so his name was omitted from that genealogical listing (*Rashi*). See comm. to 16:9, and see above, 16:10, regarding Jesse's sons.

וְהָאִישׁ בִּימֵי שָׁאוּל זָקֵן בָּא בַאֲנָשִׁים — *In the days of Saul, the man was old and would come among the elders.*

בָּא בַאֲנָשִׁים, *would come among the elders,* means that he was counted among the prominent men at major gatherings (*Targum, Rashi*).

Mahari Kara adds that he was one of Saul's distinguished followers.

The Sages derive from here that Jesse was a highly respected man who was escorted by an honorary entourage (*Berachos* 58a).

According to *Radak*, however, בָּא בַאֲנָשִׁים means that Jesse had joined the groups of elderly, weak men who could no longer come and go on their own. He therefore sent his sons to the battlefield in his stead.

13. וַיֵּלְכוּ שְׁלֹשֶׁת בְּנֵי־יִשַׁי הַגְּדֹלִים — *Jesse's three oldest sons went.*

This explains why David was not at the battlefield. Soldiers were drafted by family. Jesse sent only his three oldest sons because he was aging and needed his other sons to remain at home to assist him (*Malbim*).

הָלְכוּ אַחֲרֵי־שָׁאוּל — *Went after Saul.*

The repetition of the word *went* implies that these three brothers regularly accompanied Saul (*Radak*).

The phrase אַחֲרֵי־שָׁאוּל, *after Saul,* indicates that as his prominent followers they would stand near him (*Metzudos*).

וְשֵׁם שְׁלֹשֶׁת בָּנָיו אֲשֶׁר הָלְכוּ בַּמִּלְחָמָה אֱלִיאָב הַבְּכוֹר וּמִשְׁנֵהוּ אֲבִינָדָב וְהַשְּׁלִשִׁי שַׁמָּה — *The names of his three sons who went to war were Eliab, the firstborn; the second to him Abinadab; and the third Shammah.*

Scripture lists their names to imply that they were prominent not only as sons of Jesse, but in their own right as well (*Mishbetzos Zahav*).

14. וְדָוִד הוּא הַקָּטָן — *David was the youngest.*

The word הַקָּטָן — *the youngest* — literally means *small.* Besides being the youngest, David was exceptionally humble.

Although David had been anointed as king in the presence of his older brothers, he did not grow conceited (*Chomas Anach*).

David states in *Psalms* ה׳ לֹא־גָבַהּ לִבִּי, *HASHEM, my heart was not proud* (131:1). The Midrash explains this to mean that even after his anointment, he did not grow vain (*Bamidbar Rabbah* 4:20).

This phrase more literally means *David, he was the small.* The Talmud (*Megillah* 11a) derives from the word הוּא — *he was* — that David remained

eight sons. In the days of Saul, the man was old
and would come among the elders. [13]*Jesse's three*
oldest sons went after Saul to war. The names of
his three sons who went to war were Eliab, the
firstborn; the second to him, Abinadab; and the
third, Shammah. [14]*David was the youngest; just*
the three oldest followed Saul. [15]*David would trav-*
el back and forth from Saul's presence to tend his
father's flocks in Bethlehem.

[16]*The Philistine would approach [the Israelite*
camp] early morning and evening; he presented
himself for forty days.

humble even after he became king. Just as he lowered himself to learn from Torah scholars in his youth, so did he continue to do so after he became king.

The essence of Jewish sovereignty is a humble submission to Hashem. In this context, the king is compared to the moon, for two reasons. First, the moon diminished its size at God's command, for which reason it is called *small*: הַמָּאוֹר הַקָּטֹן, *the small light* (*Genesis* 1:16). Second, just as the moon reflects and transmits the light of the sun, so too is the role of the Jewish king to reflect and transmit the glory of Hashem (see *Chullin* 60b).

Because David excelled in both of these capacities, he was successful as king (*Mishbetzos Zahav*; see *Shabbos Malkesa* by *R' Shimshon Pincus*, Part I Ch. 2).

16. וַיִּגַּשׁ הַפְּלִשְׁתִּי הַשְׁכֵּם וְהַעֲרֵב — *The Philistine would approach [the Israelite camp] early morning and evening.*

A Jew succeeds in war when he places his trust in Hashem, a trust that he fortifies when he recites the *Shema*. The mandated times for reciting the *Shema* are morning and evening. It was thus precisely at these times that Goliath came to challenge the Jews, in order to prevent them from doing so (*Sotah* 42a-b) (*Be'er Moshe*).

וַיִּתְיַצֵּב אַרְבָּעִים יוֹם — *He presented himself for forty days.*

According to the Talmud (*Sotah* 42b) this corresponds to the forty-day period during which God gave the Jewish people the Torah. Just as it took the Jews forty days to receive the Torah, so did it take them forty days to develop the spiritual fortitude to overcome Goliath (*Radak*).

According to a Midrash (*Ruth Rabbah* 2:20), these forty days were awarded to Goliath in the merit of the forty steps that his mother Orpah took escorting her mother-in-law Naomi as she began her return to the land of Israel.

Kli Yakar explains that when a person is escorted he gains the confidence to protect himself against bandits, and thus his life is safeguarded.[1] Just as Orpah's forty steps had saved Naomi from being killed, so too was her son Goliath saved from being killed for forty days.

1. This is why, when city elders bring an *eglah arufah* (*Deuteronomy* 21:1-9), they must state that they did not allow the person who was killed to leave town without an escort — and were thus not guilty of negligence (*Sotah* 45b).

יִשַׁ֜י לְדָוִ֣ד בְּנ֗וֹ קַח־נָ֤א לְאַחֶ֙יךָ֙ אֵיפַ֤ת הַקָּלִיא֙ הַזֶּ֔ה
יח וַעֲשָׂרָ֥ה לֶ֖חֶם הַזֶּ֑ה וְהָ֥רֵץ הַֽמַּחֲנֶ֖ה לְאַחֶֽיךָ׃ וְ֠אֵת
עֲשֶׂ֜רֶת חֲרִיצֵ֤י הֶֽחָלָב֙ הָאֵ֔לֶּה תָּבִ֖יא לְשַׂ֣ר הָאָ֑לֶף
וְאֶת־אַחֶ֙יךָ֙ תִּפְקֹ֣ד לְשָׁל֔וֹם וְאֶת־עֲרֻבָּתָ֖ם תִּקָּֽח׃
יט וְשָׁא֤וּל וְהֵ֙מָּה֙ וְכָל־אִ֣ישׁ יִשְׂרָאֵ֔ל בְּעֵ֖מֶק הָאֵלָ֑ה
כ נִלְחָמִ֖ים עִם־פְּלִשְׁתִּֽים׃ וַיַּשְׁכֵּ֨ם

17. וַיֹּאמֶר יִשַׁי לְדָוִד בְּנוֹ קַח־נָא לְאַחֶיךָ ... — *Jesse said to David his son, "Please take for your brothers."*

Since Goliath had delayed the outbreak of hostilities for forty days with his daily challenge to the Jews, their provisions had been exhausted (*Malbim*).

אֵיפַת הַקָּלִיא הַזֶּה — *This ephah of toasted grain.*

This was flour made of roasted grain (*Metzudos*).

According to *Abarbanel*, this was bread that was parched so that it would be preserved.

וַעֲשָׂרָה לֶחֶם הַזֶּה — *And these ten loaves of bread.*

According to *Abarbanel*, these were fresh loaves, and Jesse urged David to deliver them quickly before they dried out.

The soldiers at the front were so pious that they ate only bread, the bare minimum required for their subsistance, and only the officers ate cheese (*Kli Yakar*).

18. חֲרִיצֵי הֶחָלָב — *Cheeses.*

Our translation follows the *Targum*.

Midrash Shmuel renders חֲרִיצֵי חָלָב as *nursing goats*, that were taken from their mothers.

תָּבִיא לְשַׂר הָאָלֶף — *Bring to the captain of the thousand.*

Soldiers were divided into thousand-man divisions, each of which was headed by a captain. Jesse sent a tribute to the captain under which his sons were assigned in order to gain his favor (*Ralbag*).

Some say that all Jews — combatants and non-combatants alike — were divided into thousand-man divisions and that Jesse sent this gift to the captain of his own group (*Radak*).

Rashi cites a view that Jesse sent this package to Jonathan, who was known to have a thousand soldiers under his command (above, 13:2).

וְאֶת אַחֶיךָ תִּפְקֹד לְשָׁלוֹם — *Inquire after the welfare of your brothers.*

Our translation follows *Metzudos*.

According to *Abarbanel*, Jesse told David to present this gift to the captain and ask him to concern himself with the welfare of his brothers.

וְאֶת־עֲרֻבָּתָם תִּקָּח — *And obtain a report of their well-being.*

The word עֲרֻבָּתָם, rendered here as *a report of their well-being*, is the subject of a wide variety of interpretations.

According to the *Targum* as understood by *Rashi*, the word עֲרֻבָּתָם is related to עָרֵב, *a guarantor*; thus, Jesse asked for assurance of their welfare.

Mahari Kara understands the *Targum* to mean that Jesse asked David to provide him with a report of what they required.

Alternatively, the word עֵרָבוֹן means *a collateral*, to back up a debt (see *Genesis* 38:17). Soldiers had to spend their own money on provisions, and when they were short of cash, they would pawn their possessions. Jesse gave David money to redeem any objects that his brothers might have pawned (*Radak, Mahari Kara*).

Ralbag states that Jesse's sons dispatched a messenger to their father

17 *Jesse said to David his son, "Please take for your brothers this ephah of toasted grain and these ten loaves of bread and hurry to the camp to your brothers,* 18 *and these ten cheeses bring to the captain of the thousand. Inquire after the welfare of your brothers, and obtain a report of their well-being."*

19 *Saul, they, and all the men of Israel were in the Terebinth Valley, fighting with the Philistines.*

with a request for provisions, and gave him an item that their father would recognize in order to authenticate their request. Jesse now sent that item back to them.

The word ערב can also mean *mix* or *mingle*. Accordingly, *Mahari Kara* interprets the phrase to mean that Jesse asked for information regarding the men whose company his sons were keeping.

The Talmud (*Kesubos* 9b) derives from this verse the protocol in King David's army — that a man going to fight would present his wife with a provisional bill of divorce,[1] which would take effect in case he was killed in battle (so that she would not be bound to a levirate marriage with his brother or be required to perform the *chalitzah* ceremony; see *Deuteronomy* 25:5-9), or if he should disappear (so that she would not be left an *agunah*, unable to remarry). The source of this practice is to be found in the present verse, in which Jesse told David to take עֲרֻבָּתָם, something from his brothers that would sever *that which binds them;* i.e., bills of divorce, which would sever the bonds of matrimony. Apparently, David learned this idea from his father, and when he became king he instituted the provisional bill of divorce as a mandatory procedure in his army (*Rashi*).

When Jacob's sons wanted to take Benjamin to Joseph in Egypt, Judah gave his guarantee that he would save Benjamin, even at great personal risk (*Genesis* 43:33). Translating the present phrase as *take your guarantee*, the Midrash (*Yalkut Shimoni*) states that Jesse told David that the time had come for him, a descendant of Judah, to fulfill Judah's guarantee and save Saul, a descendant of Benjamin. After David did so, Hashem rewarded him by situating the holy Temple partly on territory belonging to Judah and partly on territory belonging to Benjamin.

19. וְשָׁאוּל וְהֵמָּה וְכָל־אִישׁ יִשְׂרָאֵל בְּעֵמֶק הָאֵלָה — *Saul, they, and all the men of Israel were in the Terebinth Valley.*

הֵמָּה, *They,* refers to Jesse's three sons (*Metzudos*).

Malbim reads this phrase as part of Jesse's directive to David, in which he told David where to find the soldiers: *Saul, they, and all the men of Israel are in the Terebinth Valley.*

בְּעֵמֶק הָאֵלָה נִלְחָמִים עִם פְּלִשְׁתִּים — *In the Terebinth Valley, fighting with the Philistines.*

They were not actually fighting but prepared (*Metzudos*) or attempting to fight (*Ralbag*).

Daas Sofrim, however, understands this phrase literally. On the mountain, where Goliath confronted the vanguard of the Israelite troops, a tense quiet prevailed, however, skirmishes had erupted in the valley.

1. The particular stipulations, if any, included in this divorce are a subject of controversy which is beyond the scope of this work. See *Rashi, Tosafos* ad loc.

דָּוִד בַּבֹּקֶר וַיִּטֹּשׁ אֶת־הַצֹּאן עַל־שֹׁמֵר וַיִּשָּׂא וַיֵּלֶךְ
כַּאֲשֶׁר צִוָּהוּ יִשָׁי וַיָּבֹא הַמַּעְגָּלָה וְהַחַיִל הַיֹּצֵא
כא אֶל־הַמַּעֲרָכָה וְהֵרֵעוּ בַּמִּלְחָמָה: וַתַּעֲרֹךְ יִשְׂרָאֵל
כב וּפְלִשְׁתִּים מַעֲרָכָה לִקְרַאת מַעֲרָכָה: וַיִּטֹּשׁ דָּוִד
אֶת־הַכֵּלִים מֵעָלָיו עַל־יַד שׁוֹמֵר הַכֵּלִים וַיָּרָץ
כג הַמַּעֲרָכָה וַיָּבֹא וַיִּשְׁאַל לְאֶחָיו לְשָׁלוֹם: וְהוּא |
מְדַבֵּר עִמָּם וְהִנֵּה אִישׁ הַבֵּנַיִם עוֹלֶה גָּלְיָת הַפְּלִשְׁתִּי
שְׁמוֹ מִגַּת °ממערות פְּלִשְׁתִּים וַיְדַבֵּר כַּדְּבָרִים °מִמַּעַרְכוֹת ק׳
כד הָאֵלֶּה וַיִּשְׁמַע דָּוִד: וְכֹל אִישׁ יִשְׂרָאֵל בִּרְאוֹתָם
כה אֶת־הָאִישׁ וַיָּנֻסוּ מִפָּנָיו וַיִּירְאוּ מְאֹד: וַיֹּאמֶר |
אִישׁ יִשְׂרָאֵל הַרְאִיתֶם הָאִישׁ הָעֹלֶה הַזֶּה

20. וַיַּשְׁכֵּם דָּוִד בַּבֹּקֶר — *David arose early in the morning.*

He went with alacrity to fulfill his father's command (*Kli Yakar*).

הַמַּעְגָּלָה — *To the encirclement.*

A boundary was placed around the camp for two reasons: to prevent soldiers from approaching the enemy, which might instigate an attack, and to prevent soldiers from fleeing, which would damage the army's morale (*Rashi*).

Radak states that this boundary was composed of boards and chains.

Other commentators state that this *encirclement* is simply a reference to the camp. The soldiers bivouacked in a circle to prevent attacks from any direction (*Ralbag, Radak*).

22. וַיִּטֹּשׁ דָּוִד אֶת־הַכֵּלִים מֵעָלָיו עַל־יַד שׁוֹמֵר הַכֵּלִים וַיָּרָץ הַמַּעֲרָכָה — *David left his baggage with the keeper of the baggage and ran to the battle array.*

When David approached the camp, he saw that his brothers had already left for the battlefront. Since there was no longer any point in bringing the food to the camp, he deposited it with the soldier guarding the soldier's belongings, and ran to the front line to speak with them (*Abarbanel*).

In this way, Hashem caused David to hear Goliath's challenge (*Malbim*).

23. וְהִנֵּה אִישׁ הַבֵּנַיִם עוֹלֶה גָּלְיָת הַפְּלִשְׁתִּי שְׁמוֹ מִגַּת מִמַּעַרְכוֹת פְּלִשְׁתִּים — *The champion arose from the Philistine battalions, Goliath the Philistine of Gath was his name.*

Malbim observes two differences between this verse and verse 4. Verse 4 says, וַיֵּצֵא ... מִמַּחֲנוֹת פְּלִשְׁתִּים — Goliath *went forth from the camps of the Philistines.* This verse, however, says, עוֹלֶה ... מִמַּעַרְכוֹת פְּלִשְׁתִּים — Goliath *arose from the Philistine battalions.*

Previously, Goliath had left the Philistine camp on top of the mountain and descended to the valley. This time, since the opposing battalions had begun to prepare for war, he left his battalion and began to ascend the mountain on which the Jews were camped.

Be'er Moshe explains that this verse emphasizes the contrast between Goliath, who was a descendant of Orpah and epitomized evil and defilement, and David, a descendant of Ruth, who represented sactity. The verse identifies Goliath as *the Philistine*, although this fact was well known, to imply that he represented the degraded nature of the Philistine way of life. When Goliath sensed the

[20]*David arose early in the morning, left the sheep
with a watchman, and set out as Jesse had commanded him. He came to the encirclement, and the
army was going forth to the battle line, shouting
battle cries.* [21]*Israel and the Philistines deployed,
battalion facing battalion.* [22]*David left his baggage
with the keeper of the baggage and ran to the battle
array. When he arrived he inquired after the welfare of his brothers.*

[23]*As he was speaking to them, behold — the champion arose from the Philistine battalions, Goliath
the Philistine of Gath was his name, and spoke the
[above] words, and David heard.* [24]*All the men of
Israel, when they saw the man, fled from him, and
they were very frightened.* [25]*The men of Israel were
saying, "Have you seen this man who goes forth?*

sanctity of David approaching, the contamination within him *arose* to confront it. David "heard" or sensed this, and understood what he had to do.

מִמַּעַרְכוֹת פְּלִשְׁתִּים — *From the Philistine battalions.*

The word מַעַרְכוֹת — *battalions* — is written (*k'siv*) מִמְּעָרוֹת. *Radak* explains that מְעָרוֹת means *flat land* (see *Judges* 20:33). Goliath made his way from a mountaintop plateau. (*Radak*'s text of *Targum Yonasan* follows this explanation of the *k'siv*.)

However, the root of מְעָרוֹת — מְעָרָה — is generally translated as *a cave*, and so *Daas Sofrim* suggests that Goliath and the Philistines had been garrisoned in caves.

The Talmud (*Sotah* 42b) understands the *k'siv* to be an abbreviation of the phrase מִמֵּאָה עֲרָלוֹת — *from a hundred foreskins.* It derives from this that on the night after she turned away from Naomi, Orpah consorted with a hundred men and conceived Goliath.

According to *Rashi*, only one of these men impregnated Orpah, although there was no way to determine who it was. According to *Tosafos*, the semen of all one hundred men combined to form Goliath. Therefore, he was literally the child of all of them.

וַיִּשְׁמַע דָּוִד — *And David heard.*

He understood the meaning of Goliath's challenge, and in response devoted himself to avenge Hashem's honor (*Kli Yakar*).

24. *Malbim* states that they fled because, as stated in the previous verse, Goliath was climbing the mountain on which they were stationed.

25. וַיֹּאמֶר אִישׁ יִשְׂרָאֵל — *The men of Israel were saying.*

This phrase may more literally be translated as *The man of Israel said. Abarbanel* explains that one man would speak these words to his neighbor. *Kli Yakar* suggests that the verse refers to a specific, prominent individual — perhaps Jonathan or another military leader.

כִּי לְחָרֵף אֶת־יִשְׂרָאֵל עֹלֶה וְהָיָה הָאִישׁ
אֲשֶׁר־יַכֶּנּוּ יַעְשְׁרֶנּוּ הַמֶּלֶךְ | עֹשֶׁר גָּדוֹל וְאֶת־
בִּתּוֹ יִתֶּן־לוֹ וְאֵת בֵּית אָבִיו יַעֲשֶׂה חָפְשִׁי
כו בְּיִשְׂרָאֵל׃ וַיֹּאמֶר דָּוִד אֶל־הָאֲנָשִׁים
הָעֹמְדִים עִמּוֹ לֵאמֹר מַה־יֵּעָשֶׂה לָאִישׁ אֲשֶׁר יַכֶּה
אֶת־הַפְּלִשְׁתִּי הַלָּז וְהֵסִיר חֶרְפָּה מֵעַל יִשְׂרָאֵל

כִּי לְחָרֵף אֶת־יִשְׂרָאֵל עֹלֶה — *Who has ascended to disgrace Israel.*

Kli Yakar relates the verb עֹלֶה — *has ascended* — to the Midrashic teaching that any nation that persecutes the Jews will ascend to great heights (see *Eichah* 1:5; *Eichah Rabbah* 1:31). This, in effect, accords honor to the Jewish people, in that they are not subjected to lowly nations. In addition, this accords honor to Hashem when the enemy falls from its heights to the depths — as did Haman, for instance.

Accordingly, since Goliath came to disgrace the Jews, he initially rose to great prominence.

וְהָיָה הָאִישׁ אֲשֶׁר־יַכֶּנּוּ — *Whoever kills him.*

They did not say *if* he will be killed, but *whoever kills him.* They were confident that God had granted Goliath success only so that a loyal Jew could strike him down (*Kli Yakar*).

יַעְשְׁרֶנּוּ הַמֶּלֶךְ עֹשֶׁר גָּדוֹל וְאֶת־בִּתּוֹ יִתֶּן־לוֹ וְאֵת בֵּית אָבִיו יַעֲשֶׂה חָפְשִׁי בְּיִשְׂרָאֵל — *The king will greatly enrich whoever kills him and give him his daughter [in marriage], and free his father's family [from royal service] in Israel.*

We translate חָפְשִׁי — literally, *free* — as *free from royal service,* following *Metzudos.*

According to *Rashi,* this word means *exempt* — i.e., exempt from the citizens' obligations that [Samuel] had enumerated earlier (Ch. 8), one of which is the payment of taxes (*Abarbanel*).

Radak comments that יַעֲשֶׂה חָפְשִׁי means that the king would appoint that man to high office.

Saul's promises directly opposed Goliath's threats. Goliath had threatened to enslave the Jews; Saul promised freedom. Goliath intended to confiscate the Jews' belongings; Saul promised wealth. Goliath wanted to shame the Jews; Saul promised that whoever killed Goliath would have the honor of marrying his daughter (*Likkutei Yekarim*).

Simply understood, Saul offered all three rewards to the victor. Thus, the two instances of the prefix ו in this verse maintain their basic meaning of "and."

However, this prefix may also be translated as "or," and indicates that the king intended to grant only one of these rewards. *Me'am Loez* explicates that if the victor were poor, he would be accorded wealth; if he were wealthy, he would be permitted to marry the king's daughter; and if he were a slave, he would be freed.

The Talmud (*Taanis* 4a) speaks of Saul as one of those who made an ill-advised commitment, in that he promised his daughter's hand in marriage to whoever would defeat Goliath, without considering the possibility that this might be a slave or a *mamzer,* whom she would be prohibited to marry.

Later on (18:17-28), when offering his daughter to David, Saul made no reference to this promise.

Abarbanel explains that possibly this promise was made not by Saul but fabricated by the soldiers, or that Saul now spoke in an exaggerated, flowery manner and did not mean his words to be taken literally.[1]

1. Although *Abarbanel's* solution answers the question, it conflicts with the Talmud, which understands that Saul meant his stipulation seriously (*Kli Yakar;* see comm. below, 18:17).

He has ascended to disgrace Israel! The king will greatly enrich whoever kills him, and give him his daughter [in marriage], and free his father's family [from royal service] in Israel."

[26] *David spoke to the men standing with him, saying, "What will be done for the man who slays this Philistine and removes disgrace from Israel?*

26. וַיֹּאמֶר דָּוִד ... מַה־יֵּעָשֶׂה לָאִישׁ אֲשֶׁר יַכֶּה אֶת־הַפְּלִשְׁתִּי הַלָּז ... — *What will be done for the man who slays this Philistine?*

Simply understood, the proclamation recorded in the previous verse was made before David arrived. Thus, he did not hear it and had to inquire about the reward (*Abarbanel*).

Ralbag states that David inquired to ascertain that the victor would indeed marry the king's daughter, because he foresaw that this was how Hashem would bring about His desire that David ascend to the throne.

Chomas Anach explains that David was inquiring whether Saul meant to offer all three rewards or only one.

However, many commentators find it hard to believe that David was interested in this reward.

Metzudos suggests that David heard the proclamation, but made this inquiry to initiate a conversation so that he could naturally declare his desire to fight Goliath.

Sefer HaAkeidah (*Shaar* 15) presents a seminal principle. Just as Hashem invested animals with a fear of human beings (*Genesis* 9:20), so did He create a natural phenomenon that when Israel lives up to its Divine mission, all nations will be subservient to His Chosen People. Accordingly, when David heard Goliath's challenge, he understood that fighting him would entail no danger, because it was part of the nature of the world that Goliath would lose. Accordingly, David's inquiry about the reward was mean to taunt the Israelite soldiers for speaking of a reward in regard to so trifling a task.

Malbim suggests that David asked why any reward was necessary, since there could be no greater benefit than the opportunity to remove this source of national shame.

Similarly, *Be'er Moshe* states that David connoted that this conflict involved the defense of Hashem's honor and was thus obligatory. Therefore, no one had the right to request a reward.

Sefer HaTodaah states that David was still viewed by his brothers and others with disdain (see above, 16:11), and was purposely concealing his elevated spiritual level, as the time had not yet come for him to be revealed. Thus, since he wished to fight Goliath even as he appeared foolish, he inquired repeatedly about the reward, presenting himself as a mere shepherd who aspired to marry the princess.

לֵאמֹר — *Saying.*

This word is often translated as *to say to others* (see *Ramban* on *Exodus* 6:10).

That translation matches the view of *Akeidah* and *Malbim* that David did not seek the marriage, but intended to reproach the people and "spread the word" that there was no reason for reward (*Kli Yakar*).

וְהֵסִיר חֶרְפָּה מֵעַל יִשְׂרָאֵל — *And removes disgrace from Israel.*

He would succeed because his intention was to remove the source of disgrace from the Israelite nation (*Kli Yakar*).

כִּ֣י מִ֗י הַפְּלִשְׁתִּ֞י הֶעָרֵ֙ל הַזֶּ֔ה כִּ֣י חֵרֵ֔ף מַעַרְכ֖וֹת
כז אֱלֹהִ֥ים חַיִּֽים׃ וַיֹּ֤אמֶר לוֹ֙ הָעָ֔ם כַּדָּבָ֥ר הַזֶּ֖ה לֵאמֹ֑ר
כח כֹּ֥ה יֵעָשֶׂ֛ה לָאִ֖ישׁ אֲשֶׁ֥ר יַכֶּֽנּוּ׃ וַיִּשְׁמַ֤ע אֱלִיאָב֙ אָחִ֣יו
הַגָּד֔וֹל בְּדַבְּר֖וֹ אֶל־הָאֲנָשִׁ֑ים וַיִּֽחַר־אַ֨ף אֱלִיאָ֜ב בְּדָוִ֗ד
וַיֹּ֣אמֶר ׀ לָמָּה־זֶּ֣ה יָרַ֗דְתָּ וְעַל־מִ֨י נָטַ֜שְׁתָּ מְעַ֨ט הַצֹּ֤אן
הָהֵ֙נָּה֙ בַּמִּדְבָּ֔ר אֲנִ֧י יָדַ֣עְתִּי אֶת־זְדֹנְךָ֗ וְאֵת֙ רֹ֣עַ לְבָבֶ֔ךָ

הַפְּלִשְׁתִּי הֶעָרֵל הַזֶּה — *This uncircumcised Philistine.*

Scripture commonly speaks of the Philistines as being uncircumcised because circumcision represents chasteness and the Philistines were licentious.

David volunteered to go into battle as the Philistines' antithesis: a man who had been born circumcised (*Sotah* 10b) and whose his evil inclination had ceased during his lifetime (*Bava Basra* 17a). Also, in contrast to Goliath's blasphemous proclamations, David sang sweet songs of praise to Hashem (*Be'er Moshe*).

כִּי חֵרֵף מַעַרְכוֹת אֱלֹהִים חַיִּים — *That he disgraces the battalions of the living God?*

Targum renders this phrase as *the battalions of the nation of the Living God.*

However, *Kli Yakar* understands this verse literally. Although Goliath claimed that he came only to abase the battalions of Israel, David realized that since they are the "army of Hashem," Goliath was in essence disparaging Hashem.

Goliath was depending on the merits of his grandfather Eglon, Orpah's father, who had stood up to accord honor to Hashem (*Judges* 3), and on the merit of Orpah, who had escorted Naomi. David made it clear that if Goliath insulted Hashem's army, he would gain no benefit from those merits (*Me'am Loez*).

In speaking of David, *Me'am Loez* cites a Midrash (*Yalkut Shimoni, Shemos* 163) which states that whoever is prepared to sacrifice himself on behalf of Israel will attain honor and greatness.

28. וַיִּשְׁמַע אֱלִיאָב אָחִיו הַגָּדוֹל — *Eliab, his older brother, heard.*

Eliab is here referred to specifically as הַגָּדוֹל — *older* — because he felt himself responsible to protect his younger siblings from harm. Thus, he rebuked David for acting in what appeared to be a foolhardy manner.

In a more negative reading, the word הַגָּדוֹל literally means *the large,* and expresses the contrast between David, who was always humble (v. 14), and Eliab, whose anger was the result of a trace of arrogance. Similarly, the adjective *great* may indicate that Eliab had originally possessed the potential for greatness but had been disqualified due to his anger (*Kli Yakar*).

וַיִּחַר־אַף אֱלִיאָב בְּדָוִד — *Eliab became angry with David.*

Eliab grew angry because he suspected David of harboring vainglorious dreams of defeating Goliath (*Radak*).

As noted above, Eliab was a noble and worthy man, so much so that Samuel initially thought him worthy of governing the Jewish people. The Talmud derives from this verse that even if someone had been Divinely chosen for a position of leadership, he would be disqualified because of anger. This is derived from God's statement about Eliab — מְאַסְתִּיו, *I have rejected him,* which implies that he had once been chosen (*Pesachim* 66b).

But how is it that Eliab failed to respect David after seeing that Samuel had anointed him king?

Mishbetzos Zahav explains that Eliab thought that as long as Saul was alive,

For who is this uncircumcised Philistine, that he
disgraces the battalions of the Living God?'' 27 *So*
the people told him regarding this matter, say-
ing, ''Such and such shall be done for the man
who kills him.''
28 *Eliab, his older brother, heard as he was*
talking to the men, and Eliab became angry
with David, and said, ''Why did you come
down [here]? And with whom did you leave
those few sheep in the wilderness? I am
aware of your willfulness and your evil heart,

David would not reign, implying that Saul was superior to him. Also, David's modesty led him to conceal the traits that qualified him to be king and the Divine spirit that was now within him (v. 13). Eliab erred because when a person loses his temper he makes errors (see *Rashi, Numbers* 31:21).

Sefer HaTodaah (see above, 16:11) states that Eliab clung to his belief that David was an illegitimate child and not the son of Jesse. As for the fact that Eliab had heard Samuel call David Jesse's son and watched him anoint David as king, he approached these as perplexities that would eventually be resolved in accordance with his presuppositions.

וַיֹּאמֶר לָמָּה־זֶּה יָרַדְתָּ — *And said, ''Why did you come down here?''*

Apparently, David had not yet informed Eliab that Jesse had sent him (*Metzudos*).

Alternatively, Eliab knew why David had come, but he suspected that David had prevailed upon Jesse to send him so that he might enjoy the spectacle of the battle (*Mesamchei Lev*, cited by *Mishbetzos Zahav*).

וְעַל־מִי נָטַשְׁתָּ מְעַט הַצֹּאן — *And with whom did you leave those few sheep?*

Eliab's implicit rebuke was unwarranted, for — as stated earlier (v. 20) — David had left his sheep with a responsible guard (v. 20). It was in fact David's care and concern for his sheep that had proved him worthy of the throne (*Midrash Tanchuma, Shemos* 7; see above, 16:11).

בַּמִּדְבָּר — *In the wilderness?*

The sheep were in the vicinity of the wilderness, which provided the best grazing grounds. However, the wilderness was also dangerous, since it was frequented by wild animals and bandits (*Abarbanel, Metzudos*).

Alternatively, בַּמִּדְבָּר may be translated as *in the grazing area* (see *Jeremiah* 9:9; *Metzudos*).

אֲנִי יָדַעְתִּי אֶת־זְדֹנְךָ וְאֵת רֹעַ לְבָבֶךָ — *I am aware of your willfulness and your evil heart.*

Radak (based on *Targum*) renders זְדֹנְךָ as *your looseness* or *light-headedness*, implying an attitude of careless irresponsibility. *Kli Yakar* renders this word as *your insolence.*

The phrase אֲנִי יָדַעְתִּי — *I am aware* — is, more literally, *I have been aware.* Eliab was implying that he had known of these purported failings of David for some time. This phraseology, which does not describe specific failings but castigates David in all-encompassing terms, indicates that Eliab's rebuke was not disinterested and objective but born of anger (*Mishbetzos Zahav*).

כט כִּי לְמַעַן רְאוֹת הַמִּלְחָמָה יָרָדְתָּ׃ וַיֹּאמֶר דָּוִד מֶה
ל עָשִׂיתִי עָתָּה הֲלוֹא דָּבָר הוּא׃ וַיִּסֹּב מֵאֶצְלוֹ אֶל־מוּל
אַחֵר וַיֹּאמֶר כַּדָּבָר הַזֶּה וַיְשִׁבֻהוּ הָעָם דָּבָר כַּדָּבָר
לא הָרִאשׁוֹן׃ וַיִּשָּׁמְעוּ הַדְּבָרִים אֲשֶׁר דִּבֶּר דָּוִד וַיַּגִּדוּ
לב לִפְנֵי־שָׁאוּל וַיִּקָּחֵהוּ׃ וַיֹּאמֶר דָּוִד אֶל־שָׁאוּל אַל־
יִפֹּל לֵב־אָדָם עָלָיו עַבְדְּךָ יֵלֵךְ וְנִלְחַם עִם־הַפְּלִשְׁתִּי
לג הַזֶּה׃ וַיֹּאמֶר שָׁאוּל אֶל־דָּוִד לֹא תוּכַל לָלֶכֶת אֶל־
הַפְּלִשְׁתִּי הַזֶּה לְהִלָּחֵם עִמּוֹ כִּי־נַעַר אַתָּה וְהוּא

וְאֵת רֹעַ לְבָבְךָ כִּי לְמַעַן רְאוֹת הַמִּלְחָמָה יָרָדְתָּ — *And your evil heart, that you have come down here in order to watch the fighting.*

Eliab accused David of coming to enjoy the spectacle (*Metzudos*). Eliab stated that David had an evil heart because a person with a good heart is pained by the sight of death and would, given the choice, avoid a battlefield (*Daas Sofrim*).

Eliab accused David of envying his brothers as if they were having a good time, whereas in truth they were in great danger (*Kli Yakar*).

29. וַיֹּאמֶר דָּוִד מֶה עָשִׂיתִי עָתָּה הֲלוֹא דָּבָר הוּא — *David replied, "What have I done now? Was it not mere talk?"*

Even if you commonly become angry with me for doing wrong, this time I do not desrve to be censured, for all I have done is talk (*Metzudos*).

Alternatively, the phrase הֲלוֹא דָּבָר הוּא may be translated as *Is it not a [noteworthy] matter?* Although David had as yet done nothing, he intended to act because Goliath had done significant harm to the honor of the battalions of Hashem. David forbore from speaking more explicitly in order not to further antagonize Eliab (*Chomas Anach*).

David had been anointed king and had endangered himself in coming to the battlefield on behalf of his brothers. Yet, although Eliab now unjustly shamed him, he responded calmly. This self-control proved that David was indeed suited to be king (*Me'am Loez*).

David could easily have defended himself, but chose not to, in accordance with the principle that a person should not attempt to appease an angry person, who is by definition incapable of rational thought (*Avos* 4:23) (*Mishbetzos Zahav*).

The Talmud praises a person who is insulted but does not respond, and compares him to the sun as it rises with all its power (*Shabbos* 88b). Indeed, Scripture likens David to the sun (see *Psalms* 89:37, *II Samuel* 23:4; *Sefer Chassidim* 346).

Possibly in the merit of this tempered response David was infused with the strength that he needed to defeat Goliath (*Mishbetzos Zahav*).

30. וַיִּסֹּב מֵאֶצְלוֹ אֶל־מוּל אַחֵר וַיֹּאמֶר כַּדָּבָר הַזֶּה — *He then turned away from him toward someone else and said the same thing to him.*

David made the identical inquiry of many people so that his behavior would be reported to Saul, with the hope that Saul would summon him. David did so because he was embarrassed to approach Saul himself (*Abarbanel*).

31. וַיִּשָּׁמְעוּ הַדְּבָרִים אֲשֶׁר דִּבֶּר דָּוִד — *The words David was saying were heard.*

This refers to David's disparagement of Goliath and his implied readiness to confront him in battle (*Metzudos*).

32. אַל יִפֹּל לֵב־אָדָם עָלָיו — *Let no man lose heart because of him.*

Targum renders this phrase as *Let no man's heart be broken because of him.*

that you have come down here in order to watch
the fighting!" 29 *David replied, "What have I done*
now? Was it not mere talk?" 30 *He then turned*
away from him toward someone else and said the
same thing to him; and the people answered him
as before.

31 *The words David was saying were heard;*
people related [them] to Saul, and he summoned
[David]. 32 *David said to Saul, "Let no man lose*
heart because of him. Your servant will go forth
and fight this Philistine!" 33 *But Saul said to*
David, "You cannot go forth to this Philistine
to fight with him, for you are a lad, while he

Abarbanel explains David as saying that no one should fear being killed in battle, because David would fight on behalf of the entire Jewish nation.

Me'am Loez suggests that David was telling the king not to lose heart, but he spoke indirectly as a mark of respect.

Above (v. 26) we cited *Akeidah's* explanation of why David did not fear Goliath. To elaborate, Hashem's declaration נַעֲשֶׂה אָדָם בְּצַלְמֵנוּ כִּדְמוּתֵנוּ, *Let us make man in Our image after Our likeness* (*Genesis* 1:26), means that the power of control given to man is instilled only in one who masters his *image* and *likeness*, meaning that his intelligence controls his body and its instincts. Only such a person can be called אָדָם, *man*, and casts fear upon animals (*Genesis* 1:28). Accordingly David was saying a person who is in control of his body has no reason to fear Goliath.

Sig V'Siach B'Neviim adds that David himself had a particular connection to the appellation *Adam*, which is also the the name of the first human being. A well-known Midrash states that Adam was shown the history of mankind. When he saw David's soul and that he was destined to live only three hours, Adam gave him 70 years of his own life (*Yalkut Shimoni* to *Bereishis* 41). Accordingly, David literally came forth from *Adam*, and he completed his mission both in terms of living those assigned years and, more significantly, in terms of actualizing God's desire to make human beings in His image.

עַבְדְּךָ יֵלֵךְ וְנִלְחַם עִם־הַפְּלִשְׁתִּי הַזֶּה — *Your servant will go forth and fight this Philistine!*

Whether David won or lost, he would save the Jewish nation from humiliation. If David won, people would speak of how a servant of King Saul had defeated Goliath. If Goliath won, people would say that he had done no more than defeat a mere lad (*Chomas Anach*).

33. כִּי־נַעַר אַתָּה — *For you are a lad.*

Saul implied that as a lad David was unfamiliar with the stratagems of combat (*Metzudos*). Although David was 28 years old, Saul referred to him as a *lad* because he lacked military experience (*Daas Sofrim*).

Saul assumed that David intended to join the fray as an ordinary soldier and follow the rules of warfare. Thus, although it is proper to place full trust in Hashem, one must take normal precautions to protect himself from danger. Accordingly, Saul objected to David's offer because he wanted to imperil

לד אִישׁ מִלְחָמָה מִנְּעֻרָיו׃ וַיֹּאמֶר דָּוִד אֶל־
שָׁאוּל רֹעֶה הָיָה עַבְדְּךָ לְאָבִיו בַּצֹּאן וּבָא הָאֲרִי וְאֶת־
°נ״א זֶה לה הַדּוֹב וְנָשָׂא °שֶׂה מֵהָעֵדֶר׃ וְיָצָאתִי אַחֲרָיו וְהִכִּתִיו
וְהִצַּלְתִּי מִפִּיו וַיָּקָם עָלַי וְהֶחֱזַקְתִּי בִּזְקָנוֹ וְהִכִּתִיו
לו וַהֲמִיתִּיו׃ גַּם אֶת־הָאֲרִי גַּם־הַדּוֹב הִכָּה עַבְדֶּךָ

himself and, Saul felt, could not succeed (*Mishbetzos Zahav*).

34. רֹעֶה הָיָה עַבְדְּךָ לְאָבִיו בַּצֹּאן — *Your servant was a shepherd for his father among the flocks.*

Kli Yakar suggests that David mentioned *his father* to connote that he was able to overcome these animals in the merit of honoring his father.

וּבָא הָאֲרִי וְאֶת־הַדּוֹב — *The lion and the bear would come.*

The word וְאֶת, a word with no English equivalent, usually indicates the object of a verb. However, it seems misplaced here, since the phrase literally reads, *and there came the lion and* **the bear**, in which *the bear* is the subject and not the object of the sentence. Therefore *Rabbeinu Yeshayah* states that this word is extraneous [and to be ignored].

Some versions of the *Targum* render וְאֶת־הַדּוֹב as *and also the bear*. Similarly, *Radak* translates this phrase as *and with the bear*. In either case, a new discrepancy appears, for in these formulations the noun is plural, whereas the modifying verb *and came* is in the singular. However, that is not a serious objection, because in Scripture a singular verb is often used with a plural subject (see *Rashi, Bava Kamma* 54a).

Abarbanel posits that David was not describing a single episode but stating that such incidents would occur from time to time, thus affording him repeated opportunities to prove his mettle. Accordingly, this phrase should be rendered, *and the lion and the bear would come.*

וְנָשָׂא שֶׂה מֵהָעֵדֶר — *And carry off a sheep from the flock.*

Some texts have the word זֶה, *this*, instead of שֶׂה, *sheep*. Others have the *k'siv* (written version) as זֶה and the *k'ri* (oral version) as שֶׂה, *sheep. Minchas Shai*, an authoritative work on the textual variations in *Tanach*, rejects both of these readings as erroneous.

Nonetheless, the Vilna Gaon maintains the distinction between *k'ri* and *k'siv*, and explains (based on the Midrash *Lamed-beis Middos*) that after David defeated the lion and bear he wanted a token by which to recall the miracle, and so he slaughtered the sheep and made a belt of its hide. Now, as he related this story to Saul, he pointed to the belt and said, *[The lion] carried this off.*

וּבָא הָאֲרִי וְאֶת־הַדּוֹב וְנָשָׂא שֶׂה מֵהָעֵדֶר — *The lion and the bear would come and carry off a sheep from the flock.*

With these words, David stressed three details that intensified the danger. First, he had to deal with a number of adversaries. (He here mentions two but, as we will see in verse 36, there were actually more.) Second, these were the most fierce beasts of prey. And third, since the lion and the bear had already captured their prey, their motivation to hold onto it would induce them to fight with especial savagery (*Abarbanel*).

As mentioned previously (16:11), there is a view that Jesse, believing David to be a *mamzer*, deliberately sent him to an area populated by wild beasts so that they would slaughter him (*Sifsei Kohen, Parashas Vayeishev*).

35. David is here apparently speaking of a struggle with one animal, although in the previous verse he had described a confrontation with a lion and a bear.

Abarbanel suggests that here David spoke only about the one animal that had

is a warrior from his youth."
34 *David said to Saul, "Your servant was a shep-*
herd for his father among the flocks; the lion and
the bear would come and carry off a sheep from the
flock, 35 *and I would go after it, strike it down, and*
rescue [the sheep] from its mouth. If it would attack
me I would grab it by its beard and strike it and
kill it. 36 *Your servant has slain both lion and bear;*

carried away the sheep. The following verse adds that he killed the other animal as well.

Alternatively, following *Abarbanel's* suggestion that David was telling of a number of occurrences, he here described what he would do in each such instance.

Rema MiPanu (*Maamar Eim Kol Chai*, Part II §22, cited by *Be'er Moshe*) states that the first part of the verse refers to David's struggle with the lion. David struck it and it fled. The following phrase, וַיָּקָם עָלַי, *he attacked me*, refers to the bear, which David struck and killed. *Rema MiPanu* adds that this incident was symbolic of future national events. The sheep represents the Jewish nation (as in *Jeremiah* 50:17); the lion represents the gentile nations (ibid. 49:19) — in particular, Babylon's Nebuchadnezzar (see ibid. 4:7); and the bear represents Persia and Media — in particular, [Persia's] King Ahasuerus (see *Daniel* 7:5; *Megillah* 11a). David failed to kill the lion — correspondingly, Nebuchadnezzar remained in power and destroyed the Temple. However, David killed the bear — correspondingly, the kings of Persia and Media were unsuccessful in their attempts to prevent the rebuilding of the Temple. David, whose dedication to the sheep led to his choice as "shepherd" of Israel (see *Psalms* 78:70-71), understood this deeper meaning of his struggle with the lion and bear.

וְהִצַּלְתִּי מִפִּיו — *And rescue [the sheep] from its mouth.*

Taking the sheep out of the mouth of the beast of prey showed extraordinary bravery. David rescued the sheep before the wild beast had a chance to maul it with its claws and render it unkosher (*Chullin* 53a) (*Kli Yakar*).

וְהֶחֱזַקְתִּי בִּזְקָנוֹ — *I would grab it by its beard.*

The *Targum* renders בִּזְקָנוֹ as *by its jaw. Radak* explains that as David grabbed the beard, he took hold of the entire lower jaw with it.

וְהִכִּתִיו וַהֲמִתִּיו — *Strike it and kill it.*

He killed it without a sword, solely by grabbing its jaw (*Malbim*).

David's modesty is reflected in the fact that he had never related this incident until now, when it had become necessary for him to do so (*Me'am Loez*).

36. גַּם אֶת־הָאֲרִי גַּם־הַדּוֹב הִכָּה עַבְדֶּךָ — *Both lion and bear.*

The precise wording of this phrase is uncertain. Some Midrashim and commentators have texts that, although essentially identical in meaning, are worded slightly differently. Two examples are גַּם אֶת־הָאֲרִי גַּם אֶת־הַדּוֹב (*Lamed-beis Middos*, see also *Rashi*), and גַּם אֶת־הָאֲרִי וְאֶת־הַדּוֹב (*Midrash Shmuel*).

At any rate, *Minchas Shai* cites a variety of sources to persuasively argue that the version as we have it is correct.

No matter what reading one uses, the words גַּם and אֶת, as well as the definite article prefix ה, are often homiletically understood to denote additions to the literal meaning of the verse. Accordingly, Midrashim and commentators derive

וְהָיָה הַפְּלִשְׁתִּי הֶעָרֵל הַזֶּה כְּאַחַד מֵהֶם כִּי חֵרֵף
לז מַעַרְכֹת אֱלֹהִים חַיִּים: וַיֹּאמֶר
דָּוִד יהוה אֲשֶׁר הִצִּלַנִי מִיַּד הָאֲרִי וּמִיַּד הַדֹּב הוּא
יַצִּילֵנִי מִיַּד הַפְּלִשְׁתִּי הַזֶּה וַיֹּאמֶר

that David killed more than one lion and one bear. Exactly how many there were is subject to dispute: either three lions and two bears (*Lamed-beis Middos, Radak*); three lions and three bears (*Rashi*);[1] or four lions and three bears (*Midrash Shmuel*).

וְהָיָה הַפְּלִשְׁתִּי הֶעָרֵל הַזֶּה כְּאַחַד מֵהֶם כִּי חֵרֵף מַעַרְכֹת אֱלֹהִים חַיִּים — *And this uncircumcised Philistine shall be like one of them, for he has disgraced the battalions of the living God.*

David meant to say that he trusted that Hashem would condemn Goliath to the same fate as that of the beasts of prey whom David had destroyed (*Metzudos*).

He was asserting that he would find it easy to overcome Goliath, for in the past he had killed many wild beasts at one time, and Goliath was but a single individual. To counter the contention that as a human being Goliath would prove a more formidable adversary than an animal, David stated that since Goliath had insulted the battalions of Hashem, he was no longer to be considered a *man* made in God's image but an animal in human form (*Malbim;* see *Akeidah* above).

As mentioned earlier, the Talmud (*Sotah* 42b) relates that on the night that Goliath was conceived, his mother Orpah consorted with a hundred men and a dog. By blaspheming and cursing the battalions of Hashem, Goliath revealed his canine character (see v. 43), and so David fittingly compared him to an animal (*Kli Yakar*).

The Talmud (*Bava Metzia* 83b) states that in the verse, תָּשֶׁת־חֹשֶׁךְ וִיהִי לָיְלָה בּוֹ־תִרְמֹשׂ כָּל־חַיְתוֹ־יָעַר, *You make darkness and it is night, in which every forest beast stirs* (*Psalms* 104:20), the *forest beast* refers to evil people. The verse continues, תִּזְרַח הַשֶּׁמֶשׁ יֵאָסֵפוּן, *The sun rises and they are gathered in* (ibid. v. 22). The sun represents righteous people in general; when they rise up, they will put an end to the wicked. And as we have seen, the sun in particular represents David (see v. 29, comm.) (*Mishbetzos Zahav*).

37. וַיֹּאמֶר דָּוִד ה׳ אֲשֶׁר הִצִּלַנִי מִיַּד הָאֲרִי וּמִיַּד הַדֹּב הוּא יַצִּילֵנִי מִיַּד הַפְּלִשְׁתִּי הַזֶּה — *Then David said, "*H*ASHEM Who rescued me from the hand of the lion and from the hand of the bear, He will rescue me from this Philistine!"*

Kli Yakar suggests that this statement was a prayer.

However, most commentators understand David to have been predicting that he would defeat Goliath.

This raises two questions. First, how did David derive from his altercation with the beasts that he could overcome Goliath? And second, by entering into battle with Goliath, wasn't he relying on a miracle, [which is forbidden]?

The simple explanation of this verse answers both questions: David's experience in vanquishing wild animals gave him the confidence that he could overcome Goliath with no need to rely on miracles.

However, the idea that David depended on his physical strength alone misses the significance of this episode and the clear import of the verses. It is evident from David's words that he saw this confrontation not as a contest of physical might but as a conflict between Godliness and blasphemy.

Thus, according to *Yalkut Shimoni,*

1. But see comments of *R' Shlomo Buber* printed with *Midrash Shmuel.*

and this uncircumcised Philistine shall be like one of them, for he has disgraced the battalions of the Living God!" 37 *Then David said, "*Hashem *Who rescued me from the hand of the lion and from the hand of the bear, He will rescue me from this Philistine!"*

when David first saw Goliath in his heavy armor, he exclaimed in dismay, "Who can defeat him?" But when he heard Goliath cursing, he said, "I can overcome Goliath, because he does not fear Hashem." David grew confident because he believed that Hashem would support him. He understood that his victories over the lion and bear had been a message from Hashem that he had been given the gifts of bravery and strength to serve the Jewish people.[1]

But what about the fact that even a person performing a Godly task may not enter into dangerous situations, relying on miracles? (16:2; *Pesachim* 8b; see also *Exodus* 4:19, *Meshech Chochmah*). *Sig V'Siach B'Neviim* answers this objection by stating that in time of war, [which is by its very nature perilous], entering into a dangerous situation is permitted. A soldier is expected to go to war with an attitude of total self-sacrifice, setting aside all personal concerns and with complete trust in Hashem, upon Whom all wars are dependent (*Rambam, Hil. Melachim* 7:15).[2]

According to *Sefer HaAkeidah* (see above, vs. 26,32), just as the beasts fell before David, who represented the quintessential *man*, so would Goliath, who was no more than a beast in human shape. Accordingly, there would be no danger to David in confronting him.

Also, David understood that just as it had been his mission to protect his sheep from the lion and bear, so must he now begin to protect the Jewish people from foreign nations (*Be'er Moshe* to v. 35).

This verse begins with the words וַיֹּאמֶר דָּוִד, *and David said*, although David's oration had begun earlier. This verse marks a new phase in David's appeal, in which he first makes reference to Hashem. *Abarbanel* explains that previously David had attempted to persuade Saul that he was capable of defeating Goliath without recourse to miracles. Seeing that Saul was not convinced, David stated that if Hashem had performed a miracle to help him defeat the lion and the bear, He would certainly perform another miracle to help him defeat Goliath. This was an argument that Saul accepted. As *Kli Yakar* comments, if Hashem did not assist David now, then the previous miracle of David's victory over the beasts would be rendered inconsequential — something that Hashem would not allow.

הוּא יַצִּילֵנִי מִיַּד הַפְּלִשְׁתִּי הַזֶּה — *He will rescue me from this Philistine!*

This statement contained an implied prayer: even if David did not succeed in killing Goliath, Hashem should at least protect him from getting killed (*Metzudos*).

1. David was one of two people who properly interpreted messages sent to them from heaven in the form of this-worldly events. The other was Mordechai, who understood that if Esther had been taken to marry a gentile, it must be because she was being positioned to rescue the Jewish people (*Yalkut Shimoni*).
2. See *Sig V'Siach B'Neviim* and *David, King of Israel*, by R' Henry Biberfeld, for their elaborate and inspiring essays on this topic.

לח שָׁאוּל אֶל־דָּוִד לֵךְ וַיהוָה יִהְיֶה עִמָּךְ: וַיַּלְבֵּשׁ
שָׁאוּל אֶת־דָּוִד מַדָּיו וְנָתַן קוֹבַע נְחֹשֶׁת עַל־
לט רֹאשׁוֹ וַיַּלְבֵּשׁ אֹתוֹ שִׁרְיוֹן: וַיַּחְגֹּר דָּוִד אֶת־חַרְבּוֹ
מֵעַל לְמַדָּיו וַיֹּאֶל לָלֶכֶת כִּי לֹא־נִסָּה וַיֹּאמֶר
דָּוִד אֶל־שָׁאוּל לֹא־אוּכַל לָלֶכֶת בָּאֵלֶּה כִּי לֹא
מ נִסִּיתִי וַיְסִרֵם דָּוִד מֵעָלָיו: וַיִּקַּח מַקְלוֹ בְּיָדוֹ

וַיֹּאמֶר שָׁאוּל אֶל־דָּוִד לֵךְ וַה׳ יִהְיֶה עִמָּךְ — *So Saul said to David, "Go, and may* H*ASHEM be with you!"*

This phrase is preceded by a blank space — an unusual occurrence in the middle of a verse.

Daas Sofrim suggests that this indicates hesitation on Saul's part as he deliberated and then made his decision.

Ralbag explains that after deliberating, Saul decided to let David go because he saw that David placed his trust in Hashem.

Saul's words וַה׳ יִהְיֶה עִמָּךְ, *and may* H*ASHEM be with you,* recall Doeg's words (above, 16:18) that וַה׳ עִמּוֹ, H*ASHEM is with him.* Saul expressed the heartfelt wish that Hashem should continue to be with David (*Chomas Anach*).

The word וַה׳ — *and* H*ASHEM* — indicates Hashem together with His heavenly court (see *Rashi, Genesis* 19:24). David had requested that God help him in His compassion — a trait suggested by the Tetragrammaton, ה׳, H*ASHEM*. Saul responded that God's heavenly court, which represents His attribute of justice, would also support David, because Goliath had incurred the judgment of death with his insolent words (*Chomas Anach, Kli Yakar*).

38. וַיַּלְבֵּשׁ שָׁאוּל אֶת־דָּוִד מַדָּיו — *Saul dressed David in his own battle garments.*

Saul dressed David in battle gear to match that of Goliath (*Abarbanel*).

The word מַדָּיו, *his own battle garments,* is related to the word מִדָּה, *measure.* Our Sages state that although Saul was exceptionally tall (see 9:2 above), his armor fit David perfectly. This was because when a person becomes king he grows taller. The Midrash attributes this change to the action of the anointing oil.

Although David had grown taller when Samuel had anointed him, Saul noticed the change only now when he saw that his own clothing fit David perfectly (*Kli Yakar*).

Alternatively, it was only now that David grew taller. *Kli Yakar* suggests that at this point, as David's bravery came to the fore with his determination to avenge the honor of Hashem, his potential to be king blossomed into actuality.

Yefeh To'ar states that David grew fully fit to become king when he donned the royal garments.

39. וַיֹּאֶל לָלֶכֶת כִּי לֹא־נִסָּה — *But he was unwilling to go forth [that way], for he was not accustomed [to it].*

Generally, the word וַיֹּאֶל — which we translate here in accordance with the *Targum* as *he was unwilling* — means *and he wanted* (see *Exodus* 2:21). *Rashi* explains that this is an example of a word that can bear two opposite meanings.[1]

Rashi translates the word in its conventional sense, and renders the phrase as *he wanted to go, but he was unable to because he was unaccustomed.* In this rendition, the word כִּי — usually translated as *because* — is understood to mean *but* (*Abarbanel*).

1. *R' Yaakov Kamenetsky* states that when this word is spelled with a "ו" — וַיּוֹאֶל, as in *Exodus* — it means *he desired.* When it is spelled without a "ו" — as it is here — it is related to the word אַל, *not,* and means *he did not want* (*Emes L'Yaakov*).

So Saul said to David, "Go, and may HASHEM
be with you!" 38 *Saul dressed David in his own*
battle garments; he put a copper helmet on his
head and dressed him in armor. 39 *David then*
girded his sword over his battle garments. But
he was unwilling to go forth [that way], for he
was not accustomed [to it], so David said to Saul,
"I cannot walk with these, for I am not accus-
tomed [to them]," and David removed them
from on himself. 40 *He took his staff in his hand*

Malbim translates the phrase utilizing the conventional sense of both words וַיֹּאֶל and כִּי. In his reading, the phrase means that *he wanted to go [and put on the armor] because he had never tried that*, but his attempt failed.

According to other interpretations of this phrase, David attempted to wear the armor but, since he was unaccustomed to it, he felt constricted.

וַיֹּאמֶר דָּוִד אֶל־שָׁאוּל לֹא־אוּכַל לָלֶכֶת בָּאֵלֶּה כִּי לֹא נִסִּיתִי — *So David said to Saul, "I cannot walk with these, for I am not accustomed [to them]."*

The Midrash states that when Saul saw that the armor fit David, he cast an evil eye upon him, because he sensed that David was being groomed for the throne. Seeing Saul's face turn white and intuiting his evil eye, David removed the armor (*Vayikra Rabbah* 27:9; *Midrash Tanchuma, Emor* 4).

In the context of this Midrash, David's rationale here might be viewed as a mere excuse. *Mussar HaNeviim*, however, states that David was speaking truthfully. He meant to say that he was unable to wear garments that arouse envy, because he was not accustomed to causing people pain.

The root of the word נִסִּיתִי is נֵס, which may also be translated as *miracle*. Thus, the *Targum* renders the phrase כִּי לֹא נִסִּיתִי as *because there is no miracle in them*. Apparently, David wished to make the point that *not through sword and spear does HASHEM grant salvation* (v. 47).

This was not to be a contest of might or skill, but an opportunity for Hashem to avenge the desecration of His Name. That message would be transmitted only if *there was no sword in David's hand* (v. 50).[1]

40. וַיִּקַּח מַקְלוֹ בְּיָדוֹ — *He took his staff in his hand.*

Although David intended to attack Goliath with his slingshot, he took the stick to misdirect Goliath's attention (*Metzudos*).

Yalkut Shimoni (869) relates that this staff had been held by Jacob when he crossed the Jordan (*Genesis* 32:11), by Judah (ibid. 38:18), by Aaron when he performed the plagues (*Exodus* 7:9), and by Moses when he fought Amalek (ibid. 17:9). It was subsequently held by every king until the First Temple was destroyed, at which point it was hidden away,[2] and will remain so until the Messiah will regain it and use it to sub-

1. See R' Henry Biberfeld's *David, King of Israel*, which elaborates on this point.

2. The poem *Chad Gadya* at the end of the Passover Haggadah includes the stich: "The stick came and hit the dog." This is David's staff, which gave him the strength to fight Goliath, who is compared to a dog. The next stich reads, "The fire came and burned the stick," indicating that when the [First] Temple was burned, the staff was hidden away (cited by *Mishbetzos Zahav*).

וַיִּבְחַר־לוֹ חֲמִשָּׁה חַלֻּקֵי אֲבָנִים | מִן־הַנַּחַל וַיָּשֶׂם
אֹתָם בִּכְלִי הָרֹעִים אֲשֶׁר־לוֹ וּבַיַּלְקוּט וְקַלְעוֹ
מא בְיָדוֹ וַיִּגַּשׁ אֶל־הַפְּלִשְׁתִּי: וַיֵּלֶךְ הַפְּלִשְׁתִּי הֹלֵךְ
מב וְקָרֵב אֶל־דָּוִד וְהָאִישׁ נֹשֵׂא הַצִּנָּה לְפָנָיו: וַיַּבֵּט
הַפְּלִשְׁתִּי וַיִּרְאֶה אֶת־דָּוִד וַיִּבְזֵהוּ כִּי־הָיָה נַעַר
מג וְאַדְמֹנִי עִם־יְפֵה מַרְאֶה: וַיֹּאמֶר הַפְּלִשְׁתִּי אֶל־
דָּוִד הֲכֶלֶב אָנֹכִי כִּי־אַתָּה בָא־אֵלַי בַּמַּקְלוֹת וַיְקַלֵּל
מד הַפְּלִשְׁתִּי אֶת־דָּוִד בֵּאלֹהָיו: וַיֹּאמֶר הַפְּלִשְׁתִּי

due idol worshipers.

Mishbetzos Zahav states that this staff conferred upon David the power and courage to overcome the blaspheming Goliath.

וַיִּבְחַר לוֹ חֲמִשָּׁה חַלֻּקֵי אֲבָנִים מִן־הַנַּחַל — *And picked out five smooth stones from the brook.*

These were thin, smooth stones (*Rashi*).

They had been worn down by the action of the water (*Rabbeinu Yeshayah*), which made them fit for slinging (*Radak*).

The Midrash states that the first stone was associated with Hashem, Who wished His honor to be avenged. The second stone was associated with Aaron, who wished to avenge the blood of his descendants Hophni and Phinehas, who had been slain by Goliath. And the remaining three stones were associated with the forefathers, who wished to avenge themselves on Goliath for having cursed the battalions of the living God, and for attempting to uproot their offspring and the Torah (*Midrash Shmuel*).

According to *Mishbetzos Zahav*, David used only one stone, and with it he killed Goliath. This was apparently the stone associated with Hashem. Thus, David proclaimed, "I come to you with the Name of Hashem" (v. 45).

וַיָּשֶׂם אֹתָם בִּכְלִי הָרֹעִים אֲשֶׁר־לוֹ וּבַיַּלְקוּט — *And he put them in his shepherd's bag and in the knapsack.*

According to *Targum*, a יַלְקוּט is a traveler's bag made of leather or cloth (*Targum*).

Radak states that this was a bag designed to hold slingshot stones, and suggests that David put five stones into one container, and additional stones into the other.

According to *Metzudos*, David placed the stones into the shepherd's bag and then put that bag into the larger knapsack in order to conceal the stones.

Abarbanel understands the shepherd's bag and knapsack as references to the same bag, and reads the phrase as *he placed them in his shepherd's bag, which is the knapsack.* In this reading, the "ו" prefix before בַּיַּלְקוּט, meaning *and*, is extraneous.

The word יַלְקוּט is related to לקט, *gather*. The Midrash derives from this that the choice stones came together of their own accord (*Yalkut Shimoni*).

41. וַיֵּלֶךְ הַפְּלִשְׁתִּי הֹלֵךְ וְקָרֵב — *The Philistine walked, coming closer and closer.*

He walked slowly because his heavy armor weighed him down (*Abarbanel*).

42. וַיַּבֵּט הַפְּלִשְׁתִּי וַיִּרְאֶה אֶת־דָּוִד — *The Philistine peered and saw David.*

Previously, Goliath could not see David clearly because of the distance between them and because the shield-bearer obscured his view (*Me'am Loez*).

וַיִּבְזֵהוּ — *And he derided him.*

and picked out five smooth stones from the brook
and put them in his shepherd's bag and in the knap-
sack, and his slingshot was in his hand. Then he
approached the Philistine.
41 *The Philistine walked, coming closer and closer*
to David, and the man bearing his shield was before
him. 42 *The Philistine peered and saw David, and he*
derided him, for he was a youth, ruddy and hand-
some. 43 *The Philistine said to David, "Am I a dog that*
you come after me with sticks?" and the Philistine
cursed David by his gods. 44 *Then the Philistine said*

Goliath's defeat was not due to his being afraid. To the contrary, he ridiculed David (*Malbim*).

כִּי־הָיָה נַעַר — *For he was a youth.*
David appeared too youthful to have gained experience in warfare (*Mahari Kara, Metzudos*).

עִם־יְפֵה מַרְאֶה — *And handsome.*
A seasoned warrior could be expected to bear the marks of physical strain and exposure to the elements. David's soft, delicate looks made it clear that he was not accustomed to battle (*Radak, Malbim*).

A Midrash states that in general Hashem does not grant people both physical strength and good looks (*Yalkut Shimoni* 862).

43. וַיֹּאמֶר הַפְּלִשְׁתִּי אֶל־דָּוִד הֲכֶלֶב אָנֹכִי כִּי־אַתָּה בָא־אֵלַי בַּמַּקְלוֹת — *The Philistine said to David, "Am I a dog that you come after me with sticks?"*
Goliath commented only on the stick but not on the stones, which he apparently did not see (*Abarbanel*).

Alternatively, he did see the stones, but he dismissed them as unimportant, since these were a common shepherd's weapon [against wild animals and not meant for combat. Besides,] Goliath trusted that his copper helmet would protect him against any projectiles (*Kli Yakar*).

According to *Malbim* (see above, v. 9), Goliath initially proposed combat between two parties on equal terms. When he saw that David came without armor or sword, he understood that David rejected his offer. He therefore interpreted David's arrival with a stick to mean that the Jewish lad was mocking him.

הֲכֶלֶב אָנֹכִי — *Am I a dog?*
The *Targum* reads this as, *Am I a rabid dog?*

This comment of Goliath is the source of the Sages' comment that Goliath's roots can be traced to a dog since, on the night he was conceived, his mother Orpah consorted with many men and a dog (*Midrash Shmuel; Ruth Rabbah* 20:2; see *Tosafos, Sotah* 42b).

Goliath is associated with dogs, which are elsewhere characterized as being insolent (*Isaiah* 56:11) (*Be'er Moshe*).

וַיְקַלֵּל הַפְּלִשְׁתִּי אֶת־דָּוִד בֵּאלֹהָיו — *And the Philistine cursed David by his gods.*
Our translation follows the plain understanding of *by his gods* that Goliath exclaimed that David should be cursed by the Philistine gods (*Metzudos*). However, the Midrash (*Vayikra Rabbah* 17:3, see below, v. 46) implies that that Goliath cursed David's God.

אֶל־דָּוִד לְכָה אֵלַי וְאֶתְּנָה אֶת־בְּשָׂרְךָ לְעוֹף
מה הַשָּׁמַיִם וּלְבֶהֱמַת הַשָּׂדֶה׃ וַיֹּאמֶר
דָּוִד אֶל־הַפְּלִשְׁתִּי אַתָּה בָּא אֵלַי בְּחֶרֶב וּבַחֲנִית
וּבְכִידוֹן וְאָנֹכִי בָא־אֵלֶיךָ בְּשֵׁם יהוה צְבָאוֹת
מו אֱלֹהֵי מַעַרְכוֹת יִשְׂרָאֵל אֲשֶׁר חֵרַפְתָּ׃ הַיּוֹם
הַזֶּה יְסַגֶּרְךָ יהוה בְּיָדִי וְהִכִּיתִךָ וַהֲסִרֹתִי אֶת־
רֹאשְׁךָ מֵעָלֶיךָ וְנָתַתִּי פֶּגֶר מַחֲנֵה פְלִשְׁתִּים
הַיּוֹם הַזֶּה לְעוֹף הַשָּׁמַיִם וּלְחַיַּת הָאָרֶץ
וְיֵדְעוּ כָּל־הָאָרֶץ כִּי יֵשׁ אֱלֹהִים לְיִשְׂרָאֵל׃

44. וַיֹּאמֶר הַפְּלִשְׁתִּי אֶל דָּוִד לְכָה אֵלַי — *Then the Philistine said to David, "Come to me."*

Since the weight of Goliath's armor made it difficult for him to walk, he told David to approach him (*Radak*).

According to *Malbim*, Goliath considered it below his dignity to step forward in order to fight someone armed with no more than sticks and stones.

A Midrash (*Vayikra Rabbah* 21:2) states that Goliath could not step forward because the land gripped him and held him in place. Another version of the Midrash (ibid.) tells that Goliath's 248 limbs were weighed down as though by iron.[1] It was at this moment that David prayed, זְמָמוֹ אַל־תָּפֵק, *Do not loosen his muzzle* (*Psalms* 140:9) — the word *muzzle* here having the broader meaning of holding a person in check.

וְאֶתְּנָה אֶת־בְּשָׂרְךָ לְעוֹף הַשָּׁמַיִם וּלְבֶהֱמַת הַשָּׂדֶה — *So that I may offer your flesh to the fowl of the heavens and to the beast of the field.*

According to *Malbim*, had David accepted Goliath's initial challenge to a duel on equal terms, Goliath would not have uttered this threat, for protocol demanded that after a formal duel, the losing soldier would be given an honorable burial.

The word בְּהֵמָה generally refers to a *domestic animal*. Accordingly, Goliath's outburst is perplexing because domestic animals eat grass and produce, not meat. *Radak* clarifies that Goliath really meant wild animals and the word *beheimah* sometimes refers to wild animals (see *Bava Kamma* 17b et al., *Deuteronomy* 17:4,5) (*Radak*).

Nevertheless, the Midrash states that David understood from these words that Goliath's mind was befuddled, and so David triumphantly said to himself, "Now I know that he is mine."[2] As *Mussar HaNeviim* clarifies, Goliath's

1. Because Goliath prevented the Jews from reciting the 248 words of the *Shema* (above, v. 16), which correspond to a person's 248 limbs (see *Shulchan Aruch, Orach Chaim* 61:3), each of his own 248 limbs was now rooted in place (*Be'er Moshe*).

2. Why does the Midrash find it strange that Goliath spoke about feeding meat to domestic animals if the Torah does the same: וְהָיְתָה נִבְלָתְךָ לְמַאֲכָל לְכָל־עוֹף הַשָּׁמַיִם וּלְבֶהֱמַת הָאָרֶץ, *Your carcasses will be food for the birds of the sky and animals of the earth* (*Deuteronomy* 28:26). The commentators offer a variety of answers:

— Although it is not unusual for Scripture to use the word בְּהֵמָה — *domestic animal* — when referring to a wild animal, that usage is unusual and Goliath should not have spoken that way (*Kli Yakar*).

— The relevant issue is not the word itself but rather the phrase in which it appears: בֶּהֱמַת הַשָּׂדֶה,

to David, "Come to me, so that I may offer your flesh to the fowl of the heavens and to the beast of the field!"

45 David said to the Philistine, "You come to me with a sword, a spear, and a javelin — but I come to you with the Name of HASHEM, Master of Legions, the God of the battalions of Israel that you have ridiculed. 46 On this day HASHEM will deliver you into my hand. I shall smite you and I will remove your head from upon you; and I shall offer the carcass of the Philistine camp this day to the fowl of the heavens and to the beast of the earth! Then the whole earth will know that there is a God in Israel,

mind was muddled because, although he was not consciously aware that he was in danger, he must have realized on some level that his end was near. (In verse 46, when David threatens Goliath and the Philistines with a similar fate, he uses the word חַיָּה in the phrase, חַיַּת הָאָרֶץ, *wild animals of the earth.)*

45. אַתָּה בָּא אֵלַי בְּחֶרֶב — *You come to me with a sword.*

Your entire trust is in your weapons (*Metzudos*).

וּבְכִידוֹן — *And a javelin.*

See comm. above, v. 6.

וְאָנֹכִי בָא־אֵלֶיךָ בְּשֵׁם ה׳ ... — *But I come to you with the Name of HASHEM.*

Because Goliath had challenged Hashem (v. 8), David now stepped forward as Hashem's emissary (*Kli Yakar*).

46. הַיּוֹם הַזֶּה יְסַגֶּרְךָ ה׳ בְּיָדִי — *On this day, HASHEM will deliver you into my hand.*

David spoke with a confidence stemming from the infusion into him of Divine inspiration (*Daas Sofrim*).

The word יְסַגֶּרְךָ literally means *will lock you up*, and is reminiscent of the confinement of a person who has contracted *tzaraas* (*Leviticus* 13:4). The Sages derive from this that Goliath was stricken with *tzaraas* in punishment for his blasphemy (*Vayikra Rabbah* 17:3, 21:2).

וְנָתַתִּי פֶּגֶר מַחֲנֵה פְלִשְׁתִּים הַיּוֹם הַזֶּה לְעוֹף הַשָּׁמַיִם וּלְחַיַּת הָאָרֶץ — *And I shall offer the carcass of the Philistine camp this day to the fowl of the heavens and to the beast of the earth.*

David threatened that after he killed Goliath, the Philistines would flee so precipitately that some of them would fall, and then wild animals would leap upon them and tear at their flesh (*Metzudos*).

וְיֵדְעוּ כָּל־הָאָרֶץ כִּי יֵשׁ אֱלֹהִים לְיִשְׂרָאֵל — *The whole earth will know that there is a God in Israel.*

This was the ultimate goal of this confrontation: not to save the Jews from the Philistines, but to publicize

animals of the field, which indicates animals that eat from the grass of the field. The verse cited above from *Deuteronomy*, in contrast, refers to בֶּהֱמַת הָאָרֶץ, *animals of the earth* (ibid.).

— The verse in *Deuteronomy* speaks of extraordinary times of horror, in which even domestic beasts would eat human flesh (*Kli Yakar*, citing his son-in-law, and similarly *Ayalah Sheluchah*, cited by *Mussar HaNeviim*).

מז וְיֵֽדְעוּ֙ כָּל־הַקָּהָ֣ל הַזֶּ֔ה כִּֽי־לֹ֛א בְּחֶ֥רֶב וּבַחֲנִ֖ית
יְהוֹשִׁ֣יעַ יְהוָ֑ה כִּ֤י לַֽיהוָה֙ הַמִּלְחָמָ֔ה וְנָתַ֥ן אֶתְכֶ֖ם
מח בְּיָדֵֽנוּ׃ וְהָיָה֙ כִּֽי־קָ֣ם הַפְּלִשְׁתִּ֔י וַיֵּ֥לֶךְ וַיִּקְרַ֖ב
לִקְרַ֣את דָּוִ֑ד וַיְמַהֵ֣ר דָּוִ֔ד וַיָּ֥רָץ הַֽמַּעֲרָכָ֖ה לִקְרַ֥את
מט הַפְּלִשְׁתִּֽי׃ וַיִּשְׁלַ֨ח דָּוִ֜ד אֶת־יָד֗וֹ אֶל־הַכֶּ֙לִי֙ וַיִּקַּ֨ח
מִשָּׁ֥ם אֶ֙בֶן֙ וַיְקַלַּ֔ע וַיַּ֥ךְ אֶת־הַפְּלִשְׁתִּ֖י אֶל־מִצְח֑וֹ

Hashem's Name throughout the world (*Daas Sofrim*).

Goliath himself, who had disparaged the battalions of Israel and denied that Hashem would save them, would be the vehicle to bring about a sanctification of Hashem's Name.

47. וְיֵדְעוּ כָּל־הַקָּהָל הַזֶּה כִּי־לֹא בְּחֶרֶב וּבַחֲנִית יְהוֹשִׁיעַ ה׳ — *And all this assembly will know that not through sword and spear does HASHEM grant salvation.*

In the previous verse, David spoke of how the nations of the world would grow aware of Hashem's presence. Now he added that even believing Jews would come to a clearer recognition of how Hashem wins wars (*Abarbanel*).

Although the Jews believed that Hashem controls reality, they thought that He works within the laws of nature, so that human soldiers do the fighting but Hashem determines who will win. Now, however, they would see that Hashem does not work within natural boundaries, nor does He need normal armaments to win battles. In fact, strictly speaking, there is no need for an Israelite to participate in battle (*Malbim*). Of course, this does not contradict the fact that Hashem expects man to perform the normal activities of battle, as if he were fighting. As King Solomon states, סוּס מוּכָן לְיוֹם מִלְחָמָה וְלַה׳ הַתְּשׁוּעָה, *The horse is readied for the day of battle, even though salvation is HASHEM's* (*Proverbs* 21:31). Similarly, man must work to earn a living even though his income is solely in Hashem's hands (*Malbim*).

David realized that the Jewish people would be profoundly impressed by his victory over Goliath and would be liable to attribute it solely to his bravery and prowess (as in fact the women did; below, 18:7). Therefore, before going into battle he proclaimed that credit for victory was to be ascribed to Hashem alone (*Daas Sofrim*).

כִּי־לֹא בְּחֶרֶב וּבַחֲנִית יְהוֹשִׁיעַ ה׳ — *That not through sword and spear does HASHEM grant salvation.*

David had stripped himself of these accoutrements (*Metzudos*).

כִּי לַה׳ הַמִּלְחָמָה — *For unto HASHEM is the battle.*

All battles are in in the hands of Hashem. *Metzudos* adds that David meant that Hashem had the responsibility to take part in this battle because Goliath had disgraced His nation.

48. וְהָיָה כִּי־קָם הַפְּלִשְׁתִּי וַיֵּלֶךְ וַיִּקְרַב לִקְרַאת דָּוִד — *It happened that when the Philistine arose and moved closer toward David.*

The word קָם — *arose* — implies alacrity.

Although Goliath had initially summoned David to him, David's words now angered Goliath and aroused him to step forward (*Radak*).

According to the Midrashic teaching (see v. 44) that each of Goliath's limbs was weighed down as if by metal, he was only able to move slowly.

According to the Midrash that Goliath was gripped by the land (see v. 44), the land released him for a short while so that he could approach David, which would make it easier for David's stone to reach him (*Maharzu*).

[47] *and all this assembly will know that not*
through sword and spear does H*ASHEM* *grant*
salvation; for unto H*ASHEM* *is the battle, and He*
shall deliver you into our hands!"
[48] *It happened that when the Philistine arose*
and moved closer toward David that David
hurried and ran to the battle array, toward
the Philistine. [49] *David stretched his hand into*
the sack. He took a stone from there and slung
it, and struck the Philistine in the forehead.

Kli Yakar suggests that David prayed that the land should release its hold, because there would be a greater sanctification of God's Name if Goliath were given into David's hand and not defeated by the land. This is the meaning of David's statement (v. 46), *HASHEM will deliver you into my hand.* Thus, when the earth freed him, Goliath thought he had been saved, so he advanced toward David to kill him (*Kli Yakar*).

וַיָּרָץ הַמַּעֲרָכָה לִקְרַאת הַפְּלִשְׁתִּי — *And ran to the battle array, toward the Philistine.*

Our translation follows *Metzudos.* Not only did David not run away in fear, but he ran confidently toward Goliath (*Metzudos*).

Some understand that David ran back toward the Israelite battalions, לִקְרַאת הַפְּלִשְׁתִּי — which may be translated not as *toward the Philistine* but as *directly opposite the Philistine,* so that he should be able to aim better at the small exposed area on Goliath's forehead (*Malbim, Kli Yakar*).

49. וַיַּךְ אֶת־הַפְּלִשְׁתִּי אֶל־מִצְחוֹ — *And struck the Philistine in the forehead.*

The forehead represents insolence (cf. *Jeremiah* 3:3), and it is thus appropriate that Goliath was struck there (*Kli Yakar*).

The stone was able to penetrate Goliath's forehead despite the fact that he was wearing a helmet because, *Ralbag* and *Abarbanel* maintain, the helmet did not cover his forehead.

According to *Radak*, the helmet did cover Goliath's forehead. However, when Goliath said that he would feed David to the birds, he glanced up at the sky. At that moment, the helmet slipped and exposed his forehead.

A Midrash states that the stone miraculously penetrated the helmet to lodge in Goliath's forehead (see *Midrash Shmuel* 11, *Midrash Shocher Tov* 78:11), an instance in which Hashem gave a relatively soft object the power to penetrate a hard object.

The *Shulchan Aruch* (*Yoreh Deah* 264) states that although the Torah does not specify what material the implement for performing a *bris milah* should be, it is preferable to use metal. The commentary *Perishah* explains that metal is given this distinction because in the confrontation between David and Goliath the metal on Goliath's helmet did God's will by giving way to David's stone.[1]

Although it is clear that we should honor metal, why should we do so specifically by using it to perform the the mitzvah of *milah*? This may be because Goliath and the Philistines are repeatedly described as having been uncircumcised, with all of the spiritual

1. The *Shulchan Aruch* uses the word בַּרְזֶל, which means *iron,* whereas Goliath's helmet was made of נְחֹשֶׁת, *copper.* In this instance, the *Shulchan Aruch* may be using the word בַּרְזֶל as a general reference to metal.

נ וַתִּטְבַּע הָאֶבֶן בְּמִצְחוֹ וַיִּפֹּל עַל־פָּנָיו אָרְצָה: וַיֶּחֱזַק
דָּוִד מִן־הַפְּלִשְׁתִּי בַּקֶּלַע וּבָאֶבֶן וַיַּךְ אֶת־הַפְּלִשְׁתִּי
נא וַיְמִיתֵהוּ וְחֶרֶב אֵין בְּיַד־דָּוִד: וַיָּרָץ דָּוִד וַיַּעֲמֹד
אֶל־הַפְּלִשְׁתִּי וַיִּקַּח אֶת־חַרְבּוֹ וַיִּשְׁלְפָהּ מִתַּעְרָהּ

corruption that that implies. Since the metal of Goliath's helmet helped David dispatch him, metal is favored in removing the foreskin [in order to sanctify Jewish males] (*R' Kalman Krohn, R' Naftali Bassman,* cited in ArtScroll Edition of *Bris Milah*).

We noted above (v. 26) the contrast between David and Goliath in regard to circumcision. Also noteworthy is a Midrash cited by *Me'am Loez* that David's five stones had all been previously used to perform the mitzvah of *milah.* Abraham circumcised himself with one stone and circumcised Isaac his son with another; Zipporah, wife of Moses, circumcised her son with one stone (see *Exodus* 4:25); and Joshua used two stones to circumcise the Jews (see *Joshua* Ch. 5).[1]

וַיִּפֹּל עַל־פָּנָיו אָרְצָה — *And he fell upon his face, upon the ground.*

Since the stone hit Goliath in the forehead, why didn't he fall backward?

Radak and *Malbim* explain that Goliath did not fall from the impact of the blow. Rather, when the stone lodged in his head he lost his balance and fell forward.

The Midrash (*Shocher Tov* 18:32) provides a few other possible explanations.

(1) Goliath fell with his head between David's feet, as is implicit in the verse: נְאֻם ה׳ לַאדֹנִי שֵׁב לִימִינִי עַד־אָשִׁית אֹיְבֶיךָ הֲדֹם לְרַגְלֶיךָ, *The word of* HASHEM *to my master, "Wait at My right, until I make your enemies a stool for your feet"* (*Psalms* 110:1). This saved David the trouble of walking a distance to reach Goliath's head.

Why did Hashem perform this miracle for David, who was strong and swift, as is evident from the fact that he easily ran to the battlefront and afterward to Jerusalem?

Shai LaTorah addresses this question with a parable. A family had a valuable heirloom jewel. Once, it was misplaced and the distraught family searched for it tirelessly. Finally, after many days, one of the sons found it and his father gave him a thankful kiss. Although the joy of the family was great, the child's joy was doubled, because in addition to finding the jewel he had received a kiss. Finding the jewel corresponds to killing Goliath, and the father's kiss is God's gift to David that he was spared the need to walk twelve cubits and two spans (cited by *Mishbetzos Zahav*).

(2) Hashem declared that since Goliath's mouth had blasphemed, it should be filled with earth. Thus, an angel came and shoved him forward so that his mouth pressed against the earth.

(3) Goliath wore an image of his idol on his chest. When he fell forward, the retribution described in *Leviticus* (26:30) — וְנָתַתִּי אֶת־פִּגְרֵיכֶם עַל־פִּגְרֵי גִּלּוּלֵיכֶם, *I will cast your carcasses upon the carcasses of your idols* — was fulfilled.

David thanked Hashem for this miracle with the words וְאֹיְבַי נָתַתָּה לִּי עֹרֶף, *And as for my enemies, You gave me their nape* (*Psalms* 18:41).

Mussar HaNeviim adds yet another explanation. The Talmud (*Kesubos* 103b) states that if a person dies facing upward, that is a good sign, for it indicates that his life's goals had been heavenly. If, conversely, he dies facing downward, that is a bad sign, for it indicates that his life's goals had been earthly. Goliath died facing downward.

50. וַיֶּחֱזַק דָּוִד מִן־הַפְּלִשְׁתִּי בַּקֶּלַע וּבָאֶבֶן — *Thus David overpowered the Philistine with the slingshot and stone.*

1. This Midrash is inconsistent with the consensus of the commentators that Joshua used metal swords to circumcise the Jews.

The stone penetrated his forehead, and he fell
upon his face, upon the ground. [50] *Thus David*
overpowered the Philistine with the slingshot
and stone, he smote the Philistine and killed
him; there was no sword in David's hand. [51] *Da-*
vid ran and stood by the Philistine; he took
[Goliath's] sword and drew it from its sheath,

According to some commentators, the stone that David slung, as described in the previous verse, did not kill Goliath. Therefore, David continued to sling stones until he killed Goliath.

Radak explains that בַּקֶּלַע, *with the slingshot*, refers to the first stone, slung from a distance, and בָּאֶבֶן, *and stone*, to stones that David threw by hand from a closer proximity.

Other commentators state that David used just the one stone mentioned in the previous verse. The present verse recapitulates what David had done in order to underscore the fact that David overpowered the heavily armored Philistine with a mere slingshot (*Kli Yakar*, see *Metzudos*).

וַיְמִיתֵהוּ — *And killed him.*

According to *Radak*, David killed Goliath with these stones. When the next verse says וַיְמֹתְתֵהוּ, literally *he killed him*, it means *he had already killed him*. Others explain that David hit him with a stone that would soon kill him, but he was still alive when they severed his head (*Malbim*).

וְחֶרֶב אֵין בְּיַד־דָּוִד — *There was no sword in David's hand.*

Even without a sword, David was able to overpower Goliath.

Metzudos sees this sentence as an introduction to the next verse.

51. וירץ דוד ויעמד אֶל־הַפְּלִשְׁתִּי — *David ran and stood by the Philistine.*

The phrase אֶל־הַפְּלִשְׁתִּי, which we translate here as *by the Philistine*, literally means *to the Philistine*.

Radak translates this phrase as *over the Philistine*.

Kli Yakar states that the literal meaning of this phrase indicates that Goliath was still alive, and David went to him in order to make sure that he would see him and be aware of everything that was happening.

וַיִּקַּח אֶת־חַרְבּוֹ וַיִּשְׁלְפָהּ מִתַּעְרָהּ — *He took [Goliath's] sword and drew it from its sheath.*

The phrase וַיִּשְׁלְפָהּ מִתַּעְרָהּ, *and drew it from its sheath*, seems superfluous.

Kli Yakar cites a Midrash that the sheath was closed in such a way that David could not open it. Goliath's attendant was a man named Uriah, who told David that he would open it if David would give him a Jewish girl to marry. David consented and the man opened the sheath.

David was punished for making this promise, in that Uriah (who later converted and became known as Uriah the Hittite) married Bath-sheba, who had been destined from the start of creation to be David's wife (*Sanhedrin* 106a). The Talmud suggests that David made a different error, because of which he could attain Bath-sheba only through ignominious means (see *II Samuel* Ch. 11).

Otzar HaGeonim cites a disciple of R' Saadiah Gaon who takes issue with this Midrash, stating that Goliath's aide de camp could not possibly have been Uriah the Hittite, for two reasons. First, Bath-sheba's father, Eliam son of Ahitophel, would never have let his daughter marry a man of Philistine descent. Second, David would not have appointed a man of Philistine descent as his general.

וַיְמֹתְתֵ֔הוּ וַיִּכְרָת־בָּ֖הּ אֶת־רֹאשׁ֑וֹ וַיִּרְא֧וּ הַפְּלִשְׁתִּ֛ים
נב כִּֽי־מֵ֥ת גִּבּוֹרָ֖ם וַיָּנֻֽסוּ׃ וַיָּקֻ֣מוּ אַנְשֵׁ֣י יִשְׂרָאֵ֣ל
וִֽיהוּדָ֡ה וַיָּרִ֜עוּ וַֽיִּרְדְּפוּ֙ אֶת־הַפְּלִשְׁתִּ֔ים עַד־בּוֹאֲךָ֣
גַ֔יְא וְעַ֖ד שַׁעֲרֵ֣י עֶקְר֑וֹן וַיִּפְּל֞וּ חַֽלְלֵ֣י פְלִשְׁתִּים֩
נג בְּדֶ֣רֶךְ שַׁעֲרַ֔יִם וְעַד־גַּ֖ת וְעַד־עֶקְרֽוֹן׃ וַיָּשֻׁ֙בוּ֙ בְּנֵ֣י
יִשְׂרָאֵ֔ל מִדְּלֹ֖ק אַחֲרֵ֣י פְלִשְׁתִּ֑ים וַיָּשֹׁ֖סּוּ אֶת־
נד מַחֲנֵיהֶֽם׃ וַיִּקַּ֤ח דָּוִד֙ אֶת־רֹ֣אשׁ הַפְּלִשְׁתִּ֔י וַיְבִאֵ֖הוּ
נה יְרוּשָׁלִָ֑ם וְאֶת־כֵּלָ֖יו שָׂ֥ם בְּאָהֳלֽוֹ׃ וְכִרְא֨וֹת
שָׁא֜וּל אֶת־דָּוִ֗ד יֹצֵא֙ לִקְרַ֣את הַפְּלִשְׁתִּ֔י אָמַ֗ר
אֶל־אַבְנֵר֙ שַׂ֣ר הַצָּבָ֔א בֶּן־מִי־זֶ֥ה הַנַּ֖עַר אַבְנֵ֑ר

וַיְמֹתְתֵהוּ — *Having already killed him.*

Radak states that Goliath had been killed when he had been stoned (v. 50). Thus, this phrase is to be read, *he had already killed him.*

According to *Malbim,* however, Goliath died only now, when David cut off his head.

וַיִּכְרָת־בָּהּ אֶת־רֹאשׁוֹ — *And he cut off his head with it.*

David cut off Goliath's head to publicize among the Jews Goliath's death and the miraculous nature of its occurrence (*Ralbag*).

Just as Goliath used his power of speech — a gift that God infused into man (*Genesis 2:7, Targum Onkelos*) — against God, so was Goliath's sword used against Goliath (*Mussar HaNeviim*).

וַיִּרְאוּ הַפְּלִשְׁתִּים כִּי־מֵת גִּבּוֹרָם וַיָּנֻסוּ — *The Philistines saw that their hero was dead and they ran away.*

However, Goliath had stipulated that if he were killed, then the Philistines would become slaves to the Jews.

Malbim states that since the Jews had rejected this stipulation, no one was bound by it. Therefore, the Philistines now ran for their lives.

52. עַד־בּוֹאֲךָ — *Up to.*

The literal meaning of this phrase is *until you arrive at.* Scripture is addressing a reader familiar with the territory (*Metzudos;* see also above, 15:7).

וַיִּפְּלוּ חַלְלֵי פְלִשְׁתִּים — *Philistine corpses were strewn.*

From the words of the rejoicing women (below, 18:7), it appears that a substantial amount of Philistines fell during this rout and also that David was among the pursuers (*Daas Sofrim*).

The phrase חַלְלֵי פְלִשְׁתִּים, *Philistine corpses,* rather than a simple reference to חֲלָלִים, *corpses,* invites the reading, *corpses [killed by] Philistines* — that is to say, in the confusion many Philistines killed one another (*Kli Yakar*).

53. מִדְּלֹק — *From pursuing.*

This verb is associated with the word דלק, "kindling a fire."

Me'am Loez suggests that the Jews pursued the Philistines on horseback, and the hooves of the galloping horses made sparks fly.

Kli Yakar offers the explanation that the Jews were "fired up" with enthusiasm to avenge the honor of Hashem.

וַיָּשֹׁסּוּ — *And plundered.*

This word describes the gathering of spoils with joy and without compunction (*Daas Sofrim*).

54. וַיִּקַּח דָּוִד אֶת־רֹאשׁ הַפְּלִשְׁתִּי וַיְבִאֵהוּ יְרוּשָׁלִָם — *David took the head of the*

having already killed him, and he cut off his head
with it. The Philistines saw that their hero was dead
and they ran away. 52 *The men of Israel and Judah*
rose up and shouted exultantly, and pursued the
Philistines up to the approach to the valley and to
the gates of Ekron. Philistine corpses were strewn
along the Shaaraim Road, until Gath and Ekron.
53 *Then the Children of Israel returned from pursuing*
Philistines and plundered their camp. 54 *David took*
the head of the Philistine, and [eventually] brought
it to Jerusalem, and his weapons he put in his tent.
55 *When Saul had seen David going forth toward*
the Philistine, he said to Abner, the commander
of the army, "Abner, whose son is this lad?" And

Philistine, and [eventually] brought it to Jerusalem.

We insert the word *eventually* following *Radak*, who points out that first David brought the head to Saul (v. 57) and then circled among the Israelite cities to show it to the women and children, and to the men who did not go to war.

Although David made Jerusalem the capital city only later, even now he apparently had his eye on it as a city of prominence (*Daas Sofrim*).

At this time, the city of Jerusalem was in Jewish hands, with the exception of a single fortress, which was held by a group of Jebusites (see *Joshua* 15:63, *Judges* 1:21) (*Malbim*).

Radak cites his father's view that this verse is referring to the city of Nob, where the Sanctuary was then situated, and where Goliath's sword was placed (see below, 21:10). Nob was also referred to as "Jerusalem."

וְאֶת־כֵּלָיו שָׂם בְּאָהֳלוֹ — *And his weapons he put in his tent.*

David brought Goliath's weapons to his home in Bethlehem with the exception of the sword, which was wrapped in a cloth and stored in Nob (below, 21:10). The sword was put there on display so that everyone who came to bring an offering or to pray would see it, recall the miracle, offer thanks, and strengthen his trust in Hashem (*Radak*). *Malbim* states that initially the sword was placed in David's home and later on brought to Nob. According to *Abarbanel*, בְּאָהֳלוֹ — *in his tent* — refers to the Sanctuary in Nob, where David spent time communing with Hashem.

Me'am Loez cites the view that אָהֳלוֹ — *his tent* — refers to Goliath's tent. David stored the weapons there temporarily until he was ready to bring them to Nob.

55. וְכִרְאוֹת שָׁאוּל אֶת־דָּוִד יֹצֵא לִקְרַאת הַפְּלִשְׁתִּי — *When Saul saw David going forth toward the Philistine.*

Having completed describing the battle, Scripture returns to report a conversation that occurred just after Saul authorized David to fight Goliath.

אָמַר אֶל־אַבְנֵר שַׂר הַצָּבָא בֶּן־מִי־זֶה הַנַּעַר אַבְנֵר — *He said to Abner, the commander of the army, "Abner, whose son is this lad?"*

How could Saul be unaware of David's identity? We learned in the pre-

נו וַיֹּ֣אמֶר אַבְנֵ֗ר חֵֽי־נַפְשְׁךָ֥ הַמֶּ֛לֶךְ אִם־יָדָֽעְתִּי׃ וַיֹּ֣אמֶר
נז הַמֶּ֑לֶךְ שְׁאַ֣ל אַתָּ֔ה בֶּן־מִי־זֶ֖ה הָעָֽלֶם׃ וּכְשׁ֣וּב
דָּוִ֗ד מֵֽהַכּוֹת֙ אֶת־הַפְּלִשְׁתִּ֔י וַיִּקַּ֤ח אֹתוֹ֙ אַבְנֵ֔ר וַיְבִאֵ֖הוּ

vious chapter that David had been appointed Saul's armor-bearer and private musician, and that Saul loved him very much (16:21); and the present chapter informs us that David had been travelling back and forth between his home and Saul (v. 15).

Ralbag suggests that although David had frequently been present in Saul's court, the royal palace is a busy place with many people coming and going, and thus Saul did not know David by name.

Rabbeinu Yeshayah states that after Saul was gripped by an evil spirit, his memory failed him and he no longer could remember who David was.

Alternatively, says *Abarbanel*, he recognized David but had to ask who his father was.

Sefer HaAkeidah (*Shaar* 15) presents a important principle in interpeting this verse. When Hashem decides to elevate a person spiritually, He shines His "Divine light" on him, and the person then undergoes such a metamorphosis that his face glows. Thus, Saul and Abner hardly recognized David, and questioned whether he was the same man whom they had known before. However, as is apparent from the text, they were both embarrassed to ask him who he was. Thus, as we shall see in the next verse, Saul asked Abner to inquire as to his identity, something that Abner apparently did not consent to do at this point.

However, other commentators state that Saul did know who David and his father were, and his question had a different import.

Malbim suggests that since Saul had promised to give his daughter in marriage to the man who defeated Goliath, he now inquired more specifically into David's lineage.

Radak states in the name of his father that when Saul saw David's ability, he wondered whether David's father was also known for his prowess. If so, Saul thought, then David would surely be propelled to success. Abner replied to Saul's inquiry by admitting ignorance, because Jesse was an old man and Abner did not remember whether he had been physically strong.

The Talmud (*Yevamos* 76b) states that when Saul saw that his armor fit David perfectly — and thus that David was apparently destined to be king — he asked if David had the proper pedigree to be king. Such a person must be a descendant of Judah's son Perez. (This is implied in Perez's name, which means *breach*, and indicates the law that a king may breach anyone's property to let his entourage pass through.) Saul knew only that David descended from Judah, and he inquired whether David descended from Perez or from Perez's twin brother Zerah.

The Talmud relates a dialogue that is not recorded in Scripture. Doeg HaAdomi, who was David's prime detractor, said that instead of inquiring whether David was fit for the throne, Saul should ask whether David was fit to marry any Jewish woman, since he was descended from a Moabitess (see above, 16:11).

Abner rebuffed Doeg's objection with the comment that only a male Moabite is prohibited to marry a Jewish woman, but Ruth was permitted to marry a Jew and thus her descendant David was not blemished in any way.

Doeg disagreed and stated that Abner's claim was the equivalent of stating that only a male *mamzer* and not a female *mamzeres* should be prohibited from marrying into the Jewish people, something that is manifestly not the case.

 Abner replied, "By your life, O king, I do not know."
[56] *So the king instructed him, "You ask whose son this*
youth is." [57] *So when David returned from smiting*
the Philistine, Abner took him and brought him

Abner rejoined that there was a difference. The Torah provides a reason that Moabites cannot join the Jewish people: because the Moabite nation had failed to greet the Jews with bread and water on the Jews' journey from Egypt (*Deuteronomy* 23:5). Since it is not proper for a woman to offer strangers food, the Moabite women did no wrong, and so this prohibition does not extend to Moabite women.

Doeg challenged this, stating that the Moabite women should have at least proferred food to the Jewish women.

No one was able to counter this argument and the scholars present were about to assent that David was to be considered a Moabite who may not marry a Jewish woman. But then David's brother-in-law, a man named Ithra (*II Samuel* 17:25), spoke up and asserted that he had a tradition from the court of Samuel that a Moabitess is permitted. As to Doeg's argument, Ithra replied that the standards of modesty demanded that the Moabite women not go out in public even to serve other women, so the Moabite women could not be blamed.

Me'am Loez deals with the issue of Saul's apparent failure to recognize David by offering a sweeping interpretation of the previous and present chapters. The well-known rule that the Torah is not necessarily written in chronological order (see *Pesachim* 6b) applies not only to the *Chumash* but also to the Books of the Prophets as well.[1] Accordingly, the events of Chapter 17, in which David is introduced to Saul, preceded the events in Chapter 16, when David became Saul's musician. If that is the case, we must say that verse 15 in the present chapter, which speaks of David traveling repeatedly to Saul, is also out of chronological order.

וַיֹּאמֶר אַבְנֵר חֵי־נַפְשְׁךָ הַמֶּלֶךְ אִם־יָדָעְתִּי — *And Abner replied, "By your life, O king, I do not know."*

Abner did not feel that it was sufficient for him to simply state his ignorance, but that he must emphatically swear to it. He sensed how important this information was to Saul, who was concerned about whether this warrior might take the throne (*Daas Sofrim*).

Abner thus offered the assurance that Saul was the king and not David. The phrase חֵי־נַפְשְׁךָ הַמֶּלֶךְ — *by your life, O king* — may be read as *Long may you live, O king*. It is also possible that Abner knew who David was and was avoiding Saul's question. His answer, אִם־יָדָעְתִּי, translated here as *I do not know*, more literally provides the equivocal response, *if I know* (*Kli Yakar*).

56. When speaking privately to Abner (verse 55), Saul had used the term נַעַר, *lad*, which carries with it the connotation of a person who is immature or working in the capacity of a servant. In this verse, he was instructing Abner in public and so, because he wanted the masses to respect David, he referred to him by the more respectful term עֶלֶם, *a youth* (*Malbim*).

Rashi cites a Talmudic teaching that the word עֶלֶם is related to הֶעֱלֵם, *concealed*. This is a homiletic allusion to the fact that the halachah regarding the legal status of a Moabitess was at that time occluded, as a result of which Saul had instructed Abner to convene the Torah Sages so that they might issue a halachic verdict (as related in v. 55).

1. This contention is supported by *Yalkut Shimoni* 264.

יז/נח נח לִפְנֵי שָׁאוּל וְרֹאשׁ הַפְּלִשְׁתִּי בְּיָדוֹ: וַיֹּאמֶר אֵלָיו
שָׁאוּל בֶּן־מִי אַתָּה הַנָּעַר וַיֹּאמֶר דָּוִד בֶּן־עַבְדְּךָ
יח/א א יִשַׁי בֵּית הַלַּחְמִי: וַיְהִי כְּכַלֹּתוֹ לְדַבֵּר אֶל־שָׁאוּל

58. וַיֹּאמֶר דָּוִד בֶּן־עַבְדְּךָ יִשַׁי בֵּית הַלַּחְמִי — *David replied, "[I am] the son of your servant Jesse, the Bethlehemite."*

Saul wanted to obtain information about David's family background so that he might know if David was fit to be his son-in-law. David, however, did not dream of asking to be given a reward or to marry the king's daughter, so he did not elaborate on his father's lineage but simply responded that "Our significance is merely that we are servants of the king" (*Malbim*).

His answer carried the implication that since his father was Saul's servant, he was Saul's servant as well. Therefore, credit for this victory would go to the king, for people would say that a servant of Saul had killed Goliath (*Chomas Anach*).

According to the view that Saul was attempting to discern whether David descended from Perez or Zerah, David avoided providing the answer — [that he descended from Perez] — in order to keep Saul from growing jealous.

Radak cites his father's comment that Saul was inquiring into Jesse's strength (v. 55). David's response that Jesse was a *Bethlehemite* can mean either *a man of Bethlehem* or *a man of war* (according to which *lehem* is related to מִלְחָמָה, *battle*).

David chose to describe his father as בֵּית הַלַּחְמִי — *Bethlemite* — rather than with the phrase מִבֵּית לֶחֶם — *from Bethlehem.* The word הַלַּחְמִי has a ה at the beginning and a י at the end, forming a Name of Hashem. This was exactly the way that the names of the Jewish families were presented in the wilderness census (*Exodus* Ch. 26). In that case, *Rashi* explained that such a presentation indicated Hashem's testimony that these families were worthy and flawless. Here too, David indicated that his pedigree was unblemished — in regard both to his descent from Ruth and to his parentage (see 16:11) (*Me'am Loez*).

XVIII

⇐§ David and Jonathan Form a Bond

1. וַיְהִי כְּכַלֹּתוֹ לְדַבֵּר אֶל־שָׁאוּל — *It was after [David] finished speaking to Saul...*

This verse directly associates Jonathan's love for David with the completion of David's address to Saul (which closed Chapter 17) — an apparent cause and effect relationship to which the commentators assign various interpretations.

Mahari Kara states that Saul's recognition of David's unique heroism brought him to appreciate David, and this inspired Jonathan's love. This explains the connection between the present verse and the next, which states that Saul did not allow David to return home, presumably because he gained a deeper regard for David and his abilities.

Metzudos states that when Jonathan learned that, like him, David was the son of a great and noble father, he came to love him.

Me'am Loez avers that the kinship between Jonathan and David was rooted in their shared strengths and in the fact that they both had shown unusual courage on behalf of the Jewish people, with a concomitant trust in God's salvation.

According to *Ralbag*, Jonathan befriended David because he saw him as the likely successor to his father's throne.

17/58 *before Saul, while the head of the Philistine was*
[still] in his hand. 58 *Saul said to him, "Whose*
son are you, young man?" David replied, "[I am]
the son of your servant Jesse, the Bethlehem-
ite."

18/1 1 *It was after [David] finished speaking to Saul*

Finally, some commentators attribute Jonathan's love of David to two factors: first, his recognition of David's piety (after he saw how Hashem had performed a miracle through him), and second, his recognition of David's exceptional modesty (as expressed in his humble reference to himself as *the son of your servant*) (*Chomas Anach, Kli Yakar*).

וְנֶפֶשׁ יְהוֹנָתָן נִקְשְׁרָה בְּנֶפֶשׁ דָּוִד — *That Jonathan's soul became attached to David's soul.*

Maharal comments that the greatest possible love is a union between souls — this surpasses even the love between husband and wife, which possesses a physical component. Thus, when David later eulogized Jonathan, he lamented, *Your love was more wondrous to me than the love of women*! (*II Samuel* 1:26; *Derech Chaim, Avos* 5:17).

יְהוֹנָתָן — *Jonathan.*

Until now, the word *Jonathan* was spelled without a ה (with two exceptions). From this point onward, the ה is added as a rule, with but one exception (*Radak;* see also below, 19:1; *Minchas Shai*).

This change has Kabbalistic implications. Briefly, *Alshich* explains that because Jonathan loved and aided David, the letter ה of Hashem's Name was attached to his own.

נִקְשְׁרָה — *Became attached.*

נִקְשְׁרָה, lit., *was tied*, implies an intimate relationship that unifies two people (*Metzudos*).

וַיֶּאֱהָבֵהוּ יְהוֹנָתָן כְּנַפְשׁוֹ — *And Jonathan loved him as himself.*

Jonathan performed the mitzvah of loving one's fellow as oneself (*Leviticus* 19:18) to perfection (*Daas Sofrim*).

David and Jonathan's relationship is referred to by the Sages as the epitome of unconditional love, one that is eternal because it is not dependent on anything (*Avos* 5:19).

Rambam (ad loc.) explains that because material elements are transient, any love based on them will also be transient. The love between Jonathan and David, on the other hand, was of a Godly nature and was thus as eternal as God.

Also, the love of Jonathan and David was of an intrinsic nature: a love for the other person and his goodness, not for the pleasure or benefit that he provides. No other love is as powerful (*Abarbanel, Malbim*).

2. Until this point, David had returned regularly to his father's home to tend the sheep (see above, 17:15), but after witnessing David's exceptional bravery and strength, Saul no longer allowed him to do so.

In addition, since David was now slated to marry Saul's daughter, he had to be groomed for the role (*Abarbanel, Chomas Anach*).

Kli Yakar adds that Saul's high regard for David developed as he witnessed David's exemplary humility and his close relationship with Jonathan.

However, in regard to this second point *Me'am Loez* cites a comment that Saul was, to the contrary, deeply perturbed by Jonathan's love of David, and he kept David close by in order to conspire against him.

°וַיֶּאֱהָבֵהוּ ק׳

וְנֶפֶשׁ יְהוֹנָתָן נִקְשְׁרָה בְּנֶפֶשׁ דָּוִד °ויאהבו יְהוֹנָתָן
ב כְּנַפְשׁוֹ: וַיִּקָּחֵהוּ שָׁאוּל בַּיּוֹם הַהוּא וְלֹא נְתָנוֹ
ג לָשׁוּב בֵּית אָבִיו: וַיִּכְרֹת יְהוֹנָתָן וְדָוִד בְּרִית
ד בְּאַהֲבָתוֹ אֹתוֹ כְּנַפְשׁוֹ: וַיִּתְפַּשֵּׁט יְהוֹנָתָן אֶת־
הַמְּעִיל אֲשֶׁר עָלָיו וַיִּתְּנֵהוּ לְדָוִד וּמַדָּיו וְעַד־
ה חַרְבּוֹ וְעַד־קַשְׁתּוֹ וְעַד־חֲגֹרוֹ: וַיֵּצֵא דָוִד בְּכֹל אֲשֶׁר
יִשְׁלָחֶנּוּ שָׁאוּל יַשְׂכִּיל וַיְשִׂמֵהוּ שָׁאוּל עַל אַנְשֵׁי
הַמִּלְחָמָה וַיִּיטַב בְּעֵינֵי כָל־הָעָם וְגַם בְּעֵינֵי עַבְדֵי
ו שָׁאוּל: וַיְהִי בְּבוֹאָם בְּשׁוּב דָּוִד מֵהַכּוֹת
אֶת־הַפְּלִשְׁתִּי וַתֵּצֶאנָה הַנָּשִׁים מִכָּל־עָרֵי יִשְׂרָאֵל

בַּיּוֹם הַהוּא — *That day.*

Following all of the above interpretations, *that day* presents a contrast to the past — i.e., unlike earlier days, when David would travel back to his father's estate, Saul now conscripted him permanently.

Kli Yakar suggests, however, that *that day* presents a contrast with the future. On *that day,* Saul's love for David was complete; however, that state of affairs would not last long.

3. וַיִּכְרֹת יְהוֹנָתָן וְדָוִד בְּרִית — *Jonathan and David sealed a covenant.*

The word וַיִּכְרֹת, *sealed,* is in the singular, thereby implying that Jonathan initiated the treaty. Nevertheless, the fact that it says וַיִּכְרֹת יְהוֹנָתָן וְדָוִד, *Jonathan and David sealed,* rather than וַיִּכְרֹת יְהוֹנָתָן עִם דָּוִד, *Jonathan sealed with David,* indicates that although Jonathan was the initiator, the two were equally enthusiastic about completing the covenant (*Malbim, Kli Yakar*).

בְּאַהֲבָתוֹ אֹתוֹ כְּנַפְשׁוֹ — *Since each loved the other like himself.*

Usually, when two people sign a covenant they do so in order to protect themselves; this one, however, was sealed solely on the basis of love (*Malbim*).

4. וַיִּתְפַּשֵּׁט יְהוֹנָתָן אֶת־הַמְּעִיל — *And Jonathan took off the robe.*

The verb וַיִּתְפַּשֵּׁט is passive — as if to say, *Jonathan was stripped of the robe.* This connotes Jonathan's great willingness to be left bare in order to give his royal garments to David (*Radak*).

וַיִּתְּנֵהוּ לְדָוִד — *And gave it to David.*

This gesture demonstrated Jonathan's love, and signified that he accepted David as the successor to his father's throne, in his own place (*Abarbanel, Malbim*).

The *Vilna Gaon* (in his commentary to *Sefer Yetzirah,* cited by *Mishbetzos Zahav*) explains the concept of a covenant. If someone loves someone else and finds it difficult to part with him, he may leave with him something that is very dear to his heart and the two people are "bound" through that item. It is like a way of assuming that through the item they will never be apart. These garments, which represented Jonathan's royalty and were surely precious to him, were what Jonathan used to seal this covenant.

David's Popularity and Saul's Envy

5. וַיֵּצֵא דָוִד בְּכֹל אֲשֶׁר יִשְׁלָחֶנּוּ שָׁאוּל יַשְׂכִּיל — *David went forth; in everything that Saul sent him to do he was successful.*

David now emerges as a highly com-

that Jonathan's soul became attached to David's
soul, and Jonathan loved him as himself. 2 *Saul con-*
scripted him that day and did not permit him to
return to his father's home. 3 *Jonathan and David*
sealed a covenant, since each loved the other like
himself. 4 *And Jonathan took off the robe he was*
wearing and gave it to David; also his battle gar-
ments, down to his sword, his bow, and his belt.
5 *David went forth; in everything that Saul sent*
him to do he was successful. Saul appointed him
over the warriors, and it was good in the eyes of all
the people and also in the eyes of Saul's servants.
6 *It happened that when [the troops] came [back]*
— when David returned from slaying the Philistine
— that the women from all the towns of Israel came

petent and successful man, one able to perform any mission on which the king sends him, no matter how perilous and even bizarre (such as bringing Saul a hundred Philistine foreskins — see below, v. 25; *Me'am Loez*).

David now earned the approbation of the people, establishing a reputation as the *one who brought Israel out and brought them in* (*II Samuel* 5:2), which later made them amenable to his eventual ascension to the throne.

יַשְׂכִּיל — *Successful.*

This word derives from שֵׂכֶל, *intelligence.* A person who does well appears to be acting with wisdom and insight (*Metzudos;* see *Deuteronomy* 29:8, *Ibn Ezra* ad loc.).

וְגַם בְּעֵינֵי עַבְדֵי שָׁאוּל — *And also in the eyes of Saul's servants.*

Even those most likely to envy David — his compatriots above whose ranks he was promoted — were not jealous (*Radak*).

6. וַיְהִי בְּבוֹאָם בְּשׁוּב דָּוִד מֵהַכּוֹת אֶת־הַפְּלִשְׁתִּי — *It happened that when* [*the troops*] *came* [*back*] — *when David returned from slaying the Philistine.*

The following cluster of verses describes how Saul and David returned from the battlefield, at which time the accolades that David received were profoundly upsetting to Saul, who *grew very angry, and this matter was disturbing in his eyes* (v. 8).

According to *Chomas Anach,* this occurred prior to David's permanent move to Saul's palace described above (v. 2). The verses are presented out of order so as not to give the impression that Saul forced David to remain with him out of jealousy and hatred.

Malbim, however, states that these verses are presented in chronological order. While still at the Terebinth Valley after the victory over the Philistines, Saul skirmished with some neighboring armies, and it was there that David solidified his reputation as a great warrior (as in v. 5). Afterward, Saul and his troops, together with David carrying Goliath's head (see above, 17:54), returned triumphantly and were welcomed by rejoicing women.

°לָשִׁיר ק׳ °לשור וְהַמְּחֹלוֹת לִקְרַאת שָׁאוּל הַמֶּלֶךְ
ז בְּתֻפִּים בְּשִׂמְחָה וּבְשָׁלִשִׁים: וַתַּעֲנֶינָה הַנָּשִׁים
°בַּאֲלָפָיו ק׳ הַמְשַׂחֲקוֹת וַתֹּאמַרְןָ הִכָּה שָׁאוּל °באלפו וְדָוִד
ח בְּרִבְבֹתָיו: וַיִּחַר לְשָׁאוּל מְאֹד וַיֵּרַע בְּעֵינָיו
הַדָּבָר הַזֶּה וַיֹּאמֶר נָתְנוּ לְדָוִד רְבָבוֹת וְלִי

לָשִׁיר — *To sing.*

Targum renders this term as *to praise.* The written version (the כְּתִיב) is לָשׁוּר, implying *to gaze* (*Kli Yakar*).

וְהַמְּחֹלוֹת — *With timbrels.*

Our translation follows *Radak*, according to whom the מְחֹלוֹת were musical instruments. The word וְהַמְּחֹלוֹת literally means *and the timbrels* — the phrase *in their hands* is implied.

Targum, on the other hand, renders וְהַמְּחֹלוֹת as *with dances* (see *Exodus* 15:20, 32:19).

וַתֵּצֶאנָה הַנָּשִׁים מִכָּל־עָרֵי יִשְׂרָאֵל לָשִׁיר — *The women from all the towns of Israel came out to sing.*

This hero's welcome was an ancient custom. Warriors would aspire to perform great feats in order to be acclaimed publicly by the women (*Abarbanel*).

The issue of how men were permitted to hear women singing, something that is normally prohibited (*Berachos* 24a), is raised by *Sefer HaMiknah* (*Kiddushin* 70a).

Briefly, according to the view that this prohibition is a Rabbinic ordinance, it may not yet have been enacted at that time. According to the view that it is a Torah-based prohibition, it may be that it applies only when men consciously intend to listen (*Nachalas Shimon* 60:7).

לִקְרַאת שָׁאוּל הַמֶּלֶךְ — *To greet King Saul.*

Malbim derives from this verse that the women had no intention of belittling King Saul by contrasting him negatively with his subordinate, David. Their greeting was meant only to enhance his glory. (See next verse.)

וּבְשָׁלִשִׁים — *And with cymbals.*

Our translation follows *Targum.*

Other views, which note the relationship of this word to שְׁלֹשָׁה, *three*, interpret שָׁלִשִׁים as, variously, a three-stringed instrument (*Menachem the Grammarian*), a form of organized dancing in three rows (*Mahari Kara*), or a responsive choir in which one woman sings and two others respond (*Kli Yakar*).

According to *Ralbag*, שָׁלִשִׁים is related to וּמִבְחַר שָׁלִשָׁיו, *and his choice officers* — *Exodus* 15:4 (see also *Proverbs* 22:20). Thus, this phrase means that the women spoke *exceptionally glorifying words.*

7. וַתַּעֲנֶינָה — *Called out.*

Although this word most conventionally means *responded*, it is often used to indicate a raising of the voice (*Metzudos*).

הַנָּשִׁים הַמְשַׂחֲקוֹת — *The rejoicing women.*

Our translation follows *Metzudos*, which associates the root of הַמְשַׂחֲקוֹת, שְׂחוֹק, with שִׂמְחָה, *joy* (see *Genesis* 21:6).

Often, however, the word שְׂחֹק connotes *laughter* and *playfulness* (see ibid. 18:12, *II Samuel* 2:14). Accordingly, *Malbim* and *Kli Yakar* explain that it was the function of these women to make people laugh; thus, many of their comments were purposely inaccurate to the point of being comical.

Targum, on the other hand, renders הַמְשַׂחֲקוֹת as *who were praising.*

הִכָּה שָׁאוּל בַּאֲלָפָיו וְדָוִד בְּרִבְבֹתָיו — *Saul has slain his thousands, and David his tens of thousands.*

According to this translation — which is that of *Radak* — the women belittled Saul's accomplishments in comparison to those of David. This reading requires us to ignore the prefix ב, *with*, in the words בַּאֲלָפָיו, *thousands*, and בְּרִבְבֹתָיו, *tens of thousands*.

out to sing with timbrels to greet King Saul, with drums, with gladness, and with cymbals.

7 The rejoicing women called out, and said, "Saul has slain his thousands, and David his tens of thousands." 8 Saul grew very angry, and this matter was disturbing in his eyes. He said, "They have attributed to David tens of thousands, while to me

Radak offers an alternative reading, in which he makes use of the 'ב prefix, to translate this phrase as stating that when Saul fought alone it was as if he had thousands of soldiers with him, whereas when David fought alone it was as if he had tens of thousands of soldiers with him.

Both of these readings may appear forced. However, they have the virtue of rendering Saul's insulted response comprehensible.

Literally, however, this phrase would seem to favor Saul: *Saul struck with his thousands, and David with his tens of thousands.* In other words, Saul won great victories with thousands of soldiers; to achieve similar results, David needed the help of tens of thousands of soldiers (*Malbim*). This was high praise indeed — but Saul misunderstood the women's words and took offense.

According to *Kli Yakar*, even the reading that we favor, *Saul has slain his thousands, and David his tens of thousands*, does not celebrate David at Saul's expense. Rather, the women were purposely reversing the true numbers as a means of evoking laughter. Saul, however, misconstrued their intent.

A Midrash faults these women with failing to have mentioned Hashem's Name in their song of triumph, as other women did in the past (see *Exodus* 15:21, *Judges* 5:3), and were therefore held responsible for the trouble that their words caused (*Mechilta, Parashas Beshalach; Daas Sofrim*).

8. וַיִּחַר לְשָׁאוּל מְאֹד וַיֵּרַע בְּעֵינָיו הַדָּבָר הַזֶּה — *Saul grew very angry, and this matter was disturbing in his eyes.*

☙ Saul's Jealousy

Saul, who had not long before abjured publicity and any position of authority — to such a degree that *he had hidden among the baggage* (above, 10:22) — was now so upset by David's presumable threat to his crown that he was willing to kill David in order to abolish it. In this regard, the Talmud cites Rabbi Yehoshua ben Perachia's statement: "Initially, if someone would have suggested that I will rise to power, I would have bound him and cast him before a lion; now that I have achieved power, if someone would tell me to step down, I would pour water from a boiling hot urn on him — just like Saul, who first fled honor but eventually attempted to kill David in order to retain it" (*Menachos* 109b; see *Maharsha*).

Saul's fierce jealousy of David is one of the most inexplicable puzzles in all of Scripture. Although human beings are susceptible to feelings of envy and the disappointment at losing others' esteem, it is expected that a person of noble and exemplary character — such as Saul — would suppress such feelings. Yet, as described at great length in the forthcoming narrative, Saul persecuted David and pursued him with deadly intent.

Daas Sofrim explains Saul's motivation, and the nation's support of his actions, as follows. Saul saw himself as responsible for establishing a monarchy that would serve as a vehicle for the worship of God, not as a means of generating nationalistic and military pride (which was the case among the

ט נָתְנוּ הָאֲלָפִים וְעוֹד לוֹ אַךְ הַמְּלוּכָה׃ וַיְהִי שָׁאוּל
י °עון אֶת־דָּוִד מֵהַיּוֹם הַהוּא וָהָלְאָה׃ וַיְהִי
מִמָּחֳרָת וַתִּצְלַח רוּחַ אֱלֹהִים | רָעָה | אֶל־שָׁאוּל
וַיִּתְנַבֵּא בְתוֹךְ־הַבַּיִת וְדָוִד מְנַגֵּן בְּיָדוֹ כְּיוֹם | בְּיוֹם

°עוֹיֵן ק׳

other nations). From Saul's perspective, the possible advent of an individual — i.e., David — to the throne solely on the basis of his military prowess was antithetical to the Torah's design for Jewish kingship. Such a precedent would be devastating to the future of the institution of monarchy.

We must remember that Saul was not aware that David had been anointed. He was not familiar with David's outstanding attributes, and therefore was not convinced that David had any qualifications for the throne other than his success as a soldier.

Thus, Saul took a calculated, virtuous position in attacking the threat embodied by David. The problem was that Saul was seized by a melancholy that clouded his thinking; otherwise, he would have intuitively understood that David was indeed fit to reign. Moreover, his actions were triggered by underlying, possibly unconscious, feelings of jealousy. In this regard, the Sages homiletically interpret the verse קָשָׁה כִשְׁאוֹל קִנְאָה, *Envy is hard as the grave* (*Song of Songs* 8:6), as a reference to Saul, whose name [in Hebrew, *Shaul*] is alluded to in the word *grave* — *she'ol* (*Shir HaShirim Rabbah* 8:6:3).

In another explanation of Saul's persecution of David, *Be'er Moshe* states that when Saul was first anointed king, he relinquished his honor — something that he had no right to do (*Yoma* 22b), and for which he was accordingly punished (see above, 10:27). Now, in an attempt to correct that error, Saul went to the opposite extreme and staunchly protected his honor against David, whom he suspected of deliberately undermining his kingship. However, he failed to appreciate David's piety and sincerity.

Yet another explanation of these events is that on some level, Saul was deprived of the free will to suppress his natural jealousy, and Saul's persecution was a Divine test for David. David himself says to Saul (below, 26:19), *"If it is Hashem Who has incited you against me ..."* It is interesting that when the Sages list Saul's failings, his pursuit of David is not among them. Also, when Rav Nachman bar Yitzchak said something disparaging about Saul and realized that he should apologize, he said, "I spoke against you, O bones of Saul ..." *Maharsha* explains that he mentioned his bones because if one has the trait of envy, his bones will rot (*Shabbos* 152b), and since Saul's bones were still intact, Rav Nachman bar Yitzchak inferred that the king's jealousy was not sinful (*Mishbetzos Zahav*).

וַיֹּאמֶר נָתְנוּ לְדָוִד רְבָבוֹת וְלִי נָתְנוּ הָאֲלָפִים — *He said, "They have attributed to David tens of thousands, while to me they have attributed thousands!"*

Saul perceived another message in the women's words. A verse in *Psalms* states, יִפֹּל מִצִּדְּךָ אֶלֶף וּרְבָבָה מִימִינֶךָ, *A thousand may fall victim at your side, and ten thousand at your right hand* (*Psalms* 91:7). The person who fells ten thousand is associated with the right, primary hand, whereas the person who fells a thousand is represented by the left hand, which is secondary and relatively weak. Thus, Saul understood the women to be implying that David was the Jews' primary military leader and Saul a mere second-in-command (*Chomas Anach*).

Alternatively, the women's statement reminded Saul of Moses' blessing, וְהֵם רִבְבוֹת אֶפְרַיִם, *They are the tens of*

they have attributed thousands! He is lacking only the kingship." [9] *And Saul eyed David with suspicion from that day on.*

[10] *It happened the next day that an evil spirit from God came upon Saul and he raved incoherently in the house. David was playing [the harp] with his hand as [he did] every day,*

thousands of Ephraim (*Deuteronomy* 33:17). The number *ten thousand* is associated with Ephraim, the progenitor of Joshua, who ruled the nation. Saul feared that the women's paean, associating the number ten thousand with David, implied that David would eventually reign as well (*Me'am Loez*).

וְעוֹד לוֹ אַךְ הַמְּלוּכָה — *He is lacking only the kingship.*

Our translation follows *Rashi*.

Radak interprets the phrase as meaning that the only honor that the women have not yet bestowed on David is calling him king.

According to *Malbim*, Saul found this disturbing since, as he saw it, rulership is ultimately based on the people's choice, and since David was more popular than Saul, he would inevitably dispossess Saul.

These interpretations all read this phrase as a single thought: וְעוֹד לוֹ אַךְ הַמְּלוּכָה, *He is lacking only the kingship.*

Rabbi Moshe Mizrachi (cited by *Chomas Anach*), on the other hand, breaks this phrase up into two. Saul was not upset by the praise that David received. To the contrary, וְעוֹד לוֹ, *Much more to him* — i.e., let them laud him even more. What disturbed Saul was אַךְ הַמְּלוּכָה, but *the actual kingship* [*shall remain with me*]. Saul was upset that the women did not distinguish him from David, insofar as they failed to refer to him as king (*Chomas Anach*).

Similarly, *Kli Yakar* explains Saul as saying, "Although it may seem inappropriate for me to take issue over my honor, אַךְ הַמְּלוּכָה, *it is only the honor of the kingship* that I am protecting — which I do not have the authority to forgo" (*Sanhedrin* 19b).

9. וַיְהִי שָׁאוּל עוֹיֵן אֶת־דָּוִד — *And Saul eyed David with suspicion.*

The word עוֹיֵן comes from עַיִן, *eye.* Saul cast an envious and suspicious eye upon David (*Rashi*).

Ralbag explains that Saul *watched* for any opportunity to destroy David.

The written form of this word (the כְּתִיב) is עון, which may be punctuated עָוֹן, *sin.* Saul found fault in David's deeds, accusing him of attracting the nation's allegiance by means of his military prowess (*Daas Sofrim*).

◆§ Saul Attempts to Remove David, but David Prevails

10. וַיְהִי מִמָּחֳרָת וַתִּצְלַח רוּחַ אֱלֹהִים רָעָה אֶל־שָׁאוּל — *It happened the next day that an evil spirit from God came upon Saul.*

Saul's pained reflections that David might be his successor brought this *spirit of melancholy* upon him. *Abarbanel* interprets רוּחַ — literally, *spirit* — here as *will:* Saul began to perceive that it was God's will to take the throne from him and give it to David.

According to *Kli Yakar*, Saul was in the grip of two spirits, which waxed and waned alternately: a spirit of prophecy and a spirit of melancholy. When Saul loved David, Hashem loved Saul and the *spirit of melancholy* subsided. But now, a day after Saul had begun entertaining envious and suspicious thoughts of David, it returned.

וַיִּתְנַבֵּא — *And he raved incoherently.*

The word וַיִּתְנַבֵּא usually means *he*

יא וְהַחֲנִית בְּיַד־שָׁאוּל: וַיָּטֶל שָׁאוּל אֶת־הַחֲנִית
וַיֹּאמֶר אַכֶּה בְדָוִד וּבַקִּיר וַיִּסֹּב דָּוִד מִפָּנָיו פַּעֲמָיִם:
יב וַיִּרָא שָׁאוּל מִלִּפְנֵי דָוִד כִּי־הָיָה יהוה עִמּוֹ וּמֵעִם
יג שָׁאוּל סָר: וַיְסִרֵהוּ שָׁאוּל מֵעִמּוֹ וַיְשִׂמֵהוּ לוֹ
יד שַׂר־אָלֶף וַיֵּצֵא וַיָּבֹא לִפְנֵי הָעָם: וַיְהִי
טו דָוִד לְכָל־דְּרָכָו מַשְׂכִּיל וַיהוָה עִמּוֹ: וַיַּרְא שָׁאוּל

prophesied. Here *Targum* renders it as *he behaved insanely. Rashi* explains that a prophet and an insane person have two traits in common: they both speak symbolically and incoherently.

Abarbanel notes that the reflexive form of this verb indicates that Saul made a concerted effort to perceive the future. This resulted in his accurate perception that Hashem had chosen David as his successor, and consequently he fell prey to a spirit of melancholy.

וְדָוִד מְנַגֵּן בְּיָדוֹ כְּיוֹם בְּיוֹם וְהַחֲנִית בְּיַד־שָׁאוּל — *David was playing [the harp] with his hand as [he did] every day, and the spear was in Saul's hand.*

The verse implies that this scene, with David playing music and Saul holding his spear, was routine. We can thus understand why David was not alarmed when he saw Saul handling the spear (*Me'am Loez*).

11. וַיֹּאמֶר אַכֶּה בְדָוִד וּבַקִּיר — *Saying [to himself], "I will thrust it through David into the wall."*

Rashi explains that Saul was so upset that he wanted to throw the spear with enough force to pierce David's body and sink into the wall.

Sefer HaAkeidah (*Shaar* 23) and *Abarbanel*, on the other hand, state that Saul wanted to conceal his intentions, so that it would appear as if he were throwing the spear at the wall.

Daas Sofrim disagrees with both opinions, asseverating that it is inconceivable that Saul should have attempted to kill David purely out of envy. Rather, Saul foresaw prophetically that evils were coming upon the nation of Israel, for which he blamed David, who he felt was filling the people with a sense of pride in and dependence on military prowess, with a concomitant loss of dependence on Hashem. In his view, this justified removing David — even, if necessary, by putting him to death in this gory fashion.

וַיִּסֹּב דָּוִד מִפָּנָיו פַּעֲמָיִם — *But David eluded him twice.*

David noticed the spear and twice managed to elude it (*Ralbag*).

Sefer HaAkeidah, however, states that David was oblivious to this attack, and was guided by Divine providence to move just in time to avoid it. This persuaded Saul that David was the subject of Divine protection, a perception that led him to fear David, as the next verse states.

13. וַיְסִרֵהוּ שָׁאוּל מֵעִמּוֹ וַיְשִׂמֵהוּ לוֹ שַׂר־אָלֶף — *So Saul removed him from his presence and made him captain of a thousand.*

Saul's fear and envy of David led him to dismiss David from his presence. According to *Metzudos*, Saul intended for David to eventually be killed in battle.

According to *Malbim*, Saul intended this to be a demotion, lowering David's status from being a close confidant of the king to a relatively less glorious position as an army captain. Notwithstanding Saul's intentions, Scripture testifies that David was so popular with the masses that they chose him as their leader.

וַיְשִׂמֵהוּ לוֹ שַׂר־אָלֶף — *And made him captain of a thousand.*

and the spear was in Saul's hand. [11] *Then Saul*
hurled the spear, saying [to himself], "I will
thrust it through David into the wall." But David
eluded him twice.
[12] *Saul feared David, for* HASHEM *was with him,*
but He had turned away from Saul. [13] *So Saul*
removed him from his presence and made him
captain of a thousand, and he came and went
before the people. [14] *David was successful in all*
his ways, and HASHEM *was with him.* [15] *Saul saw*

וַיְשִׂמֵהוּ means *he made him.* Hence the next word, לוֹ — *to him* or *for him* — seems superfluous.

Kli Yakar suggests that Saul appointed David captain of the very unit of which he himself had previously been a soldier. Thus, לוֹ, *to his own battalion.* Then, as a gesture of honor to the king, the people raised David, who led the king's battalion, to be a leader of the entire army.

Alternatively, since each family (not only soldiers) had a "leader of thousands" (see above, 17:18), David was appointed as the leader of his family's group. Saul intended to cause the others to be resentful since David had always been of low rank, and now he rose to power, but instead they loved and respected him. These interpretations portray how people may try to carry out an agenda in opposition to Hashem's will, but His providence directs events in the way of His will. As King Solomon said, רַבּוֹת מַחֲשָׁבוֹת בְּלֶב־אִישׁ וַעֲצַת ה׳ הִיא תָקוּם, *Many thoughts are in a man's heart, but the idea of* HASHEM, *only it will prevail* (*Proverbs* 19:21, *Mishbetzos Zahav*).[1]

וַיֵּצֵא וַיָּבֹא לִפְנֵי הָעָם — *And he came and went before the people.*

This is a figure of speech that implies confident and conscientious leadership. It is a likely fulfillment of Moses' request that Hashem appoint a leader over Israel who would *go out before them and come in before them* (*Numbers* 27:17; *Abarbanel*).

14. וַיְהִי דָוִד לְכָל־דְּרָכָו מַשְׂכִּיל — *David was successful in all his ways.*

The root of the word מַשְׂכִּיל is שֶׂכֶל, *intelligence,* but it is here rendered by most commentators (including *Targum*) as *successful* (see above, v. 5).

Abarbanel, however, maintains the conventional meaning of the word. As captain, David acted with forethought and wisdom.

לְכָל דְּרָכָו — *In all his ways.*

Literally, this phrase reads *to all his ways.* David instilled within himself the necessary prerequisites that would lead him *toward* success in all his ways, and he then was able to reach success because וַה׳ עִמּוֹ, HASHEM *was with him* (*Daas Sofrim*).

וַה׳ עִמּוֹ — *And* HASHEM *was with him.*

Abarbanel understands וַה׳ עִמּוֹ to imply that David possessed an exceptional fear of Hashem.

1. *Kli Yakar* cites the not-altogether serious suggestion of his son, R' Avraham, that Saul intended poetic justice. Offended that the women had associated Saul with *thousands* and David with *tens of thousands,* Saul appointed David as a mere captain of thousands. The word לוֹ lays emphasis on that idea; they said *I* will have thousands — *he* will have thousands!

טז אֲשֶׁר־ה֖וּא מַשְׂכִּ֣יל מְאֹ֑ד וַיָּ֖גָר מִפָּנָֽיו׃ וְכָל־
יִשְׂרָאֵל֙ וִיהוּדָ֔ה אֹהֵ֖ב אֶת־דָּוִ֑ד כִּֽי־ה֛וּא יוֹצֵ֥א וָבָ֖א
יז לִפְנֵיהֶֽם׃ וַיֹּ֨אמֶר שָׁא֜וּל אֶל־דָּוִ֗ד הִנֵּה֩ בִתִּ֨י
הַגְּדוֹלָ֤ה מֵרַב֙ אֹתָהּ֙ אֶתֶּן־לְךָ֣ לְאִשָּׁ֔ה אַ֚ךְ הֱיֵה־לִּ֣י
לְבֶן־חַ֔יִל וְהִלָּחֵ֖ם מִלְחֲמ֣וֹת יְהוָ֑ה וְשָׁא֣וּל אָמַ֗ר אַל־
יח תְּהִ֤י יָדִי֙ בּ֔וֹ וּתְהִי־ב֖וֹ יַד־פְּלִשְׁתִּֽים׃ וַיֹּ֣אמֶר

As mentioned earlier, these words indicate that the halachah is always decided in accordance with David's rulings. (See above, 16:18; *Sanhedrin* 93b.)

15. Although the previous verse stated that Hashem was with David, this verse, which presents Saul's perception, does not mention that. According to *Kli Yakar*, Saul failed to recognize that David's success was due to the fact that God was with him. Thus, וַיָּגָר מִפָּנָיו — although *[Saul] was intimidated by [David],* he was not thereby aroused to fear Hashem in that context.

However, *Binah L'Itim* (cited by *Be'er Moshe*) rejects this idea, noting the earlier verse that *Saul feared David, for HASHEM was with him* (v. 12). *Binah L'Itim* thus explains that Saul, who was known to be exceptionally noble and righteous, erred a number of times when he made decisions based on his intellect (see above, 13:11-13, 15:9-15). David, on the other hand (see v. 14), saw to it that all of his actions were *with HASHEM* — i.e., in attunement with God's will. Thus, Saul acknowledged that David was מַשְׂכִּיל מְאֹד, *very intelligent*, intelligent enough to defer to God's authority. This was a trait that Saul knew he lacked, and that self-awareness caused him to feel intimidated by David.

וַיָּגָר מִפָּנָיו — *And he was intimidated by him.*

The word וַיָּגָר connotes a deeper and more intense fear than וַיִּרָא in v. 12 (*Malbim*).

Saul did not fear David's physical or military strength but his sagacity, for that showed him to be רֵעֲךָ הַטּוֹב מִמֶּךָּ — *your fellow who is better than you* (above, 15:28) — and his successor (*Abarbanel*).

16. וְכָל־יִשְׂרָאֵל וִיהוּדָה אֹהֵב אֶת־דָּוִד — *All of Israel and Judah loved David.*

Not only Judah, the tribe from which David descended, but all of Israel — including Saul's tribe of Benjamin — celebrated David's leadership, which fulfilled the people's request for a leader who would *come and go before them* (*Chomas Anach*). The verb אֹהֵב, *loved*, appears in the singular, indicating that the people loved him with one heart (*Kli Yakar*).

Alternatively, *each individual Israelite loved David* (*Mahari Kara*).

Malbim states that Saul's jealousy of David was aggravated by the latter's immense popularity, which made him practically impervious to attack.

The word אֹהֵב is in the present tense, which denotes that Israel's strong emotional bond with King David is still alive and fresh. Anyone who has something on his mind, seeks words of prayer, of praise or thanks to Hashem, or simply wishes to come closer to Hashem will find his expression in the words of David's *Psalms*. Thus, every Jew regularly feels the words that we utter in the *Kiddush Levanah* service: דָּוִד מֶלֶךְ יִשְׂרָאֵל חַי וְקַיָּם, *David King of Israel is alive and enduring!* (*Mishbetzos Zahav*)

כִּי־הוּא יוֹצֵא וָבָא לִפְנֵיהֶם — *For he came and went before them.*

The Midrash (*Shemos Rabbah* 31:3) states that the power of some men benefits them, whereas that of others harms them. David's prowess led to his great

that he was very successful, and he was intimidat-
ed by him. 16 *All of Israel and Judah loved David,*
for he came and went before them.
17 *Saul said to David, "Here is my older daughter,*
Merab; I shall give her to you for a wife, but you must
be a warrior for me and fight the wars of HASHEM.*"*
Saul said [to himself], "Let my hand not be against
him; let the hand of the Philistines be against him."

fame, whereas Goliath's might brought him to a disgraceful death, like that of a dog.

Daas Sofrim maintains that Saul was able to persuade many that David was a menace. The people's love of David was dependent on the benefit that they gained from his leadership — such a love is temporary by nature (see *Avos* 5:19), and thus Saul was able to persuade them to turn against David.

◆§ An Ill-Fated Offer of Marriage

17. הִנֵּה בִתִּי הַגְּדוֹלָה מֵרַב אֹתָהּ אֶתֶּן־לְךָ לְאִשָּׁה — *Here is my older daughter, Merab; I shall give her to you for a wife.*

During the battle against Goliath, word had spread through the camp that the warrior who defeated Goliath would be rewarded with marriage to Saul's daughter (see above, 17:25). Was Saul's present offer to David a fulfillment of that pledge? And if it was, how did Saul now justify adding a new condition?

❒ According to *Ralbag*, Saul's offer in this verse was the same as the one made earlier; *Ralbag* does not explain Saul's justification in adding a new stipulation.

❒ *Abarbanel* denies this premise. During the time of Goliath, he states, the soldiers at the battlefield fabricated the pledge or else Saul publicized it as an incentive that was not meant to be taken literally.

❒ According to *Kli Yakar* and *Malbim*, Saul's promise during the battle against Goliath did not specify which daughter he would give in marriage. If Saul chose his younger daughter, her marriage would have been delayed indefinitely until that of her older sister. Saul now specifically presented David with the opportunity to marry his older daughter.

❒ *Kli Yakar* offers an alternative approach. According to *Sefer HaAkeidah* (see above, 17:26), David stated that there was no need to reward anyone who took vengeance on Hashem's behalf. Therefore, David released Saul of the obligations of his pledge.

This is implied in Saul's words, *Be a warrior for me and fight the wars of* HASHEM. Since David was fighting solely on behalf of Hashem, Saul was not obligated to reward him. Therefore, Saul's offer of his daughter was a completely new and independent initiative. Furthermore, since David was a warrior whom Hashem used as His tool to defeat the enemy, Saul would give David credit anyway and allow him to marry Saul's daughter.

Also implicit in Saul's statement was that although his daughter Merab was גְּדוֹלָה, *old*, so that it would be inappropriate to delay her wedding, there was one factor that might take precedence over that — הִלָּחֵם מִלְחֲמוֹת ה׳ — that David would *fight the wars of* HASHEM. Of course, Saul intended to save his daughter from becoming a widow.

וְשָׁאוּל אָמַר אַל־תְּהִי יָדִי בּוֹ וּתְהִי־בוֹ יַד־פְּלִשְׁתִּים — *Saul said [to himself], "Let my hand not be against him; let the hand of the Philistines be against him."*

As the verse explicitly states, Saul intended this challenge as a ruse to bring

דָּוִד אֶל־שָׁאוּל מִי אָנֹכִי וּמִי חַיַּי מִשְׁפַּחַת אָבִי
יט בְּיִשְׂרָאֵל כִּי־אֶהְיֶה חָתָן לַמֶּלֶךְ: וַיְהִי בְּעֵת תֵּת
אֶת־מֵרַב בַּת־שָׁאוּל לְדָוִד וְהִיא נִתְּנָה לְעַדְרִיאֵל
כ הַמְּחֹלָתִי לְאִשָּׁה: וַתֶּאֱהַב מִיכַל בַּת־שָׁאוּל
אֶת־דָּוִד וַיַּגִּדוּ לְשָׁאוּל וַיִּשַׁר הַדָּבָר בְּעֵינָיו:
כא וַיֹּאמֶר שָׁאוּל אֶתְּנֶנָּה לּוֹ וּתְהִי־לוֹ לְמוֹקֵשׁ
וּתְהִי־בוֹ יַד־פְּלִשְׁתִּים וַיֹּאמֶר שָׁאוּל אֶל־דָּוִד
כב בִּשְׁתַּיִם תִּתְחַתֵּן בִּי הַיּוֹם: וַיְצַו שָׁאוּל אֶת־עֲבָדָו

about David's death.

Saul acted in this way because he wanted to avoid being punished for David's death (*Rashi*).

Daas Sofrim disagrees, stating that it is unlikely that Saul was scheming to kill David by proxy, since he had previously shown no hesitation in attempting to kill David himself. Rather, at this point Saul was not sure of Hashem's will. Thus, he placed David in the hands of the Philistines, leaving it to Hashem to determine his fate.

18. David responded in a humble and self-effacing manner. But what exactly did he mean? According to *Ralbag*, David unequivocally declined Saul's offer, considering himself unworthy. *Abarbanel*, on the other hand, interprets David's words as a conditional acceptance: although he did not believe that he deserved to be the king's son-in-law, he would be happy to go to war on Saul's behalf and make himself worthy.

מִי חַיַּי — *What is my life?*

In other words, "What is my life worth?" An honorable person's life is more valuable than that of a lowly person (*Radak*).

Literally, the word מִי does not mean *what* but *who*. Thus, according to *Daas Sofrim*, in this verse David was asking two questions. First, מִי אָנֹכִי, *Who am I [intrinsically]?* And second, מִי חַיַּי, *Who am I [based on the deeds of] my life?*

According to *Kli Yakar*, David knew that he had originally been granted only three hours of life in this world, and that Adam had donated 70 years of his own existence as a gift to David (*Yalkut Shimoni, Bereishis* §41). Thus, David now expostulated in his humility, מִי חַיַּי, *[From] whom is my life?* David's very life was sustained by an act of charity — what could be more lowly than that?

מִשְׁפַּחַת אָבִי מִיִּשְׂרָאֵל — *[And who is] my father's family in Israel?*

Following our translation, which is based on *Radak*, the earlier question מִי, *who is*, applies to this phrase as well. David described not only himself but all of his father's family as undeserving of such an honor — because, *Ralbag* explains, his family descended from Ruth the Moabitess, a factor that had always clouded its genealogy.

However, *Targum* (cited by *Radak*) interprets David's response, quite to the contrary, as a statement of family pride: *[but] my father's family in Israel [is indeed honorable*].

According to *Chomas Anach*, David deliberately referred to his family in this ambiguous fashion so that he might show the king unfettered humility, without speaking impertinently of his illustrious father.

19. When the date for the wedding arrived, even as Merab was being prepared, she married Adriel instead (*Rashi*).

[18] *David said to Saul, "Who am I and what is my
life, [and who is] my father's family in Israel
that I should become a son-in-law to the king?"*
[19] *But it happened that when the time came to
give Merab daughter of Saul to David, she was
given [instead] to Adriel the Meholathite as a
wife.*

[20] *But Michal daughter of Saul loved David. They
told [this] to Saul and it was proper in his eyes.*
[21] *Saul thought, "I will give her to him and she will
be a snare to him, and the hand of the Philistines will
act against him." So Saul said to David, "Through
[one of] my two [daughters] you will become my
son-in-law today."* [22] *Saul then commanded his*

Abarbanel explains that Saul intended to keep his word, but Merab of her own volition married Adriel.[1]

All of the commentators are in apparent agreement that, according to the simple meaning of the verse, David was never legally betrothed to Merab. This issue is the topic of debate among the Sages (*Sanhedrin* 19b). According to Rabbi Yehoshua ben Korchah, Saul rejected the legitimacy of the manner in which David betrothed Merab[2] and viewed her as being legally entitled to marry Adriel. Rabbi Yose, on the other hand, states that Merab was indeed betrothed to David, and that her marriage to Adriel was sinful.

◆§ Saul's Perilous Conditions for His Daughter's Marriage — and David's Fulfillment

21. וַיֹּאמֶר שָׁאוּל אֶתְּנֶנָּה לּוֹ וּתְהִי־לוֹ לְמוֹקֵשׁ — *Saul thought, "I will give her to him and she will be a snare to him."*

Saul hoped that David would be willing to fight the Philistines in order to earn Michal's hand in marriage; Saul confidently expected that David would fall in battle.

בִּשְׁתַּיִם תִּתְחַתֵּן בִּי הַיּוֹם — *Through* [*one of*] *my two* [*daughters*], *you will become my son-in-law today.*

Our translation follows that of *Targum*. If read literally, the verse states that David would be married to both of Saul's daughters at the same time. However, that is prohibited and, furthermore, halachically impossible, for after a man is betrothed to a woman he cannot legally betroth her sister.

Thus, Saul simply meant to say that although his plan for David to marry Merab did not materialize, David would at least marry Michal (*Radak*)

According to *Mahari Kara*, there is no need for this emendation of *Targum*, for the word בִּשְׁתַּיִם can mean not *two* but *the second*. (Similarly, בַּחֲמִשָּׁה לַחֹדֶשׁ — literally *on five of the month* — means *on the fifth of the month* [*Ezekiel* 1:1].) Thus, the verse may be translated, *Through [my] second [daughter], you will become my son-in-law today.*

1. But in that case, *Kli Yakar* objects, the word נִתְּנָה, *was given*, is inappropriate.

2. The details of that controversy are beyond the scope of this work.

דַּבְּרוּ אֶל־דָּוִד בַּלָּט לֵאמֹר הִנֵּה חָפֵץ בְּךָ הַמֶּלֶךְ
כג וְכָל־עֲבָדָיו אֲהֵבוּךָ וְעַתָּה הִתְחַתֵּן בַּמֶּלֶךְ׃ וַיְדַבְּרוּ
עַבְדֵי שָׁאוּל בְּאָזְנֵי דָוִד אֶת־הַדְּבָרִים הָאֵלֶּה
וַיֹּאמֶר דָּוִד הֲנְקַלָּה בְעֵינֵיכֶם הִתְחַתֵּן בַּמֶּלֶךְ
כד וְאָנֹכִי אִישׁ־רָשׁ וְנִקְלֶה׃ וַיַּגִּדוּ עַבְדֵי שָׁאוּל לוֹ
כה לֵאמֹר כַּדְּבָרִים הָאֵלֶּה דִּבֶּר דָּוִד׃ וַיֹּאמֶר
שָׁאוּל כֹּה־תֹאמְרוּ לְדָוִד אֵין־חֵפֶץ לַמֶּלֶךְ בְּמֹהַר
כִּי בְּמֵאָה עָרְלוֹת פְּלִשְׁתִּים לְהִנָּקֵם בְּאֹיְבֵי הַמֶּלֶךְ
וְשָׁאוּל חָשַׁב לְהַפִּיל אֶת־דָּוִד בְּיַד־פְּלִשְׁתִּים׃

According to *Malbim*, with these words Saul intended to dissociate himself from Merab's decision to marry Adriel. As far as Saul was concerned, he was saying, in a conceptual sense he and David were linked by two matrimonial ties — i.e., *through my two [daughters].*

According to both Rabbi Yose and Rabbi Yehoshua ben Korchah (see v. 19), David performed betrothal ceremonies with both of Saul's daughters. In Rabbi Yose's opinion, David's marriage to Merab was legal, and after she died David married Michal. According to Rabbi Yehoshua ben Korchah, David's attempt to marry Merab was invalid, and so he was free to marry Michal (*Sanhedrin* 19b).

22. וַיְצַו שָׁאוּל אֶת־עֲבָדָו דַּבְּרוּ אֶל־דָּוִד ... — *Saul then commanded his servants, "Speak to David ..."*

Apparently, Saul perceived that David was not eager to marry Michal.

According to most commentators, Saul realized that David had grown skeptical after the arrangement to marry Merab failed to materialize. Therefore, Saul told his servants to persuade David that Saul had had no part in Merab's marriage to Adriel, and that since Michal wished to marry David there was no impediment to their union.

Ralbag, on the other hand, states that David hesitated because of his humility, but Saul thought that David realized that he was being led to his death.

בַּלָּט — *In secret.*

Discussions held in privacy seem more sincere (*Radak*).

Daas Sofrim explains that Saul intended the servants to mention the issue casually, without appearing as if they were commissioned to persuade him.

וְכָל־עֲבָדָיו אֲהֵבוּךָ — *And all of his servants like you.*

They were to tell David, "Do not think that Saul's servants envy you and thus persuaded Merab to despise you, and that they will turn Michal against you as well. None of these things are true, for they like you."

וְעַתָּה הִתְחַתֵּן בַּמֶּלֶךְ — *So become now the king's son-in-law.*

With the word וְעַתָּה, *now*, the servants rushed David, not permitting him the time to deliberate or seek counsel but pressuring him into accepting the mission of attaining a hundred Philistine foreskins (*Kli Yakar*).

23. וְאָנֹכִי אִישׁ־רָשׁ וְנִקְלֶה — *I am a poor and simple person!*

David implied that he was unable to accept the king's offer for two reasons: first, he was poor and thus unable to afford an appropriate dowry, and second, he was a simple shepherd unworthy of marrying into the king's family (*Radak*).

However, some commentators point out in regard to the first point that

servants, "Speak to David in secret, saying, 'Be-
hold, the king desires you, and all of his servants
like you, so become now the king's son-in-law.' "
23 *So Saul's servants spoke these words in David's*
ears. And David said, "Is it a trivial matter in your
eyes to become a son-in-law to the king? I am a
poor and simple person!"
24 *Saul's servants told him saying, "David spoke*
these words." 25 *Saul said, "So shall you say to Da-*
vid: 'The king desires no dowry, only one hundred
Philistine foreskins to avenge the enemies of the
king.' " Saul thought to have David fall at the
hands of the Philistines.

David should not have been poor, since Saul had promised "great wealth" to whoever defeated Goliath (above, 17:25).

According to *Chomas Anach*, David had not received that payment, and he here took the opportunity to subtly remind Saul of that fact. In so doing, he was possibly also implying that since that promise had not been kept, David could not trust Saul's offer of Michal either.

Malbim points out that according to both Tannaic opinions cited above (v. 19), David had relinquished his claim to that prize, in order to procure Merab as a wife, and he was now left without Merab and without the wealth.

וְנִקְלֶה — *And simple.*

David resisted Saul's servants' pressure on him to rush, replying that the process of transforming himself from shepherd into nobility was necessarily a gradual one (*Kli Yakar*).

25. אֵין־חֵפֶץ לַמֶּלֶךְ בְּמֹהַר כִּי בְּמֵאָה עָרְלוֹת פְּלִשְׁתִּים — *The king desires no dowry, only one hundred Philistine foreskins.*

With this, Saul responded to both of David's protestations.

Regarding David's claim that he was too poor to marry the king's daughter, Saul replied that he desired no dowry. And regarding David's description of himself as a plain man, Saul answered that with the act of attaining a hundred enemy foreskins he would transform himself into a man fit to marry the king's daughter (*Kli Yakar*).

בְּמֵאָה עָרְלוֹת פְּלִשְׁתִּים לְהִנָּקֵם בְּאֹיְבֵי הַמֶּלֶךְ — *One hundred Philistine foreskins to avenge the enemies of the king.*

Taking the foreskins of these' warriors would shame the Philistines, and that would enhance Saul's vengeance (*Metzudos*).

As mentioned earlier, although all gentiles are referred to as *uncircumcised*, this epithet is applied particularly to the Philistines (see *Judges* 14:3, 15:18; above, 14:6, 17:26; below, 31:2; *II Samuel* 1:20).

This is possibly because the Philistine nation emerged from a society of untrammeled promiscuity (see *Rashi* to *Genesis* 10:14, *Bereishis Rabbah* 37:5; *Tanchuma, Parashas Vayeishev*). Thus, cutting off the foreskins of the Philistine soldiers would be an especially appropriate way to degrade them (*Be'er Moshe*).

Daas Sofrim speculates that the Philistines may have disgraced the Israelites in the past in regard to the commandment of circumcision (as did the Amalekites [see *Rashi, Deuteronomy* 25:18]) — if so, this act of revenge would be particularly apt.

וְשָׁאוּל חָשַׁב לְהַפִּיל אֶת־דָּוִד בְּיַד־פְּלִשְׁתִּים — *Saul thought to have David fall at the*

כו וַיַּגִּדוּ עֲבָדָיו לְדָוִד אֶת־הַדְּבָרִים הָאֵלֶּה וַיִּשַׁר
הַדָּבָר בְּעֵינֵי דָוִד לְהִתְחַתֵּן בַּמֶּלֶךְ וְלֹא
כז מָלְאוּ הַיָּמִים׃ וַיָּקָם דָּוִד וַיֵּלֶךְ | הוּא וַאֲנָשָׁיו
וַיַּךְ בַּפְּלִשְׁתִּים מָאתַיִם אִישׁ וַיָּבֵא דָוִד אֶת־
עָרְלֹתֵיהֶם וַיְמַלְאוּם לַמֶּלֶךְ לְהִתְחַתֵּן בַּמֶּלֶךְ
כח וַיִּתֶּן־לוֹ שָׁאוּל אֶת־מִיכַל בִּתּוֹ לְאִשָּׁה׃ וַיַּרְא
שָׁאוּל וַיֵּדַע כִּי יְהוָה עִם־דָּוִד וּמִיכַל בַּת־שָׁאוּל
כט אֲהֵבַתְהוּ׃ וַיֹּאסֶף שָׁאוּל לֵרֹא מִפְּנֵי דָוִד עוֹד וַיְהִי
ל שָׁאוּל אֹיֵב אֶת־דָּוִד כָּל־הַיָּמִים׃ וַיֵּצְאוּ

hands of the Philistines.

Even if David succeeded in securing a hundred Philistine foreskins, such an unprovoked attack would so infuriate the Philistines that they would do anything to kill him (*Malbim*).

According to *Mussar HaNeviim*, Saul assumed that David would lack the Divine aid that had assisted him in his battle against Goliath, since at that time he had fought on behalf of Hashem's honor, whereas now he would be fighting for no more than his own benefit.

26. וַיִּשַׁר הַדָּבָר בְּעֵינֵי דָוִד לְהִתְחַתֵּן בַּמֶּלֶךְ — *And the proposal was proper in David's eyes, to become the king's son-in-law.*

David's motivation was not his desire to marry Michal but rather his desire to attain the honor of being the king's son-in-law (*Abarbanel*).

David was confident that he would receive Divine aid in his venture against the Philistines, in order to be able to prove to Saul that Hashem was with him (*Ralbag*).

וְלֹא מָלְאוּ הַיָּמִים — *The days had not yet expired.*

Apparently, a specific time had been decided upon to bring the foreskins; however, David did not wait but acted precipitately (*Rashi*).

27. וַיָּקָם דָּוִד וַיֵּלֶךְ הוּא וַאֲנָשָׁיו וַיַּךְ — *David arose and went — he and his men — and slew.*

Although David had an escort of men, וַיַּךְ, *he slew*, the Philistines himself.

David did not allow his men to help him lest that invalidate his agreement with Saul (*Kli Yakar*).

מָאתַיִם אִישׁ — *Two hundred men.*

Although the original agreement called for only one hundred foreskins, David slew twice that amount of men in order to display a truly great success (*Ralbag*).

Me'am Loez suggests that it was customary for a prospective groom to add to the stipulated dowry. (See footnote below.)

וַיְמַלְאוּם לַמֶּלֶךְ — *And they sent them all to the king.*

The word וַיְמַלְאוּם, *and they sent them*, comes from the root מָלֵא, *full*, and implies that David took a foreskin from each of the two hundred men whom he slaughtered (*Targum, Radak*).

Rashi renders וַיְמַלְאוּם as *they presented them*. David did not bring the foreskins to Saul himself but sent them with his men or with Saul's servants. He did so either to conform to the protocol of sending a dowry through a messenger (*Radak*), or because it was

[26] *His servants told these words to David, and*
the proposal was proper in David's eyes, to be-
come the king's son-in-law. The days had not
yet expired, [27] *when David arose and went — he*
and his men — and slew two hundred Philistine
men. David brought their foreskins and they sent
them all to the king in order to become the king's
son-in-law. Then Saul gave him his daughter Mi-
chal for a wife. [28] *Saul saw and understood that*
HASHEM was with David, and that Michal, Saul's
daughter, loved him. [29] *So Saul continued to fear*
David even more; and Saul harbored enmity to-
ward David all the days.

beneath his dignity to handle the foreskins himself (*Abarbanel*).[1]

28. וַיַּרְא שָׁאוּל וַיֵּדַע כִּי ה׳ עִם־דָּוִד — *Saul saw and understood that HASHEM was with David.*

Saul had not imagined that David might prevail; David's success now deepened Saul's fear of him.

וּמִיכַל בַּת־שָׁאוּל אֲהֵבַתְהוּ — *And that Michal, Saul's daughter, loved him.*

The fact that Michal loved David amplified Saul's fear, as it underscored David's unusual popularity. Although a girl might be expected to share her father's sentiments, Michal loved a man whom her father considered to be his enemy.

Furthermore, Michal's love for David exacerbated Saul's difficulty in harming him, for by so doing he would be hurting his daughter as well. And in addition, she would reveal to David any plans to which she might be privy (*Ralbag*).

Me'am Loez adds that we see here how Hashem prepared for David's protection, for in her love of David Michal later rescued him from the hands of her father (Ch. 19).

29. וַיֹּאסֶף שָׁאוּל לֵרֹא מִפְּנֵי דָוִד עוֹד — *So Saul continued to fear David even more.*

According to *Me'am Loez,* this verse points out that although Saul was now David's father-in-law, his fear and hatred of David did not abate.

1. The text of *Genesis* 26:15 reads, *And the Philistines sealed all of the wells that the servants of his father had dug in the days of Abraham his father, and they filled them —* וַיְמַלְאוּם *— with earth.* A Masoretic note there (ibid.) notes the use of this verb both in *Genesis* and in the present verse.

But why is the same verb used to refer both to earth and to foreskins? According to *Baal HaTurim* (ad loc.) this may allude to the custom of covering the foreskin with earth after a circumcision (see *Pirkei D'Rabbi Eliezer* 29, *Tur* and *Shulchan Aruch, Yoreh Deah* 265:10). *Kli Yakar* suggests that even here, וַיְמַלְאוּם implies that David filled the foreskins with earth before sending them to the king. Alternatively, this explains why David slew an extra hundred Philistines: it was in retaliation for the Philistine's having violated their oath with Abraham by filling his wells with earth.

שָׂרֵ֣י פְלִשְׁתִּ֑ים וַיְהִ֣י ׀ מִדֵּ֣י צֵאתָ֗ם שָׂכַ֤ל דָּוִד֙ מִכֹּל֙
א עַבְדֵ֣י שָׁא֔וּל וַיִּיקַ֥ר שְׁמ֖וֹ מְאֹֽד׃ וַיְדַבֵּ֣ר
יט/א־ב שָׁא֗וּל אֶל־יוֹנָתָ֤ן בְּנוֹ֙ וְאֶל־כָּל־עֲבָדָ֔יו לְהָמִ֖ית אֶת־
ב דָּוִ֑ד וִיהֽוֹנָתָן֙ בֶּן־שָׁא֔וּל חָפֵ֥ץ בְּדָוִ֖ד מְאֹֽד׃ וַיַּגֵּ֧ד
יְהוֹנָתָ֣ן לְדָוִ֗ד לֵאמֹ֔ר מְבַקֵּ֛שׁ שָׁא֥וּל אָבִ֖י לַהֲמִיתֶ֑ךָ

30. וַיֵּצְאוּ שָׂרֵי פְלִשְׁתִּים וַיְהִי מִדֵּי צֵאתָם שָׂכַל דָּוִד — *The officers of the Philistines would venture forth — and whenever they ventured forth, David was successful.*

Rashi explains that the Philistines would occasionally enter Israelite territory, and on such occasions David would successfully overcome them.

According to *Malbim*, as Saul had expected, the Philistines attacked in order to avenge their shame. Saul had expected that these forays would frighten David and eventually result in his death. Instead, David confronted the Philistines and courageously defeated them.

שָׂכַל דָּוִד — *David was successful.*

As before (see above, v. 14), *Abarbanel* renders שָׂכַל, *successful,* in its more conventional sense as *wise;* before going forth, David prepared his battle strategy.

וַיִּיקַר שְׁמוֹ מְאֹד — *And his reputation became very outstanding.*

The word יָקָר literally means *honor* or *value.* Whoever mentioned David's name valued it highly, and held him in great esteem (*Ralbag*).

Midrash Shmuel considers David's great reputation to be in regard to matters of halachah. When the Philistines heard that David had married Michal, they considered it a perfect opportunity to attack him, because they knew that the Torah forbids a man in the first year of his marriage to participate in battle (*Deuteronomy* 24:5).[1] However, they did not know that, as a Torah scholar, David had issued a ruling that this applies only during an optional war; in the case of a *mandatory war,* however, a groom is sent to fight even from the wedding canopy (*Sotah* 44b).[2]

XIX

1. וַיְדַבֵּר שָׁאוּל אֶל־יוֹנָתָן בְּנוֹ — *Saul spoke to Jonathan his son.*

The word וַיְדַבֵּר generally connotes stern speech (*Makkos* 11a; *Kli Yakar*). Saul spoke harshly of David's exceptional popularity, hoping that this would induce Jonathan to consider David a threat to his own chances of inheriting the throne. However, Saul's plan failed utterly, as he was unable to persuade Jonathan to countenance harming David (*Abarbanel*).

1. The Midrash implies that the Philistines hoped to catch David off-guard.

Kli Yakar finds it difficult to believe that the Philistines thought that David would fail to defend himself against attack. Rather, according to *Kli Yakar*, the Philistines assumed that when David heard that they were attacking he would be unable to restrain himself from entering into battle; that would constitute a transgression, which, they thought, would remove him from Hashem's good graces, and in consequence he would fall in battle.

2. The struggle against the Philistines qualified as a *mandatory war* because their territory was part of the land that the Israelites were mandated to take over. Seizing their territory would therefore be equivalent to Joshua's conquests (*Panim Yafos, Parashas Shoftim*).

Although the Philistines were not among the seven Canaanite nations, they had taken their

18/30 [30]The officers of the Philistines would venture
forth — and whenever they ventured forth, David
was more successful than all the other servants of
Saul, and his reputation became very outstanding.

19/1-2 [1] Saul spoke to Jonathan his son and to all his
servants about killing David, but Jonathan son
of Saul liked David very much. [2]So Jonathan told
David, saying, "Saul my father is trying to kill you,

וְאֶל־כָּל־עֲבָדָיו — *And to all his servants.*

Daas Sofrim conjectures that many of the venomous comments about David quoted in *Psalms* were uttered at this time by Saul's servants.

לְהָמִית אֶת־דָּוִד — *About killing David.*

Saul planned to have his servants feign a violent struggle in David's presence, in the course of which they would kill him as though by accident, leaving no trace of Saul's involvement (*Abarbanel*).

וִיהוֹנָתָן — *But Jonathan.*

In this verse, Jonathan's name is mentioned twice: first without a ה, and then with a ה. *Chomas Anach* explains this by citing *Get Poshut's* explanation of what this letter means when it appears in Jonathan's name. Our Sages point out that the word אִישׁ, *man*, contains a י and the word אִשָּׁה, *woman*, contains a ה. Together, these two letters form יָ־הּ, one of Hashem's Names. This indicates that when a man and woman live together in harmony, Hashem's presence resides in their midst.

Similarly, says *Get Poshut*, because of the selfless nature of the love between David and Jonathan, Hashem's presence resided in their midst as well. Thus, at times David's name is spelled with a י (as דויד), and Jonathan's with a ה. In this verse, Jonathan is depicted as rejecting his father's efforts to harm David; that active measure of selfless love is highlighted by the addition of the letter ה in the middle of the verse.

וִיהוֹנָתָן בֶּן־שָׁאוּל חָפֵץ בְּדָוִד מְאֹד — *But Jonathan son of Saul liked David very much.*

Literally, חָפֵץ means *desired.*

Thus, *Mahari Kara* renders this phrase as *Jonathan desired [to save] David from his father's hands,* and *Abarbanel* reads it as *Jonathan desired David's [success].*

Daas Sofrim infers from this verse that Jonathan was the sole figure to contest Saul's will and attempt to rescue David.

2. מְבַקֵּשׁ שָׁאוּל אָבִי לַהֲמִיתֶךָ — *Saul my father is trying to kill you.*

Jonathan specifically stated his father's name to indicate that King Saul, who possessed the means to attain his goals and whom the people would not dare oppose, was actively hostile to David. It was thus imperative that David do all he could to conceal himself (*Chomas Anach*).

שָׁאוּל אָבִי — *Saul my father.*

The mitzvah of honoring one's parents prohibits a person from mentioning his father's name without an honorific

land from Canaan; therefore, the Jews were obligated to conquer it from them (*Nachalas Shimon* 40:1).

Alternatively, a war fought in self-defense after the enemy has attacked — as in the case of the Philistines — is always considered a mandatory war (*Rambam, Hil. Melachim* 5:1; *Nachalas Shimon* ibid.).

וְעַתָּה הִשָּׁמֶר־נָא בַבֹּקֶר וְיָשַׁבְתָּ בַסֵּתֶר וְנַחְבֵּאתָ׃
ג וַאֲנִי אֵצֵא וְעָמַדְתִּי לְיַד־אָבִי בַּשָּׂדֶה אֲשֶׁר
אַתָּה שָׁם וַאֲנִי אֲדַבֵּר בְּךָ אֶל־אָבִי וְרָאִיתִי מָה
ד וְהִגַּדְתִּי לָךְ׃ וַיְדַבֵּר יְהוֹנָתָן
בְּדָוִד טוֹב אֶל־שָׁאוּל אָבִיו וַיֹּאמֶר אֵלָיו אַל־
יֶחֱטָא הַמֶּלֶךְ בְּעַבְדּוֹ בְדָוִד כִּי לוֹא חָטָא לָךְ
ה וְכִי מַעֲשָׂיו טוֹב־לְךָ מְאֹד׃ וַיָּשֶׂם אֶת־נַפְשׁוֹ בְכַפּוֹ

— in this case, אָבִי, *my father* (*Yoreh Deah* 240:2, see *Beur HaGra* 242:36).

Parashas Derachim (*Derush* 15) states in regard to one's mentor that one may mention his name only if one states the honorific first — e.g., "Rabbi Reuven," but not "Reuven my Rebbi." *Chomas Anach* disputes that on the basis of the present verse, in which Jonathan first mentions the name of his father (who was also his mentor) and only afterward his title.

הִשָּׁמֶר־נָא — *So now, please be cautious.*

In his deep love for David, Jonathan pleaded with him to protect himself (*Kli Yakar*).

וְיָשַׁבְתָּ בַסֵּתֶר וְנַחְבֵּאתָ — *Stay in the secret place and conceal yourself.*

It will not suffice for David to find a secret place — even there, he will have to secrete himself (*Malbim*).

3. וְעָמַדְתִּי לְיַד־אָבִי — *And stand near my father.*

Our translation follows *Rashi*'s commentary, according to which לְיַד — lit., *at the hand of* — means *near*.

Radak, however, renders לְיַד־אָבִי as to *the place of my father*. (The word יָד not uncommonly means place [as above 15:12; *Deuteronomy* 23:13].) Thus, the verse states, *I will go out and stand at the place of my father in the field*, where Saul would take a walk each morning.

בַּשָּׂדֶה אֲשֶׁר אַתָּה שָׁם — *In the field where you will be.*

Jonathan told David to hide in the field so that he would be able to hear Jonathan and Saul converse (*Radak*). Jonathan's subsequent words, וְהִגַּדְתִּי לָךְ, *and I will tell you*, referred to the eventuality that David failed to overhear them (*Radak*).

However, *Abarbanel* disputes this interpretation, since Jonathan's comment that he will report to David seems to be an integral part of his plan and not a contingency. Rather, states *Abarbanel*, when David hid in the field, he would be unable to overhear Jonathan and Saul; the purpose of his hiding in the field is to enable Jonathan to report the results of the discussion immediately.

According to *Malbim*, the reason that Jonathan told David to hide in the field was that it was far from residential areas; should Jonathan's pleas prove unsuccessful, David would be able to readily flee.

וַאֲנִי אֲדַבֵּר בְּךָ אֶל־אָבִי — *And I will speak to my father about you.*

Jonathan promised to speak favorably on David's behalf to his father, and to sway his father's attitude.

Malbim's interpretation of this incident is unique. It is based on the contention that whenever the verb דבר — *speak* — is followed by a word employing the ב prefix, it implies disparagement (e.g., וַתְּדַבֵּר מִרְיָם וְאַהֲרֹן בְּמֹשֶׁה, *Miriam and Aaron spoke against Moses* [*Numbers* 12:1]). Thus, Jonathan told David that he intended to speak slightingly of David — in particular, he would attempt to persuade Saul that David was a thoughtless adventurer who posed no threat to Saul's position.

so now, please be cautious tomorrow morning and stay in the secret place, and conceal yourself. [3]I will go out and stand near my father in the field where you will be, and I will speak to my father about you. I will see what happens and tell you."

[4]So Jonathan spoke favorably of David to Saul his father, saying to him, "Let the king not sin against his servant David, for he has not sinned against you, and because his deeds are very good for you. [5]He put his life in his hand

וְרָאִיתִי מָה — *I will see what happens.*

Jonathan would gauge his father's attitude toward David.

Kli Yakar suggests that Jonathan intended to mention David's name in a casual fashion and carefully note his father's facial expression. Thus, Jonathan said that he would *see*, rather than *hear*.

4. וַיְדַבֵּר יְהוֹנָתָן בְּדָוִד טוֹב אֶל־שָׁאוּל — *So Jonathan spoke favorably of David to Saul.*

Jonathan urged David's virtues upon Saul and argued that Saul should not feud against him.

According to *Malbim*, Jonathan spoke derogatorily about David, claiming that he was gambling with his life in a careless and foolhardy manner. These words were טוֹב אֶל־שָׁאוּל, *good to Saul*, i.e., Saul enjoyed hearing them.

אַל־יֶחֱטָא הַמֶּלֶךְ בְּעַבְדּוֹ בְדָוִד — *Let the king not sin against his servant David.*

Jonathan asked Saul not to kill David (*Metzudos*).

By referring to David as *servant*, Jonathan implied that he was a loyal supporter; by mentioning his name *David*, Jonathan attempted to elicit in Saul's mind the image of David the virtuous Torah scholar. (*Rashi* interprets *Genesis* 21:10 עִם־בְּנִי עִם־יִצְחָק, *with my son with Isaac*, and *Numbers* 12:8, בְּעַבְדִּי בְמֹשֶׁה, *against my servant Moses* similarly [*Chomas Anach, Kli Yakar*].)

כִּי לוֹא חָטָא לָךְ וְכִי מַעֲשָׂיו טוֹב־לְךָ מְאֹד — *For he has not sinned against you, and because his deeds are very good for you.*

Not only had David not done anything to incur Saul's wrath but he had even done him good (*Abarbanel*) — i.e., he had played music to assuage Saul's spirit of melancholy (*Mahari Kara*).

According to *Malbim*, Jonathan was saying that insofar as David was impetuous and reckless, he was sinning only against himself. Furthermore, since his recklessness would inevitably claim his life, why should Saul bother pursuing him?

The language of the verse homiletically supports this interpretation: had Jonathan been praising David's good deeds, he should have stated that they are טוֹבִים, *good*, in the plural. Instead, Jonathan spoke of טוֹב, *good*, in the singular. That is to say, the result of David's many deeds would be טוֹב־לְךָ, *good for you* (*Kli Yakar*).

5. וַיָּשֶׂם אֶת־נַפְשׁוֹ בְכַפּוֹ — *He put his life in his hand.*

This figure of speech implies that David put his life in danger, like someone holding a fragile item that may be destroyed the moment he opens his hand (*Metzudos*).

In response to Saul's fear that David was encouraging the adulation of military strength, Jonathan asserted that

וַיַּ֣ךְ אֶת־הַפְּלִשְׁתִּ֗י וַיַּ֤עַשׂ יְהוָה֙ תְּשׁוּעָ֣ה גְדוֹלָ֔ה לְכָל־
יִשְׂרָאֵ֖ל רָאִ֣יתָ וַתִּשְׂמָ֑ח וְלָ֤מָּה תֶֽחֱטָא֙ בְּדָ֣ם נָקִ֔י
ו לְהָמִ֥ית אֶת־דָּוִ֖ד חִנָּֽם׃ וַיִּשְׁמַ֥ע שָׁא֖וּל בְּק֣וֹל יְהוֹנָתָ֑ן
ז וַיִּשָּׁבַע֙ שָׁא֔וּל חַי־יְהוָ֖ה אִם־יוּמָֽת׃ וַיִּקְרָ֤א יְהוֹנָתָן֙
לְדָוִ֔ד וַיַּגֶּד־לוֹ֙ יְהוֹנָתָ֔ן אֵ֥ת כָּל־הַדְּבָרִ֖ים הָאֵ֑לֶּה וַיָּבֵ֨א
יְהוֹנָתָ֤ן אֶת־דָּוִד֙ אֶל־שָׁא֔וּל וַיְהִ֥י לְפָנָ֖יו כְּאֶתְמ֥וֹל
ח שִׁלְשֽׁוֹם׃ וַתּ֥וֹסֶף הַמִּלְחָמָ֖ה לִֽהְי֑וֹת
וַיֵּצֵ֨א דָוִ֜ד וַיִּלָּ֣חֶם בַּפְּלִשְׁתִּ֗ים וַיַּ֤ךְ בָּהֶם֙ מַכָּ֣ה גְדוֹלָ֔ה
ט וַיָּנֻ֖סוּ מִפָּנָֽיו׃ וַתְּהִי֩ ר֨וּחַ יְהוָ֤ה ׀ רָעָה֙ אֶל־שָׁא֔וּל
וְהוּא֙ בְּבֵית֣וֹ יוֹשֵׁ֔ב וַחֲנִית֖וֹ בְּיָד֑וֹ וְדָוִ֖ד מְנַגֵּ֥ן בְּיָֽד׃

David had exerted his prowess solely at the risk his own life on behalf of the nation (*Daas Sofrim*).

וַיַּעַשׂ ה׳ תְּשׁוּעָה גְּדוֹלָה לְכָל־יִשְׂרָאֵל — *And HASHEM granted a great salvation to all of Israel.*

The fact that Hashem saved the nation through David, argued Jonathan, proved that Hashem favored him.

Thus, Jonathan hinted, even if Saul pursued David, he would not succeed; to the contrary, he would place his own life in danger (*Chomas Anach*).

According to *Kli Yakar*, the "innocent blood" that Jonathan was warning Saul against spilling was not that of David but that of the Israelites: killing David would deprive the innocent Israelites of the protection that David afforded them, even if it were true that he was a sinner (*Kli Yakar*).

Although David had thoughtlessly endangered his own life, Saul and the nation were the beneficiaries (*Malbim*).

רָאִיתָ וַתִּשְׂמָח — *You saw [it] and rejoiced.*

At that juncture, Saul had been happy with David's victories; why should he change his mind now (*Daas Sofrim*)?

6. וַיִּשָּׁבַע שָׁאוּל חַי־ה׳ אִם־יוּמָת — *Saul swore, "As HASHEM lives, he shall not die."*

The phrase חַי־ה׳, *as HASHEM lives*, is a standard formula for an oath.

As we will see, however, soon thereafter Saul again attempted to kill David. How could he have so cavalierly ignored his oath?

Abarbanel presents two explanations.

The first is that when Saul uttered this oath he was sincere. Afterward — probably at the instigation of his advisers — he came to believe that David was, and always had been, a mortal threat to him, and so considered that oath as having been made in error and therefore void (*Daas Sofrim*). *Kli Yakar* supports the idea that Saul's oath was sincere, and says that he could not be held responsible when he subsequently attacked David because it resulted from his being overwhelmed by an irrational "spirit of melancholy," during which Saul was not in control of his mind or heart.

In *Abarbanel's* alternative version, Saul's words constituted nothing more than an attempt to deceive Jonathan into believing that he had experienced a change of heart. According to this explanation, וַיִּשְׁמַע שָׁאוּל בְּקוֹל יְהוֹנָתָן — *And Saul heeded the voice of Jonathan* — does not mean that Saul took Jonathan's words to heart but rather that *Saul heard from Jonathan's*

and slew the Philistine and HASHEM granted a great salvation to all of Israel; you saw [it] and rejoiced — so why should you sin with innocent blood, to kill David for no reason?"

6 *Saul heeded the voice of Jonathan, and Saul swore, "As HASHEM lives, he shall not die."* 7 *So Jonathan called David, and Jonathan told him all these things. Jonathan brought David to Saul and he was before him as he had been yesterday and before.*

8 *And there was war again, and David went forth and fought against the Philistines. He smote them a great blow, and they ran from him.*

9 *Then HASHEM's evil spirit befell Saul, while he was sitting in his house with his spear in his hand and David was playing [the harp] with his hand.*

voice [that he was set on saving David], and thus uttered a misleading oath. Saul justified doing this for two reasons. First, he felt that his life was in danger at the hands of David. And second, he did not lie outright but phrased his words ambiguously. His words אִם־יוּמָת — which Jonathan understood to mean *he shall not die* — literally mean *if he will die;* as he pronounced these words, Saul had in mind *that [David] will die* (*Kli Yakar*).[1]

אִם־יוּמָת — *He shall not die.*

He would not be put to death by Saul or his agents (*Chomas Anach*).

7. וַיְהִי לְפָנָיו כְּאֶתְמוֹל שִׁלְשׁוֹם — *And he was before him as he had been yesterday and before.*

Jonathan's attempt at forging peace was so successful that in a short while David again felt that he would be secure in Saul's presence, and he returned to serve Saul and play music.

8. וַתּוֹסֶף הַמִּלְחָמָה לִהְיוֹת וַיֵּצֵא דָוִד — *And there was war again, and David went forth.*

The Philistines initiated further attacks on the Israelites in order to avenge the humiliation that they had suffered at the hands of David; as a result, David felt responsible to spearhead the defense (*Malbim, Chomas Anach*).

9. וְדָוִד מְנַגֵּן בְּיָד — *And David was playing [the harp] with his hand.*

David was only playing בְּיָד, *with his hand* — i.e., mechanically; his heart, however, was gripped by fear, for he could sense Saul's hostility. This idea is further indicated by the phraseology בְּיָד — literally, *with a hand* — rather than בְּיָדוֹ, *with his hand* — as though someone else were playing (*Kli Yakar*).

1. Under certain perilous conditions, a person is permitted to utter such an ambiguous oath. See *Nedarim* 27b, *Nachalas Shimon* 60:9.

י וַיְבַקֵּשׁ שָׁאוּל לְהַכּוֹת בַּחֲנִית בְּדָוִד וּבַקִּיר וַיִּפְטַר
מִפְּנֵי שָׁאוּל וַיַּךְ אֶת־הַחֲנִית בַּקִּיר וְדָוִד נָס
יא וַיִּמָּלֵט בַּלַּיְלָה הוּא׃ וַיִּשְׁלַח שָׁאוּל
מַלְאָכִים אֶל־בֵּית דָּוִד לְשָׁמְרוֹ וְלַהֲמִיתוֹ בַּבֹּקֶר
וַתַּגֵּד לְדָוִד מִיכַל אִשְׁתּוֹ לֵאמֹר אִם־אֵינְךָ
מְמַלֵּט אֶת־נַפְשְׁךָ הַלַּיְלָה מָחָר אַתָּה מוּמָת׃
יב וַתֹּרֶד מִיכַל אֶת־דָּוִד בְּעַד הַחַלּוֹן וַיֵּלֶךְ וַיִּבְרַח
יג וַיִּמָּלֵט׃ וַתִּקַּח מִיכַל אֶת־הַתְּרָפִים וַתָּשֶׂם אֶל־
הַמִּטָּה וְאֵת כְּבִיר הָעִזִּים שָׂמָה מְרַאֲשֹׁתָיו

10. וַיִּפְטַר מִפְּנֵי שָׁאוּל — *But he slipped away from Saul.*

Ralbag emphasizes how miraculous it was that David, who was undoubtedly concentrating deeply on the perfection of his music, was able to nonetheless notice the spear after it had been thrown and escape it.

וְדָוִד נָס וַיִּמָּלֵט בַּלַּיְלָה הוּא — *David fled and escaped that night.*

The text seems redundant. According to *Radak*, David first *fled* Saul's presence; then, with his wife's aid, he *escaped* the additional danger that he anticipated.

11. וַיִּשְׁלַח שָׁאוּל מַלְאָכִים אֶל־בֵּית דָּוִד לְשָׁמְרוֹ וְלַהֲמִיתוֹ בַּבֹּקֶר — *Saul sent messengers to David's house to keep watch over him and kill him in the morning.*

Why didn't Saul have David killed that night?

According to *Radak*, Saul did not want David to be killed in the presence of Michal.

Ralbag and *Abarbanel* state that Saul did not want to leave the assignment in the hands of his agents, for he was afraid that David might out-maneuver them.

Ralbag adds that Saul did not wish to have David killed in public for no apparent reason and thought that in his own palace he could make David's death appear accidental.

Alshich comments that this ill-planned delay was a stroke of Divine Providence that afforded David the opportunity to escape. (See *Psalms* 59:1, *ArtScroll* edition.)

The Midrash states that Saul acted more ignobly than did the wicked Jezebel, wife of Ahab (see *Ezekiel* 5:7). When she wished to have the prophet Elijah killed, she sent him a warning allowing him the opportunity to escape (*I Kings* 19:2), whereas Saul sent David no such warning (*Midrash Shmuel*).

אִם־אֵינְךָ מְמַלֵּט אֶת־נַפְשְׁךָ הַלַּיְלָה מָחָר אַתָּה מוּמָת — *If you do not [act to] escape with your life tonight, you will be killed tomorrow.*

By stating *you will be killed*, rather than *they will kill you*, Michal implied that if David did not make an effort to protect himself, his own negligence would be partially to blame for his death (*Kli Yakar*).

According to Jewish law, a calendar day begins with the onset of night. Nevertheless, it is appropriate to use the term *tomorrow* when speaking at nighttime about the following day.[1]

12. וַתֹּרֶד מִיכַל אֶת־דָּוִד בְּעַד הַחַלּוֹן — *So Michal lowered David through the window.*

1. See *Ibn Ezra* to *Leviticus* 23:11 and *Ritva* to *Rosh Hashanah* 13a, who bring support for that idea from this verse (*Nachalas Shimon* 60:10).

10 Saul tried to thrust the spear through David and
the wall, but he slipped away from Saul and the
spear hit the wall.
David fled and escaped that night.
11 Saul sent messengers to David's house to
keep watch over him and kill him in the morning.
His wife Michal told David, saying, "If you do
not [act to] escape with your life tonight, you will
be killed tomorrow." 12 So Michal lowered David
through the window, and he went and he fled and
escaped. 13 Michal then took a mannequin and placed
it in the bed, and she put a goat-skin at its head

Even as soldiers guarded the front of the house, Michal helped David escape through a back window. She did this herself so as not to confide in a confederate, who might prove false and inform Saul (*Kli Yakar*).

וַיֵּלֶךְ וַיִּבְרַח — *And he went and he fled.*

First וַיֵּלֶךְ — David *walked* slowly and quietly, in order to avoid attention. Then, when he had gone some distance, וַיִּבְרַח, he *fled* and ran (*Kli Yakar*).

13. וַתִּקַּח מִיכַל אֶת־הַתְּרָפִים וַתָּשֶׂם אֶל־הַמִּטָּה — *Michal then took a mannequin and placed it in the bed.*

Michal used a mannequin to create the impression that David was sick in bed, in order to buy time for him to escape without being noticed.

הַתְּרָפִים — *The teraphim.*

The exact nature of the *teraphim* is a matter that requires clarification. The first mention of *teraphim* in *Tanach* is in regard to the idols of Laban, which Rachel stole (*Genesis* 31:19, 30).

It is inconceivable, of course, that David possessed idols of any sort. However, most descriptions of the *teraphim* do depict it as able to predict the future. Thus, a verse states that הַתְּרָפִים דִּבְּרוּ־אָוֶן, *the teraphim have spoken vanity* (*Zechariah* 10:2). According to *Me'am Loez*, the use of such augury was halachically permissible, and Michal put such *teraphim* in David's bed, intending to claim later that it notified David about Saul's pursuit.

Radak cites approvingly the explanation of *Ibn Ezra* (to *Genesis* 31:19) that *teraphim* were statues in the form of people that were able in some mystical way to absorb higher powers. Michal simply made use of the *teraphim* shape to create the impression that David was in bed.[1]

Abarbanel's view eschews any supernatural elements. According to him, women made these mannequins in the form of their husbands so as to mitigate their loneliness when their husbands were away.

Kli Yakar cites a view that the *teraphim* was a sort of alarm clock, which David used to arouse him to perform noble deeds. Since it was evocative of David's merits, Michal placed it in his bed to evoke Divine compassion on his behalf.

וְאֵת כְּבִיר הָעִזִּים שָׂמָה מְרַאֲשֹׁתָיו — *And she put a goat-skin at its head.*

1. *Radak* cites another view that these *teraphim* were copper contrivances that could tell time and predict the future on astrological grounds. However, he rejects this explanation, questioning why Michal would have placed such an object in David's bed (see below).

יד וַתְּכַס בַּבָּגֶד׃ וַיִּשְׁלַח שָׁאוּל מַלְאָכִים
טו לָקַחַת אֶת־דָּוִד וַתֹּאמֶר חֹלֶה הוּא׃ וַיִּשְׁלַח
שָׁאוּל אֶת־הַמַּלְאָכִים לִרְאוֹת אֶת־דָּוִד לֵאמֹר
טז הַעֲלוּ אֹתוֹ בַמִּטָּה אֵלַי לַהֲמִתוֹ׃ וַיָּבֹאוּ הַמַּלְאָכִים
וְהִנֵּה הַתְּרָפִים אֶל־הַמִּטָּה וּכְבִיר הָעִזִּים
יז מְרַאֲשֹׁתָיו׃ וַיֹּאמֶר שָׁאוּל אֶל־מִיכַל
לָמָּה כָּכָה רִמִּיתִנִי וַתְּשַׁלְּחִי אֶת־אֹיְבִי וַיִּמָּלֵט
וַתֹּאמֶר מִיכַל אֶל־שָׁאוּל הוּא־אָמַר אֵלַי שַׁלְּחִנִי
יח לָמָה אֲמִיתֵךְ׃ וְדָוִד בָּרַח וַיִּמָּלֵט וַיָּבֹא אֶל־שְׁמוּאֵל
הָרָמָתָה וַיַּגֶּד־לוֹ אֵת כָּל־אֲשֶׁר עָשָׂה־לוֹ שָׁאוּל

Since the *teraphim* mannequin was hairless, Michal made it appear more like David by placing a goat-skin at its head, for goat hair resembles human hair (*Rashi*).

According to other interpretations, the כְּבִיר הָעִזִּים was a jug of wine covered by goat hair (Midrash), or a pillow made of goat hair (*Radak*).

וַתְּכַס בַּבָּגֶד — *And covered it with a cloth.*

Michal placed a bed cover over the goat-skin-covered mannequin (*Ralbag*).

Midrash Tehillim (59:3) applies the verse מָצָא אִשָּׁה מָצָא טוֹב, *One who has found a wife has found goodness* (*Proverbs* 18:22), to Michal, who rescued her husband from the hands of her father.

14. וַיִּשְׁלַח שָׁאוּל מַלְאָכִים לָקַחַת אֶת־דָּוִד — *Saul sent agents to take David.*

When David failed to leave the house in the morning, Saul sent agents to arrest him, but Michal did not let them in, claiming that David was ill (*Daas Sofrim*).

15. לִרְאוֹת אֶת־דָּוִד — *To inquire after David.*

Our translation of לִרְאוֹת (which literally means *to see*) as *to inquire* is that of *Targum*.

The word לֵאמֹר, *saying*, implies that Saul sent the agents to pretend to be paying a friendly sick call — but לֵאמֹר, *he told them* that they should bring David back in his bed to have him killed (*Kli Yakar*).

According to some commentators, Saul had seen David in perfect health earlier that day (*Daas Sofrim*) and so sent agents to investigate Michal's claim. If indeed David were malingering, Saul would have him executed on the grounds of deceiving the king. Even if he were truly ill, Saul intended to have him killed anyway (*Malbim*).

16. וַיָּבֹאוּ הַמַּלְאָכִים וְהִנֵּה הַתְּרָפִים אֶל־הַמִּטָּה — *The agents came and behold! — the mannequin was in the bed.*

It appears that the agents discovered the *teraphim* mannequin in David's room. According to the Midrash, however, the agents brought the bed back to Saul, and there the *teraphim* mannequin was discovered (*Shocher Tov* 59:4).

אֶל־הַמִּטָּה — *In the bed.*

Generally, the word אֶל denotes *to;* here, however, it means *on* or *in* (see similarly *Ezekiel* 18:6 [*Radak*]).

Daas Sofrim, however, maintains the standard translation *to*, and renders the phrase as *the agents came and behold — returned the teraphim to the bed.* According to this interpretation, the agents came at night and viewed the

and covered it with a cloth.

14 Saul sent agents to take David, but she said, "He is ill."

15 Then Saul sent the agents again to inquire after David, telling them, "Bring him up to me in the bed, to have him killed." 16 The agents came and behold! — the mannequin was in the bed and a goat-skin at its head!

17 Saul asked Michal, "Why did you deceive me this way? You sent away my enemy so that he escaped." And Michal replied, "He said to me, 'Let me go or I will kill you.' "

18 David fled and escaped, and came to Samuel at Ramah. He told him all that Saul had done to him,

teraphim, assuming it to be David. Upon their return in the morning, Michal removed the *teraphim* so that she should not be accused of deceiving her father. Nonetheless, the agents found them and, in order not to be suspected of collaborating with David, returned the *teraphim* to the bed and brought them together to Saul to "discover" that the *teraphim* was not David.

17. וַיֹּאמֶר שָׁאוּל אֶל־מִיכַל לָמָּה כָּכָה רִמִּיתִנִי — *Saul asked Michal, "Why did you deceive me this way?"*

Daas Sofrim observes that Saul's questioning of Michal is characterized by the verb וַיֹּאמֶר, a word that implies gentle, civil discourse (see *Rashi, Exodus* 19:3). Saul understood that Michal would not prevent her husband from escaping. He only asked her לָמָּה כָּכָה רִמִּיתִנִי, *Why did you deceive me this way?* — that is to say, why did you deepen the deception with the *teraphim* and the lie about his illness (*Malbim*)?

וַתֹּאמֶר מִיכַל אֶל־שָׁאוּל הוּא־אָמַר אֵלַי שַׁלְּחֵנִי לָמָה אֲמִיתֵךְ — *Michal replied, "He said to me, 'Let me go or I will kill you.'"*

Michal responded to her father's pained inquiry with the false claim that David had threatened to have her killed if she would not comply with his demands.

Rashi cites a Midrash explaining that with these words Michal shifted the blame back onto Saul. She said, "You are the one who gave me in marriage to a bandit who drew his sword and threatened to kill me unless I would help him escape." This incident earned Michal the name עֶגְלָה, *heifer* (*II Samuel* 3:5). Just as a heifer does not accept a yoke, Michal was not subservient to her father (*Shocher Tov* ibid.).

18. וַיָּבֹא אֶל־שְׁמוּאֵל הָרָמָתָה וַיַּגֶּד־לוֹ אֵת כָּל־אֲשֶׁר עָשָׂה־לוֹ שָׁאוּל — *And came to Samuel at Ramah. He told him all that Saul had done to him.*

David went to seek counsel and support from Samuel, who had anointed both Saul and himself. He hoped as well to learn what the future held in store for him — in particular, how he would escape Saul's clutches (*Abarbanel*).

Chida (*Chomas Anach*) comments that from the absence of any response from Samuel, it can be inferred that no response was necessary, for from the time that David was anointed his future

יט וַיֵּלֶךְ הוּא וּשְׁמוּאֵל וַיֵּשְׁבוּ °בנוית: וַיֻּגַּד לְשָׁאוּל °בְּנָיוֹת ק׳
כ לֵאמֹר הִנֵּה דָוִד °בנוית בָּרָמָה: וַיִּשְׁלַח שָׁאוּל °בְּנָיוֹת ק׳
מַלְאָכִים לָקַחַת אֶת־דָּוִד וַיַּרְא אֶת־לַהֲקַת
הַנְּבִיאִים נִבְּאִים וּשְׁמוּאֵל עֹמֵד נִצָּב עֲלֵיהֶם
וַתְּהִי עַל־מַלְאֲכֵי שָׁאוּל רוּחַ אֱלֹהִים וַיִּתְנַבְּאוּ
כא גַּם־הֵמָּה: וַיַּגִּדוּ לְשָׁאוּל וַיִּשְׁלַח מַלְאָכִים אֲחֵרִים
וַיִּתְנַבְּאוּ גַּם־הֵמָּה וַיֹּסֶף שָׁאוּל וַיִּשְׁלַח מַלְאָכִים
כב שְׁלִשִׁים וַיִּתְנַבְּאוּ גַּם־הֵמָּה: וַיֵּלֶךְ גַּם־הוּא הָרָמָתָה
וַיָּבֹא עַד־בּוֹר הַגָּדוֹל אֲשֶׁר בַּשֶּׂכוּ וַיִּשְׁאַל וַיֹּאמֶר
אֵיפֹה שְׁמוּאֵל וְדָוִד וַיֹּאמֶר הִנֵּה °בנוית בָּרָמָה: °בְּנָיוֹת ק׳

was assured, and Saul could not succeed with his plan.

וַיֵּלֶךְ הוּא וּשְׁמוּאֵל — *So he and Samuel went.*

The verse mentions David first out of respect for the sovereignty that he represented (*Abarbanel*).

וַיֵּשְׁבוּ בְּנָיוֹת — *And stayed at Naioth.*

In the following verse, this site is referred to as *Naioth in Ramah. Radak* explains that Naioth was an area either within or near the city of Ramah.

Targum renders *Naioth* as *a house of study*. The commentators explain that in this study hall prophets gathered to learn Torah and seek the word of Hashem.

Midrash Shmuel tells that on the night that David escaped he came to Naioth and learned more from Samuel than a gifted Torah student could ordinarily have learned in a hundred years. Some commentators, among them Chida and *Be'er Moshe*, point out David's astounding commitment to Torah study even during this most trying of times. Even as he desperately fled for his life he was able to delve deeply into the words of Torah. As David himself testified, נַפְשִׁי בְכַפִּי תָמִיד וְתוֹרָתְךָ לֹא שָׁכָחְתִּי, *My life is always at risk, but I did not forget Your Torah* (*Psalms* 119:109; see *Rashi* ad loc.).

What topic were they studying? According to our Sages (*Zevachim* 54b), Samuel and David attempted to determine the appropriate site for the Temple — in addition, *Me'am Loez* states, Samuel assured David that it would be built by his son.[1]

19. The fact that word of David's whereabouts quickly made its way to Saul indicates that David did not take pains to conceal himself. Alternatively, he did attempt to remain unnoticed, but a few informers loyal to Saul noticed him.

The Book of *Psalms* makes frequent allusion to the support that Saul received from the masses in his pursuit of David (*Daas Sofrim*).

20. וַיַּרְא — *They saw.*

The word וַיַּרְא literally means *he saw*. It refers either to the leader of Saul's agents (who had the authority to make decisions), or to each individual (*Radak*).

לַהֲקַת — *A group of.*

This is synonymous with קְהִלַּת, *an assembly of*, and consists of the same letters re-arranged. (This is a typical

1. According to our Sages, David and Samuel were in a site called Ramah. The reference to *Naioth* implies that they were discussing the Temple, which is the *splendor* — *noy* — of the world. Alternatively, they were speaking of the *central abode* — *naveh* — of the world. See *Rashi, Exodus* 15:2.

so he and Samuel went and stayed at Naioth.
19 It was told to Saul, saying, "Behold! David is
in Naioth, in Ramah." 20 Saul sent messengers
to arrest David. [When they arrived] they saw
a group of prophets prophesying with Samuel
standing erect, overseeing them, and a spirit of
God came upon Saul's messengers and they, too,
prophesied. 21 People told Saul and he sent other
messengers, but they, too, prophesied. Saul per-
sisted and sent a third group of messengers, but
they, too, prophesied. 22 So he went to Ramah
himself, arriving at the cistern in Secu. He in-
quired and said, "Where are Samuel and David?"
Someone said, "They are in Naioth, in Ramah."

phenomenon in the Hebrew language — e.g., כֶּבֶשׂ and כֶּשֶׂב, both meaning *sheep* [*Radak, Malbim*].)

The חֶבֶל הַנְּבִיאִים, *band of prophets,* mentioned earlier (10:5) was a subgroup of such a לַהֲקַת הַנְּבִיאִים (*Malbim*).

הַנְּבִיאִים — *Prophets.*

Targum renders this word as *scholars.*

נִבְּאִים — *Prophesying.*

Abarbanel understands this to mean that the prophets were predicting that David would be unscathed by Saul and would eventually reign. Hearing this and seeing that Samuel was encouraging them, Saul's messengers were inspired to fear Hashem and believed in the prophets' words. Thus, they ignored Saul's directives and joined the prophets.

Targum, on the other hand, interprets הַנְּבִיאִים נִבְּאִים as *the scholars were singing praises [to* H*ASHEM*].

וּשְׁמוּאֵל עֹמֵד נִצָּב עֲלֵיהֶם — *With Samuel standing erect, overseeing them.*

This phrase literally means, *and Samuel standing, standing over them.* However, the first of the two synonyms is read literally and the second conceptually. Thus, Samuel was on such an exalted plane that he was עֹמֵד — he *stood erect* while prophesying (unlike most prophets, who are so overwhelmed by the experience of prophecy that their limbs weaken out of fear and they fall on their faces). In addition, he was נִצָּב — he *supervised* the other prophets, influencing them with his rarefied level of prophecy (*Radak, Malbim*). (See below, 22:9, *Me'am Loez.*)

22. וַיִּשְׁאַל וַיֹּאמֶר אֵיפֹה שְׁמוּאֵל וְדָוִד וַיֹּאמֶר הִנֵּה בְּנָיוֹת בָּרָמָה — *He inquired and said, "Where are Samuel and David?" And someone said, "They are in Naioth, in Ramah."*

Kli Yakar suggests that in the phrase וַיִּשְׁאַל וַיֹּאמֶר, וַיִּשְׁאַל means that Saul *inquired* as to David's whereabouts. In order to conceal the fact that he was pursuing David, וַיֹּאמֶר, *he said* or mentioned Samuel's name as well.

Interestingly, the response he received referred solely to one person — הִנֵּה בְּנָיוֹת בָּרָמָה, *he* is in Naioth, in Ramah. Apparently, the person answering Saul intuited his intent.

כג וַיֵּ֣לֶךְ שָׁ֔ם אֶל־°נוית בָּרָמָ֑ה וַתְּהִ֨י עָלָ֜יו גַּם־ °נָיֹות ק׳
ה֤וּא ר֣וּחַ אֱלֹהִ֔ים וַיֵּ֤לֶךְ הָלוֹךְ֙ וַיִּתְנַבֵּ֔א עַד־בֹּא֖וֹ
כד °בנוית בָּרָמָֽה׃ וַיִּפְשַׁ֨ט גַּם־ה֜וּא בְּגָדָ֗יו וַיִּתְנַבֵּ֤א °בְּנָיֹות ק׳
גַם־הוּא֙ לִפְנֵ֣י שְׁמוּאֵ֔ל וַיִּפֹּ֣ל עָרֹ֔ם כָּל־הַיּ֥וֹם
הַה֖וּא וְכָל־הַלָּ֑יְלָה עַל־כֵּן֙ יֹֽאמְר֔וּ הֲגַ֥ם שָׁא֖וּל
כ/א־ב
א בַּנְּבִיאִֽם׃ וַיִּבְרַ֣ח דָּוִ֔ד °מנוות בָּרָמָ֑ה וַיָּבֹ֞א
וַיֹּ֣אמֶר ׀ לִפְנֵ֣י יְהוֹנָתָ֗ן מֶ֤ה עָשִׂ֙יתִי֙ מֶֽה־עֲוֺנִ֤י וּמֶֽה־ °מִנָּיֹות ק׳
ב חַטָּאתִי֙ לִפְנֵ֣י אָבִ֔יךָ כִּ֥י מְבַקֵּ֖שׁ אֶת־נַפְשִֽׁי׃ וַיֹּ֙אמֶר֙

23. וַיֵּלֶךְ הָלוֹךְ וַיִּתְנַבֵּא עַד־בֹּאוֹ בְּנָיוֹת בָּרָמָה — *And he kept on prophesying until he arrived in Naioth, in Ramah.*

The spirit of prophecy came upon Saul even as he was on the road (*Radak*).

Furthermore — as implied by the words הָלוֹךְ וַיִּתְנַבֵּא, *he kept on prophesying* — the closer he came to its source in Ramah the stronger it grew (*Abarbanel;* see *Genesis* 16:13).

Malbim explains that Saul was prone to attaining a prophetic spirit because he had experienced it once before (above, 10:10); therefore, it settled upon him even as he was on the road.

According to *Abarbanel,* Saul was thinking so intently about what the future held in store for David and himself that as he came closer to Samuel he almost forced prophecy upon himself.

24. וַיִּפְשַׁט גַּם־הוּא בְּגָדָיו — *He too removed his [royal] raiment.*

Rashi inserts the word *royal,* explaining that Saul changed into the clothes worn by students of prophecy. He did so in order to be like one of them and to avoid feeling superior to them (*Metzudos*).

Radak and *Ralbag,* however, read the text literally, explaining that all prophets would remove their clothing while prophesying. This is because the experience of prophecy so completely overwhelmed their senses that their physical and emotional state of consciousness vanished.

The relationship of the body to the soul is often compared to that of a garment to the body. When one wants to prepare himself for a spiritual endeavor, such as prophecy, he must experience הִתְפַּשְּׁטוּת הַגַּשְׁמִיּוּת — an "unclothing" of physicality to "expose" one's soul. Some say that this is also appropriate preparation for prayer (see *Rabbeinu Yonah* to *Berachos* 25b; *Shulchan Aruch Orach Chaim* 98:1). Accordingly, *Netziv* says that we can understand figuratively that Saul "removed his physical garments" in order to prepare for prophecy. Also, although Saul was known for his modesty and for concealing himself and his traits (see above, 10:22; *Megillah* 13b), here, when he was inspired by prophecy, he could not conceal himself, and his veils or garments were removed (*Munkatcher Rebbe,* cited by *Mishbetzos Zahav*).

וַיִּתְנַבֵּא גַם־הוּא לִפְנֵי שְׁמוּאֵל — *And he too prophesied before Samuel.*

Even in the midst of his pursuit of David and even though it meant dressing and appearing simply — like one of the disciples of Samuel — Saul seized this opportunity for spiritual growth (*Kli Yakar*).

וַיִּפֹּל — *He fell.*

This is another common effect of the state of prophecy (cf. the cases of Balaam [*Numbers* 24:4] and Daniel [*Daniel* 10:9]).

עָרֹם — *Unclothed.*

Rashi understands this to mean that Saul was stripped of royal garments,

[23] *He went there, to Naioth in Ramah, and the spirit of God came upon him, as well; and he kept on prophesying until he arrived at Naioth, in Ramah.* [24] *He too removed his [royal] raiment and he too prophesied before Samuel; he fell unclothed that entire day and night. Therefore people say, "Is Saul also among the prophets?"*

[1] *Then David fled from Naioth in Ramah. He came and said before Jonathan, "What have I done? What is my iniquity and my sin before your father, that he seeks my life?"* [2] *He said*

whereas *Radak* and *Ralbag* take it literally.

Targum translates this word as בִּרְשָׁן, which, states *R' Menachem the Grammarian,* means *mad.* (See *Rashi;* and see above, 18:10, comm.)

כָּל־הַיּוֹם הַהוּא וְכָל־הַלָּיְלָה — *That entire day and night.*

This was part of Hashem's master plan, giving David time to flee to Jonathan (*Ralbag*).

עַל־כֵּן יֹאמְרוּ הֲגַם שָׁאוּל בַּנְּבִיאִם — *Therefore people say, "Is Saul also among the prophets?"*

This is a repetition of a similar statement that had been made the last time Saul had been possessed by a spirit of prophecy (above, 10:12).[1]

Metzudos explains that now that Saul had a second experience with prophecy, the saying was repeated and grew more widespread.

According to *Daas Sofrim* and *Me'am Loez,* the first incident aroused attention because Saul was an unknown person who suddenly began to prophesy. This time, contrarily, people were surprised that even the king equated himself with Samuel's disciples.

Chomas Anach states that people were deeply impressed at the potency of Samuel's prophetic influence, which was able to dispel the spirit of melancholy that had gripped Saul.

Malbim adds that Saul's act of prophecy caught the people's interest more so than that of his agents because his began while he was still on the road and lasted an entire day and night.

XX

◆§ Jonathan and David Plan a Test of Saul's Attitude Toward David

1. וַיִּבְרַח דָּוִד מִנָּוִית בָּרָמָה — *David fled from Naioth in Ramah.*

While Saul was prophesying, David took the opportunity to escape to Naioth (*Radak*).

מֶה עָשִׂיתִי מֶה־עֲוֹנִי וּמֶה־חַטָּאתִי לִפְנֵי אָבִיךָ — *What have I done? What is my iniquity and what is my sin before your father?*

David first asked what sins he had committed in general and then what sins he had committed specifically against Saul that would be a slight to

1. As explained there, this became a standard phrase applied to anyone who suddenly performed an unexpected accomplishment.

כ/ג־ה

°לֹא־יַעֲשֶׂה ק׳

לוֹ חָלִילָה לֹא תָמוּת הִנֵּה °לו־עשה אָבִי דָּבָר
גָּדוֹל אוֹ דָּבָר קָטֹן וְלֹא יִגְלֶה אֶת־אָזְנִי וּמַדּוּעַ
ג יַסְתִּיר אָבִי מִמֶּנִּי אֶת־הַדָּבָר הַזֶּה אֵין זֹאת׃ וַיִּשָּׁבַע
עוֹד דָּוִד וַיֹּאמֶר יָדֹעַ יָדַע אָבִיךָ כִּי־מָצָאתִי חֵן
בְּעֵינֶיךָ וַיֹּאמֶר אַל־יֵדַע־זֹאת יְהוֹנָתָן פֶּן־יֵעָצֵב
וְאוּלָם חַי־יהוה וְחֵי נַפְשֶׁךָ כִּי כְפֶשַׂע בֵּינִי וּבֵין
ד הַמָּוֶת׃ וַיֹּאמֶר יְהוֹנָתָן אֶל־דָּוִד מַה־תֹּאמַר נַפְשְׁךָ
ה וְאֶעֱשֶׂה־לָּךְ׃ וַיֹּאמֶר דָּוִד אֶל־
יְהוֹנָתָן הִנֵּה־חֹדֶשׁ מָחָר וְאָנֹכִי יָשֹׁב־אֵשֵׁב עִם־

his sovereignty (*Malbim*).

2. וַיֹּאמֶר לוֹ חָלִילָה לֹא תָמוּת — *He said to him, "It would be a sacrilege. You shall not die!"*

Jonathan believed that Saul's oath not to harm David (19:6) was sincere. As for Saul's subsequent attempt to kill David (19:10), that must have been due to the influence of the spirit of melancholy over which Saul had no control. Jonathan thought that if such episodes of melancholy would be repeated, they would be rare and short-lived, and that at such times David could easily absent himself (*Radak, Ralbag*).

חָלִילָה — *It would be a sacrilege.*

Jonathan stated that his father would certainly not commit the sacrilege of transgressing his oath (*Metzudos*).

Alshich associates the word חָלִילָה with חִלּוּל, *desecration*, a word used specifically in connection with transgressing one's oath (see *Numbers* 30:3).

הִנֵּה לֹא־יַעֲשֶׂה אָבִי דָּבָר גָּדוֹל אוֹ דָּבָר קָטֹן וְלֹא יִגְלֶה אֶת־אָזְנִי — *Behold, my father does nothing, great or small, without telling me about it.*

First Jonathan alluded to Saul's oath. Now he implies, "Even if you suspect that he had his oath annulled, you can be sure that he would not conceal his plans from me" (*Chomas Anach*).

Radak adds that Jonathan's confidence was misplaced. Saul did indeed want to kill David, and he had not confided in Jonathan because he did not want to upset him.

From the text of the chapter, it seems as if some time had elapsed since the episode at Naioth and that Jonathan had succeeded in arranging for David to be welcome at Saul's table. This is apparent from the fact that David was expected to attend Saul's Rosh Chodesh feast (see below), and it explains Jonathan's confidence that the stormy past was behind them and David had nothing to fear.

As for David, he realized — either intuitively or because he had been informed by a servant of Saul — that Saul still intended to kill him (*Radak*).

3. וַיֹּאמֶר אַל־יֵדַע־זֹאת יְהוֹנָתָן פֶּן־יֵעָצֵב — *Jonathan should not know about this, lest he be saddened.*

David replied that, to the contrary, Saul had not confided in Jonathan because he had already decided to kill David and did not want to cause Jonathan distress (*Malbim*).

כִּי כְפֶשַׂע בֵּינִי וּבֵין הַמָּוֶת — *There is but a footstep between me and death!*

This was an allusion to the fact that when Saul threw the spear at David, David saved himself from death only by stepping swiftly to the side (*Rashi*).

4. מַה־תֹּאמַר נַפְשְׁךָ וְאֶעֱשֶׂה־לָּךְ — *Whatever*

to him, "It would be a sacrilege; you shall not die! Behold, my father does nothing, great or small, without telling me about it, so why should my father conceal this matter from me? It is not so!"
3 But David swore to him again and said, "Your father knows very well that I have found favor in your eyes, so he said [to himself], 'Jonathan should not know about this, lest he be saddened.' However, as HASHEM lives, and by your life, there is but a footstep between me and death."
4 Jonathan said to David, "Whatever your soul will say I shall do for you."
5 David said to Jonathan, "Behold, tomorrow is the New Moon, when I would be sitting with

your soul will say.

The intellect is seated in the soul (*Metzudos*).

Targum renders *whatever your soul desires.*

וַיֹּאמֶר יְהוֹנָתָן אֶל־דָּוִד מַה־תֹּאמַר נַפְשְׁךָ וְאֶעֱשֶׂה־לָּךְ — *Jonathan said to David, "Whatever your soul will say, I shall do for you."*

Jonathan asked David to devise a plan that would enable them to determine Saul's intentions (*Abarbanel*).

5. הִנֵּה־חֹדֶשׁ מָחָר — *Behold, tomorrow is the New Moon.*

[A brief overview of the designation of the New Moon is in order. At this period in history, Rosh Chodesh, the new month, was determined by the Sanhedrin's acceptance of testimony from witnesses that they had seen the new moon. A month might consist of 29 or 30 days. If witnesses saw the new moon on the night following the 29th day, they would testify to that effect in court the following day (witnesses could testify only during the daytime). If such witnesses did not appear, that day would belong to the previous month, giving it 30 days. In such a case, the following day would be Rosh Chodesh. If so, how could David be sure that the next day would be Rosh Chodesh? *Teshuvos Tashbetz* (Vol. I:153) explains that since it was always possible that the 30th day might be Rosh Chodesh, it was always treated in some ways as if it were Rosh Chodesh. Thus David, speaking on the 29th, could speak with certainty about a feast the next day.

Daas Sofrim observes that David did not say רֹאשׁ חֹדֶשׁ מָחָר, *tomorrow will be Rosh Chodesh*, but rather חֹדֶשׁ מָחָר, *tomorrow will be the* חֹדֶשׁ, which may be translated as *the turning point of the month*, whether the last day of the present month or the first of the next.

Rabbeinu Bachya (on *Parashas Bo*) cites the novel view of *Rabbeinu Chananel* that determining the new month never depended on the testimony of witnesses, but was solely in accordance with astronomical calculations. *Rabbeinu Chananel* supports his opinion from the present episode, in which David knew in advance when Rosh Chodesh would occur (see *Rambam, Commentary to Mishnah, Rosh Hashanah* Ch. 2, who refutes this opinion). To understand

הַמֶּלֶךְ לֶאֱכוֹל וְשִׁלַּחְתַּנִי וְנִסְתַּרְתִּי בַשָּׂדֶה עַד
ו הָעֶרֶב הַשְּׁלִשִׁית׃ אִם־פָּקֹד יִפְקְדֵנִי אָבִיךָ וְאָמַרְתָּ
נִשְׁאֹל נִשְׁאַל מִמֶּנִּי דָוִד לָרוּץ בֵּית־לֶחֶם עִירוֹ
ז כִּי זֶבַח הַיָּמִים שָׁם לְכָל־הַמִּשְׁפָּחָה׃ אִם־כֹּה
יֹאמַר טוֹב שָׁלוֹם לְעַבְדֶּךָ וְאִם־חָרֹה יֶחֱרֶה לוֹ

how *Rabbeinu Chananel* explains the Talmud's extensive discussion of the requirement that witnesses testify to having seen the new moon, see *Rabbeinu Bachya.*

וְאָנֹכִי יָשֹׁב־אֵשֵׁב עִם־הַמֶּלֶךְ לֶאֱכוֹל — *When I would be sitting with the king to eat.*

As noted above, apparently, some time had elapsed since Saul first cast his spear at David, and Jonathan had during this interval succeeded in making David welcome again at Saul's table (*Radak*).

As a regular guest at the king's table, David would be expected at this feast; his absence would be strikingly apparent (*Rashi*).

The word אֵשֵׁב, literally means I will sit. Our translation — would be sitting — reads it as indicating on-going action.

Abarbanel, however, reads this word literally. David said that he intended to sit at the king's banquet, and afterward disappear for a few days — odd behavior that would be sure to draw Saul's attention.

It seems clear from this verse and *Rashi's* designation of the meal as a *holiday feast* that Saul regularly held Rosh Chodesh banquets in his palace. From this, *Pri Chadash* derives that there is a mitzvah to eat a festive meal on Rosh Chodesh.[1]

The Jewish king is associated with the moon (see above, 17:14).[2] It was therefore appropriate for the king to arrange a feast on Rosh Chodesh.

Chasam Sofer (in *Toras Moshe* at the end of *Parashas Bereishis*) comments that this was why Saul made this feast — and when he heard that David had gone to celebrate a Rosh Chodesh feast with his family, Saul took this to mean that David considered himself king and thus worthy of celebrating the new moon. Jonathan responded that David had gone to be with his family for no other reason than that his brother had summoned him (v. 29) — implying that David had gone merely to attend a family gathering.

וְשִׁלַּחְתַּנִי — *Grant me leave.*

Jonathan [believed that,] in his capacities as army captain and son of the king, he had the authority to grant David permission to leave.

David was insistent that Saul know (*Daas Sofrim*) that he had not left without authorization (*Malbim*).

עַד הָעֶרֶב הַשְּׁלִשִׁית — *Until the third evening.*

Depending on whether witnesses testified that they had seen the new moon, Rosh Chodesh could be one of two days. David and Jonathan had this conversation the day before the new moon might be visible. The *third evening* would be the evening after both possible days of Rosh Chodesh (*Ralbag, Abarbanel*). David told Jonathan that even if Saul did not inquire about David's whereabouts the next day, he would certainly do so on the day after the next (*Malbim*).

Daas Sofrim adds that if Saul were

1. *Tur* (*Orach Chaim* 419) agrees that there is such a mitzvah, but he derives this from verses 6 and 29, which speak of the annual feast-offering of David's family.

Beis Yosef disagrees, stating that this annual feast-offering may simply have been brought to celebrate a family gathering that happened to fall on Rosh Chodesh.

2. Thus, David is mentioned in the text of *Kiddush Levanah,* the Blessing on the Moon.

the king to eat. Grant me leave and I will hide in the field until the third evening [of the month]. [6] *If your father notices my absence, you shall say to him, 'David asked me to [allow him to] hurry to his hometown of Bethlehem, for there is an annual feast there for the entire family.'* [7] *If he then says, 'Good!' then it is well for your servant. But if he grows very angry,*

to raise the topic earlier and make his attitude toward David clear, Jonathan would not wait but would immediately inform David (see v. 35).

הָעֶרֶב הַשְּׁלִשִׁית — *The third evening.*

This phrase is grammatically peculiar, for the noun is masculine, whereas the adjective is feminine.

On the basis of *Targum, Radak* explains that the adjective modifies an implied but unstated feminine noun, עֵת — *time period.* Thus, this phrase may be rendered as *the third evening time period.*

6. אִם־פָּקֹד יִפְקְדֵנִי אָבִיךָ — *If your father notices my absence.*

The phrase פָּקֹד יִפְקְדֵנִי, translated here as *notices my absence,* more simply means *notices* (or, in other contexts, *remembers*).

This phrase may literally be translated as *notice, he will notice me.* The double use of the verb refers to David's two-day absence. David's nonattendance for one day could be excused; his continued absence for a second day would not be so easily dismissed and would furthermore call his first day's nonattendance into question as well (see v. 27) (*Kehillas Yaakov*).

נִשְׁאֹל נִשְׁאַל מִמֶּנִּי דָוִד — *David asked me.*

Here too a doubled verb is employed: נִשְׁאֹל נִשְׁאַל, which means more literally *asking, asked.* This formulation indicates that David requested permission to go because his family had previously requested his presence (*Malbim*).

לָרוּץ — *To [allow him to] hurry.*

David indicated that because he was in a hurry he had no time to request authorization directly from the king (*Malbim*).

בֵּית־לֶחֶם עִירוֹ — *To his hometown of Bethlehem.*

Had David not said he was going to Bethlehem, Saul might have sent agents to search the immediate area, and they might have found him. David therefore stated that he would be in his hometown, where his family and friends would surely protect him. This would discourage Saul from sending anyone after him (*Kehillas Yaakov*).

כִּי זֶבַח הַיָּמִים שָׁם לְכָל־הַמִּשְׁפָּחָה — *For there is an annual feast there for the entire family.*

Literally, the phrase זֶבַח הַיָּמִים means *a feast of days.* We render the phrase as *an annual feast,* in accordance with *Rashi.*

Ralbag suggests that the family held an annual celebration to commemorate miracles that they had experienced (see *Magen Avraham, Orach Chaim* 686:5). *Meam Loez* conjectures that the feast may have been in honor of David's anointment.

7. אִם־כֹּה יֹאמַר טוֹב שָׁלוֹם לְעַבְדֶּךָ — *If he then says, "Good!" then it will be well for your servant.*

If Saul said "Good," that would indicate that he was not angry that David had left (*Rashi*). Alternatively, this would mean that he was not angry at Jonathan for having granted David permission to leave (*Metzudos*).

ח דַּ֕ע כִּֽי־כָלְתָ֥ה הָרָעָ֖ה מֵעִמּֽוֹ׃ וְעָשִׂ֤יתָ חֶ֙סֶד֙ עַל־
עַבְדֶּ֔ךָ כִּ֚י בִּבְרִ֣ית יהוה הֵבֵ֥אתָ אֶת־עַבְדְּךָ֖ עִמָּ֑ךְ
וְאִם־יֶשׁ־בִּ֤י עָוֺן֙ הֲמִיתֵ֣נִי אַ֔תָּה וְעַד־אָבִ֖יךָ לָמָּה־זֶּ֥ה
ט תְבִיאֵֽנִי׃ וַיֹּ֣אמֶר יְהוֹנָתָ֔ן חָלִ֖ילָה לָּ֑ךְ כִּ֣י ׀
אִם־יָדֹ֣עַ אֵדַ֗ע כִּֽי־כָלְתָ֨ה הָרָעָ֜ה מֵעִ֤ם אָבִי֙ לָב֣וֹא
י עָלֶ֔יךָ וְלֹ֥א אֹתָ֖הּ אַגִּ֥יד לָֽךְ׃ וַיֹּ֤אמֶר דָּוִד֙
אֶל־יְה֣וֹנָתָ֔ן מִ֖י יַגִּ֣יד לִ֑י א֛וֹ מַה־יַּעַנְךָ֥ אָבִ֖יךָ קָשָֽׁה׃

וְאִם־חָרֹה יֶחֱרֶה לוֹ דַּע כִּי־כָלְתָה הָרָעָה מֵעִמּוֹ — *But if he grows very angry, then know that the evil [decree] has become final with him.*

If Saul showed anger, that would show that he had intended to kill David and was now frustrated at being unable to do so (*Rashi*). *Abarbanel* adds that test was also intended to see if Saul was so angered by David's absence that he considered it reason enough to have him killed. If so, the king would not conceal his feelings.

The Hebrew for *very angry* is a doubled verb: חָרֹה יֶחֱרֶה — literally, *angry, he will get angry.*

According to *Chomas Anach*, this double usage indicates that Saul might grow angry at two people: David and Jonathan.

There were actually four possible ways in which Saul could react. David had mentioned two: that Saul would either say "good" or grow angry. The other two were that Saul would not ask about David or that he would ask but would not react to the answer that he received. According to *Malbim*, David only mentioned the possible scenarios in which Saul's position would be clear.

Rashi indicates that unless Saul grew angry it would be clear that he was at peace with David.

A person who does not wish another individual harm but is aware that he is liable to lash out at him in murderous rage will be glad when that individual is absent. Contrarily, a person who has made a calculated decision to kill another individual will maintain that intent even when that individual is absent (*Mishbetzos Zahav*).

8. וְעָשִׂיתָ חֶסֶד עַל־עַבְדֶּךָ — *Do this favor for your servant.*

David asked Jonathan to grant him permission to leave (*Rashi*).

According to *Metzudos*, David asked Jonathan to let him know how Saul would react to his (David's) absence.

וְאִם־יֶשׁ־בִּי עָוֺן הֲמִיתֵנִי — *If I am guilty of an iniquity, kill me yourself.*

David said that if he were guilty of an iniquity that voided the covenant between him and Jonathan, then Jonathan should kill David himself (*Abarbanel, Metzudos*).

וְעַד־אָבִיךָ לָמָּה־זֶּה תְבִיאֵנִי — *Why bring me to your father?*

If Saul were hostile to David and Jonathan did not tell David, David might chance coming into Saul's presence again. If Saul were then to kill David, Jonathan would be morally responsible (*Metzudos*).

If he had to be killed, David preferred death at the hands of Jonathan to death at Saul's hands. Besides that, David was concerned that should Saul kill him, he would do so out of jealousy and not due to a pure motive, such as to avenge a major sin, and would thus be held responsible for having caused the death of an innocent person (*Kli Yakar*).

then know that the evil [decree] has become fi-
nal with him. 8 *Do this favor for your servant,*
for you have brought your servant into a cov-
enant of HASHEM *with you. If I am guilty of an*
iniquity, kill me yourself; why bring me to your
father?"

9 *Jonathan said, "Far be it from you! For if I knew*
that the evil [decree] has become final with my
father, would I not tell you?"

10 *David then said to Jonathan, "Who will tell me*
[if your father answers favorably] or if your father
answers you harshly?"

9. Our rendering of the phrase וְלֹא אֹתָהּ אַגִּיד לָךְ as a question — *would I not tell you?* — is in accord with *Malbim's* reading.

Rashi, however, reads Jonathan's words as a declarative statement: *Far be it from you [to suspect me] of knowing that the evil [decree] has become final with my father, yet not telling you.*

Following *Malbim,* Jonathan's comment חָלִילָה לָךְ — *far may this be from you* — means, *far be it from you [to commit a sin so severe that it would warrant voiding the covenant between us].*

Abarbanel states that the word לָךְ — *for you* — may also be understood as *on your behalf.* With that word, Jonathan implied that he would never have revealed his father's secret to anyone else. But it would be sacrilegious for him to withhold this information from David, whom he loved like himself.

10. [David's words here are cryptic, and may be more literally translated as, *Who will tell me or what will your father answer you harshly?*]

Our translation follows *Radak,* who reads the word מַה, ordinarily translated as *what,* as *if.*

According to *Malbim,* David's question, *Who will tell me?,* is rhetorical and means that if Saul exhibited anger toward David, who would tell David? The answer is that no one would. Even Jonathan would be unable to safely tell David, whether personally or through an emissary, lest Saul learn of his betrayal. [As we will see, the commentators disagree as to when and how Jonathan would send a message, through an agent or in person.]

Mishbetzos Zahav agrees and reads this verse as referring only to a case in which Saul registered disapproval at David's absence. In that case, *Who will tell me if your father answers harshly?* Otherwise, if Saul responded favorably, Jonathan could deliver the information himself.

Some commentators explain David to be saying, *If your father answers harshly, [who will tell me] what type of harsh [sentence] he intends [to impose upon me]: to kill me or to exile me?* (*Radak*).

Sefer HaAkeidah (Shaar 23) explains David as asking rhetorically how angry Saul would have to be before [Jonathan considered] his response harsh. Because this was a matter of life and death, [David indicated,] Jonathan must view even the slightest trace on anger of Saul's part as cause for grave concern.

יא וַיֹּאמֶר יְהוֹנָתָן֙ אֶל־דָּוִ֔ד לְכָ֖ה וְנֵצֵ֣א הַשָּׂדֶ֑ה וַיֵּצְא֖וּ
יב שְׁנֵיהֶ֥ם הַשָּׂדֶֽה׃ וַיֹּאמֶר יְהוֹנָתָ֜ן אֶל־דָּוִ֗ד
יְהוָ֞ה אֱלֹהֵ֤י יִשְׂרָאֵל֙ כִּֽי־אֶחְקֹ֣ר אֶת־אָבִ֜י כָּעֵ֣ת ׀
מָחָר֙ הַשְּׁלִשִׁ֔ית וְהִנֵּה־ט֖וֹב אֶל־דָּוִ֑ד וְלֹֽא־אָז֙
יג אֶשְׁלַ֣ח אֵלֶ֔יךָ וְגָלִ֖יתִי אֶת־אָזְנֶֽךָ׃ כֹּֽה־יַעֲשֶׂה֩ יְהוָ֨ה
לִֽיהוֹנָתָ֜ן וְכֹ֣ה יֹסִ֗יף כִּֽי־יֵיטִ֨ב אֶל־אָבִ֤י אֶת־הָֽרָעָה֙
עָלֶ֔יךָ וְגָלִ֙יתִי֙ אֶת־אָזְנֶ֔ךָ וְשִׁלַּחְתִּ֖יךָ וְהָלַכְתָּ֣
לְשָׁל֑וֹם וִיהִ֤י יְהוָה֙ עִמָּ֔ךְ כַּאֲשֶׁ֥ר הָיָ֖ה עִם־אָבִֽי׃

Abarbanel suggests that the word מָה may be translated as a rhetorical exclamation (as in the phrase, מָה רַב־טוּבְךָ — *How abundant is Your goodness!* [*Psalms* 31:20]). Thus, David was exclaiming, *How [terrible it would be if] your father answered you harshly [because of me]!*

11. וַיֹּאמֶר יְהוֹנָתָן אֶל־דָּוִד לְכָה וְנֵצֵא הַשָּׂדֶה — *Jonathan said to David, "Come, let us go out to the field."*

There they would be able to speak in private, and they would notice if anyone tried to overhear them (*Ralbag*).

12. וַיֹּאמֶר יְהוֹנָתָן אֶל־דָּוִד ה׳ אֱלֹהֵי יִשְׂרָאֵל — *Jonathan said to David, "[I swear by] HASHEM, the God of Israel."*

Rashi adds the words, *I swear by.*

Kli Yakar suggests that Jonathan was reciting a prayer: [*HASHEM, God of Israel, when I probe my father at this time on the third day from now, may it be good for David.*]

אֶחְקֹר — *I will probe.*

The word חֲקִירָה implies that one doubts the truth of a statement and must *probe* what is hidden behind the words (*Daas Sofrim*).

Kehillas Yaakov comments that whereas David asked Jonathan only to take note if Saul reacted visibly to David's absence, Jonathan volunteered that if Saul were to remain quiet he would probe further into the matter.

כָּעֵת מָחָר הַשְּׁלִשִׁית — *At this time on the third day from now.*

Jonathan expressed agreement with David's previous proposal that he probe into Saul's attitude on the day after the next — i.e., the *third day.*

Targum renders this phrase as *tomorrow or the third day. Malbim* explains that to mean that Jonathan intended to wait until the next day for Saul to react to David's absence. If Saul did not on the second or third day, then Jonathan himself would bring up the topic.

וְהִנֵּה־טוֹב אֶל־דָּוִד וְלֹא־אָז אֶשְׁלַח אֵלֶיךָ וְגָלִיתִי אֶת־אָזְנֶךָ — *And if [his response] is good for David, will I not then send you [a message] and reveal it to you?*

Literally, the text reads *I will not send to you,* which is perplexing because Jonathan seems to be saying that he will *not* tell David. Our translation follows *Radak,* who renders this phrase as a rhetorical question. *Rashi* understands that it flows into the next verse and implies that Jonathan was cursing himself as follows: If Saul's reaction is positive toward you, there will be no reason not to reveal it to you, and if I do not send word to you I deserve to be cursed.

Kli Yakar maintains the literal reading and explains that if Saul reacted well, Jonathan would not send a message — rather, he would go to tell David himself.

11 *So Jonathan said to David, "Come, let us*
go out to the field," and they both went out to
the field. 12 *Jonathan said to David, "[I swear by]*
HASHEM, the God of Israel, that I will probe my
father at this time on the third day from now, and
if [his response] is good for David, will I not then
send you [a message] and reveal it to you? 13 *So shall*
HASHEM do to Jonathan and so shall He do even
further — [but] if it pleases my father to harm you
I will reveal it to you [in person], and I will send you
away that you may go to peace; and may HASHEM
be with you as He [has been] with my father.

Sefer HaAkeidah (Shaar 23) interprets Jonathan's words to mean that even if Saul's reaction seemed positive, Jonathan would not relate it to David without first establishing beyond the shadow of a doubt that Saul had no ill intentions.

13. כֹּה־יַעֲשֶׂה ה׳ לִיהוֹנָתָן וְכֹה יֹסִיף — *So shall HASHEM do to Jonathan and so shall He do even further.*

Rabbeinu Yeshayah states that this is a conventional flowery expression in which a person swears that if he does not keep his promise Hashem should punish him, in some unspecified way.

Metzudos has a contrary understanding: that this is a formula in which a person states that if he engages in a particular action then Hashem should reward him.

כִּי־יֵיטִב אֶל־אָבִי אֶת־הָרָעָה עָלֶיךָ — *[But] if it pleases my father to harm you.*

Our translation is in accord with the commentary of *Rashi.*

Above (19:4,5), we mentioned *Malbim's* comment that Jonathan intended to test his father by speaking disparagingly of David. Accordingly, this phrase may be translated as *if it will please my father [to hear] evil about you.*

Citing the grammarian *Menachem, Mahari Kara* renders כִּי־יֵיטִב as *if it will increase.* Presumably, he understands this to be a reference to Saul's *evil spirit* — i.e., *[if my father's evil spirit] in regard to you increases....*

R' M.D. Vali (cited by *Mishbetzos Zahav*) states that this phrase may be read homiletically as alluding to the concept that everything that Hashem does is for the good. Thus, כִּי־יֵיטִיב אֶל־אָבִי אֶת־הָרָעָה, *when He will do good through my father with the evil . . .*

וְגָלִיתִי אֶת־אָזְנֶךָ — *I will reveal it to you [in person].*

The previous verse addressed a hypothetical case in which Saul's reaction to David's absence would be positive. In such a case, Jonathan would send David a messenger. But now Jonathan described a case in which Saul's response would be negative — then, said Jonathan, he would deliver the information in person (*Rashi*).

וִיהִי ה׳ עִמָּךְ כַּאֲשֶׁר הָיָה עִם־אָבִי — *And may HASHEM be with you as He [has been] with my father.*

Foreseeing that David would be king, Jonathan wished him Hashem's aid in subduing his enemies, just as Hashem had helped Saul (*Radak*).

יד וְלֹא אִם־עוֹדֶנִּי חָי וְלֹא־תַעֲשֶׂה עִמָּדִי חֶסֶד
טו יהוה וְלֹא אָמוּת: וְלֹא־תַכְרִית אֶת־חַסְדְּךָ מֵעִם
בֵּיתִי עַד־עוֹלָם וְלֹא בְּהַכְרִת יהוה אֶת־אֹיְבֵי
טז דָּוִד אִישׁ מֵעַל פְּנֵי הָאֲדָמָה: וַיִּכְרֹת יְהוֹנָתָן
עִם־בֵּית דָּוִד וּבִקֵּשׁ יהוה מִיַּד אֹיְבֵי דָוִד:

14. This verse, which we translate in accordance with *Radak*, is cryptically worded. It may more literally be translated, *And not if I am yet alive, and you shall not do with me the kindness of Hashem and I shall not die.*

The verse contains three instances of the word וְלֹא — *and not*. According to *Radak*, the first וְלֹא may be translated as *I need not ask*. The second וְלֹא seems to be saying, surprisingly, that Jonathan does not expect David to perform any kindness for him. *Radak* explains this to mean that Jonathan feels no need to ask David to be kind to him, because that is self-understood.

Rashi understands the first two instances of וְלֹא to be a form of a request (see *II Kings* 5:17 and *Ezekiel* 16:47). Thus, Jonathan is asking, *While I am still alive, would you not do me the kindness of Hashem, so that I will not die?*

According to *Sefer HaAkeidah*, Jonathan is saying, *It cannot be that if I am still alive, you will refrain from doing me the kindness of Hashem* — were David to do so, he would be transgressing the covenant between himself and Jonathan, and would thus be unworthy of the throne.

Malbim understands וְלֹא as a continuation of Jonathan's previous words וִיהִי ה׳ עִמָּךְ — *Hashem shall be with you.* Jonathan is saying that God will not be with David if David does not extend kindness to Jonathan. Jonathan explicates the nature of that kindness in his next words: וְלֹא אָמוּת, *so that I will not die.* It was the custom in those days for a new monarch to kill all relatives of the previous king in order to eliminate any potential rivals to the throne, and so Jonathan asked David not to kill him.

According to *Abarbanel*, Jonathan first wished David success in becoming king (v. 13). He now adds וְלֹא. Jonathan hoped that this would not happen אִם־עוֹדֶנִּי חָי, *while I am still alive.* Notwithstanding Jonathan's boundless love for David, he felt that it would be too painful and humiliating for him to see David rise to the throne in his own place. He continued, וְלֹא־תַעֲשֶׂה עִמָּדִי חֶסֶד ה׳ — *[I hope that] you will not have to do for me the [ultimate] kindness of Hashem* — which is וְלֹא אָמוּת — *so that I will not die*, i.e., I hope I die before you become king so that it will not be necessary for you to spare my life.

Mishbetzos Zahav sees here an instance of the far-reaching foresight of Jonathan, and of great Jews in general. Jonathan should now have felt supremely secure, as the heir to the throne whose one possible rival had been branded a rebel and forced to flee for his life. Nevertheless, Jonathan saw the future correctly and spoke to David as if the situation were reversed, begging him to save his children when he rises to power. One can barely imagine how encouraging it must have been for David, the fugitive, to be preceived as the future powerful ruler.

חֶסֶד ה׳ — *The kindness of Hashem.*

Since Jonathan and David had incorporated Hashem into their covenant as a Witness by calling it בְּרִית ה׳ — a *covenant of Hashem* (v. 8) — upholding that covenant would be a kindness of Hashem (*Radak*).

According to *Daas Sofrim*, Jonathan was saying that it would be a great kindness on David's part to forget all the evil that Saul had done him and treat Saul's son Jonathan with compassion. This

[14]*I need not [ask anything of you] if I will still be alive [when you become king], for would you not do with me the kindness of* HASHEM, *so that I will not die?* [15]*But do not cut off your kindness from my descendants forever, not even when* HASHEM *cuts off David's enemies from the face of the earth."* [16]*Jonathan [also] sealed [a covenant] regarding David's household, [and added], "May* HASHEM *exact punishment from the enemies of David."*

kindness of David would be comparable to Hashem's kindness, in the following way: just as human beings cannot recompense Hashem for the kindness that He does for them, so too Jonathan would be unable to adequately repay David for the kindness that David did for him.

15. וְלֹא־תַכְרִית אֶת־חַסְדְּךָ מֵעִם בֵּיתִי עַד־עוֹלָם — *"But do not cut off your kindness from my descendants forever"* — even after my death (*Malbim*).

The translation follows *Rashi*, who says that Jonathan did not feel a need to ask for himself, but requested kindness for his children.

According to *Metzudos*, this verse continues the statement begun in verse 14 describing favors that Jonathan does *not* need to ask of David. Jonathan had no need to request that David extend kindness to his descendants, for that was clearly part of their covenant.

וְלֹא בְּהַכְרִת ה׳ אֶת־אֹיְבֵי דָוִד — *Not even when* HASHEM *cuts off David's enemies.*

Jonathan stated that he knew that Hashem would eradicate David's enemies, Saul's family among them. Nevertheless, he beseeched David to have mercy on his own descendants.

Jonathan spoke these words with Divine inspiration, for he was alluding — possibly without knowing it — to the future incident of the Gibeonites (*II Samuel* Ch. 21), in which David was compelled to deliver some of Saul's descendants to the Gibeonites to be hanged. At that time, David had mercy on Jonathan's son Mephibosheth because of this oath (ibid. v. 7; *Abarbanel*).

16. וַיִּכְרֹת יְהוֹנָתָן עִם־בֵּית דָּוִד — *Jonathan [also] sealed [a covenant] regarding David's household.*

After having pleaded with David to protect his children, Jonathan promised reciprocally that as long as his father was in power he would help David's family — particularly if David had to flee (*Radak, Ralbag, Abarbanel*).

Kli Yakar suggests that this clause obligated David's family not to harm Jonathan and his family.

Daas Sofrim comments that this covenant, which began as an agreement between two individuals, expanded into a commitment between their descendants and ultimately evolved into a long-standing bond between the tribes of Judah and Benjamin, which today survive as the principal remnants of the Jewish people.

וּבִקֵּשׁ ה׳ מִיַּד אֹיְבֵי דָוִד — *[And added], "May* HASHEM *exact punishment from the enemies of David."*

We insert the words *and added* in accordance with *Metzudos'* interpretation that these are Jonathan's words. Jonathan prayed that Hashem avenge Himself against David's enemies, even though he knew that this included his father Saul (*Rabbeinu Yeshayah*). He even intended this curse to include himself should he betray their covenant (*Ralbag*).

Some understand that the words *may* HASHEM *exact punishment* were not

יז וַיּוֹסֶף יְהוֹנָתָן לְהַשְׁבִּיעַ אֶת־דָּוִד בְּאַהֲבָתוֹ אֹתוֹ
יח כִּי־אַהֲבַת נַפְשׁוֹ אֲהֵבוֹ: וַיֹּאמֶר־לוֹ יְהוֹנָתָן
יט מָחָר חֹדֶשׁ וְנִפְקַדְתָּ כִּי יִפָּקֵד מוֹשָׁבֶךָ: וְשִׁלַּשְׁתָּ
תֵּרֵד מְאֹד וּבָאתָ אֶל־הַמָּקוֹם אֲשֶׁר־נִסְתַּרְתָּ שָּׁם

Jonathan's, but the words of the narrator. According to *Malbim*, Scripture relates that aside from committing himself to help David, Jonathan asked Hashem to aid David against his enemies.

According to *Rashi*, the phrase אֹיְבֵי דָוִד — *David's enemies* — is a euphemism for David himself: If David would not uphold the covenant, then Hashem should punish him.

Rashi elaborates that this in fact occurred. When Ziba, the servant who managed Saul and Jonathan's estate after their death, denounced Jonathan's son Mephibosheth as a traitor, David responded by taking away half of Mephibosheth's estate and giving it to Ziba (*II Samuel* 19:30).[1] That constituted a breach of the covenant between David and Jonathan.[2] At that point a Heavenly voice proclaimed that just as David had split Mephibosheth's estate in two, so too would his own kingdom be split in two: following the reign of King Solomon, there would be two contemporaneous Jewish kingdoms, of which the Davidic dynasty would control only the tribes of Judah and Benjamin.

17. וַיּוֹסֶף יְהוֹנָתָן לְהַשְׁבִּיעַ אֶת־דָּוִד בְּאַהֲבָתוֹ אֹתוֹ — *Jonathan again adjured David because of his love for him.*

Jonathan asked David to repeat the oath not because he feared that David would otherwise abrogate it, but because he loved David and enjoyed saying that David would reign and would be in a position to do kindness on his behalf (*Metzudos*).

18. וַיֹּאמֶר לוֹ יְהוֹנָתָן מָחָר חֹדֶשׁ — *Jonathan said to him, "Tomorrow is the New Moon."*

After having entered into a covenant with David, Jonathan now responded to David's earlier inquiry, *Who will tell me . . . ?* (4:10; *Metzudos*).

David's inquiry could have had one of two meanings. Not sure which one David meant, Jonathan responded to both. First, David could have been asking whether Jonathan would reliably report on his father's response. Jonathan answered (as recorded in the previous few verses) by swearing his loyalty to David. Second, David might have been asking about the mechanism whereby Jonathan would communicate with him, which Jonathan now addressed (*Abarbanel).*

מָחָר חֹדֶשׁ — *Tomorrow is the New Moon.*

David did not yet know whether Saul's actions were calculated or motivated solely by the influence of the spirit of melancholy. The test that he now proposed would answer that question. Such a spirit ceases to function on the Sabbath, festivals, and Rosh Chodesh. David thus proposed to absent himself at one of these times — Saul's response would necessarily be that of his ordinary state of mind. David chose Rosh Chodesh in particular because on the Sabbath or on a festival it would be inappropriate to hide in the fields (*Ahavas Yehonasan*).

Alternatively, David chose to absent himself on a festive Rosh Chodesh feast

1. Whether or not David was guilty of believing *lashon hara,* evil gossip or slander, is a matter of dispute (see *Shabbos* 56b).

2. This was the case even if David was not guilty of believing a slanderous report (*Mussar HaNeviim*).

17 Jonathan again adjured David because of his love
for him, for he loved him as he loved himself.
18 Jonathan said to him, "Tomorrow is the New
Moon, and you will be remembered because your
seat will be empty. 19 For three days you must re-
main far down and come to the place where you hid

as opposed to an ordinary weekday meal. Had he missed a weekly meal, Saul might have assumed that he was fasting. However, fasting is prohibited on Rosh Chodesh, and so Saul would recognize that David was purposely staying away (*Ahavas Yehonasan*).

וְנִפְקַדְתָּ כִּי יִפָּקֵד מוֹשָׁבֶךָ — *And you will be remembered because your seat will be empty.*

Jonathan here briefly reviewed David's idea for arousing Saul's reaction before going on to suggest how he intended to relay that to David (*Abarbanel*).

Mishbetzos Zahav suggests that in his present statement, Jonathan granted David the authorization to leave that David had previously requested (v. 5).

Were someone else to take David's seat, his absence might not appear particularly significant. But, the verse points out, his seat would be left vacant. That would indicate that people were refraining from sitting in it in order to accord David honor. If Saul interpreted that as being the honor that was due to an anticipated future king, he would grow angry (*Ahavas Yehonasan*).

The words וְנִפְקַדְתָּ and יִפָּקֵד apparently share the same root, פקד. Yet *Rashi* points out that they are translated differently — as, respectively, *will be remembered* and *will be empty*. We similarly find the root of this word used in the sense of *remembered* in the verse וַה׳ פָּקַד אֶת שָׂרָה — *HASHEM remembered Sarah* (*Genesis* 21:1), and in the sense of *empty*, or *lacking*, in the verse וְלֹא־נִפְקַד מִמֶּנּוּ אִישׁ — *and not a man is lacking from it* (as in *Numbers* 31:49).

19. וְשִׁלַּשְׁתָּ תֵּרֵד מְאֹד — *For three days you must remain far down.*

This translation is in accord with the interpretation of *Radak*. *Rashi*, on the other hand, reads the verses's opening phrase as *on the third day you must descend deeply*. That is to say, initially David must take reasonable pains to hide. On the third day, however, when Saul's men would be most likely to seek him since he had been "away" on Rosh Chodesh and had not yet returned, he must conceal himself carefully.

Abarbanel suggests that during his initial days of hiding David could remain in areas when he would have access to food and drink. Afterward, he would have to take greater precautions.

The commentators seem to disagree regarding which were the *three days*. For example, if they were speaking on Sunday, Jonathan may have been rerferring to Tuesday, the third day (see *Rashi*). Or he may have meant Wednesday, three full days after their conversation (*Mahari Kara, Abarbanel*; see *Radak* and comm. to v. 35).

Malbim renders וְשִׁלַּשְׁתָּ not as *for three days* but rather as *divide into three* (see *Deuteronomy* 19:3, *Makkos* 9b, for a similar translation), i.e., Jonathan told David to travel a third of the distance of the field every day.

Ahavas Yehonasan homiletically interprets this passage as meaning that after the three generations of David, Solomon, and Rehoboam, David's glory would sharply descend, because at that time his kingdom would be split. (Possibly, Jonathan alluded to this idea in conjunction with his previous comment that Hashem would avenge David's breach of this covenant, a comment that prophetically alluded to David's depriving Mephibosheth of half of his estate — see above, v. 16.)

כ בְּיוֹם הַמַּעֲשֶׂה וְיָשַׁבְתָּ אֵצֶל הָאֶבֶן הָאָזֶל: וַאֲנִי
שְׁלֹשֶׁת הַחִצִּים צִדָּה אוֹרֶה לְשַׁלַּח־לִי לְמַטָּרָה:
כא וְהִנֵּה אֶשְׁלַח אֶת־הַנַּעַר לֵךְ מְצָא אֶת־הַחִצִּים
אִם־אָמֹר אֹמַר לַנַּעַר הִנֵּה הַחִצִּים | מִמְּךָ וָהֵנָּה

Targum renders the phrase תֵּרֵד מְאֹד not as *you are to remain far down* but as *you will be heavily sought.*

Radak clarifies that after he hid for three days, Saul's men would lose respect for David, he would go *far down* in their estimation of him — and then they might feel justified in hunting him down without restraint in order to kill him. Thus, Jonathan was saying that he would easily be able to sense their feelings toward David.

וּבָאתָ אֶל־הַמָּקוֹם אֲשֶׁר־נִסְתַּרְתָּ שָּׁם בְּיוֹם הַמַּעֲשֶׂה — *Come to the place where you hid on the day of the incident.*

Simply understood, this refers to the previous incident in which David hid from Saul, at which time Jonathan's words persuaded Saul to swear that he would not harm David (19:1-6). Jonathan now told David to hide in the same place that he had hidden then (*Radak, Ralbag*).

According to *Metzudos,* בְּיוֹם הַמַּעֲשֶׂה should be rendered *on the day of implementation.* Today David should implement the first phase of the plan by hiding; on the third day, he should hide even more deeply.

Rashi states that with the phrase יוֹם הַמַּעֲשֶׂה Jonathan was referring to the present day as a *day of work,* in contrast to the next day — which, as Rosh Chodesh, was not a day of work.

Although the Torah does not prohibit work on Rosh Chodesh, women traditionally did no work on that day; they observed Rosh Chodesh as their holiday to commemorate that the women of the generation of the Exodus did not contribute their jewelry to the making of the Golden Calf (*Rashi* on *Megillah* 22b).

Men, too, would apparently curtail their activities on Rosh Chodesh. *Radak* states that they would refrain from work in order to attend the Temple *mussaf*-offering and worship Hashem. Work was not halachically forbidden, but it was customary not to work (*Tosafos, Shabbos* 24a). However, *Mordechai* (to *Megillah* #806), states that it is forbidden for men to engage in heavy agricultural labor.

Thus, Jonathan stated that David would have to hide carefully on the days preceding and following Rosh Chodesh, when workers were in the fields, but on Rosh Chodesh itself, when the fields would be empty, he need not take such pains (*Daas Sofrim*).

וְיָשַׁבְתָּ אֵצֶל הָאֶבֶן הָאָזֶל — *And stay near the marker stone.*

The word אֶזֶל — translated here as *marker* — means *go,* or *travel* in Aramaic, and is occasionally found in this sense in Hebrew (see, for instance, *Job* 14:11) (*Metzudos*).

Targum translates אֶבֶן הָאָזֶל as *the stone on the sign*; apparently, this stone was a travelers' landmark (*Rashi*).

Me'am Loez cites two versions: it was a meeting place to which people *went,* or it was marked as a target, as mentioned in the next verse, which was placed on the stone.

20. וַאֲנִי שְׁלֹשֶׁת הַחִצִּים צִדָּה אוֹרֶה — *I will shoot three arrows in that direction.*

Jonathan now began to describe how he would notify David of his father's reaction.

According to most commentators, Jonathan said that if Saul's attitude is positive, he would shoot a arrows that would fall short of the lad and call out,

on the day of the incident, and stay near the marker
stone. [20] *I will shoot three arrows in that direction*
as if I were shooting at a target. [21] *Behold, I will*
then send the lad [saying], 'Go find the arrows.' If
I tell the lad, 'Behold, the arrows are before you!'

"The arrows are before you." If, however, Saul is still angry with David, Jonathan would shoot the arrows past the lad, and call out, *"The arrows are behind you."*

Rashi, however, comments that Jonathan was proposing an omen to determine Hashem's will. He would shoot the arrows without aiming them. If Providence were to direct the lad to search for the arrows far away, that would be an omen that there was nothing to fear and Jonathan would shout that the lad should come closer. That would be a sign from Hashem that it was safe for David to return — even if Saul had reacted angrily to his absence.[1]

שְׁלֹשֶׁת הַחִצִּים — *Three arrows.*

Jonathan basically needed two arrows to convey his message: if Saul reacted positively, Jonathan would make sure to shoot a second arrow closer than the first. If Saul reacted negatively, Jonathan would make sure to shoot a second arrow farther than the first. The third arrow was simply a backup in case the second arrow did not land correctly (*Metzudos*).

Saul was surrounded by slanderers, who were liable to turn him against David. According to *Malbim,* the arrow is an allusion to a slanderous tongue, as in the verse, חֵץ שָׁחוּט לְשׁוֹנָם, *Their tongue is like a drawn arrow* (*Jeremiah* 9:7). The Talmud (*Arachin* 15b) states that a slanderer causes the deaths of three people: the subject of the slander, the recipient of the slander, and the slanderer. (The classic example of this was Doeg HaAdomi, whose slanderous report about the Kohanim of Nob [Ch. 22] caused the deaths of himself, of the Kohanim, and eventually of Saul.) The three victims of slander are represented by the three arrows.

צִדָּה אוֹרֶה — *I will shoot ... in that direction.*

The root of צִדָּה — *in that direction* — is צַד, meaning *side. Rashi* understands the suffix ה to mean *to the,* i.e., it is equivalent to the prefix ל. Thus, the word צִדָּה means *to the side* — i.e., *to the side [of the stone].*

According to *Radak,* the letter ה should be read as though it has a מַפִּיק ה (a dot in the letter), in which case it means *its.* Thus, the word צִדָּה means *to its side* — [i.e., to the side of the stone].

Malbim states that Jonathan shot the arrow slightly to the side of the stone so that the lad would not notice David, who was hiding next to it.

Targum renders the phrase צִדָּה אוֹרֶה as *I will shoot with a bow,* apparently associating the word צִדָּה with צָד, which means *to hunt,* and which may be used as a noun to mean *a bow.*

21. אִם אָמֹר אֹמַר לַנַּעַר הִנֵּה הַחִצִּים מִמְּךָ וָהֵנָּה — *If I tell the lad, "Behold, the arrows are before you."*

If Jonathan wished David to return, he would shoot the arrows short of the lad and tell him to come closer. If he wished David to flee, he would shoot the arrows past the lad and tell him to go further (*Malbim*).

1. A discussion about the halachic permissibility of interpreting omens is presented above, 14:10.

קָחֶנּוּ | וָבֹאָה כִּי־שָׁלוֹם לְךָ וְאֵין דָּבָר חַי־
כב יהוה: וְאִם־כֹּה אֹמַר לָעֶלֶם הִנֵּה הַחִצִּים מִמְּךָ
כג וָהָלְאָה לֵךְ כִּי שִׁלַּחֲךָ יהוה: וְהַדָּבָר אֲשֶׁר
דִּבַּרְנוּ אֲנִי וָאָתָּה הִנֵּה יהוה בֵּינִי וּבֵינְךָ עַד־
כד עוֹלָם: וַיִּסָּתֵר דָּוִד בַּשָּׂדֶה וַיְהִי
כה הַחֹדֶשׁ וַיֵּשֶׁב הַמֶּלֶךְ °עַל־ הַלֶּחֶם לֶאֱכוֹל: וַיֵּשֶׁב °אֶל־ ק׳
הַמֶּלֶךְ עַל־מוֹשָׁבוֹ כְּפַעַם | בְּפַעַם אֶל־מוֹשַׁב
הַקִּיר וַיָּקָם יְהוֹנָתָן וַיֵּשֶׁב אַבְנֵר מִצַּד שָׁאוּל

Here, when he refers to good news, Jonathan uses the double expression אָמֹר אֹמַר. In the next verse, however, when he refers to bad news, he uses a single verb. *Kli Yakar* explains that the double verb implies a profusion of speech — something appropriate when someone enthusiastically conveys good news (see *Pesachim* 3b).

קָחֶנּוּ וָבֹאָה — *Then you yourself may take the arrows and return.*

The word קָחֶנּוּ means *take it* or *take him.* We follow *Rashi*'s understanding that Jonathan was telling David that if everything went well, David could gather the [bundle of] arrows himself.

According to *Radak,* however, Jonathan told David that he could *take* the lad and return with him. *Daas Sofrim* explains that Jonathan suggested that David come out from hiding and greet the lad before he would have a chance to notice that David had been concealed.

Radak suggests in his father's name that Jonathan was telling David to *take,* follow, this guideline and return.

Metzudos comments that even if Saul were to react positively, Jonathan did not want to call David out of hiding himself, because then it would be apparent that he and David had engineered a system of secret communication.

חַי ה' — *As* HASHEM *lives.*

Jonathan swore that he would not mislead David but send a message that all was well only if he were sure that this was the case (*Radak*).

22. וְאִם־כֹּה אֹמַר לָעֶלֶם — *But if I say thus to the youth.*

In the previous verse, which discussed the situation in which David may return, Jonathan spoke of the attendant as a נַעַר, a *lad.* In the present verse, which speaks of a situation in which David must flee, the attendant is referred to as an עֶלֶם, a word that connotes alacrity. If David had to run away, he would have to do so expeditiously (*Malbim*).

Kli Yakar states that the word נַעַר can refer to an adult, whereas the word עֶלֶם refers solely to a young boy. Thus, if Jonathan's news was good, he would bring an older attendant; if not, he would take along a boy who would not understand Jonathan's intent. In this regard, the word עֶלֶם is related to הַעֲלָמָה, *concealment* (see above, 17:56); i.e., the matter would remain concealed.

לֵךְ כִּי שִׁלַּחֲךָ ה' — *Then go, for [this is a signal that]* HASHEM *has sent you away.*

In that case, Hashem would be telling David to escape (*Rashi*). Since this would be a directive from Hashem, it would be for David's own good (*Metzudos*).[1]

Targum renders כִּי שִׁלַּחֲךָ ה' as *because* HASHEM *has saved you.*

23. Even if David were forced to flee,

then you yourself may take the arrows and return,
for it is well with you and there is no concern, as
HASHEM lives. [22] *But if I say thus to the boy, 'Behold,*
the arrows are beyond you!' then go, for [this is a
signal that] HASHEM has sent you away. [23] *But this*
matter of which we have spoken, I and you — be-
hold, HASHEM remains [witness] between me and
you forever."
[24] *David concealed himself in the field. It was the*
New Moon and the king sat at the meal to eat. [25] *The*
king sat at his seat as at other times, on the seat by
the wall; Jonathan stood, Abner sat at Saul's side,

Hashem was witness that this covenant of friendship would remain eternally valid.

◆§ The Test, and Saul's Reaction

25. אֶל־מוֹשַׁב הַקִּיר — *On the seat by the wall.*

Saul sat with his back to the wall, on the most prominent seat in the room (*Abarbanel*).

According to *Ahavas Yehonasan,* Saul knew prophetically that he would be killed, and thus he never left his back unprotected.

וַיָּקָם יְהוֹנָתָן וַיֵּשֶׁב אַבְנֵר מִצַּד שָׁאוּל — *Jonathan stood, Abner sat at Saul's side.*

It was not considered respectful for a son to recline next to his father. Therefore, usually David would sit next to Saul, Jonathan next to David, and Abner next to Jonathan.

Now Jonathan left David's seat vacant and sat in his own place. When it was clear that David was not coming, Jonathan switched seats with Abner so as not to sit next to his father. Of course, Jonathan knew that David would not attend, but he could not reveal that, so he first sat in his customary seat and then changed places with Abner (*Abarbanel*).

Malbim adds that Jonathan switched seats in order to draw Saul's attention to David's absence.

According to *Radak,* Jonathan did not want to sit next to his father because he feared that Saul would grow enraged at David's absence, suspect Jonathan of collusion, and strike him.

וַיִּפָּקֵד מְקוֹם דָּוִד — *And David's seat was empty.*

According to *Ahavas Yehonasan,* Abner too avoided sitting in David's seat. He did so out of respect for David because he knew that David would eventually reign.

1. When Rav Elyah Meir Bloch, Rosh Yeshivah of the Telshe Yeshivah, escaped war-ravaged Europe, he came to America and immediately began building a yeshivah there. Many people expressed surprise that a fugitive had the tenacity to do this. R' Bloch responded as follows. When Jonathan told David that if his father intended to harm him he should leave, Jonathan did not use the word בְּרַח, *escape,* but rather לֵךְ, *go.* This implied that David had no reason to flee anxiously and hastily. Until this point, Hashem had wanted him to be here; now Hashem was sending him elsewhere. So too, said R' Bloch, he was not a "fugitive." Until now, Hashem had wanted him to have a yeshivah in Telshe; now He wished him to have a yeshivah in America (heard from R' Mattisyahu Salomon).

כו וַיִּפָּקֵד מְקוֹם דָּוִד: וְלֹא־דִבֶּר שָׁאוּל מְאוּמָה בַּיּוֹם
הַהוּא כִּי אָמַר מִקְרֶה הוּא בִּלְתִּי טָהוֹר הוּא כִּי־לֹא
כז טָהוֹר: וַיְהִי מִמָּחֳרַת הַחֹדֶשׁ הַשֵּׁנִי וַיִּפָּקֵד
מְקוֹם דָּוִד וַיֹּאמֶר שָׁאוּל אֶל־יְהוֹנָתָן בְּנוֹ מַדּוּעַ
לֹא־בָא בֶן־יִשַׁי גַּם־תְּמוֹל גַּם־הַיּוֹם אֶל־הַלָּחֶם:

26. כִּי אָמַר מִקְרֶה הוּא בִּלְתִּי טָהוֹר הוּא — *For he thought, "It is a coincidence; he must be impure."*

The Talmud (*Pesachim* 3a) cites this verse as an example of the extent to which Scripture will go to avoid unpleasant expressions such as טָמֵא, *contaminated,* stating instead, בִּלְתִּי טָהוֹר הוּא כִּי־לֹא טָהוֹר, an additional sixteen letters.

Saul did not make an issue over David's absence the first day, because he presumed that David had experienced a seminal emission, and was thus ritually impure. In that case, David would not attend for one of two reasons. Coming to the king's table in such a state would have been disrespectful; or it was inappropriate for people who were ritually impure to eat together with others who were pure (*Radak*).

Although it is halachically permitted to eat non-sanctified food in a state of ritual impurity, possibly the men of Saul's court refrained from doing so (see *Midrash Shocher Tov* 7:2, *Bamidbar Rabbah* 11:3). Alternatively, portions of Rosh Chodesh sacrifices were served at this meal; thus, only those in a state of ritual purity could partake of them (*Radak*).

Saul thought that David had experienced a seminal emission either because he had cohabited with his wife (*Ralbag*) or because he had had a nocturnal emission (*Rashi*).

Either way, this seems to indicate Saul's negative judgment of David — viewing him either as a man excessively drawn to engaging in marital relations (*Ralbag*) or as someone who entertained licentious thoughts (*Abarbanel*).

כִּי אָמַר מִקְרֶה הוּא בִּלְתִּי טָהוֹר הוּא כִּי־לֹא טָהוֹר — *For he thought, "It is a coincidence; he must be impure, for he has not been cleansed."*

A more literal translation of this phrase is *For he thought, "It is a coincidence; he is not pure, for he is not pure." Rabbeinu Yeshayah* thus concludes that this phrase is redundant.

Our translation follows *Metzudos,* who renders the latter wording כִּי־לֹא טָהוֹר as *for he is not yet purified.* That is to say, he has not yet immersed himself in a ritual bath.

Pnei Yehoshua (to *Pesachim* 3a) suggests that according to the view that the meat of Rosh Chodesh sacrifices was being served, even if David immersed in a ritual bath, he would still have had to wait until nighttime to join the feast. Thus, כִּי־לֹא טָהוֹר means, *for [although he had immersed] he was not yet [halachically] pure.*

Abarbanel suggests that the latter iteration of לֹא טָהוֹר refers to Saul's reading of David's general disposition. Saul thought that David was impure because he in general entertained impure thoughts.

Radak reads the word בִּלְתִּי — which we translate as *not* — as *some other [matter],* and parses the words to make the phrase מִקְרֶה הוּא בִּלְתִּי: *it is a coincidence [that he was busy with some] other matter.* Thus, the verse may be read as follows: *[Saul] thought that it was a coincidence [that David was busy with] some other matter, [and] he was pure, or possibly he was [not busy but was] not pure.*

27. וַיְהִי מִמָּחֳרַת הַחֹדֶשׁ הַשֵּׁנִי — *It was the day after the New Moon, the second [day of the month].*

More literally, this phrase may be read as *the day after the second month,*

and David's seat was empty. 26 *Saul said nothing*
on that day, for he thought, "It is a coincidence;
he must be impure, for he has not been cleansed."
27 *It was the day after the New Moon, the second*
[day of the month], and David's place was empty.
So Saul said to Jonathan, his son, "Why did the
son of Jesse not come to the feast either yesterday
or today?"

which is perplexing. Alternatively, it may be read as *the day after the second day of Rosh Chodesh.* This too is difficult, for it indicates that the episode presently being described took place on the third day [of the month,] which is inconsistent with the end of the verse.

Our translation — *It was the day after the New Moon, the second [day of the month]* — follows *Rashi,* who reads the word הַשֵּׁנִי — *the second* — as separate from the phrase מִמָּחֳרַת הַחֹדֶשׁ, *it was the day after the New Moon.* According to this reading, there was only one day of Rosh Chodesh.

Targum, however, parses the verse by placing a pause after the word מִמָּחֳרַת, and thus reads the phrase as, *It was on the next day, on the extended second day of Rosh Chodesh.* This means that, uncertain as to when Rosh Chodesh would be declared, Saul and his men celebrated the Rosh Chodesh feast on the 30th day of the month that was ending. When they received no word that the court had designated that day as Rosh Chodesh, they knew that the next day would be Rosh Chodesh, and so they celebrated this next day with a Rosh Chodesh feast as well.

From this verse, the *Talmud Yerushalmi* derives the practice of celebrating two days of Rosh Chodesh (*Taanis* 4:3). That is the precedent for the current practice of observing two days of Rosh Chodesh when the month coming to an end consists of 30 days.

וַיֹּאמֶר שָׁאוּל אֶל־יְהוֹנָתָן בְּנוֹ — *So Saul said to Jonathan, his son.*

The seemingly superfluous phrase *his son* implies that Saul felt slighted that his own son was apparently not concerned for his father's honor, in contrast to David, whom Saul referred to as בֶן־יִשַׁי, *son of Jesse,* implying that David saw himself as obligated to honor his father by attending his father's feast (*Kli Yakar*).

Daas Sofrim suggests that Saul was worried about his son-in-law David, so he questioned Jonathan, who would be expected to know of David's whereabouts.

בֶן־יִשַׁי — *The son of Jesse.*

Saul referred to David only by his father's name, thus deriding David as someone whose only claim to distinction was that his father was a righteous man (*Ahavas Yehonasan*).

Other commentators state, based on a Midrash, that in not referring to David by name Saul signified his hatred of him. Referring to someone simply as *the son of So-and-so* was a common formula of disparagement (see 10:11, where Saul is referred to as *the son of Kish*). Both Saul and Doeg (below, 22:19) referred to David in this way. David lamented this treatment of himself in the verse, בְּנֵי אִישׁ עַד־מֶה כְבוֹדִי לִכְלִמָּה — *O sons of men, how long will you put my honor to shame [by not using my name]* (*Psalms* 4:3, see *Rashi* ad loc.; *Pesikta Rabbasi* 33:1; *Abarbanel*).

גַּם־תְּמוֹל גַּם־הַיּוֹם אֶל־הַלָּחֶם — *Either yesterday or today.*

According to the view that [there

כח וַיַּ֧עַן יְהוֹנָתָ֛ן אֶת־שָׁא֖וּל נִשְׁאֹ֨ל נִשְׁאַ֥ל דָּוִ֛ד מֵעִמָּדִ֖י
כט עַד־בֵּ֥ית לָֽחֶם׃ וַיֹּ֡אמֶר שַׁלְּחֵ֣נִי נָ֠א כִּ֣י זֶ֨בַח מִשְׁפָּחָ֜ה
לָ֜נוּ בָּעִ֗יר וְה֤וּא צִוָּה־לִי֙ אָחִ֔י וְעַתָּ֗ה אִם־מָצָ֤אתִי
חֵן֙ בְּעֵינֶ֔יךָ אִמָּ֥לְטָה נָּ֖א וְאֶרְאֶ֣ה אֶת־אֶחָ֑י עַל־כֵּ֣ן
ל לֹא־בָ֔א אֶל־שֻׁלְחַ֖ן הַמֶּֽלֶךְ׃ וַיִּֽחַר־
אַ֤ף שָׁאוּל֙ בִּיה֣וֹנָתָ֔ן וַיֹּ֣אמֶר ל֔וֹ בֶּֽן־נַעֲוַ֖ת הַמַּרְד֑וּת

was one day of Rosh Chodesh and] the events described in this verse occurred on the following day, Saul argued that if for some reason David had not been able to come on Rosh Chodesh, he should have come today instead (*Metzudos*).[1]

28. נִשְׁאֹל נִשְׁאַל דָּוִד מֵעִמָּדִי עַד־בֵּית לָחֶם — *David asked me for permission to go to Bethlehem.*

As mentioned above (v. 5), Jonathan apparently had the authority to give David permission to leave. He now informed his father that he had granted David that permission (*Radak*).

Our Sages teach that Jonathan was a chief justice (*Moed Katan* 26b). *Mishbetzos Zahav* suggests that David asked Jonathan whether he was halachically permitted to honor his father [by attending the family feast] at the expense of the king's honor, i.e., because he would have to miss the royal feast. *Mishbetzos Zahav* cites the view of the *Turei Even* (to *Megillah* 29a) that since a person who learns Torah is exempt from the king's service, certainly a person engaged in a mitzvah that exempts him from learning Torah is exempt from the king's service, and honoring one's parents is such a mitzvah.

נִשְׁאֹל נִשְׁאַל דָּוִד — *David asked me.*

Saul did not want to refer to David by name. By contrast, although Jonathan could easily have referred to David by the pronoun *he*, he went out of his way to pronounce David's name. This expressed Jonathan's love for David, which Saul sensed [and resented] (*Chomas Anach*).

The phrase נִשְׁאֹל נִשְׁאַל דָּוִד is unusual in that it employs the reflexive verb. As such, *Radak* explains, it indicates that David had requested permission *for himself* to leave.

Me'am Loez states that Jonathan preferred this wording to the more conventional שָׁאוֹל שָׁאַל. That phrase sounds similar to the name of his father, Saul. A person is forbidden to call his parents by their first names, and Jonathan thought that even addressing his father in language reminiscent of his father's name would be disrespectful.

29. וְהוּא צִוָּה לִי אָחִי — *And he — my brother — has summoned me.*

Jonathan claimed that David had said that Eliab had told him to attend the

1. An analog to the phrase גַּם־תְּמוֹל גַּם־הַיּוֹם אֶל־הַלָּחֶם, *either yesterday or today to the feast,* may be found in *Exodus* (5:14), when Pharaoh's taskmasters asked, מַדּוּעַ לֹא כִלִּיתֶם חָקְכֶם לִלְבֹּן כִּתְמוֹל שִׁלְשֹׁם גַּם־תְּמוֹל גַּם־הַיּוֹם, *Why did you not complete your requirement to make bricks, as yesterday and before yesterday, either yesterday or today?* (see *Baal HaTurim* ad loc.).

Meishiv el Dal associates the two verses homiletically. Anyone who questions why Messiah — i.e., the son of Jesse — has not yet come must consider that the reason is that he himself has not completed his task to repent (the Hebrew word for לִלְבֹּן, *to make bricks,* may be read as לְלַבֵּן, *to whiten,* i.e., to repent) (cited by *Mishbetzos Zahav*).

[28]*Jonathan answered Saul, "David asked me for*
permission to go to Bethlehem. [29]*He said, 'Please*
grant me leave, for we have a family feast in the
city, and he — my brother — has summoned me;
so now, if I have found favor in your eyes, please
let me be excused so that I may see my broth-
ers.' That is why he did not come to the king's
table."

[30]*Saul's anger flared up at Jonathan, and he said*
to him, "Son of a pervertedly rebellious woman!

family feast, and the halachah obligates a person to obey his older brother (see *Kesubos* 103a; *Shulchan Aruch Yoreh Deah* 240:22; *Radak*).

There is a dispute among the halachic authorities whether a person is obligated to obey any older brother or only the oldest brother.

Although this verse refers generally to אָחִי — *my brother* — *Rashi* and *Radak* interpret that to mean specifically Eliab, David's eldest brother. From this, *Shevus Yaakov* (*Teshuvos* Vol. III #34) derives support for his view that this halachah applies only to one's oldest brother.

Radak apparently contradicts himself, for he first states that David had an obligation to heed his brother's command, but he then states that obeying an older brother is no more than customary (see *Kli Yakar* and *Kehillas Yaakov*). *Nachalas Shimon* addresses this by suggesting that in the time of David the practice of obeying one's older brother was no more than a custom; later on, it became formalized as a Rabbinic obligation (see *Mishbetzos Zahav*).[1]

Considering that Jonathan was fabricating this entire story, why didn't he just claim that David's father had commanded him to come? (*Nachalas Shimon*).

Kli Yakar provides a novel answer to this question. With the words וְהוּא צִוָּה־לִי אָחִי — *and he — my brother — summoned me* — Jonathan was not quoting David. Rather, he was speaking for himself, referring to David as his *brother*. He was stating that David had asked Jonathan to take his place and perform all of his regular offices while he was away.

אִמָּלְטָה נָּא — *Please let me be excused.*

David, Jonathan reported, had asked to be excused from serving the king for a short period of time (*Radak*).

Rabbeinu Yeshayah adds that the word אִמָּלְטָה implies speed. That is to say, David would hurry home and back.

וְאֶרְאֶה אֶת־אֶחָי — *So that I may see my brothers.*

Jonathan emphasized that David did not speak about going to eat and enjoy the feast but about going to spend time with his brothers (*Abarbanel*).

30. וַיִּחַר־אַף שָׁאוּל בִּיהוֹנָתָן — *Saul's anger flared up at Jonathan.*

According to *Daas Sofrim*, Saul was upset because he felt that only he, not Jonathan, was authorized to grant David permission to leave.

בֶּן־נַעֲוַת הַמַּרְדּוּת — *Son of a pervertedly rebellious woman!*

In his fury, Saul insulted Jonathan by using a derogatory epithet, implying that his mother was to blame for his conduct. To understand this epithet, we must translate each word; there is a variety of interpretations.

1. If *Nachalas Shimon* is correct, *Radak* would agree with the view that the obligation to obey an older brother is of Rabbinic origin (although it is associated with a Torah verse).

הֲלוֹא יָדַעְתִּי כִּי־בֹחֵר אַתָּה לְבֶן־יִשַׁי לְבָשְׁתְּךָ
לא וּלְבֹשֶׁת עֶרְוַת אִמֶּךָ׃ כִּי כָל־הַיָּמִים אֲשֶׁר בֶּן־יִשַׁי
חַי עַל־הָאֲדָמָה לֹא תִכּוֹן אַתָּה וּמַלְכוּתֶךָ וְעַתָּה
לב שְׁלַח וְקַח אֹתוֹ אֵלַי כִּי בֶן־מָוֶת הוּא׃ וַיַּעַן

Most commentators associate the word הַמַּרְדּוּת with the word מֶרֶד, *rebellion.* The word נַעֲוַת, *pervertedly*, is related to the word עוות, which means *evil, perversion,* or *corruption.* Thus, Saul claimed that just as Jonathan's mother was rebellious, so was Jonathan in that he showed love to Saul's enemy (*Radak*).

Malbim states that Saul accused Jonathan of a rebellious perversity. Saul could not understand how Jonathan could rebel (as Saul saw it) in order to place an outsider on the throne at his own expense.

Ralbag associates מַרְדּוּת with רידוי, *discipline.* Saul said that Jonathan was the son of a mother who had failed to discipline him properly. Alternatively, מַרְדּוּת means *rulership.* Saul said that just as Jonathan's mother was not qualified to be the member of a royal family, neither was Jonathan, and that is why he abdicated his right to the throne in favor of David.

Rashi relates the word נַעֲוַת to נע, *mobile*, in the sense of *outward*, and relates the following incident. Following the episode of the Concubine at Gibeah (*Judges* Ch. 21), the men of the tribe of Benjamin were given permission to take as wives young Jewish women who were dancing in the vineyards. Saul was one of the men who went to the vineyards, but he was too bashful to take a wife. Instead, one of the women boldly pursued him and she became Saul's wife and Jonathan's mother. Now, Saul called Jonathan the son of *an outward woman* who deserves to be disciplined.

Alternatively, the word נַעֲוַת may be related to the Aramaic word for *winepress*, which is reminiscent of the vineyard. Thus Saul spoke of the woman whom he had met in the vineyard, who deserved to be disciplined (*Rashi*).

הֲלוֹא יָדַעְתִּי כִּי־בֹחֵר אַתָּה לְבֶן־יִשַׁי לְבָשְׁתְּךָ וּלְבֹשֶׁת עֶרְוַת אִמֶּךָ — *Do I not know that you choose the son of Jesse, to your own shame and to the shame of your mother's nakedness?*

Saul stated that when people saw Jonathan support David, Saul's enemy, they would assume that Jonathan was the issue of an adulterous relationship (*Radak*).

Radak's explanation may be understood in one of two ways. First, people would suspect that Jonathan knew that Saul was not his father, and was for that reason not concerned about Saul's enemies. Second, a child born of an adulterous relationship tends to lack normal, decent sensibilities, and that would explain why Jonathan was seemingly unconcerned about the king's honor.[1]

Abarbanel explains that Saul knew that David would not reign during his own lifetime. Therefore, David's eventual usurpation of the throne would not shame Saul but rather Jonathan and Jonathan's mother (the former queen), who would presumably still be alive at that time.

1. This characterization of the *mamzer* is consistent with the story related in *Bava Basra* (58a) about a man who knew that of the ten sons that his wife bore, only one was his. He died, leaving a will that stated that all of his property should go to his own son. But how could that son be identified? R' Banaah directed all ten sons to strike at their father's grave until he revealed which son he meant to inherit him. Nine of the sons did so, but the tenth refused. R' Banaah declared that this must be the legitimate son, for he [possessed the instincts of decency and thus] could not bring himself to do so (*Mussar HaNeviim*).

Do I not know that you choose the son of Jesse, to your own shame and the shame of your mother's nakedness? [31] For all the days that the son of Jesse is alive on the earth, you and your kingdom will not be established! And now, send and bring him to me, for he is deserving of death!"

Ahavas Yehonasan and *Chomas Anach* present a novel approach to this phrase. The controversy regarding David's legitimacy in regard to his being a descendant of the Moabitess Ruth ended with the conclusion that a Moabitess is permitted to enter the Jewish people. Only male Moabites are prohibited, because the male Moabites in the days when the Jews were in the Wilderness did not come forward to offer the Jews bread and water. However, the female Moabites are not faulted for that, because a woman's place is in the home (see *Yevamos* 77a). Accordingly, Jonathan's support of David indicated that he agreed with this halachic conclusion and endorsed the ideal of woman's modesty. But in so doing, Jonathan would be implicitly criticizing and bringing shame upon his mother, who did not exhibit such a trait of modesty, in that she pursued Saul.

31. כִּי כָל־הַיָּמִים אֲשֶׁר בֶּן־יִשַׁי חַי עַל־הָאֲדָמָה לֹא תִכּוֹן אַתָּה וּמַלְכוּתֶךָ — *For all the days that the son of Jesse is alive on the earth, you and your kingdom will not be established.*

According to *Mishbetzos Zahav,* Saul told Jonathan that even if he became king, neither he nor his kingdom would be secure as long as David remained alive. Jonathan's only hope of surviving was to forfeit the throne.

Kli Yakar explains that Saul was warning Jonathan that he would never be able to rule justly, because he would always have to deal with the nagging worry that a nation displeased with his decisions would choose to replace him with David — and that would be to his shame. (By contrast, when Solomon executed justice for prominent leaders such as Adonijah, Joab, and Shimei, Scripture testifies that וְהַמַּמְלָכָה נָכוֹנָה בְּיַד שְׁלֹמֹה — *The kingdom was thus established in the hand of Solomon* [*I Kings* 2:46].)

וְעַתָּה שְׁלַח וְקַח אֹתוֹ אֵלַי — *And now, send and bring him to me.*

Since Jonathan had authorized David to go, he must bring him back so that Saul may kill him (*Abarbanel*).

כִּי בֶן־מָוֶת הוּא — *For he is deserving of death!*

Mahari Kara says that Saul considered David to be a rebel deserving of death because he had left without proper permission.

Rabbeinu Yeshayah avers that Saul believed that David should be considered a rebel since he was destined to reign and thereby deprive Jonathan of the throne.

According to *Mishbetzos Zahav,* Saul thought that Jonathan had to become king in order to fulfill God's prophecy to Jacob that two kings from the tribe of Benjamin would reign (see *Genesis* 35:11, *Rashi* ad loc.). Foreseeing that David could not become king unless he killed Jonathan, and therefore Jonathan would have to defend himself, Saul calculated that he would prevent this by killing David now, in accord with the principle that *If someone rises to kill you, rise and kill him first* (*Bamidbar Rabbah* 21:4).

We tend to attribute Saul's persecution of David to human foibles such as envy and anger, or to a spirit of melancholy. However, Kabbalah literature present a rational, positive

יְהוֹנָתָן אֶת־שָׁאוּל אָבִיו וַיֹּאמֶר אֵלָיו לָמָּה יוּמַת
לג מֶה עָשָׂה: וַיָּטֶל שָׁאוּל אֶת־הַחֲנִית עָלָיו לְהַכֹּתוֹ
וַיֵּדַע יְהוֹנָתָן כִּי־כָלָה הִיא מֵעִם אָבִיו לְהָמִית
לד אֶת־דָּוִד: וַיָּקָם יְהוֹנָתָן מֵעִם הַשֻּׁלְחָן
בָּחֳרִי־אָף וְלֹא־אָכַל בְּיוֹם־הַחֹדֶשׁ הַשֵּׁנִי לֶחֶם כִּי
לה נֶעְצַב אֶל־דָּוִד כִּי הִכְלִמוֹ אָבִיו: וַיְהִי

explanation for Saul's conduct. The nature of that analysis and its underlying concepts require an understanding of Kabbalah and is beyond the scope of this commentary. A short synopsis may be found in *Mishbetzos Zahav*, based on *Leshem Shevo V'Achlamah.*

32. *Mahari Kara* understands Jonathan to be saying that since he was the one who had given David permission to leave, he and not David was at fault.

According to those commentators who state that Saul considered David to be a rebel because he aspired to be king, Jonathan rejoined that David was not to blame if Hashem had chosen him (*Abarbanel*).

Daas Sofrim adds that whereas Saul wished to kill David for what he believed David would do later on (see *Mishbetzos Zahav* above), Jonathan argued that a person could not be judged for his future actions.

33. וַיָּטֶל שָׁאוּל אֶת־הַחֲנִית עָלָיו לְהַכֹּתוֹ — *Saul hurled his spear at him to strike him.*

Our translation that *Saul hurled* follows *Metzudos*. Targum renders *he raised*, implying that Saul prepared to throw the spear, but did not actually do so.

וַיֵּדַע יְהוֹנָתָן כִּי־כָלָה הִיא מֵעִם אָבִיו לְהָמִית אֶת־דָּוִד — *Jonathan then realized that his father had decided to kill David.*

Jonathan realized that if Saul would attempt to kill him for defending David, he would surely attempt to kill David himself (*Abarbanel*).[1]

Since this took place on Rosh Chodesh, Saul's behavior could not be attributed to his spirit of melancholy (*Ahavas Yehonasan*).

When Jonathan saw how upset his father was, he no longer attempted to reason with him. The Talmud (*Arachin* 16b) cites three opimions regarding the parameters of the obligation to rebuke a sinner, all of which are based on Jonathan, who had been reproving the king regarding his attitude toward David, and on Saul's angry and potentially violent response. The three opinions are as follows:

❒ One must rebuke until the other person grows very angry.

❒ One must rebuke until the other person curses him [as Saul did when he said that Jonathan's conduct should bring him shame (*Maharsha*)].

❒ One must rebuke until the other person is ready to strike him.

The commentators discuss how the Talmud can derive the laws of rebuke from this episode, which was not merely an instance of rebuke but of an attempt to save someone's life.

Mussar HaNeviim explains that the two are linked. The obligation to save a person's life is based on the verse לֹא תַעֲמֹד עַל־דַּם רֵעֶךָ, *you shall not stand*

1. According to the opinion that a person administering reproof may stop when the other person grows angry, why did Jonathan continue until his father insulted him and attempted to strike him? The Gemara explains that Jonathan went beyond the letter of the law due to his love for David.

[32] *But Jonathan spoke up to his father Saul, and said to him, "Why should he die? What has he done?"*

[33] *Saul hurled the spear at him to strike him. Jonathan then realized that his father had decided to kill David.* [34] *Jonathan arose from the table enraged; he did not partake of food on that second day of the month, for he was saddened over David, and because his father had humiliated him.*

aside while your brother's blood is shed (*Leviticus* 19:16). That verse is also the conceptual source of the obligation to rebuke another Jew (ibid., v. 17), for by rebuking him one is saving his soul. Thus, the same guidelines that apply to saving a life apply to administering rebuke.

Nachalas Shimon states that Jonathan was aware that his rebuke would have no effect on Saul's plans. Nonetheless, the halachah demands that a person administer rebuke even if he knows that it will not be accepted, until one of the three conditions mentioned previously is met (see *Rema, Orach Chaim* 608:2).[1]

34. וַיָּקָם יְהוֹנָתָן מֵעִם הַשֻּׁלְחָן בָּחֳרִי־אָף — *Jonathan arose from the table enraged.*

The phrase מֵעִם הַשֻּׁלְחָן — *from the table* — implies that this confrontation occurred in full view of all of the men attending the feast (*Kli Yakar*).

Mishbetzos Zahav cites the view of *R' M.D. Vali* that Jonathan's intentions were good, because he meant to uphold his pact with David. Nevertheless, because he caused his father pain, he lost the opportunity to conduct his own royal table.

וְלֹא־אָכַל בְּיוֹם־הַחֹדֶשׁ הַשֵּׁנִי לֶחֶם כִּי נֶעְצַב אֶל־דָּוִד כִּי הִכְלִמוֹ אָבִיו — *He did not partake of food on that second day of the month, for he was saddened over David, and because his father had humiliated him.*

Jonathan refused to eat even though that day was — in the opinion of a number of commentators — Rosh Chodesh.

Simply understood, this verse mentions two reasons that Jonathan did not eat. First, he understood that because David was in danger, the two of them would be separated, [and he mourned that eventuality]. Second, his father had humiliated him, first by calling him rebellious and second by hurling the spear at him (*Ralbag, Radak*).

According to *Malbim*, Jonathan was only upset about Saul's condemnation of David. As for the phrase, כִּי הִכְלִמוֹ אָבִיו — *because his father had humiliated him* — that may be translated as *although his father had humiliated him, [that did not bother him].*

Chomas Anach adds that Jonathan could not openly admit that he was upset about his father's condemnation of David, and so he gave the excuse that he refrained from eating because he had been humiliated.

According to *Kli Yakar*, the phrase כִּי הִכְלִמוֹ אָבִיו — *because his father had humiliated him* — means not only that Saul had humiliated Jonathan but that he had humiliated David as well by calling him *son of Jesse* and saying that he deserved to die.

1. For a broader discussion of this topic, the reader is directed to the Talmud and its commentaries, or to *Nachalas Shimon* and *Mishbetzos Zahav*, which discuss this issue at length.

בַּבֹּקֶר וַיֵּצֵא יְהוֹנָתָן הַשָּׂדֶה לְמוֹעֵד דָּוִד וְנַעַר
לו קָטֹן עִמּוֹ: וַיֹּאמֶר לְנַעֲרוֹ רֻץ מְצָא־נָא אֶת־
הַחִצִּים אֲשֶׁר אָנֹכִי מוֹרֶה הַנַּעַר רָץ וְהוּא־יָרָה
לז הַחֵצִי לְהַעֲבִרוֹ: וַיָּבֹא הַנַּעַר עַד־מְקוֹם הַחֵצִי

◆ Jonathan Delivers the Message to David

35. וַיְהִי בַבֹּקֶר וַיֵּצֵא יְהוֹנָתָן הַשָּׂדֶה לְמוֹעֵד דָּוִד — *On the next morning, Jonathan went out to the field for the meeting with David.*

Targum, Rashi, and *Radak* understand לְמוֹעֵד דָּוִד — *for the meeting with David* — to mean *at the time that David had designated.* However, this is perplexing, for David had designated that he and Jonathan should meet in the evening (v. 5), not the morning. Also, in light of the two views regarding which was the third day (see v. 19), we must clarify which morning this verse discusses. Following our abovementioned example that the two friends had met on Sunday, it is apparent from *Mahari Kara* and *Abarbanel* that although David originally proposed that he and Jonathan meet on Tuesday night (v. 5). Jonathan said (v. 19) that they should wait until Wednesday night and David agreed. However, when Saul's attitude became clear to Jonathan on Tuesday, he saw no reason to keep David in suspense. Therefore on Wednesday morning he went to deliver his information to David. Since this occurred on the designated *day* (Wednesday) that Jonathan had called for and that David had accepted, it is accurate to say that this was לְמוֹעֵד דָּוִד, *the time that David had designated.* (See also *Radak*'s citation of *Targum,* v. 19.)

Following *Rashi,* there is no discrepancy between the proposals of David and Jonathan, for both spoke of Tuesday night. Still, Jonathan set out to see him directly after the heated argument with his father, which took place on Tuesday morning.

According to *Malbim,* David and Jonathan had made two agreements. First, Jonathan would inform David of his father's attitude as soon as he could. Independent of that, David would hide until Tuesday evening. Thus, Jonathan came to David on Tuesday morning, and David remained hidden until Tuesday night.

Metzudos states that David and Jonathan had agreed to meet on Tuesday evening. But Jonathan changed his mind and waited until Wednesday morning, because he realized that his going to the field at night would attract attention, whereas his going in the morning, ostensibly to practice archery, would not be viewed askance. Thus, Jonathan did not meet David at the time that David had designated. As for the phrase לְמוֹעֵד דָּוִד, that refers to *the place that David had* designated.

Daas Sofrim, too, translates לְמוֹעֵד as *place* and not *time,* and he adds that David had originally spoken of the entire field where he would be hiding (v. 5). Jonathan then specified the marker stone as the place where they would meet in the evening (v. 19). Since it was now morning Jonathan went to the field, where David was hiding.

וְנַעַר קָטֹן עִמּוֹ — *And a young attendant was with him.*

If Jonathan were to go alone, he would arouse suspicion that he was intending to divulge secrets. Thus, he took along an aide. He made sure that this aide was a young lad who would not detect Jonathan's communication with David. As for onlook-

35 On the next morning, Jonathan went out to the
field for the meeting with David, and a young at-
tendant was with him. 36 He said to his attendant,
"Run, find now the arrows that I shoot." The atten-
dant ran, and he shot the arrow to go beyond him.
37 The attendant arrived at the place of the arrow

ers, they would assume that Jonathan was going to practice archery (*Mahari Kara*).

36. וַיֹּאמֶר לְנַעֲרוֹ רֻץ מְצָא־נָא אֶת־הַחִצִּים אֲשֶׁר אָנֹכִי מוֹרֶה — *He said to his attendant, "Run, find now the arrows that I shoot."*

This verse presents in condensed form Jonathan's instructions to his attendant, leaving out the fact that Jonathan told him that the target was the marker stone and that he should expect [to find] the arrows there (*Ralbag*).

הַנַּעַר רָץ וְהוּא־יָרָה הַחֵצִי לְהַעֲבִרוֹ — *The attendant ran, and he shot the arrow to go beyond him.*

In accordance with Jonathan and David's plans, should Saul prove hostile to David (vs. 20, 21), Jonathan shot the arrow past the lad and yelled loudly enough for David to hear, "The arrow is beyond you" (*Radak*).

According to *Metzudos*, Jonathan first shot one arrow; as the lad ran to recover it, he shot another beyond the first (see *Metzudos* to v. 20).

Rashi states that Jonathan did not aim the arrow at any particular distance but simply let it fly, in order to read its flight as an omen (see v. 20).

Abarbanel (citing *Rambam* in *Moreh Nevuchim* [Part I Ch. 21]) states that לְהַעֲבִרוֹ — lit., *to pass him* — does not mean that the arrows passed the lad, but that the communication between Jonathan and David passed him by. Initially, Jonathan had devised the scheme of shooting the arrows because he was afraid that others might be present, which would make it impossible for him and Jonathan to speak. Now that he saw that only the lad was present, he shot the arrows in order to misdirect his attention and prevent him from knowing that he meant to communicate with David.

Initially, Jonathan had said that he would shoot three arrows. Yet here the verse speaks of הַחֵצִי — *the arrow* — in the singular. *Me'am Loez* explains that initially Jonathan feared the presence of onlookers; thus, he planned to communicate with David solely via the medium of the arrows. Accordingly, he planned to use as many as three, if necessary. However, now that he saw that only his attendant was present, he decided to speak directly with David. Thus, it sufficed to shoot one arrow in order to misdirect the attendant's attention (*Me'am Loez*).

Radak states that at first Jonathan was afraid that other people might arrive, which would prevent him from speaking to David. Therefore, he shot the first arrow and called out to the lad. [After a period of time passed and it was apparent] that no one else would arrive, he went to speak with David.

Mahari Kara (citing his teacher) points out that the description of Jonathan's meeting with David does not indicate that Jonathan explicitly told David about Saul's behavior. Jonathan preferred to let David know solely through the medium of the arrows that things had gone poorly and that he must flee. This is because even when a person is permitted [or obligated] to speak negatively about someone it is preferable to avoid doing so if one can instead transmit the information by al-

אֲשֶׁר יָרָה יְהוֹנָתָן וַיִּקְרָא יְהוֹנָתָן אַחֲרֵי הַנַּעַר
לח וַיֹּאמֶר הֲלוֹא הַחֵצִי מִמְּךָ וָהָלְאָה׃ וַיִּקְרָא
יְהוֹנָתָן אַחֲרֵי הַנַּעַר מְהֵרָה חוּשָׁה אַל־תַּעֲמֹד
°הַחִצִּים ק׳ וַיְלַקֵּט נַעַר יְהוֹנָתָן אֶת־°החצי וַיָּבֹא אֶל־אֲדֹנָיו׃
לט וְהַנַּעַר לֹא־יָדַע מְאוּמָה אַךְ יְהוֹנָתָן וְדָוִד יָדְעוּ
מ אֶת־הַדָּבָר׃ וַיִּתֵּן יְהוֹנָתָן אֶת־כֵּלָיו אֶל־הַנַּעַר
מא אֲשֶׁר־לוֹ וַיֹּאמֶר לוֹ לֵךְ הָבֵיא הָעִיר׃ הַנַּעַר
בָּא וְדָוִד קָם מֵאֵצֶל הַנֶּגֶב וַיִּפֹּל לְאַפָּיו אַרְצָה
וַיִּשְׁתַּחוּ שָׁלֹשׁ פְּעָמִים וַיִּשְּׁקוּ | אִישׁ אֶת־רֵעֵהוּ

lusion — in this case, by shooting the arrow (see *Chofetz Chaim, Hil. Lashon Hara, Klal* 10:2:6, *Be'er Mayim Chaim* #11) (*Kli Yakar*).[1]

37. וַיָּבֹא הַנַּעַר עַד־מְקוֹם הַחֵצִי אֲשֶׁר יָרָה יְהוֹנָתָן — *The attendant arrived at the place of the arrow that Jonathan had shot.*

This verse seems self-contradictory. It relates that the attendant reached the place of the arrow, yet Jonathan's words indicate that the arrow lay beyond him.

Ralbag explains that the attendant arrived at the marker stone, where he *expected* to find the arrow, but Jonathan shot the arrow past that point and sent the attendant to find it.

According to *Metzudos,* Jonathan shot one arrow that the attendant reached, and then shot a subsequent arrow beyond him.

Daas Sofrim reads the verse literally. According to the original plan, the arrow was to be shot over the attendant's head, following which Jonathan would call out that the arrow lay beyond him. As it happened, the lad came upon the arrow immediately. But Jonathan still called out that the arrow lay beyond him in order to convey his message to David.

Ahavas Yehonasan states that when Jonathan saw that the lad reached the arrow with miraculous celerity, he interpreted that as a Divine message to send David on his way as swiftly as possible. Therefore, he decided not to [take the time to] shoot the remaining two arrows.

38. וַיִּקְרָא יְהוֹנָתָן אַחֲרֵי הַנַּעַר מְהֵרָה חוּשָׁה — *Jonathan then called out after the attendant, "Quickly, hurry!"*

Jonathan hurried the attendant so that David could emerge from his hiding place and flee (*Daas Sofrim*).

Malbim suggests that although Jonathan directed these words at his attendant, he also meant David to understand them as applying to him.

וַיְלַקֵּט נַעַר יְהוֹנָתָן אֶת הַחִצִּים — *Jonathan's attendant gathered the arrows.*

The word הַחִצִּים, *the arrows,* is written (*k'siv*) as הַחֵצִי — *the arrow.* Some explain that this draws attention to only one arrow because that was all that was needed to deliver the message, but that Jonathan actually shot three (see *Radak, Kli Yakar, Ta'ama D'Kra*).

1. Similarly Rabbi Yehudah HaNasi would deliver messages to the Roman emperor Antonius in a coded form without explicating them (*Avodah Zarah* 10a), so that no one might overhear them and make trouble.

that Jonathan had shot, and Jonathan called out
after the attendant and said, "Is not the arrow
beyond you?" 38 *Jonathan then called out after*
the attendant, "Quickly, hurry, do not stand
still!" Jonathan's attendant gathered the arrows
and came to his master. 39 *The attendant knew*
nothing; only Jonathan and David understood
the matter. 40 *Jonathan gave his equipment to his*
attendant and said to him, "Go, bring it to the
city."
41 *The attendant went and David stood up*
from near the south [side of the stone], and he
fell on his face to the ground and prostrated
himself three times. Each man kissed the other

Me'am Loez suggests that the lad gathered the three arrows with such alacrity that it seemed as if they were one.

As we have seen, some commentators hold that Jonathan shot only one arrow, but it is not clear how they deal with the *k'ri*, the spoken variant, *arrows*.

39. וְהַנַּעַר לֹא־יָדַע מְאוּמָה — *The attendant knew nothing.*

He did not realize that Jonathan had delivered a message via the medium of the arrows (*Metzudos*).

40. כֵּלָיו — *His equipment.*

This *equipment* is a reference to Jonathan's bow and arrows (*Radak*).

41. הַנַּעַר בָּא וְדָוִד קָם — *The attendant went and David stood up.*

The phrase, הַנַּעַר בָּא — translated here as *the attendant went* — literally means *the attendant arrived.* According to *Kehillas Yaakov*, David was afraid that when he emerged the attendant would notice him. Therefore, he waited for the amount of time that, he estimated, it would take the attendant to reach the city, and then he emerged. This verse testifies that his assessment was accurate: *when the attendant arrived [in the city], David stood up* (*Kehillas Yaakov*).

וְדָוִד קָם מֵאֵצֶל הַנֶּגֶב — *David stood up from near the south [side of the stone].*

Jonathan had made the target on the north side of the stone and told David to hide at the south side so that the attendant would not see him (*Radak*).

Ahavas Yehonasan suggests that David traveled south to fulfill the advice of the Sages that a person who wishes to grow wise should turn to the south (*Bava Basra* 25b).

וַיִּשְׁתַּחוּ שָׁלֹשׁ פְּעָמִים — *And prostrated himself three times.*

Abarbanel states when a person approaches a king he should bow three times: first upon seeing him, second while walking toward him, and third when he arrives.

וַיִּשְּׁקוּ אִישׁ אֶת־רֵעֵהוּ — *Each man kissed the other.*

They kissed each other because they found the idea of parting so difficult (*Abarbanel*).

כ/מב מב וַיִּבְכּוּ֙ אִ֣ישׁ אֶת־רֵעֵ֔הוּ עַד־דָּוִ֖ד הִגְדִּֽיל׃ וַיֹּ֧אמֶר
יְהוֹנָתָ֛ן לְדָוִ֖ד לֵ֣ךְ לְשָׁל֑וֹם אֲשֶׁר֩ נִשְׁבַּ֨עְנוּ שְׁנֵ֜ינוּ
אֲנַ֗חְנוּ בְּשֵׁ֤ם יהוה֙ לֵאמֹ֔ר יהוה֩ יִהְיֶ֨ה ׀ בֵּינִ֜י וּבֵינֶ֗ךָ
כא/א־ג א וּבֵ֥ין זַרְעִ֛י וּבֵ֥ין זַרְעֲךָ֖ עַד־עוֹלָֽם׃ וַיָּ֖קָם
ב וַיֵּלַ֑ךְ וִיהוֹנָתָ֖ן בָּ֥א הָעִֽיר׃ וַיָּבֹ֤א דָוִד֙ נֹ֔בֶה אֶל־
אֲחִימֶ֖לֶךְ הַכֹּהֵ֑ן וַיֶּחֱרַ֨ד אֲחִימֶ֜לֶךְ לִקְרַ֣את
דָּוִ֗ד וַיֹּ֤אמֶר לוֹ֙ מַדּ֤וּעַ אַתָּה֙ לְבַדֶּ֔ךָ וְאִ֖ישׁ אֵ֥ין
ג אִתָּֽךְ׃ וַיֹּ֨אמֶר דָּוִ֜ד לַאֲחִימֶ֣לֶךְ הַכֹּהֵ֗ן הַמֶּ֜לֶךְ
צִוַּ֣נִי דָבָר֒ וַיֹּ֣אמֶר אֵלַ֗י אִ֣ישׁ אַל־יֵ֤דַע מְא֙וּמָה֙
אֶת־הַדָּבָ֛ר אֲשֶׁר־אָנֹכִ֥י שֹׁלֵֽחֲךָ֖ וַאֲשֶׁ֣ר צִוִּיתִ֑ךָ

וַיִּבְכּוּ אִישׁ אֶת רֵעֵהוּ עַד דָּוִד הִגְדִּיל — *And they wept with each other, until David [wept] greatly.*

According to *Radak*, David wept more than Jonathan did.

Ralbag explains that in his fear of Saul David wept more than he should have. Seeing that, Jonathan urged him to leave.

According to *Malbim*, David raised his voice in grief, and Jonathan urged him to go before he was overheard.

42. אֲשֶׁר נִשְׁבַּעְנוּ שְׁנֵינוּ אֲנַחְנוּ בְּשֵׁם ה׳ לֵאמֹר ה׳ יִהְיֶה בֵּינִי וּבֵינֶךָ וּבֵין זַרְעִי וּבֵין זַרְעֲךָ עַד־עוֹלָם — *[Regarding this oath] that the two of us have sworn in the Name of HASHEM — saying, "HASHEM shall be [a witness] between me and you, and between my offspring and your offspring" — [that shall be] forever.*

Words seem to be missing from this cryptic statement. *Targum* and *Rashi* render *regarding the oath that we have sworn* (above, v. 23) *HASHEM shall be witness forever.*

Radak reads it as *[Remember the oath] that the two of us have sworn....*

According to *Abarbanel*, Jonathan told David that since they had sworn an oath of mutual fealty, he was now revealing everything that had occurred with his father.

Malbim explains that Jonathan assured David that although they were taking leave of each other, space could not separate them because Hashem *is between them* and will always unite them. Time could not divide them because their oath was eternal.

XXI

◆§ David Arrives Hungry in Nob

1. וַיָּקָם וַיֵּלַךְ — *[David] arose and went.*

The omission of David's name in this verse is possibly meant to indicate that he was traveling incognito (*Chomas Anach*).

The fact that it says וַיֵּלַךְ, *went* or *walked* (rather than וַיִּבְרַח, *fled* or *ran*), denotes that he was proceeding in an unhurried manner. This was due in part to his desire to avoid attracting attention and in part to his extraordinary trust that Hashem would allow no harm to come to him (*Daas Sofrim*; see footnote above, 20:22).

2. וַיָּבֹא דָוִד נֹבֶה — *David came to Nob.*

After the Philistines destroyed the Tabernacle at Shiloh, a new structure was erected at Nob where the communal sacrificial services were performed.

20/42 *and they wept with each other, until David*
[wept] greatly. 42 *Jonathan said to David, "Go*
to peace. [Regarding the oath] that the two of
us have sworn in the Name of H*ASHEM* — *say-*
*ing, '*H*ASHEM* *shall be [a witness] between me*
and you, and between my offspring and your
offspring' — [that shall be] forever!"

21/1-3 1 *[David] arose and went, and Jonathan came*
back to the city. 2 *David came to Nob, to*
Ahimelech the Kohen. Ahimelech hurried to
greet David, and said to him, "Why are you
alone, with no one accompanying you?"
3 *David said to Ahimelech the Kohen, "The*
king ordered me on a mission, and told me, 'No
man may know anything about the matter for
which I have sent you and commanded you.'

Although there was no Ark in this Sanctuary, as it was presently situated in Kiriath-je'arim (above, 7:1-2), nevertheless, it resembled the Tabernacle (see *Tosefta, Yoma* 2:11) and contained the other holy vessels, such as the Altar and Table.

David came to Nob to pray and prostrate before Hashem and seek counsel regarding his future (*Abarbanel*).

נֹבֶה — *To Nob.*

The ה suffix, a standard substitute for a ל prefix, means *to.*

אֲחִימֶלֶךְ הַכֹּהֵן — *Ahimelech the Kohen.*

Ahimelech was apparently the Kohen Gadol. He is later identified as the son of Ahitub (below, 22:9), who is probably the same Ahitub identified earlier (14:3) as a brother of Ichabod and son of Phinehas.

וַיֶּחֱרַד אֲחִימֶלֶךְ לִקְרַאת דָּוִד — *Ahimelech hurried to greet David.*

The word וַיֶּחֱרַד is usually translated as *he trembled* (see *Genesis* 27:33). Trembling is a form of movement, and that is the connotation of this word; Ahimelech hastily moved to greet the dignitary who had arrived (*Radak*). *Radak* adds that it is also correct to render the word according to its regular interpretation, since the sight of David alone frightened Ahimelech and made him tremble.

מַדּוּעַ אַתָּה לְבַדֶּךָ וְאֵין אִישׁ אִתָּךְ — *Why are you alone, with no one accompanying you?*

Ahimelech was surprised to see David — the king's son-in-law and an honored nobleman and warrior — traveling alone (*Ralbag*). If David were on a military mission, thought Ahimelech, he should have been accompanied by a military contingent; if he were engaged on some other royal assignment, he should have been attended by an appropriate retinue (*Malbim*).

3. אַל־יֵדַע מְאוּמָה אֶת־הַדָּבָר אֲשֶׁר־אָנֹכִי שֹׁלֵחֲךָ וַאֲשֶׁר צִוִּיתִךָ — *No man may know anything about the matter for which I have sent you and commanded you.*

וְאֶת־הַנְּעָרִים יוֹדַעְתִּי אֶל־מְקוֹם פְּלֹנִי אַלְמוֹנִי׃
ד וְעַתָּה מַה־יֵּשׁ תַּחַת־יָדְךָ חֲמִשָּׁה־לֶחֶם תְּנָה בְיָדִי
ה אוֹ הַנִּמְצָא׃ וַיַּעַן הַכֹּהֵן אֶת־דָּוִד וַיֹּאמֶר אֵין־
לֶחֶם חֹל אֶל־תַּחַת יָדִי כִּי־אִם־לֶחֶם קֹדֶשׁ יֵשׁ

Abarbanel explains the apparent redundancy of the phrase *I have sent you and commanded you* as follows: הַדָּבָר אֲשֶׁר־אָנֹכִי שֹׁלֵחֲךָ, *the matter for which I have sent you,* must remain a secret, וַאֲשֶׁר צִוִּיתִךָ, *and [the very fact that I have] commanded you* must remain a secret as well.

According to *Malbim,* וַאֲשֶׁר צִוִּיתִךָ refers to the destination to which David was going — that too must remain unknown. *Malbim* explains that David claimed that his attendants were stationed elsewhere so that they would not know where David was going. In addition, their own whereabouts must remain a mystery, lest someone notice David and then inform the attendants of his whereabouts.

וְאֶת־הַנְּעָרִים יוֹדַעְתִּי — *I informed my attendants.*

The word יוֹדַעְתִּי (which derives from דֵּעָה, *knowledge*) is the grammatical equivalent of הוֹדַעְתִּי, *I have informed* (*Radak*). *Targum* renders this word as *I have sent. Rashi,* based on this word's usage in *Judges* 8:16, interprets it as *I have troubled.*

אֶל־מָקוֹם פְּלֹנִי אַלְמוֹנִי — *Regarding a certain secret place.*

פְּלֹנִי means *concealed* (as in *Deuteronomy* 17:8: כִּי יִפָּלֵא, *If it is hidden* [*Rashi*]). אַלְמוֹנִי is related to אִלֵּם, *mute,* and implies that the speaker does not wish to reveal this person's identity.

Once David asserted that he was on a secret mission, he had to imbue his entire narrative with an aura of mystery (*Ralbag*).

4. וְעַתָּה מַה־יֵּשׁ תַּחַת־יָדְךָ— *And now, what do you have available?*

Having been alone and in hiding for at least three days, David was starving. Our Sages say that he was seized by *bulmos,* a deadly disease caused by extreme hunger. Thus, he requested food of Ahimelech.[1]

The Talmud (*Sanhedrin* 104a) holds Jonathan accountable for David's hunger, as he should have supplied David with two loaves of bread. Although Jonathan did not intend to ignore David's needs and was likely concerned that if he were to carry food to David his purpose would be discovered (*Daas Sofrim*), he erred. Because of that misjudgment, he is held responsible to a degree for the terrible tragedy that befell Nob.

חֲמִשָּׁה־לֶחֶם תְּנָה בְיָדִי אוֹ הַנִּמְצָא — *Five loaves of bread? Give them — or whatever there is — into my hand.*

Simply understood, David did not request any particular loaves of bread, but whatever he could obtain.

But why did he specify five loaves?

According to *Malbim,* David implied that five attendants were waiting upon him and he requested a loaf for each.

Abarbanel suggests that five was an especially meaningful number to David because it represents the five Books of the Torah.

As we will see, the only bread available was sanctified bread, most likely the לֶחֶם הַפָּנִים, show-bread that sits on the holy Table in the Inner Sanctuary and is distributed to the Kohanim on the Sabbath. The Talmud (*Yoma* 17b) cites one opinion that the Kohen Gadol received five of the twelve breads each

1. *Rema MiPanu* (*Maamar HaItim* #2) comments that David suffered the experience of lacking bread because he descended from Moab, who didn't offer bread and water to the Jews in the Wilderness (see *Deuteronomy* 23:5). *Mishbetzos Zahav* adds that there occurred another incident in which David lacked water — see *II Samuel* 23:15, *Radak* ad loc.

*Thus, I informed my attendants regarding a certain
secret place.* [4] *And now, what do you have available? Five loaves of bread? Give them — or whatever there is — into my hand."*
[5] *The Kohen answered David, saying, "I have no
ordinary bread available; there is only sacred bread,*

week. Some interpret accordingly that David assumed that Ahimelech, who was the Kohen Gadol, would be in possession of those five loaves (*Parashas Derachim, Derush* 19; *Rashash, Yoma* 17b). The service of the Kohanim in the Sanctuary was divided into 24 מִשְׁמָרוֹת, *shifts*. Each Sabbath, a different family would begin its week-long shift. The twelve show-breads were initially distributed between the out-going and in-coming families, and then each family would in turn give some of their share to the Kohen Gadol. There is a Tanna's dispute as to whether each family received six loaves, or whether the incoming group received seven loaves and the outgoing received five (*Succah* 56a). The *Talmud Yerushalmi* (end of *Succah*) cites this request of David to support the latter opinion. Apparently, the *Yerushalmi* assumes that if David asked for five breads, he must have known that Ahimelech was from the out-going shift, and he requested their breads.

The obvious perplexity is that Ahimelech was Kohen Gadol, and as such was entitled to his own portion of the show-bread that he received from the families — possibly five loaves. For a discussion of this question, see *Nachalas Shimon* 60:15.

Me'am Loez cites a view that David came as the loaves were being distributed. When he saw the five loaves being given to the outgoing family, he said, "Maybe you can give me these five breads — or anything else that may be available."

◆§ David Is Satiated by Sacred Bread

5. אֵין־לֶחֶם חֹל אֶל־תַּחַת יָדִי — *I have no ordinary bread available.*

The Kohanim in the Sanctuary ordinarily consumed only sacred bread so as not to allow it to remain uneaten beyond a certain span of time, which would have constituted a violation of a Biblical prohibition. As a result, they had no unsanctified bread available.

כִּי־אִם־לֶחֶם קֹדֶשׁ יֵשׁ — *There is only sacred bread.*

In this verse, the exact nature of the sanctity of the bread is not made clear. It seems from verse 7 that this was the show-bread, and that is indeed the understanding of our Sages, who, based on that supposition, derive many halachic conclusions from this passage.

Nevertheless, some commentators eschew our Sages' interpretation, most likely because show-bread is permitted only to Kohanim (*Leviticus* 24:9).

According to *Ralbag* and *Radak*, therefore, Ahimelech offered David loaves of the *korban todah* — the thanksgiving offering (see *Leviticus* 7:12-14) — a sacred bread that may be eaten by any Jew who is in a state of ritual purity.[1] It

1. How could the Kohanim have possessed so many loaves of the *korban todah*, which belong to their owners and are generally eaten by their families?

Malbim suggests the following answer.

When a permanent sanctuary existed (such as that in Shiloh or Jerusalem), a tenth of the *korban todah* loaves were *raised todah loaves* (*Leviticus* 7:14), which were given to the Kohanim to eat.

At this time, such a permanent sanctuary did not exist — and so, technically speaking, there

ו אִם־נִשְׁמְרוּ הַנְּעָרִים אַךְ מֵאִשָּׁה: וַיַּעַן דָּוִד אֶת־הַכֹּהֵן וַיֹּאמֶר לוֹ כִּי אִם־אִשָּׁה עֲצֻרָה־לָנוּ כִּתְמוֹל שִׁלְשֹׁם בְּצֵאתִי וַיִּהְיוּ כְלֵי־הַנְּעָרִים קֹדֶשׁ

This raises a question for those who explain that the sanctified bread was legally limited to Kohanim and that it was permitted to David because his life was in danger. Surely, in that case, the requirement for ritual purity should also have been waived.

Parashas Derachim and *Chasam Sofer* (*Teshuvos, Orach Chaim* 79) both present complicated solutions to this question. Basically, the gist of each is as follows. Had David been impure, according to *Parashas Derachim,* Ahimelech would not have given David show-bread but *terumah.* According to *Chasam Sofer,* Ahimelech would have redeemed the new batch of show-bread loaves of their sanctity and given them to David (even though that would have necessitated baking new loaves on the Sabbath).[2]

According to one version cited by *Me'am Loez,* Ahimelech made an assessment that this was not a life-threatening situation and that feeding David could be delayed until nighttime. Thus, had David been impure, Ahimelech would have expected him to immerse and wait until nightfall and then eat bread permitted to a non-Kohen.

Daas Sofrim agrees that in Ahimelech's

is true that verse 7 avers that Ahimelech possessed only show-bread — but that may mean that he possessed only show-bread in addition to the *korban todah* loaves, and since he couldn't give him the show-bread, he had no choice but to give David *korban todah* loaves.

Returning to our Sages' view that the bread in question was show-bread and thus prohibited to non-Kohanim, how could David have been permitted to eat it? The answer is that because David's life hung in the balance this prohibition was waived.[1]

אִם־נִשְׁמְרוּ הַנְּעָרִים אַךְ מֵאִשָּׁה — *Provided that your attendants have kept themselves from women.*

Targum adds the explanatory word, *from impurity of women.* Since Ahimelech was offering David sanctified bread, he stipulated that it could be eaten only in a state of ritual purity. In particular, a person who had been intimate with his wife and emitted semen was impure and remained so until he immersed himself in a *mikveh* (ritual bath) and night fell. That was not the only source of impurity that concerned Ahimelech, but he mentioned it because it is the most common.

were no *raised todah loaves* (*Zevachim* 117b). Nevertheless, the custom persisted of setting aside a tenth of one's *korban todah* loaves for the Kohanim, but since it wasn't mandated, those breads were not elevated to a higher level of sanctity and were permitted to be eaten by non-Kohanim. This explains how the Kohanim could have possessed so many loaves of the *korban todah.*

1. Why didn't Ahimelech simply give David unsanctified bread from one of the residents of Nob (*Radak*)? Doing so would not have compromised David's anonymity — Ahimelech could have sent an agent of his own to obtain it, and no one would have questioned a request of the Kohen Gadol.

Radak explains that the city of Nob was inhabited solely by Kohanim, and all of the bread that they possessed was made of *terumah,* the sanctified portion of produce. Because David was starving, Ahimelech agreed to feed him bread ordinarily forbidden to a non-Kohen. Faced with a choice between giving David show-bread or *terumah,* Ahimelech chose show-bread, the consumption of which by a non-Kohen is — for reasons beyond the scope of this work — not as severe a violation as is the consumption of *terumah.*

2. The details of these calculations are beyond the scope of this work. See also *Nachalas Shimon* 45:4,5.

provided that your attendants have kept themselves from women."

6 *David answered the Kohen and said to him, "Women have been withheld from us [since] yesterday and the day before; [moreover], when I left, the garments of the attendants were pure,*

estimation, David could wait until nighttime. He explains that Ahimelech did not wish to give David the show-bread, and therefore told David that if he was impure he must immerse in a *mikveh* and wait until nightfall, in the hope that, hearing this, David would sooner go elsewhere and seek unsanctified bread.

הַנְּעָרִים — *The attendants.*

According to *Ralbag,* Ahimelech also meant David — he referred to *the attendants* solely to avoid the appearance of speaking disrespectfully to David.

Metzudos, however, states that Ahimelech believed that David did not require bread for himself and was requesting it only on behalf of his attendants.

6. כִּי אִם־אִשָּׁה עֲצֻרָה־לָנוּ כִּתְמוֹל שִׁלְשֹׁם — *Women have been withheld from us [since] yesterday and the day before.*

David responded that he and his supposed attendants had been careful to maintain their ritual purity.

The phrase עֲצֻרָה־לָנוּ seems self-contradictory. עֲצֻרָה generally implies *restraint* (as in וְעָצַר אֶת־הַשָּׁמַיִם, *He will restrain the heavens* [*Deuteronomy* 11:17]). However, the word לָנוּ — lit., *for us* — indicates that women were *available to us. Rashi* resolves this by rendering לָנוּ as מִמֶּנּוּ, *from us,* therefore, the phrase reads, *Women were withheld from us.* David notified Ahimelech that he and his attendants had been on the road for a few days without access to women, and were therefore ritually pure.

Radak interprets this phrase in a diametrically opposite fashion. He renders עֲצֻרָה as *available* (interpreting its root meaning of *restrained* as *held on our behalf* [see below, v. 8 נֶעְצָר לִפְנֵי ה']), and translates לָנוּ literally, as *to us.* Accordingly, David told Ahimelech, "Even if any of us had a woman available and had relations recently, nevertheless, וַיִּהְיוּ כְלֵי־הַנְּעָרִים קֹדֶשׁ, *the garments of the attendants are pure,* i.e., whoever did so took care to immerse himself and regain his level of ritual purity, וְהוּא דֶּרֶךְ חֹל, *even though [we planned this to be] a mundane journey.*[1]

כִּתְמוֹל שִׁלְשֹׁם בְּצֵאתִי — *Yesterday and the day before, when I left.*

Daas Sofrim suggests that David said this to impress upon Ahimelech that he had left home three days ago and had not eaten a substantial meal since, and that the situation was therefore urgent.

וַיִּהְיוּ כְלֵי־הַנְּעָרִים קֹדֶשׁ — *The garments of the attendants were pure.*

1. Some commentators add the following insight.

A man is ordinarily obligated to be intimate with his wife before leaving on a journey (*Yevamos* 62b, *Shulchan Aruch Orach Chaim* 240:1). In addition, the standard of a Torah scholar is to be intimate with his wife only on the Sabbath, holidays and Rosh Chodesh, (see *Shulchan Aruch, Orach Chaim* 240:1; *Mishnah Berurah, Shaar HaTziyun*).

Nevertheless, stated David, that did not occur here. Women have been withheld from us כִּתְמוֹל שִׁלְשֹׁם, *even yesterday and the day before,* which were Rosh Chodesh as well as בְּצֵאתִי, *when we left* and began traveling. Although these are days when one would normally become impure וַיִּהְיוּ־כְלֵי־הַנְּעָרִים קֹדֶשׁ, *the attendants remained pure,* וְהוּא דֶּרֶךְ חֹל, and treated those days *as if they were regular [days],* by abstaining from intimacy. This was due to the critical nature of this mission.

כא/ז

וְהוּא֙ דֶּ֣רֶךְ חֹ֔ל וְאַ֕ף כִּ֥י הַיּ֖וֹם יִקְדַּ֥שׁ בַּכֶּֽלִי׃
ז וַיִּתֶּן־ל֥וֹ הַכֹּהֵ֖ן קֹ֑דֶשׁ כִּ֠י לֹא־הָ֨יָה שָׁ֥ם לֶ֙חֶם
כִּֽי־אִם־לֶ֤חֶם הַפָּנִים֙ הַמּֽוּסָרִים֙ מִלִּפְנֵ֣י
יהוה לָשׂוּם֙ לֶ֣חֶם חֹ֔ם בְּי֖וֹם הִלָּקְחֽוֹ׃

Literally, קֹדֶשׁ means *sacred*. Naturally, it would not have been of any relevance for David to say that the garments were sanctified. Thus *Targum* renders קֹדֶשׁ as *pure* — i.e., fit for sacred items.

כְּלִי can also mean *vessels*. Our translation, *garments*, is that of *Radak*.

וְהוּא דֶּרֶךְ חֹל וְאַף כִּי הַיּוֹם יִקְדַּשׁ בַּכֶּלִי — *Even though this is a mundane mission — surely today [the bread] will remain sacred, in a [proper] vessel.*

Our interpretation of this opaque phrase follows *Radak* and *Ralbag*. David assured Ahimelech that he and his men would not make the sanctified bread impure. Since it was their practice to maintain ritual purity even when coming in contact with mundane items, they would surely maintain the holiness of the sacred bread in its vessel.

The Talmud (cited by *Rashi*) offers a different explanation (*Menachos* 95b). Once the show-bread had been made available to the Kohanim by virtue of the offering of its representative frankincense on the altar (see *Leviticus* 24:7), its level of sanctity decreased.

Therefore, said David, וְהוּא, *and it*, i.e., the show-bread, was דֶּרֶךְ חֹל, *close to being mundane*. Moreover, David added, since he was suffering from *bulmos* and in imminent danger of dying, he would be justified in eating the show-bread even if it retained its original, full level of sanctity. Thus, וְאַף כִּי הַיּוֹם יִקְדַּשׁ בַּכֶּלִי, *Even if [the loaves] had been sanctified on their receptacle, [the Table,] today*, he would still have taken them and eaten them.

According to *Malbim*, the loaves that David requested were the Kohen's share of the *korban todah* (thanksgiving offerings of individual), which were permissible to non-Kohanim (see above). Thus, David stated, וְהוּא דֶּרֶךְ חֹל, *[These loaves] have the [legal] status of the mundane*, regarding their consumption by a non-Kohen and their removal from the Sanctuary territory, וְאַף כִּי הַיּוֹם יִקְדַּשׁ בַּכֶּלִי, *because they had become sanctified today — [i.e., in Nob]*. Nob had the status of a temporary altar, where many of the rules of the permanent Sanctuary did not apply.

7. וַיִּתֶּן־לוֹ הַכֹּהֵן קֹדֶשׁ — *So the Kohen gave him sacred [bread].*

According to *Midrash Yalkut Shimoni*, David was so hungry that he ate a quantity of close to seven *seah* of bread (about 80 percent of a bushel)

Each one of the show-breads was 0.2 *ephah*. All twelve show-breads therefore consisted of 2.4 *ephah* (see *Leviticus* 24:5), which is the equivalent of 7.2 *seah* (*Zayis Ra'anan*). Thus, it would seem that David consumed all twelve loaves.[1]

כִּי לֹא־הָיָה לֶחֶם כִּי־אִם־לֶחֶם הַפָּנִים — *Because there was no other bread there except the show-bread.*

As mentioned above, the Talmud states that since no other bread was

1. How could the show-bread have been available when David arrived? These loaves were distributed and eaten by the Kohanim on the Sabbath, and it is unlikely that David traveled then. If he had done so (due to the danger that threatened him), it would have been more likely for Ahimelech to comment on that, rather than on the fact that he was alone (above, v. 2; see *Kli Yakar*).

Radak explains that David arrived after the Sabbath. Since each Kohen ate only a small portion of the show-bread, some remained. (This apparently conflicts with the Midrash that David ate all of the loaves. See *Nachalas Shimon* 45:3.)

even though this is a mundane mission — surely today [the bread] will remain sacred, in a [proper] vessel." 7 *So the Kohen gave him sacred [bread], because there was no other bread there except the show-bread, which was being removed from before* HASHEM, *in order to place hot bread on the day [the old show-bread] is taken off.*

available, Ahimelech gave David the show-bread.

According to *Radak* and *Ralbag* (as noted earlier), Ahimelech gave David bread of the *korban todah*, for he had nothing else *besides the show-bread*, which Ahimelech would not give him.

לֶחֶם הַפָּנִים — *The show-bread.*

A discussion regarding the presence of the show-bread in the temporary Sanctuary in Nob may be found in *Nachalas Shimon* 60:16.

לֶחֶם הַפָּנִים הַמּוּסָרִים מִלִּפְנֵי ה׳ לָשׂוּם לֶחֶם חֹם בְּיוֹם הִלָּקְחוֹ — *The show-bread, which was being removed from before* HASHEM, *in order to place hot bread on the day [the old show-bread] is taken off.*

The Torah prescribes that show-bread must remain on the Table *always* (*Exodus* 25:30). Accordingly, every Sabbath, at the moment that the old batch was removed, the newly baked batch replaced it (*Menachos* 99b). Thus, in this phrase, לָשׂוּם לֶחֶם חֹם בְּיוֹם הִלָּקְחוֹ, *as hot bread was being placed [there] on the day [the old show-bread] was being removed*, the hot bread is the new batch.

Our Sages, however, interpret the verse as stating that the show-bread possessed the miraculous property of remaining hot for the entire week. Thus, לָשׂוּם לֶחֶם חֹם בְּיוֹם הִלָּקְחוֹ may be translated, *the [old] bread remained hot on the day of its removal.* On the festivals, our Sages state, the Kohanim would lift up these hot loaves to show the pilgrims, explaining this as a sign of Hashem's love for them (*Menachos* 96b et al.).

There is a dispute among the Sages as to whether the loaves were baked on the Sabbath or were baked on Friday and placed on the Table on the Sabbath (*Menachos* 95b).[1]

Tosafos (*Chagigah* 26b) suggests that the statement that the loaves were hot should not be understood literally, because according to the opinion that they were baked on Friday, they couldn't even have been hot when they were placed *on* the Table. Thus, it means that when they were removed they were as *soft* as when they placed. Alternatively, *Tosafos* conjectures that if they were baked on Friday, they were left in the oven, where they remained hot until they were placed on the Table on the Sabbath.

☙ Doeg HaAdomi

The following verse introduces us to one of the most infamous personalities in Jewish history. Our Sages list incidents in which Doeg was implicated prior to this point. Thus, he advised Saul not to kill Agag (above, Ch. 15), basing his argument on the verse that prohibits slaughtering a parent and child on the same day (*Leviticus* 22:28 — of course, that verse refers to kosher animals, not to Amalekites). Doeg attempted to incite Saul's envy of

1. According to *Yalkut Shimoni*, David and Doeg disagreed on this very point.

Thus, according to the view that David arrived at the Sanctuary on the Sabbath, he noticed that the Kohanim were baking the show-bread, in accordance with the ruling of Doeg HaAdomi. David reproached them and showed them a source from the Torah that this was not permitted.

ח וְשָׁם אִישׁ מֵעַבְדֵי שָׁאוּל בַּיּוֹם הַהוּא נֶעְצָר לִפְנֵי יהוה וּשְׁמוֹ דֹּאֵג הָאֲדֹמִי אַבִּיר הָרֹעִים אֲשֶׁר לְשָׁאוּל׃

David by repeating the latter's sterling attributes to Saul (above, 16:18). And Doeg challenged David's right to marry a Jewess because of his descent from Ruth the Moabitess (see above, 17:58).

Although Doeg did so much evil that he is among the few individuals named by our Sages as having no portion in the World to Come (*Sanhedrin* 90a), he was in his day renowned as a Torah scholar (see *Yerushalmi Sanhedrin* 10:2) and judge, and his word carried great weight.

The Talmud (*Sanhedrin* 106b) explains this paradox by stating that Doeg's learning was superficial, lacking the depth and emotional involvement necessary to refine a person's character. Eventually, in heavenly retribution for his wicked deeds, Doeg forgot all the Torah that he had learned.

The Talmud relates that Doeg grew jealous of David after the latter and Samuel worked together to designate the site of the Holy Temple (*Zevachim* 54b). Following that episode, Doeg focused his malicious behavior on David, who turned for solace to prayer, pouring out his heart in numerous psalms, particularly *Psalm* 52.

Doeg's life and personality are a perfect representation of the havoc that a person can wreak when he engages in gossip and slander (see *Yerushalmi Peah* 1:1, *Midrash Shocher Tov* 52:2).

8. וְשָׁם אִישׁ מֵעַבְדֵי שָׁאוּל יוֹם הַהוּא — *Now there on that day was one of Saul's servants.*

Scripture parenthetically tells us of the presence of Doeg at the Sanctuary. The relevance of his being there is not immediately apparent, but will be made clear in Chapter 22.[1] From David's comment (below, 22:22) it seems that David was familiar with Doeg's machinations, and suspected that it was not to his benefit that Doeg witnessed this episode with Ahimelech.

נֶעְצָר לִפְנֵי ה׳ — *Who lingered before* H*ASHEM*.

The root of נֶעְצָר is *restrained*, or *held back* (see v. 6). According to *Rashi*, Doeg would regularly "restrain himself" (stay) near the Tent of Meeting to study Torah.

Radak explains that Doeg had come with friends to bring offerings; when they left, he stayed behind to pray or bring more offerings.

1. This verse seems quite out of place. Aside from the fact that Doeg's role doesn't begin until the next chapter, it seems especially perplexing that in the middle of David's exchange with Ahimelech, between the discussion about the bread and the one about the sword, Scripture introduces us to Doeg. *Mishbetzos Zahav* clarifies its position here.

In the previous footnote, we cited a Midrash which states that David disagreed with Doeg regarding the baking of the show-bread. Accordingly, Doeg was incensed by what he perceived as insolence on David's part to dispute his ruling. This explains why specifically here, Scripture mentions that Doeg was the chief judge. It is even possible that Doeg's rationale for considering David deserving of death was that David stated a halachic ruling in the presence of the greatest scholar of the generation (see *Terumas HaDeshen* #138).

Mishbetzos Zahav also suggests an alternative explanation. As we will see below (22:22), David was held somewhat responsible for the demise of the Kohanim of Nob, as well as of Doeg, because he should have foreseen what would result from the requests he made of Ahimelech, particularly since they were made in the presence of the malevolent Doeg. It is possible that David could be excused for requesting bread, since his life was in danger. However, the request for the sword and to use the *Urim VeTumim* should not have been made. Accordingly, Scripture records Doeg's presence specifically prior to mention of those requests.

[8]*Now there on that day was one of Saul's servants, who lingered before* HASHEM. *His name was Doeg the Edomite; he was the chief of Saul's shepherds.*

Me'am Loez cites an alternative interpretation. As Saul's chief shepherd, Doeg went to the Sanctuary to offer the firstborn lambs and tithes of the king's sheep. A person who brings an offering is required to stay overnight, which is called עֲצִירָה, *held back*. Since this was the Sabbath (see above, v. 7), Doeg was required to remain for the entire day. This explains why it specifies בַּיּוֹם הַהוּא נֶעְצָר לִפְנֵי ה׳, *on that day [he] lingered before* HASHEM.

וּשְׁמוֹ דֹּאֵג — *His name was Doeg.*

Generally, the formula "his name was ..." rather than "... was his name" is used in the case of a righteous man (see above, 1:1, 9:1,2, 17:4). At the time that Doeg was learning Torah in the Sanctuary, he was righteous (*Kli Yakar*).

דֹּאֵג — *Doeg.*

Literally, the name דואג means *the worrier*. The Talmud relates that at first Hashem worried, as it were, that Doeg would embark on a path of evil. After he did so, he is called Doyeg, דּוֹיֵג (Chapter 22:18,22), a rendering that contains the word וַי, *Woe!*, expressing God's lamentation (*Sanhedrin* 106b).

Rabbi Avrohom Chaim Feuer suggests that since Doeg studied Torah without concomitant feelings of faith, he was not instilled with a deep sense of security in God. He was therefore left jealous and fearful, tormented by anxiety, and was hence called *the worrier* (*Psalms* 52:2, *ArtScroll Edition*).

הָאֲדֹמִי — *The Edomite.*

According to most sources, Doeg was born a Jew. He was called an *Edomite* simply because he resided in Edomite territory (similar to *Uriah the Hittite* [II *Samuel* 11:3; *Radak*]).

The Midrash (*Shocher Tov* 52:4), however, offers various homiletic reasons for this appellation.

❒ Doeg's attributes resembled those of the nation Edom. Just as Edom is full of vengeance and hatred, so was Doeg.

❒ The word *edom* also means *red*. Since Doeg was envious of David, who was *ruddy* (above, 16:12), Doeg was given a similar appellation.

❒ Doeg caused the blood of the inhabitants of Nob to be spilled (Ch. 22).

❒ Doeg called for the shedding of David's blood (see above, 20:31).

❒ Doeg kept Saul from spilling Agag's blood (see above, 15:9).

❒ Doeg reddened, or shamed, the faces of his peers when they discussed halachah because of his superior scholarship.

According to one view, Doeg was an Amalekite proselyte. His son delivered the coup de grace to Saul at the latter's request (see *II Samuel*, Chapter 1; *Midrash Tanchuma, Parashas Ki Seitzei* #11). Thus Doeg is called an Edomite, since Amalek descended from Esau, who was also called Edom.

According to another source, Doeg was the son of an Amalekite proselyte, and he himself delivered the coup de grace to Saul (*Pesikta Rabbasi* Ch. 12; *Yalkut Shimoni, Parashas Beshalach* 267; see *Rashi, II Samuel* 1:2; see also *Nachalas Shimon, I Samuel* 60:17, *II Samuel* 1:1).

אַבִּיר הָרֹעִים אֲשֶׁר לְשָׁאוּל — *Chief of Saul's shepherds.*

The word אַבִּיר means powerful (as in the verse, אֲבִיר יַעֲקֹב, *the Power of Jacob* [*Genesis* 49:24]). Doeg was appointed to a position of authority over the shepherds.

According to *Abarbanel*, *shepherds* refers to the shepherds of the nation — Doeg held a position of leadership over all the governors of the nation.

Rashi cites a Midrash that Doeg was in charge of the spiritual shepherds of the nation — i.e., he was the chief judge (*Shocher Tov* 3:4).

ט וַיֹּאמֶר דָּוִד לַאֲחִימֶלֶךְ וְאִין יֶשׁ־פֹּה תַחַת־יָדְךָ
חֲנִית אוֹ־חָרֶב כִּי גַם־חַרְבִּי וְגַם־כֵּלַי לֹא־לָקַחְתִּי
י בְיָדִי כִּי־הָיָה דְבַר־הַמֶּלֶךְ נָחוּץ׃ וַיֹּאמֶר
הַכֹּהֵן חֶרֶב גָּלְיָת הַפְּלִשְׁתִּי אֲשֶׁר־הִכִּיתָ | בְּעֵמֶק
הָאֵלָה הִנֵּה־הִיא לוּטָה בַשִּׂמְלָה אַחֲרֵי הָאֵפוֹד
אִם־אֹתָהּ תִּקַּח־לְךָ קָח כִּי אֵין אַחֶרֶת זוּלָתָהּ
בָּזֶה וַיֹּאמֶר דָּוִד אֵין כָּמוֹהָ תְּנֶנָּה
יא לִי׃ וַיָּקָם דָּוִד וַיִּבְרַח בַּיּוֹם־הַהוּא מִפְּנֵי שָׁאוּל

David Arms Himself

9. וַיֹּאמֶר דָּוִד לַאֲחִימֶלֶךְ — *David then said to Ahimelech.*

Here, for the first time, Ahimelech's name appears in a verse without the honorific *the Kohen. Kli Yakar* suggests that in this instance, in which a weapon was requested, Ahimelech's capacity as Kohen Gadol was immaterial, for it is not the function of a Kohen to involve himself with weaponry. However, in the next verse, when Ahimelech brought David Goliath's sword, Scripture again refers to him as Kohen. Since that sword was kept in the Sanctuary as a commemoration of David's miraculous victory, it was indeed appropriate for the Kohen Gadol to possess it.

וְאִין יֶשׁ־פֹּה — *Perhaps you have here.*

The word וְאִין is an uncommon one.

Targum and *Rashi* render it as equivalent to אִם, meaning *if* or *perhaps. Radak* interprets the word as if it were vocalized with a צֵירֵי — וְאֵין, meaning *there is not*. Accordingly, David asked, *Is there not here ....?*

וְאִין יֶשׁ־פֹּה תַחַת־יָדְךָ חֲנִית אוֹ־חָרֶב — *Perhaps you have here under your hand a spear or a sword.*

One reason that David wanted to be armed was that he was aware of the presence of Doeg, who — he feared — would pursue him (*Chomas Anach*).

כֵּלַי — *My weapons.*

Radak translates this word as *weapons* — based, he says, on *Targum*. However, the extant version of the *Targum Yonasan* translates כֵּלַי more literally as מָנַי, *vessels.*

10. אַחֲרֵי הָאֵפוֹד — *Behind the Ephod.*

The sword was placed behind the *Ephod* in the room where the garments of the Kohanim were stored (*Ralbag*).

Radak suggests that this was not necessarily the *Ephod* worn exclusively by the Kohen Gadol, but rather a linen apron commonly worn by any Kohen or indeed by any devoted servant of God (see above, 2:18, *II Samuel* 6:14).

Targum renders the word אַחֲרֵי, *behind,* in a chronological sense. Thus, אַחֲרֵי הָאֵפוֹד means that *after* Ahimelech had inquired of the *Urim VeTumim* (alluded to here by the word *Ephod*), he gave David the sword.[1] The *Urim VeTumim* were referred to in this colloquial fashion because they were enclosed in the *Choshen* (breastplate), which was in turn attached to the *Ephod* (*Metzudos*).

אִם־אֹתָהּ תִּקַּח־לְךָ קָח כִּי אֵין אַחֶרֶת זוּלָתָהּ — *If you wish to take it, take it, for there is none other here except for it.*

1. Ahimelech's inquiry of the *Urim VeTumim* is mentioned explicitly in the following chapter (23:10,15).

9 *David then said to Ahimelech, "Perhaps you have here under your hand a spear or a sword, for I did not take my sword and my weapons with me, since the king's mission was urgent."*

10 *The Kohen said, "The sword of Goliath, whom you slew in the Terebinth Valley, is wrapped up in a cloth behind the Ephod; if you wish to take it, take it, for there is none other here except for it."*

And David said, "There is none like it; give it to me."

11 *David arose and fled from Saul on that day,*

Ahimelech was hesitant to remove the sword, which commemorated David's miraculous victory, from the Sanctuary, and he hoped that they would find an alternative. When he saw that there were no others, he had no choice but to let David take it, particularly since it was David himself who had seized it and placed it in the Sanctuary and who thus had a right to take it (*Radak*). Indeed, as *Abarbanel* observes, the words תִּקַּח לְךָ, *take for you*, indicate that this offer was made exclusively to David.[1]

בָּזֶה — *Here.*

Literally בָּזֶה means *in this. Radak* renders it as *in this place.*

וַיֹּאמֶר דָּוִד אֵין כָּמוֹהָ תְּנֶנָּה לִּי — *And David said, "There is none like it; give it to me."*

In accordance with *Radak*'s reading, David answered that there was no reason to hesitate in removing the sword.

On the contrary, if the sword were in David's hand, it would recall the miracle more than if it rested idly in the Sanctuary (*Kli Yakar*).

Sefer HaAkeidah (Shaar 78) states that Ahimelech thought that a sword that had killed its owner (Goliath) augured ill fortune. David responded that since this sword had saved him before, it could only be to his advantage to employ it again.

☙ An Encounter and Narrow Escape at Gath

11. וַיִּבְרַח בַּיּוֹם־הַהוּא מִפְּנֵי שָׁאוּל — *And fled from Saul on that day.*

Many commentators point out that David had fled from Saul several days earlier.

Radak explains that only now that he had left the boundaries of the Land of Israel could David be said to have truly escaped. *Abarbanel* expounds that David could not have been considered to have eluded Saul as long as he remained

1. The terminology אִם־אֹתָהּ תִּקַּח־לְךָ קָח, *if you wish to take it, take it,* seems excessive. It should have said simply קָחֶנָּה, *take it.* Also, why did Ahimelech have to refer to Goliath as the one "whom you slew in the Terebinth Valley"? David definitely knew that. *Kehillas Yaakov* suggests that after having inquired of the *Urim VeTumim*, Ahimelech now understood that David was fleeing from Saul. He reminded David that this was the sword that he had used to slay Goliath, which first aroused Saul's interest in David — and his jealousy. Thus, Ahimelech said somewhat hesitantly, "If you choose to use it again, that is your choice, but if you will take my advice, you won't use it and further incite Saul's jealousy when he hears about it." David answers that, nevertheless, since he had one salvation with this sword on behalf of the nation, he preferred to use it again in the hope that he would have a personal salvation with it.

יב וַיָּבֹ֖א אֶל־אָכִ֥ישׁ מֶֽלֶךְ גַּֽת׃ וַיֹּ֨אמְר֜וּ עַבְדֵ֤י אָכִישׁ֙
אֵלָ֔יו הֲלוֹא־זֶ֥ה דָוִ֖ד מֶ֣לֶךְ הָאָ֑רֶץ הֲל֣וֹא לָזֶ֗ה
°בַּאֲלָפָ֑יו ק׳ יַעֲנ֤וּ בַמְּחֹלוֹת֙ לֵאמֹ֔ר הִכָּ֤ה שָׁאוּל֙ °באלפו
°בְּרִבְבֹתָ֑יו ק׳ יג וְדָוִ֖ד °ברבבתו׃ וַיָּ֧שֶׂם דָּוִ֛ד אֶת־הַדְּבָרִ֥ים הָאֵ֖לֶּה
יד בִּלְבָב֑וֹ וַיִּרָ֣א מְאֹ֔ד מִפְּנֵ֖י אָכִ֥ישׁ מֶֽלֶךְ־גַּֽת׃ וַיְשַׁנּ֤וֹ

within his jurisdiction; hence, מִפְּנֵי שָׁאוּל, *from before Saul.*

Abarbanel offers an alternative explanation as well. When David arrived in Nob, he was a lone fugitive, starving and unarmed. Any such escape was unrealistic. Only now that he was well-fed, equipped with a sword, and fortified with the assurance of success by the *Urim VeTumim* was he invigorated to escape. Thus, it was *now* that he fled.

בַּיּוֹם הַהוּא — *On that day.*

According to those who say that David arrived in Nob on the day, this verse emphasizes that he continued his flight on that same day, considering himself to be in mortal danger as long as he remained in the Land of Israel (*Kli Yakar*).

וַיָּבֹא אֶל־אָכִישׁ מֶלֶךְ גַּת — *And he came to Achish, king of Gath.*

Gath is one of the principal provinces in Philistia; David's decision to run there — into the hands of his mortal enemy whose hero Goliath he had recently humiliated — might therefore seem suicidal.

Kli Yakar explains that בַּיּוֹם הַהוּא, *on that day,* provides the answer to this conundrum. Now that David had secured from the *Urim VeTumim* the assurance that he would survive, he felt confident going there.

Daas Sofrim suggests that David thought he could remain unrecognized, since it was not usual for an Israelite to seek residence in Philistia. Also, he thought he could convince the Philistines that he was a renegade escaping from their mutual enemy Saul — and that, moreover, he might assist their military efforts against Saul.

אָכִישׁ מֶלֶךְ גַּת — *Achish, king of Gath.*

In *Psalms* 34:1, where David refers to this incident, he calls the king *Abimelech.* It is possible that this king had two names; alternatively, all kings of Philistia bore the generic title Abimelech, as did those in the days of Abraham and Isaac (*Genesis* 20:3, 26:1; this is similar to the Egyptian royal title, Pharaoh [*Radak*]).

Midrash Shocher Tov (*Psalms* 34:1) derives a homiletic lesson from the reference to Achish as Abimelech. Just as the Abimelech who was a contemporary of Abraham and Isaac acted righteously by not harming Sarah and by dealing pacifically with Abraham and Isaac, so too was Achish considered righteous in that he did not harm David.

12. הֲלוֹא־זֶה דָוִד מֶלֶךְ הָאָרֶץ — *Is this not David, the king of the land?*

The Philistines considered David the true king of Israel, since he was a mighty warrior and respected statesman (*Abarbanel*).

According to a Midrash (cited in part by *Rashi*), these *servants of Achish* were Goliath's brothers, and their description of David as מֶלֶךְ הָאָרֶץ, *the king of the land,* meant that he was *king of the land of Philistia.* The context is as follows.

Learning of David's presence, Goliath's brothers approached Achish and told him that they wished to kill David for having slain Goliath.

Achish responded, "Didn't David dispatch Goliath in a fair contest after Goliath challenged any Israelite to step forward and fight him?" (above, 17:9).

Goliath's brothers reminded Achish that Goliath had also stated that if anyone defeated him, *we will be slaves to*

and he came to Achish, king of Gath. 12 *The ser-*
vants of Achish said to him, "Is this not David,
the king of the land? Is it not of him that they
call out with the timbrels, saying, 'Saul has
slain his thousands, and David his tens of thou-
sands'?"
13 *David took this matter to heart and was great-*
ly afraid of Achish, king of Gath. 14 *So he changed*

you (ibid.). Thus, they said, if Achish were so scrupulous about cleaving to the particulars of this agreement, he should renounce his throne and allow David to become *king of this land (Midrash Shocher Tov, Psalms* 34:1).

According to *Malbim,* the Philistines suspected David of being on an espionage mission because a person of his stature — i.e., someone even more powerful and popular than Saul — could not possibly be running away.

הֲלוֹא לָזֶה יַעֲנוּ בַמְּחֹלוֹת לֵאמֹר הִכָּה שָׁאוּל בַּאֲלָפָיו וְדָוִד בְּרִבְבֹתָיו — *Is it not of him that they call out with the timbrels, saying, "Saul has slain his thousands and David his tens of thousands?"*

By referring to the episode in which the Israelite women lauded David to a greater degree than they did Saul (see above, 18:7), the Philistines substantiated their claim that David was like a king (*Abarbanel*).

Kli Yakar notes that the word יַעֲנוּ is written in the future tense — literally, *will call out.* Achish's servants hinted that if he allowed David to escape, the Jews would surely have reason to compose yet another paean of victory on David's behalf.

יַעֲנוּ — *Call out.*

This word usually means *answer,* but at times indicates the raising of one's voice.

בַּמְּחֹלוֹת — *With the timbrels.*

See above, 18:6.

13. וַיִּרָא מְאֹד מִפְּנֵי אָכִישׁ מֶלֶךְ־גַּת — *And was greatly afraid of Achish, king of Gath.*

This incident inspired David to intensify his reliance on God and to write Psalm 56, in which he says, יוֹם אִירָא אֲנִי אֵלֶיךָ אֶבְטָח, *The day on which I am afraid, I will trust in You* (v. 4).

Having introduced Achish as the *king of Gath* (v. 11), Scripture refers to him subsequently by name alone — with the exception of this verse. Apparently, the comment made by Goliath's brothers that Achish's throne rightfully belonged to David, thus arousing Achish's jealousy, was the main cause for David's fear (*Kli Yakar*).

14. According to *Midrash Shocher Tov* (34:1), David once commented to Hashem that all that He created — especially wisdom — was beautiful. There was one exception, one creation whose purpose David could not fathom: madness. "What benefit does the world have of a lunatic who rips his clothing and whom children run after mockingly?," he inquired of Hashem.

Hashem replied, "You question the value of insanity. I assure you that one day you will need it, and you will plead with Me to give you some of it."

In the hostile Philistine court, David grew terrified of what Achish might do to him, and so he decided to appear as a madman, so that Achish and his men would be thoroughly convinced that he could not be the intelligent and mighty warrior, David.

He thus prayed for lunacy, and as

אֶת־טַעְמוֹ֙ בְּעֵֽינֵיהֶ֔ם וַיִּתְהֹלֵ֖ל בְּיָדָ֑ם °ויתו עַל־
טו דַּלְת֣וֹת הַשַּׁ֔עַר וַיּ֥וֹרֶד רִיר֖וֹ אֶל זְקָנֽוֹ׃ וַיֹּ֥אמֶר
אָכִ֖ישׁ אֶל־עֲבָדָ֑יו הִנֵּ֤ה תִרְאוּ֙ אִ֣ישׁ מִשְׁתַּגֵּ֔עַ
טז לָ֥מָּה תָבִ֖יאוּ אֹת֥וֹ אֵלָֽי׃ חֲסַ֤ר מְשֻׁגָּעִים֙ אָ֔נִי כִּֽי־
הֲבֵאתֶ֣ם אֶת־זֶ֔ה לְהִשְׁתַּגֵּ֖עַ עָלָ֑י הֲזֶ֖ה יָב֥וֹא אֶל־
כב/א א בֵּיתִֽי׃ וַיֵּ֤לֶךְ דָּוִד֙ מִשָּׁ֔ם וַיִּמָּלֵ֖ט אֶל־מְעָרַ֣ת

°וַיְתָיו ק׳

God responded and a spirit of madness descended upon him, he approached the doors, began to scribble on them, and yelled, "Achish, king of Gath, owes me a hundred coins and his wife owes me fifty coins!"

As it happened, Achish's wife and daughter were afflicted with insanity, and locked in another room. So now, as David shouted and raved madly, they added to the din from the other chamber.

Achish responded to this cacophony in exasperation, "Do I lack madmen...?" (below, v. 16), and he chased David away (*Psalms* 34:1).

Then, as the madness drained out of him, David rejoiced, and in gratitude for this miraculous salvation composed *Psalm* 34.

וַיְשַׁנּוֹ אֶת־טַעְמוֹ — *So he changed his demeanor.*

The ו suffix at the end of וַיְשַׁנּוֹ means *it* — thus, the phrase reads literally, *he changed it, his demeanor.* This redundant usage appears elsewhere as well, as in וַתִּרְאֵהוּ אֶת הַיֶּלֶד, *She saw him, the child* (*Exodus* 2:6, *Radak*).

טַעְמוֹ — *His demeanor.*

This word implies reasonable speech, as in the verse וְטַעַם זְקֵנִים יִקָּח, *He removes sensible speech from elders* (*Job* 21:20). Thus, David began to speak madly.

The word טַעַם often means *reason.* Accordingly, *Malbim* explains that when David came to Achish, he gave one reason for being there. Now he came up with another reason, and then he continued with a string of absurdities.

וַיְשַׁנּוֹ אֶת־טַעְמוֹ בְּעֵינֵיהֶם וַיִּתְהֹלֵל בְּיָדָם — *So he changed his demeanor in their eyes and feigned madness while in their presence.*

The text offers various indications that David did not actually go mad but was only feigning madness. For instance, he was mad בְּעֵינֵיהֶם, *in their eyes;* וַיִּתְהֹלֵל, *he made himself mad;* and all this only בְּיָדָם, *while he was with them.*

That being the case, why (according to the Midrash) did David pray for actual insanity?

Yaavetz HaDoresh explains that feigned madness may be easily detected. David requested actual insanity so that he would be genuinely convincing.

According to *Kli Yakar,* David was infused with a small measure of madness, which he consciously amplified.

Zayis Ra'anan (to *Yalkut Shimoni*) has a different approach, according to which David requested that God impose madness not on himself but on Achish's daughter, for that was an essential factor in the success of his scheme. According to that, she had not previously been mad; rather, she became insane together with David — and the resulting bedlam caused Achish to cast David out.

וַיְתָיו — *And he scribbled.*

This verb indicates any action that leaves a mark, such as writing or scraping (*Metzudos*).

וַיּוֹרֶד רִירוֹ אֶל זְקָנוֹ — *And let his saliva drip into his beard.*

This phenomenon commonly charac-

21/15-16 *his demeanor in their eyes and feigned madness*
while in their presence; he scribbled on the doors
of the gateway and let his saliva drip into his
beard. 15 *Achish said to his servants, "Behold, you*
see the man is mad; why do you bring him to me?
16 *Do I lack madmen that you have brought this one*
to carry on madly before me? Should this person
enter my house?"

22/1 1 *David went from there and escaped to the cave*

terizes people who are not in control of their senses.

15. הִנֵּה תִרְאוּ אִישׁ מִשְׁתַּגֵּעַ — *Behold, you see the man is mad.*

Achish had no doubt that this was not David.

Malbim explains that in this verse and the next, Achish refuted any reason that his servants might offer for having brought David to him. They could not claim ignorance of his condition, for Achish said, *You see the man is mad.* They could not claim that they had brought him to provide entertainment for Achish, for he complained, *Do I lack madmen?* They could not disavow responsibility for having brought him, for Achish expostulated, *Should this person enter my house* — i.e., could he have entered on his own?

16. חֲסַר מְשֻׁגָּעִים אָנִי — *Do I lack madmen?*

Achish asked rhetorically, "Do I need madmen?" (*Radak*).

According to *Malbim*, Achish was saying, "There are always plenty of lunatics around" — a reference to his own wife and daughter (according to the Midrash cited earlier). "Do I need any more?"

According to *Abarbanel*, Achish insinuated that the servants who were impressed by David and brought him in must themselves have been gripped by a measure of madness.

הֲזֶה יָבוֹא אֶל־בֵּיתִי — *Should this person enter my house?*

Even if Achish's men had decided to bring in a lunatic to provide entertainment, this particular man was so far gone that he was not in the least amusing (*Ralbag*; see *Malbim* above).

Kli Yakar suggests that with this rhetorical question Achish referred back to whether or not this was David. He asked, "Is it conceivable that, knowing that he is our chief public enemy, David would come into my presence, right into the lions' den?"

David's scheme worked perfectly, and Achish chased him away in disgust. This is attested to by the verse in *Psalms*, לְדָוִד בְּשַׁנּוֹתוֹ אֶת טַעְמוֹ לִפְנֵי אֲבִימֶלֶךְ וַיְגָרְשֵׁהוּ וַיֵּלַךְ, *By David: When he disguised his sanity before Abimelech [i.e., Achish], who drove him out, and he left* (34:1).

XXII

1. וַיֵּלֶךְ דָּוִד מִשָּׁם וַיִּמָּלֵט — *David went from there and escaped.*

The word וַיֵּלֶךְ, *went*, implies calm, unhurried movement, whereas וַיִּמָּלֵט, *and escaped*, connotes frantic flight. *Daas Sofrim* explains that as he was leaving Gath, David walked at a measured pace in order not to appear as a fugitive. As soon as he was out of sight, however, he began to run.

עֲדֻלָּם וַיִּשְׁמְעוּ אֶחָיו וְכָל־בֵּית אָבִיו וַיֵּרְדוּ אֵלָיו
ב שָׁמָּה: וַיִּתְקַבְּצוּ אֵלָיו כָּל־אִישׁ מָצוֹק וְכָל־אִישׁ
אֲשֶׁר־לוֹ נֹשֶׁא וְכָל־אִישׁ מַר־נֶפֶשׁ וַיְהִי עֲלֵיהֶם
ג לְשָׂר וַיִּהְיוּ עִמּוֹ כְּאַרְבַּע מֵאוֹת אִישׁ: וַיֵּלֶךְ דָּוִד
מִשָּׁם מִצְפֵּה מוֹאָב וַיֹּאמֶר | אֶל־מֶלֶךְ מוֹאָב יֵצֵא־
נָא אָבִי וְאִמִּי אִתְּכֶם עַד אֲשֶׁר אֵדַע מַה־יַּעֲשֶׂה־לִּי
ד אֱלֹהִים: וַיַּנְחֵם אֶת־פְּנֵי מֶלֶךְ מוֹאָב וַיֵּשְׁבוּ עִמּוֹ כָּל־

מְעָרַת עֲדֻלָּם — *The cave of Adullam.*

Targum does not translate this phrase into Aramaic but retains the original Hebrew, indicating that this was a place name — and thus, states *Kli Yakar*, not necessarily an actual cave.

Alshich comments that David chose Adullam to arouse the merit of his ancestor Judah, whose descent to an Adullamite man (*Genesis* 38:1) began the episode that led to the birth of Perez, from whom the Judean kingdom was destined to descend.

וַיִּשְׁמְעוּ אֶחָיו — *His brothers heard.*

David's brothers heard of his escape from Saul and, afraid that Saul would direct his wrath onto them, they fled as well (*Abarbanel*).

Alternatively, when David's brothers heard of how he had miraculously survived his encounter with Achish, they knew that God was with him and they came to join him (*Chomas Anach, Kli Yakar*).

וְכָל־בֵּית אָבִיו — *And all his father's house.*

Verse 3 adds in particular that David's parents came — they did so out of fear that in his hatred for David Saul would lash out at them (*Radak*).

2. ... וַיִּתְקַבְּצוּ אֵלָיו כָּל־אִישׁ — *There gathered about him — every man ...*

This verse lists three categories of troubled men who came to find relief in David's company. All of them, for one reason or another, could no longer remain in their hometowns (*Metzudos*). David was a talented and successful person, and the word had spread that in his presence those in despair regained hope (*Ralbag*).

כָּל־אִישׁ מָצוֹק — *Every man in distress.*

This refers to men who were unable to fend off their enemies (*Ralbag, Abarbanel*). According to *Radak*, these men were suffering from assorted crises and had left home in an attempt to forget their difficulties.

Me'am Loez comments that these individuals were righteous men — as, for example, Gad the Prophet — for it is unlikely that David would have associated with unscrupulous people.

Our Sages offer a homiletic basis for this assertion. The word מְצוּקִים they state, indicates spiritually noble people, for the word is related to מְצֻקֵי אֶרֶץ, *the pillars of the earth* (in Hannah's song, above, 2:8) which is a reference to the righteous (*Yoma* 38b).

וְכָל־אִישׁ אֲשֶׁר־לוֹ נֹשֶׁא — *Every man with a creditor.*

These were people who did not have the means to pay their debts (*Radak*).

נֹשֶׁא — *Creditor.*

This word is usually spelled with a ה, not an א (see *Exodus* 22:24; *Radak*).

וְכָל־אִישׁ מַר־נֶפֶשׁ — *And every man with a bitter spirit.*

These were men suffering from poverty (*Radak*). The two concepts are explicitly linked in the verse: תְּנוּ־שֵׁכָר לְאוֹבֵד וְיַיִן לְמָרֵי נָפֶשׁ. יִשְׁתֶּה וְיִשְׁכַּח רִישׁוֹ, *Give strong drink to the woebegone and wine to those of embittered soul —*

of Adullam. His brothers and all his father's house
heard about this, and went down to him there. [2]*They*
gathered about him — every man in distress, every
man with a creditor, and every man with a bitter
spirit — and he became their leader. With him were
about four hundred men.

[3]*David went from there to Mizpeh of Moab, and*
he said to the king of Moab, "Let my father and
mother come out here and stay with you until I know
what God will do with me." [4]*So he escorted them*
to the king of Moab and they stayed with him all

let such a person drink and forget his poverty (*Proverbs* 31:6,7).

According to *Malbim*, this is a reference to short-tempered people.

Some commentators suggest that these people were embittered by contemplation of their sins, and David influenced them to repent (*Chomas Anach, Kli Yakar*).

3. וַיֹּאמֶר אֶל־מֶלֶךְ מוֹאָב יֵצֵא־נָא אָבִי וְאִמִּי אִתְּכֶם — *He said to the king of Moab, "Let my father and mother come out here and stay with you."*

David planned to remain in a fortress near Moab (see verse 4). Because that location might be perilous in a time of war, he wanted his elderly parents to reside in the peaceful and comfortable capital city (*Malbim*).

David had believed that the Moabite king would be hospitable toward his parents and brothers because his father was a descendant of Ruth, who was a Moabitess. Unfortunately, he was terribly wrong. After David left Moab for the forest of Hereth, the king murdered David's parents and all of his brothers save one,[1] who escaped to Nahash, king of Ammon. The king of Moab demanded David's brother's return, but Nahash refused, and it was this that David referred to when he recalled the kindness of Nahash (*II Samuel* 10:2). The details of David's revenge against Moab for having committed this horrendous crime are described in *II Samuel* 8:1,2 (*Bamidbar Rabbah* 14:1).

יֵצֵא־נָא אָבִי וְאִמִּי — *Let my father and mother come out here.*

The verb יֵצֵא, *come out*, is written in the singular form. *Kli Yakar* suggests that it refers primarily to David's father: David wanted the Moabites to appreciate that they would benefit from the counsel of this aged and wise man.

Alternatively, the singular grammar is a Scriptural expression that implies that David's mother was secondary to his father.

עַד אֲשֶׁר אֵדַע מַה־יַּעֲשֶׂה־לִּי אֱלֹהִים — *Until I know what God will do with me.*

According to *Metzudos*, David sought to obtain a stable residence for himself, to which he could then bring his parents.

1. In the *sefer Shaul B'Chir Hachom* by R' Leib Friedman, it is recorded that the Moabites judged and executed Jesse and his family as descendants of Ruth, in retribution for her betrayal in converting to Judaism.

It is also mentioned that Hashem took David to task for his unwarranted trust in the Moabite king and his assumed mercy, and that David was held somewhat responsible for the death of his relatives.

ה יְמֵי הֱיוֹת־דָּוִד בַּמְּצוּדָה: וַיֹּאמֶר גָּד הַנָּבִיא
אֶל־דָּוִד לֹא תֵשֵׁב בַּמְּצוּדָה לֵךְ וּבָאתָ־לְּךָ אֶרֶץ
ו יְהוּדָה וַיֵּלֶךְ דָּוִד וַיָּבֹא יַעַר חָרֶת: וַיִּשְׁמַע
שָׁאוּל כִּי נוֹדַע דָּוִד וַאֲנָשִׁים אֲשֶׁר אִתּוֹ וְשָׁאוּל
יוֹשֵׁב בַּגִּבְעָה תַּחַת־הָאֶשֶׁל בָּרָמָה וַחֲנִיתוֹ
ז בְיָדוֹ וְכָל־עֲבָדָיו נִצָּבִים עָלָיו: וַיֹּאמֶר שָׁאוּל
לַעֲבָדָיו הַנִּצָּבִים עָלָיו שִׁמְעוּ־נָא בְּנֵי יְמִינִי

4. כָּל־יְמֵי הֱיוֹת־דָּוִד בַּמְּצוּדָה — *All the days that David was in the fortress.*

Targum explicates *that David was hiding in the fortress.*

בַּמְּצוּדָה — *In the fortress.*

The word מְצוּדָה is a reference to any protected area — be it a tower, a large rock, or a cave (*Metzudos*).

5. וַיֹּאמֶר גָּד הַנָּבִיא אֶל־דָּוִד לֹא תֵשֵׁב בַּמְּצוּדָה לֵךְ וּבָאתָ־לְּךָ אֶרֶץ יְהוּדָה — *Gad the Prophet told David, "Do not remain in the fortress; go and get yourself to the land of Judah."*

Gad delivered Hashem's message to David that he would be safer amidst his relatives in the land of Judah, for they would warn him should Saul come to find him. In fact, that was the case, and as long as David was in the forest of Hereth, no one came to seek him. This period of respite ended when David came to Keilah, which, although located in the land of Judah, was distant from his relatives and close acquaintances. Nonetheless, David was prepared to go there when so ordered by Hashem (*Radak*).

Abarbanel adds that when the prophet told David to go to the land of Judah, he was hinting that at the beginning of David's reign he would rule only over the tribe of Judah.

Me'am Loez cites a view that Hashem did not want David to reside in Moabite territory, since with the assemblage of his four hundred followers his regime had begun to coalesce.[1]

וַיָּבֹא יַעַר חָרֶת — *And arrived at the forest of Hereth.*

According to *Midrash Shocher Tov* (*Psalms* 23:6), the name חֶרֶת is interchangeable with חֶרֶס, *a baked earthenware vessel,* and implies that when David came to this forest it was parched and arid. In David's merit, Hashem blessed it with the moisture from the best locations of the world — which, according to one view, gave it a freshness redolent of the World to Come (see *Rashi, Radak* to *Psalms* 23:2). David refers to this in the verse, בִּנְאוֹת דֶּשֶׁא יַרְבִּיצֵנִי, *In lush meadows, He lays me down* (ibid.).

Saul Accuses His Servants of Betrayal

6. וַיִּשְׁמַע שָׁאוּל כִּי נוֹדַע דָּוִד וַאֲנָשִׁים אֲשֶׁר אִתּוֹ — *Saul heard that David and the men with him had been discovered.*

Until that point, David had remained hidden from public view. Now that he had accumulated a significant following,

1. Gad told David not to remain near Moab, where he would be dependent solely on the merits of his ancestress, Ruth the Moabitess, but to go instead to Judah, where he would draw onto himself the merits of his illustrious ancestry from the tribe of Judah. Thus, the letters of the word וּבָאתָ, *get yourself,* may be rearranged into the word אָבוֹת, *ancestors.*

Furthermore, the merits of Ruth would be aroused in the land of Judah as well, because she divorced herself from her association with Moab and connected herself to the tribe of Judah when she became the mother of the Judean monarchy (*Chomas Anach*).

the days that David was in the fortress. 5*Gad the*
Prophet told David, "Do not remain in the for-
tress; go and get yourself to the land of Judah."
So David went and arrived at the forest of Hereth.
6*Saul heard that David and the men with*
him had been discovered. Saul was sitting in Gi-
beah under the tree in Ramah with his spear in
his hand, with all his servants standing about
him. 7*Saul said to his servants who were stand-*
ing about him, "Listen now, [fellow] Benjamites.

he could no longer conceal his whereabouts.

When Saul heard of David's following, he assumed that David intended to rebel against him — either by an all-out assault or by establishing a rival dominion (*Radak*).

In that spirit, *Abarbanel* reads this phrase as, וַיִּשְׁמַע שָׁאוּל כִּי נוֹדַע דָּוִד, *Saul heard that David had become known [as his foe].*

As mentioned above, *Daas Sofrim* states that Saul believed that David's leadership was predicated on reliance on military prowess, and that David therefore posed a moral threat to the Israelite nation. Accordingly, now that David had assembled a considerable number of embittered men as his followers, Saul considered that his suspicions had been confirmed, and that it would be a noble deed on his part to subdue this movement.

According to *Rashi*, כִּי נוֹדַע דָּוִד means *David had come to know [that he was being pursued with deadly intent].*

וְשָׁאוּל יוֹשֵׁב בַּגִּבְעָה תַּחַת־הָאֵשֶׁל בָּרָמָה — *Saul was sitting in Gibeah under the tree in Ramah.*

It was common for kings to sit under the shade of a tree (as above, 14:2; see also *Judges* 4:5; *Me'am Loez*).

Ramah was mentioned earlier as Samuel's hometown in Mt. Ephraim (see above, 7:17, 19:22). However, at first glance, that cannot be the Ramah of this verse, which is describing an episode that occurred in Saul's home in Gibeah, which was in the portion of Benjamin. Therefore, some commentators explain that in this verse the word *Ramah* — literally, *high spot* — is not a place name but a description; i.e., this tree was situated on a high promontory in Gibeah (*Rashi; Metzudos*).

Malbim offers another explanation. According to him, there were two sites called Ramah: one in Mt. Ephraim and one in Benjamin's territory. Saul was in the latter Ramah, and the tree under which he sat marked the boundary between Gibeah and Ramah.

The Sages, however, understand that Scripture indeed refers to Samuel's Ramah in Mount Ephraim, but in a homiletical sense. After Saul's failure to eradicate Amalek, he should have died immediately; however, Samuel prayed that Saul not die within the prophet's lifetime. Accordingly, the fact that שָׁאוּל יוֹשֵׁב בַּגִּבְעָה, *Saul resided at Gibeah* for an additional two and a half years of life, was תַּחַת־הָאֵשֶׁל בָּרָמָה, *due to [the merit of] the "great tree of Ramah"* — a reference to Samuel (*Taanis* 5b, as explained by *Rashi* here).

7. וַיֹּאמֶר שָׁאוּל לַעֲבָדָיו הַנִּצָּבִים עָלָיו שִׁמְעוּ־נָא בְּנֵי יְמִינִי ... — *Saul said to his servants who were standing around him, "Listen now, [fellow] Benjamites!"*

Discovering that David had succeeded in escaping with the collusion of his own son, Saul felt deserted. He

גַּם־לְכֻלְּכֶם יִתֵּן בֶּן־יִשַׁי שָׂדוֹת וּכְרָמִים לְכֻלְּכֶם
ח יָשִׂים שָׂרֵי אֲלָפִים וְשָׂרֵי מֵאוֹת: כִּי קְשַׁרְתֶּם
כֻּלְּכֶם עָלַי וְאֵין־גֹּלֶה אֶת־אָזְנִי בִּכְרָת־בְּנִי עִם־בֶּן־
יִשַׁי וְאֵין־חֹלֶה מִכֶּם עָלַי וְגֹלֶה אֶת־אָזְנִי כִּי הֵקִים
ט בְּנִי אֶת־עַבְדִּי עָלַי לְאֹרֵב כַּיּוֹם הַזֶּה: וַיַּעַן

thus rebuked his servants for not having communicated with him earlier and accused them of collaborating with David.

שִׁמְעוּ־נָא בְּנֵי יְמִינִי — *"Listen now, [fellow] Benjamites!"*

Most of Saul's servants were his own kin, and as such descendants of Benjamin (*Metzudos*).

Furthermore, Saul took them to task in particular, because, as his relatives, they should have exhibited greater loyalty to him (*Radak*).

גַּם־לְכֻלְּכֶם יִתֵּן בֶּן־יִשַׁי שָׂדוֹת וּכְרָמִים לְכֻלְּכֶם יָשִׂים שָׂרֵי אֲלָפִים וְשָׂרֵי מֵאוֹת — *Is the son of Jesse going to give all of you fields and vineyards? Is he going to make all of you captains of thousands and captains of hundreds?*

Saul warned his followers that if they intended to abandon him in the hope of receiving gifts of land or prestigious positions from David, their expectations would be frustrated. David could not possibly distribute wealth to everyone or appoint everyone to high office (*Radak, Abarbanel*). This is because no leader possesses sufficient abundance to make each of his subjects wealthy, nor can he appoint everyone to high office, for every leader must have a following; every captain of a thousand must have 999 adherents (*Sefer HaAkeidah, Shaar 60*).

Furthermore, by directing his words specifically to the Benjamites Saul indicated that even if David did distribute sinecures they would go first to his own kinsmen of the tribe of Judah (*Malbim*).

בֶּן־יִשַׁי — *Son of Jesse.*

See above, 20:31.

8. כִּי קְשַׁרְתֶּם כֻּלְּכֶם עָלַי — *That you have all organized against me.*

Targum renders קְשַׁרְתֶּם as *rebelled.*

The root of the word is קָשַׁר, *tied* or *combined*. The fact that people had — putatively — joined their hearts together in such common cause was itself seditious (*Radak*).

וְאֵין־גֹּלֶה אֶת־אָזְנִי ... — *And no one revealed to me ...*

If someone would have informed Saul, he argued, he would have been able to prevent matters from getting to this point (*Metzudos*).

Literally, וְאֵין־גֹּלֶה אֶת־אָזְנִי means *no one revealed to my ear*. Even if people were afraid to pass on the information openly, complained Saul, someone should have at least whispered it into his ear (*Me'am Loez*).

וְאֵין־גֹּלֶה אֶת־אָזְנִי בִּכְרָת־בְּנִי עִם־בֶּן־יִשַׁי וְאֵין־חֹלֶה מִכֶּם עָלַי וְגֹלֶה אֶת־אָזְנִי כִּי הֵקִים בְּנִי אֶת־עַבְדִּי עָלַי לְאֹרֵב — *And no one revealed to me that my son made a covenant with the son of Jesse, and none among you is distressed on my behalf or revealed to me that my son has incited my servant to rise up and ambush me.*

Most commentators explain the prefix ב of the word בִּכְרָת as meaning *that* or *when he formed a covenant*. Thus, Saul claimed that he had had no inkling of such an agreement. Similarly, in the phrase כִּי הֵקִים בְּנִי אֶת־עַבְדִּי, further on in this passage, כִּי also means *that* — i.e., no one revealed to Saul that his son had incited David.

But Saul could hardly have made this claim, objects *Abarbanel*, since he clearly did know of Jonathan's collusion with David, as evidenced by his

Is the son of Jesse going to give all of you fields and vineyards? Is he going to make all of you captains of thousands and captains of hundreds, [8] *that you have all organized against me and no one revealed to me that my son made a covenant with the son of Jesse, and none among you is distressed on my behalf or revealed to me that my son has incited my servant to rise up and ambush me, [which is as clear] as this day?"*

having earlier berated Jonathan for *choosing the son of Jesse to [his] own shame and the shame of his mother's nakedness* (above, 20:30). In light of this difficulty, *Abarbanel* translates the prefix ב and the word כִּי as *because*, and interprets Saul's intent as follows. It was *because* David forged a covenant with Saul's own son and thus compromised him that people hesitated to notify Saul of David's machinations. Furthermore, said Saul, although he was upset that no one was distressed on his behalf, he was not surprised, כִּי הֵקִים בְּנִי אֶת־עַבְדִּי עָלַי, *because my own son incited my servant to rise up against me.* Saul acknowledged that he could not expect strangers to evince loyalty to him when his own son did not.

וְאֵין־חֹלֶה מִכֶּם עָלַי — *And none among you is distressed on my behalf.*

The word חֹלֶה literally means *sick.* Saul was disappointed that his servants were not pained by his troubles.

Our Sages mandate that every Jew must empathize with the pain of a Torah scholar and pray for mercy on his behalf, and they support that injunction by citing these words of Saul (who was a Talmudic scholar; see *Rashi, Gittin* 59a).[1]

וְגֹלֶה אֶת־אָזְנִי — *Or revealed to me.*

Saul spoke repetitively, a mannerism typical of a person in distress (*Metzudos*).

כִּי הֵקִים בְּנִי אֶת־עַבְדִּי עָלַי לְאֹרֵב — *That my son has incited my servant to rise up and ambush me.*

Now that no one had stepped forward to inform Saul, he complained, the situation had deteriorated to such a degree that his servant — David — was prepared to ambush him (*Metzudos*).

כַּיּוֹם הַזֶּה — *[Which is as clear] as this day.*

The fact that David had gathered a group of followers, claimed Saul, proved beyond the shadow of a doubt that he intended to attack Saul (*Metzudos*).

◆§ Doeg's Slander

The following two verses places before us Doeg's incrimination of David, one of the most egregious acts of treachery in Jewish history, an act that led our Sages — who elaborate upon the extent of Doeg's evil speech, its effects and the punishment that he incurred — to castigate Doeg as the paradigm of a slanderer. In *Psalms* (particularly Ch. 52, but elsewhere as well), David himself describes his feeling about Doeg's

1. The Talmud ultimately deems this proof unpersuasive, because Saul was also a king and the deference he demanded might be attributed to that. However, the Talmud does find another proof to uphold this principle (*Berachos* 12b; see also *Teshuvos Chasam Sofer* Vol. 6:29, *Nachalas Shimon* 60:18).

דֹּאֵג הָאֲדֹמִי וְהוּא נִצָּב עַל־עַבְדֵי־שָׁאוּל
וַיֹּאמַר רָאִיתִי אֶת־בֶּן־יִשַׁי בָּא נֹבֶה אֶל־
י אֲחִימֶלֶךְ בֶּן־אֲחִטוּב: וַיִּשְׁאַל־לוֹ בַּיהוָה וְצֵידָה
נָתַן לוֹ וְאֵת חֶרֶב גָּלְיָת הַפְּלִשְׁתִּי נָתַן לוֹ:

malicious fabrications and distortion. Although a superficial reading of Doeg's statement gives the impression that it is a guileless report of what he witnessed, we present his words through the lens of the Sages and commentators who understood his malevolent intentions. We also mention a number of halachos regarding the prohibition of לָשׁוֹן הָרַע, *evil speech,* that are derived from this incident.[1]

9. וְהוּא נִצָּב עַל־עַבְדֵי־שָׁאוּל — *Who was appointed over Saul's servants.*

Our translation of נִצָּב, *appointed,* follows *Targum*: Doeg was appointed to a position of authority over the servants.

Metzudos, however, understands the word literally as *standing.* Doeg was standing near the servants when Saul spoke.

According to *Me'am Loez,* נִצָּב indicates that Doeg was teaching Torah — for this word was previously used in that context: וּשְׁמוּאֵל עֹמֵד נִצָּב עֲלֵיהֶם, *with Samuel standing erect, overseeing them* (19:20).

וַיֹּאמַר — *And said.*

In *Psalms* 52:2, David states that Doeg came וַיַּגֵּד לְשָׁאוּל וַיֹּאמֶר לוֹ בָּא דָוִד אֶל־בֵּית אֲחִימֶלֶךְ, *and informed Saul and said to him, "David came to the house of Ahimelech."* According to *Midrash Shocher Tov,* the word וַיַּגֵּד is related to the word אֲגַד, *joined* or *added,* and implies that Doeg did not just relate the incident but added his own implicit accusations in the following verse.

This verse from *Psalms* states that Doeg *informed Saul and said to him. Shaarei Chaim* explains the apparent redundancy: the word וַיַּגֵּד, *informed,* implies harsh speech, whereas וַיֹּאמֶר, *and said,* indicates soft words (see *Rashi, Exodus* 19:3). Doeg concluded his words by speaking sympathetically of the Kohanim of Nob, in the hope of deflecting the blame for having murdered them to Saul.

בֶּן־יִשַׁי — *The son of Jesse.*

Doeg referred to David without mentioning his name as a means of disparaging him (as had Saul; see above, 20:27; *Abarbanel*).

אֶל־אֲחִימֶלֶךְ בֶּן־אֲחִטוּב — *To Ahimelech, son of Ahitub.*

Doeg implied that David had made his way directly to Ahimelech, as if they had already been joined in conspiracy (*Abarbanel*).

In *Psalms* (ibid.), Scripture quotes Doeg as saying that David came to *the house of Ahimelech* — insinuating that they secreted themselves there in order to discuss a matter of vital importance (*Alshich*). Doeg fabricated this claim, since David had come not to

1. *R' David Cohen* (in *Sefer Ohel David* Vol. II) seeks to explain how Doeg, the head Judge of the High Court, justified speaking *lashon hara* about David. He cites *Targum Yonasan* to *Deuteronomy* 23:7, who says that even if a Moabite converts to Judaism, we are instructed to maintain our hatred toward him. Accordingly the word וְאָהַבְתָּ לְרֵעֲךָ כָּמוֹךָ, *love your fellow as yourself* (*Leviticus* 19:18) does not apply to a Moabite, even if he converts. Thus, Doeg may have assumed that, similarly, the prohibition of לֹא־תֵלֵךְ רָכִיל בְּעַמֶּיךָ, *you shall not be a gossipmonger among your people* (ibid. v. 16) would also not apply to a Moabite convert. Since Doeg didn't recognize the homiletical derivation that this law applies only to male converts but not to females, he assumed that the exceptions mentioned applied also to Ruth, and thereby to all her descendants, including David.

[9]*Then Doeg the Edomite, who was appointed over Saul's servants, [spoke up] and said, "I saw the son of Jesse come to Nob, to Ahimelech, son of Ahitub.* [10]*He inquired of* HASHEM *for him and gave him provisions, and he gave him the sword of Goliath the Philistine."*

Ahimelech's house but to the Sanctuary.

By referring to Ahimelech as "son of Ahitub," and omitting the fact that he was a Kohen, Doeg intimated that the family of Ahitub sided with David, and that David had come to Ahimelech not in regard to his official capacity but as a fellow rebel (*Malbim*).

10. וַיִּשְׁאַל־לוֹ בַּה׳ — *He inquired of* HASHEM *for him.*

The Midrash (*Yalkut Shimoni* §131) describes these words as constituting an essential component of Doeg's defamation of Ahimelech. Doeg contended that one may inquire of the *Urim VeTumim* only on behalf of the king. Ahimelech's inquiry on behalf of David therefore constituted a de facto recognition of David as king and thus flagrant defiance of Saul.

Two of Saul's trusted officers, Abner and Amasa, who were also scholars, disputed Doeg's claim and argued that it is permitted to seek counsel of the *Urim VeTumim* on behalf of any significant public servant (see *Yoma* 71b) — a description that David satisfied.

All of the major Jewish courts were consulted on this issue and they concurred unanimously with Abner and Amasa. Doeg, however, ignored them and continued to condemn Ahimelech. This constituted contempt of the court on Doeg's part and signaled the beginning of his downfall.

Thus, Hashem explained, "Because you have rebelled against Me using My own Torah, I will hereby remove it from your innards." As Doeg taught Torah to his disciples, he began misrepresenting the Torah, declaring the ritually clean unclean and vice versa. Hearing this, his students tied ropes to his feet and dragged him away.

Also, a person who speaks slander is punished with *tzaraas* (see *Numbers* Ch. 12 regarding Miriam), and the Talmud reports that Doeg was stricken with this affliction (*Sanhedrin* 106b).

וַיִּשְׁאַל־לוֹ בַּה׳ וְצֵידָה נָתַן לוֹ וְאֵת חֶרֶב גָּלְיָת הַפְּלִשְׁתִּי נָתַן לוֹ — *He inquired of* HASHEM *for him and gave him provisions, and he gave him the sword of Goliath the Philistine.*

The manner in which Doeg presented this information — including the facts that he left out — was calculated to inculpate Ahimelech.

We will here cite some of the points that *Malbim* makes in this regard.

First, Doeg omitted the fact that David had represented himself to Ahimelech as an emissary of the king on an important mission.

The truth was that Ahimelech had given David the food *before* inquiring of Hashem on his behalf (see above, 21:7-10). Had Doeg mentioned that, it would have implied that Ahimelech gave the food before he heard anything about David's flight, and was thus acting as any caring and concerned person would by supplying food to someone in need. By mentioning first that Ahimelech inquired of the *Urim VeTumim*, Doeg implied that Ahimelech knew that David was running away, and thus the offering of provisions was an act of supporting a rebel.

Doeg also failed to mention that David came in a state of starvation where his life was at risk. That information would have cleared Ahimelech from some element

יא וַיִּשְׁלַח הַמֶּלֶךְ לִקְרֹא אֶת־אֲחִימֶלֶךְ בֶּן־אֲחִיטוּב
הַכֹּהֵן וְאֵת כָּל־בֵּית אָבִיו הַכֹּהֲנִים אֲשֶׁר בְּנֹב
יב וַיָּבֹאוּ כֻלָּם אֶל־הַמֶּלֶךְ׃ וַיֹּאמֶר
שָׁאוּל שְׁמַע־נָא בֶּן־אֲחִיטוּב וַיֹּאמֶר הִנְנִי אֲדֹנִי׃
°אֵלָיו ק׳ יג וַיֹּאמֶר °אלו שָׁאוּל לָמָּה קְשַׁרְתֶּם עָלַי אַתָּה וּבֶן־
יִשָׁי בְּתִתְּךָ לוֹ לֶחֶם וְחֶרֶב וְשָׁאוֹל לוֹ בֵּאלֹהִים

of guilt, even if David were a fugitive. Instead, Doeg described the food package as צֵידָה, *provisions*, connoting that he prepared him for a long and thus more successful escape.

וְאֵת חֶרֶב גָּלְיָת הַפְּלִשְׁתִּי נָתַן לוֹ — *And he gave him the sword of Goliath the Philistine.*

With these words, Doeg justified not having confronted David and engaged him in battle. Not only was David a powerful warrior but this particular sword, which was evocative of his merit, would make him a more formidable adversary in any altercation.

◆§ Laws of Relating Evil Speech

Doeg is the classic paradigm of the gossiper/ slanderer. Even when he had previously praised David to Saul (see above, 16:18), he had done so intending to arouse Saul's envy (*Sanhedrin* 93b). In the present instance he overtly defamed David and Ahimelech.

Various ordinances regarding the laws of slander are based on this incident, and we here present a brief (and incomplete) summary.

❒ One type of prohibited speech is *rechilus*, speech that instigates ill-will, such as to say "This is what So-and-so said about you."

Kesef Mishneh (to *Rambam, Hilchos Dei'os* 7:1-2) states that if one person reports on someone else's behavior to a third party, thereby personally offending that third party, this constitutes *rechilus*. This is the case even if that behavior was objectively proper and the person who engaged in it has no regrets. To illustrate this concept, *Kesef Mishneh* cites this incident. Ahimelech meant no harm by giving food and a sword to David. He actually thought that he was *supporting* Saul by supplying his emissary. Nevertheless, Doeg's statement was considered *rechilus* because it infuriated Saul.

❒ Along the same lines, we learn from Doeg's words that a remark may be prohibited as *lashon hara, evil speech*, even if it is true. A Midrash (*Pirka D'Rabbeinu HaKadosh "Bava* of Threes" 16, cited by *Ramban, Genesis* 2:9) lists Doeg as one of three men who were banished from the World to Come for speaking the truth. Although, as noted earlier, the Sages point out inaccuracies and misleading nuances in Doeg's speech, in essence what he said was accurate (*Nachalas Shimon*).

❒ The Talmud states that slander is considered a grievous crime because it kills three individuals: the speaker, the listener, and one spoken about (*Arachin* 15b).

This particular case, which is listed as the example of that concept, was especially direful, as *four* people lost their lives: Doeg, the speaker; Saul, the listener; Ahimelech, the subject; and Abner, Saul's trusted general who could have prevented Saul's reaction but did not (*Yerushalmi Peah* 1:1).

❒ The Chofetz Chaim (in his work by that name which is devoted to the laws of evil speech) states that one may not engage in slander or gossip even if one

[11] *So the king sent for Ahimelech son of Ahitub the*
Kohen and all his father's house, the Kohanim of Nob,
and they all came to the king. [12] *Saul said, "Listen now,*
son of Ahitub!" And he said, "Here I am, my lord."
[13] *Saul said to him, "Why did you organize against*
me — you and the son of Jesse — in that you gave
him food and a sword, and inquired of God for him,

is under intense pressure to do so, even from a respectable person such as one's parent or the king. He supports his claim from Doeg, who is responsible for having spoken slander although he was responding to Saul's accusation that none of his servants had come to his aid (v. 8; *Chofetz Chaim, Be'er Mayim Chaim* 1:7).

☙ Saul's Accusation and Sentencing of Ahimelech

11. וַיִּשְׁלַח הַמֶּלֶךְ — *So the king sent.*

Here, as well as at the end of this verse, Saul is identified as *the king,* although in many other instances he is referred to simply by name. *Kli Yakar* suggests that in this verse, Saul invoked his royal authority by imperatively summoning the Kohanim, and they complied immediately in order to avoid appearing like rebels. Afterward, Scripture reverts to calling Saul by his name alone, as he then acted not as a sovereign but as a commoner who lost his claim to royalty.[1]

וְאֵת כָּל־בֵּית אָבִיו — *And all his father's house.*

Apparently, Saul suspected Ahimelech's entire family of being in collusion against him (*Ralbag, Radak*).

12. בֶּן־אֲחִיטוּב — *Son of Ahitub.*

Saul spoke to Ahimelech in a disparaging manner by referring to him only by his father's name (see above, 20:27; *Abarbanel*). *Kli Yakar* suggests that Saul called Ahimelech *son of Ahitub* in order to incorporate into his accusation all the descendants of Ahitub (*Kli Yakar*).

13. אַתָּה וּבֶן־יִשָׁי — *You and the son of Jesse.*

Saul first mentioned Ahimelech and only then David, implying that Ahimelech's guilt was the more severe of the two, since he was not influenced by self-interest but acted solely on someone else's behalf (*Kli Yakar*).

Saul referred to David only by his father's name in order to disparage him (*Abarbanel*).

בְּתִתְּךָ לוֹ לֶחֶם וְחֶרֶב וְשָׁאוֹל לוֹ בֵּאלֹהִים — *In that you gave him food and a sword, and inquired of God for him.*

Saul listed the order of events in ascending order of severity. Ahimelech's least serious malefaction was giving David bread; more deplorably, he gave David a weapon; and worst of all, he consulted the *Urim VeTumim* on David's behalf — an act that Doeg had described as illegal and even seditious (*Malbim, Kli Yakar*).

וְשָׁאוֹל לוֹ בֵּאלֹהִים — *And inquired of God for him.*

Saul accused Ahimelech of helping David determine which escape route to take (*Radak*).

1. *Daas Sofrim* views the choice of the title "king" here from a different perspective. Saul was about to make one of his most crucial decisions as king. A ruler must always find a balance between asserting control and maintaining rapport. Earlier in his career as king — soon after he had been anointed (see above, 10:27) and at the battle against Amalek (see above, Ch. 15) — Saul had erred by not sufficiently asserting his authority. Now, perhaps, Saul felt that he had to exercise control by nipping this supposed rebellion in the bud.

יד לָקוּם אֵלַי לְאֹרֵב כַּיּוֹם הַזֶּה: וַיַּעַן אֲחִימֶלֶךְ
אֶת־הַמֶּלֶךְ וַיֹּאמַר וּמִי בְכָל־עֲבָדֶיךָ כְּדָוִד נֶאֱמָן
וַחֲתַן הַמֶּלֶךְ וְסָר אֶל־מִשְׁמַעְתֶּךָ וְנִכְבָּד בְּבֵיתֶךָ:
°לִשְׁאָל־ ק׳ טו הַיּוֹם הַחִלֹּתִי °לשאול־לוֹ בֵאלֹהִים חָלִילָה לִּי
אַל־יָשֵׂם הַמֶּלֶךְ בְּעַבְדּוֹ דָבָר בְּכָל־בֵּית אָבִי כִּי

לָקוּם אֵלַי לְאֹרֵב — *So that he could arise and ambush me.*

If a person is pursuing someone else with murderous intent, one may do whatever is necessary to stop him, even killing him (see *Sanhedrin* 73a; *Rambam, Hil. Rotze'ach* Ch. 1). According to *Me'am Lo'ez*, Saul suspected David of having designs on his life and judged Ahimelech and his family as David's collaborators. Thus, in his eyes they were all deserving of execution.

Kli Yakar observes the contrast between this verse and v. 8.

Originally, Saul stated that: הֵקִים בְּנִי אֶת־עֲבְדִּי **עָלַי**, *my son has incited my servant upon me* (v. 8). Now he stated that David had come לָקוּם **אֵלַי** לְאֹרֵב, *so that he could arise toward me to ambush me*, implying an unsuccessful attempt. Saul did not believe that David could ambush him alone; David would, however, be able to do so with the aid of Jonathan.

כַּיּוֹם הַזֶּה — *[Which is as clear] as this day?*

This phrase appeared as well in v. 8.

Although each incident may have seemed innocent at the time that it occurred, on *this day* everything that Ahimelech did for David was revealed to have facilitated David's rebellion (*Malbim*).

14. וַיַּעַן אֲחִימֶלֶךְ אֶת־הַמֶּלֶךְ וַיֹּאמַר וּמִי בְּכָל־עֲבָדֶיךָ כְּדָוִד — *Ahimelech answered the king and said, "Who among all your servants is like David?"*

With deep sincerity, Ahimelech defended his actions, claiming that he had no reason to believe that David was recreant. Since Saul's accusation had incriminated both Ahimelech and David, Ahimelech first defended David and then (in the following verse) himself (*Abarbanel*).

וּמִי בְּכָל־עֲבָדֶיךָ כְּדָוִד נֶאֱמָן ... — *Who among all your servants is like David: trustworthy...?*

Ahimelech spoke of David in the present tense, implying that he believed that David had remained loyal (*Daas Sofrim*).

וְסָר אֶל־מִשְׁמַעְתֶּךָ — *A man who obeys your bidding.*

Ahimelech described David as a person who punctiliously follows orders; accordingly, he claimed that he had no reason to suspect that David was doing anything other than fulfilling the king's will (*Rashi, Radak*).

נֶאֱמָן וַחֲתַן הַמֶּלֶךְ וְסָר אֶל־מִשְׁמַעְתֶּךָ וְנִכְבָּד בְּבֵיתֶךָ — *Trustworthy, the king's son-in-law, a man who obeys your bidding, and who is honored in your household?*

Ahimelech provided four descriptions of David: (1) He was a trustworthy soldier who fought on behalf of the nation; (2) he was the king's son-in-law and therefore like the king's son; (3) he was a regular visitor to the king's table and was therefore focused on the king's words; and (4) he was honored as a leader among the masses. Thus, Ahimelech characterized David as a man who performed an essential role on behalf of the nation and for whose sake it was appropriate to inquire of the *Urim VeTumim* (*Abarbanel*).

According to *Malbim*, Ahimelech's allusion to these four attributes was an attempt to dispel any suspicion that David was a revolutionary. (1) Some people are naturally separatists and dissenters — David, on the other hand, was

so that he could arise and ambush me, [which is as
clear] as this day?"
14 Ahimelech answered the king and said,
"Who among all your servants is like David:
trustworthy, the king's son-in-law, a man who
obeys your bidding, and who is honored in your
household? 15 Did I begin today to inquire for him
of God? It would be sacrilegious for me [to betray
the king]! Let the king not accuse his servant
or my father's entire household of anything, for

loyal and trustworthy. (2) Some people belong to families that are long-time antagonists of the king — David, on the other hand, was the king's son-in-law. (3) Some people have a history of insubordination — David had always obeyed the king's bidding. (4) And some people are angry at having been unappreciated — David, however, had been honored in the king's household.

וְנִכְבָּד בְּבֵיתֶךָ — *And who is honored in your household?*

Since the king's household honored David, there was no reason for Ahimelech not to have done so as well (*Me'am Loez*).

15. הַיּוֹם הַחִלֹּתִי לִשְׁאָל־לוֹ בֵאלֹהִים — *Did I begin today to inquire for him of God?*

Doeg had accused Ahimelech of recognizing David as king, since — he argued — one may inquire of the *Urim VeTumim* only on behalf of a king (*Midrash*).

Ahimelech here justified himself by replying that he had begun inquiring of the *Urim VeTumim* on David's behalf much earlier — clearly, without acknowledging any claims of David being king — because one may inquire of the *Urim VeTumim* on behalf of someone who performs an essential national service (see above, *Yoma* 71b, *Rashi; Parashas Derachim, Derush* 13). However, Ahimelech's acknowledgment only served to inflame Saul's rage, for he considered Ahimelech to be confessing to a long-standing betrayal — and this sealed Ahimelech's fate (*Midrash Tehillim* 52:5).

This interpretation of the verse — which is the most common among commentators — translates the words הַיּוֹם הַחִלֹּתִי as a rhetorical question: *Did I begin today ...?*

Radak, however, understands these words as a statement — i.e., *Only today did I begin to inquire on his behalf.* Ahimelech argued that he had no idea that David was fleeing Saul. Had he known, he would never have consulted the *Urim VeTumim* on his behalf.

חָלִילָה לִּי — *It would be sacrilegious for me [to betray the king].*

Our translation follows *Rashi*.

Alternatively, according to *Radak* above, Ahimelech added, *It would have been sacrilegious for me* — i.e., to have consulted the *Urim VeTumim* had he known that David was fleeing Saul, and he would never do it again.

In Ahimelech's self-justification, no mention is made of the bread and the sword. Presumably, he did so, but the verse does not record these words (*Abarbanel*).

Alternatively, Saul did not allow Ahimelech to finish vindicating himself but interrupted him and peremptorily sentenced him to death (*Me'am Loez*).

אַל־יָשֵׂם הַמֶּלֶךְ בְּעַבְדּוֹ דָבָר בְּכָל־בֵּית אָבִי — *Let the king not accuse his servant or my father's entire household of anything.*

כב/טז־יח

לֹא־יָדַע עַבְדְּךָ בְּכָל־זֹאת דָּבָר קָטֹן אוֹ גָדוֹל:
טז וַיֹּאמֶר הַמֶּלֶךְ מוֹת תָּמוּת אֲחִימֶלֶךְ אַתָּה וְכָל־
יז בֵּית אָבִיךָ: וַיֹּאמֶר הַמֶּלֶךְ לָרָצִים הַנִּצָּבִים עָלָיו
סֹבּוּ וְהָמִיתוּ | כֹּהֲנֵי יהוה כִּי גַם־יָדָם עִם־דָּוִד
°אָזְנִי ק׳ וְכִי יָדְעוּ כִּי־בֹרֵחַ הוּא וְלֹא גָלוּ אֶת־°אזנו וְלֹא־
אָבוּ עַבְדֵי הַמֶּלֶךְ לִשְׁלֹחַ אֶת־יָדָם לִפְגֹעַ בְּכֹהֲנֵי
°לְדוֹאֵג ק׳ יח יהוה: וַיֹּאמֶר הַמֶּלֶךְ °לדויג

Since Saul's summons of the entire family implicated them as rebels, Ahimelech deemed it necessary to defend them as well (*Radak*).

The words בְּכָל־בֵּית אָבִי — lit., *in all of my father's household* — is to be understood as if it began with the conjunctive letter ו, *or*.

16. וַיֹּאמֶר הַמֶּלֶךְ — *But the king said.*

Here again, Scripture refers to Saul as *the king*, for with this pronouncement he spoke with sovereign authority. Also, he was acting not on his own behalf but with the intent of protecting the kingdom of Israel from David, whom he considered to be an unwelcome intruder (*Daas Sofrim*).

מוֹת תָּמוּת אֲחִימֶלֶךְ — *You must die, Ahimelech.*

Saul acted without going through a formal judicial process. Rather, he employed the right granted the king to quell rebellion by imposing the death penalty.

The phrase מוֹת תָּמוּת literally means, *die, you shall die.* This indicates Saul's intent that Ahimelech's entire family — and thus its posterity — be destroyed. It was only due to God's mercy that one son of Ahimelech, Abiathar, escaped (below, v. 20; *Kli Yakar*).

Alternatively, this double phrasing connotes Saul's belief that Ahimelech sinned both against Hashem (by inquiring of the *Urim VeTumim*) and against the king (by supporting David) (*Chomas Anach*).

17. וַיֹּאמֶר הַמֶּלֶךְ לָרָצִים הַנִּצָּבִים עָלָיו — *The king then said to the footmen who stood about him.*

רָצִים, literally *runners*, were servants who ran before the king's chariot (*Metzudos*) and who were available to execute his command.

הַנִּצָּבִים עָלָיו, literally, *standing upon him* — indicating that they were stationed near him, prepared to do his bidding (*Metzudos*).

The Midrash states (as cited by *Rashi*) that these servants were none other than Saul's highly respected warriors, Abner and Amasa, about whom we will elaborate later.

In accordance with this Midrash, *Radak* comments, the text must be understood as speaking of *runners and those standing near him*, the latter being a reference to Abner and Amasa, for Scripture would not refer to such revered noblemen as mere *runners*.

Kli Yakar, however, states that *Rashi* does not concur with this observation but considers Abner and Amasa as *runners* in the sense of men eager to perform the royal will.

סֹבּוּ וְהָמִיתוּ — *Surround and kill.*

Our translation, which follows *Targum*, is based on the relating of סֹבּוּ to סָבִיב, *around*. According to *Metzudos*, however, סֹבּוּ means *turn away* (as in the verse וַיִּסֹּב מֵעֲלֵיהֶם וַיֵּבְךְּ, *He turned away from them and wept* [Genesis 42:24]).

A Midrash cited in our commentary to v. 10 describes how Abner and Amasa consulted all the high courts across the land of Israel to seek validation of their view that any significant public figure may consult the *Urim VeTumim*. According to *Kli Yakar*, the word סֹבּוּ

your servant did not know anything small or great
about all of this."
[16] *But the king said, "You must die, Ahimelech,*
you and all your father's house!"
[17] *The king then said to the footmen who stood*
about him, "Surround and kill the Kohanim of
HASHEM, because their hand is also with David,
and because they knew that he was fleeing and
did not inform me." But the servants of the king
were not willing to send forth their hand to slay
the Kohanim of HASHEM. [18] *So the king said to Doeg,*

alludes to that incident, and means, "*Traverse* among the high courts before you kill the Kohanim."

וְלֹא גָלוּ אֶת־אָזְנִי — *And did not inform me.*

In this phrase — lit., *and did not reveal to my ear* — the word אָזְנִי, *my ear,* is written (*ksiv*) with a ו — i.e., אָזְנוֹ, *his ear.*

Saul thus implied that since his servants knew of David's treachery, they should have *informed his ear* — i.e., they should have rebuked David (*Kli Yakar*).

וְלֹא־אָבוּ עַבְדֵי הַמֶּלֶךְ לִשְׁלֹחַ אֶת־יָדָם לִפְגֹּעַ בְּכֹהֲנֵי ה׳ — *But the servants of the king were not willing to send forth their hand to slay the Kohanim of HASHEM.*

They sensed that the accusation was false (*Malbim*).

Although it is ordinarily mandatory to obey a royal command (the transgression of which is punishable by death — *Joshua* 1:18), Abner and Amasa here derived that an exception can be made if the king's imperative contravened a Torah commandment (*Rashi*).

לִפְגֹּעַ בְּכֹהֲנֵי ה׳ — *To slay the Kohanim of HASHEM.*

From the version of this story presented in *Midrash Shocher Tov* (52:5) it is evident that not only did Abner and Amasa fail to obey the king but they even protected the Kohanim against Saul's other servants. Doeg, however, prevailed and slaughtered them himself (*Kli Yakar*).

◆§ The Massacre at Nob

18. וַיֹּאמֶר הַמֶּלֶךְ לְדוֹאֵג סֹב אַתָּה וּפְגַע בַּכֹּהֲנִים — *So the king said to Doeg, "Circle around and slay the Kohanim!"*

Saul now insisted that Doeg himself, who had testified against the Kohanim, administer the death penalty, as per the Torah's command: יַד הָעֵדִים תִּהְיֶה־בּוֹ בָרִאשֹׁנָה לַהֲמִיתוֹ, *The hand of the witnesses shall be upon him first to put him to death* (*Deuteronomy* 17:7).

Doeg was chosen by Providence to commit this heinous crime in accordance with the principle that *HASHEM causes evil things to happen through evil people* (*Shabbos* 32a; *Abarbanel*).

וַיֹּאמֶר הַמֶּלֶךְ לְדוֹאֵג — *The king said to Doeg.*

The *ksiv* (written) form of the name Doeg here is דוֹיֵג. *Rashi* cites our Sages' comment (*Yerushalmi Sanhedrin* Ch. 10) that Saul trapped Doeg like a fish (דָּג), in the sense that he told him, "You denounced them; now you kill them."

Daas Sofrim comments that this implies that Doeg himself did not perform this mass murder altogether willingly but only under the pressure of Saul's insistence.

°דוֹאֵג ק׳

סֹב אַתָּה וּפְגַע בַּכֹּהֲנִים וַיִּסֹּב °דויג
הָאֲדֹמִי וַיִּפְגַּע־הוּא בַּכֹּהֲנִים וַיָּמֶת | בַּיּוֹם
הַהוּא שְׁמֹנִים וַחֲמִשָּׁה אִישׁ נֹשֵׂא אֵפוֹד
יט בַּד: וְאֵת נֹב עִיר־הַכֹּהֲנִים הִכָּה לְפִי־חֶרֶב

Just as a fish is caught by its mouth, so was Doeg assigned this horrific task because of his abusive mouth. The numerical value of the Hebrew word for mouth, פֶּה, is 85 — indicating that Doeg's mouth led to his murder of 85 people (*Kli Yakar*).

The Sages offer yet another homiletical interpretation of the dual spelling of Doeg's name. The regular spelling of the word דוֹאֵג means *worry*, whereas the spelling דוֹיֵג includes the word וַי, *woe*. Thus, initially Hashem sat and worried, as it were, that Doeg might stray onto evil pathways. Once he did so, Hashem exclaimed, "Woe, for he has strayed!" (*Sanhedrin* 106b).

סֹב אַתָּה וּפְגַע בַּכֹּהֲנִים — *Circle around and slay the Kohanim!*

The Talmud (*Yoma* 22b) comments that when Saul took pity on the animals of Amalek (above, Ch. 15), a heavenly voice told him, אַל־תְּהִי צַדִּיק הַרְבֵּה, *Do not be overly-righteous* (*Ecclesiastes* 7:16). When he commanded Doeg to slay the Kohanim, this same voice told him, אַל־תִּרְשַׁע הַרְבֵּה, *Be not overly wicked* (ibid. v. 17).

Maharsha cites the verse, וּבְכָל אֲשֶׁר־יִפְנֶה יַרְשִׁיעַ — *wherever he turned he inspired terror* (above, 14:47) — as explaining that Saul had developed a reputation as a ruthless warrior. Hashem now warned him not to misuse that trait by directing it against the Kohanim.

וַיִּסֹּב דוֹאֵג הָאֲדֹמִי — *Doeg the Edomite circled around.*

There is a tradition that this instance of the word *Doeg* also has a *keri* and *ksiv* reading, as earlier in the verse. However, some commentators deny such a tradition, and simply read the name here as דוֹיֵג (*Radak*).

וַיִּפְגַּע־הוּא בַּכֹּהֲנִים וַיָּמֶת בַּיּוֹם הַהוּא שְׁמֹנִים וַחֲמִשָּׁה אִישׁ — *And killed the Kohanim; on that day he killed eighty-five men.*

Displaying extraordinary physical strength and martial prowess, Doeg single-handedly killed 85 noblemen, and then the entire population of Nob.[1]

Regarding this incident, David addressed Doeg, מַה־תִּתְהַלֵּל בְּרָעָה הַגִּבּוֹר, *Why do you take pride in evil, O mighty warrior?* (*Psalms* 52:3; *Midrash Shocher Tov* 52:5). David asked, "Is a man truly mighty when he sees his fellow at the edge of a pit and pushes him in? To the contrary, true strength is exhibited by a person who sees his fellow about to fall into a pit and grasps his hand. Yet when you saw that Saul was angry at me, instead of defending me you persisted in vilifying me" (ibid. 52:6).

וַיִּפְגַּע־הוּא — *And killed.*

The Midrash (*Yalkut Shimoni* 131) observes that the word הוּא, *he*, is superfluous, since this pronoun is already incorporated into the word וַיִּפְגַּע. The word הוּא thus indicates that Doeg alone struck the Kohanim, since Abner and Amasa, who had first been assigned this task by Saul, refused to perform it.

According to one Midrashic opinion, Abner was eventually punished for not objecting and preventing what happened at Nob (*Yalkut Shimoni* 133).

1. From the text here, it seems that Doeg performed this mass murder entirely by himself. However, in *Otzar HaGeonim* (to Tractate *Sanhedrin*, cited by *Mishbetzos Zahav*) there is a citation of *Rav Saadiah Gaon* who says that Doeg was aided by seven of Saul's own children and grandchildren. Those were the seven that were chosen to be killed by the Gibeonites as revenge for their suffering with the destruction of Nob (see *II Samuel* Ch. 21).

"Circle around and slay the Kohanim!" Doeg
the Edomite circled around and killed the Ko-
hanim; on that day he killed eighty-five men
who wore linen robes. 19 *And Nob, the city of*
Kohanim, he struck with the blade of the sword:

שְׁמֹנִים וַחֲמִשָּׁה אִישׁ נֹשֵׂא אֵפוֹד בָּד — *Eighty-five men who wore linen robes.*

The linen robe was a garment worn only by highly respected people on an exalted spiritual and religious plane.[1]

Metzudos explains the text literally: these men were wearing linen robes.

Targum, however, amends this phrase to read, *worthy of wearing linen robes.* Possibly, *Targum* agrees that they wore the robes and is pointing out that they were intrinsically worthy of doing so.

The *Talmud Yerushalmi* (*Sanhedrin,* Chapter 8) states that this is a reference to the *Ephod* worn by the Kohen Gadol (see *Exodus* 28:6-8). Each of these eighty-five men was worthy to be the Kohen Gadol.

However, the Kohen Gadol's *Ephod* cannot be accurately described as being made of linen, since it was woven of five different types of material (*Ibn Ezra, Exodus* 28:6).

Perhaps this is why *Rambam* denies that the *Ephod* mentioned here was the one worn by the Kohen Gadol. Rather, a person who was worthy of experiencing Divine inspiration wore *a linen robe,* which indicated that he had reached the level of the Kohen Gadol, who spoke with Divine inspiration via the *Ephod* and *Choshen* (*Hil. Klei HaMikdash* 10:13; see *Kesef Mishneh;* for a resolution to *Ibn Ezra*'s query, see *Nachalas Shimon* 60:20).

According to one view, this verse is referring to the robe of the Kohen Gadol, and the conjunctive ו is to be understood as standing before the word נֹשֵׂא. Thus, Doeg killed 85 men as well as the man who wore the *Ephod* — i.e., the Kohen Gadol (*Me'am Loez*).

19. וְאֵת נֹב עִיר־הַכֹּהֲנִים הִכָּה לְפִי־חֶרֶב — *And Nob, the city of Kohanim, he struck with the blade of the sword.*

The massacre at Nob is one of the most shocking and baffling incidents in Jewish history. *Chida* writes in *Chomas Anach,* "The incident of Nob, city of Kohanim, makes one's hair stand on end," and adds that in contemplation of this incident "silence is appropriate." Nonetheless, we will cite some of the sources that attempt to shed light on this occurrence — in particular, on Saul's motives.

According to *Abarbanel,* Saul felt that he had no choice but to take this drastic step in order to instill fear in the hearts of the entire nation, so that they should not attempt to protect David. Moreover, self-preservation would be their incentive to turn David in.

Furthermore, states *Abarbanel,* Saul knew that these Kohanim were descendants of Eli, the Kohen Gadol, and as such assumed that they were unscrupulous people, just as Eli's sons had been (above, Ch. 2). Thus, he believed that they would be likely to protect a fugitive from the king. He considered them cursed by Hashem and as such deserving of annihilation.

הִכָּה לְפִי־חָרֶב — *He struck with the blade of the sword.*

Rambam rules (*Hil. Sanhedrin* 14:2) that a king who performs capital punishment is authorized to do so only with a sword. This ruling can be traced to a *Tosefta* (*Sanhedrin* 9:3).

1. We find similar references to such robes regarding Samuel (above, 2:18) and David (*I Samuel* 6:14).

מֵאִישׁ וְעַד־אִשָּׁה מֵעוֹלֵל וְעַד־יוֹנֵק וְשׁוֹר וַחֲמוֹר וָשֶׂה
כ לְפִי־חָרֶב׃ וַיִּמָּלֵט בֵּן־אֶחָד לַאֲחִימֶלֶךְ בֶּן־אֲחִטוּב
כא וּשְׁמוֹ אֶבְיָתָר וַיִּבְרַח אַחֲרֵי דָוִד׃ וַיַּגֵּד אֶבְיָתָר לְדָוִד
כב כִּי הָרַג שָׁאוּל אֵת כֹּהֲנֵי יהוה׃ וַיֹּאמֶר דָּוִד לְאֶבְיָתָר
°דוֹאֵג ק׳ יָדַעְתִּי בַּיּוֹם הַהוּא כִּי־שָׁם °דויג הָאֲדֹמִי כִּי־הַגֵּד
יַגִּיד לְשָׁאוּל אָנֹכִי סַבֹּתִי בְּכָל־נֶפֶשׁ בֵּית אָבִיךָ׃

מֵאִישׁ וְעַד־אִשָּׁה מֵעוֹלֵל וְעַד־יוֹנֵק וְשׁוֹר וַחֲמוֹר וָשֶׂה — *Man and woman alike; child and suckling alike; ox, donkey, and sheep.*

According to *Abarbanel*, Saul did not take the spoils, so that everyone would realize that he had killed the inhabitants of Nob because they were rebels, not in order to benefit from their property.

Me'am Loez adds that Saul did not want to profit from the spoils of Eli's descendants, because God's condemnation of them had been so severe.

This language of this list is strikingly similar to that of Samuel's mandate to Saul to eradicate Amalek: וְהֵמַתָּה מֵאִישׁ וְעַד־אִשָּׁה מֵעֹלֵל וְעַד־יוֹנֵק מִשּׁוֹר וְעַד־שֶׂה מִגָּמָל וְעַד־חֲמוֹר, *kill man and women alike, infant and suckling alike, ox and sheep alike, camel and donkey alike* (above, 15:3). In regard to Amalek, Saul's compassion overcame him and he failed to fulfill his mission — yet now he acted mercilessly. Our Sages comment on this contrast that whoever is compassionate when he should exhibit cruelty will eventually be cruel when compassion is due (*Midrash Koheles Rabbah* 7:16).[1]

Saul's later violent death in battle was God's retribution for this sin at Nob (*Sanhedrin* 104a; see also below, *II Samuel* 1:9, *Rashi*). However, this connection is not stated explicitly in Scripture because the Kohanim were at any rate deserving of death, seemingly because of the sins of Eli's sons (*Radak*).[2]

In *II Samuel* (Chapter 21), Scripture relates that the Israelites were held accountable for the Gibeonites that Saul killed in Nob. The Gibeonites were Canaanites who deceived Joshua into pledging that he would not harm them. When Joshua discovered their identity, he made them woodcutters and water drawers (*Joshua* Ch. 9). According to *Yerushalmi Sanhedrin*, seven Gibeonites were present when Saul killed the Kohanim of Nob, and they too were killed. However, the Sages state elsewhere that Saul did not literally have any Gibeonites killed. Rather, since the Kohanim had sustained the Gibeonites, once Saul dispatched the Kohanim, it was considered as if he had taken the Gibeonites' lives as well (*Bava Kamma* 119a).[3]

On the day that the city of Nob was destroyed, the Tabernacle was transferred to Gibeon, where it remained until the building of the Temple (*Radak*).

1. Saul killed even the children, seemingly ruling that under such circumstances a king may take the lives of children on account of their parents' sins. (For sources that discuss this issue, see *Nachalas Shimon* 60:21.)

2. When Saul made inquiry of Samuel through necromancy (below, Ch. 28), Samuel stated that Saul would lose the war to the Philistines because of his sin regarding Amalek; however, Samuel made no mention of Saul's cruelty in Nob.

Maharsha (*Sanhedrin* 104a) explains that Samuel's response provided an explanation of why Saul would lose the kingdom. However, were it not for the sin at Nob, he would not have suffered his demise at the blade of a sword.

3. For a more detailed account of this issue, see *II Samuel* Ch. 21.

man and woman alike; child and suckling alike;
ox, donkey, and sheep.
[20] *One son of Ahimelech son of Ahitub — his*
name was Abiathar — escaped, and he fled to
David. [21] *Abiathar told David that Saul had*
massacred the Kohanim of HASHEM. [22] *David*
said to Abiathar, "I knew on that day that
Doeg the Edomite was there and that he
would certainly inform Saul. I am respon-
sible for every life of your father's house!

The murder of so many Kohanim brought the service of Hashem in Nob to an end and hampered the sacrificial service for many generations to come.

This sin hung over the two tribes involved — Saul's tribe of Benjamin and David's tribe of Judah — and threatened to cause the destruction of the Temple and send the Jews into exile.

Thus, the verse עוֹד הַיּוֹם בְּנֹב לַעֲמֹד, *Yet today [Sennacherib, king of Assyria] will stand in Nob* (*Isaiah* 10:32) implies that this was the last day remaining for potential Divine retribution for the sin at Nob. Had Sennacherib immediately attacked Jerusalem, he would have succeeded. It was the Jews' dedication to Torah learning inspired by King Hezekiah that gained them their salvation (*Sanhedrin* 94b, 95a, *Maharsha* ad loc.).

◆§ Abiathar Escapes

20. וַיִּמָּלֵט בֵּן־אֶחָד לַאֲחִימֶלֶךְ בֶּן־אֲחִטוּב וּשְׁמוֹ אֶבְיָתָר — *One son of Ahimelech son of Ahitub — his name was Abiathar — escaped.*

As we will see below, David was held partially responsible for the mass murder at Nob. In retribution, therefore, his descendants should have been wiped out, and indeed, Queen Athaliah made an attempt to kill his descendants. One member of the royal family, Joash, survived (*II Kings* Ch. 11). The Sages tell us that were it not for the survival of Abiathar, the one remnant of the Kohanim of Nob, Joash would also not have survived, and there would not have remained a trace of the Davidic family (*Sanhedrin* 95b).

וּשְׁמוֹ אֶבְיָתָר — *His name was Abiathar.*

The formula "his name was ..." rather than "... was his name" is used in the case of a righteous man (*Bamidbar Rabbah* 10:5).

22. וַיֹּאמֶר דָּוִד לְאֶבְיָתָר יָדַעְתִּי בַּיּוֹם הַהוּא כִּי־ ... שָׁם דּוֹאֵג — *David said to Abiathar, "I knew on that day that Doeg the Edomite was there ..."*

David lamented that his actions had precipitated the massacre at Nob, for he should have foreseen the consequences of Doeg witnessing his receipt of provisions from Abimelech.

Our Sages concur that David was to a degree culpable (*Sanhedrin* 95a) — and not only for the deaths of the Kohanim at Nob but also for the subsequent demise of Doeg (who also lost his share in the World to Come), Saul, and Saul's three sons.

In *II Samuel* (21:16), Scripture tells of a Philistine named Ishbi-benob (which may be read as *Ishbi in Nob*), who attempted to kill David (but who was struck down by the warrior Abishai, brother of Joab).

The Talmud relates that the name Ishbi-benob indicates that this man's attack was related to the incident in Nob. Hashem offered David two ways of atoning: either he would be delivered into the hands of the enemy or else

כב/כג כג שְׁבָה אִתִּי אַל־תִּירָא כִּי אֲשֶׁר־יְבַקֵּשׁ אֶת־נַפְשִׁי
א יְבַקֵּשׁ אֶת־נַפְשֶׁךָ כִּי־מִשְׁמֶרֶת אַתָּה עִמָּדִי: וַיַּגִּדוּ
כג/א־ב לְדָוִד לֵאמֹר הִנֵּה פְלִשְׁתִּים נִלְחָמִים בִּקְעִילָה
ב וְהֵמָּה שֹׁסִים אֶת־הַגְּרָנוֹת: וַיִּשְׁאַל דָּוִד בַּיהוה לֵאמֹר
הַאֵלֵךְ וְהִכֵּיתִי בַּפְּלִשְׁתִּים הָאֵלֶּה וַיֹּאמֶר

his offspring would die. David initially chose the former punishment, and thus Ishbi attacked him. As David was on the verge of death, Abishai persuaded him to choose instead the death of his descendants. Thus Queen Athaliah exterminated the entire Davidic family with the exception of one descendant, Joash — just as one person, Abiathar, survived the massacre at Nob.

According to one view, the fact that David was charged with the deaths that he unintentionally caused has broader implications. Thus, if a person's agent is harmed or killed in the execution of his duties, the dispatcher must assume some measure of responsibility and repent (*Mahari Veil* 125, *Be'er Sheva*).

Others deny that we can derive such a rule from this episode, for in this particular case David had acted irresponsibly in that he failed to realize that Abimelech's supplying him with provisions would arouse suspicion — particularly in the mind of a witness as vicious as Doeg. In addition, David misled Abimelech by not telling him that he was escaping from Saul (although he had impeccable motives for doing so). In typical circumstances, on the other hand, a person who dispatches an agent on his behalf has no reason to suspect that any danger will befall him. (A comprehensive discussion about this topic is found in *Nachalas Shimon* 49.)

23. כִּי אֲשֶׁר־יְבַקֵּשׁ אֶת־נַפְשִׁי יְבַקֵּשׁ אֶת־נַפְשֶׁךָ — *For the man who seeks my life seeks your life, as well.*

Most commentators concur with *Targum* that David here referred to Saul. Just as Saul sought to kill David, he said, so did he seek to kill Abiathar. Therefore, David suggested that they join together.

Rashi cites an alternative interpretation. Sometimes the phrase, *seeking a life*, has a positive connotation (as in the verse: אַנְשֵׁי דָמִים יִשְׂנְאוּ־תָם וִישָׁרִים יְבַקְשׁוּ נַפְשׁוֹ, *Bloody men hate an innocent person, but the upright seek [to cleave to] his soul [Proverbs* 29:10]). Therefore, the present phrase may be translated, *The man who seeks to protect my life will seek to protect yours as well.*

Radak and *Abarbanel* read the latter part of this phrase as נַפְשִׁי יְבַקֵּשׁ אֵת אֲשֶׁר יְבַקֵּשׁ אֶת־נַפְשֶׁךָ, *I will seek [to protect you from] anyone who seeks your life.*

כִּי־מִשְׁמֶרֶת אַתָּה עִמָּדִי — *You are safe with me.*

"I will watch you as I watch myself" (*Radak*).

Chomas Anach adds that Divine protection offered to a group — in this case two people — is greater than that enjoyed by an individual — therefore, their chances of survival would be enhanced if they would join together.

Ralbag explains that Abiathar was in possession of the *Urim VeTumim*, and David promised to protect both him and it.

According to *Kli Yakar*, David told Abiathar that he would safeguard him כִּי מִשְׁמֶרֶת אַתָּה עִמָּדִי, "Because you — Abiathar — are a source of protection for me." Abiathar's spiritual stature would protect David, as well as the fact that he had survived Doeg's onslaught, in consequence of which one of David's descendants would survive Queen Athaliah's onslaught (as mentioned above).

Malbim notes that in regard to their *being pursued*, David mentioned himself first: אֲשֶׁר־יְבַקֵּשׁ אֶת־נַפְשִׁי יְבַקֵּשׁ אֶת־נַפְשֶׁךָ, *Whoever seeks my life seeks your life.* However, in regard to their security, David mentioned Abiathar first: כִּי־מִשְׁמֶרֶת אַתָּה עִמָּדִי, *You are safe with me.* David thus implied that he

22/23 [23]*Stay with me and fear not, for the man who seeks my life seeks your life, as well. You are safe with me."*

23/1-2 [1]*They told David, saying, "Behold, the Philistines are battling against Keilah and they are pillaging the granaries."* [2]*David then inquired of HASHEM, saying, "Shall I go and strike down these Philistines?"*

was in greater danger but that Abiathar had greater merits, because he was a Kohen who performed the service of Hashem (and was thus more likely to be saved). This comment was intended to reassure Abiathar and give him hope.[1]

XXIII

☙§ David Saves Keilah

1. קְעִילָה — *Keilah.*

Keilah was a heavily fortified Jewish city (see v. 7) on the border separating Israelite from Philistine territory (*Eruvin* 45a). It was in the territory of Judah (*Mahari Kara; see Joshua* 15:44 and v. 3 below).

נִלְחָמִים בִּקְעִילָה וְהֵמָּה שֹׁסִים אֶת־הַגְּרָנוֹת — *Are battling against Keilah and they are pillaging the granaries.*

The Philistines appeared during the harvest season to plunder straw and hay. Although their purpose was not to invade Israelite territory, such an attack was an act of war, since Keilah was a border city, the breach of whose security opened the entire land to assault (*Eruvin* ibid., *Rashi, Tosafos* ad loc.).

2. וַיִּשְׁאַל דָּוִד בַּה׳ לֵאמֹר הַאֵלֵךְ וְהִכֵּיתִי בַּפְּלִשְׁתִּים הָאֵלֶּה — *David then inquired of HASHEM, saying, "Shall I go and strike down these Philistines?"*

Scripture does not specify how David made this inquiry. Below, however (v. 6), we learn that Abiathar the Kohen possessed the *Ephod* (which included the *Urim VeTumim*), and it was this medium that David presumably used (*Radak*).

Daas Sofrim, however, disagrees, contending that if that were the case, the *Ephod* would have been mentioned here. Rather, David posed his question in the form of a prayer, and he received his answer through Divine Inspiration.

הַאֵלֵךְ וְהִכֵּיתִי בַּפְּלִשְׁתִּים — *Shall I go and strike down these Philistines?*

David could have raised a number of halachic questions regarding such a venture. For example, since the Philistines were interested only in material plunder, did he have a right to risk his life and that of his men by attacking them? And did he have a right to engage in battle on the Sabbath?

However, David apparently harbored no doubts regarding his right to engage in this mission, because (as stated above) any attack on a border city poses a mortal risk to the entire nation. Besides that, the Talmud relates, David would not have made such inquiry of the *Urim VeTumim,* since the proper venue for such questions is a qualified judge.

David thus had only one inquiry: would he succeed? That this was in fact his question may be inferred from the response that he received: וְהוֹשַׁעְתָּ אֶת־קְעִילָה — *you will [succeed] in saving Keilah* (*Eruvin* 45a, *Tosafos* ad loc.).

1. *Chomas Anach* offers a homiletical interpretation of this verse. The numerical value of the name *Abiathar* is 613. Thus, David said, "Because of you, I will remember to keep the 613 commandments."

כג/ג־ו

יְהֹוָה אֶל־דָּוִד לֵךְ וְהִכִּיתָ בַפְּלִשְׁתִּים וְהוֹשַׁעְתָּ
ג אֶת־קְעִילָה: וַיֹּאמְרוּ אַנְשֵׁי דָוִד אֵלָיו הִנֵּה אֲנַחְנוּ
פֹה בִּיהוּדָה יְרֵאִים וְאַף כִּי־נֵלֵךְ קְעִלָה אֶל־
ד מַעַרְכוֹת פְּלִשְׁתִּים: וַיּוֹסֶף עוֹד דָּוִד
לִשְׁאֹל בַּיהוָֹה וַיַּעֲנֵהוּ יְהוָֹה וַיֹּאמֶר קוּם
ה רֵד קְעִילָה כִּי־אֲנִי נֹתֵן אֶת־פְּלִשְׁתִּים בְּיָדֶךָ: וַיֵּלֶךְ
דָּוִד °ואנשו קְעִילָה וַיִּלָּחֶם בַּפְּלִשְׁתִּים וַיִּנְהַג אֶת־ °וַאֲנָשָׁיו ק׳
מִקְנֵיהֶם וַיַּךְ בָּהֶם מַכָּה גְדוֹלָה וַיֹּשַׁע דָּוִד אֵת יֹשְׁבֵי
ו קְעִילָה: וַיְהִי בִּבְרֹחַ אֶבְיָתָר בֶּן־אֲחִימֶלֶךְ אֶל־דָּוִד

וַיֹּאמֶר ה׳ אֶל־דָּוִד לֵךְ וְהִכִּיתָ בַפְּלִשְׁתִּים וְהוֹשַׁעְתָּ אֶת־קְעִילָה — *HASHEM said to David, "Go and strike the Philistines, and save Keilah."*

As long as David had remained in the forest of Hereth, Saul had not pursued him. Still, when Hashem commanded him to leave this enclave and go to Keilah — which, although in Judean territory, was far from his friends and relatives — he did not hesitate (*Radak*).

David's extraordinary dedication to the Jewish people expressed itself in the fact that, although he was fleeing Saul, he possessed the strength and composure to engage in battle on behalf of Keilah. Possibly he felt some measure of personal responsibility, surmising that the Philistines only dared attack because King Saul was preoccupied with pursuing him (*Me'am Loez*).

3. וַיֹּאמְרוּ אַנְשֵׁי דָוִד אֵלָיו הִנֵּה אֲנַחְנוּ פֹה בִּיהוּדָה יְרֵאִים וְאַף כִּי־נֵלֵךְ קְעִילָה — *But David's men said to him, "Behold, we are afraid [even] here in Judah; how much more so if we go to Keilah."*

They argued that they were in great danger among their own people — surely they should not take even further risks by attempting to fight the Philistines (*Radak*).

Me'am Loez adds that they were afraid that if they entered Keilah, a walled city, they might be locked in and rendered vulnerable to an assault by Saul.

הִנֵּה אֲנַחְנוּ פֹה בִּיהוּדָה יְרֵאִים וְאַף כִּי־נֵלֵךְ קְעִילָה — *Behold, we are afraid [even] here in Judah; how much more so if we go to Keilah.*

Although the Book of *Joshua* lists Keilah as a Judean city, the present text implies that it lay outside of Judah (*Malbim*).

Possibly there were two cities named Keilah.

Alternatively, there was just the one Keilah in Judah, and David's men meant to say, "If here in a Judean area free of gentile presence we are frightened, how much worse will our situation be in Keilah, in the midst of the Philistines."

מַעַרְכוֹת פְּלִשְׁתִּים — *The Philistine lines.*

עָרוּךְ means *prepared or organized.* Thus, when army troops are are properly organized for war they are called מַעַרְכוֹת, *lines* (*Metzudos*).

4. וַיּוֹסֶף עוֹד דָּוִד לִשְׁאֹל בַּה׳ — *David inquired again of HASHEM.*

Naturally David felt secure after the first message from the *Urim VeTumim,* but when he saw that his men were still apprehensive, he inquired again on their behalf. When they heard that Hashem's promise was repeated and reinforced, they were ready to proceed (*Radak*). According to *Me'am Loez,* David's first inquiry was made privately, but he made the second inquiry in their presence

Hashem said to David, "Go and strike the Philistines,
and save Keilah." [3]*But David's men said to him,*
"Behold, we are afraid [even] here in Judah; how
much more so if we go to Keilah to the Philistine
lines!" [4]*David inquired again of Hashem, and Hashem*
answered him, "Arise, go down to Keilah, for I am
delivering the Philistines into your hand." [5]*David*
and his men went to Keilah and battled the Philis-
tines; he led away their livestock and struck them a
great blow. Thus David saved the residents of Keilah.
[6]*When Abiathar son of Ahimelech fled to David*

Why didn't David's men trust the first response he had received?

Ralbag explains that that answer was vague. It could be interpreted to mean that the only way to save Keilah was to fight the Philistines, but it did not promise victory.[1]

Chomas Anach suggests that although the *Urim VeTumim's* first response did imply that the Jews would win the war, it left room for the possibility of casualties. The second response promised that Hashem would *deliver the Philistines into your hand* — meaning, without injury.

Daas Sofrim proves from here that in his first inquiry David was not consulting the *Urim VeTumim*, but praying to God. If he had indeed inquired and been answered, his men would surely not have doubted the veracity of the Divine response (see also *Malbim* and *Kli Yakar*).

5. וַיֵּלֶךְ דָּוִד וַאֲנָשָׁיו — *David and his men went.*

The *ksiv*, or written, form of the word וַאֲנָשָׁיו — *and his men* — is וַאֲנָשׁוֹ — literally, *and his man*. This indicates that only a few of his elite men followed him into battle.

וַיִּנְהַג אֶת־מִקְנֵיהֶם — *He led away their livestock.*

מִקְנֶה, *livestock*, is a reference to domestic farm animals.

If the Philistines were encamped for war or pillaging purposes, why would they have their animals with them? *Radak* explains that they did not. Rather, David chased the Philistines back to their homeland, where he took some livestock as booty.

וַיֹּשַׁע דָּוִד אֵת יֹשְׁבֵי קְעִילָה — *Thus David saved the residents of Keilah.*

Although David's men benefited by taking the livestock, Scripture testifies that David's sole motivation was to save Keilah (*Likkutei Yekarim*).

Hashem had told David, וְהוֹשַׁעְתָּ אֶת־קְעִלָה, *Save Keilah* (v. 2). The verse here states that David saved the *residents* of Keilah. This may imply that following David's victory the Philistines grew hesitant about provoking anyone who came from Keilah — even those who were presently situated elsewhere (*Kli Yaakov*).

◆§ David Avoids Confrontation With Saul at Keilah

6. וַיְהִי בִּבְרֹחַ אֶבְיָתָר בֶּן־אֲחִימֶלֶךְ אֶל־דָּוִד קְעִילָה — *When Abiathar son of Ahimelech fled to David to Keilah.*

1. The episode of the concubine in Gibeah had taught the Jews never to rely on an ambiguous statement from the *Urim VeTumim*. In that instance, they had twice asked if they should go to war, and were twice answered in the affirmative. Only after they lost those battles did they realize that they had never asked if they would win (see *Judges* 20:18,23).

ז קְעִילָה אֵפוֹד יָרַד בְּיָדוֹ: וַיֻּגַּד לְשָׁאוּל כִּי־בָא דָוִד
קְעִילָה וַיֹּאמֶר שָׁאוּל נִכַּר אֹתוֹ אֱלֹהִים בְּיָדִי

Most commentators state that this verse does not appear in chronological order, for Abiathar had joined David in the forest of Hereth (above, 22:20), before they came to Keilah. This verse merely provides background information, in order to explain how it was that David had access to the *Urim VeTumim.* Such a non-chronological presentation is quite common, and indeed our Sages state that *there is no particular chronological order in Torah* (*Me'am Loez*).

וַיְהִי בִּבְרֹחַ אֶבְיָתָר ... קְעִילָה — *When Abiathar fled . . . to Keilah.*

We learned earlier (22:20) that Abiathar had joined David in the forest of Hereth, from which they proceeded together to Keilah. Yet this verse states that Abiathar fled directly to Keilah.

Varying solutions are proposed to reconcile these two narratives.

❒ *Metzudos* explains that Abiathar met David at the border between Hereth and Keilah.

❒ According to *Malbim,* Abiathar and David met in the forest of Hereth. This verse mentions Keilah to connote that the fact Abiathar had the *Ephod* with him was an act of Providence, so that David would be informed to save Keilah.

❒ Similarly, *Kli Yakar* explains that Abiathar would never have risked taking the sacred *Ephod* into the wilderness. He was persuaded to carry it with him only because he knew that the fortified city of Keilah was nearby.

❒ *Daas Sofrim,* in accordance with its opinion that David made his first inquiry in prayer, explains that David launched his attack on Keilah without Abiathar. Only after David entered Keilah did Abiathar join him. Accordingly, verse 20 in the previous chapter is not in chronological order.

אֵפוֹד יָרַד בְּיָדוֹ — *He brought the Ephod with him.*

Rashi (*Exodus* 28:30) explains that the *Urim VeTumim* consisted of a parchment inserted into the Kohen Gadol's *Choshen* (Breastplate), on which the Name of Hashem was written; when it was consulted, the letters carved into the twelve stones mounted on the *Choshen* would shine and convey messages.

Here, Scripture refers to the *Urim VeTumim* as the *Ephod,* because the *Choshen* was attached to the *Ephod* (see *Ramban, Exodus* 25:7).

However, Saul, too, consulted the *Urim VeTumim* (below, 28:6). How was this possible if it was in David's camp? Various solutions have been proposed.

❒ *Radak* (ibid.) contends that Saul sent emissaries to Abiathar.

❒ *Ibn Ezra* states that the *Urim VeTumim* remained with Saul. Abiathar did not bring the *Urim VeTumim,* but one of the many *ephods* that the Kohanim possessed (see above, 22:18). A person accustomed to communicating with the *Urim VeTumim* could at times receive a Divine response from an ordinary *ephod* alone, and that is what occurred here. In support of this contention, *Ibn Ezra* points out that Scripture here refers not to הָאֵפוֹד, *the Ephod,* but rather to אֵפוֹד, *an ephod.*

❒ *Ramban* agrees with *Ibn Ezra* that the *Urim VeTumim* remained with Saul, and that the Kohanim possessed multiple *ephods.* He adds that certain scholars knew the text of the *Urim VeTumim* and had the authority to make copies of it, of the *Ephod,*[1] and of the *Choshen.* When a Kohen wore these garments, they would sometimes respond to questions, just as the original *Urim VeTumim* did.

❒ According to *Rambam,* the *Urim VeTumim* comprised an indivisible part

1. Although the copy was made only of linen, and not of the original five types of thread.

to Keilah, he brought the Ephod with him.
7 Saul was told that David had come to Keilah, and
Saul said, "God has delivered him into my hand,

of the Kohen Gadol's wardrobe, without which he may not serve.[1]

Thus, it was possible that Abiathar had the *Urim VeTumim*, and when Saul appointed a new Kohen Gadol, they made a new *Urim VeTumim* for him.

Alternatively, since many people possessed Divine Inspiration, both sets of *Urim VeTumim* functioned simultaneously (*Nachalas Shimon;* see *Ritva* to *Yoma* 73b).

According to the view that David was inquiring of the original *Urim VeTumim*, Abiathar was apparently the Kohen Gadol (see *Rambam, Commentary to Mishnayos, Yoma*, Chapter 7).

But how can that be, since a Kohen Gadol must be appointed by the king and the Kohanim (see *Tosafos, Yoma* 12b), a ceremony that Scripture does not record? Moreover, Saul would certainly not have appointed Abiathar after liquidating his family (see *Nachalas Shimon* 60:23).

One possible answer is that since David had been anointed king by Samuel he considered himself authorized to appoint Abiathar as Kohen Gadol.

Alternatively, since Abiathar was the son of the deceased Kohen Gadol, all that was necessary was that a competent authority — i.e., David — determine that he was fit for the position (see *Exodus* 29:30, *Rashi; Toras Kohanim* 16:5; *Rambam, Hil. Klei HaMikdash* 4:20).

אֵפוֹד יָרַד — *He brought the Ephod.*

Literally, the phrase אֵפוֹד יָרַד means *an ephod came down. Targum Yonasan*, however, renders the verb as *brought down.*

Radak comments that this verb implies that Abiathar did not plan to bring the *Ephod*. Rather, it "came down" by chance. In a rush to escape Saul, Abiathar grabbed whatever he could. It was by Divine Providence that the *Ephod* was among those items, so that David would be able to consult the *Urim VeTumim.*

Ibn Ezra cites the use of this verb to support his claim (above) that Abiathar did not bring *the Ephod* of Moses. By chance, among his belongings, was *an ephod* — i.e., some other *ephod.*

The word יָרַד, *went down* (rather than הָלַךְ, *went*), connotes that the *Urim VeTumim* suffered a spiritual descent as it left the Sanctuary and entered into exile.

7. וַיֹּאמֶר שָׁאוּל נִכַּר אֹתוֹ אֱלֹהִים בְּיָדִי — *And Saul said, "God has delivered him into my hand."*

Our translation of נִכַּר as *delivered* follows *Targum.*

Rashi, on the other hand, renders נִכַּר as *trapped.*

Ralbag relates the word נִכַּר to פֶּן־יְנַכְּרוּ צָרֵימוֹ, *lest his tormentors misinterpret* (*Deuteronomy* 32:27). Accordingly, Saul exclaimed that Hashem had caused David to misjudge the situation, for any discerning person would have understood that it would be all but suicidal to seek refuge in a walled city, from which he could not easily escape.

According to *Malbim*, נִכַּר is the verb form of נָכְרִי, *foreigner* or *stranger*. Thus, Saul claimed that since David had escaped to a fortified city and was unequivocally conducting himself like a rebel, Saul had the right to treat him not as an Israelite but as a foreigner.

נִיכַּר אֹתוֹ אֱלֹהִים בְּיָדִי — *God has delivered him into my hand.*

This statement shows that Saul believed that Hashem endorsed his pursuit of David (*Me'am Loez*). Saul here refers to God by the Name אֱלֹהִים, which represents the Attribute of Justice, attesting to his perception that when justice would

1. Thus, during the Second Temple era, even though no one possessed Divine Inspiration with which to decipher the *Urim VeTumim*, it nevertheless had to be devised for each Kohen Gadol's outfit (*Rambam, Hilchos Beis HaBechirah* 4:1, *Hilchos Klei HaMikdosh* 10:10; see *Kesef Mishneh* in both locations).

ח כִּי נִסְגַּר לָבוֹא בְּעִיר דְּלָתַיִם וּבְרִיחַ: וַיְשַׁמַּע שָׁאוּל
אֶת־כָּל־הָעָם לַמִּלְחָמָה לָרֶדֶת קְעִילָה לָצוּר
ט אֶל־דָּוִד וְאֶל־אֲנָשָׁיו: וַיֵּדַע דָּוִד כִּי עָלָיו שָׁאוּל
מַחֲרִישׁ הָרָעָה וַיֹּאמֶר אֶל־אֶבְיָתָר הַכֹּהֵן הַגִּישָׁה
י הָאֵפוֹד: וַיֹּאמֶר דָּוִד יהוה אֱלֹהֵי יִשְׂרָאֵל שָׁמֹעַ
שָׁמַע עַבְדְּךָ כִּי־מְבַקֵּשׁ שָׁאוּל לָבוֹא אֶל־קְעִילָה
יא לְשַׁחֵת לָעִיר בַּעֲבוּרִי: הֲיַסְגִּרֻנִי בַעֲלֵי קְעִילָה
בְיָדוֹ הֲיֵרֵד שָׁאוּל כַּאֲשֶׁר שָׁמַע עַבְדֶּךָ יהוה אֱלֹהֵי
יִשְׂרָאֵל הַגֶּד־נָא לְעַבְדֶּךָ וַיֹּאמֶר יהוה יֵרֵד:

prevail, he would triumph over David (*Daas Sofrim*).

כִּי נִסְגַּר לָבוֹא בְּעִיר דְּלָתַיִם וּבְרִיחַ — *For he has been trapped by coming into a city of gates and bar.*

By entering a fortified city, David would place his trust in its walls and not try to escape or hide (*Rashi*).

According to *Radak*, it is relatively easy to trap someone in a walled city since there is no room for escape. Moreover, Saul did not think that anyone would warn David of Saul's approach.

Kli Yakar explains Saul's hope as follows. Until this point, David had placed his trust in Hashem and had therefore earned Divine protection. Now that David sought security behind gates, Hashem would remove His protection, leaving David vulnerable.

וּבְרִיחַ — *And bar.*

This secures the gates (*Metzudos*).

8. וַיְשַׁמַּע שָׁאוּל — *So Saul summoned.*

Targum renders וַיְשַׁמַּע as *gathered.*

Radak explains the word as being related to שׁוֹמֵעַ, *hear*. In order to assemble a crowd, one must issue a proclamation that everyone can *hear* (see above, 15:4).

לַמִּלְחָמָה לָרֶדֶת קְעִילָה לָצוּר אֶל־דָּוִד — *For war, to go down to Keilah to besiege David.*

Saul did not inform the people of his purpose, so that those who had not heard of David's victory thought that they were going to fight the Philistines. The latter part of the verse, לָצוּר אֶל־דָּוִד וְאֶל־אֲנָשָׁיו, *to besiege David and his men*, reveals Saul's real and secret intention (*Kli Yakar, Malbim*).

9. וַיֵּדַע דָּוִד כִּי עָלָיו שָׁאוּל מַחֲרִישׁ הָרָעָה — *David learned that Saul was plotting evil against him.*

Literally, וַיֵּדַע means *he knew*. David realized that Saul's offensive was directed solely against him (*Metzudos*).

מַחֲרִישׁ — *Plotting.*

The word מַחֲרִישׁ usually indicates *silence* (see *Genesis* 24:21) or *secrecy* (see *Joshua* 2:1). (It is thus related to חֵרֵשׁ, *deaf*.) In this case, however, commentators relate it to the verse, אַל־תַּחֲרֹשׁ עַל־רֵעֲךָ רָעָה, *Do not devise evil against your neighbor* (*Proverbs* 3:29). They render our verse as *Saul is plotting . . .*

Following *Kli Yakar* and *Malbim* above, Saul was indeed secretive about the motive of his pursuit, so that מַחֲרִישׁ can mean *secretly plotting*.

Targum, however, renders the word as *ambush*, seemingly followed by *Radak*.

10. ה׳ אֱלֹהֵי יִשְׂרָאֵל — *HASHEM, God of Israel.*

By referring to the Deity as the *God of Israel*, David implicitly entreated that no Israelite be injured — in particular, he asked to be given the wherewithal to escape, so that hostilities would not even ensue (*Kli Yakar*).

for he has been trapped by coming into a city
of gates and bar." [8] *So Saul summoned all the*
people for war, to go down to Keilah to besiege
David and his men. [9] *David learned that Saul was*
plotting evil against him, and he said to Abiathar
the Kohen, "Bring forth the Ephod." [10] *David*
said, "HASHEM, God of Israel, Your servant has
heard that Saul seeks to come to Keilah to destroy
the city on my account. [11] *Will the inhabitants*
of Keilah deliver me into his hand? Will Saul
come down here, as Your servant has heard?
HASHEM, God of Israel, please tell Your servant!"
And HASHEM said, "He will come down."

Mishbetzos Zahav suggests that David emphasizes that Hashem, Who had crowned him as king, would not allow him to be killed through the treachery of Keilah.

לְשַׁחֵת לָעִיר בַּעֲבוּרִי — *To destroy the city on my account.*

David feared that just as Saul had killed the people of Nob so would he execute those of Keilah (*Daas Sofrim*).

11. הֲיַסְגִּרֻנִי בַעֲלֵי קְעִילָה בְיָדוֹ הֲיֵרֵד שָׁאוּל ... וַיֹּאמֶר ה׳ יֵרֵד — *"Will the inhabitants of Keilah deliver me into his hand? Will Saul come down here . . .?" And HASHEM said, "He will come down."*

From this episode, the Talmud (*Yoma* 73) derives various rules regarding making inquiry of the *Urim VeTumim.*

First, one should not ask two questions at one time. Should one do so, the *Urim VeTumim* will respond only to the first.[1]

It is true that in this instance God answered David's second question. But that is only because it should logically have been the first. That is to say, David should first have asked if Saul would come; then, if God answered affirmatively, he should have asked if the people of Keilah would hand him over. When David saw that he received a response only to his second question, he repeated the first one, and was answered.

Why, indeed, did David present his queries "out of order"? *Malbim* offers an explanation that deviates somewhat from that of the Talmud. Initially, David thought that Saul would not come to Keilah himself but would dispatch agents to capture him. Thus, he had to know whether the people of Keilah would hand him over. He asked only about himself and not his men, because to quell the rebellion it would be enough for them to arrest the leader. Also, the people of Keilah would not risk the danger of betraying his entire force, because that would surely trigger a civil war.

David's second question was that in case the people of Keilah acquiesced to the demand of Saul's army, would Saul himself come to Keilah? Hashem's response was that Saul himself would come immediately; that answered both questions and prompted David's question in the next verse: *Will the inhabitants of Keilah deliver me and my men over . . .?* David suspected that if Saul and his army were allowed to enter Keilah, Saul would attack both David and his men.

1. However, when time is limited, one may ask two questions, as occurred in the case of David's battle at Ziklag (below, 30:8).

יב וַיֹּאמֶר דָּוִד הֲיַסְגִּרוּ בַּעֲלֵי קְעִילָה אֹתִי וְאֶת־אֲנָשַׁי
יג בְּיַד שָׁאוּל וַיֹּאמֶר יהוה יַסְגִּירוּ׃ וַיָּקָם
דָּוִד וַאֲנָשָׁיו כְּשֵׁשׁ־מֵאוֹת אִישׁ וַיֵּצְאוּ מִקְּעִלָה
וַיִּתְהַלְּכוּ בַּאֲשֶׁר יִתְהַלָּכוּ וּלְשָׁאוּל הֻגַּד כִּי־נִמְלַט
יד דָּוִד מִקְּעִילָה וַיֶּחְדַּל לָצֵאת׃ וַיֵּשֶׁב דָּוִד בַּמִּדְבָּר
בַּמְּצָדוֹת וַיֵּשֶׁב בָּהָר בְּמִדְבַּר־זִיף וַיְבַקְשֵׁהוּ
שָׁאוּל כָּל־הַיָּמִים וְלֹא־נְתָנוֹ אֱלֹהִים בְּיָדוֹ׃

הֲיַסְגִּרֻנִי ... הֲיֵרֵד — *Will [they] deliver me? ... Will [he] come down...?*

The Talmud (*Yoma* ibid.) states that a prediction made by the *Urim VeTumim* can never be reversed. Yet the *Urim VeTumim* foretold that Saul would come (v. 11) and the people of Keilah would hand David over to him (v. 12), but neither of those things happened, because David escaped in time (v. 13).

Abarbanel explains that David was asking not whether these events would take place but rather whether the inhabitants of Keilah and Saul planned to do so. This apparently mirrors the view of *Targum*, which renders this phrase as *Do they plan to give me over? Does he plan to come down*?

Malbim and *Kli Yakar* explain somewhat differently, that David's question was conditional — i.e., *If I stay here, will they hand me over? If I stay, will Saul come*?

בַּעֲלֵי קְעִילָה — *The inhabitants of Keilah.*

Our translation follows *Targum.*

Generally, the word בְּעָלִים denotes an *owner* or *authority*. Thus, *Radak* renders the phrase as *the lords of Keilah.*

12. וַיֹּאמֶר דָּוִד הֲיַסְגִּרוּ בַּעֲלֵי קְעִילָה אֹתִי וְאֶת־אֲנָשַׁי — *David then said, "Will the inhabitants of Keilah deliver me and my men ... ?"*

David realized that he had posed his questions out of order, as a result of which only his second question had been answered (v. 11), and so he now repeated his inquiry regarding the people of Keilah.

However, *Malbim* disagrees and avers that David was not merely repeating his previous question. Originally, when he thought that Saul would send agents to apprehend him, David had asked only about himself — now, fearing that Saul would come himself, he expressed concern for the well-being of his men as well (see *Malbim* above).

וַיֹּאמֶר ה׳ יַסְגִּירוּ — *And* H*ASHEM said, "They will deliver [you]."*

Although David had just saved the people of Keilah from the Philistines, the *Urim VeTumim* testified that they would betray him to Saul — either because their allegiance to Saul outweighed their sense of gratitude to him or because they would be swayed by the fear of suffering the same fate as had befallen the people of Nob.

Since Hashem testified that the people of Keilah were prepared to betray David, the Sages branded them as בְּנֵי־אָדָם שִׁנֵּיהֶם חֲנִית וְחִצִּים, *people whose teeth are spears and arrows* (*Psalms* 57:5; *Vayikra Rabbah* 26:2; *Midrash Shocher Tov* 7:7). Even if that betrayal were motivated by fear, they had no right to turn over an innocent man (*Yefeh Toar*).

13. וַיִּתְהַלְּכוּ בַּאֲשֶׁר יִתְהַלָּכוּ — *And went wherever they could go.*

Our translation follows *Targum*. As *Rashi* explains, David and his men went to whatever haven they could find.

12 *David then said, "Will the inhabitants of Keilah*
deliver me and my men over into the hand of
Saul?" And Hashem *said, "They will deliver*
[you]." 13 *So David and his men — about six hun-*
dred men — arose and left Keilah and went wher-
ever they could go. When Saul was told that David
had escaped from Keilah, he stopped advancing.
14 *David then dwelled in the wilderness in*
strongholds, or he dwelled in the mountain, in the
Wilderness of Ziph. Saul searched for him all the
days, but God did not deliver him into his hand.

Radak understands the verse to mean that they wandered aimlessly and settled wherever it was convenient for them to do so.

The standard verb for *went* is וַיֵּלְכוּ, whereas the word used here — וַיִּתְהַלְּכוּ — has a reflective connotation, implying that they were the objects of some unknown force that moved them about.

Alternatively, *Kli Yakar* suggests that David knew that he had been endangered by staying in a walled city, so he now chose to go to a location where he would have unlimited flexibility. Thus וַיִּתְהַלְּכוּ בַּאֲשֶׁר יִתְהַלָּכוּ may be translated as *they went to wherever they could continue to be mobile.*

וּלְשָׁאוּל הֻגַּד כִּי־נִמְלַט דָּוִד מִקְּעִילָה וַיֶּחְדַּל לָצֵאת — *When Saul was told that David had escaped from Keilah, he stopped advancing.*

Possibly, Saul harbored the intent of attacking the people of Keilah for having hosted David. But when Saul was told that David had fled because the people planned to betray him, Saul felt assured of their loyalty to him (*Kli Yakar*).

☙ David Renews the Covenant with Jonathan

14. בַּמְּצָדוֹת — *In strongholds.*

The word מְצָדוֹת — *strongholds* — is apparently related to מְצוּדוֹת, *fortresses,* and indicates well-protected areas (*Metzudos*).

Radak describes these as high, rocky areas in the wilderness.

וַיֵּשֶׁב דָּוִד בַּמִּדְבָּר בַּמְּצָדוֹת וַיֵּשֶׁב בָּהָר בְּמִדְבַּר־זִיף — *David then dwelled in the wilderness in strongholds, or he dwelled in the mountain, in the Wilderness of Ziph.*

According to *Abarbanel,* whose commentary our translation follows, each instance of וַיֵּשֶׁב — *dwelled* — refers to a different habitation. Sometimes David settled in *strongholds* and sometimes in *the mountain, in the Wilderness of Ziph.*

Radak disagrees and comments that the latter instance of וַיֵּשֶׁב — *dwelled* — explicates the meaning of the first — i.e., the elevated rocks were located *in the mountain, in the Wilderness of Ziph.*

וְלֹא־נְתָנוֹ אֱלֹהִים בְּיָדוֹ — *But God did not deliver him into his hand.*

Abarbanel assumes that some of Saul's servants would warn David each time Saul set out to find him.

Considering the fact that David simply alternated between these two sites (see *Abarbanel* above), it is surprising that Saul never caught up with him (*Malbim*). Indeed, as the text implies, David would have been caught easily were it not that he enjoyed Divine protection (*Daas Sofrim*).

טו וַיַּרְא דָוִד כִּי־יָצָא שָׁאוּל לְבַקֵּשׁ אֶת־נַפְשׁוֹ וְדָוִד
טז בְּמִדְבַּר־זִיף בַּחֹרְשָׁה: וַיָּקָם יְהוֹנָתָן
בֶּן־שָׁאוּל וַיֵּלֶךְ אֶל־דָּוִד חֹרְשָׁה וַיְחַזֵּק אֶת־יָדוֹ
יז בֵּאלֹהִים: וַיֹּאמֶר אֵלָיו אַל־תִּירָא כִּי לֹא תִמְצָאֲךָ
יַד־שָׁאוּל אָבִי וְאַתָּה תִּמְלֹךְ עַל־יִשְׂרָאֵל וְאָנֹכִי
אֶהְיֶה־לְּךָ לְמִשְׁנֶה וְגַם־שָׁאוּל אָבִי יֹדֵעַ כֵּן:
יח וַיִּכְרְתוּ שְׁנֵיהֶם בְּרִית לִפְנֵי יְהוָה וַיֵּשֶׁב דָּוִד
יט בַּחֹרְשָׁה וִיהוֹנָתָן הָלַךְ לְבֵיתוֹ: וַיַּעֲלוּ

15. According to *Radak*, this verse — which imparts no new information — constitutes an introduction to the following verse. While *in the Wilderness of Ziph, in the forest*, David discovered that the Ziphites had informed Saul of his whereabouts, and that Saul was coming to apprehend him. David undertook to leave, but just then Jonathan arrived.

Kli Yakar offers an alternative interpretation (based on *Ralbag*'s words) to this verse. David and his men were stationed in the treeless Wilderness of Ziph — which, although relatively uninhabited, was exposed and conspicuous. Whenever David had reason to suspect that Saul was pursuing him, he would escape to the forest by himself.

בַּחֹרְשָׁה — *In the forest.*

The more common rendering of חֹרְשָׁה is *forest. Radak* mentions this, and also an alternative view that *Chorshah* was a place name (*Radak*).

16. וַיָּקָם יְהוֹנָתָן בֶּן־שָׁאוּל וַיֵּלֶךְ אֶל־דָּוִד חֹרְשָׁה — *Jonathan son of Saul arose and went to see David in the forest.*

This illustrates the depth of the love between David and Jonathan — one described by the mishnah (*Avos* 5:16) as *not dependent on a specific cause* — i.e., as utterly selfless. Jonathan imperiled his own life to bring David encouragement, even as his own father was in deadly pursuit of David (*Me'am Loez*).

Daas Sofrim notes that Jonathan seems to have had no trouble finding David. Clearly, Saul could have as well had God not prevented him from doing so.

וַיְחַזֵּק אֶת־יָדוֹ בֵּאלֹהִים — *And he encouraged him with the word of God.*

Literally, בֵּאלֹהִים means *with God.* Jonathan told David that no creature of flesh and blood could frustrate God's assurances that he would inherit the throne (*Radak*).

Rashi renders *and he encouraged him*, meaning that Jonathan *reinforced their covenant*. Thus, the word בֵּאלֹהִים, *with God*, means that they sealed their covenant with Hashem as witness (see above, 20:23; below, v. 18).

Daas Sofrim suggests that Jonathan assuaged David by reminding him that that all his tribulations had been brought about by Hashem, and they would surely soon come to an end. Since Jonathan was speaking of difficult times, he used the Name אֱלֹהִים, which represents the Attribute of Justice that sometimes tests a person through hardship.

17. וְאַתָּה תִּמְלֹךְ עַל־יִשְׂרָאֵל וְאָנֹכִי אֶהְיֶה־לְּךָ לְמִשְׁנֶה — *You will reign over Israel, and I will be second to you.*

Jonathan requested that David appoint him as his second-in-command, after he became king (*Radak*).

Previously, Jonathan had expressed the hope that he not live to see the day that David reigned (*Abarbanel* to 20:14

[15] *David saw that Saul had gone forth to seek his
life, and David was in the Wilderness of Ziph, in
the forest.* [16] *Jonathan son of Saul arose and went
to see David in the forest, and he encouraged him
with the word of God.* [17] *He said to him, "Fear not,
for the hand of my father Saul will not find you;
you will reign over Israel and I will be second to
you, and even my father Saul knows it."* [18] *The two
of them sealed a covenant before* HASHEM. *David
remained on in the forest, and Jonathan went to
his home.*

— see there). Now, *Abarbanel* explains, Jonathan changed his mind.

Alternatively, Jonathan simply stated that if he were to remain alive — much against his will — he wished at least to be David's second-in-command.

Generally speaking, two parties in an intimate relationship grow uncertain if one of them advances in status, fearing that this will adversely affect their friendship. Jonathan, on the other hand, gladly proclaimed that he wished David to become king. However, so that the bond between them might easily retain its vigor, he expressed his hope that David would choose him as his second-in-command (*Sefer HaAkeidah, Shaar* 8).

The Talmud (*Bava Metzia* 85a) names Jonathan as one of three especially humble people — a title that he earned when he relinquished his sovereign inheritance and agreed to accept a position subordinate to that of David.

וְגַם־שָׁאוּל אָבִי יֹדֵעַ כֵּן — *And even my father Saul knows it.*

Even Saul recognized that David would reign, because they had heard rumors that David had been anointed (*Radak*). Also, when David had killed Goliath, Saul himself had said that if the boy was a descendant of Perez he would surely one day be king (see above, 17:55, *Rashi*; *Yevamos* 76b; *Kli Yakar*).

That Jonathan said *my father Saul knows it* immediately after saying *I will be second to you* implies that Saul himself knew both that David would reign and that Jonathan was prepared to relinquish his rights to the throne in David's favor (*Kli Yakar*).

18. וַיִּכְרְתוּ שְׁנֵיהֶם בְּרִית לִפְנֵי ה׳ — *The two of them sealed a covenant before* HASHEM.

This implies that Hashem was a witness to that covenant (as mentioned in 20:25).

Alternatively the first covenant between David and Jonathan had been made privately. Now they reinforced and renewed that covenant in the presence of Abiathar and the *Urim VeTumim* — hence, they did so *before* HASHEM (*Radak, Abarbanel*).[1]

וַיֵּשֶׁב דָּוִד בַּחֹרְשָׁה — *David remained in the forest.*

And he was not afraid that Jonathan would reveal his whereabouts to Saul, especially now that they had renewed their covenant (*Ralbag*). *Kli Yakar* adds that David did not escort Jonathan in order to avoid attracting attention.

1. *Netziv* comments that this is the source of the custom to take an oath or to make a commitment to another person in a sacred place, such as a synagogue, preferably near the Ark (cited by *Mishbetzos Zahav*).

זִפִים֙ אֶל־שָׁא֔וּל הַגִּבְעָ֖תָה לֵאמֹ֑ר הֲל֣וֹא דָ֠וִד
מִסְתַּתֵּ֨ר עִמָּ֜נוּ בַמְּצָד֤וֹת בַּחֹ֙רְשָׁה֙ בְּגִבְעַ֣ת
כ הַחֲכִילָ֔ה אֲשֶׁ֖ר מִימִ֥ין הַיְשִׁימֽוֹן׃ וְעַתָּ֗ה לְכָל־
אַוַּ֨ת נַפְשְׁךָ֥ הַמֶּ֛לֶךְ לָרֶ֖דֶת רֵ֑ד וְלָ֥נוּ הַסְגִּיר֖וֹ בְּיַ֥ד
כא הַמֶּֽלֶךְ׃ וַיֹּ֣אמֶר שָׁא֔וּל בְּרוּכִ֥ים אַתֶּ֖ם לַיהוָ֑ה כִּ֥י
כב חֲמַלְתֶּ֖ם עָלָֽי׃ לְכוּ־נָ֞א הָכִ֣ינוּ ע֗וֹד וּדְע֤וּ וּרְאוּ֙
אֶת־מְקוֹמוֹ֙ אֲשֶׁ֣ר תִּהְיֶ֣ה רַגְל֔וֹ מִ֥י רָאָ֖הוּ שָׁ֑ם

◆§ The Ziphites' Treacherous Betrayal of David

19. וַיַּעֲלוּ זִפִים — *Some Ziphites went up.*

The Talmud offers two interpretations of the word זִפִים (*Sotah* 48b). According to one view, it refers to the residents of Ziph. This city was within the boundaries of the tribe of Judah (see *Joshua* 15:24); accordingly, David was betrayed by members of his own tribe.

Alternatively, the word זִפִים is cognate with זִיוּף, *forgery*, indicating that these men were liars, in that they claimed falsely that they could easily locate David and deliver him to the king (*Maharasha* [*Sotah* 48b]; see *Kli Yakar* below).

וַיַּעֲלוּ זִפִים אֶל־שָׁאוּל — *Some Ziphites went up to Saul.*

The commentators disagree as to when this episode occurred.

Radak contends that this took place before Jonathan came to see David in the Wilderness, and is alluded to in v. 15, when *David saw that Saul had gone forth to seek his life, and David was in the Wilderness of Ziph, in the forest.*

Abarbanel, on the other hand, states that only after Jonathan met David did the Ziphites betray him.

לֵאמֹר הֲלוֹא דָוִד מִסְתַּתֵּר עִמָּנוּ — *Saying, "David is hiding among us."*

The Ziphites were motivated either by fear or by loyalty to Saul. Either way, they had no right to inform on David, who was innocent of wrongdoing, and our Sages censure their deed as treacherous slander.

Midrash Shocher Tov (54:1) applies the verse, *If a ruler hearkens to falsehood, all his servants are wicked* (*Proverbs* 29:12), to this episode. Since the Ziphites saw that *the ruler* Saul believed Doeg's *falsehood* and evil speech, they too decided to become Saul's *wicked servants.*

David denounced the Ziphites' לְשׁוֹנָם חֶרֶב חַדָּה, *tongue [as] a sharp sword* (*Psalm* 57:5; *Vayikra Rabbah* 26:2; *Yerushalmi Peah* 1:1).

And *Psalm* 54 records the prayer that he composed when the Ziphites betrayed him — a treachery so profound that David employed special musical instruments to accompany that psalm, in order to lift his spirits so that he might attain prophetic ecstasy.

דָוִד מִסְתַּתֵּר עִמָּנוּ — *David is hiding among us.*

Literally, this phrase states that *David is hiding with us.* The Ziphites deceived David by acting so friendly that he would never have suspected that they would turn against him. Then they assured Saul that he would find it easy to seize David because he viewed them as his allies. This perfidious behavior constitutes another reason that they are branded as זִיפִים, *liars* (*Kli Yakar*).

בַּמְּצָדוֹת בַּחֹרְשָׁה בְּגִבְעַת הַחֲכִילָה אֲשֶׁר מִימִין הַיְשִׁימוֹן — *In the strongholds in the forest of Hachilah Hill, south of Jeshimon.*

19 Some Ziphites went up to Saul in Gibeah, say-
ing, "David is hiding among us in the strongholds
in the forest in Hachilah Hill, south of Jeshimon.
20 So now, however your soul desires to come
down, O king, come down — and we undertake
to deliver him into the hand of the king." 21 Saul
said, "Blessed are you unto HASHEM, for you
have shown me compassion! 22 Go now and pre-
pare further, ascertain and observe his location,
where he dwells, and who has seen him there,

These sinister people specified David's whereabouts in detail so that Saul might the more easily apprehend him.

מִימִין הַיְשִׁימוֹן — *South of Jeshimon.*

Literally, this phrase states, *to the right of Jeshimon.* In Scriptural nomenclature, the principal cardinal point is east, which is called *forward* (קֶדֶם); west, therefore, is *backward* (אָחוֹר). When a person faces east, his right hand is toward the south.[1]

20. לְכָל־אַוַּת נַפְשְׁךָ הַמֶּלֶךְ לָרֶדֶת רֵד וְלָנוּ הַסְגִּירוֹ בְּיַד הַמֶּלֶךְ — *However your soul desires to come down, O king, come down — and we undertake to deliver him into the hand of the king.*

The Ziphites volunteered to seize David upon Saul's arrival.

According to *Abarbanel,* the Ziphites presented Saul with two options. Either רֵד — he could *come down* himself and capture David, or לָנוּ הַסְגִּירוֹ, *let us arrest him,* and Saul would have no need to come himself.

וְלָנוּ הַסְגִּירוֹ — *And we undertake to deliver him.*

Our translation follows *Targum. Rashi* interprets the phrase as *we deem ourselves responsible to deliver him.*

21. וַיֹּאמֶר שָׁאוּל בְּרוּכִים אַתֶּם לַה׳ — *Saul said, "Blessed are you unto HASHEM."*

Saul invoked Hashem's blessing upon them (*Metzudos*). This heartfelt exclamation shows that Saul believed that he was acting in accordance with God's will.

Generally, a person who incriminates others will himself be cursed. As the verse states, אָרוּר מַכֵּה רֵעֵהוּ בַּסָּתֶר — *Accursed is one who strikes his fellow stealthily* (*Deuteronomy* 27:24; see *Rashi* ad loc.; also see *Sefer Chofetz Chaim, Introduction, "Arurim"* 1,3). Saul saw it necessary to assure the Ziphites that their denunciation of David would not cause them to be cursed — to the contrary, because they were helping Saul apprehend a criminal rebel, they would be blessed (*Kli Yakar*).

22. לְכוּ־נָא הָכִינוּ עוֹד ... — *Go now and prepare further ...*

Aware that David was an agile and wily warrior, Saul was not satisfied with the sketchy details that the Ziphites had provided. He requested that they search more diligently for David and describe his exact location (*Radak*).

מִי רָאָהוּ שָׁם — *And who has seen him there.*

Saul told them not to rely on hearsay but to obtain a firsthand report (*Abarbanel*).

According to *Malbim,* Saul suspected

1. We find similarly צָפוֹן וְיָמִין — literally, *north and right* — i.e., *north and south* (*Psalms* 89:13, *Metzudos* ad loc.).

כג כִּי אָמַר אֵלַי עָרוֹם יַעְרִם הוּא: וּרְאוּ וּדְעוּ
מִכֹּל הַמַּחֲבֹאִים אֲשֶׁר יִתְחַבֵּא שָׁם וְשַׁבְתֶּם
אֵלַי אֶל־נָכוֹן וְהָלַכְתִּי אִתְּכֶם וְהָיָה אִם־יֶשְׁנוֹ
בָאָרֶץ וְחִפַּשְׂתִּי אֹתוֹ בְּכֹל אַלְפֵי יְהוּדָה:
כד וַיָּקוּמוּ וַיֵּלְכוּ זִיפָה לִפְנֵי שָׁאוּל וְדָוִד וַאֲנָשָׁיו
כה בְּמִדְבַּר מָעוֹן בָּעֲרָבָה אֶל יְמִין הַיְשִׁימוֹן: וַיֵּלֶךְ
שָׁאוּל וַאֲנָשָׁיו לְבַקֵּשׁ וַיַּגִּדוּ לְדָוִד וַיֵּרֶד הַסֶּלַע

that one of David's supporters might provide false information. Thus, Saul stated, *Ascertain ... who has seen him there* — i.e., they should make sure that whoever provided them with information was trustworthy.

כִּי אָמַר אֵלַי עָרוֹם יַעְרִם הוּא — *For someone has told me that he acts with great cunning.*

Literally, אָמַר אֵלַי means *he told me.* Our translation follows *Rashi,* who explains that it refers to some insignificant figure (see similarly *Genesis* 48:1).

Ralbag interprets the phrase as meaning, *My heart tells me* — i.e., Saul had a strong sense that David was exceedingly cunning.

According to *Radak,* this phrase means that David himself had told this to Saul. Saul informed the Ziphites, "When David was in my service, I asked him how he managed to avoid capture by the Philistines. He described his many stratagems for convincing the enemy that he is to be found in one place as he swiftly makes his way elsewhere. I know he can do the same now, and so it is essential that you discover every one of his hiding places."

עָרוֹם יַעְרִם הוּא — *He acts with great cunning.*

He is seen in one place today and in another tomorrow, so that it is all-but-impossible to apprehend him (*Rashi*).

23. וּרְאוּ וּדְעוּ — *Observe and ascertain.*

In the previous verse, Saul used these two verbs in reverse order: וּדְעוּ וּרְאוּ, *ascertain and observe.*

Kli Yakar explains that earlier Saul urged the Ziphites not to accept second-hand reports but to rely solely on eyewitnesses; thus, he emphasized the word רְאוּ, *see,* by placing it at the end of the phrase. In this verse, on the other hand, Saul discussed the necessity of searching for David in his hiding places. A cursory survey of those places would not suffice. Therefore, he emphasized the necessity of דְעוּ, *ascertain,* the different entrances to David's hiding places.

אֶל־נָכוֹן — *With an accurate report.*

The word נָכוֹן means *truthful* or *accurate.* The word אֶל, which is usually translated *to,* in this verse means *with* (*Targum;* see *Metzudos*).

וְהָלַכְתִּי אִתְּכֶם . . . וְחִפַּשְׂתִּי אֹתוֹ — *I shall go with you . . . I will search him out.*

Saul made it clear that he had no intention of leaving the task to the Ziphites. Once he possessed accurate information of David's whereabouts, he would invest the effort necessary to find him (*Malbim*).

וְהָיָה אִם־יֶשְׁנוֹ בָאָרֶץ וְחִפַּשְׂתִּי אֹתוֹ בְּכֹל אַלְפֵי יְהוּדָה — *And it will be that if he is in the land, I will search him out from among all the thousands of Judah.*

If David were *anywhere* in the land, Saul said, he would discover him.

Alternatively, if after a thorough search of David's hiding places the Ziphites failed to discover him, it would be clear that he was living in the *land* belonging to the people of his tribe, and

for someone has told me that he acts with great
cunning. [23]*Observe and ascertain all the hiding*
places where he conceals himself and come back
to me with an accurate report, and then I shall go
with you. And it will be that if he is in the land, I
will search him out from among all the thousands
of Judah."

[24]*So they arose and returned to Ziph, ahead*
of Saul. David and his men were in the Wil-
derness of Maon in the plains, south of Jeshi-
mon. [25]*Saul and his men went to search, and*
people told David, so he descended to the rock

Saul would seek him there (*Kli Yakar, Metzudos*).

וְחִפַּשְׂתִּי אֹתוֹ בְּכֹל אַלְפֵי יְהוּדָה — *I will search him out from among all the thousands of Judah.*

The word אַלְפֵי, *thousands,* is used particularly in regard to soldiers, who are organized in regiments of thousands. Thus, Saul said, "I will order all of the captains of thousands in the tribe of Judah to search among their regiments until David is discovered" (*Radak*).

24. וַיָּקוּמוּ וַיֵּלְכוּ זִיפָה לִפְנֵי שָׁאוּל — *So they arose and returned to Ziph, ahead of Saul.*

Saul directed the Ziphites to search for David and determine his precise location, and then come back to Gibeah to notify him, following which he would accompany them to David's retreat.

Rashi and *Radak* state that the present verse tells how the Ziphites set out on that search for David. The phrase לִפְנֵי שָׁאוּל, *ahead of Saul,* means that they went to Ziph while Saul remained in Gibeah. Scripture does not describe how the Ziphites found David and returned to inform Saul — that, however, may be inferred from the next verse, which tells that Saul and his men proceeded to search for David.

Malbim agrees that Scripture skips the narrative of how the Ziphites found David and returned to Saul to inform him. According to him, however, this verse describes what occurred after that: the Ziphites went to Ziph, לִפְנֵי שָׁאוּל, *followed closely by Saul.*

According to both of these interpretations, Scripture omits crucial elements of the narrative — to wit, that the Ziphites found David and returned to Saul in Gibeah to notify him.

This is a serious difficulty that *Kli Yakar* circumscribes by interpreting the verses as follows. Saul did not remain in Gibeah to await the Ziphites' report on David's whereabouts. Rather, when they returned to Ziph he followed them close behind. Then, when the Ziphites located David, they only had to retreat a short distance in order to inform Saul.

וְדָוִד וַאֲנָשָׁיו בְּמִדְבַּר מָעוֹן — *David and his men were in the Wilderness of Maon.*

At this point, they had left the forest (*Malbim*).

Maon is situated in the territory of Judah (see *Joshua* 15:55).

✎ A Miraculous Escape

25. וַיֵּרֶד הַסֶּלַע — *So he descended to the rock.*

סֶלַע — *rock* — generally refers to a flinty or mountainous area.

וַיֵּשֶׁב בְּמִדְבַּר מָעוֹן וַיִּשְׁמַע שָׁאוּל וַיִּרְדֹּף אַחֲרֵי־
כו דָוִד מִדְבַּר מָעוֹן: וַיֵּלֶךְ שָׁאוּל מִצַּד הָהָר מִזֶּה
וְדָוִד וַאֲנָשָׁיו מִצַּד הָהָר מִזֶּה וַיְהִי דָוִד נֶחְפָּז
לָלֶכֶת מִפְּנֵי שָׁאוּל וְשָׁאוּל וַאֲנָשָׁיו עֹטְרִים
כז אֶל־דָּוִד וְאֶל־אֲנָשָׁיו לְתָפְשָׂם: וּמַלְאָךְ בָּא אֶל־
שָׁאוּל לֵאמֹר מַהֲרָה וְלֵכָה כִּי־פָשְׁטוּ פְלִשְׁתִּים
כח עַל־הָאָרֶץ: וַיָּשָׁב שָׁאוּל מִרְדֹף אַחֲרֵי דָוִד

But how could David descend from a plain to a mountain?

Radak explains that a valley separated the plain from the mountain. He thus went down into the valley in order to ascend the mountain.

David left the plain because it was an open space where he might be easily detected.

Abarbanel explains this verse differently, that David had been in a mountainous area. וַיֵּרֶד הַסֶּלַע, *He went down from the rock,* because he believed that he would enjoy greater flexibility on level ground.

וַיֵּשֶׁב בְּמִדְבַּר מָעוֹן — *And stayed in the Wilderness of Maon.*

David remained in the Wilderness of Maon because he had no time to escape any farther (*Radak, Malbim*).

וַיֵּלֶךְ שָׁאוּל וַאֲנָשָׁיו ... וַיִּשְׁמַע שָׁאוּל — *Saul and his men went ... Saul heard.*

As noted above, *Kli Yakar* interprets the narrative as stating that immediately after Saul directed the Ziphites to search for David, he followed close behind.

According to that, these words are to be understood as follows: וַיֵּלֶךְ שָׁאוּל וַאֲנָשָׁיו, *Saul and his men went to search,* following directly behind the Ziphites. Then וַיִּשְׁמַע שָׁאוּל, *Saul heard [from the Ziphites],* who were slightly ahead of him, of David's whereabouts, whom he proceeded to pursue.

26. וַיֵּלֶךְ שָׁאוּל מִצַּד הָהָר מִזֶּה — *Saul went on this side of the mountain.*

This *mountain* is identical with the *rock* of the previous verse (*Radak*).

This was all that separated Saul from David.

וַיְהִי דָוִד נֶחְפָּז לָלֶכֶת מִפְּנֵי שָׁאוּל — *David hastened to get away from Saul.*

Scripture describes David here as acting in haste. *Midrash Shocher Tov* (18:7) applies to this incident David's self-reproach (*Psalm* 116:11), אֲנִי אָמַרְתִּי בְחָפְזִי כָּל־הָאָדָם כֹּזֵב — *I said in my haste, "All man is deceitful."* The Midrash explicates that when David saw that he had almost no chance of escaping, he exclaimed bitterly, "Samuel anointed me and proclaimed me king, but for nothing! What will come of his anointment and his promise?" Hashem responded, "You are calling Samuel false, but I can testify that he is trustworthy. As the verse states *All of Israel, from Dan to Beer-sheba, knew that Samuel was faithful as a prophet to HASHEM*" (above, 3:20). Immediately Hashem sent an agent to miraculously save David (as described in the following verses; see *Radak* to *Psalms* ibid.; see also footnote to *Psalms* 18:24, *ArtScroll Tanach Series*).

מִפְּנֵי שָׁאוּל — *From Saul.*

Me'am Loez states that although David was a seasoned warrior who had previously sought combat with large and mighty armies, in this case he fled in order to avoid harming Hashem's anointed king, Saul (see below, 24:7).

וְשָׁאוּל וַאֲנָשָׁיו עֹטְרִים אֶל דָוִד — *But Saul and his men surrounded David.*

and stayed in the Wilderness of Maon. Saul
heard and pursued David to the Wilderness of
Maon. [26] *Saul went on this side of the mountain*
while David and his men were on that side of
the mountain; David hastened to get away
from Saul, but Saul and his men surrounded
David and his men, to capture them. [27] *Then a*
messenger came to Saul saying, "Hurry and go
— for the Philistines have spread out over the
land!" [28] *So Saul retreated from pursuing David,*

The word עֹטְרִים — *surrounded* — derives from עֲטָרָה, *crown.* Saul's men encircled David and his men like a crown.

Targum renders עֹטְרִים as *ambushing.*

Kli Yakar suggests that Scripture employs the image of a crown, because it sits on top of one's head. Similarly, Saul's men stood on the peaks of the mountain surrounding David, thus putting him in an extremely exposed position.

The beginning of the verse describes the forces of Saul and David as stationed on opposite sides of the mountain. But when Saul's men noticed David, they surrounded him to block his escape.

לְתָפְשָׂם — *To capture them.*

Saul's men came so close to David that all they had to do was seize him.

Although David had been in many perilous situations before, never had he been so close to death.

According to the Midrash (*Shocher Tov* 23:6), David alluded to this episode in the words, גַּם כִּי־אֵלֵךְ בְּגֵיא צַלְמָוֶת לֹא־אִירָא רָע, *Even though I walk in the valley overshadowed by death, I will fear no evil* (*Psalms* 23:4).

27. וּמַלְאָךְ בָּא אֶל־שָׁאוּל — *Then a messenger came to Saul.*

The Midrash cites two opinions regarding the identity of this *messenger.*

According to one sage, this was a human emissary, who was dispatched by Divine Providence at this moment to rescue David. Another sage objects that such a messenger would lack the authority to offer the king advice (i.e., "hurry and go"). Therefore, this *messenger* must have been an angel. This idea is supported by the verse, יִשְׁלַח מִמָּרוֹם יִקָּחֵנִי, *He sent from on high and took me* (*Psalms* 18:17; *Midrash Shocher Tov* 18:7).[1]

It is striking to see the extraordinary ways in which Hashem protects those closest to Him, miraculously saving them from danger (*Ralbag*).

28. וַיָּשָׁב שָׁאוּל מִרְדֹף אַחֲרֵי דָוִד — *So Saul retreated from pursuing David.*

David expressed his gratitude to Hashem in the words, אֲזַמְּרָה שִׁמְךָ עֶלְיוֹן בְּשׁוּב־אוֹיְבַי אָחוֹר, *I will sing praise to Your Name, Most High, when my enemies retreat* (*Psalms* 9:3,4; *Midrash Shocher Tov* 9:6). And, in an allusion to the fact that he had been saved at the *rock,* David praised God as ה׳ סַלְעִי, *HASHEM, my Rock* (*Psalms* 18:3; *Midrash Shocher Tov* 18:7).

Mussar HaNeviim notes Saul's bravery, selflessness, and sense of responsibilty to the nation. He was finally able to apprehend his enemy, yet he dropped everything in order to defend his people against the Philistines.

1. In *Radak*'s reading of this Midrash, the verse quoted is יִשְׁלַח מִשָּׁמַיִם וְיוֹשִׁיעֵנִי, *He will dispatch from heaven and save me* (*Psalms* 57:4).

וַיֵּלֶךְ לִקְרַאת פְּלִשְׁתִּים עַל־כֵּן קָרְאוּ לַמָּקוֹם
א הַהוּא סֶלַע הַמַּחְלְקוֹת: וַיַּעַל דָּוִד מִשָּׁם וַיֵּשֶׁב
ב בִּמְצָדוֹת עֵין־גֶּדִי: וַיְהִי כַּאֲשֶׁר שָׁב שָׁאוּל
מֵאַחֲרֵי פְּלִשְׁתִּים וַיַּגִּדוּ לוֹ לֵאמֹר הִנֵּה דָוִד
ג בְּמִדְבַּר עֵין גֶּדִי: וַיִּקַּח שָׁאוּל שְׁלֹשֶׁת
אֲלָפִים אִישׁ בָּחוּר מִכָּל־יִשְׂרָאֵל וַיֵּלֶךְ לְבַקֵּשׁ
ד אֶת־דָּוִד וַאֲנָשָׁיו עַל־פְּנֵי צוּרֵי הַיְּעֵלִים: וַיָּבֹא
אֶל־גִּדְרוֹת הַצֹּאן עַל־הַדֶּרֶךְ וְשָׁם מְעָרָה

עַל־כֵּן קָרְאוּ לַמָּקוֹם הַהוּא סֶלַע הַמַּחְלְקוֹת — *That is why that place is called "the Rock of Divisions."*

The commentators and Midrash provide a variety of explanations for this name, of which we list a few.

❒ *Radak* interprets the text as stating that here the camps of Saul and David separated from each other. This interpretation fits best with the flow of the text, which associates this name with Saul's departure.

❒ *Targum* (cited by *Rashi*) explains that here Saul's mind was divided about whether he should continue his pursuit of David or turn back and confront the Philistines.

The following three explanations appear in *Midrash Shocher Tov* (18:7).

❒ Saul's warriors disagreed with one another, some insisting that they not leave before capturing David, and others contending that they could find David any time but that it was now crucial that they protect the Israelites from the onslaught of the Philistines.

❒ The mountain was miraculously sundered, with Saul and his men on one half, and David and his men on the other, so that Saul could not gain access to David.

❒ In the future, whenever David and his army would pass this location, David and those men who had been saved here would dismount their horses, prostrate themselves and recite the blessing, "Blessed are You, Hashem . . . Who performed a miracle for us at this place" (see *Berachos* 54a; *Shulchan Aruch, Orach Chaim* 218:4), whereas those who had not been present would not recite the blessing. Thus, there would be a *division* among David's men.

❒ Finally, *Kli Yakar* observes that the word מַחְלְקוֹת is in the plural and describes two *divisive battles* that took place: that between Saul and David and that between the Philistines and the Jews. This name celebrates the miraculous fact that the Philistines launched their attack just as Saul was preparing to seize David.

XXIV

◆§ Saul Continues His Pursuit of David

1. וַיַּעַל דָּוִד מִשָּׁם — *David ascended from there.*

Homiletically interpreted, וַיַּעַל דָּוִד, *David ascended*, means that he was spiritually elevated after God miraculously saved him מִשָּׁם, *from there*, as described at the end of the previous chapter (*Rashi*, cited by *Kli Yakar; most texts of Rashi*, however, do not contain this comment).

עֵין־גֶּדִי — *En-gedi.*

En-gedi, also known as *Hazazon Tamar* (*Genesis* 14:7; *Targum* ad loc.; *II Chronicles* 20:2), is situated in Judah (*Joshua* 15:62).

and went toward the Philistines. This is why that
place is called "the Rock of Divisions."

24/1-4 1 *David ascended from there and dwelt in*
the strongholds of En-gedi. 2 *When Saul*
returned from [chasing] after the Philistines,
people told him, saying, "Behold, David is in
the Wilderness of En-gedi." 3 *So Saul took three*
thousand chosen men, from all of Israel, and
went to seek David and his men on the rocks
of the wild goats. 4 *He came to sheep enclosures*
along the road, where a cavern was situated,

2. וַיְהִי כַּאֲשֶׁר שָׁב שָׁאוּל מֵאַחֲרֵי פְּלִשְׁתִּים — *When Saul returned from [chasing] after the Philistines.*

The verse implies that Saul only pursued the Philistines, but never engaged them in battle.

According to *Kli Yakar*, the messenger's warning that the Philistines were about to attack (23:27) was false. God had arranged for Saul to hear such a rumor so that he would halt his pursuit of David. Even after he saw that the report was false — and according to one tradition, he saw the mountain split — he did not realize that these were messages for him to stop pursuing David. He continued his pursuit with a vengeance.

וַיַּגִּדוּ לוֹ לֵאמֹר הִנֵּה דָוִד בְּמִדְבַּר עֵין גֶּדִי — *People told him, saying, "Behold, David is in the Wilderness of En-gedi."*

According to *Kli Yakar*, these were the warriors who had previously advised him to capture David before engaging the Philistines. Now they argued that events had proven them correct. Saul had gone to battle the Philistines and accomplished nothing, as in the meantime David had escaped to En-gedi.

3. וַיִּקַּח שָׁאוּל — *So Saul took.*

Saul did not need to gather his soldiers together (as he had done previously — 23:8), because they were already assembled to battle the Philistines (*Me'am Loez*).

אִישׁ בָּחוּר מִכָּל־יִשְׂרָאֵל — *Chosen men, from all of Israel.*

Saul gained the support of the entire nation in his undertaking against David (*Daas Sofrim*).

עַל־פְּנֵי צוּרֵי הַיְּעֵלִים — *On the rocks of the wild goats.*

The יָעֵל is a wild animal mentioned numerous times in Scripture and in the Mishnah. Most sources agree that it is a wild goat. It is a weak creature that resides on the highest and most remote peaks (see *Psalms* 104:18, *Bereishis Rabbah* 12:9). Saul assumed that David would conceal himself in mountainous areas. David, however, intuited Saul's thoughts and instead hid in a cavern alongside the road (*Malbim*).

The fact that Saul passed by David's hiding place as he went to seek him on distant crags was clearly an act of Providence (*Kli Yakar*).

Targum renders צוּרֵי הַיְּעֵלִים as *domed rocks* — i.e., rocks with cavities that form dome-shaped ceilings.

Radak questions how *Targum* derives this meaning from the word הַיְּעֵלִים. *Kli Yakar* offers the suggestion that הַיְּעֵלִים may be related to הָעֱלִים, *concealed* — i.e., a secluded mountain area.

◆§ David's Opportunity to Harm Saul — and His Self-Restraint

4. וַיָּבֹא אֶל־גִּדְרוֹת הַצֹּאן עַל־הַדֶּרֶךְ וְשָׁם מְעָרָה

וַיָּבֹא שָׁאוּל לְהָסֵךְ אֶת־רַגְלָיו וְדָוִד וַאֲנָשָׁיו בְּיַרְכְּתֵי
ה הַמְּעָרָה יֹשְׁבִים׃ וַיֹּאמְרוּ אַנְשֵׁי דָוִד אֵלָיו הִנֵּה
הַיּוֹם אֲשֶׁר־אָמַר יהוה אֵלֶיךָ הִנֵּה אָנֹכִי נֹתֵן אֶת־
°איביך בְּיָדֶךָ וְעָשִׂיתָ לּוֹ כַּאֲשֶׁר יִטַב בְּעֵינֶיךָ וַיָּקָם
דָּוִד וַיִּכְרֹת אֶת־כְּנַף־הַמְּעִיל אֲשֶׁר־לְשָׁאוּל בַּלָּט׃

°אֹיִבְךָ ק׳

וַיָּבֹא שָׁאוּל לְהָסֵךְ אֶת־רַגְלָיו — *He came to sheep enclosures along the road, where a cavern was situated, which Saul entered to relieve himself.*

Saul had no reason to suspect that David would be hiding in a conspicuous cavern along the road. Therefore, when he had to relieve himself, he incautiously entered the cavern alone (*Malbim*).

The cavern must have been a large one, since all of David's men were hiding in it (*Abarbanel*).

The Talmud (*Berachos* 62b) observes that the plural formation of the word גְּדֵרוֹת, *enclosures* (related to גֶּדֶר, *fence*), implies that the cavern lay within two concentric enclosures. Furthermore, the Talmud asseverates that the cavern itself consisted of one cave within another. (*Ben Yehoyada* suggests that this latter inference may be based on Scripture's repetition of the word וַיָּבֹא, *he came.*)

All of this illustrates the exceptional nature of Saul's modesty.

לְהָסֵךְ אֶת־רַגְלָיו — *To relieve himself.*

The word רַגְלָיו, *his feet*, is a euphemism. The word לְהָסֵךְ is related to נֶסֶךְ, *pouring*, i.e., urinating (*Radak*, see *Rashi, Yevamos* 103a).

However, according to most commentators, including *Rashi* and *Targum*, the word לְהָסֵךְ derives from סוּכָּה or סִיכּוּךְ, *a covering* or *protective overlay*, for when a person relieves himself, he should cover himself.

The Sages (*Berachos* ibid.) derive from this that Saul avoided exposing any part of his body. This modesty saved his life (as we will see below, v. 11; see also *Yerushalmi Succah* 5:4; *Pnei Moshe* ad loc.; *Bamidbar Rabbah* 4:21).

וְדָוִד וַאֲנָשָׁיו בְּיַרְכְּתֵי הַמְּעָרָה יֹשְׁבִים — *David and his men were sitting at the far end of the cavern.*

Providentially, Saul did not proceed to the far end of the cavern, despite his unusual sense of decorousness (*Kli Yakar*).

When David and his men heard Saul entering, they moved to the far end of the cavern. This may be derived from the verse, בְּבָרְחוֹ מִפְּנֵי־שָׁאוּל בַּמְּעָרָה, *When [David] fled from Saul, in the cavern* (*Psalms* 57:1) — indicating that, unbeknownst to Saul, David fled from Saul while they were both in the cavern (*Kli Yakar*).

One can imagine how David must have felt when he saw Saul entering the very cavern where David had been confident he was safe. This was when David composed *Psalm* 142, which begins with the introductory verse, מַשְׂכִּיל לְדָוִד בִּהְיוֹתוֹ בַמְּעָרָה תְפִלָּה, *A maskil by David, when he was in the cavern — a prayer.* The Midrash (*Shocher Tov* 142:1) explains the word מַשְׂכִּיל as meaning *comprehension.* David comprehended that at such a moment a person cannot rely on his money, wisdom, or strength. All that he has is prayer.

In that psalm, David states, קוֹלִי אֶל־ה׳ אֶזְעָק קוֹלִי אֶל־ה׳ אֶתְחַנָּן, *With my voice I cry out to* HASHEM*, with my voice I plead with* HASHEM (v. 2). The Midrash (*Shocher Tov* 142:2) explains this repetition as follows: David first prayed not to fall into Saul's hands, and then that Saul not fall into his hands (see also *Psalms* 57:2, *Rashi*).

A Midrash relates an extraordinary incident that occurred at this point.

David once said to Hashem, "Master of the Universe, I understand the purpose of all of your creations except for the spider, who spins all year long but whose web is worthless, and the madman, who harms people." Hashem answered,

which Saul entered to relieve himself. David and
his men were sitting at the far end of the cavern.
5 *David's men said to him, "Behold, this is the*
day of which Hashem *said to you, 'Behold, I am*
delivering your enemy into your hand, and you
may do to him as you please'!" So David arose
and stealthily cut off the corner of Saul's robe.

"There will come a time when you will need each of these."

We have already seen how David was saved from Achish when he entered a state of delirium (madness) (above, 21:14-16).

Regarding the spider, the Midrash relates that while David was hiding in the cavern, Hashem sent a spider to spin a web across its entrance. Seeing this, Saul assumed that no one had entered the cavern for some time (*Aleph Beis d'Ben Sira; Otzar HaMidrashim* 47).

5. וַיֹּאמְרוּ אַנְשֵׁי דָוִד אֵלָיו הִנֵּה הַיּוֹם ... — *David's men said to him, "Behold, this is the day ..."*

Angry and vengeful because Saul was pursuing them with deadly intent although they were innocent of any wrongdoing, David's men interpreted Saul's sudden appearance as a God-given opportunity to him, and were certain that David would agree. He would have been halachically justified to do so, for Saul qualified as a רוֹדֵף, a murderous *pursuer* (*Sanhedrin* 72a).

אֲשֶׁר־אָמַר ה׳ אֵלֶיךָ הִנֵּה אָנֹכִי נֹתֵן אֶת־אֹיִבְךָ בְּיָדֶךָ — ... *of which* Hashem *said to you, "Behold, I am delivering your enemy into your hand."*

There is no record of such a statement in Scripture. Apparently, when one of the prophets — whether Samuel, Gad, or Nathan — told David that he would be king, he also informed him that his enemies would be delivered into his hand. David's men knew of this prophecy and understood it to be a reference to Saul, who, at that time, was David's primary enemy.

Accordingly, although the *kesiv* (written version) of the verse states אֹיְבֶיךָ, *your enemies*, in the plural — because that was the actual promise — the *k'ri* (read version) is אֹיִבְךָ, *your enemy*, in the singular, representing the understanding of David's men (*Radak*).

וְעָשִׂיתָ לוֹ כַּאֲשֶׁר יִטַב בְּעֵינֶיךָ — *And you may do to him as you please.*

David might either harm or kill Saul (*Mahari Kara*).

וַיָּקָם דָּוִד וַיִּכְרֹת אֶת־כְּנַף־הַמְּעִיל אֲשֶׁר־לְשָׁאוּל בַּלָּט — *So David arose and stealthily cut off the corner of Saul's robe.*

When Samuel tore Saul's tunic (according to one version) after the incident with Amalek, Samuel told him that this was an omen that whoever would sever his garment would become king (*Midrash*, see 15:27,28). Now David had done it.[1]

Chomas Anach suggests that this idea is homiletically implicit in the phrase וַיָּקָם דָּוִד, *so David arose*. David *arose*

1. There is a custom that when one is angry, it is helpful to suppress the anger by grasping the corner of one's garment, because the numerical value of כָּנָף, *corner* (150), is the same as that of כַּעַס, *anger*. Accordingly, David cut off a corner of Saul's garment to remind the king that he was acting cruelly, out of unjustified anger. Earlier, when Samuel tore Saul's tunic, he was hinting that since Saul had wrongly taken pity on Amalek, he would one day be furious when he should be merciful, and the severing of his garment would remind him of his grievous error and its destined outcome (*Chasam Sofer* to *Haftarah of Chayei Sarah*).

ו וַיְהִי֙ אַחֲרֵי־כֵ֔ן וַיַּ֥ךְ לֵב־דָּוִ֖ד אֹת֑וֹ עַ֚ל אֲשֶׁ֣ר
ז כָּרַ֔ת אֶת־כָּנָ֖ף אֲשֶׁ֥ר לְשָׁאֽוּל׃ וַיֹּ֨אמֶר לַאֲנָשָׁ֜יו

in status since there was a publicly displayed sign that he would become king.

וַיִּכְרֹת אֶת־כְּנַף־הַמְּעִיל אֲשֶׁר־לְשָׁאוּל בַּלָּט — *And stealthily cut off the corner of Saul's robe.*

David could easily have killed Saul — something that many commentators say was his original intent — but chose instead to cut Saul's robe.

Possibly the manner in which Saul draped his robe over his body for reasons of modesty made it easier for David to remain unnoticed, for the edges of Saul's garment may have been dragging along the ground (*Daas Sofrim*).

◆§ Why Didn't David Kill Saul?

As mentioned above, David had a right to kill Saul in self-defense. Various explanations are offered for why David did not kill Saul.

❒ The Talmud (*Berachos* 62b) states that when David witnessed Saul's extraordinary modesty, he said, "It is not appropriate to touch such a chaste body" (*Bamidbar Rabbah* 4:21, see below, v. 11).

❒ *Ralbag* explains that David's exceptional piety led him to refrain from killing Saul.

Also, David felt that he had to teach by example that an assassination may not be undertaken lightly. (David had a personal interest in setting such a precedent, because he knew that he and his descendants would eventually reign.) David did so later as well when he put to death the Amalekite convert (*II Samuel* Ch. 1) who had killed Saul (at Saul's request), since in so doing he had laid his hands on Hashem's anointed king. David's handling of the assassins of King Ish-bosheth (*II Samuel* Ch. 4) also exemplifies this concept.

❒ David knew that he would be king after Saul's reign came to an end, but he did not know if that time had now come. Thus, he profaned Saul's garment as he monitored his own emotions, knowing that if he sensed remorse, he must be doing the wrong thing — since if a righteous person proceeds on a wrong path, Hashem fills him with feelings of contrition (*Alshich, Malbim*).

Yet seemingly David had an obligation to kill Saul. According to the halachah, if someone is pursuing a fellow-Jew with deadly intent, one is obligated to kill him (*Rambam, Hil. Rotze'ach* 1:6-15; *Tosafos, Sanhedrin* 73a).

What gave David the right to ignore this mandate?

❒ *Hagahos Yaavetz* (to *Berachos* 62b) states that Samuel's prophecy that David would eventually reign meant that Saul could not pose a mortal risk to him, and therefore was not deemed an assailant.

❒ Saul would have had one of his soldiers kill David, as in the case of Nob; he would not have done so himself. Accordingly, Saul personally was not actually a *pursuer*. It may be that in such a case, one *may* kill the commander to prevent him from issuing the order, but the fugitive is not required to do so (*Galia Masechta* (*Teshuvos Yoreh Deah,* 5).

❒ The Talmud (*Sanhedrin* 74a) rules that one does not have the right to kill such a *pursuer* if one can stop him by less lethal means. However, according to *Mishneh LaMelech* (cited in a parenthetic comment to *Rambam, Hil. Chovel U'Mazik* 8:10), this limitation applies only to a bystander. The potential victim may under any circumstances kill his *pursuer*. Possibly, this means that the potential victim has the right to kill *his pursuer* but is not obliged to do so. David may have believed that although he had the right to kill Saul (as is clear from *Berachos*), he was not required to do so (*Nachalas Shimon* 49), and that he might put an end to Saul's persecution of him by cutting off a corner of his garment.

[6] *Afterward, however, David's conscience troubled him for having cut off the corner of Saul's [garment].* [7] *He said to his men,*

By cutting off a corner of Saul's robe, David demonstrated an element of disdain for garments. He later suffered Divine retribution in that as an old man he remained cold no matter how many garments his retainers put on him (*I Kings* 1:1; *Berachos* 62b, see *Maharsha* ad loc.).[1]

6. וַיַּךְ לֵב־דָּוִד אֹתוֹ — *David's conscience troubled him.*

Literally, וַיַּךְ — *troubled* — means *struck*.

When a person is frightened or troubled, his heart palpitates rapidly and, as it were, strikes him (*Metzudos*).

עַל אֲשֶׁר כָּרַת אֶת־כָּנָף אֲשֶׁר לְשָׁאוּל — *For having cut off the corner of Saul's [garment].*

David now regretted even the realtively minor damage that he had caused. Despite being a fugitive, he believed that he should have exhibited great deference to Hashem's anointed king, and so should not have touched Saul's garment (*Radak*).

As mentioned above, *Alshich* states that David ripped Saul's garment in order to monitor his own emotions — for (in *Malbim*'s words), a person whose heart is whole is intuitively filled with regret should he do something wrong. Now that David felt remorseful, he realized that Saul must still remain king.

Psalm 7 begins שִׁגָּיוֹן לְדָוִד אֲשֶׁר־שָׁר לַה׳ עַל־דִּבְרֵי־כוּשׁ בֶּן־יְמִינִי — *A shigayon of David, which he sang to Hashem concerning Kush ben Yemini.*

Our Sages state that *shigayon* is related to מִשְׁגֶּה — *a mistake* — and that *Kush* is a reference to Saul. Thus, David expressed his regret over the mistake he had made in regard to Saul — that being, according to a view cited by *Rashi* (to *Psalms* ad loc.), cutting off the corner of Saul's garment.

According to *Midrash Shocher Tov* (7:4), David exclaimed in remorse, "What difference is there between cutting off Saul's garment and cutting off his head?"[2]

David sensed that once he allowed himself to tamper with the property of the king, he was susceptible to eventually assassinating him (*Mussar HaNeviim*).

According to another sage, the emphasis on the word *corner* implies a connection to *tzitzis*, the mitzvah that is performed on four-cornered garments. By cutting off a corner of Saul's garment, David disqualified it from the commandment of *tzitzis*, and that is what he regretted.[3]

7. וַיֹּאמֶר לַאֲנָשָׁיו חָלִילָה לִּי מֵה׳ אִם אֶעֱשֶׂה אֶת־הַדָּבָר הַזֶּה — *He said to his men, "It would be sacrilegious before Hashem for me to do this thing."*

1. Although David acted with extreme piety by sparing Saul, and he hoped that he could make peace between them by showing the cut corner to the king (v. 14), his good intention did not spare him from the effect of his action, for in his old age, he could not be warmed by garments (*I Kings* 1:1; *Berachos* 62b). This was not so much a punishment, as a natural phenomenon, for if one shows disdain for something — in this case damaging a garment — he cannot benefit from it , notwithstanding his noble intentions (*Mishnas R' Aharon*, Vol. 1).

Although David repented (v. 6), his remorse was limited to his having laid hands on the king, not for showing disdain for garments in general (*Mishbetzos Zahav*).

2. According to *Zayis Ra'anan* (to *Yalkut Shimoni* §133), Hashem spoke these words to David.

3. It is not clear how David cut the garment. If he cut the corner in such a way that formed a new corner, the garment would still require *tzitzis*. If he cut off the *tzitzis* with the corner (as the Midrash implies), he would have caused Saul to unwittingly transgress the positive commandment of placing *tzitzis* on all four corners. It is unlikely that David would do such a thing. Possibly, he rounded the corner, or cut it in another way that left the garment with only three corners, so that it was no longer obligated in *tzitzis*. If so, Saul would not be transgressing the mitzvah, but would have been deprived of the opportunity to fulfill it, and this is what David regretted.

חָלִילָה לִּי מֵיהוָה אִם־אֶעֱשֶׂה אֶת־הַדָּבָר הַזֶּה
לַאדֹנִי לִמְשִׁיחַ יְהוָה לִשְׁלֹחַ יָדִי בּוֹ כִּי־מְשִׁיחַ
ח יְהוָה הוּא׃ וַיְשַׁסַּע דָּוִד אֶת־אֲנָשָׁיו בַּדְּבָרִים וְלֹא
נְתָנָם לָקוּם אֶל־שָׁאוּל וְשָׁאוּל קָם מֵהַמְּעָרָה וַיֵּלֶךְ
ט בַּדָּרֶךְ׃ וַיָּקָם דָּוִד אַחֲרֵי־כֵן וַיֵּצֵא °מִן־המערה
°מֵהַמְּעָרָה ק׳
וַיִּקְרָא אַחֲרֵי־שָׁאוּל לֵאמֹר אֲדֹנִי הַמֶּלֶךְ וַיַּבֵּט
שָׁאוּל אַחֲרָיו וַיִּקֹּד דָּוִד אַפַּיִם אַרְצָה וַיִּשְׁתָּחוּ׃
י וַיֹּאמֶר דָּוִד לְשָׁאוּל לָמָּה תִשְׁמַע אֶת־דִּבְרֵי אָדָם
יא לֵאמֹר הִנֵּה דָוִד מְבַקֵּשׁ רָעָתֶךָ׃ הִנֵּה הַיּוֹם הַזֶּה
רָאוּ עֵינֶיךָ אֵת אֲשֶׁר־נְתָנְךָ יְהוָה | הַיּוֹם | בְּיָדִי

David's men had suggested that he injure or kill Saul — *you may do to him as you please* (v. 5). According to *Rashi*, David said this before his remorse for cutting the garment.[1]

Other commentators, including *Radak*, interpret this verse as appearing in correct chronological order. When David returned to his men with the corner of Saul's garment, he explained why he had refrained from killing Saul.

חָלִילָה לִי מֵה׳ — *It would be sacrilegious before HASHEM for me.*

David mentioned Hashem's Name to indicate that he had spared Saul solely in order to avoid debasing the Name of Hashem. Had he assassinated Saul in a concealed location and then succeeded him as king, that would have been an immense desecration of Hashem's Name (*Daas Sofrim*).

According to *Me'am Loez*, David's use of the Name of Hashem indicates that he had committed himself with an oath not to harm Saul.

לַאדֹנִי לִמְשִׁיחַ ה׳ — *To my lord, the anointed of HASHEM.*

David stated that killing Saul would have been sinful for two reasons. First, he would have been rebelling against his master, and second, he would have killed the representative of the kingdom of Hashem (*Abarbanel*).

Alternatively, David implied that he must desist from hurting Saul for two reasons: on a personal level, because Saul was his father-in-law; and on a national level, because Saul was the anointed king of Hashem (*Chomas Anach*).

אִם־אֶעֱשֶׂה אֶת־הַדָּבָר הַזֶּה לַאדֹנִי לִמְשִׁיחַ ה׳ ... לִשְׁלֹחַ יָדִי בּוֹ כִּי־מְשִׁיחַ ה׳ הוּא — *For me to do this thing to my lord, the anointed of HASHEM, to send forth my hand against him, for he is the anointed of HASHEM.*

Abarbanel explains this repetitiveness — *to do this thing to my lord, the anointed of HASHEM, to send forth my hand* — as follows.

First, David stated that he could not strike Saul out of fear and respect for *the anointed of HASHEM*. Then, he implicitly rejected the argument that he owed Saul no respect because he, David, had been anointed and Saul's time had presumably passed. In response to that, David said כִּי־מְשִׁיחַ הוּא, *for he is*, i.e., although

1. His reply is presented out of chronological order because once Scripture describes how he ripped Saul's garment (v. 5), it goes on to describe his remorse for doing so (v. 6), and then returns to his response.

"It would be sacrilegious before HASHEM *for*
me to do this thing to my lord, the anointed of
HASHEM, *to send forth my hand against him,*
for he is the anointed of HASHEM*!"* [8] *David split*
up his men with rhetoric, and did not permit
them to rise up against Saul. Then Saul rose
up from the cavern and continued on the way.
[9] *After that David arose and stepped out of*
the cavern, calling after Saul, saying, "My lord,
the king!" Saul looked behind him, and David
bowed down on his face to the ground and pros-
trated himself. [10] *David said to Saul, "Why do*
you listen to the words of someone who says,
'Behold, David seeks to harm you'? [11] *Behold!*
This day your eyes have seen that HASHEM *de-*
livered you into my hand in the cavern today,

I will succeed Saul, at the moment *he is [still] the anointed of* HASHEM (see *Malbim*).

8. וַיְשַׁסַּע דָּוִד אֶת־אֲנָשָׁיו — *David split up his men.*

The word וַיְשַׁסַּע means *cut* or *severed* (as in the verse, וְשִׁסַּע אֹתוֹ, *He shall split it* [*Leviticus* 1:17]).

David's men had unanimously decided to kill Saul. But David *broke* their alliance (*Metzudos*) and *severed* them from their plan (*Ralbag*), thereby *keeping them away* from Saul (*Rashi, Radak*).

Targum renders וַיְשַׁסַּע as *he pacified.*

בַּדְּבָרִים — *With rhetoric.*

This may be literally translated as *with the words.* David persuaded his men with the words cited in v. 7 that Saul was *the anointed of* HASHEM (*Radak*).

וְשָׁאוּל קָם מֵהַמְּעָרָה וַיֵּלֶךְ בַּדָּרֶךְ — *Then Saul rose up from the cavern and continued on the way.*

According to some commentators, David kept his men's attention on his oration long enough to allow Saul time to get away (*Malbim, Kli Yakar*).

◆§ David's Impassioned Self-Vindication and Call for Justice

9. וַיִּקֹּד דָּוִד אַפַּיִם אַרְצָה וַיִּשְׁתָּחוּ — *David bowed down on his face to the ground and prostrated himself.*

This verse gives us a glimpse into David's humility and self-control. Not only did he refuse to harm Saul but he even bowed down to him (*Me'am Loez*).

David believed that although Saul was mistaken, his intentions were noble (*Daas Sofrim*).

10. לָמָּה תִשְׁמַע אֶת־דִּבְרֵי אָדָם לֵאמֹר הִנֵּה דָוִד מְבַקֵּשׁ רָעָתֶךָ — *Why do you listen to the words of someone who says, "Behold, David seeks to harm you"?*

David was referring specifically to Doeg; he asked Saul why he believed Doeg's slanderous imputations (*Rashi*).

The word אָדָם — *someone* — is an allusion to Doeg in that this word (*adam*) is similar to the description of Doeg as the Edomite — *HaAdomi* (*Kli Yakar*).

בַּמְּעָרָה וְאָמַר לַהֲרָגְךָ וַתָּחָס עָלֶיךָ וָאֹמַר
לֹא־אֶשְׁלַח יָדִי בַּאדֹנִי כִּי־מְשִׁיחַ יהוה הוּא:
יב וְאָבִי רְאֵה גַּם רְאֵה אֶת־כְּנַף מְעִילְךָ בְּיָדִי
כִּי בְּכָרְתִי אֶת־כְּנַף מְעִילְךָ וְלֹא הֲרַגְתִּיךָ

11. וְאָמַר לַהֲרָגְךָ וַתָּחָס עָלֶיךָ — *And [although] someone said to kill you, [my soul] took pity on you.*

Scripture does not identify the *someone.*

Rashi renders simply *someone said. Radak* renders *each one of my men said.* According to *Ralbag,* it means, *my heart said.* And *Targum* renders it in the plural as *others said.*

The word וַתָּחָס, *took pity,* can be rendered in the *second-person* masculine **you** *took pity,* or in the third-person feminine **she** *took pity.* Obviously, our verse is not in the second person, so the subject of the word must be something in the feminine gender. *Rashi* and *Ralbag* translate it as *my soul took pity.*

According to *Mahari Kara,* it means *my eye pitied* (see *Deuteronomy* 7:16 et al.).

Abarbanel explains this as a continuation of the earlier part of the verse, in which David referred to his *hand.* Thus, *Although* HASHEM *delivered you into my hand, my hand took pity on you.*

Each of these nouns —*soul, eye,* and *hand* — is feminine

According to most commentators, other than *Ralbag,* David did not acknowledge to Saul that he had ever considered killing him — because, states *Daas Sofrim,* he did not want to allow Saul the opportunity to claim that he was David's victim, and that David had initiated the dispute.

The Sages interpret this phrase as follows.

וְאָמַר — *and said* — means that *the Torah has said* — i.e., the Torah teaches that a victim has the right to kill his *pursuer* (see above, v. 5).

And וַתָּחָס means *you took pity* — i.e., *Saul took pity* on himself (unwittingly) by acting in an exceptionally modest manner that persuaded David to spare him (see v. 4).[1]

Malbim states that in this verse David addressed the slanderer who had claimed that David was seeking to harm Saul (v. 10). According to this slanderer, David had presumably tried to attack Saul. However, he had been frustrated for one of three possible reasons: 1. He was incapable. 2. He feared human intervention or revenge. 3. He feared Hashem's punishment if he were to kill Saul.

David now refuted these three points. First, he was capable and could very easily have killed Saul, had he wanted to. Second, since Saul was *in a cavern,* David had no reason to fear human intervention, for the only witnesses would have been his loyal followers. And third, he had no reason to fear Divine punishment, since the Torah gave him the right to kill Saul. Thus the accusation had no basis.

12. וְאָבִי רְאֵה גַּם רְאֵה — *See now, my father, indeed, see.*

By stressing the word רְאֵה, *see,* David emphasizes that Saul can *see* clearly and indisputably that David is innocent (*Metzudos*).

Targum renders this repetition as *Look and see.*

According to *Rashi,* the first instance of רְאֵה means *Take this* [matter] *to heart,* whereas the second adds, *And gaze upon the evidence.*

Radak, however, reads this phrase as having the opposite meaning: David told Saul to first *look* at the torn garment and then *appreciate* David's righteousness.

The Midrash (*Shocher Tov* 7:4) presents two interpretations of this phrase, both of them in agreement that David

1. Alternatively, this phrase might be translated as *she took pity* in that *Saul's modesty* took pity on him, as it were (*Berachos* 62b, *Maharsha* ad loc.).

and [although] someone said to kill you, [my
soul] took pity on you, and I said, 'I shall not
send forth my hand against my lord, for he
is the anointed of HASHEM*!'* [12]*See now, my fa-*
ther, indeed, see the corner of your coat that
is in my hand, for since I have cut off the cor-
ner of your garment and have not killed you,

was addressing two men. According to Rabbi Yehudah, David first addressed Saul with the words, אָבִי רְאֵה, *See, my father,* and then appealed to Abner, Saul's general, with the words, *indeed, see.* The other Sages, however, reverse the order: David first addressed Abner, calling him *my father,* since Abner had taught him Torah (see *Rashi, Deuteronomy* 6:7), and then he turned to Saul.

According to one Midrashic version, when Saul emerged from the cavern, he noticed that his garment was torn and he asked Abner, "Where is the corner of my robe?"

Abner replied, "It must have been caught by a thorn."

At that point, David proclaimed, רְאֵה גַּם רְאֵה ... כִּי בְּכָרְתִי אֶת־כְּנַף מְעִילְךָ — *See now ... see ... that I cut off the corner of your garment* (*Shocher Tov* ibid.).

According to a different text (see *Vayikra Rabbah* 26:2), David first exhibited the corner of Saul's garment, at which point Abner told Saul, "Perhaps a thorn tore it off, and David then found it."

Our Sages agree that Abner was punished for thus dissuading Saul of the truth of David's contention. And so shortly before Abner was killed, Scripture describes him as having been returned from *Bor-hassirah* (*II Samuel* 3:26), the literal meaning of which — *The Pit of the Thorn* — recalls this episode (*Sanhedrin* 49a).

וְאָבִי — *My father.*

According to *Targum, my father* is a term of respect indicating *my master.*

The Midrash (*Shocher Tov* ibid.), on the other hand, states that David was addressing Saul as his *father* since Saul was his father-in-law. From this, [the Midrash] infers that "a person is as obligated to honor his father-in-law as his father."

The *Tur* (end of *Yoreh Deah,* 240) and *Shulchan Aruch* (*Yoreh Deah* 240:24) cite this verse as proof that a person is obligated to honor his father-in-law.[1]

The *Tur* omits the words of the Midrash, "as his father," from which *Bach* concludes that the *Tur* interprets the word אָבִי — *my father* — in this verse as a reference to Abner, and it thus has no bearing on honoring one's father-in-law. Nevertheless, the close proximity between this and David's reference to Saul indicates that some element of paternal respect applies to a father-in-law.

Thus, *Bach,* as well as *Shach,* rules that a person must accord his father-in-law the same degree of respect that he must give an honorable elder (such as by rising in his presence — see *Rashi, Leviticus* 19:32), but not as much as he gives his father (see *Chomas Anach, Nachalas Shimon*).

By addressing Saul as *father,* David hoped to remind him that while it is clear David will reign, Saul could take consolation in the knowledge that the next king would be his own son-in-law (*Me'am Loez*).

Chomas Anach adds another implication of David's use of the word אָבִי, *my father.* Generally speaking, a person is permitted to kill a thief who tunnels into his house (see *Exodus* 22:1-2). However, if it is clear that the thief is not potentially murderous — e.g., if

1. And, *Bach* and *Taz* add, his mother-in-law as well.

דַּע וּרְאֵה כִּי אֵין בְּיָדִי רָעָה וָפֶשַׁע וְלֹא־
חָטָאתִי לָךְ וְאַתָּה צֹדֶה אֶת־נַפְשִׁי לְקַחְתָּהּ׃
יג יִשְׁפֹּט יהוה בֵּינִי וּבֵינֶךָ וּנְקָמַנִי יהוה מִמֶּךָּ וְיָדִי
יד לֹא תִהְיֶה־בָּךְ׃ כַּאֲשֶׁר יֹאמַר מְשַׁל הַקַּדְמֹנִי
מֵרְשָׁעִים יֵצֵא רֶשַׁע וְיָדִי לֹא תִהְיֶה־בָּךְ׃

he is the householder's father — the householder may not kill him. Thus, David hinted to Saul that even though a person had a right to kill his *pursuer,* David considered Saul to be his father and thus refrained from harming him.

דַּע וּרְאֵה כִּי אֵין בְּיָדִי רָעָה וָפֶשַׁע וְלֹא־חָטָאתִי לָךְ — *You should know and see that there is no evil or rebellion in my hand, and that I have not sinned against you.*

David proved that he was not hostile to Saul by not harming him.

Aside from stating that וְלֹא־חָטָאתִי לָךְ, *"I have not sinned against you,"* David added the words, אֵין בְּיָדִי רָעָה וָפֶשַׁע, *There is no evil or iniquity in my hand at all.* Had David been guilty of other sins, the principle that *one sin leads to another sin* (*Avos* 4:2) would have influenced him to harm Saul (*Malbim*).

13. יִשְׁפֹּט ה׳ בֵּינִי וּבֵינֶךָ — *May Hashem judge between me and you.*

Despite the persuasive evidence of his innocence, David did not expect to influence Saul; he therefore merely asserted that he had no intention of harming Saul and was leaving matters in Hashem's hands.

David apparently anticipated that Saul's men would minimize his proof involving the garment — as indeed Abner did (see above, *Daas Sofrim*). Similarly, a Midrash records that after Saul left the cavern, his warriors asked him, "Is David to be considered righteous because he didn't kill you in the cavern? He knew full well that had he harmed you, we would have immediately annihilated him" (*Shocher Tov* 58:1, *Yalkut Shimoni*).

As a general rule, states the Talmud, a person should not relegate a dispute between himself and someone else to adjudication in the Heavenly Court; one who does so is liable to be punished himself, even before his opponent (*Bava Kamma* 93a).

However, this is so only if he has the opportunity to seek justice in a human court. Since David lacked that opportunity, he was permitted to call on heaven to settle his dispute.[1] Furthermore, since David had the right to take Saul's life but refrained from doing so (see above, v. 5), he could justifiably ask God to administer justice (*Me'am Loez*).

וּנְקָמַנִי ה׳ מִמֶּךָּ — *And may Hashem avenge me from you.*

The phrase וּנְקָמַנִי ה׳ מִמֶּךָּ was not a prayer (as is the similar formula, יִנְקוֹם ה׳ לִי). David would not have prayed for Saul's downfall (see below, 26:10). Rather, he expressed his confidence that Hashem was aware of his suffering and would exact justice (*Daas Sofrim*).

The word מִמֶּךָּ — literally, *from you* — can also mean *through you.* David thus prophetically intimated that Saul himself would be the tool through which David's vengeance would come, and so it was, for Saul cast himself on his own sword (below, 31:4) (*Kli Yakar*).

14. כַּאֲשֶׁר יֹאמַר מְשַׁל הַקַּדְמֹנִי — *As the ancient proverb says ...*

Our translation represents the simplest understanding of these words. Grammatically, however, the more accurate Hebrew for that term would be מְשַׁל הַקַּדְמוֹן. As it appears in the verse,

1. *Kli Yakar* claims that David was indeed punished first — when, prior to Saul's death, David's wives were temporarily taken into captivity (below, Chs. 30, 31). (*Nachalas Shimon* raises and discusses the point that David was unable to attain earthly justice.)

you should know and see that there is no evil or rebellion in my hand, and that I have not sinned against you — yet you ambush my soul to take it! [13] *May* HASHEM *judge between me and you, and may* HASHEM *avenge me from you — but my hand will not act against you.* [14] *As the ancient proverb says, 'Wickedness issues from the wicked'; but my hand will not act against you.*

the words would be more accurately translated as *proverb of the Ancient One* or *proverb of the early one.* Therefore, *Metzudos* renders *a proverb of the ancient times.*

According to *Radak,* קַדְמוֹנִי — *the ancient one* — is a reference to the first person who spoke this parable.

The Talmudic Sages, on the other hand, state (*Makkos* 10b, cited by *Rashi*) that קַדְמוֹנִי is a reference to Hashem, the *Ancient One* Who preceded the world, Whose "proverbs" are the Torah. It is the Torah itself that — in the halachah regarding an accidental killer — teaches that *wickedness issues from the wicked.*

The Torah teaches that if a person unintentionally kills a Jew, he is exiled to a city of refuge. Scripture describes such an accidental death as something that *God has caused to come to [the killer's] hand* (*Exodus* 21:13). But why would God cause a person to accidentally kill someone else? Our Sages answer that in this way God advances the cause of justice, and illustrate the principle with the following scenario.

Reuven committed a murder for which he deserved capital punishment, and Shimon committed an act of accidental manslaughter for which he deserved exile — however, because there were no witnesses in either case, both men remained at large.

One day as Shimon was descending a ladder under which Reuven was sitting, he fell onto Reuven and killed him — this time, in the presence of witnesses. Thus, Reuven the murderer met his death and Shimon the accidental killer had to flee to a city of refuge.

We learn from here that *wickedness issues from the wicked* — Hashem employs unscrupulous people as His emissaries to bring misfortune to those who deserve it.[1]

Me'am Loez suggests that the saying, *wickedness issues from the wicked,* is called an "ancient proverb" insofar as it is a *proverb about an ancient event* — i.e., the avenging of Cain's murder of Abel, which occurred when Cain was killed (albeit erroneously) by his descendant Lemech (see *Genesis* 4:23, *Rashi*).

מֵרְשָׁעִים יֵצֵא רֶשַׁע וְיָדִי לֹא תִהְיֶה־בָּךְ — *"Wickedness issues from the wicked" — but my hand will not act against you.*

David would not take revenge, because he trusted that Hashem would send wicked people to punish Saul.

Other explanations of this proverb follow.

❒ Wicked people generate evil in the world, which eventually causes their own destruction (*Radak*).

❒ David told Saul that the wickedness of a person's heart may be inferred from his deeds. David recognized Saul's heart

1. Why should the accidental killer be considered *wicked*? The answer is that it was his unpardonable negligence that caused the accidental death of his victim, and betrayed insufficient regard for human life.

טו אַחֲרֵי מִי יָצָא מֶלֶךְ יִשְׂרָאֵל אַחֲרֵי מִי אַתָּה רֹדֵף
טז אַחֲרֵי כֶּלֶב מֵת אַחֲרֵי פַּרְעֹשׁ אֶחָד: וְהָיָה יהוה לְדַיָּן
וְשָׁפַט בֵּינִי וּבֵינֶךָ וְיֵרֶא וְיָרֵב אֶת־רִיבִי וְיִשְׁפְּטֵנִי
יז מִיָּדֶךָ: וַיְהִי | כְּכַלּוֹת דָּוִד לְדַבֵּר אֶת־הַדְּבָרִים
הָאֵלֶּה אֶל־שָׁאוּל וַיֹּאמֶר שָׁאוּל הֲקֹלְךָ זֶה בְּנִי דָוִד

and knew that he would not have mercy on David; nevertheless, David would not strike him (*Radak*).

Similarly, *Abarbanel* explains that David told Saul, "You are wicked and so you can perform wicked deeds if you please — but I will not."

❐ A Midrash (*Shir HaShirim Rabbah* 1:1:6) cites this verse to illustrate the concept that wicked people often have wicked descendants (*Daas Sofrim*).

❐ According to *Sefer HaAkeidah* (*Shaar* 26), David here referred prophetically to a later incident in his life. When David ran for refuge to Achish, King of Gath (below, Ch. 27), he was accepted and enlisted as a Philistine soldier. When Achish prepared to battle Saul, David was placed in a dilemma. On the one hand, he had to demonstrate his loyalty to Achish — yet on the other, how could he enter into battle against his fellow Israelites — in particular, against his father-in-law, King Saul? Much to his relief, the Philistine officers objected to David's participation and refused to let him fight (see below, Ch. 29). In that war, Saul eventually lost his life. Thus, David now exclaimed, "The wicked men of Achish were wickedly suspicious of me — but as a result יָדִי לֹא תִהְיֶה־בָּךְ, *my hand did not have to harm you.*"

וְיָדִי לֹא תִהְיֶה־בָּךְ — *But my hand will not act against you.*

This phrase appeared in the previous verse as well. Why did David repeat it?

Some suggest that the words form part of the ancient proverb — i.e., "Let wickedness issue from the wicked, but my hand will not act against you" (*Kli Yakar, Daas Sofrim*).

Kli Yakar cites another explanation (in the name of his son). By repeating these words, David indicated that he would play no role, whether direct or indirect, in harming Saul.

15. אַחֲרֵי מִי יָצָא מֶלֶךְ יִשְׂרָאֵל — *After whom has the king of Israel gone forth?*

After declaring his innocence, David took Saul to task for the manner in which he had pursued him, one that detracted from Saul's dignity (*Malbim*).

According to *Abarbanel*, David told Saul that if he were guilty, the king should not personally have taken part in the pursuit of such a lowly person (*Abarbanel*).

אַחֲרֵי כֶּלֶב מֵת אחרי פַּרְעֹשׁ אֶחָד — *After a dead dog, after a single flea.*

This phrase means, *someone as insignificant as a dead dog or a single flea.*

Targum renders כֶּלֶב מֵת as *a weakling*, and פַּרְעֹשׁ as a *simple person.*

When a dead dog decays, it produces a repulsive stench. David portrayed himself in that light in concurrence with the vile, slanderous remarks spoken about him (*Abarbanel*).

A dog is loyal only until it dies. Similarly, David implied, his ability to demonstrate his loyalty to Saul ended when he was forced to flee (*Malbim*).

David compared himself to a flea with the hope of impressing upon Saul the degradation to which he had been subjected. Saul had tried to capture David like a person who tries to snatch a flea, which escapes by jumping about wildly from one place to another (*Radak*).

[15] *After whom has the king of Israel gone forth? Whom
are you pursuing? After [someone as insignificant as]
a dead dog, after a single flea!* [16] *May* HASHEM *be an
arbiter, and judge between me and you; may He see
and take up my grievance, and vindicate me from
your hand."*

[17] *And when David finished speaking these words to
Saul, Saul said, "Is that your voice, my son David?"* —

David's use of these self-abasing metaphors illustrates his absolute humility, and that reflects upon the entire nation — thus, our Sages state that Hashem tells the Jewish people, "I cherish you because even when I bestow greatness upon you, you belittle yourselves before Me — for instance, David said, 'I am a worm and not a man' "(*Psalms* 22:7) (*Chullin* 98a).

16. וְהָיָה ה׳ לְדַיָּן וְשָׁפַט בֵּינִי וּבֵינֶךָ — *May* HASHEM *be an arbiter, and judge between me and you.*

Malbim explains that the word דַיָּן — *arbiter* — is used in conjunction with weighing the litigants' claims, whereas שׁוֹפֵט — *judge* — is associated with determining the verdict. Thus, prayed David, may Hashem *take up my cause,* i.e., present my claims on my behalf, as it were, and then deliver His judgment and *vindicate me from [Saul's] hand.*

David's sentiments here apparently repeat his earlier words, *May* HASHEM *judge between me and you and may* HASHEM *avenge me from you* (v. 13).

According to *Abarbanel*, however, there is no redundancy. Earlier, David had expressed his hope that Hashem would perceive his innocence and punish Saul. Now, after David had showed Saul how ludicrous it was for the king to degrade himself by pursuing someone as lowly as David, he concluded by praying that Saul's view of David come true: "May Hashem increase my significance while reducing yours."

וְשָׁפַט בֵּינִי וּבֵינֶךָ ... וְיִשְׁפְּטֵנִי מִיָּדֶךָ — *And judge between me and you ... and vindicate me from your hand.*

In the Hebrew, the words *judge* and *vindicate* share the same root: שפט. *Judge* is followed by בֵּינִי — *between me,* denoting arbitration between two parties. *Vindicated* is followed by the prefix מ, *from,* implying that justice is being performed (see also *II Samuel* 18:19).

Targum renders וְיִשְׁפְּטֵנִי מִיָּדֶךָ — *vindicate me from your hand* — as *[God] will take vengeance upon you for my shame.*[1]

◆§ Saul Admits Guilt and Pleads for Compassion.

17. וַיְהִי כְּכַלּוֹת דָּוִד לְדַבֵּר אֶת־הַדְּבָרִים הָאֵלֶּה אֶל־שָׁאוּל וַיֹּאמֶר שָׁאוּל — *And when David finished speaking these words to Saul, Saul said ...*

Our Sages teach that the word דִּבּוּר — *speech* — describes harsh and strong words, whereas אֲמִירָה describes a gentle tone and message (see *Makkos* 11a; *Exodus* 19:3, *Rashi*). Thus, although David spoke harshly (לְדַבֵּר), Saul answered gently (וַיֹּאמֶר). Apparently, Saul was moved by and recognized the truth of David's declamation.

הֲקֹלְךָ זֶה בְּנִי דָוִד — *Is that your voice, my son David?*

Saul referred to David as his son, since David had treated him with filial

1. See *Kli Yakar*, who explains that in the two parts of this verse David directed his speech to both Saul and Abner.

יח וַיִּשָּׂא שָׁאוּל קֹלוֹ וַיֵּבְךְּ: וַיֹּאמֶר אֶל־דָּוִד צַדִּיק
אַתָּה מִמֶּנִּי כִּי אַתָּה גְּמַלְתַּנִי הַטּוֹבָה וַאֲנִי גְּמַלְתִּיךָ
יט הָרָעָה: °ואת הִגַּדְתָּ הַיּוֹם אֵת אֲשֶׁר־עָשִׂיתָה אִתִּי °וְאַתָּה ק׳
טוֹבָה אֵת אֲשֶׁר סִגְּרַנִי יהוה בְּיָדְךָ וְלֹא הֲרַגְתָּנִי:
כ וְכִי־יִמְצָא אִישׁ אֶת־אֹיְבוֹ וְשִׁלְּחוֹ בְּדֶרֶךְ טוֹבָה
וַיהוה יְשַׁלֶּמְךָ טוֹבָה תַּחַת הַיּוֹם הַזֶּה אֲשֶׁר
כא עָשִׂיתָה לִי: וְעַתָּה הִנֵּה יָדַעְתִּי כִּי מָלֹךְ תִּמְלוֹךְ

compassion. Alternatively, Saul called David his *son* because David was his son-in-law (*Abarbanel*).

According to *Chomas Anach,* with these words Saul delivered an implicit rebuke to David. Although David addressed Saul respectfully and intimately by calling him אָבִי — *my father,* his words were sharp and biting, Saul riposted, "הֲקֹלְךָ זֶה — *Is that your voice?* Can this harsh voice be that of בְּנִי דָוִד — *my son David* — who calls me אָבִי — *my father?*"

וַיִּשָּׂא שָׁאוּל קֹלוֹ וַיֵּבְךְּ — *And Saul raised his voice and wept.*

Saul wept as he realized David was innocent and that he had persecuted David without justification.

Alternatively, when Saul saw his ripped garment, he understood that he would lose the kingship and that David would succeed him (*Kli Yakar*).

According to *Chomas Anach,* he wept over what he now understood to be the unjustified massacre of the Kohanim at Nob. As *Daas Sofrim* elaborates, Saul had devoted much effort into his belief that David was a menace to the nation and that he sought to assassinate his king. Now, if David was really innocent, then Saul had wrongfully taken Michal away from him, destroyed Nob, and agitated the leaders of the nation against him.

18. צַדִּיק אַתָּה מִמֶּנִּי — *You are more righteous than I.*

This phrase may be translated homiletically as *you are righteous because of me.* According to a Midrash (*Shocher Tov* 58:1). Saul told David, "I made you righteous because although I would have killed you, you refrained from killing me." That is to say, explains *Kli Yakar,* through his struggles with Saul, David's potential righteousness and virtues were realized.

כִּי אַתָּה גְּמַלְתַּנִי הַטּוֹבָה וַאֲנִי גְּמַלְתִּיךָ הָרָעָה — *For you have repaid me with goodness, whereas I have repaid you with wickedness.*

The verb — גמל — is generally translated as *repaid* (*Metzudos*).

According to *Malbim,* it connotes an action motivated by the love or hatred of another.

גְּמַלְתַּנִי הַטּוֹבָה — *You have repaid me with goodness.*

Abarbanel explains that Saul was not referring here to David's sparing his life, which he mentions in the next verse. Rather, Saul was speaking of David's heroic victory over Goliath and his other military exploits against the Philistines.

19. וְאַתָּה הִגַּדְתָּ הַיּוֹם — *You have proven today.*

This phrase literally means, *and today you told.* Our translation is that of *Targum.*

Be'er Moshe, citing *Binah L'Itim,* offers an interpretation that satisfies the literal meaning of this phrase. Generally, a person who performs a noble deed should not publicize it, because an aspiration for fame diminishes the value of the deed. But there is an exception to this

and Saul raised his voice and wept. [18] *He said*
to David, "You are more righteous than I, for
you have repaid me with goodness, whereas I
have repaid you with wickedness. [19] *You have*
proven today that you have done [only] good
with me, for H*ASHEM* *delivered me into your*
hand but you did not kill me. [20] *Does a man*
find his enemy and then send him off in a good
way? May H*ASHEM* *repay you with beneficence*
for what you have done to me this day. [21] *Now*
behold! I know that you will certainly reign,

rule — namely, when a general awareness of the deed will influence others to emulate it. Thus, Saul lauded David for *telling* what he had done — because, as the following verse explicates, others would be inspired by David's behavior to refrain from harming their enemies under similar circumstances.

20. וְכִי־יִמְצָא אִישׁ אֶת־אֹיְבוֹ וְשִׁלְּחוֹ בְּדֶרֶךְ טוֹבָה וַה׳ יְשַׁלֶּמְךָ טוֹבָה — *Does a man find his enemy and then send him off in a good way? May* H*ASHEM* *repay you.*

We present this phrase as a rhetorical question, as does *Abarbanel.* Other commentators, however, render these words as an abridged sentence: "If a man finds his enemy and sends him off on a good way, *he deserves to be rewarded by* H*ASHEM* — and so may Hashem repay you ..." (*Radak, Ralbag*).

According to *Be'er Moshe* (preceding verse), the verse states that once David made his self-restraint inspired by his compassion known, when others would be moved to act in a similar manner, Hashem would reward David (see also *Malbim*).

וְשִׁלְּחוֹ בְּדֶרֶךְ טוֹבָה— *And then send him off in a good way.*

Lev Shalom (cited by *Mishbetzos Zahav*) explains the implication of *in a good way.* David and his men could easily have captured Saul in the cavern, expressed their innocence and then set him free. They did not do so because the brief time of his captivity would have been an affront to his dignity. David chose to cut off a piece of Saul's garment — even though people could have claimed that it had been caught on a thorn — to preserve Saul's honor and have him leave *in a good way.* It was this that Saul now acknowledged.

21. וְעַתָּה הִנֵּה יָדַעְתִּי כִּי מָלֹךְ תִּמְלוֹךְ — *Now behold! I know that you will certainly reign.*

Saul now understood that since Hashem had consistently saved David from Saul's hands, Hashem must be grooming David for the throne (*Rashi*).

Radak and *Abarbanel* suggest that Saul heard that Samuel had anointed David as king.

Also (as mentioned earlier), Saul had another indication that David would serve as king. After Saul's failure in regard to the war with Amalek, Samuel had told him that whoever would rip his garment in the future would succeed him as king (see above, 15:27) (*Shocher Tov* 57:3).

Malbim adds that Saul was convinced that David was fit to be king because of his exceptional display of self-control. This is consistent with the verse, טוֹב אֶרֶךְ אַפַּיִם מִגִּבּוֹר וּמֹשֵׁל בְּרוּחוֹ מִלֹּכֵד עִיר — *He who is slow to anger is better than a strong man, and a master of his passions [is better] than a conqueror of a city* (*Proverbs* 16:32).

כב וְקָמָה֙ בְּיָ֣דְךָ֔ מַמְלֶ֖כֶת יִשְׂרָאֵֽל׃ וְעַתָּ֗ה הִשָּׁ֤בְעָה
לִּי֙ בַּֽיהוָ֔ה אִם־תַּכְרִ֥ית אֶת־זַרְעִ֖י אַחֲרָ֑י וְאִם־
כג תַּשְׁמִ֥יד אֶת־שְׁמִ֖י מִבֵּ֥ית אָבִֽי׃ וַיִּשָּׁבַ֥ע דָּוִ֖ד לְשָׁא֑וּל
וַיֵּ֤לֶךְ שָׁאוּל֙ אֶל־בֵּית֔וֹ וְדָוִד֙ וַאֲנָשָׁ֔יו עָל֖וּ עַל־
כה/א א הַמְּצוּדָֽה׃ וַיָּ֣מָת שְׁמוּאֵ֔ל וַיִּקָּבְצ֤וּ כָל־יִשְׂרָאֵל֙

Saul had always known that David was a warrior. Now that he saw that David possessed the attribute of compassion, he knew that he possessed the qualifications for kingship (*Kli Yakar*).

Mishbetzos Zahav suggests that since Saul was told that his successor would be *your fellow who is better than you* (15:28), he now realized that that person must be David, who, as he now admitted, was *more righteous than I* (v. 18).

מָלֹךְ תִּמְלוֹךְ — *You will certainly reign.*

מָלֹךְ תִּמְלוֹךְ literally means, *Reign, you will reign.* This double language implies that David and his offspring will be kings both in the present era and in the era of the Messiah, who will also be a descendant of David (*Midrash Shocher Tov* ibid.).

וְקָמָה בְּיָדְךָ מַמְלֶכֶת יִשְׂרָאֵל — *And the kingship over Israel shall be established in your hand.*

The word קָמָה is usually associated with קָם, *rise.* In this case, however, *Targum* relates it to קִיּוּם, *endurance.* Hence, Saul told David, "Although my own kingship will cease, yours will endure" (*Radak*).

22. אִם־תַּכְרִית אֶת־זַרְעִי אַחֲרָי וְאִם־תַּשְׁמִיד אֶת־שְׁמִי מִבֵּית אָבִי — *That you will not annihilate my descendants after me and that you will not destroy my name from my father's house.*

It was common practice for a newly appointed king to wipe out the entire family of his predecessor (*Abarbanel*).

By annihilating the former king's descendants, one has effectively destroyed his name. Thus, *Radak* explains, the two clauses in Saul's statement are essentially one.

Kli Yakar suggests, however, that the latter clause does not merely reiterate the first.

First, Saul asked David to swear that he would not destroy his children, and then that David would not destroy his name — meaning that David would not kill him. If David allowed Saul to live out his years, his good name as king would be preserved.

23. וַיִּשָּׁבַע דָּוִד לְשָׁאוּל — *David swore to Saul.*

According to *Me'am Loez,* David swore only in regard to *Saul,* not in regard to his offspring. This may explain how it is that he subsequently delivered seven descendants of Saul into the hands of the Gibeonites to be killed (*II Samuel* Ch. 21).

Malbim disagrees and contends that the oath included Saul's descendants. As for the Gibeonites, it was they and not David who performed the executions.

וַיֵּלֶךְ שָׁאוּל אֶל־בֵּיתוֹ — *Saul went to his house.*

Saul left feeling not like a king but rather dejected, like a man stripped of his power and glory (*Kli Yakar*).

As mentioned earlier, after Saul made his sincere and emotional admission of guilt, his warriors scoffed at the idea of David's heroism, telling Saul that David had refrained from harming him out of fear of what they would do to him in revenge.[1]

וַאֲנָשָׁיו עָלוּ עַל־הַמְּצוּדָה — *And his men ascended to the stronghold.*

Rather than the conventional אֶל, *to,*

1. As we will see in Chapter 26, Saul was apparently affected by their skepticism, for he returned to his pursuit of David.

24/22-23 *and the kingship over Israel shall be established*
in your hand. [22] *So now, swear to me by* Hashem
that you will not annihilate my descendants af-
ter me and that you will not destroy my name
from my father's house."
[23] *David swore to Saul. Saul went to his house*
and David and his men ascended to the strong-
hold.

25/1 [1] *Samuel died, and all of Israel gathered*

Scripture uses the word עַל — literally, *on* or *upon.* Apparently, David's men mistrusted Saul, and so they ascended to an elevation higher than the stronghold (*Kli Yakar*).

Alternatively, because these *strongholds* were not buildings but concealed spots atop the mountains and cliffs, the word עַל is appropriate here (*Daas Sofrim*).

XXV

1. וַיָּמָת שְׁמוּאֵל — *Samuel died.*

Scripture describes Samuel's death here and in Chapter 28 as well (v. 3). According to many commentators, the present verse appears in correct chronological order. As for the description of Samuel's death in Ch. 28, that is a brief reprise introducing the narrative in which Saul summons Samuel from the grave.

Thus, as described at the end of the previous chapter, Saul admitted that David would prevail over him — acknowledging, in effect, Samuel's anointment of David as king. And directly following that episode, Samuel died (*Radak*).

This understanding of the narrative fits in well with our Sages' statement that Samuel died seven months before Saul did. For a little over four of those months preceding Saul's death, David resided in the Philistine countryside (below, 27:7). During the previous two and a fraction months, David and Abigail met and David stayed at Hachilah Hill (see Ch. 26) (*Radak*).[1]

The Midrash (*Midrash Shmuel, Koheles Rabbah* 7:1:4) states that the main place where Scripture reports Samuel's death is in Chapter 28. It is mentioned here, before the story of Nabal, only to show that while the people of Israel were mourning Samuel, Nabal was engaged in gaiety and self-gratification. This was such an egregious violation of civilized behavior that it was tantamount to a denial of Hashem's existence.[2]

According to *Abarbanel,* Scripture records Samuel's demise here to contrast the deaths

1. *Rashi* (below, 27:7, and to *Nazir* 5a; also *Tosafos, Temurah* 5a), however, cites Midrashic sources that Samuel died only four months before Saul. Those were the four months that David spent in Philistia.

2. It seems clear that the Midrash agrees that Samuel died before the incident of Nabal. The Midrash means to emphasize that the primary narrative of Samuel's death is in Chapter 28, but it is briefly mentioned here to associate it with the description of Nabal's boorishness. A different source (*Tosefta Sotah*) seems to say the opposite: that the main record of Samuel's death is here and that the one in Chapter 28 is secondary (see *Chasdei David, Chazon Yechezkel* to the *Tosefta*).

וַיִּסְפְּדוּ־לוֹ וַיִּקְבְּרֻהוּ בְּבֵיתוֹ בָּרָמָה וַיָּקָם דָּוִד
ב וַיֵּרֶד אֶל־מִדְבַּר פָּארָן: וְאִישׁ
בְּמָעוֹן וּמַעֲשֵׂהוּ בַכַּרְמֶל וְהָאִישׁ גָּדוֹל מְאֹד

of these two men. Nabal died ignominiously and received no eulogies, whereas Samuel was lauded before multitudes.

The Date of Samuel's Death

As discussed above (8:1), Samuel died at the age of 52. There is a disagreement regarding the exact date of his passing.

Megillas Taanis, which records various dates on which it is appropriate to fast, lists the 29th of Iyar as the date on which he died. However, the *Shulchan Aruch* (*Orach Chaim* 580:2) lists it as the 28th.[1]

וַיִּקָּבְצוּ כָל־יִשְׂרָאֵל וַיִּסְפְּדוּ לוֹ — *And all of Israel gathered and eulogized him.*

Since it had been Samuel's practice to circulate throughout Israel to judge the people and nurture peace among them (*I Samuel* 7:17), it was appropriate that people should gather from all corners of the land to extend their last respects (*Midrash Shmuel*).

Also, by gathering en masse to honor Samuel, the people of Israel corrected a mistake that they had made after Joshua died. Scripture records Joshua's burial place as being north of Mt. Gaash — literally, Mt. Eruption (*Joshua* 24:30). Our Sages say that there is no site called Mt. Gaash; this name is an allusion to the following occurrence. When Joshua died, the people continued in their quotidian tasks: one was preoccupied in his field, another in his vineyard, and so forth. Hashem thus caused a mountain to *erupt* and almost bury them (*Midrash Shmuel*). The Talmud (*Shabbos* 105b) derives from this episode that anyone who is lax in eulogizing a Torah scholar deserves to be buried alive. Thus, when Samuel died, the Jews feared provoking God's wrath and gathered to pay their respects.[2]

וַיִּקְבְּרֻהוּ בְּבֵיתוֹ בָּרָמָה — *And they buried him at his home in Ramah.*

Simply understood, this reference to Samuel's hometown of *Ramah* is unnecessary. It may thus be understood as bearing a deeper meaning — to wit, that Samuel was eulogized in all cities of Israel to the same extent that he was in his own home of Ramah (*Tosefta, Sotah* 11:6).

וַיָּקָם דָּוִד וַיֵּרֶד אֶל־מִדְבַּר פָּארָן — *David arose and descended to the Wilderness of Paran.*

As long as Samuel was alive, he did not divulge that he had anointed David, apprehensive lest Saul attack him (see above, 16:2). But prior to his death, that information became known — either through Samuel or one of his disciples. Thus, in the midst of the national mourning and eulogizing of Samuel, David learned of this added cause for concern and he fled.

Metzudos conjectures that David's camp in the wilderness of Ein Gedi was flocked with passersby on their way to and from the eulogies for Samuel; fearful that he would be noticed by one of Saul's supporters, David left *and descended to the Wilderness of Paran.*

According to *Midrash Shmuel*, David attended the eulogies for Samuel at the risk of his life, performing a "kindness" on behalf of the great prophet.

1. This date is perplexing because the Sages (*Rosh Hashanah* 18a) say that Nabal died ten days after Samuel, which would put Samuel's death on the day before Rosh Hashanah (see *Targum Yerushalmi, Bikkurim* 2:1; *Rashi* below, v. 38; *Kaf HaChaim, Orach Chaim* 580; *Mishbetzos Zahav*).

2. Our Sages compare this behavior to that of a person who has been bitten by a snake and who is subsequently terrified whenever he sees a rope, which resembles a snake.

and eulogized him, and they buried him at his home in Ramah.

David arose and descended to the Wilderness of Paran.

[2]There was a man in Maon whose business was in Carmel. The man was very wealthy;

◆§ David Seeks Provisions in the Wilderness

2. This verse introduces us to the ignoble Nabal. The commentators infer a number of details regarding Nabal's venality from the present verse, and subsequent verses explicitly impeach him.

וְאִישׁ בְּמָעוֹן וּמַעֲשֵׂהוּ בַכַּרְמֶל — *There was a man in Maon whose business was in Carmel.*

Maon and Carmel are cities in the territory of Judah (*Joshua* 15:55).

The word וּמַעֲשֵׂהוּ — literally, *whose actions* or *whose work* — is translated by *Targum* as *whose property* or *whose business.*

This word often refers to *livestock* (similar to *Genesis* 33:14, לְרֶגֶל הַמְּלָאכָה), because animal husbandry absorbs all of a person's attention (*Radak*).

Nabal exploited his dual residency to excuse himself from discharging his civic obligations. In Maon, he refused to donate to local charities on the grounds that he was paying in Carmel, and vice versa (*Me'am Loez,* quoting the Sages).

This verse mentions Nabal's hometown to emphasize his dereliction in not coming to David's aid. He could not claim unfamiliarity with David and his men, because they had been residing in the wilderness of Maon (above, 23:25; *Malbim* ad loc.).

Maon can also mean *home* or *abode.*

Accordingly, *Ralbag* explains וְאִישׁ בְּמָעוֹן וּמַעֲשֵׂהוּ בַכַּרְמֶל as meaning, *there was a man whose home and business were located in Carmel.* Nabal had so much real estate in the form of fields, vineyards, and so forth that he placed his home next to it.

Alternatively, וְאִישׁ בְּמָעוֹן — *there was a man whose home* — means that Nabal possessed an impressive mansion that was far from his business in Carmel.

As for כַּרְמֶל, it can be interpreted as referring either to the city of *Carmel* or to a *verdant agricultural area* (*Radak*).

וְהָאִישׁ גָּדוֹל מְאֹד — *This man was very wealthy.*

The use of the word גָּדוֹל — literally, *great* — for *wealth* indicates Nabal's arrogance (*Be'er Moshe*). The next phrase, וְלוֹ צֹאן שְׁלֹשֶׁת־אֲלָפִים — literally, *to him were three thousand sheep* — connotes that these animals were his alone, for he shared his wealth with no one. This was the case even בִּגְזֹז אֶת־צֹאנוֹ, *when he was shearing his sheep,* which is traditionally a festive time during which people act generously.

According to *Me'am Loez,* גָּדוֹל indicates that Nabal came from a *great* — i.e., a *prestigious* — family. His family lineage was as follows.

Judah had a grandson Hezron, who had three sons: Jerahmeel, Ram, and Chelubai (another name for Caleb). Nabal was a direct descendant of Caleb (v. 3), and his lineage was unblemished. As for Jerahmeel, he had married a gentile (see *I Chronicles* 2:26, *Rashi*) and thus disqualified his descendants from attaining the crown. And Ram's descendant was David — who, Nabal thought, was unfit to be king since his great-grandmother was a Moabitess. Thus, Nabal considered that he possessed the purest genealogy of anyone in the tribe of Judah and was therefore worthy of the throne. Accordingly, Nabal treated David with contempt, asking, "Who is David and who is the son of Jesse?" (below, v. 10; *Rashi* to *I Chronicles* [2:9]).

וְלוֹ צֹאן שְׁלֹשֶׁת־אֲלָפִים וְאֶלֶף עִזִּים וַיְהִי בִּגְזֹז
ג אֶת־צֹאנוֹ בַּכַּרְמֶל׃ וְשֵׁם הָאִישׁ נָבָל וְשֵׁם אִשְׁתּוֹ
אֲבִגָיִל וְהָאִשָּׁה טוֹבַת־שֶׂכֶל וִיפַת תֹּאַר וְהָאִישׁ
ד קָשֶׁה וְרַע מַעֲלָלִים וְהוּא °כלבו׃ וַיִּשְׁמַע דָּוִד
ה בַּמִּדְבָּר כִּי־גֹזֵז נָבָל אֶת־צֹאנוֹ׃ וַיִּשְׁלַח דָּוִד
עֲשָׂרָה נְעָרִים וַיֹּאמֶר דָּוִד לַנְּעָרִים עֲלוּ כַרְמֶלָה
וּבָאתֶם אֶל־נָבָל וּשְׁאֶלְתֶּם־לוֹ בִשְׁמִי לְשָׁלוֹם׃

°כָּלִבִּי ק׳

וְלוֹ צֹאן שְׁלֹשֶׁת אֲלָפִים — *He owned three thousand sheep.*

The word צֹאן is a general term for sheep and goats. Whenever it is mentioned in association with shearing, it refers solely to sheep; thus, goats are listed separately in this verse (*Radak*).

וַיְהִי בִּגְזֹז אֶת־צֹאנוֹ בַּכַּרְמֶל — *[The following episode] occurred at the shearing of his sheep in Carmel.*

As was the general custom, Nabal feasted when he sheared his sheep (*Rashi*).

The Midrash comments that whenever wool-shearing is mentioned in *Tanach*, it is associated with adversity — i.e., in regard to Laban (*Genesis* 31:19), Judah (*Genesis* Ch. 38), Absalom (*II Samuel* Ch. 13), and here. The reason is that shearing prompts revelry focused on material success, in consequence of which the Satan is aroused to tempt its celebrants to sin and then to prosecute them (see *Midrash Shmuel; Bereishis Rabbah* 74:6, *Yefeh Toar, Yedei Moshe* ad loc.; *Bereishis Rabbah* 85:6, *Maharzu* ad loc.).

3. וְשֵׁם הָאִישׁ נָבָל — *The man's name was Nabal.*

The word נָבָל means *base* or *degraded* — a name that, as Nabal's wife Abigail attested (below, v. 25) — accurately described his character.

Radak cites the view of his father that Nabal was not a given name but a sobriquet created by those who knew him well.

וְשֵׁם אִשְׁתּוֹ אֲבִגָיִל — *And his wife's name was Abigail.*

The word גִּיל means *joy*. Thus, she was אֲב הַגִּיל — literally, *father of happiness* — i.e., she possessed a radiant and content disposition (*Abarbanel*).

וְהָאִשָּׁה טוֹבַת שֶׂכֶל וִיפַת תֹּאַר — *The woman was intelligent and beautiful.*

טוֹבַת שֶׂכֶל — *intelligent* — means that Abigail possessed a superior character (*Abarbanel*).

Alternatively, the phrase refers to her physical attributes. שֶׂכֶל can imply *scrutiny*, and thus, טוֹבַת שֶׂכֶל means that under scrutiny Abigail's countenance was attractive to look upon. The next phrase, יְפַת תֹּאַר — *beautiful* — refers to her figure (similar to Scripture's descriptions of Rachel [*Genesis* 29:13] and Joseph [ibid. 39:6] — *Radak*).

וְהָאִישׁ קָשֶׁה וְרַע מַעֲלָלִים — *But the man was difficult and an evildoer.*

קָשֶׁה, *difficult*, means that he was verbally abusive, and רַע מַעֲלָלִים, *an evildoer*, that his deeds were repugnant (*Abarbanel*).

According to *Malbim*, on the other hand, קָשֶׁה, *difficult*, denotes Nabal's inborn traits, and רַע מַעֲלָלִים, *an evildoer*, his lack of self-control. A person with a difficult nature can learn to overcome it, and a person who lacks self-control can, when under the influence of emotions such as pity or fear, overcome his primitive impulses. Nabal, however, was capable of neither; thus, he could not be relied upon to behave in a moral fashion.

וְהוּא כָלִבִּי — *He was a descendant of Caleb.*

he owned three thousand sheep and a thousand
goats. [The following episode] occurred at the
shearing of his sheep in Carmel: 3*(The man's*
name was Nabal and his wife's name was Abi-
gail; the woman was intelligent and beautiful, but
the man was difficult and an evildoer; he was a
descendant of Caleb.) 4*David heard in the wil-*
derness that Nabal was shearing his sheep, 5*so*
David sent ten attendants, and David said to
the attendants, "Go up to Carmel and approach
Nabal, inquiring after his welfare, in my name.

Caleb was known for the heroic integrity that he displayed during the episode of the spies (*Numbers* Chs. 13,14). Nabal took pride in his illustrious lineage, which may have contributed to his arrogance.

Because Nabal had such a noble lineage, David expected him to respond magnanimously to David's request for assistance (*Malbim*).[1]

Ralbag reads כָלִבִּי not as *Caleb* but as related to כֶּלֶב, *dog*. Nabal acted in a cruel and miserly fashion — like a dog, which barks aggressively when approached by other dogs, and which will not share its food with them, even if it has more than enough for itself.

Evidence for the miserly nature of the canine species is found in *Isaiah*: *The dogs are greedy; they do not know satiation* (56:11). Also, the Talmud describes a dog as "a creature that benefits from you but will not provide benefit for you" (*Nedarim* 24a; see *Abarbanel, Be'er Moshe*).

The word that is read (*k'ri*) as כָלִבִּי is written (*k'siv*) as כלבו. *Radak* suggests that the word is pronounced כְּלִבּוֹ — *as his heart*. This means that Nabal's actions reflected his feelings — he was evil through and through.

Along the same lines, *Radak* interprets the *k'ri* as כְּלִבִּי, meaning *as my heart*. A person who observed him would say, *Nabal turned out to be as bad as as my heart told me he would.*

4. It was customary to celebrate during the time of sheep-shearing, and so David hoped that this would be an opportune moment to ask Nabal for provisions.

Nabal's celebrations were so vast that David heard about them *in the wilderness*, yet Nabal refused to share his abundant provisions with David's men (*Kli Yakar*).

5. וַיִּשְׁלַח דָּוִד עֲשָׂרָה נְעָרִים — *So David sent ten attendants.*

Apparently, David anticipated a substantial gift, one that would require ten attendants to transport (*Daas Sofrim*).

According to *Me'am Loez*, David sent ten attendants as a gesture of respect toward Nabal.

וּשְׁאֶלְתֶּם־לוֹ בִשְׁמִי לְשָׁלוֹם — *Inquiring after his welfare, in my name.*

In the next verse, David again told his attendants to wish Nabal *peace*. Simply understood, the present verse describes how David told his attendants to inquire as to Nabal's well-being, and the following verse describes how he instructed them to send Nabal his blessing for peace.

1. Caleb's name alludes to the word כֶּלֶב, *dog*. Since Caleb had an ignominious name yet possessed a a sterling character, David hoped that Nabal would be no different (*Chomas Anach*, citing *Mahari De Seguvia*).

ו וַאֲמַרְתֶּם כֹּה לֶחָי וְאַתָּה שָׁלוֹם וּבֵיתְךָ שָׁלוֹם
ז וְכֹל אֲשֶׁר־לְךָ שָׁלוֹם: וְעַתָּה שָׁמַעְתִּי כִּי גֹזְזִים
לָךְ עַתָּה הָרֹעִים אֲשֶׁר־לְךָ הָיוּ עִמָּנוּ לֹא
הֶכְלַמְנוּם וְלֹא־נִפְקַד לָהֶם מְאוּמָה כָּל־יְמֵי
ח הֱיוֹתָם בַּכַּרְמֶל: שְׁאַל אֶת־נְעָרֶיךָ וְיַגִּידוּ לָךְ
וְיִמְצְאוּ הַנְּעָרִים חֵן בְּעֵינֶיךָ כִּי־עַל־יוֹם טוֹב °בנו °בָּאנוּ ק׳

Kli Yakar, on the other hand, suggests that the present verse describes how David told his attendants to convey his words solely to Nabal — as one leader to another. The next verse describes how David told his attendants to convey his words to Nabal's family and entourage as well.

Alternatively, the *Zohar* states that whereas this verse describes David's words to Nabal, the next verse describes David's prayer to Hashem. Thus, David now told his attendants, וּשְׁאֶלְתֶּם לוֹ בִשְׁמִי לְשָׁלוֹם, the only words that he should direct to Nabal were the inquiry of the present verse. The words of the following verse, however, were directed to Hashem (*Zohar*).

6. וַאֲמַרְתֶּם כֹּה לֶחָי — *And say, "Such [success] for life."*

Literally, כֹּה לֶחָי means *so for the living* — a cryptic phrase that has inspired a variety of interpretations.

Our translation — *such success for life* — is that of *Targum,* which explains this phrase as David's blessing that the prosperity that Nabal was now enjoying should continue throughout his life.

Rashi explains כֹּה לֶחָי to mean, *So shall it be next year* (similar to the phrase, כָּעֵת חַיָּה, *at this time when you will all be alive and well,* or *at this time next year* [*Genesis* 18:10]).

Alternatively, *Rashi* interprets חַי as a reference to a person who is *alive* in the sense that he is active and worthy of respect. Thus, כֹּה לֶחָי means that the blessing enjoyed by Nabal was appropriate for a person who possessed these attributes.

Mahari Kara renders וַאֲמַרְתֶּם כֹּה as meaning, *You shall say as follows,* and לֶחָי as *To life!* — i.e., may you be remembered for life.

In *Ecclesiastes* (6:8), a wealthy man is referred to as חַי, *alive.* Thus, כֹּה לֶחָי means, *Such [a blessing] is appropriate for an affluent man [such as yourself]* (*Radak*).

The above interpretations see this verse as David's greeting to Nabal.

The *Zohar* (*Parashas Vayishlach,* p. 171b; *Parashas Va'eira,* p. 23b), however, points out that it is forbidden to extend greetings to an unscrupulous man, and denies that David would have violated this prohibition. Accordingly, the *Zohar* explains that while speaking to Nabal David mentally directed his words to Hashem.[1]

The following interpretations avoid this issue, for they do not construe the verse as a greeting to Nabal.

According to *Me'am Loez,* David was attempting to persuade Nabal to help him and his men. כֹּה לֶחָי thus means, *Such is the way of the living* — i.e., people should be concerned about others. The following phrase, וְאַתָּה שָׁלוֹם — *and peace upon you* — means that just

1. And this, the *Zohar* explicates, is not considered deceitful.

The Talmud (*Gittin* 62a) relates that whenever Rav Kahana met a gentile he would say, "Peace unto my master." *Rashi* explains that when he did so he would have in mind that this blessing should apply to his teacher. *Tosafos* reject *Rashi*'s interpretation on the grounds that it would be improper for Rav Kahana to engage in such misleading behavior. But *Chomas Anach* defends *Rashi* on the basis of the above-mentioned *Zohar*.

6 And say, 'Such [success] for life! Peace be upon you,
peace be upon your household, and peace be upon all
that is yours! 7 And now, I have heard that they are
shearing for you. Now, your shepherds stayed with
us, we did not shame them and they did not lack
anything all the days they were in Carmel — 8 ask
your attendants and they will tell you [so]. [There-
fore] let my attendants find favor in your eyes,
for we have come because of [your] celebration —

as Nabal enjoyed peace because David's men protected his possessions, so must he reciprocate and share his wealth (*Me'am Loez*).

According to *Kli Yakar*, וַאֲמַרְתֶּם, means *Tell them [that]* כֹּה — *such [is the text of my prayer]* לֶחָי, *to the Source of Life [of the world]:* וְאַתָּה שָׁלוֹם, *that you should have peace....*

וְאַתָּה שָׁלוֹם וּבֵיתְךָ שָׁלוֹם וְכֹל אֲשֶׁר־לְךָ שָׁלוֹם — *Peace be upon you, peace be upon your household, and peace be upon all that is yours.*

In a novel homiletical approach, *Be'er Moshe* explains David's blessing as follows. First, Nabal should be *at peace with himself* by conquering his evil inclination. Then he should extend that serenity to his household. And that will eventually bring peace to all Israel — which is, essentially, לְךָ, *yours*, in that all Jews are part of a unified whole.

Kli Yakar suggests that David's words constituted not a blessing but rather an assurance: he and his men would do their best to maintain the well-being of Nabal's property. And this carried an implicit expectation — i.e., that Nabal would extend to them a small portion of his possessions.

7. וְעַתָּה שָׁמַעְתִּי כִּי גֹזְזִים לָךְ — *And now, I have heard that they are shearing for you.*

At this moment of festivity and abundance, David argued, Nabal surely had some food to spare.

Me'am Loez adds that David implied that at this feast all of Nabal's shepherds would be available to confirm the integrity and beneficence of David's men.

לֹא הֶכְלַמְנוּם — *We did not shame them.*

Soldiers commonly took advantage of shepherds, mocking and robbing them, because they considered them to be weak and held their profession in low esteem. This would deepen the shame of the shepherds when they had to tell Nabal that his flocks had been diminished. But David testified that his men had not engaged in such behavior (*Ralbag, Abarbanel*).

Rashi, however, avoids this interpretation — possibly because it was unlikely that David would demand compensation merely because his men had not abused the shepherds. Instead, *Rashi* explains לֹא הֶכְלַמְנוּם as meaning, *We did not shame them [by rejecting their requests for aid].*

The phrase, הָרֹעִים אֲשֶׁר־לְךָ הָיוּ עִמָּנוּ — *your shepherds were with us* — can be understood as implying that David guarded the flocks together with the shepherds, לֹא הֶכְלַמְנוּם — *so as not to make them feel ashamed [of their inferior profession].*

וְלֹא־נִפְקַד לָהֶם מְאוּמָה — *And they did not lack anything.*

This was because David's men protected their belongings (*Rashi*).

Although David and his men were in dire need of provisions themselves, they did not lay their hands on any of Nabal's possessions (*Metzudos, Me'am Loez*).

8. כִּי־עַל־יוֹם טוֹב בָּאנוּ — *For we have come because of [your] celebration.*

תְּנָה־נָּא אֵת אֲשֶׁר תִּמְצָא יָדְךָ לַעֲבָדֶיךָ וּלְבִנְךָ
ט לְדָוִד: וַיָּבֹאוּ נַעֲרֵי דָוִד וַיְדַבְּרוּ אֶל־נָבָל כְּכָל־
י הַדְּבָרִים הָאֵלֶּה בְּשֵׁם דָּוִד וַיָּנוּחוּ: וַיַּעַן נָבָל
אֶת־עַבְדֵי דָוִד וַיֹּאמֶר מִי דָוִד וּמִי בֶן־יִשָׁי הַיּוֹם
רַבּוּ עֲבָדִים הַמִּתְפָּרְצִים אִישׁ מִפְּנֵי אֲדֹנָיו:

David implied that his request would not place a burden on Nabal's resources, since Nabal had prepared an appreciable amount of food for the feast (*Radak*). Furthermore, the Torah specifically demands that a person share his festival provisions with the poor (see *Deuteronomy* 16:14; *Me'am Loez*).

Metzudos adds that it is appropriate at a time of celebration to receive guests with a cheerful disposition.

According to *Rashi,* David sent this message on the day before Rosh Hashanah (see below, v. 38, *Rashi* ad loc.), and thus was referring literally to *a holiday*. He was hoping Nabal would send food, so that his men could have a feast in honor of the holiday.[1]

A verse in *Proverbs* admonishes, אַל־תִּלְחַם אֶת־לֶחֶם רַע עָיִן, *Do not eat the bread of the miserly* (23:6) — which the Talmud interprets not as advice but rather as a prohibition (*Sotah* 38b). Were it not for the fact that David and his men were mandated to eat on Rosh Hashanah, David would never have dreamed of benefiting from the miserly Nabal (*Kli Yakar*).

וּלְבִנְךָ לְדָוִד — *And to your son, to David.*

David referred to himself as *your son,* since he considered Nabal a close relative who, despite his hard heart, would be sympathetic (*Daas Sofrim*). ...

9. וַיְדַבְּרוּ אֶל־נָבָל כְּכָל הַדְּבָרִים הָאֵלֶּה ... וַיָּנוּחוּ — *And spoke in accordance with all these words to Nabal ... and then rested.*

The word וַיָּנוּחוּ, *and they rested,* implies that they were silent and awaited Nabal's response (*Rashi*). Thus Scripture emphasizes that David's attendants said nothing to incite Nabal's anger — instead, they communicated David's peaceful and humble message exactly as he had spoken it, and then וַיָּנוּחוּ, *they rested* — i.e., they did not add a word (*Rambam,* cited by *Abarbanel; Malbim*).

According to *Rashi,* וַיָּנוּחוּ means that although they were exhausted from traveling, they did not rest until they had delivered David's message, and only then did they rest.

Ralbag explains that since they knew Nabal was a difficult person, they did not deliver the message immediately, but *rested,* i.e., waited, until an opportune time.

According to *Abarbanel,* the messengers put down their belongings in Nabal's home and rested. When the miserly Nabal saw ten unwelcome guests making themselves at home in his house, he was enraged.

The Talmud (*Rosh Hashanah* 18a, *Rashi*) states that Nabal did, indeed, serve a meal to the ten attendants. *Kli Yakar* suggests that וַיָּנוּחוּ may be Scripture's allusion to that meal. We find the word נָח alluding to food in *Exodus* 23:12: לְמַעַן יָנוּחַ שׁוֹרְךָ וַחֲמֹרֶךָ, *so that your ox and donkey may rest* — meaning, states the *Mechilta* (cited by *Rashi*) that, among other things, the ox must have food to eat (*Maharsha;* see also below, v. 38).

The Mishnah (*Eruvin* 17a) gives four halachic leniencies that apply to army troops that lack readily available provisions. *Midrash Shmuel* and *Talmud Yerushalmi* (*Eruvin* Ch. 1) cite varying views regarding how many soldiers constitute a "camp." One

1. For a comprehensive discussion on the obligation to eat on Rosh Hashanah and the custom among some people to fast, see *Nachalas Shimon* 60:27.

please give whatever you can to your servants and to your son, to David.' "

*[9]David's attendants came and spoke in ac-
cordance with all these words to Nabal in David's name, and then rested. [10]Nabal replied to
David's servants, saying, "Who is David and who is the son of Jesse? These days the rebellious servants have increased, each against his master!*

opinion refers to וַיָּנוּחוּ, *and they camped,* as employed here, as proof that ten men are constitute a "camp."

◆§ Nabal's Insolent Rejection

10. וַיֹּאמֶר מִי דָוִד וּמִי בֶן־יִשָׁי — *Saying, "Who is David and who is the son of Jesse?"*

Neither David nor his family, intimated Nabal, were at all significant to him (*Mahari Kara*).

Rashi explicates that Nabal asked why David, as a descendant of Ruth the Moabitess, should deserve Nabal's largesse. With these words, Nabal showed his concurrence with the opinion of many, including Doeg, that David's lineage was tainted — and so his denial of Samuel's prophecy that David would be king (*Me'am Loez*).

But even if Nabal were correct that Boaz's marriage to Ruth was prohibited, how was that relevant to David's request for supplies?

Nachalas Shimon explains that if it were forbidden to marry a female Moabite, then the descendants of such a woman would be subject to the interdiction prohibiting a Jew from "pursuing peace" (see *Deuteronomy* 23:7) — which, according to Nabal, included doing favors (see *Bamidbar Rabbah* 21:5).

On the other hand, there is reason to say that even so Nabal would not have been prohibited from helping David, either because Nabal would be repaying David's kindness or because David had requested aid — in either case, Nabal's assistance would not technically be considered "pursuing peace" (for sources, see *Nachalas Shimon* 60:28).

According to *Midrash Shmuel*, Nabal exclaimed, "David is relying on the two droplets of anointing oil with which Samuel anointed him. But where is Samuel and where are those droplets?"[1]

If that were the case, then Abigail's defense of Nabal that he was unaware of David's fame (see *Megillah* 14b) was in error. (See *Be'er Moshe* [below, v. 13], which elaborates on this point.)

הַיּוֹם רַבּוּ עֲבָדִים הַמִּתְפָּרְצִים, אִישׁ מִפְּנֵי אֲדֹנָיו — *These days the rebellious servants have increased, each against his master!*

Our translation of הַמִּתְפָּרְצִים as *rebellious* follows *Radak*, who apparently relates the word to *breach* (see *Proverbs* 25:28).

Targum similarly translates this word as *break away and hide.*

However, the root of this word, פרץ, is also commonly associated with *strength* (see *Genesis* 28:14, *Targum Onkelos*).

Thus, *Metzudos* interprets עֲבָדִים הַמִּתְפָּרְצִים אִישׁ מִפְּנֵי אֲדֹנָיו as *servants who strengthen themselves against their masters and claim to be greater than they.*

Perach Levanon (cited by *Chomas Anach*) states that הַמִּתְפָּרְצִים is a form of the name פֶּרֶץ, *Perez* — the son of Judah, from whom the dynasty of Jewish kings was destined to descend. Nabal bemoaned the fact that there was an abundance of servants who flaunted their descent from Perez and claimed a right to the throne.

1. According to this Midrash, Nabal was aware that Samuel had appointed David king.

יא וְלָקַחְתִּ֤י אֶת־לַחְמִי֙ וְאֶת־מֵימַ֔י וְאֵת֙ טִבְחָתִ֔י
אֲשֶׁ֥ר טָבַ֖חְתִּי לְגֹֽזְזָ֑י וְנָֽתַתִּי֙ לַאֲנָשִׁ֔ים אֲשֶׁר֙ לֹ֣א
יב יָדַ֔עְתִּי אֵ֥י מִזֶּ֖ה הֵֽמָּה׃ וַיַּהַפְכ֥וּ נַעֲרֵֽי־דָוִ֖ד לְדַרְכָּ֑ם
וַיָּשֻׁ֙בוּ֙ וַיָּבֹ֔אוּ וַיַּגִּ֣דוּ ל֔וֹ כְּכֹ֖ל הַדְּבָרִ֥ים הָאֵֽלֶּה׃
יג וַיֹּ֨אמֶר דָּוִ֜ד לַאֲנָשָׁ֗יו חִגְר֣וּ ׀ אִ֣ישׁ אֶת־חַרְבּ֗וֹ
וַֽיַּחְגְּרוּ֙ אִ֣ישׁ אֶת־חַרְבּ֔וֹ וַיַּחְגֹּ֥ר גַּם־דָּוִ֖ד אֶת־חַרְבּ֑וֹ

מִי דָוִד וּמִי בֶן־יִשָׁי הַיּוֹם רַבּוּ עֲבָדִים הַמִּתְפָּרְצִים, אִישׁ מִפְּנֵי אֲדֹנָיו — *Who is David and who is the son of Jesse? These days the rebellious servants have increased, each against his master!*

Malbim explains Nabal's words as follows: David was not fit for glory either on his own or on his family's account. His only claim to repute was that he was a renegade — nowadays, however, that constituted no distinction, since there were many such rebellious servants.

According to *Abarbanel*, however, with these words Nabal was not denigrating David. On the contrary, his question, מִי דָוִד, *Who is David?*, meant that if David were seeking assistance for himself alone, Nabal would have gladly helped him. The problem was that there were *many rebels* — i.e., David's 600 followers — for whom Nabal could not provide.

Nabal's statement that there were many rebellious servants was possibly an allusion to Ahimelech, and Nabal signified his fear that if he aided David he would suffer Ahimelech's fate (*Me'am Loez*).

According to *Daas Sofrim*, had Nabal said that he was afraid of incurring Saul's wrath, David would have reacted differently. David was upset not by Nabal's refusal but by his insolence.

11. וְלָקַחְתִּי אֶת־לַחְמִי — *Should I take my bread?*

לֶחֶם — translated here as *bread* — can also refer to *food* in general (*Radak*, citing *Targum*).

וְאֶת מֵימַי — *And my water.*

Water is a valuable commodity in desert areas (*Radak*). So miserly was Nabal that he would not even offer water to thirsty people (*Me'am Loez*).

Midrash Shmuel interprets מֵימַי — *my water* — as *my wine*. Similarly, the Talmud (*Eruvin* 65a) renders מֵימֶיךָ (*Exodus* 23:25) as *your wine* (see also *Mahari Kara*, who finds support for this rendition from *Hosea* 2:8-11). *Kli Yakar* explains that the reason for such a translation might be that it was customary to dilute wine with an ample amount of water (as much as three parts water to one part wine — see *Shabbos* 77a).

Alternatively, *Targum* renders מֵימַי as *my drinks* in general.

וְאֵת טִבְחָתִי אֲשֶׁר טָבַחְתִּי — *And my meat that I have slaughtered.*

Targum translates טִבְחָתִי as a reference to any processed food.

וְנָתַתִּי לַאֲנָשִׁים אֲשֶׁר לֹא יָדַעְתִּי אֵי מִזֶּה הֵמָּה — *And give them to men whose origin I do not know?*

This disparaging statement was transparently dishonest, for all of Israel was familiar with David and his men (*Daas Sofrim*).

12. וַיַּהַפְכוּ נַעֲרֵי־דָוִד לְדַרְכָּם — *David's attendants turned around to their way.*

The word וַיַּהַפְכוּ — *turned about abruptly* — is a stronger terminology than the usual וַיָּשֻׁבוּ, *they returned.*

David's attendants felt so humiliated that they refused to hear any more insults or even look at Nabal's face, but stormed out. Also, they wished to see whether Nabal would reconsider his words when he saw them leave furiously — which he did not (*Me'am Loez*).

11 Should I take from my bread and my water and
my meat that I have slaughtered for my shearers
and give them to men whose origin I do not know?"
12 David's attendants turned around to their way,
and they went back, arrived and reported to him
in accordance with all these words. 13 David said
to his men, "Each man gird his sword!" Each man
girded his sword, and David, too, girded his sword.

וַיַּגִּדוּ לוֹ כְּכֹל הַדְּבָרִים הָאֵלֶּה — *And reported to him in accordance with all these words.*

The כ in כְּכֹל — *in accordance with all* — is a preposition that implies כְּכֹל הַדְּבָרִים — *like these words.* They merely paraphrased Nabal, for they could not bring themselves to repeat his tirade verbatim (*Kli Yakar*).

◈ David's Planned Attack

13. וַיֹּאמֶר דָּוִד לַאֲנָשָׁיו חִגְרוּ אִישׁ אֶת־חַרְבּוֹ וַיַּחְגְּרוּ אִישׁ אֶת־חַרְבּוֹ וַיַּחְגֹּר גַּם־דָּוִד אֶת־חַרְבּוֹ — *David said to his men, "Each man gird his sword!" Each man girded his sword, and David, too, girded his sword.*

After deliberating on this episode, David and his supporters came to the conclusion that, since Nabal had referred to David as a *servant* — although he was aware that David had been anointed king — he qualified as *a rebel to the throne* and was therefore liable to the death penalty.

According to the Sages, as learned scholars, David and his men convened an impromptu court of law and rendered a legal decision (*Radak*).

Kli Yakar observes that for this reason Scripture here refers to David's supporters as אֲנָשָׁיו, *his men* (rather than, as earlier, נְעָרִים, *attendants*), since אֲנָשִׁים is a common title for *judges* (see *Deuteronomy* 1:13).

The Talmud (*Sanhedrin* 36a) derives from this verse an important ruling regarding the judicial voting process, which is that the most eminent judges vote last. Girding one's sword expressed the view that Nabal deserved capital punishment. Thus, David told his men to gird their swords — if they viewed Nabal as guilty — and then did so as well. Were David to have voted first, the other judges would not have been permitted to disagree with him, and the defendant would thus have been deprived of the possibility of being acquitted.

This episode raises many questions, among them: If the Talmud draws a conclusion from this incident regarding judicial proceedings, it would seem as if conviction of a rebel requires a trial. Is this so? Must an accused rebel against the king be tried formally by a court? Must he be present when witnesses testify against him (as is the case in other trials)? May a king act as judge? Did David already possess the legal status of a king?

Some of these issues are discussed by *Tosafos* (*Sanhedrin* ibid.; *Megillah* 14a) and they are dealt with comprehensively by *Nachalas Shimon* 52.

Why was Nabal any more culpable than the other Israelites who wanted to hand David over to Saul, and whom David did not seek to execute?

Be'er Moshe explains that those Israelites may have been unaware that David had been anointed king, whereas Nabal did know (see commentary on v. 10).

Furthermore, there is evidence that Nabal himself harbored the ambition of being king (ibid.). Thus, even as the Jewish nation mourned Samuel's death, Nabal engaged

וַיַּעֲלוּ | אַחֲרֵי דָוִד כְּאַרְבַּע מֵאוֹת אִישׁ וּמָאתַיִם
יד יָשְׁבוּ עַל־הַכֵּלִים: וְלַאֲבִיגַיִל אֵשֶׁת נָבָל הִגִּיד
נַעַר־אֶחָד מֵהַנְּעָרִים לֵאמֹר הִנֵּה שָׁלַח דָּוִד
מַלְאָכִים | מֵהַמִּדְבָּר לְבָרֵךְ אֶת־אֲדֹנֵינוּ וַיָּעַט בָּהֶם:
טו וְהָאֲנָשִׁים טֹבִים לָנוּ מְאֹד וְלֹא הָכְלַמְנוּ וְלֹא־
פָקַדְנוּ מְאוּמָה כָּל־יְמֵי הִתְהַלַּכְנוּ אִתָּם בִּהְיוֹתֵנוּ
טז בַּשָּׂדֶה: חוֹמָה הָיוּ עָלֵינוּ גַּם־לַיְלָה גַּם־יוֹמָם כָּל־יְמֵי
יז הֱיוֹתֵנוּ עִמָּם רֹעִים הַצֹּאן: וְעַתָּה דְּעִי וּרְאִי מַה־
תַּעֲשִׂי כִּי־כָלְתָה הָרָעָה אֶל־אֲדֹנֵינוּ וְעַל־כָּל־בֵּיתוֹ

in celebratory revels (*Yalkut Shimoni* 134). Nabal was rejoicing because he had viewed Samuel as an obstacle to his ascension to the throne, since Samuel had anointed David and, if alive, would oppose Nabal's ambitions.

Thus, David felt it necessary to prevent Nabal from developing a following. For the same reason, David brought 400 men with him when he went to execute Nabal, for they constituted an imposing entourage that would make a public display of his sovereignty. In addition, David went before them, since one of the primary functions of an Israelite monarch is to lead the nation to war (see *Rambam, Hil. Melachim* 4:10; see also below vs. 31,32).

The fact that David accompanied his men, although they could legally have executed Nabal without him, is an indication of his agitation at Nabal's insolence (*Radak*).

וּמָאתַיִם יָשְׁבוּ עַל־הַכֵּלִים — *And two hundred others remained with the belongings.*

They remained to guard the tents and other property (*Rashi*).

14. וְלַאֲבִיגַיִל אֵשֶׁת נָבָל הִגִּיד נַעַר־אֶחָד מֵהַנְּעָרִים — *One young man from the attendants spoke to Abigail, Nabal's wife.*

This was Abigail's attendant (*Rashi*).

נַעַר־אֶחָד מֵהַנְּעָרִים — *One young man from the attendants.*

The verse could simply have referred to נַעַר, *an attendant*. This phrase implies that he was אֶחָד, *one*, in the sense of being unique: he was far-sighted enough to recognize impending danger, and so he notified Abigail.

הִנֵּה שָׁלַח דָּוִד מַלְאָכִים — *Behold! David sent messages.*

Mishbetzos Zahav cites *R' M.D. Vali* that the attendant used the word מַלְאָכִים to imply that David's men acted like *angels*, both in the respectful way they spoke to Nabal and in their tolerance in not reacting to his tirade.

לְבָרֵךְ אֶת־אֲדֹנֵינוּ — *To greet our master.*

Literally, לְבָרֵךְ means *to bless.* Greetings were commonly referred to as *blessings*, since they were wishes for well-being (*Radak*). Additionally, David's greeting included the words כֹּה לֶחָי — *such success for life* (above, v. 6) — an explicit blessing for prosperity (*Abarbanel*).

מֵהַמִּדְבָּר לְבָרֵךְ אֶת־אֲדֹנֵינוּ — *From the wilderness to greet our master.*

Why was it relevant for the attendant to relate David's location?

Kli Yakar suggests that he was implying that since David was in the wilderness, he qualified as an עָנִי, a *desperately needy person*, who deserved assistance.

Additionally, a benefactor who supports a poor man in his time of need brings blessing into his own home (see *Ezekiel* 44:30). David's request could

About four hundred men went after David, and
two hundred others remained with the belongings.
14 *One young man from the attendants told*
Abigail, Nabal's wife, saying, "Behold! David
sent messengers from the wilderness to greet our
master and he drove them off. 15 *These men were*
very good to us; we were not shamed, nor were
we lacking anything all the days that we traveled
with them, when we were in the field. 16 *They were*
a [protective] wall over us, both by night and by
day, all the days we were with them tending the
sheep. 17 *And now be aware and determine what to*
do, for the evil [decree] has been made final against
our master and against his entire household,

have brought Nabal a blessing — לְבָרֵךְ אֶת־אֲדֹנֵינוּ, *to bless our master* — but Nabal chose to reject it (*Kli Yakar*).

וַיָּעַט בָּהֶם — *And he drove them off.*

The word וַיָּעַט is related to עַיִט, *bird of prey* (*Genesis* 15:11). Nabal dismissed them with his words, making them "fly" away like birds of prey (*Midrash Shmuel, Rashi*).

Not only did Nabal not answer them respectfully but he acted as cruelly as a bird of prey (*Ralbag*).

According to *Targum*, וַיָּעַט בָּהֶם means *he despised them.*

Finally, *Mahari Kara* relates the word וַיָּעַט to וַיִּבְעַט: *he kicked them.*

15. וְהָאֲנָשִׁים טֹבִים לָנוּ מְאֹד — *These men were very good to us.*

The attendant averred that even if David did not possess a royal status, he and his men still should be treated well in reciprocation for what they had done for Nabal.

Although David's followers had come to Nabal as embittered souls (above, 22:2), they were noble and honest in their dealings with others (*Daas Sofrim*).

According to *Kli Yakar*, the phrase טֹבִים לָנוּ מְאֹד — *were very good to us* — implies that David's men were not only helpful in regard to their material needs but also exerted a positive spiritual influence.

וְלֹא הָכְלַמְנוּ — *We were not shamed.*

The קָמַץ vowel under the ה׳ makes the word reflexive; with a חִירִיק, the word would have meant, *we did not shame [them].*

The attendant confirmed the testimony of David's men (above, v. 7).

16. חוֹמָה הָיוּ עָלֵינוּ — *They were a [protective] wall over us.*

Not only did David and his men not harm Nabal's shepherds, but they prevented others from doing so as well.

Since David's men performed a necessary service for Nabal's shepherds, David could legally demand compensation, even if that help had not been previously stipulated (see *Rema* 264:4; *Machaneh Ephraim, Hil. Nizkei Mammon* 2; *Me'am Loez; Nachalas Shimon* 54, Part 1).

From this verse we see that righteous people are called *walls,* since their merits protect the world from harmful decrees (*Midrash*).

17. וְעַתָּה דְּעִי וּרְאִי מַה־תַּעֲשִׂי — *And now be aware and determine what to do.*

יח וְהוּא בֶּן־בְּלִיַּעַל מִדַּבֵּר אֵלָיו: וַתְּמַהֵר °אבוגיל
וַתִּקַּח מָאתַיִם לֶחֶם וּשְׁנַיִם נִבְלֵי־יַיִן וְחָמֵשׁ צֹאן
°עשוות וְחָמֵשׁ סְאִים קָלִי וּמֵאָה צִמֻּקִים וּמָאתַיִם
יט דְּבֵלִים וַתָּשֶׂם עַל־הַחֲמֹרִים: וַתֹּאמֶר לִנְעָרֶיהָ
עִבְרוּ לְפָנַי הִנְנִי אַחֲרֵיכֶם בָּאָה וּלְאִישָׁהּ נָבָל
כ לֹא הִגִּידָה: וְהָיָה הִיא | רֹכֶבֶת עַל־הַחֲמוֹר וְיֹרֶדֶת
בְּסֵתֶר הָהָר וְהִנֵּה דָוִד וַאֲנָשָׁיו יֹרְדִים לִקְרָאתָהּ

°אֲבִיגַיִל ק׳

°עֲשׂוּיֹת ק׳

They must decide how to rectify the damage that had been done and pacify David (*Metzudos*).

וְהוּא בֶּן־בְּלִיַּעַל מִדַּבֵּר אֵלָיו — *And he is too base a person even to talk to.*

The phrase, *he is too base a person even to talk to* is generally understood to be a reference to Nabal.

Our translation follows *Rashi*, who states that with this description, the attendant explained to Abigail why he was approaching her and not Nabal.

According to *Mahari Kara*, the attendant called Nabal a base person for having made such denigrating comments about David.

Ralbag explains that the word בְּלִיַּעַל — *base person*, but literally, "without the yoke [of Hashem]" — may be used to describe a miserly person in particular (see *Job* 34:18), and that is its meaning here.

Arizal states (as cited by *Chomas Anach*) that Nabal was a reincarnation of Balaam. This is alluded to in the fact that the name *Balaam*, בִּלְעָם, has the same numerical value as the word בְּלִיַּעַל — 142.

Arizal also states that in the context of reincarnation, the soul's first body is called אָב, *father*, and the subsequent body is called בֵּן, *son*.

Accordingly, says *Chomas Anach*, Nabal was called בֶּן בְּלִיַּעַל, a *son of Belial* — i.e., Balaam.

However, *Abarbanel* states that the attendant was referring not to Nabal but to David. Although David was a decent and noble human being, Nabal's insolent response might lead him to respond in a base fashion (see also *Radak*).

⇐§ Abigail Hastens and Meets David

18. וַתְּמַהֵר אֲבִיגַיִל — *So Abigail hurried.*

Abigail understood the severity of the danger and hastened to correct the damage that her husband had wrought.

וְחָמֵשׁ צֹאן עֲשׂוּיֹת — *Five cooked sheep.*

Literally, עֲשׂוּיֹת means *made* or *prepared.* Accordingly, *Radak* states that the sheep were *cooked.*

Rashi explains that עֲשׂוּיֹת means that the sheep were *stuffed* with thin strands of meat and eggs — apparently a culinary delicacy in those days. *Rashi* draws his interpretation from the *Targum*, which renders עֲשׂוּיֹת as תַּכְבְּרָא — a word that *Rashi* explains as meaning תּוֹכוֹ לְבָרוֹ, *what was inside is brought to the outside* — i.e., the meat from the innards of the animal is visible. (See also *Rashi* to *Pesachim* 74a.)

Abarbanel, on the other hand, reads עֲשׂוּיֹת as *plump and healthy.*

One of the gifts that an Israelite must give to a Kohen is רֵאשִׁית הַגֵּז, *the first of the wool shearings* (*Deuteronomy* 18:4). According to one view, based on this verse, an Israelite is obligated to do so when he shears a minimum of five sheep (*Chullin* 135a,137a).

קָלִי — *Toasted grain.*

This is flour made of toasted grain (*Metzudos*).

לֶחֶם ... יַיִן ... צֹאן עֲשׂוּיֹת ... קָלִי ... צִמֻּקִים ... דְּבֵלִים — *Breads ... wine ... cooked sheeps ... toasted grain ... clusters of raisins ... cakes of pressed figs.*

and he is too base a person even to talk to."
18 So Abigail hurried and took two hundred
breads, two containers of wine, five cooked sheep,
five se'ahs of toasted grain, a hundred clusters
of raisins, and two hundred cakes of pressed
figs, and she put them on the donkeys. 19 She said
to her attendants, "Go on ahead of me; behold,
I am coming behind you." But she did not tell
Nabal her husband. 20 Then it happened, as she
was riding on the donkey, clandestinely descend-
ing the mountain, behold — David and his men
were descending [the other mountain] toward her,

Abigail took pains to assure that her gift would provide David and his men with the succor that they required. Thus, the first three items — bread, wine, and cooked meat — were prepared for immediate consumption, and the last three — toasted grain, raisins, and pressed figs — were processed so that they would not spoil in the desert heat.

Nabal had hoped to preserve his resources by rejecting David's request — yet had he acceded, he would have had to give him only half the amount that Abigail sent (*Me'am Loez*).

As to how Abigail was legally entitled to give such a gift against her husband's wishes, see v. 35 below.

19. וַתֹּאמֶר לִנְעָרֶיהָ עִבְרוּ לְפָנַי הִנְנִי אַחֲרֵיכֶם בָּאָה — *She said to her attendants, "Go on ahead of me; behold, I am coming behind you."*

Abigail's strategy was similar to that of Jacob when he went to meet Esau (*Genesis* 32:14-21).

By sending her gift first, she hoped to appease David even before she met him (*Abarbanel*).

According to *Malbim*, Abigail asked the attendants to precede her so that their relationship with her would not be apparent and news of what she was doing would not be relayed to her husband.

Mishbetzos Zahav comments that by asking the attendant to go before her, Abigail followed the Torah's directive that a man should not follow a woman.

וּלְאִישָׁהּ נָבָל לֹא הִגִּידָה — *But she did not tell her husband, Nabal.*

She knew that he would have objected.

20. וְיֹרֶדֶת בְּסֵתֶר הָהָר וְהִנֵּה דָוִד וַאֲנָשָׁיו יֹרְדִים לִקְרָאתָהּ — *Clandestinely descending the mountain, behold — David and his men were descending [the other mountain] toward her.*

As Abigail descended one mountain, David was descending another directly opposite her (*Rashi*).

Literally, בְּסֵתֶר הָהָר means *in the clandestine part of the mountain,* implying that the mountain hid Abigail so that she and David did not see each other until they met (*Mahari Kara;* see *Radak*).

According to *Targum* and *Metzudos*, this *clandestine part* was the valley separating the two mountains.

The Talmud (*Megillah* 14a), however, explains בְּסֵתֶר as an adverb describing the nature of Abigail's descent (an understanding that is reflected in our translation).

Accordingly, however, the verse should have stated, מִן הָהָר, *from the*

mountain, rather than simply הָהָר — *the mountain*. To vindicate the wording of the verse, the Talmud expounds it homiletically to tell how Abigail cunningly drew David into a dialogue in which she persuaded him not to execute Nabal.

When Abigail met David, she asked him about a *concealed* and private matter — i.e., concerning a bloodstain.

David replied that since it was nighttime (see v. 22), he could not legally make a determination (see *Niddah* 20b, *Nachalas Shimon* 60:29).

Abigail then challenged him, "But could you legally issue a death sentence against Nabal at night?"

David replied that he was authorized to do so, because protocols regarding a rebel against the king do not need to conform to ordinary court procedures.

Abigail, however, refuted David's words on two counts. First, since Saul was still alive, David's kingdom had not yet begun. And second, since David's fame had not yet spread, Nabal could not be considered a rebel.

Hearing this, David acknowledged the justice of Abigail's arguments and thanked her for having prevented him from unjustly spilling blood (see below, vs. 32-34).

Many issues are raised in this Talmudic passage, some of them too complex to be dealt with here. We refer the reader to *Tosafos* (*Megillah* 14b, *Sanhedrin* 36a) and *Nachalas Shimon* 52.

One of the topics discussed there is a disagreement regarding whether David possessed the legal status of a king.

The end of this dialogue indicates that David conceded that his kingdom had not yet begun.

However, some commentaries — among them *Be'er Moshe* — maintain that David's kingdom had commenced either when he was anointed or when Samuel died.

According to *Be'er Moshe*, neither of Abigail's arguments was correct. First, although Saul was still alive, the right to the monarchy had already been withdrawn from him and transferred to David.[1] And second, Abigail's representation that David's fame had not yet spread — seemingly an attempt to absolve Nabal by alleging that he was unaware of David's status — was inaccurate, for Nabal was well-aware of David's appointment (see commentary above).

But although Abigail's contentions were insubstantial, David decided to suspend execution anyway, on different grounds suggested by her. Abigail conveyed her prophetic knowledge that after Nabal's death she would be married to David. If David were to kill Nabal and shortly afterward marry Nabal's widow, ugly suspicions would be raised (see *Yevamos* 25b, *Nachalas Shimon* 52, fn. 21). Thus, Abigail advised David to wait for Nabal to die of natural causes — something that, she knew, would soon occur (below, v. 26, *Rashi* ad loc.).

וַתִּפְגֹּשׁ אֹתָם — *And she met them.*

These seemingly superfluous words (*Radvaz*) are referred to by *Talmud Yerushalmi* (*Sanhedrin* 2:3) as an allusion to the following incident.[2]

As Abigail — one of history's most beautiful women (*Megillah* 15a) — traveled, she momentarily uncovered her leg, which produced such a bright light that David could travel a distance of three *parsaos* away (roughly 7-1/2 miles) by its illumination. Attracted by what he saw, David proposed that they have relations, but Abigail persuaded

1. Saul deserved to lose the kingdom immediately after he sinned in regard to Agag and the Amalekites (above, Ch. 15). His life and kingdom were salvaged for a short period because of Samuel's prayer that his handiwork not be nullified during his lifetime (*Taanis* 5b). Accordingly, once Samuel died there was no reason for Saul's reign to continue; thus, *Be'er Moshe* contends, it ceased at that point. Saul lived another four months only so that he could gain atonement by accepting God's judgment that he would die in battle.

2. *Talmud Bavli* (*Megillah* 14b) also relates this occurrence but associates it with v. 33 below.

and she met them.

[21]*Now David had said, "It was for naught*

him to change his mind (see v. 33 below).

Tosafos (*Megillah* ad loc.) raise two questions regarding this story. First, how could Abigail, a righteous prophetess, have exposed her leg to David? Second, the idea that her leg emanated a light that shone for three *parsaos* seems excessive.

Maharsha answers *Tosafos'* initial question by stating that Abigail did not intend to expose her leg to David. Rather, as she was walking in the concealed part of the mountain — where, she assumed, no one could see her — she uncovered her leg for a moment. Although David was at a distance of three *parsaos*, the light that emanated allowed him to see her until he reached her.

In regard to the question of the extent of light emanating from Abigail's leg, *Tosafos* state that David did not literally travel by its illumination. Rather, he was filled with a burning desire that lasted as he traveled the entire three *parsaos*. *Rashash* clarifies the Talmud's statement. It does not mean that David traveled לְאוֹרָה, *by the light* of Abigail's leg, but rather לְאוּרָה, *by the heat of* his desire (see also *Pnei Moshe*, *Yerushalmi Sanhedrin* 2:3).

Tosafos does not answer the question as to why she would have uncovered her leg, because it can obviously be answered by saying that she did not do so intentionally, but that the wind uncovered it (*Radvaz*).

Sefer Imrei Moshe to *Megillas Esther* explains that Abigail saw a menstrual stain on her leg and had to show it to David for a halachic ruling. *Me'am Loez* suggests a different version. The word שׁוֹקָהּ as used in this Talmudic passage does not bear its usual meaning of *leg* but derives from the word הִשְׁתּוֹקְקוּת, *thirst*. Abigail revealed her eagerness to be married to David.[1]

21. וְדָוִד אָמַר — *Now David had said.*

David said this to himself after his attendants reported Nabal's words (*Rashi*).[2]

According to *Abarbanel*, David spoke these words to his men by chance as they were approaching Abigail, which explains why Scripture inserts it at this point.

Malbim explains that when David saw Abigail's attendants and their load, he thought that they were transporting these foodstuffs to Nabal's party, and so he commented that he and his men had protected those very items for nothing.

1. *Rema MiPanu* (*Asarah Maamaros, Maamar Em Kol Chai* II:I) explains this Midrash on a mystical level. The seven prophetesses listed in the Talmud (*Megillah* 14a) correspond to the seven *sefiros*, or emanations of God, mentioned in Kabbalistic literature. Accordingly, Abigail, who was the fifth prophetess, corresponds to the attribute of הוֹד, *glory*, which is called the "left leg." Thus, our Sages' statement that Abigail revealed her leg means that she revealed her prophetic knowledge.

The three *parsaos* hint at the three prophetic revelations that she made: (a) Nabal would soon die (v. 26); (b) David would get involved with Bathsheba (see v. 31); and (c) David's royal dynasty would be everlasting (v. 28).

2. *Mishbetzos Zahav* infers an important lesson from *Rashi*. Although David felt that Nabal deserved to die as a rebel, and he even convened a court to try him (above, v. 13), he was not motivated by anger or personal bias; otherwise he would have said so audibly. *Rashi* means that David spoke to *himself*, i.e., he deliberated to come to a rational decision whether Nabal should be killed according to Torah law. Thus although David's brother Eliab was rejected as king because of his temper, David overcame this trait. Accordingly, when Samuel hesitated to anoint David because his ruddy complexion suggested that he would shed blood, Hashem reassured him that David would kill only with the consent of the court (*Bereishis Rabbah* 63:8; see above, 16:12).

שָׁמַרְתִּי אֶת־כָּל־אֲשֶׁר לָזֶה בַּמִּדְבָּר וְלֹא־נִפְקַד
מִכָּל־אֲשֶׁר־לוֹ מְאוּמָה וַיָּשֶׁב־לִי רָעָה תַּחַת
כב טוֹבָה׃ כֹּה־יַעֲשֶׂה אֱלֹהִים לְאֹיְבֵי דָוִד וְכֹה יֹסִיף
אִם־אַשְׁאִיר מִכָּל־אֲשֶׁר־לוֹ עַד־הַבֹּקֶר מַשְׁתִּין
כג בְּקִיר׃ וַתֵּרֶא אֲבִיגַיִל אֶת־דָּוִד וַתְּמַהֵר וַתֵּרֶד
מֵעַל הַחֲמוֹר וַתִּפֹּל לְאַפֵּי דָוִד עַל־פָּנֶיהָ וַתִּשְׁתַּחוּ
כד אָרֶץ׃ וַתִּפֹּל עַל־רַגְלָיו וַתֹּאמֶר בִּי־אֲנִי אֲדֹנִי הֶעָוֹן
וּתְדַבֶּר־נָא אֲמָתְךָ בְּאָזְנֶיךָ וּשְׁמַע אֵת דִּבְרֵי אֲמָתֶךָ׃

Me'am Loez suggests that when David spoke these words, Abigail was nearby (although concealed), a fact of which David was aware. He deliberately spoke these words so that she would hear him and understand why he had sentenced Nabal to death.

אַךְ לַשֶּׁקֶר שָׁמַרְתִּי — *It was for naught that I guarded.*

לַשֶּׁקֶר literally means *for falsehood.* Our translation follows *Radak,* who renders it here as *for nothing. Kli Yakar* retains the literal translation, explaining that had Nabal humiliated David with accusations that could not be impeached, David would have been less upset. But in asking, וּמִי בֶן־יִשַׁי, *Who is the son of Jesse?* Nabal had impugned the stature of David's noble and righteous father, an abasement that David could not forgive.[1]

וַיָּשֶׁב־לִי רָעָה תַּחַת טוֹבָה — *Yet he has repaid my kindness with evil.*

Not only did Nabal refuse to provide for David's men but he even showered them with abusive words (*Daas Sofrim*).

22. כֹּה יַעֲשֶׂה אֱלֹהִים לְאֹיְבֵי דָוִד וְכֹה יֹסִיף — *Such shall God do to David's enemies and such shall He do further.*

David used a standard formula to commit himself to a task and curse himself should he fail to perform it. His proclamation that the curse should fall upon אוֹיְבֵי דָוִד, *the enemies of David,* is a conventional euphemistic device.

According to *Metzudos,* David explicitly spoke of the curse devolving upon him. Scripture, however, altered his words because he did not fulfill his commitment.

Ultimately, David had no compunctions about not fulfilling his oath, since Abigail showed him that it contradicted the Torah (see commentary above; *Daas Sofrim*).

Some commentators understand this verse as the expression of the fact that God punish his enemies in general, just as he planned to punish Nabal.

According to *Abarbanel,* David invited God to shower David's enemies with blessings equal to those that Nabal enjoyed — and even more — should he fail to keep his word. This would be like a curse upon David.

אִם־אַשְׁאִיר מִכָּל־אֲשֶׁר־לוֹ — *If I leave over of all that belongs to him.*

1. *Mishbetzos Zahav* cites the *Steipler Gaon* (*Birkas Peretz, Bamidbar*), who comments that some people always impugn the motives of those who help them, claiming that they were motivated by selfish considerations of glory and power. Accordingly, they feel that they are justified in repaying their benefactor with bad for good. On the other hand, if the benefactor sincerely meant to help, the beneficiary will recognize and appreciate it. Thus, David may have been trying to find a justification for Nabal's abysmal behavior, saying, "Perhaps Nabal thought that I guarded his sheep not as an act of kindness, but לַשֶּׁקֶר, *for falsehood,* i.e., for a selfish, ulterior motive."

that I guarded all of this man's possessions in
the desert and there was not missing anything
from all that belonged to him; yet he has repaid
my kindness with evil. [22]*Such shall God do to*
David's enemies and such shall He do further,
if I leave over until morning of all that belongs
to him so much as a dog!''
[23]*When Abigail saw David she hurried*
and dismounted from the donkey, and fell on
her face before David and prostrated herself
to the ground. [24]*She fell at his feet and said,*
''With me myself, my lord, lies the sin. Let
your maidservant please speak in your ears,
and hear out the words of your maidservant.

David had a legal right to all of Nabal's belongings, since the latter was a traitor to the crown (*Sanhedrin* 48b).

מַשְׁתִּין בְּקִיר — *So much as a dog* [lit. *one who urinates against the wall*].

Our translation follows *Rashi,* who understands David as saying that he would not even leave Nabal's dog alive.

Alternatively, *Ralbag* explains מַשְׁתִּין בְּקִיר as a reference to men of Nabal's household. *Ralbag* explains that since Nabal had denigrated someone who had been anointed as king, he was guilty of shaming the kingship, and so were those who supported him.

Targum, however, renders מַשְׁתִּין בְּקִיר as *one who has intelligence,* apparently deriving מַשְׁתִּין from מֵשִׁית, *placing,* and קִיר, *wall,* referring to the "walls of the heart" — hence, *one who brings thoughts into the chambers of his heart.*

⚜ Abigail's Impassioned Plea

24. וַתֹּאמֶר בִּי־אֲנִי אֲדֹנִי הֶעָוֹן וּתְדַבֶּר נָא אֲמָתְךָ בְּאָזְנֶיךָ — *And said, ''With me myself, my lord, lies the sin. Let your maidservant please speak in your ears.''*

Abigail's acceptance of blame for Nabal's offenses is perplexing, as is her vindication of herself in the following verse.

These points are the subject of a variety of interpretations.

❒ *Rashi* explains that first Abigail admitted guilt in order to attract David's attention. Afterward, she exculpated herself, because in truth she had known nothing of Nabal's deeds.

❒ According to *Radak,* Abigail did not mean to say that she was actually guilty. Rather, she asked David to take heed of her, just as he would listen to a culpable person defending himself.

❒ *Abarbanel* explains that the word עָוֹן here does not bear the usual meaning of *sin.* Rather, it refers to *punishment* (as the verse, וַאֲנַחְנוּ עֲוֹנֹתֵיהֶם סָבָלְנוּ, *we have suffered their punishments* [*Lamentations* 5:7]). Abigail pleaded that since she would suffer much of the pain that would result from David's vengeance, she had the right to attempt to prevent it.

❒ According to *Metzudos,* David did not know who Abigail was. Her words were her way of notifying David that Nabal was her husband and asking permission to plead on his behalf.

כה אַל־נָא יָשִׂים אֲדֹנִי | אֶת־לִבּוֹ אֶל־אִישׁ הַבְּלִיַּעַל
הַזֶּה עַל־נָבָל כִּי כִשְׁמוֹ כֶּן־הוּא נָבָל שְׁמוֹ וּנְבָלָה
עִמּוֹ וַאֲנִי אֲמָתְךָ לֹא רָאִיתִי אֶת־נַעֲרֵי אֲדֹנִי
כו אֲשֶׁר שָׁלָחְתָּ׃ °וְעַתָּה אֲדֹנִי חַי־יְהֹוָה וְחֵי־נַפְשְׁךָ

There are other interpretations of this verse as well.

❐ It is apparent from Abigail's words that she was able to dissuade her husband from engaging in certain deeds; thus, she considered herself responsible for not having prevented Nabal's insolent response to David. However, she then went on to vindicate herself by saying that she had not been aware that David's men had gone to see him. Had she known, she would have done all in her power to influence Nabal's actions (*Daas Sofrim*).

❐ The sin that Abigail referred to was not that of Nabal, but rather that of David, i.e., his intent to wipe out Nabal and his family. Abigail told David that he would not be absolved of guilt for killing her, since she was innocent of any wrongdoing (*Kli Yakar*).

❐ Possibly, Abigail referred here to her sin of carelessly revealing her leg (*Me'am Loez*).

25. אַל־נָא יָשִׂים אֲדֹנִי אֶת־לִבּוֹ אֶל־אִישׁ הַבְּלִיַּעַל הַזֶּה — *Let my lord not set his heart against this base man.*

Abigail told David that anger is justified only if one is offended by a respectable person, but it was beneath David's dignity to grow angry at Nabal, who was — as indicated by his very name — a base individual (*Abarbanel*).

Alternatively, although it is sometimes useful to rebuke and punish someone who refuses to accept constructive criticism in order to set an example for others, this is only when there is a fear that others will be influenced be the evildoer. But since everyone held Nabal in contempt, there is no reason to punish him so harshly (*Minchas Elazar*).

אַל־נָא יָשִׂים אֲדֹנִי אֶת־לִבּוֹ ... כִּי כִשְׁמוֹ כֶּן־הוּא נָבָל שְׁמוֹ וּנְבָלָה עִמּוֹ — *Let not my lord set his heart ... for he is as his name implies — Nabal is his name and revulsion is his trait.*

According to the Midrash (*Shocher Tov, Psalm* 53), Abigail placed responsibility for this incident on David's shoulders, for he should have realized from Nabal's name how he would act.

Kli Yakar explains that Abigail told David not to complain of Nabal's refusal to give his men provisions. David should have realized from his name that he would — in David's words — "repay his kindness with evil." The word נָבָל is used in *Deuteronomy* (32:6, see *Ramban* ad loc.) to denote a person who repays kindness with evil, and a person who benefits an individual of this sort must anticipate such a reaction.[1]

The Talmud (*Yoma* 83b) relates that Rabbi Meir would evaluate someone's nature based on his name. For instance, when he came to an inn and discovered that the innkeeper's name was Kidor, Rabbi Meir refused to trust him, because his name implied evil, as in the verse, כִּי דוֹר תַּהְפֻּכֹת הֵמָּה — *for they are a generation (ki dor) of reversals* (*Deuteronomy* 32:20).

אֶל־אִישׁ הַבְּלִיַּעַל הַזֶּה — *Against this base man.*

See above, v. 17.

The word בְּלִיַּעַל — literally, *without the yoke [of heaven]* — is used many times in Scripture to describe a variety of iniquities. It may indicate a person who is selfish, stingy, and covetous (*Deuteronomy* 15:9), a person who engages in illicit relations, or a person

1. The word for *revulsion* — נְבָלָה — is the feminine form of נָבָל, *Nabal.* Thus, the verse may be translated, *Let not my lord think that Nabal is his name and Nabalah is with him* — i.e., that his wife too is base. On the contrary, she proclaimed, had she only known of the arrival of David's attendants, she would have done all that she could to influence Nabal for the good (*Kli Yakar*).

25Let my lord not set his heart against this base
man — against Nabal — for he is as his name
implies — Nabal is his name and revulsion is
his trait; and I, your maidservant, did not see
my lord's attendants whom you sent. 26Now,
my lord, as HASHEM lives — and by your life —

who entertains idolatrous thoughts (*Deuteronomy* 13:14; *Midrash Shocher Tov* [*Psalms* 53]).

Psalm 53 contains the following verse, אָמַר נָבָל בְּלִבּוֹ אֵין אֱלֹהִים הִשְׁחִיתוּ וְהִתְעִיבוּ עָוֶל אֵין עֹשֵׂה־טוֹב, *The degraded man — nabal — says in his heart, "There is no God!" They acted corruptly and despicably through iniquity; not one does good* (v. 2).

Midrash Shocher Tov explains that *the degraded man* in this verse is Nabal. This verse identifies him as having denied God's existence. And this is because he rejected the legitimacy of the Davidic dynasty — belief in which *Rambam* lists as a constituent of his "Thirteen Principles of Faith" (see Commentary to *Mishnah, Sanhedrin* Ch. 11). Denying this is tantamount to denying Hashem and His prophets (see *Psalms*, ArtScroll edition, commentary to 2:2, 53:2).

The *Talmud Yerushalmi* (*Sanhedrin* 2:3) states that when Abigail asked David why he intended to destroy Nabal's family he answered, "Because he denigrated the kingdom of David."

כִּי כִשְׁמוֹ כֶּן־הוּא נָבָל שְׁמוֹ וּנְבָלָה עִמּוֹ — *For he is as his name implies — Nabal is his name and revulsion is his trait.*

Abigail implied, "Do not reject the implication of his name because he is a descendant of Caleb (see above, v. 3). In this case Nabal's name accurately reflects his character.

Furthermore, even though at times a miserly person may perform an act of kindness, that was not the case with Nabal. In his case, נְבָלָה עִמּוֹ, *revulsion is constantly with him.* Moreover, the feminine nature of the word נְבָלָה implies the idea of reproduction — i.e., Nabal constantly expanded and intensified his selfishness (*Chomas Anach*).

נָבָל שְׁמוֹ — *Nabal is his name.*

Midrash Shocher Tov (*Psalms* 53) comments that the letters of נָבָל rearranged form the name לָבָן, *Laban*, thus establishing that the two men were one and the same: just as Laban was a deceitful person, so was Nabal.

The Midrash apparently means to say that Nabal was a reincarnation of Laban. As mentioned above, he was also a reincarnation of Balaam. Thus, the letters of לָבָן (and of נָבָל) form the acrostic: נָבָל, בִּלְעָם, לָבָן — *Nabal, Balaam, Laban* (*Sefer HaNeemarim BeEmes*, citing *Shaar HaPesukim*).

Generally, the formula "... was his name" (rather than "his name was ...") is used to describe a wicked man (see above, 1:1; *Ruth Rabbah* 4:3, *Esther Rabbah* 6:2).

וַאֲנִי אֲמָתְךָ — *And I, your maidservant.*

According to *Pnei Moshe* (*Yerushalmi Sanhedrin* 2:3), these words were Abigail's response to David's proposal that he have relations with her. She protested, "I am only fit to be your maidservant."

26. חַי־ה׳ וְחֵי־נַפְשְׁךָ — *As HASHEM lives — and by your life.*

This phrase is generally understood to be a formula for an oath. חַי־ה׳ — *as HASHEM lives* — means that just as Hashem's life is an absolute, so is the matter being attested to.[1] *Ralbag* states

1. However, the concept of equating the truth of Hashem's existence with any other truth is subject to controversy. See *Radvaz* (*Teshuvos* Vol. I:17) and *Nachalas Shimon* (53:2).

The validity of an oath dependent on something other than God — such as *by your life* or *by Pharaoh's life* (see *Genesis* 42:15, *Rashi* ad loc.), as well as the problem involved in

כה/כו אֲשֶׁר מְנָעֲךָ יהוה מִבּוֹא בְדָמִים וְהוֹשֵׁעַ יָדְךָ לָךְ וְעַתָּה יִהְיוּ כְנָבָל אֹיְבֶיךָ וְהַמְבַקְשִׁים אֶל־אֲדֹנִי רָעָה:

that Abigail swore that (as she had stated in the previous verse) she had not seen the attendants whom David had sent to Nabal.

In referring to Hashem, Abigail used the word חַי, a verb implying *He lives,* whereas regarding David, she used the word חֵי, a possessive noun meaning *the life of. Rambam* (*Hil. Yesodei HaTorah* 2:10) explains that Hashem's life is inseparable from Himself, and accordingly חַי־ה׳ means *HASHEM is living.* But as a mortal human being, David's life was not intrinsic to him, and so Abigail used the phrase, *the life of* (see also *Tosafos Yom Tov,* end of *Mishnayos Tamid, Nachalas Shimon* 43:4).

וְעַתָּה אֲדֹנִי חַי־ה׳ וְחֵי־נַפְשְׁךָ אֲשֶׁר מְנָעֲךָ ה׳ מִבּוֹא בְדָמִים — *Now, my lord, as HASHEM lives — and by your life — as HASHEM has prevented you from coming to bloodshed.*

It is clear that Abigail was confident that David would be appeased by her words and not harm Nabal or his household (*Ralbag*).

According to *Metzudos,* Abigail understood that it was God's will that she prevent David from spilling blood. She considered all the circumstances of her involvement — her learning of Nabal's confrontation with David's attendants, her speedy journey, and her overhearing David's words to his men — as evidence that Hashem had sent her to stop him.

In this context, *Mahari Kara* renders חַי־ה׳ — *as HASHEM lives* — not as an oath but rather as praise: *Blessed is HASHEM Who prevented you from coming to bloodshed.*

Our Sages state that Hashem is pained, as it were, when blood is spilled — even that of the wicked (see *Sanhedrin* 46a). Thus, חַי־ה׳ may be translated as *HASHEM will live [without that pain],* so to speak, now that He prevented this execution (*Kli Yakar*).

Kli Yakar suggests that the words חֵי־נַפְשְׁךָ — *by your life* — are to be understood as *you will live.* Thus, Abigail told David, "Now that Hashem has prevented you from shedding blood, *you will live* as well."

אֲשֶׁר מְנָעֲךָ ה׳ — *As HASHEM has prevented you.*

In these words, Abigail told David that Hashem had sent her to stop him (*Rashi*).

מִבּוֹא בְדָמִים — *From coming to bloodshed.*

Hashem prevented David from spilling innocent blood (*Targum*).

As mentioned earlier, although David had convened a court and determined that Nabal was guilty of rebelling against the king, Abigail disputed the decision on the grounds that Saul was still alive and that David's claim to the throne was as yet unknown, in consequence of which Nabal's disrespect could not legally be considered as an affront to the throne (*Megillah* 14b).[1]

The *Talmud Yerushalmi* (*Sanhedrin* 2:3) elaborates that Abigail pleaded, "My master, David, what did I do? What did my children do? What did my animals do?"

However, a court is not permitted to take into consideration the effect of issuing a death sentence on the guilty man's family. What then was Abigail's intent?

Mussar HaNeviim provides a resolution to this question based on a homiletic

invoking the Name of Hashem in association with some mundane matter, is the topic of a comprehensive essay by *Nachalas Shimon* 53.

1. We have already cited *Be'er Moshe's* view that David's ruling was correct but that Abigail had other reasons with which she persuaded David not to carry out his sentence.

as HASHEM has prevented you from coming to bloodshed and your hand from acting on your behalf, may your enemies and all those who wish evil upon my lord be like Nabal!

reading of the verse: כְּבֹד אֱלֹהִים הַסְתֵּר דָּבָר וּכְבֹד מְלָכִים חֲקֹר דָּבָר, *It is the honor to God to conceal a matter, but it is the honor of kings to investigate a matter* (*Proverbs* 25:2). The word אֱלֹהִים can sometimes refer to judges (see *Exodus* 22:8). Thus, when *judges* punish, they must *conceal* their feelings for the criminal's family. However, when the punitive measure comes from the authority of a *king*, he must *investigate* whether the family of the convicted man also deserves to suffer. If not, he may choose to waive execution.

This apparently contradicts the principle that *a king has no right to forgive an affront to his honor* (*Sanhedrin* 19b). Nevertheless, it seems from *Rambam* (*Hil. Melachim* 3:8) that indeed a king is not required to kill those who oppose him (see *Minchas Chinuch* §497, *Nachalas Shimon* 24).

As per our translation, מִבּוֹא בְדָמִים means *from coming to bloodshed. Alshich*, on the other hand, renders this phrase as *[HASHEM prevented you] from coming to the throne through [the fears induced in the populace by] bloodshed.* A Jewish monarch must enter into the sovereignty through mitzvos and good deeds, not violence.

בְדָמִים — *To bloodshed.*

The word דָּמִים — *bloodshed* — is written in the plural.

According to the Talmud, this implies that not only would Nabal's blood be shed but also that of all the generations that might have otherwise descended from him. (The Talmud [*Sanhedrin* 37a] similarly interprets the verse in *Genesis* [4:10] about Abel: קוֹל דְּמֵי אָחִיךָ צֹעֲקִים אֵלַי, *the bloods of your brother cry out to Me — Kli Yakar.*)

Alternatively, by refraining from killing Nabal, David saved his own life (*Kli Yakar*) — thus, the plural nature of דָּמִים refers to the blood of Nabal and David.

וְהוֹשֵׁעַ יָדְךָ לָךְ — *And your hand from acting on your behalf.*

Had David killed Nabal, he would have been punished by God (*Rashi*).

Daas Sofrim explains that it is inappropriate for a person to take the law into his own hands, lest others suspect his motives (see *Bava Kamma* 27b). David himself expressed this idea in the previous chapter: מֵרְשָׁעִים יֵצֵא רֶשַׁע וְיָדִי לֹא תִהְיֶה־בָּךְ, *Wickedness issues from the wicked, but my hand will not act against you* (24:14).

According to this, the words מְנָעֲךָ ה׳ וְהוֹשֵׁעַ יָדְךָ לָךְ form an extended phrase: *HASHEM kept you from taking vengeance with your own hands.*

Alternatively, *Me'am Loez* explains וְהוֹשֵׁעַ יָדְךָ לָךְ — *and your hand from acting on your behalf* — as meaning that by not spilling blood, David saved himself from sinning.

וְעַתָּה יִהְיוּ כְנָבָל אֹיְבֶיךָ — *May your enemies be like Nabal.*

That is to say, Abigail blessed David that all his enemies would be as powerless against him as was Nabal (*Radak*).

A person need be concerned only if he is shamed by a man of standing. *If everyone who tries to discredit David is as disreputable as Nabal, he need not be concerned* (*Mahari Kara*).

According to *Rashi*, this statement intimated Abigail's prophetic knowledge that Nabal would soon die.

Metzudos adds that Abigail told David that Hashem, Who had prevented David from spilling blood, would take up David's cause and put Nabal to death. She then added to this prophecy her hope that the same fate would befall David's other enemies as well (*Metzudos*).

כז וְעַתָּה֙ הַבְּרָכָ֣ה הַזֹּ֔את אֲשֶׁר־הֵבִ֥יא שִׁפְחָתְךָ֖
לַֽאדֹנִ֑י וְנִתְּנָה֙ לַנְּעָרִ֔ים הַמִּֽתְהַלְּכִ֖ים בְּרַגְלֵ֥י
כח אֲדֹנִֽי׃ שָׂ֥א נָ֖א לְפֶ֣שַׁע אֲמָתֶ֑ךָ כִּ֣י עָשֹֽׂה־יַעֲשֶׂ֣ה
יְהוָ֣ה לַֽאדֹנִ֗י בַּ֚יִת נֶאֱמָ֔ן כִּֽי־מִלְחֲמ֤וֹת יְהוָה֙
אֲדֹנִ֣י נִלְחָ֔ם וְרָעָ֛ה לֹא־תִמָּצֵ֥א בְךָ֖ מִיָּמֶֽיךָ׃

27. וְעַתָּה הַבְּרָכָה הַזֹּאת ... — *And now, this homage ...*

In the previous verse, Abigail stated וְעַתָּה, *and now*, twice, and once in the present verse. According to *Abarbanel*, Abigail was refuting three motives that David might have in attacking Nabal. First, David might have intended to do God's will by executing Nabal as a rebel. Thus, Abigail stated, וְעַתָּה ... מְנָעֲךָ ה׳ מִבּוֹא בְדָמִים — *and now, HASHEM prevented you from engaging in bloodshed* — meaning that the time had not yet come for David to attack Nabal.

Second, David may have wished to demonstrate his prowess. In response to that, Abigail stated, וְעַתָּה יִהְיוּ כְנָבָל אֹיְבֶיךָ, *and now, may your enemies be like Nabal* — meaning that David need not exercise his might, for Nabal was a lowly and powerless person.

Finally, David may have desired to gain desperately needed provisions, to which he felt he had a right. Therefore, together with the statement, וְעַתָּה הַבְּרָכָה הַזֹּאת, Abigail brought a substantial gift of food.

הַבְּרָכָה הַזֹּאת — *This homage.*

The word בְּרָכָה, usually *blessing*, is sometimes used to denote a *tribute* (such as in the verse, קַח־נָא אֶת־בִּרְכָתִי, *Please accept my gift* [*Genesis* 33:11]).

Abigail used this word since it implies a gesture of respect and precludes any implication that she was bestowing charity (*Daas Sofrim*).

אֲשֶׁר־הֵבִיא שִׁפְחָתְךָ — *That your maidservant has brought.*

Although Abigail did not physically bring this gift herself, since it came from her the attendants who carried it were not mentioned (*Radak*).

However, the word הֵבִיא, *brought*, is written in the masculine form. Thus, *Me'am Loez* explains, it is as if the verse stated, אֲשֶׁר־הֵבִיא נַעַר שִׁפְחָתְךָ, *that the attendant of your maidservant brought.*

According to *Malbim*, Abigail used the masculine verb to connote that David should consider the gift as having come from Nabal, since it came from his property.

וְנִתְּנָה לַנְּעָרִים — *Let it be given to the attendants.*

So as not to imply that David needed her gift, Abigail said that it should be given to his attendants (*Radak, Metzudos*).

Also, in case the quantity or quality of the gift was not congruent with David's honor, it should at least suffice for the attendants (*Abarbanel*).

וְנִתְּנָה — *Let it be given.*

The word נִתְּנָה is in the past tense — the prefix ו׳ changes it to the future tense (*Rashi*).

Daas Sofrim, however, maintains that the verb remains in the past tense. Abigail told David that these provisions had already been designated for his attendants, and it was as if they had already been given.

הַמִּתְהַלְּכִים בְּרַגְלֵי אֲדֹנִי — *Who are traveling with my lord.*

Literally, בְּרַגְלֵי אֲדֹנִי means *at my lord's feet* — meaning, states *Metzudos*, following after him.

Targum renders this phrase as *who serve before my master*. Presumably, *Targum* understands *feet* as a figurative word for service, similar to its usage in the mishnah, וֶהֱוֵי מִתְאַבֵּק בַּעֲפַר רַגְלֵיהֶם, *Sit in the dust of their feet* (*Avos* 1:4).

[27] *And now, this homage that your maidservant has brought to my lord — let it be given to the attendants who are traveling with my lord.* [28] *Please forgive the sin of your maidservant, for HASHEM shall certainly make for my lord an enduring house, for my lord fights the wars of HASHEM; and no blame has been found in you in your days.*

28. After presenting David with supplies, Abigail provided yet another reason that he not harm Nabal — i.e., it was not proper for an idealistic, blameless king with an illustrious future before him to engage in such an ugly deed.

שָׂא נָא לְפֶשַׁע אֲמָתֶךָ — *Please forgive the sin of your maidservant.*

According to *Abarbanel,* Abigail apologized for speaking to him at length, which might be seen as disrespectful (*Abarbanel*).

Alternatively, she apologized lest she inadvertently say something unbecoming (*Metzudos*).

According to *Daas Sofrim,* Abigail took responsibility for Nabal's actions and sought David's forgiveness.

Finally, *Abarbanel* suggests that Abigail apologized for having brought a gift not in keeping with David's honor.

בַּיִת נֶאֱמָן — *An enduring house.*

Although the word בַּיִת usually means *house* or *family,* here it apparently connotes a royal *dynasty* (*Targum;* see below, *II Samuel,* Ch. 7).

The word נֶאֱמָן — literally, *trusted* — is sometimes used to denote *permanence.*

As mentioned earlier, the Sages state that when David and Abigail met, he proposed that they engage in an act of intimacy — a proposal that she rejected. *Kli Yakar* suggests that Abigail excused herself by stating that David was destined to have a בַּיִת נֶאֱמָן, *an enduring house.* Although most commentators interpret this to mean his royal dynasty, nonetheless the word בַּיִת is commonly used to refer to one's household, which would be tainted if he were to commit such a deed.

כִּי עָשֹׂה־יַעֲשֶׂה ה׳ לַאדֹנִי בַּיִת נֶאֱמָן — *For HASHEM shall certainly make for my lord an enduring house.*

The fact that David was anointed king seems to have been common knowledge.

Here, Abigail prophesied that his kingdom would endure (*Radak*).

כִּי עָשֹׂה־יַעֲשֶׂה ה׳ לַאדֹנִי בַּיִת נֶאֱמָן כִּי־מִלְחֲמוֹת ה׳ אֲדֹנִי נִלְחָם וְרָעָה לֹא־תִמָּצֵא בְךָ מִיָּמֶיךָ — *For HASHEM shall certainly make for my lord an enduring house, for my lord fights the wars of HASHEM; and no blame has been found in you in your days.*

The phrase וְרָעָה לֹא־תִמָּצֵא בְךָ literally means *and no blame should be found in you.* Our translation — *and no blame has been found in you* — follows *Radak,* who renders these words in the past tense, noting that this is congruent with the word מִיָּמֶיךָ, *in your days* — i.e., in past days. Accordingly, this verse reviews David's history, and serves as an introduction to verses 30-31, which describe how Abigail urged David to proceed on his path of probity.

David was destined to attain an everlasting dynasty, stated Abigail, because מִלְחֲמוֹת ה׳ אֲדֹנִי נִלְחָם, *my lord fights the wars of HASHEM;* he only fought battles on behalf of Hashem. Abigail was implicitly contrasting David with Saul, who lost his right to the throne after killing the residents of Nob. Since David waged only Hashem's wars, we can be confident that just as no blame *has been* found in his family heretofore, so it will continue — unless he were to ruin it by his treatment of Nabal. Accordingly,

כט וַיָּקָם אָדָם לִרְדָפְךָ וּלְבַקֵּשׁ אֶת־נַפְשֶׁךָ וְהָיְתָה
נֶפֶשׁ אֲדֹנִי צְרוּרָה | בִּצְרוֹר הַחַיִּים אֵת יהוה
אֱלֹהֶיךָ וְאֵת נֶפֶשׁ אֹיְבֶיךָ יְקַלְּעֶנָּה בְּתוֹךְ כַּף הַקָּלַע:

the following phrase, וְרָעָה לֹא־תִמָּצֵא, is to be understood as *no blame is found* — encompassing both past and future (*Abarbanel*).

According to *Rashi*, on the other hand, the phrase וְרָעָה לֹא־תִמָּצֵא בְךָ is to be understood as *blame will not be found in you*, and constitutes part of Abigail's advice. Since Hashem was going to make *an enduring house* for David, it would be unbecoming if he were to sin.

Malbim interprets this verse similarly. David had acquired a reputation for fighting only מִלְחֲמוֹת ה׳, *the wars of* HASHEM. If he would attack Nabal, people would say that he was an inveterate troublemaker who on previous occasions had only happened to engage in Divinely ordained battles.

Rambam (*Hil. Melachim* 7:15) interprets this verse as teaching that a person who fearlessly enters into battle in order to sanctify Hashem's Name may be assured that no harm will befall him. Hashem will build him a secure house, he will draw merit to himself and his descendants forever, and he will attain the life of the World to Come. Thus, וְרָעָה לֹא תִמָּצֵא בְךָ is a promise that *no evil will befall you* — a promise that no misfortune would come David's way.

Mussar HaNeviim translates רָעָה לֹא־תִמָּצֵא בְךָ similarly, seeing it as a promise that David would be rewarded for forgiving Abigail. As the Sages say, "If someone overcomes his nature and forgives another, Heaven will forgive him for his sins as well" (*Rosh Hashanah* 17a).[1]

כִּי־מִלְחֲמוֹת ה׳ — *The wars of* HASHEM.

Targum renders this as *the wars of the nation of* HASHEM.

29. Simply understood, this verse continues Abigail's petition; however, the

1. *Chomas Anach* provides a novel interpretation of this verse.

The Tannaim disagree as to whether it is permissible to assign a reason for a mitzvah and then, should that reason not apply under certain circumstances, alter one's observance of that mitzvah.

As a rule, this is permitted only if the Torah itself has indicated the reason for the mitzvah (see *Sanhedrin* 21a).

When Abigail requested that David not kill Nabal, she was asking that he alter — in this case, suspend — the rule that a king may not relinquish his honor.

To bolster her request, she offered two arguments that such an alteration was legitimate.

First, she addressed the issue itself. The halachah that forbids a king from relinquishing his honor is based on the verse שׂוֹם תָּשִׂים עָלֶיךָ מֶלֶךְ, *You shall set a king over yourself* (*Deuteronomy* 17:15). The Sages interpret the word עָלֶיךָ, *over yourself*, to mean that "his fear shall be upon you" (*Sanhedrin* 19a). Abigail argued that since Saul was still king, this law was not germane because awe of David was not required of them.

Second, she showed David that he himself had chosen to alter the basic meaning of a mitzvah on the basis of the rationale provided by the Torah. The Torah prohibits a Jew from marrying a descendant of Moab. This restriction would have included female Moabites, had the Torah not provided a reason for the mitzvah: *Because [the Moabites] did not greet you with bread and water on the road when you were leaving Egypt* (*Deuteronomy* 23:5). Since only men and not women are expected to offer food to wayfarers, the Moabitesses were considered blameless and it was thus permissible to marry them (*Yevamos* 76b). Thus, Boaz was permitted to marry Ruth, and their descendant David was fit to be king.

If David could interpret the law regarding Moab on the basis of the reason that the Torah provides, argued Abigail, then she could do the same and interpret the law about a king relinquishing his honor, and thus demonstrate that Nabal was legally blameless.

David responded to this argument, בָּרוּךְ טַעְמֵךְ (v. 33) — *Blessed is your advice* — but, literally, *Blessed is your reasoning*.

[29] *A man has risen up to pursue you and to seek your life! May my lord's soul be bound up in the bond of life, with HASHEM, your God, and may He hurl away the soul of your enemies as one shoots a stone from a slingshot.*

Sages and commentators derive from it essential principles of Jewish belief regarding the afterlife. We will first present the straightforward meaning of the verse and then discuss its deeper implications.

וַיָּקָם אָדָם לִרְדָפְךָ וּלְבַקֵּשׁ אֶת־נַפְשֶׁךָ — *A man has risen up to pursue you and seek your life.*

Most commentators consider this to be a reference to Saul (*Radak; Ralbag; Abarbanel*), who pursued David even though וְרָעָה לֹא־תִמָּצֵא בְךָ, *no blame has been found in you.* Although David had had the opportunity to kill Saul in self-defense (the incident at the cave [discussed in Ch. 24] was well-known), he had refrained from doing so.

וַיָּקָם אָדָם לִרְדָפְךָ — *A man has risen up to pursue you.*

Although referring to Saul, Abigail did not speak of him as *king* but simply as a *man* — intimating that Saul would not succeed against David (*Radak*).

וְהָיְתָה נֶפֶשׁ אֲדֹנִי צְרוּרָה בִּצְרוֹר הַחַיִּים אֵת ה׳ אֱלֹהֶיךָ — *May my lord's soul be bound up in the bond of life, with HASHEM, your God.*

Abarbanel explains that in leading up to her concluding point, she spoke of two independent elements of David's future, one in this world and one in the next. First, by saying *a man has risen up . . .* she concludes her thought in the previous verse by saying that his impeccable behavior would earn him an *enduring house.* Then she speaks of the incomparable pleasure that awaits him in the World to Come, while his enemies would not merit the same. However, should he engage in an unwarranted act of violence — i.e., should he kill Nabal — he would forfeit this exalted reward.

According to some commentators, in this verse Abigail attempted to dissuade David from killing Nabal by reminding him of how he had remained blameless even as Saul was persecuting him, and that in reward for that, his soul would be bound up in God, even as his enemies suffered the fate their sins had earned them (*Metzudos*).

Alshich and *Malbim* explain that Abigail told David that the tribulations he had suffered would refine him, making his soul worthy of enjoying eternal delight.

Radak, however, understands Abigail's promise of felicity as referring to *this* world. Although Saul had pursued David, she stated, וְהָיְתָה נֶפֶשׁ אֲדֹנִי צְרוּרָה בִּצְרוֹר הַחַיִּים, *my lord's life will be bound to those alive* — i.e., Saul would be unable to kill him, and David would continue to walk אֵת ה׳ אֱלֹהֶיךָ — *in HASHEM's ways* — throughout his life (*Radak*). *Mahari Kara* elaborates that צְרוּרָה, *bound,* means *wrapped* and *protected.* David would be as carefully guarded by God as a precious treasure.

These explanations of the verse understand the words וַיָּקָם אָדָם לִרְדָפְךָ, *a man has risen up to pursue you,* as referring to Saul. Some commentators, however, state that they refer to anyone who might rise up against David in the future. David need never fear, because Hashem would surely guard his soul — i.e., his *life* — by binding it with Himself (*Me'am Loez*).

Abigail presented this blessing with certainty, because it was in the nature of a prophecy (*Daas Sofrim*).

וְאֵת נֶפֶשׁ אֹיְבֶיךָ יְקַלְּעֶנָּה בְּתוֹךְ כַּף הַקָּלַע — *And may He hurl away the soul of your enemies as one shoots a stone from a slingshot.*

ל וְהָיָה כִּי־יַעֲשֶׂה יהוה לַאדֹנִי כְּכֹל אֲשֶׁר־דִּבֶּר
אֶת־הַטּוֹבָה עָלֶיךָ וְצִוְּךָ לְנָגִיד עַל־יִשְׂרָאֵל׃

Aside from understanding the nature of this punishment, we must identify the *enemies* and whether they will be punished in this world or the next.

Many commentators state that *enemies* refers to Saul — i.e., he will fall to the Philistines (*Mahari Kara*).

Me'am Loez observes that this figurative slingshot is reminiscent of the actual slingshot with which David killed Goliath. Saul would suffer this retribution for having forgotten what David had accomplished with his slingshot.

However, *Maharsha* (to *Shabbos* 152b) denies that Abigail was referring to Saul, a righteous man, with these words. Rather, she was speaking either of Doeg HaAdomi or Nabal.

According to *Rema MiPanu* (*Maamar Em Kol Chai* 2:1), Abigail was referring to Nabal. She described his punishment in terms of a hurled stone because he had slandered David, and the Sages state that a slanderer deserves to be stoned.

According to *Kli Yakar*, Abigail was speaking of Doeg and the Ziphites, whose slanderous words had forced David to wander like a nomad. In direct retribution, their souls would be hurled forth as a stone that never comes to rest (see below).

Me'am Loez states that the *enemies* are people who may in the future pursue David (see above). They are destined to be *hurled about* — i.e., to constantly wander as they fruitlessly pursue him.

יְקַלְּעֶנָּה בְּתוֹךְ כַּף הַקָּלַע — *As one shoots a stone from a slingshot.*

The כַּף הַקָּלַע is the *palm* of the slingshot — i.e., a long, leather strip indented in the middle to hold the stone, which bears a similarity to the palm of the hand (*Rashi*).

בְּתוֹךְ כַּף הַקָּלַע literally means *into the midst of the palm of the slingshot. Malbim* explains that when a person flings a stone from a slingshot, it eventually comes to rest. This verse compares the judgment on the enemy's soul to a stone thrown into an elastic slingshot, from which it is constantly flies back and forth between two slingshots, never coming to rest (*Shabbos* 152b).

Contrarily, *Kli Yakar* cites a comment by *Ri Di Kuriel* that the stone will constantly remain בְּתוֹךְ כַּף הַקָּלַע, *inside the palm of the slingshot*. The soul will undergo pain and unrest as it is rotated within the slingshot and never set free. This is part of the process of purifying a tainted soul that Hashem has not completely rejected.

Binyan Yehoshua (to *Avos D'Rabbi Nassan* 12:4) cites the view of *Raavad* and *Ritva* that the כַּף הַקָּלַע is a fiery wheel in which the souls of the wicked are placed.

וְהָיְתָה נֶפֶשׁ אֲדֹנִי צְרוּרָה בִּצְרוֹר הַחַיִּים אֵת ה׳ אֱלֹהֶיךָ וְאֵת נֶפֶשׁ אֹיְבֶיךָ יְקַלְּעֶנָּה בְּתוֹךְ כַּף הַקָּלַע — *May my lord's soul be bound up in the bond of life, with* HASHEM, *your God, and may He hurl away the soul of your enemies as one shoots a stone from a slingshot.*

Targum renders חַיִּים — *life* — as the everlasting life of the World to Come.[1]

The Talmud (*Shabbos* 152b) derives from this verse that the souls of righteous people are stored beneath God's Throne of Glory, whereas the souls of the wicked are cast from angel to angel across the span of the world, never coming to rest.

Kli Yakar elaborates that every soul desires to return to its source in the Throne of Glory (see *Chagigah* 12b). The perfectly righteous suffer no impediment and immediately reach it after death. Others, however, are

1. This phrase serves as the basis for a common epitaph, cited at funerals and carved into tombstones — תְּהֵא נַפְשׁוֹ צְרוּרָה בִּצְרוֹר הַחַיִּים, *His soul shall be bound up in the bond of life.*

[30] *And may it be that when HASHEM performs for my lord all the beneficence of which He has spoken regarding you, and appoints you as leader over Israel,*

hurled down by their sins. Those of an intermediate moral cast are cleansed and ascend, whereas the wicked are hurled down for eternity despite their constant attempts to elevate themselves.

Rabbeinu Yonah (*Shaarei Teshuvah* 2:18) cites a Midrash (*Koheles Rabbah* 3:21) stating that initially the souls of the righteous and of the wicked are brought to the Throne of Glory and judged. The righteous remain, whereas the wicked are cast back down.

Rabbeinu Yonah explains that the wicked person has so degraded his nature that after he dies his soul naturally sinks to earth, the source of its desires. It is only brought up to the heights so that it will be able to perceive what it forfeited — how it traded eternal elevation for the deepest depths — and is then cast back down, just as a stone drops to the ground after it has been raised.

Maharsha (to *Shabbos* ibid.) interprets the words of the Talmud that the righteous remain with the Throne of Glory whereas the wicked are cast from angel to angel as a reference to the stressful and painful passage of reincarnation. The soul of the righteous person who has completed his task in this world returns to its heavenly source. The soul of an immoral person, however, is hurled back into another body so it may complete its unfinished work (receiving three chances to do so).

Pirkei D'Rabbi Eliezer (Ch. 34) considers the צְרוֹר הַחַיִּים — *bond of life* — to be a reference to the *Land of the Living* — i.e., the Land of Israel (see *Psalms* 116:9,142:6, *Radak* ad loc.). The souls of righteous people who die and are buried outside the Land of Israel will be brought into the land, where they will be brought closer to Hashem. Contrarily, the souls of iniquitous people who die in the Land of Israel are "hurled out with the slingshot."

Abigail foresaw that David would be expelled from the Land of Israel (Ch. 26), and prophesied that since his soul was bound to the Land of Israel, he would return (*Radal; Be'er Moshe*).

Tanna D'Vei Eliyahu Rabbah (Ch. 4) derives from this verse that a scholar who toils in Torah during his lifetime is considered to be alive even after death (and in that way shares God's attribute of unending life).

With this, *Be'er Moshe* explains the words of the Talmud (*Berachos* 64a) that "Torah scholars have no rest — neither in this world nor in the next." Even after they die, they continue to live with the Torah, composing new insights and rising from level to level.

Abarbanel derives seven particulars regarding the fate of the soul after death.

(1) The soul remains intact so that it may be rewarded or punished.

(2) Each soul is independent, and thus benefits or suffers according to its individual deeds. This refutes the notion that all souls are joined after death.

(3) Reward in the World to Come is not extended to people for their intellectual insights. Rather, Hashem awards those whose lives are saturated with Torah and mitzvos, and who refrain from evil. This is indicated in the flow of the last two verses. First, כִּי־מִלְחֲמוֹת ה׳ אֲדֹנִי נִלְחָם, *for my lord fights the wars of HASHEM* — meaning that a person performs Hashem's mitzvos; at the same time, וְרָעָה לֹא־תִמָּצֵא בְךָ, *and no blame has been found in you* — he does not transgress any prohibitions; and even though וַיָּקָם אָדָם לִרְדָפְךָ, *a man has risen up to pursue you* — he undergoes the difficulties of this world, they cleanse his soul and make it ready for eternal delight, so that finally וְהָיְתָה נֶפֶשׁ צְרוּרָה, *his soul shall be bound up....*

(4) Eternal reward consists of attachment to one's Father in Heaven.

(5) The soul's greatest pleasure — which

לא וְלֹא תִהְיֶה זֹאת | לְךָ לְפוּקָה וּלְמִכְשׁוֹל לֵב לַאדֹנִי
וְלִשְׁפָּךְ־דָּם חִנָּם וּלְהוֹשִׁיעַ אֲדֹנִי לוֹ וְהֵיטִב
לב יהוה לַאדֹנִי וְזָכַרְתָּ אֶת־אֲמָתֶךָ׃ וַיֹּאמֶר

is called חַיִּים, *life* — is its perception of God, something that it cannot experience in this world.

(6) The soul of the righteous person survives in order to receive reward, whereas the soul of the evil person survives in order to suffer retribution.

(7) The punishment suffered by the wicked is not merely an absence of the pleasures enjoyed by the righteous. Rather, their souls suffer an all-but-unimaginable, eternal agony.

31. וְלֹא תִהְיֶה זֹאת לְךָ — *That this not be for you.*

זֹאת — *it* — was a reference to David's plan to execute Nabal. Thus, it is in the feminine form, for it implies the word נְקָמָה, *revenge* (*Radak*).

לְפוּקָה — *A stumbling block.*

A similar word in *Nahum* (2:11), פַּק בִּרְכַּיִם, refers to buckling knees (*Rashi*).

Elsewhere, the word יָפֵק connotes *extraction* (as in *Proverbs* 8:35; also, the Aramaic word for *take out* is מַפִּיק). Thus, *Malbim* explains that if David killed Nabal, his deed would be interpreted as being an *extraction* or *realization* of his inner self — i.e., he would be perceived as having the character of a murderer.

According to the Talmud, the word פוּקָה is a reference to גֵּיהִנֹּם, *purgatory* (*Megillah* 15b).

לְפוּקָה וּלְמִכְשׁוֹל לֵב — *A stumbling block and a moral hindrance.*

Simply understood, פוּקָה means *obstacle*, and the following phrase, מִכְשׁוֹל לֵב, is a synonym that emphasizes her point (*Radak*).

According to *Abarbanel*, מִכְשׁוֹל לֵב means *a source of regret.*

וְלֹא תִהְיֶה זֹאת לְךָ לְפוּקָה וּלְמִכְשׁוֹל לֵב לַאדֹנִי — *That this not be for you a stumbling block and a moral hindrance — for my lord....*

If David killed Nabal and the people reacted with abhorrence, the glowing future that Abigail had outlined would in whole or in part be compromised.

Also, were David to kill Nabal he would, as king, lack the authority to subdue acts of bloodshed. This idea is portrayed graphically by *Midrash Shocher Tov* (53:1). Abigail told David, "One day, the following case may come before you. A poor man had requested alms from a rich person, and, upon being refused, killed him. How will you be able to judge this case? People will say that you did the same to Nabal!" According to this Midrash, the word פוּקָה derives from פִּקְפּוּק, *hesitation.* David would be forced to hesitate in judgment.[1]

Metzudos explains this verse differently. Abigail intimated that as long as he was a fugitive, David was more concerned about Nabal's offense than by how the people viewed him. However, she stated, once David became king, לֹא תִהְיֶה זֹאת לְךָ לְפוּקָה וּלְמִכְשׁוֹל לֵב, *[The words of the lowly Nabal] would not bother you a bit.* Abigail continued, וְלִשְׁפָּךְ־דָּם חִנָּם וּלְהוֹשִׁיעַ אֲדֹנִי לוֹ, "If you refrain from killing Nabal, you will prevent the people from saying that *you spilled innocent blood and took matters into your own hands* — which is something that would concern you as king."

In verses 28-31, *Abarbanel* offered David four other incentives to refrain from harming Nabal.

(a) עָשֹׂה־יַעֲשֶׂה ה׳ לַאדֹנִי בַּיִת נֶאֱמָן, *Hashem will*

1. David responded, "This is not your initiative. Hashem sent you to me" (see v. 32). Nevertheless, he agreed that she should be blessed for what she had done (v. 33).

31 *that this not be for you a stumbling block and a moral hindrance — for my lord to have shed innocent blood, for my lord to have avenged himself! And may* HASHEM *act beneficently toward my lord, and may you [then] remember your maidservant."*

make for my lord an enduring house. Abigail intimated that since David was not yet king, therefore Nabal could not be tried as a rebel (see above, verses 13,20).

(b) כִּי־מִלְחֲמוֹת ה׳ אֲדֹנִי נִלְחָם, *For my lord fights the wars of* HASHEM. A warrior, who is always in danger and needs to elicit Divine protection, must remain noble and unsullied.

(c) וַיָּקָם אָדָם לִרְדָפְךָ, *A man has risen up to pursue you.* In order to gain Hashem's help in battling his enemy, David required the merit gained via impeccable behavior.

(d) וְלֹא תִהְיֶה זֹאת לְךָ לְפוּקָה, *Let this not be for you a stumbling block.* If David submitted to his inclination to kill Nabal, he would be drawn to commit other sins as well — for, as our Sages state (*Avos* 4:2), *one sin leads to another.*

וְלִשְׁפָּךְ־דָּם חִנָּם — *To have shed innocent blood.*

We have already mentioned the view that Nabal was in fact not innocent (see *Be'er Moshe* above, v. 20). Accordingly, *Kli Yakar* translates this phrase as *to have shed blood for nothing* — since Nabal would soon die of natural causes.

וּלְהוֹשִׁיעַ אֲדֹנִי לוֹ — *For my lord to have avenged himself.*

Our translation presents *Rashi*'s interpretation of this phrase — i.e., these words speak of what David should *not* do: personally avenge himself.

Radak explains that with these words, Abigail implied, "My lord would save himself much trouble by not spilling innocent blood" (see similarly above, v. 26).

וְזָכַרְתָּ אֶת־אֲמָתֶךָ — *May you [then] remember your maidservant.*

Our translation follows *Ralbag*, who understands these words as a request: "When Hashem acts beneficently toward you, do not forget me."

According to *Abarbanel*, Abigail beseeched David to bear in mind that anything he did to Nabal would harm her as well (see above, v. 26).

Many commentators interpret these words not as a request but as a prediction, that when Hashem made David king, he would remember Abigail favorably and appreciate that she had prevented him from acting violently (*Radak*).

The Midrash (ibid.) applies to Abigail the verse: מָצָא אִשָּׁה מָצָא טוֹב, *One who has found a wife has found goodness* (*Proverbs* 18:22). Had David killed Nabal, all the offerings in the world would not have atoned for him — but she came and saved him from incurring such guilt. Accordingly, David's introduction to his psalm about Nabal reads: לַמְנַצֵּחַ עַל־מָחֲלַת מַשְׂכִּיל לְדָוִד, *For the conductor on the machalas, a maskil of David* (*Psalms* 53:1). Simply understood, the *machalas* was a type of musical instrument (see *Rashi* ad loc.). However, this word is related to מְחִילָה, *forgiveness.* Just as offerings provide forgiveness, so did Abigail gain forgiveness for David.

The Talmud (*Megillah* 14b) teaches that with the words וְזָכַרְתָּ אֶת־אֲמָתֶךָ — *remember your maidservant* — Abigail requested that David marry her following Nabal's death.

According to *Ralbag*, Abigail's statement that David would marry her was in the nature of a prophecy.

The Talmud comments that "women, while still speaking, will spin" — i.e., even as Abigail was asking David to spare her husband's life, she was hinting to David that he should marry her after Nabal died.

דָּוִד לַאֲבִיגַל בָּרוּךְ יהוה אֱלֹהֵי יִשְׂרָאֵל אֲשֶׁר
לג שְׁלָחֵךְ הַיּוֹם הַזֶּה לִקְרָאתִי: וּבָרוּךְ טַעְמֵךְ וּבְרוּכָה
אָתְּ אֲשֶׁר כְּלִתִנִי הַיּוֹם הַזֶּה מִבּוֹא בְדָמִים וְהֹשֵׁעַ
לד יָדִי לִי: וְאוּלָם חַי־יהוה אֱלֹהֵי יִשְׂרָאֵל אֲשֶׁר מְנָעַנִי
מֵהָרַע אֹתָךְ כִּי | לוּלֵי מִהַרְתְּ °ותבאתי לִקְרָאתִי

°וַתָּבֹאת ק׳

From this Talmudic passage (and from a teaching in the *Talmud Yerushalmi* that will be cited in the commentary on the following verse), we see that the Sages frowned upon a married woman discussing her plans for future marriage. Why then did the righteous Abigail do so?

Sefer Ein Eliyahu (cited by *Mussar HaNeviim*) justifies Abigail's behavior as follows. The Talmud (*Sotah* 7a) states that a man's passion for a woman who is forbidden to him is likely to be moderated if he knows that she will eventually be permitted to him. Seeing that David was overcome by his attraction to her, Abigail informed him that he would soon be allowed to marry her.

The Talmud (*Megillah* 14b, *Bava Kamma* 92b) derives from Abigail's request that a person should never allow humility to interfere with meeting his needs, be they material or spiritual. Although Abigail humbly referred to herself as אֲמָתֶךָ, *your maidservant*, she nevertheless gathered the courage to ask David to marry her (see *Rashi, Bava Kamma* ibid.).

Be'er Moshe extrapolates that a person should assume the same attitude in regard to prayer. As small and undeserving as he may be, he should never hesitate to ask Hashem to fulfill his every need.

◆§ David Refrains From Acting, and Thanks Abigail

32. וַיֹּאמֶר דָּוִד לַאֲבִיגַל — *David then said to Abigail.*

Abigail's name is here written אֲבִיגַל, without a *yud* before the *lamed*. *Talmud Yerushalmi* (*Sanhedrin* 2:3) explains that Scripture shortened her name because of her inappropriate allusion that David should marry her after Nabal died, which was a breach of the moral code.

According to many texts, only the written (*k'siv*) version of this word is altered — the read (*k'ri*) version remains אֲבִיגַיִל. Other editions, however, change the *k'ri* text as well to אֲבִיגַל.

וַיֹּאמֶר דָּוִד לַאֲבִיגַל בָּרוּךְ ה׳ אֱלֹהֵי יִשְׂרָאֵל אֲשֶׁר שְׁלָחֵךְ — *David then said to Abigail, "Blessed is HASHEM, God of Israel, Who sent you."*

David admitted that Abigail was right, insofar as that he should not kill Nabal. This does not, however, necessarily mean that he agreed that Nabal was innocent — only that killing Nabal was not appropriate at present.

David first thanked Hashem and only then Abigail. Possibly, he had learned from the error made by Malchizedek, who first blessed Abraham and only then Hashem (*Genesis* 14:19,20, see *Rabbeinu Bachya*), as a result of which he lost his rights to the priesthood (*Nedarim* 32b; *Me'am Loez*).

Daas Sofrim comments that David had much to be thankful for — in particular, that someone had come to dissuade him from killing Nabal, whereas no one had tried to stop Saul from killing the inhabitants of Nob.

בָּרוּךְ ה׳ אֱלֹהֵי יִשְׂרָאֵל — *Blessed is HASHEM, God of Israel.*

The use of the phrase אֱלֹהֵי יִשְׂרָאֵל — *the God of Israel* — indicates that David and Abigail's sole concern was fulfilling the needs of the nation of Israel (*Daas Sofrim*).

33. וּבָרוּךְ טַעְמֵךְ — *And blessed is your advice.*

Our translation follows *Radak*.

Alternatively, טַעְמֵךְ may be translated

³²David then said to Abigail, "Blessed is
HASHEM, God of Israel, Who sent you this day to
meet me. ³³And blessed is your advice and blessed
are you, who have restrained me on this day
from coming to bloodshed and avenging myself
by my own hand. ³⁴Truly, as HASHEM, God of Is-
rael, lives — Who has prevented me from harming
you — had you not hurried and come to meet me,

as *your words* (*Mahari Kara*), or *your reasoning* (see footnote, v. 28).

וּבָרוּךְ טַעְמֵךְ וּבְרוּכָה אָתְּ — *And blessed is your advice and blessed are you.*

Although David credited Hashem for orchestrating this meeting and preventing him from killing Nabal, he also praised Abigail for the role she played (*Midrash Shocher Tov* 53:1), in accordance with the principle that *Heaven arranges for meritorious people to perform meritorious deeds* (*Shabbos* 32a).

In these two verses, David listed three factors that led him to retract his plan to kill Nabal: (1) בָּרוּךְ ה׳, *Blessed is HASHEM* — God's providence arranged matters so that David realized that he should not continue; (2) בָּרוּךְ טַעְמֵךְ, *blessed is your advice* — Abigail's arguments were clear and sound; and (3) בְּרוּכָה אָתְּ — *Blessed are you* — Abigail was so meritorious that her request was sufficient a reason for David to rescind his decision.

אֲשֶׁר כְּלִתִנִי הַיּוֹם הַזֶּה מִבּוֹא בְדָמִים — *Who have restrained me on this day from coming to bloodshed.*

Targum translates מִבּוֹא בְדָמִים — *from coming to bloodshed* — as *from shedding innocent blood.*

The word דָּמִים — *blood* — is in the plural form, referring to two different blood related sins that David could have committed (*Megillah* 14b): that of murder and that of engaging in relations with a menstruant woman (*Rashi*; see also *Yerushalmi Sanhedrin* 2:3).

However, *Maharsha* suggests that the two blood-related crimes to which the Talmud alludes are murder and adultery — the latter, like murder, is punishable by death (and thus more severe than the sin of engaging in relations with a menstruant woman).[1]

וְהֹשֵׁעַ יָדִי לִי — *And avenging myself by my own hand.*

According to our translation, which follows *Rashi*, the prefix מ, *from*, in the phrase מִבּוֹא בְדָמִים — *from coming to bloodshed* — applies as well to the words הוֹשֵׁעַ יָדִי לִי — *avenging myself by my own hand.* Thus, the phrase should be read as, *And [you have restrained me] from avenging myself by my own hand.* (See above, vs. 26,31.)

34. אֲשֶׁר מְנָעַנִי מֵהָרַע אֹתָךְ — *Who has prevented me from harming you.*

With the word אֹתָךְ, *you*, David referred to Abigail's family and belongings (*Abarbanel*).

David restrained himself because of Abigail, not because of his concern for Nabal (*Malbim*).

וַתָּבֹאת לִקְרָאתִי — *And come to meet me.*

The word וַתָּבֹאת is a combination of the future tense תָּבֹא, *she will come*, and the past tense בָּאת, *you came.* This conjunction of past and future connotes Abigail's swiftness and zeal (*Radak*).

Mishbetzos Zahav suggests that the

1. To understand why the *Yerushalmi* may have ignored the sin of adultery, see *Mareh Panim* ad loc. and commentary above, v. 31.

כִּי אִם־נוֹתַר לְנָבָל עַד־אוֹר הַבֹּקֶר מַשְׁתִּין
לה בְּקִיר: וַיִּקַּח דָּוִד מִיָּדָהּ אֵת אֲשֶׁר־הֵבִיאָה לוֹ וְלָהּ
אָמַר עֲלִי לְשָׁלוֹם לְבֵיתֵךְ רְאִי שָׁמַעְתִּי בְקוֹלֵךְ
לו וָאֶשָּׂא פָּנָיִךְ: וַתָּבֹא אֲבִיגַיִל | אֶל־נָבָל וְהִנֵּה־לוֹ
מִשְׁתֶּה בְּבֵיתוֹ כְּמִשְׁתֵּה הַמֶּלֶךְ וְלֵב נָבָל טוֹב
עָלָיו וְהוּא שִׁכֹּר עַד־מְאֹד וְלֹא־הִגִּידָה לּוֹ דָּבָר

future tense implies that he agree to her request because of her prophecy that they would marry after Nabal died. He also implied that he would not kill Nabal lest people think that the only reason he did so was to be able to marry the widow.

35. וַיִּקַּח דָּוִד מִיָּדָהּ אֵת אֲשֶׁר־הֵבִיאָה לוֹ — *David then accepted from her what she had brought to him.*

David's acceptance of this gift is halachically complicated. Generally speaking, a family's property is assumed to belong to the husband, especially if he is the chief breadwinner. Therefore, a wife requires her husband's permission to spend or give items away. Thus, the Talmud (*Bava Kamma* 119a) cautions charity collectors not to take sizable gifts from women without ascertaining that they have obtained their husbands' permission. Furthermore, the *Shulchan Aruch* (*Yoreh Deah* 248:4) rules that a woman may not give even a small amount to charity if her husband explicitly objects. In a case involving a known miser whose wife distributed money to the poor according to her own judgment, *Noda BiYehudah* (Vol. II, *Yoreh Deah* 158) ruled that she was guilty of theft and that it was forbidden to accept gifts from her.

How then did David have the right to take these items from Abigail, since she was acting against her husband's wishes? (We do not question Abigail's decision, which she apparently believed was necessary to save Nabal's life.)

It is not feasible to say that David considered Nabal's belongings as those of a rebel, and thus the property of the king — for once David decided not to kill Nabal, his property remained his own (see *Nachalas Shimon* 54:1).

Various solutions to this problem have been proposed, of which we cite four, the first three from *Noda BiYehudah.*

❒ David possibly believed that he deserved payment for guarding Nabal's sheep. This is a complicated halachic matter, beyond the scope of this work. See *Nachalas Shimon* 54.

❒ Possibly, Abigail's gift came solely from her own funds — either as an allotment from her husband, or because the principle that a husband controls his wife's property is a rabbinic decree that had not yet been enacted (see *Sefer Chassidim* 315).

❒ Although a miser, Nabal was generous to his wife and gave her a free hand to spend money as she wished.

❒ *Maharatz Chayes* (*Toras HaNeviim*, addendum 21) suggests that David had the right to take provisions for his men from Nabal because soldiers are permitted to forcibly provide for themselves during wartime.[1]

רְאִי שָׁמַעְתִּי בְקוֹלֵךְ וָאֶשָּׂא פָּנָיִךְ — *See, I have heeded your advice, and I shall show you grace.*

Our translation follows *Abarbanel,* who understands שָׁמַעְתִּי בְקוֹלֵךְ — *I have heeded your advice* — as being in the past tense, and וָאֶשָּׂא פָּנָיִךְ — *I shall show you grace [and fulfill your requests]* — in the future tense.

1. For more information on this topic, see *Nachalas Shimon* 20, 27 (footnote #12), 54.

by morning's light there would not have remained to Nabal as much as a dog."
35 *David then accepted from her what she had brought to him. He said to her, "Go up in peace to your house. See, I have heeded your advice, and I shall show you grace."*
36 *Abigail then came to Nabal and behold, he was having himself a feast in his house — a feast [fit] for the king. Nabal's heart was pleased about himself, and he was very drunk, so she did not tell him anything*

However, it would seem that the ו prefix with the *kametz* vowel should convert the word וָאֶשָּׂא to the past tense — *I have shown you grace* (as in *Genesis* 31:10).[1] If so, David implied that in Abigail's honor, he took the gift for himself and not for his attendants, as she had suggested (*Kli Yakar*).

According to *Metzudos*, David simply meant that he was honoring her by fulfilling her request not to kill Nabal.

Chomas Anach notes that the word וָאֶשָּׂא is related to נִישּׂוּאִין, *marriage*. Thus, David hinted that he would consent to Abigail's proposal and marry her.

☙ Nabal Dies and David Marries Abigail

36. וְהִנֵּה־לוֹ מִשְׁתֶּה — *And behold, he was having himself a feast in his house.*

The seemingly superfluous word לוֹ — *himself* — indicates that Nabal was rejoicing privately. He did not invite the poor to join him (*Kli Yakar*).

בְּבֵיתוֹ — *In his house.*

Nabal's home was in Maon, whereas the shearing took place in Carmel (v. 2). Thus, he either returned home to Maon for the feast, or he had a second house in Carmel (*Daas Sofrim*).

כְּמִשְׁתֵּה הַמֶּלֶךְ — *A feast [fit] for the king.*

Although miserly people generally spend sparingly even on themselves, Nabal seems to have been parsimonious solely with the poor (*Me'am Loez*). Nabal's feasting shows that his unwillingness to give David provisions was not due to a lack of funds (*Chomas Anach*).

וְהוּא שִׁכֹּר עַד מְאֹד — *And he was very drunk.*

Were it not for his drunkenness, Nabal would have been upset that other people were celebrating at his expense (*Chomas Anach*).

וְלֹא־הִגִּידָה לּוֹ דָּבָר — *So she did not tell him anything.*

Abigail did not want to disturb Nabal's joy. Additionally, she feared that if he heard about what had happened while he was intoxicated, he would react violently (*Abarbanel*).

Malbim adds that initially Abigail may have been concerned that Nabal would notice the absence of the items that she had taken to David; however, noticing that Nabal's table was fully laden with food, she decided that there was no reason to tell him now.

1. Had Scripture wanted to add the prefix ו for *and* while maintaining the future tense, it would have used the שְׁוָא vowel.

לז קָטֹן וְגָדוֹל עַד־אוֹר הַבֹּקֶר׃ וַיְהִי בַבֹּקֶר בְּצֵאת
הַיַּיִן מִנָּבָל וַתַּגֶּד־לוֹ אִשְׁתּוֹ אֶת־הַדְּבָרִים הָאֵלֶּה
לח וַיָּמָת לִבּוֹ בְּקִרְבּוֹ וְהוּא הָיָה לְאָבֶן׃ וַיְהִי כַּעֲשֶׂרֶת
לט הַיָּמִים וַיִּגֹּף יהוה אֶת־נָבָל וַיָּמֹת׃ וַיִּשְׁמַע דָּוִד

דָּבָר קָטֹן וְגָדוֹל — *Anything small or great.*

קָטֹן, *small,* refers to the gift that she gave David, whereas גָּדוֹל, *great,* is a reference to the fact that she had persuaded David not to kill Nabal (*Kli Yakar*).

37. וַתַּגֶּד־לוֹ אִשְׁתּוֹ — *His wife told him.*

The verb וַתַּגֶּד, *told,* often connotes harsh, stern words (see *Shabbos* 87a; *Rashi, Exodus* 19:3). Abigail used a brusque tone to relate frightening information (*Daas Sofrim*).

וַיָּמָת לִבּוֹ בְּקִרְבּוֹ וְהוּא הָיָה לְאָבֶן — *His heart died within him, and he was like a stone.*

Nabal was so distressed that he grew numb (*Abarbanel*).

Rashi states that Nabal was upset about the extravagant gift that Abigail had given David. *Ralbag* and *Abarbanel* explain that Nabal was also aggrieved over the possibility that David would still attack him.[1]

Rambam (*Moreh Nevuchim* Vol. 1, Ch. 42) derives from this verse that וַיָּמָת — *died* — may be used to connote a severe illness.

וְהוּא הָיָה לְאָבֶן — *And he was like a stone.*

It is not entirely clear whether the verse is stating that Nabal's heart was like a stone, or Nabal himself was like a stone.

Many commentators adapt the former view, and read the phrase וַיָּמָת לִבּוֹ בְּקִרְבּוֹ וְהוּא הָיָה לְאָבֶן as: *[Nabal's] heart died within him and was like stone.*

Be'er Moshe explains that a person's heart turns stone-like when his emotions are obstructed — often as a result of having sinned (*Yoma* 39a). (The Torah refers to this phenomenon in the verse, וּמַלְתֶּם אֵת עָרְלַת לְבַבְכֶם וְעָרְפְּכֶם לֹא תַקְשׁוּ עוֹד, *You shall cut away the barrier of your heart and no longer stiffen your neck* [*Deuteronomy* 10:16].)

Other commentators opine that if the verse meant to refer solely to Nabal's heart, it would have stated וַיְהִי לְאָבֶן. The addition of the word וְהוּא, *and he,* implies that it is speaking of Nabal himself. Either way, the implication is that Nabal was emotionally dulled.[2]

38. As Abigail had prophesied, Nabal died for his sins.

Tanna DeVei Eliyahu Zuta (Chapter 1) states that Nabal was punished for not having provided David with food, and concludes from this verse that a person who is able to give charity but does not do so brings death upon himself.

Tanna DeVei Eliyahu Rabbah (Ch. 18)

1. Why doesn't *Rashi* state that Abigail told Nabal that David had planned to kill him? Perhaps this would not have shocked Nabal, since she would also have told him that David had retracted his plans.

2. According to Kabbalistic tradition, a person who abuses the gift of speech is reincarnated as a stone, which is inanimate and speechless. Considering the previously mentioned tradition that Nabal was a reincarnation of Balaam, it would stand to reason that before his soul arrived in the world as Nabal, it was reincarnated as a stone in retribution for Balaam's curses.

Thus, Scripture's statement that Nabal's heart died within him means that he did not respond to Abigail with abusive words about David because הוּא הָיָה לְאָבֶן, *he had been a stone* — i.e., his soul remembered the punishment it had undergone for having previous engaged in the sin of abusive speech (*Likkutei Torah,* from the *Arizal*).

small or great until the morning's light. [37] *And it*
was in the morning, when Nabal had become sober,
his wife told him of these matters, his heart died
within him, and he was like a stone.
[38] *It happened after ten days that* HASHEM
struck Nabal and he died. [39] *When David heard*

tells that Nabal's sin consisted of offering David's men poisoned provisions[1] (which they refused to eat). For attempting to kill them — in particularly because they were Torah scholars — he lost his life.

וַיְהִי כַּעֲשֶׂרֶת הַיָּמִים — *It happened after ten days.*

Simply understood, Nabal suffered for ten days and then died.[2] The prefix כ in כַּעֲשֶׂרֶת does not imply *like* but rather *after*, as in כַּאֲשֶׁר, *when* (*Radak*).

However, the Sages offer three other explanations for these ten days.

❒ As is evident from the beginning of the chapter, Nabal rebuffed David's messengers immediately after Samuel's death (see comm. v. 1). Hashem waited seven days for the mourning period for Samuel to come to an end, so that it not coincide with the mourning period for the detestable Nabal. Finally, those seven days began a three-day period, which is the standard preface to a plague-type (מַגֵּפָה) death (*Midrash Shmuel*).

❒ These were the Ten Days of Repentance, from Rosh Hashanah through Yom Kippur. They afforded Nabal a final opportunity — but one that he rejected — to repent. Support for this idea may be found in the seemingly superfluous prefix ה — *the* — in כַּעֲשֶׂרֶת הַיָּמִים — *after the ten days* — i.e., a specific, well-known unit of ten days (*Maharsha*). *Radak* wonders how Nabal could be expected to repent, since he was emotionally numb.

In keeping with this view, *Rashi* (above, v. 8) comments that David's attendants came to Nabal on the day preceding Rosh Hashanah.

Others, however, translate כַּעֲשֶׂרֶת הַיָּמִים as *like the ten days.* Hashem gave Nabal a ten-day period in which to repent, similar to the annual ten-day period of repentance. (See *Midrash Shmuel*, *Radak* and, at length, *Daas Sofrim.*)

❒ Nabal was given an extra ten days of life as a reward for having served a meal to David's attendants (*Rosh Hashanah* ibid.). Although Scripture does not explicitly relate that Nabal fed them this meal, an allusion to this may be found in the word וַיָּנוּחוּ, *and they rested* (above, v. 9, see commentary; *Maharsha).*[3]

1. *Yeshuos Yaakov* comments that Nabal was a reincarnation of Laban. Just as Laban attempted to poison Eliezer, so did Nabal attempt to poison David's attendants.

2. *Sefer Chassidim* (#185) derives from this incident the ignominious nature of ingratitude. Shimei ben Gera committed a worse offense than did Nabal, yet he did not die (see *II Samuel* 16:5-13, 19:19-24). Nabal lost his life because he did not appreciate the favors that David had done for him, as is alluded to in the verse, מֵשִׁיב רָעָה תַּחַת טוֹבָה לֹא תָמוּשׁ רָעָה מִבֵּיתוֹ, *If a person repays good with evil, evil will not depart from his house* (*Proverbs* 17:13). The word תָמוּשׁ — *depart* — is written as תָמִישׁ, with a י. The י, which has the numerical value of 10, alludes to the ten days of respite that Nabal was granted.

3. *Me'am Loez* combines the latter two Midrashic versions with a homiletic approach. The Talmud (*Rosh Hashanah* 16b) relates that the Ten Days of Repentance are meant for the average person. Those who are righteous are sealed on Rosh Hashanah for life, whereas those who are wicked are sealed for death. Elsewhere, the Talmud (*Sanhedrin* 102b) classifies King Ahab as an average person. Although he was an idolater, half of his misdeeds were forgiven because he supported Torah scholars. Thus, Nabal's punishment too was ameliorated because he fed Torah scholars, and that moved the scale of judgment until he was considered "average," and earned him a ten-day opportunity to repent.

כִּֽי־מֵת נָבָל וַיֹּאמֶר בָּר֣וּךְ יְהֹוָ֡ה אֲשֶׁ֣ר רָב֩ אֶת־
רִ֨יב חֶרְפָּתִ֜י מִיַּ֣ד נָבָ֗ל וְאֶת־עַבְדּוֹ֙ חָשַׂ֣ךְ מֵֽרָעָ֔ה
וְאֵת֙ רָעַ֣ת נָבָ֔ל הֵשִׁ֥יב יְהֹוָ֖ה בְּרֹאשׁ֑וֹ וַיִּשְׁלַ֣ח
דָּוִד֙ וַיְדַבֵּ֣ר בַּאֲבִיגַ֔יִל לְקַחְתָּ֥הּ ל֖וֹ לְאִשָּֽׁה׃
מ וַיָּבֹ֜אוּ עַבְדֵ֥י דָוִ֛ד אֶל־אֲבִיגַ֖יִל הַכַּרְמֶ֑לָה וַיְדַבְּר֤וּ
אֵלֶ֙יהָ֙ לֵאמֹ֔ר דָּוִד֙ שְׁלָחָ֣נוּ אֵלַ֔יִךְ לְקַחְתֵּ֥ךְ ל֖וֹ
מא לְאִשָּֽׁה׃ וַתָּ֕קָם וַתִּשְׁתַּ֥חוּ אַפַּ֖יִם אָ֑רְצָה וַתֹּ֗אמֶר
הִנֵּ֤ה אֲמָֽתְךָ֙ לְשִׁפְחָ֔ה לִרְחֹ֕ץ רַגְלֵ֖י עַבְדֵ֥י אֲדֹנִֽי׃

39. וַיֹּאמֶר בָּרוּךְ ה׳ אֲשֶׁר רָב אֶת רִיב חֶרְפָּתִי — *He said, "Blessed is* Hashem*, Who has taken up the cause of my disgrace."*

Scripture presents two apparently contradictory views in regard to rejoicing over the fall of one's enemies. One verse in *Proverbs* states, בִּנְפֹל אוֹיִבְךָ אַל־תִּשְׂמָח, *When your foe falls, do not be glad* (24:16), yet another avers, וּבַאֲבֹד רְשָׁעִים רִנָּה, *and when the wicked perish, there is glad song* (11:10).

Tanna D'Vei Eliyahu Rabbah (Ch. 18) explains that a person should not rejoice when his "foe" is his Torah learning partner, whom he has bested in argument. However, if his enemy is a genuinely wicked man, upon that man's downfall he may rejoice and thank Hashem.

חֶרְפָּתִי — *My disgrace.*

Nabal shamed David when he stated, מִי דָוִד וּמִי בֶן־יִשָׁי הַיּוֹם רַבּוּ עֲבָדִים הַמִּתְפָּרְצִים, *Who is David and who is the son of Jesse? These days the rebellious servants have increased ...* (v. 10) (*Rashi, Radak*).

וְאֶת־עַבְדּוֹ חָשַׂךְ מֵרָעָה — *And has prevented his servant from wrongdoing.*

David thanked Hashem for having prevented him from killing Nabal (*Rashi*) — and, *Kli Yakar* adds, from committing adultery with Abigail.

וְאֵת רָעַת נָבָל הֵשִׁיב ה׳ בְּרֹאשׁוֹ — *And* Hashem *has returned Nabal's evil upon his head.*

Since David already mentioned the retribution that Nabal suffered, this phrase seems redundant.

Abarbanel explains that David was expressing his appreciation that Hashem had punished Nabal בְּרֹאשׁוֹ — *on his head* alone — without affecting his wife and property. David was especially appreciative of this, since he intended to marry Abigail and take possession of Nabal's belongings.

According to *Me'am Loez*, David mentioned Nabal's punishment twice in order to allude to Nabal's two sins: refusing to help the needy and rebelling against the king.

Malbim states that David was thanking Hashem for punishing Nabal for other iniquities that he had committed, so that David would not be considered the cause of his death — a fate to be avoided since, as the Talmud says, "Anyone whose fellow gets punished on his account is not allowed to enter into Hashem's domain" (*Shabbos* 149b). Nabal died not only because of the way he had treated David but because he was, in general, "shorthanded in mitzvos" (*Midrash Shocher Tov* 53:1). See above, v. 24.

וַיְדַבֵּר בַּאֲבִיגַיִל לְקַחְתָּהּ לוֹ לְאִשָּׁה — *And spoke regarding Abigail, to take her to himself as a wife.*

Our Sages enjoin a woman who has been widowed or divorced from remarrying for at least three months, in order

*that Nabal had died, he said, "Blessed is HASHEM,
Who has taken up the cause of my disgrace from
the hand of Nabal, and has prevented His servant
from wrongdoing; and HASHEM has returned Nabal's evil upon his head." Then David sent [agents]
and spoke regarding Abigail to take her to himself
as a wife.*

*40 David's servants came to Abigail to Carmel
and spoke to her saying, "David has sent us to you,
to take you for himself as a wife." 41 She arose and
prostrated herself to the ground and said, "Your
maidservant is merely a handmaid to wash the
feet of the servants of my lord."*

to avoid any ambiguity about the paternity of a child conceived at that general period (see *Yevamos* 41a).

Me'am Loez cites a Midrash stating that each word in the phrase, לְקַחְתָּהּ לוֹ לְאִשָּׁה — *to take her to himself as a wife,* begins with the letter ל — which has the numerical value of thirty, indicating thirty days. David waited three periods of thirty days each — i.e., a total of ninety days — before marrying Abigail.[1]

40. הַכַּרְמֶלָה — *To Carmel.*

Apparently, Nabal died in Carmel, where he had held his feast (and where his business was located), and Abigail remained there following his death (*Malbim;* see above, v. 36).

41. וַתָּקָם — *She arose.*

In a homiletic sense, Abigail was *elevated* from wife of the lowly Nabal to wife of King David (*Chomas Anach*).[2]

וַתִּשְׁתַּחוּ אַפַּיִם אָרְצָה — *And prostrated herself to the ground.*

Simply understood, Abigail bowed in respect for David and his emissaries.

Chomas Anach, however, suggests that she bowed down to Hashem in gratitude for His benevolence in arranging this marriage.

וַתֹּאמֶר הִנֵּה אֲמָתְךָ לְשִׁפְחָה — *And said, "Your maidservant is merely a handmaid ..."*

Abigail spoke to David's messengers as if she were speaking to David himself, in accordance with the principle that a person's agent is like himself (*Abarbanel*).

Kli Yakar adds an observation that explains why, particularly here, Abigail spoke to the emissaries this way. Generally, a matchmaker does not state that he is acting on behalf of the person whom he is recommending, so as to avoid embarrassment if his recommendation is rejected. However, in

1. Even though three months had passed since Nabal's death, there were still cynics who said that Nabal was the father of Abigail's first child. To discredit them, Hashem made the child look exactly like David. The child was named כִּלְאָב [Chileab], a contraction of כֻּלּוֹ אָב, *he is entirely like his father* (*Midrash Tanchuma, Toldos;* see also *Rashi, Genesis* 25:19).

2. This is similar to the Midrashic interpretation (*Bereishis Rabbah* 58:8) of the verse regarding the sale of the the Cave of Machpelah, in which וַיָּקָם שְׂדֵה עֶפְרוֹן ... לְאַבְרָהָם, *the field of Ephron was confirmed for Abraham as a purchase.* Literally, *was confirmed for* is *rose to* — i.e., when the property was transferred from Ephron to Abraham, it was spiritually *elevated.*

מב וַתְּמַהֵר וַתָּקָם אֲבִיגַיִל וַתִּרְכַּב עַל־הַחֲמוֹר וְחָמֵשׁ
נַעֲרֹתֶיהָ הַהֹלְכוֹת לְרַגְלָהּ וַתֵּלֶךְ אַחֲרֵי מַלְאֲכֵי דָוִד
מג וַתְּהִי־לוֹ לְאִשָּׁה׃ וְאֶת־אֲחִינֹעַם לָקַח דָּוִד מִיִּזְרְעֶאל
מד וַתִּהְיֶיןָ גַּם־שְׁתֵּיהֶן לוֹ לְנָשִׁים׃ וְשָׁאוּל נָתַן אֶת־
מִיכַל בִּתּוֹ אֵשֶׁת דָּוִד לְפַלְטִי בֶן־לַיִשׁ אֲשֶׁר מִגַּלִּים׃

this case David told his messengers to inform Abigail that he had sent them, because it was clear to him that since he was king Abigail would not refuse his offer.

וַתֹּאמֶר הִנֵּה אֲמָתְךָ לְשִׁפְחָה לִרְחֹץ רַגְלֵי עַבְדֵי אֲדֹנִי — *And said, "Your maidservant is merely a handmaid to wash the feet of the servants of my lord."*

Abigail replied that she regarded herself as fit only to be David's maidservant (*Metzudos*), after which she identified one of the roles of a maidservant as washing the feet of her master's servants. However, our Sages consider the act of washing a man's feet to be an intimate service to be performed only by his wife, not by a maidservant. Probably for this reason, *Ralbag* interprets Abigail's words as meaning that she did not deserve to be married to David, but at best to one of his servants, whose feet she would wash.

42. וַתְּמַהֵר — *Hurried...*

This phrase describes Abigail's zeal to fulfill the king's wishes.

וַתִּרְכַּב עַל־הַחֲמוֹר וְחָמֵשׁ נַעֲרֹתֶיהָ הַהֹלְכוֹת לְרַגְלָהּ וַתֵּלֶךְ אַחֲרֵי מַלְאֲכֵי דָוִד — *And mounted the donkey, her five maids accompanying her, and she followed David's messengers.*

This verse describes three instances of Abigail's exceptional modesty. First, she mounted the donkey on her own rather than with the aid of any men. Second, she traveled together with her maids so as not to be alone with David's men. And third, she rode behind the men — a virtuous practice commended by the Talmud (*Berachos* 61a).

הַהֹלְכוֹת לְרַגְלָהּ — *Accompanying her.*

Literally, לְרַגְלָהּ means *at her feet*, implying that the men rode behind her (*Metzudos*).

43. וַתִּהְיֶיןָ גַּם־שְׁתֵּיהֶן לוֹ לְנָשִׁים — *And they were, both of them, his wives.*

The apparently superfluous word גַּם, *both of them*, means that both women were David's wives in addition to Michal, his first wife (*Metzudos*). Furthermore, "in addition to" implies that David cherished Michal more than these two women (*Kli Yakar*).

Although Scripture does not describe Ahinoam's nature, the word גַּם, *both of them*, implies that she was, like Abigail, a noble woman (*Kli Yakar*).

The information here leads to the next verse, indicating that Abigail and Ahinoam remained David's wives, in contrast to Michal, who Saul gave away to another man (*Radak*).

44. וְשָׁאוּל נָתַן אֶת־מִיכַל בִּתּוֹ ... — *Saul had given his daughter Michal ...*

Saul was offended by David's two additional marriages, considering them an affront to the honor due his daughter, who was a princess (*Malbim*).

וְשָׁאוּל נָתַן אֶת־מִיכַל בִּתּוֹ אֵשֶׁת דָּוִד לְפַלְטִי בֶן־לַיִשׁ אֲשֶׁר מִגַּלִּים — *Saul had given his daughter Michal, David's wife, to Palti, son of Laish of Gallim.*

This incident, in which Saul retrieved his daughter Michal from David and offered her to another man is one of the most perplexing events recorded in *Tanach*, involving many complicated halachic issues beyond the scope of this work. The reader is urged to study some of the original Talmudic texts and *Nachalas Shimon's* in-depth study treating Merav and Michal (Chapters 34-38).

[42] *Abigail then hurried, arose and mounted the*
donkey, her five maids accompanying her, and she
followed David's messengers and became his wife.
[43] *David also married Ahinoam of Jezreel, and they*
were, both of them, his wives. [44] *Saul had given*
his daughter Michal, David's wife, to Palti, son of
Laish of Gallim.

Saul had promised wealth and the hand of his daughter in marriage to whoever would defeat Goliath (17:25). After David did so, Saul was about to give his daughter Merav to him but she married Adriel instead (see 18:17,18). Later on, Saul promised David his other daughter Michal if David brought a hundred foreskins of Philistine men. David did so — in fact, he brought back twice that number — and married Michal (see ibid. vs. 25-27). Later on, when Saul turned against David, she helped him escape (see Ch. 19), and since then, David had been roaming the country as a fugitive — during which time Michal was taken away from him, apparently without a divorce, and given to another man.

The following chapters of *Samuel* describe how, after David became king, recognized only by his own tribe of Judah, Saul died, following which Saul's son Ish-bosheth offered David peace terms. David agreed to consider them on condition that his wife Michal be returned to him, and Ish-bosheth complied. As Michal traveled to David, her interim husband Palti (there called Paltiel) escorted her for part of the way weeping until he was told to turn back; and Michal thereafter remained with David (*II Samuel* 3:16).

This series of events raises many questions, principally:

❒ How could Saul have sent a married woman to live with another man without first procuring a *get*, a contract of divorce?

❒ How could Palti and Michal — two exceptionally righteous people — have lived together under such circumstances?

❒ If they were living together in sin, how could David have taken Michal back as his wife? A married woman who commits adultery is forbidden both to the adulterer and to her husband. And even if we posit that Michal had obtained a *get* from David, a woman who has been divorced and remarried can never return to her first husband (see *Deuteronomy* 24:4).

Having mentioned some of the questions, we now present a variety of explanations.

❒ According to the Talmud (*Sanhedrin* 19b), Saul and David had a halachic disagreement regarding the validity of David's betrothal to Michal. The Torah requires a man to perform a legally binding acquisition to marry a woman; usually, he gives her an item of value. David implied that he had acquired Michal with a hundred Philistine foreskins (*II Samuel* 3:14). Did these really have intrinsic value? Or did David give her something else to betroth her?

Saul felt that the foreskins had no monetary value and therefore Michal was not legally bound to David, whereas David contended that the foreskins had worth because they could be fed to dogs and cats.[1]

Because Saul considered Michal to be unmarried, he had no hesitation in giving her to Palti. David, however, believed her to be his wife.

1. The Talmud mentions an alternative, more complicated version of their argument, also pertaining to the method of betrothal.

א וַיָּבֹאוּ הַזִּפִים אֶל־שָׁאוּל הַגִּבְעָתָה לֵאמֹר
הֲלוֹא דָוִד מִסְתַּתֵּר בְּגִבְעַת הַחֲכִילָה עַל
ב פְּנֵי הַיְשִׁימֹן: וַיָּקָם שָׁאוּל וַיֵּרֶד אֶל־מִדְבַּר־
זִיף וְאִתּוֹ שְׁלֹשֶׁת־אֲלָפִים אִישׁ בְּחוּרֵי יִשְׂרָאֵל

As for Palti, in order to honor Saul he presented the appearance of being married to Michal. Yet at the same time, he considered the possibility that David was right. Accordingly, the Talmud states, he placed a sword in his bed that separated him from Michal and said, "Whoever tries to engage in the marital act shall be stabbed by this sword," and he lived with Michal for years without touching her. The Sages laud Palti for his extraordinary self-control, which they consider to be even greater than that demonstrated by Joseph (with Potiphar's wife) and Boaz (with Ruth). For this reason, he is called Paltiel (*II Samuel*), meaning, *God has saved him [from sin]* (*Vayikra Rabbah* 23:10). The Talmud states that when Paltiel wept while escorting Michal back to David, he was regretting the loss of opportunity to continue performing this mitzvah of self-restraint.

Be'er Moshe suggests that Michal and Palti were afraid that if Palti would refuse, a less scrupulous person would accept Saul's offer.

Be'er Moshe also cites a comment by *Rama MiPano* in *Gilgulei Neshamos* that although Palti reached an astounding level of purity he still enjoyed the forbidden pleasure of gazing at Michal, and consequently was reincarnated as Rabbi Masia ben Cheresh. The Midrash (*Yalkut Shimoni, Vayechi* 161) relates that R' Masia was an exceptionally pure person who never laid eyes on a woman. One time Satan tried to seduce him by appearing as a beautiful woman who stood in his line of sight wherever he looked. When R' Masia realized that he could not turn his eyes aside from her, he blinded himself, an act that stunned Satan himself. Hashem then sent Raphael to heal R' Masia, but he refused until Hashem promised that the evil inclination would no longer bother him. Thus, in the body of R' Masia, Palti's soul achieved an even higher level of purity and corrected the damage he had caused when he had looked at Michal.

It is now clear why David took Michal back. As he saw it, his original betrothal of her had been valid, and Paltiel had never touched her. But how did David know that Palti and Michal had not lived together? *Ralbag* states that this was public knowledge; *Teshuvos HaRashba* (#10) suggests that he was informed of this by a prophet.

Radak, however, suggests that Saul, upset that his daughter Michal was left alone, insisted that David give her a *get*, after which Saul arranged her marriage to Palti. However, David's *get* was not valid, for one of three possible reasons.

(a) David had been coerced into giving it, which invalidated it (*Gittin* 88b).

(b) David explicitly stated that he was being forced into sending Michal the *get* and did not mean to divorce her.

(c) After sending an emissary to Michal with the *get*, David disqualified it (see *Gittin* 32a). According to this third explanation, although Michal remained married to David, neither she nor Palti were aware of the fact. Accordingly, although they cohabited, that did not disqualify her from returning to David, for it was not considered an act of intentional adultery.

Abarbanel, however, finds it difficult to believe that David gave Michal a *get*, since there is no allusion to this in the text. Also, whether it was legally acceptable or not, David would not have taken Michal back after she had lived together with Palti as his wife.

Therefore, *Abarbanel* proposes a novel approach. Nowhere does the verse state that Michal had been given to Palti *as a wife*. Rather, to keep Michal from engaging in lewd behavior, growing

[1] The Ziphites came to Saul at Gibeah, saying, "Is David not hiding himself in Hachilah Hill, which faces Jeshimon?" [2] So Saul
arose and went down to the Wilderness of
Ziph, with three thousand choice men of Israel,

depressed, or running away to David, Saul appointed Palti as her guardian. (He also sent her the children of her sister Merav to keep her busy so that she should not get depressed [see *II Samuel* 21:8, *Sanhedrin* 19b].)

Accordingly, David had no hesitation in taking her back. Although Scripture refers to Paltiel as אִישָׁהּ (*II Samuel* 3:16), which usually means *her husband*, in this case the word means *her man*.

Understandably, some commentators — notably, *Kli Yakar* and *Chomas Anach* — reject any such historical hypotheses that differ from the words of our Sages, "from whose words we drink."

XXVI

◆§ The Ziphites Again Betray David

1. וַיָּבֹאוּ הַזִּפִים אֶל־שָׁאוּל הַגִּבְעָתָה לֵאמֹר הֲלוֹא דָוִד מִסְתַּתֵּר ... — *The Ziphites came to Saul at Gibeah, saying, "Is David not hiding himself..."*

The Ziphites had similarly betrayed David once before (above, 23:19). At that time, Saul would have captured David had God not intervened and sent him a dire warning about an impending Philistine attack. Later, after David spared Saul's life in the cave (Ch. 24), Saul apologized for having persecuted David and committed himself to do so no more. What then prompted the Ziphites to think that they could instigate Saul to pursue David yet again?

According to *Kli Yakar*, the fact that David remained in hiding even though Saul had pledged himself to peace indicated — so the Ziphites told Saul — that David was preparing to attack him.

Chomas Anach states that, unsure of Saul's reaction to the idea of reneging on his pact, the Ziphites did not offer to help him capture David, as they had previously, but merely told him where David was hiding. If Saul responded to their implicit betrayal with indignation, they would backtrack and explain that they meant only to notify him that David was preparing to ambush the Philistines (*Chomas Anach*).

Me'am Loez suggests that the proximate cause of the Ziphites' new betrayal was the death of Samuel. Previously, the Ziphites argued, Samuel's merit had protected David. This time, with Samuel gone, David would fall easily to Saul.

What was the Ziphites' motive in seeking David's ruin? Initially, they may have feared that if they concealed David, Saul would massacre them, as he had the inhabitants of Nob. Now, however, that Saul and David had come to terms, that was no longer a concern, and their incitement could only be malicious. Thus, in *Psalm* 54, David denounced them as malevolent "strangers who have risen against me" (v. 5).

How may we know that *Psalm* 54 refers to this episode and not to the Ziphites' first denunciation of David? The answer is implicit in the language of the psalm's opening verse.

The first time that the Ziphites had informed on David, Scripture states: וַיַּעֲלוּ זִפִים, *Ziphites went up*. The present verse, on the other hand, states, וַיָּבֹאוּ הַזִּפִים, *the Ziphites came*. *Psalm* 54 mirrors that latter expression, opening with the words, בְּבוֹא הַזִּיפִים וַיֹּאמְרוּ לְשָׁאוּל הֲלֹא דָוִד מִסְתַּתֵּר עִמָּנוּ — *When the Ziphites came and said to Saul, "Is David not hiding among us?"* (v. 2) (*Kli Yakar*).

2. אִישׁ בְּחוּרֵי יִשְׂרָאֵל — *Choice men of Israel.*

Had the word בְּחוּרֵי been vowelized with a פַּתָח as בַּחוּרֵי, it would have meant *young men* (as in *Ezekiel* 23:6,

ג לְבַקֵּשׁ אֶת־דָּוִד בְּמִדְבַּר־זִיף׃ וַיִּחַן שָׁאוּל בְּגִבְעַת
הַחֲכִילָה אֲשֶׁר עַל־פְּנֵי הַיְשִׁימֹן עַל־הַדָּרֶךְ וְדָוִד
יֹשֵׁב בַּמִּדְבָּר וַיַּרְא כִּי בָא שָׁאוּל אַחֲרָיו הַמִּדְבָּרָה׃
ד וַיִּשְׁלַח דָּוִד מְרַגְּלִים וַיֵּדַע כִּי־בָא שָׁאוּל אֶל־
ה נָכוֹן׃ וַיָּקָם דָּוִד וַיָּבֹא אֶל־הַמָּקוֹם אֲשֶׁר חָנָה־שָׁם
שָׁאוּל וַיַּרְא דָּוִד אֶת־הַמָּקוֹם אֲשֶׁר שָׁכַב־שָׁם
שָׁאוּל וְאַבְנֵר בֶּן־נֵר שַׂר־צְבָאוֹ וְשָׁאוּל שֹׁכֵב
ו בַּמַּעְגָּל וְהָעָם חֹנִים °סביבתו׃ וַיַּעַן דָּוִד וַיֹּאמֶר | °סְבִיבֹתָיו ק׳
אֶל־אֲחִימֶלֶךְ הַחִתִּי וְאֶל־אֲבִישַׁי בֶּן־צְרוּיָה
אֲחִי יוֹאָב לֵאמֹר מִי־יֵרֵד אִתִּי אֶל־שָׁאוּל אֶל־
ז הַמַּחֲנֶה וַיֹּאמֶר אֲבִישַׁי אֲנִי אֵרֵד עִמָּךְ׃ וַיָּבֹא
דָוִד וַאֲבִישַׁי | אֶל־הָעָם לַיְלָה וְהִנֵּה שָׁאוּל שֹׁכֵב
יָשֵׁן בַּמַּעְגָּל וַחֲנִיתוֹ מְעוּכָה־בָאָרֶץ °מראשתו °מְרַאֲשֹׁתָיו ק׳

בַּחוּרֵי חֶמֶד — *pleasant young men*). Since it is vowelized with a שְׁוָא, its root is בָּחַר — *chose* — and it means *choice men* (*Malbim*).

David's Restrained Preemptive Strike

4. Although the previous verse related that David *saw that Saul was coming after him,* he sent men to ascertain Saul's identity.

According to *Kli Yakar*, David knew that the camp was that of Saul but he found it hard to believe that after he and Saul had made peace, the king *himself* would come to attack him.

Alternatively, David wished to determine whether Saul was anxious and apprehensive, or confident that David would flee from him. His inquiry indicated that Saul was coming אֶל־נָכוֹן — which may be translated as *confidently*.

אֶל־נָכוֹן — *Indeed.*

Our translation follows *Targum*. Possibly, however, נָכוֹן is a place-name; hence, David discovered that Saul had come to the district called *Nachon* (*Kli Yakar*).

5. וַיָּקָם דָּוִד וַיָּבֹא אֶל־הַמָּקוֹם אֲשֶׁר חָנָה־שָׁם שָׁאוּל — *David then arose and came to the place where Saul was encamped.*

David must have learned through Divine Inspiration that he would be successful, for he would otherwise not have taken such a risky step (*Daas Sofrim*).

וְשָׁאוּל שֹׁכֵב בַּמַּעְגָּל — *Saul lay within the circle.*

A camp of soldiers was commonly referred to as a *circle*, since they formed a circle for any one of several reasons: to protect their commander (*Abarbanel*), to see in all directions (*Ralbag*), or to prevent desertion (*Mahari Kara*).

וְשָׁאוּל שֹׁכֵב בַּמַּעְגָּל וְהָעָם חֹנִים סְבִיבֹתָיו — *Saul lay within the circle, with the people encamped all around him.*

Whereas Saul and Abner were lying down, the soldiers were only *encamped* — i.e., they stood on guard (*Malbim*, *Me'am Loez*).

6. אֲבִישַׁי בֶּן־צְרוּיָה אֲחִי יוֹאָב — *Abishai son of Zeruiah, Joab's brother.*

Abishai was David's nephew, the son of David's sister, Zeruiah.

He was a mighty warrior and a highly

to search for David in the Wilderness of Ziph. 3 Saul
encamped at Hachilah Hill, which faces Jeshimon,
beside the road. David was staying in the wilder-
ness, and he saw that Saul was coming after him,
toward the wilderness. 4 David sent out scouts and
ascertained that Saul was indeed coming.
5 David then arose and came to the place
where Saul was encamped. David saw the place
where Saul and Abner, the commander of his
army, lay; Saul lay within the circle, with the
people encamped all around him. 6 David spoke
up and said to Ahimelech the Hittite and Abi-
shai son of Zeruiah, Joab's brother, saying, "Who
will go down with me to Saul, to the camp?"
And Abishai said, "I will go down with you."
7 So David and Abishai came to the people at
night, and behold, Saul lay asleep in the circle,
his spear plunged into the ground by his head,

accomplished Torah scholar — who, our Sages state, was equal to the greater part of the Sanhedrin (*Berachos* 62b).

מִי־יֵרֵד אִתִּי אֶל־שָׁאוּל אֶל־הַמַּחֲנֶה — *Who will go down with me to Saul, to the camp?*

David disdained to refer to Saul as "king," because Saul had violated his oath to no longer pursue David (*Chomas Anach*).

וַיֹּאמֶר אֲבִישַׁי אֲנִי אֵרֵד עִמָּךְ — *Abishai said, "I will go down with you."*

Either David desired only one attendant and Abishai responded first, or else Ahimelech was afraid to join this venture (*Abarbanel*).

7. וַיָּבֹא דָוִד וַאֲבִישַׁי — *So David and Abishai came.*

The word וַיָּבֹא — *came* — is written in the singular, to connote that they came separately, so as not to arouse attention (*Kli Yakar*).

אֶל־הָעָם — *To the people.*

In the previous verse, Saul's men were referred to as a *camp*, one of whose attributes is that it is guarded. Here, Scripture calls them *the people* because, since they had all fallen asleep, they could no longer be characterized as a camp (*Malbim*).

Alternatively, the phrase אֶל־הָעָם, *to the people*, implies that David and Abishai infiltrated Saul's camp as if they were his soldiers (*Kli Yakar*).

וְהִנֵּה שָׁאוּל שֹׁכֵב יָשֵׁן — *And behold, Saul lay asleep.*

The word, הִנֵּה, *behold*, implies something sudden. Apparently, Saul had been lying down — but awake — when he suddenly fell into a deep sleep (*Kli Yakar*).

וַחֲנִיתוֹ מְעוּכָה־בָאָרֶץ — *His spear plunged into the ground.*

The spear was plunged so deeply that normally no one could have removed it without attracting notice, but since all the soldiers had fallen into a deep sleep, David was able to seize it inconspicuously (*Kli Yakar*).

°סְבִיבֹתָיו ק׳

ח וְאַבְנֵר וְהָעָם שֹׁכְבִים °סביבתו: וַיֹּאמֶר
אֲבִישַׁי אֶל־דָּוִד סִגַּר אֱלֹהִים הַיּוֹם אֶת־אוֹיִבְךָ
בְּיָדֶךָ וְעַתָּה אַכֶּנּוּ נָא בַּחֲנִית וּבָאָרֶץ פַּעַם
ט אַחַת וְלֹא אֶשְׁנֶה לוֹ: וַיֹּאמֶר דָּוִד אֶל־אֲבִישַׁי
אַל־תַּשְׁחִיתֵהוּ כִּי מִי שָׁלַח יָדוֹ בִּמְשִׁיחַ יְהוָה
י וְנִקָּה: וַיֹּאמֶר דָּוִד חַי־יְהוָה כִּי אִם־יְהוָה יִגָּפֶנּוּ
אוֹ־יוֹמוֹ יָבוֹא וָמֵת אוֹ בַמִּלְחָמָה יֵרֵד וְנִסְפָּה:

Daas Sofrim comments that David located Saul when he saw the royal spear, which never left Saul's side.

וְאַבְנֵר וְהָעָם שֹׁכְבִים סְבִיבֹתָיו — *And Abner and the people lay all around him.*

Scripture does not say that they were lying *asleep*, as it says of Saul. They had been awake until they, too, were suddenly plunged into a deep sleep (*Kli Yakar*).

8. וַיֹּאמֶר אֲבִישַׁי אֶל־דָּוִד סִגַּר אֱלֹהִים הַיּוֹם אֶת־אוֹיִבְךָ בְּיָדֶךָ — *Abishai said to David, "God has delivered your enemy into your hand this day."*

Abishai interpreted the fact that all the men were asleep as a sign that he and David should kill Saul (*Malbim*).

Abishai assumed that David wanted to kill Saul (*Abarbanel*). Although previously (above, 24:5-7) David had chosen not to do so, now that Saul had continued to pursue David even after acknowledging his blamelessness, David might have decided to have Saul executed as a *pursuer* (*Kli Yakar*).

פַּעַם אַחַת וְלֹא אֶשְׁנֶה לוֹ — *With a single thrust — I will not need to [to strike] a second time!*

David need not worry that Saul would awaken and scream, because Abishai would kill him with the first blow (*Malbim*).

9. Although Saul was a *pursuer*, who is as a rule subject to the death penalty, it was forbidden to lay one's hands on him since he was Hashem's *anointed one* (*Malbim*; see below, v. 11). Only Hashem, Who appointed him, had a right to remove him (*Daas Sofrim*).

According to *Kli Yakar*, David was referring here to his own destiny. He understood that because he had ripped Saul's garment, he would be punished (*Kli Yakar*; see *Berachos* 62b).

10. וַיֹּאמֶר דָּוִד... — *David said...*

Although Scripture already established in the previous verse that David was speaking, this verse repeats the words וַיֹּאמֶר דָּוִד, *David said*. Apparently, Abishai was not convinced by David's first warning, and so David spoke again.

Furthermore, David's first words could be construed as meaning that as a commoner Abishai should not harm Saul, but that as presumptive king David had a right to do so. When Abishai expressed this view, David replied that that was not the case (*Abarbanel, Kli Yakar*; see below, *Yefeh Anaf*).

חַי־ה׳... — *As* Hashem *lives...*

This phrase generally signifies an oath. However, that is not pertinent to David's following words, which listed possible ways in which God might cause Saul to die (*Maharzu* to *Vayikra Rabbah* 23:11). Thus, the Sages explain that David was vowing that he himself would not put Saul to death.

According to the Midrash, the redundant use of the phrase, וַיֹּאמֶר דָּוִד, *David said*, indicates that David was addressing his own conscience and not Abishai. David felt tempted to kill Saul, and to restrain himself took an oath not to do so. The Midrash commends such an approach to conquering

and Abner and the people lay all around him!
[8] *Abishai said to David, "God has delivered your*
enemy into your hand this day! Now let me strike
him with the spear, [driving it] into the ground
with a single thrust — I will not need [to strike]
a second time!" [9] *But David said to Abishai, "Do*
not destroy him, for who can send forth his hand
against the anointed one of HASHEM *and be ab-*
solved?" [10] *David said, "As* HASHEM *lives,* HASHEM
will strike him with illness, or his day will come
and he will die, or he will go into battle and perish.

one's impulses, and lists other righteous men who used this technique, such as Abraham, Joseph, Boaz, and Elisha (*Yalkut Shimoni* 137, citing *Sifrei; Vayikra Rabbah* ibid.; *Yefeh Anaf* to *Ruth Rabbah* 6:4; see above).

Another Midrash states that David directed his oath to Abishai, stating that if Abishai killed Saul, David would kill him in turn (*Vayikra Rabbah* ibid., *Ruth Rabbah* ibid.). Accordingly, David mentioned Hashem's Name twice — חַי־ה׳ כִּי אִם־ה׳ יִגָּפֶנּוּ — *as* HASHEM *lives,* HASHEM *will strike him* — to connote a twofold oath: first, Abishai may not kill Saul; and second, if he does, David will kill Abishai (*Midrash Shocher Tov* 58:1).

חַי־ה׳ כִּי אִם־ה׳ יִגָּפֶנּוּ אוֹ־יוֹמוֹ יָבוֹא... — *As* HASHEM *lives,* HASHEM *will strike him with illness, or his day will come...*

David told Abishai that there was no reason to kill Saul, since he would meet his demise in the near future anyway. David knew this either because Samuel had told him so, or because he realized that since Hashem had rejected Saul as king and chosen David to succeed him, this transition must be imminent (*Radak*).

According to *Malbim,* David saw that Abishai wanted to kill Saul in order to realize Hashem's desire that David become king. David assured him that Hashem's word would be realized without Abishai's intervention.

כִּי אִם־ה׳ יִגָּפֶנּוּ אוֹ־יוֹמוֹ יָבוֹא וָמֵת אוֹ בַמִּלְחָמָה יֵרֵד וְנִסְפָּה — HASHEM *will strike him with illness, or his day will come and he will die, or he will go into battle and perish.*

Either Saul's preordained life span would soon end and he would die a natural death, or else his sins would cause him to die prematurely, through disease or in battle — the latter if he had committed a particularly egregious sin (*Radak*).[1]

According to *Ralbag,* if Saul endangered himself by entering into battle, he might bring death upon himself even if it had not been previously decreed from heaven. As our Sages teach, the Satan takes advantage of a person's vulnerability to indict him (*Bereishis Rabbah* 91:9, *Shabbos* 32a).

כִּי אִם־ה׳ יִגָּפֶנּוּ — HASHEM *will strike him with illness.*

Although the four-letter Name of Hashem represents His Attribute of Mercy, a person's sins can induce even that attribute to effectuate strict judgment (*Chomas Anach*).

כִּי אִם־ה׳ יִגָּפֶנּוּ אוֹ יוֹמוֹ יָבוֹא וָמֵת אוֹ בַמִּלְחָמָה יֵרֵד וְנִסְפָּה — HASHEM *will strike him with illness, or his day will come and*

1. A discussion regarding man's allotment of days, its decrease because of sin, and a disagreement about a possible increase because of merit, may be found in the Talmud in *Yevamos* 49b.

°מְרַאֲשֹׁתָיו ק׳

יא חָלִ֣ילָה לִּ֗י מֵֽיהוָ֔ה מִשְּׁלֹ֥חַ יָדִ֖י בִּמְשִׁ֣יחַ יְהוָ֑ה
וְעַתָּ֗ה קַח־נָ֨א אֶת־הַחֲנִ֜ית אֲשֶׁ֤ר °מראשתו
יב וְאֶת־צַפַּ֥חַת הַמַּ֖יִם וְנֵ֥לְכָה לָּֽנוּ׃ וַיִּקַּ֨ח דָּוִ֜ד אֶת־
הַחֲנִ֗ית וְאֶת־צַפַּ֣חַת הַמַּ֔יִם מֵרַאֲשֹׁתֵ֖י שָׁא֑וּל
וַיֵּלְכ֣וּ לָהֶ֑ם וְאֵ֨ין רֹאֶ֜ה וְאֵ֤ין יוֹדֵ֙עַ֙ וְאֵ֣ין מֵקִ֔יץ כִּ֤י
כֻלָּם֙ יְשֵׁנִ֔ים כִּ֚י תַּרְדֵּמַ֣ת יְהוָ֔ה נָפְלָ֖ה עֲלֵיהֶֽם׃

he will die, or he will go into battle and perish.

According to the simple meaning of the text, David intended only to predict Saul's inevitable demise.

However, a Midrash states that David cursed Saul to suffer these tribulations. Thus, when David introduced *Psalm* 7 with the words, שִׁגָּיוֹן לְדָוִד, *An error to David* (*Psalms* 7:1), he was pleading with Hashem to consider his utterance here not a deliberate sin but a mere error (*Midrash Shocher Tov* 7:18).

At any rate, the three possibilities that David mentioned eventually befell Saul (ibid. 7:2). (1) יוֹמוֹ יָבוֹא — *his day will come.* Saul's death came in its time. (2) בַּמִּלְחָמָה יֵרֵד וְנִסְפָּה — *he will go forth into battle and perish.* Saul was killed at war. And (3) ה׳ יִגָּפֶנּוּ — *HASHEM will strike him with illness.* Before Saul died on the battlefield, he complained (*II Samuel* 1:9), אֲחָזַנִי הַשָּׁבָץ, *the throes of death have gripped me* (*Kli Yakar*).

When David sought atonement for the sin of taking a census improperly (*II Samuel*, Ch. 24), Hashem gave him a choice of three punishments — these corresponded to the three judgments that he had decreed upon Saul (*Midrash Shocher Tov* 17:4).

11. חָלִילָה לִי מֵה׳ מִשְּׁלֹחַ יָדִי בִּמְשִׁיחַ ה׳ — *It would be sacrilegious before HASHEM for me to send forth my hand against HASHEM's anointed one.*

David repeated his oath not to kill Saul with the words, חָלִילָה לִי מֵה׳ — *"It would be sacrilegious before HASHEM for me...."* This was to prevent himself from killing Saul on the grounds that Saul was a *pursuer* (which he would be justified in doing) (*Bamidbar Rabbah* 15:16, *Matnos Kehunah* ad loc.).

Homiletically, David stated that he had learned to avoid harming the king מִשְּׁלֹחַ יָדִי בִּמְשִׁיחַ ה׳ — *from [the last time] that I sent forth my hand against HASHEM's anointed one.* That is to say, David expressed his regret at having cut Saul's garment (above, Ch. 24), and he resolved never to do such a thing again (*Kli Yakar*).

וְעַתָּה קַח־נָא אֶת־הַחֲנִית אֲשֶׁר מְרַאֲשֹׁתָיו וְאֶת־צַפַּחַת הַמַּיִם וְנֵלְכָה לָּנוּ — *Now, please take the spear that is near Saul's head and the flask of water, and let us go.*

The phrases *now* and *let us go* connote that David wanted to leave hastily so that he would not be tempted to change his mind and harm Saul (*Kli Yakar*).

קַח־נָא אֶת־הַחֲנִית אֲשֶׁר מְרַאֲשֹׁתָיו וְאֶת־צַפַּחַת הַמַּיִם — *Please take the spear that is near Saul's head and the flask of water.*

With this, David explained to Abishai that he could not justify killing Saul, since he could as fully accomplish his goal of protecting himself by taking the spear and water (*Malbim*).

Alternatively, David calculated that although he would save his own life by killing Saul, he would thereby endanger the lives of all the Jews, since the surrounding gentile nations would take advantage of a people left without a ruler to protect them (*Sefer Chassidim* 45; see above, 24:5).

12. וַיִּקַּח דָּוִד אֶת־הַחֲנִית — *So David took the spear.*

Initially, David told Abishai to take

26/11-12

[11] *It would be sacrilegious before* HASHEM *for me to send forth my hand against* HASHEM*'s anointed one. Now, please take the spear that is near Saul's head and the flask of water, and let us go."*

[12] *So David took the spear and the flask of water from near Saul's head and they left. No one saw, no one knew, and no one awoke, for they were all asleep, for a deep sleep from* HASHEM *had fallen upon them.*

Saul's spear and water flask. But he changed his mind, afraid that Abishai would harm Saul. Therefore, as described here, he did so himself (*Radak*).

According to *Abarbanel*, when David told Abishai that he did not have permission to kill Saul, Abishai refused to go.

וַיִּקַּח דָּוִד אֶת־הַחֲנִית וְאֶת־צַפַּחַת הַמַּיִם — *So David took the spear and the flask of water.*

By taking Saul's spear and water, David symbolically demonstrated that Saul's end was near: his weapons would no longer protect him and his supplies would dwindle (*Chomas Anach*).

וְאֵין רֹאֶה וְאֵין יוֹדֵעַ וְאֵין מֵקִיץ — *No one saw, no one knew, and no one awoke.*

אֵין רֹאֶה — *no one saw.* No one was awake to see.

אֵין יוֹדֵעַ — *no one knew.* No one sensed — in particular, heard (*Metzudos*).

And אֵין מֵקִיץ — *and no one awoke.* Saul and his men were sleeping so soundly that none of them were awakened by the movement and conversation of David and Avishai (*Radak*).

כִּי תַּרְדֵּמַת ה׳ נָפְלָה עֲלֵיהֶם — *For a deep sleep from* HASHEM *had fallen upon them.*

It was Divinely ordained that Saul and his men should not awaken (*Abarbanel*).

Alternatively, this phrase simply means, *a profoundly deep sleep,* for Hashem's Name is at times used to indicate a superlative. (Similarly, we find phrases such as צִדְקָתְךָ כְּהַרְרֵי־אֵל, *Your righteousness is like the mighty mountains* — lit., *Your righteousness is like the mountains of God* [*Psalms* 36:7], and וְנִינְוֵה הָיְתָה עִיר־גְּדוֹלָה לֵאלֹהִים — *Nineveh was an enormously great city* — lit., *Nineveh was a city great to God* [*Jonah* 3:3; *Radak*].)

The Midrash states that there are three types of תַּרְדֵּמָה: *a deep sleep,* as Adam experienced (*Genesis* 2:21); prophecy, as Abraham experienced (ibid. 15:12); and a sleep that resembles death, as described here (*Bereishis Rabbah* 17:15). The Midrash refers to the sleep in this verse as מַרְמִיטָה, which *Maharzu* interprets as a state similar to death (see also *Yedei Moshe*).[1]

1. Above (24:4), we cited a Midrash regarding David's questioning the need for spiders and madmen.

An alternative version of that Midrash (cited in *Otzar HaMidrashim* I, p. 47) also refers to the flea. According to that, David once saw a flea attacking a spider, and then watched as a madman chased both of them away with a stick. Following that, he asked God the purpose of these three creatures. We told earlier how God taught David the purpose of spiders and madmen.

Regarding the flea, the Midrash relates that during this episode Abner was lying asleep with his knees bent and raised, protecting Saul. David slipped beneath Abner's knees and grabbed the spear and jug when suddenly Abner stretched his legs out flat, trapping David beneath them. David silently prayed to Hashem, whereupon Hashem sent a flea, which bit Abner's leg. Abner raised his legs and David was able to escape.

יג וַיַּעֲבֹר דָּוִד הָעֵבֶר וַיַּעֲמֹד עַל־רֹאשׁ־הָהָר מֵרָחֹק
יד רַב הַמָּקוֹם בֵּינֵיהֶם: וַיִּקְרָא דָוִד אֶל־הָעָם וְאֶל־
אַבְנֵר בֶּן־נֵר לֵאמֹר הֲלוֹא תַעֲנֶה אַבְנֵר וַיַּעַן
טו אַבְנֵר וַיֹּאמֶר מִי אַתָּה קָרָאתָ אֶל־הַמֶּלֶךְ: וַיֹּאמֶר
דָּוִד אֶל־אַבְנֵר הֲלוֹא־אִישׁ אַתָּה וּמִי כָמוֹךָ
בְּיִשְׂרָאֵל וְלָמָּה לֹא שָׁמַרְתָּ אֶל־אֲדֹנֶיךָ הַמֶּלֶךְ כִּי־

David Accuses Abner

13. וַיַּעֲמֹד עַל־רֹאשׁ־הָהָר מֵרָחֹק רַב הַמָּקוֹם בֵּינֵיהֶם — *And stood on a mountaintop from afar; there was a considerable distance between them.*

David was concerned about being captured and so kept his distance. He climbed to the top of the mountain so that his voice would be heard (*Ralbag*).

Daas Sofrim explains that David is described as standing *from afar* because of the height of the mountain. Contrarily, *Malbim* deduces from the redundancy of מֵרָחֹק, *from afar*, and רַב הַמָּקוֹם, *a considerable distance*, that a considerable breadth of territory separated David from Saul.

14. וַיִּקְרָא דָוִד אֶל־הָעָם וְאֶל־אַבְנֵר בֶּן־נֵר לֵאמֹר הֲלוֹא תַעֲנֶה אַבְנֵר — *David called out to the people and to Abner son of Ner, saying, "Won't you answer, Abner?"*

David first called to the nation as a whole. When he received no response, he addressed Abner (*Radak*).

הֲלוֹא תַעֲנֶה אַבְנֵר — *Won't you answer, Abner?*

Simply understood, David solicited Abner's attention and then addressed him, as recorded in the following verses.

The Sages, however, associate this phrase with the incident at the cave, when David cut off a corner of Saul's garment (Ch. 24) and then informed Saul of how he had spared his life, exhibiting the cloth as proof. Abner had at that time dismissed David's words and told Saul that David had merely found a fragment of Saul's garment that had gotten caught on a thorn. Abner then added that had David attempted to approach Saul, Abner and his men would have cut him up limb by limb (or would have roasted, cooked, and eaten him — see *Yalkut Shimoni* 136).

Having now taken Saul's spear and water jug, David called to Abner: "When I cut Saul's garment, you reacted with skepticism and threats. But now you must acknowledge that I could have harmed Saul but refrained from doing so. And so won't you speak to him on my behalf?"

Abner, however, could not bring himself to do so. Thus, as recorded in *Psalms*, David protested, הַאֻמְנָם אֵלֶם צֶדֶק תְּדַבֵּרוּן, *Do you indeed remain silent? Justice should you speak!* (*Psalms* 58:2; *Midrash Shocher Tov* 58:1, *Vayikra Rabbah* 26:2, *Radak*, *Abarbanel*).

According to the Talmud, Abner did respond to David, but again with a far-fetched refutation of his words, claiming that one of Saul's soldiers had brought David the spear and water flask (*Sanhedrin* 49a, *Rashi* ad loc.). For going out of his way to maintain the rift between Saul and David, Abner was condemned by Hashem to an untimely and tragic death. Thus, our Sages state that Abner died at בּוֹר הַסִּרָה, *Bor-hassirah* (*II Samuel* 3:26) — i.e., on account of a *bor* — literally, a *water pit* but in this case a flask of water — and a *sirah*, or *thorn*.

וַיַּעַן אַבְנֵר וַיֹּאמֶר מִי אַתָּה קָרָאתָ אֶל־הַמֶּלֶךְ — *Abner replied and said, "Who are you that you shout at the king?"*

[13] *David then crossed the ford and stood on a*
mountaintop from afar; there was considerable
distance between them. [14] *David called out to the*
people and to Abner son of Ner, saying, "Won't
you answer, Abner?" Abner replied and said,
"Who are you that you shout at the king!"
[15] *David said to Abner, "Are you not a great*
man? Who is your equal in Israel? So why did you
not guard your lord, the king? For someone from

But David had not addressed the king. Rather, Abner was asking who had the temerity to shout while the king lay asleep. The phrase אֶל־הַמֶּלֶךְ — lit., *to the king* — is to be read as *regarding the king* (*Radak*) or *near the head of the king* (*Targum*).

מִי אַתָּה, *Who are you?* is a dismissive phrase, connoting, "How dare a person as insignificant as yourself call out toward the king?" (*Me'am Loez*).

Generally speaking, protocol demands that a person of lowly rank approach a person of high standing through his subordinate. Accordingly, a person who wishes to speak to a general goes to his subaltern, and a person who wishes to speak with the king goes to his general.

Because David was anointed king, when he wished to speak with Abner he did not hesitate to address him directly. Abner, however, assumed that David must want to speak with Saul, and so he responded, "Who are you to call out to the king?" David replied that he wished to speak to Abner, and added that he chose to address him directly because the matter was urgent, involving the safety of the king (*Sefer HaAkeidah, Shaar* 103).

15. הֲלוֹא־אִישׁ אַתָּה — *Are you not a great man?*

The word אִישׁ generally means *a man*, but it is often used to denote a highly respected, dignified person (cf. *Numbers* 13:3: כֻּלָּם אֲנָשִׁים, *they were all distinguished men*) (*Radak*).

According to *Targum*, אִישׁ אַתָּה connotes, *You are a powerful man.*

The Midrash states that Abner was so powerful that it was easier to move a six-cubit-wide wall than to displace one of his feet (*Koheles Rabbah* 9:11; see above, v. 12 fn.).

הֲלוֹא־אִישׁ אַתָּה וּמִי כָמוֹךָ בְּיִשְׂרָאֵל — *Are you not a great man? Who is your equal in Israel?*

David faulted Abner for being lax in guarding the king — in particular, because he was a *great man* with a correspondingly great measure of responsibility (*Abarbanel*).

Kli Yakar explains that David rebuked Abner on two counts. First, אִישׁ אַתָּה, *you are a human being*, and any person should be concerned enough about the king not to leave him inadequately protected. Furthermore, מִי כָמוֹךָ, *Who is your equal?;* it was unbecoming of a man of Abner's stature to be so negligent.

According to *Malbim*, הֲלוֹא־אִישׁ אַתָּה means that *you are the man* who is expected to appoint guards over the king. מִי כָמוֹךָ adds that if Abner had appointed watchmen who were subsequently negligent, then *who else is as responsible as you* to discipline them?

וְלָמָּה לֹא שָׁמַרְתָּ אֶל־אֲדֹנֶיךָ הַמֶּלֶךְ — *So why did you not guard your lord, the king?*

Although here David addressed Abner, much of the following verse is stated in the plural form, laying blame

טז בָא אַחַד הָעָם לְהַשְׁחִית אֶת־הַמֶּלֶךְ אֲדֹנֶיךָ׃ לֹא־
טוֹב הַדָּבָר הַזֶּה אֲשֶׁר עָשִׂיתָ חַי־יהוה כִּי בְנֵי־מָוֶת
אַתֶּם אֲשֶׁר לֹא־שְׁמַרְתֶּם עַל־אֲדֹנֵיכֶם עַל־מְשִׁיחַ
יהוה וְעַתָּה | רְאֵה אֵי־חֲנִית הַמֶּלֶךְ וְאֶת־צַפַּחַת
°מְרַאֲשֹׁתָיו ק׳ יז הַמַּיִם אֲשֶׁר °מראשתו׃ וַיַּכֵּר שָׁאוּל אֶת־קוֹל דָּוִד
וַיֹּאמֶר הֲקוֹלְךָ זֶה בְּנִי דָוִד וַיֹּאמֶר דָּוִד קוֹלִי אֲדֹנִי
יח הַמֶּלֶךְ׃ וַיֹּאמֶר לָמָּה זֶּה אֲדֹנִי רֹדֵף אַחֲרֵי עַבְדּוֹ

on all the soldiers. If Abner had not assigned guards to watch the king at night, then he was solely responsible. But if he had done so, then they were guilty of neglect (*Abarbanel*).

According to *Kli Yakar*, David told Abner, אִישׁ אַתָּה — *You are only human;* therefore, if you alone were guarding the king, it can be understood that you fell asleep, even though לֹא־טוֹב הַדָּבָר הַזֶּה אֲשֶׁר עָשִׂיתָ, *it is not proper what you have done,* i.e., assume sole responsibility; Abner should have realized that he might fall asleep. David then addressed the soldiers more harshly, telling them, בְּנֵי־מָוֶת אַתֶּם, *You deserve to die* (v. 16). They had no excuse for having fallen asleep, because they should have scheduled consecutive shifts through the night.

Abner had justified his persecution of David by claiming that he was protecting the king. David now challenged him: "It is clear that you have not been guarding the king properly. Therefore, you must have had some other motive in pursuing me" — and that, stated David, was jealousy (*Mussar HaNeviim*).

וְלָמָּה לֹא שָׁמַרְתָּ אֶל־אֲדֹנֶיךָ — *So why did you not guard your lord?*

The phrase אֶל־אֲדֹנֶיךָ literally means *to your lord.*

Kli Yakar makes use of the word אֶל by explaining that David blamed only Abner for not having assigned his soldiers to guard Saul — i.e., for not sending them *to* his master.

Daas Sofrim, alternatively, suggests that David asked Abner why he didn't protect the roads and passages leading *to* Saul.

Targum, cited by *Radak,* renders אֶל, *to,* as *over.* Thus, the phrase may be translated as *over your lord.*

כִּי־בָא אַחַד הָעָם לְהַשְׁחִית אֶת־הַמֶּלֶךְ אֲדֹנֶיךָ — *For someone from among the people came to assassinate the king, your master!*

According to *Metzudos,* there is a dual implication here. You should have guarded your master *lest someone come,* and therefore the past tense of the words כִּי־בָא implies that indeed someone — Abishai — did come intending to do harm.

16. לֹא־טוֹב הַדָּבָר הַזֶּה אֲשֶׁר עָשִׂיתָ — *This thing that you have done is not proper.*

Although Abner had only been guilty of a passive failure to protect the king, his neglect was tantamount to a misdeed, and so David accused him of something that he had *done* (*Malbim*).

כִּי בְנֵי־מָוֶת אַתֶּם — *You [all] deserve to die.*

David now addressed the soldiers. According to *Metzudos,* he did so out of respect for Abner, in order to avoid the implication that only Abner was to blame.

כִּי בְנֵי־מָוֶת אַתֶּם אֲשֶׁר לֹא־שְׁמַרְתֶּם עַל־אֲדֹנֵיכֶם — *You [all] deserve to die, for you have not kept watch over your master.*

Simply understood, this means that because Saul's soldiers had fallen asleep, they deserved to die.

among the people came to assassinate the king,
your master! [16] *This thing that you have done is*
not proper! As Hashem *lives, you [all] deserve to die*
for you have not kept watch over your master, over
the anointed one of Hashem. *Now, look — where are*
the king's spear and the flask of water that were
near his head?"
[17] *Saul recognized David's voice and said, "Is*
that your voice, my son David?" David replied,
"It is my voice, my lord, the king." [18] *And he said*
[further], "Why does my lord pursue his servant?

Less drastically, it might mean that had an intruder killed Saul, then they would have been subject to the death penalty. Alternatively, David meant only that they themselves might easily have been killed (*Abarbanel*).

וְעַתָּה רְאֵה אֵי־חֲנִית הַמֶּלֶךְ ... — *Now, look — where are the king's spear ....*

If you claim that you did protect the king, where is his spear? How was it taken from him? (*Metzudos*).

Abner had not noticed on his own that these items were missing because it was still night (*Daas Sofrim*).

With these words, David again demonstrated that he intended Saul no harm.

David devoted an entire psalm to this topic, in which he expressed his grievances about being misjudged, concluding יִשְׂמַח צַדִּיק כִּי־חָזָה נָקָם, *The righteous one shall rejoice when he sees vengeance,* וְיֹאמַר אָדָם אַךְ־פְּרִי לַצַּדִּיק אַךְ יֵשׁ־אֱלֹהִים שֹׁפְטִים בָּאָרֶץ, *And people shall say, "There is indeed a reward for the righteous; there is indeed a God judging the land"* (*Psalms* 58:11,12).

☙ David's Impassioned Questioning of Saul's Motives

17. וַיַּכֵּר שָׁאוּל אֶת־קוֹל דָּוִד — *Saul recognized David's voice.*

Abner had not recognized David's voice (*Abarbanel*). But Saul, who had spent much time with David (who was his son-in-law and former attendant), did.

וַיֹּאמֶר הֲקוֹלְךָ זֶה בְּנִי דָוִד — *And he said, "Is that your voice, my son David?"*

Saul referred to David as his son, since David had twice shown him a filial mercy (*Abarbanel*).

Saul's question was not intended to ascertain David's identity. Rather, he asked if David's tone of voice and words, which indicated that he viewed Saul as a father, were sincere. הֲקוֹלְךָ זֶה בְּנִי דָוִד may thus be translated as, *Are those sincere words of my son David?* (*Kli Yakar*).

18. לָמָּה זֶּה אֲדֹנִי רֹדֵף אַחֲרֵי עַבְדּוֹ — *Why does my lord pursue his servant?*

The Midrash comments: When one rebukes an inferior, one should criticize him directly and explicitly. Thus, David rebuked Abner, "This thing that you have done is not proper." When criticizing a superior, however, the criticism should be indirect and respectful. Thus, David did not accuse Saul directly of wronging him; he implied it in his question, where he respectfully asked Saul, "Why does my lord pursue his servant?" (Moses acted similarly with Aharon and his sons — see *Leviticus* 10:12; *Yalkut Shimoni* 139.)

יט כִּי מֶה עָשִׂיתִי וּמַה־בְּיָדִי רָעָה: וְעַתָּה יִשְׁמַע־
נָא אֲדֹנִי הַמֶּלֶךְ אֵת דִּבְרֵי עַבְדּוֹ אִם־יהוה
הֱסִיתְךָ בִי יָרַח מִנְחָה וְאִם | בְּנֵי הָאָדָם אֲרוּרִים
הֵם לִפְנֵי יהוה כִּי־גֵרְשׁוּנִי הַיּוֹם מֵהִסְתַּפֵּחַ
בְּנַחֲלַת יהוה לֵאמֹר לֵךְ עֲבֹד אֱלֹהִים אֲחֵרִים:

מֶה עָשִׂיתִי וּמַה־בְּיָדִי רָעָה — *What have I done and what evil is in my hand?*

David asked what wrong he had committed since the incident at the cave, at which time Saul had made a commitment to no longer pursue him (*Kli Yakar*).

According to *Malbim*, David was asking two separate questions: *What have I done [against Saul's kingdom], and what evil is in my hand [regarding any other issue]?*

19. יִשְׁמַע־נָא אֲדֹנִי הַמֶּלֶךְ אֵת דִּבְרֵי עַבְדּוֹ — *Let my lord the king listen to the words of his servant.*

In the previous verse, David spoke appeasingly, and so the verb, וַיֹּאמֶר, *and said [softly],* was used. Here, as David's tone grew more scathing, he referred to his words as דִּבְרֵי — *[harsh] words* (see *Makkos* 11a; *Me'am Loez*).

אִם־ה׳ הֱסִיתְךָ בִי — *If it is HASHEM Who has incited you against me ...*

David did not believe that Saul had decided on his own to break his word and attack him. Thus, it must be that Saul had been persuaded to do so either by God or by his followers.

If the former was the case and God wished to punish David, using Saul as His emissary, David accepted His decision. However, if Saul's followers had influenced him, they would be cursed (based on *Mahari Kara*).

David entertained the possibility that Hashem was to blame for Saul's unjust pursuit of him. Although David held no grudge against Hashem and, to the contrary, sought to appease Him, our Sages consider his attitude improper. Thus, a Midrash states that Hashem reproved David, "You state that I incited Saul. I will therefore incite you to transgress a law with which even schoolchildren are familiar." Thus, וַיָּסֶת אֶת־דָּוִד, *[HASHEM] incited David* (*II Samuel* 24:1) to take a head count of the Jews, which is clearly prohibited (see above, 11:8, 15:4; *Berachos* 62b).[1]

יָרַח מִנְחָה — *He will be appeased by an offering.*

The word יָרַח is related to רֵיחַ, *fragrance.* Hashem will, as it were, enjoy the רֵיחַ נִחוֹחַ, the pleasing fragrance of the מִנְחָה — literally, *gift* (see *Genesis* 32:19), but referring here to an *offering* (*Targum*) — in particular, a meal-offering.

Such a meal-offering was generally brought as a secondary offering accompanying an animal sacrifice (see *Numbers* Ch. 15). David's sparing of Saul's life in the cave had been the equivalent of an elevation-offering (an animal sacrifice), and his sparing of Saul's life again now was the equivalent of the secondary meal-offering (*Malbim*).

1. David's unbending faith in Hashem and his ability to see only good in His ways was legendary. When Shimei cursed him, he reacted by saying, "Hashem has said to him, 'Curse David' " (*II Samuel* 16:10). Even here, he insisted that Avishai should not take action against Saul, for it was clear to him that Saul's pursuit was God's will. Nevertheless, he used the word *incite,* which implied that what was transpiring was not correct. Hashem then showed him that if not for Heavenly protection from sin, he could err even in a simple matter that schoolchildren know. This supports the concept that when Hashem judges the righteous punctiliously (see *Bava Kamma* 50a), He does so particularly regarding matters in which they excel, demanding ever higher levels of performance from them. Thus, David, who excelled in accepting God's judgment, was punished for implying that he was being persecuted wrongly (*Mishbetzos Zahav*).

For what have I done and what evil is in my hand?
[19] *And now, let my lord the king listen to the words of his servant: If it is* HASHEM *Who has incited you against me, He will be appeased by an offering — but if it is men, may they be cursed before* HASHEM*, for they have driven me away this day from attaching myself to the heritage of* HASHEM*, [as if] to say, 'Go worship the gods of others!'*

According to *Rashi*, David was referring to his prayers, which constituted a substitute for an offering, and which he hoped would arouse Hashem's mercy and calm His wrath.

וְאִם בְּנֵי אָדָם ... — *But if it is men ...*

If human beings incited Saul, they deserved to be cursed.

This verse raises a major philosophical issue, for it implies that although Hashem may not have intended for David to be hurt, human beings had the capacity to harm him anyway. Indeed, *Metzudos* comments that man's free will is unrestrained (see *Ohr HaChaim, Genesis* 37:21). This is clearly a perplexing idea.

According to *Daas Sofrim*, everything is directed by Hashem. However, there is a difference between the decrees He performs directly and those He effects via the actions of human beings. If Hashem Himself carries out a decree, the dynamics of the universe that He has instituted allow it to be ameliorated by His Attribute of Mercy more easily than if He effects a decree via the actions of man. This concept is referred to in the verse, *Let us fall into the hands of* HASHEM*, for His mercies are abundant; but let me not fall into human hands* (*II Samuel* 24:14).

אֲרוּרִים הֵם לִפְנֵי ה׳ — *May they be cursed before* HASHEM*!*

David could overlook his pain but he could not forgive these men for the effect that their actions had לִפְנֵי ה׳ — *before* HASHEM — in that they frustrated his spiritual pursuits (*Malbim*).

This phrase is expressed in the present tense — literally, *they are cursed*. Their actions had already incurred the imprecation, אָרוּר מַכֵּה רֵעֵהוּ בַּסָּתֶר — *Accursed is the person who strikes his friend stealthily* (*Deuteronomy* 27:24) — which, our Sages state (see *Rashi* ad loc.), is directed at a slanderer (*Kli Yakar*).

כִּי־גֵרְשׁוּנִי הַיּוֹם מֵהִסְתַּפֵּחַ בְּנַחֲלַת ה׳ לֵאמֹר לֵךְ עֲבֹד אֱלֹהִים אֲחֵרִים — *For they have driven me away this day from attaching myself to the heritage of* HASHEM*, [as if] to say, "Go worship the gods of others!"*

Since David could no longer trust Saul to leave him in peace, he felt that he had to forsake the land of Israel — a fate that he viewed as tantamount to worshiping idols.[1]

Targum renders לֵךְ עֲבֹד אֱלֹהִים אֲחֵרִים — *Go worship the gods of others* — as *Go and dwell among the nations that serve idols.* A person forced to dwell among idol worshipers will find it difficult to resist their influence (*Mussar Haneviim*).

Furthermore, even if he merely works for idol worshipers, he is considered as though he is serving their idols as well

1. David eventually fled to Philistine territory, settling in the city of Ziklag (see Ch. 24). There are sources that recognize Philistia as part of *Eretz Yisrael* (see *Tosafos, Gittin* 2a), and Ziklag is listed in the Book of *Joshua* (15:31) as in the territory of Judah (see below, 27:6). Apparently, however, David considered himself as having left the Holy Land because Ziklag was under Philistine control. See *Mishbetzos Zahav* for a fuller discussion.

כ וְעַתָּה אַל־יִפֹּל דָּמִי אַרְצָה מִנֶּגֶד פְּנֵי יהוה כִּי־
יָצָא מֶלֶךְ יִשְׂרָאֵל לְבַקֵּשׁ אֶת־פַּרְעֹשׁ אֶחָד כַּאֲשֶׁר
כא יִרְדֹּף הַקֹּרֵא בֶּהָרִים׃ וַיֹּאמֶר שָׁאוּל חָטָאתִי שׁוּב

(*Rabbeinu Yeshayah*; see *Deuteronomy* 4:28, 28:64, *Targum*, *Rashi* ad loc.).[1]

However, this issue goes beyond the issue of being influenced by one's neighbors. Thus, the Talmud (*Kesubos* 110b) states that it is preferable to live in the land of Israel, even if the majority of one's neighbors are gentiles, than to live outside the land of Israel, even if the majority of one's neighbors are Jews (see *Meiri* to *Kesubos*; *Mishbetzos Zahav*).

Ramban (*Genesis* 24:3, *Leviticus* 18:25) explains that God appointed celestial ministers to superintend the lands of the world. [Thus, the Book of *Daniel* speaks of *the [heavenly] prince of the Persian kingdom* and *the [heavenly] prince of Greece* (10:13,20).] The only land ruled directly by God, as it were, is that of Israel. Accordingly, it is called נַחֲלַת ה׳, *the heritage of HASHEM*, and when Hashem is called אֱלֹהֵי הָאָרֶץ, *God of the Land*, it refers to the Land of Israel.

Someone who willingly leaves the land of Israel forfeits this special Divine connection, and his choice to subject himself to the power of foreign angels is tantamount to serving other gods (*Maharsha*, *Maharal* to *Kesubos* 110b; *Malbim*).

Thus, the Talmud (*Kesubos* 110b) derives from this verse that a person who lives outside the land of Israel is considered as if he has no God. (In some versions, *Rashi* paraphrases this statement so that it applies to a person who leaves the land of Israel during the time that the Temple is standing.)

Malbim adds that by leaving the land of Israel, David would relinquish the opportunity to perform mitzvos that apply only in the land of Israel (e.g., agricultural laws such as *shemittah*, *terumos*, *maasros*, etc.).

Alternatively, נַחֲלַת ה׳ — *the heritage of HASHEM* — refers to the study of Torah (*Sifrei* 43, *Yalkut Shimoni* 139, cited by *Rashi* to *Deuteronomy* 11:16). Because he was constantly pursued, David was forced to refrain from Torah study, and a person who strays from Torah eventually becomes attached to idol worship.

David expresses this complaint again in *Psalms:* סוּרוּ־מִמֶּנִּי מְרֵעִים וְאֶצְּרָה מִצְוֹת אֱלֹהָי, *Depart from me, you evildoers, and I will guard the commandments of my God* (119:115). According to *Midrash Shocher Tov*, in this verse David was pleading with Doeg and Ahithophel to give him the wherewithal to devote his time to Torah study.

Abarbanel suggests that נַחֲלַת ה׳, *the heritage of HASHEM*, refers to Saul and his family (since Saul was Hashem's anointed king).

Alternatively, it refers to David's wife Michal and his household, based on the verse: בַּיִת וָהוֹן נַחֲלַת אָבוֹת וּמֵה׳ אִשָּׁה מַשְׂכָּלֶת, *A house and wealth are an inheritance from fathers, and an intelligent woman comes from HASHEM* (*Proverbs* 19:14). Thus, *Abarbanel* explains, David bemoaned the fact that he had been cast away from the king and his family.

Daas Sofrim suggests that *"the heritage"* is the nation of Israel (as in the verse, יַעֲקֹב חֶבֶל נַחֲלָתוֹ, *Jacob is the measure of His inheritance* [*Deuteronomy* 32:9]).

מֵהִסְתַּפֵּחַ בְּנַחֲלַת ה׳ — *From attaching myself to the heritage of HASHEM.*

Targum paraphrases this phrase as *from living in the inherited [land] of the nation of HASHEM.*

The word מֵהִסְתַּפֵּחַ often connotes

1. This idea is possibly derived from an application of the principle that "whatever a servant owns is automatically owned by his master." In this case, the "servant" is the idolater and the "master" is his god, so the Jew who works for the idolater is, in effect, working for the idol (*Shaarei Aharon*).

[20] *And now, let my blood not be cast to the ground,*
away from HASHEM*'s attention, for the king of Is-*
rael has gone to seek out a single flea as one hunts
the partridge in the mountains."
[21] *Saul then said, "I have sinned! Come back,*

something *secondary* or *offshoot*, as in סַפַּחַת, a shade of *tzaraas* that is not as white as the primary color (see *Leviticus* 13:2 and *Shevuos* 6b). Accordingly, David said that he was not seeking a position of honor or a significant portion of the land of Israel; he merely wanted to be a "subordinate attachment," and now he is deprived even of that (*Malbim*).

20. וְעַתָּה אַל־יִפֹּל דָּמִי אַרְצָה מִנֶּגֶד פְּנֵי ה׳ — *And now, let my blood not be cast to the ground, away from* HASHEM*'s attention.*

According to *Radak*, David begged God not to overlook the attempts made to kill him but to punish his enemies as if they had succeeded in spilling his blood.

Malbim, however, understands these words not as a prayer but as a statement that "now my blood will not be spilled — because I will flee away from *Eretz Yisrael* — away from the 'Face of Hashem'" (*Mishbetzos Zahav*).

כִּי־יָצָא מֶלֶךְ יִשְׂרָאֵל לְבַקֵּשׁ אֶת־פַּרְעֹשׁ אֶחָד כַּאֲשֶׁר יִרְדֹּף הַקֹּרֵא בֶּהָרִים — *For the king of Israel has gone to seek out a single flea as one hunts the partridge in the mountains.*

The קֹרֵא, *partridge*, was commonly hunted by kings for sport.

The פַּרְעֹשׁ is a small insect — a *flea* or, according to *Metzudos*, a *black louse* — which leaps about to avoid being caught.

David compared Saul to a person who hunts a flea instead of a partridge. Saul was chasing a lowly man as if he were pursuing some illustrious personality (*Abarbanel*).

Because a flea can only bite a person, he should not bother to kill it but only chase it away. Similarly, David had no interest in harming Saul. At worst, Saul might be "bitten" by jealousy if David became king in his place — but that was not a reason to kill him (*Likkutei Yekarim*).

Mishbetzos Zahav offers a homiletical interpretation of David's reference to a flea. King Solomon states, בִּרְצוֹת ה׳ דַּרְכֵי־אִישׁ גַּם־אוֹיְבָיו יַשְׁלִם אִתּוֹ, *When* HASHEM *favors a man's ways, even his foes will make peace with him* (*Proverbs* 16:7). The Midrash (*Bereishis Rabbah* 54:1) explicates that when a man is favored by Hashem, even nuisances such as mosquitoes and fleas will no longer bother him. Thus, if Saul earned Hashem's favor, he would no longer suffer from David.

כַּאֲשֶׁר יִרְדֹּף הַקֹּרֵא בֶּהָרִים — *As one hunts the partridge in the mountains.*

Our translation represents the view shared by the majority of commentators that David compared Saul to the hunter.

However, the antecedent of the verb יִרְדֹּף — *he will hunt* — seems to be הַקֹּרֵא, *the partridge*. Thus, the phrase should read, *as the partridge hunts in the mountains.*

To avoid this reading, *Targum* renders יִרְדֹּף not in its conventional active form as *he will chase* but reflexively as *he will be chased* (*Radak*). Thus, the phrase reads, *as the partridge is hunted in the mountains.*

Radak and others render *as [the hunter] hunts the partridge*. The word *hunter* is understood.

Rashi comments that the קֹרֵא seeks the nests of other birds and broods on their eggs (see *Chullin* 140b). As indicated by Scripture (*Jeremiah* 17:11), it whistles to attract the chicks of other birds to itself. It is perhaps for this reason that it is called a קוֹרֵא — lit., *a caller*. *Rashi* apparently understands the verse as reading, *as the partridge hunts [and chases]* other birds.

The verse in *Jeremiah* cited above goes on to say that although the partridge initially gathers other birds' chicks, they

בְּנִי־דָוִד כִּי לֹא־אָרַע לְךָ עוֹד תַּחַת אֲשֶׁר יָקְרָה
נַפְשִׁי בְּעֵינֶיךָ הַיּוֹם הַזֶּה הִנֵּה הִסְכַּלְתִּי וָאֶשְׁגֶּה
כב הַרְבֵּה מְאֹד: וַיַּעַן דָּוִד וַיֹּאמֶר הִנֵּה °החנית הַמֶּלֶךְ
כג וְיַעֲבֹר אֶחָד מֵהַנְּעָרִים וְיִקָּחֶהָ: וַיהוה יָשִׁיב לָאִישׁ
אֶת־צִדְקָתוֹ וְאֶת־אֱמֻנָתוֹ אֲשֶׁר נְתָנְךָ יהוה | הַיּוֹם
בְּיָד וְלֹא אָבִיתִי לִשְׁלֹחַ יָדִי בִּמְשִׁיחַ יהוה:

°חֲנִית ק׳

eventually desert their seducer and return to their mothers. Similarly, although Saul was pursuing David to prevent him from seizing his kingdom, in the end his efforts would fail (*Me'am Loez*, see also *Likkutei Yekarim*).

Malbim translates הַקֹּרֵא בֶּהָרִים simply as *the one who calls in the mountains* — a reference to David, who was calling aloud from the mountaintop. Thus, David says, "The king chases the flea as he chases [me], who calls from the mountains," i.e., he chases me as one chases a flea.[1]

☙ David and Saul Are Again Reconciled

21. שׁוּב בְּנִי־דָוִד — *Come back, my son David.*

Saul asked David to return home (*Abarbanel*) and not leave the land of Israel (*Malbim*), for Saul no longer intended to harm him.

תַּחַת אֲשֶׁר יָקְרָה נַפְשִׁי בְּעֵינֶיךָ הַיּוֹם הַזֶּה — *Because my life has been precious in your eyes this day.*

Saul promised not to hurt David, for David had shown how much he valued Saul's life. Accordingly, we translate תַּחַת — literally, *under* or *in place of* — as *because.*

According to *Kli Yakar,* Saul stated that God would not allow Saul to harm David — תַּחַת, *in exchange for* — the fact that Saul's life had been precious in David's eyes.

הִנֵּה הִסְכַּלְתִּי וָאֶשְׁגֶּה הַרְבֵּה מְאֹד — *Behold, I have been foolish and have greatly erred.*

Saul acknowledged that he had been foolish to overlook the special Providence that protected David, and that he had erred in not recalling how David had spared his life at the cave (*Ralbag*).

Saul now grew cognizant of the many wrongs that he had committed in the course of his persecution of David, including the massacre of the Kohanim at Nob and the nullifying of David's marriage to Michal (*Daas Sofrim*).

הִסְכַּלְתִּי — *I have been foolish* — refers to Saul's misjudgment of David, which generated a host of errors in its wake. He thus goes on to state, וָאֶשְׁגֶּה הַרְבֵּה מְאֹד — *and have greatly erred.* Due to Saul's initial foolishness, he *greatly erred.* And a person is held responsible for all such errors, in accordance with the principle תְּחִלָּתוֹ בִּפְשִׁיעָה וְסוֹפוֹ בְּאוֹנֶס חַיָּב, *if someone begins to sin willfully, even if he ends by acting against his will, he is held accountable* (*Chomas Anach*).

Although Saul admitted to foolishness and errors, he denied any intent to knowingly harm an innocent man (*Daas Sofrim*).[2]

22. הִנֵּה חֲנִית הַמֶּלֶךְ — *Here is the spear of the king.*

The word חֲנִית is written with an unpronounced ה prefix, which acts as the definite article: *the.*[3] With this, David alluded to why he would not accept Saul's offer to return home. This spear, he said,

1. *Malbim* must also alter the grammar, as did *Targum* and *Radak.*

2. In order to describe the deep awareness that a person must have of his sin in order to properly repent (*Shaarei Teshuvah, Shaar* 3:2), *Rabbeinu Yonah* cites these words of Saul.

3. In the Hebrew, this is superfluous, since the phrase *spear of the king* requires only one definite article, which is placed before the word *king.*

my son David, for I will no longer cause you
harm, because my life has been precious in your
eyes this day. Behold, I have been foolish and
have very greatly erred.'' [22]David then spoke up
and said, "Here is the spear of the king; let one
of the attendants cross over and take it. [23]May
HASHEM repay every man his righteousness and
his faithfulness; for HASHEM delivered you into
[my] hand today, but I had no desire to send forth
my hand against the anointed one of HASHEM.

was the same that Saul had flung at him while under the influence of the spirit of melancholy, even after having specifically sworn not to do so (*Kli Yakar*).

וְיַעֲבֹר אֶחָד מֵהַנְּעָרִים וְיִקָּחֶהָ — *Let one of the attendants cross over and take it.*

David did not trust Saul enough to bring the spear himself (*Abarbanel*). Furthermore, he stipulated that only one of Saul's men should come take it (*Daas Sofrim*).

No mention is made of the flask of water, for it would be below the king's dignity to send a lad to retrieve so petty an item (*Abarbanel*).

Not only had David experienced Saul's unpredictable changes of heart too often to trust him, he was also aware that many people would continue to urge Saul to harm him — especially if he came back into their midst and they had reason to fear his revenge for past wrongdoings.

23. וַה׳ יָשִׁיב לָאִישׁ אֶת־צִדְקָתוֹ וְאֶת־אֱמֻנָתוֹ — *May HASHEM repay every man his righteousness and his faithfulness.*

David's words implied that although Saul would not repay him, God would (*Abarbanel*).

In his humility, David did not refer to himself as righteous (*Daas Sofrim*) but merely spoke in a general manner of God repaying the righteous (*Rashi, Radak, Metzudos*).

אֶת־צִדְקָתוֹ וְאֶת־אֱמֻנָתוֹ — *His righteousness and his faithfulness.*

Righteousness refers to a good deed, whereas *faithfulness* is a deeply-rooted conviction, an internal commitment that only Hashem can discern, which prompts that good deed (*Daas Sofrim*).

וה׳ יָשִׁיב לָאִישׁ אֶת־צִדְקָתוֹ וְאֶת־אֱמֻנָתוֹ אֲשֶׁר נְתָנְךָ ה׳ הַיּוֹם בְּיָד — *May HASHEM repay every man his righteousness and his faithfulness, for HASHEM delivered you into [my] hand today.*

Simply understood, David prayed that God reward him for not having harmed His anointed king.

Malbim understands this verse in accordance with the mishnah that *one mitzvah draws another in its wake* (*Avos* 4:2). Because David had succeeded in overcoming his desire to harm Saul in the cave, Hashem sent him another such opportunity so that he might gain even greater merit. David now prayed that Hashem should give everyone the opportunity to confirm his righteousness and faithfulness in a similar manner.

אֲשֶׁר נְתָנְךָ ה׳ הַיּוֹם בְּיָד — *For HASHEM delivered you into [my] hand today.*

The word בְּיָד literally means *into a hand.* Nonetheless, *Targum* renders the phrase as if it read *my hand.*

Alternatively, *Radak* suggests that David meant *in the hand of one of my men.*[1]

David stated simply בְּיָד — *in a hand* — because he could not state with cer-

1. Although we should then have expected the vowel to be a פַּתָּח and not a קָמַץ.

כו/כד־כה כד וְהִנֵּה כַּאֲשֶׁר גָּדְלָה נַפְשְׁךָ הַיּוֹם הַזֶּה בְּעֵינָי כֵּן־
תִּגְדַּל נַפְשִׁי בְּעֵינֵי יהוה וְיַצִּלֵנִי מִכָּל־צָרָה׃
כה וַיֹּאמֶר שָׁאוּל אֶל־דָּוִד בָּרוּךְ אַתָּה בְּנִי דָוִד גַּם
עָשֹׂה תַעֲשֶׂה וְגַם יָכֹל תּוּכָל וַיֵּלֶךְ דָּוִד לְדַרְכּוֹ
כז/א א וְשָׁאוּל שָׁב לִמְקוֹמוֹ׃ וַיֹּאמֶר דָּוִד
אֶל־לִבּוֹ עַתָּה אֶסָּפֶה יוֹם־אֶחָד בְּיַד־שָׁאוּל אֵין־

tainty that God had delivered Saul into his power, since God might change that circumstance at any moment. However, later in the verse David does refer explicitly to *my hand*, stating: וְלֹא אָבִיתִי לִשְׁלֹחַ יָדִי בִּמְשִׁיחַ ה׳ — *I had no desire to send forth my hand against the anointed one of Hashem*. In that phrase, David is discussing free will, which is indeed in a person's hand (*Daas Sofrim*).

24. David prayed that Hashem protect him in recompense for having refrained from harming Saul (*Malbim*).

Mishbetzos Zahav adds that David's prayer implied that just as he had saved Saul, notwithstanding the pain the king had caused him, so too, Hashem should ignore David's sins and save him from misfortune.

According to *Kli Yakar*, these words are not a prayer but a statement: "Just as your life was important to me this day [because you are the anointed of Hashem], so will my life be important in the eyes of Hashem, [for I too am the anointed of Hashem,] and so will He save me from all misfortune."

25. בָּרוּךְ אַתָּה בְּנִי דָוִד — *Blessed are you, my son David.*

Although בָּרוּךְ אַתָּה is often translated as "May you be blessed," the word בָּרוּךְ is actually an adjective meaning *blessed*.[1]

Accordingly, *Metzudos* interprets Saul's words to mean, "I can discern that you are blessed and that you will therefore succeed."

גַּם עָשֹׂה תַעֲשֶׂה וְגַם יָכֹל תּוּכָל — *May you accomplish much and may you be very successful.*

Our translation presents these words as a blessing. Many commentators, however, understand it as Saul's prediction made on the basis of the good fortune with which God had until now favored David (*Abarbanel, Metzudos*).

Targum renders עָשֹׂה תַעֲשֶׂה as *you will reign as king*; and the phrase יָכֹל תּוּכָל as *you will be successful*, related to the word יָכוֹל, *capable.*

וַיֵּלֶךְ דָּוִד לְדַרְכּוֹ וְשָׁאוּל שָׁב לִמְקוֹמוֹ — *Then David went on his way and Saul returned to his place.*

Exhibiting considerable sensitivity, Saul waited for David to leave before himself moving, so as not to frighten him (*Kli Yakar*).

XXVII

◈ David Flees for Asylum among the Philistines

1. וַיֹּאמֶר דָּוִד אֶל־לִבּוֹ — *David said to himself.*

This phrase literally means, *David spoke to his heart.*

Scripture states of righteous people, whose rational thinking controls the desires of their hearts, that they speak *to* their hearts. We find this in the cases of

1. For this reason (among others), many commentators on the *siddur* explain the formula בָּרוּךְ אַתָּה ה׳ as *You are the Source of blessings, Hashem* (see *Abudraham, Sefer HaChinuch* 430; see also *Appendix* to *Pathway to Prayer*).

26/24-25 [24] *Behold, just as your life was important to me this*
day, so may my life be important in the eyes of
HASHEM, and may He save me from all misfortune."
[25] *Saul then said to David, "Blessed are you, my*
son David. May you accomplish much and may
you be very successful." Then David went on his
way and Saul returned to his place.

27/1 [1] *David said to himself, "Now I may well perish*
one day at the hand of Saul. There is nothing

David, Hannah (above, 1:13) and Daniel (*Daniel* 1:5). By doing so, they emulate Hashem, about whom the verse states that וַיֹּאמֶר ה׳ אֶל־לִבּוֹ — *HASHEM spoke to His heart* (*Genesis* 8:21).

Contrarily, because evil people are controlled by their hearts and desires, Scripture states that they speak *in* their hearts. This phraseology is applied to Esau (וַיֹּאמֶר עֵשָׂו בְּלִבּוֹ — *Genesis* 27:41), Jeroboam (*I Kings* 12:26), and Haman (*Esther* 6:6; *Bereishis Rabbah* 34:10, 67:8).

עַתָּה אֶסָּפֶה יוֹם־אֶחָד בְּיַד־שָׁאוּל — *Now I may well perish one day at the hand of Saul.*

David mistrusted Saul's assurances, all of which had hitherto been short-lived.

Abarbanel adds that David's success had always aroused Saul's jealousy. David could thus expect that this would be the case now as well, since in their last two encounters David had escaped Saul's forces, to the point that Saul had predicted that David would succeed (or — according to an alternative reading of the verses — had blessed him to succeed).

Malbim states that David knew that he had been supernaturally rescued from Saul repeatedly, and that he could not expect such miracles to continue uninterrupted. Furthermore, being rescued with Divine assistance diminishes a person's worthiness (see *Genesis* 32:11, *Rashi*), and David was afraid that he had exhausted all his merits.

Kli Yakar suggests that David was particularly apprehensive now that he had told Saul that he did not intend to do him harm, for now Saul might feel that he could pursue David with impunity.

Alternatively, David had always been confident that he could prevail upon himself not to kill Saul. Now, however, he feared that if Saul ambushed him yet again, he would have no choice but to kill him in self-defense. His desire to avoid this contingency impelled him to flee (see *Genesis* 32:8, *Rashi*).

David's fears that Saul would continue to pursue him were apparently justified, for a verse states further on that when *it was told to Saul that David had fled to Gath, he no longer searched for him* (below, v. 4) — implying that if David would not have fled, Saul would have continued to persecute him (*Me'am Loez*).

עַתָּה אֶסָּפֶה יוֹם־אֶחָד — *Now, I may well perish.*

We translate אֶסָּפֶה as *I may well perish*, following *Radak*. (This is similar to its usage in the phrase, פֶּן תִּסָּפֶה, *lest you be swept away* [*Genesis* 19:15; see *Rashi* ad loc.].)

Possibly, however, the word is related to סוֹף, *end*, as it indicates complete destruction.

Finally, *Targum* renders אֶסָּפֶה as *I will be given over*, seemingly associating it with אָסַף — *gather.*

יוֹם־אֶחָד — *One day.*

David feared that Saul might suddenly ambush him (*Rashi*).

לִי טוֹב כִּי הִמָּלֵט אִמָּלֵט | אֶל־אֶרֶץ פְּלִשְׁתִּים
וְנוֹאַשׁ מִמֶּנִּי שָׁאוּל לְבַקְשֵׁנִי עוֹד בְּכָל־גְּבוּל יִשְׂרָאֵל
ב וְנִמְלַטְתִּי מִיָּדוֹ׃ וַיָּקָם דָּוִד וַיַּעֲבֹר הוּא וְשֵׁשׁ־מֵאוֹת
ג אִישׁ אֲשֶׁר עִמּוֹ אֶל־אָכִישׁ בֶּן־מָעוֹךְ מֶלֶךְ גַּת׃ וַיֵּשֶׁב
דָּוִד עִם־אָכִישׁ בְּגַת הוּא וַאֲנָשָׁיו אִישׁ וּבֵיתוֹ דָּוִד
וּשְׁתֵּי נָשָׁיו אֲחִינֹעַם הַיִּזְרְעֵאלִית וַאֲבִיגַיִל אֵשֶׁת־
ד נָבָל הַכַּרְמְלִית׃ וַיֻּגַּד לְשָׁאוּל כִּי־בָרַח דָּוִד גַּת וְלֹא־
ה °יוסף עוֹד לְבַקְשׁוֹ׃ וַיֹּאמֶר דָּוִד אֶל־אָכִישׁ
אִם־נָא מָצָאתִי חֵן בְּעֵינֶיךָ יִתְּנוּ־לִי מָקוֹם בְּאַחַת

°יָסַף ק׳

אֵין־לִי טוֹב כִּי הִמָּלֵט אִמָּלֵט — *There is nothing better for me than to escape.*

In this phrase, the word כִּי — which has a number of meanings, depending on the context — functions as אֶלָּא, *but* (see *Gittin* 90a, *Rashi* ad loc.; *Rashi, Genesis* 18:15). Thus, אֵין־לִי טוֹב כִּי הִמָּלֵט אִמָּלֵט means, *There is nothing good for me but that I should escape.* The word כִּי is thus an abbreviated form of the phrase כִּי אִם, *only* (see *Abarbanel).*

הִמָּלֵט אִמָּלֵט אֶל־אֶרֶץ פְּלִשְׁתִּים — *To escape to the land of the Philistines.*

Although the Philistines had been long-term enemies of Israel and particularly of David — who had killed Goliath — David seemed confident that he could persuade them of his allegiance (*Daas Sofrim*).

David probably chose to go to their land because it retained some of the sanctity of the land of Israel (ibid.).

Malbim lists three reasons for David's flight to Philistia. (1) Since David would be unable to attract more rebels, Saul would feel no need to continue pursuing him. (2) It was unlikely that Saul would venture into Philistine territory to pursue David. (3) Even if Saul did enter Philistine territory, the Philistine king might come to David's defense.

כִּי הִמָּלֵט אִמָּלֵט ... וְנִמְלַטְתִּי מִיָּדוֹ — *Than to escape...and I will have escaped from his hand.*

The repetition of the word *escape* (it appears three times in the Hebrew) denotes the intensity of the danger that David sensed (*Daas Sofrim*).

2. וַיָּקָם דָּוִד — *So David arose.*

The word וַיָּקָם often connotes not only a physical ascent but also an elevated status (see *Genesis* 23:20, *Rashi*).

Chomas Anach suggests that David escaped because he was afraid that his sins would inhibit his success — and this humility marked an elevation in his spiritual stature.

וַיַּעֲבֹר הוּא וְשֵׁשׁ־מֵאוֹת אִישׁ אֲשֶׁר עִמּוֹ אֶל־אָכִישׁ בֶּן־מָעוֹךְ מֶלֶךְ גַּת — *And crossed over, with the six hundred men who were with him, to Achish son of Maoch, king of Gath.*

But how could David have sought asylum with Achish, whom he had barely escaped by feigning madness (above, Ch. 21)?

The difference was that previously David had come alone, which caused the Philistines to suspect him of being a spy. This time, he arrived in the company of 600 men, which precluded any chance of their being spies (*Malbim*).

Also, this time David sent a message to Achish, explaining that he was out of favor with Saul and requesting political asylum (*Radak, Rabbeinu Yeshayah*).

In addition, it was public knowledge that Saul had repeatedly sought to kill

better for me than to escape to the land of the
Philistines; then Saul will despair of search-
ing for me again anywhere in the borders of Is-
rael, and I will have escaped from his hand."
2 *So David arose and crossed over, with the six*
hundred men who were with him, to Achish
son of Maoch, king of Gath. 3 *David dwelt with*
Achish in Gath, he and his men, each man with his
household; David with his two wives, Ahinoam of
Jezreel and Abigail, the [former] wife of Nabal, the
Carmelite. 4 *It was told to Saul that David had fled*
to Gath, so he no longer searched for him.
5 *David said to Achish, "If I have found fa-*
vor in your eyes, let them give me a place in one

David (*Abarbanel*), and the men with whom David came substantiated his claim that he was a rebel leader (*Chomas Anach*).

Alternatively, the fact that Scripture mentions the name of Achish's father indicates that this was not the same Achish as before (*Chomas Anach*).

3. וַיֵּשֶׁב דָּוִד עִם־אָכִישׁ בְּגַת — *David dwelt with Achish in Gath.*

Hashem's unfailing benevolence to David impelled Achish to trust David so wholeheartedly that he allowed him and his men to dwell freely with their families and gain relief from their constant persecution (*Kli Yakar*).

הוּא וַאֲנָשָׁיו אִישׁ וּבֵיתוֹ — *He and his men, each man with his household.*

The fact that David and his men brought their families further proved to Achish that they were not merely seeking temporary asylum (*Malbim*).

וּשְׁתֵּי נָשָׁיו אֲחִינֹעַם הַיִּזְרְעֵאלִית וַאֲבִיגַיִל אֵשֶׁת־נָבָל הַכַּרְמְלִית — *With his two wives, Ahinoam of Jezreel, and Abigail, the [former] wife of Nabal, the Carmelite.*

It has already been established that Abigail was a noble and righteous woman. This verse lists Ahinoam before her to indicate that she too was a woman of sterling worth (*Chomas Anach*).

Daas Sofrim suggests that the arrival of the prophetess Abigail shows that she approved of David's decision to live among the Philistines.

4. Apparently, Saul was not prepared to risk war with the Philistines in order to pursue David.

The word וַיֻּגַּד, *It was told,* is derived from the word הַגָּדָה, implying that the teller came to Saul with a narrative calculated to please him with "words of wisdom." He persuaded Saul that David had fallen into a trap of his own making, since the Philistines would surely execute him for having killed Goliath. This seemed to be an intelligent analysis of David's plight, so for this reason, Saul was saw no further reason to continue his pursuit; the Philistines would put an end to David's threat (*Chomas Anach;* see also *Kli Yaakov*).

5. וַיֹּאמֶר דָּוִד אֶל־אָכִישׁ אִם־נָא מָצָאתִי חֵן בְּעֵינֶיךָ יִתְּנוּ־לִי מָקוֹם — *David said to Achish, "If I have found favor in your eyes, let them give me a place."*

David was planning to raid the sur-

עָרֵ֣י הַשָּׂדֶ֔ה וְאֵ֥שְׁבָה שָּׁ֑ם וְלָ֨מָּה יֵשֵׁ֧ב עַבְדְּךָ֛ בְּעִ֥יר
ו הַמַּמְלָכָ֖ה עִמָּֽךְ׃ וַיִּתֶּן־ל֥וֹ אָכִ֛ישׁ בַּיּ֥וֹם הַה֖וּא אֶת־
צִֽקְלָ֑ג לָכֵ֞ן הָיְתָ֤ה צִֽקְלַג֙ לְמַלְכֵ֣י יְהוּדָ֔ה עַ֖ד הַיּ֥וֹם
ז הַזֶּֽה׃ וַיְהִי֙ מִסְפַּ֣ר הַיָּמִ֔ים אֲשֶׁר־יָשַׁ֥ב
דָּוִ֖ד בִּשְׂדֵ֣ה פְלִשְׁתִּ֑ים יָמִ֖ים וְאַרְבָּעָ֥ה חֳדָשִֽׁים׃

rounding territories (see below), and therefore asked permission to live in the outlying areas, far from the capital city, where his movements would not arouse Achish's attention (*Radak*).

It is also possible that David wanted to segregate himself from the influence of the idolatrous Philistines (*Me'am Loez*).

בְּאַחַת עָרֵי הַשָּׂדֶה — *In one of the towns of the countryside.*

This phrase literally means, *in one of the cities of the field.*

This is a reference to a non-walled city (*Ralbag*).

David refrained from asking for a place in a walled city, lest Achish refuse his request, fearful that David would take advantage of its fortifications to stage a coup (*Abarbanel*).

וְלָמָּה יֵשֵׁב עַבְדְּךָ בְּעִיר הַמַּמְלָכָה עִמָּךְ — *Why should your servant dwell in the royal city with you?*

David stated that it would be an imposition for him to live in close proximity to Achish (*Rashi*), since it is impossible for two kings to live together (*Abarbanel*).

Kli Yakar explains David to mean that it would be arrogant for him to remain in Achish's jurisdiction. His request, *Let "them" give me a place,* implied that people other than Achish should do so. He meant that the populate would gladly give David a place so that he would not encroach on Achish's territory and diminish his glory.

6. וַיִּתֶּן־לוֹ אָכִישׁ — *So Achish gave him.*

Although David had requested no more than a *place* in one of Achish's cities, Achish granted him an entire city. Also, David assumed that he would require the consent of the populace. However, Achish did not wait for anyone's approval but gave David this city immediately.

Hence, the verse continues, לָכֵן הָיְתָה צִקְלַג לְמַלְכֵי יְהוּדָה *This is why Ziklag belongs to the kings of Judah.* Had David received the city through a public election or had he shared it with the Philistines it would never have become the possession of the Judean kings. That occurred only because David acquired this city as a royal gift, and because it was reserved for him and his people (*Kli Yakar*).

בַּיּוֹם הַהוּא — *On that day.*

David merited extraordinary Providential assistance in that Achish did not hesitate to agree to his bold request (and in fact exceeded it) — thus verifying the dictum that לֶב־מֶלֶךְ בְּיַד ה׳, *the heart of a king is in the hand of* HASHEM (*Proverbs* 21:1). Achish's generosity indicates his nobility, and thus Scripture calls him Abimelech (see *Psalms* 34:1, *Rashi* ad loc.) to connote his righteousness (*Daas Sofrim*).

וַיִּתֶּן־לוֹ אָכִישׁ בַּיּוֹם הַהוּא אֶת־צִקְלָג — *So Achish gave him Ziklag on that day.*

This seemingly contradicts the statement in the Book of *Joshua* (15:31) that Ziklag was a city belonging to the tribe of Judah.

Radak offers two explanations. First, following the Book of *Joshua's* description of Ziklag as a city of Judah, the Philistines conquered it. Alternatively, that description was in fact a prediction that one day Ziklag would become a Judean city — as was occurring now.

לָכֵן הָיְתָה צִקְלַג לְמַלְכֵי יְהוּדָה — *This is why Ziklag belongs to the kings of Judah.*

of the towns of the countryside that I may settle there. Why should your servant dwell in the royal city with you?" [6]*So Achish gave him Ziklag on that day; this is why Ziklag belongs to the kings of Judah to this day.* [7]*The number of days that David dwelled in the Philistine countryside was four months and two days.*

It remained in the possession of the kings, for they did not transfer it to the entire tribe (*Metzudos*).

לָכֵן הָיְתָה צִקְלַג לְמַלְכֵי יְהוּדָה עַד הַיּוֹם הַזֶּה — *This is why Ziklag belongs to the kings of Judah to this day.*

Kli Yakar suggests homiletically that this verse indicates that Ziklag remained a historical landmark because it was where David lived in relative tranquility for the first time and began his ascent to the throne.

The Talmud (*Bava Basra* 14b) records that the author of the majority of the Book of *Samuel* was Samuel himself. After he died, it was completed by Nathan the Prophet and Gad the Seer.

In his monumental and controversial introduction to the Early Prophets, *Abarbanel* cites the present verse to challenge this contention, asking how Samuel could have referred to the kings of Judah, since the Israelite nation was not split into two separate kingdoms — Israel and Judah — until after his death. *Abarbanel* concludes that Jeremiah compiled and edited the words of Samuel, Nathan, and Gad, and added his own occasional comments.

Nachalas Shimon (31:25) defends the Talmud, however, suggesting that Nathan or Gad was still living during the days of Rehoboam and wrote this verse.

7. יָמִים וְאַרְבָּעָה חֳדָשִׁים — *Four months and two days.*

We translate the word יָמִים — literally, *days* — as *two days*, following the rule that an unspecified plural is assumed to mean *two* (*Rashi*).

However, this word may also be rendered as *a year* (see *Genesis* 24:55, *Leviticus* 25:29, *Rashi* ad loc.; *Kesubos* 57b), a reading propounded by *Rabbeinu Yeshayah* (above, 13:1), *Mahari Kara*, and *Targum*.[1]

Finally, *Abarbanel* offers a third view, translating יָמִים as *two years* (as in *Genesis* [41:1]: שְׁנָתַיִם יָמִים).

The translation of יָמִים as *year* or *two years* is problematic, for two principal reasons.

First, this entire episode took place after Samuel's death (see above, 25:1) and before that of Saul. The period of time separating those deaths was less than a year — four months according to *Rashi* (citing *Seder Olam*, Ch. 13), and seven months according to *Radak* (see comm. above, 25:1). Second, Scripture states that Saul's kingdom lasted two years (above, 13:1). If יָמִים means a *year*, then all of the events that transpired from the beginning of Saul's reign (Ch. 10) until the present took place within a span of eight months — a highly implausible scenario. And if יָמִים means *two years*, as *Abarbanel* proposes, then this explanation is completely incredible.

Rabbeinu Yeshayah addresses this point and explains that Scripture's comment that Saul's reigned for two years refers only to the time before David was anointed. The period after that is no longer counted as belonging to Saul's kingdom, since it had been technically superseded by that of David.

Abarbanel and *Ralbag* explain in a similar vein that the statement about

1. However, an alternative reading of *Targum*, cited by *Radak*, translates יָמִים as יוֹמִין, *days.*

ח וַיַּעַל דָּוִד וַאֲנָשָׁיו וַיִּפְשְׁטוּ אֶל־הַגְּשׁוּרִי °והגרזי
וְהָעֲמָלֵקִי כִּי הֵנָּה יֹשְׁבוֹת הָאָרֶץ אֲשֶׁר מֵעוֹלָם בּוֹאֲךָ
ט שׁוּרָה וְעַד־אֶרֶץ מִצְרָיִם: וְהִכָּה דָוִד אֶת־הָאָרֶץ
וְלֹא יְחַיֶּה אִישׁ וְאִשָּׁה וְלָקַח צֹאן וּבָקָר וַחֲמֹרִים
י וּגְמַלִּים וּבְגָדִים וַיָּשָׁב וַיָּבֹא אֶל־אָכִישׁ: וַיֹּאמֶר
אָכִישׁ אַל־פְּשַׁטְתֶּם הַיּוֹם וַיֹּאמֶר דָּוִד עַל־נֶגֶב יְהוּדָה

°וְהַגִּזְרִי ק׳

Saul ruling for two years refers solely to the events prior to verse 13:1.

Abarbanel challenges *Rashi* and *Radak's* interpretation of יָמִים as *days* on the basis of the fact that, when Scripture mentions a larger and smaller figure together, it conventionally presents the larger figure first. Thus, if יָמִים means *days*, the verse should have stated *four months and two* יָמִים (not, as it does, *two* יָמִים *and four months*).

But *Malbim* provides an explanation for the wording by commenting that David and his men spent two days in Gath, followed by four months in Ziklag; thus, the days are mentioned first and the months second.

Abarbanel cites further support for his view that יָמִים means *two years* by citing the words of Achish, הֲלוֹא־זֶה דָוִד עֶבֶד שָׁאוּל מֶלֶךְ־יִשְׂרָאֵל אֲשֶׁר הָיָה אִתִּי זֶה יָמִים אוֹ־זֶה שָׁנִים — *Is this not David, the servant of Saul, king of Israel, who has been with me for these days or these years...* (below, 29:3).

Radak, however, counters that this statement should not be read literally. Achish appreciated David as if he had been in Ziklag for years; in truth, however, David had been there only a few months.

Kli Yakar resolves both verses according to the literal understanding. David spent four months in Ziklag *inactive*, before beginning his conquests of the surrounding territory; but including the period of conquest, he spent a few years there. Alternatively, David spent four months in Ziklag, but a much longer period of time in Gath.[1]

◆§ David Raids the Neighbors While Earning Achish's Trust

8. וַיַּעַל דָּוִד וַאֲנָשָׁיו — *David and his men went up.*

Rashi comments that this is to be understood in the past continuous tense: David and his men were regularly going up.

וַיַּעַל דָּוִד וַאֲנָשָׁיו וַיִּפְשְׁטוּ אֶל־הַגְּשׁוּרִי וְהַגִּזְרִי וְהָעֲמָלֵקִי — *David and his men went up and spread out against the Geshurite and the Gizrite and the Amalekite.*

They did this because they had nothing to eat.

Since these three nations were Achish's enemies, they did not complain to him, and he did nothing to prevent these incursions.

אֶל־הַגְּשׁוּרִי — *Against the Geshurite.*

The Talmud (*Sanhedrin* 107a) relates that David wed a *woman of beautiful form*, a gentile woman whom a soldier may marry under certain conditions (*Deuteronomy* 21:10-14). That woman was Maacah, daughter of Talmai, king of Geshur, and the mother of Absalom (see *II Samuel* 3:3) and Tamar (ibid. 13:1).

It is likely that David met her in the course of a battle against the nation of Geshur (*Daas Sofrim*).

כִּי הֵנָּה יֹשְׁבוֹת הָאָרֶץ אֲשֶׁר מֵעוֹלָם — *For they were the original inhabitants of the land.*

The words הֵנָּה, *they* and יֹשְׁבוֹת, *inhabitants*, are written in the feminine form. *Radak* explains that the subject of this phrase is the feminine word מִשְׁפָּחוֹת, *families*, and the families listed lived in these lands.

1. These interpretations, *Kli Yakar* concedes, are inconsistent with the Sages' view (echoed by *Rashi*) that Saul's reign lasted a total of two years, and he concludes that he will not dispute the Sages.

8 David and his men went up and spread out
against the Geshurite and the Gizrite and the
Amalekite, for they were the original inhabitants of
the land, from where you approach Shur until the
land of Egypt. 9 David would smite the land, and
would not leave a man or woman alive; he would
take sheep, cattle, donkeys, camels, and clothing,
and would return and come to Achish. 10 Achish
would ask, "Where did you raid today?" And
David would say, "Against the south of Judah,"

כִּי הֵנָּה יֹשְׁבוֹת הָאָרֶץ אֲשֶׁר מֵעוֹלָם — *For they were the original inhabitants of the land.*

That is to say, since they were nearby (*Rabbeinu Yeshayah*).

Furthermore, since they had been dwelling there peacefully for many years, they grew complacent and were not prepared for David's offensive (*Radak*).

Malbim adds that these nations were among the seven Canaanite nations that the Israelites were commanded to annihilate (*Deuteronomy* 20:16). Accordingly, David was performing a mitzvah.

בּוֹאֲךָ שׁוּרָה — *From where you approach Shur.*

Scripture describes the location as if speaking to a person familiar with the area (*Metzudos*).

9. וְלֹא יְחַיֶּה אִישׁ וְאִשָּׁה — *And would not leave a man or woman alive.*

David acted in this fashion even though it was the practice for raiding parties to take captives, because he meant to leave no survivors who could tell who had attacked them (*Radak*) — an element that was crucial to David's plans (see following verse).

Midrash Esther Rabbah (7:13) mentions that in Haman's campaign to gain support for his plan to annihilate the Jews, he cited this verse to show David's "lack of mercy" in killing the men and woman of "all the kingdoms."

וְלָקַח צֹאן וּבָקָר וַחֲמֹרִים וּגְמַלִּים — *He would take sheep, cattle, donkeys, and camels.*

Since David did not kill the livestock, it appears that the commandment to destroy Amalek does not apply to their animals (see *Mechilta, Rashi,* and *Meshech Chochmah* to *Deuteronomy* 25:19; see comm. above, 15:3,9).

10. וַיֹּאמֶר אָכִישׁ אַל־פְּשַׁטְתֶּם הַיּוֹם — *Achish would ask, "Where did you raid today?"*

This phrase includes the word אַל, which generally signifies, *let not* or *do not*. But that meaning does not seem to fit the present context — literally, *Achish said, "al did you raid today?"*

Rashi explains אַל here, to mean אָן — *where* — as the letter ל sometimes substitutes for a נ. Thus, Achish asked David, *Where did you raid?*

According to *Ralbag*, the word אַל is to be read as if it were spelled עַל, *on*, and the word מִי, *who*, is implied. Thus, the phrase reads עַל מִי, *Upon whom did you raid?*

Ibn Ezra maintains the conventional meaning of אַל, understanding Achish's comment as a rhetorical question: *Did you not raid today?*

Chomas Anach adds that according to this, Achish was induced by Providence to express himself as he did, so that David might answer him without overtly lying. David did not have to say "Yes, I did." Rather, by merely listing his victims, it would imply that he had raided those places, which is what Achish

כז/יא־יב

יא וְעַל־נֶגֶב הַיְּרַחְמְאֵלִי וְאֶל־נֶגֶב הַקֵּינִי׃ וְאִישׁ וְאִשָּׁה
לֹא־יְחַיֶּה דָוִד לְהָבִיא גַת לֵאמֹר פֶּן־יַגִּדוּ עָלֵינוּ
לֵאמֹר כֹּה־עָשָׂה דָוִד וְכֹה מִשְׁפָּטוֹ כָּל־הַיָּמִים
יב אֲשֶׁר יָשַׁב בִּשְׂדֵה פְלִשְׁתִּים׃ וַיַּאֲמֵן אָכִישׁ בְּדָוִד
לֵאמֹר הַבְאֵשׁ הִבְאִישׁ בְּעַמּוֹ בְיִשְׂרָאֵל וְהָיָה
כח/א א לִי לְעֶבֶד עוֹלָם׃ וַיְהִי
בַּיָּמִים הָהֵם וַיִּקְבְּצוּ פְלִשְׁתִּים אֶת־מַחֲנֵיהֶם
לַצָּבָא לְהִלָּחֵם בְּיִשְׂרָאֵל וַיֹּאמֶר אָכִישׁ אֶל־דָּוִד
יָדֹעַ תֵּדַע כִּי אִתִּי תֵּצֵא בַמַּחֲנֶה אַתָּה וַאֲנָשֶׁיךָ׃

understood. However, since Achish said, "You did not raid," David's reply can also mean that he had *not* raided the south of Judah, the south of the Jerahmeelite, or the south of the Kenite.

וְעַל־נֶגֶב הַיְּרַחְמְאֵלִי — *Or "Against the south of the Jerahmeelite."*

The Judean clan of Jerahmeel was descended from Hezron, son of Perez (see *I Chronicles* (2:9).

וְאֶל־נֶגֶב הַקֵּינִי — *Or "Against the south of the Kenite."*

The Kenites were the descendants of Jethro, Moses' father-in-law. They settled among the families of the tribes of Judah, as recorded in *Judges* (1:16).

וַיֹּאמֶר דָּוִד עַל־נֶגֶב יְהוּדָה וְעַל־נֶגֶב הַיְּרַחְמְאֵלִי וְאֶל־נֶגֶב הַקֵּינִי — *And David would say, "Against the south of Judah," or "Against the south of the Jerahmeelite," or "Against the south of the Kenite."*

By impressing upon Achish the idea that he had become an enemy to his own people, David gained his confidence.

Although Achish would eventually hear about David's conquests in Geshur, David would explain that he had conducted those raids in passing, on his return from Judah (*Abarbanel*).

עַל־נֶגֶב יְהוּדָה וְעַל־נֶגֶב הַיְּרַחְמְאֵלִי וְאֶל־נֶגֶב הַקֵּינִי — *"Against the south of Judah," or "Against the south of the Jerahmeelite," or "Against the south of the Kenite."*

These three territories were near one another (*Radak*).

Kli Yakar observes that regarding Judah and Jerahmeel, David's word for *against* is עַל — lit., *upon* — whereas regarding the Kenites, it uses the word אֶל — *to*. By using this terminology, David implied that he had assaulted his own kinsmen more forcefully than he did the Kenites.

11. פֶּן־יַגִּדוּ עָלֵינוּ לֵאמֹר כֹּה־עָשָׂה דָוִד — *Lest they inform about us, saying, "This is what David did."*

David wanted Achish to believe that he was attacking Israelites.

Me'am Loez suggests that David was concerned that fugitives might meet Saul's allies and inform them of his whereabouts.

12. וַיַּאֲמֵן אָכִישׁ בְּדָוִד לֵאמֹר הַבְאֵשׁ הִבְאִישׁ בְּעַמּוֹ — *And Achish believed David, thinking, "He has really come to abhor his people."*

Since David regularly staged these raids, apparently against his own people, he clearly despised them and would would never make peace with them (*Radak*).

בְּעַמּוֹ בְיִשְׂרָאֵל — *His people Israel.*

Had David attacked only Kenites or Jews who did not belong to his tribe, one might suspect that he could still garner the support of his tribe of Judah.

27/11-12 *or "Against the south of the Jerahmeelite," or*
"Against the south of the Kenite." [11] *And David*
would not leave alive any man or woman to bring
back [captive] to Gath, saying [to himself], "Lest
they inform about us, saying, 'This is what David
did and this has been his practice all the days that
he has been dwelling in the Philistine countryside.'"
[12] *And Achish believed David, thinking, "He has*
really come to abhor his people Israel, and he will
be my servant always."

28/1 [1] *It happened in those days that the Philistines mo-*
bilized their camps to the army, to fight against
Israel, and Achish said to David, "Know that you will
go forth with me to the camp — you and your men."

On the other hand, had he raided Judah alone, one might argue that he wished to persuade the rest of Israel that he was not partial to his own tribe — but that he had not spurned his people as a whole. By attacking both עַמּוֹ — *his people*, i.e., his tribe — as well as יִשְׂרָאֵל — *[non-Judean] Israelites* — he demonstrated that he had alienated himself from them all (*Malbim*).

XXVIII

❧ David Is Invited to Join Achish at War

1. וַיְהִי — *It happened.*

This word generally denotes a troublesome time (see *Megillah* 10b). It is used here because this episode would prove to be dolorous for Saul and his sons, and for the nation of Israel as a whole.

In addition, this constituted a time of crisis for David, presenting him with the quandary of whether to fight against his brethren or, by refraining from doing so, lose Achish's painstakingly procured trust. In the end, Hashem kindly saved David from this dilemma when the officers of Achish's army refused to allow him to fight with them (*Kli Yakar*).

וַיְהִי בַּיָּמִים הָהֵם וַיִּקְבְּצוּ פְלִשְׁתִּים אֶת־מַחֲנֵיהֶם לַצָּבָא לְהִלָּחֵם בְּיִשְׂרָאֵל — *It happened in those days that the Philistines mobilized their camps to the army, to fight against Israel.*

Although Samuel's death is not mentioned until v. 3, *Tosefta* (to *Sotah* 11:6) states that he died somewhat earlier, and that his death prompted this offensive. The Philistines believed, based on their experience, that Samuel's merit had protected Israel. Now that he was no longer alive, they were optimistic that an assault on Israel would meet with success.

Kli Yakar adds that the Philistines' confidence was bolstered as well by the fact that David was absent from the Israelite army.

וַיֹּאמֶר אָכִישׁ אֶל־דָּוִד יָדֹעַ תֵּדַע כִּי אִתִּי תֵּצֵא בַמַּחֲנֶה — *Achish said to David, "Know that you will go forth with me to the camp."*

In the next verse, Achish invites David to be his personal bodyguard.

ב וַיֹּאמֶר דָּוִד אֶל־אָכִישׁ לָכֵן אַתָּה תֵדַע אֵת אֲשֶׁר־
יַעֲשֶׂה עַבְדֶּךָ וַיֹּאמֶר אָכִישׁ אֶל־דָּוִד לָכֵן שֹׁמֵר
לְרֹאשִׁי אֲשִׂימְךָ כָּל־הַיָּמִים:
ג וּשְׁמוּאֵל מֵת וַיִּסְפְּדוּ־לוֹ כָּל־יִשְׂרָאֵל וַיִּקְבְּרֻהוּ
בָרָמָה וּבְעִירוֹ וְשָׁאוּל הֵסִיר הָאֹבוֹת וְאֶת־
ד הַיִּדְּעֹנִים מֵהָאָרֶץ: וַיִּקָּבְצוּ פְלִשְׁתִּים וַיָּבֹאוּ וַיַּחֲנוּ

According to *Malbim*, Achish was already making that offer here, in the words, אִתִּי תֵּצֵא, *you will go forth with me*. When David did not respond to this oblique offer, Achish inferred that David did not understand him and repeated his offer explicitly.

2. וַיֹּאמֶר דָּוִד אֶל־אָכִישׁ לָכֵן אַתָּה תֵדַע אֵת אֲשֶׁר־יַעֲשֶׂה עַבְדֶּךָ — *David replied to Achish, "Therefore, you shall see what your servant will do!"*

David responded with deliberate ambiguity in order to give the impression that he would demonstrate his loyalty by attacking the Israelites, whereas he intended to do no more than protect Achish without harming any Israelite (*Abarbanel*).

לָכֵן אַתָּה תֵדַע אֵת אֲשֶׁר־יַעֲשֶׂה עַבְדֶּךָ — *Therefore, you shall see what your servant will do!*

David promised that he would now vindicate the trust that Achish had placed in him (*Metzudos*).

Achish had heretofore known of David's abilities from hearsay. Now he would see them demonstrated with his own eyes (*Malbim*).

וַיֹּאמֶר אָכִישׁ אֶל־דָּוִד לָכֵן שֹׁמֵר לְרֹאשִׁי אֲשִׂימְךָ כָּל־הַיָּמִים — *Achish then said to David, "Therefore I will appoint you as my permanent bodyguard."*

According to *Rabbeinu Yeshayah*, the word לָכֵן, *therefore*, implies a reward. Once David fulfilled his promise to attack the Israelites, he would be appointed the king's personal bodyguard.

Other commentators, however, state that Achish immediately appointed David as his bodyguard. Accordingly, *Malbim* explains that Achish was assuring David that he did not question his loyalty or strength. On the contrary, לָכֵן, *therefore*, it was precisely due to Achish's confidence that he offered David the post. It was common for a king to appoint an outsider, rather than one of his own soldiers, as his bodyguard, becasue he needed protection not only from foreign enemies, but from his own people who might have reason to overthrow him.

According to *Abarbanel*, Achish liked David and thus wanted him in his vicinity. This was a manifestation of the principle later noted by Solomon, *When HASHEM favors a man's ways, even his foes will make peace with him* (*Proverbs* 16:7).

Me'am Loez states that Achish appointed David as his bodyguard because he did not want people to say that he had conscripted David in order to have him killed.

According to *Kli Yakar*, Achish had two motives in keeping David with him. First, he wanted to save David the pain of killing people. And second, he was afraid that David would have mercy on his own kinsmen.

Saul Begins to Fear the Philistine Attack

3. וּשְׁמוּאֵל מֵת וַיִּסְפְּדוּ־לוֹ כָּל־יִשְׂרָאֵל — *Samuel had died and all Israel eulogized him.*

Samuel's death was reported earlier in Chapter 25 (25:1), and there we cited differing opinions regarding the chronology. Here, *Rashi* comments that Samuel

[2]*David replied to Achish, "Therefore you shall see*
what your servant will do!" Achish then said to
David, "Therefore I will appoint you as my per-
manent bodyguard."
[3]*Samuel had died and all Israel eulogized him*
and buried him in Ramah, in his hometown. Saul
had banished the ov-necromancers and the yidoni-
diviners from the land.
[4]*The Philistines mobilized, they came and en-*

died in the context of the events narrated in Chapter 25. His death is restated here to explain the following episode, when Saul resorted to necromancy, because he had no prophet to guide him. This also clarifies the connection beteen Samuel's death and the end of this verse, which states that it was hard for Saul to find a necromancer because he had banished them. Had Samuel been alive, Saul would have gone to him.

Abarbanel adds that Samuel's presence made it possible for others to achieve prophecy. Now that he was gone, other prophets were not available to Saul.

Malbim explains that Samuel's death is noted here because it was the cause of four events mentioned in the following verses. First, it created the need for a public statement prohibiting recourse to sorcerers; in Samuel's lifetime, no one had dreamed of seeking advice from a sorcerer, since it was possible to speak with Samuel. Second, the Philistines gathered for war, since they were no longer concerned that Samuel's merit would protect the Jews. Third, Saul grew fearful, for the same reason. And fourth, he sought out a necromancer because he could not speak to Samuel.

וַיִּסְפְּדוּ־לוֹ כָּל־יִשְׂרָאֵל וַיִּקְבְּרֻהוּ בָרָמָה וּבְעִירוֹ — *And all Israel eulogized him and buried him in Ramah, in his hometown.*

The phrase בָרָמָה וּבְעִירוֹ — literally, *in Ramah and in his hometown* — is perplexing for two reasons. First, Samuel obviously was buried in one site, not two. And second, Ramah was itself Samuel's hometown.

Thus, our translation, based on *Rabbeinu Yeshayah,* renders the word וּבְעִירוֹ as if it read simply בְּעִירוֹ, *in his hometown.*

Radak explains this phrase to mean that there was more than one locale called Ramah. This phrase specifies the Ramah in which Samuel was buried.

Alternatively, *Radak* states that this phrase informs us that the burial took place inside the city limits, which was an unusual procedure.

Targum renders the word וּבְעִירוֹ as modifying the word וַיִּסְפְּדוּ, *and they eulogized.* Thus, the phrase reads, *All of Israel eulogized him and buried him in Ramah, and each person eulogized him in his own city.* This reading also appears in *Tosefta* (*Sotah* 11:5), which states that the people eulogized Saul in every city just as they did at his burial site in Ramah.

Radak explains that this was in compensation for Samuel's having traveled across the land of Israel to judge the people (see above, 7:16).

וְשָׁאוּל הֵסִיר הָאֹבוֹת וְאֶת הַיִּדְּעֹנִים מֵהָאָרֶץ — *Saul had banished the ov-necromancers and the yidoni-diviners from the land.*

Necromancers (*ovos*) and diviners (*yidonim*) were magicians who predicted the future by communicating with the dead. The Torah severely warns against such techniques, and practitioners are punishable by ston-

בְּשׁוּנֵם וַיִּקְבֹּץ שָׁאוּל אֶת־כָּל־יִשְׂרָאֵל וַיַּחֲנוּ
ה בַּגִּלְבֹּעַ: וַיַּרְא שָׁאוּל אֶת־מַחֲנֵה פְלִשְׁתִּים וַיִּרָא
ו וַיֶּחֱרַד לִבּוֹ מְאֹד: וַיִּשְׁאַל שָׁאוּל בַּיהוָה וְלֹא
עָנָהוּ יהוה גַּם בַּחֲלֹמוֹת גַּם בָּאוּרִים גַּם בַּנְּבִיאִם:

ing (*Leviticus* 20:27). According to the mishnah (*Sanhedrin* 65a), a necromancer *(ov)* raised voices of the spirits of the deceased through his armpit, whereas a diviner (*yidoni*) placed a bone of an animal called a *yadua* in his mouth, and a voice emanated from the bone. (Below, we will discuss necromancy in greater detail.)

Abarbanel comments that the verse mentions this action of Saul to his disrepute, for although he had initially banished these abominations, he then himself made use of them.

4. וַיַּחֲנוּ בְשׁוּנֵם — *Encamped at Shunem.*

Shunem was a city in the portion of Issachar (*Joshua* 19:18). Possibly, the Philistines advanced there because the people of Issachar, scholars heavily involved in Torah learning, were not known to possess military prowess (*Daas Sofrim*).

5. ...וַיַּרְא שָׁאוּל אֶת־מַחֲנֵה פְלִשְׁתִּים — *When Saul saw the Philistine camp...*

Gilboa was an elevated mountainous area, which allowed Saul a panoramic view of the Philistine army.

וַיִּרָא וַיֶּחֱרַד לִבּוֹ מְאֹד — *He was afraid and his heart trembled greatly.*

Saul was terrified for a number of reasons, which have already been delineated — one of them being that he no longer could count on Samuel's prayers on his behalf (*Abarbanel*).

The Midrash (*Bamidbar Rabbah* 11:3) states that a man who has not sinned is awarded the gift of instilling fear in others. Conversely, after a man sins, he is afraid of others. Until Saul sinned, he was a warrior filled with confidence (see above, 14:47), but now his heart trembled as he contemplated the Philistines' impending attack.

6. וְלֹא עָנָהוּ ה׳ — *But* H*ASHEM* *did not answer him.*

Targum renders this phrase as H*ASHEM* *did not accept his prayers.* Apparently, any inquiry made of Hashem must be accompanied by a prayer that it be answered (*Daas Sofrim*).

וְלֹא עָנָהוּ ה׳ גַּם בַּחֲלֹמוֹת גַּם בָּאוּרִים גַּם בַּנְּבִיאִם — *But* H*ASHEM* *did not answer him — not in dreams, nor through the Urim [VeTumim], nor through the prophets.*

This phrase repeats the word גַּם three times — which, following *Radak*, we interpret as enumerating items on a list (see also *Judges* 8:22). Thus, Hashem did not answer him in any of the following three ways.

According to *Kli Yakar*, however, the word גַּם here retains its more usual meaning of *also*, and the phrase H*ASHEM* *did not answer him* refers to a different means of communication; Saul had once experienced prophecy (19:24), and he tried to enter this elevated state again, but failed. Then, he tried to inquire through dreams, through the *Urim*, and through other prophets.

גַּם בַּחֲלֹמוֹת — *Not in dreams.*

Radak and *Ralbag* explain that certain people were known to have the ability to make "dream inquiries." They would focus on a question in a waking state and would be given a response in a dream.

Some commentators imply that Saul himself attempted to engage in such a dream inquiry.

גַּם בָּאוּרִים — *Nor through the Urim [VeTumim].*

The *Urim VeTumim*, which were worn by the Kohen Gadol (see *Exodus* 28:30), answered the questions of petitioners.

camped at Shunem, and Saul mobilized all Israel
and they encamped at Gilboa. 5 *When Saul saw the*
Philistine camp he was afraid and his heart trem-
bled greatly. 6 *Saul inquired of* HASHEM, *but* HASHEM
did not answer him — not in dreams, nor through
the Urim [VeTumim], nor through the prophets.

According to *Rashi*, the *Urim VeTumim* did not respond to Saul because he had caused the death of the Kohanim at Nob.

Ralbag suggests that after Saul killed those Kohanim, no Kohen worthy of Divine Inspiration necessary to understand the *Urim VeTumim* remained. Alternatively, such Kohanim may have been found only in David's camp.

Radak states that the *Urim VeTumim* were in the possession of Abiathar, who was with David, and that Saul sent messengers to David's camp to inquire of them.

This is one of the few verses in which Scripture uses the word *Urim* without the word *Tumim* (see also *Numbers* 27:21).

The Talmud explains that the word *Urim* (from the word אוֹר, *light*) indicates that the letters shone, and *Tumim* (from תָּם, *complete*) that they brought their words to completion, in the sense that their decrees came true (*Yoma* 73b, *Rashi* ad loc.). Possibly, Saul only desired their function as *Urim*, in that he sought advice on how to act,[1] not a prediction of the future (*Mishbetzos Zahav*).

גַּם בַּנְּבִיאִם — *Nor through the prophets.* This is a reference to Samuel's disciples (see above, 19:20; *Radak, Ralbag*).

Targum renders נְבִיאִם as סַפְרַיָא — *scribes. Daas Sofrim* sees in this translation an implication that Saul did not seek the preeminent prophets of the generation such as Gad or Nathan, but rather sought those on a lower level.

גַּם בַּחֲלֹמוֹת גַּם בָּאוּרִים גַּם בַּנְּבִיאִם — *Not in dreams, nor through the Urim [VeTumim], nor through the prophets.*

According to *Ralbag*, this verse mentions three elements in ascending order of effectiveness. First, dream inquiries were least likely to produce a response. Second, the *Urim VeTumim* could be expected to answer any question unless blocked by an impediment caused by sin. And third, because of the abundance of prophets alive at the time, Saul might have been expected with almost total certitude to receive prophetic assistance. Thus, with each subsequent example, it became more surprising that he had no response.

Abarbanel states that Saul's inquiries were made in ascending order of Divine power. Lowest are dreams; then come the *Urim VeTumim*, which stand at a level of Divine Inspiration; and finally prophecy is the highest level of communication with God.

וַיִּשְׁאַל שָׁאוּל בַּה׳ וְלֹא עָנָהוּ ה׳ גַּם בַּחֲלֹמוֹת גַּם בָּאוּרִים גַּם בַּנְּבִיאִם — *Saul inquired of* HASHEM, *but* HASHEM *did not answer him — not in dreams, nor through the Urim [VeTumim], nor through the prophets.*

A verse in *I Chronicles* (10:14) states that Saul died because he consulted a necromancer — וְלֹא־דָרַשׁ בַּה׳ — *and did not seek out* HASHEM. Yet we see here that Saul did initially seek out Hashem. However, his recourse to a necromancer shows that he effectively equated that with seeking the word of Hashem. Therefore, his search for Hashem's word was tantamount to not inquiring of Hashem at all (*Radak*).

According to *Abarbanel*, the state-

1. This was all that Saul asked of Samuel — לְהוֹדִיעֵנִי מָה אֶעֱשֶׂה, *to tell me what to do.* Thus, we can infer that this was the question that he would have posed to the *Urim VeTumim.*

ment that Saul did not inquire of Hashem refers not to the present incident but to the episodes involving Gilgal (see above, Ch. 13) and Amalek (Ch. 15).

Scripture relates here that וַיִּשְׁאַל שָׁאוּל בַּה' — *Saul inquired of HASHEM*, whereas in *Chronicles* he is described as וְלֹא־דָרַשׁ בַּה' — *he did not seek out HASHEM*. That is to say, even when Saul inquired of Hashem, he did so in a desultory manner. Only a refusal to accept failure is called truly *seeking* Hashem; but Saul did not devote his entire heart to this endeavor, and instead easily gave up (*Malbim* and *Kli Yakar*).

Malbim adds that Saul proved that he had not committed himself to eliciting an answer from Hashem by the fact that he inquired in an ascending order of holiness: first dreams, then the *Urim VeTumim*, and finally prophets. Had he been determined to seek Hashem's word, he would have prepared himself properly and gone directly to the prophets.

Daas Sofrim states that the fact that Saul inquired of a prophet last constituted a disparagement of the value of prophecy. Thus, Saul was considered as if he had not sought out Hashem at all.

☙ Preface: Saul's Inquiry of the Ov Necromancer

The following incident is one of the most perplexing in all of Scripture. After Saul had rid the nation of *ov* necromancy and *yidoni* divination, he himself resorted to necromancy in order to communicate with Samuel. Various questions immediately come to mind — for instance:

❒ How could Saul, a righteous man, justify engaging in a prohibited mode of witchcraft that he himself had zealously extirpated? The question is how Saul himself could have erroneously rationalized what he did; not that it was permissible, for Scripture clearly calls it a sin (*I Chronicles* 10:13).

❒ How could the profane powers of witchcraft have brought back the holy soul of Samuel?

❒ In the course of the narrative, why was the sorceress surprised to see Samuel, if it was her expertise that had raised him? And how did she know that the person making the inquiry was Saul?

This topic is the subject of a wide of range of explanations, found both in the Midrash and in the commentaries. To facilitate a clear understanding, before proceeding to the verse-by-verse elucidation, we will outline the various views regarding this episode.

☙ How Are Ov Necromancy and Yidoni Divination Performed?

Above (v. 3), we cited the mishnah's description of *ov* necromancy and *yidoni* divination.

Radak adds that the sorcerer would wave his hand. Others say that he would burn incense. According to *Rambam*, the sorcerer would wave a wand of myrtle. Following the necessary preparations, a demon would come and speak in a soft voice.

The mishnah cited earlier mentions a type of necromancy in which the voice emanates from a joint of the sorcerer or from his underarm.

The Talmud (*Sanhedrin* 65b) mentions two other types of necromancy: נִשְׁאַל בְּגוּלְגּוֹלֶת and מַעֲלֶה בִּזְכוּרוֹ. *Rashi* explains מַעֲלֶה בִּזְכוּרוֹ as meaning *raising with his male organ*, for the sorcerer raised a spirit that spoke from the vicinity of his male organ.

However, *Tosafos* (ibid.) contest this interpretation on the basis of the incident described here, in which the magician was a woman (see *Maharsha*). *Tosafos* therefore explain that זְכוּרוֹ does not mean *male organ* but is simply the name of this sorcery.

According to *Radak*, the voice seems to come from under the ground at a burial site.

נִשְׁאַל בְּגוּלְגּוֹלֶת — *consulting a skull* — is a process whereby the sorcerer communicates with the skull of a dead body (*Rashi*) — or, according to *Radak*, receives information from a voice that emanates from a *shoham* stone or a crystal ball.

☙ The Efficacy of Ov Necromancy

Our Sages apparently consider the power of necromancy to be genuine, albeit proscribed and involving unclean spiritual forces (see *Sanhedrin* 65 and *Vayikra Rabbah* 26:7).

They state that the sorceress whom Saul consulted was able to summon Samuel's soul because during the first twelve months after a person dies, his soul periodically returns to his body (*Shabbos* 152b).

However, some highly respected commentators consider witchcraft a hoax. The most extreme view is held by *Rabbi Shmuel ben Chophni* (cited by *Radak*). According to him, there was no validity to this type of magic; they were all merely deceptions performed by their practitioners. Even in Saul's case, Samuel never actually rose from the dead. Rather, an accomplice of the sorceress pretended to be the prophet. She recognized Saul and her exhibition of surprise was entirely feigned. The sorceress and her confederate were able to predict Saul's demise because it was common knowledge that David had been chosen to succeed Saul, and that the Jews feared the impending confrontation with the Philistine army. Scripture's statement that Samuel spoke with Saul only reflects Saul's perspective.

However, *Radak* and *Abarbanel* dismiss this theory as farfetched. Aside from the fact that it disputes the Sages' view that this necromancy was authentic, Saul would not be deceived by such a fabrication. Also, it is not feasible that the sorceress would know about private conversations between Samuel and Saul and that she would so accurately guess the following day's events.

Rav Saadia Gaon and *Rav Hai Gaon* (cited by *Radak*) state that in general necromancy is a fraud, and in this case too the woman had planned to deceive Saul. However, to her surprise, Hashem brought Samuel back to inform Saul of his fate. That is why she screamed in bewilderment and fear.

However, *Radak* and *Abarbanel* question this view as well. First, this would mean that Saul was naive enough to believe in the efficacy of a fraudulent technique — a proposition that they reject. Besides, it is hard to understand why Hashem would choose to communicate words of prophecy in this manner, rather than through living prophets or the *Urim VeTumim*. Furthermore, Scripture implies that the woman screamed (v. 12) not because she was surprised to see her witchcraft work but because she realized that Saul was standing before her.

Ralbag (here, and in greater detail in his *Sefer Milchamos HASHEM*) and *Rambam* explain that the communication of the *ov* came not via a vision or voice but via the imaginative faculty. It therefore required both the practitioner and inquirer to plunge deeply into their imaginations. This explains our Sages' comment that the practitioner sees but does not hear, and the inquirer hears but does not see — because each perceives what he strives to imagine. (Thus, bystanders neither see nor hear anything.)

Abarbanel understands *Ralbag* to mean that, like sick people or people with limited intelligence, Saul experienced a hallucination. *Abarbanel* disputes this view — first, because there are sources that demonstrate that necromancy is real, and second, because it is inconceivable that the intelligent, wise, and healthy king would hallucinate. Moreover, if this were the case, why would Scripture present a conversation in which Samuel speaks? And furthermore, how could Saul's imagination have so accurately predicted the future?

However, *Kli Yakar* defends the explanation of *Ralbag* and *Rambam*, clarifying that they do not mean to say that Saul was hallucinating. Rather, genuine messages are being communicated not, however, through sound, but through the medium of the imagination.

Rambam (*Hil. Avodas Kochavim* 11:16) explicitly states that all of the types of witchcraft and omens mentioned in the Torah and the Talmud are frauds, in which a Jew

should place no credence.

The *Vilna Gaon* (see *Beur HaGra* to *Yoreh Deah* 179:13) sharply critiques *Rambam* for making this statement, and accuses him of having been unduly influenced by the philosophers who did not take the words of the Sages literally. The Vilna Gaon cites many stories recorded in the Talmud that tell of the practice of omens and magic.

Abarbanel's interpretation of the *ov* is based on the belief that demons exist and have the power to foretell the future. Such entities seek entry into dead bodies — whether those of simple folk or of righteous people. Thus, the sorcerer has the ability to draw demons into bodies, which then appear to rise up from the ground and impart information.

Accordingly, in this instance a demon was speaking. However, Scripture refers to it as *Samuel* since it was residing in Samuel's body. No sorceress could have brought Samuel's exalted soul back down to earth, nor did Saul expect her to. He intended only to use the body of Samuel because the accuracy of the information imparted by a demon is dependent upon the virtue of the person from whose corpse the demon is speaking. Scripture's comment that Samuel was disturbed by this (v. 15) means that it was as if Samuel's body, which had been an abode for the Divine presence, was itself complaining about this ill association.

Radvaz (*Teshuvah,* Vol. I, 1067) states that there exist "evil powers" in the world that seek entry into dead bodies and, having gained entry, foretell events. This idea is supported by the fact that the voice emanates from the armpit or male organ, which are known to be habitations of evil power. Typically, the body rises feet first, in a manner antithetical to that of holiness.

However, the body of a prophet or righteous man is a throne for sanctity, which remains after death. Therefore, after the sorceress began her ritual to bring forth the evil powers that would enter Samuel's body, Hashem interceded and allowed Samuel's own soul to reenter his body. As a result, he rose in the natural way, head first. Seeing this, the sorceress was stunned and recognized that this was not her work but that of Hashem. Thus, she said, אֱלֹהִים רָאִיתִי עֹלִים מִן־הָאָרֶץ — lit., *I have seen God rising from the ground.*

According to *Sefer HaAkeidah* (*Shaar* 60), Saul did not ask the sorceress to use her powers of necromancy to communicate with Samuel. Rather, he requested only, קָסֳמִי־נָא לִי בָּאוֹב וְהַעֲלִי לִי — *Please divine for me through necromancy and raise up for me* (v. 8). His sole request was that she raise Samuel's body, after which he intended to communicate directly with Samuel himself.

However, *Malbim* states, quite to the contrary, that Saul originally intended to deputize the sorceress to question Samuel on his behalf.

Saul was loath to tell the witch exactly whom he wanted because she would have laughed at him. Therefore, he commanded her, *Raise Samuel up for me* (v. 11), hoping that she would think that he was referring to another person named Samuel.

When the sorceress saw the prophet Samuel, she was shocked, for she realized that only Saul would have the temerity to refer to the prophet by his first name alone.

According to *Baal HaAkeidah,* Saul thought that he was doing no wrong by using necromancy to summon Samuel. Indeed, Saul was held accountable not for the sin of *ov,* but rather for not repenting, and instead seeking alternate methods of procuring the word of Hashem without repentance.

Kli Yakar disagrees with the view of *Baal HaAkeidah* on two points. First, although he agrees that Saul utilized necromancy only to reach Samuel, he states that this too was forbidden, at least in a minor sense. Second, he states that Saul made it clear that he wanted to speak specifically to Samuel the prophet.

7 *So Saul said to his servants, "Seek out a woman who practices necromancy, and I will go*

The woman screamed not in surprise but in fear, for as Samuel rose up he wore a disapproving look on his face.

☙ What Was Saul's Rationalization for Consulting the Ov?

The Torah forbids both engaging in necromancy and consulting a necromancer (*Sanhedrin* 53a). Of all the interpretations presented above, only the last two — those of the *Baal Akeidah* and *Kli Yakar* — address the question of how King Saul justified his consultation of a necromancer.[1]

Possibly, Saul justified his behavior as being a matter of saving lives — *pikuach nefesh.* Generally speaking, one may commit any transgression — with the exception of the three cardinal sins of idolatry, adultery, and murder — in order to save a life. Saul apparently considered it essential to his survival or the survival of his troops to know what the coming battle against the Philistines held in store. Indeed, it seems to be generally accepted that prohibitions relating to magic and witchcraft are waived in life-threatening situations (see *Yoreh Deah* 179:7, *Shach* 1,9).

However, *Sefer HaChinuch* (511) argues that such dispensation is questionable since it may be argued that magical devices intrinsically possess at least a trace of idolatry (*Sefer HaChinuch* 511, *Minchas Chinuch*). In that case, comments *Minchas Chinuch,* perhaps prohibitions of magic would be deferred because of danger.

At any rate, Saul was wrong — either because necromancy qualifies as idolatry, or because he should have realized that no practical good would come of his seeking information from the ov (*Nachalas Shimon, Daas Sofrim*).[2]

Ohr HaChaim explains Saul's error as being based on his misinterpretation of the verse, *For these nations that you are possessing hearken to astrologers and diviners; but as for you, not so has* HASHEM, *your God given you. A prophet from your midst, from your brethren, like me, shall* HASHEM, *your God establish for you — to him shall you hearken* (*Deuteronomy* 18:14-15). From this, Saul deduced that the Torah prohibits a person only from consulting with necromancers when he has the option to consult prophets or the *Urim VeTumim.*

Netziv (*Haamek Davar, Deuteronomy* ibid.) ratifies this idea and adds that in perilous times — such as war — it is permitted to seek advice from an *ov* if no information may be gleaned from prophets or the *Urim VeTumim.*

According to *Netziv,* Saul was held accountable only because he should have repented and asked Hashem to answer him through more sanctified means.[3]

We now return to the verse-by-verse commentary.

☙ Saul Consults With the Sorceress

7. בַּקְשׁוּ־לִי אֵשֶׁת בַּעֲלַת־אוֹב — *Seek out a woman who practices necromancy.*

It was more common for women than men to engage in sorcery, for they were more frivolous (*Radak*) and their minds, being less involved in intellectual pursuits, were more prone to matters of the imagination (*Abarbanel*).

The Midrash (*Midrash Shmuel* 24:1, *Vayikra Rabbah* 26:7) compares Saul to a king who, after decreeing that all roosters be destroyed, complained that there were no roosters to crow and announce the time. His servants remonstrated with him, "Wasn't it

1. An act for which he was held accountable — *I Chronicles* 10:13.
2. See *Nachalas Shimon* 56.
3. See *Akeidah* above and *Malbim* below.

וְאֵלְכָה אֵלֶיהָ וְאֶדְרְשָׁה־בָּהּ וַיֹּאמְרוּ עֲבָדָיו
ח אֵלָיו הִנֵּה אֵשֶׁת בַּעֲלַת־אוֹב בְּעֵין דּוֹר: וַיִּתְחַפֵּשׂ
שָׁאוּל וַיִּלְבַּשׁ בְּגָדִים אֲחֵרִים וַיֵּלֶךְ הוּא וּשְׁנֵי
אֲנָשִׁים עִמּוֹ וַיָּבֹאוּ אֶל־הָאִשָּׁה לָיְלָה וַיֹּאמֶר
°קסומי־נָא לִי בָּאוֹב וְהַעֲלִי לִי אֵת אֲשֶׁר־אֹמַר
ט אֵלָיִךְ: וַתֹּאמֶר הָאִשָּׁה אֵלָיו הִנֵּה אַתָּה יָדַעְתָּ

°קָסֳמִי־ ק׳

you who legislated their slaughter?"

Yet, states the Midrash, at his request his servants went to find a necromancer. *Mussar HaNeviim* elucidates that although they feared revealing their knowledge of a sorceress lest they be punished for not having denounced her earlier, they were so moved by the sight of Saul's desperation that they were prepared to accept that punishment.

וְאֶדְרְשָׁה־בָּהּ — *And I will ... inquire through her.*

Saul did not intend to inquire of the *ov* himself, but rather ask the sorceress what the *ov* told her. Saul apparently assumed that in this way he would not be violating the prohibition. Although that was his original intention, once Samuel began speaking to him, Saul responded (*Malbim*).

וַיֹּאמְרוּ עֲבָדָיו אֵלָיו — *His servants told him.*

Daas Sofrim observes that Saul's servants did not hesitate to obey. Apparently, they were convinced that his behavior was justified.

הִנֵּה אֵשֶׁת בַּעֲלַת־אוֹב — *Behold, there is a woman who practices necromancy.*

According to *Pirkei D'Rabbi Eliezer* (Ch. 33), this woman was the wife of Zephaniah, the mother of Abner (general of Saul's army) and an aunt of Saul.

She had studied how to utilize the *ov* not for practical purposes but to learn about its use (as did the members of the Sanhedrin). Apparently, her son persuaded her that the dire circumstances justified its use (*Chomas Anach*).

בְּעֵין דּוֹר — *In En-dor.*

En-dor was a city in the territory of Issachar, owned by the tribe of Manasseh (*Joshua* 17:11).

8. וַיִּתְחַפֵּשׂ שָׁאוּל — *Saul disguised himself.*

Targum renders this phrase as *Saul changed himself.*

Some commentators interpret וַיִּתְחַפֵּשׂ as meaning that *he changed his clothing* (*Rashi, Ralbag*). Since the subsequent phrase tells that he *donned different clothing,* it seems likely that וַיִּתְחַפֵּשׂ means that he removed his royal garments.

Malbim sees in this verse four actions that Saul undertook to conceal his identity: (1) He changed his clothing. (2) He went accompanied by two people only — something unusual for a king. (3) He went at night, also uncommon for a king. (4) He did not state immediately that he sought Samuel, for if he were to mention that, the sorceress would sense that he was Saul, since no one else would dare summon the prophet.

Reading the word וַיִּתְחַפֵּשׂ as if it contains not a *sin* שׂ but a *shin* שׁ, the Midrash (ibid.) homiletically interprets it to mean that Saul became חָפְשִׁי — *free* — from royalty. *Mussar HaNeviim* explains this as meaning that as a result of consulting with the *ov*, Saul lost his kingdom.

Yefeh Toar, on the other hand, explains that by donning simple clothing, Saul failed to uphold the dignity of the king and thus abased himself.

וַיִּלְבַּשׁ בְּגָדִים אֲחֵרִים — *And donned different clothing.*

The Midrash (*Midrash Shmuel* 24:1, *Vayikra Rabbah* 26:7) describes these garments as the clothes of a commoner,

to her and inquire through her." His servants told
him, "Behold, there is a woman who practices nec-
romancy in En-dor."
[8] *Saul disguised himself and donned different*
clothing; he went with two men accompanying
him. They came to the woman at night, and he said
to her, "Please divine for me through necromancy,
and raise up whomever I shall tell you." [9] *But the*
woman said to him, "Behold, you surely know

or, alternatively, as shameful garments (see *Matnos Kehunah*).

The prophet Zechariah tells of a vision in which the Kohen Gadol Joshua stands in "filthy [spiritual] garments" because of the sins of his sons (*Zechariah* 3:3). Accordingly, *Kli Yakar* suggests that the present verse figuratively records that as Saul entered on this profane mission, he clothed himself in inferior spiritual garb.

וַיֵּלֶךְ הוּא וּשְׁנֵי אֲנָשִׁים עִמּוֹ — *He went, with two men accompanying him.*

According to the Midrash (ibid.), these two men were Abner and Amasa. Abner was Saul's cousin from the tribe of Benjamin, and Amasa was David's nephew from the tribe of Judah. Both were accomplished Torah scholars and mighty warriors.[1]

The Midrash adds that we learn from Saul's actions that a person should never travel with less than two escorts. A man who travels with only one aide will be forced to serve him — i.e., to attend to his needs should he grow sick or wait for him when he performs his bodily functions. (The same lesson may also be learned from Abraham [*Genesis* 22:3].)

וַיָּבֹאוּ אֶל־הָאִשָּׁה לָיְלָה — *They came to the woman at night.*

The Midrash (ibid.) states that Saul and his men actually came to her during the day — however, "the difficulty of the times darkened their daytime as if it were night."

How did the Midrash know that the verse is not to be understood literally?

❒ *Radal* states, citing *Shir HaShirim Rabbah* 3:5, that magic cannot be practiced at night

❒ *Matnos Kehunah* avers that since Saul and his men had changed their clothing and were well disguised, there would be no reason for them to specifically go at night.

❒ As mentioned above, *ov* necromancy is possible only during the first twelve months after a person's death, when his soul on occasion visits his body (*Shabbos* 15b). According to the *Zohar* (cited by *Mishbetzos Zahav*), the soul comes to earth during the day and returns to heaven at night; thus, *ov* necromancy would have worked only during the day.

❒ The phrase reads, literally, *They came to the woman — night.* That phraseology implies that this was a time "like night" (*Kli Yakar*). Had Scripture wished to say that Saul and his men went *at night*, it would have said so explicitly — i.e., בַּלַּיְלָה.

קָסֳמִי־נָא לִי בָּאוֹב — *Please divine for me through necromancy.*

The word קָסֳמִי — *divine* — refers to a specific type of sorcery (see *Deuteronomy* 18:10), but is also used more generally to refer to all types of magic (*Radak*).

This word is related to קֵיסָם, a *stick* or *splinter*, because the magician would

1. A possible source for the Midrash's conclusion is that these two men are also referred to as אֲנָשִׁים, in the sense of *distinguished men*, as in *I Kings* 2:32 (*Rashash*).

אֵת אֲשֶׁר־עָשָׂה שָׁאוּל אֲשֶׁר הִכְרִית אֶת־הָאֹבוֹת
וְאֶת־הַיִּדְּעֹנִי מִן־הָאָרֶץ וְלָמָה אַתָּה מִתְנַקֵּשׁ
י בְּנַפְשִׁי לַהֲמִיתֵנִי׃ וַיִּשָּׁבַע לָהּ שָׁאוּל בַּיהוָה
לֵאמֹר חַי־יהוָה אִם־יִקְּרֵךְ עָוֺן בַּדָּבָר הַזֶּה׃
יא וַתֹּאמֶר הָאִשָּׁה אֶת־מִי אַעֲלֶה־לָּךְ וַיֹּאמֶר
יב אֶת־שְׁמוּאֵל הַעֲלִי־לִי׃ וַתֵּרֶא הָאִשָּׁה אֶת־
שְׁמוּאֵל וַתִּזְעַק בְּקוֹל גָּדוֹל וַתֹּאמֶר הָאִשָּׁה
אֶל־שָׁאוּל לֵאמֹר לָמָּה רִמִּיתָנִי וְאַתָּה שָׁאוּל׃
יג וַיֹּאמֶר לָהּ הַמֶּלֶךְ אַל־תִּירְאִי כִּי מָה רָאִית

wave sticks in order to arouse the spirits (*Me'am Loez*).

9. וְלָמָּה אַתָּה מִתְנַקֵּשׁ בְּנַפְשִׁי לַהֲמִיתֵנִי — *So why do you seek to entrap me, in order to have me killed?*

מִתְנַקֵּשׁ is related to מוֹקֵשׁ, *obstacle* or *trap*. (See also *Psalms* 109:11.)

מִתְנַקֵּשׁ is not an active, but a reflexive verb. Thus, the woman asked, *Why do you seek to remove from yourself the "obstacle" of your troubles by transferring it to me?* (*Metzudos*).

10. Saul would swear in Hashem's Name that what he was asking for was not a sin only if he genuinely believed his actions to be justified (*Daas Sofrim*). Saul persuaded the woman that, under the circumstances, necromancy was permitted (for one of the reasons presented above).

Saul spoke specifically of בַּדָּבָר הַזֶּה — *this thing* — implying that the same practice under other conditions would be forbidden (*Kli Yakar*).

In truth, Saul was betraying Hashem — yet as he did so he swore by Hashem's Name. The Midrash (ibid.) notes the irony of this, comparing it to an adulterous woman who swears by the life of her husband.

According to *Yefeh Toar*, this Midrash intends to mitigate Saul's guilt. He was not rebelling against God; however, under the stress of worry and pain, he committed an error.

According to *Metzudos*, עָוֺן, literally, *sin*, is to be read as *punishment*. Saul promised the woman that she would not be harmed. This is consistent with the verb יִקְּרֵךְ — literally, *happen to you*.

According to *Me'am Loez*, the disguised Saul assured the woman that she need not worry that King Saul would punish her, because he would keep this matter a secret.

Abarbanel disagrees, stating that Saul spoke as the king who had abolished sorcery and had the power to let her engage in it safely. (It is unclear whether *Abarbanel* means to say that Saul revealed his identity to the woman. At any rate, she did not realize who he was until v. 12.)

11. וַתֹּאמֶר הָאִשָּׁה אֶת־מִי אַעֲלֶה־לָּךְ — *The woman said, "Whom shall I raise up for you?"*

The woman was persuaded to accommodate Saul's request, apparently under the influence of her son Abner (*Daas Sofrim*).

The Midrash homiletically explains her question as, "Which type of person shall I raise up for you? A gentile who uses the word מִי, *who*, to disparage God, like Pharaoh, who said מִי ה׳, *Who is HASHEM that I should heed His voice*! (*Exodus* 5:2), or a Jew who uses the word *who* in order to laud God, like Moses, who said *Who is like You among the heavenly powers, HASHEM!* (ibid. 15:11)?"

The woman's methodology would depend on whether she had to raise a

what Saul has done — that he has eliminated the
necromancers and Yidoni-diviner from the land —
so why do you seek to entrap me, in order to have
me killed?" [10] *Saul then swore to her by* HASHEM*,*
saying, "As HASHEM *lives, this thing will not be*
held against you as an iniquity."
[11] *The woman said, "Whom shall I raise up for*
you?" And he said, "Raise up Samuel for me."
[12] *The woman then saw Samuel, and she screamed*
in a loud voice. The woman said to Saul, "Why
did you deceive me? You are Saul!" [13] *The king*
then said to her, "Fear not. What did you see?"

holy or a wicked person (*Daas Sofrim*).

Scripture does not state that *the woman asked,* but rather *the woman said;* she was making a statement — i.e., that Saul was a hypocrite. Although Saul swore in Hashem's Name, by making use of sorcery he appeared to be a heretic like Pharaoh (*Maharzu*).

וַיֹּאמֶר אֶת־שְׁמוּאֵל הַעֲלִי־לִי — *And he said, "Raise up Samuel for me."*

As mentioned in the preface above, *Ralbag* and *Baal HaAkeidah* state that Saul did not specify which Samuel he wanted raised, and the woman did not immediately understand that he meant the prophet. This is derived either from the fact that Saul did not refer to Samuel as a prophet, or from the woman's surprised reaction (v. 12), which can be interpreted as her shock at seeing *which* Samuel she had summoned.

Other commentators, however, such as *Abarbanel,* disagree and find it hard to believe that she did not know whom she was summoning.

12. וַתֵּרֶא הָאִשָּׁה אֶת־שְׁמוּאֵל וַתִּזְעַק בְּקוֹל גָּדוֹל — *The woman then saw Samuel, and she screamed in a loud voice.*

Rashi cites a Midrash stating that the woman was astonished because spirits raised through *ov* necromancy usually rise feet first, whereas Samuel rose head first. She knew that this would happen only in honor of the king — thus, she realized that her inquirer must be Saul.

According to *Rav Saadia Gaon,* she had never before been successful in raising spirits, and was shocked to see this really happen.

In the view of *Radvaz,* the fact that Samuel rose head first proved that it was not her sorcery that had brought Samuel but the summons of Hashem.

וַתֹּאמֶר הָאִשָּׁה אֶל־שָׁאוּל לֵאמֹר לָמָּה רִמִּיתָנִי וְאַתָּה שָׁאוּל — *The woman said to Saul, "Why did you deceive me? You are Saul!"*

Rabbeinu Yeshayah cites a view that Samuel informed the woman of Saul's identity.

Daas Sofrim observes that the woman called Saul by his first name, without an honorific title. This supports the Midrash that she was his aunt (the mother of Abner) and therefore treated him with familiarity.

13. וַיֹּאמֶר לָהּ הַמֶּלֶךְ אַל־תִּירְאִי — *The king then said to her, "Fear not."*

Saul sensed that the woman was afraid that he had entrapped her into violating his edict and would have her executed. Saul confirmed his identity, but reassured her that, as he had already sworn, he would not harm her (*Radak*).

כִּי מָה רָאִית — *What did you see?*

The words מָה רָאִית — *What did you see?* — are proceeded by the word כִּי, usually rendered *because,* which is out

וַתֹּאמֶר הָאִשָּׁה אֶל־שָׁאוּל אֱלֹהִים רָאִיתִי עֹלִים
יד מִן־הָאָרֶץ: וַיֹּאמֶר לָהּ מַה־תָּאֳרוֹ וַתֹּאמֶר אִישׁ
זָקֵן עֹלֶה וְהוּא עֹטֶה מְעִיל וַיֵּדַע שָׁאוּל כִּי־שְׁמוּאֵל
טו הוּא וַיִּקֹּד אַפַּיִם אַרְצָה וַיִּשְׁתָּחוּ: וַיֹּאמֶר
שְׁמוּאֵל אֶל־שָׁאוּל לָמָּה הִרְגַּזְתַּנִי לְהַעֲלוֹת אֹתִי
וַיֹּאמֶר שָׁאוּל צַר־לִי מְאֹד וּפְלִשְׁתִּים | נִלְחָמִים בִּי

of place here and which our translation elides.

Radak translates this word as *but*. Thus, Saul told the woman, *Fear not, but what did you see [that led you to discover my identity]?*

וַתֹּאמֶר הָאִשָּׁה אֶל־שָׁאוּל אֱלֹהִים רָאִיתִי עֹלִים מִן־הָאָרֶץ — *The woman said to Saul, "I saw a great man ascending from the earth."*

Although the woman used the word אֱלֹהִים, which usually refers to God, most commentators explain that she referred to a *great man* or a *judge*. (Similarly, אֱלֹקִים לֹא תְקַלֵּל [*Exodus* 22:27] may be translated as *Do not curse a judge* [see *Sanhedrin* 66a].)

The fact that the woman used the verb in the plural form is not surprising, since the noun אֱלֹהִים is technically plural (figures of authority are commonly referred to in the plural).

Nevertheless, the Sages derive from the plural form of the verb that two people rose — Samuel and Moses, the latter being referred to in Scripture as אֱלֹהִים (*Exodus* 7:1). The reason for this is that when Samuel heard that he was being summoned, he was afraid that he was being called to a Grand Judgment, and so he brought Moses to testify that he had kept all the words of the Torah.

The Sages comment that if a man as great as Samuel was fearful of the Day of Judgment, how much more so must we be (*Chagigah* 4b, *Vayikra Rabbah* 26:7). According to *Kli Yakar*, it was this thought that roused the woman to scream in fear when she saw Samuel.

Midrash Shocher Tov (138:1) comments that from this incident we see that prophets are called אֱלֹהִים even after their deaths.

Targum renders אֱלֹהִים רָאִיתִי as *I saw an angel of* H*ASHEM*.

14. וַיֹּאמֶר לָהּ מַה־תָּאֳרוֹ — *He then said to her, "What does he look like?"*

Apparently, Saul was not able to see Samuel. The Midrash (*Vayikra Rabbah* ibid.) explains that as a rule, in the case of the necromancy called מַעֲלֶה בִּזְכוּרוֹ — which was presumably employed here (see preface) — the sorceress can see the raised spirit but cannot hear it, the inquirer can hear it but cannot see it, and others present — in this case, Abner and Amasa — can neither hear nor see it.

וַיֹּאמֶר לָהּ מַה־תָּאֳרוֹ וַתֹּאמֶר אִישׁ זָקֵן עֹלֶה וְהוּא עֹטֶה מְעִיל — *He then said to her, "What does he look like?" She said, "An elderly man is ascending, and he is garbed in a cloak."*

After the woman described the rising man as אֱלֹהִים, implying that he was a great personage, Saul asked her what led her to that conclusion. She answered that he wore a type of cloak that was worn only by distinguished people (*Metzudos*).

Samuel was particularly known for his robe — he began wearing one at an early age, when his mother brought him to study with Eli (above, 2:19). The Sages tell that since he was buried with it, he rose with it. In general, people will rise at the Resurrection of the Dead wearing the clothing in which they were buried. As the verse states, תִּתְהַפֵּךְ כְּחֹמֶר חוֹתָם וְיִתְיַצְּבוּ כְּמוֹ לְבוּשׁ, *Their form will change like clay [at death], and they will stand up [again] as they had been*

The woman said to Saul, "I saw a great man as-
cending from the earth." [14]*He then said to her,*
"What does he look like?" She said, "An elderly
man is ascending, and he is garbed in a cloak."
Saul realized that it was Samuel, and he bowed
down upon his face to the ground and prostrated
himself.
[15]*Samuel said to Saul, "Why did you disturb*
me, to raise me up?" Saul replied, "I am in great
distress, and the Philistines are at war against me;

clothed (*Job* 38:14; see *Bereishis Rabbah* 95:1; *Midrash Tanchuma, Emor* 63b; see also *Kesubos* 111b, *Sanhedrin* 90b).

אִישׁ זָקֵן עֹלֶה וְהוּא עֹטֶה מְעִיל — *An elderly man is ascending, and he is garbed in a cloak.*

Although Samuel had died at the relatively young age of 52, he appeared as an old man since the symptoms of old age had crept up on him toward the end of his life (*Taanis* 5b; *Kli Yakar*).

Malbim states that the woman referred here to two people. אִישׁ זָקֵן עֹלֶה — *an elderly man ascending* — refers to Moses, who died at the age of 120, and וְהוּא עֹטֶה מְעִיל — *he is garbed in a cloak* — refers to Samuel.

וַיִּקֹּד אַפַּיִם אַרְצָה וַיִּשְׁתָּחוּ — *And he bowed upon his face to the ground and prostrated himself.*

Simply understood, Saul respectfully bowed to Samuel.

However, *Abarbanel* interprets the verse as stating that Samuel bowed to Saul, since he was king. In this way, the woman discovered that her inquirer was Saul.

Samuel's Frightening Prophecy

15. וַיֹּאמֶר שְׁמוּאֵל אֶל־שָׁאוּל לָמָּה הִרְגַּזְתַּנִי לְהַעֲלוֹת אֹתִי — *Samuel said to Saul, "Why did you disturb me, to raise me up?"*

Our translation of הִרְגַּזְתַּנִי *disturb* follows *Radak*, who states that Samuel complained that he had been *disturbed* from his resting place.

However, this word is generally associated with a trembling or agitated movement. *Rashi* thus renders it as *you made me tremble.* This interpretation is based on the Sages' comment that Samuel was frightened because he thought that he was being brought to judgment.[1]

A Midrash (*Vayikra Rabbah* 26:7) relates the word הִרְגַּזְתַּנִי to anger. Samuel chastised Saul, "Not only did you anger Hashem by inquiring of the *ov*, but you did so through me. Your use of me for sorcery was tantamount to turning me into an idol — and just as an idolater is punished, so is the object of his worship."[2]

וַיֹּאמֶר שָׁאוּל צַר־לִי מְאֹד וּפְלִשְׁתִּים נִלְחָמִים בִּי — *Saul replied, "I am in great distress, and the Philistines are at war against me."*

Daas Sofrim observes that the conjunctive ו, *and*, indicates that Saul had two problems. First, he was suffering from personal distress, possibly because

1. *Beis Yosef* (*Yoreh Deah* 363), citing *Kolbo*, mentions this as a source for not moving the remains of the deceased, since doing so instills fear in him.

2. Thus, Jacob requested that he not be buried in Egypt (*Genesis* 47:29, see *Rashi* ad loc.), fearing that his deceased body would be the object of veneration (*Bereishis Rabbah* 96:5).

וֵאלֹהִים סָר מֵעָלַי וְלֹא־עָנָנִי עוֹד גַּם בְּיַד־
הַנְּבִיאִם גַּם־בַּחֲלֹמוֹת וָאֶקְרָאֶה לְךָ לְהוֹדִיעֵנִי
טז מָה אֶעֱשֶׂה: וַיֹּאמֶר שְׁמוּאֵל וְלָמָּה תִּשְׁאָלֵנִי
יז וַיהוָה סָר מֵעָלֶיךָ וַיְהִי עָרֶךָ: וַיַּעַשׂ יהוה לוֹ כַּאֲשֶׁר
דִּבֶּר בְּיָדִי וַיִּקְרַע יהוה אֶת־הַמַּמְלָכָה מִיָּדֶךָ
יח וַיִּתְּנָהּ לְרֵעֲךָ לְדָוִד: כַּאֲשֶׁר לֹא־שָׁמַעְתָּ בְּקוֹל

of the spirit of melancholy that had descended upon him, and second, the Philistines were preparing for war.

וְלֹא־עָנָנִי עוֹד גַּם בְּיַד־הַנְּבִיאִם גַּם־בַּחֲלֹמוֹת — *And does not answer me anymore — not through the hand of the prophets nor in dreams.*

Simply understood, the phrase גַּם בְּיַד־הַנְּבִיאִם גַּם־בַּחֲלֹמוֹת — *not through the hand of the prophets nor in dreams* — modifies וְלֹא־עָנָנִי עוֹד — *He does not answer me anymore.*

However, *Abarbanel* notes that וְלֹא־עָנָנִי עוֹד — *He does not answer me anymore* — can also be understood as having a self-contained meaning: although Saul had once been among the prophets, God was no longer answering him, nor had God responded to Saul's inquiries via other prophets or dreams.

Targum renders וְלֹא־עָנָנִי עוֹד as *He has no longer accepted my prayers.*

The Sages (*Vayikra Rabbah* 26:7) state that Saul omitted reporting his attempt to inquire of the *Urim VeTumim.* He knew that if he did so Samuel would remind him that they had failed to respond because he had arranged the murder of the Kohanim of Nob, and Saul was ashamed of that sin.

The Talmud (*Berachos* 12b) derives from here that a person who suffers shame for his sin is forgiven for all his sins (we see that Saul was forgiven, for Samuel subsequently told Saul that they would share the same realm in heaven).

Although the Talmud states that when a person grows ashamed, he is pardoned for all his sins, some commentators assert that he is pardoned only for the particular sin of which he is ashamed (see *Radak* below, v. 19; *Meiri, Shitah Mikubetzes* to *Berachos* 12b; see also *Nachalas Shimon, Mishbetzos Zahav*).

16. וַיֹּאמֶר שְׁמוּאֵל וְלָמָּה תִּשְׁאָלֵנִי... — *Samuel said, "But why do you ask me...?"*

Since Saul could see that Hashem had refused to answer him through living prophets, how could he expect to get an answer from Samuel? (*Rashi*).

According to *Metzudos*, Samuel told Saul that since Hashem had already turned away from him, the answer to his question was self-evident; thus, he had no reason to question Samuel.

...וַה׳ סָר מֵעָלֶיךָ וַיְהִי עָרֶךָ — *...Since HASHEM has turned away from you and has become your adversary?*

We follow *Rashi* in translating the unusual word עָרֶךָ as *your adversary* (*Rashi*).

Targum renders this phrase as, *The word [and support] of HASHEM has been distanced from you and has come to the aid of the man whose enemy you are.* Thus, in this rendition the verse does not say that Hashem was Saul's adversary — presumably because, as we will see, Saul was still considered a righteous man.

Also, *Targum* implies that although Saul was David's enemy, David was not Saul's enemy. Whereas Saul hated David, David held no grudge against Saul (*Mishbetzos Zahav*).

When Saul said, וֵאלֹהִים סָר מֵעָלַי — *God has turned away from me* — he used the Name connoting justice. But in his answer, וַה׳ סָר מֵעָלֶיךָ, Samuel used the Name that connotes mercy. Furthermore, the term וַה׳ — *and HASHEM* — represents Hashem together with His heavenly courts — i.e., a combination of

God has turned away from me and does not answer
me anymore — not through the hand of the proph-
ets nor in dreams — so I called upon you to inform
me what I should do."
[16] *Samuel said, "But why do you ask me, since*
HASHEM has turned away from you and has become
your adversary. [17] *HASHEM has done for him that*
which He spoke through me, for HASHEM has torn
the kingship from your hand and given it to your fel-
low, to David. [18] *Because you did not obey the word*

Mercy and Justice (see *Rashi, Genesis* 19:24). Thus, Samuel indicated to Saul that Hashem was employing mercy to make it possible for him to atone for his sins (*Mishbetzos Zahav*).

The phrase מֵעָלֶיךָ — *from you* — literally means *from over you.* According to *Rav Yishai Chasidah,* it alludes to our Sages' explanation of the verse, שׂוֹם תָּשִׂים עָלֶיךָ מֶלֶךְ — *You shall surely set a king over you* (*Deuteronomy* 17:15) — as meaning that the *fear* of the king shall rest *over you.* This fear was aroused by the Divine Presence resting upon the king. But now וַה׳ סָר מֵעָלֶיךָ — *HASHEM has removed His Divine Presence from over you.* Since the Divine Presence no longer rested upon Saul, the nation would no longer fear him.

The word עָרֶךָ reverses the letters of the word רֵעַ, *friend.* The worst hatred may at times exist between people who had formerly been close friends, as in the case of Saul and David (*Mishbetzos Zahav*).

17. וַיַּעַשׂ ה׳ לוֹ כַּאֲשֶׁר דִּבֶּר בְּיָדִי — *HASHEM has done for him that which He spoke through me.*

According to *Targum,* this phrase means that *HASHEM acted on behalf of David* (who had been referred to at the end of the previous verse) by making him king.

Radak comments that the phrase states that *HASHEM had acted against [Saul].* It is not uncommon for Scripture to use a third person pronoun although speaking directly to the person.

Kli Yakar translates differently: *HASHEM has done for Himself,*[1] i.e., Hashem acted on His own behalf, as it were, by replacing Saul with David.

Alternatively, Hashem felt the pain that He was inflicting on Saul by removing him from power, so it can be said that He inflicted this pain on Himself, as well as on Saul.

וַיִּתְּנָהּ לְרֵעֲךָ לְדָוִד — *And given it to your fellow, to David.*

This is the first time that Saul was told explicitly that David would succeed him.

The Midrash (*Vayikra Rabbah* 26:7, cited by *Rashi*) states that Samuel had not previously revealed this to Saul, fearful that Saul would kill him for having anointed David.

According to the Midrash, Saul asked why previously Samuel had only told him that sovereignty would be given to a better man[2] but had not divulged that man's name.

Samuel replied, "When I was with you, I was in a world of falsehood, so you heard false words from me. But now I am in the world of truth, so you will only hear the

1. This phrase is thus similar to that above, בִּקֵּשׁ ה׳ לוֹ אִישׁ — *HASHEM has sought for Himself a man* (13:14).

2. *[HASHEM] has given it to your fellow who is better than you* (15:28).

יהוה וְלֹא־עָשִׂיתָ חֲרוֹן־אַפּוֹ בַּעֲמָלֵק עַל־כֵּן הַדָּבָר
יט הַזֶּה עָשָׂה־לְךָ יהוה הַיּוֹם הַזֶּה: וְיִתֵּן יהוה גַּם אֶת־
יִשְׂרָאֵל עִמְּךָ בְּיַד־פְּלִשְׁתִּים וּמָחָר אַתָּה וּבָנֶיךָ עִמִּי

truth from me."

Mussar HaNeviim explains this colloquy as follows.

Rambam (*Hil. Yesodei HaTorah* 10:4) states that if a prophet predicts chastisement, even if it does not materialize he is still considered to be legitimate, because it is possible that the object of his rebuke repented and gained forgiveness (as in the case of Nineveh). However, if a prophet's prediction of good tidings is not realized, he is proven to be false, because Hashem does not retract His good resolve.

Saul thus stated that since Samuel's prophecy to him had not named a specific candidate for king, it apparently had only a negative meaning: i.e., it was detrimental to Saul. Thus, he had the possibility of changing the decree by repenting. But in fact a specific person — David — had been chosen king. Consequently, this prophecy had a positive meaning as well as far as David was concerned, and therefore it was immutable. Saul now claimed that had he known this, he would never have pursued David.

Samuel responded that he had not mentioned David's name out of fear that Saul would kill him.

Mussar HaNeviim notes that Samuel did not state, "In the world of falsehood, I spoke false words," but rather, "You heard false words from me." Samuel would never have spoken or even intimated a falsehood. But because Samuel concealed David's identity, Saul persuaded himself that he could change Samuel's prophecy.

According to *Mishbetzos Zahav*, Samuel's comment about different worlds has another meaning as well. At the incident with Amalek, Samuel had told Saul that *[Hashem] has given [your sovereignty] to your fellow who is better than you.* But here no mention is made of David being better than Saul. Only in the world of falsehood, where there is a need for an effective leader who can suppress evil, was David considered better than Saul. In the land of truth, however, Saul might be considered the more righteous man (see *Moed Katan* 16b, *Rashi* ad loc.).

Although Samuel had not named David in his prophecy, Saul had amassed sufficient information to deduce that David would be his successor. *Midrash Shocher Tov* (57:2) states that when Samuel ripped Saul's garment (above, 15:27-28) he was hinting that whoever next tore his garment would take over as king. And indeed when David did so (above, 24:5), Saul recalled that comment.

18. הַדָּבָר הַזֶּה — *This thing.*

This thing refers to the Philistines' attack and Hashem's ignoring of Saul's frantic appeals for information (*Metzudos*).

Samuel said that Saul knew very well why he was being punished, and so there had been no reason for Hashem to answer him (*Malbim*).

According to *Kli Yakar, this thing* refers to a precisely calibrated punishment. Just as Saul had not heeded Hashem's voice, Hashem did not heed Saul's voice. And since Saul had not poured God's wrath onto Amalek, God vented it upon Saul.

Daas Sofrim observes that the words עָשָׂה לְךָ may be read both as *done to you* and *done for you* — implying that everything that occurred was meted out to cleanse Saul of his sins.

19. וְיִתֵּן ה׳ גַּם אֶת־יִשְׂרָאֵל עִמְּךָ בְּיַד־פְּלִשְׁתִּים — *Hashem will deliver Israel with you into the hand of the Philistines.*

Although the nation as a whole had not sinned, its success at war was dependent upon the merits of its king (*Abarbanel*).

According to Hillel the Elder, Samuel told Saul, "Not only did you previously disobey My command to destroy Amalek but you now made inquiry of the *ov*. Woe to such a shepherd and woe to his flock! Because of you, Hashem will deliver Israel into the hands of the Philistines" (*Yalkut Shimoni* 141).

According to *Malbim*, however, the

of HASHEM *and did not carry out His wrath against*
Amalek, therefore HASHEM *has done this thing*
to you this day. 19 HASHEM *will deliver Israel*
with you into the hand of the Philistines; to-
morrow you and your sons will be with me,

nation had participated in the sin of the Amalekite incident, when *the people took pity on the best of the sheep and cattle* (above, 15:15).

Mahari Kara states that this calamity fulfilled Samuel's warning that *both you [the nation] and your king will perish* (above, 12:25).

וּמָחָר אַתָּה וּבָנֶיךָ עִמִּי — *Tomorrow you and your sons will be with me.*

Simply understood, Samuel stated that Saul and his sons too would die (*Radak*).

The Sages (*Vayikra Rabbah* 26:7) relate that Saul asked, "Will I be able to escape?" Samuel answered, "Yes, but if you will accept God's justice upon yourself, then you and your sons will be with me within the same confines — i.e., you will be forgiven for your sins and you will be with me in the Garden of Eden."[1]

At this, Saul grew frightened. Abner and Amasa asked him what he had heard; not wanting to undermine their morale, he told them that the Jews would be victorious and that his sons would be appointed to honorable positions. He then took his three sons with him to the battlefield, with full knowledge of the death that lay in store for them all.

Hashem summoned the angels and told them, "Look at this creature that I have created. Normally, a father will protect his offspring so carefully that he will not even bring them to a festive gathering for fear of the evil eye of envy. Yet this man, knowing that he and his three sons are doomed, goes to war and rejoices with the Attribute of Justice that will meet him there."

Saul was punished for the incident with Amalek and not for his slaughter of the Kohanim of Nob, because, as mentioned above (v. 15), Saul had been forgiven for his sin at Nob, since he was ashamed of that sin (*Berachos* 12b). *Maharal* (*Nesivos Olam, Nesiv HaTeshuvah* Ch. 5) explains that a person's shame creates a distance between him and his sin, and that grants him atonement.

Since death confers atonement even for major sins (see *Yoma* 86a), why do the Sages assert that Saul merited to be at Samuel's level in the Next World only because he felt shame?

❐ *Melo HaR'oim* explains that since Samuel told Saul of his reward while he was still alive, he must have been worthy of the future reward even at this point

❐ *Imrei Emes* (*Sefer HaLikkutim*) adds that it must have been Saul's shame that elicited God's forgiveness, since he could not have

1. Surely, Samuel had a glorious share in the next world. How could Saul have earned the same reward simply by accepting upon himself the Attribute of Justice?

Mussar HaNeviim suggests that although Saul could have avoided death by leaving the field of battle, he would have severely damaged the morale of his people, who would have been left like "sheep without a shephaerd." Thus, he willingly gave his life for the good of the nation, and this earned him a level of sanctity equal to Samuel's.

Furthermore, the judgment he accepted upon himself was a fitting retribution for his previous error. By permitting the survival of elements of Amalek, he had lost the throne because his weakness demonstrated a lack of leadership (see 15:1,11). Now that Saul led his people in battle, even though he knew it would cost him his life and the lives of his sons, he redeemed himself and gained atonement for his earlier sin.

גַּם אֶת־מַחֲנֵה יִשְׂרָאֵל יִתֵּן יהוה בְּיַד פְּלִשְׁתִּים׃
כ וַיְמַהֵר שָׁאוּל וַיִּפֹּל מְלֹא־קוֹמָתוֹ אַרְצָה וַיִּרָא
מְאֹד מִדִּבְרֵי שְׁמוּאֵל גַּם־כֹּחַ לֹא־הָיָה בוֹ כִּי
כא לֹא אָכַל לֶחֶם כָּל־הַיּוֹם וְכָל־הַלָּיְלָה׃ וַתָּבוֹא
הָאִשָּׁה אֶל־שָׁאוּל וַתֵּרֶא כִּי־נִבְהַל מְאֹד
וַתֹּאמֶר אֵלָיו הִנֵּה שָׁמְעָה שִׁפְחָתְךָ בְּקוֹלֶךָ
וָאָשִׂים נַפְשִׁי בְּכַפִּי וָאֶשְׁמַע אֶת־דְּבָרֶיךָ

gained atonement via his death, which came as a result of his taking his life (see below Ch. 31).

However, some sources state that because Saul had killed the Kohanim at Nob by the sword, he had to be put to death by the sword (see *II Samuel* 1:9, *Rashi; Maharsha, Sanhedrin* 104a). Thus, Saul did require death to gain atonement for that crime.

❒ *Beer Mayim Chaim* (*Bereishis*) explains that a person who harms someone else has committed two offenses: one against the person and one against Hashem. The shame that Saul suffered was enough to atone for his disobedience of Hashem's word, but in order to earn forgiveness for having harmed others, he had to be killed by the sword.

❒ *Mishbetzos Zahav* suggests that Saul did gain God's comprehensive pardon because of his shame, which he felt so deeply that he was willing to die. His death by the sword was merely a culmination of that powerful sense of self-abasement. Thus, the concept of atonement through death is the acknowledgment of sin and *acceptance* of death as atonement.

Whereas all other prophets related their auguries during their lifetimes, Samuel prophesied even after his death. In addition, he gave advice to Saul — which Saul heeded — on how to atone (*Yalkut Shimon* 141).

גַּם אֶת־מַחֲנֵה יִשְׂרָאֵל יִתֵּן ה׳ בְּיַד פְּלִשְׁתִּים — *And* HASHEM *will also deliver the Israelite camp into the hand of the Philistines.*

Ostensibly, this seems to be a repetition of the first part of the verse. According to *Abarbanel*, in the first half of this verse — HASHEM *will deliver Israel with you into the hand of the Philistines* — Saul spoke of the army base. Here — *and* HASHEM *will also deliver the Israelite camp* — Samuel was referring to the surrounding cities. The Israelites would abandon their dwellings and the Philistines would settle in them (see below, 31:7).

According to *Maharzu*, at the beginning of the verse, Saul was told that the Israelites would perish עִמְּךָ, *with you*, i.e., because of his sins.

Saul asked, "If I escape, will the rest of the nation be spared?" Samuel responded with the words of this latter part of the verse, which omits the word perish עִמְּךָ, *with you* — implying that the Jews would not be spared. Hearing this, Saul decided to go to his death together with them.

Malbim explains that the text from verse 16 until וּמָחָר אַתָּה וּבָנֶיךָ עִמִּי, *Tomorrow you and your sons will be with me*, presents Samuel's reproach against Saul for having raised him from the grave, since Saul should have been able to answer his question himself. The word וּמָחָר — *tomorrow* — begins Samuel's response to Saul's question and his notification of the impending doom. Accordingly, there is no redundancy.

◆§ A Broken and Weak Saul Eats to Regain Strength

20. וַיְמַהֵר שָׁאוּל וַיִּפֹּל מְלֹא־קוֹמָתוֹ אַרְצָה וַיִּרָא מְאֹד מִדִּבְרֵי שְׁמוּאֵל — *Saul quickly fell his full height to the ground and he was exceedingly frightened by Samuel's words.*

and HASHEM will also deliver the Israelite camp
into the hand of the Philistines."
[20] *Saul quickly fell his full height to the ground*
and he was exceedingly frightened by Samuel's
words; also he had no strength for he had not
eaten any food all the day and all the night.
[21] *The woman came over to Saul and saw that he*
was greatly terrified, and she said to him, "Be-
hold, your maidservant heeded your voice. I put
my life in my hand, and listened to your words

Frightened by Samuel's dread prophecy, Saul bowed down before Samuel. (Although he could not see Samuel, as mentioned above, he bowed down in the direction of the voice that he heard [*Radak*].)

Abarbanel comments that Saul was not frightened by Samuel's words, but rather was stunned by the fact that it was indeed Samuel's own voice. The word וַיְמַהֵר, *and he hastened*, implies that he did not wait until the *ov* finished speaking, but bowed as soon as he recognized the prophet's voice.

According to *Kli Yakar*, Saul bowed in submissive humility to show his remorse for having agitated Samuel by raising him up. Also, Saul's fright was a reaction to Samuel's fear of being judged. If Samuel dreaded the day of reckoning, thought Saul, how much more should everyone else.

According to the Midrash (*Vayikra Rabbah* 26:7), Saul grew afraid when he heard the sorceress pronounce the name אֱלֹהִים (v. 13).

☙ Why Didn't Saul Pray for Mercy?

As a rule, a person can escape a prophetic sentence of death by pleading for forgiveness (as Hezekiah escaped Isaiah's prophetic sentence of death — *II Kings* Ch. 20). However, Saul knew that this was not the case here, since that principle is applicable only if the prophet is alive (*Rabbi Yishai Chasidah* citing *Sefer Sod Yesharim*).

גַּם־כֹּחַ לֹא־הָיָה בוֹ — *Also, he had no strength.*

He was unable to lift himself off the ground (*Radak*)

כִּי לֹא אָכַל לֶחֶם — *Since he had not eaten any food.*

Daas Sofrim suggests that Saul fasted to show that he had not meant to rebel against God by inquiring of the *ov*, but had done so in desperation.

Alternatively, Saul did not eat due to bitterness and depression.

כִּי לֹא אָכַל לֶחֶם כָּל־הַיּוֹם וְכָל־הַלָּיְלָה — *Since he had not eaten any food all the day and all the night.*

He had not eaten until this point. As Scripture relates, he did subsequently eat that night (see *Nachalas Shimon* 60:41)

21. וַתָּבוֹא הָאִשָּׁה אֶל־שָׁאוּל — *The woman came over to Saul.*

Seeing that Saul was terrified, the sorceress brought the conversation with Samuel's spirit to a halt in order to address Saul's needs (*Abarbanel*).

וַתֵּרֶא כִּי־נִבְהַל מְאֹד — *And saw that he was greatly terrified.*

The woman had not heard what Samuel had said (see above, v. 14). She only understood from perceiving Saul that something had frightened him (*Mahari Kara*).

וַתֹּאמֶר אֵלָיו הִנֵּה שָׁמְעָה שִׁפְחָתְךָ בְּקוֹלֶךָ וָאָשִׂים נַפְשִׁי בְּכַפִּי וָאֶשְׁמַע אֶת־דְּבָרֶיךָ — *And she said to him, "Behold, your maidservant heeded your voice. I put my life in my hand and listened to your words."*

כח/כב־כה כב אֲשֶׁר דִּבַּרְתָּ אֵלָי: וְעַתָּה שְׁמַע־נָא גַם־אַתָּה
בְּקוֹל שִׁפְחָתֶךָ וְאָשִׂמָה לְפָנֶיךָ פַּת־לֶחֶם וֶאֱכוֹל
כג וִיהִי בְךָ כֹּחַ כִּי תֵלֵךְ בַּדָּרֶךְ: וַיְמָאֵן וַיֹּאמֶר לֹא
אֹכַל וַיִּפְרְצוּ־בוֹ עֲבָדָיו וְגַם־הָאִשָּׁה וַיִּשְׁמַע
כד לְקֹלָם וַיָּקָם מֵהָאָרֶץ וַיֵּשֶׁב אֶל־הַמִּטָּה: וְלָאִשָּׁה
עֵגֶל־מַרְבֵּק בַּבַּיִת וַתְּמַהֵר וַתִּזְבָּחֵהוּ וַתִּקַּח־
כה קֶמַח וַתָּלָשׁ וַתֹּפֵהוּ מַצּוֹת: וַתַּגֵּשׁ לִפְנֵי־שָׁאוּל
וְלִפְנֵי עֲבָדָיו וַיֹּאכֵלוּ וַיָּקֻמוּ וַיֵּלְכוּ בַּלַּיְלָה
כט/א א הַהוּא: וַיִּקְבְּצוּ פְלִשְׁתִּים אֶת־כָּל־מַחֲנֵיהֶם

Noting the apparent redundancy, *Kli Yakar* explains that first the woman had *heeded [Saul's] voice* — his proclamation that sorcery must cease. Now she risked her life by engaging in it at his bequest.

וָאָשִׂים נַפְשִׁי בְּכַפִּי — *I put my life in my hand.*

This is a figurative way of saying that she risked her life. Something that a person holds in his hand is vulnerable, for if he opens his hand it may be easily lost (*Metzudos*).

The woman stated that she was in danger because Saul himself (whom she had not at first recognized) could have killed her for engaging in *ov* necromancy (*Radak, Metzudos*).

Alternatively, the act of performing necromancy is intrinsically dangerous (*Radak*).

22. וְעַתָּה שְׁמַע־נָא גַם־אַתָּה בְּקוֹל שִׁפְחָתֶךָ — *Now you, too, listen to the voice of your maidservant.*

Just as she had heeded him, so should he listen to her (*Abarbanel*).

23. וַיְמָאֵן וַיֹּאמֶר לֹא אֹכַל וַיִּפְרְצוּ־בוֹ עֲבָדָיו — *But he refused and said, "I shall not eat." His servants urged him strongly.*

At first Saul refused to eat because his soldiers were at war. This had been his policy at a previous encounter with the Philistines (above, 14:24). But his servants persuaded him that the nation's security was at risk and he must have the strength to prevail (*Me'am Loez*).

וַיִּפְרְצוּ — *Urged strongly.*

The usual word for *urged strongly* is וַיִּפְצְרוּ (see *Genesis* 19:3,9). Apparently, this is one of the words in which two letters can be interchanged without changing the meaning — such as כֶּבֶשׂ and כֶּשֶׂב, both of which mean *sheep* (*Radak*).

Daas Sofrim, however, understands וַיִּפְרְצוּ in its conventional sense as *they breached*. Saul's soldiers broke through to his soul.

וַיֵּשֶׁב אֶל־הַמִּטָּה — *And sat on the bed.*

This phrase literally means *and sat to the bed*, but the word אל is treated as עַל, *on* (*Targum, Radak*).

24. עֵגֶל־מַרְבֵּק — *A fattened calf.*

Our translation follows *Targum*.

Radak explains that the place where the calves were customarily *fattened* was called מַרְבֵּק.

According to *Daas Sofrim*, the woman was in the process of fattening the calf, and in Saul's honor slaughtered it earlier than she would have otherwise.

וַתִּזְבָּחֵהוּ — *And slaughtered it.*

There is a major halachic controversy regarding the validity of *shechitah* — kosher slaughter — performed by a woman (see *Tosafos, Chullin* 2a; *Shulchan Aruch, Yoreh Deah* 1:1). Some

28/22-25 *that you spoke to me.* [22] *Now you, too, listen to the*
voice of your maidservant. I will place before you a
piece of bread so that you may eat, so that you may
have strength when you go on your way." [23] *But he*
refused, and said, "I shall not eat." His servants,
and also the woman, urged him strongly, and he lis-
tened to their voice. He arose from the ground and
sat on the bed. [24] *The woman had a fattened calf in*
her house, she hurried and slaughtered it; and she
took flour and kneaded it and baked it into matzos.
[25] *She set it before Saul and before his servants*
and they ate; and they arose and left that night.

29/1 [1] *The Philistines mobilized their entire army*

authorities cite this instance to show that it is permitted. However, *Hagahos Yad Shaul* questions this proof, as follows. The Talmud (*Avodah Zarah* 27a) attempts to demonstrate that a woman may perform circumcision from the incident in which Zipporah (*Exodus* 4:25) is described as circumcising her son. Yet that proof is refuted because it is possible that Scripture means to say that she sent an emissary to perform the circumcision. The same logic may be applied here. Although Scripture attributes the slaughtering to the woman, that may mean that she assigned the task to a man. (See *Nachalas Shimon* 57.)

וַתֹּפֵהוּ מַצּוֹת — *And baked it into matzos.*

She baked matzos so that she could feed Saul quickly. The word וַתֹּפֵהוּ is spelled in an abbreviated fashion (leaving out the א) to indicate that she acted quickly (*Radak*).

25. וַתַּגֵּשׁ לִפְנֵי־שָׁאוּל וְלִפְנֵי עֲבָדָיו וַיֹּאכֵלוּ — *She set it before Saul and before his servants and they ate.*

Kli Yakar notes that Scripture could have stated more succinctly that וַתַּגֵּשׁ לִפְנֵי־שָׁאוּל וַעֲבָדָיו, *she set it before Saul and his servants.* The apparently unnecessary second use of the word לִפְנֵי, *before,* may indicate that Saul ate by himself and the servants by themselves, either because of respect for the king or since he was pained by the revelation, he chose to eat by himself.

Abarbanel comments that no mention is made of Saul paying for either the necromancy or the food. It was likely understood that these were the king's prerogative.

Daas Sofrim adds that the woman did not perform necromancy for money, but rather because her son Abner had persuaded her to do so.

XXIX

Philistine Officers Reject David

1. וַיִּקְבְּצוּ פְלִשְׁתִּים אֶת־כָּל־מַחֲנֵיהֶם אֲפֵקָה — *The Philistines gathered their entire army to Aphek.*

The Philistines had previously gathered in Shunem, prior to the time that Saul had consulted with the *ov* (above, 28:4). Now they advanced closer to the Jews and camped at Aphek (*Malbim*).

When describing the mustering of troops in Shunem, Scripture had employed the reflexive form of *gathered* —

אֲפֵקָה וְיִשְׂרָאֵל חֹנִים בַּעַיִן אֲשֶׁר בְּיִזְרְעֶאל׃
ב וְסַרְנֵי פְלִשְׁתִּים עֹבְרִים לְמֵאוֹת וְלַאֲלָפִים
וְדָוִד וַאֲנָשָׁיו עֹבְרִים בָּאַחֲרֹנָה עִם־אָכִישׁ׃
ג וַיֹּאמְרוּ שָׂרֵי פְלִשְׁתִּים מָה הָעִבְרִים הָאֵלֶּה
וַיֹּאמֶר אָכִישׁ אֶל־שָׂרֵי פְלִשְׁתִּים הֲלוֹא־זֶה דָוִד
עֶבֶד | שָׁאוּל מֶלֶךְ־יִשְׂרָאֵל אֲשֶׁר הָיָה אִתִּי זֶה
יָמִים אוֹ־זֶה שָׁנִים וְלֹא־מָצָאתִי בוֹ מְאוּמָה

וַיִּקָּבְצוּ (*vayikavzu*) — implying that the Philistines were reacting to the news of Samuel's death. In this verse, however, the verb is presented in the active form — וַיִּקְבְּצוּ (*vayikb'zu*) — indicating that the Philistine army officers took initiative: i.e., they carried out a census of the soldiers on the field (*Kli Yakar*).

אֲפֵקָה — *To Aphek.*

There seems to have been more than one city named Aphek (see *Joshua* 12:18, 19:30).

According to *Tevuos HaAretz*, this particular city was located in Issachar's territory.

It is noteworthy that in the war in which the Philistines captured the Ark, their first encampment was also at Aphek (above, 4:1).

2. וְסַרְנֵי פְלִשְׁתִּים עֹבְרִים לְמֵאוֹת וְלַאֲלָפִים — *The governors of the Philistines were passing by with hundreds and thousands.*

Translated literally, this phrase means that *the governors of the Philistines were passing by in the hundreds and thousands.* That is obviously impossible, as there were only five governors (one to each Philistine province) (*Malbim*). Clearly Scripture means to state that the governors were passing by together with hundreds and thousands of fighters (*Radak*). The Philistine soldiers first formed hundred-man units, and these in turn gathered together to form thousand-man units (*Metzudos*). Each group — whether of a hundred or a thousand men — was assigned an officer.

וְדָוִד וַאֲנָשָׁיו עֹבְרִים בָּאַחֲרֹנָה עִם־אָכִישׁ — *And David and his men were passing at the rear with Achish.*

As Achish's bodyguard, David traveled with him at the rear of the army.

But how could David have even entertained the notion of accompanying the Philistines to fight against Saul and the Israelites?

Ralbag explains that David had no choice but to go, in order to persuade the Philistines of his continued allegiance to Achish. Furthermore, he intended to foil the Philistines' plans by giving them faulty advice, which he knew they would accept because of the trust that they had invested in him.

However, *Abarbanel* finds it hard to accept the idea that David would practice such duplicity, especially in light of the kindness that Achish had shown him. Rather, he states, David intended to do no more than protect Achish from harm. As for his commitment to the Philistine cause, he had never promised them that he would fight the Jews but had only made the ambiguous statement, *You shall see what your servant will do* (above, 28:2).

According to *Abarbanel*, David referred to this incident in *Psalms* 139. That Psalm begins with the words, ה׳ חֲקַרְתַּנִי וַתֵּדָע, *Hashem, You have scrutinized me and You know* (v. 1). Although David seemed to have sided with Achish, he asked Hashem to appreciate the purity of his intentions.

David concluded this psalm with an expression of his hatred for the Philistines (ibid. vs. 21-23) and the request, וּנְחֵנִי בְּדֶרֶךְ

to Aphek, and Israel was encamped by the
spring that is in Jezreel. 2 *The governors of the*
Philistines were passing by with hundreds and
thousands, and David and his men were passing
at the rear with Achish. 3 *The Philistine officers*
said, "What are these Hebrews [doing here]?"
And Achish replied to the Philistine officers,
"Is this not David, the servant of Saul, king of
Israel, who has been with me for these days or
these years, and I have found no fault with him

עוֹלָם, *And lead me in the way of eternity* (v. 24) — i.e., Hashem should direct him to leave Achish if what he was doing was wrong. Hashem accepted David's prayer, and the Philistines rejected David's assistance.

This was a great boon for David, for two reasons. First, it made it possible for him to save his family from Amalek's assault and in so doing fight Hashem's war against Amalek (Ch. 30). Second, had David remained in the Philistine camp, he would have been accused of bringing about Saul's death in order to usurp his position. Now he remained blameless in the eyes of all Israel.

3. מָה הָעִבְרִים הָאֵלֶּה — *What are these Hebrews [doing here]?*

עִבְרִים, *Hebrews,* was a term used often by the Philistines to refer to the Israelites (see above, 4:6, 14:11). It had a derogatory connotation, implying that the Israelites were foreign interlopers who had come from *across* (עֵבֶר) the river (see *Rashi, Genesis* 14:13; *Daas Sofrim*).

הֲלוֹא־זֶה דָוִד עֶבֶד שָׁאוּל מֶלֶךְ־יִשְׂרָאֵל — *Is this not David, the servant of Saul, king of Israel...*

Achish meant to imply that as a former servant of Saul who had rebelled against him, David would presumably be happy to take this opportunity to challenge him in battle (*Malbim*).

אֲשֶׁר הָיָה אִתִּי זֶה יָמִים אוֹ־זֶה שָׁנִים — *...Who has been with me for these days or these years ...*

Considering how long David had been with the Philistines, they could no longer consider him a Hebrew; he was now one of them (*Abarbanel*).

Above (27:7), we cited the controversy regarding the extent of David's sojourn among the Philistines and the significance of this verse in making that determination.

To review briefly, *Radak*, who insists that David's stay lasted not much more than a few months, interprets Achish as saying, "Although David has been with me only a few days (i.e., months), I feel as though I have known him for years."

Other commentators, however, interpret *years* literally (see above).

According to *Metzudos*, Achish was referring to the *days* that David had lived in Gath and to the *years* that he had resided in the countryside, i.e., Ziklag (see above, 27:5,6).

Malbim suggests that *days* refers to the span of time following David's relatively recent arrival in Gath (Ch. 27) (following which he remained in Philistine territory), whereas *years* includes the period of time beginning with David's first visit to Gath as a rebel fugitive (21:11-16).

Daas Sofrim denies that any evidence may be gleaned from this verse regarding the length of David's stay, because Achish did not intend to speak precisely, but merely wished to impart that David had been with them for quite some time.

וְלֹא־מָצָאתִי בוֹ מְאוּמָה — *And I have found no fault with him.*

The word מְאוּמָה generally means

ד מִיּוֹם נָפְלוֹ עַד־הַיּוֹם הַזֶּה: וַיִּקְצְפוּ עָלָיו
שָׂרֵי פְלִשְׁתִּים וַיֹּאמְרוּ לוֹ שָׂרֵי פְלִשְׁתִּים הָשֵׁב
אֶת־הָאִישׁ וְיָשֹׁב אֶל־מְקוֹמוֹ אֲשֶׁר הִפְקַדְתּוֹ שָׁם
וְלֹא־יֵרֵד עִמָּנוּ בַּמִּלְחָמָה וְלֹא־יִהְיֶה־לָּנוּ לְשָׂטָן
בַּמִּלְחָמָה וּבַמֶּה יִתְרַצֶּה זֶה אֶל־אֲדֹנָיו הֲלוֹא
ה בְּרָאשֵׁי הָאֲנָשִׁים הָהֵם: הֲלוֹא־זֶה דָוִד אֲשֶׁר יַעֲנוּ־
לוֹ בַּמְּחֹלוֹת לֵאמֹר הִכָּה שָׁאוּל בַּאֲלָפָיו וְדָוִד
ו °ברבבתו: וַיִּקְרָא אָכִישׁ אֶל־דָּוִד וַיֹּאמֶר
אֵלָיו חַי־יהוה כִּי־יָשָׁר אַתָּה וְטוֹב בְּעֵינַי צֵאתְךָ
וּבֹאֲךָ אִתִּי בַּמַּחֲנֶה כִּי לֹא־מָצָאתִי בְךָ רָעָה מִיּוֹם

°בְּרִבְבֹתָיו ק׳

anything, but sometimes, such as here, the *Targum* renders it as *anything bad* or *any fault* (above, 12:4; see also *Genesis* 40:15).

מִיּוֹם נָפְלוֹ — *From the day he encamped.*
Although נָפְלוֹ usually means *fell,* it is here understood to mean *dwelled* or *resided* (as in *Genesis* 25:18, עַל־פְּנֵי כָל־אֶחָיו נָפָל — *over all his brothers he dwelt* [*Radak*]).

Mishbetzos Zahav, however, citing *R' M.D. Vali,* translates the word in its conventional sense. Achish apparently imagined that since David joined them he had *fallen* from his spiritual heights.

4. וַיִּקְצְפוּ עָלָיו שָׂרֵי פְלִשְׁתִּים וַיֹּאמְרוּ לוֹ שָׂרֵי פְלִשְׁתִּים — *But the Philistine officers were angry with him, and the Philistine officers said to him....*

Scripture refers twice to the *Philistine officers,* although the second time it could have used the pronoun *they.* This usage indicates that the officers were united on this point. Furthermore, they were not speaking only in the heat of the moment but their opinion remained unchanged even after their anger died down (*Chomas Anach*).

הָשֵׁב אֶת־הָאִישׁ וְיָשֹׁב אֶל־מְקוֹמוֹ — *Send this man back and let him return to his place.*

The officers urged Achish to offer David two options. He could return either to Saul or, at the very least, to his residence in Ziklag (*Likkutei Yekarim*).

וְלֹא־יֵרֵד עִמָּנוּ בַּמִּלְחָמָה וְלֹא־יִהְיֶה־לָּנוּ לְשָׂטָן בַּמִּלְחָמָה — *Do not let him go down to battle with us, so that he will not be an antagonist to us in the battle.*

According to *Malbim,* the officers told Achish not to allow David to accompany them, even as Achish's bodyguard. They were insistent on this point because they had had experience with Jews who had fought on their behalf and then betrayed them (above, 14:21) (*Daas Sofrim*).

However, although the officers opposed David's involvement, they did not object to that of his men (*Malbim*).

וְלֹא־יִהְיֶה־לָּנוּ לְשָׂטָן בַּמִּלְחָמָה — *So that he will not be an antagonist to us in the battle.*

The word שָׂטָן means an *antagonist* or *enemy,* and indicates that the officers were afraid that David would ally himself with their enemies (*Abarbanel*).

However, this word is sometimes used in regard to an impediment, particularly one that is not discernible. Accordingly, the Philistines were voicing their concern that David would frustrate their success through deceitful means (*Daas Sofrim*).

from the day he encamped [with me] until this
very day.” 4 But the Philistine officers were an-
gry with him, and the Philistine officers said to
him, “Send this man back and let him return to
the place that you assigned to him. Do not let
him go down to battle with us, so that he will not
be an antagonist to us in the battle. With what
can this person ingratiate himself to his master?
Is it not with the heads of these [our] men? 5 Is
this not David, of whom they sing with the tim-
brels, saying, ‘Saul has slain his thousands and
David his tens of thousands’?”
6 So Achish called David and said to him, “As
Hashem lives, you are an upright person, and
your going forth and coming in with me in the
camp would have been fine with me, for I have
found nothing wrong with you from the day

Mishbetzos Zahav comments that this is an example of evil people refusing to join with those who are noble and good.

הֲלוֹא בְּרָאשֵׁי הָאֲנָשִׁים הָהֵם — *Is it not with the heads of these* [*our*] *men?*

הָאֲנָשִׁים הָהֵם literally means *those men.* Although the officers were referring to themselves, it was common usage to attribute misfortune meant for oneself to someone else (*Radak*).

5. הֲלוֹא־זֶה דָוִד אֲשֶׁר יַעֲנוּ־לוֹ בַּמְּחֹלוֹת — *Is this not David, of whom they sing with the timbrels...*

Since David was so powerful, the officers argued, he might take advantage of the situation to ingratiate himself with Saul (*Radak*).

Abarbanel adds that these words of praise had been prompted by David's victory over the Philistines (18:8). Thus, the officers were warning Achish that David was an old enemy, and that he probably still hated them.

According to *Chomas Anach*, the officers implied that even if David were sincere and he would fight against Saul, credit for victory would go to him and not to the Philistines.

Achish Bids David Farewell

6. וַיִּקְרָא אָכִישׁ אֶל־דָּוִד וַיֹּאמֶר אֵלָיו חַי־ה׳ — *So Achish called David and said to him, “As Hashem lives...”*

Radak states that in order to show David respect, Achish swore by the Deity in Whom David believed.

Other commentators aver, however, that David's association with Achish had had such a positive spiritual affect that Achish believed in Hashem and sincerely took oaths in His Name (*Kli Yakar, Daas Sofrim*).

וְטוֹב בְּעֵינַי צֵאתְךָ וּבֹאֲךָ אִתִּי ... וּבְעֵינֵי הַסְּרָנִים לֹא־טוֹב אָתָּה — *And your going forth and coming in with me would have been fine with me ... but in the eyes of the governors you are not good.*

Malbim explains that Achish was reluctant to tell David that the officers

בֹּאֲךָ אֵלַי עַד־הַיּוֹם הַזֶּה וּבְעֵינֵי הַסְּרָנִים לֹא־
ז טוֹב אָתָּה: וְעַתָּה שׁוּב וְלֵךְ בְּשָׁלוֹם וְלֹא־תַעֲשֶׂה
ח רָע בְּעֵינֵי סַרְנֵי פְלִשְׁתִּים: וַיֹּאמֶר
דָּוִד אֶל־אָכִישׁ כִּי מֶה עָשִׂיתִי וּמַה־מָּצָאתָ
בְעַבְדְּךָ מִיּוֹם אֲשֶׁר הָיִיתִי לְפָנֶיךָ עַד הַיּוֹם הַזֶּה
כִּי לֹא אָבוֹא וְנִלְחַמְתִּי בְּאֹיְבֵי אֲדֹנִי הַמֶּלֶךְ:
ט וַיַּעַן אָכִישׁ וַיֹּאמֶר אֶל־דָּוִד יָדַעְתִּי כִּי טוֹב אַתָּה
בְּעֵינַי כְּמַלְאַךְ אֱלֹהִים אַךְ שָׂרֵי פְלִשְׁתִּים אָמְרוּ
י לֹא־יַעֲלֶה עִמָּנוּ בַּמִּלְחָמָה: וְעַתָּה הַשְׁכֵּם בַּבֹּקֶר
וְעַבְדֵי אֲדֹנֶיךָ אֲשֶׁר־בָּאוּ אִתָּךְ וְהִשְׁכַּמְתֶּם
יא בַּבֹּקֶר וְאוֹר לָכֶם וָלֵכוּ: וַיַּשְׁכֵּם דָּוִד הוּא
וַאֲנָשָׁיו לָלֶכֶת בַּבֹּקֶר לָשׁוּב אֶל־אֶרֶץ פְּלִשְׁתִּים
ל/א א וּפְלִשְׁתִּים עָלוּ יִזְרְעֶאל: וַיְהִי

mistrusted him. Therefore, he told David instead that the *governors* objected to his presence — presumably out of jealousy that he had been chosen to be the king's bodyguard, an assignment that would otherwise have gone to one of them or someone of comparable stature. This is implied in the fact that Achish made no mention of the warfront — instead, he spoke only of David's "coming and going with him."

7. וְעַתָּה שׁוּב — *So now return.*

Initially, Achish ordered only David and not his men to leave, for it was only he whom the officers mistrusted (*Abarbanel*).

וְלֹא־תַעֲשֶׂה רָע בְּעֵינֵי סַרְנֵי פְלִשְׁתִּים — *And do not do what is wrong in the eyes of the Philistine governors.*

Achish did not want to provoke the officers against David (*Malbim*).

8. וַיֹּאמֶר דָּוִד אֶל־אָכִישׁ כִּי מֶה עָשִׂיתִי — *David then said to Achish, "But what have I done ..."*

David's question begins with כִּי, usually translated as *because*. David asked, *[Why should I return] — because what have I done...?* (*Metzudos*).

David made sure to express disappointment so that no one should realize that he was actually glad to have been dismissed (*Me'am Loez*).

Alternatively, David was genuinely saddened. He had wanted to accompany the Philistines so that he could covertly aid the Israelites (*Daas Sofrim*).

According to *Abarbanel*, David was upset that he was asked to leave, whereas his men were welcome to remain.

Such a public dismissal would be intensely shameful, because it would imply that David was fearful and faint-hearted (*Kli Yakar*).

9. אַךְ שָׂרֵי פְלִשְׁתִּים אָמְרוּ לֹא־יַעֲלֶה עִמָּנוּ בַּמִּלְחָמָה — *But the Philistine officers have said, "He shall not go up with us into battle."*

Embarrassed to tell David why the officers objected to him, Achish omitted any explanation whatsoever (*Abarbanel*).

According to *Malbim*, Achish now felt that he had no choice but to admit that it was really the officers and not the

of your coming to me until this very day; but in
the eyes of the governors you are not good. 7 *So*
now return, and go in peace, and do not do what
is wrong in the eyes of the Philistine governors."
8 *David then said to Achish, "But what have I*
done, and what [fault] have you found with your
servant from the day I have been before you to this
very day, that I should not come and fight against
the enemies of my lord the king?"
9 *So Achish answered, and said to David, "I*
know — for in my eyes you are as good as an angel
of God — but the Philistine officers have said, 'He
shall not go up with us into battle.' 10 *So now, arise*
early in the morning along with the servants of
your master who came with you; all of you arise
early in the morning, and, when it becomes light
enough for you, go." 11 *So David and his men arose*
early, to leave in the morning to return to the land
of the Philistines, while the Philistines ascended
to Jezreel.

governors who had voiced their opposition — and not on grounds of envy but of suspicion.

10. וְעַתָּה הַשְׁכֵּם בַּבֹּקֶר — *So now, arise early in the morning.*

By rising early, David would avoid any dangerous encounters with hostile Philistines (*Ralbag*).

Alternatively, he would avoid the shame of publicly leaving the battlefront (*Abarbanel*).

Achish told David not to resist leaving, because such resistance would serve only to ratify the officers' belief that he was scheming against them (*Chomas Anach*).

וְעַבְדֵי אֲדֹנֶיךָ — *Along with the servants of your master.*

This is a reference to David's followers, who had previously been servants of David's master, Saul (*Radak*).

With these words, Achish hinted that his officers' objection was based on their suspicion that David's men secretly remained loyal to Saul and intended to support him in battle (*Abarbanel*). As mentioned above, at first David had rebuffed Achish's request that he leave because it was limited to him. Now that Achish suggested that they all leave, David agreed.

It is possible that David's initial request to be allowed to remain was part of a strategy in which he maneuvered Achish into ordering not only him but his men as well to leave (*Mishbetzos Zahav*).

בְּבֹא דָוִד וַאֲנָשָׁיו צִקְלַג בַּיּוֹם הַשְּׁלִישִׁי וַעֲמָלֵקִי
פָשְׁטוּ אֶל־נֶגֶב וְאֶל־צִקְלַג וַיַּכּוּ אֶת־צִקְלַג
ב וַיִּשְׂרְפוּ אֹתָהּ בָּאֵשׁ׃ וַיִּשְׁבּוּ אֶת־הַנָּשִׁים אֲשֶׁר־
בָּהּ מִקָּטֹן וְעַד־גָּדוֹל לֹא הֵמִיתוּ אִישׁ וַיִּנְהֲגוּ
ג וַיֵּלְכוּ לְדַרְכָּם׃ וַיָּבֹא דָוִד וַאֲנָשָׁיו אֶל־הָעִיר וְהִנֵּה
שְׂרוּפָה בָּאֵשׁ וּנְשֵׁיהֶם וּבְנֵיהֶם וּבְנֹתֵיהֶם נִשְׁבּוּ׃
ד וַיִּשָּׂא דָוִד וְהָעָם אֲשֶׁר־אִתּוֹ אֶת־קוֹלָם וַיִּבְכּוּ

XXX

☙ The Amalekites Strike and Plunder David's Territory

1. בַּיּוֹם הַשְּׁלִישִׁי — *On the third day.*

This was the third day since David and his men had Left Ziklag in order to accompany Achish (*Radak*).

וַעֲמָלֵקִי פָּשְׁטוּ — *That the Amalekite had spread out.*

The word פָּשְׁטוּ implies that they *spread out* with the specific intent to plunder and gather spoils (*Metzudos*).

There is a difficulty here. Saul had been commanded to eradicate Amalek, and the verse states: וַיִּתְפֹּשׂ אֶת־אֲגַג מֶלֶךְ עֲמָלֵק חָי וְאֶת־כָּל־הָעָם הֶחֱרִים לְפִי־חָרֶב, *[Saul] captured Agag, king of Amalek, alive, and he destroyed all the people by the edge of the sword* (15:8). Since Agag was the lone survivor, how could an army of Amalekites have remained? Although the Midrash relates that Agag consorted with a maid that night and she conceived progenitor of Haman, that took place no more than two years before this war — therefore, there could not have been even one adult alive, not to mention a band.

Perhaps some Amalekites were allowed to live because they accepted the seven Noahide laws and agreed to serve and pay taxes to the Jews (*Rambam, Hil. Melachim* 6:4). These Amalekites had now reneged on their commitment and raided the Jewish area of Ziklag (*Nachalas Shimon*).

It is also possible that in Saul's campaign against Amalek, while Saul's army was collecting the spoils, some Amalekites escaped (*Nachalas Shimon,* from *Moadim U'Zemanim* 162). However, that seems to contradict the above-cited verse.

Finally (as mentioned earlier, see 15:3, *Rashi*), a Midrash states that the Amalekites were able to transform themselves into animal shapes. It is possible that some Amalekites did so at that time, and afterward returned to human form (*Mishbetzos Zahav,* from *Siach Mordechai*).

וַעֲמָלֵקִי פָּשְׁטוּ אֶל־נֶגֶב וְאֶל־צִקְלַג — *That the Amalekite had spread out to the south and to Ziklag.*

The Amalekites discovered that the raiders who had attacked them came from Ziklag. Since David's men never left survivors, the Amalekites could have been expected to do the same, and massacre everyone they found. They did not do so only due to Divine Providence (*Radak*).

אֶל־נֶגֶב — *To the south.*

This phrase literally means, *to south.* Later (v. 14), we will see that the Amalekites' looting occurred south of the Cherethite and south of Caleb. Apparently the word *south* here is an abbreviated reference to those locations. Had Scripture wanted to refer to the south in general it would have added the definite article and stated, הַנֶּגֶב — *the south.* The absence of that article implies that the verse is referring to the south *of something.*

30/1-4

[1] *It happened that when David and his men ar-*
rived in Ziklag on the third day, that the Ama-
lekite had spread out to the south and to Ziklag.
They had attacked Ziklag and burned it with fire.
[2] *They had captured the women in it, [everyone]*
from small to great, they did not kill a person but
led them off and went their way. [3] *When David and*
his men arrived at the city — and, behold, it was
burned in fire, and their wives and sons and daugh-
ters had been captured! — [4] *David and the people*
who were with him raised their voices and wept,

Alternatively, this is a reference to a city named נֶגֶב, Negev (*Radak*).

וַיַּכּוּ אֶת־צִקְלַג — *They had attacked Ziklag.*

Although the word וַיַּכּוּ normally indicates a massacre, here it means only that the Amalekites destroyed the city infrastructure (*Radak*).

However, *Kli Yakar* suggests that this verb may be understood in its typical sense. There were Philistines living in Ziklag as well as Jews. It did not occur to the Amalekites that the foreign, fugitive Israelites would have the audacity to loot other nations. The Amalekites thus assumed that the raiders were Philistines. They therefore killed all of the local Philistines, and they then took the Jewish women into captivity for not having prevented the Philistines from attacking them.

וַיִּשְׂרְפוּ אֹתָהּ בָּאֵשׁ — *And burned it with fire.*

They burned it so that their attackers should not be able to resettle it and attack them again (*Abarbanel*).

2. וַיִּשְׁבּוּ אֶת־הַנָּשִׁים אֲשֶׁר־בָּהּ מִקָּטֹן וְעַד־גָּדוֹל — *They had captured the women in it, [everyone] from small to great.*

Since the men were away at war, the Amalekites were able to easily capture the women and children (*Radak*).

This episode presents an instance of the Amalekites' tactic of attacking the weak and vulnerable (just as they had waged war against the Jewish נֶחֱשָׁלִים, *weaklings* [*Deuteronomy* 25:18] in the wilderness) (*Me'am Loez*).

מִקָּטֹן וְעַד־גָּדוֹל — *From small to great.*

The word קָטֹן, *small*, refers to the *sons and daughters*, who are mentioned specifically in the following verse (*Daas Sofrim*).

3. According to *Sefer HaAkeidah* (*Shaar* 26), this episode demonstrates Hashem's kindness in arranging a necessary mission for David to fulfill — i.e., restore the kidnaped family members and the property — so that he would not be condemned for failing to come to the aid of the Jewish people during their war against Achish.

Also, this incident showed the Jews how David was able to heroically save his family and defeat the Amalekites. This instilled within the people trust in David and fear of his military prowess, and thus paved the way for him to gain the monarchy.

The fact that Amalekites remained alive to attack the Jews could be blamed on Saul, since he had failed to destroy them. This aroused God's judgment against him, which was soon to come (*Mussar HaNeviim*)

4. וַיִּשָּׂא דָוִד וְהָעָם אֲשֶׁר־אִתּוֹ אֶת־קוֹלָם וַיִּבְכּוּ — *David and the people who were with him raised their voices and wept.*

Although the fact that the Amalekites

ה עַד אֲשֶׁר אֵין־בָּהֶם כֹּחַ לִבְכּוֹת׃ וּשְׁתֵּי נְשֵׁי־דָוִד
נִשְׁבּוּ אֲחִינֹעַם הַיִּזְרְעֵלִית וַאֲבִיגַיִל אֵשֶׁת נָבָל
ו הַכַּרְמְלִי׃ וַתֵּצֶר לְדָוִד מְאֹד כִּי־אָמְרוּ הָעָם לְסָקְלוֹ
כִּי־מָרָה נֶפֶשׁ כָּל־הָעָם אִישׁ עַל־°בנו וְעַל־בְּנֹתָיו °בָּנָיו ק׳
ז וַיִּתְחַזֵּק דָּוִד בַּיהוָה אֱלֹהָיו׃ וַיֹּאמֶר דָּוִד אֶל־
אֶבְיָתָר הַכֹּהֵן בֶּן־אֲחִימֶלֶךְ הַגִּישָׁה־נָּא לִי הָאֵפֹד
ח וַיַּגֵּשׁ אֶבְיָתָר אֶת־הָאֵפֹד אֶל־דָּוִד׃ וַיִּשְׁאַל דָּוִד
בַּיהוה לֵאמֹר אֶרְדֹּף אַחֲרֵי הַגְּדוּד־הַזֶּה הַאַשִּׂגֶנּוּ

had not massacred these families was a miracle, the men were in anguish because they feared that the Amalekites planned to commit atrocities against their families and forcibly assimilate them into the Amalekite nation — both of which could be considered fates worse than death (*Kli Yakar, Me'am Loez*).

5. וּשְׁתֵּי נְשֵׁי־דָוִד נִשְׁבּוּ — *Both of David's wives had been captured.*

It was an added element of satisfaction for the Amalekites that they had captured David's wives.

This wording indicates that notwithstanding their exceptional beauty, David's wives had only been captured and not violated (*Chomas Anach*).

☙ David Seeks Guidance From Hashem

6. וַתֵּצֶר לְדָוִד מְאֹד כִּי־אָמְרוּ הָעָם לְסָקְלוֹ — *David was very distressed, because the people were ready to stone him.*

Aside from the grief that he was suffering because his wives had been captured, David was even more distressed by the fact that his men blamed him for this debacle (*Metzudos*).

What fault did they find in his behavior?

Abarbanel suggests that David's men held him responsible since he had joined Achish, which had led to the Amalekite attack because the city had been left unprotected.

According to *Malbim*, they felt that he should have assigned a guard to remain in Ziklag and protect the families.

Alternatively, *Abarbanel* suggests that the word כִּי does not mean, as it usually does, *because*, but rather *but*. The verse may then be understood as follows. וַתֵּצֶר לְדָוִד מְאֹד, *David was very distressed* over the kidnaping of his wives. So overwhelmed was he by his anguish that he did not make an effort to rescue them. כִּי־אָמְרוּ הָעָם לְסָקְלוֹ, *But the people said they would stone him* for not taking action. David drew strength from Hashem so that he could ignore his distress and prepare to fight.

According to *Kli Yakar*, it is possible that David's men had no substantial claim against him. They wished to stone him merely כִּי־מָרָה נֶפֶשׁ כָּל־הָעָם, *because they were embittered* by what had happened and were therefore not thinking rationally.

Alternatively, the word אָמְרוּ — *they said* — implies that they only *said* that they wanted to stone David, in order to influence him to renew his trust in Hashem. And, as the end of the verse testifies, they succeeded.

וַתֵּצֶר לְדָוִד — *David was ... distressed.*

Literally, these words mean, *and it was distressing to David*. The word וַתֵּצֶר is written in the feminine form, as it refers to הָרָעָה, a *crisis*, which is a feminine noun (*Radak*).

אִישׁ עַל־בָּנָיו וְעַל־בְּנֹתָיו — *Each man for his sons and his daughters.*

No mention is made here of their wives. Apparently, the concern of these noble Jews was that their children would

until they had no strength to weep. [5] Both of Da-
vid's wives had been captured — Ahinoam of Jez-
reel and Abigail, the [former] wife of Nabal the
Carmelite. [6] David was very distressed, because the
people were ready to stone him, for the soul of all
the people was embittered, each man for his sons
and his daughters; but David drew strength from
HASHEM, his God.
[7] David said to Abiathar the Kohen, son of Ahime-
lech, "Bring the Ephod to me now," so Abiathar brought
the Ephod to David. [8] David inquired of HASHEM, say-
ing, "Shall I pursue this band? Will I overtake them?"

be drawn to immorality or forced to assimilate. As for their wives, they trusted that they would be strong enough to withstand the Amalekites — even, if need be, at the cost of their lives (*Me'am Loez*).

וַיִּתְחַזֵּק דָּוִד בַּה׳ אֱלֹהָיו — *But David drew strength from HASHEM, his God.*

David did not despair but trusted that Hashem would enable him to recover the captives and the booty (*Abarbanel*).

Chomas Anach observes that this verse speaks of God as Hashem, a Name that represents His Attribute of Kindness. David acknowledged God's clemency in arranging that the Philistine governors should insist on his dismissal, so that he would have the opportunity to save the captives.

According to the Midrash (*Vayikra Rabbah* 21:3), David referred to this incident in *Psalm* 27. There he states, בִּקְרֹב עָלַי מְרֵעִים לֶאֱכֹל אֶת־בְּשָׂרִי צָרַי וְאֹיְבַי לִי הֵמָּה כָּשְׁלוּ וְנָפָלוּ, *When evildoers approach me to devour my flesh, my tormentors and my foes against me, it is they who stumble and fall* (v. 2). *To devour my flesh* refers to the Amalekites who had seized his wives, for a man's wife is considered to be his own flesh (see *Genesis* 2:23,24).

In his *Sefer Machaneh Yisrael* (Ch. 39), which was written as encouragement and guidance for Jewish young men who were drafted into the army, the *Chofetz Chaim* expounds on the message of this incident. David's actions here serve as a lesson for a soldier faced with a fearful massive opposition. That is the time for a person to strengthen his trust in Hashem and realize that אֵין־הַמֶּלֶךְ נוֹשָׁע בְּרָב־חָיִל, *the king is not saved by a great army* (*Psalms* 33:16). David did just that, and only afterward inquired of the *Urim VeTumim*. He received the response that he would succeed only because of his sense of security in Hashem.

7. וַיֹּאמֶר דָּוִד אֶל־אֶבְיָתָר הַכֹּהֵן בֶּן־אֲחִימֶלֶךְ הַגִּישָׁה־נָּא לִי הָאֵפֹד — *David said to Abiathar the Kohen, son of Ahimelech, "Bring the Ephod to me now."*

It would have been more appropriate for David to go to the *Ephod*. Apparently, David was so exhausted from crying that he felt compelled to ask the Kohen Gadol to bring it to him (*Kli Yakar*).

8. וַיִּשְׁאַל דָּוִד בַּה׳ לֵאמֹר אֶרְדֹּף אַחֲרֵי הַגְּדוּד הַזֶּה הַאַשִּׂגֶנּוּ — *David inquired of HASHEM, saying, "Shall I pursue this band? Will I overtake them?"*

The word אֶרְדֹּף is generally understood to constitute a statement: *I will pursue* (as in *Exodus* 15:9). Nevertheless, most commentators understand it here as a question: *Shall I pursue?* Ordinarily, such a verb only becomes a question when it possesses the prefix ה.

וַיֹּאמֶר לוֹ רְדֹף כִּי־הַשֵּׂג תַּשִּׂיג וְהַצֵּל תַּצִּיל׃
ט וַיֵּלֶךְ דָּוִד הוּא וְשֵׁשׁ־מֵאוֹת אִישׁ אֲשֶׁר אִתּוֹ
י וַיָּבֹאוּ עַד־נַחַל הַבְּשׂוֹר וְהַנּוֹתָרִים עָמָדוּ׃ וַיִּרְדֹּף
דָּוִד הוּא וְאַרְבַּע־מֵאוֹת אִישׁ וַיַּעַמְדוּ מָאתַיִם
אִישׁ אֲשֶׁר פִּגְּרוּ מֵעֲבֹר אֶת־נַחַל הַבְּשׂוֹר׃
יא וַיִּמְצְאוּ אִישׁ־מִצְרִי בַּשָּׂדֶה וַיִּקְחוּ אֹתוֹ אֶל־דָּוִד
יב וַיִּתְּנוּ־לוֹ לֶחֶם וַיֹּאכַל וַיַּשְׁקֻהוּ מָיִם׃ וַיִּתְּנוּ־לוֹ

However, that is not an unbending rule, and there are other instances when such a prefix is omitted (e.g., *Genesis* 3:1).

Our translation is based on the Talmud (*Yoma* 73b), which explains that David asked two questions: *Shall I pursue?* and *Will I overtake them?* It is generally inappropriate to ask two inquiries of the *Urim VeTumim* at once, but David was pressed for time.

According to *Ritva* (to *Yoma* ad loc.), an exception was made here because the two questions were interrelated, and the answer to one without the other would be almost worthless.

Malbim, however, reads this phrase as a statement: *I will pursue*. David insisted that he would pursue Amalek, and asked only what the result would be. Hashem responded to his question and in addition gave him Divine approval of his plan.

כִּי־הַשֵּׂג תַּשִּׂיג וְהַצֵּל תַּצִּיל — *For you will surely overtake them and you will surely rescue.*

הַשֵּׂג תַּשִּׂיג, *you will surely overtake them*, means that David would be successful, and וְהַצֵּל תַּצִּיל, *you will surely rescue*, that he was *obligated* to go (*Malbim*).

The doubled verb of the phrase הַשֵּׂג תַּשִּׂיג — literally, *overtake, you will overtake* — implies that the Israelites would first meet the Egyptian lad, who would help them find the band of Amalekites (*Mishbetzos Zahav*). The doubled verb of the next phrase, הַצֵּל תַּצִּיל — literally, *rescue, you will rescue* — teaches that David would save both the people and their belongings (*Kli Yakar*).

David Sets Out to Rescue

9. וַיֵּלֶךְ דָּוִד הוּא וְשֵׁשׁ־מֵאוֹת אִישׁ — *So David went, he and the six hundred men.*

The seemingly superfluous word הוּא, *he*, indicates that David traveled at the front of the troops to lead them (*Kli Yakar*).

וְהַנּוֹתָרִים עָמָדוּ — *Where some men remained behind.*

Most commentators explain that the men who remained behind were the two hundred mentioned in the following verse. They were either too exhausted to fight (*Rashi*) or afraid (*Ralbag*). They did not return to Ziklag; rather, they stayed at Besor Brook to guard the baggage of those who advanced to engage in battle (*Radak*).

Abarbanel questions this interpretation for two reasons. First, it means that the same information is presented twice (i.e., here and in the next verse). And second, the word וְהַנּוֹתָרִים, *some men*, implies that these were men who remained in addition to the 600 men. Therefore, *Abarbanel* explains that aside from the 600 men, there were additional men, some of them unhealthy or elderly, who stayed in Ziklag. The next verse mentions that, in addition, of the 600, 200 remained at Besor Brook.

Malbim also states that these men were not part of the contingent of 600 men. He explains that they were among the mighty men of the tribes of Manasseh and Benjamin, who had come

And He said to him, "Pursue, for you will surely overtake them and you will surely rescue."
[9] *So David went, he and the six hundred men who were with him, and they came to the Besor Brook, where some men remained behind.*
[10] *David pursued, he together with four hundred men, while two hundred men remained, who were too exhausted to cross the Besor Brook.* [11] *They found an Egyptian man in the field and took him to David; they gave him bread and he ate, and they gave him water to drink.* [12] *They gave him*

to join David at Ziklag (as described in *I Chronicles* Ch. 12). Because these men came without their families, their wives had not been captured. Thus, they felt no need to join David's pursuit and remained in Ziklag.

10. וַיַּעַמְדוּ מָאתַיִם אִישׁ אֲשֶׁר פִּגְּרוּ מֵעֲבֹר אֶת־נַחַל הַבְּשׂוֹר — *While two hundred men remained, who were too exhausted to cross the Besor Brook.*

The word פִּגְּרוּ is an uncommon verb. Our translation — *too exhausted* — follows *Radak*, who understands it as implying inactivity caused by weakness or fatigue. A similar word is found in the Talmudic phrase, יוֹמָא דְמִפַּגְרֵי בָהּ רַבָּנָן — *a day on which the Torah scholars were too weak and tired [to learn]* (*Shabbos* 129b; see *Tosafos* ad loc.).

However, that Talmudic phrase can also be understood as referring to a day on which the students were *lax* in coming in study and the word פִּגְּרוּ here can similarly be interpreted as meaning *lazy*.

Rashi renders פִּגְּרוּ simply as *who refrained.*

The noun form of this word, פֶּגֶר, means *body* (or, more commonly, *carcass*). *Abarbanel* thus states that these 200 men joined forces *as one body* to protect David and the other men. There was a mountain overlooking the Besor Brook, from which the enemy could have pummeled them with stones. David stationed these 200 men atop the mountain to keep the enemy from doing so. Accordingly, their inactivity was not due to laziness.

◆§ An Informer Appears

11. וַיִּמְצְאוּ — *They found.*

It is not clear who *they* refers to — perhaps some of the men who had remained behind at the brook (who were wandering about before David had gone very far), or, perhaps some of the men who were accompanying David (*Ralbag*).

וַיִּתְּנוּ־לוֹ לֶחֶם וַיֹּאכַל וַיַּשְׁקֻהוּ מָיִם — *They gave him bread and he ate, and they gave him water to drink.*

The Talmud (*Yoma* 83b) derives from this phrase that although a starving person is invigorated when he is given sweets (see 14:29) — as indeed was done here (next verse), he should first be given bread or other simple food, otherwise, the sweets will only aggravate his hunger.

Regarding the bread, וַיֹּאכַל, *he ate.* However, regarding the water, וַיַּשְׁקֻהוּ, *they gave him ... to drink.* The soldiers regulated the amount of water, because when a person is famished, drinking too much can cause his stomach to burst (*Malbim, Kli Yakar*).

Mussar HaNeviim comments on the extraordinary kindness of David's men. Although they were desperately preoccupied with rescuing their families, they took the time and trouble to nurse this stranger back

פֶּלַח דְּבֵלָה וּשְׁנֵי צִמֻּקִים וַיֹּאכַל וַתָּשָׁב רוּחוֹ אֵלָיו
כִּי לֹא־אָכַל לֶחֶם וְלֹא־שָׁתָה מַיִם שְׁלֹשָׁה יָמִים
יג וּשְׁלֹשָׁה לֵילוֹת: וַיֹּאמֶר לוֹ
דָוִד לְמִי־אַתָּה וְאֵי מִזֶּה אָתָּה וַיֹּאמֶר נַעַר מִצְרִי
אָנֹכִי עֶבֶד לְאִישׁ עֲמָלֵקִי וַיַּעַזְבֵנִי אֲדֹנִי כִּי חָלִיתִי
יד הַיּוֹם שְׁלֹשָׁה: אֲנַחְנוּ פָּשַׁטְנוּ נֶגֶב הַכְּרֵתִי וְעַל־
אֲשֶׁר לִיהוּדָה וְעַל־נֶגֶב כָּלֵב וְאֶת־צִקְלַג שָׂרַפְנוּ
טו בָאֵשׁ: וַיֹּאמֶר אֵלָיו דָּוִד הֲתוֹרִדֵנִי אֶל־הַגְּדוּד
הַזֶּה וַיֹּאמֶר הִשָּׁבְעָה לִּי בֵאלֹהִים אִם־תְּמִיתֵנִי
וְאִם־תַּסְגִּרֵנִי בְּיַד־אֲדֹנִי וְאוֹרִדְךָ אֶל־הַגְּדוּד הַזֶּה:

to life. Since kindness is one of the mitzvos whose "fruits" are given in this world, it may be that the merit of this deed helped them recover their families and possessions.

12. פֶּלַח דְּבֵלָה — *A cake of pressed figs.*

According to *Radak*, a פֶּלַח is a slice of such a cake.

וַתָּשָׁב רוּחוֹ אֵלָיו — *And his spirit returned to him.*

Simply understood, he was returned to his full vigor.

However, the *Zohar* (Vol. 1, 175) seems to interpret this as meaning that his life-spirit had left him, and he was now restored to life.

13. אֵי מִזֶּה אָתָּה — *And where are you from?*

The word מִזֶּה — *where ... from* — literally means *from here*. Thus, אֵי מִזֶּה may be understood as, *Where [is the nation from which you can state], "I am from here"?* (*Metzudos*).

נַעַר מִצְרִי אָנֹכִי עֶבֶד לְאִישׁ עֲמָלֵקִי — *I am an Egyptian youth, the slave of an Amalekite man.*

The boy answered the second question first.

וַיַּעַזְבֵנִי אֲדֹנִי כִּי חָלִיתִי — *My master abandoned me because I became ill.*

Me'am Loez observes the contrast between the Israelites and the Amalekites. Whereas the slave's master had abandoned him when he grew ill, the Jews nursed him back to health.

הַיּוֹם שְׁלֹשָׁה — *Three days ago.*

Literally, *today is the third day* (*Metzudos*).

14. נֶגֶב — *South.*

South is the conventional translation of נֶגֶב. The root of the word is *dry*, and the lands to the south of the land of Israel are generally dry.

Alternatively, *Radak* states that נֶגֶב here may refer to *plains*, which are also dry.

נֶגֶב הַכְּרֵתִי — *South of the Cherethite.*

Rashi states that *Cherethite* is a reference to the Philistines.

Thus, נֶגֶב הַכְּרֵתִי means *the south of the Cherethites.*

According to *Radak*, this phrase refers to a specific Philistine family (see *Zephaniah* 2:5). *Radak* adds that the Amalekites raided the southern area of the Cherethites as well, as we will see below (v. 16), and that the Amalekites raided Philistine territory as well.

וְעַל־אֲשֶׁר לִיהוּדָה וְעַל־נֶגֶב כָּלֵב — *And the territory of Judah and the south of Caleb.*

Although Caleb was a member of the

a cake of pressed figs and two raisin-clusters and
he ate, and his spirit returned to him, for he had
not eaten bread nor drunk water for three days
and three nights. [13]*David said to him, "To whom*
do you belong? And where are you from?" He re-
plied, "I am an Egyptian youth, the slave of an
Amalekite man. My master abandoned me because
I became ill, three days ago. [14]*We raided the south*
of the Cherethite and the territory of Judah and
the south of Caleb, and we burned down Ziklag
with fire." [15]*So David asked him, "Will you lead*
me to that band?" He replied, "Swear to me by
God that you will not kill me nor hand me over
to my master, and I will lead you to that band."

tribe of Judah, his land was significant in itself and was thus referred to separately. This was possibly because Caleb earned Hebron (in addition to his regular allotment in the land) with the courage and faithfulness that he exhibited in the incident of the Spies (see *Numbers* 14:24, *Joshua* 14:9; *Daas Sofrim*).

וְאֶת־צִקְלַג שָׂרַפְנוּ בָאֵשׁ — *And we burned down Ziklag with fire.*

Hashem guided the man to tell David exactly what he wanted to know (*Daas Sofrim*).

15. וַיֹּאמֶר הִשָּׁבְעָה לִּי בֵאלֹהִים אִם־תְּמִיתֵנִי וְאִם תַּסְגִּרֵנִי בְּיַד־אֲדֹנִי — *He replied, "Swear to me by God that you will not kill me nor hand me over to my master."*

The slave did not know the nature of David's relationship with the Amalekites. In case David viewed him as the slave of an enemy, he asked David not to kill him. And in case David was an ally of the Amalekites, he asked him not to act on their behalf and return him to them (*Malbim*).

Meshech Chochmah (to *Exodus* 20:7) states that David did not accede to the slave's request to swear. Although it is permitted to swear to perform a mitzvah (in order to fill oneself with added enthusiasm — *Nedarim* 8a), this applies only to an active mitzvah (*Ritva*). In regard to refraining from action (as here), such an oath would be considered to be *an oath taken in vain.*

Also, the slave asked David to swear that he would not hand him back to his Amalekite master. But since a Jew is commanded to destroy an Amalekite and his belongings, David was already bound not to return the slave to his master. Accordingly, David refused to swear to that, because such an oath would be superfluous and thus in vain.

However, why was David not obligated to kill the slave, since he constituted a portion of the spoils of Amalek, which must be destroyed? *Nachalas Shimon* (60:44) answers by pointing out that a gentile master does not own the *body* of his slave; rather, he possesses only monetary rights to him (see *Gittin* 38a). Thus, a slave is not legally considered Amalekite *property*, and therefore there was no obligation to kill him. However, it was forbidden to return him to his master.

Alternatively, *Nachalas Shimon* conjectures that under normal circumstances a Jew might indeed be obligated to kill the slave of an Amalekite. In this case, however, since the Amalekite master abandoned his slave, he apparently relinquished all ownership of him. Thus David was permitted to let him live.

טז וַיֹּרִדֵהוּ וְהִנֵּה נְטֻשִׁים עַל־פְּנֵי כָל־הָאָרֶץ
אֹכְלִים וְשֹׁתִים וְחֹגְגִים בְּכֹל הַשָּׁלָל הַגָּדוֹל
אֲשֶׁר לָקְחוּ מֵאֶרֶץ פְּלִשְׁתִּים וּמֵאֶרֶץ יְהוּדָה:
יז וַיַּכֵּם דָּוִד מֵהַנֶּשֶׁף וְעַד־הָעֶרֶב לְמָחֳרָתָם
וְלֹא־נִמְלַט מֵהֶם אִישׁ כִּי אִם־אַרְבַּע מֵאוֹת
אִישׁ־נַעַר אֲשֶׁר־רָכְבוּ עַל־הַגְּמַלִּים וַיָּנֻסוּ:

16. נְטֻשִׁים עַל־פְּנֵי כָל־הָאָרֶץ — *Spread out across the face of the entire land.*

That is, across the area of land that they had occupied (*Metzudos*).

וְחֹגְגִים — *And celebrating.*

The word חֹגְגִים implies that they were leaping and dancing (*Radak*).

נְטֻשִׁים עַל־פְּנֵי כָל־הָאָרֶץ אֹכְלִים וְשֹׁתִים וְחֹגְגִים — *Spread out across the face of the entire land, eating and drinking and celebrating.*

David now had two indications that the Amalekites felt secure. First, they were spread out and not camped close together next to their guards. And second, they were celebrating their victory (*Malbim*).

אֲשֶׁר לָקְחוּ מֵאֶרֶץ פְּלִשְׁתִּים וּמֵאֶרֶץ יְהוּדָה — *That they had taken from the land of the Philistines and the land of Judah.*

They were particularly joyful because they had conducted successful raids against two such mighty nations as Philistia and Judah (*Kli Yakar*).

☙ David's Rescue and Distribution of Spoils

17. וַיַּכֵּם דָּוִד — *David smote them.*

We learn from the prophet Obadiah that Esau will be defeated only by the descendants of Joseph (see *Obadiah* 1:18). How then could David — who was from the tribe of Judah — have successfully overpowered Amalek, a nation descended from Esau?

The Talmud explains that David was aided in this battle by soldiers from the tribe of Manasseh (see *I Chronicles* 12:21; *Bava Basra* 123b).

מֵהַנֶּשֶׁף וְעַד־הָעֶרֶב לְמָחֳרָתָם — *From twilight until the evening of the next day.*

This short phrase lends itself to a variety of interpretations.

In particular, two points are unclear.

First, it is not clear whether נֶשֶׁף refers to the end of the day or the end of the night.

Second, the word לְמָחֳרָתָם — translated here as *of the next day* — literally means *to their morrow.* This word is perplexing for two reasons: it is unclear which day the verse is referring to, and the construction of the word (it is a plural noun) is unusual.

❒ The Talmud (ibid.) seems to conclude that here נֶשֶׁף means *morning.* Thus, David smote the Amalekites from morning to evening.

The Talmud offers no explanation for לְמָחֳרָתָם. However, *Rashi* (ad loc.) states that it means the day after their (the Amalekites) setting up camp, which accounts for the plural form.

❒ *Malbim* explains that David chose not to attack on the day that he arrived because he was heavily outnumbered. Instead, he waited until early the next morning when he could stage a surprise attack, and then smote the Amalekites from morning until evening.

❒ *Rabbeinu Yeshayah* also translates נֶשֶׁף as *morning.* David began his attack in the morning and continued until the evening following the *next day.* Thus, מֵהַנֶּשֶׁף וְעַד־הָעֶרֶב לְמָחֳרָתָם means *from morning until the evening of the next day.*

[16] *So he led him and there they were! — spread
out across the face of the entire land, eating
and drinking and celebrating with all the great
spoils that they had taken from the land of the
Philistines and the land of Judah.* [17] *David smote
them from twilight until the evening of the next
day; not a man of them survived, except four
hundred youths who rode camels, who fled.*

❒ The Midrash (*Vayikra Rabbah* 21:3, *Shocher Tov* 18:23) disagrees with the Talmud, and translates נֶשֶׁף as *evening*. Accordingly, David began his assault in the evening and continued through the next day and the next night until the second morning.

Hence, לְמָחֳרָתָם means *to the morrow of the two [evenings]*. As *Radak* translates this phrase, *from evening to evening and then until the next day*.

❒ *Rashi* interprets this passage homiletically, citing a Midrash to do so. לְמָחֳרָתָם means *to the morrow [of the Amalekites]*. The defeat of the Amalekites was associated with the concept of "tomorrow." Thus, when Moses and Joshua fought Amalek after the Exodus, Moses stated, *Tomorrow I will stand on top of the hill* (*Exodus* 17:9) (see *Pachad Yitzchak, Purim* 5, which expands this idea to explain the significance of "tomorrow" in *Megillas Esther* 5:8, 9:13).

Mussar HaNeviim explains that Amalek's hold on the world, which is represented by the proliferation of evil, should be viewed as a temporary condition, because *tomorrow* Amalek and evil will be defeated, and Israel and justice will prevail. As Balaam stated, *Amalek is the first among nations, but its end will be eternal destruction* (*Numbers* 24:20).

מֵהַנֶּשֶׁף וְעַד־הָעֶרֶב — *From twilight until the evening.*

Most of the interpretations cited above assume that David fought during the nighttime. How then was he provided with light? The Midrash (*Vayikra Rabbah* ibid., *Shocher Tov* ibid.) explains that Hashem miraculously illuminated the night with lightning and shooting stars. David referred to this with the words, כִּי־אַתָּה תָּאִיר נֵרִי, *For it is You Who will light my lamp* (*Psalms* 18:29).

Mishbetzos Zahav cites the comment of *Sefer Torah SheBe'al Peh* in the name of *Midrash HaGadol* that Hashem stopped the sun in the sky for David, just as he had done for Joshua (see *Joshua* 10:13).

וְלֹא נִמְלַט מֵהֶם אִישׁ — *Not a man of them survived.*

Metzudos explains אִישׁ here to mean *a man on foot*. Apparently *Metzudos* provides this explanation since it is unusual for Scripture to present an inclusive statement followed by an exception.

כִּי אִם־אַרְבַּע מֵאוֹת אִישׁ־נַעַר — *Except four hundred youths.*

When Esau went to fight his brother Jacob (*Genesis* Ch. 32), he brought along four hundred men. Later, when Esau departed from Jacob, no mention is made of these men (ibid. 33:15). The reason they had slipped away from Esau was out of fear of being "burnt by the coals of Jacob." They were rewarded here when exactly four hundred of Amalek's men, who descended from Esau, survived David's attack (*Bereishis Rabbah* 78:15; *Rashi, Genesis* ad loc.).

אִישׁ־נַעַר אֲשֶׁר־רָכְבוּ עַל־הַגְּמַלִּים — *Youths who rode camels.*

As *Malbim* explains, the only survivors were those who had two advantages: youth and camels. Either one without the other would not have sufficed.

יח וַיַּצֵּל דָּוִד אֵת כָּל־אֲשֶׁר לָקְחוּ עֲמָלֵק וְאֶת־שְׁתֵּי נָשָׁיו
יט הִצִּיל דָּוִד: וְלֹא נֶעְדַּר־לָהֶם מִן־הַקָּטֹן וְעַד־הַגָּדוֹל
וְעַד־בָּנִים וּבָנוֹת וּמִשָּׁלָל וְעַד כָּל־אֲשֶׁר לָקְחוּ לָהֶם
כ הַכֹּל הֵשִׁיב דָּוִד: וַיִּקַּח דָּוִד אֶת־כָּל־הַצֹּאן וְהַבָּקָר
נָהֲגוּ לִפְנֵי הַמִּקְנֶה הַהוּא וַיֹּאמְרוּ זֶה שְׁלַל דָּוִד:

18. וַיַּצֵּל דָּוִד — *So David rescued.*

Although David was aided by his men, he is given credit for the rescue, because it occurred in his merit — in particular, in the merit of the extraordinary humility that he displayed when he tolerated the anger of his men who wanted to stone him (*Chomas Anach*).

וַיַּצֵּל דָּוִד אֵת כָּל־אֲשֶׁר לָקְחוּ עֲמָלֵק וְאֶת־שְׁתֵּי נָשָׁיו — *So David rescued everything that Amalek had taken, and ... his two wives.*

Scripture mentions David's wives separately to teach us his greatness. He made the belongings of others his priority and preceded to save those before his own wives.

Alternatively, they are listed separately because of their regal stature (*Chomas Anach*).

Kli Yakar suggests that Scripture mentions David's wives to indicate that their rescue was complete — i.e., they had not been violated.[1]

וְאֶת־שְׁתֵּי נָשָׁיו הִצִּיל דָּוִד — *And David rescued his two wives.*

According to *Malbim*, Scripture repeats David's name to indicate that although he was aided by others in salvaging the other people and their belongings, he rescued his wives himself.

David referred to this victory in *Psalms*: אִם־תַּחֲנֶה עָלַי מַחֲנֶה לֹא־יִירָא לִבִּי אִם־תָּקוּם עָלַי מִלְחָמָה בְּזֹאת אֲנִי בוֹטֵחַ, *Though an army would besiege me, my heart would not fear; though war would arise against me, in this I trust* (*Psalms* 27:3). בְּזֹאת אֲנִי בוֹטֵחַ, *In this I trust*, refers to Moses' blessing to the tribe of Judah — David's tribe — which begins with the words, וְזֹאת לִיהוּדָה, *And this to Judah*. In that blessing, Moses stated about Judah, יָדָיו רָב לוֹ וְעֵזֶר מִצָּרָיו תִּהְיֶה, *May his hands fight his grievance, and may You [HASHEM] be a Helper against his enemies* (*Deuteronomy* 33:7).

19. וְלֹא נֶעְדַּר־לָהֶם — *No one among them was missing.*

The fact that the Amalekites did no damage to either people or property was extraordinary. David and his followers thus experienced a fulfillment of the verse, יִפֹּל מִצִּדְּךָ אֶלֶף וּרְבָבָה מִימִינֶךָ אֵלֶיךָ לֹא יִגָּשׁ, *A thousand will fall at your side and a myriad at your right hand, but to you it shall not approach* (*Psalms* 91:7) (*Daas Sofrim*).

וּמִשָּׁלָל וְעַד כָּל־אֲשֶׁר לָקְחוּ לָהֶם — *As well as the spoils, including everything they had taken for themselves.*

שָׁלָל, *spoils*, refers to whatever had been taken by the army but not yet distributed to individuals. כָּל־אֲשֶׁר לָקְחוּ, *everything they had taken*, is a reference to those items that had already been distributed (*Malbim*).

1. *Me'am Loez* avers that there were witnesses to testify that they had remained pure, because their own claims that their captors did not violate them would not have been believed (*Kesubos* 22a) — and as a result David would have been prohibited to remain married to them.

Me'am Loez does not specify why that would have been the case. Possibly, this alludes to the ruling that a king may not remain with a woman who was violated (a ruling that is the subject of dispute in *Yerushalmi Sanhedrin* 2:3; see *II Samuel* 20:3, *Radak*; see also *Nachalas Shimon* to *II Samuel* 35).

18 So David rescued everything that Amalek had
taken, and David rescued his two wives. 19 No one
among them was missing, from small to great,
sons and daughters, as well as the spoils, includ-
ing everything they had taken for themselves;
David returned everything. 20 David took all the
[Amalekite] sheep and cattle; they led them before
all that livestock and said, "This is the booty of
David."

According to *Metzudos*, כָּל־אֲשֶׁר לָקְחוּ, *everything they had taken*, included what the Amalekites had taken from the Philistines, Judah, and the south of Caleb.

הַכֹּל הֵשִׁיב דָּוִד — *David returned everything.*

In the previous verse, Scripture used the word הִצִּיל, *rescued*. The verb used here, הֵשִׁיב, *returned*, adds that he made sure that every item was brought back to its original owner (*Mishbetzos Zahav*).

20. The meaning of this verse is unclear and subject to a wide variety of interpretations. Among the issues that must be clarified are:

❒ Are the *sheep and cattle* mentioned here the property of David and his men from Ziklag, or other spoils that they recovered from the Amalekites?

❒ Who are *they*?

❒ What is *that livestock?*

❒ What was the purpose of announcing, *This is the booty of David?*

We cite interpretations of the commentators as well as explanations based on the Talmud.

❒ *Rashi* states that the *sheep and cattle* were spoils that the Amalekites had taken from Judah and Caleb. David's men now led these animals in order to proclaim his conquest over Amalek. Thus, נָהֲגוּ לִפְנֵי הַמִּקְנֶה הַהוּא means that David's men *led [and walked] before that [above-mentioned] livestock.*[1]

❒ *Rabbeinu Yeshayah* follows this view, and adds that the announcement was meant to publicize David's name.

❒ *Radak* quotes his father as stating that this verse is referring to two groups of animals. The *sheep and cattle* had belonged to the Amalekites. The *other livestock* was comprised of the animals that had previously been their own. David's men proclaimed regarding those in front, *This is the booty of David.*

❒ *Radak* adds his own understanding of this verse.

The Mishnah in *Sanhedrin* (20b) states that a king has the right to breach private fences to make a route for himself, and he has the right to take the best of the spoils captured in war.

Talmud Yerushalmi (*Sanhedrin* 2:5) comments that the present verse serves as the source of that Mishnah. Presumably, the Talmud is referring to the statement in the Mishnah that the king may breach fences, since that is the part that is quoted in the Talmud.

Accordingly, *Radak* explains our verse as follows. David's men led the livestock before the soldiers (as was common). When the animals breached fences surrounding private property, David's men told the property owners,

1. It is apparently left unstated but understood that the livestock taken from David and his men was restored to them.

כא וַיָּבֹא דָוִד אֶל־מָאתַיִם הָאֲנָשִׁים אֲשֶׁר־פִּגְּרוּ | מִלֶּכֶת |
אַחֲרֵי דָוִד וַיֹּשִׁיבֻם בְּנַחַל הַבְּשׂוֹר וַיֵּצְאוּ לִקְרַאת
דָּוִד וְלִקְרַאת הָעָם אֲשֶׁר־אִתּוֹ וַיִּגַּשׁ דָּוִד אֶת־הָעָם
כב וַיִּשְׁאַל לָהֶם לְשָׁלוֹם: וַיַּעַן כָּל־אִישׁ־רָע
וּבְלִיַּעַל מֵהָאֲנָשִׁים אֲשֶׁר הָלְכוּ עִם־דָּוִד וַיֹּאמְרוּ יַעַן

This is the booty of David — i.e., the king may act in such a manner when necessary.[1]

It is noteworthy that not all agree with *Radak's* interpretation of the Talmudic passage. According to *Pnei Moshe* and *Sheyurei Korban* (two commentaries on *Talmud Yerushalmi*), the Talmud was referring to the other ruling in the Mishnah: i.e., that a king has the right to the best part of the booty. Thus, the verse relates that David took for himself the *cattle and sheep* that had belonged to the Philistines. These were led before the animals that had belonged to the people of Judah and which had now been returned. The people proclaimed regarding the animals at the front, *This is the booty of David*.[2]

❒ *Abarbanel* presents an alternative approach. וַיִּקַּח דָּוִד אֶת־כָּל־הַצֹּאן means that *David took all the sheep*, and וְהַבָּקָר נָהֲגוּ לִפְנֵי הַמִּקְנֶה הַהוּא means that *the cattle he placed in front of those livestock.* David placed the cattle in front of the sheep, a common practice meant to protect the sheep.[3]

The end of the verse, states *Abarbanel*, is to be understood as follows. When the people of southern Judah and Caleb and the Cherethites came to reclaim their belongings, they were told, *This is the booty of David* — i.e., they had no claim to it. This is based on the Mishnaic law that a person who recovers property from bandits may keep it because there is a presumption that the original owner has given up hope of regaining it and has thereby relinquished claims to ownership (*Bava Kamma* 114a).

❒ This view that David had a legal right to all the spoils is shared by *Malbim*, *Chomas Anach*, and *Metzudos* (although they differ from *Abarbanel* in their understanding of the beginning of the verse).

❒ According to *Malbim*, *David took for himself even the livestock* that his men had possessed in Ziklag, and it was regarding this that his men proclaimed, *this is the booty of David*.

❒ *Metzudos* explains that David took all the *sheep and cattle* that had originally belonged to the Philistines and Judah; his men led them and prevented the original owners from retrieving them.[4]

Considering the fact that the Amalekites had legally acquired the plunder in the sense that the original owners were presumed to have given up hope of recovery, how could David have benefited from these animals, since he was mandated to destroy Amalekite

1. However, *Abarbanel* objects to this interpretation on two counts. First, the verses here give no indication that any fences were breached. Second, since David was not king of the Philistines, how could he claim monarchial rights in Philistine territory?

2. According to either interpretation, this statement of *Talmud Yerushalmi* supports the idea that David already possessed the legal status of a king, even though Saul was still alive. See above, comm. to 25:26, *Nachalas Shimon* 52:5.

3. However, *Abarbanel's* interpretation deviates from the sentence structure indicated by the cantillation, according to which *the sheep and the cattle* constitute one phrase.

4. It seems that *Rashi* agrees that the booty from Judah was not returned to the owners. However, according to *Rashi* the proclamation of זֶה שְׁלַל דָּוִד — *this is the booty of David* — was not made in this regard.

[21] *David then came to the two hundred men
who were too exhausted to go follow after
David, whom he had stationed at the Besor Brook,
and they went to meet David and to meet the
people who were with him. David approached the
people and inquired after their welfare.* [22] *Every
mean-spirited and base person of the men who
had gone with David spoke up and said, "Since*

belongings? *Sefer Ner Mitzvah,* a commentary on *Rambam's Sefer HaMitzvos,* cites this incident to buttress the opinion (apparently held by *Rambam*) that there is no long-term commandment to destroy Amalek's livestock. The directive to Saul to do so (above, 15:3) did not apply to anyone else.

Rashi, however, states on *Deuteronomy* (25:19) that the dictum to eradicate Amalek applies to their livestock as well.

Meshech Chochmah (ibid.) demonstrates that *Rashi* must therefore hold the opinion that the commandment to destroy Amalek is not incumbent on an individual Jew but rather on the nation at large. Therefore, as an individual, David was allowed to take from the spoils.

However, *Sefer HaChinuch* disagrees and says that the commandment is directed at each individual. How then does *Sefer HaChinuch* reconcile this question? Possibly, the mandate to destroy Amalekite possessions takes effect only after the Amalekites have been annihilated (*Oneg Yom Tov*) — which had not occurred.

Alternatively, as *Moadim U'Zemanim* (162) rules, the command to destroy Amalek applies only if one can complete the task. This was not possible here, because some Amalekites had dispersed after Saul's failed attempt (*Nachalas Shimon* 60:45; see also 30:1).

21. וַיָּבֹא דָוִד אֶל־מָאתַיִם הָאֲנָשִׁים — *David came to the two hundred men.*

David did not go all the way to them, because they set out to receive him (*Metzudos*).

וַיֹּשִׁיבֻם בְּנַחַל הַבְּשׂוֹר — *Whom he had stationed at the Besor Brook.*

We translate וַיֹּשִׁיבֻם as describing a previous action: *whom he had stationed* (and not as describing a new action — i.e., *and he stationed them*). The two hundred men who had previously been stationed by David at Besor Brook now came out to greet him upon his return (*Radak*).

Abarbanel asserts that this underscores the fact that these men had been assigned by David to stay back and guard the utensils.

וַיִּגַּשׁ דָּוִד אֶת־הָעָם — *David approached the people.*

The word וַיִּגַּשׁ means *he came close;* the word אֵת here substitutes for אֶל, *to* (*Radak*).

וַיִּשְׁאַל לָהֶם לְשָׁלוֹם — *And inquired after their welfare.*

David greeted these men happily. Although he may have deplored the fact that they had chosen not to join in battle, he understood that they had suffered many tribulations because of their devotion to him (*Daas Sofrim*).

David's initiative to greet his men was a characteristic example of his sterling character (*Chomas Anach*).

22. וַיַּעַן כָּל־אִישׁ־רָע וּבְלִיַּעַל — *Every mean-spirited and base person spoke up.*

רָע literally means *evil,* and בְלִיַּעַל, *base,* literally means *without a yoke* — i.e., without a sense of responsibility. Often this latter word is associated with casting off *the yoke of HASHEM's sovereignty,* as in the case of idolaters (see *Deuteronomy* 13:14).

The men were called רָע in regard to

אֲשֶׁר לֹא־הָלְכוּ עִמִּי לֹא־נִתֵּן לָהֶם מֵהַשָּׁלָל אֲשֶׁר
הִצַּלְנוּ כִּי־אִם־אִישׁ אֶת־אִשְׁתּוֹ וְאֶת־בָּנָיו וְיִנְהֲגוּ
כג וְיֵלֵכוּ׃ וַיֹּאמֶר דָּוִד לֹא־תַעֲשׂוּ כֵן אֶחָי אֵת אֲשֶׁר־
נָתַן יהוה לָנוּ וַיִּשְׁמֹר אֹתָנוּ וַיִּתֵּן אֶת־הַגְּדוּד הַבָּא
כד עָלֵינוּ בְּיָדֵנוּ׃ וּמִי יִשְׁמַע לָכֶם לַדָּבָר הַזֶּה כִּי כְּחֵלֶק ׀
הַיֹּרֵד בַּמִּלְחָמָה וּכְחֵלֶק הַיֹּשֵׁב עַל־הַכֵּלִים יַחְדָּו
כה יַחֲלֹקוּ׃ וַיְהִי מֵהַיּוֹם הַהוּא וָמָעְלָה וַיְשִׂמֶהָ
כו לְחֹק וּלְמִשְׁפָּט לְיִשְׂרָאֵל עַד הַיּוֹם הַזֶּה׃ וַיָּבֹא

their interpersonal attitude of selfishness, and בְּלִיַּעַל because they failed to realize that it was not their own strength that gained them these spoils but the hand of Hashem (*Kli Yakar*).

Although these men spoke out of ignorance of the law, they were deemed to be evil and base because their greedy character led them to suggest this idea (*Mishbetzos Zahav*).

וַיֹּאמְרוּ יַעַן אֲשֶׁר לֹא־הָלְכוּ עִמִּי — *And said, "Since they did not go with me..."*

Each one spoke in the singular, since each thought only about himself (see *Me'am Loez*).

לֹא־נִתֵּן לָהֶם מֵהַשָּׁלָל אֲשֶׁר הִצַּלְנוּ כִּי־אִם־אִישׁ אֶת־אִשְׁתּוֹ וְאֶת־בָּנָיו — *We will not give them of the spoils that we rescued, except for each man's wife and children.*

They did not want the men who had stayed behind to receive even that which had previously been theirs. Since (as stated above) the owner of plundered goods presumably abandons hope of repossessing his belongings, the combatants believed that they deserved to keep everything.

23. וַיֹּאמֶר דָּוִד לֹא־תַעֲשׂוּ כֵן אֶחָי — *But David said, "Do not act so, my brothers ..."*

Although David was the commander and could have harshly enforced the law, he spoke to his men softly like a brother and explained to them why their reasoning was flawed (*Abarbanel*).

אֵת אֲשֶׁר־נָתַן ה׳ לָנוּ — *With what* Hashem *has given us.*

David gave two explanations of why their reasoning was faulty — the first here and the second in the next verse.

Here, David stated that a person who claimed that he deserved a greater share of the spoils because he had engaged in battle was denying Hashem's hand. The fighters had been enabled to retrieve these goods solely due to Hashem's benevolence. These were a gift from Him, and consequently everyone should receive an equal portion.

Malbim comments that since Hashem's intervention achieved this success, the people who did *not* choose to fight exhibited a superior level of trust that Hashem would return their belongings. Thus, it was *their* merit that brought about the victory.

24. וּמִי יִשְׁמַע לָכֶם לַדָּבָר הַזֶּה ... — *Who could hearken to you regarding such a thing!...*

David's second point was that even if one claimed that the soldiers were responsible for the victory, it was still wrong to deprive the others who had remained behind of an equal share in the spoils, because the warriors could not have succeeded without the service of the non-combatants (*Abarbanel*).

25. וַיְהִי מֵהַיּוֹם הַהוּא וָמָעְלָה וַיְשִׂמֶהָ לְחֹק וּלְמִשְׁפָּט — *And it was from that day onward that [David] made this a decree and a law.*

they did not go with me, we will not give them
of the spoils that we rescued, except for each
man's wife and children; let them take them and
go." 23 *But David said, "Do not act so, my broth-*
ers, with what HASHEM *has given us, for He has*
watched over us and delivered into our hands
the band that had come upon us. 24 *Who could*
hearken to you regarding such a thing! Rather,
like the portion of the one who went into battle,
so is the portion of the one who remained with
the baggage; they shall divide [it] equally." 25 *And*
it was from that day onward that [David] made
this a decree and a law in Israel, until this day.

Rashi cites a Midrash (*Bereishis Rabbah* 43:9) that the verse might have more conventionally used the word וְהָלְאָה to indicate *onward*. The word וָמָעְלָה used here literally means *above*. The choice of this word implies that dividing spoils with non-combatants had once been an accepted practice — i.e., *above*, in the meaning of "in the past." And David had now re-introduced that practice. The Midrash explains that this custom had been established by Abraham, when he had insisted that a share of the spoils of his battle against the Four Kings go to his friends Aner, Eshkol, and Mamre (*Genesis* 14:24).

As *Malbim* adds, Abraham also reasoned that spoils are a gift from Hashem. Therefore, no one participant deserves a share greater than another. Abraham expressed this idea when, upon being offered the spoils, he responded, הֲרִמֹתִי יָדִי אֶל־ה', *I lift up my hand to* HASHEM (ibid., v. 22) — i.e., he gave all of the credit to Hashem. He then proceeded to state that he would not take anything for himself but asked that his friends receive their share.

Abarbanel proves at length that this incident serves as a perfect paradigm for David's decree. *Abarbanel* demonstrates that Aner, Eshkol, and Mamre had not engaged in battle but had remained behind with the baggage. The verse states, וַיָּרֶק אֶת־חֲנִיכָיו יְלִידֵי בֵיתוֹ (ibid., v. 14) — which *Abarbanel* renders as [*Abraham*] *armed his hired soldiers* [*and*] *the slaves born in his house*. This excludes Aner, Eshkol, and Mamre, his three friends; they remained unarmed, for they did not go to fight. After the battle, there were four contingents who deserved a portion of the spoils: Abraham, his slaves, his hired workers, and his three friends. Abraham elected to forego his share and the share of his slaves (which belonged to him). The only two remaining groups were the soldiers and his friends, and both groups received equal portions. That mode of conduct David now renewed.

But there is another incident that the Midrash could have referred to — one that would seem to be a clearer precedent, in which the Jews were explicitly instructed to divide the spoils equally between the soldiers and the rest of the nation. Following the war against Midian, the Jews were told, *Divide the spoils in half between those who undertook the battle, who went out as part of the army, and the entire assembly*

דָוִד֙ אֶל־צִקְלַ֔ג וַיְשַׁלַּ֥ח מֵהַשָּׁלָ֛ל לְזִקְנֵ֥י יְהוּדָ֖ה
לְרֵעֵ֣הוּ לֵאמֹ֑ר הִנֵּ֤ה לָכֶם֙ בְּרָכָ֔ה מִשְּׁלַ֖ל אֹיְבֵ֥י
כז יְהוָֽה׃ לַאֲשֶׁ֥ר בְּבֵֽית־אֵ֖ל וְלַאֲשֶׁ֥ר בְּרָמֽוֹת־נֶ֖גֶב
כח וְלַאֲשֶׁ֥ר בְּיַתִּֽר׃ וְלַאֲשֶׁ֥ר בַּעֲרֹעֵ֛ר וְלַאֲשֶׁ֥ר בְּשִׂפְמ֖וֹת
כט וְלַאֲשֶׁ֥ר בְּאֶשְׁתְּמֹֽעַ׃ וְלַאֲשֶׁ֥ר בְּרָכָ֔ל וְלַאֲשֶׁר֙
ל בְּעָרֵ֣י הַיְּרַחְמְאֵלִ֔י וְלַאֲשֶׁ֕ר בְּעָרֵ֖י הַקֵּינִֽי׃ וְלַאֲשֶׁ֥ר
בְּחָרְמָ֛ה וְלַאֲשֶׁ֥ר °בְּבוֹר־עָשָׁ֖ן וְלַאֲשֶׁ֥ר בַּעֲתָֽךְ׃

(*Numbers* 31:27). Why, then, asks *Abarbanel*, did the Midrash not cite this straightforward precedent?

Abarbanel provides three answers.

First, in the war against Midian the soldiers were emissaries of the nation — it thus stood to reason that the noncombatants would receive a share of the spoils. In David's case, on the other hand, each man who fought did so on his own behalf, in order to rescue his own family, not as anyone else's agent.

Second, there is no reason to assume that the directives given at the war with Midian were intended to apply to future generations.

And third, in the war against Midian, the spoils were divided evenly between the 12,000 soldiers and the almost 600,000 other Jews. Therefore, each soldier received close to fifty times as much as each of the other Jews did. David, on the other hand, gave an equal share to each person who remained behind.

Furthermore, adds *Abarbanel*, the non-combatants in the war against Midian were not involved in the war effort at all, so that everything that they received was more than they deserved. Here, on the other hand, the non-combatants aided the soldiers by guarding the baggage.

וַיְשִׂמֶהָ לְחֹק וּלְמִשְׁפָּט לְיִשְׂרָאֵל — [*David*] *made this a decree and a law in Israel.*

Establishing this law would commemorate this episode — in this way, David publicized the miracle of their victory (*Ralbag*).

David promulgated this law to remind people that the results of war are in the hands of Hashem. No warrior may lay claim to the spoils on the grounds that the war was won through his might. Thus, the verse states that the decree was *for Israel* — i.e., for them alone, because only the Israelites possessed such an awareness.

לְחֹק וּלְמִשְׁפָּט — *A decree and a law.*

These terms are generally thought to be contradictory. A חֹק is an edict whose reasoning is beyond comprehension, whereas a מִשְׁפָּט is a law that may be logically understood. David's decision to divide the spoils equally between the combatants and non-combatants initially appeared to be an irrational decree. After David explained his reasoning, however, it was seen to be a rational law (*Malbim*).

According to *Daas Sofrim*, מִשְׁפָּט is a *judgment* — i.e., something that may be claimed in a court of law. Although the decision to divide the spoils was outside the scope of the law, once it was established as a חֹק, *decree*, it become a מִשְׁפָּט, a judicially enforcable law.

עַד הַיּוֹם הַזֶּה — *Until this day.*

Until the Jews went into exile and were no longer involved in wars (*Metzudos*).

26. וַיְשַׁלַּח מֵהַשָּׁלָל לְזִקְנֵי יְהוּדָה — *He sent some of the spoils to the elders of Judah.*

[26] When David arrived at Ziklag, he sent some
of the spoils to the elders of Judah, to his al-
lies, saying, "Here is a gift for you from the
spoils of the enemies of HASHEM*!" [27] [He sent]*
to those in Beth-el, to those in Ramot of the
South, and to those in Jattir; [28] and to those in
Aroer and to those in Siphmoth and to those
in Eshtemoa; [29] and to those in Rachal and to
those in the Jerahmeelite cities and to those in
the Kenite cities; [30] and to those in Hormah and
to those in Cor Ashan and to those in Athach,

Although some of the spoils originally came from the cities of Judah (above, v. 14), David was not legally obligated to return them (as mentioned above).

Nevertheless, states *Malbim,* David went beyond the letter of the law and returned what had been stolen from them.

According to *Daas Sofrim,* David lost the trust of the men of Judah when he had gone to dwell among the Philistines, and he wished to regain that trust by returning their goods.

Other commentators, however, make no association between these gifts and the items that had been captured from the Judean cities.

Thus, *Ralbag* opines that there is no evidence that David sought to determine who the original owners of the spoils had been. Rather, he sent these gifts out of sheer benevolence.

Abarbanel adds another motive as well: the desire to publicize Hashem's miracle and kindness.

According to a Midrash (*Shocher Tov* 15:6), David sent tributes to the righteous, God-fearing men who study Torah. In this regard, the Midrash quotes the verse, וְאֶת־יִרְאֵי ה׳ יְכַבֵּד, *he honors those who fear* HASHEM (*Psalms* 15:4). *Mussar HaNeviim* explains that David understood that the merits of the Torah scholars had led him and his men to victory, and he expressed that awareness by giving them a share of the spoils of war.

לְרֵעֵהוּ — *To his allies.*

Although the word רֵעֵהוּ usually means *to his ally,* most commentators render it here in the plural, citing various precedents (e.g., וַאֲחֻזַּת מֵרֵעֵהוּ, *and a group of his friends* [*Genesis* 26:26]) (*Rabbeinu Yeshayah*).

Metzudos renders this word as meaning, *he gave to each of his friends.*

הִנֵּה לָכֶם בְּרָכָה מִשְּׁלַל אֹיְבֵי ה׳ — *Here is a gift for you from the spoils of the enemies of* HASHEM.

According to *Abarbanel,* David emphasized that he was not returning items to their rightful owners, but rather distributing gifts.

In *Malbim's* opinion (see above), David did return people's property, and added his own gift in order to commemorate the miracle.

מִשְּׁלַל אֹיְבֵי ה׳ — *From the spoils of the enemies of* HASHEM.

In this comment, David taught the people that they need not worry that by consuming the enemy's spoils they would arouse him to curse them — to the contrary, eating the booty of Hashem's enemies would evoke heavenly blessings (*Abarbanel*).

ל/לא לא וְלַאֲשֶׁר בְּחֶבְרוֹן וּלְכָל־הַמְּקֹמוֹת אֲשֶׁר־הִתְהַלֶּךְ־
שָׁם דָּוִד הוּא וַאֲנָשָׁיו׃
לא/א־ב א וּפְלִשְׁתִּים נִלְחָמִים בְּיִשְׂרָאֵל וַיָּנֻסוּ אַנְשֵׁי יִשְׂרָאֵל
ב מִפְּנֵי פְלִשְׁתִּים וַיִּפְּלוּ חֲלָלִים בְּהַר הַגִּלְבֹּעַ׃ וַיַּדְבְּקוּ
פְלִשְׁתִּים אֶת־שָׁאוּל וְאֶת־בָּנָיו וַיַּכּוּ פְלִשְׁתִּים אֶת־
יְהוֹנָתָן וְאֶת־אֲבִינָדָב וְאֶת־מַלְכִּי־שׁוּעַ בְּנֵי שָׁאוּל׃

31. וּלְכָל־הַמְּקֹמוֹת אֲשֶׁר־הִתְהַלֶּךְ־שָׁם דָּוִד — *And to all the places where David had traveled.*

When David had fled Saul, the people in these places had helped him hide and done other favors for him. David now repaid those kindnesses (*Rashi, Radak*).

XXXI

The Death of Saul and His Sons

1. וּפְלִשְׁתִּים נִלְחָמִים בְּיִשְׂרָאֵל — *The Philistines were battling with Israel.*

Scripture interrupted its description of the war between Israel and the Philistines to relate the incidents of David and Achish and, following that, of David and the Amalekites. Now it comes back to the account of the war, introducing its return with these words (*Rashi*).

Kli Yakar explains this phrase as indicating that David was victorious due to his merits, whereas Saul failed as a result of his sins.

וַיָּנֻסוּ אַנְשֵׁי יִשְׂרָאֵל מִפְּנֵי פְלִשְׁתִּים — *And the men of Israel fled from before the Philistines.*

Although news of Samuel's dire prophecy had probably been withheld from the Israelite soldiers so that they would not lose heart, they apparently sensed the calamitous Divine decree and fled (*Chomas Anach, Me'am Loez*).

Daas Sofrim points out that there was no natural reason for Israel to have ever defeated the powerful Philistines. Now that they lacked the merit to achieve miraculous victory, they ran away.

וַיָּנֻסוּ אַנְשֵׁי יִשְׂרָאֵל מִפְּנֵי פְלִשְׁתִּים וַיִּפְּלוּ חֲלָלִים — *And the men of Israel fled from before the Philistines and fell slain.*

This phrase implies that the soldiers fell slain because they fled — from which the Talmud (*Sotah* 44b) infers that the primary cause of wartime casualties is fearful retreat. Thus, in order to prevent a rout, officers have the right (see *Deuteronomy* 20:9) to punish deserters harshly — even to chop off their feet.

וַיִּפְּלוּ חֲלָלִים — *And fell slain.*

A Midrash relates that in Saul's generation the Jews suffered casualties in war because their ranks were riddled by informers and gossipers. By contrast, although the populace in the time of Ahab included many idol worshipers, they were victorious because they did not engage in slander (*Devarim Rabbah* 5:10[1]). The Talmud *Yerushalmi* (*Peah* 1:1) makes a similar statement, but contrasts Ahab's generation with that of David. *S'mag* (Prohibition #9) reconciles these two sources by stating that both refer to the present episode, which marks a transitional period between the kingdoms of Saul and David. *Dina D'Chayi* explicates that the Talmud

1. The standard Vilna edition of *Midrash Rabbah* erroneously numbers this paragraph as ו, rather than י. Also, the letter ט of the previous paragraph is omitted.

30/31 [31] *and to those in Hebron; and to all the places where*
David had traveled — he and his men.

[1] *The Philistines were battling with Israel, and the*
31/1-2 *men of Israel fled from before the Philistines and*
fell slain upon Mount Gilboa. [2] *The Philistines caught*
Saul and his sons, and the Philistines slew Jona-
than, Abinadab, and Malchi-shua, the sons of Saul.

Yerushalmi could only be referring to this episode because during David's reign the Jews did not lose any wars (*Nachalas Shimon* 60:48).

2. וַיַּדְבְּקוּ פְלִשְׁתִּים אֶת־שָׁאוּל וְאֶת־בָּנָיו — *The Philistines caught Saul and his sons.*

Saul and his sons did not flee. Had they done so, Scripture would have stated וַיַּשִּׂיגוּ — that the Philistines *overtook*. Scripture's use of the word וַיַּדְבְּקוּ — *caught* — which is related to דבק — *attached* — implies that the two groups converged upon each other. As brave warriors Saul and his sons did not retreat; rather, they fought unrelentingly until the Philistines overcame them (*Abarbanel, Malbim*).

וַיַּכּוּ פְלִשְׁתִּים אֶת־יְהוֹנָתָן וְאֶת־אֲבִינָדָב וְאֶת־מַלְכִּי־שׁוּעַ — *And the Philistines slew Jonathan, Abinadab and Malchi-shua.*

The tragedy of their deaths illustrates the Divine Providence that eased David's way to the throne. Had Jonathan survived, David may not have consented to bypass him and become king. Also, David's victory at the head of only a small force, at the same time that Saul's army was crushed, convinced people that he was the most effective leader in the nation, and the best choice for the kingship (*Ralbag*'s lessons, after *II Samuel* Ch. 1).

Saul's fourth son and eventual successor, Ish-bosheth, did not join the battle (*Radak*), either because of physical weakness or for some other reason (see comm. above, 14:4). Or he may have escaped together with Abner (*Abarbanel*).

אֲבִינָדָב — *Abinadab.*

Above (14:48), he is called *Ishvi* (see comm. ad loc.).

Me'am Loez (to *II Samuel* 1:4) cites a Midrash that Abinadab was given this name because of an incident. Although Saul had been told that after the battle he would join Samuel in the Garden of Eden, when he was at the front he had second thoughts. Realizing that if he were killed, the Philistines would use his death to taunt Israel, he wondered whether it would be better to escape. Abinadab convinced him that entry into the Garden of Eden was worth the sacrifice. Therefore he was called אֲבִי, *My father*, נָדָב, *dedicated*, i.e., he convinced his father to dedicate his heart in repentance to be worthy of the World to Come.

בְּנֵי שָׁאוּל — *The sons of Saul.*

This redundancy indicates that these men were righteous and died only because, as Saul's sons, their fate was bound up with his (*Mishbetzos Zahav* from *Kehillas Yaakov*).

The Midrash (*Vayikra Rabbah* 26:7) relates that after Samuel's spirit told Saul that he and his sons would die in battle, Abner and Amasa asked Saul, "What did Samuel tell you?"

He answered, "I was told that I would be victorious at war and my sons would be appointed to high positions." With that, he took his sons and went to war.

At that time, Hashem called the heavenly angels and told them, "Come and see this creature that I have created in My world. Generally, a person will not even bring his children to a celebration because he is concerned about the evil eye of envious

ג וַתִּכְבַּ֤ד הַמִּלְחָמָה֙ אֶל־שָׁא֔וּל וַיִּמְצָאֻ֥הוּ
הַמּוֹרִ֖ים אֲנָשִׁ֣ים בַּקָּ֑שֶׁת וַיָּ֥חֶל מְאֹ֖ד מֵהַמּוֹרִֽים׃
ד וַיֹּ֣אמֶר שָׁא֡וּל לְנֹשֵׂ֣א כֵלָיו֩ שְׁלֹ֨ף חַרְבְּךָ֜ ׀
וְדָקְרֵ֣נִי בָ֗הּ פֶּן־יָ֩בוֹאוּ֩ הָעֲרֵלִ֨ים הָאֵ֜לֶּה וּדְקָרֻ֙נִי֙
וְהִֽתְעַלְּלוּ־בִ֔י וְלֹ֤א אָבָה֙ נֹשֵׂ֣א כֵלָ֔יו כִּ֥י יָרֵ֖א
מְאֹ֑ד וַיִּקַּ֤ח שָׁאוּל֙ אֶת־הַחֶ֔רֶב וַיִּפֹּ֖ל עָלֶֽיהָ׃

onlookers. Yet this man goes to war and takes his three sons with him, rejoicing in the Attribute of Justice that will strike him down" (see below, v. 3).

3. וַתִּכְבַּד הַמִּלְחָמָה אֶל־שָׁאוּל — *The battle bore down on Saul.*

Having killed Saul's sons, the Philistines turned to Saul.

Even after the Israelite soldiers had retreated and Saul's sons were killed, Saul continued fighting, prepared to sacrifice his life in order to earn the atonement he had been promised (*Chomas Anach*).

Targum Yonasan renders this phrase as *the warriors overpowered Saul.*

Above, we cited the Midrash that Saul rejoiced in the knowledge that God's Attribute of Justice would deal with him.

According to *Maharzu*, that Midrash is based on the use of the word וַתִּכְבַּד in this verse, which can be homiletically understood as implying כָּבוֹד, *honor*. Saul perceived the present debacle and death of his sons — which was Hashem's will — as a source of honor, and thus joy.

הַמּוֹרִים אֲנָשִׁים בַּקָּשֶׁת — *The archers — the men with bows...*

Our translation follows *Targum*, which interprets the phrase אֲנָשִׁים בַּקָּשֶׁת — literally, *men with bows* — as modifying the word הַמּוֹרִים, *the archers*. More specifically, *Targum* renders אֲנָשִׁים בַּקָּשֶׁת as *experts with the bow*, reading אֲנָשִׁים not simply as *men* but *distinguished men* (as in *Numbers* 13:3 and *Deuteronomy* 1:13; see *Kli Yakar*).

According to *Radak* and *Rabbeinu Yeshayah*, this phrase is to be understood as if the words were rearranged to read אֲנָשִׁים הַמּוֹרִים בַּקָּשֶׁת, *men who shoot with bows.*

וַיָּחֶל מְאֹד — *And he was terrified.*

Our translation follows *Targum*. Alternatively, *Mahari Kara* cites an opinion that relates וַיָּחֶל to חוֹלִי, *illness* — meaning that Saul's body was damaged by the arrows. (See also *Malbim*.)

וַיָּחֶל מְאֹד מֵהַמּוֹרִים — *And he was terrified of the archers.*

Abarbanel comments that Saul was not afraid of death, as he knew that his end was imminent. Rather (as we will see in the next verse), he feared that the Philistines would abuse him while he was still alive.

4. וְדָקְרֵנִי — *And stab me.*

Targum renders this phrase as *and kill me.*

פֶּן־יָבוֹאוּ הָעֲרֵלִים הָאֵלֶּה וּדְקָרֻנִי וְהִתְעַלְּלוּ־בִי — *Lest these uncircumcised men come and stab me and make sport of me.*

Because he had in the past inflicted considerable damage upon the Philistines, Saul was afraid that they would take their revenge by making a mockery of him (*Targum*) or by brutally tormenting him (*Ralbag*).

According to *Abarbanel*, Saul feared that before they killed him, the cruel Philistines would blind him and sever his limbs. Similarly, they made sport of Samson to humiliate him (*Judges* 16:20,25). Therefore, he preferred to be killed by a compatriot.

Kli Yakar explains that Saul was afraid that if he were killed by the Philistines, they would credit this victory to their gods, which

[3]The battle bore down on Saul. The archers —
the men with bows — found him, and he was
terrified of the archers. [4]Saul said to his armor-
bearer, "Draw your sword and stab me with it,
lest these uncircumcised men come and stab me
and make sport of me." But his armor-bearer
did not consent, for he was very frightened, so
Saul took the sword himself and fell upon it.

would constitute a desecration of Hashem's Name. In alluding to this possibility, Saul referred to the Philistines in terms of their religion, describing them as *uncircumcised men.*[1]

וְלֹא אָבָה נֹשֵׂא כֵלָיו כִּי יָרֵא מְאֹד — *But his armor-bearer did not consent, for he was very frightened.*

The armor-bearer was frightened of Hashem (*Mahari Kara, Metzudos*). Although Saul himself was absolved of guilt for killing himself (see below), his armor-bearer was not prepared to kill the anointed of God.

וַיִּקַּח שָׁאוּל אֶת־הַחֶרֶב וַיִּפֹּל עָלֶיהָ — *So Saul took the sword himself and fell upon it.*

The prohibition against suicide derives from the verse, *However, your blood which belongs to your souls I will demand* (*Genesis* 9:5). From the exclusionary word אַךְ, *however,* the Sages derive that in Saul's situation, what he did is permitted.

The prohibition against homicide, however, which is derived from the command, *Do not murder* (*Exodus* 20:13), has no such exclusionary clause, which explains why the armor-bearer declined (*Mishbetzos Zahav*).

It is possible that Saul felt that he was permitted to kill himself because he was clear about his reasoning and motives. The armor-bearer, however, could not be sure of Saul's intentions, and thus had no right to end his life (*Shevus Yaakov* Vol. 3:10,11, from *R' Yechezkel of Hamburg*; see *Mishbetzos Zahav*).

וַיִּקַּח שָׁאוּל אֶת־הַחֶרֶב וַיִּפֹּל עָלֶיהָ — *So Saul took the sword himself and fell upon it.*

As noted above, the Sages (*Bereishis Rabbah* 34:13) make allowance for suicide under such exceptionable circumstances. See also *Yoreh Deah* 345:3, where Saul's suicide is described as having been an אָנוּס, forced upon him. We present some explanations of this Midrash:

❒ According to *Radak* and *Yefeh Toar* (on *Bereishis Rabbah* ibid.), Saul was permitted to kill himself because he had been prophetically foretold that he would die. Seeing that he could not escape the archers, he preferred to commit suicide rather than be killed and in all likelihood mocked by the Philistines.

Similarly, the Vilna Gaon (in *Beur HaGra to Shulchan Aruch* ibid.) cites a text of the Midrash that exonerates Saul because he was being pursued with no hope of escape.

❒ *Daas Zekeinim MiBaalei HaTosafos* (*Genesis* ibid.) and *Tosafos* (*Avodah Zarah* 18a) state that if a person is afraid he will not be able to withstand torture, he may take his life. *Tosafos (Avodah*

1. Similarly, after David killed Uriah, Nathan admonished him with the words, *You have killed him by the sword of the children of Ammon* (*II Samuel* 12:9). David's sin was augmented by the fact that Uriah had been killed by the Ammonites, who consequently thanked their gods.

ה וַיַּ֥רְא נֹשֵֽׂא־כֵלָ֖יו כִּ֣י מֵ֣ת שָׁא֑וּל וַיִּפֹּ֥ל גַּם־ה֛וּא
ו עַל־חַרְבּ֖וֹ וַיָּ֥מָת עִמּֽוֹ׃ וַיָּ֣מָת שָׁא֡וּל וּשְׁלֹ֣שֶׁת בָּנָיו֩
וְנֹשֵׂ֨א כֵלָ֜יו גַּ֧ם כָּל־אֲנָשָׁ֛יו בַּיּ֥וֹם הַה֖וּא יַחְדָּֽו׃

Zarah 18a) rule that it is also permittted if one fears that torture will force him to sin. The Talmud (*Gittin* 57b) relates an incident after the destruction of the Second Temple in which many boys and girls jumped into the sea rather than allow themselves to be forced to sin, and they were awarded a share in the World to Come.

However, other authorities rule that it is preferable to suffer at the hands of gentiles than to inflict death upon oneself (as in the story of Rabbi Chanina ben Tradyon — *Avodah Zarah* 18a; this opinion is endorsed by *Yam Shel Shlomo, Bava Kamma*, Ch. 8 §59).

Yam Shel Shlomo offers two other ways of justifying Saul's action.

First, a person may take his life if that will save the lives of other Jews. Saul thought that if the Philistines tortured him, the Jews would be unable to restrain their desire for revenge and attack the Philistines recklessly, putting their lives in danger.

Second, as the anointed king of Hashem, Saul had the right to commit suicide rather than die a disgraceful death at the hands of uncircumcised men, which would have caused a desecration of God's Name.

According to *Mahari Kara*, the archers had injured Saul grievously. Since he was dying of his wounds, it would not be considered murder to kill him (*Sanhedrin* 78a).

A person who commits manslaughter of this type is responsible before the Heavenly Court, but doing so here might have been permissible, considering the other factors involved (*Nachalas Shimon, Mishbetzos Zahav*).[1]

The Talmud (*Sotah* 10a) lists five people, each of whom was blessed with an extraordinary feature. And each suffered through that very gift.

One of these people was Saul. His neck was considered exceptional, as he stood "taller than any of his people from his shoulder upward" (10:23), and his downfall came by the sword, which normally kills at the neck (*Rashi* ad loc.).

A Midrash (*Vayikra Rabbah* 26:7) relates that Hashem showed Moses a sweeping view of history, including each generation's kings, judges, and wise men. When Moses saw Saul's death, he asked, "How is it that the first king You will appoint will be killed by the sword?"

Hashem responded, "Do not complain to Me. Instead, speak to the Kohanim of Nob whom Saul killed, because it is they who are prosecuting him." This is homiletically implicit in the words, *Hashem said to Moses, "Say to the Kohanim"* (*Leviticus* 21:1).

The Midrash (*Midrash Shmuel* 24:7) enumerates five sins for which Saul deserved death (homiletically based on the verse in *I Chronicles* [10:13,14]): (1) authorizing the murder of the Kohanim of Nob; (2) having mercy on Agag; (3) not hearkening to Samuel's command to wait for him (above, 13:8-14); (4) inquiring of the *ov* sorceress; and (5) not inquiring of the *Urim VeTumim* in the war against the Philistines (14:19,20).[2]

5. וַיַּרְא נֹשֵׂא־כֵלָיו כִּי־מֵת שָׁאוּל — *When the armor-bearer saw that Saul was dying.*

Literally, כִּי־מֵת שָׁאוּל means *that Saul had died*. However, Scripture relates (*II Samuel*, Ch. 1) that an Amalekite convert came to David and informed him that he himself, at Saul's request,

1. For more on the topic of suicide, see *Nachalas Shimon* 58.

2. Regarding Saul's fifth sin, see also *Vayikra Rabbah* 26:7, *Radak, Maharzu*.

[5]*When the armor-bearer saw that Saul was dying*
he also fell upon his sword to die with him. [6]*So*
Saul and his three sons and his armor-bearer, as
well as all of his men, died together on that day.

had dispatched Saul. Accordingly, this phrase means that the armor-bearer saw that Saul was nearing his death (*Radak*).

Alternatively, Saul died immediately; as for the Amalekite convert, he fabricated his story about killing Saul in an unsuccessful attempt to curry favor with David (*Radak*).

וַיִּפֹּל גַּם־הוּא עַל־חַרְבּוֹ וַיָּמָת עִמּוֹ — *He also fell upon his sword to die with him.*

Thus, he escorted Saul in life and in death, as had Saul's sons (*Abarbanel*).

Since the commentaries to the previous verse indicate that the armor-bearer was a God-fearing man, we must assume that he had noble intentions in taking his life. Possibly, he feared a desecration of God's Name should the Philistines make a mockery of him. It is also possible that he was experiencing such overwhelming stress that he was not fully responsible for his actions (*Daas Sofrim*).

6. וַיָּמָת שָׁאוּל וּשְׁלֹשֶׁת בָּנָיו וְנֹשֵׂא כֵלָיו גַּם כָּל־אֲנָשָׁיו — *So Saul and his three sons and his armor-bearer, as well as all of his men, died.*

This verse, which repeats information that has just been presented, functions as a brief elegy to stress the painful tragedy of the day (*Daas Sofrim*).

It also confirms the fulfillment of Samuel's prophecy that וְיִתֵּן ה׳ גַּם אֶת־יִשְׂרָאֵל עִמְּךָ בְּיַד־פְּלִשְׁתִּים — HASHEM *will deliver Israel with you into the hand of the Philistines* (above, 28:19) (*Mishbetzos Zahav*).

וַיָּמָת שָׁאוּל וּשְׁלֹשֶׁת בָּנָיו — *So Saul and his three sons ... died.*

A Midrash (*Koheles Rabbah* 7:15) comments that whoever acts with mercy when harshness is called for will be subjected to the Divine Attribute of Justice. Because Saul had pity on Agag when he should have been cruel to him, he and his sons died a brutal death. The Midrash seems to be teaching that if a person is supposed to make use of the Attribute of Justice and fails to do so, Hashem's Attribute of Justice will take its revenge upon him, as it were.

Maharzu explains that Saul's death was unusually brutal, for the Torah does not even allow the slaughter of a mother animal and her offspring on the same day (*Leviticus* 22:29), yet here Saul died together with his three sons.

Abarbanel reiterates that although Saul lost his kingdom for having sinned in regard to Agag, he would not have died so violently were it not for his murder of the Kohanim. For that deed, he was punished measure for measure, in that he and all of his sons met their deaths at the hands of man. In addition to his three sons who were killed with him, Ish-bosheth was assassinated in his sleep (*II Samuel* 4:6,7), and two other sons — born to Rizpah, daughter of Aiah — were hanged by the Gibeonites (*II Samuel* 21:8,9).

גַּם כָּל־אֲנָשָׁיו — *As well as all of his men.*

That is, his men who were near him. Other soldiers were able to escape (*Radak*).

Daas Sofrim suggests that those of Saul's men who died were thus punished for not having attempted to prevent Saul's wrongdoing in the past. On the other hand, although Abner and Amasa were strong supporters of Saul and likely at the battlefront, they escaped death, possibly because they had opposed Saul's decision to kill the Kohanim at Nob (see above, 22:17).

ז וַיִּרְאוּ אַנְשֵׁי־יִשְׂרָאֵל אֲשֶׁר־בְּעֵבֶר הָעֵמֶק וַאֲשֶׁר |
בְּעֵבֶר הַיַּרְדֵּן כִּי־נָסוּ אַנְשֵׁי יִשְׂרָאֵל וְכִי־מֵתוּ
שָׁאוּל וּבָנָיו וַיַּעַזְבוּ אֶת־הֶעָרִים וַיָּנֻסוּ וַיָּבֹאוּ
ח פְלִשְׁתִּים וַיֵּשְׁבוּ בָּהֶן׃ וַיְהִי
מִמָּחֳרָת וַיָּבֹאוּ פְלִשְׁתִּים לְפַשֵּׁט אֶת־הַחֲלָלִים
וַיִּמְצְאוּ אֶת־שָׁאוּל וְאֶת־שְׁלֹשֶׁת בָּנָיו נֹפְלִים
ט בְּהַר הַגִּלְבֹּעַ׃ וַיִּכְרְתוּ אֶת־רֹאשׁוֹ וַיַּפְשִׁטוּ אֶת־
כֵּלָיו וַיְשַׁלְּחוּ בְאֶרֶץ־פְּלִשְׁתִּים סָבִיב לְבַשֵּׂר
י בֵּית עֲצַבֵּיהֶם וְאֶת־הָעָם׃ וַיָּשִׂמוּ אֶת־כֵּלָיו בֵּית
עַשְׁתָּרוֹת וְאֶת־גְּוִיָּתוֹ תָּקְעוּ בְּחוֹמַת בֵּית שָׁן׃

◈ The Philistines' Dishonorable Post-War Behavior

7. אֲשֶׁר בְּעֵבֶר־הָעֵמֶק וַאֲשֶׁר בְּעֵבֶר הַיַּרְדֵּן — *Those who were on the other side of the valley and on the other side of the Jordan.*

Targum renders הָעֵמֶק — *valley* — as *the plains*. This was the site of the cities closest to the Philistines. Since these cities were not fortified, their inhabitants abandoned them and fled (*Radak*).

According to *Metzudos*, these cities were the closest to the battlefield.

כִּי־נָסוּ אַנְשֵׁי יִשְׂרָאֵל וְכִי־מֵתוּ שָׁאוּל וּבָנָיו — *That the men of Israel had fled and that Saul and his sons had died.*

Without the heroic warriors or the king and his royal family to count on, the inhabitants of these cities lost hope (*Abarbanel, Malbim*).

8. נֹפְלִים — *Fallen.*

Targum renders the word as *murdered*.

9. וַיִּכְרְתוּ אֶת־רֹאשׁוֹ — *They severed his head.*

Although the Philistines who found Saul realized that he had committed suicide, they cut off his head to persuade the populace that the Philistine army had killed him (*Chomas Anach*).

Daas Sofrim comments that from the disgraceful way that the Philistines handled Saul's body, we can infer how they would have treated him had they discovered him alive.

וַיַּפְשִׁיטוּ אֶת־כֵּלָיו — *And stripped off his gear.*

This refers to his clothing, armor, and weapons. The Amalekite convert had already taken Saul's crown and bracelet (see below, *II Samuel* 1:10; *Radak*).

וַיְשַׁלְּחוּ בְאֶרֶץ פְּלִשְׁתִּים — *And sent [heralds] all about the land.*

The word *messengers* does not appear in the Hebrew, which does not specify what they sent. Our insertion of the word follows *Metzudos*, that messengers were sent to inform the people of the tragedy.

However, *Kli Yakar* states that they sent Saul's head to the Philistine cities to demonstrate their victory.

לְבַשֵּׂר בֵּית עֲצַבֵּיהֶם — *To inform [those in] the temple of their idols.*

We follow *Radak* in adding the words *those in* to this phrase. Presumably, the Philistines believed that their idols knew of what had occurred; thus, they needed only to inform the populace.

Abarbanel, however, understands the verse literally: that the Philistines informed their idols. *Me'am Loez* points out the difference between Jewish and Philistine beliefs reflected here. Whereas the *Urim VeTumim* were able to predict

[7]When the men of Israel, who were on the other
side of the valley and on the other side of the Jordan,
saw that the men of Israel had fled and that Saul and
his sons had died, they abandoned their cities and
fled, and the Philistines came and settled in them. [8]It
happened the next day, when the Philistines came
to plunder the corpses, that they found Saul and his
three sons, fallen on Mount Gilboa. [9]They severed
his head and stripped off his gear, and sent [heralds]
all about the land of the Philistines to inform [those
in] the temple of their idols and the people. [10]They
placed his gear in the temple of Ashtaroth, and they
hanged his remains upon the wall of Beth-shan.

events, the Philistines had to notify their idols of events after the fact.

According to *Malbim*, this phrase means that the Philistines went to *thank* their idols.

עֲצַבֵּיהֶם — *Their idols.*

Scripture here uses this particular term for the first time (*Daas Sofrim*). It is a demeaning word derived from עָצֵב — *sad* or *disappointed* — implying that an idol leaves its worshipers dejected when they cry out to it, for it does not even respond to them, much less save them.

10. וַיָּשִׂמוּ אֶת־כֵּלָיו בֵּית עַשְׁתָּרוֹת — *They placed his gear in the temple of Ashtaroth.*

There is a parallel narrative in *I Chronicles* (10:10), which states that the gear was placed in בֵּית אֱלֹהֵיהֶם — *the temple of their gods*, thus clarifying that Ashtaroth was the name of a Philistine god. The idols representing this god were in the form of sheep. They were therefore called *ashtaroth* — meaning *flocks* (see *Deuteronomy* 7:13; *Radak*).

וְאֶת גְּוִיָּתוֹ תָּקְעוּ בְּחוֹמַת בֵּית שָׁן — *And they hanged his remains upon the wall of Beth-shan.*

תָּקְעוּ — *hanged* — means *secured with nails* (*Radak*).

I Chronicles (ibid.) makes no mention of Saul's body, but records that his head was hanged in the temple of the idol Dagon. This verse, on the other hand, speaks only of Saul's body — his *remains* — and not his head. Thus, the information in these two texts is complementary (*Radak*).

The previous verse mentioned that the Philistines publicized Saul's death in the temples and before the people. More specifically, Saul's gear and head were hanged in the temples, while his body was hanged in Beth-shan, where its presence informed the people of his death (*Malbim*).

In accordance with *Kli Yakar's* opinion that Saul's head was initially sent to all the cities of the Philistines (above), *Kli Yakar* explains that Scripture here omits telling how his head was hanged because it reports only what the Philistines did immediately after they found him.

It is possible that the Philistines deliberately put Saul's severed head in the house of Dagon as an expression of revenge for the incident in which the Holy Ark caused Dagon's head to be severed (above, 5:4; *Malbim*).

This verse omits the fact that the bodies of Saul's sons were hanged as well, because that is mentioned below in v. 12 (*Radak*).

יא וַיִּשְׁמְעוּ אֵלָיו יֹשְׁבֵי יָבֵישׁ גִּלְעָד אֵת אֲשֶׁר־עָשׂוּ
יב פְלִשְׁתִּים לְשָׁאוּל׃ וַיָּקוּמוּ כָּל־אִישׁ חַיִל וַיֵּלְכוּ
כָל־הַלַּיְלָה וַיִּקְחוּ אֶת־גְּוִיַּת שָׁאוּל וְאֵת גְּוִיֹּת
בָּנָיו מֵחוֹמַת בֵּית שָׁן וַיָּבֹאוּ יָבֵשָׁה וַיִּשְׂרְפוּ אֹתָם
יג שָׁם׃ וַיִּקְחוּ אֶת־עַצְמֹתֵיהֶם וַיִּקְבְּרוּ תַחַת־הָאֶשֶׁל
בְּיָבֵשָׁה וַיָּצֻמוּ שִׁבְעַת יָמִים׃

Me'am Loez cites a Midrash stating that no animal or bird touched the bodies of Saul and his sons.

☙ A Daring Rescue

11. וַיִּשְׁמְעוּ אֵלָיו יֹשְׁבֵי יָבֵישׁ גִּלְעָד — *The inhabitants of Jabesh-gilead heard about him.*

The word אֵלָיו usually means *to him,* but here means *about him,* as if it were the similar word, עָלָיו (*Targum, Radak*).

The usage of this word implies that these men heard what had been done to Saul and recalled what he had done for them. When the king of Ammon had once threatened to take out the right eye of each inhabitant of Jabesh-gilead (above, 11:3), Saul had come to the townspeople's rescue and defeated Ammon. Since he had saved them from disgrace, they felt indebted to him and accordingly rescued his remains from shame.

According to *Abarbanel,* this phrase means that *they gathered on his behalf. Kli Yakar* ratifies this rendering, demonstrating that the word וַיִּשְׁמַע is sometimes used in this sense (see above, 15:4).

Daas Sofrim suggests a different interpretation. A single individual brought Jabesh-gilead the news about Saul's corpse and impressed its inhabitants with the urgency of redeeming it. וַיִּשְׁמְעוּ אֵלָיו thus means that *they listened to him,* and acted.

12. וַיָּקוּמוּ כָּל־אִישׁ חַיִל וַיֵּלְכוּ כָל־הַלַּיְלָה וַיִּקְחוּ אֶת־גְּוִיַּת שָׁאוּל — *All the daring men arose and traveled throughout the night. They took the remains of Saul...*

These heroes risked their lives to save Saul's body from disgrace and recompense the good that Saul had done for them.

For this deed, states a Midrash, Hashem promised them that when He will assemble the Jewish people at the time of the Redemption, He will first gather the people of Gilead and the half-tribe of Manasseh that dwelled on the eastern bank of the Jordan, where Gilead is located. This is alluded to in the verse, לִי גִלְעָד וְלִי מְנַשֶּׁה *Mine is Gilead, and Mine is Manasseh* (*Psalms* 60:9; *Pirkei DeRabbi Eliezer* Ch. 17).

וַיִּשְׂרְפוּ אֹתָם שָׁם — *They burned them there.*

The commentators interpret this phrase in four ways, each one involving a halachic issue. Here we will focus on the aspects of their interpretations germane to understanding the narrative.[1]

Targum renders וַיִּשְׂרְפוּ אֹתָם שָׁם not literally — that *they burned them* — but rather that *they burned on them. Radak* offers two explanations of this interpretation.

❒ First, *Radak* states that they burned Saul's belongings, in accordance with the prohibition against benefiting from a king's possessions.

This is referred to as burning עַל הַמְּלָכִים — *on* or *over* the kings (*Tosefta,*

1. For a comprehensive discussion of the halachic matters involved, the reader is directed to *Nachalas Shimon* 59.

[11]*The inhabitants of Jabesh-gilead heard about
him — about what the Philistines had done to
Saul —* [12]*and all the daring men arose and traveled throughout the night. They took the remains
of Saul and the remains of his sons from the wall of
Beth-shan, and came back to Jabesh. They burned
them there.* [13]*They then took their bones and buried them under the tamarisk tree in Jabesh, and
they fasted seven days.*

Shabbos 8:9; *Sanhedrin* 52b; *Avodah Zarah* 11a).[1]

It is a matter of dispute whether the Talmud merely *permits* such burning (which would otherwise have been proscribed as an Amoraic custom) or mandates it.

❐ Alternatively, the *burning* consisted of embalming the remains, similar to the treatment that Jacob (*Genesis* 50:2) and Joseph (ibid. 50:26) received.

Radak seems to understand (as does *Rashi* on *Genesis* 50:2, and *Rabbeinu Bachya* ibid. [based on *II Chronicles* 16:14]) that the embalming process did not involve cutting or otherwise tampering with the body. Rather, spices and perfumes were burned near or on the body in order to prevent — or at least limit — decomposition.

This would explain *Targum's* words that *they burned on him.* The permissibility of such an embalming processes is questionable, as it delays the natural decomposition of the body.[2]

Tosafos Yom Tov (to *Pesachim* 4:9) cites *Abarbanel's* description of the embalming process, according to which many organs of the deceased are removed and replaced with spices and perfumes. These have the effect of "burning" the flesh off the body without stench or decay.

Thus, Scripture's statement וַיִּשְׂרְפוּ אֹתָם means that the Jews burned the bodies of Saul and his sons by using these chemicals with the purpose of protecting their bodies from shame.

Whether or not it was necessary to cut open parts of the body to perform this process is the subject of dispute — with a related halachic ramification in regard to the permissibility of conducting an autopsy for a beneficial purpose.[3]

Radak mentions another interpretation: that the flesh of Saul's body had begun to decompose and was infested with worms; accordingly, the Jews felt that it would be appropriate to burn the flesh and bury the bones. Although there is an obligation to bury an entire corpse, according to one view the purpose of doing so is to protect the dignity of the body. In the present case, the dignity of the body would be protected by burning more than by burial.

Kli Yakar adds that the Jews may have chosen to burn Saul's flesh so that the Philistines would not be able to disinter his body and hang it up again. The halachic parameters of this topic are discussed in *Nachalas Shimon.*

13. וַיִּקְבְּרוּ תַחַת־הָאֵשֶׁל — *And buried them under the tamarisk tree.*

In *I Chronicles* (10:12), Scripture states that the tree was an אֵלָה. *Radak*

1. King Zedekiah was promised that he would not be deprived of this honor (*Jeremiah* 34:5).
2. See *ArtScroll Edition* of *Genesis* by Rabbi Meir Zlotowitz, *Genesis* 50:2.
3. See *Nachalas Shimon* and *Igros Moshe, Yoreh Deah* II §151.

explains that אֵשֶׁל — the word used in this verse — is the name of a family of trees, whereas אֵלָה is the name of the particular species.

Kli Yakar cites the homiletic interpretation of Abraham's אֵשֶׁל (*Genesis* 21:33) as an inn, the word functioning as an acrostic of אֲכִילָה, *food*, שְׁתִיָּה, *drink*, and לְוָיָה, *escort*: the three services that a host should provide for his guest (see *Rashi, Sotah* 10a).

Accordingly, *Kli Yakar* suggests that the burial took place at a center for guests, where many passersby would be present day and night, in order to maximize the honor to Saul.

This would not be Saul's permanent burial plot, as David eventually reinterred Saul and Jonathan's bones in the burial plot of Saul's father Kish (*II Samuel* 21:14).

Although David composed an elegy (*II Samuel* Ch. 1), Saul's death otherwise went largely unremarked. For having failed to eulogize this great man properly, the Jewish people were eventually punished by being subjected to a famine (see *II Samuel* Ch. 21, *Yevamos* 78b).

וַיָּצֻמוּ — *And they fasted.*

They fasted to mourn the loss of their first king, who had saved them from the hands of the Ammonites (*Metzudos*).

According to *Meshech Chochmah* (*Deuteronomy* 21:23), they fasted because of the defeat that they had suffered, and their consequent vulnerability.

Kli Yakar suggests that although it had been necessary to burn the king's flesh, doing so disgraced him, and that prompted them to fast.

Me'am Loez comments that this verse is the source of the custom to fast on the day of a great man's death.

שִׁבְעַת יָמִים — *Seven days.*

This seven-day period corresponds to the seven-day grace period that the Jews of Jabesh-gilead received from Nahash, king of Ammon, before Saul came to their aid (above, 11:3). They paid their last respects to Saul by commemorating his salvation.

Some commentators suggest that they fasted seven days as do the mourners of a close relative (*Daas Sofrim;* see *I Chronicles* 10:12, ArtScroll edition).

✤ *Appendix*

TIMELINE
(based on Seder Olam)

<table>
<tr><th>YEAR</th><th colspan="2">LEADER OF JEWS</th><th>STATION OF TABERNACLE</th><th>STATION OF ARK</th></tr>
<tr><td></td><td colspan="2">Eli
40 Years ↓</td><td>Shiloh
369 Years ↓</td><td>Shiloh
369 Years ↓</td></tr>
<tr><td>2871</td><td colspan="2">Samuel Alone
10 Years</td><td rowspan="3">Nob
13 Years</td><td rowspan="4">Philistia — 7 Months
Kiriath-je'arim
20 Years</td></tr>
<tr><td>2881</td><td colspan="2">Samuel and Saul
1 Year</td></tr>
<tr><td>2882</td><td colspan="2">King Saul
2 Years</td></tr>
<tr><td>2884</td><td rowspan="2">King David
40 Years</td><td>7 years in Hebron</td><td rowspan="3">Gibeon
44 Years</td></tr>
<tr><td>2891</td><td>33 years in Jerusalem</td><td rowspan="2">House of Obed-edom
3 Months
"City of David"
(Jerusalem) 37 Years</td></tr>
<tr><td>2924</td><td colspan="2" rowspan="2">King Solomon 40 Years ↓</td></tr>
<tr><td>2928</td><td>Temple ↓</td><td>Temple ↓</td></tr>
</table>

TIMELINE

Calculations to Prove Samuel's Life Span

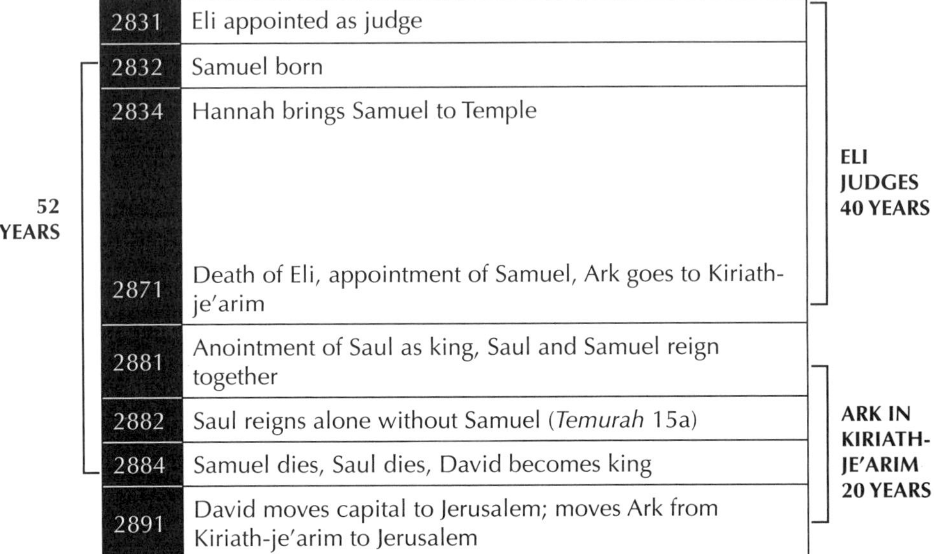

Year	Event
2831	Eli appointed as judge
2832	Samuel born
2834	Hannah brings Samuel to Temple
2871	Death of Eli, appointment of Samuel, Ark goes to Kiriath-je'arim
2881	Anointment of Saul as king, Saul and Samuel reign together
2882	Saul reigns alone without Samuel (*Temurah* 15a)
2884	Samuel dies, Saul dies, David becomes king
2891	David moves capital to Jerusalem; moves Ark from Kiriath-je'arim to Jerusalem

I. RASHI:

1. Two years after Samuel was weaned, he was brought to serve Eli in Shiloh (1:23,24).
2. Samuel remained in the House of God for *an entire lifetime* (1:22), which means 50 years, until his death at age 52.

II. TOSAFOS (Taanis 5b):

1. Eli became judge on the day of Hannah's prayer, six months prior to the birth of Samuel (1:9, *Rashi* ad loc.; 1:20, *Rashi* ad loc.).
2. Eli judged for 40 years (4:18); Samuel then succeeded him when he was 39 1/2 years old.
3. Samuel judged for 10 years until he was 49 1/2 prior to coronation of King Saul (*Seder Olam* Ch. 13; see preface to 13:1).
4. Samuel lived for 2 1/2 years of King Saul's reign, until he was 52.

III. TOSAFOS (ibid.)

See steps 1 & 2 above.

3. After Eli's death, the Ark went to Philistia for seven months (5:1) until Samuel turned 40 years old, at which time the Ark was transferred to Kiriath-je'arim.
4. The Ark remained in Kiryath-je'arim for 20 years (7:2), the last 7 1/2 of which were the years of David's reign in Hebron. Thus, for 12 years, Samuel was still alive (until 52) and David became king one-half year later.

This volume is part of
THE ARTSCROLL SERIES®
an ongoing project of
translations, commentaries and expositions on
Scripture, Mishnah, Talmud, Midrash, Halachah,
liturgy, history, the classic Rabbinic writings,
biographies and thought.

For a brochure of current publications
visit your local Hebrew bookseller
or contact the publisher:

Mesorah Publications, ltd

4401 Second Avenue
Brooklyn, New York 11232
(718) 921-9000
www.artscroll.com